W9-BNH-363

Advertising and Promotion

AN INTEGRATED MARKETING COMMUNICATIONS PERSPECTIVE

The McGraw-Hill/Irwin Series in Marketing

Arens
CONTEMPORARY ADVERTISING
NINTH EDITION

Arnould, Price & Zinkhan
CONSUMERS
SECOND EDITION

Bearden, Ingram & LaForge
MARKETING: PRINCIPLES & PERSPECTIVES
FOURTH EDITION

Belch & Belch
ADVERTISING & PROMOTION: AN INTEGRATED MARKETING COMMUNICATIONS APPROACH
SIXTH EDITION

Bingham & Gomes
BUSINESS MARKETING MANAGEMENT
SECOND EDITION

Boyd, Walker, Mullins & Larreche
MARKETING MANAGEMENT: A STRATEGIC DECISION-MAKING APPROACH
FOURTH EDITION

Cateora & Graham
INTERNATIONAL MARKETING
ELEVENTH EDITION

Cole & Mishler
CONSUMER AND BUSINESS CREDIT MANAGEMENT
ELEVENTH EDITION

Cravens, Lamb & Crittenden
STRATEGIC MARKETING MANAGEMENT CASES
SEVENTH EDITION

Cravens & Piercy
STRATEGIC MARKETING
SEVENTH EDITION

Crawford & Di Benedetto
NEW PRODUCTS MANAGEMENT
SEVENTH EDITION

Dolan
MARKETING MANAGEMENT: TEXT AND CASES
FIRST EDITION

Duncan
IMC: USING ADVERTISING AND PROMOTION TO BUILD BRANDS
FIRST EDITION

Dwyer & Tanner
BUSINESS MARKETING
SECOND EDITION

Eisenmann
INTERNET BUSINESS MODELS: TEXT AND CASES
FIRST EDITION

Etzel, Walker & Stanton
MARKETING
TWELFTH EDITION

Forrest
INTERNET MARKETING INTELLIGENCE
FIRST EDITION

Futrell
ABC'S OF RELATIONSHIP SELLING
EIGHTH EDITION

Futrell
FUNDAMENTALS OF SELLING
SEVENTH EDITION

Hair, Bush & Ortinau
MARKETING RESEARCH
SECOND EDITION

Hawkins, Best & Coney
CONSUMER BEHAVIOR
NINTH EDITION

Johansson
GLOBAL MARKETING
THIRD EDITION

Johnston & Marshall
CHURCHILL/FORD/WALKER'S SALES FORCE MANAGEMENT
SEVENTH EDITION

Kerin, Berkowitz, Hartley & Rudelius
MARKETING
SEVENTH EDITION

Kerin, Hartley & Rudelius
MARKETING: THE CORE
FIRST EDITION

Lehmann & Winer
ANALYSIS FOR MARKETING PLANNING
FIFTH EDITION

Lehmann & Winer
PRODUCT MANAGEMENT
THIRD EDITION

Levy & Weitz
RETAILING MANAGEMENT
FIFTH EDITION

Mason & Perreault
THE MARKETING GAME!
THIRD EDITION

McDonald
DIRECT MARKETING: AN INTEGRATED APPROACH
FIRST EDITION

Mohammed, Fisher, Jaworski & Paddison
INTERNET MARKETING: BUILDING ADVANTAGE IN A NETWORKED ECONOMY
SECOND EDITION

Monroe
PRICING
THIRD EDITION

Pelton, Strutton & Lumpkin
MARKETING CHANNELS: A RELATIONSHIP MANAGEMENT APPROACH
SECOND EDITION

Peppers & Rogers
MANAGING CUSTOMER RELATIONSHIPS TO BUILD COMPETITIVE ADVANTAGE
FIRST EDITION

Perreault & McCarthy
BASIC MARKETING: A GLOBAL MANAGERIAL APPROACH
FOURTEENTH EDITION

Perreault & McCarthy
ESSENTIALS OF MARKETING: A GLOBAL MANAGERIAL APPROACH
NINTH EDITION

Peter & Donnelly
A PREFACE TO MARKETING MANAGEMENT
NINTH EDITION

Peter & Donnelly
MARKETING MANAGEMENT: KNOWLEDGE AND SKILLS
SEVENTH EDITION

Peter & Olson
CONSUMER BEHAVIOR
SIXTH EDITION

Purvis & Burton
WHICH AD PULLED BEST?
NINTH EDITION

Rayport & Jaworski
INTRODUCTION TO E-COMMERCE
SECOND EDITION

Rayport & Jaworski
E-COMMERCE
FIRST EDITION

Rayport & Jaworski
CASES IN E-COMMERCE
FIRST EDITION

Richardson
INTERNET MARKETING
FIRST EDITION

Roberts
INTERNET MARKETING: INTEGRATING ONLINE AND OFFLINE STRATEGIES
FIRST EDITION

Spiro, Stanton & Rich
MANAGEMENT OF A SALES FORCE
ELEVENTH EDITION

Stock & Lambert
STRATEGIC LOGISTICS MANAGEMENT
FOURTH EDITION

Ulrich & Eppinger
PRODUCT DESIGN AND DEVELOPMENT
SECOND EDITION

Walker, Boyd, Mullins & Larreche
MARKETING STRATEGY: A DECISION-FOCUSED APPROACH
FOURTH EDITION

Weitz, Castleberry & Tanner
SELLING: BUILDING PARTNERSHIPS
FIFTH EDITION

Zeithaml & Bitner
SERVICES MARKETING
THIRD EDITION

Advertising and Promotion

AN INTEGRATED MARKETING COMMUNICATIONS PERSPECTIVE

SIXTH EDITION

George E. Belch & Michael A. Belch

BOTH OF SAN DIEGO STATE UNIVERSITY

McGraw Hill Irwin

Boston Burr Ridge IL Dubuque, IA Madison, WI New York San Francisco St. Louis
Bangkok Bogotá Caracas Kuala Lumpur Lisbon London Madrid Mexico City
Milan Montreal New Delhi Santiago Seoul Singapore Sydney Taipei Toronto

ADVERTISING AND PROMOTION:
AN INTEGRATED MARKETING COMMUNICATIONS PERSPECTIVE

Published by McGraw-Hill/Irwin, a business unit of The McGraw-Hill Companies, Inc. 1221 Avenue of the Americas, New York, NY, 10020. Copyright © 2004, 2001, 1998, 1995, 1993, 1990 by The McGraw-Hill Companies, Inc. All rights reserved. No part of this publication may be reproduced or distributed in any form or by any means, or stored in a database or retrieval system, without the prior written consent of The McGraw-Hill Companies, Inc., including, but not limited to, in any network or other electronic storage or transmission, or broadcast for distance learning. Some ancillaries, including electronic and print components, may not be available to customers outside the United States.

This book is printed on acid-free paper.

domestic 1 2 3 4 5 6 7 8 9 0 DOW/DOW 0 9 8 7 6 5 4 3
international 1 2 3 4 5 6 7 8 9 0 DOW/DOW 0 9 8 7 6 5 4 3

ISBN 0-07-253676-4

Publisher: *John E. Biernat*
Associate sponsoring editor: *Barrett Koger*
Managing developmental editor: *Nancy Barbour*
Marketing manager: *Kimberly Kanakes*
Media producer: *Craig Atkins*
Project manager: *Natalie J. Ruffatto*
Production supervisor: *Debra R. Sylvester*
Director of design: *Keith J. McPherson*
Photo research coordinator: *Judy Kausal*
Photo researcher: *Charlotte Goldman*
Supplement producer: *Joyce J. Chappetto*
Senior digital content specialist: *Brian Nacik*
Cover and Interior design: *Kiera Cunningham*
Cover Images: *Courtesy of United States Army Recruiting Command and the Department of the Army; © 2004 BMW of North America, LLC, used with permission. The BMW name and logo are registered trademarks; © 2002 Dell Computer Corporation; Courtesy of American Advertising Federation; Courtesy of MINI USA; Courtesy of Covering Kids; Courtesy of NIKE, Inc.*
Typeface: *10.5/12 Times Roman*
Compositor: *Precision Graphics Services, Inc.*
Printer: *R. R. Donnelley*

Library of Congress Cataloging-in-Publication Data

Belch, George E. (George Edward)
Advertising and promotion : an integrated marketing communications perspective / George E. Belch & Michael A. Belch.—6th ed.
p. cm.—(The McGraw-Hill/Irwin series in marketing)
Includes bibliographical references and index.
ISBN 0-07-253676-4 (alk. paper)—ISBN 0-07-121438-0 (international : alk. paper)
1. Advertising. 2. Sales promotion. 3. Communication in marketing. I. Belch, Michael A. II. Title. III. Series

HF5823.B387 2004
659.1—dc21

2003042015

INTERNATIONAL EDITION ISBN 0-07-121438-0
Copyright © 2004. Exclusive rights by The McGraw-Hill Companies, Inc., for manufacture and export. This book cannot be re-exported from the country to which it is sold by McGraw-Hill. The International Edition is not available in North America.

www.mhhe.com

To Mom

To whom we dedicate this book and a great deal more

Preface

The Changing World of Advertising and Promotion

Nearly everyone in the modern world is influenced to some degree by advertising and other forms of promotion. Organizations in both the private and public sectors have learned that the ability to communicate effectively and efficiently with their target audiences is critical to their success. Advertising and other types of promotional messages are used to sell products and services as well as to promote causes, market political candidates, and deal with societal problems such as alcohol and drug abuse. Consumers are finding it increasingly difficult to avoid the efforts of marketers, who are constantly searching for new ways to communicate with them.

Most of the people involved in advertising and promotion will tell you that there is no more dynamic and fascinating a field to either practice or study. However, they will also tell you that the field is undergoing dramatic changes that are changing advertising and promotion forever. The changes are coming from all sides—clients demanding better results from their advertising and promotional dollars; lean but highly creative smaller ad agencies; sales promotion and direct-marketing firms, as well as interactive agencies, which want a larger share of the billions of dollars companies spend each year promoting their products and services; consumers who no longer respond to traditional forms of advertising; and new technologies that may reinvent the very process of advertising. As the new millennium begins, we are experiencing perhaps the most dynamic and revolutionary changes of any era in the history of marketing, as well as advertising and promotion. These changes are being driven by advances in technology and developments that have led to the rapid growth of communications through interactive media, particularly the Internet.

For decades the advertising business was dominated by large, full-service Madison Avenue–type agencies. The advertising strategy for a national brand involved creating one or two commercials that could be run on network television, a few print ads that would run in general interest magazines, and some sales promotion support such as coupons or premium offers. However, in today's world there are a myriad of media outlets—print, radio, cable and satellite TV, and the Internet—competing for consumers' attention. Marketers are looking beyond the traditional media to find new and better ways to communicate with their customers. They no longer accept on faith the value of conventional advertising placed in traditional media. The large agencies are recognizing that they must change if they hope to survive in the 21st century. Keith Reinhard, chairman and CEO of DDB Worldwide, notes that the large agencies "have finally begun to acknowledge that this isn't a recession we're in, and that we're not going back to the good old days."

In addition to redefining the role and nature of their advertising agencies, marketers are changing the way they communicate with consumers. They know they are operating in an environment where advertising messages are everywhere, consumers channel-surf past most commercials, and brands promoted in traditional ways often fail. New-age advertisers are redefining the notion of what an ad is and where it runs. Stealth messages are being woven into the culture and embedded into movies and TV shows or made into their own form of entertainment. Many experts argue that "branded content" is the wave of the future, and there is a growing movement to reinvent advertising and other forms of marketing communication to be more akin to entertainment. Companies such as BMW, Levi Straus & Co., Nike, and Skyy Spirits are among the marketers using "advertainment" as a way of reaching consumers: They create short films or commercials that are shown on their websites.

Marketers are also changing the ways they allocate their promotional dollars. Spending on sales promotion activities targeted at both consumers and the trade has surpassed advertising media expenditures for years and continues to rise. In his book *The End of Marketing as We Know It,* Sergio Zyman, the former head of marketing for Coca-Cola, declares traditional marketing is "not dying, but dead." He argues that advertising in general is overrated as part of the marketing mix and notes that all elements of the marketing mix communicate, such as brand names, packaging, pricing, and the way a product is distributed. The information revolution is exposing consumers to all types of communications, and marketers need to better understand this process.

A number of factors are impacting the way marketers communicate with consumers. The audiences that marketers seek, along with the media and methods for reaching them, have become increasingly fragmented. Advertising and promotional efforts have become more regionalized and targeted to specific audiences. Retailers have become larger and more powerful, forcing marketers to shift money from advertising budgets to sales promotion. Marketers expect their promotional dollars to generate immediate sales and are demanding more accountability from their agencies. The Internet revolution is well under way and the online audience is growing rapidly, not only in the United States and Western Europe but in many other countries as well. Many companies are coordinating all their communications efforts so that they can send cohesive messages to their customers. Some companies are building brands with little or no use of traditional media advertising. Many

advertising agencies have acquired, started, or become affiliated with sales promotion, direct-marketing, interactive agencies, and public relations companies to better serve their clients' marketing communications needs. Their clients have become "media-neutral" and are asking that they consider whatever form of marketing communication works best to target market segments and build long-term reputations and short-term sales.

This text will introduce students to this fast-changing field of advertising and promotion. While advertising is its primary focus, it is more than just an introductory advertising text because there is more to most organizations' promotional programs than just advertising. The changes discussed above are leading marketers and their agencies to approach advertising and promotion from an integrated marketing communications (IMC) perspective, which calls for a "big picture" approach to planning marketing and promotion programs and coordinating the various communication functions. To understand the role of advertising and promotion in today's business world, one must recognize how a firm can use all the promotional tools to communicate with its customers.

To the Student: Preparing You for the New World of Advertising and Promotion

Some of you are taking this course to learn more about this fascinating field; many of you hope to work in advertising or some other promotional area. The changes in the industry have profound implications for the way today's student is trained and educated. You will not be working for the same kind of communication agencies that existed 5 or 10 years ago. If you work on the client side of the business, you will find that the way they approach advertising and promotion is changing dramatically.

Today's student is expected to understand all the major marketing communication functions: advertising, direct marketing, the Internet, interactive media, sales promotion, public relations, and personal selling. You will also be expected to know how to research and evaluate a company's marketing and promotional situation and how to use these various functions in developing effective communication strategies and programs. This book will help prepare you for these challenges.

As professors we were, of course, once students ourselves. In many ways we are perpetual students in that we are constantly striving to learn about and explain how advertising and promotion work. We share many of your interests and concerns and are often excited (and bored) by the same things. Having taught in the advertising and promotion area for a combined 50-plus years, we have developed an understanding of what makes a book in this field interesting to students. In writing this book, we have tried to remember how we felt about the various texts we used throughout the years and to incorporate the good things and minimize those we felt were of little use. We have tried not to overburden you with definitions, although we do call out those that are especially important to your understanding of the material.

We also remember that as students we were not really excited about theory. But to fully understand how integrated marketing communications works, it is necessary to establish some theoretical basis. The more you understand about how things are supposed to work, the easier it will be for you to understand why they do or do not turn out as planned.

Perhaps the question students ask most often is, "How do I use this in the real world?" In response, we provide numerous examples of how the various theories and concepts in the text can be used in practice. A particular strength of this text is the integration of theory with practical application. Nearly every day an example of advertising and promotion in practice is reported in the media. We have used many sources, such as *Advertising Age, Adweek, Brandweek, The Wall Street Journal, BusinessWeek, Fortune, Forbes, Sales & Marketing Management, Business 2.0, eMarketer, The Internet Advertising Report, Promo,* and many others, to find practical examples that are integrated throughout the text. We have spoken with hundreds of people about the strategies and rationale behind the ads and other types of promotions we use as examples. Each chapter begins with a vignette that presents an example of an advertising or promotional campaign or other interesting insights. Every chapter also contains several **IMC Perspectives** that present in-depth discussions of particular issues related to the chapter material and show how companies are using integrated marketing communications. **Global Perspectives** are presented throughout the text in recognition of the increasing importance of international marketing and the challenges of advertising and promotion and the role they play in the marketing programs of multinational marketers. **Ethical Perspectives** focus attention on important social issues and show how advertisers must take ethical considerations into account when planning and implementing advertising and promotional programs. **Diversity Perspectives** discuss the opportunities, as well as the challenges, associated with marketers' efforts to reach culturally and ethnically diverse target markets. There are also a number of **Career Profiles,** which highlight successful individuals working in various areas of the field of advertising and promotion.

Each chapter features beautiful four-color illustrations showing examples from many of the most current and best-integrated marketing communication campaigns being used around the world. We have included more than 350 advertisements and examples of numerous other types of promotion, all of which were carefully chosen to illustrate a particular idea, theory, or practical application. Please take time to read the opening vignettes to each chapter, the IMC, Global, Ethical, and Diversity Perspectives, and the Career Profiles and study the diverse ads and illustrations. We think they will stimulate

your interest and relate to your daily life as a consumer and a target of advertising and promotion.

To the Instructor: A Text That Reflects the Changes in the World of Advertising and Promotion

Our major goal in writing the sixth edition of *Advertising and Promotion* was to continue to provide you with the most comprehensive and current text on the market for teaching advertising and promotion from an IMC perspective. This sixth edition focuses on the many changes that are occurring in areas of marketing communications and how they influence advertising and promotional strategies and tactics. We have done this by continuing with the *integrated marketing communications perspective* we introduced in the second edition. More and more companies are approaching advertising and promotion from an IMC perspective, coordinating the various promotional mix elements with other marketing activities that communicate with a firm's customers. Many advertising agencies are also developing expertise in direct marketing, sales promotion, event sponsorship, the Internet, and other areas so that they can meet all their clients' integrated marketing communication needs—and, of course, survive.

The text is built around an integrated marketing communications planning model and recognizes the importance of coordinating all of the promotional mix elements to develop an effective communications program. Although media advertising is often the most visible part of a firm's promotional program, attention must also be given to direct marketing, sales promotion, public relations, interactive media, and personal selling.

This text integrates theory with planning, management, and strategy. To effectively plan, implement, and evaluate IMC programs, one must understand the overall marketing process, consumer behavior, and communications theory. We draw from the extensive research in advertising, consumer behavior, communications, marketing, sales promotion, and other fields to give students a basis for understanding the marketing communications process, how it influences consumer decision making, and how to develop promotional strategies.

While this is an introductory text, we do treat each topic in some depth. We believe the marketing and advertising student of today needs a text that provides more than just an introduction to terms and topics. The book is positioned primarily for the introductory advertising, marketing communications, or promotions course as taught in the business/marketing curriculum. It can also be used in journalism/communications courses that take an integrated marketing communications perspective. Many schools also use the text at the graduate level. In addition to its thorough coverage of advertising, this text has chapters on sales promotion, direct marketing and marketing on the Internet, personal selling, and publicity/public relations. These chapters stress the integration of advertising with other promotional mix elements and the need to understand their role in the overall marketing program.

Organization of This Text

This book is divided into seven major parts. In Part One we examine the role of advertising and promotion in marketing and introduce the concept of integrated marketing communications. Chapter 1 provides an overview of advertising and promotion and its role in modern marketing. The concept of IMC and the factors that have led to its growth are discussed. Each of the promotional mix elements is defined, and an IMC planning model shows the various steps in the promotional planning process. This model provides a framework for developing the integrated marketing communications program and is followed throughout the text. Chapter 2 examines the role of advertising and promotion in the overall marketing program, with attention to the various elements of the marketing mix and how they interact with advertising and promotional strategy. We have also included coverage of market segmentation and positioning in this chapter so that students can understand how these concepts fit into the overall marketing programs as well as their role in the development of an advertising and promotional program.

In Part Two we cover the promotional program situation analysis. Chapter 3 describes how firms organize for advertising and promotion and examines the role of ad agencies and other firms that provide marketing and promotional services. We discuss how ad agencies are selected, evaluated, and compensated as well as the changes occurring in the agency business. Attention is also given to other types of marketing communication organizations such as direct marketing, sales promotion, and interactive agencies as well as public relations firms. We also consider whether responsibility for integrating the various communication functions lies with the client or the agency. Chapter 4 covers the stages of the consumer decision-making process and both the internal psychological factors and the external factors that influence consumer behavior. The focus of this chapter is on how advertisers can use an understanding of buyer behavior to develop effective advertising and other forms of promotion.

Part Three analyzes the communications process. Chapter 5 examines various communication theories and models of how consumers respond to advertising messages and other forms of marketing communications. Chapter 6 provides a detailed discussion of source, message, and channel factors.

In Part Four we consider how firms develop goals and objectives for their integrated marketing communications programs and determine how much money to spend trying to achieve them. Chapter 7 stresses the importance of knowing what to expect from advertising and promotion,

the differences between advertising and communication objectives, characteristics of good objectives, and problems in setting objectives. We have also integrated the discussion of various methods for determining and allocating the promotional budget into this chapter. These first four sections of the text provide students with a solid background in the areas of marketing, consumer behavior, communications, planning, objective setting, and budgeting. This background lays the foundation for the next section, where we discuss the development of the integrated marketing communications program.

Part Five examines the various promotional mix elements that form the basis of the integrated marketing communications program. Chapter 8 discusses the planning and development of the creative strategy and advertising campaign and examines the creative process. In Chapter 9 we turn our attention to ways to execute the creative strategy and some criteria for evaluating creative work. Chapters 10 through 13 cover media strategy and planning and the various advertising media. Chapter 10 introduces the key principles of media planning and strategy and examines how a media plan is developed. Chapter 11 discusses the advantages and disadvantages of the broadcast media (TV and radio) as well as issues regarding the purchase of radio and TV time and audience measurement. Chapter 12 considers the same issues for the print media (magazines and newspapers). Chapter 13 examines the role of support media such as outdoor and transit advertising and some of the many new media alternatives.

In Chapters 14 through 17 we continue the IMC emphasis by examining other promotional tools that are used in the integrated marketing communications process. Chapter 14 looks at the rapidly growing areas of direct marketing. This chapter examines database marketing and the way by which companies communicate directly with target customers through various media. Chapter 15 provides a detailed discussion of interactive media and marketing on the Internet and how companies are using the World Wide Web as a medium for communicating with customers. We discuss how this medium is being used for a variety of marketing activities including advertising, sales promotion and even the selling of products and services. Chapter 16 examines the area of sales promotion including both consumer-oriented promotions and programs targeted to the trade (retailers, wholesalers and other middlemen). Chapter 17 covers the role of publicity and public relations in IMC as well as corporate advertising. Basic issues regarding personal selling and its role in promotional strategy are presented in Chapter 18.

Part Six of the text consists of Chapter 19, where we discuss ways to measure the effectiveness of various elements of the integrated marketing communications program, including methods for pretesting and posttesting advertising messages and campaigns. In Part Seven we turn our attention to special markets, topics, and perspectives that are becoming increasingly important in contemporary marketing. In Chapter 20 we examine the global marketplace and the role of advertising and other promotional mix variables such as sales promotion, public relations, and the Internet in international marketing.

The text concludes with a discussion of the regulatory, social, and economic environments in which advertising and promotion operate. Chapter 21 examines industry self-regulation and regulation of advertising by governmental agencies such as the Federal Trade Commission, as well as rules and regulations governing sales promotion, direct marketing, and marketing on the Internet. Because advertising's role in society is constantly changing, our discussion would not be complete without a look at the criticisms frequently levied, so in Chapter 22 we consider the social, ethical, and economic aspects of advertising and promotion.

Chapter Features

The following features in each chapter enhance students' understanding of the material as well as their reading enjoyment.

Chapter Objectives

Objectives are provided at the beginning of each chapter to identify the major areas and points covered in the chapter and guide the learning effort.

Chapter Opening Vignettes

Each chapter begins with a vignette that shows the effective use of integrated marketing communications by a company or ad agency or discusses an interesting issue that is relevant to the chapter. These opening vignettes are designed to draw the students into the chapter by presenting an interesting example, development, or issue that relates to the material covered in the chapter. Some of the companies, brands, and organizations profiled in the opening vignettes include the U.S. Army, BMW, Samsung, TiVo, Red Bull, Nike, Skyy Spirits, and *Rolling Stone* magazine. In addition, some of the chapter openers discuss current topics and issues such as branding, convergence, the role of advertising versus public relations, and the controversy over the advertising of hard liquor on network television.

IMC Perspectives

These boxed items feature in-depth discussions of interesting issues related to the chapter material and the practical application of integrated marketing communications. Each chapter contains several of these insights into the world of integrated marketing communications. Some of the companies/brands whose IMC programs are discussed in these perspectives include Jet Blue, Dell Computer, Jupiter Media Matrix, BMW Mini-Cooper, Intel, *USA Today,* PT-Cruiser, and Dunkin' Donuts. Issues such as the use of music to enhance the effectiveness of commercials, the value of stadium naming rights,

public relations blunders, and problems that companies have encountered when using contests and sweepstakes are also discussed in the IMC Perspectives.

Global Perspectives

These boxed sidebars provide information similar to that in the IMC Perspectives, with a focus on international aspects of advertising and promotion. Some of the companies/brands whose international advertising programs are covered in the Global Perspectives include MTV, Microsoft, Sony, McDonald's, and Nike. Topics such as the Cannes international advertising awards, celebrities who appear in commercials in Japan while protecting their image in the United States, advertising in China, and the challenges of communicating with consumers in Third World countries are also discussed.

Ethical Perspectives

These boxed items discuss the moral and/or ethical issues regarding practices engaged in by marketers and are also tied to the material presented in the particular chapter. Issues covered in the Ethical Perspectives include subliminal advertising, the battle between television networks and advertisers over tasteful advertising, and controversies arising from the increase in direct-to-consumer advertising of prescription drugs and the commercialization of schools.

Diversity Perspectives

These boxed items discuss topics related to the opportunities and challenges facing companies as they develop integrated marketing communications programs for markets that are becoming more ethnically diverse. The Diversity Perspectives include the rapid growth of the Hispanic market and issues involved in communicating with this important segment, the emergence of Spanish-language television stations in the United States, and the use of sales promotion to target the African-American market.

Career Profiles

Also included are Career Profiles of successful individuals working in the communications industry. The individuals featured in Career Profiles include an account executive for the Leo Burnett advertising agency, a director of corporate communications for JetBlue airlines, the vice president of the iDeutsch interactive agency, the manager of Corporate Communications and Creative Services for Savin Corporation, a media salesperson for *Rolling Stone* magazine, the vice president of marketing and communication for Cox Target Media, a marketing and sales promotion analyst for Chicken of the Sea International, the president of *eMarketer,* and the president of the Ipsos-ASI, Inc., global marketing and advertising research firm.

Key Terms

Important terms are highlighted in boldface throughout the text and listed at the end of each chapter with a page reference. These terms help call students' attention to important ideas, concepts, and definitions and help them review their learning progress.

Chapter Summaries

These synopses serve as a quick review of important topics covered and a very helpful study guide.

Discussion Questions

Questions at the end of each chapter give students an opportunity to test their understanding of the material and to apply it. These questions can also serve as a basis for class discussion or assignments.

Four-Color Visuals

Print ads, photoboards, and other examples appear throughout the book. More than 400 ads, charts, graphs, and other types of illustrations are included in the text.

Changes in the Sixth Edition

We have made a number of changes in the sixth edition to make it as relevant and current as possible, as well as more interesting to students:

- **Updated Coverage of the Emerging Field of Integrated Marketing Communications** The sixth edition continues to place a strong emphasis on studying advertising and promotion from an integrated marketing communications perspective. We examine developments that are impacting the way marketers communicate with their customers, such as the movement toward "branded content," whereby marketers and agencies are becoming more involved in creating an entertainment product and integrating their messages into it. New technologies such as personal video recorders and the convergence of television, computers, and the Internet are changing the way companies are using advertising along with other marketing tools to communicate with their customers. In this new edition we examine how these cutting-edge developments are impacting the IMC program of marketers.
- **Updated Chapter on the Internet and Interactive Media** The sixth edition includes up-to-date information on the Internet and other forms of interactive media and how they are being used by marketers. We also discuss developments such as wireless communications as well as regulations affecting the use of the Internet and important issues such as privacy. This chapter also discusses the latest developments in areas such as audience

measurement and methods for determining the effectiveness of Internet advertising. Discussion of the emerging role of the Internet as an important integrated marketing communications tool and of the ways it is being used by marketers is integrated throughout the sixth edition.

- **Diversity Perspectives—New to This Edition** In this edition we introduce a new feature called *Diversity Perspectives.* These boxed items are designed to focus attention on the increase in the diversity of the consumer market in the United States. The 2000 census showed that the Hispanic market grew by 58 percent over the past decade, and another 35 percent increase is forecast over the next 10 years. Marketers are recognizing the importance of being able to communicate with a diverse market that includes Hispanics, African-Americans, Asian-Americans, and other ethnic groups. This new feature focuses on the opportunities and challenges facing companies as they develop integrated marketing communications programs for markets that are becoming more ethnically diverse.
- **Online Cases** Six short cases written to correspond to various sections of the text are available online and can be downloaded for classroom use and assignments. These cases are designed to build on the material presented in the text and provide students with the opportunity to apply various IMC tools and concepts. The cases include companies and organizations such as Gateway, the U.S. Armed Forces, Chicken of the Sea International, the Partnership for a Drug Free America, and the U.S. Office of National Drug Control Policy. The online cases include information beyond that provided in the text and require that students evaluate an advertising and promotional issue and make a decision and recommendation.
- **New Chapter Opening Vignettes** *All* of the chapter opening vignettes in the sixth edition are new and were chosen for their currency and relevance to students. They demonstrate how various companies and advertising agencies use advertising and other IMC tools. They also provide interesting insights into some of the current trends and developments that are taking place in the advertising world.
- **New and Updated IMC Perspectives** All of the boxed items focusing on specific examples of how companies and their communications agencies are using integrated marketing communications are new or updated, and they provide insight into many of the most current and popular advertising and promotional campaigns being used by marketers. The IMC Perspectives also address interesting issues related to advertising, sales promotion, direct marketing, marketing on the Internet, and personal selling.
- **New and Updated Global and Ethical Perspectives** Nearly all of the boxed items focusing on global and ethical issues of advertising and promotion are new; those retained from the fifth edition have been updated. The Global Perspectives examine the role of advertising and other promotional areas in international markets. The Ethical Perspectives discuss specific issues, developments, and problems that call into question the ethics of marketers and their decisions as they develop and implement their advertising and promotional programs.
- **New Career Profiles** The sixth edition has all new Career Profiles that discuss the career path of successful individuals working in various areas of advertising and promotion, including clients, advertising agencies, and the media. These profiles provide students with insight into various types of careers that are available in the area of advertising and promotion on the client and agency side as well as in media. They discuss the educational backgrounds of the individuals profiled, some of the responsibilities and requirements of their positions, and their career paths. This feature has been very popular among students and in this edition we provide eight new profiles. These profiles have been written by the individuals themselves and provide students with insight into the educational background of the persons profiled, how they got started in the field of advertising and promotion, their current responsibilities, and interesting aspects of their jobs as well as experiences.
- **Contemporary Examples** The field of advertising and promotion changes very rapidly, and we continue to keep pace with it. Wherever possible we updated the statistical information presented in tables, charts, and figures throughout the text. We reviewed the most current academic and trade literature to ensure that this text reflects the most current perspectives and theories on advertising, promotion, and the rapidly evolving area of integrated marketing communications. We also updated most of the examples and ads throughout the book. *Advertising and Promotion* continues to be the most contemporary text on the market, offering students as timely a perspective as possible.

Support Material

A high-quality package of instructional supplements supports the sixth edition. Nearly all of the supplements have been developed by the authors to ensure their coordination with the text. We offer instructors a support package that facilitates the use of our text and enhances the learning experience of the student.

Instructor's Manual

The instructor's manual is a valuable teaching resource that includes learning objectives, chapter and lecture outlines, answers to all end-of-chapter discussion questions, transparency masters, and further insights and teaching suggestions. Additional discussion questions are also presented for each chapter. These questions can be used for class discussion or as short-answer essay questions for exams.

Manual of Tests

A test bank of more than 1,500 multiple-choice questions has been developed to accompany the text. The questions provide thorough coverage of the chapter material, including opening vignettes and IMC, Global, Diversity, and Ethical Perspectives.

Computerized Test Bank

A computerized version of the test bank is available to adopters of the text.

Instructor CD-ROM

This exciting presentation CD-ROM allows the professor to customize a multimedia lecture with original material from the supplements package. It includes video clips, commercials, ads and art from the text, electronic slides and acetates, the computerized test bank, and the print supplements.

Electronic Slides

A disk containing nearly 300 PowerPoint® slides is available to adopters of the sixth edition for electronic presentations. These slides contain lecture notes, charts, graphs, and other instructional materials.

Home Page

A home page on the Internet can be found at

www.mhhe.business/marketing/

It contains Web Exploration Links (hot links to other websites) as well as various other items of interest. For instructors, the home page will offer updates of examples, chapter opener vignettes and IMC, Global, and Ethical Perspectives; additional sources of advertising and promotion information; and downloads of key supplements. Adopters will be able to communicate directly with the authors through the site (contact your McGraw-Hill/ Irwin representative for your password).

Four-Color Transparencies

Each adopter may request a set of over 100 four-color acetate transparencies that present print ads, photoboards, sales promotion offers, and other materials that do not appear in the text. A number of important models or charts appearing in the text are also provided as color transparencies. Slip sheets are included with each transparency to give the instructor useful background information about the illustration and how it can be integrated into the lecture.

Video Supplements

A video supplement package has been developed specifically for classroom use with this text. The first set of videos contains nearly 200 television and radio commercials that are examples of creative advertising. It can be used to help the instructor explain a particular concept or principle or give more insight into how a company executes its advertising strategy. Most of the commercials are tied to the chapter openings, IMC and Global Perspectives, or specific examples cited in the text. Insights and/or background information about each commercial are provided in the instructor's manual written specifically for the videos. The second set of videos contains longer segments on the advertising and promotional strategies of various companies and industries. Included on this video are three segments showing campaigns chosen as Ogilvy Award Winners by the Advertising Research Foundation. Each segment shows how research was used to guide the development of an effective advertising campaign. Other segments include highlights of promotions that won Reggie Awards (given each year to the best sales promotion campaigns) and case studies of the integrated marketing communications programs used by the U.S. Army, Skyy Spirits, Mazda, and Chicken of the Sea International.

Acknowledgments

While this sixth edition represents a tremendous amount of work on our part, it would not have become a reality without the assistance and support of many other people. Authors tend to think they have the best ideas, approach, examples, and organization for writing a great book. But we quickly learned that there is always room for our ideas to be improved on by others. A number of colleagues provided detailed, thoughtful reviews that were immensely helpful in making this a better book. We are very grateful to the following individuals who worked with us on earlier editions. They include

Lauranne Buchanan, *University of Illinois*
Roy Busby, *University of North Texas*
Lindell Chew, *University of Missouri–St. Louis*
Catherine Cole, *University of Iowa*
John Faier, *Miami University*
Raymond Fisk, *Oklahoma State University*
Geoff Gordon, *University of Kentucky*
Donald Grambois, *Indiana University*
Stephen Grove, *Clemson University*
Ron Hill, *University of Portland*
Paul Jackson, *Ferris State College*

Don Kirchner, *California State University–Northridge*
Clark Leavitt, *Ohio State University*
Charles Overstreet, *Oklahoma State University*
Paul Prabhaker, *Depaul University, Chicago*
Scott Roberts, *Old Dominion University*
Harlan Spotts, *Northeastern University*
Mary Ann Stutts, *Southwest Texas State University*
Terrence Witkowski, *California State University–Long Beach*
Robert Young, *Northeastern University*
Terry Bristol, *Oklahoma State University*
Roberta Ellins, *Fashion Institute of Technology*
Robert Erffmeyer, *University of Wisconsin–Eau Claire*
Alan Fletcher, *Louisiana State University*
Jon B. Freiden, *Florida State University*
Patricia Kennedy, *University of Nebraska*
Susan Kleine, *Arizona State University*
Tina Lowry, *Rider University*
Elizabeth Moore-Shay, *University of Illinois*
Notis Pagiavlas, *University of Texas–Arlington*
William Pride, *Texas A&M University*
Joel Reedy, *University of South Florida*
Denise D. Schoenbachler, *Northern Illinois University*
James Swartz, *California State University–Pomona*
Robert H. Ducoffe, *Baruch College*
Robert Gulonsen, *Washington University*
Craig Andrews, *Marquette University*
Subir Bandyopadhyay, *University of Ottawa*
Beverly Brockman, *University of Alabama*
John H. Murphy II, *University of Texas–Austin*
Glen Reicken, *East Tennessee State University*
Michelle Rodriquez, *University of Central Florida*
Elaine Scott, *Bluefield State College*

We are particularly grateful to the individuals who provided constructive comments on how to make this edition better: Craig Andrews, *Marquette University;* Christopher Cakebread, *Boston University;* Robert Cutter, *Cleveland State University;* Don Dickinson, *Portland State University;* Karen James, *Louisiana State University–Shreveport;* Robert Kent, *University of Delaware;* Herbert Jack Rotfield, *Auburn University;* Lisa Sciulli, *Indiana University of Pennsylvania;* Janice Taylor, *Miami University,* and Richard Wingerson, *Florida Atlantic University.* A very special thank-you goes to Roberta Elins and the faculty at the Fashion Institute of Technology, who provided many useful insights and interesting examples.

We would also like to acknowledge the cooperation we received from many people in the business, advertising, and media communities. This book contains several hundred ads, illustrations, charts, and tables that have been provided by advertisers and/or their agencies, various publications, and other advertising and industry organizations. Many individuals took time from their busy schedules to provide us with requested materials and gave us permission to use them. A special thanks to all of you.

A manuscript does not become a book without a great deal of work on the part of a publisher. Various individuals at Irwin/McGraw-Hill have been involved with this project over the past several years. Our sponsoring editor on the sixth edition, Barrett Koger, provided valuable guidance and was instrumental in making sure this was much more than just a token revision. A special thanks goes to Nancy Barbour, our developmental editor, for all of her efforts and for being so great to work with. Thanks also to Natalie Ruffatto for doing a superb job of managing the production process. We also want to acknowledge the outstanding work of Charlotte Goldman for her help in obtaining permissions for most of the ads that appear throughout the book. Thanks to the other members of the product team, Keith McPherson, Judy Kausal, Joyce Chappetto, Debra Sylvester, and Craig Atkins, for all their hard work on this edition.

We would like to acknowledge the support we have received from the College of Business at San Diego State University. As always, a great deal of thanks goes to our families for putting up with us while we were revising this book. Once again we look forward to returning to normal. Finally, we would like to acknowledge each other for making it through this ordeal again. Our mother to whom we dedicate this edition, will be happy to know that we still get along after all this—though it is definitely getting tougher and tougher.

George E. Belch
Michael A. Belch

Your guide through the exciting

Why It's a Powerful Learning Tool

The sixth edition continues to provide you with the most comprehensive and current text on the market in the area of advertising and promotion from an integrated marketing communications perspective. The following features in each chapter enhance students' understanding of the material as well as their reading enjoyment.

Chapter Openers

Chapter Objectives are provided at the beginning of each chapter to identify the major areas and points covered in the chapter and guide the learning effort. Each chapter also begins with a **Chapter Opening Vignette** that shows the effective use of Integrated Marketing Communications by a company or ad agency or discusses an interesting issue that is relevant to the chapter. Some of the companies profiled in the opening vignettes include the U.S. Army, BMW, Samsung, TiVo, Red Bull, Nike, Skyy Spirits, and *Rolling Stone* magazine.

An Introduction to Integrated Marketing Communications

1

Chapter Objectives

1. To examine the promotional function and the growing importance of advertising and other promotional elements in the marketing programs of domestic and foreign companies.
2. To introduce the concept of integrated marketing communications (IMC) and consider how it has evolved.
3. To examine reasons for the increasing importance of the IMC perspective in planning and executing advertising and promotional programs.
4. To introduce the various elements of the promotional mix and consider their roles in an IMC program.
5. To examine how various marketing and promotional elements must be coordinated to communicate effectively.
6. To introduce a model of the IMC planning process and examine the steps in developing a marketing communications program.

"An Army of One" Campaign Accomplishes Its Mission

During the early to mid 1990s, the U.S. Army had little trouble attracting enough young men to enlist for military service. The collapse of the Soviet Union had all but ended, and the cold war and military warfare was becoming more high-

tech, which meant that fewer soldiers were needed. Thus, the Army was downsized by 40 percent, making it easy to reach modest recruitment goals. Recruitment advertising used the "Be All That You Can Be" tagline and relied primarily on expensive television commercials to deliver the self-actualization message. The ads also emphasized how joining the Army provided opportunities for career training, college scholarships, and other financial incentives.

While its recruitment marketing strategy worked well in the early to mid '90s, by the later part of the decade the Army found itself losing the battle to recruit America's youth. The military recruiting environment had changed as the booming economy of the '90s created many other opportunities for high school graduates. The Army's financial package was not enough to attract qualified recruits, and many high school graduates were not willing to endure the demands of basic training. However, the core challenge facing the Army was deeply rooted negative perceptions of the military. Research showed that 63 percent of young adults 17–24 said there was no way they would enlist in the military, and only 12 percent indicated an interest in military service. Comments such as, "not for people like me," "for losers," and, "only for those with no other options" were typical of the feelings young people held toward military service. Moreover, even for many of those who would consider enlisting in the service, the Army was their fourth choice among the branches of the military as it had major image problems on key attributes considered important in a post-high school opportunity.

All of these factors resulted in the Army missing its recruiting goals three out of the five years during the late '90s, despite spending more money on recruitment advertising than any branch of the military. In early 2000, Secretary of the Army Louis Caldera announced that: "We are totally changing the way we do Army advertising. We have to adopt the kinds of practices that the best marketing companies use to attract today's youth." His new marketing strategy called for a new advertising campaign and a new media strategy that included less reliance on television ads and greater use of the Internet, and "e-recruiting" to complement the Army's transformation into a more mobile, high-tech force. In June of 2000, Caldera announced the hiring of Leo Burnett USA, Chicago, as its new agency, replacing Young & Rubicam which had created Army ads since 1987.

One of the first decisions facing Leo Burnett was whether to continue with the long running "Be All That You Can Be" tagline. Although highly recognizable, the agency felt that the

WALKTHROUGH PREFACE

world of advertising and promotion.

Exhibit 2-21 Advertising for designer clothing

Branding Choosing a brand name for a product is important from a promotional perspective because brand names communicate attributes and meaning. Marketers search for brand names that can communicate product concepts and help position the product in customers' minds. Names such as Safeguard (soap), I Can't Believe It's Not Butter! (margarine), Easy-Off (oven cleaner), Arrid (antiperspirant), and Spic and Span (floor cleaner) all clearly communicate the benefits of using these products and at the same time create images extending beyond the names themselves. (What about La-Z-Boy?)

One important role of advertising in respect to branding strategies is creating and maintaining **brand equity,** which can be thought of as an intangible asset of added value or goodwill that results from the favorable image, impressions of differentiation, and/or the strength of consumer attachment to a company name, brand name, or trademark. Brand equity allows a brand to earn greater sales volume and/or higher margins than it could without the name, providing the company with a competitive advantage. The strong equity position a company and/or its brand enjoys is often reinforced through advertising. For example, Rado watches command a premium price because of their high quality as well as the strong brand equity they have developed through advertising (Exhibit 2-22).

Exhibit 2-22 Rado creates strong brand equity through advertising

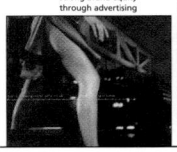

Packaging Packaging is another aspect of product strategy that has become incre
tional benefit
role and funct
emphasis of
sions are mad
as two-thirds
The package
must make a

59 Chapter Two The Role of IMC in the Marketing Process

Exhibit 8-9 The major selling idea behind this Polaroid commercial is that the picture is only the beginning of the story

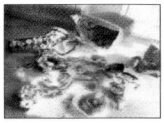

home for lunch. But in a sultry voice she tells him to look in his briefcase, saying "I left you something this morning." He pulls out a Polaroid photo, his eyes widen, and he says, "I'll be there in 10 minutes."[7] Another humorous spot from the campaign shows a dog, wrongfully being scolded for upsetting the trash while an evil-looking cat sneers from the other side of the kitchen. The owner leaves, and the cat goes for the trash once again. However, this time the dog takes a Polaroid snapshot of the cat, astride the trash with a chicken bone in its mouth, and then patiently waits, incriminating photo in mouth, as the door opens and the owner returns. "Oh dear," we hear as the picture fades (Exhibit 8-9).

Many copy platforms also include supporting information and requirements (brand identifications, disclaimers, and the like) that should appear in any advertising message. This information may be important in ensuring uniformity across various executions of the ads used in a campaign or in meeting any legal requirements. One of the major challenges for the creative team is determining the major selling idea that will be used as the basis of the campaign. We examine below some approaches often used for determining the major selling idea and campaign theme.

The Search for the Major Selling Idea

An important part of creative strategy is determining the central theme that will become the **major selling idea** of the ad campaign. As A. Jerome Jeweler states in his book *Creative Strategy in Advertising*:

> The major selling idea should emerge as the strongest singular thing you can say about your product or service. This should be the claim with the broadest and most meaningful appeal to your target audience. Once you determine this message, be certain you can live with it; be sure it stands strong enough to remain the central issue in every ad and commercial in the campaign.[27]

Some advertising experts argue that for an ad campaign to be effective it must contain a big idea that attracts the consumer's attention, gets a reaction, and sets the advertiser's product or service apart from the competition's. Well-known adman John O'Toole describes the *big idea* as "that flash of insight that synthesizes the purpose of the strategy, joins the product benefit with consumer desire in a fresh, involving way, brings the subject to life, and makes the reader or audience stop, look, and listen."[28]

255 Chapter Eight Creative Strategy, Planning and Development

Chapter Pedagogy

Four-Color visuals throughout the book consist of photoboards, commercial shots, charts, graphs, and over 400 print ads. **Key terms** are highlighted in boldface throughout the text and listed at the end of each chapter with a page reference. **Chapter summaries** serve as a quick review of important topics covered and as a study guide. **Discussion questions** at the end of each chapter give students an opportunity to test their understanding of the material and to apply it. These questions can also serve as a basis for class discussion or assignments.

A Basic Model of Communication

Over the years, a basic model of the various elements of the communication process has evolved, as shown in Figure 5-1.[2] Two elements represent the major participants in the communication process, the sender and the receiver. Another two are the major communication tools, message and channel.

Figure 5-1 A model of the communication process

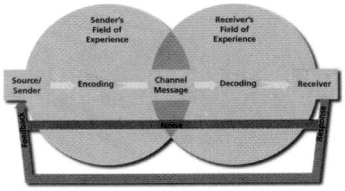

Five The Communication Process

Key Terms

selectivity, 395
gatefolds, 398
bleed pages, 398
split runs, 401
controlled-circulation basis, 405
pass-along readership, 405
total audience/readership, 406
magazine networks, 408
multimagazine deals, 411
cross-media advertising, 411
selective binding, 411
ink-jet imaging, 412
display advertising, 416
classified advertising, 416
preprinted inserts, 416
city zone, 421
retail trading zone, 421
general advertising rates, 422
retail advertising rates, 422
standard advertising units (SAUs), 423
flat rates, 424
open-rate structure, 424
run of paper (ROP), 424
preferred position rate, 425
combination rates, 425

Discussion Questions

1. The vignette at the beginning of the chapter discusses how *Rolling Stone* magazine is undergoing major changes to update its image and make it more appealing to a younger audience. Evaluate the changes being made by *Rolling Stone* to reposition itself and the challenges the magazine faces in trying to compete against other magazines that are targeting young adults.

2. Discuss the role of newspapers and magazines in the development and implementation of an integrated marketing communications program. What advantages are offered by each medium?

3. What is meant by selectivity with regard to the purchase of advertising media? Discuss the various ways magazines offer selectivity to advertisers.

4. Choose a specific target market that an advertiser might want to reach. Discuss how magazines and/or newspapers might be used to reach this particular market in a cost effective manner.

5. IMC Perspective 12-1 discusses the challenges marketers targeting products and services to the young male market face in trying to reach this segment. Why do you think teenage males are such a difficult market to reach with magazines? Do you think a magazine such as *Stance* will be successful in appealing to the teen male market?

6. Discuss why many companies such as Nike, Kodak, Ford, Ikea and others are choosing to publish their own custom magazines. Do you think these custom publications are an effective way to reach their customers?

7. If you were purchasing magazine advertising space for a manufacturer of golf clubs such as Taylor-Made or Calloway, what factors would you consider? Would your selection of magazines be limited to golf publications? Why or why not?

8. Discuss how the use of newspapers as an advertising medium would differ for national versus local advertisers. Find examples of newspaper advertising used by a national and a local advertiser and evaluate the type of ad used by each.

9. Discuss the reasons why *USA Today* has become the leading national newspaper. What challenges do other national newspapers such as *The Wall Street Journal* and the *New York Times* face in trying to compete against *USA Today* for national advertising?

10. Why has newspaper readership in the United States been declining over the past decade? Do you think campaigns such as the Newspaper Association of America's "It all starts with newspapers" can help reverse the decline in newspaper readership among young people?

Real life examples

The authors have used many sources to find practical examples to use throughout the text. In addition to the integration of the strategy and rationale behind the ads and other types of promotion that are used for current examples of industry practice, there are special in-depth discussions highlighted in boxed sections. **IMC Perspectives** present in-depth discussion of particular issues related to the chapter material and show how companies are using integrated marketing communications. **Global Perspectives** are presented throughout the text in recognition of the increasing important of international marketing and the challenges of advertising and promotion and the role they play in the marketing programs of multinational marketers. **Ethical Perspectives** focus attention on important social issues and show how advertisers must take ethical considerations into account then planning and implementing advertising and promotional programs. **Diversity Perspectives** discuss the opportunities, as well as the challenges associated with marketers' efforts to reach culturally and ethnically diverse target markets. There are also a number of **Career Profiles** which highlight successful individuals working in various areas of the field of advertising and promotion.

IMC PERSPECTIVE 19-1

The ARF David Ogilvy Research Awards—No Longer Just Ad Campaign Awards

One of the most prestigious awards an advertiser can receive is the David Ogilvy Award. The award is given by the Advertising Research Foundation (ARF) in honor of researcher-turned-adman David Ogilvy, whose own work always stressed the role of research in developing, evaluating, and improving advertising. To win an Ogilvy Award, the candidate must demonstrate how research was used in developing a program and show marketing success. Awards are given in three areas—(1) services, (2) durables, and (3) packaged goods—and an overall grand-prize winner is announced. Judges come from academia, advertising agencies, companies, and research firms. This year's winners included:

- *Grand Winner: Robert Wood Johnson Foundation—"The Covering Kids Campaign."* In 1997 the federal government allocated money to each state to offer health coverage to children in low-income families. Unfortunately, much of this money went unused. The Robert Wood Johnson Foundation used its own monies to determine why this was the case, as well as to develop a campaign to communicate to parents. The foundation worked with Wirthlin Worldwide, a marketing research company, to determine the motivations, or lack of motivations, for taking advantage of this opportunity. The research demonstrated that financial aid and emotional issues were involved and that while low-income families were concerned with insuring their children, there was a lack of knowledge of the program as well as a number of misperceptions regarding qualifications. In addition, semantics mattered, as many families felt that "insurance" was synonymous with high cost and that if it was free, it was a "handout."

Based on this research, the advertising agency of Greer, Margolis, Mitchell, Burns and Associates developed a "values approach" in which ad messages stated "You could be eligible" and funneled callers directly into the program. The campaign included TV, outdoor, radio, and print ads differentiated for various ethnic groups. An Internet site was also included, as was a toll-free number to call for more assistance.

The results reflected the value of the research, as 8 out of every 10 persons who called the national hotline did so after seeing a Covering Kids ad, and the number of calls doubled during the time the ad campaign ran. Calls to regional toll-free numbers increased by as much as 745 percent!

- *Distinguished Finalist: United States Navy—"An URL in Every Port."* Joining the armed services is not an easy decision. The U.S. Navy had found that its competition included colleges, trade schools, the workforce, and other branches of military services. To compete successfully, the Navy felt that it had to conduct research into the motivations and attitudes of high school students—its primary target audience. Working with advertising agency Campbell-Ewald, the Navy created an extensive research portfolio that included interviews with Navy personnel, recruiters, and decision influencers such as parents and teachers. Focus groups, brand metaphor exercises, and a quantitative survey of teens were all used to explore the values and attitudes of teens. The resulting psychographic profile showed that "Adventurers" (active, fun-oriented outdoor types), "Vocationalists" (concerned about the future and looking for vocational skills to improve their job prospects), and "Independent Skill Seekers" (uncertain about their future, looking for vocational

Aprendiendo
Aprendiendo
Aprendiendo

WALKTHROUGH PREFACE

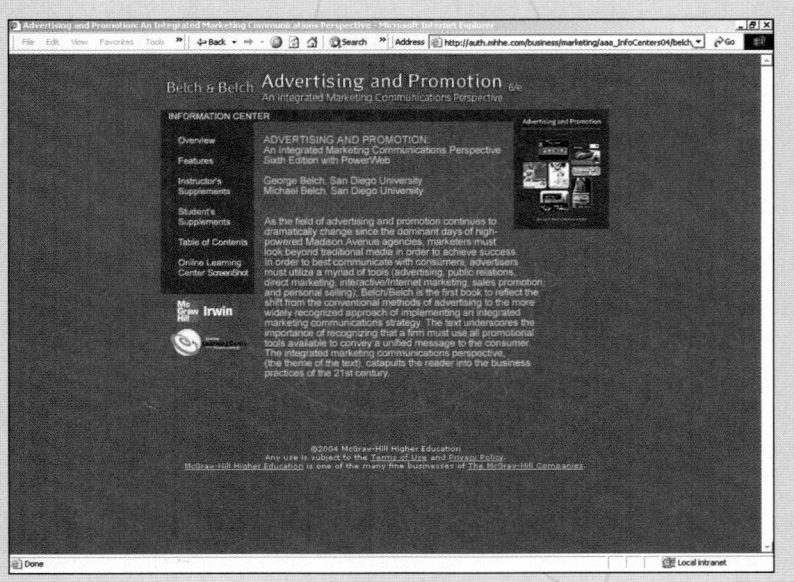

Online Learning Center

www.mhhe.com/belch04

For Instructors

The resources available online for Instructors include downloadable versions of the Instructor's Manual, Video Instructor's Manual, Cases and case teaching notes, Video Clips, and notes for using the Campaign Planner.

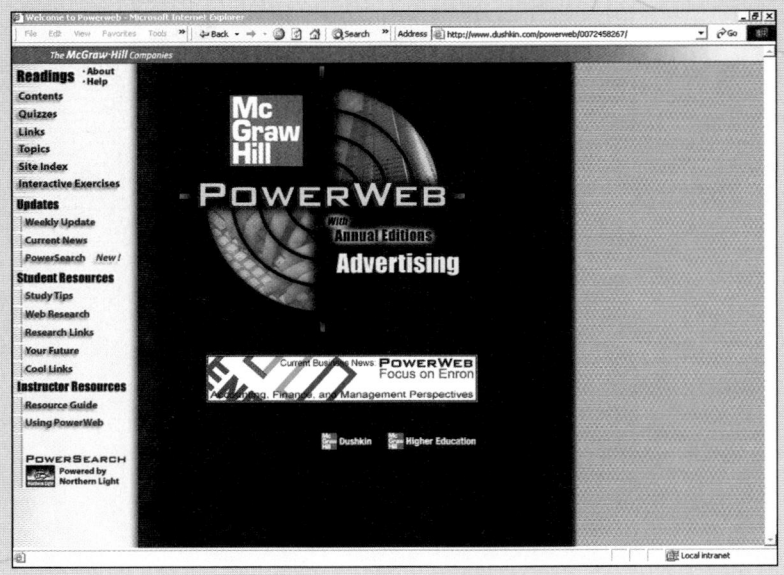

For Students

A wealth of study tools is available for students at the site including self-assessing quizzes, an online Campaign Planner, key terms drills, and cases.

Both instructors and students also have the opportunity to access **PowerWeb for Advertising** through our website. Daily news feeds, chapter specific article updates, and quizzes, are only a few of the resources available there.

Contents in Brief

Part One

Introduction to Integrated Marketing Communications

Chapter One
An Introduction to Integrated Marketing Communications 2

Chapter Two
The Role of IMC in the Marketing Process 36

Part Two

Integrated Marketing Program Situation Analysis

Chapter Three
Organizing for Advertising and Promotion: The Role of Ad Agencies and Other Marketing Communication Organizations 66

Chapter Four
Perspectives on Consumer Behavior 102

Part Three

Analyzing the Communication Process

Chapter Five
The Communication Process 136

Chapter Six
Source, Message, and Channel Factors 164

Part Four

Objectives and Budgeting for Integrated Marketing Communications Programs

Chapter Seven
Establishing Objectives and Budgeting for the Promotional Program 192

Part Five

Developing the Integrated Marketing Communications Program

Chapter Eight
Creative Strategy: Planning and Development 234

Chapter Nine
Creative Strategy: Implementation and Evaluation 264

Chapter Ten
Media Planning and Strategy 298

Chapter Eleven
Evaluation of Broadcast Media 348

Chapter Twelve
Evaluation of Print Media 390

Chapter Thirteen
Support Media 430

Chapter Fourteen
Direct Marketing 460

Chapter Fifteen
The Internet and Interactive Media 484

Chapter Sixteen
Sales Promotion 510

Chapter Seventeen
Public Relations, Publicity, and Corporate Advertising 562

Chapter Eighteen
Personal Selling 596

Part Six

Monitoring, Evaluation, and Control

Chapter Nineteen
Measuring the Effectiveness of the Promotional Program 618

Part Seven

Special Topics and Perspectives

Chapter Twenty
International Advertising and Promotion 656

Chapter Twenty-one
Regulation of Advertising and Promotion 708

Chapter Twenty-two
Evaluating the Social, Ethical, and Economic Aspects of Advertising and Promotion 748

Glossary of Advertising and Promotion Terms GL1

Endnotes EN1

Credits and Acknowledgments CR

Name and Company Index IN

Subject Index IN13

Contents

Part One

Introduction to Integrated Marketing Communications 2

Chapter One
An Introduction to Integrated Marketing Communications 2

The Growth of Advertising and Promotion 5
CAREER PROFILE: Thomas L. Aiello, Vice President, Account Supervisor—Leo Burnett, USA 6
What Is Marketing? 7
Marketing Focuses on Exchange 7
Relationship Marketing 7
The Marketing Mix 8
Integrated Marketing Communications 9
The Evolution of IMC 9
Reasons for the Growing Importance of IMC 11
The Role of IMC in Branding 14
The Promotional Mix: The Tools for IMC 16
Advertising 16
Direct Marketing 18
Interactive/Internet Marketing 20
Sales Promotion 21
Publicity/Public Relations 22
Personal Selling 23
Promotional Management 24
The IMC Planning Process 25
Review of the Marketing Plan 25
Promotional Program Situation Analysis 25
Analysis of the Communications Process 29
Budget Determination 31
Developing the Integrated Marketing Communications Program 31
Monitoring, Evaluation, and Control 32
Perspective and Organization of This Text 32

Chapter Two
The Role of IMC in the Marketing Process 36

Marketing Strategy and Analysis 40
Opportunity Analysis 40
Competitive Analysis 41
Target Market Selection 42
The Target Marketing Process 43
Identifying Markets 43
Market Segmentation 44
Selecting a Target Market 50
Market Positioning 51
Developing the Marketing Planning Program 58
Product Decisions 58
Price Decisions 60
Distribution Channel Decisions 62
Developing Promotional Strategies: Push or Pull? 62
CAREER PROFILE: Fiona Morrisson, Director, Corporate Communications, JetBlue Airways 63
The Role of Advertising and Promotion 64

Part Two

Integrated Marketing Program Situation Analysis 66

Chapter Three
Organizing for Advertising and Promotion: The Role of Ad Agencies and Other Marketing Communication Organizations 66

Participants in the Integrated Marketing Communications Process: An Overview 69

Organizing for Advertising and Promotion in the Firm: The Client's Role 71
The Centralized System 71
The Decentralized System 72
In-House Agencies 75
Advertising Agencies 77
The Ad Agency's Role 78
Types of Ad Agencies 79
Other Types of Agencies and Services 83
Agency Compensation 85
Commissions from Media 85
Fee, Cost, and Incentive-Based Systems 87
Percentage Charges 88
The Future of Agency Compensation 88
Evaluating Agencies 88
Gaining and Losing Clients 90
Specialized Services 94
Direct-Response Agencies 94
Sales Promotion Agencies 94
Public Relations Firms 95
Interactive Agencies 95
Collateral Services 96
CAREER PROFILE: Josh Rose, Senior Vice President, Director of iDeutsch 97
Marketing Research Companies 98
Integrated Marketing Communications Services 98
Pros and Cons of Integrated Services 98
Responsibility for IMC: Agency versus Client 99

Chapter Four
Perspectives on Consumer Behavior 102

An Overview of Consumer Behavior 105
The Consumer Decision-Making Process 107
Problem Recognition 107
Examining Consumer Motivations 109
Information Search 112
Perception 113
Alternative Evaluation 114
Attitudes 117
Integration Processes and Decision Rules 119
Purchase Decision 120
Postpurchase Evaluation 120
Variations in Consumer Decision Making 122
The Consumer Learning Process 123
Behavioral Learning Theory 123
Cognitive Learning Theory 126
Environmental Influences on Consumer Behavior 127
Culture 127
Subcultures 128
Reference Groups 129
Situational Determinants 130
Alternative Approaches to Consumer Behavior 131
New Methodologies 131
New Insights 131

Part Three
Analyzing the Communication Process 136

Chapter Five
The Communication Process 136

The Nature of Communication 139
A Basic Model of Communication 139
Source Encoding 141
Message 141
Channel 143
Receiver/Decoding 143
Noise 145
Response/Feedback 145
Analyzing the Receiver 145
Identifying the Target Audience 146
The Response Process 147
Traditional Response Hierarchy Models 147
Alternative Response Hierarchies 150
Implications of the Alternative Response Models 153
Understanding Involvement 153
The FCB Planning Model 154
Cognitive Processing of Communications 157
The Cognitive Response Approach 157
The Elaboration Likelihood Model 158
Summarizing the Response Process and the Effects of Advertising 161

Chapter Six
Source, Message, and Channel Factors 164

Promotional Planning through the Persuasion Matrix 166

Source Factors 168
Source Credibility 168
Source Attractiveness 172
Source Power 177
Message Factors 179
Message Structure 179
Message Appeals 183
Channel Factors 187
Personal versus Nonpersonal Channels 187
Effects of Alternative Mass Media 187
Effects of Context and Environment 188
Clutter 188

Part Four

Objectives and Budgeting for Integrated Marketing Communications Programs 192

Chapter Seven
Establishing Objectives and Budgeting for the Promotional Program 192

The Value of Objectives 195
Communications 195
Planning and Decision Making 196
Measurement and Evaluation of Results 196
Determining Promotional Objectives 196
Marketing versus Communications Objectives 196
Sales versus Communications Objectives 198
Sales-Oriented Objectives 198
Communications Objectives 202
DAGMAR: An Approach to Setting Objectives 206
Characteristics of Objectives 206
Assessment of DAGMAR 208
Problems in Setting Objectives 209
Improving Promotional Planners' Use of Objectives 209
Setting Objectives for the IMC Program 210
Establishing and Allocating the Promotional Budget 211
Establishing the Budget 211
Budgeting Approaches 217
Allocating the Budget 228

Part Five

Developing the Integrated Marketing Communications Program 234

Chapter Eight
Creative Strategy: Planning and Development 234

The Importance of Creativity in Advertising 237
Advertising Creativity 239
What Is Creativity? 239
Different Perspectives on Advertising Creativity 239
Planning Creative Strategy 243
The Creative Challenge 243
Taking Creative Risks 243
Creative Personnel 244
The Creative Process 244
Account Planning 246
Inputs to the Creative Process: Preparation, Incubation, Illumination 247
Inputs to the Creative Process: Verification, Revision 251
Creative Strategy Development 251
Advertising Campaigns 251
Copy Platform 254
The Search for the Major Selling Idea 255

Chapter Nine
Creative Strategy: Implementation and Evaluation 264

Appeals and Execution Styles 266
Advertising Appeals 267
Advertising Execution 275
Creative Tactics 283
Creative Tactics for Print Advertising 283
Creative Tactics for Television 286
Client Evaluation and Approval of Creative Work 291
Guidelines for Evaluating Creative Output 292
CAREER PROFILE: Louise Stix, Manager of Corporate Communications and Creative Services, Savin Corporation 295

Chapter Ten
Media Planning and Strategy 298

An Overview of Media Planning 301
Some Basic Terms and Concepts 301
The Media Plan 303
Problems in Media Planning 303
Developing the Media Plan 306
Market Analysis and Target Market Identification 306
To Whom Shall We Advertise? 306
What Internal and External Factors Are Operating? 309
Where to Promote? 310
Establishing Media Objectives 312
Developing and Implementing Media Strategies 313
The Media Mix 313
Target Market Coverage 313
Geographic Coverage 314
Scheduling 314
Reach versus Frequency 316
Creative Aspects and Mood 321
Flexibility 323
Budget Considerations 323
Evaluation and Follow-Up 326
Computers in Media Planning 326
Computers in Market Analysis 328
Computers in Media Strategy Development 328
Characteristics of Media 331
APPENDIX A: Sources of Media Information 334
APPENDIX B: Media Plan for Bumble Bee Tuna 335

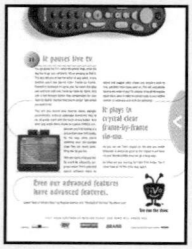

Chapter Eleven
Evaluation of Broadcast Media 348

Television 351
Advantages of Television 351
Limitations of Television 353
Buying Television Time 357
Network versus Spot 357
Methods of Buying Time 362
Selecting Time Periods and Programs 364
Cable Television 364
Measuring the TV Audience 370
Radio 377
Advantages of Radio 377
Limitations of Radio 380
Buying Radio Time 383
Time Classifications 383
Audience Information 385

Chapter Twelve
Evaluation of Print Media 390

The Role of Magazines and Newspapers 393
Magazines 393
Classifications of Magazines 393
Advantages of Magazines 395
Disadvantages of Magazines 401
Magazine Circulation and Readership 403
Audience Information and Research for Magazines 406
CAREER PROFILE: Greg Hancock, Sales Representative for *Rolling Stone* magazine 407
Purchasing Magazine Advertising Space 408
The Future for Magazines 409
Newspapers 413
Types of Newspapers 413
Types of Newspaper Advertising 416
Advantages of Newspapers 417
Limitations of Newspapers 420
The Newspaper Audience 421
Purchasing Newspaper Space 422
Newspaper Rates 423
The Future for Newspapers 425

Chapter Thirteen
Support Media 430

The Scope of the Support Media Industry 432
Out-of-Home Media 432
Outdoor Advertising 433
Additional Out-of-Home Media 436

In-Store Media 437
Miscellaneous Outdoor Media 437
Audience Measurement in Out-of-Home Media 437
Transit Advertising 440
Promotional Products Marketing 443
Advantages and Disadvantages of Promotional Products Marketing 443
Audience Measurement in Promotional Products Marketing 445
Yellow Pages Advertising 446
Other Media 448
Advertising in Movie Theaters 448
Product Placements in Movies and on TV 450
In-Flight Advertising 453
Miscellaneous Other Media 456

Chapter Fourteen
Direct Marketing 460

Direct Marketing 462
Defining Direct Marketing 463
The Growth of Direct Marketing 463
The Role of Direct Marketing in the IMC Program 465
CAREER PROFILE: Melissa L. Fisher, Vice President, Marketing and Communications Cox Target Media, Inc. 466
Direct-Marketing Objectives 467
Developing a Database 467
Direct-Marketing Strategies and Media 471
Direct Selling 478
Evaluating the Effectiveness of Direct Marketing 480
Advantages and Disadvantages of Direct Marketing 480

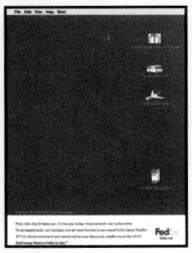

Chapter Fifteen
The Internet and Interactive Media 484

Defining the Internet 486
Developing an Internet Program 488
Web Participants 488
Web Objectives 490
Developing and Maintaining a Website 490
Communications Objectives 492
E-Commerce 494
The Internet and Integrated Marketing Communications 496
Advertising 496
Sales Promotion on the Internet 498
Personal Selling on the Internet 499
Public Relations on the Internet 499
Direct Marketing on the Internet 500
Measuring Effectiveness of the Internet 501
Audience Measures and Measures of Effectiveness 501
Sources of Measurement Data 504
Advantages and Disadvantages of the Internet 504
Additional Interactive Media 506
Wireless 508

Chapter Sixteen
Sales Promotion 510

The Scope and Role of Sales Promotion 513
The Growth of Sales Promotion 514
Reasons for the Increase in Sales Promotion 515
Concerns about the Increased Role of Sales Promotion 520
Consumer Franchise-Building versus Nonfranchise-Building Promotions 520
Consumer-Oriented Sales Promotion 522
Objectives of Consumer-Oriented Sales Promotion 522
Consumer-Oriented Sales Promotion Techniques 526
Sampling 526
Couponing 529
Premiums 535
Contests and Sweepstakes 537
Refunds and Rebates 540
Bonus Packs 541
Price-Off Deals 541
Frequency Programs 541
Event Marketing 543
Summary of Consumer-Oriented Promotions and Marketer Objectives 543
Trade-Oriented Sales Promotion 544
Objectives of Trade-Oriented Sales Promotion 544
Types of Trade-Oriented Promotions 546
CAREER PROFILE: John Boyle, Marketing Analyst, Chicken of the Sea International 548

Coordinating Sales Promotion and Advertising 554
Budget Allocation 554
Coordination of Ad and Promotion Themes 555
Media Support and Timing 555
Sales Promotion Abuse 557

Chapter Seventeen
Public Relations, Publicity, and Corporate Advertising 562

Public Relations 564
The Traditional Definition of PR 564
The New Role of PR 565
Integrating PR into the Promotional Mix 566
Marketing Public Relations (MPR) Functions 566
The Process of Public Relations 568
Determining and Evaluating Public Attitudes 568
Establishing a PR Plan 569
Developing and Executing the PR Program 569
Advantages and Disadvantages of PR 576
Measuring the Effectiveness of PR 577
Publicity 579
The Power of Publicity 579
The Control and Dissemination of Publicity 581
Advantages and Disadvantages of Publicity 583
Measuring the Effectiveness of Publicity 583
Corporate Advertising 583
Objectives of Corporate Advertising 585
Types of Corporate Advertising 585
Advantages and Disadvantages of Corporate Advertising 592
Measuring the Effectiveness of Corporate Advertising 593

Chapter Eighteen
Personal Selling 596

The Scope of Personal Selling 598
The Role of Personal Selling in the IMC Program 599
Determining the Role of Personal Selling 599
The Nature of Personal Selling 600
Advantages and Disadvantages of Personal Selling 606
Combining Personal Selling with Other Promotional Tools 608
Combining Personal Selling and Advertising 608
Combining Personal Selling and Public Relations 609
Combining Personal Selling and Direct Marketing 610
Combining Personal Selling and Sales Promotion 611
Combining Personal Selling with the Internet 611
Evaluating the Personal Selling Effort 613
Criteria for Evaluating Personal Selling 613

Part Six

Monitoring, Evaluation, and Control

Chapter Nineteen
Measuring the Effectiveness of the Promotional Program 618

Arguments for and Against Measuring Effectiveness 621
Reasons to Measure Effectiveness 621
Reasons Not to Measure Effectiveness 623
Conducting Research to Measure Advertising Effectiveness 625
What to Test 625
When to Test 626
Where to Test 627
How to Test 628
The Testing Process 629
Concept Generation and Testing 629
Rough Art, Copy, and Commercial Testing 631
Pretesting of Finished Ads 633
CAREER PROFILE: John Hallward, President, Global Product Development Ipsos-ASI Inc, "The Advertising Research Company" 637
Market Testing of Ads 638
Establishing a Program for Measuring Advertising Effects 647
Problems with Current Research Methods 647
Essentials of Effective Testing 648

Measuring the Effectiveness of Other Program Elements 648
Measuring the Effectiveness of Sales Promotions 648
Measuring the Effectiveness of Nontraditional Media 650
Measuring the Effectiveness of Sponsorships 650
Measuring the Effectiveness of Other IMC Program Elements 651

Part Seven

Special Topics and Perspectives

Chapter Twenty
International Advertising and Promotion 656

The Importance of International Markets 659
The Role of International Advertising and Promotion 660
The International Environment 661
The Economic Environment 661
The Demographic Environment 664
The Cultural Environment 664
The Political/Legal Environment 666
Global versus Localized Advertising 668
Advantages of Global Marketing and Advertising 669
Problems with Global Advertising 670
When Is Globalization Appropriate? 672
Global Products, Local Messages 674
Decision Areas in International Advertising 677
Organizing for International Advertising 677
Agency Selection 678
Advertising Research 682
Creative Decisions 683
Media Selection 685
The Roles of Other Promotional Mix Elements in International Marketing 690
Sales Promotion 690
Personal Selling 693
Public Relations 694
The Internet 695
Appendix C: Promoting Overseas: What's Legal and What's Not 700

Chapter Twenty-one
Regulation of Advertising and Promotion 708

Self-Regulation 712
Self-Regulation by Advertisers and Agencies 712
Self-Regulation by Trade Associations 714
Self-Regulation by Businesses 715
The National Advertising Review Council and the NAD/NARB 716
Self-Regulation by Media 718
Appraising Self-Regulation 721
Federal Regulation of Advertising 722
Advertising and the First Amendment 722
Background on Federal Regulation of Advertising 723
The Federal Trade Commission 723
The Concept of Unfairness 724
Deceptive Advertising 725
The FTC's Handling of Deceptive Advertising Cases 730
Current Status of Federal Regulation by the FTC 733
Additional Federal Regulatory Agencies 734
The Lanham Act 738
State Regulation 740
Regulation of Other Promotional Areas 740
Sales Promotion 740
Marketing on the Internet 744

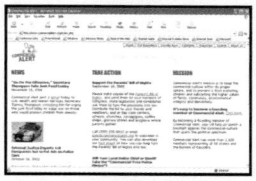

Chapter Twenty-two
Evaluating the Social, Ethical, and Economic Aspects of Advertising and Promotion 748

Advertising and Promotion Ethics 751
Social and Ethical Criticisms of Advertising 753
Advertising as Untruthful or Deceptive 754
Advertising as Offensive or in Bad Taste 754
Advertising and Children 758
Social and Cultural Consequences 762
Summarizing Social Effects 771
Economic Effects of Advertising 772
Effects on Consumer Choice 774
Effects on Competition 775
Effects on Product Costs and Prices 776
Summarizing Economic Effects 777

Glossary of Advertising and Promotion Terms GL1

Endnotes EN1

Credits and Acknowledgments CR

Name and Company Index IN

Subject Index IN13

Advertising and Promotion

AN INTEGRATED MARKETING COMMUNICATIONS PERSPECTIVE

An Introduction to Integrated Marketing Communications

1

Chapter Objectives

1. To examine the promotional function and the growing importance of advertising and other promotional elements in the marketing programs of domestic and foreign companies.
2. To introduce the concept of integrated marketing communications (IMC) and consider how it has evolved.
3. To examine reasons for the increasing importance of the IMC perspective in planning and executing advertising and promotional programs.
4. To introduce the various elements of the promotional mix and consider their roles in an IMC program.
5. To examine how various marketing and promotional elements must be coordinated to communicate effectively.
6. To introduce a model of the IMC planning process and examine the steps in developing a marketing communications program.

"An Army of One" Campaign Accomplishes Its Mission

During the early to mid 1990s, the U.S. Army had little trouble attracting enough young men to enlist for military service. The collapse of the Soviet Union had all but ended, and the cold war and military warfare was becoming more high-

tech, which meant that fewer soldiers were needed. Thus, the Army was downsized by 40 percent, making it easy to reach modest recruitment goals. Recruitment advertising used the "Be All That You Can Be" tagline and relied primarily on expensive television commercials to deliver the self-actualization message. The ads also emphasized how joining the Army provided opportunities for career training, college scholarships, and other financial incentives.

While its recruitment marketing strategy worked well in the early to mid '90s, by the later part of the decade the Army found itself losing the battle to recruit America's youth. The military recruiting environment had changed as the booming economy of the '90s created many other opportunities for high school graduates. The Army's financial package was not enough to attract qualified recruits, and many high school graduates were not willing to endure the demands of basic training. However, the core challenge facing the Army was deeply rooted negative perceptions of the military. Research showed that 63 percent of young adults 17–24 said there was no way they would enlist in the military, and only 12 percent indicated an interest in military service. Comments such as, "not for people like me," "for losers," and, "only for those with no other options" were typical of the feelings young people held toward military service. Moreover, even for many of those who would consider enlisting in the service, the Army was their fourth choice among the branches of the military as it had major image problems on key attributes considered important in a post-high school opportunity.

All of these factors resulted in the Army missing its recruiting goals three out of the five years during the late '90s, despite spending more money on recruitment advertising than any branch of the military. In early 2000, Secretary of the Army Louis Caldera announced that: "We are totally changing the way we do Army advertising. We have to adopt the kinds of practices that the best marketing companies use to attract today's youth." His new marketing strategy called for a new advertising campaign and a new media strategy that included less reliance on television ads and greater use of the Internet, and "e-recruiting" to complement the Army's transformation into a more mobile, high-tech force. In June of 2000, Caldera announced the hiring of Leo Burnett USA, Chicago, as its new agency, replacing Young & Rubicam which had created Army ads since 1987.

One of the first decisions facing Leo Burnett was whether to continue with the long running "Be All That You Can Be" tagline. Although highly recognizable, the agency felt that the

tagline had lost its relevance with young adults and could not be used to reposition the Army and forge a connection with this target audience. The agency came up with a new advertising and positioning theme that would be the basis for the integrated marketing campaign—"An Army of One." The creative strategy behind the theme is that it would bring to the forefront the idea that soldiers are the Army's most important resource and highlight that each individual can and does make a difference; that his/her contributions are important to the success of the whole team. The "An Army of One" campaign would send a message that a soldier is not nameless or faceless, but part of a unified group of individuals who together create the strength of the U.S. Army.

A major goal of the "An Army of One" campaign is to provide young adults with an accurate look into what it means to be a soldier in today's Army. A key phase of the campaign was called "Basic Training" which uses a reality based television format made popular by the hit show *Survivor.* The unscripted TV spots feature brief profiles of six actual army recruits as they progress through basic training, giving viewers a glimpse of their personal experiences and opinions as they transform from civilians into soldiers. The ads also encourage prospective recruits to visit the Army website (GoArmy.com) to experience a complete, in-depth multimedia "webisode" presentation including commentary from the recruits. The Web site was re-designed in early 2001 by Chemistri, an interactive agency which is a subsidiary of Leo Burnett, with the goal of making it a more effective recruitment tool. The site serves as a resource for potential recruits interested in learning about the Army and helps them overcome fears about basic training, increases their understanding of career opportunities available, and introduces them to soldiers similar to themselves.

The "An Army of One" campaign has been a great success. Although its media budget was 20 percent lower than the previous year, the Army fulfilled its 2001 recruiting goal of 115,000 new recruits one month early. Television, print, radio and online ads were effective in driving traffic to GoArmy.com as visits to the Web site doubled and online leads were up by 75 percent. The Web site has won several awards including a prestigious Cannes Cyber Lion and has become a focal point for the Army's recruitment efforts. The overall "An Army of One" integrated campaign also won an Effie Award as one of the most effective marketing programs of the year. Mission accomplished.

Sources: 2002 Effie Awards Brief of Effectiveness, Leo Burnett USA; Kate MacArthur, "The 'Army of One' meets 'Survivor,'" *Advertising Age,* www.AdAge.com February 02, 2001; Michael McCarthy, "Army enlists Net to be all it can be," *USA Today,* April 19, 2000, p. 10B.

The opening vignette illustrates how the roles of advertising and other forms of promotion are changing in the modern world of marketing. In the past, marketers such as the U.S. Army relied primarily on advertising through traditional mass media to promote their products. Today many companies are taking a different approach to marketing and promotion: They integrate their advertising efforts with a variety of other communication techniques such as websites on the Internet, direct marketing, sales promotion, publicity and public relations (PR), and event sponsorships. They are also recognizing that these communication tools are most effective when they are coordinated with other elements of the marketing program.

The various marketing communication tools used by the U.S. Army as part of its recruitment efforts exemplify how marketers are using an *integrated marketing communications* approach to reach their customers. The U.S. Army runs recruitment advertising in a variety of media including television, radio, magazines, newspapers, and billboards. Banner ads on the Internet as well as in other media encourage consumers to visit the GoArmy.com website which provides valuable information about the U.S. Army such as career paths, the enlistment process, and benefits (Exhibit 1-1). Direct marketing efforts include mailings to high school seniors and direct response

television ads which encourage young people to request more information and help generate leads for Army recruiters. Publicity for the U.S. Army is generated through press releases and public relation activities as well as in movies and television shows. At the local level the Army sponsors athletic events and participates in activities such as career fairs to reach its target audience as well as other groups or individuals who can influence its brand image. Recruiters work in local recruitment offices and are available to meet individually with potential recruits to answer questions and provide information about the Army. Recruitment efforts for the U.S. Army also include promotional incentives such as cash enlistment bonuses and educational benefits.

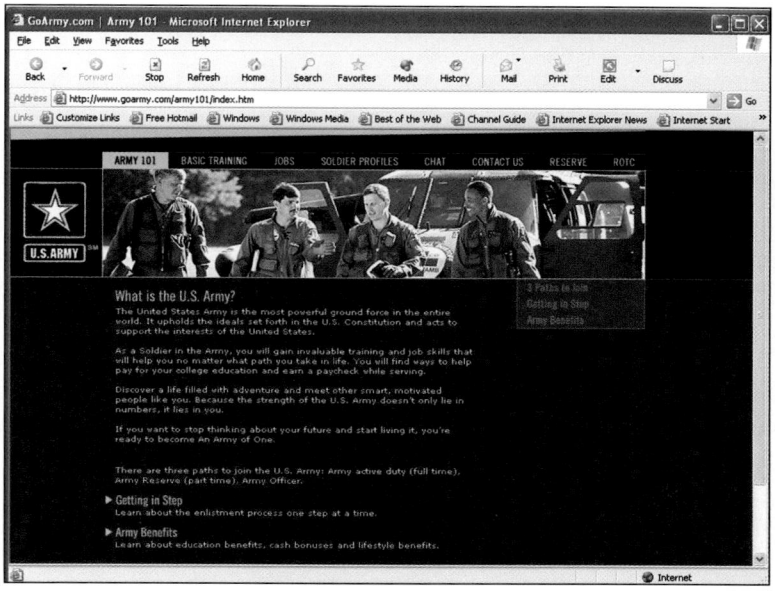

Exhibit 1-1 The U.S. Army provides potential recruits with valuable information through the GoArmy.com website on the Internet

The U.S. Army and thousands of other companies and organizations recognize that the way they must communicate with consumers and promote their products and services is changing rapidly. The fragmentation of mass markets, the explosion of new technologies that are giving consumers greater control over the communications process, the rapid growth of the Internet and electronic commerce, the emergence of global markets, and economic uncertainties are all changing the way companies approach marketing as well as advertising and promotion. Developing marketing communications programs that are responsive to these changes is critical to the success of every organization. However, advertising and other forms of promotion will continue to play an important role in the integrated marketing programs of most companies.

The Growth of Advertising and Promotion

Advertising and promotion are an integral part of our social and economic systems. In our complex society, advertising has evolved into a vital communications system for both consumers and businesses. The ability of advertising and other promotional methods to deliver carefully prepared messages to target audiences has given them a major role in the marketing programs of most organizations. Companies ranging from large multinational corporations to small retailers increasingly rely on advertising and promotion to help them market products and services. In market-based economies, consumers have learned to rely on advertising and other forms of promotion for information they can use in making purchase decisions.

Evidence of the increasing importance of advertising and promotion comes from the growth in expenditures in these areas. In 1980, advertising expenditures in the United States were $53 billion, and $49 billion was spent on sales promotion techniques such as product samples, coupons, contests, sweepstakes, premiums, rebates, and allowances and discounts to retailers. By 2002, nearly $240 billion was spent on local and national advertising, while spending on sales promotion programs targeted toward consumers and retailers increased to more than $250 billion.[1] Companies bombarded the U.S. consumer with messages and promotional offers, collectively spending more than $30 a week on every man, woman, and child in the country—nearly 50 percent more per capita than in any other nation.

Promotional expenditures in international markets have grown as well. Advertising expenditures outside the United States increased from $55 billion in 1980 to nearly $214 billion by 2002.[2] Both foreign and domestic companies spend billions more on sales promotion, personal selling, direct marketing, event sponsorships, and public relations, all important parts of a firm's marketing communications program.

The tremendous growth in expenditures for advertising and promotion reflects in part the growth of the U.S. and global economies and the efforts of expansion-minded marketers to take advantage of growth opportunities in various regions of the world.

CAREER PROFILE

Thomas L. Aiello

Vice President, Account Supervisor—Leo Burnett, USA

I graduated from the U.S. Military Academy in 1993 with a bachelor's of science degree in engineering management. After West Point, I spent five years serving in the U.S. Army in the armored cavalry where I led groups of 50 or more soldiers. As a Captain, I was awarded the Army Commendation Medal for my accomplishments during real-world deployment to Panama, Korea, and Kuwait. My military training and experiences taught me valuable skills about leadership, project management, and strategic decision making. But the most valuable thing the Army taught me was about people and what makes them tick—this human insight is the core of all good advertising.

In 1998, I transitioned to the corporate world and accepted a position with Leo Burnett in Chicago. I had interviewed with Fortune-500 companies for careers in sales, operations and even manufacturing. When I interviewed with Leo Burnett, the advertising job seemed the best fit for my skills and I was attracted to the strong values and culture of the agency. Working at a major agency like Leo Burnett has many advantages. We have big agency resources with a small agency attitude in terms of our adaptability to move the client's business forward. My first position at Leo Burnett was in the Client Service Department working with the Chicagoland McDonald's account team. I played an integral role in helping Chicago become one of McDonald's top sales regions.

In 1999, I began working on national assignments for McDonald's and was the catalyst in winning new McDonald's business for the agency. After a promotion to account supervisor, I took the lead role on the McDonald's Happy Meal calendar team. I helped develop programs to launch new products such as Mighty Kids Meals and the Kid Dessert Menu.

Although I was learning through experience and Leo Burnett's training program, I felt a need to expand my business skills. I began night school and in early 2002 I finished my MBA from Northwestern University's Kellogg Graduate School of Management evening program with majors in marketing and finance. The undertaking of working full-time and going to business school was tasking, but I was able to directly apply my class work to my job at Leo Burnett. I then moved to the U.S. Army account, where I supervise the ROTC business and all local advertising and field marketing. Working on an account like the U.S. Army is very rewarding given its importance in a post 9/11 world. Personally, it seemed like my years of military experience, advertising, and business school had come together.

"The Army is a great account because of the diversity of people I get to work with."

The Army is a great account because of the diversity of people I get to work with. My client partners are Army officers and Department of Defense civilians. They bring a great deal of experience and drive to the business. Our approach on Army is integrated, so I get to work with a diverse cross-functional team spanning creative, planning, media, web, PR, direct mail, sports marketing, and ethnic experts. Coordinating all of these areas into flawless execution is half art, half science, and a lot of hard work. My peers on the Army account created the Army of One integrated campaign. It has helped the Army achieve their recruiting mission over the last two years and won many ad industry awards.

I also do volunteer work for various organizations which help promote the advertising business such as the Ad Council which is a leading producer of public service advertisements (PSAs) since 1942. I am also an ambassador for the Advertising Education Foundation (AEF). The AEF is a not-for-profit organization created and supported by ad agencies to improve the perception and understanding of the social, historical, and economic roles of advertising. As an ambassador I visit students and faculty of various colleges and universities to talk on the advertising process and issues such as global advertising and ethics, gender, and ethnicity in advertising.

The growth in promotional expenditures also reflects the fact that marketers around the world recognize the value and importance of advertising and promotion. Promotional strategies play an important role in the marketing programs of companies as they attempt to communicate with and sell their products to their customers. To understand the roles advertising and promotion play in the marketing process, let us first examine the marketing function.

What Is Marketing?

Before reading on, stop for a moment and think about how you would define marketing. Chances are that each reader of this book will come up with a somewhat different answer, since marketing is often viewed in terms of individual activities that constitute the overall marketing process. One popular conception of marketing is that it primarily involves sales. Other perspectives view marketing as consisting of advertising or retailing activities. For some of you, market research, pricing, or product planning may come to mind.

While all these activities are part of marketing, it encompasses more than just these individual elements. The American Marketing Association (AMA), which represents marketing professionals in the United States and Canada, defines **marketing** as

> the process of planning and executing the conception, pricing, promotion, and distribution of ideas, goods, and services to create exchanges that satisfy individual and organizational objectives.[3]

Effective marketing requires that managers recognize the interdependence of such activities as sales and promotion and how they can be combined to develop a marketing program.

Marketing Focuses on Exchange

The AMA definition recognizes that **exchange** is a central concept in marketing.[4] For exchange to occur, there must be two or more parties with something of value to one another, a desire and ability to give up that something to the other party, and a way to communicate with each other. Advertising and promotion play an important role in the exchange process by informing consumers of an organization's product or service and convincing them of its ability to satisfy their needs or wants.

Not all marketing transactions involve the exchange of money for a tangible product or service. Nonprofit organizations such as charities, religious groups, the arts, and colleges and universities (probably including the one you are attending) receive millions of dollars in donations every year. Nonprofits often use ads like the one in Exhibit 1-2 to solicit contributions from the public. Donors generally do not receive any material benefits for their contributions; they donate in exchange for intangible social and psychological satisfactions such as feelings of goodwill and altruism.

Exhibit 1-2 Nonprofit organizations use advertising to solicit contributions and support

Relationship Marketing

Today, most marketers are seeking more than just a one-time exchange or transaction with customers. The focus of market-driven companies is on developing and sustaining *relationships* with their customers. This has led to a new emphasis on **relationship marketing,** which involves creating, maintaining, and enhancing long-term relationships with individual customers as well as other stakeholders for mutual benefit.[5]

The movement toward relationship marketing is due to several factors. First, companies recognize that customers have become much more demanding. Consumers desire *superior customer value,* which includes quality products and services that are competitively priced, convenient to purchase, delivered on time, and supported by excellent customer service. They also want personalized products and services that are tailored to their specific needs and wants. Advances in information technology, along with flexible manufacturing systems and new marketing processes, have led to **mass customization,** whereby a company can make a product or deliver a service in response to a particular customer's needs in a cost-effective

way.[6] New technology is making it possible to configure and personalize a wide array of products and services including computers, automobiles, clothing, golf clubs, cosmetics, mortgages, and vitamins. Consumers can log on to websites such as Mattel Inc.'s barbie.com and design their own Barbie pal doll or Fingerhut's myjewelry.com to design their own rings. Technological developments are also likely to make the mass customization of advertising more practical as well.[7]

Another major reason why marketers are emphasizing relationships is that it is often more cost-effective to retain customers than to acquire new ones. Marketers are giving more attention to the *lifetime value* of a customer because studies have shown that reducing customer defections by just 5 percent can increase future profit by as much as 30 to 90 percent.[8] Exhibit 1-3 shows an ad for Dell Computer, a company that recognizes the importance of developing long-term relationships with its customers.

The Marketing Mix

Marketing facilitates the exchange process and the development of relationships by carefully examining the needs and wants of consumers, developing a product or service that satisfies these needs, offering it at a certain price, making it available through a particular place or channel of distribution, and developing a program of promotion or communication to create awareness and interest. These four Ps—product, price, place (distribution), and promotion—are elements of the **marketing mix.** The basic task of marketing is combining these four elements into a marketing program to facilitate the potential for exchange with consumers in the marketplace.

The proper marketing mix does not just happen. Marketers must be knowledgeable about the issues and options involved in each element of the mix. They must also be aware of how these elements can be combined to provide an effective marketing program. The market must be analyzed through consumer research, and the resulting information must be used to develop an overall marketing strategy and mix.

The primary focus of this book is on one element of the marketing mix: the promotional variable. However, the promotional program must be part of a viable marketing strategy and be coordinated with other marketing activities. A firm can spend large sums on advertising or sales promotion, but it stands little chance of success if the product is of poor quality, is priced improperly, or does not have adequate distribution to consumers. Marketers have long recognized the importance of combining the elements of the marketing mix into a cohesive marketing strategy. Many companies also recognize the need to integrate their various marketing communications efforts, such as media advertising, direct marketing, sales promotion, and public relations, to achieve more effective marketing communications.

Exhibit 1-3 Dell Computer recognizes the importance of developing relationships with customers

For many years, the promotional function in most companies was dominated by mass-media advertising. Companies relied primarily on their advertising agencies for guidance in nearly all areas of marketing communication. Most marketers did use additional promotional and marketing communication tools, but sales promotion and direct-marketing agencies as well as package design firms were generally viewed as auxiliary services and often used on a per-project basis. Public relations agencies were used to manage the organization's publicity, image, and affairs with relevant publics on an ongoing basis but were not viewed as integral participants in the marketing communications process.

Many marketers built strong barriers around the various marketing and promotional functions and planned and managed them as separate practices, with different budgets, different views of the market, and different goals and objectives. These companies failed to recognize that the wide range of marketing and promotional tools must be coordinated to communicate effectively and present a consistent image to target markets.

The Evolution of IMC

During the 1980s, many companies came to see the need for more of a strategic integration of their promotional tools. These firms began moving toward the process of **integrated marketing communications (IMC),** which involves coordinating the various promotional elements and other marketing activities that communicate with a firm's customers.[9] As marketers embraced the concept of integrated marketing communications, they began asking their ad agencies to coordinate the use of a variety of promotional tools rather than relying primarily on media advertising. A number of companies also began to look beyond traditional advertising agencies and use other types of promotional specialists to develop and implement various components of their promotional plans.

Many agencies responded to the call for synergy among the promotional tools by acquiring PR, sales promotion, and direct-marketing companies and touting themselves as IMC agencies that offer one-stop shopping for all their clients' promotional needs.[10] Some agencies became involved in these nonadvertising areas to gain control over their clients' promotional programs and budgets and struggled to offer any real value beyond creating advertising. However, the advertising industry soon recognized that IMC was more than just a fad. Terms such as *new advertising, orchestration,* and *seamless communication* were used to describe the concept of integration.[11] A task force from the American Association of Advertising Agencies (the "4As") developed one of the first definitions of integrated marketing communications:

> a concept of marketing communications planning that recognizes the added value of a comprehensive plan that evaluates the strategic roles of a variety of communication disciplines—for example, general advertising, direct response, sales promotion, and public relations—and combines these disciplines to provide clarity, consistency, and maximum communications impact.[12]

The 4As' definition focuses on the process of using all forms of promotion to achieve maximum communication impact. However, advocates of the IMC concept, such as Don Schultz of Northwestern University, argue for an even broader perspective that considers *all sources of brand or company contact* that a customer or prospect has with a product or service.[13] Schultz and others note that the process of integrated marketing communications calls for a "big-picture" approach to planning marketing and promotion programs and coordinating the various communication functions. It requires that firms develop a total marketing communications strategy that recognizes how all of a firm's marketing activities, not just promotion, communicate with its customers.

Consumers' perceptions of a company and/or its various brands are a synthesis of the bundle of messages they receive or contacts they have, such as media advertisements, price, package design, direct-marketing efforts, publicity, sales promotions, websites, point-of-purchase displays, and even the type of store where a product or service is sold. The integrated marketing communications approach seeks to have all

of a company's marketing and promotional activities project a consistent, unified image to the marketplace. It calls for a centralized messaging function so that everything a company says and does communicates a common theme and positioning.

Many companies have adopted this broader perspective of IMC. They see it as a way to coordinate and manage their marketing communications programs to ensure that they give customers a consistent message about the company and/or its brands. For these companies, the IMC approach represents an improvement over the traditional method of treating the various marketing and communications elements as virtually separate activities. However, as marketers become more sophisticated in their understanding of IMC, they recognize that it offers more than just ideas for coordinating all elements of the marketing and communications programs. The IMC approach helps companies identify the most appropriate and effective methods for communicating and building relationships with their customers as well as other stakeholders such as employees, suppliers, investors, interest groups, and the general public.

Tom Duncan and Sandra Moriarty note that IMC is one of the "new-generation" marketing approaches being used by companies to better focus their efforts in acquiring, retaining, and developing relationships with customers and other stakeholders. They have developed a communication-based marketing model that emphasizes the importance of managing *all* corporate or brand communications, as they collectively create, maintain, or weaken the customer and stakeholder relationships that drive brand value.[14] Messages can originate at three levels—corporate, marketing, and marketing communications—since all of a company's corporate activities, marketing-mix activities, and marketing communications efforts have communication dimensions and play a role in attracting and keeping customers.

At the corporate level, various aspects of a firm's business practices and philosophies, such as its mission, hiring practices, philanthropies, corporate culture, and ways of responding to inquiries, all have dimensions that communicate with customers and other stakeholders and affect relationships. For example, Ben & Jerry's is a company that is rated very high in social responsibility and is perceived as a very good corporate citizen in its dealings with communities, employees, and the environment.[15] Ben & Jerry's capitalizes on its image as a socially responsible company by supporting various causes as well as community events (Exhibit 1-4).

At the marketing level, as was mentioned earlier, companies send messages to customers and other stakeholders through all aspects of their marketing mixes, not just promotion. Consumers make inferences about a product on the basis of elements such as its design, appearance, performance, pricing, service support, and where and how it is distributed. For example, a high price may symbolize quality to customers, as may the shape or design of a product, its packaging, its brand name, or the image of the stores in which it is sold. Montblanc uses classic design and a distinctive brand name as well as a

Exhibit 1-4 Ben & Jerry's has a very strong image and reputation as a socially responsible company

high price to position its watches and pens as high-quality, high-status products. This upscale image is enhanced by the company's strategy of distributing its products only through boutiques, jewelry stores, and other exclusive retail shops. Notice how the marketing-mix elements that help shape the brand's distinctive image are reflected in the Montblanc ad shown in Exhibit 1-5.

At the marketing communications level, Duncan and Moriarty note that all messages should be delivered and received on a platform of executional and strategic consistency in order to create coherent perceptions among customers and other stakeholders. This requires the integration of the various marketing communication's messages and the functions of various promotional facilitators such as ad agencies, public relations firms, sales promotion specialists, package design firms, direct-response specialists, and interactive agencies. The goal is to communicate with one voice, look, and image across all the marketing communications functions and to identify and position the company and/or the brand in a consistent manner.

Many companies are realizing that communicating effectively with customers and other stakeholders involves more than traditional marketing communications tools. Many marketers, as well as advertising agencies, are embracing the IMC approach and adopting total communication solutions to create and sustain relationships between companies or brands and their customers. Some academics and practitioners have questioned whether the IMC movement is just another management fad.[16] However, the IMC approach is proving to be a permanent change that offers significant value to marketers in the rapidly changing communications environment they are facing in the new millennium.[17] We will now discuss some of the reasons for the growing importance of IMC.

Exhibit 1-5 Montblanc uses a variety of marketing mix elements including price, product design, brand name, and distribution strategy to create a high-quality, upscale image for its watches

Reasons for the Growing Importance of IMC

The move toward integrated marketing communications is one of the most significant marketing developments that occurred during the 1990s, and the shift toward this approach is continuing as we begin the new century. The IMC approach to marketing communications planning and strategy is being adopted by both large and small companies and has become popular among firms marketing consumer products and services as well as business-to-business marketers. There are a number of reasons why marketers are adopting the IMC approach. A fundamental reason is that they understand the value of strategically integrating the various communications functions rather than having them operate autonomously. By coordinating their marketing communications efforts, companies can avoid duplication, take advantage of synergy among promotional tools, and develop more efficient and effective marketing communications programs. Advocates of IMC argue that it is one of the easiest ways for a company to maximize the return on its investment in marketing and promotion.[18]

The move to integrated marketing communications also reflects an adaptation by marketers to a changing environment, particularly with respect to consumers, technology, and media. Major changes have occurred among consumers with respect to demographics, lifestyles, media use, and buying and shopping patterns. For example, cable TV and more recently digital satellite systems have vastly expanded the number of channels available to households. Some of these channels offer 24-hour shopping networks; others contain 30- or 60-minute direct-response appeals known as *infomercials,* which look more like TV shows than ads. Every day more consumers are surfing the Internet's World Wide Web. Online services such as America Online and Microsoft Network provide information and entertainment as well as the opportunity to shop for and order a vast array of products and services. Marketers are responding by developing home pages on which they can advertise their products and services interactively as well as transact sales. For example, travelers can use American Airlines' AA.com website to plan flights, check for special fares, purchase tickets, and reserve seats, as well as make hotel and car-rental reservations (Exhibit 1-6).

Even as new technologies and formats create new ways for marketers to reach consumers, they are affecting the more traditional media. Television, radio, magazines,

Exhibit 1-6 Travelers can use American Airlines' website to purchase tickets and reserve seats

and newspapers are becoming more fragmented and reaching smaller and more selective audiences. A recent survey of leading U.S. advertising executives on trends that will shape the industry identified the segmentation of media audiences by new media technologies as the most important development.[19]

In addition to facing the decline in audience size for many media, marketers are facing the problem of consumers' being less responsive to traditional advertising. They recognize that many consumers are turned off by advertising and tired of being bombarded with sales messages. These factors are prompting many marketers to look for alternative ways to communicate with their target audiences, such as making their selling messages part of popular culture. For example, marketers often hire product placement firms to get their brands into TV shows and movies. MGM/United Artists created special scenes in the recent James Bond movie *Die Another Day* to feature the Aston Martin V12 Vanquish sports car. It is estimated that the British automaker, which is owned by Ford Motor Company, paid $70 million to have the car featured in the movie. In an arrangement with Columbia Pictures, Daimler-Benz agreed to spend several million dollars on commercials, private screenings, and other promotions to have the redesigned Mercedes-Benz E500 automobile featured in the movie *Men in Black II.*[20] IMC Perspective 1-1 discusses how marketers are finding new ways to reach consumers and disguise their promotional messages by making them part of popular culture.

The integrated marketing communications movement is also being driven by changes in the ways companies market their products and services. A major reason for the growing importance of the IMC approach is the ongoing revolution that is changing the rules of marketing and the role of the traditional advertising agency.[21] Major characteristics of this marketing revolution include:

- *A shifting of marketing dollars from media advertising to other forms of promotion, particularly consumer- and trade-oriented sales promotions.* Many marketers feel that traditional media advertising has become too expensive and is not cost-effective. Also, escalating price competition in many markets has resulted in marketers' pouring more of their promotional budgets into price promotions rather than media advertising.
- *A movement away from relying on advertising-focused approaches, which emphasize mass media such as network television and national magazines, to solve communication problems.* Many companies are turning to lower-cost, more targeted communication tools such as event marketing and sponsorships, direct mail, sales promotion, and the Internet as they develop their marketing communications strategies.
- *A shift in marketplace power from manufacturers to retailers.* Due to consolidation in the retail industry, small local retailers are being replaced by regional, national, and international chains. These large retailers are using their clout to demand larger promotional fees and allowances from manufacturers, a practice that often siphons money away from advertising. Moreover, new technologies such as checkout scanners give retailers information on the effectiveness of manufacturers' promotional programs. This is leading many marketers to shift their focus to promotional tools that can produce short-term results, such as sale promotion.
- *The rapid growth and development of database marketing.* Many companies are building databases containing customer names; geographic, demographic, and psychographic profiles; purchase patterns; media preferences; credit ratings; and other characteristics. Marketers are using this information to target consumers through a variety of

IMC PERSPECTIVE 1-1

What's the Buzz?

Consumers have long had a love-hate relationship with advertising. We enjoy watching music- and celebrity-laden commercials that are often more entertaining, humorous, or interesting than the programs they are sponsoring. We purchase magazines such as *Glamour, Vogue,* and *GQ,* which contain more ad pages than articles. But many consumers are tired of being bombarded with sales messages and are turned off by advertising. This is especially true of Generation Y, the age cohort born between 1979 and 1994, which is 60 million strong. The Generation Y cohort is three times the size of its Gen X predecessor, and its members constitute the biggest group to hit the U.S. market since the 72 million baby boomers, who are their parents. Having grown up in an even more media-saturated, brand-conscious world than their parents did, they respond to advertising differently and prefer to encounter marketing messages in different places or from different sources.

Marketers recognize that to penetrate the skepticism and capture the attention of the Gen Ys they have to bring their messages to these people in a different way. To do so, many companies are turning to a stealth-type strategy known as *buzz marketing,* whereby brand come-ons become part of popular culture and consumers themselves are lured into spreading the message. Marketers are turning their brands into carefully guarded secrets that are revealed to only a few people in each community. Each carefully cultivated recipient of the brand message becomes a powerful carrier, spreading the word to yet more carriers, who tell a few more, and so on. The goal of the marketer is to identify the trendsetters in each community and push them into talking up the brand to their friends and admirers. As the senior vice president at Bates U.S.A., who developed a buzz campaign for Lucky Strike cigarettes, notes, "Ultimately, the brand benefits because an accepted member of the social circle will always be far more credible than any communication that could come directly from the brand."

A number of marketers have used buzz marketing successfully. Rather than blitzing the airways with 30-second commercials for its new Focus subcompact, Ford Motor Company recruited 120 trendsetters in five key markets and gave them each a Focus to drive for six months. According to Ford's marketing communications manager, who planned and implemented the program, "We weren't looking for celebrities. We were looking for the assistants to celebrities, party planners, disc jockeys—the people who really seemed to influence what was cool." The recruits' duties were simply to be seen with the car, to hand out Focus-themed trinkets to anyone who expressed an interest

in the car, and to keep a record of where they took the car. The program helped Ford get the Focus off to a brisk start, selling 286,166 units in its first full year.

Vespa motor scooter importer Piagio U.S.A. hired a group of attractive models to find the right cafes in and around Los Angeles and to interact with people over a cup of coffee or iced latte and generate buzz for the European bikes.

Even ad agencies that are heavily invested in traditional brand-building techniques acknowledge that buzz marketing has become a phenomenon. Malcolm Gladwell's book *The Tipping Point: How Little Things Can Make a Big Difference*—which describes how a small number of consumers can ignite a trend, if they're the right ones—has become must reading among ad agency personnel. The chairperson and CEO of Grey Global Group notes, "Everybody has read *The Tipping Point* and is trying to figure out the underground streams to reach consumers. Everybody is experimenting with it." For example, Reebok conducted more than 1,000 interviews to identify young Canadian women who were trendsetters among their peers. The company then gave 90 of these women a pair of $150 U-Shuffle DMX cross-trainers to get the funky shoes on the feet of these urban trendsetters. The product seeding campaign helped make the product-line launch one of the most successful in the company's history.

Some experts note that the growing popularity of buzz marketing could well spell its downfall. If everyone does it, it will no longer be buzz; it will simply be obscure and annoying advertising. And when consumers recognize that every company is trying to create a buzz for its brand, they are likely to be turned off to the technique. By then, of course, marketers will have found another stealth way to deliver their sales messages.

Sources: Garry Khermouch and Jeff Green, "Buzz Marketing," *BusinessWeek,* July 30, 2001, pp. 50–56; "Firms Reap Fruits of Product Seeding," *The Montreal Gazette,* Sept. 11, 2001, p. D6.

direct-marketing methods such as telemarketing, direct mail, and direct-response advertising, rather than relying on mass media. Advocates of the approach argue that database marketing is critical to the development and practice of effective IMC.[22]

- *Demands for greater accountability from advertising agencies and changes in the way agencies are compensated.* Many companies are moving toward incentive-based systems whereby compensation of their ad agencies is based, at least in part, on objective measures such as sales, market share, and profitability. Demands for accountability are motivating many agencies to consider a variety of communication tools and less expensive alternatives to mass-media advertising.
- *The rapid growth of the Internet, which is changing the very nature of how companies do business and the ways they communicate and interact with consumers.* The Internet revolution is well under way, and the Internet audience is growing rapidly. The Internet is an interactive medium that is becoming an integral part of communication strategy, and even business strategy, for many companies.

This marketing revolution is affecting everyone involved in the marketing and promotional process. Companies are recognizing that they must change the ways they market and promote their products and services. They can no longer be tied to a specific communication tool (such as media advertising); rather, they should use whatever contact methods offer the best way of delivering the message to their target audiences. Ad agencies continue to reposition themselves as offering more than just advertising expertise; they strive to convince their clients that they can manage all or any part of clients' integrated communications needs. Most agencies recognize that their future success depends on their ability to understand all areas of promotion and help their clients develop and implement integrated marketing communications programs.

The Role of IMC in Branding

One of the major reasons for the growing importance of integrated marketing communications over the past decade is that it plays a major role in the process of developing and sustaining brand identity and equity. As branding expert Kevin Keller notes, "Building and properly managing brand equity has become a priority for companies of all sizes, in all types of industries, in all types of markets."[23] With more and more products and services competing for consideration by customers who have less and less time to make choices, well-known brands have a major competitive advantage in today's marketplace. Building and maintaining brand identity and equity require the creation of well-known brands that have favorable, strong, and unique associations in the mind of the consumer.[24] IMC Perspective 1-2 discusses the important role that branding now plays in the marketing process.

Brand identity is a combination of many factors, including the name, logo, symbols, design, packaging, and performance of a product or service as well as the image or type of associations that comes to mind when consumers think about a brand. It encompasses the entire spectrum of consumers' awareness, knowledge, and image of the brand as well as the company behind it. It is the sum of all points of encounter or contact that consumers have with the brand, and it extends beyond the experience or outcome of using it. These contacts can also result from various forms of integrated marketing communications activities used by a company, including mass-media advertising, sales promotion offers, sponsorship activities at sporting or entertainment events, websites on the Internet, and direct-mail pieces such as letters, brochures, catalogs, or videos. Consumers can also have contact with or receive information about a brand in stores at the point of sale; through articles or stories they see, hear, or read in the media; or through interactions with a company representative, such as a salesperson.

Marketers recognize that in the modern world of marketing there are many different opportunities and methods for *contacting* current and prospective customers to provide them with information about a company and/or brands. The challenge is to understand how to use the various IMC tools to make such contacts and deliver the branding message effectively and efficiently. A successful IMC program requires that marketers find the right combination of communication tools and techniques, define their role and the extent to which they can or should be used, and coordinate their use. To accomplish this, the persons responsible for the company's communication efforts must have an understanding of the IMC tools that are available and the ways they can be used.

IMC PERSPECTIVE 1-2

The Power of Brands

Consider for a moment what consumers' reactions would be to a pair of running or basketball shoes if the Nike name or "swoosh" was taken off of them or to a bottle of cola without the Coke or Pepsi name. Would a Godiva chocolate by any other name taste as sweet? Do plain blue jeans carry the same cachet as those bearing the Diesel or Calvin Klein label? There was a time when consumers were proudly declaring their independence from the appeal of name-brand names by favoring the more practical generics and private labels. However, in today's marketplace the appeal of brand names is greater than ever, and marketers recognize that building and reinforcing the image of their brands is a key to profitability and growth. Many companies now know that brand equity is as important an asset as factories, inventory, and cash because strong brands have the power to command a premium price from consumers as well as investors. The table below shows the world's most valuable brands as measured by Interbrand Corp., a leading brand consultancy company.

There are a number of reasons why brands are more important than ever before. Consumers have a tremendous number of choices available in nearly every product and service category but have less and less time to shop and make selections. Well-known and trusted brand names are a touchstone for consumers and help simplify their decision-making process. Branding guru Larry Light notes that the key to all successful brands is that they stand for something and are much more than simply trademarks or logos. A brand is a promise to the customer. As one executive has stated: "Consumers don't go shopping for a 24-valve, 6-cylinder, 200-horsepower, fuel-injected engine. They shop for a Taurus, a Lexus, a BMW, a Jeep Cherokee, a Hummer, whatever. They shop for well-known, trusted brands."

Having a strong brand name and identity is also important to companies competing in the global economy as they must reach customers far from their home base. Companies such as Nokia, which is based in Finland, or Samsung, which is headquartered in South Korea, rely heavily on markets outside their home countries to sell their cellular phones and other electronic products. A strong brand name is also important for companies entering new markets or introducing new products. For example, Boeing recently began its first-ever corporate branding campaign as part of its overall strategy to expand beyond the commercial-aviation market and into new industries such as military aircraft, rockets, satellites, and broadband communications. Everything from Boeing's logo to its decision to relocate its corporate headquarters from Seattle to Chicago has been devised with the Boeing brand in mind.

While marketers recognize the importance of brand building, many are finding it difficult to commit themselves to the effort as the global economy slows and budgets tighten. Media sales staff, advertising agencies, and other marketing communications specialists have been doing their best to convince companies not to cut back on their spending but, rather, to continue to support their brands. They point to the last economic downturn, in the early 1990s, during which private-label brands leaped to prominence when many packaged-goods companies slashed their advertising budgets. Today, while many companies are avoiding the temptation to cut back on advertising and promotion to help meet earnings forecasts, others have shown less willingness to support their brands. Experts note that these firms run the risk of losing their pricing power and, more important, their connection with their customers. Moreover, they run the risk of losing market share to well-funded competitors that are eager to grab market share from weaker rivals. As marketing professor Kevin Keller notes, "People who starve their brands now will be paying in the future."

The world's 10 most valuable brands, 2002

Rank	Brand	2002 Brand Value (Billions)
1	Coca-Cola	$69.6
2	Microsoft	64.1
3	IBM	51.2
4	GE	41.3
5	Intel	30.9
6	Nokia	30.0
7	Disney	29.3
8	McDonald's	26.4
9	Marlboro	24.2
10	Mercedes	21.0

Source: Interbrand Corp., J.P. Morgan Chase & Co.

Sources: Gerry Khermouch, "The Best Global Brands," *BusinessWeek,* Aug. 5, 2002, pp. 92–94; Gerry Khermouch, "Why Advertising Matters More than Ever," *BusinessWeek,* Aug. 6, 2001, pp. 50–57; Scott Ward, Larry Light, and Jonathon Goldstine, "What High-Tech Managers Need to Know about Brands," *Harvard Business Review,* July–August, 1999, pp. 85–95.

Advertising investments undeniably help build a brand. The American Advertising Federation reminds companies of this through its Great Brands campaign. The parent companies of these brands gave unprecedented permission to modify their logos for use in this campaign.

The Promotional Mix: The Tools for IMC

Promotion has been defined as the coordination of all seller-initiated efforts to set up channels of information and persuasion in order to sell goods and services or promote an idea.[25] While implicit communication occurs through the various elements of the marketing mix, most of an organization's communications with the marketplace take place as part of a carefully planned and controlled promotional program. The basic tools used to accomplish an organization's communication objectives are often referred to as the **promotional mix** (Figure 1-1).

Traditionally the promotional mix has included four elements: advertising, sales promotion, publicity/public relations, and personal selling. However, in this text we view direct marketing as well as interactive media as major promotional-mix elements that modern-day marketers use to communicate with their target markets. Each element of the promotional mix is viewed as an integrated marketing communications tool that plays a distinctive role in an IMC program. Each may take on a variety of forms. And each has certain advantages.

Advertising

Advertising is defined as any paid form of nonpersonal communication about an organization, product, service, or idea by an identified sponsor.[26] The *paid* aspect of this definition reflects the fact that the space or time for an advertising message generally must be bought. An occasional exception to this is the public service announcement (PSA), whose advertising space or time is donated by the media.

The *nonpersonal* component means that advertising involves mass media (e.g., TV, radio, magazines, newspapers) that can transmit a message to large groups of individuals, often at the same time. The nonpersonal nature of advertising means that there is generally no opportunity for immediate feedback from the message recipient (except in direct-response advertising). Therefore, before the message is sent, the advertiser must consider how the audience will interpret and respond to it.

Advertising is the best-known and most widely discussed form of promotion, probably because of its pervasiveness. It is also a very important promotional tool, particu-

Figure 1-1 Elements of the promotional mix

larly for companies whose products and services are targeted at mass consumer markets. More than 200 companies each spend over $100 million a year on advertising in the United States. Figure 1-2 shows the advertising expenditures of the 25 leading national advertisers in 2001.

There are several reasons why advertising is such an important part of many marketers' promotional mixes. First, it can be a very cost-effective method for communicating with large audiences. For example, the average 30-second spot on the four major networks during prime-time network television reaches nearly 10 million households. The cost per thousand households reached is around $14.[27]

Advertising can be used to create brand images and symbolic appeals for a company or brand, a very important capability for companies selling products and services that are difficult to differentiate on functional attributes. For example, since 1980 Absolut has used creative advertising to position its vodka as an upscale, fashionable, sophisticated drink and differentiate it from other brands. The advertising strategy has been to focus attention on two unique aspects of the product: the Absolut name and the distinctive shape of the bottle (Exhibit 1-7). Most of the print ads used in this long-running campaign are specifically tailored for the magazine or region where they appear. The campaign, one of the most successful and recognizable in advertising history, has made the Absolut brand nearly synonymous with imported vodka. While all other spirits sales have declined by more than 40 percent over the past 15 years, Absolut sales have increased 10-fold and the various Absolut brands have a combined 70 percent market share.[28]

Figure 1-2 25 leading advertisers in the United States, 2001

Rank	Advertiser	Ad Spending (Millions)
1	General Motors Corp.	$3,374.4
2	Procter & Gamble	2,540.6
3	Ford Motor Co.	2,408.2
4	PepsiCo	2,210.4
5	Pfizer	2,189.5
6	DaimlerChrysler	1,985.3
7	AOL Time Warner	1,885.3
8	Philip Morris Cos.	1,815.7
9	Walt Disney Co.	1,757.3
10	Johnson & Johnson	1,618.1
11	Unilever	1,483.6
12	Sears, Roebuck & Co.	1,480.1
13	Verizon Communications	1,461.6
14	Toyota Motor Corp.	1,399.1
15	AT&T Corp.	1,371.9
16	Sony Corp.	1,310.1
17	Viacom	1,282.8
18	McDonald's Corp.	1,194.7
19	Diageo	1,180.8
20	Sprint Corp.	1,160.1
21	Merck & Co.	1,136.6
22	Honda Motor Co.	1,102.9
23	J.C. Penney Corp.	1,085.7
24	U.S. government	1,056.8
25	L'Oreal	1,040.7

Source: Advertising Age, June 24, 2002, p. S-2.

Exhibit 1-7 Creative advertising has made Absolut the most popular brand of imported vodka in the United States

Exhibit 1-8 Eveready uses the popularity of its pink bunny campaign to generate support from retailers

Another advantage of advertising is its ability to strike a responsive chord with consumers when differentiation across other elements of the marketing mix is difficult to achieve. Popular advertising campaigns attract consumers' attention and can help generate sales. These popular campaigns can also sometimes be leveraged into successful integrated marketing communications programs. For example, Eveready used the popularity of its Energizer Bunny campaign to generate support from retailers in the form of shelf space, promotional displays, and other merchandising activities (Exhibit 1-8). Consumer promotions such as in-store displays, premium offers, and sweepstakes feature the pink bunny. Pictures of the Energizer Bunny appear on Energizer packages to ensure brand identification and extend the campaign's impact to the point of purchase. Eveready has extended its integrated marketing efforts to include tie-ins with sports marketing and sponsorships.

Exhibit 1-9 The goals of the "milk mustache" campaign are to change the image of milk and increase sales of the product

The nature and purpose of advertising differ from one industry to another and/or across situations. The targets of an organization's advertising efforts often vary, as do advertising's role and function in the marketing program. One advertiser may seek to generate immediate response or action from the customer; another may want to develop awareness or a positive image for its product or service over a longer period. For example, Exhibit 1-9 shows one of the ads from the popular "milk mustache" campaign. The goal of this campaign, which began in 1995, has been to change the image of milk and help reverse the decline in per-capita milk consumption in the United States.

Marketers advertise to the consumer market with national and retail/local advertising, which may stimulate primary or selective demand. For business/professional markets, they use business-to-business, professional, and trade advertising. Figure 1-3 describes the most common types of advertising.

Direct Marketing

One of the fastest-growing sectors of the U.S. economy is **direct marketing,** in which organizations communicate directly with target customers to generate a response and/or a transaction. Traditionally, direct marketing

Figure 1-3 Classifications of advertising

ADVERTISING TO CONSUMER MARKETS

National Advertising
Advertising done by large companies on a nationwide basis or in most regions of the country. Most of the ads for well-known companies and brands that are seen on prime-time TV or in other major national or regional media are examples of national advertising. The goals of national advertisers are to inform or remind consumers of the company or brand and its features, benefits, advantages, or uses and to create or reinforce its image so that consumers will be predisposed to purchase it.

Retail/Local Advertising
Advertising done by retailers or local merchants to encourage consumers to shop at a specific store, use a local service, or patronize a particular establishment. Retail or local advertising tends to emphasize specific patronage motives such as price, hours of operation, service, atmosphere, image, or merchandise assortment. Retailers are concerned with building store traffic, so their promotions often take the form of direct-action advertising designed to produce immediate store traffic and sales.

Primary- versus Selective-Demand Advertising
Primary-demand advertising is designed to stimulate demand for the general product class or entire industry. Selective-demand advertising focuses on creating demand for a specific company's brands. Most advertising for products and services is concerned with stimulating selective demand and emphasizes reasons for purchasing a particular brand.

An advertiser might concentrate on stimulating primary demand when, for example, its brand dominates a market and will benefit the most from overall market growth. Primary-demand advertising is often used as part of a promotional strategy to help a new product gain market acceptance, since the challenge is to sell customers on the product concept as much as to sell a particular brand. Industry trade associations also try to stimulate primary demand for their members' products, among them cotton, milk, orange juice, pork, and beef.

ADVERTISING TO BUSINESS AND PROFESSIONAL MARKETS

Business-to-Business Advertising
Advertising targeted at individuals who buy or influence the purchase of industrial goods or services for their companies. Industrial goods are products that either become a physical part of another product (raw material or component parts), are used in manufacturing other goods (machinery), or are used to help a company conduct its business (e.g., office supplies, computers). Business services such as insurance, travel services, and health care are also included in this category.

Professional Advertising
Advertising targeted to professionals such as doctors, lawyers, dentists, engineers, or professors to encourage them to use a company's product in their business operations. It might also be used to encourage professionals to recommend or specify the use of a company's product by end-users.

Trade Advertising
Advertising targeted to marketing channel members such as wholesalers, distributors, and retailers. The goal is to encourage channel members to stock, promote, and resell the manufacturer's branded products to their customers.

Exhibit 1-10 The Bose Corporation uses direct-response advertising to promote its audio products

has not been considered an element of the promotional mix. However, because it has become such an integral part of the IMC program of many organizations and often involves separate objectives, budgets, and strategies, we view direct marketing as a component of the promotional mix.

Direct marketing is much more than direct mail and mail-order catalogs. It involves a variety of activities, including database management, direct selling, telemarketing, and direct-response ads through direct mail, the Internet, and various broadcast and print media. Some companies, such as Tupperware, Discovery Toys, and Amway, do not use any other distribution channels, relying on independent contractors to sell their products directly to consumers. Companies such as L.L. Bean, Lands' End, and J. Crew have been very successful in using direct marketing to sell their clothing products. Dell Computer and Gateway have experienced tremendous growth in the computer industry by selling a full line of personal computers through direct marketing.

One of the major tools of direct marketing is **direct-response advertising,** whereby a product is promoted through an ad that encourages the consumer to purchase directly from the manufacturer. Traditionally, direct mail has been the primary medium for direct-response advertising, although television and magazines have become increasingly important media. For example, Exhibit 1-10 shows a direct-response ad for the Bose Corporation's Acoustic Waveguide products. Direct-response advertising and other forms of direct marketing have become very popular over the past two decades, owing primarily to changing lifestyles, particularly the increase in two-income households. This has meant more discretionary income but less time for in-store shopping. The availability of credit cards and toll-free phone numbers has also facilitated the purchase of products from direct-response ads. More recently, the rapid growth of the Internet is fueling the growth of direct marketing. The convenience of shopping through catalogs or on a company's website and placing orders by mail, by phone, or online has led the tremendous growth of direct marketing.

Direct-marketing tools and techniques are also being used by companies that distribute their products through traditional distribution channels or have their own sales force. Direct marketing plays a big role in the integrated marketing communications programs of consumer-product companies and business-to-business marketers. These companies spend large amounts of money each year developing and maintaining databases containing the addresses and/or phone numbers of present and prospective customers. They use telemarketing to call customers directly and attempt to sell them products and services or qualify them as sales leads. Marketers also send out direct-mail pieces ranging from simple letters and flyers to detailed brochures, catalogs, and videotapes to give potential customers information about their products or services. Direct-marketing techniques are also used to distribute product samples or target users of a competing brand.

Interactive/Internet Marketing

As the new millennium begins, we are experiencing perhaps the most dynamic and revolutionary changes of any era in the history of marketing, as well as advertising and promotion. These changes are being driven by advances in technology and developments that have led to dramatic growth of communication through interactive media, particularly the Internet. **Interactive media** allow for a back-and-forth flow of information whereby users can participate in and modify the form and content of the information they receive in real time. Unlike traditional forms of marketing communications such as advertising, which are one-way in nature, the new media allow users to perform a variety of functions such as receive and alter information and images, make inquiries, respond to questions, and, of course, make purchases. In addition to the Internet, other forms of interactive media include CD-ROMs, kiosks, and

interactive television. However, the interactive medium that is having the greatest impact on marketing is the Internet, especially through the component known as the World Wide Web.

While the Internet is changing the ways companies design and implement their entire business and marketing strategies, it is also affecting their marketing communications programs. Thousands of companies, ranging from large multinational corporations to small local firms, have developed websites to promote their products and services, by providing current and potential customers with information, as well as to entertain and interact with consumers. Perhaps the most prevalent perspective on the Internet is that it is an advertising medium, as many marketers advertise their products and services on the websites of other companies and/or organizations. Actually, the Internet is a medium that can be used to execute all the elements of the promotional mix. In addition to advertising on the Web, marketers offer sales promotion incentives such as coupons, contests, and sweepstakes online, and they use the Internet to conduct direct marketing, personal selling, and public relations activities more effectively and efficiently. For example, Exhibit 1-11 shows a page from the Web site for Lands' End which informs consumers how they can get personalized service when they shop online.

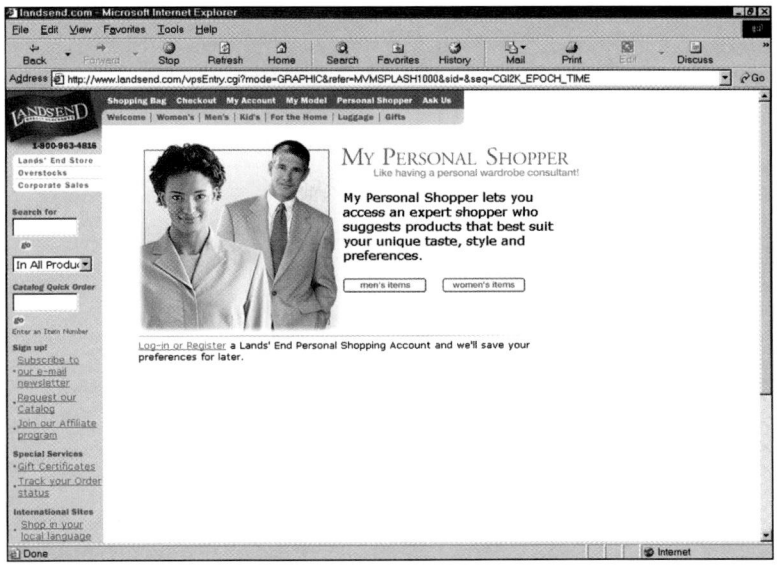

Exhibit 1-11 Lands' End uses its website as part of its direct-marketing efforts

While the Internet is a promotional medium, it can also be viewed as a marketing communications tool in its own right. Because of its interactive nature, it is a very effective way of communicating with customers. Many companies recognize the advantages of communicating via the Internet and are developing Web strategies and hiring interactive agencies specifically to develop their websites and make them part of their integrated marketing communications program. However, companies that are using the Internet effectively are integrating their Web strategies with other aspects of their IMC programs.

An excellent example of this is the award-winning "Whatever" campaign developed by Nike and its advertising agency, Weiden & Kennedy, to introduce the Air Cross Trainer II shoes. The ads featured star athletes such as sprinter Marion Jones in dramatic situations, and as each spot ended, the words "Continue at Whatever.Nike.com" appeared on the screen (Exhibit 1-12). When viewers visited the site, they could select from six or seven possible endings to the commercial, read information on the sports and athletes featured in the ads, or purchase the shoes. The integrated campaign was very effective in driving traffic to both Nike's main website and the whatever.nike.com site created specifically for the campaign. The "Whatever" campaign was also very effective in terms of sales as it helped make the Air Cross Trainer II Nike's best-selling shoe soon after the ads debuted.[29]

Exhibit 1-12 Nike's "Whatever" campaign creatively integrated the use of television advertising and the Internet

Sales Promotion

The next variable in the promotional mix is **sales promotion,** which is generally defined as those marketing activities that provide extra value or incentives to the sales force, the distributors, or the ultimate consumer and can stimulate immediate sales. Sales promotion is generally broken into two major categories: consumer-oriented and trade-oriented activities.

Consumer-oriented sales promotion is targeted to the ultimate user of a product or service and includes couponing, sampling, premiums, rebates, contests, sweepstakes,

Exhibit 1-13 Coupons are a popular consumer-oriented sales promotion tool

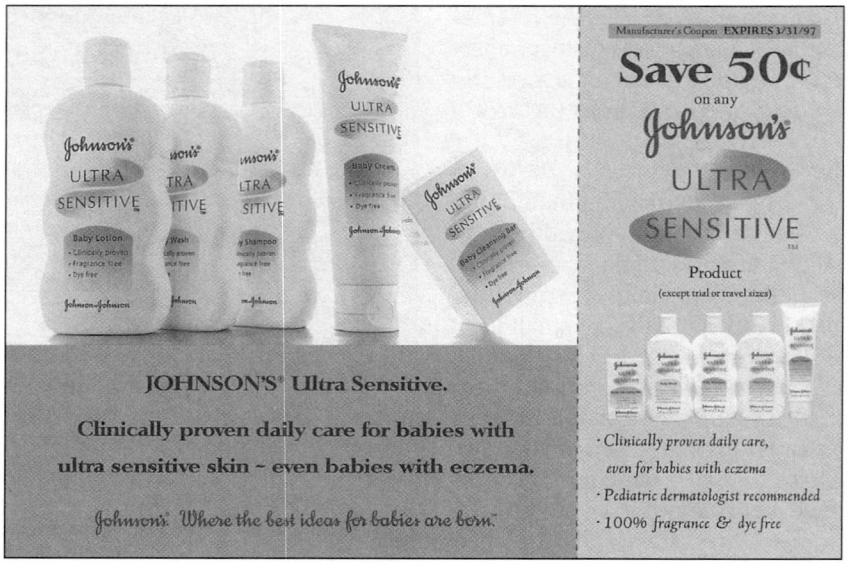

and various point-of-purchase materials (Exhibit 1-13). These promotional tools encourage consumers to make an immediate purchase and thus can stimulate short-term sales. *Trade-oriented sales promotion* is targeted toward marketing intermediaries such as wholesalers, distributors, and retailers. Promotional and merchandising allowances, price deals, sales contests, and trade shows are some of the promotional tools used to encourage the trade to stock and promote a company's products.

Among many consumer packaged-goods companies, sales promotion is often 60 to 70 percent of the promotional budget.[30] In recent years many companies have shifted the emphasis of their promotional strategy from advertising to sales promotion. Reasons for the increased emphasis on sales promotion include declining brand loyalty and increased consumer sensitivity to promotional deals. Another major reason is that retailers have become larger and more powerful and are demanding more trade promotion support from companies.

Promotion and *sales promotion* are two terms that often create confusion in the advertising and marketing fields. As noted, promotion is an element of marketing by which firms communicate with their customers; it includes all the promotional-mix elements we have just discussed. However, many marketing and advertising practitioners use the term more narrowly to refer to sales promotion activities to either consumers or the trade (retailers, wholesalers). In this book, *promotion* is used in the broader sense to refer to the various marketing communications activities of an organization.

Publicity/Public Relations

Another important component of an organization's promotional mix is publicity/public relations.

Publicity

Publicity refers to nonpersonal communications regarding an organization, product, service, or idea not directly paid for or run under identified sponsorship. It usually comes in the form of a news story, editorial, or announcement about an organization and/or its products and services. Like advertising, publicity involves nonpersonal communication to a mass audience, but unlike advertising, publicity is not directly paid for by the company. The company or organization attempts to get the media to cover or run a favorable story on a product, service, cause, or event to affect awareness, knowledge, opinions, and/or behavior. Techniques used to gain publicity include news releases, press conferences, feature articles, photographs, films, and videotapes.

An advantage of publicity over other forms of promotion is its credibility. Consumers generally tend to be less skeptical toward favorable information about a product or service when it comes from a source they perceive as unbiased. For example, the success (or failure) of a new movie is often determined by the reviews it receives from film critics, who are viewed by many moviegoers as objective evaluators.

Another advantage of publicity is its low cost, since the company is not paying for time or space in a mass medium such as TV, radio, or newspapers. While an organization may incur some costs in developing publicity items or maintaining a staff to do so, these expenses will be far less than those for the other promotional programs.

Publicity is not always under the control of an organization and is sometimes unfavorable. Negative stories about a company and/or its products can be very damaging. For example, a few years ago negative stories about abdominal exercise machines appeared on ABC's "20/20" and NBC's "Dateline" newsmagazine TV shows. Before these stories aired, more than $3 million worth of the machines were being sold each week, primarily through infomercials. After the negative stories aired, sales of the machines dropped immediately; within a few months the product category was all but dead.[31]

Public Relations

It is important to recognize the distinction between publicity and public relations. When an organization systematically plans and distributes information in an attempt to control and manage its image and the nature of the publicity it receives, it is really engaging in a function known as public relations. **Public relations** is defined as "the management function which evaluates public attitudes, identifies the policies and procedures of an individual or organization with the public interest, and executes a program of action to earn public understanding and acceptance."[32] Public relations generally has a broader objective than publicity, as its purpose is to establish and maintain a positive image of the company among its various publics.

Public relations uses publicity and a variety of other tools—including special publications, participation in community activities, fund-raising, sponsorship of special events, and various public affairs activities—to enhance an organization's image. Organizations also use advertising as a public relations tool. For example, in Exhibit 1-14 a corporate ad for DuPont shows how the company uses science to make life better.

Traditionally, publicity and public relations have been considered more supportive than primary to the marketing and promotional process. However, many firms have begun making PR an integral part of their predetermined marketing and promotional strategies. PR firms are increasingly touting public relations as a communications tool that can take over many of the functions of conventional advertising and marketing.[33]

Personal Selling

The final element of an organization's promotional mix is **personal selling,** a form of person-to-person communication in which a seller attempts to assist and/or persuade prospective buyers to purchase the company's product or service or to act on an idea. Unlike advertising, personal selling involves direct contact between buyer and seller, either face-to-face or through some form of telecommunications such as telephone sales. This interaction gives the marketer communication flexibility; the seller can see

Exhibit 1-14 Advertising is often used to enhance companies' corporate images

or hear the potential buyer's reactions and modify the message accordingly. The personal, individualized communication in personal selling allows the seller to tailor the message to the customer's specific needs or situation.

Personal selling also involves more immediate and precise feedback because the impact of the sales presentation can generally be assessed from the customer's reactions. If the feedback is unfavorable, the salesperson can modify the message. Personal selling efforts can also be targeted to specific markets and customer types that are the best prospects for the company's product or service.

Promotional Management

In developing an integrated marketing communications strategy, a company combines the promotional-mix elements, balancing the strengths and weaknesses of each, to produce an effective promotional campaign. **Promotional management** involves coordinating the promotional-mix elements to develop a controlled, integrated program of effective marketing communications. The marketer must consider which promotional tools to use and how to combine them to achieve its marketing and promotional objectives. Companies also face the task of distributing the total promotional budget across the promotional-mix elements. What percentage of the budget should they allocate to advertising, sales promotion, the Internet, direct marketing, and personal selling?

Companies consider many factors in developing their IMC programs, including the type of product, the target market, the buyer's decision process, the stage of the product life cycle, and the channels of distribution. Companies selling consumer products and services generally rely on advertising through mass media to communicate with ultimate consumers. Business-to-business marketers, who generally sell expensive, risky, and often complex products and services, more often use personal selling. Business-to-business marketers such as Honeywell do use advertising to perform important functions such as building awareness of the company and its products, generating leads for the sales force, and reassuring customers about the purchase they have made (see Exhibit 1-15).

Exhibit 1-15 Business-to-business marketers such as Honeywell use advertising to build awareness

Conversely, personal selling also plays an important role in consumer-product marketing. A consumer-goods company retains a sales force to call on marketing intermediaries (wholesalers and retailers) that distribute the product or service to the final consumer. While the company sales reps do not communicate with the ultimate consumer, they make an important contribution to the marketing effort by gaining new distribution outlets for the company's product, securing shelf position and space for the brand, informing retailers about advertising and promotion efforts to users, and encouraging dealers to merchandise and promote the brand at the local market level.

Advertising and personal-selling efforts vary depending on the type of market being sought, and even firms in the same industry may differ in the allocation of their promotional efforts. For example, in the cosmetics industry, Avon and Mary Kay Cosmetics concentrate on direct selling, whereas Revlon and Max Factor rely heavily on consumer advertising. Firms also differ in the relative emphasis they place on advertising and sales promotion. Companies selling high-quality brands use advertising to convince consumers of their superiority, justify their higher prices, and maintain their image. Brands of lower quality, or those that are hard to differentiate, often compete more on a price or "value for the money" basis and may rely more on sales promotion to the trade and/or to consumers.

The marketing communications program of an organization is generally developed with a specific purpose in mind and is the end product of a detailed marketing and promotional planning process. We will now look at a model of the promotional planning process that shows the sequence of decisions made in developing and implementing the IMC program.

The IMC Planning Process

As with any business function, planning plays a fundamental role in the development and implementation of an effective promotional program. The individuals involved in promotion design a **promotional plan** that provides the framework for developing, implementing, and controlling the organization's integrated marketing communications programs and activities. Promotional planners must decide on the role and function of the specific elements of the promotional mix, develop strategies for each element, and implement the plan. Promotion is but one part of, and must be integrated into, the overall marketing plan and program.

A model of the IMC planning process is shown in Figure 1-4. The remainder of this chapter presents a brief overview of the various steps involved in this process.

Review of the Marketing Plan

The first step in the IMC planning process is to review the marketing plan and objectives. Before developing a promotional plan, marketers must understand where the company (or the brand) has been, its current position in the market, where it intends to go, and how it plans to get there. Most of this information should be contained in the **marketing plan,** a written document that describes the overall marketing strategy and programs developed for an organization, a particular product line, or a brand. Marketing plans can take several forms but generally include five basic elements:

1. A detailed situation analysis that consists of an internal marketing audit and review and an external analysis of the market competition and environmental factors.
2. Specific marketing objectives that provide direction, a time frame for marketing activities, and a mechanism for measuring performance.
3. A marketing strategy and program that include selection of target market(s) and decisions and plans for the four elements of the marketing mix.
4. A program for implementing the marketing strategy, including determining specific tasks to be performed and responsibilities.
5. A process for monitoring and evaluating performance and providing feedback so that proper control can be maintained and any necessary changes can be made in the overall marketing strategy or tactics.

For most firms, the promotional plan is an integral part of the marketing strategy. Thus, the promotional planners must know the roles advertising and other promotional-mix elements will play in the overall marketing program. The promotional plan is developed similarly to the marketing plan and often uses its detailed information. Promotional planners focus on information in the marketing plan that is relevant to the promotional strategy.

Promotional Program Situation Analysis

After the overall marketing plan is reviewed, the next step in developing a promotional plan is to conduct the situation analysis. In the IMC program, the situation analysis focuses on the factors that influence or are relevant to the development of a promotional strategy. Like the overall marketing situation analysis, the promotional program situation analysis includes both an internal and an external analysis.

Internal Analysis The **internal analysis** assesses relevant areas involving the product/service offering and the firm itself. The capabilities of the firm and its ability to develop and implement a successful promotional program, the organization of the promotional department, and the successes and failures of past programs should be reviewed. The analysis should study the relative advantages and disadvantages of

Figure 1-4 An integrated marketing communications planning model

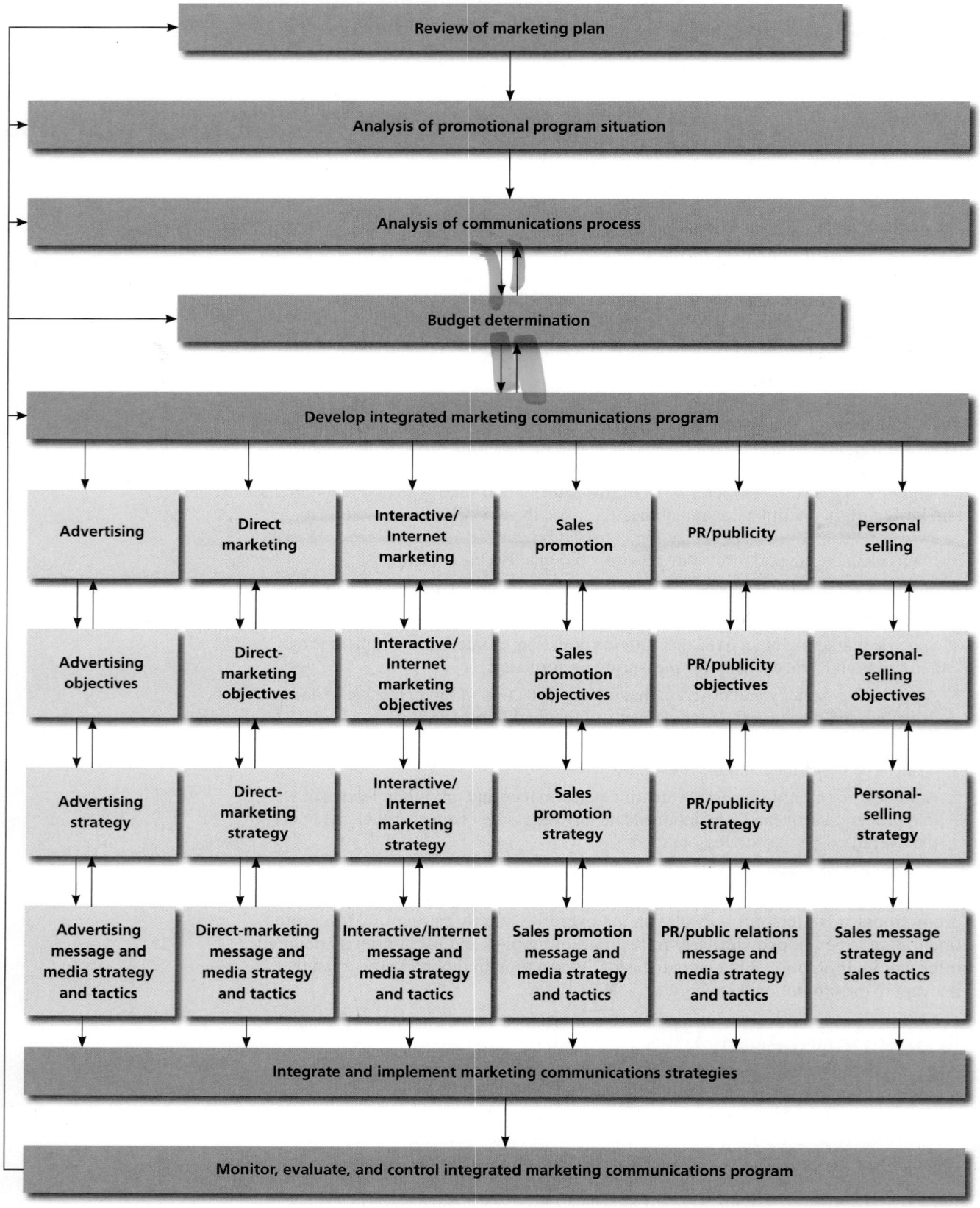

Review of Marketing Plan
Examine overall marketing plan and objectives
Role of advertising and promotion
Competitive analysis
Assess environmental influences

Analysis of Promotional Program Situation
Internal analysis
- Promotional department organization
- Firm's ability to implement promotional program
- Agency evaluation and selection
- Review of previous program results

External analysis
- Consumer behavior analysis
- Market segmentation and target marketing
- Market positioning

Analysis of Communications Process
Analyze receiver's response processes
Analyze source, message, channel factors
Establish communications goals and objectives

Budget Determination
Set tentative marketing communications budget
Allocate tentative budget

Develop Integrated Marketing Communications Program
Advertising
- Set advertising objectives
- Determine advertising budget
- Develop advertising message
- Develop advertising media strategy

Direct marketing
- Set direct-marketing objectives
- Determine direct-marketing budget
- Develop direct-marketing message
- Develop direct-marketing media strategy

Interactive/Internet marketing
- Set interactive/Internet marketing objectives
- Determine interactive/Internet marketing budget
- Develop interactive/Internet message
- Develop interactive/Internet media strategy

Sales promotion
- Set sales promotion objectives
- Determine sales promotion budget
- Determine sales promotion tools and develop messages
- Develop sales promotion media strategy

Public relations/publicity
- Set PR/publicity objectives
- Determine PR/publicity budget
- Develop PR/publicity messages
- Develop PR/publicity media strategy

Personal selling
- Set personal-selling and sales objectives
- Determine personal-selling/sales budget
- Develop sales message
- Develop selling roles and responsibilities

Integrate and Implement Marketing Communications Strategies
Integrate promotional-mix strategies
Create and produce ads
Purchase media time, space, etc.
Design and implement direct-marketing programs
Design and distribute sales promotion materials
Design and implement public relations/publicity programs
Design and implement interactive/Internet marketing programs

Monitor, Evaluate, and Control Integrated Marketing Communications Program
Evaluate promotional program results/effectiveness
Take measures to control and adjust promotional strategies

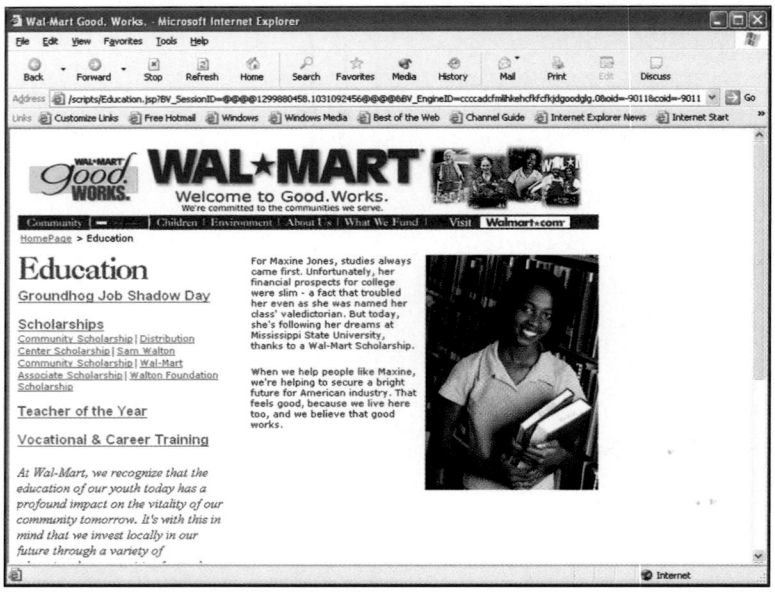

Exhibit 1-16 Wal-Mart has a very strong image and reputation as a socially responsible company

performing the promotional functions in-house as opposed to hiring an external agency (or agencies). For example, the internal analysis may indicate the firm is not capable of planning, implementing, and managing certain areas of the promotional program. If this is the case, it would be wise to look for assistance from an advertising agency or some other promotional facilitator. If the organization is already using an ad agency, the focus will be on the quality of the agency's work and the results achieved by past and/or current campaigns.

In this text we will examine the functions ad agencies perform for their clients, the agency selection process, compensation, and considerations in evaluating agency performance. We will also discuss the role and function of other promotional facilitators such as sales promotion firms, direct-marketing companies, public relations agencies, and marketing and media research firms.

Another aspect of the internal analysis is assessing the strengths and weaknesses of the firm or the brand from an image perspective. Often the image a firm brings to the market will have a significant impact on the way the firm can advertise and promote itself as well as its various products and services. Companies or brands that are new to the market or those for whom perceptions are negative may have to concentrate on their images, not just the benefits or attributes of the specific product or service. On the other hand, a firm with a strong reputation and/or image is already a step ahead when it comes to marketing its products or services. For example, a nationwide survey found that the companies with the best overall reputations among American consumers include Johnson & Johnson, Coca-Cola, Hewlett-Packard, Intel, Ben & Jerry's, and Wal-Mart.[34] Wal-Mart was rated very high in the area of social responsibility, which involves perceptions of the company as a good citizen in its dealings with communities, employees, and the environment. Wal-Mart enhances its image as a socially responsible company by supporting various causes at both local and national levels (Exhibit 1-16).

The internal analysis also assesses the relative strengths and weaknesses of the product or service; its advantages and disadvantages; any unique selling points or benefits it may have; its packaging, price, and design; and so on. This information is particularly important to the creative personnel who must develop the advertising message for the brand.

Figure 1-5 is a checklist of some of the areas one might consider when performing analyses for promotional planning purposes. Addressing internal areas may require information the company does not have available internally and must gather as part of the external analysis.

External Analysis

The **external analysis** focuses on factors such as characteristics of the firm's customers, market segments, positioning strategies, and competitors, as shown in Figure 1-5. An important part of the external analysis is a detailed consideration of customers' characteristics and buying patterns, their decision processes, and factors influencing their purchase decisions. Attention must also be given to consumers' perceptions and attitudes, lifestyles, and criteria for making purchase decisions. Often, marketing research studies are needed to answer some of these questions.

A key element of the external analysis is an assessment of the market. The attractiveness of various market segments must be evaluated and the segments to target must be identified. Once the target markets are chosen, the emphasis will be on determining how the product should be positioned. What image or place should it have in consumers' minds?

This part of the promotional program situation analysis also includes an in-depth examination of both direct and indirect competitors. While competitors were analyzed in the overall marketing situation analysis, even more attention is devoted to promo-

Figure 1-5 Areas covered in the situation analysis

Internal Factors	External Factors
Assessment of Firm's Promotional Organization and Capabilities	***Customer Analysis***
Organization of promotional department	Who buys our product or service?
Capability of firm to develop and execute promotional programs	Who makes the decision to buy the product?
Determination of role and function of ad agency and other promotional facilitators	Who influences the decision to buy the product?
Review of Firm's Previous Promotional Programs and Results	How is the purchase decision made? Who assumes what role?
Review previous promotional objectives	What does the customer buy? What needs must be satisfied?
Review previous promotional budgets and allocations	Why do customers buy a particular brand?
Review previous promotional-mix strategies and programs	Where do they go or look to buy the product or service?
Review results of previous promotional programs	When do they buy? Any seasonality factors?
Assessment of Firm or Brand Image and Implications for Promotion	What are customers' attitudes toward our product or service?
Assessment of Relative Strengths and Weaknesses of Product or Service	What social factors might influence the purchase decision?
What are the strengths and weaknesses of product or service?	Do the customers' lifestyles influence their decisions?
What are its key benefits?	How is our product or service perceived by customers?
Does it have any unique selling points?	How do demographic factors influence the purchase decision?
Assessment of packaging, labeling, and brand image	***Competitive Analysis***
How does our product or service compare with competition?	Who are our direct and indirect competitors?
	What key benefits and positioning are used by our competitors?
	What is our position relative to the competition?
	How big are competitors' ad budgets?
	What message and media strategies are competitors using?
	Environmental Analysis
	Are there any current trends or developments that might affect the promotional program?

tional aspects at this phase. Focus is on the firm's primary competitors: their specific strengths and weaknesses; their segmentation, targeting, and positioning strategies; and the promotional strategies they employ. The size and allocation of their promotional budgets, their media strategies, and the messages they are sending to the marketplace should all be considered.

The external phase also includes an analysis of the marketing environment and current trends or developments that might affect the promotional program. IMC Perspective 1-3 discusses how marketers responded to the marketing environment that emerged after the terrorist attacks on September 11, 2002.

Analysis of the Communications Process

This stage of the promotional planning process examines how the company can effectively communicate with consumers in its target markets. The promotional planner must think about the process consumers will go through in responding to marketing communications. The response process for products or services for which consumer decision making is characterized by a high level of interest is often different from that for low-involvement or routine purchase decisions. These differences will influence the promotional strategy.

Communication decisions regarding the use of various source, message, and channel factors must also be considered. The promotional planner should recognize the different effects various types of advertising messages might have on consumers and whether they are appropriate for the product or brand. Issues such as whether a celebrity spokesperson should be used and at what cost may also be studied. Preliminary discussion of media-mix options (print, TV, radio, newspaper, direct marketing) and their cost implications might also occur at this stage.

IMC PERSPECTIVE 1-3

Marketers Respond to 9/11

Marketers often have to deal with events that have a significant impact on the economy as well as the psyche of the consumer. However, the tragedy created by the horrific events of September 11, 2001, caused an environment unlike anything most businesspeople have ever experienced. The aftershocks of the terrorist attacks rippled through nearly every sector of the U.S. economy, with certain industries, such as travel, tourism, media, and entertainment, being particularly hard hit.

After the attacks, the major television networks, including CBS, NBC, ABC, and Fox, went commercial-free for several days, an approach costing them a combined $35 to $40 million a day in lost revenue. Adding in cable news networks and local stations, the television industry's cost for covering the attacks and their immediate aftermath was more than $700 million in canceled advertising. The major broadcast and cable news operations face growing expenses to cover the war on terrorism, including the costs of creating new bureaus abroad, improving technology, and widening coverage.

The terrorist attacks also have had a significant impact on the advertising industry and created major problems for ad agencies as well as media companies, both of which were already reeling from the soft economy and dot-com bust that resulted in lower advertising spending. Advertising agencies and their clients have had to determine how to appeal to consumers facing economic uncertainty, rethinking their priorities, and feeling anxious about their safety. Marketing after a tragedy is always a tricky business and was even more so because of the scale of the September 11 events. Marketers who alluded to the tragedy risked alienating consumers who might think they were trying to capitalize on it, while those who ignored it ran the risk of seeming insensitive and out of touch.

Consumers emitted mixed signals regarding their feelings about the terrorist attacks. Researchers found a resurgence of patriotism, a renewed desire to connect with family and friends, and a strengthened belief in old-fashioned values such as community service and charity. In a survey conducted six months after the attacks, 80 percent of the consumer respondents indicated that 9/11 was still affecting their professional and personal lives. Though their lives were returning to normal and few people radically modified their day-to-day activities, changes included keeping cell phones handy, installing more locks, watching more 24-hour news channels, and looking more for products that were made in the United States.

Some marketers decided that the best way to respond to the new times was with messages offering appeals to patriotism, the promise of escape, or tribute to those who died or were involved with the tragedy. One of the most popular commercials during the 2002 Super Bowl was an Anheuser Busch spot featuring stately Clydesdales trotting across serene snowy landscapes and over the Brooklyn Bridge to pause before the Manhattan skyline and bow in tribute to New York City. Not surprisingly, New York City firefighters and police officers became popular advertising spokespersons.

WHAT WE STAND FOR IS MORE IMPORTANT THAN WHAT WE STAND IN.
-KENNETH COLE

The U.S. government used the public's outrage over the terrorist attacks as part of its efforts to fight drug abuse. The White House Office of National Drug Control Policy developed an advertising campaign suggesting that illegal drug sales have become a major means of raising money for terrorism. The idea behind the campaign is that people will be less likely to use drugs if they understand that by using them they may be supporting terrorism.

Marketers have now had time to reflect on how they responded to the nation's worst terrorist tragedy and how their marketing communications during the chaotic months after the attacks were received by consumers. Appeals to patriotism were unwelcome if they were seen as attempts to cash in on the tragedy. However, companies whose advertising programs were already identified with patriotism, the flag, and other U.S. symbols and those whose marketing efforts were tied to charitable donations destined to help the recovery effort were perceived favorably.

Sources: Steve Jarvis, "Red, White and the Blues," *Marketing News*, May 27, 2002, pp. 1, 9; Hillary Chura, "The New Normal," *Advertising Age*, Mar. 11, 2002, pp. 1, 4; Gwendolyn Bounds, "Marketers Tread Precarious Terrain," *The Wall Street Journal*, Feb. 5, 2002, pp. B1, 4; Jon E. Hilsenrath, "Terror's Toll on the Economy," *The Wall Street Journal*, Oct. 9, 2002, pp. B1, 4.

An important part of this stage of the promotional planning process is establishing communication goals and objectives. In this text, we stress the importance of distinguishing between communication and marketing objectives. **Marketing objectives** refer to what is to be accomplished by the overall marketing program. They are often stated in terms of sales, market share, or profitability.

Communication objectives refer to what the firm seeks to accomplish with its promotional program. They are often stated in terms of the nature of the message to be communicated or what specific communication effects are to be achieved. Communication objectives may include creating awareness or knowledge about a product and its attributes or benefits; creating an image; or developing favorable attitudes, preferences, or purchase intentions. Communication objectives should be the guiding force for development of the overall marketing communications strategy and of objectives for each promotional-mix area.

Budget Determination

After the communication objectives are determined, attention turns to the promotional budget. Two basic questions are asked at this point: What will the promotional program cost? How will the money be allocated? Ideally, the amount a firm needs to spend on promotion should be determined by what must be done to accomplish its communication objectives. In reality, promotional budgets are often determined using a more simplistic approach, such as how much money is available or a percentage of a company's or brand's sales revenue. At this stage, the budget is often tentative. It may not be finalized until specific promotional-mix strategies are developed.

Developing the Integrated Marketing Communications Program

Developing the IMC program is generally the most involved and detailed step of the promotional planning process. As discussed earlier, each promotional-mix element has certain advantages and limitations. At this stage of the planning process, decisions have to be made regarding the role and importance of each element and their coordination with one another. As Figure 1-4 shows, each promotional-mix element has its own set of objectives and a budget and strategy for meeting them. Decisions must be made and activities performed to implement the promotional programs. Procedures must be developed for evaluating performance and making any necessary changes.

For example, the advertising program will have its own set of objectives, usually involving the communication of some message or appeal to a target audience. A budget will be determined, providing the advertising manager and the agency with some idea of how much money is available for developing the ad campaign and purchasing media to disseminate the ad message.

Two important aspects of the advertising program are development of the message and the media strategy. Message development, often referred to as *creative strategy,* involves determining the basic appeal and message the advertiser wishes to convey to the target audience. This process, along with the ads that result, is to many students the most fascinating aspect of promotion. *Media strategy* involves determining which communication channels will be used to deliver the advertising message to the target audience. Decisions must be made regarding which types of media will be used (e.g., newspapers, magazines, radio, TV, billboards) as well as specific media selections (e.g., a particular magazine or TV program). This task requires careful evaluation of the media options' advantages and limitations, costs, and ability to deliver the message effectively to the target market.

Once the message and media strategies have been determined, steps must be taken to implement them. Most large companies hire advertising agencies to plan and produce their messages and to evaluate and purchase the media that will carry their ads. However, most agencies work very closely with their clients as they develop the ads and select media, because it is the advertiser that ultimately approves (and pays for) the creative work and media plan.

A similar process takes place for the other elements of the IMC program as objectives are set, an overall strategy is developed, message and media strategies are determined,

and steps are taken to implement them. While the marketer's advertising agencies may be used to perform some of the other IMC functions, they may also hire other communication specialists such as direct-marketing and interactive and/or sales promotion agencies, as well as public relations firms.

Monitoring, Evaluation, and Control

The final stage of the promotional planning process is monitoring, evaluating, and controlling the promotional program. It is important to determine how well the promotional program is meeting communications objectives and helping the firm accomplish its overall marketing goals and objectives. The promotional planner wants to know not only how well the promotional program is doing but also why. For example, problems with the advertising program may lie in the nature of the message or in a media plan that does not reach the target market effectively. The manager must know the reasons for the results in order to take the right steps to correct the program.

This final stage of the process is designed to provide managers with continual feedback concerning the effectiveness of the promotional program, which in turn can be used as input into the planning process. As Figure 1-3 shows, information on the results achieved by the promotional program is used in subsequent promotional planning and strategy development.

Perspective and Organization of This Text

Traditional approaches to teaching advertising, promotional strategy, or marketing communications courses have often treated the various elements of the promotional mix as separate functions. As a result, many people who work in advertising, sales promotion, direct marketing, or public relations tend to approach marketing communications problems from the perspective of their particular specialty. An advertising person may believe marketing communications objectives are best met through the use of media advertising; a promotional specialist argues for a sales promotion program to motivate consumer response; a public relations person advocates a PR campaign to tackle the problem. These orientations are not surprising, since each person has been trained to view marketing communications problems primarily from one perspective.

In the contemporary business world, however, individuals working in marketing, advertising, and other promotional areas are expected to understand and use a variety of marketing communications tools, not just the one in which they specialize. Ad agencies no longer confine their services to the advertising area. Many are involved in sales promotion, public relations, direct marketing, event sponsorship, and other marketing communications areas. Individuals working on the client or advertiser side of the business, such as brand, product, or promotional managers, are developing marketing programs that use a variety of marketing communications methods.

This text views advertising and promotion from an integrated marketing communications perspective. We will examine all the promotional-mix elements and their roles in an organization's integrated marketing communications efforts. Although media advertising may be the most visible part of the communications program, understanding its role in contemporary marketing requires attention to other promotional areas such as the Internet and interactive marketing, direct marketing, sales promotion, public relations, and personal selling. Not all the promotional-mix areas are under the direct control of the advertising or marketing communications manager. For example, personal selling is typically a specialized marketing function outside the control of the advertising or promotional department. Likewise, publicity/public relations is often assigned to a separate department. All these departments should, however, communicate to coordinate all the organization's marketing communications tools.

The purpose of this book is to provide you with a thorough understanding of the field of advertising and other elements of a firm's promotional mix and show how they are combined to form an integrated marketing communications program. To plan, develop, and implement an effective IMC program, those involved must understand marketing, consumer behavior, and the communications process. The first part of this book is designed to provide this foundation by examining the roles of advertising and other forms of promotion in the marketing process. We examine the process of market

segmentation and positioning and consider their part in developing an IMC strategy. We also discuss how firms organize for IMC and make decisions regarding ad agencies and other firms that provide marketing and promotional services.

We then focus on consumer behavior considerations and analyze the communications process. We discuss various communications models of value to promotional planners in developing strategies and establishing goals and objectives for advertising and other forms of promotion. We also consider how firms determine and allocate their marketing communications budget.

After laying the foundation for the development of a promotional program, this text will follow the integrated marketing communications planning model presented in Figure 1-4. We examine each of the promotional-mix variables, beginning with advertising. Our detailed examination of advertising includes a discussion of creative strategy and the process of developing the advertising message, an overview of media strategy, and an evaluation of the various media (print, broadcast, and support media). The discussion then turns to the other areas of the promotional mix: direct marketing, interactive/Internet marketing, sales promotion, public relations/publicity, and personal selling. Our examination of the IMC planning process concludes with a discussion of how the promotional program is monitored, evaluated, and controlled. Particular attention is given to measuring the effectiveness of advertising and other forms of promotion.

The final part of the text examines special topic areas and perspectives that have become increasingly important in contemporary marketing. We will examine the area of international advertising and promotion and the challenges companies face in developing IMC programs for global markets as well as various countries around the world. The text concludes with an examination of the environment in which integrated marketing communications operates, including the regulatory, social, and economic factors that influence, and in turn are influenced by, an organization's advertising and promotional program.

Summary

Advertising and other forms of promotion are an integral part of the marketing process in most organizations. Over the past decade, the amount of money spent on advertising, sales promotion, direct marketing, and other forms of marketing communication has increased tremendously, both in the United States and in foreign markets. To understand the role of advertising and promotion in a marketing program, one must understand the role and function of marketing in an organization. The basic task of marketing is to combine the four controllable elements, known as the marketing mix, into a comprehensive program that facilitates exchange with a target market. The elements of the marketing mix are the product or service, price, place (distribution), and promotion.

For many years, the promotional function in most companies was dominated by mass-media advertising. However, more and more companies are recognizing the importance of integrated marketing communications, coordinating the various marketing and promotional elements to achieve more efficient and effective communication programs. A number of factors underlie the move toward IMC by marketers as well as ad agencies and other promotional facilitators. Reasons for the growing importance of the integrated marketing communications perspective include a rapidly changing environment with respect to consumers, technology, and media. The IMC movement is also being driven by changes in the ways companies market their products and services. A shift in marketing dollars from advertising to sales promotion, the rapid growth and development of database marketing, and the fragmentation of media markets are among the key changes taking place.

Promotion is best viewed as the communication function of marketing. It is accomplished through a promotional mix that includes advertising, personal selling, publicity/public relations, sales promotion, direct marketing, and interactive/Internet marketing. The inherent advantages and disadvantages of each of these promotional-mix elements influence the roles they play in the overall marketing program. In developing the promotional program, the marketer must decide which tools to use and how to combine them to achieve the organization's marketing and communication objectives.

Promotional management involves coordinating the promotional-mix elements to develop an integrated program of effective marketing communication. The model of the IMC planning process in Figure 1-4 contains a number of steps: a review of the marketing plan; promotional program situation analysis; analysis of the communications process; budget determination; development of an integrated marketing communications program; integration and implementation of marketing communications strategies; and monitoring, evaluation, and control of the promotional program.

Key Terms

marketing, 7
exchange, 7
relationship marketing, 7
mass customization, 7
marketing mix, 8
integrated marketing communications (IMC), 9
promotion, 16
promotional mix, 16
advertising, 16
direct marketing, 18
direct-response advertising, 20
interactive media, 20
sales promotion, 21
publicity, 22
public relations, 23
personal selling, 23
promotional management, 24
promotional plan, 25
marketing plan, 25
internal analysis, 25
external analysis, 28
marketing objectives, 31
communication objectives, 31

Discussion Questions

1. Analyze the role of integrated marketing communications in the recruitment efforts of various branches of the military such as the U.S. Army. How can each element of the promotional mix be used by the military in its recruitment marketing?

2. Discuss the role integrated marketing communications plays in relationship marketing. How might the mass customization of advertising and other forms of marketing communication be possible?

3. Choose a company or organization and discuss how it communicates with its customers at the corporate, marketing and the marketing communications levels.

4. Discuss how the integrated marketing communications perspective differs from traditional advertising and promotion. What are some of the reasons more marketers and more companies are taking an integrated marketing communications perspective in their advertising and promotional programs?

5. Discuss the concept of buzz marketing and some of the reasons markets are using the technique. Do you think there are any ethical issues that should be considered in using buzz marketing techniques?

6. Why are marketers putting so much emphasis on developing strong brands? Choose one of the top 10 brands listed in IMC Perspective 1-2 and discuss how the company has used integrated marketing communications to build a strong brand image.

7. Discuss the role of direct marketing as an IMC tool, giving attention to the various forms of direct marketing.

8. Analyze the role of the Internet in the integrated marketing communications program of a company. Discuss how the Internet can be used to execute the various elements of the promotional mix.

9. IMC Perspective 1-3 discusses how marketers responded to the tragedy resulting from the terrorist attack of September 11, 2001. Do you think that companies are still being influenced by this tragedy with respect to the planning and execution of their integrated marketing communication programs? If so, how are they being affected?

10. Why is it important for those who work in the field of advertising and promotion to understand and appreciate all various integrated marketing communications tools, not just the area in which they specialize?

The Role of IMC in the Marketing Process

2

Chapter Objectives

1. To understand the marketing process and the role of advertising and promotion in an organization's integrated marketing program.
2. To know the various decision areas under each element of the marketing mix and how they influence and interact with advertising and promotional strategy.
3. To understand the concept of target marketing in an integrated marketing communications program.
4. To recognize the role of market segmentation and its use in an integrated marketing communications program.
5. To understand the use of positioning and repositioning strategies.

Look Out Sony—The Koreans Are Coming!

Have you ever heard of Samsung? Probably not, unless you own a microwave oven (the company's preeminent U.S. brand presence). But then again, not too many people had heard of Sony back in the early 1960s. Like Sony, which was initially known for its clock radios and small black-and-white TVs and was a secondary player relative to Motorola, Philips, and Zenith, Samsung has been known in the United States for low-end products, such as VCRs, TVs, and microwave ovens. Now the company wants to be like Sony in another way—by becoming a well-known, market-leading electronics brand. In fact, Korea-based Samsung has Sony in its crosshairs—its goal is to be a stronger brand name than Sony by the year 2005.

Not likely, you say? Well, don't tell that to Samsung. Consider this: While the Japanese companies Fujitsu, Hitachi, Matsushita, NEC, and Toshiba have all been losing money and Sony has been struggling, Samsung has been on a roll, turning a $2.2 billion profit on sales of $24.7 billion in 2001. Not only that, but Samsung now manufactures laptops, DVDs, cell phones, and flat-screen TVs (among many other products) and is ranked fifth in the world in patents, behind IBM, NEC, Canon, and Micron Technology. The firm's growth has caught the attention of the competition, who now no longer doubt that Samsung can do it.

Samsung's strategy is to reposition its current brands upward. The company's most well known brand, Sanyo, produced copycat products—cheaper versions of Sony or Mitsubishi products. But since 1997, the company has changed its image by producing more upscale, top-of-the line offerings. It is pulling out of big discount chains like Kmart and Wal-Mart, which focus on price over quality, and moving in to Best Buy, Circuit City, and other specialty stores. And while its brands are still slightly lower priced than the very top names, the Samsung label is right there with them in quality.

The change in image has been supported by changes in advertising and promotion. A new campaign, "DigitAll:Everyone's Invited," attempts to position Samsung products as exciting, cutting edge, and reasonably priced. The company's 55 different advertising agencies were consolidated into one. Over $900 million was to be spent on global IMC marketing campaigns in 2002, $70 million of it in the United States, including the cost of a redesigned 65-foot-high electronic billboard in New York's Times Square and a high-profile presence at the Olympic Games in Salt Lake City. The

current advertising campaign is designed to raise awareness, as well as to enhance the brand image. The focus of the ads is surreal, many featuring the "snow woman"—a hauntingly beautiful woman who imparts an expensive and classy feeling to the viewer and, hopefully, to the brand. The ads will appear on television, in print, and on retail and outdoor billboards.

Samsung's Olympic sponsorship typifies the repositioning strategy the company has undertaken. Samsung's objectives in Salt Lake were "to provide Olympic fans, athletes and their families with entertaining and memorable Olympic experiences" and "to showcase [its] leadership in digital convergence by letting spectators touch and feel products that will soon be unveiled to the U.S. market" (Il-Hyung Chang, head of Samsung's Olympic projects). The Olympic Rendezvous was the centerpiece of the sponsorship. Located in Salt Lake Olympic Square, the sponsorship provided daily entertainment shows, athlete appearances, future product displays, free phone calls, and other forms of entertainment. More than 240,000 people visited the Rendezvous during the 16-day period, and it was rated the top attraction in Olympic Square by visiting fans. Perhaps more important, 74 percent of the visitors stated they now had a more positive image of Samsung, and 76 percent indicated a willingness to purchase a Samsung product in the future.

The Internet is also a major part of the new IMC program. Samsung will have front-page sponsorships on 50 major websites, including Fortune.com, Forbes.com, BusinessWeek.com, and other business publication sites. CNN.com and EW.com will also be included in an attempt to reach 300 million "hits" per month. By being on these sites, Samsung hopes to associate its brand with other well-known, and well-expected, brands. Joint product development ventures with strong-brand-image companies such as Sprint, Texas Instruments, and Dell are also working to reposition the brand.

So far, the efforts appear to have gone well. According to Interbrand—a brand consulting firm in New York—Samsung's brand-value rank is 43 (Sony's is 18). While still behind Sony, the brand's value rose 22 percent in 2001, with only Starbucks doing better. The Samsung brand ranks number 1 in flat-panel monitors and DRAM semiconductor memory chips. It is number 2, behind Sony, in DVD players and number 3 in mobile handsets. Samsung is, by far, the largest corporate presence in South Korea. Overall, Samsung is the second most recognizable consumer electronics brand in the world, according to Interbrand. A very strong player in China, Russia, and Korea, Samsung has now become a global brand as well, with 70 percent of its sales outside these three countries.

Can Samsung overtake Sony? As of now, the company has less than half the revenue of Sony, but it is no longer just making cheaper versions of Sony products. Robert Batt, of Nebraska Furniture Mart, thinks Samsung can outstrip Sony. To quote the $300 million retailer, "Someone shook that company up. It's moving up with the big boys." Look out big boys!

Sources: Christopher Saunders, "Samsung Ramps Up Web Efforts in New Campaign," InternetNews.com, May 24, 2002, pp.1–2; William J. Holstein, "Samsung's Golden Touch," *Fortune,* Apr. 1, 2002, pp. 89–94; Frank Gibney, Jr., "Samsung Moves Upmarket," *Time,* Mar. 25, 2002, pp. 49–52; Heidi Brown, "Look Out, Sony," *Forbes,* June 11, 2001, pp. 96–98.

The Samsung example is just one of many image-creating strategies that demonstrate a number of important marketing strategies that will be discussed in this chapter. These include the identification of market opportunities, market segmentation, target marketing and positioning, and marketing program development. Samsung's recognition of the importance of a strong brand image coupled with a strong IMC program reflects the solid marketing orientation required to be successful in today's marketplace.

In this chapter, we take a closer look at how marketing strategies influence the role of promotion and how promotional decisions must be coordinated with other areas of the marketing mix. In turn, all elements of the marketing mix must be consistent in a

strategic plan that results in an integrated marketing communications program. We use the model in Figure 2-1 as a framework for analyzing how promotion fits into an organization's marketing strategy and programs.

This model consists of four major components: the organization's marketing strategy and analysis, the target marketing process, the marketing planning program development (which includes the promotional mix), and the target market. As the model shows, the marketing process begins with the development of a marketing strategy and analysis in which the company decides the product or service areas and particular markets where it wants to compete. The company must then coordinate the various elements of the marketing mix into a cohesive marketing program that will reach the target market effectively. Note that a firm's promotion program is directed not only to the final buyer but also to the channel or "trade" members that distribute its products to the ultimate consumer. These channel members must be convinced there is a demand for the company's products so they will carry them and will aggressively merchandise and promote them to consumers. Promotions play an important role in the marketing program for building and maintaining demand not only among final consumers but among the trade as well.

As noted in Chapter 1, all elements of the marketing mix—price, product, distribution, and promotions—must be integrated to provide consistency and maximum communications impact. Development of a marketing plan is instrumental in achieving this goal.

As Figure 2-1 shows, development of a marketing program requires an in-depth analysis of the market. This analysis may make extensive use of marketing research as an input into the planning process. This input, in turn, provides the basis for the development of marketing strategies in regard to product, pricing, distribution, and promotion decisions. Each of these steps requires a detailed analysis, since this plan serves as the road map to follow in achieving marketing goals. Once the detailed market analysis has been completed and marketing objectives have been established, each element in the marketing mix must contribute to a comprehensive integrated marketing program. Of course, the promotional program element (the focus of this text) must be combined with all other program elements in such a way as to achieve maximum impact.

Figure 2-1 Marketing and promotions process model

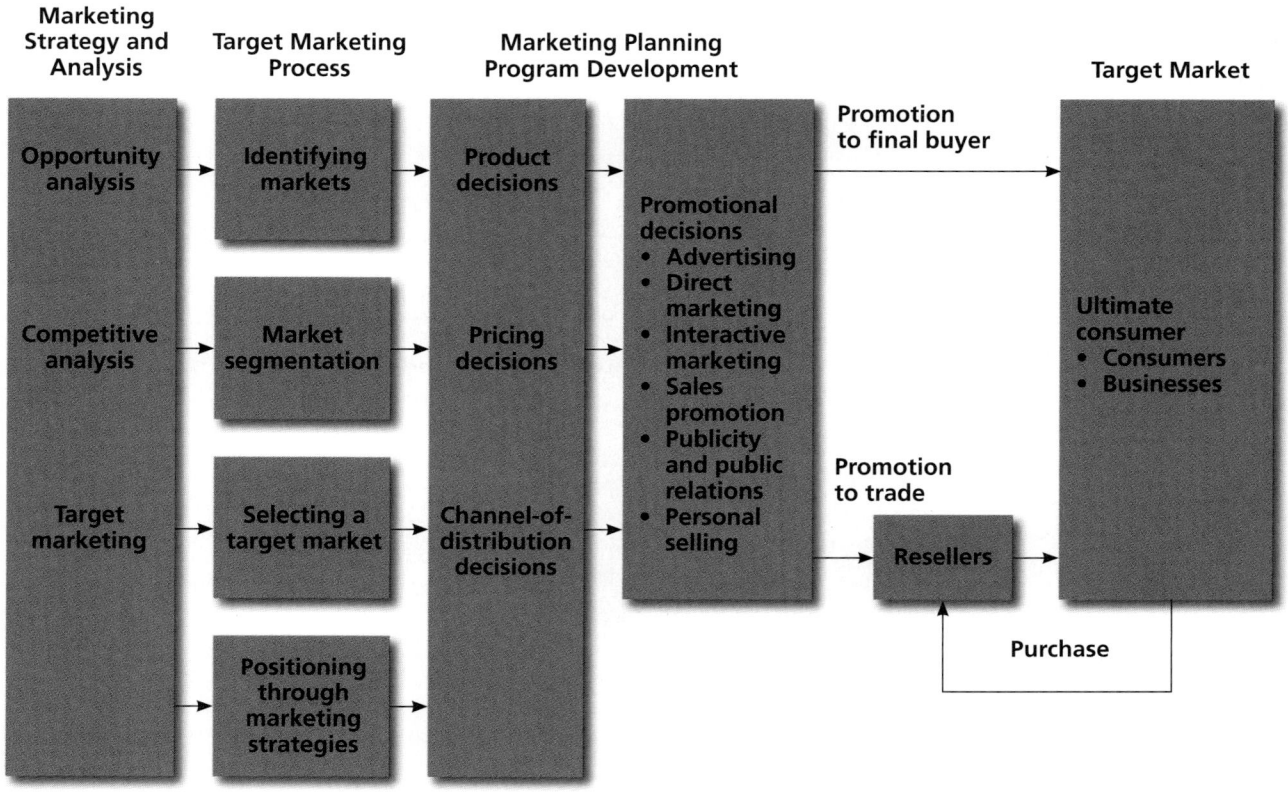

Marketing Strategy and Analysis

Any organization that wants to exchange its products or services in the marketplace successfully should have a **strategic marketing plan** to guide the allocation of its resources. A strategic marketing plan usually evolves from an organization's overall corporate strategy and serves as a guide for specific marketing programs and policies. For example, a few years ago Abercrombie & Fitch decided to reposition the brand as part of the overall corporate effort to attract a younger audience. As we noted earlier, marketing strategy is based on a situation analysis—a detailed assessment of the current marketing conditions facing the company, its product lines, or its individual brands. From this situation analysis, a firm develops an understanding of the market and the various opportunities it offers, the competition, and the **market segments** or target markets the company wishes to pursue. We examine each step of the marketing strategy and *planning* in this chapter.

Opportunity Analysis

A careful analysis of the marketplace should lead to alternative market opportunities for existing product lines in current or new markets, new products for current markets, or new products for new markets. **Market opportunities** are areas where there are favorable demand trends, where the company believes customer needs and opportunities are not being satisfied, and where it can compete effectively. For example, the number of people who exercise has increased tremendously in recent years, and the market for athletic footwear has reached over $13.5 billion.[1] Athletic-shoe companies such as Nike, Reebok, and others see the shoe market as an opportunity to broaden their customer base both domestically and internationally. To capitalize on this growth, some companies spend millions of dollars on advertising alone. In 2001 New Balance spent "only" $13 million, Reebok spent $49 million and Nike spent over $155 million. All told, athletic-footwear companies spent over $5.9 billion on advertising and celebrity endorsements in 2001.[2] Changes in lifestyles have seen changes in the market for trail, running, basketball, and "lifestyle" shoes such as slip-ons (Exhibit 2-1).

A company usually identifies market opportunities by carefully examining the marketplace and noting demand trends and competition in various market segments. A market can rarely be viewed as one large homogeneous group of customers; rather, it consists of many heterogeneous groups, or segments. In recent years, many companies have recognized the importance of tailoring their marketing to meet the needs and demand trends of different market segments.

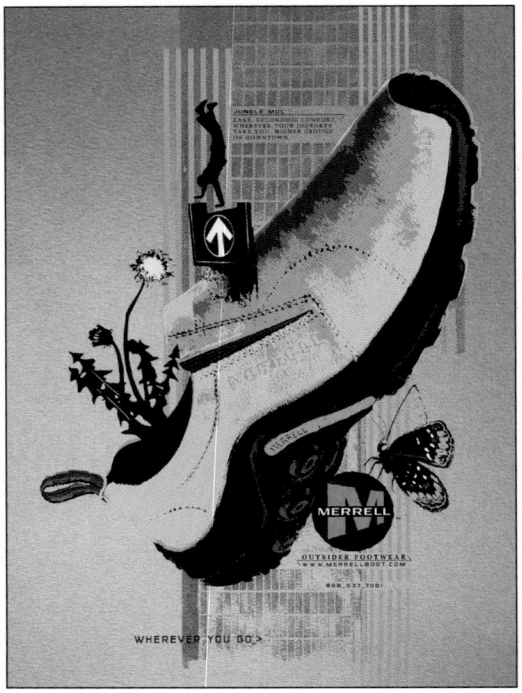

Exhibit 2-1 Merrell sees market opportunities for "lifestyle" shoes

For example, different market segments in the personal computer (PC) industry include the home, education, science, and business markets. These segments can be even further divided. The business market consists of both small companies and large corporations; the education market can range from elementary schools to colleges and universities. A company that is marketing its products in the auto industry must decide in which particular market segment or segments it wishes to compete. This decision depends on the amount and nature of competition the brand will face in a particular market. For example, a number of companies that have been successful in the luxury-car segment have now introduced SUVs. Lincoln, Cadillac, Lexus, BMW, and Mercedes now offer models in this line. Porsche—a successful participant in the sports-car segment—will introduce its SUV in 2004. A competitive analysis is an important part of marketing strategy development and warrants further consideration.

Competitive Analysis

In developing the firm's marketing strategies and plans for its products and services, the manager must carefully analyze the competition to be faced in the marketplace. This may range from direct brand competition (which can also include its own brands) to more indirect forms of competition, such as product substitutes. For example, when Lay's introduced Baked Lay's low-fat chips, the product ended up taking away sales from the regular Lay's potato chip brand. At the same time, new consumers were gained from competing brands of potato chips.

In addition to having direct potato chip competitors, Lay's faces competition from other types of snack foods, such as pretzels and crackers. One might argue that other low-fat products also offer the consumer a choice and compete with Lay's as well (e.g., fruits). The sale of bagels has declined in recent years as competitors have introduced breakfast bars (Nutri-Grain and Quaker Oats) and breakfast snacks such as Chex Morning Mix.

At a more general level, marketers must recognize they are competing for the consumer's discretionary income, so they must understand the various ways potential customers choose to spend their money. For example, sales of motorcycles in the United States had declined significantly in the late 1980s and early 1990s. This decline reflected shifting demographic patterns; aging baby boomers are less inclined to ride motorcycles, and the number of 18- to 34-year-old males has been declining. The drop in sales could also be attributed to the number of other options consumers could spend their discretionary income on, including Jet Skis, dirt bikes, home fitness equipment, spas, and home entertainment systems such as large-screen TVs and stereos. Thus, motorcycle marketers like Honda and Harley-Davidson had to convince potential buyers that a motorcycle was worth a sizable portion of their disposable income in comparison to other purchase options. Through successful marketing strategies, the industry was effective in reversing the downturn, increasing sales by over 25 percent by the late 1990s.[3]

An important aspect of marketing strategy development is the search for a **competitive advantage,** something special a firm does or has that gives it an edge over competitors. Ways to achieve a competitive advantage include having quality products that command a premium price, providing superior customer service, having the lowest production costs and lower prices, or dominating channels of distribution. Competitive advantage can also be achieved through advertising that creates and maintains product differentiation and brand equity, an example of which was the long-running advertising campaign for Michelin tires, which stressed security as well as performance. For example, the strong brand images of Colgate toothpaste, Campbell's soup, Nike shoes, Kodak, and McDonald's give them a competitive advantage in their respective markets (Exhibit 2-2).

Recently, there has been concern that some marketers have not been spending enough money on advertising to allow leading brands to sustain their competitive edge. Advertising proponents have been calling for companies to protect their brand equity and franchises by investing more money in advertising instead of costly trade promotions. Some companies, recognizing the important competitive advantage strong brands provide, have been increasing their investments in them. Capital One and McDonald's are just two of many examples. Capital One used public relations,

Exhibit 2-2 Campbell's campaign stresses taste and convenience

Exhibit 2-3 Capital One's new branding campaign also uses celebrities

direct marketing and $96 million in media spending on a new branding campaign designed to show the protection offered by their credit cards (Exhibit 2-3).

Companies must be concerned with the ever-changing competitive environment. Competitors' marketing programs have a major impact on a firm's marketing strategy, so they must be analyzed and monitored. The reactions of competitors to a company's marketing and promotional strategy are also very important. Competitors may cut price, increase promotional spending, develop new brands, or attack one another through comparative advertising. One of the more intense competitive rivalries is the battle between Coca-Cola and Pepsi. A number of other intense competitive rivalries exist in the marketplace, including Hertz and Avis and Ford and GM among others.

A final aspect of competition is the growing number of foreign companies penetrating the U.S. market and taking business from domestic firms. In products ranging from beer to cars to electronics, imports are becoming an increasingly strong form of competition with which U.S. firms must contend. As we move to a more global economy, U.S. companies must not only defend their domestic markets but also learn how to compete effectively in the international marketplace.

Target Market Selection

After evaluating the opportunities presented by various market segments, including a detailed competitive analysis, the company may select one, or more, as a target market. This target market becomes the focus of the firm's marketing effort, and goals and objectives are set according to where the company wants to be and what it hopes to accomplish in this market. As noted in Chapter 1, these goals and objectives are set in terms of specific performance variables such as sales, market share, and profitability. The selection of the target market (or markets) in which the firm will compete is an important part of its marketing strategy and has direct implications for its advertising and promotional efforts.

Recall from our discussion of the integrated marketing communications planning program that the situation analysis is conducted at the beginning of the promotional planning process. Specific objectives—both marketing and communications—are derived from the situation analysis, and the promotional-mix strategies are developed to achieve these objectives. Marketers rarely go after the entire market with one product, brand, or service offering. Rather, they pursue a number of different strategies, breaking the market into segments and targeting one or more of these segments for marketing and promotional efforts. This means different objectives may be established, different budgets may be used, and the promotional-mix strategies may vary, depending on the market approach used.

Figure 2-2 The target marketing process

The Target Marketing Process

Because few, if any, products can satisfy the needs of all consumers, companies often develop different marketing strategies to satisfy different consumer needs. The process by which marketers do this (presented in Figure 2-2) is referred to as **target marketing** and involves four basic steps: identifying markets with unfulfilled needs, segmenting the market, targeting specific segments, and positioning one's product or service through marketing strategies.

Identifying Markets

When employing a target marketing strategy, the marketer identifies the specific needs of groups of people (or segments), selects one or more of these segments as a target, and develops marketing programs directed to each. This approach has found increased applicability in marketing for a number of reasons, including changes in the market (consumers are becoming much more diverse in their needs, attitudes, and lifestyles); increased use of segmentation by competitors; and the fact that more managers are trained in segmentation and realize the advantages associated with this strategy. Perhaps the best explanation, however, comes back to the basic premise that you must understand as much as possible about consumers to design marketing programs that meet their needs most effectively.

Target market identification isolates consumers with similar lifestyles, needs, and the like, and increases our knowledge of their specific requirements. The more marketers can establish this common ground with consumers, the more effective they will be in addressing these requirements in their communications programs and informing and/or persuading potential consumers that the product or service offering will meet their needs.

Let's use the beer industry as an example. Years ago, beer was just beer, with little differentiation, many local distributors, and few truly national brands. The industry began consolidating; many brands were assumed by the larger brewers or ceased to exist. As the number of competitors decreased, competition among the major brewers increased. To compete more effectively, brewers began to look at different tastes, lifestyles, and so on, of beer drinkers and used this information in their marketing strategies. This process resulted in the identification of many market segments, each of which corresponds to different customers' needs, lifestyles, and other characteristics.

As you can see in Figure 2-3, the beer market has become quite segmented, offering superpremiums, premiums, populars (low price), imports, lights (low calorie), and

Figure 2-3 Market breakdown by product in the beer industry

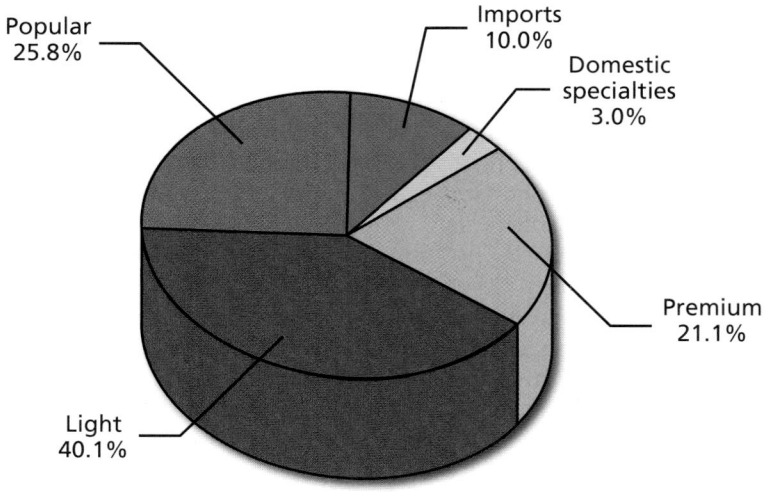

Exhibit 2-4 Grupo Modelo offers a variety of products to market

malts. Low-alcohol and nonalcoholic brands have also been introduced, as has draft beer in bottles and cans. And there are now imported lights, superpremium drafts, dry beers, and on and on. As you can see in Exhibit 2-4, to market to these various segments, Grupo Modelo pursues a strategy whereby it offers a variety of products from which consumers can choose, varying the marketing mix for each. Each appeals to a different set of needs. Taste is certainly one; others include image, cost, and the size of one's waistline. A variety of other reasons for purchasing are also operating, including the consumer's social class, lifestyle, and economic status.

Marketers competing in nearly all product and service categories are constantly searching for ways to segment their markets in an attempt to better satisfy customers' needs. Diversity Perspective 2-1 discusses the increasing emphasis being placed on marketing to ethnic groups. The remainder of this section discusses ways to approach this task.

Market Segmentation

It is not possible to develop marketing strategies for every consumer. Rather, the marketer attempts to identify broad classes of buyers who have the same needs and will respond similarly to marketing actions. As noted by Eric N. Berkowitz, Roger A. Kerin, and William Rudelius, **market segmentation** is "dividing up a market into distinct groups that (1) have common needs and (2) will respond similarly to a marketing action."[4] The segmentation process involves five distinct steps:

1. Finding ways to group consumers according to their needs.
2. Finding ways to group the marketing actions—usually the products offered—available to the organization.
3. Developing a market-product grid to relate the market segments to the firm's products or actions.
4. Selecting the target segments toward which the firm directs its marketing actions.
5. Taking marketing actions to reach target segments.

The more marketers segment the market, the more precise is their understanding of it. But the more the market becomes divided, the fewer consumers there are in each segment. Thus, a key decision is, How far should one go in the segmentation process? Where does the process stop? As you can see by the strategy taken in the beer industry, it can go far!

In planning the promotional effort, managers consider whether the target segment is substantial enough to support individualized strategies. More specifically, they consider whether this group is accessible. Can it be reached with a communications program? For example, you will see in Chapter 10 that in some instances there are no media that can be used to reach some targeted groups. Or the promotions manager may identify a number of segments but be unable to develop the required programs to reach them. The firm may have insufficient funds to develop the required advertising campaign, inadequate sales staff to cover all areas, or other promotional deficiencies. After determining that a segmentation strategy is in order, the marketer must establish the basis on which it will address the market. The following section discusses some of the bases for segmenting markets and demonstrates advertising and promotions applications.

DIVERSITY PERSPECTIVE 2-1

Marketers Reach Out to Hispanics—A Multidimensional Segment

It seems that U.S. marketers have finally discovered the Hispanic market. Not that it hasn't been here for some time; it has. And not that it isn't of substantial size; it is. So what has suddenly woken Madison Avenue to the potential in this market? A number of things.

First, consider the size of the Hispanic market—35.3 million people. Second, consider the growth rate—58 percent in the past decade (four times that of the overall population). Third, throw in the estimated $400 billion in buying power, which "seems impervious to the Nasdaq's swoons" according to Marci McDonald of *U.S. News & World Report.* The end result is an extremely attractive market. And, unlike the case in the past, this market has finally attracted the attention of some big-time marketers.

CBS has noticed. Hoping that the Hispanic market will help reverse the downward trend in the size of its soap opera audience, the network has introduced a Spanish simulcast of *The Bold and the Beautiful* titled *Belleza y Poder* ("Beauty and Power"). Liz Claiborne Cosmetics introduced its new perfume, Mambo, with a $20 million campaign targeting Latinos (among others), and the American Association of Retired Persons (AARP) has more specifically targeted the over-50 Hispanic market with a $3 million campaign. Among the other firms now increasing their efforts in this market are MasterCard International, Reader's Digest, and Tillamook Cheese.

Even though there has been a significant increase in spending in the Hispanic market, Spanish-language and bilingual campaigns still account for only about one percent of the $200 billion advertisers spend yearly on broadcast media (another $250 million goes to magazines and newspapers). While some companies already spend heavily to attract this segment (e.g., Sears has targeted this market for over 10 years, and AT&T spent about $35 million on it in 2001), most have simply ignored the segment—until now. The fact that young Hispanics will become the largest ethnic youth population in the United States by 2005 has made more marketers take notice.

Reaching this segment may not be as easy as it seems, however. Roberto Ramos, president of the Ruido Group, a Hispanic-youth-focused communication agency in New York, notes: "One of the biggest misconceptions about Hispanic youth is that they are a homogeneous group. Puerto Ricans, Colombians and Cubans are not all the same. What works to attract one group may not work for another." Erasmo Arteaga, a

Sears store manager in West Covina, California, adds: "People think Hispanic means one thing, . . . But it's different from Miami to Southern California. And here in California, it's not just Mexicans; it's Guatemalans, Salvadorans, and other people from Central America." Arteaga notes that two Hispanic-designated stores in Los Angeles only 20 miles apart reflect very different buying motives. While this segment is certainly a challenging market, there is no doubt among many marketers that Hispanics are worth the effort. Consider some of the efforts being taken:

- Reader's Digest has launched *Selecciones* magazine, a magazine showcasing Latinos.
- MasterCard International maintains a Spanish-language website to encourage Latinos to apply for credit cards.
- AC Nielsen formed a Southern California Hispanic-consumer panel to learn more about the likes and dislikes of this audience.
- American Airlines has an in-flight magazine titled *NEXOS* that is targeted at Hispanics.
- The "Got Milk" campaign now includes Spanish versions of the ads.
- Galavision, a Spanish-language cable station, launched five youth programs aimed at bilingual and bicultural Hispanic youth.
- Throughout its bilingual TV, print, and radio campaigns, the Office of National Drug Control Policy focuses its antidrug message on the strong family values inherent in Hispanic cultures.

The above are just a few examples of the many companies and organizations targeting the Hispanic market. With the segment's strong growth rates in population and in spending power, you can be sure that many more will join in. The question is, will they

take the time and effort required to understand the diversity of this market, or will they simply attempt to reach Hispanics through the appeals and media they employ for other ethnic groups. One thing is sure: If they pursue the latter strategy, they won't be in the Hispanic market for very long.

Sources: John Kerrigan "Playing to Hispanics garners rewards," *Marketing News*, July 22, 2002, p. 20; Jennifer Gonzalez McPherson, "Targeting Teens," *Hispanic Magazine*, September 2001, pp. 33-36; Marci McDonald, "Madison Avenue's New Latin Beat," *U.S. News & World Report*, June 4, 2001, p. 42; Greg Johnson, "Gaining Insight into the Latino Middle Class," *Los Angeles Times*, June 11, 2001, p. C-1.

Exhibit 2-5 Big Red markets to a specific geographic region

Bases for Segmentation As shown in Figure 2-4, several methods are available for segmenting markets. Marketers may use one of the segmentation variables or a combination of approaches. Consider the market segmentation strategy that might be employed to market snow skis. The consumer's lifestyle—active, fun-loving, enjoys outdoor sports—is certainly important. But so are other factors, such as age (participation in downhill skiing drops off significantly at about age 30) and income (Have you seen the price of a lift ticket lately?), as well as marital status. Let us review the bases for segmentation and examine some promotional strategies employed in each.

Geographic Segmentation In the **geographic segmentation** approach, markets are divided into different geographic units. These units may include nations, states, counties, or even neighborhoods. Consumers often have different buying habits depending on where they reside. For example, General Motors, among other car manufacturers, considers California a very different market from the rest of the United States and has developed specific marketing programs targeted to the consumers in that state. Other companies have developed programs targeted at specific regions. Exhibit 2-5 shows an ad for Big Red, just one of the regional soft-drink "cult" brands—along with Cheerwine (the Carolinas), Vernors (Michigan), and Moxie (New England)—that have found success by marketing in regional areas (in this case, Texas). One company—Olde Brooklyn Beverage Company—has even gone so far as to promote a brand based on a specific section of New York City, differentiating it from bigger brands by promoting the product's "Brooklyn Attitude."

Demographic Segmentation Dividing the market on the basis of demographic variables such as age, sex, family size, education, income, and social class is called **demographic segmentation.** Secret deodorant and the Lady Schick shaver are products that have met with a great deal of success by using the demographic variable of sex as a basis for segmentation. iVillage, a website targeting women, may be one of the most successful websites on the Internet (Exhibit 2-6).

Although market segmentation on the basis of demographics may seem obvious, companies sometimes discover that they need to focus more attention on a specific demographic group. For example, Kodak and Procter & Gamble, among others, have had to redo their images for younger markets. Abercrombie changed its image to reach the "echo-boomer" (18- to 22-year-old) segment (Exhibit 2-7). Magazines like *Modern Maturity* are targeted to the estimated 76 million people in the "Be Generation," who are now in their fifties or older or are from the baby-boomer generation, the cohort born between 1946 and 1964, and *Segunda Juventud* to the 50+ Hispanic market (Exhibit 2-8).

Other products that have successfully employed demographic segmentation include Virginia Slims cigarettes (sex), Doan's Pills (age), JCPenney Co. (race), Mercedes-Benz and BMW cars (income), and prepackaged dinners (family size).

While demographics may still be the most common method of segmenting markets, it is important to recognize that other factors may be the underlying basis for homogeneity and/or consumer behavior. The astute marketer will identify additional bases for segmenting and will recognize the limitations of demographics.

Figure 2-4 Some bases for market segmentation

Main Dimension	Segmentation Variables	Typical Breakdowns
Customer Characteristics		
Geographic	Region	Northeast; Midwest; South; West; etc.
	City size	Under 10,000; 10,000–24,999; 25,000–49,999; 50,000–99,999; 100,000–249,999; 250,000–499,999; 500,000–999,999; 1,000,000 or more
	Metropolitan area	Metropolitan statistical area (MSAs); etc.
	Density	Urban; suburban; small town; rural
Demographic	Gender	Male; female
	Age	Under 6 yrs; 6–11 yrs; 12–17 yrs; 18–24 yrs; 25–34 yrs; 35–44 yrs; 45–54 yrs; 55–64 yrs; 65–74 yrs; 75 yrs plus
	Race	African-American; Asian; Hispanic; White/Caucasian; etc.
	Life stage	Infant; preschool; child; youth; collegiate; adult; senior
	Birth era	Baby boomer (1949–1964); Generation X (1965–1976); baby boomlet/Generation Y (1977–present)
	Household size	1; 2; 3–4; 5 or more
	Residence tenure	Own home; rent home
	Marital status	Never married; married; separated; divorced; widowed
Socioeconomic	Income	<$15,000; $15,000–$24,999; $25,000–$34,999; $35,000–$49,999; $50,000–$74,999; $75,000+
	Education	Some high school or less; high school graduate (or GED); etc.
	Occupation	Managerial and professional specialty; technical, sales, and administrative support; service; farming, forestry, and fishing; etc.
Psychographic	Personality	Gregarious; compulsive; introverted; aggressive; ambitious; etc.
	Values (VALS)	Actualizers; fulfilleds; achievers; experiencers; believers; strivers; makers; strugglers
	Lifestyle (Claritas)	Settled in; white picket fence; and 46 other household segments
Buying Situations		
Outlet type	In-store	Department; specialty; outlet; convenience; supermarket; superstore/mass merchandiser; catalog
	Direct	Mail order/catalog; door-to-door; direct response; Internet
Benefits sought	Product features	Situation specific; general
	Needs	Quality; service; price/value; financing; warranty; etc.
Usage	Usage rate	Light user; medium user; heavy user
	User status	Nonuser; ex-user; prospect; first-time user; regular user
Awareness and intentions	Product knowledge	Unaware; aware; informed; interested; intending to buy; purchaser; rejection
Behavior	Involvement	Minimum effort; comparison; special effort

Exhibit 2-6 iVillage initiated a website targeted at women

Psychographic Segmentation Dividing the market on the basis of personality and/or lifestyles is referred to as **psychographic segmentation.** While there is some disagreement as to whether personality is a useful basis for segmentation, lifestyle factors have been used effectively. Many consider lifestyle the most effective criterion for segmentation.

The determination of lifestyles is usually based on an analysis of the activities, interests, and opinions (AIOs) of consumers. These lifestyles are then correlated with the consumers' product, brand, and/or media usage. For many products and/or services, lifestyles may be the best discriminator between use and nonuse, accounting for differences in food, clothing, and car selections, among numerous other consumer behaviors.[5]

Exhibit 2-7 Abercrombie & Fitch changed its image to appeal to echo boomers

Exhibit 2-8 *Segunda Juventud* targets the 50+ Hispanic segment

Psychographic segmentation has been increasingly accepted with the advent of the values and lifestyles (VALS) program. Although marketers employed lifestyle segmentation long before VALS and although a number of alternatives—for example, PRIZM—are available, VALS remains one of the more popular options. Developed by the Stanford Research Institute (SRI), VALS has become a very popular method for applying lifestyle segmentation. VALS 2 divides Americans into eight lifestyle segments that exhibit distinctive attitudes, behaviors, and decision-making patterns.[6] SRI believes that when combined with an estimate of the resources the consumer can draw on (education, income, health, energy level, self-confidence, and degree of consumerism), the VALS 2 system is an excellent predictor of consumer behaviors. A number of companies, including Chevron, Mercedes, and Eastman Kodak, have employed the VALS 2 program for a variety of purposes, including advertising, positioning, and media planning.

Behavioristic Segmentation Dividing consumers into groups according to their usage, loyalties, or buying responses to a product is **behavioristic segmentation.** For example, product or brand usage, degree of use (heavy versus light), and/or brand loyalty are combined with demographic and/or psychographic criteria to develop profiles of market segments. In the case of usage, the marketer assumes that nonpurchasers of a brand or product who have the same characteristics as purchasers hold greater potential for adoption than nonusers with different characteristics. A profile (demographic or psychographic) of the user is developed, which serves as the basis for promotional strategies designed to attract new users. For example, teenagers share certain similarities in their consumption behaviors. Those who do not currently own a Sony Discman are more likely to be potential buyers than people in other age groups.

Degree of use relates to the fact that a few consumers may buy a disproportionate amount of many products or brands. Industrial marketers refer to the **80-20 rule,** meaning 20 percent of their buyers account for 80 percent of their sales volume. Again, when the characteristics of these users are identified, targeting them allows for a much greater concentration of efforts and less wasted time and money. The same heavy-half strategy is possible in the consumer market as well. The majority of purchases of many products (e.g., soaps and detergents, shampoos, cake mixes, beer, dog food, colas, bourbon, and toilet tissue—yes, toilet tissue!) are accounted for by a small proportion of the population. Perhaps you can think of some additional examples.

Benefit Segmentation In purchasing products, consumers are generally trying to satisfy specific needs and/or wants. They are looking for products that provide specific benefits to satisfy these needs. The grouping of consumers on the basis of attributes sought in a product is known as **benefit segmentation** and is widely used (Exhibit 2-9).

Exhibit 2-9 Estrostep takes a unique approach in its dual-benefit ads

Consider the purchase of a wristwatch. While you might buy a watch for particular benefits such as accuracy, water resistance, or stylishness, others may seek a different set of benefits. Watches are commonly given as gifts for birthdays, Christmas, and graduation. Certainly some of the same benefits are considered in the purchase of a gift, but the benefits the purchaser derives are different from those the user will obtain. Ads that portray watches as good gifts stress different criteria to consider in the purchase decision. The next time you see an ad or commercial for a watch, think about the basic appeal and the benefits it offers.

Another example of benefit segmentation can be seen in the toothpaste market. Some consumers want a product with fluoride (Crest, Colgate); others prefer one that freshens their breath (Close-Up, Aqua-Fresh). More recent benefit segments offer tartar control (Crest) and plaque reduction (Viadent). The Den-Mat Corp. introduced Rembrandt whitening toothpaste for consumers who want whiter teeth, and other brands followed with their own whitening attributes.

The Process of Segmenting a Market

The segmentation process develops over time and is an integral part of the situation analysis. It is in this stage that marketers attempt to determine as much as they

can about the market: What needs are not being fulfilled? What benefits are being sought? What characteristics distinguish among the various groups seeking these products and services? A number of alternative segmentation strategies may be used. Each time a specific segment is identified, additional information is gathered to help the marketer understand this group.

For example, once a specific segment is identified on the basis of benefits sought, the marketer will examine lifestyle characteristics and demographics to help characterize this group and to further its understanding of this market. Behavioristic segmentation criteria will also be examined. In the purchase of ski boots, for example, specific benefits may be sought—flexibility or stiffness—depending on the type of skiing the buyer does. All this information will be combined to provide a complete profile of the skier.

A number of companies now offer research services to help marketing managers define their markets and develop strategies targeting them. The VALS and PRIZM systems discussed earlier are just a few of the services offered; others use demographic, socioeconomic, and geographic data to cluster consumer households into distinct "microgeographic" segments.

Whether these microunits meet the criteria for useful segmentation is determined by the user of the system. A national company might not attempt to define such small segments, but it could be useful for companies operating within one city or geographic area.

After completing the segmentation analysis, the marketer moves to the third phase shown in Figure 2-2: targeting a specific market.

Selecting a Target Market

The outcome of the segmentation analysis will reveal the market opportunities available. The next phase in the target marketing process involves two steps: (1) determining how many segments to enter and (2) determining which segments offer the most potential.

Determining How Many Segments to Enter

Three market coverage alternatives are available. **Undifferentiated marketing** involves ignoring segment differences and offering just one product or service to the entire market. For example, when Henry Ford brought out the first assembly-line automobile, all potential consumers were offered the same basic product: a black Ford. For many years, Coca-Cola offered only one product version. While this standardized strategy saves the company money, it does not allow the opportunity to offer different versions of the product to different markets.

Differentiated marketing involves marketing in a number of segments, developing separate marketing strategies for each. The Viagra ads in Exhibit 2-10 reflect this strategy. Notice how the two ads differ given alternate target markets and media.

Exhibit 2-10 Viagra uses different appeals for the same product in different segments

While an undifferentiated strategy offers reduced costs through increased production, it does not allow for variety or tailoring to specific needs. Through differentiation, products—or advertising appeals—may be developed for the various segments, increasing the opportunity to satisfy the needs and wants of various groups.

The third alternative, **concentrated marketing,** is used when the firm selects one segment and attempts to capture a large share of this market. Volkswagen used this strategy in the 1950s when it was the only major automobile company competing in the economy-car segment in the United States. While Volkswagen has now assumed a more differentiated strategy, other companies have found the concentrated strategy effective. For example, Maxwell Business Systems has focused its business exclusively on providing software for job cost accounting/MIS systems for government contractors through its JAMIS product line (Exhibit 2-11).

Exhibit 2-11 Maxwell Business Systems pursues a concentrated marketing strategy with JAMIS

Determining Which Segments Offer Potential

The second step in selecting a market involves determining the most attractive segment. The firm must examine the sales potential of the segment, the opportunities for growth, the competition, and its own ability to compete. Then it must decide whether it can market to this group. Stories abound of companies that have entered new markets only to find their lack of resources or expertise would not allow them to compete successfully. For example, Royal Crown (RC) Cola has often been quite successful in identifying new segment opportunities but because of limited resources has been less able to capitalize on them than Coke and Pepsi. RC was the first to bring to market diet colas and caffeine-free colas, but it has not been able to establish itself as a market leader in either market. After selecting the segments to target and determining that it can compete, the firm proceeds to the final step in Figure 2-2: the market positioning phase.

Market Positioning

Positioning has been defined as "the art and science of fitting the product or service to one or more segments of the broad market in such a way as to set it meaningfully apart from competition."[7] As you can see, the position of the product, service, or even store is the image that comes to mind and the attributes consumers perceive as related to it. This communication occurs through the message itself, which explains the benefits, as well as the media strategy employed to reach the target group. Take a few moments to think about how some products are positioned and how their positions are conveyed to you. For example, what comes to mind when you hear the name Mercedes, Dr. Pepper, or Sony? What about department stores such as Neiman Marcus, Sears, and JCPenney? Now think of the ads for each of these products and companies. Are their approaches different from their competitors'? When and where are these ads shown?

Exhibit 2-12 Positioning that focuses on the consumer

Approaches to Positioning

Positioning strategies generally focus on either the consumer or the competition. While both approaches involve the association of product benefits with consumer needs, the former does so by linking the product with the benefits the consumer will derive or creating a favorable brand image, as shown in Exhibit 2-12. The latter approach positions the product by comparing it and the benefit it offers with the competition, as shown in Exhibit 2-13. Products like Scope mouthwash (positioning itself as better tasting than Listerine) and Poweraid (comparing their rehydration capabilities and caloric content to the leading brand) have employed this strategy successfully.

Many advertising practitioners consider market positioning the most important factor in establishing a brand in the marketplace.

Exhibit 2-13 Positioning that focuses on the competition

David Aaker and John Myers note that the term *position* has been used to indicate the brand's or product's image in the marketplace.[8] Jack Trout and Al Ries suggest that this brand image must contrast with competitors. They say, "In today's marketplace, the competitors' image is just as important as your own. Sometimes more important."[9] Thus, *positioning,* as used in this text, relates to the image of the product and or brand relative to competing products or brands. The position of the product or brand is the key factor in communicating the benefits it offers and differentiating it from the competition. Let us now turn to strategies marketers use to position a product.

Developing a Positioning Strategy

To create a position for a product or service, Trout and Ries suggest that managers ask themselves six basic questions:[10]

1. What position, if any, do we already have in the prospect's mind? (This information must come from the marketplace, not the managers' perceptions.)
2. What position do we want to own?
3. What companies must be outgunned if we are to establish that position?
4. Do we have enough marketing money to occupy and hold the position?
5. Do we have the guts to stick with one consistent positioning strategy?
6. Does our creative approach match our positioning strategy?

A number of positioning strategies might be employed in developing a promotional program. David Aaker and J. Gary Shansby discuss six such strategies: positioning by product attributes, price/quality, use, product class, users, and competitor.[11] Aaker and Myers add one more approach, positioning by cultural symbols.[12]

Positioning by Product Attributes and Benefits A common approach to positioning is setting the brand apart from competitors on the basis of the specific characteristics or benefits offered. Sometimes a product may be positioned on more than one product benefit. Marketers attempt to identify **salient attributes** (those that are important to consumers and are the basis for making a purchase decision). For example, when Apple first introduced its computers, the key benefit stressed was ease of use—an effective strategy, given the complexity of computers in the market at that time.

Positioning by Price/Quality Marketers often use price/quality characteristics to position their brands. One way they do this is with ads that reflect the image of a high-quality brand where cost, while not irrelevant, is considered secondary to the quality benefits derived from using the brand. Premium brands positioned at the high end of the market use this approach to positioning.

Another way to use price/quality characteristics for positioning is to focus on the quality or value offered by the brand at a very competitive price. For example, the Lands' End ad shown in Exhibit 2-14 uses this strategy by suggesting that quality need not be unaffordable. Remember that although price is an important consideration, the product quality must be comparable to, or even better than, competing brands for the positioning strategy to be effective.

Positioning by Use or Application Another way to communicate a specific image or position for a brand is to associate it with a specific use or application. For example, Black & Decker introduced the Snakelight as an innovative solution to the problem of trying to hold a flashlight while working. A TV commercial showed various uses for the product, while creative packaging and in-store displays were used to communicate the uses (Exhibit 2-15).

Exhibit 2-14 Lands' End positions its brand as having high quality for the right price

Exhibit 2-15 Black & Decker shows the various uses of the Snakelight

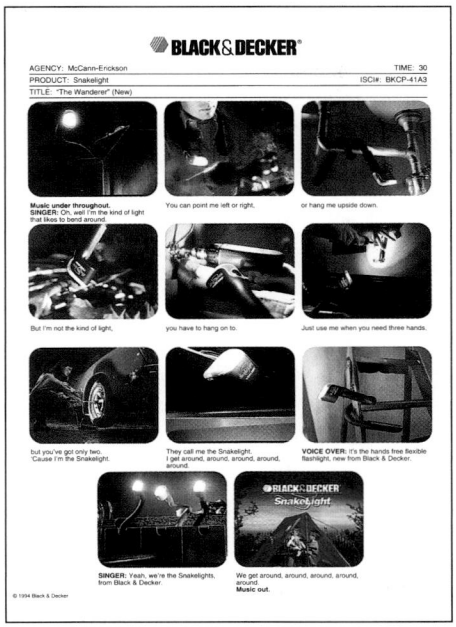

While this strategy is often used to enter a market on the basis of a particular use or application, it is also an effective way to expand the usage of a product. For example, Arm & Hammer baking soda has been promoted for everything from baking to relieving heartburn to eliminating odors in carpets and refrigerators (Exhibit 2-16).

Positioning by Product Class Often the competition for a product comes from outside the product class. For example, airlines know that while they compete with other airlines, trains and buses are also viable alternatives. Amtrak has positioned itself as an alternative to airplanes, citing cost savings, enjoyment, and other advantages. Manufacturers of music CDs must compete with MP3 players; many margarines position themselves against butter. Rather than positioning against another brand, an alternative

Exhibit 2-16 Arm & Hammer baking soda demonstrates numerous product uses

Exhibit 2-17 An example of positioning by product class

strategy is to position oneself against another product category, as shown in Exhibit 2-17.

Positioning by Product User Positioning a product by associating it with a particular user or group of users is yet another approach. An example would be the Valvoline ad shown in Exhibit 2-18. This campaign emphasizes identification or association with a specific group, in this case, people who receive pleasure from working on their cars.

Positioning by Competitor Competitors may be as important to positioning strategy as a firm's own product or services. As Trout and Ries observe, the old strategy of ignoring one's competition no longer works.[13] (Advertisers used to think it was a cardinal sin to mention a competitor in their advertising.) In today's market, an effective positioning strategy for a product or brand may focus on specific competitors. This approach is similar to positioning by product class, although in this case the competition is within the same product category. Perhaps the best-known example of this strategy was Avis, which positioned itself against the car-rental leader, Hertz, by stating, "We're number two, so we try harder." The Powerade ad shown earlier (Exhibit 2-13) is an example of positioning a brand against the competition. When positioning by competitor, a marketer must often employ another positioning strategy as well to differentiate the brand.

Positioning by Cultural Symbols Aaker and Myers include an additional positioning strategy in which cultural symbols are used to differentiate brands. Examples are the Jolly Green Giant, the Keebler elves, Speedy Alka-Seltzer, the Pillsbury Doughboy, Buster Brown, Ronald McDonald, Chiquita Banana, and Mr. Peanut. Each of these symbols has successfully differentiated the product it represents from competitors' (Exhibit 2-19).

Exhibit 2-18 Valvoline positions by product user

Exhibit 2-19 The Jolly Green Giant is a cultural symbol

Exhibit 2-20 This ad is one of a series used in the successful campaign to reposition *Rolling Stone* magazine

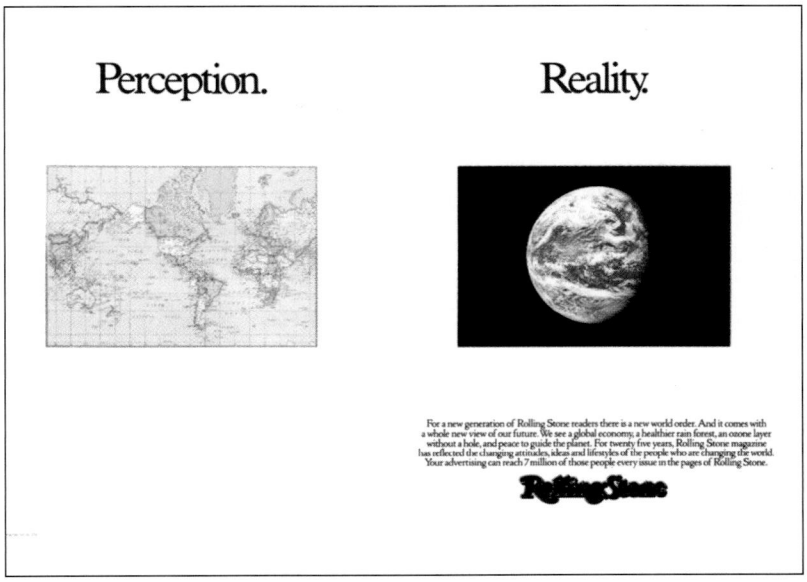

Repositioning One final positioning strategy involves altering or changing a product's or brand's position. **Repositioning** a product usually occurs because of declining or stagnant sales or because of anticipated opportunities in other market positions. Repositioning is often difficult to accomplish because of entrenched perceptions about and attitudes toward the product or brand. Many companies' attempts to change their positions have met with little or no success. For example, Kmart (the store) and Aurora (the Oldsmobile) have both attempted to reposition themselves to a level of higher quality, appealing to younger and more well-to-do customers. Both have met with limited success. (Kmart is in bankruptcy and the Oldsmobile line will be discontinued). Nutri-Grain Bars—originally positioned as a convenience snack ("Good food to go")—have been repositioned as a breakfast substitute ("Respect yourself in the morning"). Buick has repositioned in an attempt to reach a younger market (using Tiger Woods, in his twenties, as a spokesperson), while La-Z-Boy is attempting to move away from its blue-collar image and to a more affluent one. Sears has changed its positioning so often in recent years that consumers may not know exactly what image the company is trying to convey.

One extremely successful effort at repositioning was employed by *Rolling Stone* magazine. In an attempt to change advertisers' image of the type of person who reads *Rolling Stone,* the company embarked on an extensive advertising campaign directed at potential advertisers. The ad shown in Exhibit 2-20 is just one example of how this strategy was successfully implemented.

IMC Perspective 2-1 describes how Jet Blue has been successful in its positioning efforts in a very competitive market.

Determining the Positioning Strategy

Having explored the alternative positioning strategies available, the marketer must determine which strategy is best suited for the firm or product and begin developing the positioning platform. As you remember from the promotional planning process in Chapter 1, the input into this stage will be derived from the situation analysis—specifically, the marketing research conducted therein. Essentially, the development of a positioning platform can be broken into a six-step process:[14]

1. *Identifying competitors.* This process requires broad thinking. Competitors may not be just those products and/or brands that fall into our product class or with which we compete directly. For example, a red wine competes with other red wines of various positions. It may also compete with white, sparkling, and nonalcoholic wines. Wine coolers provide an alternative, as do beer and other alcoholic drinks. Other

IMC PERSPECTIVE 2-1

JetBlue—the "Unairline"

At a time when most of the airlines of the world are struggling, one carrier is seeing nothing but "blue skies." Despite the simultaneous problems of September 11, a recession, and war, the airline—aptly named JetBlue—has continued to succeed where competitors have faltered. For the second quarter of 2002, JetBlue reported a net income of $14.6 million on operating revenues of $149.3 million, while nearly all major airlines reported record losses.

What's the secret behind JetBlue's success? It's a combination of successful branding, unique positioning, and integrated marketing communications that transcends seemingly every aspect of the "antiairline" approach. JetBlue flies at about 80 percent full on every flight (versus the industry average of 64 percent) and attracts travelers from all segments—students, grandmothers, and business travelers (Everybody who likes low fares and a great flying experience). JetBlue has adopted a unique positioning in the industry, and takes every effort conceivable to maintain that image and attitude.

First, there is the unique positioning. Initially positioned as a low-fare, all-coach carrier, the airline has evolved into what one writer has described as a cross between Southwest Airlines (low price, all coach) and Virgin Atlantic (hip and sassy). This means that fares generally are lower than those of competitors flying the same routes but the product itself is more attractive. The planes are new and feature leather seats, each of which offers free satellite TV on a personal video screen. The pilots are efficient and honest about delays, and the flight attendants offer excellent service and go about with a "fun" attitude. JetBlue claims to bring pleasure and style back into flying—and they usually do.

JetBlue has also focused on branding. Its strategy has been to emphasize the things that distinguish the brand from other carriers but cost little—things like courtesy, comfort, and punctuality—while paying less attention to those items that do not, like food. Service is a top priority, including updates on flight status every 15 minutes. *Vanity Fair* magazine named JetBlue its top airline of 2000, and readers of *Condé Nast Traveler* and *Zagat* rated it number 2 behind Midwest Express—an all-business airline that charges much higher prices.

The communication mix for JetBlue supports the brand image and positioning. From the blue potato chips to the stylish blue uniforms, all communications attempt to appeal to its "aspirational audience"—frugal, yet style-conscious consumers. For example, the JetBlue website is simple, functional, and user-friendly. It doesn't look like other airlines' sites, nor does it have the same impact. (More than 60 percent of JetBlue's customers book on the airline's website, while other airlines average about 10 percent.) The original advertising message—"Somebody up there likes you"—attempted to be "un-airline," focusing on big-city swagger and wit rather than the typical "small-world" theme used by others. The post-September 11 campaign—"reasons to fly," which included both TV and radio spots, featured sentimental and nonsentimental reasons for flying—but did so in a humorous style to maintain JetBlue's personality.

The question in the minds of many travelers and industry pundits is, How long can JetBlue keep this up? With its strong identity, positioning, and brand image, and consumers' increasing hatred for other airlines, the future looks pretty bright. Let's hope so!

Sources: Amy Goldwasser, "Something Stylish, Something Blue," *Business 2.0,* February 2002, pp. 94-95; Sally B. Donnelly, "Blue Skies," *Time,* July 30, 2001, pp. 24-27; Scott Donaton, "Flying Lessons: JetBlue Soars When Front Lines Value Brand," *Advertising Age,* Feb. 11, 2002, p.16.

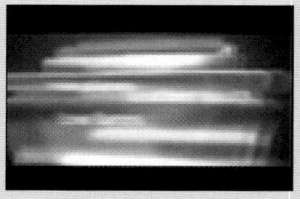

nonalcoholic drinks may come into consideration at various times and/or in certain situations. The marketer must consider all likely competitors, as well as the diverse effects of use and situations on the consumer.

2. *Assessing consumers' perceptions of competitors.* Once we define the competition, we must determine how they are perceived by consumers. Which attributes are important to consumers in evaluating a product and/or brand? As you might expect, for many products, consumers consider a wide variety of attributes or product benefits—most if not all of which are important. Much of marketing firms' research is directed at making such determinations. Consumers are asked to take part in focus groups and/or complete surveys indicating which attributes are important in their purchase decisions. For example, attributes considered important in the selection of a bank may include convenience, teller friendliness, financial security, and a host of other factors. This process establishes the basis for determining competitive positions.

3. *Determining competitors' positions.* After identifying the relevant attributes and their relative importance to consumers, we must determine how each competitor (including our own entry) is positioned with respect to each attribute. This will also show how the competitors are positioned relative to each other. Consumer research is required to make this assessment.

4. *Analyzing the consumers' preferences.* Our discussion of segmentation noted various factors that may distinguish among groups of consumers, including lifestyles, purchase motivations, and demographic differences. Each of these segments may have different purchase motivations and different attribute importance ratings. One way to determine these differences is to consider the *ideal brand* or *product,* defined as the object the consumer would prefer over all others, including objects that can be imagined but do not exist. Identifying the ideal product can help us identify different ideals among segments or identify segments with similar or the same ideal points.

5. *Making the positioning decision.* Going through the first four steps should let us decide which position to assume in the marketplace. Such a decision is not always clear and well defined, however, and research may provide only limited input. In that case, the marketing manager or groups of managers must make some subjective judgments. These judgments raise a number of questions:

- *Is the segmentation strategy appropriate?* Positioning usually entails a decision to segment the market. Consider whether the market segment sought will support an entry and whether it is in the best interests of the company to de-emphasize the remaining market. When a specific position is chosen, consumers may believe this is what the product is for. Those not looking for that specific benefit may not consider the brand. If the marketer decides on an undifferentiated strategy, it may be possible to be general in the positioning platform. For example, Toyota's slogan, "Get the feeling" allows receivers to project their feelings about the brand—all of which (hopefully) involve a positive image of Toyota.

- *Are there sufficient resources available to communicate the position effectively?* It is very expensive to establish a position. One ad, or even a series of ads, is not likely to be enough. The marketer must commit to a long-range effort in all aspects of the marketing campaign to make sure the objectives sought are obtained. Too often, the firm abandons a position and/or advertising campaign long before it can establish a position successfully. The *Rolling Stone* repositioning discussed earlier is an excellent example of sticking with a campaign: The basic theme ran for a number of years. In contrast, Sears has switched campaigns so often in the past few years that it has been impossible to establish a distinct position in the consumer's mind. Further, once a successful position is attained, it is likely to attract competitors. It may become expensive to ward off "me-too" brands and continue to hold on to the brand distinction.

- *How strong is the competition?* The marketing manager must ask whether a position sought is likely to be maintained, given the strengths of the competition. For example, General Foods often made it a practice not to be the first entry into a market. When competitors developed new markets with their entries, General Foods would simply improve on the product and capture a large percentage of the

market share. This leads to two basic questions: First, if our firm is first into the market, will we be able to maintain the position (in terms of quality, price, etc.)? Second, if a product is positioned as finest quality, it must be. If it is positioned as lowest cost, it has to be. Otherwise, the position claimed is sure to be lost.

- *Is the current positioning strategy working?* There is an old saying, "If it ain't broke, don't fix it." If current efforts are not working, it may be time to consider an alternative positioning strategy. But if they are working, a change is usually unwise. Sometimes executives become bored with a theme and decide it is time for a change, but this change causes confusion in the marketplace and weakens a brand's position. Unless there is strong reason to believe a change in positioning is necessary, stick with the current strategy.

6. *Monitoring the position.* Once a position has been established, we want to monitor how well it is being maintained in the marketplace. Tracking studies measure the image of the product or firm over time. Changes in consumers' perceptions can be determined, with any slippage immediately noted and reacted to. At the same time, the impact of competitors can be determined.

Before leaving this section, you might stop to think for a moment about the positioning (and repositioning) strategies pursued by different companies. Any successful product that comes to mind probably occupies a distinct market position.

Developing the Marketing Planning Program

The development of the marketing strategy and selection of a target market(s) tell the marketing department which customers to focus on and what needs to attempt to satisfy. The next stage of the marketing process involves combining the various elements of the marketing mix into a cohesive, effective marketing program. Each marketing-mix element is multidimensional and includes a number of decision areas. Likewise, each must consider and contribute to the overall IMC program. We now examine product, price, and distribution channels and how each influences and interacts with the promotional program.

Product Decisions

An organization exists because it has some product, service, or idea to offer consumers, generally in exchange for money. This offering may come in the form of a physical product (such as a soft drink, pair of jeans, or car), a service (banking, airlines, or legal assistance), a cause (United Way, March of Dimes), or even a person (a political candidate). The product is anything that can be marketed and that, when used or supported, gives satisfaction to the individual.

A *product* is not just a physical object; it is a bundle of benefits or values that satisfies the needs of consumers. The needs may be purely functional, or they may include social and psychological benefits. For example, the campaign for Michelin tires shown earlier stresses the quality built into Michelin tires (value) as well as their performance and durability (function). The term **product symbolism** refers to what a product or brand means to consumers and what they experience in purchasing and using it.[15] For many products, strong symbolic features and social and psychological meaning may be more important than functional utility.[16] For example, designer clothing such as Versace, Gucci, and Bebe is often purchased on the basis of its symbolic meaning and image, particularly by teenagers and young adults. Advertising plays an important role in developing and maintaining the image of these brands (Exhibit 2-21).

Product planning involves decisions not only about the item itself, such as design and quality, but also about aspects such as service and warranties as well as brand name and package design. Consumers look beyond the reality of the product and its ingredients. The product's quality, branding, packaging, and even the company standing behind it all contribute to consumers' perceptions.[17] In an effective IMC program, advertising, branding, and packaging are all designed to portray the product as more than just a bundle of attributes. All are coordinated to present an image or positioning of the product that extends well beyond its physical attributes. Think for a minute about the ads for Nike; the product benefits and attributes are usually not even mentioned—yet information about the brand is communicated effectively.

Exhibit 2-21 Advertising for designer clothing

Branding Choosing a brand name for a product is important from a promotional perspective because brand names communicate attributes and meaning. Marketers search for brand names that can communicate product concepts and help position the product in customers' minds. Names such as Safeguard (soap), I Can't Believe It's Not Butter! (margarine), Easy-Off (oven cleaner), Arrid (antiperspirant), and Spic and Span (floor cleaner) all clearly communicate the benefits of using these products and at the same time create images extending beyond the names themselves. (What about La-Z-Boy?)

One important role of advertising in respect to branding strategies is creating and maintaining **brand equity,** which can be thought of as an intangible asset of added value or goodwill that results from the favorable image, impressions of differentiation, and/or the strength of consumer attachment to a company name, brand name, or trademark. Brand equity allows a brand to earn greater sales volume and/or higher margins than it could without the name, providing the company with a competitive advantage. The strong equity position a company and/or its brand enjoys is often reinforced through advertising. For example, Rado watches command a premium price because of their high quality as well as the strong brand equity they have developed through advertising (Exhibit 2-22).

Exhibit 2-22 Rado creates strong brand equity through advertising

Packaging Packaging is another aspect of product strategy that has become increasingly important. Traditionally, the package provided functional benefits such as economy, protection, and storage. However, the role and function of the package have changed because of the self-service emphasis of many stores and the fact that more and more buying decisions are made at the point of purchase. One study estimated that as many as two-thirds of all purchases made in the supermarket are unplanned. The package is often the consumer's first exposure to the product, so it must make a favorable first impression. A typical supermarket has more

Exhibit 2-23 Listerine communicates through effective packaging

than 20,000 items competing for attention. Not only must a package attract and hold the consumer's attention, but it must also communicate information on how to use the product, divulge its composition and content, and satisfy any legal requirements regarding disclosure. Moreover, many firms design the package to carry a sales promotion message such as a contest, sweepstakes, or premium offer.

Many companies view the package as an important way to communicate with consumers and create an impression of the brand in their minds. In other instances packages can extend the brand by offering new uses. For example, Listerine's PocketPaks (Exhibit 2-23) have created new opportunities for the mouthwash. Design factors such as size, shape, color, and lettering all contribute to the appeal of a package and can be as important as a commercial in determining what goes from the store shelf to the consumer's shopping cart. Many products use packaging to create a distinctive brand image and identity. The next time you walk by a perfume counter, stop to look at the many unique package designs (see Exhibit 2-24). Packaging can also serve more functional purposes. For example, Tylenol's Safe-Ty-Lock bottle protects children from consuming the medicine when they shouldn't (Exhibit 2-25).

Price Decisions

The *price variable* refers to what the consumer must give up to purchase a product or service. While price is discussed in terms of the dollar amount exchanged for an item, the cost of a product to the consumer includes time, mental activity, and behavioral effort.[18] The marketing manager is usually concerned with establishing a price level, developing pricing policies, and monitoring competitors' and consumers' reactions to prices in the marketplace. A firm must consider a number of factors in determining the price it charges for its product or service, including costs, demand factors, competi-

Exhibit 2-24 The packaging creates product image

Exhibit 2-25 Packaging may also add product benefits

tion, and perceived value. From an IMC perspective, the price must be consistent with the perceptions of the product, as well as the communications strategy. Higher prices, of course, will communicate a higher product quality, while lower prices reflect bargain or "value" perceptions (Exhibit 2-26). A product positioned as highest quality but carrying a lower price than competitors will only confuse consumers. In other words, the price, the advertising, and the distribution channels must present one unified voice speaking to the product's positioning.

Relating Price to Advertising and Promotion Factors such as product quality, competition, and advertising all interact in determining what price a firm can and should charge. The relationship among price, product quality, and advertising was examined in one study using information on 227 consumer businesses from the Profit Impact of Marketing Strategies (PIMS) project of the Strategic Planning Institute.[19] Several interesting findings concerning the interaction of these variables emerged from this study:

- Brands with high relative advertising budgets were able to charge premium prices, whereas brands that spent less than their competitors on advertising charged lower prices.
- Companies with high-quality products charged high relative prices for the extra quality, but businesses with high quality and high advertising levels obtained the highest prices. Conversely, businesses with low quality and low advertising charged the lowest prices.
- The positive relationship between high relative advertising and price levels was stronger for products in the late stage of the product life cycle, for market leaders, and for low-cost products (under $10).
- Companies with relatively high prices and high advertising expenditures showed a higher return on investment than companies with relatively low prices and high advertising budgets.
- Companies with high-quality products were hurt the most, in terms of return on investment, by inconsistent advertising and pricing strategies.

Exhibit 2-26 Some products compete on the basis of quality rather than price

The study concluded that pricing and advertising strategies go together. High relative ad expenditures should accompany premium prices, and low relative ad expenditures should be tailored to low prices. These results obviously support the IMC perspective that one voice must be conveyed.

Distribution Channel Decisions

As consumers, we generally take for granted the role of marketing intermediaries or channel members. If we want a six-pack of soda or a box of detergent, we can buy it at a supermarket, a convenience store, or even a drugstore. Manufacturers understand the value and importance of these intermediaries.

One of a marketer's most important marketing decisions involves the way it makes its products and services available for purchase. A firm can have an excellent product at a great price, but it will be of little value unless it is available where the customer wants it, when the customer wants it, and with the proper support and service. **Marketing channels,** the place element of the marketing mix, are "sets of interdependent organizations involved in the process of making a product or service available for use or consumption."[20]

Channel decisions involve selecting, managing, and motivating intermediaries such as wholesalers, distributors, brokers, and retailers that help a firm make a product or service available to customers. These intermediaries, sometimes called **resellers,** are critical to the success of a company's marketing program.

The distribution strategy should also take into consideration the communication objectives and the impact that the channel strategy will have on the IMC program. Stewart and colleagues discuss the need for "integrated channel management," which "reflects the blurring of the boundaries of the communications and distribution functions."[21] Consistent with the product and pricing decisions, where the product is distributed will send a communications message. Does the fact that a product is sold at Neiman Marcus or Saks convey a different message regarding its image than if it were distributed at Kmart or Wal-Mart? If you think about it for a moment, the mere fact that the product is distributed in these channels communicates an image about it in your mind. (Think about the Samsung discussion at the beginning of this chapter.) Stewart gives examples of how channel elements contribute to communication—for example, grocery store displays, point-of-purchase merchandising, and shelf footage. The distribution channel in a well-integrated marketing program serves as a form of reminder advertising. The consumer sees the brand name and recalls the advertising. (Think about the last time you passed a McDonald's. Did it remind you of any of McDonald's ads?)

A company can choose not to use any channel intermediaries but, rather, to sell to its customers through **direct channels.** This type of channel arrangement is sometimes used in the consumer market by firms using direct-selling programs, such as Avon, Tupperware, and Mary Kay, or firms that use direct-response advertising or telemarketing to sell their products. Direct channels are also frequently used by manufacturers of industrial products and services, which are often selling expensive and complex products that require extensive negotiations and sales efforts, as well as service and follow-up calls after the sale. The ad for Titleist putters shown earlier reflects the higher cost and quality associated with the brand.

Chapter 15 provides a discussion of the role of the Internet in an IMC program. As will be seen, the Internet is relied upon by many companies as a direct channel of distribution, since they offer products and services for sale on their websites. Amazon.com and Barnes&Noble.com are just two of the many examples of such efforts.

Most consumer-product companies distribute through **indirect channels,** usually using a network of wholesalers (institutions that sell to other resellers) and/or retailers (which sell primarily to the final consumer).

Developing Promotional Strategies: Push or Pull?

Most of you are aware of advertising and other forms of promotion directed toward ultimate consumers or business customers. We see these ads in the media and are often part of the target audience for the promotions. In addition to developing a consumer

CAREER PROFILE

Fiona Morrisson

Director, Corporate Communications JetBlue Airways

My career-path, especially the first ten years of it, has been one that text books never recommend, guidance counselors are paid to discourage, and parents fear the most.

I grew up in a small country town in Australia where it wasn't a given that everyone would graduate from high school and go on to university. I left school after grade ten and spent the next eight years of my working life in jobs that provided me with an extremely useful work skill: a typing speed of 120 words per minute. I held positions in everything from dental clinics to multinational computing companies, with a myriad of temporary jobs in between.

In my early twenties, I headed to Japan. My first real job in Tokyo was with a science publishing company where I worked "polishing" English language research papers submitted by Japanese scientists before the reports were sent for publication in Europe.

After leaving then returning to Tokyo, I was fortunate to find work in two industries that have since become the foundation for my career: media and travel.

Every morning I was employed by a travel tour consolidator to write English language marketing plans and proposals aimed at their U.S., Australian, and South East Asian airline and tour partners. Every afternoon, I worked in the International Relations department of Nihon Television (NTV), Japan's oldest network station.

At NTV, my job was to "culturally translate" scripts for programs that the station was hoping to sell overseas.

While I loved living in Japan, I began to feel that there was something that school could offer me. I felt that a university degree would give me a theoretical base from which to understand and utilize the experiences and skills I'd gained.

"A friend's recommendation and successful interviews landed me the JetBlue job."

I returned to Australia to earn a BA in Communications from the University of Technology in Sydney. After graduation, I was off to New York.

My first job in New York was with an Australian corporate finance company. I soon realized that I was not suited to the finance industry, so when the opportunity to interview at a public relations agency came along, I jumped at it.

Porter Novelli had just won the Australian Tourist Commission (ATC) account and was looking for an account executive with a knowledge of the country. Thanks to my nationality, my writing skills and my experience "translating" between two cultures, I got the job. Along with the ATC, I worked on the Princess Cruises, Bermuda Tourism, and Southwest Airlines accounts, learning media relations, co-ordinating major events, and organizing press trips.

I spent two happy years with Porter Novelli before landing the position of Manager of Corporate Communications with JetBlue Airways.

The first day with JetBlue I worked on the inauguration of new service to Orlando, Florida, the fourth city on the route network. By the end of my first year, we'd launched ten more destinations around the country. Since then JetBlue has gone from being an "upstart" to a successful low-fare competitor to being voted the Best US Airline by Conde Nast Traveler readers. Three of us handle all JetBlue's PR in-house—which means that we do everything, from media pitching to event planning to internal communications.

So while it might not have been as fast as the traditional route, my career path, with its roundabout ways and spontaneous detours, has brought me to a job and a company that I love, and given me some unique experiences along the way. I'm excited about where it could take me next.

marketing mix, a company must have a program to motivate the channel members. Programs designed to persuade the trade to stock, merchandise, and promote a manufacturer's products are part of a **promotional push strategy.** The goal of this strategy is to push the product through the channels of distribution by aggressively selling and promoting the item to the resellers, or trade.

Promotion to the trade includes all the elements of the promotional mix. Company sales representatives call on resellers to explain the product, discuss the firm's plans for building demand among ultimate consumers, and describe special programs being offered to the trade, such as introductory discounts, promotional allowances, and cooperative ad programs. The company may use **trade advertising** to interest wholesalers and retailers and motivate them to purchase its products for resale to their customers. Trade advertising usually appears in publications that serve the particular industry.

A push strategy tries to convince resellers they can make a profit on a manufacturer's product and to encourage them to order the merchandise and push it through to their customers. Sometimes manufacturers face resistance from channel members who do not want to take on an additional product line or brand. In these cases, companies may turn to a **promotional pull strategy,** spending money on advertising and sales promotion efforts directed toward the ultimate consumer. The goal of a pull strategy is to create demand among consumers and encourage them to request the product from the retailer. Seeing the consumer demand, retailers will order the product from wholesalers (if they are used), which in turn will request it from the manufacturer. Thus, stimulating demand at the end-user level pulls the product through the channels of distribution.

Whether to emphasize a push or a pull strategy depends on a number of factors, including the company's relations with the trade, its promotional budget, and demand for the firm's products. Companies that have favorable channel relationships may prefer to use a push strategy and work closely with channel members to encourage them to stock and promote their products. A firm with a limited promotional budget may not have the funds for advertising and sales promotion that a pull strategy requires and may find it more cost-effective to build distribution and demand by working closely with resellers. When the demand outlook for a product is favorable because it has unique benefits, is superior to competing brands, or is very popular among consumers, a pull strategy may be appropriate. Companies often use a combination of push and pull strategies, with the emphasis changing as the product moves through its life cycle.

The Role of Advertising and Promotion

As shown in the marketing model in Figure 2-1, the marketing program includes promotion both to the trade (channel members) and to the company's ultimate customers. And interactive marketers use the various promotional-mix elements—advertising, sales promotion, direct marketing, publicity/public relations, and personal selling—to inform consumers about their products, their prices, and places where the products are available. Each promotional-mix variable helps marketers achieve their promotional objectives, and all variables must work together to achieve an integrated marketing communications program.

To this point, we have discussed the various elements of the marketing plan that serves as the basis for the IMC program. The development and implementation of an IMC program is based on a strong foundation that includes market analysis, target marketing and positioning, and coordination of the various marketing-mix elements. Throughout the following chapters of this text, we will explore the role of advertising and promotion in helping to achieve marketing objectives.

Summary

Promotion plays an important role in an organization's efforts to market its product, service, or ideas to its customers. Figure 2-1 shows a model for analyzing how promotions fit into a company's marketing program. The model includes a marketing strategy and analysis, target marketing, program development, and the target market. The marketing process begins with a marketing strategy that is based on a detailed situation analysis and guides for target market selection and development of the firm's marketing program.

In the planning process, the situation analysis requires that the marketing strategy be assumed. The promotional program is developed with this strategy as a guide. One of the key decisions to be made pertains to the target marketing process, which includes identifying, segmenting, targeting, and positioning to target markets. There are several bases for segmenting the market and various ways to position a product.

Once the target marketing process has been completed, marketing program decisions regarding product, price, distribution, and promotions must be made. All of these must be coordinated to provide an integrated marketing communications perspective, in which the positioning strategy is supported by one voice. Thus all product strategies, pricing strategies, and distribution choices must be made with the objective of contributing to the overall image of the product or brand. Advertising and promotion decisions, in turn, must be integrated with the other marketing-mix decisions to accomplish this goal.

Key Terms

strategic marketing plan, 40
market segments, 40
market opportunities, 40
competitive advantage, 41
target marketing, 43
market segmentation, 44
geographic segmentation, 46
demographic segmentation, 46
psychographic segmentation, 48
behavioristic segmentation, 49
80-20 rule, 49
benefit segmentation, 49
undifferentiated marketing, 50
differentiated marketing, 50
concentrated marketing, 51
positioning, 51
salient attributes, 52
repositioning, 55
product symbolism, 58
brand equity, 59
marketing channels, 62
resellers, 62
direct channels, 62
indirect channels, 62
promotional push strategy, 64
trade advertising, 64
promotional pull strategy, 64

Discussion Questions

1. Recently, some marketers have noted that it is easier to develop communications programs to Generation X members than Generation Y. Briefly describe the characteristics of Gen X and Gen Y, and whether or not you believe this to be true.

2. The text discusses Samsung's attempt to reposition to be competitive with companies like Sony. Discuss what factors might promote and/or inhibit their success in this endeavor.

3. As companies increase their efforts to target the Hispanic segment, they are likely to encounter differences from other subcultural groups. Discuss some of the differences that they might expect to notice in the Hispanic subculture.

4. Changing lifestyles can create both opportunities and threats for the marketer. Provide an example of a change in lifestyle that poses a threat to marketers, and one that provides an opportunity. Give an example of a product or brand that has been affected in both of these ways.

5. The text discusses the positioning of JetBlue and their success so far. Describe some of the things that JetBlue has done effectively to lead to their success. What will JetBlue need to do in the future to maintain this success?

6. Some marketers contend that demographics is not really a basis for segmentation but is a descriptor of the segment. Discuss examples to support both positions.

7. Establishing brand image is often difficult for new companies. Explain what these companies must do to establish a strong brand image.

8. More and more business-to-business companies have gone away from purely trade advertising to advertising on consumer media. Is this likely to be a successful strategy? Why or why not?

9. A number of approaches to segmentation have been cited in the text. Provide examples of companies and/or brands that employ each.

10. Describe how the positioning strategy adopted for a brand would need to be supported by all other elements of the marketing mix.

Organizing for Advertising and Promotion: The Role of Ad Agencies and Other Marketing Communication Organizations

3

Chapter Objectives

1. To understand how companies organize for advertising and other aspects of integrated marketing communications.
2. To examine methods for selecting, compensating, and evaluating advertising agencies.
3. To explain the role and functions of specialized marketing communications organizations.
4. To examine various perspectives on the use of integrated services and responsibilities of advertisers versus agencies.

Madison Avenue Goes Hollywood

In the spring of 2000, the creative group at the Fallon Worldwide agency assigned to the BMW North America account was in the process of developing a new branding campaign for the German automaker. Both the BMW and Fallon people were becoming increasingly concerned with their ability to reach their core market of overachieving, hard-working consumers via traditional methods such as network television. BMW had done three different campaigns recently emphasizing responsive performance with product-focused ads designed to show what it's like behind the wheel of a BMW. However, from the perspective of both the client and the agency, the look and feel of the ads had begun to be copied by competitors and wannabes, making them less distinctive than before. Meanwhile, their research indicated that many Bimmer buyers were tech-savvy and had fast, reliable access to the Internet; most importantly, 85 percent of them had researched their car purchase on the Web before stepping into a dealer showroom.

As the creative team worked to develop a new branding campaign for BMW, concern over the effectiveness of traditional media advertising and curiosity over how to exploit the popularity of the Internet among car buyers were two key factors they were considering. Another creative team at Fallon had recently completed a campaign for Timex that incorporated an Internet element by featuring short video clips developed specifically for the Web. So the idea emerged of doing something for the Web that would be not only entertaining but also cinematic. However, the associative creative director for the BMW group at Fallon noted that the goal was to do a different level of web film—one that by its very nature would call attention to itself and could be promoted like regular films. The agency took the web film concept to Anonymous Content, a Hollywood production company, where director David Fincher is a partner. Fincher took the original concept for a longer film that would be shot in segments and suggested instead a series of stand-alone shorts, each directed by a marquee name. He also came up with the idea for a central character, the Driver, played by young British actor Clive Owen, who appears in all the films as a James Bond–type driver who takes such costars as Madonna, Mickey Rourke, and Stellan Skarsgaard for the ride of their lives in a BMW.

The series of five- to seven-minute films created by Fallon and Anonymous Content is called "The Hire," and the films have been directed by big names such as Ang Lee, John Franeheimer,

and Guy Ritchie. The most popular film in the series was Ritchie's seven-minute short called "Star," which starred his wife, Madonna, portraying a spoiled pop diva who is taken on a wild ride to her hotel in a BMW 540i by the hired driver. Each film shows a different BMW model pushing the envelope of performance by showing what the car can do in extreme conditions and situations that could never be conveyed in a traditional TV commercial.

A special website, BMWFilms.com, was created to show the five films in "The Hire" series. The site also includes five "substories," which are two-minute vignettes that introduce additional characters, as well as a behind-the-scenes look at how the films were made, interviews with the stunt drivers, and commentaries by the directors on their individual shoots. Fallon also created an integrated campaign to drive consumers to the website that included television, print and Internet ads, viral marketing efforts, and an aggressive public relations effort. "The Hire" film series has been singled out as the first high-profile, big-budget, celebrity-laden marriage of advertising and entertainment. Since its launch in April 2001, more than 13 million people have logged on to BMWFilms.com to view the five films in the series, and its success prompted BMW to commission three new films, which debuted in fall 2002.

BMW Films was awarded the Super Reggie Award in 2002 by the Promotion Marketing Association (PMA) for the best promotional campaign. The PMA director noted: "BMW Films has truly established a creative benchmark in integrated and interactive promotions, allowing consumers to interact with the BMW name on their own terms. The promotion helped drive increases in brand measures and dealership visits as well as vehicle sales numbers." The film series also won the Cyber Grand Prix award at the 2002 Cannes Advertising Festival for the best online marketing campaign.

BMW is not the only marketer that has turned to the *advertainment* genre to promote its products. Skyy Vodka, which has a history of support for independent filmmakers and film festivals, was one of the first companies to use the genre, with its "Skyy Short Film Series." The three short films, which were created by the company's ad agency Lambesis, also used top directors and talent including model-actress Claudia Schiffer and Dian Merrill. The short films, which are featured on the "Skyy Cinema" section of the company's website, are seen as a way to build its brand image with its primary target audience of young, technologically savvy adults. Bartle Bogle Hegarty, a London agency, has also created short films for several clients including Levi's jeans and Microsoft's Xbox video game. The long-form ad for the Xbox, called "Champagne," shows a baby being shot out of a window at birth and morphing into old age and has been downloaded more than 4 million times.

Experts note that these digital short films signal the way toward the long-awaited convergence of television and the personal computer. They note that other technological developments such as the personal video recorder, digital cable, and satellite TV will allow consumers to watch what they want when they want to and this will change how they relate to advertisers. Thus, advertisers and their agencies will continue to use the short-film advertainments as a way to make their messages more compelling and to encourage consumers to actually choose to view their ads rather than avoid them.

Sources: Michael McCarthy, "Ads Go Hollywood with Short Films," *USA Today,* June 20, 2002, p. 3b; Anthony Vagnoi, "Behind the Wheel," *Advertising Age,* July 23, 2001, pp. 10, 12; Benny Evangelista, "Marketers Turn to Web Films to Push Their Products," *San Francisco Chronicle,* July 23, 2001, p. E2.

Developing and implementing an integrated marketing communications program is usually a complex and detailed process involving the efforts of many persons. As consumers, we generally give little thought to the individuals or organizations that create the clever advertisements that capture our attention or the contests or sweepstakes we hope to win. But for those involved in the marketing process, it is important to understand the nature of the industry and the structure and functions of the organizations involved. As can be seen from the opening vignette, the advertising and promotions business is changing as marketers search for better ways to communicate with their customers. These changes are impacting the way marketers organize for marketing communications, as well as their relationships with advertising agencies and other communication specialists.

This chapter examines the various organizations that participate in the IMC process, their roles and responsibilities, and their relationship to one another. We discuss how companies organize internally for advertising and promotion. For most companies, advertising is planned and executed by an outside ad agency. Many large agencies offer a variety of other IMC capabilities, including public relations, sales promotion, and direct marketing. Thus, we will devote particular attention to the ad agency's role and the overall relationship between company and agency.

Other participants in the promotional process (such as direct-response, sales promotion, and interactive agencies and public relations firms) are becoming increasingly important as more companies take an integrated marketing communications approach to promotion. We examine the role of these specialized marketing communications organizations in the promotional process as well. The chapter concludes with a discussion of whether marketers are best served by using the integrated services of one large agency or the separate services of a variety of communications specialists.

Participants in the Integrated Marketing Communications Process: An Overview

Before discussing the specifics of the industry, we'll provide an overview of the entire system and identify some of the players. As shown in Figure 3-1, participants in the integrated marketing communications process can be divided into five major groups: the advertiser (or client), advertising agencies, media organizations, specialized communication services, and collateral services. Each group has specific roles in the promotional process.

The advertisers, or **clients,** are the key participants in the process. They have the products, services, or causes to be marketed, and they provide the funds that pay for advertising and promotions. The advertisers also assume major responsibility for developing the marketing program and making the final decisions regarding the advertising and promotional program to be employed. The organization may perform most of these efforts itself, either through its own advertising department or by setting up an in-house agency.

However, many organizations use an **advertising agency,** an outside firm that specializes in the creation, production, and/or placement of the communications message and that may provide other services to facilitate the marketing and promotions

Figure 3-1 Participants in the integrated marketing communications process

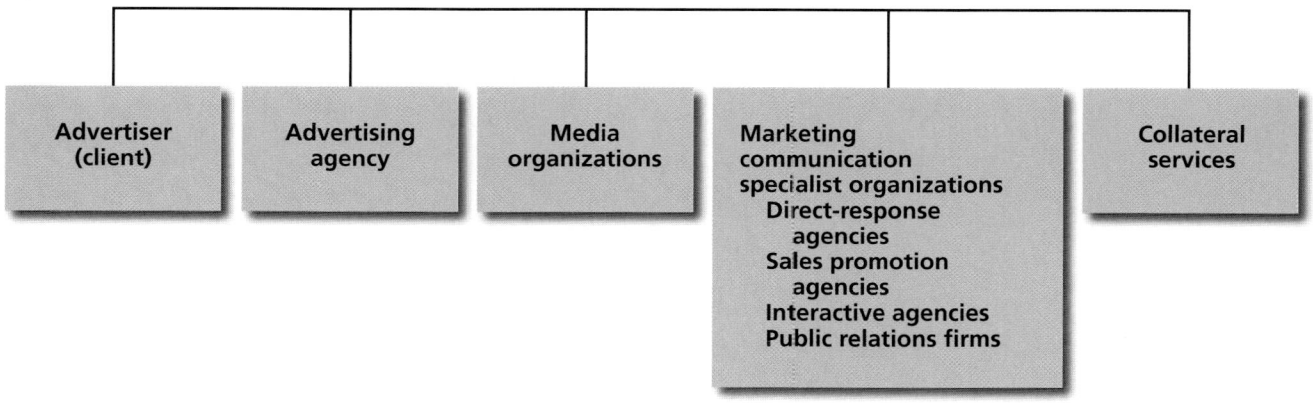

process. Many large advertisers retain the services of a number of agencies, particularly when they market a number of products. For example, Kraft Foods uses as many as 8 advertising agencies for its various brands, while Procter & Gamble uses 12 ad agencies and 2 major media buying services companies. More and more, ad agencies are acting as partners with advertisers and assuming more responsibility for developing the marketing and promotional programs.

Media organizations are another major participant in the advertising and promotions process. The primary function of most media is to provide information or entertainment to their subscribers, viewers, or readers. But from the perspective of the promotional planner, the purpose of media is to provide an environment for the firm's marketing communications message. The media must have editorial or program content that attracts consumers so that advertisers and their agencies will want to buy time or space with them. Exhibit 3-1 shows an ad run in advertising trade publications promoting the value of The History Channel magazine as a media vehicle for reaching men. While the media perform many other functions that help advertisers understand their markets and their customers, a medium's primary objective is to sell itself as a way for companies to reach their target markets with their messages effectively.

The next group of participants are organizations that provide **specialized marketing communications services.** They include direct-marketing agencies, sales promotion agencies, interactive agencies, and public relations firms. These organizations provide services in their areas of expertise. A direct-response agency develops and implements direct-marketing programs, while sales promotion agencies develop promotional programs such as contests and sweepstakes, premium offers, or sampling programs. Interactive agencies are being retained to develop websites for the Internet and help marketers as they move deeper into the realm of interactive media. Public relations firms are used to generate and manage publicity for a company and its products and services as well as to focus on its relationships and communications with its relevant publics.

The final participants shown in the promotions process of Figure 3-1 are those that provide **collateral services,** the wide range of support functions used by advertisers,

Exhibit 3-1 The History Channel advertises its ability to reach male television viewers

agencies, media organizations, and specialized marketing communications firms. These individuals and companies perform specialized functions the other participants use in planning and executing advertising and other promotional functions. We will now examine the role of each participant in more detail. (Media organizations will be examined in Chapters 10 through 14.)

Organizing for Advertising and Promotion in the Firm: The Client's Role

Virtually every business organization uses some form of marketing communications. However, the way a company organizes for these efforts depends on several factors, including its size, the number of products it markets, the role of advertising and promotion in its marketing mix, the advertising and promotion budget, and its marketing organization structure. Many individuals throughout the organization may be involved in the promotions decision-making process. Marketing personnel have the most direct relationship with advertising and are often involved in many aspects of the decision process, such as providing input to the campaign plan, agency selection, and evaluation of proposed programs. Top management is usually interested in how the advertising program represents the firm, and this may also mean being involved in advertising decisions even when the decisions are not part of its day-to-day responsibilities.

While many people both inside and outside the organization have some input into the advertising and promotion process, direct responsibility for administering the program must be assumed by someone within the firm. Many companies have an advertising department headed by an advertising or communications manager operating under a marketing director. An alternative used by many large multiproduct firms is a decentralized marketing (brand management) system. A third option is to form a separate agency within the firm, an in-house agency. Each of these alternatives is examined in more detail in the following sections.

The Centralized System

In many organizations, marketing activities are divided along functional lines, with advertising placed alongside other marketing functions such as sales, marketing research, and product planning, as shown in Figure 3-2. The **advertising manager** is responsible for all promotions activities except sales (in some companies this individual has the title of Marketing Communications Manager). In the most common example of a **centralized system,** the advertising manager controls the entire promotions operation, including budgeting, coordinating creation and production of ads, planning media schedules, and monitoring and administering the sales promotions programs for all the company's products or services.

The specific duties of the advertising manager depend on the size of the firm and the importance it places on promotional programs. Basic functions the manager and staff perform include the following.

Figure 3-2 The advertising department under a centralized system

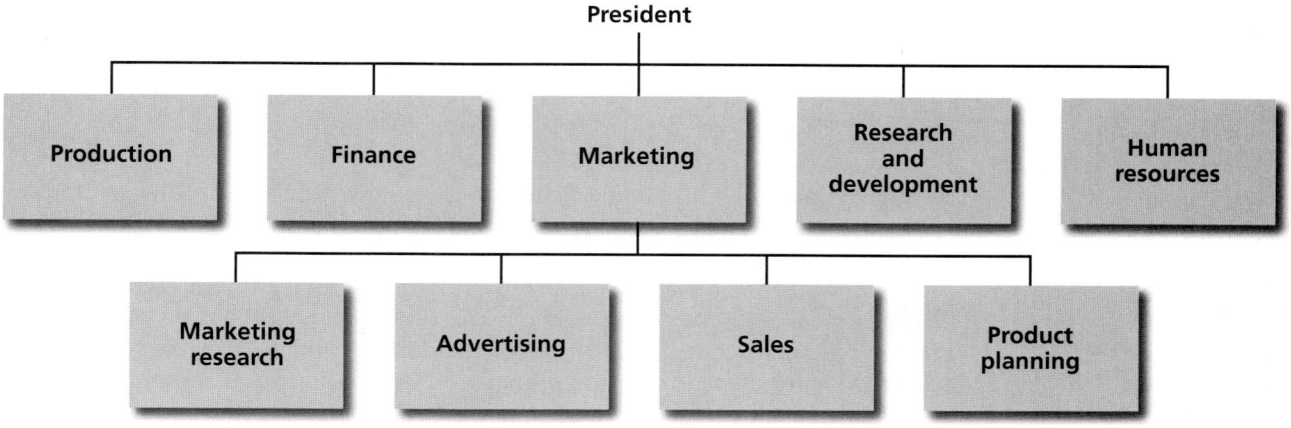

Planning and Budgeting

The advertising department is responsible for developing advertising and promotions plans that will be approved by management and recommending a promotions program based on the overall marketing plan, objectives, and budget. Formal plans are submitted annually or when a program is being changed significantly, as when a new campaign is developed. While the advertising department develops the promotional budget, the final decision on allocating funds is usually made by top management.

Administration and Execution

The manager must organize the advertising department and supervise and control its activities. The manager also supervises the execution of the plan by subordinates and/or the advertising agency. This requires working with such departments as production, media, art, copy, and sales promotion. If an outside agency is used, the advertising department is relieved of much of the executional responsibility; however, it must review and approve the agency's plans.

Coordination with Other Departments

The manager must coordinate the advertising department's activities with those of other departments, particularly those involving other marketing functions. For example, the advertising department must communicate with marketing research and/or sales to determine which product features are important to customers and should be emphasized in the company's communications. Research may also provide profiles of product users and nonusers for the media department before it selects broadcast or print media. The advertising department may also be responsible for preparing material the sales force can use when calling on customers, such as sales promotion tools, advertising materials, and point-of-purchase displays.

Coordination with Outside Agencies and Services

Many companies have an advertising department but still use many outside services. For example, companies may develop their advertising programs in-house while employing media buying services to place their ads and/or use collateral services agencies to develop brochures, point-of-purchase materials, and so on. The department serves as liaison between the company and any outside service providers and also determines which ones to use. Once outside services are retained, the manager will work with other marketing managers to coordinate their efforts and evaluate their performances.

A centralized organizational system is often used when companies do not have many different divisions, product or service lines, or brands to advertise. For example, airlines such as Southwest, American, and Continental have centralized advertising departments. Many companies prefer a centralized advertising department because developing and coordinating advertising programs from one central location facilitates communication regarding the promotions program, making it easier for top management to participate in decision making. A centralized system may also result in a more efficient operation because fewer people are involved in the program decisions, and as their experience in making such decisions increases, the process becomes easier.

At the same time, problems are inherent in a centralized operation. First, it is difficult for the advertising department to understand the overall marketing strategy for the brand. The department may also be slow in responding to specific needs and problems of a product or brand. As companies become larger and develop or acquire new products, brands, or even divisions, the centralized system may become impractical.

The Decentralized System

In large corporations with multiple divisions and many different products, it is very difficult to manage all the advertising, promotional, and other functions through a centralized department. These types of companies generally have a **decentralized system,** with separate manufacturing, research and development, sales, and marketing departments for various divisions, product lines, or businesses. Many companies that use a decentralized system, such as Procter & Gamble, Gillette Co., and Nestlé, assign each product or brand to a **brand manager** who is responsible for the total management of the brand, including planning, budgeting, sales, and profit performance. (The

Exhibit 3-2 Many of Procter & Gamble's brands compete against each other

term *product manager* is also used to describe this position.) The brand manager, who may have one or more assistant brand managers, is also responsible for the planning, implementation, and control of the marketing program.[1]

Under this system, the responsibilities and functions associated with advertising and promotions are transferred to the brand manager, who works closely with the outside advertising agency and other marketing communications specialists as they develop the promotional program.[2] In a multiproduct firm, each brand may have its own ad agency and may compete against other brands within the company, not just against outside competitors. For example, Exhibit 3-2 shows ads for Tide and ERA, which are both Procter & Gamble products that compete for a share of the laundry detergent market.

As shown in Figure 3-3, the advertising department is part of marketing services and provides support for the brand managers. The role of marketing services is to assist the brand managers in planning and coordinating the integrated marketing communications program. In some companies, the marketing services group may include sales promotion. The brand managers may work with sales promotion people to develop budgets, define strategies, and implement tactical executions for both trade and consumer promotions. Marketing services may also provide other types of support services, such as package design and merchandising.

Some companies may have an additional layer(s) of management above the brand managers to coordinate the efforts of all the brand managers handling a related group of products. An example is the organizational structure of Procter & Gamble, shown in Figure 3-4. This system—generally referred to as a **category management system**—includes category managers as well as brand and advertising managers. The category manager oversees management of the entire product category and focuses on the strategic role of the various brands in order to build profits and market share.[3]

The advertising manager may review and evaluate the various parts of the program and advise and consult with the brand managers. This person may have the authority to override the brand manager's decisions on advertising. In some multiproduct firms that spend a lot on advertising, the advertising manager may coordinate the work of the various agencies to obtain media discounts for the firm's large volume of media purchases.

An advantage of the decentralized system is that each brand receives concentrated managerial attention, resulting in faster response to both problems and opportunities. The brand manager system is also more flexible and makes it easier to adjust various aspects of the advertising and promotional program, such as creative platforms and media and sales promotion schedules.[4] For example, General Motors began using a brand manager system in 1996 as a way to create stronger identities and positioning platforms for its 40-plus models of cars, trucks, minivans, and sport utility vehicles. The brand managers have full responsibility for the marketing of their vehicles,

Figure 3-3 A decentralized brand management system

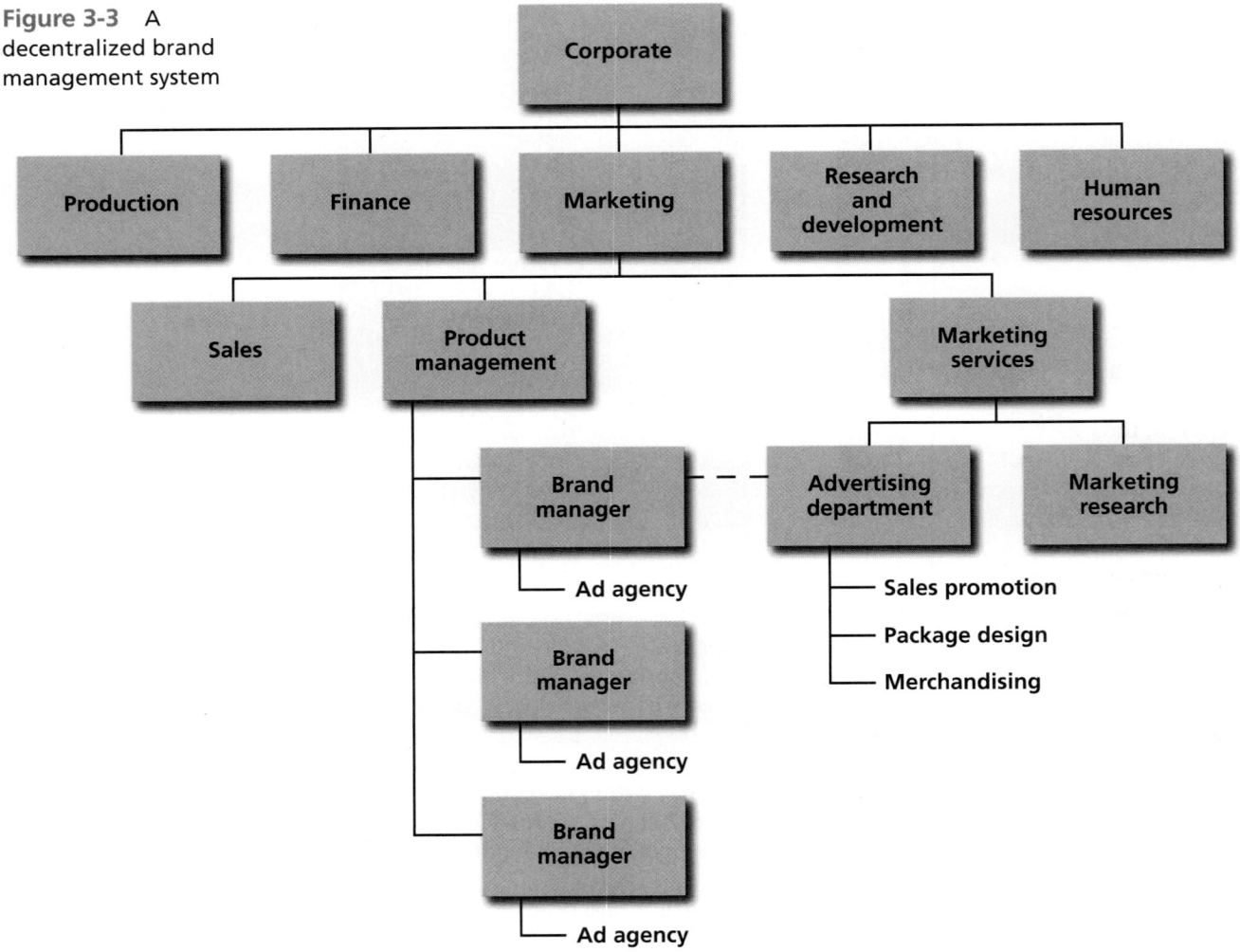

Figure 3-4 A Procter & Gamble division, using the category management system

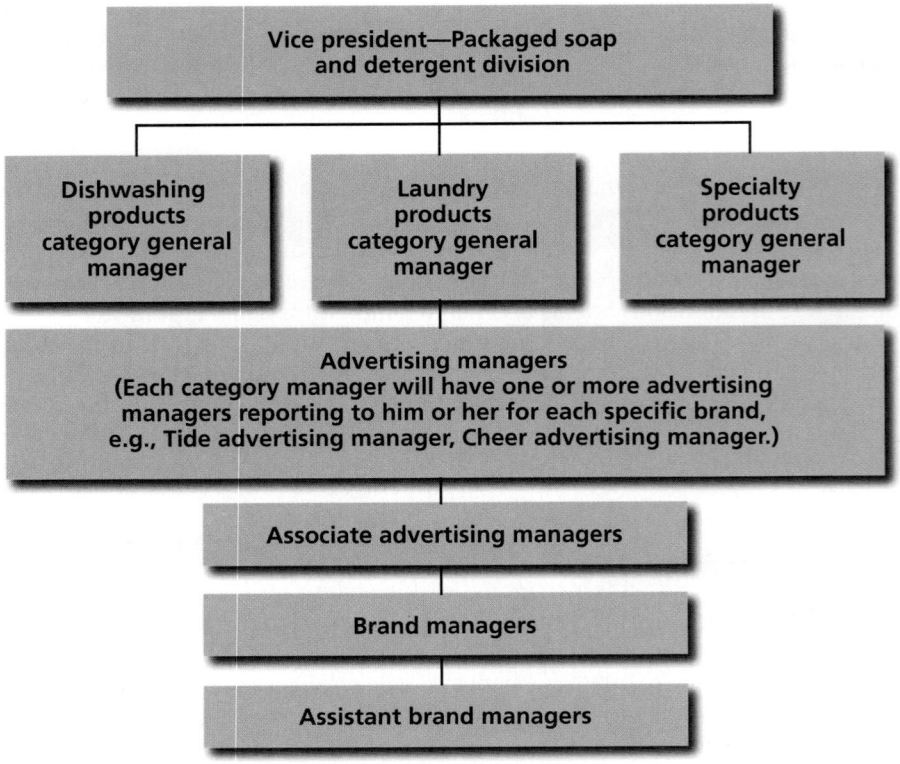

including the identification of target markets as well as the development of integrated marketing communications programs that will differentiate the brand.[5]

There are some drawbacks to the decentralized approach. Brand managers often lack training and experience. The promotional strategy for a brand may be developed by a brand manager who does not really understand what advertising or sales promotion can and cannot do and how each should be used. Brand managers may focus too much on short-run planning and administrative tasks, neglecting the development of long-term programs.

Another problem is that individual brand managers often end up competing for management attention, marketing dollars, and other resources, which can lead to unproductive rivalries and potential misallocation of funds. The manager's persuasiveness may become a bigger factor in determining budgets than the long-run profit potential of the brands. These types of problems were key factors in Procter & Gamble's decision to switch to a category management system.

Finally, the brand management system has been criticized for failing to provide brand managers with authority over the functions needed to implement and control the plans they develop.[6] Some companies have dealt with this problem by expanding the roles and responsibilities of the advertising and sales promotion managers and their staff of specialists. The staff specialists counsel the individual brand managers, and advertising or sales promotion decision making involves the advertising and/or sales promotion manager, the brand manager, and the marketing director.

In-House Agencies

Some companies, in an effort to reduce costs and maintain greater control over agency activities, have set up their own advertising agencies internally. An **in-house agency** is an advertising agency that is set up, owned, and operated by the advertiser. Some in-house agencies are little more than advertising departments, but in other companies they are given a separate identity and are responsible for the expenditure of large sums of advertising dollars. Large advertisers that use in-house agencies include Calvin Klein, The Gap, Avon, Revlon, and Benetton. Many companies use in-house agencies exclusively; others combine in-house efforts with those of outside agencies. For example, No Fear handles most of its advertising in-house, but it does use an outside agency for some of its creative work (Exhibit 3-3). (The specific roles performed by in-house agencies will become clearer when we discuss the functions of outside agencies.)

A major reason for using an in-house agency is to reduce advertising and promotion costs. Companies with very large advertising budgets pay a substantial amount to outside agencies in the form of media commissions. With an internal structure, these commissions go to the in-house agency. An in-house agency can also provide related work such as sales presentations and sales force materials, package design, and public

Exhibit 3-3 Most of the advertising for No Fear is done by an in-house agency

relations at a lower cost than outside agencies. A study by M. Louise Ripley found that creative and media services were the most likely functions to be performed outside, while merchandising and sales promotion were the most likely to be performed in-house.[7]

Saving money is not the only reason companies use in-house agencies. Time savings, bad experiences with outside agencies, and the increased knowledge and understanding of the market that come from working on advertising and promotion for the product or service day by day are also reasons. Companies can also maintain tighter control over the process and more easily coordinate promotions with the firm's overall marketing program. Some companies use an in-house agency simply because they believe it can do a better job than an outside agency could.[8]

Opponents of in-house agencies say they can give the advertiser neither the experience and objectivity of an outside agency nor the range of services. They argue that outside agencies have more highly skilled specialists and attract the best creative talent and that using an external firm gives a company a more varied perspective on its advertising problems and greater flexibility. In-house personnel may become narrow or grow stale while working on the same product line, but outside agencies may have different people with a variety of backgrounds and ideas working on the account. Flexibility is greater because an outside agency can be dismissed if the company is not satisfied, whereas changes in an in-house agency could be slower and more disruptive.

The cost savings of an in-house agency must be evaluated against these considerations. For many companies, high-quality advertising is critical to their marketing success and should be the major criterion in determining whether to use in-house services. Companies like Rockport and Redken Laboratories have moved their in-house work to outside agencies in recent years. Redken cited the need for a "fresh look" and objectivity as the reasons, noting that management gets too close to the product to come up with different creative ideas. Companies often hire outside agencies as they grow and their advertising budgets and needs increase. For example, Gateway hired a full-service outside agency to handle its advertising as the personal computer company experienced rapid growth during the 90s.[9]

The ultimate decision as to which type of advertising organization to use depends on which arrangement works best for the company. The advantages and disadvantages of the three systems are summarized in Figure 3-5. We now turn our attention to the functions of outside agencies and their roles in the promotional process.

Figure 3-5 Comparison of advertising organization systems

Organizational system	Advantages	Disadvantages
Centralized	• Facilitated communications • Fewer personnel required • Continuity in staff • Allows for more top-management involvement	• Less involvement with and understanding of overall marketing goals • Longer response time • Inability to handle multiple product lines
Decentralized	• Concentrated managerial attention • Rapid response to problems and opportunities • Increased flexibility	• Ineffective decision making • Internal conflicts • Misallocation of funds • Lack of authority
In-house agencies	• Cost savings • More control • Increased coordination	• Less experience • Less objectivity • Less flexibility

Advertising Agencies

Many major companies use an advertising agency to assist them in developing, preparing, and executing their promotional programs. An ad agency is a service organization that specializes in planning and executing advertising programs for its clients. Over 13,000 U.S. and international agencies are listed in the *Standard Directory of Advertising Agencies* (the "Red Book"); however, most are individually owned small businesses employing fewer than five people. The U.S. ad agency business is highly concentrated. Nearly two-thirds of the domestic **billings** (the amount of client money agencies spend on media purchases and other equivalent activities) are handled by the top 500 agencies. In fact, just 10 U.S. agencies handle nearly 30 percent of the total volume of business done by the top 500 agencies in the United States. The top agencies also have foreign operations that generate substantial billings and income. The top 25 agencies, ranked by their U.S. gross incomes, are listed in Figure 3-6. The table shows that the advertising business is also geographically concentrated, with 20 of the top 25 agencies headquartered in New York City or the surrounding area. Nearly 40 percent of U.S. agency business is handled by New York–based agencies. Other leading advertising centers in the United States include Boston, Chicago, Los Angeles, Detroit, San Francisco, and Minneapolis.[10]

During the late 1980s and into the 90s, the advertising industry underwent major changes as large agencies merged with or acquired other agencies and support organizations to form large advertising organizations, or superagencies. These **superagencies**

Figure 3-6 Top 25 agencies ranked by U.S. gross income, 2001

Rank	Agency	Headquarters	Gross Income (Millions)
1	Grey Worldwide	New York	$581.0
2	J. Walter Thompson	New York	565.5
3	McCann-Erickson Worldwide	New York	528.1
4	Leo Burnett Worldwide	Chicago	472.1
5	BBDO Worldwide	New York	458.9
6	Y&R Advertising	New York	432.2
7	DDB Worldwide Communications	New York	428.9
8	Euro RSCG Worldwide	New York	418.2
9	Ogilvy & Mather Worldwide	New York	384.8
10	Foote, Cone & Belding Worldwide	New York	376.3
11	D'Arcy Masius Benton & Bowles	New York	316.8
12	TMP Worldwide	New York	227.9
13	Campbell-Ewald	Warren, MI	214.0
14	TBWA Worldwide	New York	206.1
15	Deutsch	New York	202.5
16	Arnold Worldwide	Boston	193.8
17	CommonHealth	Parsippany, N.J.	190.8
18	Lowe & Partners Worldwide	New York	184.9
19	Saatchi & Saatchi	New York	176.0
20	Bates U.S.A.	New York	154.5
21	Publicis U.S.A.	New York	139.6
22	Nelson Communications Worldwide	New York	131.9
23	Hill, Holliday, Connors, Cosmopulos	Boston	125.0
24	Low Healthcare Worldwide	Parsippany, N.J.	124.0
25	Campbell Mithun	Minneapolis	118.0

Source: *Advertising Age*, Apr. 22, 2002, p. S-4.

were formed so that agencies could provide clients with integrated marketing communications services worldwide. Some advertisers became disenchanted with the superagencies and moved to smaller agencies that were flexible and more responsive.[11] However, during the mid-90s the agency business went through another wave of consolidation as a number of medium-size agencies were acquired and became part of large advertising organizations such as Omnicom Group, WPP Group, and the Interpublic Group of Cos. Many of the mid-size agencies were acquired by or forged alliances with larger agencies because their clients wanted an agency with international communications capabilities and their alignment with larger organizations gave them access to a network of agencies around the world. For example, TBWA and Chiat/Day merged and became part of the TBWA Worldwide agency, which is part of the Omnicom Group, the world's largest agency holding company. The acquisition of mid-size agencies by large advertising organizations has continued into the new millenium. In early 2000, Fallon McElligott, one of the largest and hottest independent U.S. ad agencies, was acquired by French advertising giant Publicis Groupe, as was London-based Saatchi & Saatchi. In 2002 Publicis acquired the Bcom3 Group, whose holdings include the Leo Burnett Co.; D'Arcy Masius Benton & Bowles; Manning Selvage & Lee; Bartle Bogel Hegarty; and the Starcom Media Vest Group. The deal also includes a partnership with Dentsu, Japan's largest advertising agency.[12]

Many of the advertising organizations and major agencies have been acquiring companies specializing in areas such as interactive communications, public relations, direct marketing, and sales promotion so that they can offer their clients an ever-broader range of integrated marketing communication services.[13] Recently the activity of the advertising holding companies has moved in a new direction as they have begun pursuing alliances with talent agencies. A new agreement negotiated between the Screen Actors Guild and the Association of Talent Agents in 2002 allows outside investors such as advertising agencies to own stakes in talent agencies that seek and negotiate work on behalf of actors, directors, and writers as well as some athletes.[14] By having a stake in the talent business, ad agencies can negotiate deals with current, as well as up-and-coming, celebrities for their clients.

Exhibit 3-4 Mentus Communications specializes in creating ads for high-tech companies

The Ad Agency's Role

The functions performed by advertising agencies might be conducted by the clients themselves through one of the designs discussed earlier in this chapter, but most large companies use outside firms. This section discusses some reasons advertisers use external agencies.

Reasons for Using an Agency

Probably the main reason outside agencies are used is that they provide the client with the services of highly skilled individuals who are specialists in their chosen fields. An advertising agency staff may include artists, writers, media analysts, researchers, and others with specific skills, knowledge, and experience who can help market the client's products or services. Many agencies specialize in a particular type of business and use their knowledge of the industry to assist their clients. For example, Mentus Inc. is an agency that specializes in integrated marketing communications for the high-technology, e-commerce, and bioscience industries (Exhibit 3-4).

An outside agency can also provide an objective viewpoint of the market and its business that is not subject to internal company policies, biases, or other limitations. The agency can draw on the broad range of experience it has gained while working on a diverse set of marketing problems for various clients. For example, an ad agency that is handling a travel-related account may have individuals who have worked with airlines,

cruise ship companies, travel agencies, hotels, and other travel-related industries. The agency may have experience in this area or may even have previously worked on the advertising account of one of the client's competitors. Thus, the agency can provide the client with insight into the industry (and, in some cases, the competition).

Types of Ad Agencies

Since ad agencies can range in size from a one- or two-person operation to large organizations with over 1,000 employees, the services offered and functions performed will vary. This section examines the different types of agencies, the services they perform for their clients, and how they are organized.

Full-Service Agencies

Many companies employ what is known as a **full-service agency,** which offers its clients a full range of marketing, communications, and promotions services, including planning, creating, and producing the advertising; performing research; and selecting media. A full-service agency may also offer nonadvertising services such as strategic market planning; sales promotions, direct marketing, and interactive capabilities; package design; and public relations and publicity.

The full-service agency is made up of departments that provide the activities needed to perform the various advertising functions and serve the client, as shown in Figure 3-7.

Account Services

Account services, or account management, is the link between the ad agency and its clients. Depending on the size of the client and its advertising budget, one or more account executives serve as liaison. The **account executive** is responsible for understanding the advertiser's marketing and promotions needs and interpreting them to agency personnel. He or she coordinates agency efforts in planning, creating, and producing ads. The account executive also presents agency recommendations and obtains client approval.

Figure 3-7 Full-service agency organizational chart

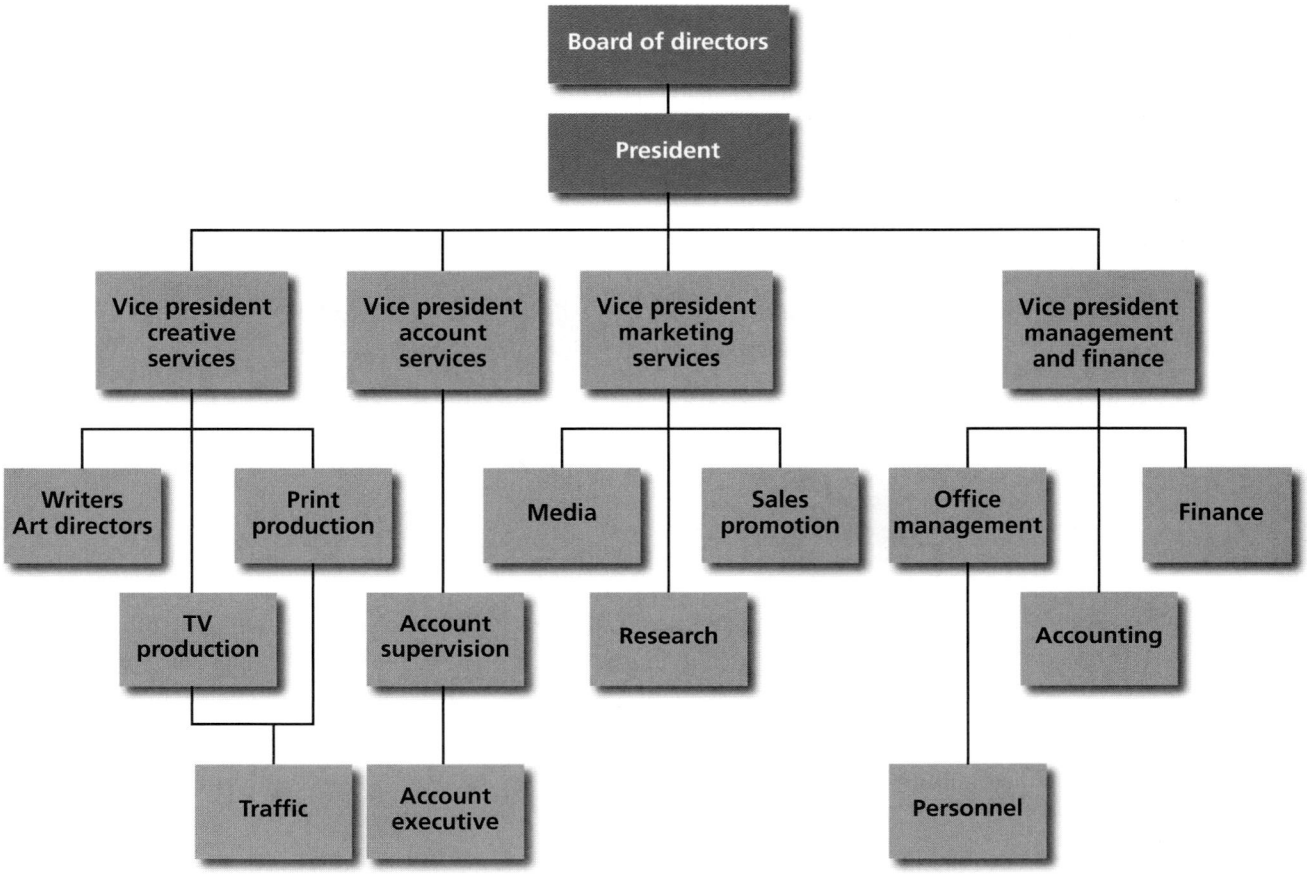

As the focal point of agency-client relationships, the account executive must know a great deal about the client's business and be able to communicate this to specialists in the agency working on the account.[15] The ideal account executive has a strong marketing background as well as a thorough understanding of all phases of the advertising process.

Marketing Services Over the past two decades, use of marketing services has increased dramatically. One service gaining increased attention is research, as agencies realize that to communicate effectively with their clients' customers, they must have a good understanding of the target audience. As shown in Chapter 1, the advertising planning process begins with a thorough situation analysis, which is based on research and information about the target audience.

Most full-service agencies maintain a *research department* whose function is to gather, analyze, and interpret information that will be useful in developing advertising for their clients. This can be done through primary research—where a study is designed, executed, and interpreted by the research department—or through the use of secondary (previously published) sources of information. Sometimes the research department acquires studies conducted by independent syndicated research firms or consultants. The research staff then interprets these reports and passes on the information to other agency personnel working on that account.

The research department may also design and conduct research to pretest the effectiveness of advertising the agency is considering. For example, copy testing is often conducted to determine how messages developed by the creative specialists are likely to be interpreted by the receiving audience.

The *media department* of an agency analyzes, selects, and contracts for space or time in the media that will be used to deliver the client's advertising message. The media department is expected to develop a media plan that will reach the target market and effectively communicate the message. Since most of the client's ad budget is spent on media time and/or space, this department must develop a plan that both communicates with the right audience and is cost-effective.

Media specialists must know what audiences the media reach, their rates, and how well they match the client's target market. The media department reviews information on demographics, magazine and newspaper readership, radio listenership, and consumers' TV viewing patterns to develop an effective media plan. The media buyer implements the media plan by purchasing the actual time and space.

The media department is becoming an increasingly important part of the agency business. An agency's ability to negotiate prices and effectively use the vast array of media vehicles, as well as other sources of customer contact, is becoming as important as its ability to create ads. Some of the major agencies and/or their holding companies have formed independent media services companies to better serve their clients. For example, the Leo Burnett agency formed Starcom as a full service media planning and buying company, while McCann Erickson Worldwide formed Universal McCann, and Foote Cone and Belding Worldwide formed Horizon.FCB. These media companies primarily serve the agency's clients but may also offer media services separately to other clients as well. A number of large advertisers have consolidated their media buying with these large media services companies to save money and improve media efficiency. General Motors consolidated its $3.6 billion media business with Starcom, while the Interpublic Group's Universal McCann handles close to $1 billion in Nestlé media business around the world.[16]

The research and media departments perform most of the functions that full-service agencies need to plan and execute their clients' advertising programs. Some agencies offer additional marketing services to their clients to assist in other promotional areas. An agency may have a sales promotion department, or merchandising department, that specializes in developing contests, premiums, promotions, point-of-sale materials, and other sales materials. It may have direct-marketing specialists and package designers, as well as a PR/publicity department. Many agencies have developed interactive media departments to create websites for their clients. The growing popularity of integrated marketing communications has prompted many full-function agencies to develop capabilities and offer services in these other promotional areas. IMC Perspective 3-1 discusses how traditional advertising agencies are developing integrated marketing capabilities that extend beyond media advertising.

IMC PERSPECTIVE 3-1

Agencies Learn That It's about More Than Advertising

During the late 1980s many of the world's largest advertising agencies recognized that their clients were shifting more and more of their promotional budgets away from traditional media advertising to other areas of marketing communication such as direct marketing, public relations, sales promotion, and event sponsorship. In response to this trend, many of these agencies began acquiring companies that were specialists in these areas and ended up turning them into profit-centered departments or subsidiaries that often ended up battling one another for a piece of their client's promotional budget. While the agencies could point to these specialists when touting their IMC capabilities, there was really little emphasis on integrating the various communication functions.

During the 90s some agencies began taking steps to place more of an emphasis on IMC by truly integrating it into all aspects of their operations. For example, the Leo Burnett agency brought in direct-marketing, sales promotion, event marketing, and public relations professionals and dispersed them throughout the agency. Burnetters were expected to interact with clients not as advertising specialists who happened to know about sales promotion, direct marketing, or public relations but as generalists able to work with a variety of integrated marketing tools. Another agency that embraced IMC was Fallon McElligott, which hired a president of integrated marketing and expanded its capabilities in areas such as PR, events, and interactive advertising.

As we begin the new millennium, the shift toward IMC is taking place at a number of major ad agencies that are recognizing they must embrace a way of doing business that doesn't always involve advertising. Many companies are developing campaigns and strategies using event marketing, sponsorships, direct marketing, targeted radio, and the Internet with only peripheral use of print and TV advertising. The Internet poses a particular threat to traditional agencies as it is not well understood by many agency veterans and is taking yet another slice from the marketing communications budget pie.

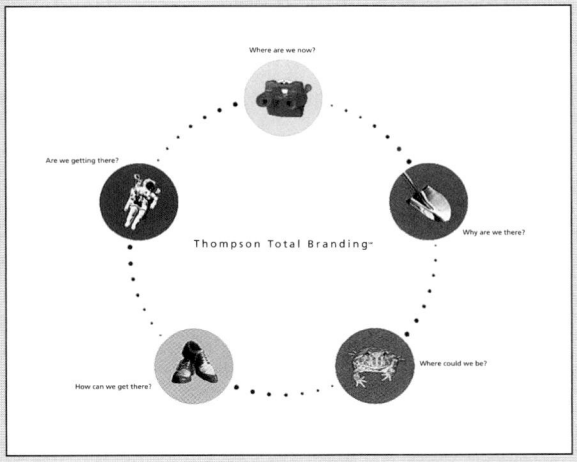

Foote, Cone & Belding is remaking itself as a New Economy ad agency by building up its capabilities in areas such as direct marketing, interactive, customer relationship, management/database, event marketing, and sports marketing. FCB touts its ability to offer clients a broad spectrum of integrated marketing communications services through its "Model of One," which ensures that all these services are seamlessly integrated and unified. All efforts are managed under one team and based on one strategy and one broad creative idea.

At J. Walter Thompson, the agency's CEO, Chris Jones, has championed a program called Thompson Total Branding (TTB) that makes JWT the manager of a client's brand. TTB involves taking what the agency calls a "Branding Idea" and developing a total communications plan that helps decide which integrated marketing tools can most powerfully and persuasively communicate it. One of the company executives notes, "Agencies are finally realizing that our job is creating branding solutions and, while those may involve advertising, it's not necessarily about advertising. That's a fundamental change in the way we operate." The ability to use various IMC tools has helped the agency secure new accounts and strengthen relationships with existing clients.

While traditional agencies have been preaching integrated marketing for years, many have not been really practicing it. However, these agencies are realizing they must alter their course if they plan to be competitive in the future. They are retraining their staffers in the use and best practices of various IMC tools and getting them, at long last, to focus on total communications solutions to their clients' businesses. The move toward integrated marketing communications appears to be for real this time around.

Sources: Laura Q. Hughes, "Measuring Up," *Advertising Age,* Feb. 5, 2001, pp. 1, 34; Kathryn Kranhold, "FCB Makes Itself a New Economy Shop," *The Wall Street Journal,* June 14, 2000, p. B8; Ellen Newborne, "Mad Ave: A Star Is Reborn," *BusinessWeek,* July 26, 1999, pp. 54–64.

Creative Services The creative services department is responsible for the creation and execution of advertisements. The individuals who conceive the ideas for the ads and write the headlines, subheads, and body copy (the words constituting the message) are known as **copywriters.** They may also be involved in determining the basic appeal or theme of the ad campaign and often prepare a rough initial visual layout of the print ad or television commercial.

While copywriters are responsible for what the message says, the *art department* is responsible for how the ad looks. For print ads, the art director and graphic designers prepare *layouts,* which are drawings that show what the ad will look like and from which the final artwork will be produced. For TV commercials, the layout is known as a *storyboard,* a sequence of frames or panels that depict the commercial in still form.

Members of the creative department work together to develop ads that will communicate the key points determined to be the basis of the creative strategy for the client's product or service. Writers and artists generally work under the direction of the agency's creative director, who oversees all the advertising produced by the organization. The director sets the creative philosophy of the department and may even become directly involved in creating ads for the agency's largest clients.

Once the copy, layout, illustrations, and mechanical specifications have been completed and approved, the ad is turned over to the *production department.* Most agencies do not actually produce finished ads; they hire printers, engravers, photographers, typographers, and other suppliers to complete the finished product. For broadcast production, the approved storyboard must be turned into a finished commercial. The production department may supervise the casting of people to appear in the ad and the setting for the scenes as well as choose an independent production studio. The department may hire an outside director to turn the creative concept into a commercial. For example, several companies, including Nike and Kmart, have used film director Spike Lee to direct their commercials; Airwalk shoes has used John Glen, who directed many of the James Bond films, for its TV spots. Copywriters, art directors, account managers, people from research and planning, and representatives from the client side may all participate in production decisions, particularly when large sums of money are involved.

Creating an advertisement often involves many people and takes several months. In large agencies with many clients, coordinating the creative and production processes can be a major problem. A *traffic department* coordinates all phases of production to see that the ads are completed on time and that all deadlines for submitting the ads to the media are met. The traffic department may be located in the creative services area of the agency, or be part of media or account management, or be separate.

Management and Finance Like any other business, an advertising agency must be managed and perform basic operating and administrative functions such as accounting, finance, and human resources. It must also attempt to generate new business. Large agencies employ administrative, managerial, and clerical people to perform these functions. The bulk of an agency's income (approximately 64 percent) goes to salary and benefits for its employees. Thus, an agency must manage its personnel carefully and get maximum productivity from them.

Agency Organization and Structure Full-function advertising agencies must develop an organizational structure that will meet their clients' needs and serve their own internal requirements. Most medium-size and large agencies are structured under either a departmental or a group system. Under the **departmental system,** each of the agency functions shown in Figure 3-7 is set up as a separate department and is called on as needed to perform its specialty and serve all of the agency's clients. Ad layout, writing, and production are done by the creative department, marketing services is responsible for any research or media selection and purchases, and the account services department handles client contact. Some agencies prefer the departmental system because it gives employees the opportunity to develop expertise in servicing a variety of accounts.

Many large agencies use the **group system,** in which individuals from each department work together in groups to service particular accounts. Each group is headed by an account executive or supervisor and has one or more media people, including

media planners and buyers; a creative team, which includes copywriters, art directors, artists, and production personnel; and one or more account executives. The group may also include individuals from other departments such as marketing research, direct marketing, or sales promotion. The size and composition of the group varies depending on the client's billings and the importance of the account to the agency. For very important accounts, the group members may be assigned exclusively to one client. In some agencies, they may serve a number of smaller clients. Many agencies prefer the group system because employees become very knowledgeable about the client's business and there is continuity in servicing the account.

Other Types of Agencies and Services

Not every agency is a large full-service agency. Many smaller agencies expect their employees to handle a variety of jobs. For example, account executives may do their own research, work out their own media schedule, and coordinate the production of ads written and designed by the creative department. Many advertisers, including some large companies, are not interested in paying for the services of a full-service agency but are interested in some of the specific services agencies have to offer. Over the past few decades, several alternatives to full-service agencies have evolved, including creative boutiques and media buying services.

Creative Boutiques

A **creative boutique** is an agency that provides only creative services. These specialized companies have developed in response to some clients' desires to use only the creative talent of an outside provider while maintaining the other functions internally. The client may seek outside creative talent because it believes an extra creative effort is required or because its own employees do not have sufficient skills in this regard. Some advertisers have been bypassing traditional agencies and tapping into the movie industry for creative ideas for their commercials.[17] For example, a few years ago Coca-Cola entered into a joint venture with Disney and three former employees of Creative Artists Agency (CAA), a Hollywood talent agency, to create an in-house agency called Edge Creative. The agency created several commercials for Coca-Cola's flagship brand, including the popular polar bears spot (Exhibit 3-5). However, in 2000 the Coca-Cola Company sold off its interest in Edge Creative and shifted the Coke account back to a traditional agency.

Full-service agencies often subcontract work to creative boutiques when they are very busy or want to avoid adding full-time employees to their payrolls. Creative boutiques are usually founded by members of the creative departments of full-service agencies who leave the firm and take with them clients who want to retain their creative talents. These boutiques usually perform the creative function on a fee basis. IMC Perspective 3-2 discusses the challenges faced by creative boutiques and some of the small shops that have been successful recently.

Exhibit 3-5 This popular Coca-Cola spot was done by the company's in-house creative boutique

Media Buying Services

Media buying services are independent companies that specialize in the buying of media, particularly radio and television time. The task of purchasing advertising media has grown more complex as specialized media proliferate, so media buying services have found a niche by specializing in the analysis and purchase of advertising time and space. Agencies and clients usually develop their own media strategies and hire the buying service to execute them. Some media buying services do help advertisers plan their media strategies. Because media buying services purchase such large amounts of time and space, they receive large discounts and can save the small agency or client money on media purchases. Media buying services are paid a fee or commission for their work.

Media buying services have been experiencing strong growth in recent years as clients seek alternatives to full-service agency

IMC PERSPECTIVE 3-2

Tough Times for Creative Boutiques

Creative boutiques have long been an important part of the advertising industry. The competitive advantage for boutiques has always been their ability to turn out inventive creative work quickly, without the cumbersome bureaucracy and politics of larger agencies. Large and small shops coexisted successfully because boutiques usually pursued smaller accounts than large agencies were interested in. And even as the agency business was reshaped by consolidation and the creation of large mega-agencies that now dominate the industry, creative boutiques were riding high on the dot-com boom of the late 90s that provided a boost in billings, profile, and morale for small shops. However, the dot-com wave crashed even faster than it appeared, and then came the terrorist attacks of September 11, which were followed by the worst advertising recession in decades.

Today's creative boutiques are facing major challenges, and many are struggling to identify and differentiate themselves and attract clients. They find themselves competing against the larger agencies for accounts that would have been passed over by top-tier shops during better economic times. Moreover, selling the creativity of a boutique's work is not enough, as many clients want the range of services that larger agencies provide. Creative work does not capture the imagination of the industry the way it used to, as marketers are looking for business-building ideas rather than creative home runs. As the new business director at a large New York agency notes: "Boutiques can't compete in terms of offering integrated solutions, and don't have the resources to mount serious pitches for even the smaller pieces of business that might go to a mid-size agency. They will be forever mired in project work."

Despite these obstacles, there are still those brave or foolhardy enough to believe that with a dollar and a dream they can open their own creative boutique, and they are hanging out shingles. The advertising business has always been grounded in creativity and entrepreneurship, and most boutique partners see the small shop as still relevant in an age of consolidation and multinational clients. They note that there still is a niche for creative boutiques, citing the number of big-client–small-agency relationships across the industry. Anheuser Busch, which has large multinational agencies on its roster, also works with small hybrid shops such as Fusion Idea Lab in Chicago on project assignments for Bud Light. Target parcels out project work to small shops like Peterson Milla Hooks in Minneapolis, while Boston-based Velocity's clients include Just For

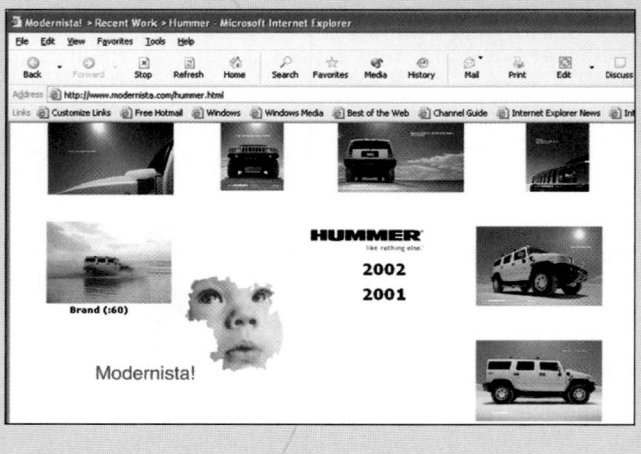

Feet and the Bruegger's Bagels chain. Many of these hope to become the Next Modernista!, the Boston shop that was founded by former creative directors from Arnold Advertising and Wieden & Kennedy, New York, and in less than two years has managed to land clients such as the Gap, MTV, and General Motors' Hummer.

Many clients recognize the benefits of working directly with a smaller creative boutique where they can get more attention and better access to creative talent than they would at a larger agency. For example, the marketing director for Culver Franchising System, the parent of Culver's Frozen Custard, hired the small One and All Shop because the company was looking for an agency where the partners would be involved and there would not be a lot of layers of bureaucracy with which to deal. Creative duties on the Boston Beer Co.'s $30 million account went to a former Lowe Lintas & Partners creative director who left to form his own agency, called Big Chair. The vice president of brand development at Boston Beer explained: "I was looking for people who had beer experience, who had good experience with humor, and a shop that was unconventional and small. The creative so far has met my expectations and so has the relationship with very quick response time a very high level of thinking."

Many creative boutique owners still feel they can beat the odds and carve out a niche for themselves in the advertising agency business. Those who can survive the tough times facing the advertising industry may find a bright future, as there will always be clients who want key-principal involvement and creative people who are doing breakthrough creative work.

Sources: Anthony Vagnoni, "Small Fries," *Advertising Age,* March 4, 2002, pp. 20, 22; Eleftheria Parpis, "The Little League," *Adweek,* Nov. 26, 2001, p. 3.

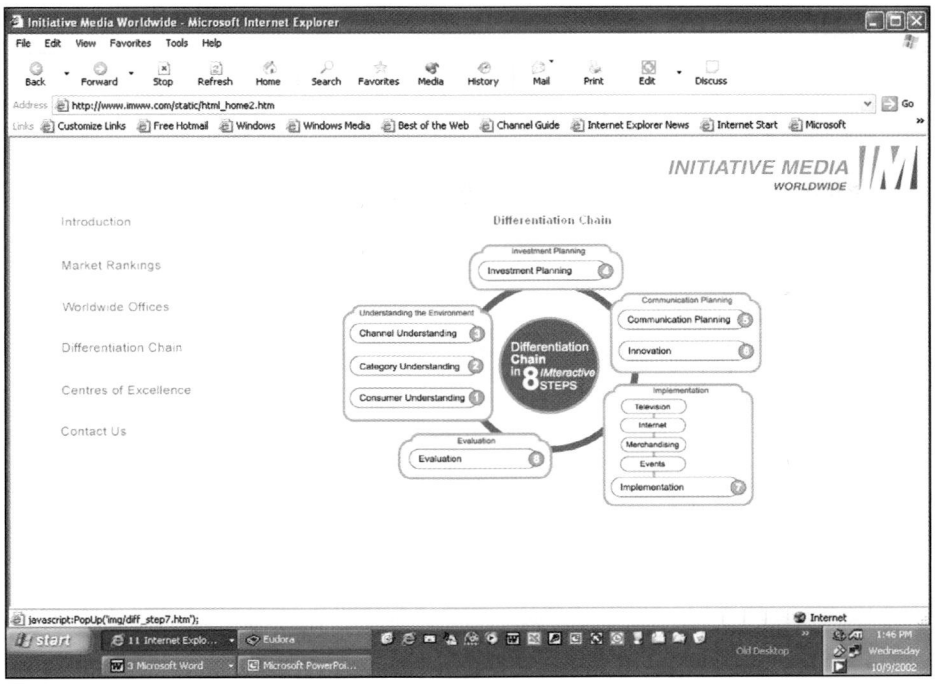

Exhibit 3-6 Initiative Media is the leading independent media buying service

relationships. Many companies have been unbundling agency services and consolidating media buying to get more clout from their advertising budgets. Nike, Maytag, and Gateway are among those that have switched some or all of their media buying from full-service agencies to independent media buyers. As noted earlier, many of the major agencies have formed independent media services companies that handle the media planning and buying for their clients and also offer their services separately to companies interested in a more specialized or consolidated approach to media planning, research, and/or buying. Exhibit 3-6 shows a page from the website of Initiative Media Worldwide, the largest media services company in the world.

Agency Compensation

As you have seen, the type and amount of services an agency performs vary from one client to another. As a result, agencies use a variety of methods to get paid for their services. Agencies are typically compensated in three ways: commissions, some type of fee arrangement, or percentage charges.

Commissions from Media

The traditional method of compensating agencies is through a **commission system,** where the agency receives a specified commission (usually 15 percent) from the media on any advertising time or space it purchases for its client. (For outdoor advertising, the commission is 16⅔ percent.) This system provides a simple method of determining payments, as shown in the following example.

Assume an agency prepares a full-page magazine ad and arranges to place the ad on the back cover of a magazine at a cost of $100,000. The agency places the order for the space and delivers the ad to the magazine. Once the ad is run, the magazine will bill the agency for $100,000, less the 15 percent ($15,000) commission. The media will also offer a 2 percent cash discount for early payment, which the agency may pass along to the client. The agency will bill the client $100,000 less the 2 percent cash discount on the net amount, or a total of $98,300, as shown in Figure 3-8. The $15,000 commission represents the agency's compensation for its services.

Appraisal of the Commission System Use of the commission system to compensate agencies has been quite controversial for many years. A major problem centers on whether the 15 percent commission represents equitable compensation for services performed. Two agencies may require the same amount of effort to create

Figure 3-8 Example of commission system payment

Media Bills Agency		Agency Bills Advertiser	
Costs for magazine space	$100,000	Costs for magazine space	$100,000
Less 15% commission	−15,000	Less 2% cash discount	−1,700
Cost of media space	85,000	Advertiser pays agency	$ 98,300
Less 2% cash discount	−1,700		
Agency pays media	$ 83,300	Agency income	$ 15,000

and produce an ad. However, one client may spend $2 million on commissionable media, which results in a $300,000 agency income, while the other spends $20 million, generating $3 million in commissions. Critics argue that the commission system encourages agencies to recommend high media expenditures to increase their commission level.

Another criticism of the commission system is that it ties agency compensation to media costs. In periods of media cost inflation, the agency is (according to the client) disproportionately rewarded. The commission system has also been criticized for encouraging agencies to ignore cost accounting systems to justify the expenses attributable to work on a particular account. Still others charge that this system tempts the agency to avoid noncommissionable media such as direct mail, sales promotions, or advertising specialties, unless they are requested by the client.

Defenders of the commission system argue that it is easy to administer and it keeps the emphasis in agency competition on nonprice factors such as the quality of the advertising developed. Proponents argue that agency services are proportional to the size of the commission, since more time and effort are devoted to the large accounts that generate high revenue for the agency. They also say the system is more flexible than it appears because agencies often perform other services for large clients at no extra charge, justifying such actions by the large commission they receive.

The commission system has been a highly debated topic among advertisers and agencies for years. Critics of the system have argued that it provides an incentive for agencies to do the wrong thing, such as recommending mass-media advertising when other forms of communication such as direct marketing or public relations might do a better job.[18] They argue that the commission system is outdated and must be changed. This does indeed appear to be happening. A recent study of agency compensation conducted by the Association of National Advertisers (ANA) indicates that agency compensation based on the traditional 15 percent commission is becoming rare.[19] The survey found that only 21 percent of advertisers paid commissions to their agencies and only 16 percent paid the standard 15 percent. The clients who have stuck with commissions do so either from inertia or from administrative simplicity. However, the survey also found that most clients and agencies use the 15 percent commission standard as a starting point for determining other compensation agreements such as labor- and performance-based plans.

While the use of the 15 percent commission is on the wane, many advertisers still use some form of media commission to compensate their agencies. Many advertisers have gone to a **negotiated commission** system to compensate their agencies. This commission structure can take the form of reduced percentage rates, variable commission rates, and commissions with minimum and maximum profit rates. Negotiated commissions are designed to consider the needs of the clients as well as the time and effort exerted by the agency, thereby avoiding some of the problems inherent in the traditional 15 percent sytem. Some of the leading agencies now receive a commission based on a sliding rate that becomes lower as the clients' media expenditures increase and end up receiving average commissions of 8 to 10 percent versus the traditional 15 percent.[20] Agencies are also relying less on media commissions for their income as their clients expand their integrated marketing communications programs to include other forms of promotion and cut back on mass-media advertising. The percentage of

agency income from media commissions is declining, and a greater percentage is coming through other methods such as fees and performance incentives.

Fee, Cost, and Incentive-Based Systems

Since many believe the commission system is not equitable to all parties, many agencies and their clients have developed some type of fee arrangement or cost-plus agreement for agency compensation. Some are using incentive-based compensation, which is a combination of a commission and a fee system.

Fee Arrangement

There are two basic types of fee arrangement systems. In the straight or **fixed-fee method,** the agency charges a basic monthly fee for all of its services and credits to the client any media commissions earned. Agency and client agree on the specific work to be done and the amount the agency will be paid for it. Sometimes agencies are compensated through a **fee-commission combination,** in which the media commissions received by the agency are credited against the fee. If the commissions are less than the agreed-on fee, the client must make up the difference. If the agency does much work for the client in noncommissionable media, the fee may be charged over and above the commissions received.

Both types of fee arrangements require that the agency carefully assess its costs of serving the client for the specified period, or for the project, plus its desired profit margin. To avoid any later disagreement, a fee arrangement should specify exactly what services the agency is expected to perform for the client. Fee arrangements have become the primary type of agreement used by advertisers with their agencies, accounting for 68 percent of the compensation plans in the recent ANA survey.

Cost-Plus Agreement

Under a **cost-plus system,** the client agrees to pay the agency a fee based on the costs of its work plus some agreed-on profit margin (often a percentage of total costs). This system requires that the agency keep detailed records of the costs it incurs in working on the client's account. Direct costs (personnel time and out-of-pocket expenses) plus an allocation for overhead and a markup for profits determine the amount the agency bills the client.

Fee agreements and cost-plus systems are commonly used in conjunction with a commission system. The fee-based system can be advantageous to both the client and the agency, depending on the size of the client, advertising budget, media used, and services required. Many clients prefer fee or cost-plus systems because they receive a detailed breakdown of where and how their advertising and promotion dollars are being spent. However, these arrangements can be difficult for the agency, as they require careful cost accounting and may be difficult to estimate when bidding for an advertiser's business. Agencies are also reluctant to let clients see their internal cost figures.

Incentive-Based Compensation

Many clients these days are demanding more accountability from their agencies and tying agency compensation to performance through some type of **incentive-based system.** While there are many variations, the basic idea is that the agency's ultimate compensation level will depend on how well it meets predetermined performance goals. These goals often include objective measures such as sales or market share as well as more subjective measures such as evaluations of the quality of the agency's creative work. Companies using incentive-based systems determine agency compensation through media commissions, fees, bonuses, or some combination of these methods. The use of performance incentives varies by the size of the advertiser, with large advertisers the most likely to use them. Figure 3-9 shows the various performance criteria used along with the basis for the incentive and the use of performance incentives by advertiser size.

Recognizing the movement toward incentive-based systems, most agencies have agreed to tie their compensation to performance.[21] Agency executives note that pay for performance works best when the agency has complete control over a campaign. Thus, if a campaign fails to help sell a product or service, the agency is willing to assume complete responsibility and take a reduction in compensation. On the other hand, if sales increase, the agency can receive greater compensation for its work.

Figure 3-9 Use of performance incentives by advertisers

Performance Criteria Used for Incentive Systems	
Sales goals	73%
Market share	29
Profit	25
Brand/ad awareness	50
Brand perceptions	23
Copy test results	25
Performance reviews	58
Other criteria	11
Basis for Incentive	
Agency performance	14%
Company performance	17
Both agency and company performance	69
Performance incentive use by size of advertiser	
Under $4 million	13%
$4 million–$20 million	10
$20 million–$100 million	33
More than $100 million	44

Source: Association of National Advertisers: Trend in Compensation Survey: 2000.

Percentage Charges

Another way to compensate an agency is by adding a markup of **percentage charges** to various services the agency purchases from outside providers. These may include market research, artwork, printing, photography, and other services or materials. Markups usually range from 17.65 to 20 percent and are added to the client's overall bill. Since suppliers of these services do not allow the agency a commission, percentage charges cover administrative costs while allowing a reasonable profit for the agency's efforts. (A markup of 17.65 percent of costs added to the initial cost would yield a 15 percent commission. For example, research costs of $\$100{,}000 \times 17.65\% = \$100{,}000 + \$17{,}650 = \$117{,}650$. The $17,650 markup is about 15 percent of $117,650.)

The Future of Agency Compensation

As you can see there is no one method of agency compensation to which everyone subscribes. The recent ANA survey found that nearly half of advertisers made significant changes in their compensation plans in the past three years, while 21 percent plan more changes soon. One of the most significant findings from the recent ANA survey is the rapid rise in incentive-based compensation agreements, as 35 percent of advertisers are using some type of performance-based system versus only 13 percent 10 years ago.

As more companies adopt IMC approaches, they are reducing their reliance on traditional media advertising, and this is leading to changes in the way they compensate their agencies. For example, Procter & Gamble, which has traditionally been a heavy user of television advertising, was one of the largest major advertisers to move away from the standard 15 percent commission system. In 2000 P&G implemented a major change in its compensation structure from one based entirely on media commissions to one based entirely on sales-based incentives. One of the reasons for the change in P&G's compensation system is to encourage agencies to focus less on expensive commissionable media such as television and magazines and make use of other IMC tools such as direct mail, event marketing, public relations, and the Internet.[22] P&G joins a list of other major consumer products advertisers, such as Colgate-Palmolive, Unilever, and Campbell Soup, that have changed their systems to more closely link agency compensation to a product's performance in the market. Many automobile advertisers, including Nissan, Ford, BMW, and General Motors, are also using incentive-based systems.[23] GM made the change to encourage its agencies to look beyond traditional mass-media advertising and develop other ways of reaching consumers.[24]

Many companies are changing their compensation systems as they move away from traditional mass media and turn to a wider array of marketing communication tools. They are also trying to make their agencies more accountable and reduce agency compensation costs. However, advertisers must recognize that their compensation policies should provide agencies with a reasonable profit if they want quality work and the best results from their agencies.

Evaluating Agencies

Given the substantial amounts of money being spent on advertising and promotion, demand for accountability of the expenditures has increased. Regular reviews of the agency's performance are necessary. The agency evaluation process usually involves two types of assessments, one financial and operational and the other more qualitative. The **financial audit** focuses on how the agency conducts its business. It is designed to verify costs and expenses, the number of personnel hours charged to an account, and payments to media and outside suppliers. The **qualitative audit** focuses on the agency's efforts in planning, developing, and implementing the client's advertising programs and considers the results achieved.

The agency evaluation is often done on a subjective, informal basis, particularly in smaller companies where ad budgets are low or advertising is not seen as the most critical factor in the firm's marketing performance. However some companies have developed formal, systematic evaluation systems, particularly when budgets are large and the advertising function receives much emphasis. The top management of these companies wants to be sure money is being spent efficiently and effectively. As the costs of advertising and other forms of promotion rises, more companies are adopting formal procedures for evaluating the performance of their agencies.

One example of a formal agency evaluation system is that used by Whirlpool, which markets a variety of consumer products. Whirlpool management meets once a year with the company's agencies to review their performance. Whirlpool managers complete an advertising agency performance evaluation, part of which is shown in Exhibit 3-7. These reports are compiled and reviewed with the agency at each annual meeting. Whirlpool's evaluation process covers six areas of performance. The company and the agency develop an action plan to correct areas of deficiency.

Companies develop evaluation procedures that emphasize different areas. For example, R. J. Reynolds emphasizes creative development and execution, marketing counsel and ideas, promotion support, and cost controls, without any mention of sales figures. Sears focuses on the performance of the agency as a whole in an effort to establish a partnership between the agency and the client. These and other evaluation methods are being used more regularly by advertisers. As fiscal controls tighten, clients will require more accountability from their providers and adopt formal evaluation procedures.

Exhibit 3-7 Whirlpool's ad agency performance evaluation

CREATIVE SERVICES

	Always 4	Often 3	Occasionally 2	Seldom 1	Never 0	NA	Marks Scored
1. Agency produces fresh ideas and original approaches							
2. Agency accurately interprets facts, strategies and objectives into usable advertisements and plans							
3. Creative group is knowledgeable about company's products, markets and strategies							
4. Creative group is concerned with good advertising communications and develops campaigns and ads that exhibit this concern							
5. Creative group produces on time							
6. Creative group performs well under pressure							
7. Creative group operates in a businesslike manner to control production costs and other creative charges							
8. Agency presentations are well organized with sufficient examples of proposed executions							
9. Creative group participates in major campaign presentations							
10. Agency presents ideas and executions not requested but felt to be good opportunities							
11. Agency willingly accepts ideas generated by other locations/agency offices vs. being over-protective of its own creative product							
12. Other areas not mentioned							
13. Agency demonstrates commitment to client's business							
14. Agency creative proposals are relevant and properly fulfill creative brief							

Value—(marks)

Rating:			
	Excellent	90–100%	Total marks scored
	Good	80–89%	
	Average	70–79%	Total possible marks
	Fair	60–69%	
	Poor	below 60%	Score

ACCOUNT REPRESENTATION & SERVICE

	Always 4	Often 3	Occasionally 2	Seldom 1	Never 0	NA	Marks Scored
1. Account representatives act with personal initiative							
2. Account representatives anticipate needs in advance of direction by client (ie: are proactive)							
3. Account group takes direction well							
4. Agency is able to demonstrate results of programs implemented							
5. Account representatives function strategically rather than as creative advisors only							
6. Account representatives are knowledgeable about competitive programs and share this information along with their recommendations in a timely manner							
7. Account representatives respond to client requests in a timely fashion							
8. Account group operates in a business-like manner to control costs							
9. Agency recommendations are founded on sound reasoning and supported factually, and appropriately fit within budget constraints							
10. Agency is able to advise the client on trends and developments in technology							
11. Account representatives demonstrate a high degree of professionalism in both written and oral communication							
12. Agency presents ideas and executions not requested by felt to be good opportunities							
13. Agency makes reasoned recommendations on allocation of budgets							
14. Agency demonstrates commitment to client's business							
15. There is a positive social relationship between client and agency							

Value—(marks)

Rating:			
	Excellent	90–100%	Total marks scored
	Good	80–89%	
	Average	70–79%	Total possible marks
	Fair	60–69%	
	Poor	below 60%	Score

Exhibit 3-8 Young & Rubicam has been the agency for Dr Pepper for more than three decades

Gaining and Losing Clients

The evaluation process described above provides valuable feedback to both the agency and the client, such as indicating changes that need to be made by the agency and/or the client to improve performance and make the relationship more productive. Many agencies have had very long-lasting relationships with their clients. For example, General Electric has been with the BBDO Worldwide agency for over 80 years. Other well-known companies or brands that have had long-lasting relationships include Marlboro/Leo Burnett (50 years), McDonald's/DDB Needham Worldwide (34 years), and PepsiCo/BBDO (44 years). Exhibit 3-8 shows an ad run by Dr Pepper/Seven Up Inc. celebrating its long-term relationship with the Young & Rubicam agency.

While many successful client-agency relationships go on for a number of years, long-term relationships are becoming less common. A survey conducted a few years ago by the American Association of Advertising Agencies found that the average tenure of client-agency relationships declined from 7.2 years in 1984 to 5.3 years in the late 90s.[25] In recent years a number of long-standing client-agency relationships were terminated. Levi Strauss & Co. terminated its 68-year relationship with Foote, Cone & Belding, of San Francisco, in 1998 when it transferred its U.S. jeans account to TBWA/Chiat/Day. However, just three years later the company moved the account to Bartle Bogle Hegarty, the agency that handles its advertising in Europe.[26] In 2002 Saturn Corp. ended its long relationship with Hal Riney & Partners, the agency that had been with the automaker since its debut in 1990, and moved to Goodby Silverstein & Partners, San Francisco.[27] IMC Perspective 3-3 discusses how Gateway has changed agencies four times in the past 10 years.

There are a number of reasons clients switch agencies. Understanding these potential problems can help the agency avoid them.[28] In addition, it is important to understand the process agencies go through in trying to win new clients.

Why Agencies Lose Clients

Some of the more common reasons agencies lose clients follow:

- *Poor performance or service.* The client becomes dissatisfied with the quality of the advertising and/or the service provided by the agency.
- *Poor communication.* The client and agency personnel fail to develop or maintain the level of communication necessary to sustain a favorable working relationship.
- *Unrealistic demands by the client.* The client places demands on the agency that exceed the amount of compensation received and reduce the account's profitability.
- *Personality conflicts.* People working on the account on the client and agency sides do not have enough rapport to work well together.
- *Personnel changes.* A change in personnel at either the agency or the advertiser can create problems. New managers may wish to use an agency with which they have established ties. Agency personnel often take accounts with them when they switch agencies or start their own.
- *Changes in size of the client or agency.* The client may outgrow the agency or decide it needs a larger agency to handle its business. If the agency gets too large, the client may represent too small a percentage of its business to command attention.
- *Conflicts of interest.* A conflict may develop when an agency merges with another agency or when a client is part of an acquisition or merger. In the United States, an agency cannot handle two accounts that are in direct competition with each other. In some cases, even indirect competition will not be tolerated.
- *Changes in the client's corporate and/or marketing strategy.* A client may change its marketing strategy and decide that a new agency is needed to carry out the new program. As more companies adapt an integrated marketing communications

IMC PERSPECTIVE 3-3

Gateway Searches for the Right Ad Agency

While some companies have long-lasting relationships with their advertising agencies, others often find themselves changing agencies more frequently. Decisions to switch ad agencies can be driven by a variety of factors including increases in the client's size, changes in the markets it serves, reorganizations that lead to changes in top management, and/or changes in its advertising strategy or philosophy. One company that found itself changing agencies quite frequently during the past 10 years is Gateway, which is one of the world's largest computer companies.

Founded in 1985, Gateway was a pioneer in the build-to-order, direct-marketing segment of the personal computer business. The company's chairman and CEO, Ted Waitt, started Gateway on his family's cattle farm in Iowa and built it into a multibillion-dollar company. The Holstein dairy cows on the Waitt farm inspired the company's distinctive and nationally recognized logo and the cow-spot patterns on its boxes. The spots serve as a constant reminder of Gateway's midwestern roots and the company's values: hard work, honesty, friendliness, quality—and putting people first.

Until 1993, Gateway relied solely on print advertising that was produced in-house. However, as the company's rapid growth continued, it decided to add television ads to the media mix and to retain the services of an outside agency to work with its in-house advertising department. The agency, Carmichael Lynch of Minneapolis, hired a New York commercial director and filmmaker, Henry Corra, to direct the first Gateway commercials. Ted Waitt liked the unscripted, folksy ads that Corra was shooting, with their emphasis on "real people," and the visionary entrepreneur and artist developed a strong personal relationship.

As Gateway grew and its international sales increased, the company decided it needed a global agency. In 1997 the company moved its account to D'Arcy Masius Benton & Bowles. However, Waitt quickly became dissatisfied with DMB&B's traditional campaigns and dropped the agency after a year. He brought back Henry Corra to work on Gateway's advertising with a new agency, DiMassimo Brand Advertising, a small but aggressive creative boutique. Corra and the new agency produced a number of unscripted TV commercials throughout 1998. However, that same year Jeff Weitzen, a former AT&T executive, was brought in to run Gateway when Waitt decided to step back from the day-to-day operations of the company. The new CEO quickly moved the entire Gateway account again—this time to McCann-Erickson, one of the largest agencies in the world.

McCann worked on the Gateway account for three years and developed the "People Rule" campaign, which included actor Michael J. Fox as a spokesperson and also featured Waitt touting the company's services for small businesses. However, in January 2001, Weitzen resigned as CEO and Waitt once again took the helm. A few days after Waitt resumed control of the company, Gateway dismissed McCann-Erickson as its agency. A Gateway spokesman described the parting as "amicable," while McCann viewed the dismissal as part of the wholesale changes and management shake-up that accompanied Ted Waitt's return.

A few days later several agencies made presentations to Waitt and the vice president of advertising for Gateway's consumer business, including former agency DiMassimo Brand Advertising; Fallon, Minneapolis; and Siltanen/Keehn. However, Gateway decided to move its advertising back in-house. Once again, Ted Waitt turned to his friend Henry Corra to direct the company's commercials. While Corra continued to direct and shoot the TV commercials for Gateway, the company also began working with yet another agency, Siltanen/Keehn, whose founders worked on Apple Computer's "Think Different" campaign at TBWA/Chiat/Day. After working with Gateway on a project basis for five months, Siltanen/Keehn became the company's agency of record for print and broadcast advertising in early 2002.

The relationship with Siltanen/Keehn was also short-lived as Gateway parted ways with the agency after only 10 months and moved its account to the Arnell Group, New York. The change was part of Gateway's decision to move away from the folksy, rural image and brand itself as a more modern and hip company. The

new advertising tagline is "Gateway a better way" and the ads show computer users in a series of vignettes with an urban look and feel. Gateway is also touting a new logo as the old one, which featured a cow-spotted shipping box, has been replaced. The new logo is a computer power button rotated on its side to form a stylized "G" but still retains a hint of a cow spot. However, the talking cow has been retired and Gateway feels that it has found the right image for the future as well as the right agency. Hopefully the company will no longer have to keep looking for an udder agency.

Sources: Bruce V. Bigelow, "How now Gateway cow?," *The San Diego Union Tribune,* December 8, 2002, pp. H1, 10; Richard Linnett, "Regarding Henry," *Advertising Age,* Mar. 26, 2001, pp. 1, 37, 41; Tobi Elkin, "Troubled Gateway Turns to New Shop as Earnings Fall," *Advertising Age,* Feb. 12, 2001, p. 4.

approach, they are looking for agencies that have integrated capabilities and can handle more than just their media advertising.

- *Declining sales.* When sales of the client's product or service are stagnant or declining, advertising may be seen as contributing to the problem. A new agency may be sought for a new creative approach.
- *Conflicting compensation philosophies.* Disagreement may develop over the level or method of compensation. As more companies move toward incentive-based compensation systems, disagreement over compensation is becoming more commonplace.
- *Changes in policies.* Policy changes may result when either party reevaluates the importance of the relationship, the agency acquires a new (and larger) client, or either side undergoes a merger or acquisition.

If the agency recognizes these warning signs, it can try to adapt its programs and policies to make sure the client is satisfied. Some of the situations discussed here are unavoidable, and others are beyond the agency's control. But to maintain the account, problems within the agency's control must be addressed.

The time may come when the agency decides it is no longer in its best interest to continue to work with the client. Personnel conflicts, changes in management philosophy, and/or insufficient financial incentives are just a few of the reasons for such a decision. Then the agency may terminate the account relationship.

How Agencies Gain Clients

Competition for accounts in the agency business is intense, since most companies have already organized for the advertising function and only a limited number of new businesses require such services each year. While small agencies may be willing to work with a new company and grow along with it, larger agencies often do not become interested in these firms until they are able to spend at least $1 million per year on advertising. Many of the top 15 agencies won't accept an account that spends less than $5 million per year. Once that expenditure level is reached, competition for the account intensifies.

In large agencies, most new business results from clients that already have an agency but decide to change their relationships. Thus, agencies must constantly search and compete for new clients. Some of the ways they do this follow.

Referrals Many good agencies obtain new clients as a result of referrals from existing clients, media representatives, and even other agencies. These agencies maintain

good working relationships with their clients, the media, and outside parties that might provide business to them.

Solicitations One of the more common ways to gain new business is through direct solicitation. In smaller agencies, the president may solicit new accounts. In most large agencies, a new business development group seeks out and establishes contact with new clients. The group is responsible for writing solicitation letters, making cold calls, and following up on leads. The cutbacks in ad spending by many companies during the recent recession have resulted in many agencies' pitching their services on an unsolicited basis to marketers who are satisfied with their agencies. Senior executives recognize that new business is the lifeblood of their agencies and are encouraging their business development teams to pursue advertisers who have not even put their accounts up for review.[29]

Presentations A basic goal of the new business development group is to receive an invitation from a company to make a presentation. This gives the agency the opportunity to sell itself—to describe its experience, personnel, capabilities, and operating procedures, as well as to demonstrate its previous work.

The agency may be asked to make a speculative presentation, in which it examines the client's marketing situation and proposes a tentative communications campaign. Because presentations require a great deal of time and preparation and may cost the agency a considerable amount of money without a guarantee of gaining the business, many firms refuse to participate in "creative shootouts." They argue that agencies should be selected on the basis of their experience and the services and programs they have provided for previous clients.[30] Nevertheless, most agencies do participate in this form of solicitation, either by choice or because they must do so to gain accounts.

Due in part to the emphasis on speculative presentations, a very important role has developed for *ad agency review consultants,* who specialize in helping clients choose ad agencies. These consultants are often used to bring an objective perspective to the agency review process and to assist advertisers who may lack the resources, experience, or organizational consensus needed to successfully conduct a review.[31] Because their opinions are respected by clients, the entire agency review process may be structured according to their guidelines. As you might imagine, these consultants wield a great deal of power with both clients and agencies.

Public Relations Agencies also seek business through publicity/public relations efforts. They often participate in civic and social groups and work with charitable organizations pro bono (at cost, without pay) to earn respect in the community. Participation in professional associations such as the American Association of Advertising Agencies and the Advertising Research Foundation can also lead to new contacts. Successful agencies often receive free publicity throughout the industry as well as in the mass media.

Image and Reputation Perhaps the most effective way an agency can gain new business is through its reputation. Agencies that consistently develop excellent campaigns are often approached by clients. Agencies may enter their work in award competitions or advertise themselves to enhance their image in the marketing community. In some cases the clients themselves may provide valuable testimonials. For example, Exhibit 3-9 shows an ad from IBM congratulating its agency, Ogilvy & Mather, for winning the Grand EFFIE in the annual competition sponsored by the New York American Marketing Association that recognizes the most effective advertising campaigns.

Exhibit 3-9 IBM congratulates its agency for developing an award-winning campaign

THE BOOK OF @ BUSINESS

"IF IT DOESN'T SELL, IT ISN'T CREATIVE."

–*David Ogilvy*

Touffou – the Ogilvy castle. "Just throw those Chos and Lions in the basement."

WE WOULD LIKE to congratulate Ogilvy & Mather for this year's Grand EFFIE–winning e-business Infrastructure campaign and the Silver-winning "Easy to Buy" campaign. The work was impressive. The numbers, staggering. Your friends and partners at IBM thank you for a year of incredible success.

IBM.

IBM is a registered trademark of International Business Machines Corp. in the United States and/or other countries. © 2002 IBM Corporation. All rights reserved.

Specialized Services

Many companies assign the development and implementation of their promotional programs to an advertising agency. But several other types of organizations provide specialized services that complement the efforts of ad agencies. Direct-response agencies, sales promotion agencies, and public relations firms are important to marketers in developing and executing IMC programs in the United States as well as international markets. Let us examine the functions these organizations perform.

Direct-Response Agencies

One of the fastest-growing areas of IMC is direct marketing, where companies communicate with consumers through telemarketing, direct mail, and other forms of direct-response advertising. As this industry has grown, numerous direct-response agencies have evolved that offer companies their specialized skills in both consumer and business markets. Figure 3-10 shows the top 10 direct-response agencies (several of which, including OgilvyOne, DraftWorldwide, and Grey Direct Marketing, are divisions or subsidiaries of large ad agencies).

Direct-response agencies provide a variety of services, including database management, direct mail, research, media services, and creative and production capabilities. While direct mail is their primary weapon, many direct-response agencies are expanding their services to include such areas as infomercial production and database management. Database development and management is becoming one of the most important services provided by direct-response agencies. Many companies are using database marketing to pinpoint new customers and build relationships and loyalty among existing customers.[32]

A typical direct-response agency is divided into three main departments: account management, creative, and media. Some agencies also have a department whose function is to develop and manage databases for their clients. The account managers work with their clients to plan direct-marketing programs and determine their role in the overall integrated marketing communications process. The creative department consists of copywriters, artists, and producers. Creative is responsible for developing the direct-response message, while the media department is concerned with its placement.

Like advertising agencies, direct-response agencies must solicit new business and have their performance reviewed by their existing clients, often through formal assessment programs. Most direct-response agencies are compensated on a fee basis, although some large advertisers still prefer the commission system.

Sales Promotion Agencies

Developing and managing sales promotion programs such as contests, sweepstakes, refunds and rebates, premium and incentive offers, and sampling programs is a very complex task. Most companies use a **sales promotion agency** to develop and administer

Figure 3-10 Top 10 direct-response agencies

Rank	Agency (Affiliation)	Headquarters
1	Euro RSCG Marketing Services	New York
2	Draft Worldwide	Chicago
3	OgilvyOne Worldwide Interactive	New York
4	Rapp Collins Worldwide	New York
5	Wunderman	New York
6	Digitas	New York
7	MRM Partners Worldwide	New York
8	Brann Worldwide	New York
9	Proximity Worldwide	New York
10	Grey Direct Marketing Group	New York

these programs. Some large ad agencies have created their own sales promotion department or acquired a sales promotion firm. However, most sales promotion agencies are independent companies that specialize in providing the services needed to plan, develop, and execute a variety of sales promotion programs.

Sales promotion agencies often work in conjunction with the client's advertising and/or direct-response agencies to coordinate their efforts with the advertising and direct-marketing programs. Services provided by large sales promotion agencies include promotional planning, creative, research, tie-in coordination, fulfillment, premium design and manufacturing, catalog production, and contest/sweepstakes management. Many sales promotion agencies are also developing direct/database marketing and telemarketing to expand their integrated marketing services capabilities. Sales promotion agencies are generally compensated on a fee basis. Exhibit 3-10 shows an ad for DVC, which was selected as the promotional agency of the decade a few years ago by *Promo Magazine.*

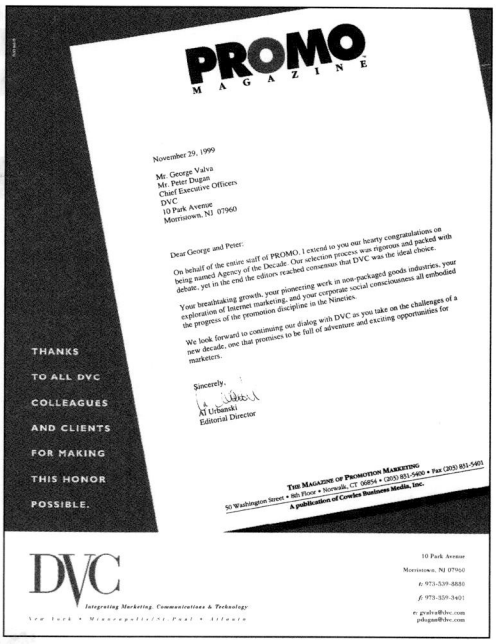

Exhibit 3-10 DVC is one of the leading promotional agencies

Public Relations Firms

Many large companies use both an advertising agency and a PR firm. The **public relations firm** develops and implements programs to manage the organization's publicity, image, and affairs with consumers and other relevant publics, including employees, suppliers, stockholders, government, labor groups, citizen action groups, and the general public. The PR firm analyzes the relationships between the client and these various publics, determines how the client's policies and actions relate to and affect these publics, develops PR strategies and programs, implements these programs using various public relations tools, and evaluates their effectiveness.

The activities of a public relations firm include planning the PR strategy and program, generating publicity, conducting lobbying and public affairs efforts, becoming involved in community activities and events, preparing news releases and other communications, conducting research, promoting and managing special events, and managing crises. As companies adopt an IMC approach to promotional planning, they are coordinating their PR activities with advertising and other promotional areas. Many companies are integrating public relations and publicity into the marketing communications mix to increase message credibility and save media costs.[33] Public relations firms are generally compensated by retainer. We will examine their role in more detail in Chapter 17.

Interactive Agencies

With the rapid growth of the Internet and other forms of interactive media, a new type of specialized marketing communications organization has evolved—the interactive agency. Many marketers are using **interactive agencies** that specialize in the development and strategic use of various interactive marketing tools such as websites for the Internet, banner ads, CD-ROMs, and kiosks. They recognize that the development of successful interactive marketing programs requires expertise in technology as well as areas such as creative website design, database marketing, digital media, and customer relationship management. Many traditional advertising agencies have established interactive capabilities, ranging from a few specialists within the agency to an entire interactive division. Some of the largest interactive agencies such as EuroRSCG Interaction, Grey Digital Marketing, and Ogilvy Interactive are affiliates of major agencies, while others such as Agency.com, Modern Media, and R/GA are owned by major holding companies (see Figure 3-11). Many agencies work closely with their interactive affiliates in developing integrated marketing campaigns for their clients. For example, iDeutsch, the interactive arm of the Deutsch agency, has developed the websites and online campaigns for clients such as Snapple, Almay, Mitsubishi automobiles and the California Milk Processor Board; the parent agency handles the off-line campaign in traditional media for these companies (Exhibit 3-11).

While many agencies have or are developing interactive capabilities, a number of marketers are turning to more specialized interactive agencies to develop websites and

Figure 3-11 Top 10 U.S. interactive agencies

Rank	Agency (Affiliation)	Headquarters
1	EuroRSCG Worldwide Interaction	New York
2	Grey Digital Marketing	New York
3	Ogilvy Interactive (WPP Group)	New York
4	Digitas	Boston
5	Modem Media (Interpublic Group)	Norwalk, Conn.
6	Answerthink Interactive Marketing	Miami
7	Agency.com (Omnicom Group)	New York
8	Tribal DDB (Omnicom Group)	New York
9	Dentropy Partners (Interpublic Group)	Cambridge, Mass.
10	R/GA (Interpublic Group)	New York

interactive media. They feel these companies have more expertise in designing and developing websites as well as managing and supporting them. Interactive agencies range from smaller companies that specialize in website design and creation to full-service interactive agencies that provide all the elements needed for a successful Internet/interactive marketing program. These services include strategic consulting regarding the use of the Internet and online branding, technical knowledge, systems integration, and the development of electronic commerce capabilities.

Full-service interactive agencies, such as AGENCY.COM, have created successful Internet marketing programs for a number of companies, including Nike, MetLife, Ford Motor Company, McDonald's, and British Airways. For example, AGENCY.COM developed the website and various online promotions that support the new global brand positioning strategy for British Airways. As the Internet becomes an increasingly important marketing tool, more companies will be turning to interactive agencies to help them develop successful interactive marketing programs. The number of interactive agencies will continue to grow, as will their importance in the development and implementation of Internet-based strategies and initiatives.

Collateral Services

The final participants in the promotional process are those that provide various collateral services. They include marketing research companies, package design firms, consultants, photographers, printers, video production houses, and event marketing services companies.

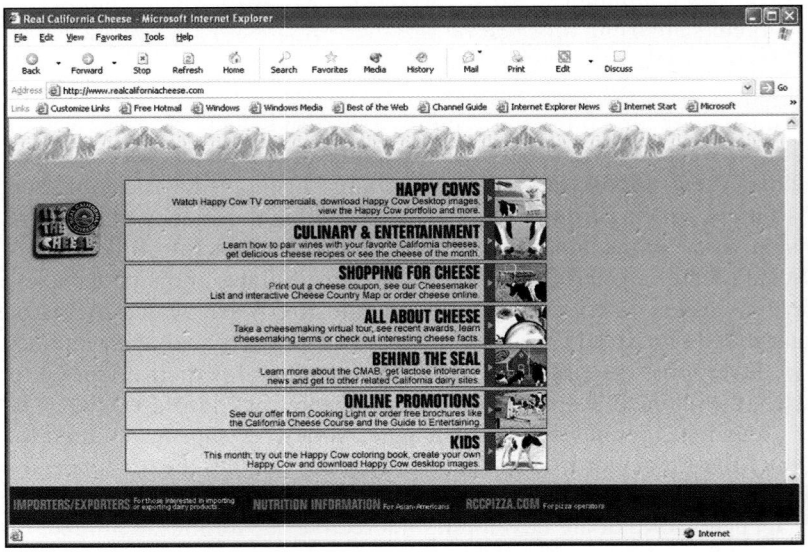

Exhibit 3-11 iDeutsch developed the website and various online promotions for its California Cheese account

CAREER PROFILE

Josh Rose

Senior Vice President, Director of iDeutsch

I graduated from the University of California at Santa Cruz in 1991. And only a year late! I got my bachelor's degree in fine art, determined to make it as an artist. I moved to Los Angeles that same year and took a temp job with The Walt Disney Company in the marketing department for their motion picture division which includes Walt Disney Pictures, Hollywood Pictures and Touchstone. It was supposed to just be a temporary job but I stayed for 4 years. My time at Disney allowed me to learn about marketing and promotion at one of the biggest marketing machines in the world. I spent much of my time with the artists and got them to teach me the basics of graphic design: photo-retouching, typography, layout and color. I bought my first Mac in 1994 and I stayed up every night teaching myself every application I could get my hands on: Photoshop, Illustrator, Freehand and Quark. I would go to Kinko's and print my work and, in about 6 months, I had a modest little portfolio of mock ads and photo-retouching work.

I was unsure as to what I wanted to do with my newfound skills but doing graphic art work gave me as much pleasure as working with clay or chalk pastels. In 1995 I offered to work for free at a small photo retouching shop called Outerspace in Santa Monica. I apprenticed there under the tutelage of a renowned re-toucher named Tom Slatky. Through the fine details of graphic design and art direction, Tom taught me how to really see and I had the opportunity to work with just about every ad agency in Los Angeles on their image-intensive movie posters and print ads. I learned how to work quick and in front of clients. I also learned how to pull the all-nighter (Hint: 7-11 Big Gulps).

Eventually, I was hired by American Cybercast which was a division of the Fattal & Collins advertising agency. I basically reinvented myself and many more opportunities began to open for me. I became very involved with the Internet, working on the first online "shows", *The Spot* and *EON-4* (a sci-fi episodic web show) and eventually became the creative director for the largest Internet consulting firm in the country, iXL. Along the way, I created online brands for The Experience Music Project (Microsoft co-founder Paul Allen's multi-million dollar interactive music museum in Seattle), Spinner (the internet's largest streaming music site), Playboy.com, Alanis Morissette.com, Wherehouse Music, Nike.com, and many others.

"My role is to ensure that all of our clients are getting the most out of the Internet."

My work at iXL made it relatively easy for me to transition to Deutsch, one of the most prominent advertising agencies in the country. My role as the head of the agency's interactive division, iDeutsch, is to ensure that all of our clients are getting the most out of the Internet. This can mean different things to different accounts. For example, one of the agency's clients is The California Milk Advisory Board for whom we have developed a campaign touting Real California Cheese. Maybe you've seen the talking cows on TV in the commercials which use the tagline "Great cheese comes from happy cows. Happy cows come from California." The goal of the website (www.realcaliforniacheese.com) is to support the branding effort for California cheese so we integrated the talking cow concept into the site.

Creating a website for a company is a lot like creating an ad. You have to develop a thorough understanding of your client's business, marketing objectives and consumer goals. When you do it well, you create something that's really entertaining as well as useful. And it sure beats flippin' burgers.

Marketing Research Companies

One of the more widely used collateral service organizations is the marketing research firm. Companies are increasingly turning to marketing research to help them understand their target audiences and to gather information that will be of value in designing and evaluating their advertising and promotions programs. Even companies with their own marketing research departments often hire outside research agencies to perform some services. Marketing research companies offer specialized services and can gather objective information that is valuable to the advertiser's promotional programs. They conduct *qualitative* research such as in-depth interviews and focus groups, as well as *quantitative* studies such as market surveys.

Integrated Marketing Communications Services

You have seen that marketers can choose from a variety of specialized organizations to assist them in planning, developing, and implementing an integrated marketing communications program. But companies must decide whether to use a different organization for each marketing communications function or consolidate them with a large advertising agency that offers all of these services under one roof.

As noted in Chapter 1, during the 1980s many of the large agencies realized that their clients were shifting their promotional dollars away from traditional advertising to other forms of promotion and began developing IMC capabilities. Some did this through mergers and acquisitions and became superagencies consisting of advertising, public relations, sales promotion, and direct-response agencies.

Many large agencies are continuing to expand their IMC capabilities by acquiring specialists in various fields. All the major agency holding companies either own or have substantial investments in interactive and direct-response agencies as well as public relations firms. For example, Omnicom Group acquired Fleishman-Hillard Inc.; WPPGroup bought Hill & Knowlton; and Interpublic Group purchased Golin/Harris International. Nonadvertising business accounts for nearly half of Interpublic's revenue, and the company, along with its competitors, continues to acquire public relations firms, direct-marketing companies, interactive agencies, and other specialized marketing services firms.[34]

Pros and Cons of Integrated Services

It has been argued that the concept of integrated marketing is nothing new, particularly in smaller companies and communication agencies that have been coordinating a variety of promotional tools for years. And larger advertising agencies have been trying to gain more of their clients' promotional business for over 20 years. However, in the past, the various services were run as separate profit centers. Each was motivated to push its own expertise and pursue its own goals rather than develop truly integrated marketing programs. Moreover, the creative specialists in many agencies resisted becoming involved in sales promotion or direct marketing. They preferred to concentrate on developing magazine ads or television commercials rather than designing coupons or direct-mail pieces.

Proponents of integrated marketing services contend that past problems are being solved and the various individuals in the agencies and subsidiaries are learning to work together to deliver a consistent message to the client's customers. They argue that maintaining control of the entire promotional process achieves greater synergy among each of the communications program elements. They also note that it is more convenient for the client to coordinate all of its marketing efforts—media advertising, direct mail, special events, sales promotions, and public relations—through one agency. An agency with integrated marketing capabilities can create a single image for the product or service and address everyone, from wholesalers to consumers, with one voice.

But not everyone wants to turn the entire IMC program over to one agency. Opponents say the providers become involved in political wrangling over budgets, do not communicate with each other as well and as often as they should, and do not achieve synergy. They also claim that agencies' efforts to control all aspects of the promotional program are nothing more than an attempt to hold on to business that might otherwise

be lost to independent providers. They note that synergy and economies of scale, while nice in theory, have been difficult to achieve and competition and conflict among agency subsidiaries have been a major problem.[35]

Many companies use a variety of vendors for communication functions, choosing the specialist they believe is best suited for each promotional task, be it advertising, sales promotion, or public relations. While many ad agencies are working to master integration and compete against one another, they still must compete against firms that offer specialized services. As marketing consultant Jack Trout notes, "As long as there are a lot of specialized players, integrating an agency will be tricky. Specialists walk in the door and say 'this is all we do and we're good at it,' which is a hell of an argument. An agency that has all marketing operations in-house will never be perceived as the best in breed."[36]

Responsibility for IMC: Agency versus Client

Surveys of advertisers and agency executives have shown that both groups believe integrated marketing is important to their organizations' success and that it will be even more important in the future.[37] One agency executive recently noted that 75 percent of the requests for proposals the agency now receives are from clients seeking total communication solutions.[38] However, marketers and agency executives have very different opinions regarding who should be in charge of the integrated marketing communications process. Many advertisers prefer to set strategy for and coordinate their own IMC campaigns, but most agency executives see this as their domain.

While agency executives believe their shops are capable of handling the various elements an integrated campaign requires, many marketers, particularly larger firms, disagree. Marketing executives say the biggest obstacle to implementing IMC is the lack of people with the broad perspective and skills to make it work. Internal turf battles, agency egos, and fear of budget reductions are also cited as major barriers to successful integrated marketing campaigns.[39]

Many ad agencies are adding more resources to offer their clients a full line of services. They are expanding their agencies' capabilities in interactive and multimedia advertising, database management, direct marketing, public relations, and sales promotion. However, many marketers still want to set the strategy for their IMC campaigns and seek specialized expertise, more quality and creativity, and greater control and cost efficiency by using multiple providers.

Most marketers do recognize that ad agencies will no longer stick primarily to advertising and will continue to expand their IMC capabilities. There is an opportunity for agencies to broaden their services beyond advertising—but they will have to develop true expertise in a variety of integrated marketing communications areas. They will also have to create organizational structures that make it possible for individuals with expertise in a variety of communications areas to work well together both internally and externally. One thing is certain: as companies continue to shift their promotional dollars away from media advertising to other IMC tools, agencies will continue to explore ways to keep these monies under their roofs.

Summary

The development, execution, and administration of an advertising and promotions program involve the efforts of many individuals, both within the company and outside it. Participants in the integrated marketing communications process include the advertiser or client, ad agencies, media organizations, specialized marketing communications firms, and providers of collateral services.

Companies use three basic systems to organize internally for advertising and promotion. Centralized systems offer the advantages of facilitated communications, lower personnel requirements, continuity in staff, and more top-management involvement. Disadvantages include a lower involvement with overall marketing goals, longer response times, and difficulties in handling multiple product lines.

Decentralized systems offer the advantages of concentrated

managerial attention, more rapid responses to problems, and increased flexibility, though they may be limited by ineffective decision making, internal conflicts, misallocation of funds, and a lack of authority. In-house agencies, while offering the advantages of cost savings, control, and increased coordination, have the disadvantage of less experience, objectivity, and flexibility.

Many firms use advertising agencies to help develop and execute their programs. These agencies may take on a variety of forms, including full-service agencies, creative boutiques, and media buying services. The first offers the client a full range of services (including creative, account, marketing, and financial and management services); the other two specialize in creative services and media buying, respectively. Agencies are compensated through commission systems, percentage charges, and fee- and cost-based systems. Recently, the emphasis on agency accountability has increased. Agencies are being evaluated on both financial and qualitative aspects, and some clients are using incentive-based compensation systems that tie agency compensation to performance measures such as sales and market share.

In addition to using ad agencies, marketers use the services of other marketing communication specialists, including direct-marketing agencies, sales promotion agencies, public relations firms, and interactive agencies. A marketer must decide whether to use a different specialist for each promotional function or have all of its integrated marketing communications done by an advertising agency that offers all of these services under one roof.

Recent studies have found that most marketers believe it is their responsibility, not the ad agency's, to set strategy for and coordinate IMC campaigns. The lack of a broad perspective and specialized skills in nonadvertising areas is seen as the major barrier to agencies' increased involvement in integrated marketing communications.

Key Terms

clients, 69
advertising agency, 69
media organizations, 70
specialized marketing communications services, 70
collateral services, 70
advertising manager, 71
centralized system, 71
decentralized system, 72
brand manager, 72
category management system, 73
in-house agency, 75
billings, 77
superagencies, 77
full-service agency, 79
account executive, 79
copywriters, 82
departmental system, 82
group system, 82
creative boutique, 83
media buying services, 83
commission system, 85
negotiated commission, 86
fixed-fee method, 87
fee-commission combination, 87
cost-plus system, 87
incentive-based system, 87
percentage charges, 88
financial audit, 88
qualitative audit, 88
direct-response agency, 94
sales promotion agency, 94
public relations firm, 95
interactive agencies, 95

Discussion Questions

1. Evaluate the decision by BMW and its advertising agency, Fallon Worldwide, to develop short-films that can be viewed at the BMWFilms.com website. Do you think more companies will be using the "advertainment" concept to promote their products?

2. Identify the various organizations that participate in the integrated marketing communications process and briefly discuss their roles and responsibilities.

3. What are some of the specific responsibilities and duties of an advertising manager under a centralized advertising department structure? Why is an advertising manager needed if a company uses an outside agency?

4. Discuss the pros and cons of using an in-house advertising agency. What are some of the reasons why companies might change from using an in-house agency and hire an outside agency?

5. Discuss some of the reasons why traditional advertising agencies have been developing more integrated marketing communication capabilities. What changes might traditional agencies have to make to improve their IMC capabilities?

6. Why might a company choose to use a creative boutique rather than a larger, full-service agency? Find an example of a company that uses a creative boutique and discuss why the decision to use a smaller agency may be appropriate for this firm.

7. Discuss the various methods by which advertising agencies are compensated. What factors will determine the type of compensation arrangement a company uses with an agency?

8. Why are many companies moving away from the traditional commission system and using

incentive-based compensation for their advertising agencies? Why might an ad agency be reluctant to accept an incentive-based compensation system?

9. IMC Perspective 3-2 discusses how Gateway has changed advertising agencies five times in the past ten years. Discuss the various reasons why Gateway has changed agencies so often and how the changes may have impacted its advertising.

10. Discuss the role of agencies that perform specialized marketing communication services such as public relations firms, direct response, sales promotion, and interactive agencies. Why might a company choose to use these specialized agencies rather than using a full service agency for all of its integrated marketing communication functions?

Perspectives on Consumer Behavior

4

Chapter Objectives

1. To understand the role consumer behavior plays in the development and implementation of advertising and promotional programs.
2. To understand the consumer decision-making process and how it varies for different types of purchases.
3. To understand various internal psychological processes, their influence on consumer decision making, and implications for advertising and promotion.
4. To recognize the various approaches to studying the consumer learning process and their implications for advertising and promotion.
5. To recognize external factors such as culture, social class, group influences, and situational determinants and how they affect consumer behavior.
6. To understand alternative approaches to studying consumer behavior.

Energy Drinks: The Real Thing or Just Bull?

Forget about the cola wars between Pepsi and Coke. The new threat to the stagnant cola market is an international cult drink—and that's no bull—it's Red Bull, actually. And the large soft-drink manufacturers have taken notice.

Red Bull is just one of the many "energy" drinks now on the market. Others include Extreme Energy Shot, Venom, Dark Dog, Energy, AMP, and KMX, just to mention a few. In fact, it seems that every company wants to introduce its own energy drink in an attempt to take advantage of a new market that is growing at an amazing rate. Consider that when Red Bull first introduced its product in 1997, there was no such thing as an energy-drink category. By 2001, estimates are that the market was somewhere between $140 million to $200 million, with forecasts that it will be $500 million in just a few years. Also consider that Red Bull has about 70 percent of the market share. While these figures may pale in comparison to the overall carbonated-beverage market (approximately $45 billion), there is enough concern for competitors to take notice.

Red Bull has been variously described as "an international cult drink," "a kinky concoction," and "the new sex drink," all of which suit the company just fine. It is exactly the mystique attributed to the drink that helps create the "buzz" that makes it sell. Many marketers feel that it is Red Bull's alternative image that accounts for much of its success. Even the company's marketing department likes to maintain the illusions while claiming the product is a "nonmarketed brand."

But while the mystique part of Red Bull may be true, the "nonmarketed" claims may not necessarily be so. As noted by the *Economist,* it takes a lot of marketing money to sustain this image. The magazine notes that Red Bull's founder, Dietrich Mateschitz (an Austrian) "spent three years developing the drink's image, its packaging and its low-key, grassroots marketing strategy." Further, Red Bull puts about 35 percent of its revenues back into advertising—about $19 million according to *Advertising Age.* And advertising is not the only IMC component the company successfully employs. At launch in Europe, students were persuaded to drive around in Volkswagen Beetles or Minis with a Red Bull can strapped on the top and to conduct Red Bull parties using wild and unusual themes. A marketing director from Procter & Gamble was hired to oversee strategic planning for the brand in North America (he later was named one of *Brandweek*'s Marketers of the Year).

At present, Red Bull's marketing efforts still employ grassroots efforts but have expanded to include more traditional media as well. What seems to make Red Bull successful, however, is that the efforts assume a very nontraditional approach to its messages—essentially attempting to do the opposite of what everyone else does. The first order of business in any market is to determine four or five accounts in a particular market area that sustain the image—underage discos, surf shops, and so on—rather than attempting to gain widespread distribution. Spokespeople (deejays, alternative sports stars, etc.) are recruited to spread the word and to be seen using the product. Sponsorship of alternative sports like the Red Bull Streets of San Francisco (a street luge event) and Red Bull Rampage (a free-ride mountain bike competition) has also been shown to be effective, as has the use of "education teams"—hip locals who drive around in a Red Bull auto handing out samples and promoting the brand.

The more mainstream media are also used—though on a market-by-market basis rather than through mass media. And even these traditional efforts may take on a less traditional form. For example, the advertising campaign ("Red Bull gives you wings") uses animated television and radio spots featuring the devil trying the product and sprouting wings. The company also sponsors a number of more traditional events ranging from soapbox derbies to Formula 1 racing cars, as well as extensive public relations programs to reach youth.

Now that Mateschitz and Red Bull have created a new beverage category, can they hold on to it? Success attracts competitors—many who have the potential to provide more marketing clout than Red Bull. Coca-Cola, Pepsi, and Anheuser Busch have all recently introduced their own energy drinks. Hansen Beverage's "Energy" and Sobe have both been gaining sales, and Snapple's "Venom" is getting more marketing support from Cadbury. Mateschitz is not oblivious to the competition. He and his marketing team are continually developing more wacky ideas to maintain Red Bull's alternative and mystical image. Others feel that expanding the category can only benefit Red Bull. It may depend on how large the cult grows!

Sources: "Selling Energy," *Economist,* May 11, 2002, p. 62; Kenneth Hein, "Red Bull Charging Ahead," *Brandweek,* Oct. 15, 2001, pp. 38–42; Hillary Chula, "Grabbing Bull by Tail," *Advertising Age,* June 11, 2001, pp. 4-6; David Noonan, "Red Bull's Good Buzz," *Newsweek,* May 14, 2001, p. 39.

The Red Bull introduction to this chapter demonstrates how products and/or brands become successful due to their adoption by certain segments of society. In this instance, a whole new category of drinks has developed as a result of consumer needs. What is important for marketers to know is how and why these needs develop, what they are, and who is likely to use the product or service. Specifically, marketers will study consumer behaviors in an attempt to understand the many factors that lead to and impact purchase decisions. Those who develop advertising and other promotional strategies begin by identifying relevant markets and then analyzing the relationship between target consumers and the product/service or brand. Often, in an attempt to gain insights, marketers will employ techniques borrowed from other disciplines. Research methods used in psychology, anthropology, and sociology are becoming more popular in businesses as managers attempt to explore consumers' purchasing motives. The motives for purchasing, attitudes, and lifestyles need to be understood before effective marketing strategies can be formulated.

These are just a few of the aspects of consumer behavior that promotional planners must consider in developing integrated marketing communications programs. As you will see, consumer choice is influenced by a variety of factors.

It is beyond the scope of this text to examine consumer behavior in depth. However, promotional planners need a basic understanding of consumer decision making, factors that influence it, and how this knowledge can be used in developing promotional strategies and programs. We begin with an overview of consumer behavior.

An Overview of Consumer Behavior

A challenge faced by all marketers is how to influence the purchase behavior of consumers in favor of the product or service they offer. For companies like American Express, this means getting consumers to charge more purchases on their AmEx cards. For BMW, it means getting them to purchase or lease a car; for business-to-business marketers like Canon or Ricoh, it means getting organizational buyers to purchase more of their copiers or fax machines. While their ultimate goal is to influence consumers' purchase behavior, most marketers understand that the actual purchase is only part of an overall process.

Consumer behavior can be defined as the process and activities people engage in when searching for, selecting, purchasing, using, evaluating, and disposing of products and services so as to satisfy their needs and desires. For many products and services, purchase decisions are the result of a long, detailed process that may include an extensive information search, brand comparisons and evaluations, and other activities. Other purchase decisions are more incidental and may result from little more than seeing a product prominently displayed at a discount price in a store. Think of how many times you have made impulse purchases in stores.

Marketers' success in influencing purchase behavior depends in large part on how well they understand consumer behavior. Marketers need to know the specific needs customers are attempting to satisfy and how they translate into purchase criteria. They need to understand how consumers gather information regarding various alternatives and use this information to select among competing brands. They need to understand how customers make purchase decisions. Where do they prefer to buy a product? How are they influenced by marketing stimuli at the point of purchase? Marketers also need to understand how the consumer decision process and reasons for purchase vary among different types of customers. For example, purchase decisions may be influenced by the personality or lifestyle of the consumer.[1] Notice how the ad shown in Exhibit 4-1 reflects the various roles in the life of the target audience members. IMC Perspective 4-1 describes how marketers target specific demographic and lifestyle groups.

The conceptual model in Figure 4-1 will be used as a framework for analyzing the consumer decision process. We will discuss what occurs at the various stages of this model and how advertising and promotion can be used to influence decision making. We will also examine the influence of various psychological concepts, such as motivation, perception, attitudes, and integration processes. Variations in the consumer decision-making process will be

Exhibit 4-1 Ashworth appeals to the active lifestyle

Figure 4-1 A basic model of consumer decision making

A. Stages in the Consumer Decision-Making Process

B. Relevant Internal Psychological Processes

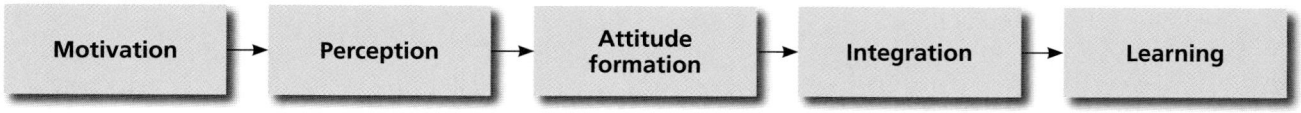

IMC PERSPECTIVE 4-1

Retailers Seek Bonanza in Tweens and Female Surfers

Tweens—the age group so named because its members are between early childhood and the teenage years, (7 to 14)—spend an estimated $90 billion a year, and they are doing so with a newfound independence. The days of mom bringing home new school clothes for the tween are in the past. Due in part to dual working parents' spending less time on their kids as well as indulging them more when they do, youngsters in this age group have more freedom to choose their own clothes. Add in television, magazines, the Internet, and other media, and girls in particular, have become more fashion-conscious and trendy. Clothing manufacturers and retailers have taken notice—to the chagrin of many parents.

Retail giant Wal-Mart has doubled floor space for preteen girls over the past year. Sears now offers trendier clothes for the age group and has sponsored concert tours for Christina Aguilera and Backstreet Boys—both popular with preteens. While these chains are doing well, it is the specialty retailers that are really capturing the market. Limited Too, which offers trendy clothes, glittery makeup, and extras like in-store ear piercing, dominates the apparel niche. Girl Mania offers hairstyling and birthday parties, while Club Libby Lu in Chicago greets customers with a glittering of "fairy dust" and allows them to mix their own shower gel, moisturizer, and lip gloss. Bath & Body Works offers pedicure kits for the 4- to 12-year-old set.

Many of these tweens are driving another retail niche market upward—surf apparel. The changing profile of the surfer—the number of young females has substantially increased—has led to opportunities for brands previously only marketed to males. Quicksilver Inc., a Huntington Beach, California, surf wear company, recently predicted that revenue for girls' products will eclipse sales to men and boys by the year 2004. Another southern California company, Billabong USA, has seen a 50 percent increase in girls' surf wear over the last three years. While already on the increase, the $2.4 billion market was expected to explode in the summer of 2002 when the girls' surf movie "Blue Crush" was released. (Just the release of movie trailers has already led to surf schools being swamped with enrollments.) The big winner is expected to be Billabong, whose name will be prominently displayed on the girls' wetsuit shirt as a result of a product placement arrangement with Universal Studios. Many of those in the industry consider the placement a major coup. Others like Pacific Sunwear have invested in other promotional opportunities. PacSun will spend a record $10 million on marketing in magazines such as *Seventeen, Teen People,* and *YM.*

Not everyone is happy, however. Many parents and consumer advocates feel that the companies are taking advantage of tweens, who they contend are overly impressionable and insecure at this stage of their lives. They contend that girls who are "barely past Beanie Babies" are being pushed too quickly toward mascara and navel rings. Consider Abercrombie & Fitch, for example. In just one of the recent controversies surrounding the retailer, thong underwear bearing the words "wink wink" and "eye candy" were being marketed to 9- and 10-year-olds. The company was deluged with e-mails from people enraged with the strategy. While Marshal Cohen of *NPDFashion-World* notes that Abercrombie is "all about selling sex, even to the younger kid," the company response was that sex is in the eye of the beholder and their products are designed with only prurient purposes in mind.

However, a number of people are concerned enough to fight back. One organization, Girls, Inc., a New York-based nonprofit, holds meetings in schools, in homes, and elsewhere to talk with tween girls about the messages they receive from TV, videos, and magazine ads. The organization recently offered a program called Body IMAGEination intended to help girls age 7 to 11 deal with peer pressures to dress more provocatively. The organization has a huge battle ahead!

Sources: Leslie Earnest, "Apparel Retailers Catch New Girls' Surfing Wave," *Los Angeles Times,* July 5, 2002, latimes.com, pp. 1–3; Leslie Earnest, "'Tweens: From Dolls to Thongs," *Los Angeles Times,* June 27, 2002, p. 1.

explored, as will perspectives regarding consumer learning and external influences on the consumer decision process. The chapter concludes with a consideration of alternative means of studying consumer behavior.

The Consumer Decision-Making Process

As shown in Figure 4-1, the consumer's purchase decision process is generally viewed as consisting of stages through which the buyer passes in purchasing a product or service. This model shows that decision making involves a number of internal psychological processes. Motivation, perception, attitude formation, integration, and learning are important to promotional planners, since they influence the general decision-making process of the consumer. We will examine each stage of the purchase decision model and discuss how the various subprocesses influence what occurs at this phase of the consumer behavior process. We will also discuss how promotional planners can influence this process.

Problem Recognition

Figure 4-1 shows that the first stage in the consumer decision-making process is **problem recognition,** which occurs when the consumer perceives a need and becomes motivated to solve the problem. The problem recognition stage initiates the subsequent decision processes.

Problem recognition is caused by a difference between the consumer's *ideal state* and *actual state.* A discrepancy exists between what the consumer wants the situation to be like and what the situation is really like. (Note that *problem* does not always imply a negative state. A goal exists for the consumer, and this goal may be the attainment of a more positive situation.)

Sources of Problem Recognition The causes of problem recognition may be very simple or very complex and may result from changes in the consumer's current and/or desired state. These causes may be influenced by both internal and external factors.

Out of Stock Problem recognition occurs when consumers use their existing supply of a product and must replenish their stock. The purchase decision is usually simple and routine and is often resolved by choosing a familiar brand or one to which the consumer feels loyal.

Dissatisfaction Problem recognition is created by the consumer's dissatisfaction with the current state of affairs and/or the product or service being used. For example, a consumer may think her ski boots are no longer comfortable or stylish enough. Advertising may be used to help consumers recognize when they have a problem and/or need to make a purchase. The Rogaine ad shown in Exhibit 4-2 helps women realize that hair thinning is not just a man's problem.

New Needs/Wants Changes in consumers' lives often result in new needs and wants. For example, changes in one's financial situation, employment status, or lifestyle may create new needs and trigger problem recognition. As you will see, when you graduate from college and begin your professional career, your new job may necessitate a change in your wardrobe. (Good-bye blue jeans and T-shirts, hello suits and ties.)

Not all product purchases are based on needs. Some products or services sought by consumers are not essential but are nonetheless desired. A **want** has been defined as a felt need that is shaped by a person's knowledge, culture, and personality.[2] Many products sold to consumers satisfy their wants rather than their basic needs.

Exhibit 4-2 Rogaine helps women recognize hair loss problems

Related Products/Purchases Problem recognition can also be stimulated by the purchase of a product. For example, the purchase of a new camera may lead to the recognition of a need for accessories, such as additional lenses or a carrying case. The purchase of a personal computer may prompt the need for software programs, upgrades, printers, and so on.

Marketer-Induced Problem Recognition Another source of problem recognition is marketers' actions that encourage consumers not to be content with their current state or situation. Ads for personal hygiene products such as mouthwash, deodorant, and foot sprays may be designed to create insecurities that consumers can resolve through the use of these products. Marketers change fashions and clothing designs and create perceptions among consumers that their wardrobes are out of style. The Orajel ad in Exhibit 4-3 demonstrates the special needs of children's baby teeth to stimulate problem recognition.

Marketers also take advantage of consumers' tendency toward *novelty-seeking behavior,* which leads them to try different brands. Consumers often try new products or brands even when they are basically satisfied with their regular brand. Marketers encourage brand switching by introducing new brands into markets that are already saturated and by using advertising and sales promotion techniques such as free samples, introductory price offers, and coupons.

New Products Problem recognition can also occur when innovative products are introduced and brought to the attention of consumers. Marketers are constantly introducing new products and services and telling consumers about the types of problems they solve. For example, the Hidden Mind ad shown in Exhibit 4-4 introduces a new mobile technology that allows the businessperson to continue working with or without a connection to a mobile network.

Marketers' attempts to create problem recognition among consumers are not always successful. Consumers may not see a problem or need for the product the mar-

Exhibit 4-3 This ad for Baby Orajel shows that baby teeth have special needs

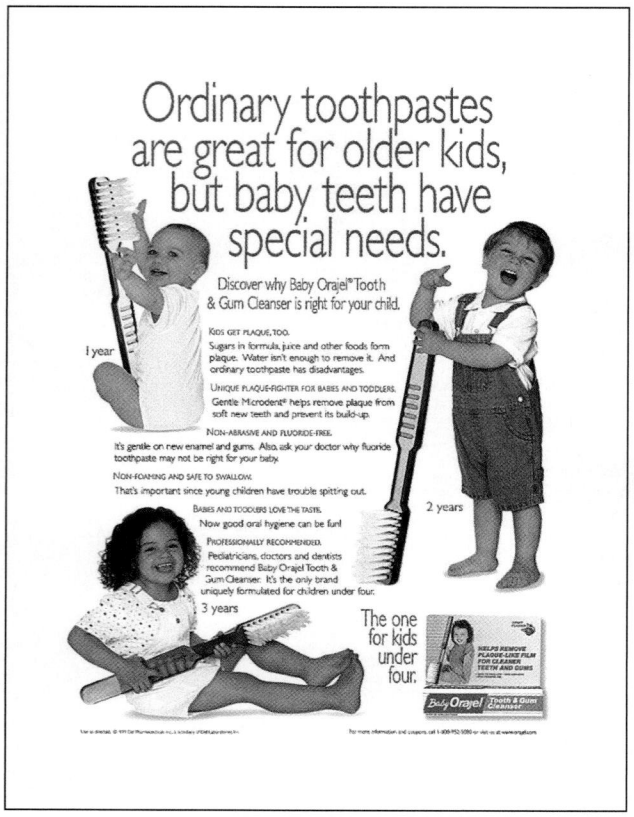

Exhibit 4-4 Hidden Mind introduces active technology

keter is selling. A main reason many consumers were initially reluctant to purchase personal computers was that they failed to see what problems owning one would solve. One way PC manufacturers successfully activated problem recognition was by stressing how a computer helps children improve their academic skills and do better in school.

Examining Consumer Motivations

Marketers recognize that while problem recognition is often a basic, simple process, the way a consumer perceives a problem and becomes motivated to solve it will influence the remainder of the decision process. For example, one consumer may perceive the need to purchase a new watch from a functional perspective and focus on reliable, low-priced alternatives. Another consumer may see the purchase of a watch as more of a fashion statement and focus on the design and image of various brands. To better understand the reasons underlying consumer purchases, marketers devote considerable attention to examining **motives**—that is, those factors that compel a consumer to take a particular action.

Hierarchy of Needs

One of the most popular approaches to understanding consumer motivations is based on the classic theory of human motivation popularized many years ago by psychologist Abraham Maslow.[3] His **hierarchy of needs** theory postulates five basic levels of human needs, arranged in a hierarchy based on their importance. As shown in Figure 4-2, the five needs are (1) *physiological*—the basic level of primary needs for things required to sustain life, such as food, shelter, clothing, and sex; (2) *safety*—the need for security and safety from physical harm; (3) *social/love and belonging*—the desire to have satisfying relationships with others and feel a sense of love, affection, belonging, and acceptance; (4) *esteem*—the need to feel a sense of accomplishment and gain recognition, status, and respect from others; and (5) *self-actualization*—the need for self-fulfillment and a desire to realize one's own potential.

According to Maslow's theory, the lower-level physiological and safety needs must be satisfied before the higher-order needs become meaningful. Once these basic needs are satisfied, the individual moves on to attempting to satisfy higher-order needs such as self-esteem. In reality, it is unlikely that people move through the needs hierarchy in a stairstep manner. Lower-level needs are an ongoing source of motivation for consumer purchase behavior. However, since basic physiological needs are met in most

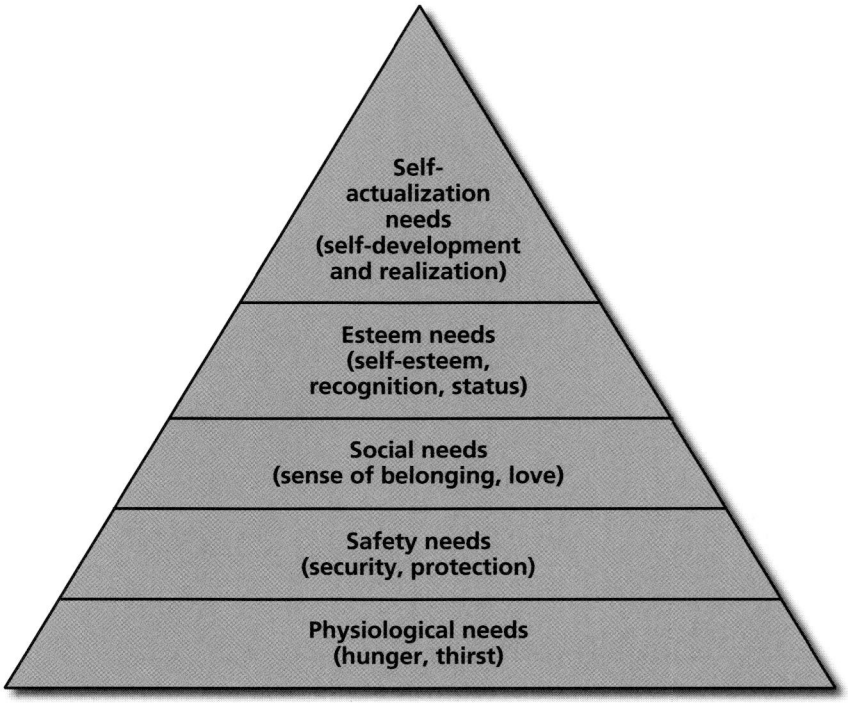

Figure 4-2 Maslow's hierarchy of needs

developed countries, marketers often sell products that fill basic physiological needs by appealing to consumers' higher-level needs. For example, in marketing its wipes, Pampers focuses on the love between parent and child (social needs) in addition to the gentleness of the product (Exhibit 4-5).

While Maslow's need hierarchy has flaws, it offers a framework for marketers to use in determining what needs they want their products and services to be shown satisfying. Advertising campaigns can then be designed to show how a brand can fulfill these needs. Marketers also recognize that different market segments emphasize different need levels. For example, a young single person may be attempting to satisfy social or self-esteem needs in purchasing a car, while a family with children will focus more on safety needs. Jeep used ads like the one in Exhibit 4-6 to position its cars as meeting the security needs of consumers.

Psychoanalytic Theory

A somewhat more controversial approach to the study of consumer motives is the **psychoanalytic theory** pioneered by Sigmund Freud.[4] Although his work dealt with the structure and development of personality, Freud also studied the underlying motivations for human behavior. Psychoanalytic theory had a strong influence on the development of modern psychology and on explanations of motivation and personality. It has also been applied to the study of consumer behavior by marketers interested in probing deeply rooted motives that may underlie purchase decisions.

Those who attempt to relate psychoanalytic theory to consumer behavior believe consumers' motivations for purchasing are often very complex and unclear to the casual observer—and to the consumers themselves. Many motives for purchase and/or consumption may be driven by deep motives one can determine only by probing the subconscious.

Among the first to conduct this type of research in marketing, Ernest Dichter and James Vicary were employed by a number of major corporations to use psychoanalytic techniques to determine consumers' purchase motivations. The work of these researchers and others who continue to use this approach assumed the title of **motivation research.**

Motivation Research in Marketing

Motivation researchers use a variety of methodologies to gain insight into the underlying causes of consumer behavior.

Exhibit 4-5 Pampers appeals to needs for love and belonging in this ad

Exhibit 4-6 Jeep uses an appeal to security needs

Methods employed include in-depth interviews, projective techniques, association tests, and focus groups in which consumers are encouraged to bring out associations related to products and brands (see Figure 4-3). As one might expect, such associations often lead to interesting insights as to why people purchase. For example:

- Consumers prefer large cars because they believe such cars protect them from the "jungle" of everyday driving.[5]
- A man buys a convertible as a substitute mistress.
- Women like to bake cakes because they feel like they are giving birth to a baby.
- Women wear perfume to "attract a man" and "glorify their existence."
- Men like frankfurters better than women do because cooking them (frankfurters, not men!) makes women feel guilty. It's an admission of laziness.
- When people shower, their sins go down the drain with the soap as they rinse.[6]

As you can see from these examples, motivation research has led to some very interesting, albeit controversial, findings and to much skepticism from marketing managers. However, major corporations and advertising agencies continue to use motivation research to help them market their products.

Problems and Contributions of Psychoanalytic Theory and Motivation Research

Psychoanalytic theory has been criticized as being too vague, unresponsive to the external environment, and too reliant on the early development of the individual. It also uses a small sample for drawing conclusions. Because of the emphasis on the unconscious, results are difficult if not impossible to verify, leading motivation research to be criticized for both the conclusions drawn and its lack of experimental validation. Since motivation research studies typically use so few participants, there is also concern that it really discovers the idiosyncracies of a few individuals and its findings are not generalizable to the whole population.

Still, it is difficult to ignore the psychoanalytic approach in furthering our understanding of consumer behavior. Its insights can often be used as a basis for advertising messages aimed at buyers' deeply rooted feelings, hopes, aspirations, and fears. Such strategies are often more effective than rationally based appeals.

In-depth interviews
Face-to-face situations in which an interviewer asks a consumer to talk freely in an unstructured interview using specific questions designed to obtain insights into his or her motives, ideas, or opinions.

Projective techniques
Efforts designed to gain insights into consumers' values, motives, attitudes, or needs that are difficult to express or identify by having them project these internal states upon some external object.

Association tests
A technique in which an individual is asked to respond with the first thing that comes to mind when he or she is presented with a stimulus; the stimulus may be a word, picture, ad, and so on.

Focus groups
A small number of people with similar backgrounds and/or interests who are brought together to discuss a particular product, idea, or issue.

Figure 4-3 Some of the marketing research methods used to probe the mind of the consumer

Exhibit 4-7 212 Men uses sex appeal in its advertising

Some corporations and advertising agencies have used motivation research to gain further insights into how consumers think. Examples include the following:[7]

- Chrysler had consumers sit on the floor, like children, and use scissors to cut words out of magazines to describe a car.[8]
- McCann-Erickson asked women to draw and describe how they felt about roaches. The agency concluded that many women associated roaches with men who had abandoned them and that this was why women preferred roach killers that let them see the roaches die.
- Saatchi & Saatchi used psychological probes to conclude that Ronald McDonald created a more nurturing mood than did the Burger King (who was perceived as more aggressive and distant).
- Foote, Cone & Belding gave consumers stacks of photographs of faces and asked them to associate the faces with the kinds of people who might use particular products.

While often criticized, motivation research has also contributed to the marketing discipline. The qualitative nature of the research is considered important in assessing how and why consumers buy. Focus groups and in-depth interviews are valuable methods for gaining insights into consumers' feelings, and projective techniques are often the only way to get around stereotypical or socially desirable responses. In addition, motivation research is the forerunner of psychographics (discussed in Chapter 2).

Finally, we know that buyers are sometimes motivated by symbolic as well as functional drives in their purchase decisions. At least one study has shown that two-thirds of all prime-time TV shows present an average of 5.2 scenes per hour that contain talk about sex. Thus, we see the use of sexual appeals and symbols in ads like Exhibit 4-7.

Information Search

The second stage in the consumer decision-making process is *information search.* Once consumers perceive a problem or need that can be satisfied by the purchase of a product or service, they begin to search for information needed to make a purchase decision. The initial search effort often consists of an attempt to scan information stored in memory to recall past experiences and/or knowledge regarding various purchase alternatives.[9] This information retrieval is referred to as **internal search.** For many routine, repetitive purchases, previously acquired information that is stored in memory (such as past performance or outcomes from using a brand) is sufficient for comparing alternatives and making a choice.

If the internal search does not yield enough information, the consumer will seek additional information by engaging in **external search.** External sources of information include:

- *Personal sources,* such as friends, relatives, or co-workers.
- *Marketer-controlled (commercial) sources,* such as information from advertising, salespeople, or point-of-purchase displays and the Internet.
- *Public sources,* including articles in magazines or newspapers and reports on TV.
- *Personal experience,* such as actually handling, examining, or testing the product.

Determining how much and which sources of external information to use involves several factors, including the importance of the purchase decision, the effort needed to acquire information, the amount of past experience relevant, the degree of perceived risk associated with the purchase, and the time available. For example, the selection of a movie to see on a Friday night might entail simply talking to a friend or checking the movie guide in the daily newspaper. A more complex purchase such as a new car might use a number of information sources—perhaps a review of *Road & Track,*

Motortrend, or *Consumer Reports;* discussion with family members and friends; and test-driving of cars. At this point in the purchase decision, the information-providing aspects of advertising are extremely important.

Perception

Knowledge of how consumers acquire and use information from external sources is important to marketers in formulating communication strategies. Marketers are particularly interested in (1) how consumers sense external information, (2) how they select and attend to various sources of information, and (3) how this information is interpreted and given meaning. These processes are all part of **perception,** the process by which an individual receives, selects, organizes, and interprets information to create a meaningful picture of the world.[10] Perception is an individual process; it depends on internal factors such as a person's beliefs, experiences, needs, moods, and expectations. The perceptual process is also influenced by the characteristics of a stimulus (such as its size, color, and intensity) and the context in which it is seen or heard.

Sensation

Perception involves three distinct processes. **Sensation** is the immediate, direct response of the senses (taste, smell, sight, touch, and hearing) to a stimulus such as an ad, package, brand name, or point-of-purchase display. Perception uses these senses to create a representation of the stimulus. Marketers recognize that it is important to understand consumers' physiological reactions to marketing stimuli. For example, the visual elements of an ad or package design must attract consumers' favorable attention.

Marketers sometimes try to increase the level of sensory input so that their advertising messages will get noticed. For example, marketers of colognes and perfumes often use strong visuals as well as scent strips to appeal to multiple senses and attract the attention of magazine readers. Some advertisers have even inserted microcomputer chips into their print ads to play a song or deliver a message.

Selecting Information

Sensory inputs are important but are only one part of the perceptual process. Other determinants of whether marketing stimuli will be attended to and how they will be interpreted include internal psychological factors such as the consumer's personality, needs, motives, expectations, and experiences. These psychological inputs explain why people focus attention on some things and ignore others. Two people may perceive the same stimuli in very different ways because they select, attend, and comprehend differently. An individual's perceptual processes usually focus on elements of the environment that are relevant to his or her needs and tune out irrelevant stimuli. Think about how much more attentive you are to advertising for personal computers, tires, or stereos when you are in the market for one of these products (a point that is made by the message from the American Association of Advertising Agencies in Exhibit 4-8).

Exhibit 4-8 This ad reminds consumers of how advertising responds to their needs

ISN'T IT FUNNY HOW STEREO ADS ARE BORING UNTIL YOU WANT A STEREO?

We admit it. There are times when advertising isn't especially interesting.

For instance, stereo ads when you're not looking for a new stereo. Or insurance ads when you're not looking for a new insurance company. Or detergent ads when you're not looking for a new detergent.

But suppose your stereo breaks down. Or your insurance rates go up. Or your laundry comes out gray.

All of a sudden, stereo ads, insurance ads and detergent ads start looking a lot more interesting.

It's one of the basic truths of advertising. We try to be entertaining, but that's not really our job. Our job is to help you make the right choices when you're in the market for any kind of product or service.

Of course, when you're not in the market, we recognize that advertising may seem beside the point. In that case, you're free to pretend it isn't there.

In fact, you're free to ignore advertising for as long as you choose.

Right up until your stereo breaks down.

ADVERTISING.
ANOTHER WORD FOR FREEDOM OF CHOICE.
American Association of Advertising Agencies

Interpreting the Information

Once a consumer selects and attends to a stimulus, the perceptual process focuses on organizing, categorizing, and interpreting the incoming information. This stage of the perceptual process is very individualized and is influenced by internal psychological factors. The interpretation and meaning an individual assigns to an incoming stimulus also depend in part on the nature of the stimulus. For example, many ads are objective, and their message is clear and straightforward. Other ads are more ambiguous, and their meaning is strongly influenced by the consumer's individual interpretation.

Selectivity occurs throughout the various stages of the consumer's perceptual process. Perception may be viewed as a filtering process in which internal and external factors influence what is received and how it is processed and interpreted. The sheer number and complexity of the marketing stimuli a person is exposed to in any given day require that

Figure 4-4 The selective perception process

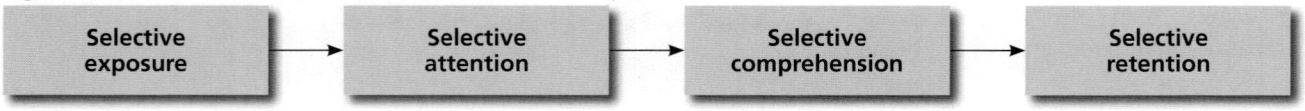

this filtering occur. **Selective perception** may occur at the exposure, attention, comprehension, or retention stage of perception, as shown in Figure 4-4.

Selective Perception

Selective exposure occurs as consumers choose whether or not to make themselves available to information. For example, a viewer of a television show may change channels or leave the room during commercial breaks.

Selective attention occurs when the consumer chooses to focus attention on certain stimuli while excluding others. One study of selective attention estimates the typical consumer is exposed to nearly 1,500 ads per day yet perceives only 76 of these messages.[11] Other estimates range as high as 3,000 exposures per day. This means advertisers must make considerable effort to get their messages noticed. Advertisers often use the creative aspects of their ads to gain consumers' attention. For example, some advertisers set their ads off from others by showing their products in color against a black-and-white background (Exhibit 4-9). This creative tactic has been used in advertising for many products, among them Cherry 7UP, Nuprin, and Pepto-Bismol.[12]

Even if the consumer does notice the advertiser's message, there is no guarantee it will be interpreted in the intended manner. Consumers may engage in **selective comprehension,** interpreting information on the basis of their own attitudes, beliefs, motives, and experiences. They often interpret information in a manner that supports their own position. For example, an ad that disparages a consumer's favorite brand may be seen as biased or untruthful, and its claims may not be accepted.

The final screening process shown in Figure 4-4 is **selective retention,** which means consumers do not remember all the information they see, hear, or read even after attending to and comprehending it. Advertisers attempt to make sure information will be retained in the consumer's memory so that it will be available when it is time to make a purchase. **Mnemonics** such as symbols, rhymes, associations, and images that assist in the learning and memory process are helpful. Many advertisers use telephone numbers that spell out the company name and are easy to remember. Eveready put pictures of its pink bunny on packages to remind consumers at the point of purchase of its creative advertising.

Exhibit 4-9 Tropicana attempts to create attention with this ad

Subliminal Perception

Advertisers know consumers use selective perception to filter out irrelevant or unwanted advertising messages, so they employ various creative tactics to get their messages noticed. One controversial tactic advertisers have been accused of using is appealing to consumers' subconscious. **Subliminal perception** refers to the ability to perceive a stimulus that is below the level of conscious awareness. Psychologists generally agree it is possible to perceive things without being consciously aware of them.

As you might imagine, the possibility of using hidden persuaders such as subliminal audio messages or visual cues to influence consumers might be intriguing to advertisers but would not be welcomed by consumers. The idea of marketers influencing consumers at a subconscious level has strong ethical implications. Ethical Perspective 4-2 discusses researchers' mixed opinions as to whether subliminal messages are likely to be effective in influencing consumer behavior. The use of subliminal techniques is *not* a creative tactic we would recommend to advertisers.

Alternative Evaluation

After acquiring information during the information search stage of the decision process, the consumer moves to alternative evaluation. In this stage, the consumer compares the various brands or products and

ETHICAL PERSPECTIVE 4-2

Subliminal Rats or Purely Coincidence?

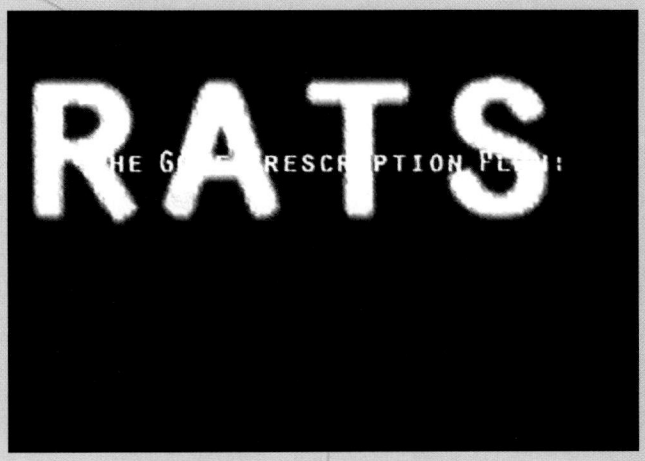

One of the most controversial topics in all of advertising is subliminal advertising. Rooted in psychoanalytic theory, subliminal advertising supposedly influences consumer behaviors by subconsciously altering perceptions or attitudes toward products without the knowledge—or consent—of the consumer. Marketers have promoted subliminal self-help audiotapes, weight-loss videos, and golf game improvement tapes. Studies have shown that the majority of American consumers believe that advertisers sometimes use subliminal advertising and that it works.

The controversy hit national proportions in the last presidential election. In the Bush-Gore campaign, Democratic officials and some advertising experts accused the Republican National Committee of running a subliminal advertisement on television by having the phrase "bureaucrats decide" flashing around the screen and then, in larger print, flashing the word "rats" for a fraction of a second while an announcer criticized candidate Gore's Medicare plan. Republicans argued that the word appeared for one-thirtieth of a second on only one frame out of 900 and was purely an accident. Advertising analysts, including two experts on political advertising, disagreed, contending that there is no way such a thing could happen by accident. At least one noted that the word was "carefully superimposed." A Federal Communications Commission (FCC) investigation concluded that no further action would be taken.

The concept of subliminal advertising was introduced in 1957 when James Vicary, a motivational researcher, reported that he increased the sales of popcorn and Coke by subliminally flashing "Eat popcorn" and "Drink Coca-Cola" across the screen during a movie in New Jersey. Since then, numerous books and research studies have been published regarding the effectiveness of this advertising form. Some of these have reported on the use of this technique by advertisers to manipulate consumers.

Numerous articles have reviewed the research in this area. Timothy Moore, after reviewing the literature three times (1982, 1988, 1992), has concluded that there is no evidence to support the fact that subliminal messages can affect consumers' motivations, perceptions, or attitudes. Joel Saegart and Jack Haberstroh have supported Moore's conclusions in their studies. On the other hand, in 1994 Kathryn Theus concluded after an extensive review of the literature that "certain themes might be effectively applied by advertising or marketing specialists."

In more recent writings, opposite positions are again taken. In a study conducted in Australia by an ad agency and Mindtec (a consulting firm), 12 groups of television viewers were hypnotized and asked questions about specific commercials and programs. According to the study, 75 percent of the hypnotized subjects stated that sexy images were the main attraction for viewing, as opposed to only 22 percent of the nonhypnotized subjects. The researchers were surprised by the subliminal details that hypnotized participants were able to recall. In the ads, names and slogans that were visible only when the commercial was paused had high levels of recall, even when the brands recalled were not those being advertised. On the other hand, in his book, *Ice Cube Sex: The Truth about Subliminal Advertising,* Haberstroh reviews research and discussions with practitioners and concludes that subliminal advertising does not influence consumer behaviors, advertising recall, attitudes, or any other marketplace behavior.

When Haberstroh asked ad agency executives if they had ever deliberately used subliminal advertising, 96 percent said no, 94 percent said they had never supervised the use of implants, and 91 percent denied knowing anyone who had ever used this technique. A study by Rogers and Seiler supported these results, with over 90 percent denying any use of subliminal implants.

Going even further, Haberstroh contends that subliminal advertising does not even exist except for a few pranksters playing around with artwork for fun. But not so fast! Fashion retailer French Connection is not only employing subliminal advertising but incorporating it into a tagline. Using print and posters, the tagline "subliminal advertising experiment" is arranged in such a way as to spell out the word *sex* if one reads vertically. Likewise, Master Lock has become the first company to run a one-second national print commercial. The goal of the ad is to reinforce the brand name. And, in upstate New York, a personal-injury lawyer paid $35 each for one-second spots in an attempt to gain new clients. At this time, no one knows if any of these efforts have been successful.

Thus, while most consumers believe subliminal techniques are used and effective, researchers are divided as to their effects. It seems few people in the advertising world think subliminal advertising works and even fewer claim to use it, but there are still those who feel they are wrong. Will there ever be an end to this controversy?

Sources: "Hypnosis Reveals Ad Effects," *Adweek Asia,* Jan. 29, 1999, p. 4; "Breaking French Connection," *Ad Age,* Mar. 22, 1999, p. 52; "Blink of an Ad," *Time,* Aug. 3, 1998, p. 51; Jack Haberstroh, *Ice Cube Sex: The Truth about Subliminal Advertising,* New York Times Publishing, 1996; Kathryn Theus, "Subliminal Advertising and the Psychology of Processing Unconscious Stimuli: A Review of Research," *Psychology & Marketing* 11, no. 3, 1994, pp. 271–90; Timothy Moore, "Subliminal Advertising: What You See Is What You Get," *Journal of Marketing* 46, no. 2 (Spring 1982), pp. 38–47; Timothy Moore, "The Case against Subliminal Manipulation," *Psychology and Marketing* 5, no. 4 (Winter 1988), pp. 297–316; Kalpana Srinivasan, "FCC Ends Probe on Republican Ad," www.individual.com, Mar. 12, 2001, pp. 1–2; George E. Condon Jr. and Toby Eckert, "Flap over 'RATS' Latest to Plague Bush's Drive," *San Diego Tribune,* Sept. 13, 2000, p. A1; Bob Garfield, "Subliminable Seduction and Other Urban Myths," *Advertising Age,* Sept. 18, 2000, p. 4.

services he or she has identified as being capable of solving the consumption problem and satisfying the needs or motives that initiated the decision process. The various brands identified as purchase options to be considered during the alternative evaluation process are referred to as the consumer's *evoked set.*

The Evoked Set The evoked set is generally only a subset of all the brands of which the consumer is aware. The consumer reduces the number of brands to be reviewed during the alternative evaluation stage to a manageable level. The exact size of the evoked set varies from one consumer to another and depends on such factors as the importance of the purchase and the amount of time and energy the consumer wants to spend comparing alternatives.

The goal of most advertising and promotional strategies is to increase the likelihood that a brand will be included in the consumer's evoked set and considered during alternative evaluation. Marketers use advertising to create *top-of-mind awareness* among consumers so that their brands are part of the evoked set of their target audiences. Popular brands with large advertising budgets use *reminder advertising* to maintain high awareness levels and increase the likelihood they will be considered by consumers in the market for the product. Marketers of new brands or those with a low market share need to gain awareness among consumers and break into their evoked sets. The ad promoting Spokane as a better place to live and do business (Exhibit 4-10) shows this strategy being used in a different context from products and brands. The ad presents the many benefits of Spokane and encourages prospective businesses to consider it in their evoked set of places to locate or relocate.

Advertising is a valuable promotional tool for creating and maintaining brand awareness and making sure a brand is included in the evoked set. However, marketers also work to promote their brands in the actual environment where purchase decisions are made. Point-of-purchase materials and promotional techniques such as in-store sampling, end-aisle displays, or shelf tags touting special prices encourage consumers to consider brands that may not have initially been in their evoked set.

Evaluative Criteria and Consequences Once consumers have identified an evoked set and have a list of alternatives, they must evaluate the various brands. This involves comparing the choice alternatives on specific criteria important to the consumer. **Evaluative criteria** are the dimensions or attributes of a product or service that are used to compare different alternatives. Evaluative criteria can be objective or subjective. For example, in buying an automobile, consumers use objective attributes such as price, warranty, and fuel economy as well as subjective factors such as image, styling, and performance.

Exhibit 4-10 Spokane wants to be in the evoked set of business locations

Evaluative criteria are usually viewed as product or service attributes. Many marketers view their products or services as *bundles of attributes,* but consumers tend to think about products or services in terms of their *consequences* instead. J. Paul Peter and Jerry Olson define consequences as specific events or outcomes that consumers experience when they purchase and/or consume a product or service.[13] They distinguish between two broad types of consequences. **Functional consequences** are concrete outcomes of product or service usage that are tangible and directly experienced by consumers. The taste of a soft drink or a potato chip, the acceleration of a car, and the clarity of a fax transmission are examples of functional consequences. **Psychosocial consequences** are abstract outcomes that are more intangible, subjective, and personal, such as how a product makes you feel or how you think others will view you for purchasing or using it.

Marketers should distinguish between product/service attributes and consequences, because the importance and meaning consumers assign to an attribute are usually determined by its consequences for them. Moreover, advertisers must be sure consumers understand the link between a particular attribute and a consequence. For example, the Callaway golf ad in Exhibit 4-11 focuses on the consequences of using the new Hawkeye VFT Clubs, such as getting the ball airborne with less effort. Notice how the detail drawings reinforce that the clubs can help golfers enjoy the game more.

Exhibit 4-11 This ad emphasizes the positive consequences of using Callaway golf clubs

Product/service attributes and the consequences or outcomes consumers think they will experience from a particular brand are very important, for they are often the basis on which consumers form attitudes and purchase intentions and decide among various choice alternatives. Two subprocesses are very important during the alternative evaluation stage: (1) the process by which consumer attitudes are created, reinforced, and changed and (2) the decision rules or integration strategies consumers use to compare brands and make purchase decisions. We will examine each of these processes in more detail.

Attitudes

Attitudes are one of the most heavily studied concepts in consumer behavior. According to Gordon Allport's classic definition, "attitudes are learned predispositions to respond to an object."[14] More recent perspectives view attitudes as a summary construct that represents an individual's overall feelings toward or evaluation of an object.[15] Consumers hold attitudes toward a variety of objects that are important to marketers, including individuals (celebrity endorsers such as Tiger Woods or Andre Agassi), brands (Cheerios, Kix), companies (Intel, Microsoft), product categories (beef, pork, tuna), retail stores (Kmart, Sears), or even advertisements (Nike ads).

Attitudes are important to marketers because they theoretically summarize a consumer's evaluation of an object (or brand or company) and represent positive or negative feelings and behavioral tendencies. Marketers' keen interest in attitudes is based on the assumption that they are related to consumers' purchase behavior. Considerable evidence supports the basic assumption of a relationship between attitudes and behavior.[16] The attitude-behavior link does not always hold; many other factors can affect behavior.[17] But attitudes are very important to marketers. Advertising and promotion are used to create favorable attitudes toward new products/services or brands, reinforce existing favorable attitudes, and/or change negative attitudes. An approach to studying and measuring attitudes that is particularly relevant to advertising is multiattribute attitude models.

Multiattribute Attitude Models

Consumer researchers and marketing practitioners have been using multiattribute attitude models to study consumer attitudes for two decades.[18] A **multiattribute attitude model** views an attitude object, such as a product or brand, as possessing a number of attributes that provide the basis on which consumers form their attitudes. According to this model, consumers have beliefs about

specific brand attributes and attach different levels of importance to these attributes. Using this approach, an attitude toward a particular brand can be represented as

$$A_B = \sum_{i=1}^{n} B_i \times E_i$$

where A_B = attitude toward a brand
B_i = beliefs about the brand's performance on attribute i
E_i = importance attached to attribute i
n = number of attributes considered

For example, a consumer may have beliefs (B_i) about various brands of toothpaste on certain attributes. One brand may be perceived as having fluoride and thus preventing cavities, tasting good, and helping control tartar buildup. Another brand may not be perceived as having these attributes, but consumers may believe it performs well on other attributes such as freshening breath and whitening teeth.

To predict attitudes, one must know how much importance consumers attach to each of these attributes (E_i). For example, parents purchasing toothpaste for their children may prefer a brand that performs well on cavity prevention, a preference that leads to a more favorable attitude toward the first brand. Teenagers and young adults may prefer a brand that freshens their breath and makes their teeth white and thus prefer the second brand.

Consumers may hold a number of different beliefs about brands in any product or service category. However, not all of these beliefs are activated in forming an attitude. Beliefs concerning specific attributes or consequences that are activated and form the basis of an attitude are referred to as **salient beliefs.** Marketers should identify and understand these salient beliefs. They must also recognize that the saliency of beliefs varies among different market segments, over time, and across different consumption situations.

Attitude Change Strategies

Multiattribute models help marketers understand and diagnose the underlying basis of consumers' attitudes. By understanding the beliefs that underlie consumers' evaluations of a brand and the importance of various attributes or consequences, the marketer is better able to develop communication strategies for creating, changing, or reinforcing brand attitudes. The multiattribute model provides insight into several ways marketers can influence consumer attitudes, including:

- Increasing or changing the strength or belief rating of a brand on an important attribute (Southwest Airlines has the most on-time arrivals).
- Changing consumers' perceptions of the importance or value of an attribute (demonstrating safety in Mercedes' ads).
- Adding a new attribute to the attitude formation process (American Airlines' increased leg room).
- Changing perceptions of belief ratings for a competing brand (Volvo's ads that show Volvo as stylish).

The first strategy is commonly used by advertisers. They identify an attribute or consequence that is important and remind consumers how well their brand performs on this attribute. In situations where consumers do not perceive the marketer's brand as possessing an important attribute or the belief strength is low, advertising strategies may be targeted at changing the belief rating. Even when belief strength is high, advertising may be used to increase the rating of a brand on an important attribute. BMW's "The Ultimate Driving Machine" campaign is a good example of a strategy designed to create a belief and reinforce it through advertising.

Marketers often attempt to influence consumer attitudes by changing the relative importance of a particular attribute. This second strategy involves getting consumers to attach more importance to the attribute in forming their attitude toward the brand. Marketers using this strategy want to increase the importance of an attribute their particular brand has.

The third strategy for influencing consumer attitudes is to add or emphasize a new attribute that consumers can use in evaluating a brand. Marketers often do this by improving their products or focusing on additional benefits or consequences associated with using the brand. Exhibit 4-12 shows how Panasonic is introducing wireless technology in an attempt to influence consumers' attitudes.

A final strategy marketers use is to change consumer beliefs about the attributes of competing brands or product categories. This strategy has become much more common with the increase in comparative advertising, where marketers compare their brands to competitors' on specific product attributes. An example of this is the Progresso ad shown in Exhibit 4-13, where the company compares what it has to offer to what Campbell's offers.

Integration Processes and Decision Rules

Another important aspect of the alternative evaluation stage is the way consumers combine information about the characteristics of brands to arrive at a purchase decision. **Integration processes** are the way product knowledge, meanings, and beliefs are combined to evaluate two or more alternatives.[19] Analysis of the integration process focuses on the different types of *decision rules* or strategies consumers use to decide among purchase alternatives.

Consumers often make purchase selections by using formal integration strategies or decision rules that require examination and comparison of alternatives on specific attributes. This process involves a very deliberate evaluation of the alternatives, attribute by attribute. When consumers apply such formal decision rules, marketers need to know which attributes are being considered so as to provide the information the consumers require.

Sometimes consumers make their purchase decisions using more simplified decision rules known as **heuristics.** Peter and Olson note that heuristics are easy to use and are highly adaptive to specific environmental situations (such as a retail store).[20] For familiar products that are purchased frequently, consumers may use price-based heuristics (buy the least expensive brand) or promotion-based heuristics (choose the

Exhibit 4-12 Panasonic adds a new attribute for customers to consider

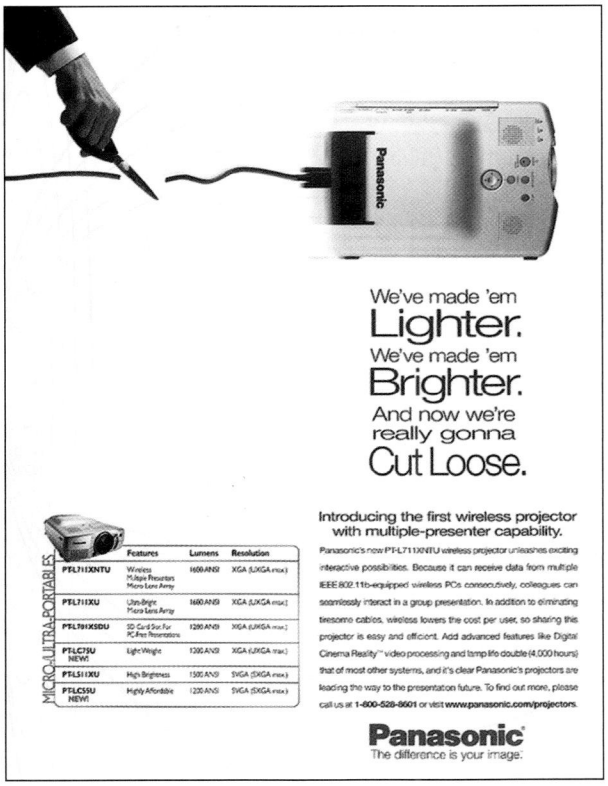

Exhibit 4-13 Progresso compares its products to those offered by Campbell's

brand for which I can get a price reduction through a coupon, rebate, or special deal).

One type of heuristic is the **affect referral decision rule,**[21] in which consumers make a selection on the basis of an overall impression or summary evaluation of the various alternatives under consideration. This decision rule suggests that consumers have affective impressions of brands stored in memory that can be accessed at the time of purchase. How many times have you gone into a store and made purchases based on your overall impressions of the brands rather than going through detailed comparisons of the alternatives' specific attributes?

Marketers selling familiar and popular brands may appeal to an affect referral rule by stressing overall affective feelings or impressions about their products. Market leaders, whose products enjoy strong overall brand images, often use ads that promote the brand as the best overall. Pepsi's "Joy of Pepsi," Jeep's "There's only one," and Budweiser's "The king of beers" are all examples of this strategy (Exhibit 4-14).

Exhibit 4-14 Market leaders such as Budweiser can appeal to consumer affect

Purchase Decision

At some point in the buying process, the consumer must stop searching for and evaluating information about alternative brands in the evoked set and make a *purchase decision.* As an outcome of the alternative evaluation stage, the consumer may develop a **purchase intention** or predisposition to buy a certain brand. Purchase intentions are generally based on a matching of purchase motives with attributes or characteristics of brands under consideration. Their formation involves many of the personal subprocesses discussed in this chapter, including motivation, perception, attitude formation, and integration.

A purchase decision is not the same as an actual purchase. Once a consumer chooses which brand to buy, he or she must still implement the decision and make the actual purchase. Additional decisions may be needed, such as when to buy, where to buy, and how much money to spend. Often, there is a time delay between the formation of a purchase intention or decision and the actual purchase, particularly for highly involved and complex purchases such as automobiles, personal computers, and consumer durables.

For nondurable products, which include many low-involvement items such as consumer package goods, the time between the decision and the actual purchase may be short. Before leaving home, the consumer may make a shopping list that includes specific brand names because the consumer has developed **brand loyalty**—a preference for a particular brand that results in its repeated purchase. Marketers strive to develop and maintain brand loyalty among consumers. They use reminder advertising to keep their brand names in front of consumers, maintain prominent shelf positions and displays in stores, and run periodic promotions to deter consumers from switching brands.

Maintaining consumers' brand loyalty is not easy. Competitors use many techniques to encourage consumers to try their brands, among them new product introductions and free samples. As Figure 4-5 shows, for many products fewer than 50 percent of consumers are loyal to one brand. Marketers must continually battle to maintain their loyal consumers while replacing those who switch brands.

Purchase decisions for nondurable, convenience items sometimes take place in the store, almost simultaneous with the purchase. Marketers must ensure that consumers have top-of-mind awareness of their brands so that they are quickly recognized and considered. These types of decisions are influenced at the actual point of purchase. Packaging, shelf displays, point-of-purchase materials, and promotional tools such as on-package coupons or premium offers can influence decisions made through constructive processes at the time of purchase.

Postpurchase Evaluation

The consumer decision process does not end with the purchase. After using the product or service, the consumer compares the level of performance with expectations and is either satisfied or dissatisfied. *Satisfaction* occurs when the consumer's expectations

Figure 4-5 Faithful or fickle? Percentage of users of these products who are loyal to one brand

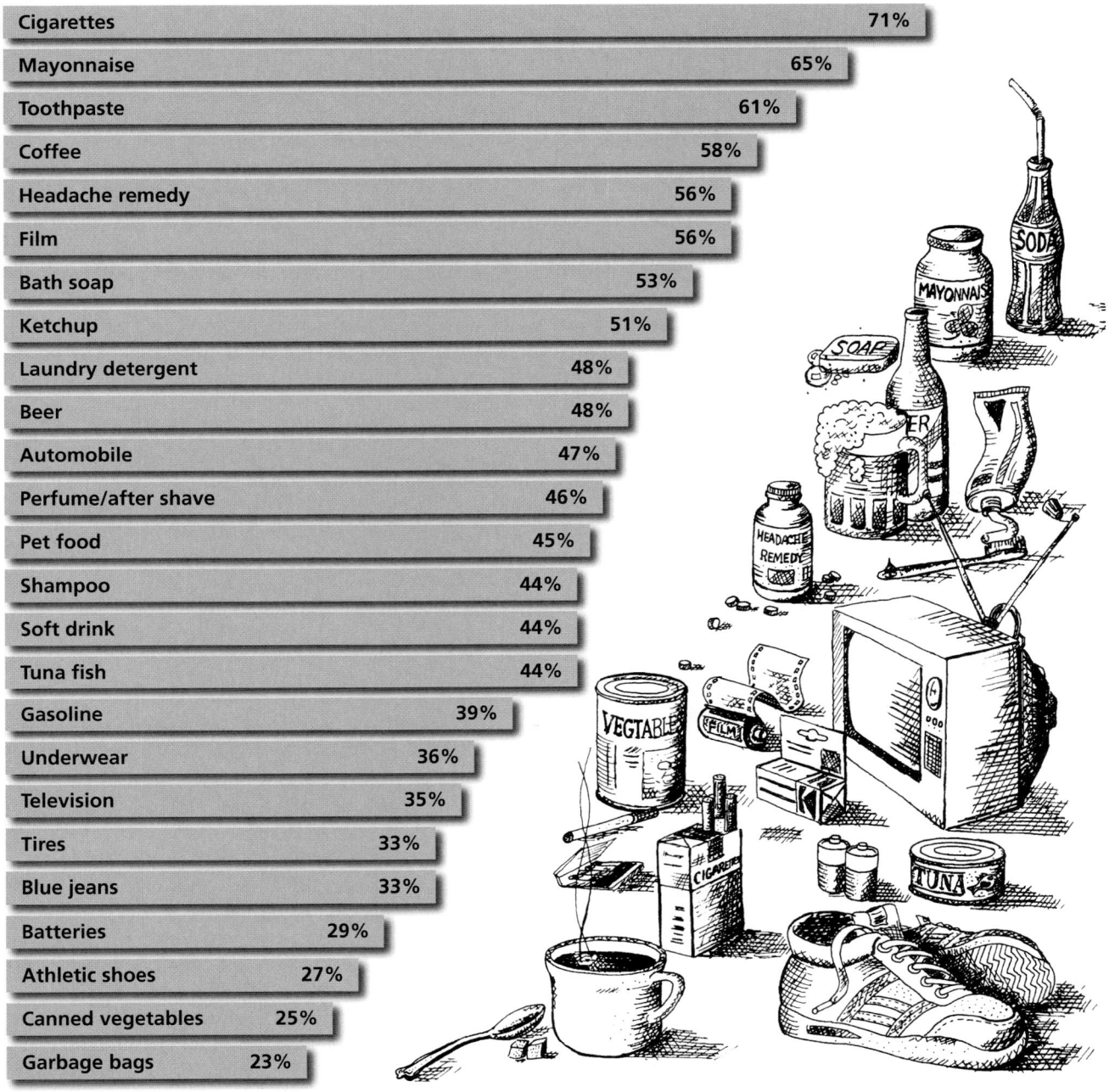

are either met or exceeded; *dissatisfaction* results when performance is below expectations. The postpurchase evaluation process is important because the feedback acquired from actual use of a product will influence the likelihood of future purchases. Positive performance means the brand is retained in the evoked set and increases the likelihood it will be purchased again. Unfavorable outcomes may lead the consumer to form negative attitudes toward the brand, lessening the likelihood it will be purchased again or even eliminating it from the consumer's evoked set.

Another possible outcome of purchase is **cognitive dissonance,** a feeling of psychological tension or postpurchase doubt that a consumer experiences after making a difficult purchase choice. Dissonance is more likely to occur in important decisions where the consumer must choose among close alternatives (especially if the unchosen alternative has unique or desirable features that the selected alternative does not have).

Consumers experiencing cognitive dissonance may use a number of strategies to attempt to reduce it. They may seek out reassurance and opinions from others to confirm

Exhibit 4-15 UUNET attempts to capitalize on consumer dissatisfaction

the wisdom of their purchase decision, lower their attitudes or opinions of the unchosen alternative, deny or distort any information that does not support the choice they made, or look for information that does support their choice. An important source of supportive information is advertising; consumers tend to be more attentive to advertising for the brand they have chosen.[22] Thus, it may be important for companies to advertise to reinforce consumer decisions to purchase their brands.

Marketers must recognize the importance of the postpurchase evaluation stage. Dissatisfied consumers who experience dissonance not only are unlikely to repurchase the marketer's product but may also spread negative word-of-mouth information that deters others from purchasing the product or service. The best guarantee of favorable postpurchase evaluations is to provide consumers with a quality product or service that always meets their expectations. Marketers must be sure their advertising and other forms of promotion do not create unreasonable expectations their products cannot meet.

Marketers have come to realize that postpurchase communication is also important. Some companies send follow-up letters and brochures to reassure buyers and reinforce the wisdom of their decision. Many companies have set up toll-free numbers or e-mail addresses for consumers to call if they need information or have a question or complaint regarding a product. Marketers also offer liberalized return and refund policies and extended warranties and guarantees to ensure customer satisfaction. Some have used customers' postpurchase dissatisfaction as an opportunity for gaining new business, as is reflected in the ad for UUNET (Exhibit 4-15).

Variations in Consumer Decision Making

The preceding pages describe a general model of consumer decision making. But consumers do not always engage in all five steps of the purchase decision process or proceed in the sequence presented. They may minimize or even skip one or more stages if they have previous experience in purchasing the product or service or if the decision is of low personal, social, or economic significance. To develop effective promotional strategies and programs, marketers need some understanding of the problem-solving processes their target consumers use to make purchase decisions.[23]

Many of the purchase decisions we make as consumers are based on a habitual or routine choice process. For many low-priced, frequently purchased products, the decision process consists of little more than recognizing the problem, engaging in a quick internal search, and making the purchase. The consumer spends little or no effort engaging in external search or alternative evaluation.

Marketers of products characterized by a routine response purchase process need to get and/or keep their brands in the consumer's evoked set and avoid anything that may result in their removal from consideration. Established brands that have strong market share position are likely to be in the evoked set of most consumers. Marketers of these brands want consumers to follow a routine choice process and continue to purchase their products. This means maintaining high levels of brand awareness through reminder advertising, periodic promotions, and prominent shelf positions in retail stores.

Marketers of new brands or those with a low market share face a different challenge. They must find ways to disrupt consumers' routine choice process and get them to consider different alternatives. High levels of advertising may be used to encourage trial or brand switching, along with sales promotion efforts in the form of free samples, special price offers, high-value coupons, and the like.

A more complicated decision-making process may occur when consumers have limited experience in purchasing a particular product or service and little or no knowledge of the brands available and/or the criteria to use in making a purchase decision. They may have to learn what attributes or criteria should be used in making a purchase decision and how the various alternatives perform on these dimensions. For products or services characterized by problem solving, whether limited or extensive, marketers should make information available that will help consumers decide. Advertising that provides consumers with detailed information about a brand and

how it can satisfy their purchase motives and goals is important. Marketers may also want to give consumers information at the point of purchase, through either displays or brochures. Distribution channels should have knowledgeable salespeople available to explain the features and benefits of the company's product or service and why it is superior to competing products.

The Fidelity Investments ad in Exhibit 4-16 is a good example of how advertising can appeal to consumers who may be engaging in extended problem solving when considering retirement investing. Notice how the ad communicates with consumers who may feel they know little about how to plan for retirement. The ad helps the consumer by offering expert advice and planning a variety of options. The ad also makes more detailed information available by offering a toll-free number and a website.

Exhibit 4-16 This ad for Fidelity Investments shows how marketers can appeal to consumers engaging in extended problem solving

The Consumer Learning Process

The discussion of the decision process shows that the way consumers make a purchase varies depending on a number of factors, including the nature of the product or service, the amount of experience they have with the product, and the importance of the purchase. One factor in the level of problem solving to be employed is the consumer's *involvement* with the product or brand. Chapter 5 examines the meaning of involvement, the difference between low- and high-involvement decision making, and the implications of involvement for developing advertising and promotional strategies.

Our examination of consumer behavior thus far has looked at the decision-making process from a *cognitive orientation.* The five-stage decision process model views the consumer as a problem solver and information processor who engages in a variety of mental processes to evaluate various alternatives and determine the degree to which they might satisfy needs or purchase motives. There are, however, other perspectives regarding how consumers acquire the knowledge and experience they use in making purchase decisions. To understand these perspectives, we examine various approaches to learning and their implications for advertising and promotion.

Consumer learning has been defined as "the process by which individuals acquire the purchase and consumption knowledge and experience they apply to future related behavior."[24] Two basic approaches to learning are the behavioral approach and cognitive learning theory.

Behavioral Learning Theory

Behavioral learning theories emphasize the role of external, environmental stimuli in causing behavior; they minimize the significance of internal psychological processes. Behavioral learning theories are based on the *stimulus–response orientation* (S–R), the premise that learning occurs as the result of responses to external stimuli in the environment. Behavioral learning theorists believe learning occurs through the connection between a stimulus and a response. We will examine the basic principles of two behavioral learning theory approaches: classical conditioning and operant conditioning.

Classical Conditioning

Classical conditioning assumes that learning is an *associative process* with an already existing relationship between a stimulus and a response. Probably the best-known example of this type of learning comes from the studies done with animals by the Russian psychologist Pavlov.[25] Pavlov noticed that at feeding times, his dogs would salivate at the sight of food. The connection between food and salivation is not taught; it is an innate reflex reaction. Because this relationship exists before the conditioning process, the food is referred to as an *unconditioned stimulus* and salivation is an *unconditioned response.* To see if salivation could be conditioned to occur in response to another neutral stimulus, Pavlov paired the ringing of a bell with the presentation of the food. After a number of trials, the dogs learned to salivate at the sound of the bell alone. Thus, the bell became a **conditioned stimulus** that elicited a **conditioned response** resembling the original unconditioned reaction.

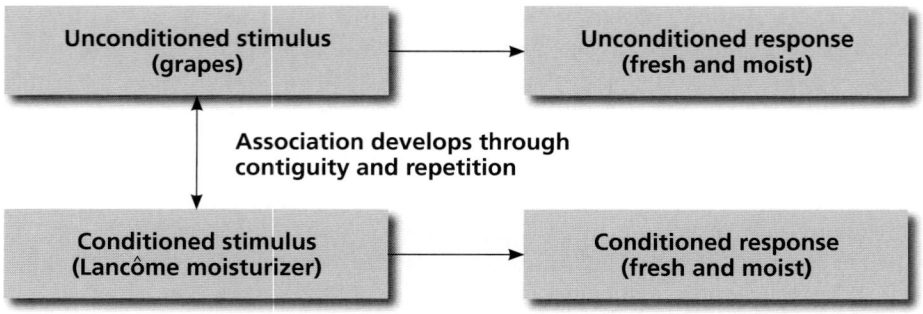

Figure 4-6 The classical conditioning process

Two factors are important for learning to occur through the associative process. The first is contiguity, which means the unconditioned stimulus and conditioned stimulus must be close in time and space. In Pavlov's experiment, the dog learns to associate the ringing of the bell with food because of the contiguous presentation of the two stimuli. The other important principle is *repetition,* or the frequency of the association. The more often the unconditioned and conditioned stimuli occur together, the stronger the association between them will be.

Applying Classical Conditioning Learning through classical conditioning plays an important role in marketing. Buyers can be conditioned to form favorable impressions and images of various brands through the associative process. Advertisers strive to associate their products and services with perceptions, images, and emotions known to evoke positive reactions from consumers. Many products are promoted through image advertising, in which the brand is shown with an unconditioned stimulus that elicits pleasant feelings. When the brand is presented simultaneously with this unconditioned stimulus, the brand itself becomes a conditioned stimulus that elicits the same favorable response.

Figure 4-6 provides a diagram of this process, and the ad for Lancôme in Exhibit 4-17 shows an application of this strategy. Notice how this ad associates Lancôme with the freshness and moisture of grapes. The brand's positioning plays off this association.

Classical conditioning can also associate a product or service with a favorable emotional state. A study by Gerald Gorn used this approach to examine how background music in ads influences product choice.[26] He found that subjects were more likely to choose a product when it was presented against a background of music they liked

Exhibit 4-17 Lancôme associates itself with moisture

rather than music they disliked. These results suggest the emotions generated by a commercial are important because they may become associated with the advertised product through classical conditioning. Kellaris and colleagues also showed that music that was congruent with the message enhanced both ad recall and recognition.[27] Richard Yalch also has demonstrated that music can be used effectively as a mnemonic device to enhance the recall of advertising slogans. Advertisers often attempt to pair a neutral product or service stimulus with an event or situation that arouses positive feelings, such as humor, an exciting sports event, or popular music.

Exhibit 4-18 This Energizer batteries ad shows how to avoid negative consequences

Operant Conditioning

Classical conditioning views the individual as a passive participant in the learning process who simply receives stimuli. Conditioning occurs as a result of exposure to a stimulus that occurs before the response. In the **operant conditioning** approach, the individual must actively *operate* or act on some aspect of the environment for learning to occur. Operant conditioning is sometimes referred to as *instrumental conditioning* because the individual's response is instrumental in getting a positive reinforcement (reward) or negative reinforcement (punishment).

Reinforcement, the reward or favorable consequence associated with a particular response, is an important element of instrumental conditioning. Behavior that is reinforced strengthens the bond between a stimulus and a response. Thus, if a consumer buys a product in response to an ad and experiences a positive outcome, the likelihood that the consumer will use this product again increases. If the outcome is not favorable, the likelihood of buying the product again decreases.

The principles of operant conditioning can be applied to marketing, as shown in Figure 4-7. Companies attempt to provide their customers with products and services that satisfy their needs and reward them to reinforce the probability of repeat purchase. Reinforcement can also be implied in advertising; many ads emphasize the benefits or rewards a consumer will receive from using a product or service. Reinforcement also occurs when an ad encourages consumers to use a particular product or brand to avoid unpleasant consequences. For example, the ad for Energizer batteries in Exhibit 4-18 shows how using this product will help avoid negative consequences—that is, being without a working cell phone when you need it.

Two concepts that are particularly relevant to marketers in their use of reinforcement through promotional strategies are schedules of reinforcement and shaping. Different **schedules of reinforcement** result in varying patterns of learning and behavior. Learning occurs most rapidly under a *continuous reinforcement schedule,* in which every response is rewarded—but the behavior is likely to cease when the reinforcement stops. Marketers must provide continuous reinforcement to consumers or risk their switching to brands that do.

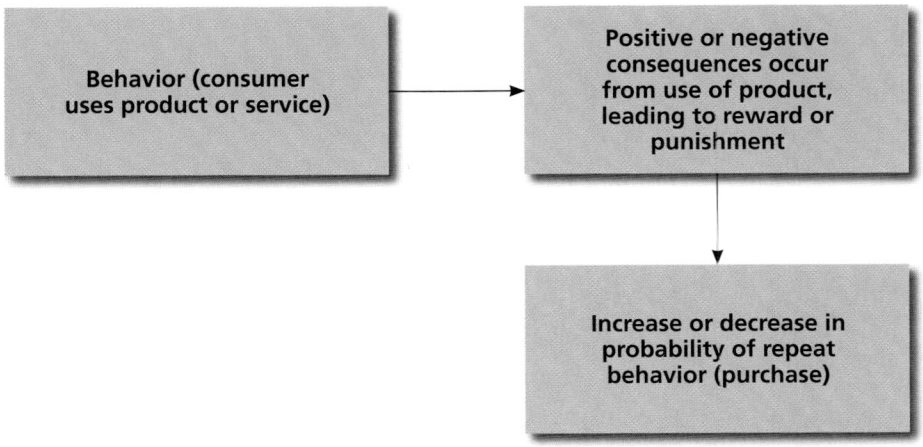

Figure 4-7 Instrumental conditioning in marketing

Learning occurs more slowly but lasts longer when a *partial* or *intermittent reinforcement schedule* is used and only some of the individual's responses are rewarded. Promotional programs have partial reinforcement schedules. A firm may offer consumers an incentive to use the company's product. The firm does not want to offer the incentive every time (continuous reinforcement), because consumers might become dependent on it and stop buying the brand when the incentive is withdrawn. A study that examined the effect of reinforcement on bus ridership found that discount coupons given as rewards for riding the bus were as effective when given on a partial schedule as when given on a continuous schedule.[28] The cost of giving the discount coupons under the partial schedule, however, was considerably less.

Reinforcement schedules can also be used to influence consumer learning and behavior through a process known as **shaping,** the reinforcement of successive acts that lead to a desired behavior pattern or response. Rothschild and Gaidis argue that shaping is a very useful concept for marketers:

> Shaping is an essential process in deriving new and complex behavior because a behavior cannot be rewarded unless it first occurs; a stimulus can only reinforce acts that already occur. New, complex behaviors rarely occur by chance in nature. If the only behavior to be rewarded were the final complex sought behavior, one would probably have to wait a long time for this to occur by chance. Instead, one can reward simpler existing behaviors; over time, more complex patterns evolve and these are rewarded. Thus the shaping process occurs by a method of successive approximations.[29]

In a promotional context, shaping procedures are used as part of the introductory program for new products. Figure 4-8 provides an example of how samples and discount coupons can be used to introduce a new product and take a consumer from trial to repeat purchase. Marketers must be careful in their use of shaping procedures: If they drop the incentives too soon, the consumer may not establish the desired behavior; but if they overuse them, the consumer's purchase may become contingent on the incentive rather than the product or service.

Cognitive Learning Theory

Behavioral learning theories have been criticized for assuming a mechanistic view of the consumer that puts too much emphasis on external stimulus factors. They ignore internal psychological processes such as motivation, thinking, and perception; they

Figure 4-8 Application of shaping procedures in marketing

Terminal Goal: Repeat Purchase Behavior

Approximation Sequence	Shaping Procedure	Reinforcement Applied
Induce product trial	Free samples distributed; large discount coupon	Product performance; coupon
Induce purchase with little financial obligation	Discount coupon prompts purchase with little cost; coupon good for small discount on next purchase enclosed	Product performance; coupon
Induce purchase with moderate financial obligation	Small discount coupon prompts purchase with moderate cost	Product performance
Induce purchase with full financial obligation	Purchase occurs without coupon assistance	Product performance

Figure 4-9 The cognitive learning process

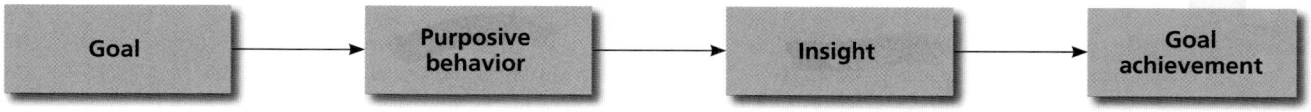

assume that the external stimulus environment will elicit fairly predictable responses. Many consumer researchers and marketers disagree with the simplified explanations of behavioral learning theories and are more interested in the complex mental processes that underlie consumer decision making. The cognitive approach to studying learning and decision making has dominated the field of consumer behavior in recent years. Figure 4-9 shows how cognitive theorists view the learning process.

Since consumer behavior typically involves choices and decision making, the cognitive perspective has particular appeal to marketers, especially those whose product/service calls for important and involved purchase decisions. Cognitive processes such as perception, formation of beliefs about brands, attitude development and change, and integration are important to understanding the decision-making process for many types of purchases. The subprocesses examined during our discussion of the five-stage decision process model are all relevant to a cognitive learning approach to consumer behavior.

Environmental Influences on Consumer Behavior

The consumer does not make purchase decisions in isolation. A number of external factors have been identified that may influence consumer decision making. They are shown in Figure 4-10 and examined in more detail in the next sections.

Culture

The broadest and most abstract of the external factors that influence consumer behavior is **culture,** or the complexity of learned meanings, values, norms, and customs shared by members of a society. Cultural norms and values offer direction and guidance to members of a society in all aspects of their lives, including their consumption behavior. It is becoming increasingly important to study the impact of culture on consumer behavior as marketers expand their international marketing efforts. Each country has certain cultural traditions, customs, and values that marketers must understand as they develop marketing programs.

Marketers must also be aware of changes that may be occurring in a particular culture and the implications of these changes for their advertising and promotional strategies and programs. American culture continually goes through many changes that

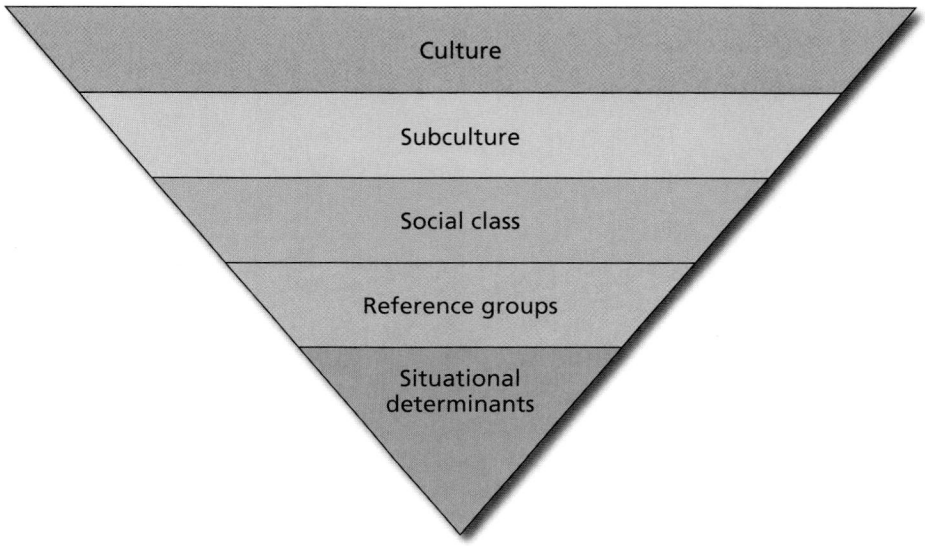

Figure 4-10 External influences on consumer behavior

have direct implications for advertising. Marketing researchers monitor these changes and their impact on the ways companies market their products and services.

While marketers recognize that culture exerts a demonstrable influence on consumers, they often find it difficult to respond to cultural differences in different markets. The subtleties of various cultures are often difficult to understand and appreciate, but marketers must understand the cultural context in which consumer purchase decisions are made and adapt their advertising and promotional programs accordingly.

Subcultures

Within a given culture are generally found smaller groups or segments whose beliefs, values, norms, and patterns of behavior set them apart from the larger cultural mainstream. These **subcultures** may be based on age, geographic, religious, racial, and/or ethnic differences. A number of subcultures exist within the United States. The three largest racial/ethnic subcultures are African-Americans, Hispanics, and various Asian groups. These racial/ethnic subcultures are important to marketers because of their size, growth, purchasing power, and distinct purchasing patterns. Marketers develop specific marketing programs for various products and services for these target markets. The ads in Exhibit 4-19 are just two of the many specifically designed to appeal to U.S. subcultures—in these cases, blacks and Hispanics. Many others can easily be found that target teens, Generations X and Y, the elderly, and so on.

Social Class

Virtually all societies exhibit some form of stratification whereby individuals can be assigned to a specific social category on the basis of criteria important to members of that society. **Social class** refers to relatively homogeneous divisions in a society into which people sharing similar lifestyles, values, norms, interests, and behaviors can be grouped. While a number of methods for determining social class exist, class structures in the United States are usually based on occupational status, educational attainment, and income. Sociologists generally agree there are three broad levels of social classes in the United States: the upper (14 percent), middle (70 percent), and lower (16 percent) classes.[30]

Social class is an important concept to marketers, since consumers within each social stratum often have similar values, lifestyles, and buying behavior. Thus, the various social class groups provide a natural basis for market segmentation. Consumers in the different social classes differ in the degree to which they use various products and services and in their leisure activities, shopping patterns, and media habits. Marketers respond to these differences through the positioning of their products and services, the

Exhibit 4-19 Ads targeted to subcultures

media strategies they use to reach different social classes, and the types of advertising appeals they develop. The ad for New York Palace in Exhibit 4-20 shows how a product attempts to appeal to the upper classes in both copy and illustration.

Reference Groups

Think about the last time you attended a party. As you dressed for the party, you probably asked yourself (or someone else) what others would be wearing. Your selection of attire may have been influenced by those likely to be present. This simple example reflects one form of impact that groups may exert on your behavior.

A group has been defined as "two or more individuals who share a set of norms, values, or beliefs and have certain implicitly or explicitly defined relationships to one another such that their behavior is interdependent."[31] Groups are one of the primary factors influencing learning and socialization, and group situations constitute many of our purchase decisions.

A **reference group** is "a group whose presumed perspectives or values are being used by an individual as the basis for his or her judgments, opinions, and actions." Consumers use reference groups as a guide to specific behaviors, even when the groups are not present.[32] In the party example, your peers—although not present—provided a standard of dress that you referred to in your clothing selection. Likewise, your college classmates, family, and co-workers, or even a group to which you aspire, may serve as referents, and your consumption patterns will typically conform to the expectations of the groups that are most important to you.

Marketers use reference group influences in developing advertisements and promotional strategies. The ads in Exhibit 4-21 are examples of *aspirational* reference groups (to which we might like to belong) and *disassociative* groups (to which we do not wish to belong), respectively.

Exhibit 4-20 New York Palace targets upper classes

Family Decision Making: An Example of Group Influences

In some instances, the group may be involved more directly than just as a referent. Family members may serve as referents to each other, or they may actually be involved in the purchase decision process—acting as an individual buying unit. As shown in Figure 4-11, family members may assume a variety of roles in the decision-making process.[33] Each role has implications for marketers.

The initiator. The person responsible for initiating the purchase decision process; for example, the mother who determines she needs a new car.

The information provider. The individual responsible for gathering information to be used in making the decision; for example, the teenage car buff who knows where to find product information in specific magazines or collects it from dealers.

The influencer. The person who exerts influence as to what criteria will be used in the selection process. All members of the family may be involved. The mother may have her criteria, whereas others may each have their own input.

The decision maker(s). That person(s) who actually makes the decision. In our example, it may be the mother alone or in combination with another family member.

The purchasing agent. The individual who performs the physical act of making the purchase. In the case of a car, a husband and wife may decide to choose it together and sign the purchase agreement.

The consumer. The actual user of the product. In the case of a family car, all family members are consumers. For a private car, only the mother might be the consumer.

Figure 4-11 Roles in the family decision-making process

Exhibit 4-21 The ad on the left shows an aspirational reference group; the one on the right stresses a disassociative reference group

First, the advertiser must determine who is responsible for the various roles in the decision-making process so messages can be targeted at that person (or those people). These roles will also dictate media strategies, since the appropriate magazines, newspapers, or TV or radio stations must be used. Second, understanding the decision-making process and the use of information by individual family members is critical to the design of messages and choice of promotional program elements. In sum, to create an effective promotional program, a marketer must have an overall understanding of how the decision process works and the role that each family member plays.

Situational Determinants

The final external factor is the purchase and usage situation. The specific situation in which consumers plan to use the product or brand directly affects their perceptions, preferences, and purchasing behaviors.[34] Three types of **situational determinants** may have an effect: the specific usage situation, the purchase situation, and the communications situation.

Usage refers to the circumstance in which the product will be used. For example, purchases made for private consumption may be thought of differently from those that will be obvious to the public. The *purchase* situation more directly involves the environment operating at the time of the purchase. Time constraints, store environments, and other factors may all have an impact. The *communications* situation is the condition in which an advertising exposure occurs (in a car listening to the radio, with friends, etc.). This may be most relevant to the development of promotional strategies, because the impact on the consumer will vary according to the particular situation. For example, a consumer may pay more attention to a commercial that is heard alone at home than to one heard in the presence of friends, at work, or anywhere distractions may be present. If advertisers can isolate a particular time when the listener is likely to be attentive, they will probably earn his or her undivided attention.

In sum, situational determinants may either enhance or detract from the potential success of a message. To the degree that advertisers can assess situational influences that may be operating, they will increase the likelihood of successfully communicating with their target audiences.

Alternative Approaches to Consumer Behavior

In addition to the perspectives discussed, consumer researchers complement these psychological approaches with perspectives driven from other scientific disciplines, such as sociology, anthropology, philosophy, or history. These cross-disciplinary perspectives have broadened the realm of methodologies used to study consumers and have provided additional insights into consumer decision processes. IMC Perspective 4-3 provides a few examples of applications of these approaches.

New Methodologies

Whereas psychologists often study consumer responses to advertising and other forms of communication in controlled settings, where environmental variables can be kept constant, sociologists and anthropologists study behavior in context. For this reason, they often employ qualitative methodologies such as individual interviews, participant observation studies, and/or ethnographies. These methods help capture the social, cultural, and environmental influences that may affect consumer behavior.

The humanities have also been a source of new methodologies for consumer research. Historians and semioticians focus their analyses on the advertising messages and other forms of communications themselves. These researchers examine the significance of communications from a linguistic or historical perspective. Research methods such as semiotic and structural analyses examine the symbolic meanings of advertising and different facets of consumption.

New Insights

These alternative perspectives and methodologies provide additional insights and expand our knowledge of consumers. For example, the cultural significance of advertising messages in shaping cultures and triggering communities is now better understood. Likewise, marketers now have a better understanding of how advertising campaigns like "Got Milk" become popular and help shape our culture. Thanks to the many interpretive analyses of advertisements over recent years, we are also more aware of the influence of advertising images on society.

Some consumer researchers believe that cross-disciplinary research is better suited for the study of consumers because it takes into account their complexity and multidimensionality. When considered along with psychological research, these alternative approaches help us better understand the impact of communications.

IMC PERSPECTIVE 4-3

Want to Name a Car or Develop an Ad Campaign? Try Archetype Research, Hypnosis, or Something Else Unconventional

Marketers are constantly trying to determine what goes on in the mind of consumers when they consider purchase decisions, view advertisements, and so on. Packages, brand names, ads, and commercials are commonly researched in an attempt to improve their likelihood of success. Surveys, focus groups, in-depth discussions, and a variety of other methods have been employed to find the "holy grail" of research that will provide insight into consumer's minds. Recently some companies have turned to mind probing through less traditional methods, including hypnosis and "archetype research."

Take DaimlerChrysler, for example. In searching for a "breakthrough" car, the company shunned traditional marketing research techniques and instead employed an unconventional approach known as *archetype research.* With billions of dollars of investments on the line, Chrysler recently shifted the bulk of its research to this methodology, which was developed by a French-born medical anthropologist, G. Clotaire Rapaille, whose previous work involved working with autistic children. To gain insights from deep inside consumers' minds, Rapaille conducted three-hour focus group sessions, in which—with lights dimmed and mood music in the background—consumers were asked to look at a prototype of the newly designed PT Cruiser and to go far back into their childhood to discuss what emotions were evoked, as well as to write stories about their feelings. After the sessions, Rapaille and a team of Chrysler employees read the stories, looking for what they refer to as "reptilian hot buttons," or nuggets of revealing emotions. According to Rapaille, remembering a new concept is dependent upon associating it with an emotion, and the more emotions evoked, the greater the likelihood of recall. The process led to significant design changes that resulted in a less-than-traditional-looking car that won an award as North America's Car of the Year.

Actually, Chrysler was not the first to employ archetype research. Archetype research has also been applied to the naming of SUVs. What comes to your mind when you hear Bronco, Cherokee, Wrangler, Blazer, Yukon, Navigator, or Denali? What about Tahoe, Explorer, Range Rover, or Bravada? As SUVs are increasingly adopted by women (men are going for trucks), it is important to convey some image of the vehicles that meets the target market's needs—conscious or subconscious. According to archetype research, these SUV names conjure up the wilderness, ruggedness, and the new frontier. To women, the size and safety of these vehicles are what they need to compete in this "less than civilized" environment. Does it work? No other product class has seen greater growth over the last 10 years.

But don't think that it's only the auto companies that want to know what's in your head. The list of subscribers to archetype research includes AT&T, Boeing, GE, Lego, Kellogg, and Samsonite, just to name a few. At least 10 years prior to Chrysler's use of the technique, Procter & Gamble employed Rapaille to determine that aroma sells more coffee than taste because of the emotional ties to home. The Folger's coffee ad in which a young soldier returns home and brews a pot of coffee that causes his sleeping mother to wake up and sense that he has returned is a direct result of that research. General Motors has also used this research methodology.

In an equally unconventional approach, California wine maker Domain Chandon and its ad agency D'Arcy

Masius Benton & Bowles of Los Angeles conducted focus groups of hypnotized consumers. In the groups, participants were asked to discuss their experiences and feelings about the first time they drank champagne and/or sparkling wine. According to Chandon and D'Arcy, traditional focus groups lead to "surface" discussions whereas drinking champagne involves more of an "inside"-driven and emotional response. By hypnotizing the participants, they felt they could get behind the barriers set up in conscious minds. The approach apparently worked; as noted by Diane Dreyer, senior VP at D'Arcy, some participants revealed romantic and sexual experiences that "I'm sure they wouldn't share in the waking state." The input from the groups was used in the development of a new advertising campaign that featured a sexual and passionate appeal, as well as a new logo. Essentially, the research led to a whole new positioning for the brand, with ads placed on billboards and in travel and epicurean magazines, as well as a move into e-commerce.

In his book *Why We Buy: The Science of Shopping,* retail consultant Paco Underhill attempts to explain why consumers buy. With a degree in Chinese history, Underhill shifted his emphasis to environmental psychology and, like Rapaille, found the consulting world much more lucrative. Equating the modern-day shopper with the "hunter-gatherer" mentality of the past, he sees men as shopping because of an obsession with a single item. Women, on the other hand, look upon shopping as a social occasion that provides a sense of liberation. At the mall they can escape their husbands and families, exercise their judgments, and see and be seen. Is this what women did in the caveman days?

Traditional or not, millions of dollars are now being invested in previously unheard-of techniques. Billions more are riding on the results. Are you willing to take the risk?

Sources: Phil Patton, "Car Shrinks" *Fortune,* March 18, 2002, pp. 187–190; Alice Z. Cuneo, "Domain Chandon Looks beyond the Celebrations," *Advertising Age,* July 19, 1999, p. 9; Abigail Goldman, "Expert Offers Retailers Glimpse into Shoppers' Minds," *Los Angeles Times,* June 3, 1999, p. C5; Jeffrey Ball, "But How Does It Make You Feel?" *The Wall Street Journal,* May 3, 1999, p. B1.

Summary

This chapter introduced you to the field of consumer behavior and examined its relevance to promotional strategy. Consumer behavior is best viewed as the process and activities that people engage in when searching for, selecting, purchasing, using, evaluating, and disposing of products and services to satisfy their needs and desires. A five-stage model of the consumer decision-making process consists of problem recognition, information search, alternative evaluation, purchase, and postpurchase evaluation. Internal psychological processes that influence the consumer decision-making process include motivation, perception, attitude formation and change, and integration processes.

The decision process model views consumer behavior primarily from a cognitive orientation. The chapter considered other perspectives by examining various approaches to consumer learning and their implications for advertising and promotion. Behavioral learning theories such as classical conditioning and operant (instrumental) conditioning were discussed. Problems with behavioral learning theories were noted, and the alternative perspective of cognitive learning was discussed.

The chapter also examined relevant external factors that influence consumer decision making. Culture, subculture, social class, reference groups, and situational determinants were discussed, along with their implications for the development of promotional strategies and programs. The chapter concluded with an introduction to alternative perspectives on the study of consumer behavior (also called interpretive, postmodern, or postpositivist perspectives).

Key Terms

consumer behavior, 105
problem recognition, 107
want, 107
motives, 109
hierarchy of needs, 109
psychoanalytic theory, 110
motivation research, 110
internal search, 112
external search, 112
perception, 113
sensation, 113
selective perception, 114
selective exposure, 114
selective attention, 114
selective comprehension, 114
selective retention, 114
mnemonics, 114
subliminal perception, 114
evaluative criteria, 116
functional consequences, 117
psychosocial consequences, 117
multiattribute attitude model, 117
salient beliefs, 118
integration processes, 119
heuristics, 119
affect referral decision rule, 120
purchase intention, 120
brand loyalty, 120
cognitive dissonance, 121
classical conditioning, 123
conditioned stimulus, 123
conditioned response, 123
operant conditioning, 125
reinforcement, 125
schedules of reinforcement, 125
shaping, 126
culture, 127
subcultures, 128
social class, 128
reference group, 129
situational determinants, 130

Discussion Questions

1. A number of factors may lead to problem recognition among consumers. Discuss the various causes of problem recognition, and give an example of each.

2. Explain the concept of an *evoked set.* Why is this concept important to marketers? Give examples of an evoked set, and how marketers might attempt to influence consumers to gain consideration.

3. Jerry Olson and J. Paul Peter define two broad categories of evaluative consequences. Describe each of these and provide examples.

4. Figure 4-10 details a number of external influences on consumer behavior. Describe each of these influences, explaining how it might have an impact on consumer behavior, and provide an example of each.

5. Psychoanalytic theory has been criticized for its problems with validity and reliability. How do the current methods discussed in the lead-in—for example, hypnosis—fare in regard to these criteria?

6. Explain how consumers might engage in each of the processes of selective perception described in the chapter. Provide examples.

7. Describe how cultural differences might impact viewers' perceptions of advertisements. Provide examples.

8. In the text it was indicated that families may influence the consumer decision-making process. Describe how various family members may assume the different roles described in Figure 4-11. Also explain how these roles might change depending upon the product under consideration.

9. The text discusses alternative approaches to studying consumer behavior. Explain how these approaches differ from those described earlier in the chapter.

10. Postmodern research often involves a sociological perspective to understanding consumer behavior. Give examples of how sociology might impact purchase behaviors.

The Communication Process

5

Chapter Objectives

1. To understand the basic elements of the communication process and the role of communications in marketing.
2. To examine various models of the communication process.
3. To analyze the response processes of receivers of marketing communications, including alternative response hierarchies and their implications for promotional planning and strategy.
4. To examine the nature of consumers' cognitive processing of marketing communications.

EDS Rebuilds Its Image

Until 2000, if you asked the average person what, if anything, he or she knew about a company called Electronic Data Systems (EDS), you would probably get a blank stare. Some might associate the company with Ross Perot, the company's founder and former presidential candidate, and know that he later sold EDS to General Motors, but it is unlikely they would know anything more. Perot founded EDS in Dallas, Texas, in 1962 with the somewhat radical notion that organizations would hire an outside company to handle all of their computer operations. At the time, the word "outsourcing" had not even entered the business lexicon. However, the idea caught on quickly and EDS came to rule the industry it created, which was evolving beyond just computers into information technology services (ITS). EDS grew exponentially after being acquired by General Motors in 1984 and became a $14 billion giant before splitting off from the automaker in 1996 and becoming an independent company. In many ways the success EDS had under General Motors' wing turned out to be a competitive handicap. A hefty annuity from GM provided a steady revenue stream that lulled the company into complacency and fostered an unwillingness to change even though the world was changing all around it, particularly with the rapid growth of the Internet.

In early 1999, EDS hired a new CEO, Dick Brown, who realized that he and his management team had to do more than reinvent the company—they had to remake its identity and brand image. EDS was perceived as a stodgy, old-economy firm in a new-economy industry and was being eclipsed by flashier firms such as Razorfish, Scient, and Viant, which focused purely on e-services, as well as a reinvented IBM, which had rebuilt its identity around the themes of e-business. Brown hired Don Uzzi, whose record included leading a marketing turnaround for Gatorade in the 90s, as EDS's senior vice president of global marketing and advertising and put him in charge of rebuilding the company's image. Brown wanted Uzzi to build awareness of EDS and make the company a household name. However, there was also a second, equally critical goal: to market EDS to its own employees and make them feel good about working at the company.

The first area Brown turned to in establishing EDS as a power brand was advertising. EDS began working with the Fallon McElligott agency, which came up with a new tagline, "EDS Solved," that was chosen to position the company as a problem solver in the complicated, ever-changing world of e-business. While print work broke in the fall of 1999 with full-page ads in *The Wall Street Journal, New York Times,* and other major publications, the company did not limit its newfound boldness to advertising. Uzzi decided the Y2K fervor provided an opportunity for EDS, which had a thriving year-2000 conversion practice in place, as a publicity opportunity. He arranged for EDS's strategic command center

in Plano, Texas, to be opened to the media on New Year's Eve night. More than a dozen journalists showed up, and CNBC and CNN did live feeds from the command center, as did local TV crews. Uzzi noted: "We showed the world what EDS does and how we do it. That's something the company never would have done before." Once the new year passed with few glitches, EDS celebrated with a full-page "Y2KO" ad in *The Wall Street Journal,* calling attention to the role the company played in helping the world get ready for the date change.

The risk taking continued when EDS ran its now-famous "Cat Herders" ad during the 2000 Super Bowl. The Super Bowl is advertising's biggest showcase and is usually reserved for major advertisers rather than companies such as EDS, which was nearly invisible in the ad world. The commercial was shot in the style of a John Ford old-style western—big sky, big country, stirring musical score—and featured cowboys herding 10,000 house cats. Uzzi noted that herding cats is an information management metaphor for organizing an overwhelming amount of varied data and captures perfectly what EDS does: "We ride herd on complexity. We make technology go where clients want it to go." The commercial was one of the most popular of the Super Bowl ads, and the EDS website received 2 million hits in the first 24 hours after the ad ran and 10 million hits in the first week. Clients called from all over the world, asking for tapes of the commercial to play at meetings, and EDS parlayed the ad's success into a high-profile presence at trade shows.

EDS followed the "Cat Herders" spot with two more high-profile commercials including an ad that debuted on the 2001 Super Bowl called "Running with the Squirrels," which was a spoof of the traditional running of the bulls in Pamplona, Spain, and sent a message about the importance of staying nimble in business. The second commercial was called "Airplane," and it compared what EDS does to building an airplane while it is in the air. Follow-up research shows that the trilogy of commercials resulted in a doubling of the percentage of people associating EDS with e-business solutions and a 50 percent increase in overall brand awareness.

In 2002, EDS moved its advertising in a new direction with a series of commercials and print ads designed to move beyond creating awareness and provide businesses with a better understanding of each of the EDS lines of business—information technology outsourcing, hosting, and security/privacy.

In just two years, a lot more people in the corporate world have become aware of EDS and now view it as a hip, hardworking company that can provide solutions to information technology problems. In addition to helping generate business, EDS's advertising has created excitement among its employees and helped attract new talent to the company. EDS wants its advertising to continue to lead, surprise, and impress its customers as well as its own employees. It is likely that it will.

Sources: Suzanne Vranica, "Cats Corralled: EDS Ads Go Back to Basics," *The Wall Street Journal,* Feb. 8, 2002, p. B9; Tom Wasserman, "Brand Builders," *Brandweek,* Feb. 11, 2002, pp. 17, 18; "Reinventing the Brand," *Fortune,* October 2001, p. 112.

The function of all elements of the integrated marketing communications program is to communicate. An organization's IMC strategy is implemented through the various communications it sends to current or prospective customers as well as other relevant publics. Organizations send communications and messages in a variety of ways, such as through advertisements, brand names, logos and graphic systems, websites, press releases, package designs, promotions, and visual images. Thus, those involved in the planning and implementation of an IMC program need to understand the communications process and how it occurs. As you can see from the opening vignette on the EDS Company, the way marketers communicate with their target audiences depends on many factors, including how much customers know and what they think about the company and the image it hopes to create. Developing an effective marketing communications program is far more complicated than just choosing a product feature or attribute to emphasize. Marketers must understand how consumers will perceive and

interpret their messages and how these reactions will shape consumers' responses to the company and/or its product or service.

This chapter reviews the fundamentals of communication and examines various perspectives and models regarding how consumers respond to advertising and promotional messages. Our goal is to demonstrate how valuable an understanding of the communication process can be in planning, implementing, and evaluating the marketing communications program.

The Nature of Communication

Communication has been variously defined as the passing of information, the exchange of ideas, or the process of establishing a commonness or oneness of thought between a sender and a receiver.[1] These definitions suggest that for communication to occur, there must be some common thinking between two parties and information must be passed from one person to another (or from one group to another). As you will see in this chapter, establishing this commonality in thinking is not always as easy as it might seem; many attempts to communicate are unsuccessful.

The communication process is often very complex. Success depends on such factors as the nature of the message, the audience's interpretation of it, and the environment in which it is received. The receiver's perception of the source and the medium used to transmit the message may also affect the ability to communicate, as do many other factors. Words, pictures, sounds, and colors may have different meanings to different audiences, and people's perceptions and interpretations of them vary. For example, if you ask for a soda on the East Coast or West Coast, you'll receive a soft drink such as Coke or Pepsi. However, in parts of the Midwest and South, a soft drink is referred to as pop. If you ask for a soda, you may get a glass of pop with ice cream in it. Marketers must understand the meanings that words and symbols take on and how they influence consumers' interpretation of products and messages. This can be particularly challenging to companies marketing their products in foreign countries.

Language is one of the major barriers to effective communication, as there are different languages in different countries, different languages or dialects within a single country, and more subtle problems of linguistic nuance and vernacular. The growth of bilingual, multicultural ethnic markets in the United States is also creating challenges for domestic marketers. Diversity Perspective 5-1 discusses issues advertisers must consider in developing messages for young Hispanics, who are a very fast growing market segment.

A Basic Model of Communication

Over the years, a basic model of the various elements of the communication process has evolved, as shown in Figure 5-1.[2] Two elements represent the major participants in the communication process, the sender and the receiver. Another two are the major communication tools, message and channel.

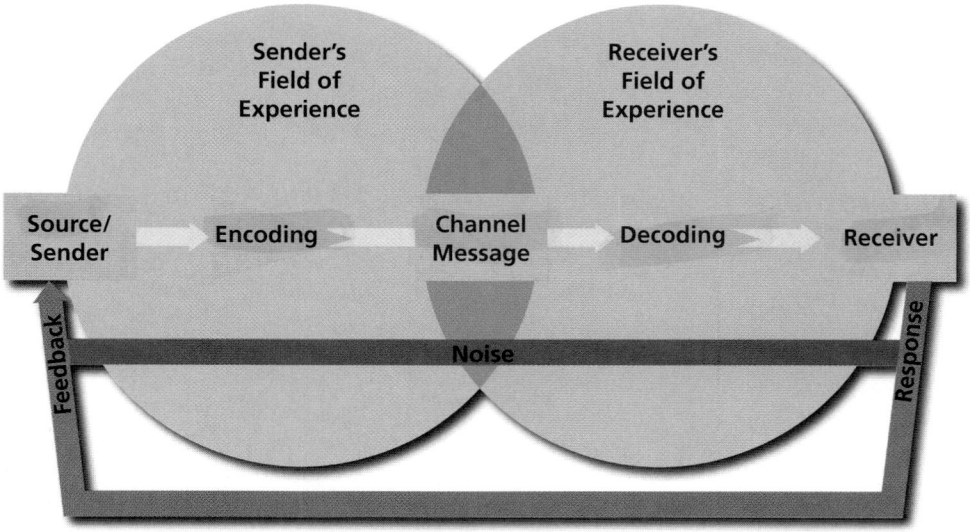

Figure 5-1 A model of the communication process

DIVERSITY PERSPECTIVE 5-1

Communicating with the Hispanic Teen Market

A few years ago, Jeff Manning, the executive director of the California Milk Processor Board (CMPB), was considering ways to reverse a decline in milk sales in the heavily Hispanic southern California market. As he reviewed a report on the Latino market, a potential solution to the problem came to him: target one of the fastest-growing market segments in the United States, which is Hispanic teenagers. The results from the 2000 census show that over the past decade the Hispanic market grew by 58 percent, compared with only 3 percent for the non-Hispanic white segment, and another 35 percent jump for Hispanics is forecast over the next 10 years. Moreover, the ranks of Hispanic teenagers are projected to swell to 18 percent of the U.S. teen population over the next decade, up from 12 percent in 2000. Nearly one in five children born in the United States today is of Latin American descent, and more than half of all children in Los Angeles alone are born to Latino mothers.

While marketers are recognizing the importance of appealing to the Hispanic market, they are also finding that communicating with this fast-growing segment can be very challenging and requires more than creating an ad in the Spanish with tried-and-true Hispanic themes. They have to decide whether to use ads with a Hispanic-focused creative, dub or remake general market campaigns into Spanish, or run English-language ads and trust that they will be picked up by bilingual Hispanics. Contributing to the challenge is the fact that Hispanic teens often live in two worlds: one rich in traditional Latino values, such as strong commitment to family and religion, and the other in which they eagerly participate in mainstream teen America. They bounce between hip-hop and *rock en Espanol;* watch *Buffy the Vampire Slayer* with their friends and Spanish *telenovelas* (night-time soap operas) with their parents; and blend Mexican rice with spaghetti sauce and spread peanut butter and jelly on tortillas.

Advertising and marketing executives have different perspectives on how to best reach these "young biculturals." For example, research Manning conducted for the California Milk Processor Board on targeting English versions of its popular "Got Milk?" ads to Hispanic teens found that they reacted enthusiastically to the ads. The CMPB had considered doing the ads in Spanglish (a combination of English and Spanish) but found that the language used was not a major issue for teens, as they reacted to ideas, not language. However, a 2000 study of Hispanic teens by the Roslow Research Group found that advertising to bilingual Hispanics in Spanish is significantly more effective than advertising to them in English. English ads were 28 percent less effective than Spanish ads in terms of

ad recall, 54 percent less effective in terms of persuasion, and 14 percent less effective in terms of communication.

The California Milk Processor Board has decided that it is important to develop ads that appeal to bicultural teens. Recently its ad agency worked with Latino students from the Art Center College of Design in Pasadena to develop a commercial based on a Hispanic cultural myth that has long been used to scare kids straight. When Hispanic kids misbehave, their parents threaten that *La Llorona* ("the weeping woman") will come to claim them. Basically she's a boogiewoman for bambinos. In the spot the ghostly figure, clad in flowing gown and veil, wails as she wanders through a house. Walking through a wall, the specter enters the kitchen and opens the refrigerator. Rather abruptly, her tears terminate. "Leche!" she exclaims, lunging at the half gallon of milk needed to wash down the Mexican pastry she clutches. But sadly for *La Llorona,* the carton is empty, so the tears resume and the "Got milk?" tagline appears.

While the *La Llorona* ad targets bicultural teens through mainstream media, it relies on only one word of dialogue and thus may appeal to non-Hispanics as well. In fact, marketers are finding that by targeting Hispanic youth they may also attract the more general teen market. Many have noted the tremendous popularity of Hispanic entertainers such as Ricky Martin, Jennifer Lopez, Marc Anthony, and Shakira, and their crossover appeal to non-Hispanic teens. As one agency executive notes: "It's very cool to be Hispanic at this age. It almost makes them more attractive, exotic."

Sources: Becky Ebenkamp, "A House Lacking in Lactose? Intolerable," *Brandweek,* Jan. 21, 2002, p. 23; Jeffery D. Zbar, "Hispanic Teens Set Urban Beat," *Advertising Age,* June 25, 2001, p. S6; Rick Wartzman, "When You Translate 'Got Milk' for Latinos, What Do You Get?" *The Wall Street Journal,* June 3, 1999, pp. A1, 10.

Four others are the major communication functions and processes: encoding, decoding, response, and feedback. The last element, noise, refers to any extraneous factors in the system that can interfere with the process and work against effective communication.

Exhibit 5-1 Picabo Street is a source in this Rolex ad

Source Encoding

The sender, or **source,** of a communication is the person or organization that has information to share with another person or group of people. The source may be an individual (say, a salesperson or hired spokesperson, such as a celebrity, who appears in a company's advertisements) or a nonpersonal entity (such as the corporation or organization itself). For example, the source of the ad shown in the opening vignette is the EDS company, since no specific spokesperson or source is shown. However, in the Rolex ad shown in Exhibit 5-1, Olympic gold medalist Picabo Street is also a source since she appears as a spokesperson for the company.

Because the receiver's perceptions of the source influence how the communication is received, marketers must be careful to select a communicator the receiver believes is knowledgeable and trustworthy or with whom the receiver can identify or relate in some manner. (How these characteristics influence the receiver's responses is discussed further in Chapter 6.)

The communication process begins when the source selects words, symbols, pictures, and the like, to represent the message that will be delivered to the receiver(s). This process, known as **encoding,** involves putting thoughts, ideas, or information into a symbolic form. The sender's goal is to encode the message in such a way that it will be understood by the receiver. This means using words, signs, or symbols that are familiar to the target audience. Many symbols have universal meaning, such as the familiar circle with a line through it to denote no parking, no smoking, and so forth. Many companies also have highly recognizable symbols—such as McDonald's golden arches, Nike's swoosh, or the Coca-Cola trademark—that are known to consumers around the world.

Message

The encoding process leads to development of a **message** that contains the information or meaning the source hopes to convey. The message may be verbal or nonverbal, oral or written, or symbolic. Messages must be put into a transmittable form that is appropriate for the channel of communication being used. In advertising, this may range from simply writing some words or copy that will be read as a radio message to producing an expensive television commercial. For many products, it is not the actual words of the message that determine its communication effectiveness but rather the impression or image the ad creates. Notice how Spellbound perfume in Exhibit 5-2 uses only a picture

Exhibit 5-2 The image projected by an ad often communicates more than words

to deliver its message. However, the product name and picture help communicate a feeling of attraction and fascination between the man and woman shown in the ad.

To better understand the symbolic meaning that might be conveyed in a communication, advertising and marketing researchers have begun focusing attention on **semiotics,** which studies the nature of meaning and asks how our reality—words, gestures, myths, signs, symbols, products/services, theories—acquire meaning.[3] Semiotics is important in marketing communications since products and brands acquire meaning through the way they are advertised and consumers use products and brands to express their social identities. Consumer researcher Michael Solomon notes: "From a semiotic perspective, every marketing message has three basic components: an object, a sign or symbol and an interpretant. The object is the product that is the focus of the message (e.g., Marlboro cigarettes). The sign is the sensory imagery that represents the intended meanings of the object (e.g., the Marlboro cowboy). The interpretant is the meaning derived (e.g., rugged, individualistic, American)."[4]

Marketers may use individuals trained in semiotics and related fields such as cultural anthropology to better understand the conscious and subconscious meanings the nonverbal signs and symbols in their ads transmit to consumers. For example, Levi Strauss & Co.'s former agency, TBWA/Chiat/Day, hired a cultural anthropologist to help it better understand the image and meaning of clothing and fashion among young consumers. As part of the process, the agency research team recruited hip-looking young people in the streets of the East Village section of New York City, an area picked because they felt it is the best reflection of today's youth life. Those chosen were handed a piece of red cardboard and a white marker and asked to "write down something you believe in; something that's true about you or your world." The process provided the agency with insight into the teen market and was the impetus for an ad campaign featuring teenagers holding placards inscribed with their philosophical messages.[5] Exhibit 5-3 shows the thinking behind the various elements of one of the ads used in the campaign as explained by Sean Dee, the director of the Levi's brand.

Some advertising and marketing people are skeptical about the value of semiotics. They question whether social scientists read too much into advertising messages and are overly intellectual in interpreting them. However, the meaning of an advertising

Exhibit 5-3 Semiotic analysis is used to describe the various elements of this Levi's ad

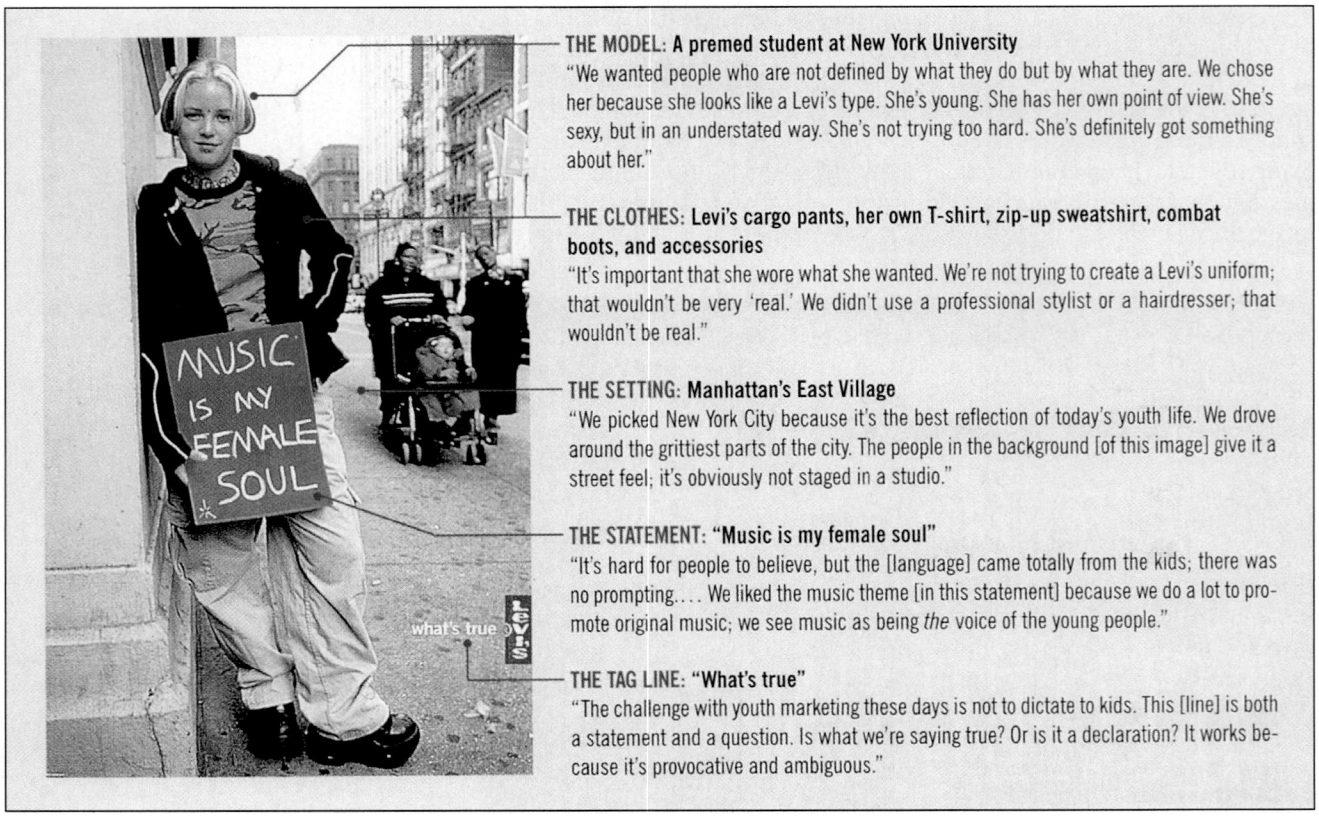

message or other form of marketing communication lies not in the message but with the people who see and interpret it. Moreover, consumers behave on the basis of meanings they ascribe to marketplace stimuli. Thus, marketers must consider the meanings consumers attach to the various signs and symbols. Semiotics may be helpful in analyzing how various aspects of the marketing program—such as advertising messages, packaging, brand names, and even the nonverbal communications of salespeople (gestures, mode of dress)—are interpreted by receivers.[6]

Channel

The **channel** is the method by which the communication travels from the source or sender to the receiver. At the broadest level, channels of communication are of two types, personal and nonpersonal. *Personal channels* of communication are direct interpersonal (face-to-face) contact with target individuals or groups. Salespeople serve as personal channels of communication when they deliver their sales message to a buyer or potential customer. Social channels of communication such as friends, neighbors, associates, co-workers, or family members are also personal channels. They often represent *word-of-mouth communication,* a powerful source of information for consumers.[7]

Nonpersonal channels of communication are those that carry a message without interpersonal contact between sender and receiver. Nonpersonal channels are generally referred to as the **mass media** or mass communications, since the message is sent to many individuals at one time. For example, a TV commercial broadcast on a prime-time show may be seen by 20 million households in a given evening. Nonpersonal channels of communication consist of two major types, print and broadcast. Print media include newspapers, magazines, direct mail, and billboards; broadcast media include radio and television.

Receiver/Decoding

The **receiver** is the person(s) with whom the sender shares thoughts or information. Generally, receivers are the consumers in the target market or audience who read, hear, and/or see the marketer's message and decode it. **Decoding** is the process of transforming the sender's message back into thought. This process is heavily influenced by the receiver's frame of reference or **field of experience,** which refers to the experiences, perceptions, attitudes, and values he or she brings to the communication situation.

For effective communication to occur, the message decoding process of the receiver must match the encoding of the sender. Simply put, this means the receiver understands and correctly interprets what the source is trying to communicate. As Figure 5-1 showed, the source and the receiver each have a frame of reference (the circle around each) that they bring to the communication situation. Effective communication is more likely when there is some *common ground* between the two parties. (This is represented by the overlapping of the two circles.) The more knowledge the sender has about the receivers, the better the sender can understand their needs, empathize with them, and communicate effectively.

While this notion of common ground between sender and receiver may sound basic, it often causes great difficulty in the advertising communications process. Marketing and advertising people often have very different fields of experience from the consumers who constitute the mass markets with whom they must communicate. Most advertising and marketing people are college-educated and work and/or reside in large urban areas such as New York, Chicago, or Los Angeles. Yet they are attempting to develop commercials that will effectively communicate with millions of consumers who have never attended college, work in blue-collar occupations, and live in rural areas or small towns. The executive creative director of a large advertising agency described how advertising executives become isolated from the cultural mainstream: "We pull them in and work them to death. And then they begin moving in sushi circles and lose touch with Velveeta and the people who eat it."[8]

Another factor that can lead to problems in establishing common ground between senders and receivers is age. IMC Perspective 5-2 discusses the youth bias in advertising and some interesting findings from a study that considered problems younger advertising professionals have in developing ads for older consumers.

IMC PERSPECTIVE 5-2

Does Advertising Ignore Older Consumers?

In early 2002, a battle was waged between two of the major television networks, CBS and ABC, over *The Late Show with David Letterman.* ABC was trying to lure Letterman's show away from CBS to replace *Nightline,* the news show hosted by Ted Koppel, which it had been airing in the late-night time slot for 22 years. The battle was being fought mainly because *Letterman* is more popular among younger viewers between the key ages of 18 to 32 and brings in $100 million more in advertising revenue each year than *Nightline.* Observers argued that the tug-of-war over *Letterman* is just another example of advertisers' obsession with younger consumers. While aging baby boomers may argue they are more active, more fit, more adventurous, and more experimental than their predecessors, they are still of less interest to advertisers than younger consumers.

It has often been argued that people who work in advertising are different from the typical consumers who represent the target markets for their clients' products and services. Some say advertising may better reflect those who work in the industry than the consuming public, as it is really about the people who create it, not about the consumers who actually buy the products being advertised. A study conducted a few years ago on ageism in advertising considered potential problems that might arise because of age differences between agency personnel and older consumers. The study found that professionals who work in advertising agencies are much younger than the U.S. adult population. Nearly 40 percent of ad agency professional staff are between the ages of 30 and 39, while only 20 percent of all adults are in their 30s.

The youth bias is particularly evident in the creative departments. Agency employment drops like a rock after age 40, particularly among those involved in creating the ads. As a result, agencies rarely have creative professionals with a true understanding of life after age 40, not to mention life after 50 or 60. Richard Lee, a principal of High-Yield Marketing, the company that conducted the study, notes: "Most young agency staff, reflective of their life phase, are fixated on creating advertising that is hip, cool, impressive to their peers, and award-winning. This is more fulfilling than creating advertising for people with dated tastes who wouldn't know Smashing Pumpkins if they stepped on them."

Advertisers who are unable to connect with older consumers may be squandering opportunities to reach a valuable market. While nearly 40 percent of American adults are 50 or older and they control more than 50 percent of the U.S.'s discretionary income, they receive only 10 percent of the advertising messages. Many observers wonder why advertisers remain focused on consumers in their teens, 20s, and early 30s when spending power is becoming progressively more concentrated among those age 50 and older. Some point to the conventional wisdom in marketing and advertising that brand loyalties and consumer preferences form early and once formed, stay pretty much the same. Older people are stereotyped as unlikely to change brands and try something new.

Another reason for the youth bias stems from the problem of advertisers' not wanting to have their brands perceived as being for older consumers for fear of damaging their image among younger people. As the senior vice president of Zenith Media notes: "For a lot of brands we work with, it's sexier to advertise to the younger consumers who are trendier, much more fashion forward, very social and very in the public eye. With marketing dollars so limited and precious, you want to bet on the future."

Of course, not everyone in the advertising industry agrees with the findings of the ageism study. One agency executive calls the conclusions ridiculous, noting that "we have people of every age segment here." There are, of course, examples of excellent advertising targeted at mature consumers, and new media are being introduced to reach the over-50 crowd.

Many believe, however, that the youth bias in advertising is still a major problem. They note that the best hope for the demise of the primary focus on youth in advertising is the marketing people who are growing and maturing themselves. Some feel that it has finally dawned on advertisers that they ought to follow the green, which is quickly going gray, and that older consumers are more hip. As one ad executive noted: "Sixty-year-olds don't think like they did in the last generation. Sixty-year-olds in the last generation wore plaid pants."

Sources: Hillary Chura, "Boomers Hope to Break Age-Old Ad Myth," *Advertising Age,* May 13, 2002, p. 16; Richard Lee, "The Youth Bias in Advertising," *American Demographics,* January 1997, pp. 47–50.

Advertisers spend millions of dollars every year to understand the frames of reference of the target markets who receive their messages. They also spend much time and money pretesting messages to make sure consumers understand and decode them in the manner the advertiser intended.

Noise

Throughout the communication process, the message is subject to extraneous factors that can distort or interfere with its reception. This unplanned distortion or interference is known as **noise.** Errors or problems that occur in the encoding of the message, distortion in a radio or television signal, or distractions at the point of reception are examples of noise. When you are watching your favorite commercial on TV and a problem occurs in the signal transmission, it will obviously interfere with your reception, lessening the impact of the commercial.

Noise may also occur because the fields of experience of the sender and receiver don't overlap. Lack of common ground may result in improper encoding of the message—using a sign, symbol, or words that are unfamiliar or have different meaning to the receiver. The more common ground there is between the sender and the receiver, the less likely it is this type of noise will occur.

Response/Feedback

The receiver's set of reactions after seeing, hearing, or reading the message is known as a **response.** Receivers' responses can range from nonobservable actions such as storing information in memory to immediate action such as dialing a toll-free number to order a product advertised on television. Marketers are very interested in **feedback,** that part of the receiver's response that is communicated back to the sender. Feedback, which may take a variety of forms, closes the loop in the communications flow and lets the sender monitor how the intended message is being decoded and received.

For example, in a personal-selling situation, customers may pose questions, comments, or objections or indicate their reactions through nonverbal responses such as gestures and frowns.[9] The salesperson has the advantage of receiving instant feedback through the customer's reactions. But this is generally not the case when mass media are used. Because advertisers are not in direct contact with the customers, they must use other means to determine how their messages have been received. While the ultimate form of feedback occurs through sales, it is often hard to show a direct relationship between advertising and purchase behavior. So marketers use other methods to obtain feedback, among them customer inquiries, store visits, coupon redemptions, and reply cards. Research-based feedback analyzes readership and recall of ads, message comprehension, attitude change, and other forms of response. With this information, the advertiser can determine reasons for success or failure in the communication process and make adjustments.

Successful communication is accomplished when the marketer selects an appropriate source, develops an effective message or appeal that is encoded properly, and then selects the channels or media that will best reach the target audience so that the message can be effectively decoded and delivered. In Chapter 6, we will examine the source, message, and channel decisions and see how promotional planners work with these controllable variables to develop communication strategies. Since these decisions must consider how the target audience will respond to the promotional message, the remainder of this chapter examines the receiver and the process by which consumers respond to advertising and other forms of marketing communications.

Analyzing the Receiver

To communicate effectively with their customers, marketers must understand who the target audience is, what (if anything) it knows or feels about the company's product or service, and how to communicate with the audience to influence its decision-making process. Marketers must also know how the market is likely to respond to various sources of communication or different types of messages. Before they make decisions regarding source, message, and channel variables, promotional planners must understand the potential effects associated with each of these factors. This section focuses

on the receiver of the marketing communication. It examines how the audience is identified and the process it may go through in responding to a promotional message. This information serves as a foundation for evaluating the controllable communication variable decisions in the next chapter.

Identifying the Target Audience

The marketing communication process really begins with identifying the audience that will be the focus of the firm's advertising and promotional efforts. The target audience may consist of individuals, groups, niche markets, market segments, or a general public or mass audience (Figure 5-2). Marketers approach each of these audiences differently.

The target market may consist of *individuals* who have specific needs and for whom the communication must be specifically tailored. This often requires person-to-person communication and is generally accomplished through personal selling. Other forms of communication, such as advertising, may be used to attract the audience's attention to the firm, but the detailed message is carried by a salesperson who can respond to the specific needs of the individual customer. Life insurance, financial services, and real estate are examples of products and services promoted this way.

A second level of audience aggregation is represented by the *group.* Marketers often must communicate with a group of people who make or influence the purchase decision. For example, organizational purchasing often involves buying centers or committees that vary in size and composition. Companies marketing their products and services to other businesses or organizations must understand who is on the purchase committee, what aspect of the decision each individual influences, and the criteria each member uses to evaluate a product. Advertising may be directed at each member of the buying center, and multilevel personal selling may be necessary to reach those individuals who influence or actually make decisions.

Marketers look for customers who have similar needs and wants and thus represent some type of market segment that can be reached with the same basic communication strategy. Very small, well-defined groups of customers are often referred to as *market niches.* They can usually be reached through personal-selling efforts or highly targeted media such as direct mail. The next level of audience aggregation is *market segments,* broader classes of buyers who have similar needs and can be reached with similar messages. As we saw in Chapter 2, there are various ways of segmenting markets and reaching the customers in these segments. As market segments get larger, marketers usually turn to broader-based media such as newspapers, magazines, and TV to reach them.

Marketers of most consumer products attempt to attract the attention of large numbers of present or potential customers (*mass markets*) through mass communication such as advertising or publicity. Mass communication is a one-way flow of information from the marketer to the consumer. Feedback on the audience's reactions to the message is generally indirect and difficult to measure.

TV advertising, for example, lets the marketer send a message to millions of consumers at the same time. But this does not mean effective communication has

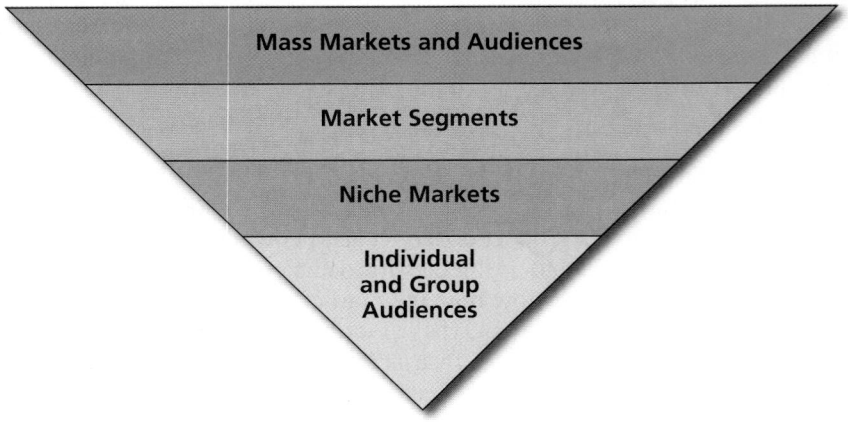

Figure 5-2 Levels of audience aggregation

occurred. This may be only one of several hundred messages the consumer is exposed to that day. There is no guarantee the information will be attended to, processed, comprehended, or stored in memory for later retrieval. Even if the advertising message is processed, it may not interest consumers or may be misinterpreted by them. Studies by Jacob Jacoby and Wayne D. Hoyer have shown that nearly 20 percent of all print ads and even more TV commercials are miscomprehended by readers.[10]

Unlike personal or face-to-face communications, mass communications do not offer the marketer an opportunity to explain or clarify the message to make it more effective. The marketer must enter the communication situation with knowledge of the target audience and how it is likely to react to the message. This means the receiver's response process must be understood, along with its implications for promotional planning and strategy.

The Response Process

Perhaps the most important aspect of developing effective communication programs involves understanding the *response process* the receiver may go through in moving toward a specific behavior (like purchasing a product) and how the promotional efforts of the marketer influence consumer responses. In many instances, the marketer's only objective may be to create awareness of the company or brand name, which may trigger interest in the product. In other situations, the marketer may want to convey detailed information to change consumers' knowledge of and attitudes toward the brand and ultimately change their behavior.

Traditional Response Hierarchy Models

A number of models have been developed to depict the stages a consumer may pass through in moving from a state of not being aware of a company, product, or brand to actual purchase behavior. Figure 5-3 shows four of the best-known response hierarchy models. While these response models may appear similar, they were developed for different reasons.

The **AIDA model** was developed to represent the stages a salesperson must take a customer through in the personal-selling process.[11] This model depicts the buyer as passing successively through attention, interest, desire, and action. The salesperson must first get the customer's attention and then arouse some interest in the company's

Figure 5-3 Models of the response process

	Models			
Stages	**AIDA model[a]**	**Hierarchy of effects model[b]**	**Innovation adoption model[c]**	**Information processing model[d]**
Cognitive stage	Attention	Awareness	Awareness	Presentation
				Attention
		Knowledge		Comprehension
Affective stage	Interest	Liking	Interest	Yielding
		Preference		
	Desire	Conviction	Evaluation	Retention
Behavioral stage			Trial	
	Action	Purchase	Adoption	Behavior

product or service. Strong levels of interest should create desire to own or use the product. The action stage in the AIDA model involves getting the customer to make a purchase commitment and closing the sale. To the marketer, this is the most important stage in the selling process, but it can also be the most difficult. Companies train their sales reps in closing techniques to help them complete the selling process.

Perhaps the best known of these response hierarchies is the model developed by Robert Lavidge and Gary Steiner as a paradigm for setting and measuring advertising objectives.[12] Their **hierarchy of effects model** shows the process by which advertising works; it assumes a consumer passes through a series of steps in sequential order from initial awareness of a product or service to actual purchase. A basic premise of this model is that advertising effects occur over a period of time. Advertising communication may not lead to immediate behavioral response or purchase; rather, a series of effects must occur, with each step fulfilled before the consumer can move to the next stage in the hierarchy. As we will see in Chapter 7, the hierarchy of effects model has become the foundation for objective setting and measurement of advertising effects in many companies.

The **innovation adoption model** evolved from work on the diffusion of innovations.[13] This model represents the stages a consumer passes through in adopting a new product or service. Like the other models, it says potential adopters must be moved through a series of steps before taking some action (in this case, deciding to adopt a new product). The steps preceding adoption are awareness, interest, evaluation, and trial. The challenge facing companies introducing new products is to create awareness and interest among consumers and then get them to evaluate the product favorably. The best way to evaluate a new product is through actual use so that performance can be judged. Marketers often encourage trial by using demonstration or sampling programs or allowing consumers to use a product with minimal commitment (Exhibit 5-4). After trial, consumers either adopt the product or reject it.

The final hierarchy model shown in Figure 5-3 is the **information processing model** of advertising effects, developed by William McGuire.[14] This model assumes the receiver in a persuasive communication situation like advertising is an information processor or problem solver. McGuire suggests the series of steps a receiver goes through in being persuaded constitutes a response hierarchy. The stages of this model are similar to the hierarchy of effects sequence; attention and comprehension are similar to awareness and knowledge, and yielding is synonymous with liking. McGuire's model includes a stage not found in the other models: retention, or the receiver's ability to retain that portion of the comprehended information that he or she accepts as valid or relevant. This stage is important since most promotional campaigns are designed not to motivate consumers to take immediate action but rather to provide information they will use later when making a purchase decision.

Each stage of the response hierarchy is a dependent variable that must be attained and that may serve as an objective of the communication process. As shown in Figure 5-4, each stage can be measured, providing the advertiser with feedback regarding the effectiveness of various strategies designed to move the consumer to purchase. The information processing model may be an effective framework for planning and evaluating the effects of a promotional campaign.

Exhibit 5-4 Sampling or demonstration programs encourage trial of new products such as disposable contact lenses

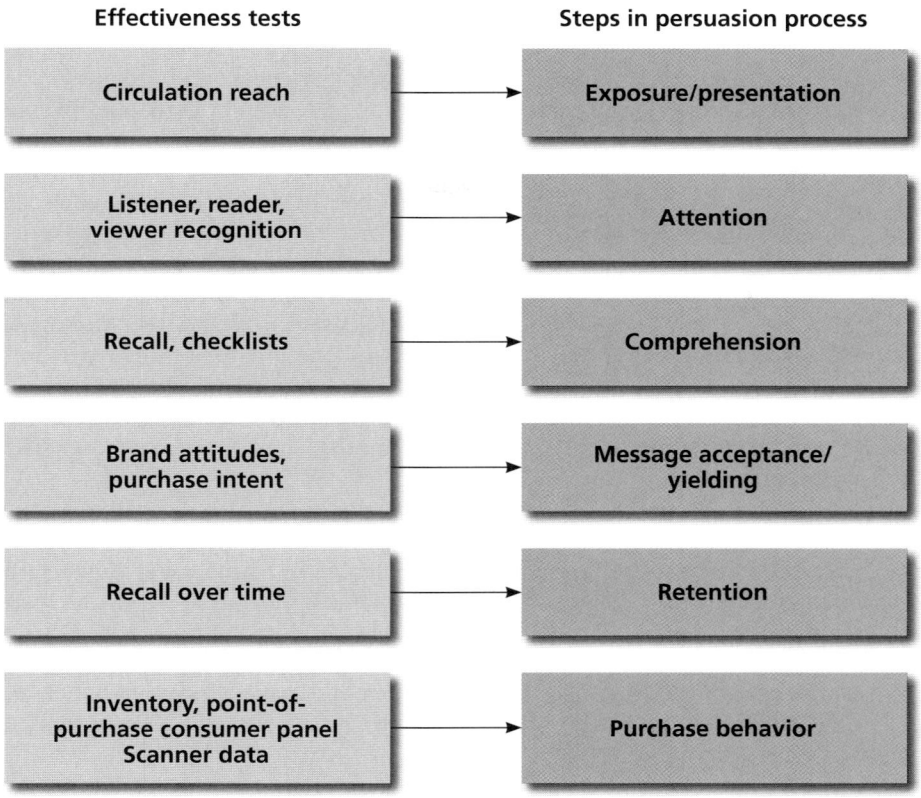

Figure 5-4 Methods of obtaining feedback in the response hierarchy

Implications of the Traditional Hierarchy Models

The hierarchy models of communication response are useful to promotional planners from several perspectives. First, they delineate the series of steps potential purchasers must be taken through to move them from unawareness of a product or service to readiness to purchase it. Second, potential buyers may be at different stages in the hierarchy, so the advertiser will face different sets of communication problems. For example, a company introducing an innovative product like Zenith's plasma high-definition television (HDTV) may need to devote considerable effort to making people aware of the product, how it works, and its benefits (Exhibit 5-5). Marketers of a mature brand that enjoys customer loyalty may need only supportive or reminder advertising to reinforce positive perceptions and maintain the awareness level for the brand.

The hierarchy models can also be useful as intermediate measures of communication effectiveness. The marketer needs to know where audience members are on the response hierarchy. For example, research may reveal that one target segment has low awareness of the advertiser's brand, whereas another is aware of the brand and its various attributes but has a low level of liking or brand preference.

For the first segment of the market, the communication task involves increasing the awareness level for the brand. The number of ads may be increased, or a product sampling program may be used. For the second segment, where awareness is already high but liking and preference are low, the advertiser must determine the

Exhibit 5-5 Advertising for innovative new products such as HDTV must make consumers aware of their features and benefits

reason for the negative feelings and then attempt to address this problem in future advertising.

When research or other evidence reveals a company is perceived favorably on a particular attribute or performance criterion, the company may want to take advantage of this in its advertising.

Evaluating Traditional Response Hierarchy Models

As you saw in Figure 5-3, the four models presented all view the response process as consisting of movement through a sequence of three basic stages. The *cognitive stage* represents what the receiver knows or perceives about the particular product or brand. This stage includes awareness that the brand exists and knowledge, information, or comprehension about its attributes, characteristics, or benefits. The *affective stage* refers to the receiver's feelings or affect level (like or dislike) for the particular brand. This stage also includes stronger levels of affect such as desire, preference, or conviction. The *conative* or *behavioral stage* refers to the consumer's action toward the brand: trial, purchase, adoption, or rejection.

All four models assume a similar ordering of these three stages. Cognitive development precedes affective reactions, which precede behavior. One might assume that consumers become aware of and knowledgeable about a brand, develop feelings toward it, form a desire or preference, and then make a purchase. While this logical progression is often accurate, the response sequence does not always operate this way.

Over the past two decades, considerable research in marketing, social psychology, and communications has led to questioning of the traditional cognitive → affective → behavioral sequence of response. Several other configurations of the response hierarchy have been theorized.

Alternative Response Hierarchies

Michael Ray has developed a model of information processing that identifies three alternative orderings of the three stages based on perceived product differentiation and product involvement.[15] These alternative response hierarchies are the standard learning, dissonance/attribution, and low-involvement models (Figure 5-5).

The Standard Learning Hierarchy

In many purchase situations, the consumer will go through the response process in the sequence depicted by the traditional communication models. Ray terms this a **standard learning model,** which consists of a learn → feel → do sequence. Information and knowledge acquired or *learned* about the various brands are the basis for developing affect, or *feelings,* that guide what the

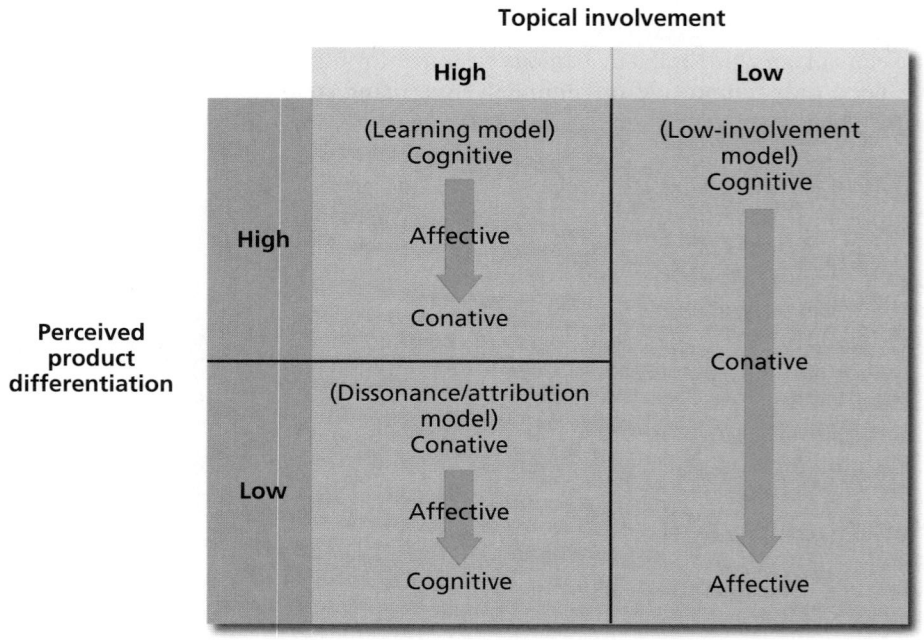

Figure 5-5 Alternative response hierarchies: the three-orders model of information processing

consumer will *do* (e.g., actual trial or purchase). In this hierarchy, the consumer is viewed as an active participant in the communication process who gathers information through active learning.

Ray suggests the standard learning hierarchy is likely when the consumer is highly involved in the purchase process and there is much differentiation among competing brands. High-involvement purchase decisions such as those for industrial products and services and consumer durables like personal computers, printers, cameras, appliances, and cars are areas where a standard learning hierarchy response process is likely. Ads for products and services in these areas are usually very detailed and provide customers with information that can be used to evaluate brands and help them make a purchase decision (Exhibit 5-6).

Exhibit 5-6 Ads for high-involvement products provide consumers with information to help them evaluate brands

The Dissonance/Attribution Hierarchy A second response hierarchy proposed by Ray involves situations where consumers first behave, then develop attitudes or feelings as a result of that behavior, and then learn or process information that supports the behavior. This **dissonance/attribution model,** or do → feel → learn, occurs in situations where consumers must choose between two alternatives that are similar in quality but are complex and may have hidden or unknown attributes. The consumer may purchase the product on the basis of a recommendation by some nonmedia source and then attempt to support the decision by developing a positive attitude toward the brand and perhaps even developing negative feelings toward the rejected alternative(s). This reduces any *postpurchase dissonance* or anxiety the consumer may experience resulting from doubt over the purchase (as discussed in Chapter 4). Dissonance reduction involves *selective learning,* whereby the consumer seeks information that supports the choice made and avoids information that would raise doubts about the decision.

According to this model, marketers need to recognize that in some situations, attitudes develop *after* purchase, as does learning from the mass media. Ray suggests that in these situations the main effect of the mass media is not the promotion of original choice behavior and attitude change but rather the reduction of dissonance by reinforcing the wisdom of the purchase or providing supportive information. For example, the ad shown in Exhibit 5-7 reinforces consumers' decisions to purchase Michelin tires by showing the number of awards the brand has received for customer satisfaction.

Exhibit 5-7 This ad reinforces the wisdom of the decision to purchase Michelin tires

As with the standard learning model, this response hierarchy is likely to occur when the consumer is involved in the purchase situation; it is particularly relevant for post-purchase situations. For example, a consumer may purchase tires recommended by a friend and then develop a favorable attitude toward the company and pay close attention to its ads to reduce dissonance.

Some marketers resist this view of the response hierarchy because they can't accept the notion that the mass media have no effect on the consumer's initial purchase decision. But the model doesn't claim the mass media have no effect—just that their major impact occurs after the purchase has been made. Marketing communications planners must be aware of the need for advertising and promotion efforts not just to encourage brand selection but to reinforce choices and ensure that a purchase pattern will continue.

The Low-Involvement Hierarchy

Perhaps the most intriguing of the three response hierarchies proposed by Ray is the **low-involvement hierarchy,** in which the receiver is viewed as passing from cognition to behavior to attitude change. This learn → do → feel sequence is thought to characterize situations of low consumer involvement in the purchase process. Ray suggests this hierarchy tends to occur when involvement in the purchase decision is low, there are minimal differences among brand alternatives, and mass-media (especially broadcast) advertising is important.

The notion of a low-involvement hierarchy is based in large part on Herbert Krugman's theory explaining the effects of television advertising.[16] Krugman wanted to find out why TV advertising produced a strong effect on brand awareness and recall but little change in consumers' attitudes toward the product. He hypothesized that TV is basically a low-involvement medium and the viewer's perceptual defenses are reduced or even absent during commercials. In a low-involvement situation, the consumer does not compare the message with previously acquired beliefs, needs, or past experiences. The commercial results in subtle changes in the consumer's knowledge structure, particularly with repeated exposure. This change in the consumer's knowledge does not result in attitude change but is related to learning something about the advertised brand, such as a brand name, ad theme, or slogan. According to Krugman, when the consumer enters a purchase situation, this information may be sufficient to trigger a purchase. The consumer will then form an attitude toward the purchased brand as a result of experience with it. Thus, in the low-involvement situation the response sequence is as follows:

Message exposure under low involvement →

Shift in cognitive structure → Purchase →

Positive or negative experience → Attitude formation

Exhibit 5-8 Advertising promoting taste quality has helped Heinz dominate the ketchup market

In the low-involvement hierarchy, the consumer engages in passive learning and random information catching rather than active information seeking. The advertiser must recognize that a passive, uninterested consumer may focus more on nonmessage elements such as music, characters, symbols, and slogans or jingles than actual message content. The advertiser might capitalize on this situation by developing a catchy jingle that is stored in the consumer's mind without any active cognitive processing and becomes salient when he or she enters the actual purchase situation.

Advertisers of low-involvement products also repeat simple product claims such as a key copy point or distinctive product benefit. A study by Scott Hawkins and Stephen Hoch found that under low-involvement conditions, repetition of simple product claims increased consumers' memory of and belief in those claims.[17] They concluded that advertisers of low-involvement products might find it more profitable to pursue a heavy repetition strategy than to reach larger audiences with lengthy, more detailed messages. For example, Heinz has dominated the ketchup market for over 20 years by repeatedly telling consumers that its brand is the thickest and richest. Heinz has used a variety of advertising campaigns over the years. However, they all have communicated the same basic message that Heinz is the best and most preferred brand of ketchup (Exhibit 5-8).

Low-involvement advertising appeals prevail in much of the advertising we see for frequently purchased consumer products: Wrigley's Doublemint gum invites consumers to "Double your pleasure." Bounty paper towels claim to be the "quicker picker-upper." Oscar Mayer uses the catchy jingle, "I wish I were an Oscar Mayer wiener." Each of these appeals is designed to help consumers make an association without really attempting to formulate or change an attitude.

Another popular creative strategy used by advertisers of low-involvement products is what advertising analyst Harry McMahan calls *VIP,* or *visual image personality.*[18] Advertisers often use symbols like the Pillsbury doughboy, Morris the cat, Tony the tiger, Speedy Alka-Seltzer, and Mr. Clean to develop visual images that will lead consumers to identify and retain ads. Eveready began using the pink bunny in ads for its Energizer batteries in 1989, and he has helped sales of the brand keep going and going for over 14 years.

Implications of the Alternative Response Models

Advertising and consumer researchers recognize that not all response sequences and behaviors are explained adequately by either the traditional or the alternative response hierarchies. Advertising is just one source of information consumers use in learning about products, forming attitudes, and/or making a purchase decision. Consumers are likely to integrate information from advertising and other forms of marketing communication as well as direct experience in forming judgments about a brand. For example, a study by Robert Smith found that advertising can lessen the negative effects of an unfavorable trial experience on brand evaluations when the ad is processed before the trial. However, when a negative trial experience precedes exposure to an ad, cognitive evaluations of the ad are more negative.[19] More recent research has also shown that advertising can affect consumers' objective sensory interpretation of their experiences with a brand and what they remember about it.[20]

The various response models offer an interesting perspective on the ways consumers respond to advertising and other forms of marketing communications. They also provide insight into promotional strategies marketers might pursue in different situations. A review of these alternative models of the response process shows that the traditional standard learning model does not always apply. The notion of a highly involved consumer who engages in active information processing and learning and acts on the basis of higher-order beliefs and a well-formed attitude may be inappropriate for some types of purchases. Sometimes consumers make a purchase decision on the basis of general awareness resulting from repetitive exposure to advertising, and attitude development occurs after the purchase, if at all. The role of advertising and other forms of promotion may be to induce trial, so consumers can develop brand preferences primarily on the basis of their direct experience with the product.

From a promotional planning perspective, it is important that marketers examine the communication situation for their product or service and determine which type of response process is most likely to occur. They should analyze involvement levels and product/service differentiation as well as consumers' use of various information sources and their levels of experience with the product or service. Once the manager has determined which response sequence is most likely to operate, the integrated marketing communications program can be designed to influence the response process in favor of the company's product or service. Because this requires that marketers determine the involvement level of consumers in their target markets, we examine the concept of involvement in more detail.

Understanding Involvement

Over the past two decades, consumer behavior and advertising researchers have extensively studied the concept of involvement.[21] Involvement is viewed as a variable that can help explain how consumers process advertising information and how this information might affect message recipients. One problem that has plagued the study of involvement has been agreeing on how to define and measure it. Advertising managers must be able to determine targeted consumers' involvement levels with their products.

Some of the problems in conceptualizing and measuring involvement have been addressed in extensive review by Judith Zaichkowsky. She has noted that although there is no single precise definition of involvement, there is an underlying theme focusing on *personal relevance.*[22] Zaichkowsky developed an involvement construct that includes three antecedents, or variables proposed to precede involvement (Figure 5-6). The first is traits of the person (value system, unique experiences, needs). The second factor is characteristics of the stimulus, or differences in type of media (TV, radio, or print), content of the communication, or product class variations. The third antecedent is situational factors, such as whether one is or is not in the market for a particular product.

The various antecedents can influence the consumer's level of involvement in several ways, including the way the consumer responds to the advertising, the products being advertised, and the actual purchase decision. This involvement conceptualization shows that a variety of outcomes or behaviors can result from involvement with advertising, products, or purchase decisions.

Several other advertising planning grids have been developed that consider involvement levels as well as other factors, including response processes and motives that underlie attitude formation and subsequent brand choice.

The FCB Planning Model

An interesting approach to analyzing the communication situation comes from the work of Richard Vaughn of the Foote, Cone & Belding advertising agency. Vaughn and his associates developed an advertising planning model by building on traditional response theories such as the hierarchy of effects model and its variants and research on high and low involvement.[23] They added the dimension of thinking versus feeling processing at each involvement level by bringing in theories regarding brain specialization. The right/left brain theory suggests the left side of the brain is more capable of rational, cognitive thinking, while the right side is more visual and emotional and

Figure 5-6 Involvement concept

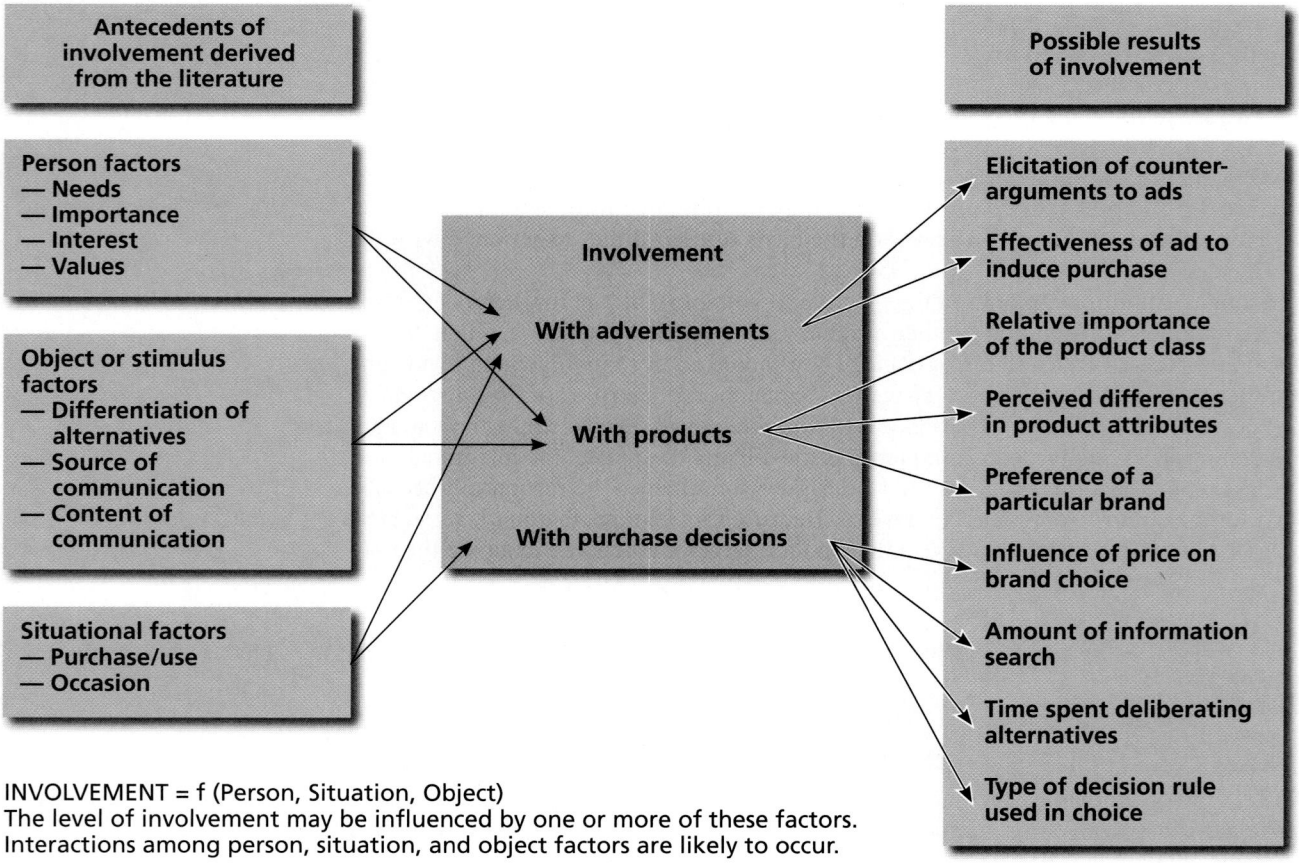

INVOLVEMENT = f (Person, Situation, Object)
The level of involvement may be influenced by one or more of these factors. Interactions among person, situation, and object factors are likely to occur.

engages more in the affective (feeling) functions. Their model, which became known as the FCB grid, delineates four primary advertising planning strategies—informative, affective, habit formation, and satisfaction—along with the most appropriate variant of the alternative response hierarchies (Figure 5-7).

Vaughn suggests that the *informative strategy* is for highly involving products and services where rational thinking and economic considerations prevail and the standard learning hierarchy is the appropriate response model. The *affective strategy* is for highly involving/feeling purchases. For these types of products, advertising should stress psychological and emotional motives such as building self-esteem or enhancing one's ego or self-image.

The *habit formation strategy* is for low-involvement/thinking products with such routinized behavior patterns that learning occurs most often after a trial purchase. The response process for these products is consistent with a behavioristic learning-by-doing model (remember our discussion of operant conditioning in Chapter 4?). The *self-satisfaction strategy* is for low-involvement/feeling products where appeals to sensory pleasures and social motives are important. Again, the do → feel or do → learn hierarchy is operating, since product experience is an important part of the learning process. Vaughn acknowledges that some minimal level of awareness (passive learning) may precede purchase of both types of low-involvement products, but deeper, active learning is not necessary. This is consistent with the low-involvement hierarchy discussed earlier (learn → do → feel).

The FCB grid provides a useful way for those involved in the advertising planning process, such as creative specialists, to analyze consumer–product relationships and develop appropriate promotional strategies. Consumer research can be used to determine how consumers perceive products or brands on the involvement and thinking/feeling dimensions.[24] This information can then be used to develop effective creative options such as using rational versus emotional appeals, increasing involvement levels, or even getting consumers to evaluate a think-type product on the basis of feelings. IMC Perspective 5-3 discusses how Whirlpool has used creative advertising to get women to develop an emotional connection to its appliances.

	Thinking	Feeling
High involvement	**1. Informative (thinker)** Car–house–furnishings–new products model: Learn–feel–do (economic?) **Possible implications** Test: Recall Diagnostics Media: Long copy format Reflective vehicles Creative: Specific information Demonstration	**2. Affective (feeler)** Jewelry–cosmetics–fashion apparel–motorcycles model: Feel–learn–do (psychological?) **Possible implications** Test: Attitude change Emotional arousal Media: Large space Image specials Creative: Executional Impact
Low involvement	**3. Habit formation (doer)** Food–household items model: Do–learn–feel (responsive?) **Possible implications** Test: Sales Media: Small space ads 10-second I.D.s Radio; POS Creative: Reminder	**4. Self-satisfaction (reactor)** Cigarettes–liquor–candy model: Do–feel–learn (social?) **Possible implications** Test: Sales Media: Billboards Newspapers POS Creative: Attention

Figure 5-7 The Foote, Cone & Belding (FCB) grid

IMC PERSPECTIVE 5-3

Whirlpool Connects with 21st-Century Women

Household appliances are a product category where the advertising has traditionally been pretty bland, with most ads appealing to consumers' rational, functional motives. Television commercials generally would show the capacity of a refrigerator, explain how a washer or dryer works, or tout their reliability; while print ads would feature a shot of the appliance and give a detailed description of how it functions. For example, among the most memorable appliance ads are those from the campaign featuring the Maytag repairman who would wait in vain for a repair call. The campaign was created more than 30 years ago, and the lonely Maytag repairman is still waiting for the phone to ring.

In recent years appliance companies have been focusing on form as well as function and have been touting the design of their products as much as their functionality in their ads. However, one company that has taken a very unique approach to its advertising is Whirlpool, whose "Just Imagine" campaign features Household Goddesses—five ethereal female figures who use water, fire, or air to take control of their environments while promoting various Whirlpool appliances. The campaign is designed to connect with the modern-day "supermoms," working women between the ages of 25 and 54 with children. These women's homes are very important to them; the women are challenged, yet capable of handling a very demanding and busy lifestyle, and they want control of their lives and acknowledgment for all they do and for being very capable. They set new standards and appreciate beauty in their environments. They do not give appliances a great deal of thought until there is a moment of need, such as a broken appliance or a home renovation. Innovation, style, and time saving are all important factors to these women.

The idea for the "Just Imagine" campaign originated in the late 90s in Europe, where Whirlpool was eager to build its brand name and capture a larger share of the appliance market, having acquired the appliance division of the Dutch firm Philips Electronics. The campaign connected well with women in Europe, so in 1999 Whirlpool and its French agency Publicis decided to adapt it to women in the U.S. market. However, before bringing the campaign to the States, Whirlpool conducted more than 20 focus groups with women throughout the country to test their reaction to the goddesses.

According to Whirlpool's manager of brand communication, the ads with the goddesses celebrate the growing power of women in the 21st century. They are aimed at striking an emotional cord with modern-day women, showing them as strong females in control of their environments who can be made even stronger through the latest Whirlpool technology. The mythical figures in the ads include a blue-skinned ice diva who represents the Whirlpool Conquest refrigerator, a silken-robed water nymph who appears in commercials for the Catalyst washer, a heat maiden in cascading red robes who promotes the Senson and Duet dryers, a fire-breathing goddess who helps sell the Speed Cook range, and a flying blonde clean-air angel who extols the virtues of Whirlpool's dehumidifiers and air-conditioners. The goddesses promote many of the innovative features found on Whirlpool appliances, such as a dryer that gently dries clothes in the time it takes to wash them, a washing machine that does not require pretreating because concentrated water and detergent spray through clothes before they are washed, and a refrigerator with more space inside.

The goal of the "Just Imagine" campaign is to use the stylish and dramatic commercials to get consumers to take notice of Whirlpool appliances and make them feel the brand is in tune with their changing needs and values and thus has something more to offer than competing brands. In addition to being in the television commercials, the goddesses appear in print ads, on the Whirlpool website, on company brochures, on billboards on the side of the company's trucks, and in point-of-purchase displays for local retailers. The campaign is the biggest in the appliance maker's history. To many women, using a washing machine or dryer means nothing more than cleaning clothes. However, Whirlpool hopes this campaign will help them feel they are taking control of their lives when they use its appliances.

Sources: "Whirlpool's Worship-Worthy Goddess," *Brand Marketing,* June 2000, p. 33; Katheryn Dranhold, "Whirlpool Conjures Up Appliance Divas," *The Wall Street Journal,* Apr. 27, 2000, p. B14.

Cognitive Processing of Communications

The hierarchical response models were for many years the primary focus of approaches for studying the receivers' responses to marketing communications. Attention centered on identifying relationships between specific controllable variables (such as source and message factors) and outcome or response variables (such as attention, comprehension, attitudes, and purchase intentions). This approach has been criticized on a number of fronts, including its black-box nature, since it can't explain what is causing these reactions.[25] In response to these concerns, researchers began trying to understand the nature of cognitive reactions to persuasive messages. Several approaches have been developed to examine the nature of consumers' cognitive processing of advertising messages.

The Cognitive Response Approach

One of the most widely used methods for examining consumers' cognitive processing of advertising messages is assessment of their **cognitive responses,** the thoughts that occur to them while reading, viewing, and/or hearing a communication.[26] These thoughts are generally measured by having consumers write down or verbally report their reactions to a message. The assumption is that these thoughts reflect the recipient's cognitive processes or reactions and help shape ultimate acceptance or rejection of the message.

The cognitive response approach has been widely used in research by both academicians and advertising practitioners. Its focus has been to determine the types of responses evoked by an advertising message and how these responses relate to attitudes toward the ad, brand attitudes, and purchase intentions. Figure 5-8 depicts the three basic categories of cognitive responses researchers have identified—product/message, source-oriented, and ad execution thoughts—and how they may relate to attitudes and intentions.

Exhibit 5-9 Consumers often generate support arguments in response to ads for quality products

Product/Message Thoughts

The first category of thoughts comprises those directed at the product or service and/or the claims being made in the communication. Much attention has focused on two particular types of responses, counterarguments and support arguments.

Counterarguments are thoughts the recipient has that are opposed to the position taken in the message. For example, consider the ad for Ultra Tide shown in Exhibit 5-9. A consumer may express disbelief or disapproval of a claim made in an ad. ("I don't believe that any detergent could get that stain out!") Other consumers who see this ad may generate **support arguments,** or thoughts that affirm the claims made in the message. ("Ultra Tide looks like a really good product—I think I'll try it.")

Figure 5-8 A model of cognitive response

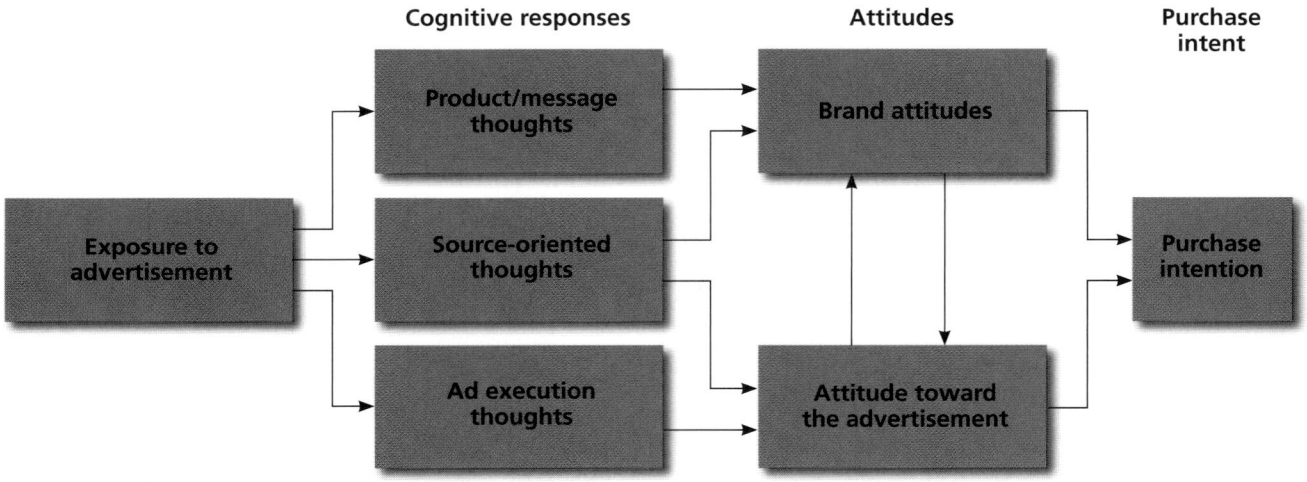

The likelihood of counterarguing is greater when the message makes claims that oppose the receiver's beliefs. For example, a consumer viewing a commercial that attacks a favorite brand is likely to engage in counterarguing. Counterarguments relate negatively to message acceptance; the more the receiver counterargues, the less likely he or she is to accept the position advocated in the message.[27] Support arguments, on the other hand, relate positively to message acceptance. Thus, the marketer should develop ads or other promotional messages that minimize counterarguing and encourage support arguments.

Source-Oriented Thoughts

A second category of cognitive responses is directed at the source of the communication. One of the most important types of responses in this category is **source derogations,** or negative thoughts about the spokesperson or organization making the claims. Such thoughts generally lead to a reduction in message acceptance. If consumers find a particular spokesperson annoying or untrustworthy, they are less likely to accept what this source has to say.

Of course, source-related thoughts are not always negative. Receivers who react favorably to the source generate favorable thoughts, or **source bolsters.** As you would expect, most advertisers attempt to hire spokespeople their target audience likes so as to carry this effect over to the message. Considerations involved in choosing an appropriate source or spokesperson will be discussed in Chapter 6.

Ad Execution Thoughts

The third category of cognitive responses shown in Figure 5-8 consists of the individual's thoughts about the ad itself. Many of the thoughts receivers have when reading or viewing an ad do not concern the product and/or message claims directly. Rather, they are affective reactions representing the consumer's feelings toward the ad. These thoughts may include reactions to ad execution factors such as the creativity of the ad, the quality of the visual effects, colors, and voice tones. **Ad execution-related thoughts** can be either favorable or unfavorable. They are important because of their effect on attitudes toward the advertisement as well as the brand.

In recent years, much attention has focused on consumers' affective reactions to ads, especially TV commercials.[28] **Attitude toward the ad** (A → ad) represents the receivers' feelings of favorability or unfavorability toward the ad. Advertisers are interested in consumers' reactions to the ad because they know that affective reactions are an important determinant of advertising effectiveness, since these reactions may be transferred to the brand itself or directly influence purchase intentions. One study found that people who enjoy a commercial are twice as likely as those who are neutral toward it to be convinced that the brand is the best.[29]

Consumers' feelings about the ad may be just as important as their attitudes toward the brand (if not more so) in determining an ad's effectiveness.[30] The importance of affective reactions and feelings generated by the ad depend on several factors, among them the nature of the ad and the type of processing engaged in by the receiver.[31] Many advertisers now use emotional ads designed to evoke feelings and affective reactions as the basis of their creative strategy. The success of this strategy depends in part on the consumers' involvement with the brand and their likelihood of attending to and processing the message.

We end our analysis of the receiver by examining a model that integrates some of the factors that may account for different types and levels of cognitive processing of a message.

The Elaboration Likelihood Model

Differences in the ways consumers process and respond to persuasive messages are addressed in the **elaboration likelihood model (ELM)** of persuasion, shown in Figure 5-9.[32] The ELM was devised by Richard Petty and John Cacioppo to explain the process by which persuasive communications (such as ads) lead to persuasion by influencing *attitudes.* According to this model, the attitude formation or change process depends on the amount and nature of *elaboration,* or processing, of relevant information that occurs in response to a persuasive message. High elaboration means the receiver engages in careful consideration, thinking, and evaluation of the informa-

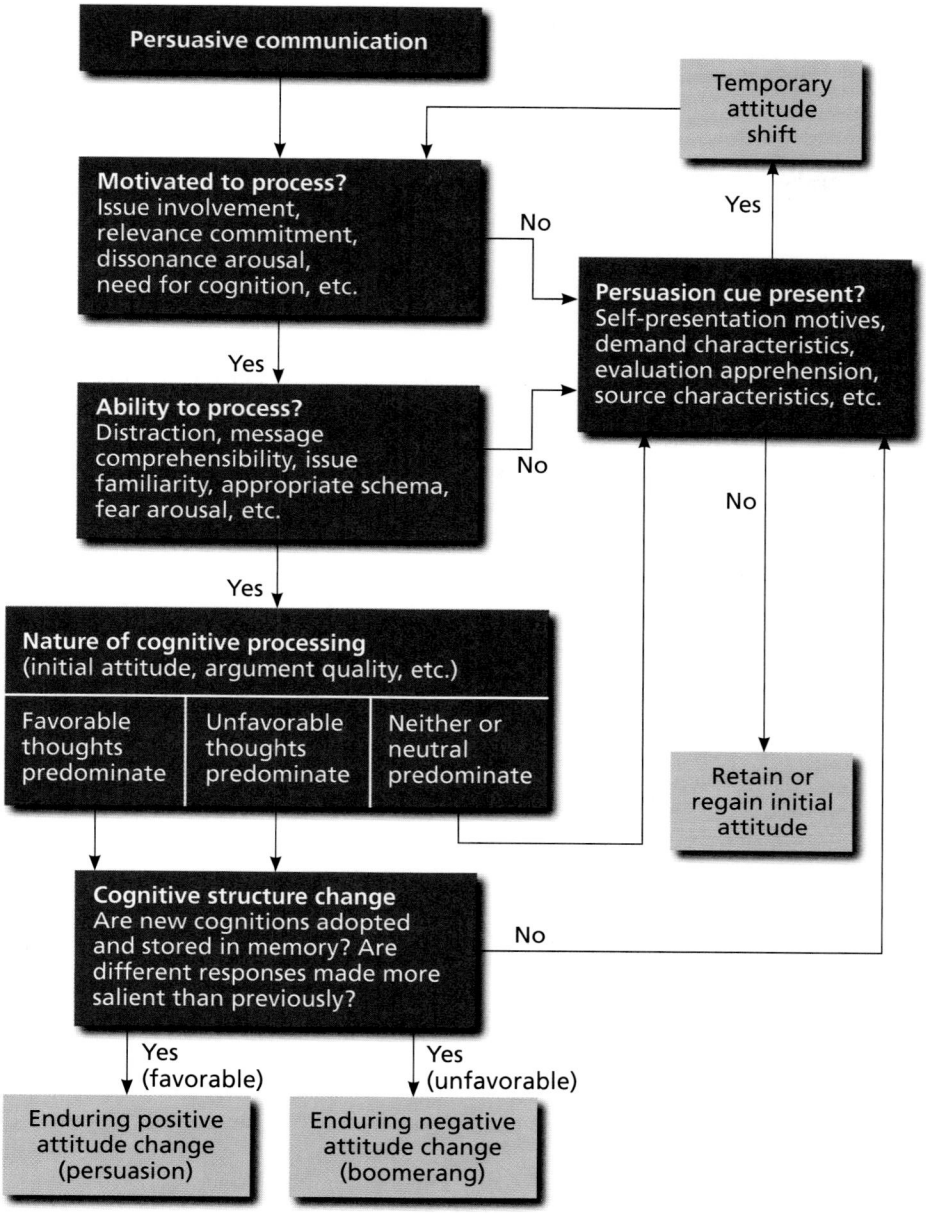

Figure 5-9 The elaboration likelihood model of persuasion

tion or arguments contained in the message. Low elaboration occurs when the receiver does not engage in active information processing or thinking but rather makes inferences about the position being advocated in the message on the basis of simple positive or negative cues.

The ELM shows that elaboration likelihood is a function of two elements, motivation and ability to process the message. *Motivation* to process the message depends on such factors as involvement, personal relevance, and individuals' needs and arousal levels. *Ability* depends on the individual's knowledge, intellectual capacity, and opportunity to process the message. For example, an individual viewing a humorous commercial or one containing an attractive model may be distracted from processing the information about the product.

According to the ELM, there are two basic routes to persuasion or attitude change. Under the **central route to persuasion,** the receiver is viewed as a very active, involved participant in the communication process whose ability and motivation to attend, comprehend, and evaluate messages are high. When central processing of an advertising message occurs, the consumer pays close attention to message content and scrutinizes the message arguments. A high level of cognitive response activity or processing occurs,

and the ad's ability to persuade the receiver depends primarily on the receiver's evaluation of the quality of the arguments presented. Predominantly favorable cognitive responses (support arguments and source bolsters) lead to favorable changes in cognitive structure, which lead to positive attitude change, or persuasion.

Conversely, if the cognitive processing is predominantly unfavorable and results in counterarguments and/or source derogations, the changes in cognitive structure are unfavorable and *boomerang,* or result in negative attitude change. Attitude change that occurs through central processing is relatively enduring and should resist subsequent efforts to change it.

Under the **peripheral route to persuasion,** shown on the right side of Figure 5-9, the receiver is viewed as lacking the motivation or ability to process information and is not likely to engage in detailed cognitive processing. Rather than evaluating the information presented in the message, the receiver relies on peripheral cues that may be incidental to the main arguments. The receiver's reaction to the message depends on how he or she evaluates these peripheral cues.

The consumer may use several types of peripheral cues or cognitive shortcuts rather than carefully evaluating the message arguments presented in an advertisement.[33] Favorable attitudes may be formed if the endorser in the ad is viewed as an expert or is attractive and/or likable or if the consumer likes certain executional aspects of the ad such as the way it is made, the music, or the imagery. Notice how the ad in Exhibit 5-10 for Maxfli golf balls contains several positive peripheral cues, including a popular celebrity endorser (golfer Fred Couples) and excellent visual imagery. These cues might help consumers form a positive attitude toward the brand even if they do not process the message portion of the ad.

Peripheral cues can also lead to rejection of a message. For example, ads that advocate extreme positions, use endorsers who are not well liked or have credibility problems, or are not executed well (such as low-budget ads for local retailers) may be rejected without any consideration of their information or message arguments. As shown in Figure 5-9, the ELM views attitudes resulting from peripheral processing as temporary. So favorable attitudes must be maintained by continual exposure to the peripheral cues, such as through repetitive advertising.

Exhibit 5-10 This ad contains peripheral cues, most notably a celebrity endorser

Implications of the ELM

The elaboration likelihood model has important implications for marketing communications, particularly with respect to involvement. For example, if the involvement level of consumers in the target audience is high, an ad or sales presentation should contain strong arguments that are difficult for the message recipient to refute or counterargue. If the involvement level of the target audience is low, peripheral cues may be more important than detailed message arguments.

An interesting test of the ELM showed that the effectiveness of a celebrity endorser in an ad depends on the receiver's involvement level.[34] When involvement was low, a celebrity endorser had a significant effect on attitudes. When the receiver's involvement was high, however, the use of a celebrity had no effect on brand attitudes; the quality of the arguments used in the ad was more important.

The explanation given for these findings was that a celebrity may serve as a peripheral cue in the low-involvement situation, allowing the receiver to develop favorable attitudes based on feelings toward the source rather than engaging in extensive processing of the message. A highly involved consumer, however, engages in more detailed central processing of the message content. The quality of the message claims becomes more important than the identity of the endorser.

The ELM suggests that the most effective type of message depends on the route to persuasion the consumer follows. Many marketers recognize that involvement levels are low for their product categories and consumers are not motivated to process advertising messages in any detail. That's why marketers of low-involvement products often rely on creative tactics that emphasize peripheral cues

and use repetitive advertising to create and maintain favorable attitudes toward their brand.

Summarizing the Response Process and the Effects of Advertising

As you have seen from our analysis of the receiver, the process consumers go through in responding to marketing communications can be viewed from a number of perspectives. Vakratsas and Ambler recently reviewed more than 250 journal articles and books in an effort to better understand how advertising works and affects the consumer.[35] On the basis of their review of these studies, they concluded that although effects hierarchies have been actively employed for nearly 100 years, there is little support for the concept of a hierarchy of effects in the sense of temporal sequence. They note that in trying to understand the response process and the manner in which advertising works, there are three critical intermediate effects between advertising and purchase (Figure 5-10). These include *cognition,* the "thinking" dimension of a person's response; *affect,* the "feeling" dimension; and *experience,* which is a feedback dimension based on the outcomes of product purchasing and usage. They conclude that individual responses to advertising are mediated or filtered by factors such as motivation and ability to process information, which can radically alter or change the individual's response to advertising. They suggest that the effects of advertising should be evaluated using these three dimensions, with some intermediate variables being more important than others, depending on factors such as the product category, stage of the product life cycle, target audience, competition, and impact of other marketing-mix components.

Other researchers have been critical of the hierarchy models as well. For example, Hall argues that advertisers need to move away from explicit and implicit reliance on hierarchical models of advertising effects and develop models that place affect and experience at the center of the advertising process.[36] The implication of these criticisms is that marketers should focus on cognition, affect, and experience as critical variables that advertising may affect. However, they should not assume a particular sequence of responses but, rather, engage in research and analysis to better understand how advertising and other forms of promotion may affect these intermediate variables in various product/market situations.

Those responsible for planning the IMC program need to learn as much as possible about their target audience and how it may respond to advertising, along with other forms of marketing communication. For example, William Weilbacher has noted that

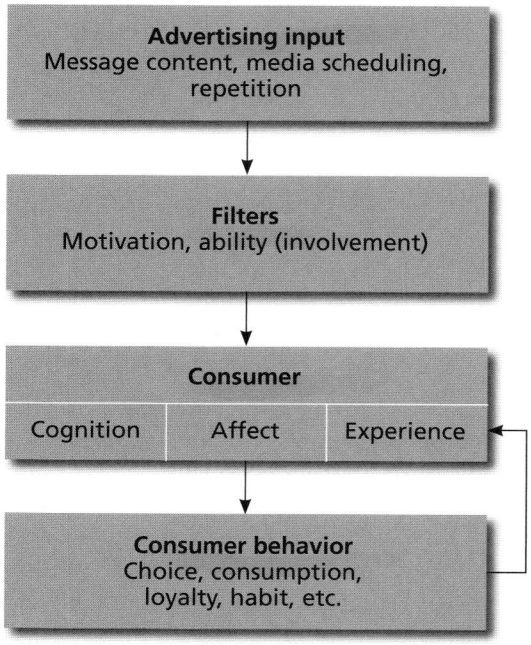

Figure 5-10 A framework for studying how advertising works

marketing communications programs include more than just advertising.[37] Consumers are continually immersed in brand-sponsored communications that include public relations, a broad range of sales promotion activities, websites, direct marketing, event sponsorships, movie and TV show product placements, and other forms of marketing communication. He argues that hierarchy models must move beyond just explaining the effects of advertising and consider how, and with what effects, consumers synthesize information from all the various integrated marketing communications activities for a brand. The various communication models presented in this chapter provide insight into how consumers may process and respond to persuasive messages and hopefully help marketers make better decisions in planning and implementing their integrated marketing communications programs.

Summary

The function of all elements of the promotional mix is to communicate, so promotional planners must understand the communication process. This process can be very complex; successful marketing communications depend on a number of factors, including the nature of the message, the audience's interpretation of it, and the environment in which it is received. For effective communication to occur, the sender must encode a message in such a way that it will be decoded by the receiver in the intended manner. Feedback from the receiver helps the sender determine whether proper decoding has occurred or whether noise has interfered with the communication process.

Promotional planning begins with the receiver or target audience, as marketers must understand how the audience is likely to respond to various sources of communication or types of messages. For promotional planning, the receiver can be analyzed with respect to both its composition (i.e., individual, group, or mass audiences) and the response process it goes through. Different orderings of the traditional response hierarchy include the standard learning, dissonance/attribution, and low-involvement models. The information response model integrates concepts from both the high- and low-involvement response hierarchy perspectives and recognizes the effects of direct experience with a product.

The cognitive response approach examines the thoughts evoked by a message and how they shape the receiver's ultimate acceptance or rejection of the communication. The elaboration likelihood model of attitude formation and change recognizes two forms of message processing, the central and peripheral routes to persuasion, which are a function of the receiver's motivation and ability to process a message. There are three critical intermediate effects between advertising and purchase including cognition, affect, and experience. Those responsible for planning the IMC program should learn as much as possible about their target audience and how it may respond to advertising and other forms of marketing communications.

Key Terms

communication, 139
source, 141
encoding, 141
message, 141
semiotics, 142
channel, 143
mass media, 143
receiver, 143
decoding, 143
field of experience, 143
noise, 145
response, 145
feedback, 145
AIDA model, 147
hierarchy of effects model, 148
innovation adoption model, 148
information processing model, 148
standard learning model, 150
dissonance/attribution model, 151
low-involvement hierarchy, 152
cognitive responses, 157
counterarguments, 157
support arguments, 157
source derogations, 158
source bolsters, 158
ad execution-related thoughts, 158
attitude toward the ad, 158
elaboration likelihood model (ELM), 158
central route to persuasion, 159
peripheral route to persuasion, 160

Discussion Questions

1. The opening vignette to the chapter discusses how EDS developed a new branding and positioning campaign around the "EDS Solved" theme. Analyze the decision by EDS to use high profile commercials such as "Cat Herders," "Running with the Squirrels," and the "Airplane" spots as part of its efforts to remake its identity and change the image of the company.

2. Discuss the challenges marketers face as they develop advertisements and other forms of marketing communications for young Hispanics. Do you think marketers should advertise to bilingual Hispanics teens in English or Spanish?

3. What is meant by encoding and decoding? Discuss how these two processes differ for radio versus television commercials.

4. Discuss how semiotics can be of value to the field of integrated marketing communications. Select a marketing stimulus such as an advertisement, package, or other relevant marketing symbol and conduct a semiotic analysis of it such as the one shown in Exhibit 5-3.

5. The study discussed in IMC Perspective 5-2 suggests that ageism is a problem in the advertising business. Do you think young creative professionals can connect with and create ads that are effective for communicating with the mature market? What are some things that might be done to ensure that agencies do create ads that are relevant to older consumers?

6. Discuss how a company introducing an innovative new product might use the innovation adoption model in planning its ingegrated marketing communications program.

7. Assume that you are the marketing communications manager for a brand of paper towels. Discuss how the low-involvement hierarchy could be of value in developing an advertising and promotion strategy for this brand.

8. Evaluate the "Just Imagine" campaign for Whirlpool appliances discussed in IMC Perspective 5-3. Do you think this campaign will be effective in connecting with the working women Whirlpool is targeting? Why or why not?

9. Find an example of a print ad and evaluate it using the cognitive response model shown in Figure 5-8. Identify the specific types of cognitive responses that the ad might elicit from consumers and discuss why they might occur.

10. Explain what is meant by a central versus peripheral route to persuasion and the factors that would determine when each might be used by consumers in response to an advertisement.

Source, Message, and Channel Factors

Chapter Objectives

1. To study the major variables in the communication system and how they influence consumers' processing of promotional messages.
2. To examine the considerations involved in selecting a source or communicator of a promotional message.
3. To examine different types of message structures and appeals that can be used to develop a promotional message.
4. To consider how the channel or medium used to deliver a promotional message influences the communication process.

Bad Boys Become Pitchmen for Athletic Shoes

Athletic-shoe companies have been using popular athletes to endorse their products and serve as advertising pitchmen for years. Traditionally these companies would stay away from controversial athletes and sign players with a clean-cut image who could create a favorable association for the product as well as the company. Superstars such as Michael Jordan, Derek Jeter, Grant Hill, and Kobe Bryant have been used by companies such as Nike, Fila, and Adidas because of their likable personalities and their image as positive role models. However, in recent years many athletic-shoe marketers have been moving away from athletes with squeaky-clean images and hiring spokespersons who are known as much for their alleged misdeeds off the court or field as for their accomplishments on it.

Among the first of the "bad-boy" pitchmen was former basketball star Charles Barkley, who appeared in a Nike commercial in the mid-90s in which he glowered at the camera and declared, "I am not a role model." Basketball star Dennis Rodman was also able to parlay his irreverent and rebellious image into an endorsement contract with Nike, as well as a number of other companies, although his antics eventually became too much for most of these companies. The new generation of bad-boy pitchmen includes NBA stars such as Allan Iverson and Lattrell Sprewell as well as retired athletes such as baseball star Pete Rose and former Oakland Raider football players Ken Stabler and Jack Tatum.

Iverson, who came into the NBA in 1996 as a first-round draft pick, is among the best known as well as the most controversial of the new generation of endorsers. The Philadelphia 76ers star is viewed by many as the poster boy for a generation of unruly young players who many feel are damaging the image of professional sports: a rap-loving, inner-city type with too many tattoos, a closet full of gang wear, and a history of run-ins with the law and the league. Coca-Cola let a one-year deal with him lapse after he was arrested in 1997 on gun and drug charges and placed on probation. However, Iverson led the 76ers to the NBA finals in 2001 and was named the league's most valuable player, and he began changing his image into a model of courage, toughness, caring, and humility. In December 2001, Reebok signed Iverson to a lifetime contract guaranteeing him he would remain a Reebok endorser throughout his pro career. The company began developing an extensive line of Iverson's signature I-3 products as well as extensively promoting his signature shoe, the Answer, by increasing his role in print and TV ads. However, just seven months later Iverson was charged with multiple felonies after he allegedly went on a gun-wielding rampage in pursuit of his wife. Most of the charges were later dropped and Reebok has expressed unwavering support for Iverson.

Upstart basketball sneaker and apparel brand And 1 also decided to go the bad-boy route by hiring New York Knicks star Latrell Sprewell to

endorse its shoes. Sprewell became one of the most vilified athletes in sports a few years ago when he choked and assaulted his Golden State Warrior's coach after becoming upset with his sarcasm during a practice. And 1 featured Sprewell in a controversial TV commercial showing a tight spot of him getting his hair braided. In the spot, Sprewell says, "People say I'm what's wrong with the sport. I say I'm a three-time NBA All-Star. I say I'm the American dream." Jay Gilbert, And 1's vice president of marketing, defended the spot by stating that it brings the company's target market closer to Latrell and the And 1 brand. He noted, "It will make a lot of people uncomfortable, but he represents the dream to the ballplayers that are our core consumers."

Urban sports brand Pony decided to go a slightly different route in using bad-boy athletes as endorsers with its "Why Not?" campaign, which addresses why three athletes have not been named to the Hall of Fame in their respective sports. The ads feature baseball legend Pete Rose, who was banned from the sport for gambling; former NFL quarterback Kenny "the Snake" Stabler; and Jack "the Assassin" Tatum, the former Oakland Raider who was known for his crushing hits while playing on the team in the 1970s, including one that paralyzed an opposing player. Rose appears in three ads featuring the question "Why isn't Pete Rose in the Hall of Fame?" while the ad featuring Tatum in Pony attire asks, "Why is the Assassin not in the Hall of Fame?"

So what's behind the decisions by these companies to use bad-boy pitchmen? One explanation is that athletic-shoe companies are trying to reach young, trendsetting urban males who identify with the rebellious and scandalous image these athletes represent. One sports marketing expert notes that when a company attaches its brand to these antiheroes. "it's a way of saying we're in touch with someone who is street real." Gilbert of And 1 argues that personalities like Iverson and Sprewell can slowly change society and notes that "they really force people to look at them without blinking and say, 'Can you accept this?'" Perhaps the ultimate reason companies use such spokespersons is that they help the firms sell their shoes and apparel. Iverson's shoe line has consistently been among the top two or three basketball sneakers and his 76ers jersey is the NBA's top seller. Even after his most recent arrest, sales of Reebok products continued to increase. In the current market for athletic shoes, it appears that the nice guys do finish last and it is the bad boys who are winning the endorsement game.

Sources: Rebecca Winters, "Bad-Boy Pitchmen," *Time,* Aug. 19, 2002, p. 18; Hilary Cassidy, "Pete Rose, Ken "Snake" Stabler Star in Pony Ads," *Adweek,* May 14, 2002; Stefan Fatsis, "Can Iverson Pitch to the Mainstream?" *The Wall Street Journal,* June 8, 2001, pp. B1, 4.

In this chapter, we analyze the major variables in the communication system: the source, the message, and the channel. We examine the characteristics of sources, how they influence reactions to promotional messages, and why one type of communicator is more effective than another. We then focus on the message itself and how structure and type of appeal influence its effectiveness. Finally, we consider how factors related to the channel or medium affect the communication process.

Promotional Planning through the Persuasion Matrix

To develop an effective advertising and promotional campaign, a firm must select the right spokesperson to deliver a compelling message through appropriate channels or media. Source, message, and channel factors are controllable elements in the communications model. The **persuasion matrix** (Figure 6-1) helps marketers see how each controllable element interacts with the consumer's response process.[1] The matrix has two sets of variables. *Independent variables* are the controllable components of the communication process, outlined in Chapter 5; *dependent*

variables are the steps a receiver goes through in being persuaded. Marketers can choose the person or source who delivers the message, the type of message appeal used, and the channel or medium. And although they can't control the receiver, they can select their target audience. The destination variable is included because the initial message recipient may pass on information to others, such as friends or associates, through word of mouth.

Promotional planners need to know how decisions about each independent variable influence the stages of the response hierarchy so that they don't enhance one stage at the expense of another. A humorous message may gain attention but result in decreased comprehension if consumers fail to process its content. Many ads that use humor, sexual appeals, or celebrities capture consumers' attention but result in poor recall of the brand name or message. The following examples, which correspond to the numbers in Figure 6-1, illustrate decisions that can be evaluated with the persuasion matrix.

1. *Receiver/comprehension: Can the receiver comprehend the ad?* Marketers must know their target market to make their messages clear and understandable. A less educated person may have more difficulty interpreting a complicated message. Jargon may be unfamiliar to some receivers. The more marketers know about the target market, the more they see which words, symbols, and expressions their customers understand.

2. *Channel/presentation: Which media will increase presentation?* A top-rated, prime-time TV program is seen by nearly 12 million households each week. *TV Guide* and *Reader's Digest* reach nearly 12 million homes with each issue. But the important point is how well they reach the marketer's target audience. CNN's financial show *Lou Dobbs Moneyline* reaches only around a million viewers each weekday evening, but its audience consists mostly of upscale businesspeople who are prime prospects for expensive cars, financial services, and business-related products.

3. *Message/yielding: What type of message will create favorable attitudes or feelings?* Marketers generally try to create agreeable messages that lead to positive feelings toward the product or service. Humorous messages often put consumers in a good mood and evoke positive feelings that may become associated with the brand being advertised. Music adds emotion that makes consumers more receptive to the message. Many advertisers use explicit sexual appeals designed to arouse consumers

Figure 6-1 The persuasion matrix

	Independent variables: The communication components				
Dependent variables: Steps in being persuaded	Source	Message	Channel	Receiver	Destination
Message presentation			(2)		
Attention	(4)				
Comprehension				(1)	
Yielding		(3)			
Retention					
Behavior					

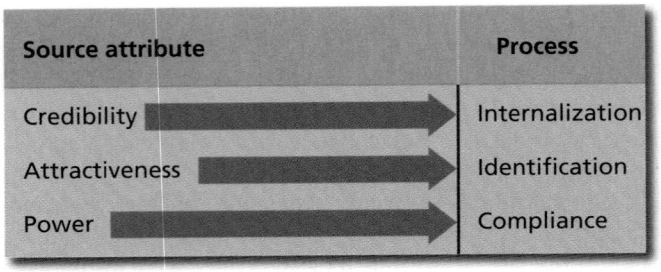

Figure 6-2 Source attributes and receiver processing modes

or suggest they can enhance their attractiveness to the opposite sex. Some marketers compare their brands to the competition.

4. *Source/attention: Who will be effective in getting consumers' attention?* The large number of ads we are bombarded with every day makes it difficult for advertisers to break through the clutter. Marketers deal with this problem by using sources who will attract the target audience's attention—actors, athletes, rock stars, or attractive models.

Source Factors

The source component is a multifaceted concept. When Tiger Woods appears in a commercial for Nike, is the source Woods himself, the company, or some combination of the two? And, of course, consumers get information from friends, relatives, and neighbors; in fact, personal sources may be the most influential factor in a purchase decision. Word-of-mouth information transmitted from one individual to another is often perceived as more reliable and trustworthy than that received through more formal marketing channels such as advertising. As was discussed in Chapter 1, marketers are using buzz and stealth marketing methods to generate favorable word-of-mouth discussion and recommendations for their products and services.[2]

We use the term **source** to mean the person involved in communicating a marketing message, either directly or indirectly. A *direct source* is a spokesperson who delivers a message and/or demonstrates a product or service, like tennis star Andre Agassi who endorses Head tennis rackets in Exhibit 6-1. An *indirect source,* say, a model, doesn't actually deliver a message but draws attention to and/or enhances the appearance of the ad. Some ads use neither a direct nor an indirect source; the source is the organization with the message to communicate. Since most research focuses on individuals as a message source, our examination of source factors follows this approach.

Exhibit 6-1 Tennis star Andre Agassi serves as a spokesperson for Head

Companies are very careful when selecting individuals to deliver their selling messages. Many firms spend huge sums of money for a specific person to endorse their product or company. They also spend millions recruiting, selecting, and training salespeople to represent the company and deliver sales presentations. They recognize that the characteristics of the source affect the sales and advertising message.

Marketers try to select individuals whose traits will maximize message influence. The source may be knowledgeable, popular, and/or physically attractive; typify the target audience; or have the power to reward or punish the receiver in some manner. Herbert Kelman developed three basic categories of source attributes: credibility, attractiveness, and power.[3] Each influences the recipient's attitude or behavior through a different process (see Figure 6-2).

Source Credibility

Credibility is the extent to which the recipient sees the source as having relevant knowledge, skill, or experience and trusts the source to give unbiased, objective information. There are two important dimensions to credibility, expertise and trustworthiness.

A communicator seen as knowledgeable—someone with expertise—is more persuasive than one with less expertise. But the source also has to be trustworthy—honest, ethical, and believable. The influence of a knowledgeable source will be lessened if audience members think he or she is biased or has underlying personal motives for advocating a position (such as being paid to endorse a product).

One of the most reliable effects found in communications research is that expert and/or trustworthy sources are more persuasive than sources who are less expert or trustworthy.[4] Information from a credible source influences beliefs, opinions, attitudes, and/or behavior through a process known as **internalization,** which occurs when the receiver adopts the opinion of the credible communicator since he or she believes information from this source is accurate. Once the receiver internalizes an opinion or attitude, it becomes integrated into his or her belief system and may be maintained even after the source of the message is forgotten.

A highly credible communicator is particularly important when message recipients have a negative position toward the product, service, company, or issue being promoted, because the credible source is likely to inhibit counterarguments. As discussed in Chapter 5, reduced counterarguing should result in greater message acceptance and persuasion.

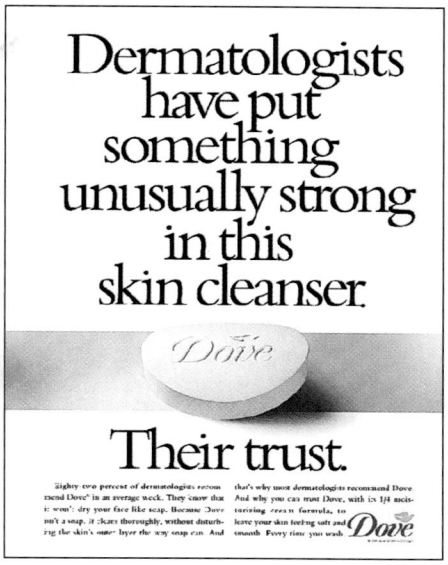

Exhibit 6-2 Dove promotes the fact that it is recommended by experts in skin care

Applying Expertise Because attitudes and opinions developed through an internalization process become part of the individual's belief system, marketers want to use communicators with high credibility. Companies use a variety of techniques to convey source expertise. Sales personnel are trained in the product line, which increases customers' perceptions of their expertise. Marketers of highly technical products recruit sales reps with specialized technical backgrounds in engineering, computer science, and other areas to ensure their expertise.

Spokespeople are often chosen because of their knowledge, experience, and expertise in a particular product or service area. Endorsements from individuals or groups recognized as experts, such as doctors or dentists, are also common in advertising (Exhibit 6-2). The importance of using expert sources was shown in a study by Roobina Ohanian, who found that the perceived expertise of celebrity endorsers was more important in explaining purchase intentions than their attractiveness or trustworthiness. She suggests that celebrity spokespeople are most effective when they are knowledgeable, experienced, and qualified to talk about the product they are endorsing.[5]

Applying Trustworthiness While expertise is important, the target audience must also find the source believable. Finding celebrities or other figures with a trustworthy image is often difficult. Many trustworthy public figures hesitate to endorse products because of the potential impact on their reputation and image. It has been suggested that former CBS news anchor Walter Cronkite, who has repeatedly been rated one of the most trusted people in America, could command millions of dollars as a product spokesperson. Global Perspective 6-1 discusses how some American celebrities protect their image by endorsing products in Japan rather than in the United States.

Advertisers use various techniques to increase the perception that their sources are trustworthy. Hidden cameras are used to show that the consumer is not a paid spokesperson and is making an objective evaluation of the product. Disguised brands are compared. (Of course, the sponsor's brand always performs better than the consumer's regular brand, and he or she is always surprised.) Advertisers also use the overheard-conversation technique to enhance trustworthiness. This involves creating a situation in a commercial where a person is shown overhearing a conversation in which favorable claims are made about a product or service. Most consumers are skeptical of these techniques, so they may have limited value in enhancing perceptions of an advertiser's credibility.

Marketers can also deal with the source-trustworthiness issue by using other IMC tools such as publicity. Information received from sources such as newscasters is often very influential because these individuals are perceived as unbiased and thus more

GLOBAL PERSPECTIVE 6-1

Celebrities Sell Out—But Only in Japan

Many American celebrities make huge sums of money endorsing products and serving as advertising spokespeople. Other big stars won't appear in ads because they don't want fans to think they've sold out. But many celebrities who resist the temptation to cash in on their fame in the United States are only too happy to appear in ads in foreign countries. And nowhere are ads starring American celebrities more prevalent than in Japan. Even the rich and famous have trouble saying no to Japanese advertisers who will pay them between $1 million and $3 million for a few hours' work to make 15- to 30-second spots that their Western fans across the Pacific will never see.

Megastars like Meg Ryan, Brad Pitt, Demi Moore, and Harrison Ford are paid millions for appearing in Japanese commercials. Ryan endorses cosmetics and tea, Pitt appears in ads for canned coffee and blue jeans, while Demi Moore hawks protein drinks. Ford received several million dollars for appearing sweaty and bare-chested in Kirin beer commercials and print ads. Sometimes celebrities are forced to change their images or personalities to suit the advertising style of Japanese companies and the tastes of audiences in Japan. Japanese commercials have a totally different feel than those in the United States and Europe and have often been described as "tacky" or "cheesy" by Western standards. For example, one ad showed actor Dennis Hopper sitting in a tub with a rubber ducky to promote a brand of shampoo and body wash.

There are several reasons why Japanese companies are willing to shell out huge sums of money for these stars. Many Japanese are fascinated by American culture and its celebrities, and endorsement of a brand by a star gives it a certain international cachet. Also, Japanese advertising emphasizes style and mood rather than substance; consumers expect to be entertained, rather than bored by product information or testimonials. Because most Japanese commercials last only 15 seconds, advertisers feel that an instantly recognizable Western celebrity who can capture viewers' attention is well worth the money. Some movie studios encourage celebrities to do ads in Japan because it boosts their visibility and helps the marketing of their films in Japan and other Asian countries. Advertising campaigns featuring U.S. celebrities often coincide with the release of their films in Asia.

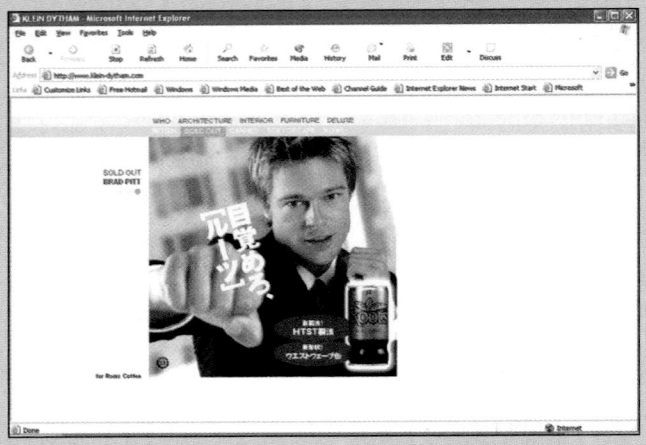

While many celebrities are cashing in on endorsement deals in Japan, they still try to protect their image at home. The stars commonly have nondisclosure clauses in their contracts, specifying that the ads cannot be shown—or sometimes even discussed (oops!)—outside Japan. However, with the growth of the Internet, stars like Arnold Schwarzenegger may have to say *hasta la vista* to keeping their endorsements secret and preventing people back home from seeing the Japanese ads. A small Canadian web company, Zero One Design, is dedicated to showing U.S. celebrities pitching products in Japan at www.gaijinagogo.com. Recently, several celebrities, including Schwarzenegger and Leonardo DiCaprio, threatened legal action against the site for showing their commercials, arguing that it infringed on the star's intellectual-property rights. Ironically, the site went from about 500 hits a month to nearly 4 million in the two weeks following the publicity surrounding the controversy over the posting of the commercial Schwarzenegger made for DirecTV in Japan. Other websites, such as www.klein-dytham.com, also provide examples of U.S. celebrities who appear in commercials in Japan but would not be caught dead endorsing products back home. Celebrities are used to getting their way, and most want knowledge of their Japanese endorsements to stay across the Pacific. Sorry about that.

Sources: Debra Lau, "Movie Stars Moonlight in Japan," Forbes.com, Mar. 14, 2001; Kim Lunman, "Arnold Terminates Site Leaking Foreign TV Ad," Globetechnology.com, Aug. 11, 2000; Stephen Rae, "How Celebrities Make Killings on Commercials," *Cosmopolitan,* January 1997, pp. 14, 67.

credible, even though they are often presenting stories that stem from press releases. In some situations celebrities may appear on news programs or talk shows and promote an upcoming cause or event such as the release of a new movie or music CD. With the increase in stealth marketing techniques, many consumers are becoming wary of endorsements made by celebrities on news programs and talk shows. For example, a *New York Times* article revealed that drug companies were making payments to celebrities or their favorite charities in return for the celebrities' touting the companies' pharmaceutical products on news and talk shows. As a result of the controversy from the article, CNN and the major broadcast networks announced that they would disclose any such financial deals during an interview.[6]

Using Corporate Leaders as Spokespeople Another way of enhancing source credibility is to use the company president or chief executive officer as a spokesperson in the firm's advertising. Many companies believe the use of their president or CEO is the ultimate expression of the company's commitment to quality and customer service. In some cases, these ads have not only increased sales but also helped turn the company leaders into celebrities.[7] Lee Iacocca appeared in more than 60 commercials for Chrysler Corp. and became a national business hero for guiding the successful turnaround of the company. One of the most popular corporate spokespersons ever was Dave Thomas, the founder of Wendy's fast-food restaurants. Thomas appeared in more than 800 ads for Wendy's, which is a Guinness record for the longest-running campaign by a company founder, between 1989 and early 2002 when he passed away[8] (Exhibit 6-3). Other well-known corporate leaders who sometimes appear in ads for their companies include Dell computer founder and CEO Michael Dell, Gateway founder Ted Wait, and Charles Schwab, who founded the investment company that bears his name. The practice of using company founders, owners, and presidents as advertising spokespersons is particularly prevalent among small and mid-size companies such as retailers and auto dealers serving local markets. For these companies, the decision to have the owner or president become a quasi actor has to do with advertising budgets too small to accommodate professional actors or announcers, who may charge thousands of dollars to tape a few commercials.

Many marketing and advertising experts question the strategy of using company presidents or owners in ads and note that it is often ego rather than logic that results in their use.[9] The experts suggest that businesspeople should get in front of the camera only if they exude credibility and possess the intangible quality of provoking a warm, fuzzy feeling in viewers. They also note that CEO spokespeople who become very popular may get more attention than their company's product/service or advertising message. And if a firm's image becomes too closely tied to a popular leader, there can be problems if that person leaves the company.

Major corporations are likely to continue to use their top executives in their advertising, particularly when they have celebrity value that helps enhance the firm's image. Some research suggests the use of a company president or CEO can improve attitudes and increase the likelihood that consumers will inquire about a company's product or service.[10] Defenders of the practice argue that the use of top executives or business owners in ads is an effective way of projecting an image of trust and honesty and, more importantly, the idea that the company isn't run by some faceless corporate monolith. As one expert notes: "These guys come into people's living rooms every night and, over the course of weeks and years, become like members of the family. It gets to the point that when you think of a certain product category, you think of the guy you see all the time on TV."[11]

Limitations of Credible Sources Several studies have shown that a high-credibility source is not always an asset, nor is a low-credibility source always a liability. High- and low-credibility sources are equally effective when they are arguing for a position

Exhibit 6-3 Dave Thomas was a very effective spokesperson for Wendy's for many years

On January 8th our friend R. David Thomas passed away.

Of course no one called him that. To everyone, employees, customers, business associates, friends, members of Congress, American Presidents, and people who only knew him from his commercials, he was simply Dave.

He was the Senior Chairman and founder of Wendy's. But he was a lot more than that. He was an adopted child who never finished high school. So when he became famous and successful, he used that to promote the causes of adoption and staying in school.

He created the Dave Thomas Foundation for Adoption and lobbied Congress to get laws changed so adoption could become more available to thousands of kids and parents. Then he lobbied boardrooms to get adoption benefits placed alongside traditional maternity/paternity benefits. "If we can get just one child, just one boy or girl adopted into a loving family," Dave said, "all our work will be worth it."

When high school kids asked him why he didn't stay in school, he went back to school and earned his GED. He said he didn't think it was right asking them to do something that he hadn't done. When he finally got his diploma at age 60, he went to the Coconut Creek High School senior prom in Ft. Lauderdale with his wife Lorraine. They voted him most likely to succeed. That was Dave.

He believed simply in being nice and giving back. He was never so happy as when he could help someone else succeed.

So from all of us who were lucky enough to be touched by his life we send our prayers to Lorraine and their family and we join them in saying, thanks Dave.

With love and affection,

Jack Schuessler
Chairman & CEO Wendy's International, Inc.

opposing their own best interest.[12] A very credible source is more effective when message recipients are not in favor of the position advocated in the message.[13] However, a very credible source is less important when the audience has a neutral position, and such a source may even be less effective than a moderately credible source when the receiver's initial attitude is favorable.[14]

Another reason a low-credibility source may be as effective as a high-credibility source is the **sleeper effect,** whereby the persuasiveness of a message increases with the passage of time. The immediate impact of a persuasive message may be inhibited because of its association with a low-credibility source. But with time, the association of the message with the source diminishes and the receiver's attention focuses more on favorable information in the message, resulting in more support arguing. However, many studies have failed to demonstrate the presence of a sleeper effect.[15] Many advertisers hesitate to count on the sleeper effect, since exposure to a credible source is a more reliable strategy.[16]

Source Attractiveness

A source characteristic frequently used by advertisers is **attractiveness,** which encompasses similarity, familiarity, and likability.[17] *Similarity* is a supposed resemblance between the source and the receiver of the message, while *familiarity* refers to knowledge of the source through exposure. *Likability* is an affection for the source as a result of physical appearance, behavior, or other personal traits. Even when the sources are not athletes or movie stars, consumers often admire their physical appearance, talent, and/or personality.

Source attractiveness leads to persuasion through a process of **identification,** whereby the receiver is motivated to seek some type of relationship with the source and thus adopts similar beliefs, attitudes, preferences, or behavior. Maintaining this position depends on the source's continued support for the position as well as the receiver's continued identification with the source. If the source changes position, the receiver may also change. Unlike internalization, identification does not usually integrate information from an attractive source into the receiver's belief system. The receiver may maintain the attitudinal position or behavior only as long as it is supported by the source or the source remains attractive.

Marketers recognize that receivers of persuasive communications are more likely to attend to and identify with people they find likable or similar to themselves. Similarity and likability are the two source characteristics marketers seek when choosing a communicator.

Applying Similarity

Marketers recognize that people are more likely to be influenced by a message coming from someone with whom they feel a sense of similarity.[18] If the communicator and receiver have similar needs, goals, interests, and lifestyles, the position advocated by the source is better understood and received. Similarity is used in various ways in marketing communications. Companies select salespeople whose characteristics match well with their customers'. A sales position for a particular region may be staffed by someone local who has background and interests in common with the customers. Global marketers often hire foreign nationals as salespeople so customers can relate more easily to them.

Companies may also try to recruit former athletes to sell sporting goods or beer, since their customers usually have a strong interest in sports. Several studies have shown that customers who perceive a salesperson as similar to themselves are more likely to be influenced by his or her message.[19]

Similarity is also used to create a situation where the consumer feels empathy for the person shown in the commercial. In a slice-of-life commercial, the advertiser usually starts by presenting a predicament with the hope of getting the consumer to think, "I can see myself in that situation." This can help establish a bond of similarity between the communicator and the receiver, increasing the source's level of persuasiveness. Many companies feel that the best way to connect with consumers is by using regular-looking, everyday people with whom the average person can easily identify. For example, some of the most popular commercials in recent years have been those from the "Whassup?" campaign for Budweiser beer. In these ads the

agency cast a group of real-life friends from Philadelphia, rather than actors, who greet each other with an exaggerated "Whassup?" when they speak with one another or get together to watch a game and enjoy a Bud. IMC Perspective 6-2 discusses how an unknown, aspiring actor with an easygoing manner that appeals to consumers became a very popular spokesperson for Dell Computer.

Applying Likability: Using Celebrities Advertisers recognize the value of using spokespeople who are admired: TV and movie stars, athletes, musicians, and other popular public figures. It is estimated that nearly 20 percent of all TV commercials feature celebrities, and advertisers pay hundreds of millions of dollars for their services. The top celebrity endorser is golfer Tiger Woods, who makes more than $60 million a year from endorsement contracts with Nike, Disney, American Express, General Mills, and Buick (Exhibit 6-4). Michael Jordan is also among the highest-paid and most sought-after celebrity endorsers, along with singer Brittany Spears and cyclist Lance Armstrong.

Why do companies spend huge sums to have celebrities appear in their ads and endorse their products? They think celebrities have *stopping power.* That is, they draw attention to advertising messages in a very cluttered media environment. Marketers think a popular celebrity will favorably influence consumers' feelings, attitudes, and purchase behavior. And they believe celebrities can enhance the target audience's perceptions of the product in terms of image and/or performance. For example, a well-known athlete may convince potential buyers that the product will enhance their own performance.

A number of factors must be considered when a company decides to use a celebrity spokesperson, including the dangers of overshadowing the product and being overexposed, the target audience's receptivity, and risks to the advertiser.

Overshadowing the Product How will the celebrity affect the target audience's processing of the advertising message? Consumers may focus their attention on the celebrity and fail to notice the brand. Advertisers should select a celebrity spokesperson who will attract attention and enhance the sales message, yet not overshadow the brand. For example, actress Lindsay Wagner served as the spokesperson for Ford Motor Co. dealers in Southern California for a number of years and was very popular and effective. She brought a star power and presence to the advertising that attracted attention and made it memorable, yet she never overshadowed the Ford vehicles she was promoting.[20]

Overexposure Consumers are often skeptical of endorsements because they know the celebrities are being paid.[21] This problem is particularly pronounced when a celebrity endorses too many products or companies and becomes overexposed. For example, cyclist Lance Armstrong has endorsement contracts with nearly 20 different companies, including the U.S. Postal Service, Nike, PowerBar, General Mills, Oakley, and many others, and has recently limited his endorsements so he does not become overexposed.[22] Advertisers can protect themselves against overexposure with an exclusivity clause limiting the number of products a celebrity can endorse. However, such clauses are usually expensive, and most celebrities agree not to endorse similar products anyway. Many celebrities, knowing their fame is fleeting, try to earn as much endorsement money as possible, yet they must be careful not to damage their credibility by endorsing too many products. For example, singer/actress Cher damaged her credibility as an advertising spokesperson by appearing in too many infomercials. When she realized that appearing in so many infomercials was devastating to her acting career as well, she ceased doing them.[23]

Target Audiences' Receptivity One of the most important considerations in choosing a celebrity endorser is how well the individual matches with and is received by the advertiser's target audience.

Exhibit 6-4 Tiger Woods has endorsement contracts with a number of companies, including Buick

IMC PERSPECTIVE 6-2

The Dell Dude Connects With PC Buyers

Every so often an advertising character jumps out of the television screen and into the hearts of consumers. A few years ago it was "Stuart"—the geeky, red-headed know-it-all who appeared in commercials for online stock trading company Ameritrade—who struck a chord with viewers. The latest ad spokesperson generating the buzz is "Steven," the lovable blond surfer dude who gives expert advice to people shopping for a home computer. The "Dell Dude" is played by Ben Curtis, a 21-year-old student who studies acting at New York University and hails from Chattanooga, Tennessee. Curtis got the role after an audition, and his first appearances in a Dell commercial came in late 2000 in a spot in which he makes a video for his parents explaining why they should buy him a Dell personal computer. Although Dell switched ad agencies a few months after Curtis was hired, the company and its new agency, DDB Chicago, knew they had a star in the making and retained the Steven character as its "spokesdude."

Over the past two years "Steven" has appeared in more than 10 commercials for Dell including a popular spot where he hawks Dells while driving his dad's convertible with a hot brunette seated next to him. The commercials use a clever blend of humor and salesmanship by portraying Steven as a hip teenager who convinces his parents, his friends' parents, and even random people he meets to buy computers from Dell. Shortly after taking over the account, DDB's creative group added the quip: "Dude, you're gettin' a Dell" to Steven's pitch and the phrase has slowly been seeping into pop-culture vernacular. The ad campaign has helped Dell put a friendly face on its personal computers—a product category that is often intimidating to consumers. Dell's senior manager of consumer advertising says that Steven "has changed our image into that of an approachable company, a company that makes technology easy and fun." The ads have also helped sales, as Dell's share of the home segment of the personal computer market has increased significantly since the campaign was launched.

Curtis's success as the Dell Dude demonstrates the importance of casting in creating effective advertising. The creative director at DDB notes that the right casting is as important as the right message since you need somebody to bring it to life. Curtis clearly brings the Dell Dude to life as "Steven" is described as a modern-day Tom Sawyer who appeals to a broad range of consumers. He receives fan mail from teenybopper girls who want to date him as well as from seniors who like his Eddie Haskell-like charm. The "Dell Guy," as he is often referred to, boasts one of the largest advertising fan-club message boards on Yahoo, with over 500 members as well as numerous fan websites. Curtis has been interviewed on the *Today Show, CNN,* and ABC's *20/20 Downtown* and been featured in articles in *The Wall Street Journal, USA Today,* and many other publications. Curtis also makes appearances at Dell events to rally employees as well as at industry trade shows such as Comdex. In recognition of his celebrity status, Dell created a new web "sitelet" that fans can visit to find out more about Curtis and his latest ads.

In late 2002 Dell announced that "Steven" would be playing a smaller role in its advertising, although the company still plans to use him in the future. However, some analysts note that the company may not want to use "the Dell Dude" as it focuses more on selling its computers to businesses. Curtis knows that the fame he is currently enjoying may be short-lived but hopes he can use it as a launchpad for his ultimate goal of becoming an actor. He worries somewhat about being typecast as a surfer dude but says that the pay helps with school and the expense of living in New York. So goes the life of Madison Avenue's newest mini-celebrity.

Sources: Michael McCarthy, "Goofy Dell Guy Exudes Star Power; 'Steven' Wins Over Bunches of Computer Buyers," *USA Today,* Jan. 14, 2002, p. B5; Suzanne Vranica, "Dell, Starting New Campaign, Plans for Life Without Steven," *The Wall Street Journal,* October 16, 2002, p. B3.

Many former athletes such as Arnold Palmer and Nolan Ryan are effective endorsers because they have very favorable images among aging baby boomers and seniors. Pop star Brittany Spears is a very effective spokesperson for Pepsi as she is very popular among young teens, who are the heavy users of soft drinks.

Consumers who are particularly knowledgeable about a product or service or have strongly established attitudes may be less influenced by a celebrity than those with little knowledge or neutral attitudes. One study found that college-age students were more likely to have a positive attitude toward a product endorsed by a celebrity than were older consumers.[24] The teenage market has generally been very receptive to celebrity endorsers, as evidenced by the frequent use of entertainers and athletes in ads targeted to this group for products such as apparel, cosmetics, and beverages. However, many marketers are finding that teenage consumers are more skeptical and cynical toward the use of celebrity endorsers and respond better to ads using humor, irony, and unvarnished truth.[25] Some marketers targeting teenagers have responded to this by no longer using celebrities in their campaigns or by poking fun at their use. For example, Sprite has developed a very effective campaign using ads that parody celebrity endorsers and carry the tagline "Image is nothing. Obey your thirst" (Exhibit 6-5).

Exhibit 6-5 Sprite parodies the use of celebrity endorsers in this ad

Risk to the Advertiser A celebrity's behavior may pose a risk to a company.[26] A number of entertainers and athletes have been involved in activities that could embarrass the companies whose products they endorsed. For example, Hertz used O. J. Simpson as its spokesperson for 20 years and lost all that equity when he was accused of murdering his ex-wife and her friend. Pepsi had a string of problems with celebrity endorsers; it severed ties with Mike Tyson, after his wife accused him of beating her, and with singer Michael Jackson, after he was accused of having sex with a 12-year-old boy. Pepsi dropped a TV commercial featuring Madonna when some religious groups and consumers objected to her "Like a Prayer" video and threatened to boycott Pepsi products. More recently, several companies including Pizza Hut and the Carl's Jr. fast-food chain terminated the endorsement contract with controversial basketball star Dennis Rodman because of his unpredictable behavior both on and off the court.[27]

To avoid these problems, companies often research a celebrity's personal life and background. Many endorsement contracts include a morals clause allowing the company to terminate the contract if a controversy arises. Callaway Golf terminated its endorsement deal with well-known and popular golfer John Daly a few years ago on the grounds that he violated a clause in his contract prohibiting him from drinking or gambling.[28] As discussed in the opening vignette to this chapter, basketball star Allan Iverson has been involved in several controversies that have resulted in some companies' refraining from using him as an endorser and led to criticism of those that continue to do so, such as Reebok.[29] However, marketers should remember that adding morals clauses to their endorsement contracts only gets them out of a problem; it does not prevent it.

Understanding the Meaning of Celebrity Endorsers Advertisers must try to match the product or company's image, the characteristics of the target market, and the personality of the celebrity.[30] The image celebrities project to consumers can be just as important as their ability to attract attention. An interesting perspective on celebrity endorsement was developed by Grant McCracken.[31] He argues that credibility and attractiveness don't sufficiently explain how and why celebrity endorsements work and offers a model based on meaning transfer (Figure 6-3).

According to this model, a celebrity's effectiveness as an endorser depends on the culturally acquired meanings he or she brings to the endorsement process. Each celebrity contains many meanings, including status, class, gender, and age as well as

Figure 6-3 Meaning movement and the endorsement process

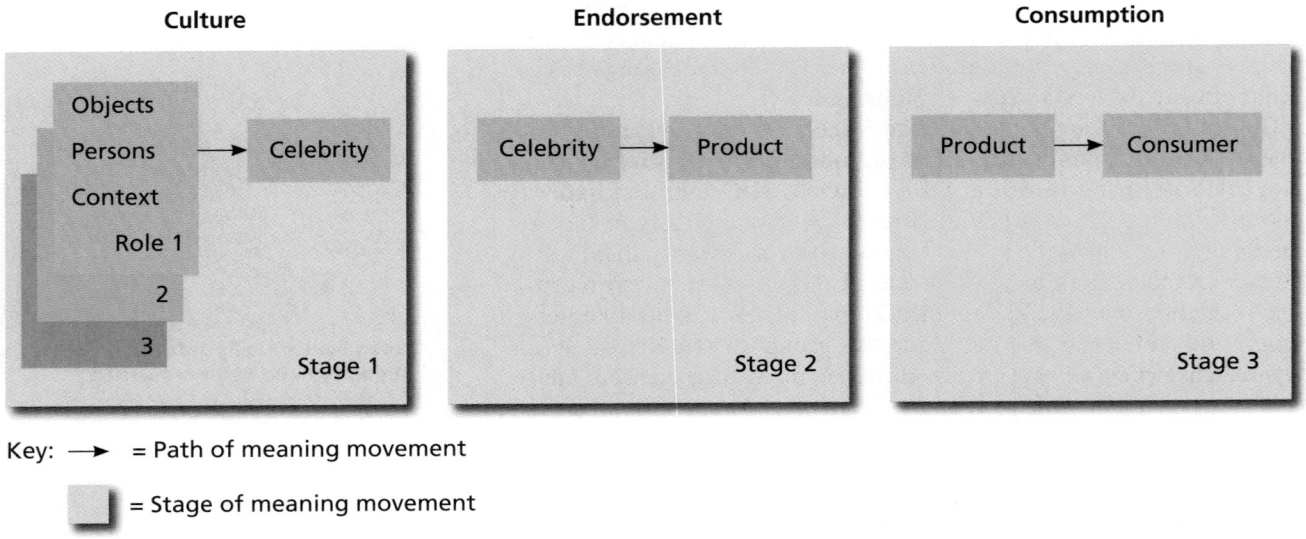

personality and lifestyle. In explaining stage 1 of the meaning transfer process, McCracken notes:

> Celebrities draw these powerful meanings from the roles they assume in their television, movie, military, athletic, and other careers. Each new dramatic role brings the celebrity into contact with a range of objects, persons, and contexts. Out of these objects, persons, and contexts are transferred meanings that then reside in the celebrity.[32]

Examples of celebrities who have acquired meanings include actor Bill Cosby as the perfect father (from his role on *The Cosby Show*) and actor Jerry Seinfeld as the quirky comedian (from his role on the sitcom *Seinfeld*). Cyclist Lance Armstrong has developed a very favorable image as a fierce competitor and an All-American superhero by winning the grueling Tour de France cycling race four times after overcoming a life-threatening form of testicular cancer.

McCracken suggests celebrity endorsers bring their meanings and image into the ad and transfer them to the product they are endorsing (stage 2 of the model in Figure 6-3). For example, PowerBar, the leading brand of energy performance bars, takes advantage of Armstrong's image as a competitor and champion with great determination in ads such as the one shown in Exhibit 6-6. He is also an effective endorser for the product since he competes in a very grueling and demanding sport where the benefits of sustained energy are very important.

Exhibit 6-6 Cyclist Lance Armstrong helps position PowerBar as a product that provides energy to athletes

In the final stage of McCracken's model, the meanings the celebrity has given to the product are transferred to the consumer. By using Armstrong in its ads, PowerBar hopes to enhance its image as a product that can provide extra energy to athletes and enhance their performance. McCracken notes that this final stage is complicated and difficult to achieve. The way consumers take possession of the meaning the celebrity has transferred to a product is probably the least understood part of the process.

The meaning transfer model has some important implications for companies using celebrity endorsers. Marketers must first decide on the image or symbolic meanings important to the target audience for the particular product, service, or company. They must then determine which celebrity best represents the meaning or image to be projected. An advertising campaign must be designed that captures that meaning in the product and moves it to the consumer. Marketing and advertising personnel often rely on intuition in choosing celebrity endorsers for their companies or products, but some companies conduct research studies to determine consumers' perceptions of celebrities' meaning.

Marketers may also pretest ads to determine whether they transfer the proper meaning to the product. When celebrity endorsers are used, the marketer should track the campaign's effectiveness. Does the celebrity continue to be effective in communicating the proper meaning to the target audience? Celebrities who are no longer in the limelight may lose their ability to transfer any significant meanings to the product.

As we have seen, marketers must consider many factors when choosing a celebrity to serve as an advertising spokesperson for the company or a particular brand. Studies have shown that advertising and marketing managers take these various factors into account when choosing a celebrity endorser.[33] Among the most important factors are the celebrity's match with the target audience and the product/service or brand, the overall image of the celebrity, the cost of acquiring the celebrity, trustworthiness, the risk of controversy, and the celebrity's familiarity and likability among the target audience. IMC Perspective 6-3 discusses how marketers and advertising agencies use research data and other types of information in choosing celebrity endorsers.

Applying Likability: Decorative Models

Advertisers often draw attention to their ads by featuring a physically attractive person who serves as a passive or decorative model rather than as an active communicator. Research suggests that physically attractive communicators generally have a positive impact and generate more favorable evaluations of both ads and products than less attractive models.[34] The gender appropriateness of the model for the product being advertised and his or her relevance to the product are also important considerations.[35] Products such as cosmetics or fashionable clothing are likely to benefit from the use of an attractive model, since physical appearance is very relevant in marketing these items. For example, Revlon has used supermodel Cindy Crawford in advertising for various cosmetics products such as its Fire & Ice fragrance (Exhibit 6-7).

Some models draw attention to the ad but not to the product or message. Studies show that an attractive model facilitates recognition of the ad but does not enhance copy readership or message recall. Thus, advertisers must ensure that the consumer's attention will go beyond the model to the product and advertising message.[36] Marketers must also consider whether the use of highly attractive models might negatively impact advertising effectiveness. Several recent studies have shown that some women experience negative feelings when comparing themselves with beautiful models used in ads and the images of physical perfection they represent.[37]

Source Power

The final characteristic in Kelman's classification scheme is **source power.** A source has power when he or she can actually administer rewards and punishments to the receiver. As a result of this power, the source may be able to induce another person(s) to respond to the request or position he or she is advocating. The power of the source depends on several factors. The source must be perceived as being able to administer positive or negative sanctions to the receiver *(perceived control)* and the receiver must think the source cares about whether or not the receiver conforms *(perceived concern).* The receiver's estimate of the source's ability to observe conformity is also important *(perceived scrutiny).*

When a receiver perceives a source as having power, the influence process occurs through a process known as **compliance.** The receiver accepts the persuasive influence of the source and acquiesces to his or her position in hopes of obtaining a favorable reaction or avoiding punishment. The receiver may show public agreement with the source's position but not have an internal or private commitment to this position. Persuasion induced through compliance may be superficial and last only as long as the receiver perceives that the source can administer some reward or punishment.

Power as a source characteristic is very difficult to apply in a nonpersonal influence situation such as advertising. A communicator in an ad generally cannot apply any sanctions to the receiver or

Exhibit 6-7 Revlon makes effective use of supermodel Cindy Crawford in this ad

IMC PERSPECTIVE 6-3

Using Q Scores and the Fame Index to Help Choose a Celebrity Endorser

Obviously many marketers believe strongly in the value of celebrity spokespeople, as the amount of money paid to them continues to soar to record levels. Companies look for a celebrity who will attract viewers' attention and enhance the image of the company or brand. But how do they choose the right one? While some executives rely on their own intuition and gut feeling, many turn to research that measures a celebrity's appeal as well as other factors that will provide insight into his or her warmth, trust, and credibility among the target audience.

To help select a celebrity endorser, many companies and their advertising agencies rely on *Q ratings* that are commercially available from the New York-based firm known as Marketing Evaluations/TVQ, Inc. To determine its Performer Q ratings for TV and movie personalities, the company surveys a representative national panel of 1,800 people twice a year and asks them to evaluate over 1,500 performers. For its Sports Q rating, which is conducted once a year, the company surveys 2,000 teens and adults and asks them about approximately 500 active and retired players, coaches, managers, and sportscasters. In both studies respondents are asked to indicate whether they have ever seen or heard of the performer or sports personality and, if they have, to rate him or her on a scale that includes "one of my favorites," "very good," "good," "fair," or "poor." The *familiarity* score indicates the percentage of people who have heard of the person, while the *one-of-my-favorite* score is an absolute measure of the appeal or popularity of the celebrity. The well-known Q rating is calculated by taking the percentage of respondents who indicate that a person is "one of my favorites" and dividing that number by the percentage of respondents who indicate that they have heard of that person. The Q score thus answers the question "How appealing is the person among those who do know him or her?"

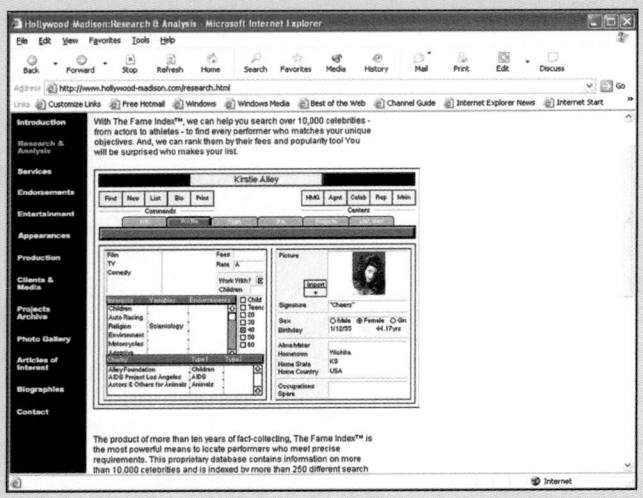

Results from a 2002 Performer Q study found that Tom Hanks was familiar to 92 percent of those surveyed and was considered "one of my favorites" by 48 percent. Thus, his Q rating was 52 (48/92) which was the highest score among all performers measured. Other performers in the top 10 along with their Q ratings included Bill Cosby (50), Mel Gibson (47), Harrison Ford (45), Sean Connery (45), Denzel Washington (42), Robert DeNiro (41), Michael J. Fox (40), and Will Peterson (30). The 2002 Sports Q survey for active and retired athletes, coaches, managers, and sportscasters showed that Michael Jordan was familiar to 90 percent of those surveyed and considered "one of my favorites" by 47 percent, for a leading Q rating of 52. Other sports personalities in the top 10 included Tiger Woods (43), Nolan Ryan (40), Cal Ripken Jr. (39), Joe Montana (39), Wayne Gretzky (37), Jerry Rice (36), Sarah Hughes (36), Jackie Joyner-Kersey (36), and John Madden (35). The average Q score is generally around 18 for performers and 17 for sports personalities. Marketing Evaluation's Q ratings are also broken down on the basis of various demographic criteria such as a respondent's age, income, occupation, education, and race so that marketers have some idea of how a celebrity's popularity varies among different groups of consumers.

In addition to using Q ratings, marketers are using information provided by other firms to match celebrities with their products. Hollywood-Madison Avenue Group, a firm that arranges celebrity endorsements, has poured over 10 years of research into its Fame Index, which is a database listing more than 10,000 celebrities by 250 criteria such as age, sex, residence, career highlights, charity affiliations, fears, interests, and addictions. The database is updated daily with information from the Internet, magazines, and newspaper articles as well as television. Information in the Fame Index reveals that actors Tom Cruise, Jim Belushi, and Jason Alexander are big hockey fans, while Carol Burnett and Rosie O'Donnell collect dolls. Kirstie Alley's interests include Scientology, the environment, and motorcycles, and she supports charities concerned with AIDS, children's welfare, and animal rights. Hollywood-Madison has helped a number of companies choose celebrities to serve as their advertising spokespersons. For example, Philips Consumer Elec-

tronics used the company to help with the selection of a celebrity to promote high-definition, wide-screen televisions. The Fame Index identified director Martin Scorsese as a film preservationist who supports the wide-screen format, and Hollywood-Madison helped broker a deal with him to participate in a public education campaign supporting the introduction of Philips new line of wide-screen HDTV.

As more and more companies court celebrities to endorse their products or businesses, appear at events, or support causes, they no longer are relying solely on intuition or brainstorming sessions to select such spokespersons. Companies such as Marketing Evaluations/TVQ and Hollywood-Madison are providing information that helps them find the ideal candidate.

Sources: Marketing Evaluations/TVQ, Inc., www.qscores.com; Kristina Saurwein, "Finding the Right Pitch," *Los Angeles Times*, July 30, 2001, p. B3; www.hollywood-madison.com.

determine whether compliance actually occurs. An indirect way of using power is by using an individual with an authoritative personality as a spokesperson. Actor Charles Bronson, who typifies this image, has appeared in public service campaigns commanding people not to pollute or damage our natural parks (Exhibit 6-8).

The use of source power applies more in situations involving personal communication and influence. For example, in a personal selling situation, the sales rep may have some power over a buyer if the latter anticipates receiving special rewards or favors for complying with the salesperson. Some companies provide their sales reps with large expense accounts to spend on customers for this very purpose. Representatives of companies whose product demand exceeds supply are often in a position of power; buyers may comply with their requests to ensure an adequate supply of the product. Sales reps must be very careful in their use of a power position, since abusing a power base to maximize short-term gains can damage long-term relationships with customers.

Message Factors

The way marketing communications are presented is very important in determining their effectiveness. Promotional managers must consider not only the content of their persuasive messages but also how this information will be structured for presentation and what type of message appeal will be used. Advertising, in all media except radio, relies heavily on visual as well as verbal information. Many options are available with respect to the design and presentation of a message. This section examines the structure of messages and considers the effects of different types of appeals used in advertising.

Exhibit 6-8 Actor Charles Bronson's authoritative image makes him an effective source

Message Structure

Marketing communications usually consist of a number of message points that the communicator wants to get across. An important aspect of message strategy is knowing the best way to communicate these points and overcome any opposing viewpoints audience members may hold. Extensive research has been conducted on how the structure of a persuasive message can influence its effectiveness, including order of presentation, conclusion drawing, message sidedness, refutation, and verbal versus visual message characteristics.

Order of Presentation A basic consideration in the design of a persuasive message is the arguments' order of presentation. Should the most important message points be placed at the beginning of the message, in the middle, or at the end? Research on learning and memory generally indicates that items presented first and last are remembered better than those presented in the middle (see Figure 6-4).[38] This suggests that a communicator's strongest arguments should be presented early or late in the message but never in the middle.

Presenting the strongest arguments at the beginning of the message assumes a **primacy effect** is operating, whereby information presented first is most effective. Putting the strong points at the end assumes a **recency effect,** whereby the last arguments presented are most persuasive.

Whether to place the strongest selling points at the beginning or the end of the message depends on several factors. If the target audience is opposed to the communicator's

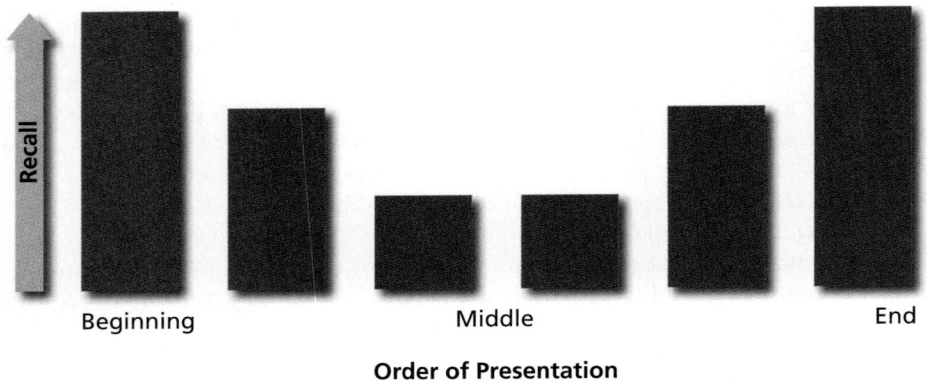

Figure 6-4 Ad message recall as a function of order of presentation

position, presenting strong points first can reduce the level of counterarguing. Putting weak arguments first might lead to such a high level of counterarguing that strong arguments that followed would not be believed. Strong arguments work best at the beginning of the message if the audience is not interested in the topic, so they can arouse interest in the message. When the target audience is predisposed toward the communicator's position or is highly interested in the issue or product, strong arguments can be saved for the end of the message. This may result in a more favorable opinion as well as better retention of the information.

The order of presentation can be critical when a long, detailed message with many arguments is being presented. Most effective sales presentations open and close with strong selling points and bury weaker arguments in the middle. For short communications, such as a 15- or 30-second TV or radio commercial, the order may be less critical. However, many product and service messages are received by consumers with low involvement and minimal interest. Thus, an advertiser may want to present the brand name and key selling points early in the message and repeat them at the end to enhance recall and retention. Order of presentation is also an important consideration in other forms of marketing communication. For example, many press releases use the "pyramid style" of writing, whereby most of the important information is presented up front to ensure that it is read since editors often cut from the end of articles.

Conclusion Drawing Marketing communicators must decide whether their messages should explicitly draw a firm conclusion or allow receivers to draw their own conclusions. Research suggests that, in general, messages with explicit conclusions are more easily understood and effective in influencing attitudes. However, other studies have shown that the effectiveness of conclusion drawing may depend on the target audience, the type of issue or topic, and the nature of the situation.[39]

More highly educated people prefer to draw their own conclusions and may be annoyed at an attempt to explain the obvious or to draw an inference for them. But stating the conclusion may be necessary for a less educated audience, who may not draw any conclusion or may make an incorrect inference from the message. Marketers must also consider the audience's level of involvement in the topic. For highly personal or ego-involving issues, message recipients may want to make up their own minds and resent any attempts by the communicator to draw a conclusion. One study found that open-ended ads (without explicit conclusions) were more effective than closed-ended arguments that did include a specific conclusion—but only for involved audiences.[40]

Whether to draw a conclusion for the audience also depends on the complexity of the topic. Even a highly educated audience may need assistance if its knowledge level in a particular area is low. Does the marketer want the message to trigger immediate action or a more long-term effect? If immediate action is an objective, the message should draw a definite conclusion. This is a common strategy in political advertising, particularly for ads run close to election day. When immediate impact is not the objective and repeated exposure will give the audience members opportunities to draw their own conclusions, an open-ended message may be used.

Drawing a conclusion in a message may make sure the target audience gets the point the marketer intended. But many advertisers believe that letting customers draw their own conclusions reinforces the points being made in the message. For example, a health services agency in Kentucky found that open-ended ads were more memorable and more effective in getting consumers to use health services than were ads stating a conclusion. Ads that posed questions about alcohol and drug abuse and left them unanswered resulted in more calls by teenagers to a help line for information than did a message offering a resolution to the problem.[41] The ad for Silk Soymilk in Exhibit 6-9 is a very good example of an open-ended message. The question in the headline encourages consumers to be open to the idea of drinking soymilk.

Exhibit 6-9 This ad makes effective use of an open-ended approach

Message Sidedness Another message structure decision facing the marketer involves message sidedness. A **one-sided message** mentions only positive attributes or benefits. A **two-sided message** presents both good and bad points. One-sided messages are most effective when the target audience already holds a favorable opinion about the topic. They also work better with a less educated audience.[42]

Two-sided messages are more effective when the target audience holds an opposing opinion or is highly educated. Two-sided messages may enhance the credibility of the source.[43] A better-educated audience usually knows there are opposing arguments, so a communicator who presents both sides of an issue is likely to be seen as less biased and more objective.

Most advertisers use one-sided messages. They are concerned about the negative effects of acknowledging a weakness in their brand or don't want to say anything positive about their competitors. There are exceptions, however. Sometimes advertisers compare brands on several attributes and do not show their product as being the best on every one.

In some situations marketers may focus on a negative attribute as a way of enhancing overall perceptions of the product. For example, W. K. Buckley Limited has become one of the leading brands of cough syrup in Canada by using a blunt two-sided slogan, "Buckley's Mixture. It tastes awful. And it works." Ads for the brand poke fun at the cough syrup's terrible taste but also suggest that the taste is a reason why the product is effective (Exhibit 6-10). Buckley's is using the humorous two-sided message strategy in its entry into the U.S. market.[44]

Refutation In a special type of two-sided message known as a **refutational appeal,** the communicator presents both sides of an issue and then refutes the opposing viewpoint. Since refutational appeals tend to "inoculate" the target audience against a competitor's counterclaims, they are more effective than one-sided messages in making consumers resistant to an opposing message.[45]

Refutational messages may be useful when marketers wish to build attitudes that resist change and must defend against attacks or criticism of their products or the company. For example, Exhibit 6-11 shows an ad used by the Almond Board of California to refute nutritional concerns about almonds regarding their fat content. Market leaders, who are often the target of comparative messages, may find that acknowledging competitors' claims and then refuting them can help build resistant attitudes and customer loyalty.

Verbal versus Visual Messages Thus far our discussion has focused on the information, or verbal, portion of the message. However, the nonverbal, visual elements of an ad are also very important. Many ads provide minimal amounts of information and rely on visual elements to communicate. Pictures are commonly used in advertising to convey information or reinforce copy or message claims.

Both the verbal and visual portions of an ad influence the way the advertising message is processed.[46] Consumers may develop images or impressions based on visual elements such as an illustration in an ad or the scenes in a TV commercial. In some

Exhibit 6-10 Buckley's Cough Syrup uses a two-sided message to promote the product's effectiveness

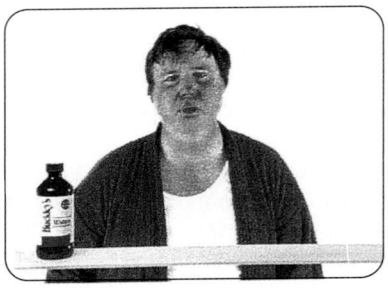

SFX: Man with cold.
ANNCR: You'll be amazed...

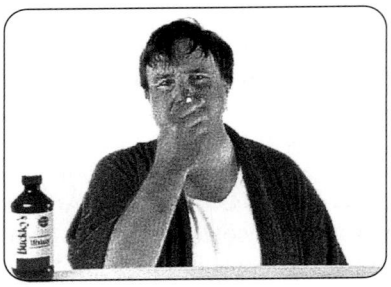

...at how quickly Buckley's Mixture relieves coughs due to colds.

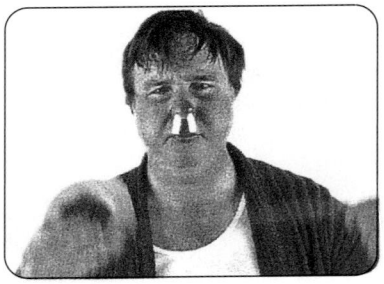

SFX: Duct tape rip.

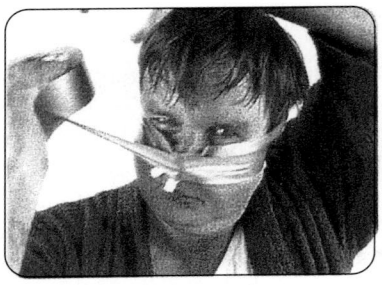

ANNCR: You'll also be amazed...

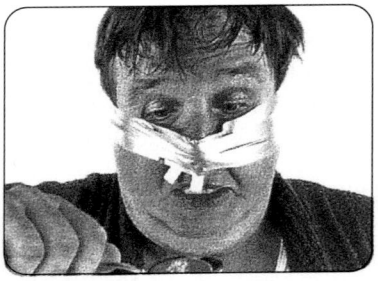

...at how it tastes.

SFX: Scream.

Exhibit 6-11 A refutational appeal is used to address nutritional concerns about almonds

cases, the visual portion of an ad may reduce its persuasiveness, since the processing stimulated by the picture may be less controlled and consequently less favorable than that stimulated by words.[47]

Pictures affect the way consumers process accompanying copy. A recent study showed that when verbal information was low in imagery value, the use of pictures providing examples increased both immediate and delayed recall of product attributes.[48] However, when the verbal information was already high in imagery value, the addition of pictures did not increase recall. Advertisers often design ads where the visual image supports the verbal appeal to create a compelling impression in the consumer's mind. Notice how the ad for the CamelBak SnoBowl uses visual elements to support the claims made in the copy regarding the importance of being hydrated when skiing (Exhibit 6-12).

Sometimes advertisers use a different strategy; they design ads in which the visual portion is incongruent with or contradicts the verbal information presented. The logic behind this strategy is that the use of an unexpected picture or visual image will grab consumers' attention and get them to engage in more effortful or elaborative processing.[49] A number of studies have shown that the use of a visual that is inconsistent with the verbal content leads to more recall and greater processing of the information presented.[50]

Exhibit 6-12 Visual images are often designed to support verbal appeals

Message Appeals

One of the advertiser's most important creative strategy decisions involves the choice of an appropriate appeal. Some ads are designed to appeal to the rational, logical aspect of the consumer's decision-making process; others appeal to feelings in an attempt to evoke some emotional reaction. Many believe that effective advertising combines the practical reasons for purchasing a product with emotional values. In this section we will examine several common types of message appeals, including comparative advertising, fear, and humor.

Comparative Advertising

Comparative advertising is the practice of either directly or indirectly naming competitors in an ad and comparing one or more specific attributes.[51] This form of advertising became popular after the Federal Trade Commission (FTC) began advocating its use in 1972. The FTC reasoned that direct comparison of brands would provide better product information, giving consumers a more rational basis for making purchase decisions. Television networks cooperated with the FTC by lifting their ban on comparative ads, and the result was a flurry of comparative commercials.

Initially, the novelty of comparative ads resulted in greater attention. But since they have become so common, their attention-getting value has probably declined. Some studies show that recall is higher for comparative than noncomparative messages, but comparative ads are generally not more effective for other response variables, such as brand attitudes or purchase intentions.[52] Advertisers must also consider how comparative messages affect credibility. Users of the brand being attacked in a comparative message may be especially skeptical about the advertiser's claims.

Comparative advertising may be particularly useful for new brands, since it allows a new market entrant to position itself directly against the more established brands and to promote its distinctive advantages. Direct comparisons can help position a new brand in the evoked, or choice, set of brands the customer may be considering.

Comparative advertising is often used for brands with a small market share. They compare themselves to an established market leader in hopes of creating an association and tapping into the leader's market. For example, Savin Corp. used comparative ads for a number of years that were aimed directly at Xerox, the market leader in the copier industry. The campaign was very effective in convincing decision makers at small and mid-size companies that Savin should be considered as an alternative to Xerox as well as other copier companies such as Canon, Konica, and Mita (Exhibit 6-13). Market leaders, on the

Exhibit 6-13 Savin used a comparative ad to position itself against Xerox

other hand, often hesitate to use comparison ads, as most believe they have little to gain by featuring competitors' products in their ads. There are exceptions, of course; Coca-Cola resorted to comparative advertising in response to challenges made by Pepsi that were reducing Coke's market share.

Another area where comparative messages are quite commonly used is political advertising. Political advertising is viewed as an important component of political speech and thus enjoys more First Amendment protection than commercial speech and less regulation by either government or self-policing agencies. Thus, it has become quite common for political ads to contain negative, one-sided attacks on an opposing candidate's weaknesses such as character flaws, voting record, public misstatements, broken promises, and the like.[53] The goal of these ads is to discredit the character, record, or position of an opponent and create doubt in voters' minds about his or her ability to govern effectively. A major reason why negative political ads are used successfully is that voters often tend to weight negative information more heavily than positive information when forming impressions of political candidates.[54] However, studies have shown that the use of "attack advertising" by politicians can result in negative perceptions of both candidates.[55]

Fear Appeals

Fear is an emotional response to a threat that expresses, or at least implies, some sort of danger. Ads sometimes use **fear appeals** to evoke this emotional response and arouse individuals to take steps to remove the threat. Some, like the antidrug ads used by the Partnership for a Drug-Free America, stress physical danger that can occur if behaviors are not altered. Others—like those for deodorant, mouthwash, or dandruff shampoos—threaten disapproval or social rejection.

How Fear Operates Before deciding to use a fear appeal–based message strategy, the advertiser should consider how fear operates, what level to use, and how different target audiences may respond. One theory suggests that the relationship between the level of fear in a message and acceptance or persuasion is curvilinear, as shown in Figure 6-5.[56] This means that message acceptance increases as the amount of fear used rises—to a point. Beyond that point, acceptance decreases as the level of fear rises.

This relationship between fear and persuasion can be explained by the fact that fear appeals have both facilitating and inhibiting effects.[57] A low level of fear can have facilitating effects; it attracts attention and interest in the message and may motivate the receiver to act to resolve the threat. Thus, increasing the level of fear in a message from low to moderate can result in increased persuasion. High levels of fear, however, can produce inhibiting effects; the receiver may emotionally block the message by tuning it out, perceiving it selectively, or denying its arguments outright. Figure 6-5 illustrates how these two countereffects operate to produce the curvilinear relationship between fear and persuasion.

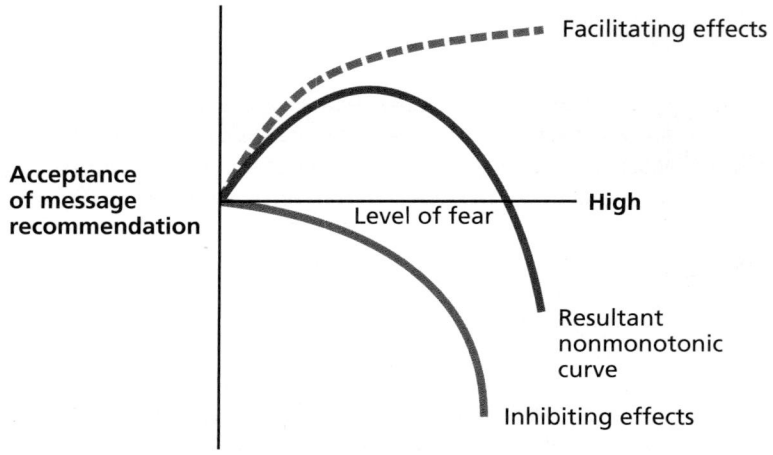

Figure 6-5 Relationship between fear levels and message acceptance

A study by Anand-Keller and Block provides support for this perspective on how fear operates.[58] They examined the conditions under which low- and high-fear appeals urging people to stop smoking are likely to be effective. Their study indicated that a communication using a low level of fear may be ineffective because it results in insufficient motivation to elaborate on the harmful consequences of engaging in the destructive behavior (smoking). However, an appeal arousing high levels of fear was ineffective because it resulted in too much elaboration on the harmful consequences. This led to defensive tendencies such as message avoidance and interfered with processing of recommended solutions to the problem.

Another approach to the curvilinear explanation of fear is the protection motivation model.[59] According to this theory, four cognitive appraisal processes mediate the individual's response to the threat: appraising (1) the information available regarding the severity of the perceived threat, (2) the perceived probability that the threat will occur, (3) the perceived ability of a coping behavior to remove the threat, and (4) the individual's perceived ability to carry out the coping behavior.

This model suggests that both the cognitive appraisal of the information in a fear appeal message and the emotional response mediate persuasion. An audience is more likely to continue processing threat-related information, thereby increasing the likelihood that a coping behavior will occur.

Exhibit 6-14 This ad uses a mild fear appeal but reduces anxiety by offering a solution to the problem

The protection motivation model suggests that ads using fear appeals should give the target audience information about the severity of the threat, the probability of its occurrence, the effectiveness of a coping response, and the ease with which the response can be implemented.[60] For example, the Havrix ad in Exhibit 6-14 discusses how tourists can pick up hepatitis A when traveling to high-risk areas outside the United States and describes the severity of the problem. However, the ad reduces anxiety by offering a solution to the problem—a vaccination with Havrix.

It is also important to consider how the target audience may respond. Fear appeals are more effective when the message recipient is self-confident and prefers to cope with dangers rather than avoid them.[61] They are also more effective among nonusers of a product than among users. Thus, a fear appeal may be better at keeping nonsmokers from starting than persuading smokers to stop.

In reviewing research on fear appeals, Herbert Rotfeld has argued that some of the studies may be confusing different types of threats and the level of potential harm portrayed in the message with fear, which is an emotional response.[62] He concludes that the relationship between the emotional responses of fear or arousal and persuasion is not curvilinear but rather is monotonic and positive, meaning that higher levels of fear do result in greater persuasion. However, Rotfeld notes that not all fear messages are equally effective, because different people fear different things. Thus they will respond differently to the same threat, so the strongest threats are not always the most persuasive. This suggests that marketers using fear appeals must consider the emotional responses generated by the message and how they will affect reactions to the message.

Exhibit 6-15 This clever ad is an example of how humor can be executed in print media

Humor Appeals Humorous ads are often the best known and best remembered of all advertising messages. Many advertisers, including FedEx, Little Caesar's pizza, Pepsi, and Budweiser, have used humor appeals effectively. Humor is usually presented through radio and TV commercials as these media lend themselves to the execution of humorous messages. However, humor is occasionally used in print ads as well. The clever PayDay ad shown in Exhibit 6-15 is an excellent example of how humor can be used to attract attention and convey a key selling point in a magazine ad.

Advertisers use humor for many reasons. Humorous messages attract and hold consumers' attention. They enhance effectiveness by putting consumers in a positive mood, increasing their liking of the ad itself and

IMC PERSPECTIVE 6-4

Do Humorous Ads Wear Out Too Fast?

An issue of much concern to advertisers is the problem of commercial wearout, or the tendency of a message to lose its effectiveness when it is seen repeatedly. Wearout may occur for several reasons. One is inattention; consumers may no longer attend to an ad after several exposures, so the message loses its effectiveness. Another reason is that consumers may become annoyed at seeing an ad many times.

While wearout is a problem for any type of commercial, some advertising experts argue that humorous ads wear out much sooner than other formats because once the viewer gets the joke, the ad becomes boring. However, advocates of humor argue that ads filled with yuks are effective longer because consumers can tolerate a well-executed humorous commercial again and again.

So who is right? Well, a study conducted by Research Systems Corp. concludes that neither view is correct. Humorous ads wear out at the same rate as other types of ads, whether the commercials include comparative messages, celebrity spokespeople, or other approaches. According to the study, the average ad's effectiveness wears out within eight weeks.

Not everyone agrees with this study. Another research firm, Video Storyboard Tests, claims that humorous ads lose their effectiveness faster than other ads. Says the company's president, "The first time the ad is funny, the second time the ad is acceptable, and the third time it is a bore."

While individual humorous ads may get old fast, advertisers often get around this problem by using humorous campaigns consisting of many different commercials. For example, the Little Caesar's pizza chain, FedEx, Energizer batteries, Pepsi, and Anheuser-Busch (Budweiser and Bud Light beer) have made effective use of humor by constantly developing new commercials and working them into the ad rotation.

One media consultant argues that it's quite simple to determine if a humorous spot or campaign is wearing out. "If the viewers laugh with you, you can be in it for the long haul. It's when they laugh at you that you're in trouble."

Sources: Dottie Enrico, "Humorous Touch Resonates with Consumers," *USA Today,* May 13, 1996, p. 3B; Kevin Goldman, "Ever Hear the One about the Funny Ad?" *The Wall Street Journal,* Nov. 2, 1993, p. B11.

their feeling toward the product or service. And humor can distract the receiver from counterarguing against the message.[63]

Critics argue that funny ads draw people to the humorous situation but distract them from the brand and its attributes. Also, effective humor can be difficult to produce and some attempts are too subtle for mass audiences. And, as discussed in IMC Perspective 6-4, there is concern that humorous ads may wear out faster than serious appeals.

Clearly, there are valid reasons both for and against the use of humor in advertising. Not every product or service lends itself to a humorous approach. A number of studies have found that the effectiveness of humor depends on several factors, including the type of product and audience characteristics.[64] For example, humor has been more prevalent and more effective with low-involvement, feeling products than high-involvement, thinking products.[65] An interesting study surveyed the research and creative directors of the top 150 advertising agencies.[66] They were asked to name which communications objectives are facilitated through the appropriate situational use of

- Humor does aid awareness and attention, which are the objectives best achieved by its use.
  - Humor may harm recall and comprehension in general.
  - Humor may aid name and simple copy registration.
  - Humor may harm complex copy registration.
  - Humor may aid retention.
- Humor does not aid persuasion in general.
  - Humor may aid persuasion to switch brands.
  - Humor creates a positive mood that enhances persuasion.
- Humor does not aid source credibility.
- Humor is generally not very effective in bringing about action/sales.
- Creatives are more positive on the use of humor to fulfill all the above objectives than research directors are.
- Radio and TV are the best media in which to use humor; direct mail and newspapers are least suited.
- Consumer nondurables and business services are best suited to humor; corporate advertising and industrial products are least suited.
- Humor should be related to the product.
- Humor should not be used with sensitive goods or services.
- Audiences that are younger, better educated, upscale, male, and professional are best suited to humor; older, less educated, and downscale groups are least suited to humor appeals.

Figure 6-6 Summary of top ad agency research and creative directors' opinions regarding humor

humor in terms of media, product, and audience factors. The general conclusions of this study are shown in Figure 6-6.

Channel Factors

The final controllable variable of the communication process is the channel, or medium, used to deliver the message to the target audience. While a variety of methods are available to transmit marketing communications, as noted in Chapter 5 they can be classified into two broad categories, personal and nonpersonal media.

Personal versus Nonpersonal Channels

There are a number of basic differences between personal and nonpersonal communications channels. Information received from personal influence channels is generally more persuasive than information received via the mass media. Reasons for the differences are summarized in the following comparison of advertising and personal selling:

> From the standpoint of persuasion, a sales message is far more flexible, personal, and powerful than an advertisement. An advertisement is normally prepared by persons having minimal personal contact with customers. The message is designed to appeal to a large number of persons. By contrast, the message in a good sales presentation is not determined in advance. The salesman has a tremendous store of knowledge about his product or service and selects appropriate items as the interview progresses. Thus, the salesman can adapt this to the thinking and needs of the customer or prospect at the time of the sales call. Furthermore, as objections arise and are voiced by the buyer, the salesman can treat the objections in an appropriate manner. This is not possible in advertising.[67]

Effects of Alternative Mass Media

The various mass media that advertisers use to transmit their messages differ in many ways, including the number and type of people they reach, costs, information processing requirements, and qualitative factors. The mass media's costs and efficiency in exposing a target audience to a communication will be evaluated in Chapters 10 through 12. However, we should recognize differences in how information is processed and how communications are influenced by context or environment.

Differences in Information Processing There are basic differences in the manner and rate at which information from various forms of media is transmitted and can be processed. Information from ads in print media, such as newspapers, magazines, or direct mail, is *self-paced;* readers process the ad at their own rate and can study it as long as they desire. In contrast, information from the broadcast media of radio and television is *externally paced;* the transmission rate is controlled by the medium.

The difference in the processing rate for print and broadcast media has some obvious implications for advertisers. Self-paced print media make it easier for the message recipient to process a long, complex message. Advertisers often use print ads when they want to present a detailed message with a lot of information. Broadcast media are more effective for transmitting shorter messages or, in the case of TV, presenting pictorial information along with words.

While there are limits to the length and complexity of broadcast messages, advertisers can deal with this problem. One strategy is to use a radio or TV ad to get consumers' attention and direct them to specific print media for a more detailed message. For example, home builders use radio ads to draw attention to new developments and direct listeners to the real estate section of the newspaper for more details. Some advertisers develop broadcast and print versions of the same message. The copy portion is similar in both media, but the print ad can be processed at a rate comfortable to the receiver.

Effects of Context and Environment

Interpretation of an advertising message can be influenced by the context or environment in which the ad appears. Communication theorist Marshall McLuhan's thesis, "The medium is the message," implies that the medium communicates an image that is independent of any message it contains.[68] A **qualitative media effect** is the influence the medium has on a message. The image of the media vehicle can affect reactions to the message. For example, an ad for a high-quality men's clothing line might have more of an impact in a fashion magazine like *GQ* than in *Sports Afield.* Airlines, destination resorts, and travel-related services advertise in publications such as *Travel & Leisure* partly because the articles, pictures, and other ads help to excite readers about travel (Exhibit 6-16).

A media environment can also be created by the nature of the program in which a commercial appears. One study found that consumers reacted more positively to commercials seen during a happy TV program than a sad one.[69] Advertisers pay premium dollars to advertise on popular programs that create positive moods, like the Olympic Games and Christmas specials. Conversely, advertisers tend to avoid programs that create a negative mood among viewers or may be detrimental to the company or its products. Many companies won't advertise on programs with excessive violence or sexual content. As a corporate policy, Coca-Cola never advertises on TV news programs because it thinks bad news is inconsistent with Coke's image as an upbeat, fun product. A study by Andrew Aylesworth and Scott MacKenzie found that commercials placed in programs that induce negative moods are processed less systematically than ads placed in programs that put viewers in positive moods.[70] They suggest that media buyers might be well advised to follow the conventional wisdom of placing their ads during "feel-good" programming, especially if the message is intended to work through a central route to persuasion. However, messages intended to operate through a peripheral route to persuasion might be more effective if they are shown during more negative programs, where presumably viewers will not analyze the ad in detail because of their negative mood state.

Clutter

Another aspect of the media environment, which is important to advertisers, is the problem of **clutter,** which has been defined as the amount of advertising in a medium.[71] However, for television, clutter is often viewed as including all the nonprogram material that appears in the broadcast environment—commercials, promotional

Exhibit 6-16 *Travel & Leisure* magazine creates an excellent reception environment for travel-related ads

messages for shows, public service announcements (PSAs), and the like. Clutter is of increasing concern to advertisers since there are so many messages in various media competing for the consumer's attention. Half of the average magazine's pages contain ads and in some publications the ratio of ads to editorial content is even higher. On average, around a quarter of a broadcast hour on TV is devoted to commercials, while most radio stations carry an average of 10 to 12 minutes of commercial time per hour. The high level of advertising often annoys consumers and makes it difficult for ads to communicate effectively.

Clutter has become a major concern among television advertisers as a result of increases in nonprogram time and the trend toward shorter commercials. While the 30-second commercial replaced 60-second spots as the industry standard in the 1970s, many advertisers are now using 15-second spots. The advertising industry continues to express concern over the highly cluttered viewing environment on TV, as the amount of clutter increased as much as 30 percent during the 1990s. An industry-sponsored study found that commercial clutter on the television broadcast networks reached record levels during the 2001 season in some day parts such as early morning, daytime, and local news.[72] The amount of nonprogramming time ranged from just over 16 minutes per hour during prime time to nearly 21 minutes per hour in daytime. The study also found that clutter levels are even higher on many cable networks and during syndicated programs. The problem is even greater during popular shows, to which the networks add more commercials because they can charge more. And, of course, advertisers and their agencies perpetuate the problem by pressuring the networks to squeeze their ads into top-rated shows with the largest audiences.

Advertisers and agencies want the networks to commit to a minimum amount of program time and then manage the nonprogram portion however they see fit. If the networks wanted to add more commercials, it would come out of their promos, PSAs, or program credit time. The problem is not likely to go away, however, and advertisers will continue to search for ways to break through the clutter, such as using humor, celebrity spokespeople, or novel, creative approaches.[73]

Summary

This chapter focused on the controllable variables that are part of the communication process—source, message, and channel factors. Decisions regarding each of these variables should consider their impact on the various steps of the response hierarchy the message receiver passes through. The persuasion matrix helps assess the effect of controllable communication decisions on the consumer's response process.

Selection of the appropriate source or communicator to deliver a message is an important aspect of communications strategy. Three important attributes are source credibility, attractiveness, and power. Marketers enhance message effectiveness by hiring communicators who are experts in a particular area and/or have a trustworthy image. The use of celebrities to deliver advertising messages has become very popular; advertisers hope they will catch the receivers' attention and influence their attitudes or behavior through an identification process. The chapter discusses the meaning a celebrity brings to the endorsement process and the importance of matching the image of the celebrity with that of the company or brand.

The design of the advertising message is a critical part of the communication process. There are various options regarding message structure, including order of presentation of message arguments, conclusion drawing, message sidedness, refutation, and verbal versus visual traits. The advantages and disadvantages of different message appeal strategies were considered, including comparative messages and emotional appeals such as fear and humor.

Finally, the channel or medium used to deliver the message was considered. Differences between personal and nonpersonal channels of communication were discussed. Alternative mass media can have an effect on the communication process as a result of information processing and qualitative factors. The context in which an ad appears and the reception environment are important factors to consider in the selection of mass media. Clutter has become a serious problem for advertisers, particularly on TV, where commercials have become shorter and more numerous.

Key Terms

persuasion matrix, 166
source, 168
credibility, 168
internalization, 169
sleeper effect, 172
attractiveness, 172
identification, 172
source power, 177
compliance, 177
primacy effect, 179
recency effect, 179
one-sided message, 181
two-sided message, 181
refutational appeal, 181
comparative advertising, 183
fear appeals, 184
qualitative media effect, 188
clutter, 188

Discussion Questions

1. The opening vignette discusses how a number of companies are using athletes with a "bad-boy" image as endorsers for their athletic shoes. Why do you think companies such as Reebok, And 1, and Pony use controversial athletes such as Alan Iverson, Latrell Sprewell, and Pete Rose as their spokesperson? What risks are they taking by using these athletes to endorse their products?

2. Discuss how marketers could use the persuasion matrix to plan their communication programs. Choose a print ad or TV commercial and use the persuasion matrix to analyze how it might influence consumers' response processes.

3. What are the differences between the source credibility components of expertise and trustworthiness? Provide an example of an ad or other form of marketing communications that uses these source characteristics.

4. Discuss why companies might use their founder, president or CEO as an advertising spokesperson. Discuss the pros and cons of this practice for both major corporations and smaller companies, such as a local retailer.

5. Discuss the ethics of celebrities endorsing products in foreign countries but not in the United States to protect their image. Do you think celebrities hurt their reputations by endorsing products and appearing in ads? Why or why not?

6. IMC Perspective 6-2 discusses Dell Computer use of Steven "The Dell Dude" as its advertising spokesperson. Discuss why Steven was such an effective spokesperson for Dell. Why do you think the company has decided to phase him out of its advertising?

7. Find a celebrity who is currently appearing in ads for a particular company or brand and use McCracken's meaning transfer model (shown in Figure 6-3) to analyze the use of the celebrity as a spokesperson.

8. What is meant by one-sided versus two-sided messages? Discuss some of the reasons marketers may or may not want to use a two-sided message.

9. Discuss the pros and cons of using a comparative advertising message. Find an example of a current campaign where a marketer is using a comparative ad and evaluate the decision to do so.

10. Evaluate the pros and cons of using humor as the basis for an advertising campaign. Find an example of an advertising campaign that supports your arguments for and against the use of humor.

11. What is meant by a qualitative media effect? Choose a specific magazine and discuss the nature of the media environment in that publication.

Establishing Objectives and Budgeting for the Promotional Program

7

Chapter Objectives

1. To recognize the importance and value of setting specific objectives for advertising and promotion.
2. To understand the role objectives play in the IMC planning process and the relationship of promotional objectives to marketing objectives.
3. To know the differences between sales and communications objectives and the issues regarding the use of each.
4. To recognize some problems marketers encounter in setting objectives for their IMC programs.
5. To understand the process of budgeting for IMC.
6. To understand theoretical issues involved in budget setting.
7. To know various methods of budget setting.

Does It Really Matter What We Spend on Advertising?

As you can imagine, marketers have probably always wondered whether their advertising dollars have an impact. This is particularly true now, as advertising budgets are being slashed in virtually every industry due to the downturn in the U.S. economy. Simply put, marketers want to know whether it is worth advertising their brand, and how much they should be spending if it is.

There are some out there who think that the amount spent on media has little or no impact—at least as it relates to consumers' perceptions of the brand's quality. In a study commissioned by *Brandweek* magazine, a Princeton-based research company concluded: "Consumer opinions pertaining to quality bear little correlation to the amount of time and money companies spend advertising their wares on *Friends,* FM radio or Foxsports.com." According to Total Research Corp., none of the 10 brands most heavily advertised in the United States were recognized as among the top 100 "quality" brands—even though they accounted for over $3.5 billion in expenditures. On the other hand, the brands considered in the top 10 spent only approximately $150 million. The top three media spenders—McDonald's, Burger King, and Circuit City—didn't make the top 100 list! (List numbers 1 to 3 were Waterford Crystal, Craftsman tools, and the Discovery Channel.)

When asked why this might be the case, some consultants noted that advertising may be less effective than initially thought or that it lacked credibility in general. Others argued that advertising is too weak to establish a brand and that word of mouth or customer experience is far more valuable in establishing quality.

But not everyone is ready to dismiss advertising as ineffective. Even those that conclude that advertising is not effective in creating a quality image are not yet ready to recommend that companies stop advertising. They agree that while advertising may be weak for this objective, it is (if well designed and placed) quite effective, particularly when it comes to creating awareness and reinforcing the product's message. Further, Robert Passikoff, president of the Brand Keys consulting agency, notes that advertising has different objectives depending on the product category. He notes that "quality is less important in hamburgers than in crystal" and if the list was about fun, "Waterford would be down at the bottom."

Others agree with Passikoff, contending that stressing quality may be only one objective of advertising and that many companies do not use

metrics to measure the ROI on advertising expenditures or—if they do—use the wrong ones. The result is that these expenditures are easy to cut, even when they should not be. As noted by Keith Woodward, VP of finance at General Mills, Inc., most managers want to see the direct returns to volume or revenue, and "you can't do that with advertising." He suggests the consideration of new forms of metrics.

Woodward notes that brand value is important but investments must consider other objectives as well. Factors such as opportunity for growth, historical performance, growth versus the competition, and previous advertising effectiveness metrics must also be taken into consideration. Once the campaign is launched, revenue, market data, and other proprietary data are considered. Woodward notes that while there is no absolute metric for advertising ROI, he feels that General Mills has some good insights and that advertising does work.

Carol Gee of Du Pont (Lycra, Cordura, and other brands) agrees. As global director of brands, Gee notes that it is difficult to track the effectiveness of advertising on the end consumer, "but if we just advertised to our direct (OEM) customers we would be a commodity overnight." While most consultants and experts agree that creating awareness and reinforcing the brand's image are both necessary and measurable, most do not agree on what other factors should be considered in computing ROI. Brand revenues, sales, and even contributions to stock values have been suggested—though there are certainly some limitations to each.

For their part, advertising agencies are also offering their opinions. In addition to awareness, factors such as valuation, ability of the campaign to differentiate the brand name, and other "response components" are suggested. Getting the ad to prompt the consumer to call a toll-free number, visit a website, or request additional information about the brand is also a valuable objective, they contend.

While the experts and consultants may disagree as to the real value of advertising—and perhaps even the real objectives—they do agree on a couple of things. First, it is hard to measure the direct impact of advertising. Second, a variety of objectives might be used in the evaluation process. And third, so far as determining the ability of advertising to demonstrate positive ROI, we aren't exactly there yet.

Sources: Kris Frieswick, "New Brand Day," *CFO,* November 2001, pp. 97–99; Kenneth Hein, "Can't Buy Me Love," *Brandweek,* June 4, 2001, pp. S20–S22.

The lead-in to this chapter reports on an issue that has perplexed marketers seemingly forever—what is the value of advertising? As you can see, there is no 100 percent agreement on what the objectives of advertising are or if it works. As this chapter will demonstrate, success can be measured by both marketing and communications objectives. This chapter will examine how the goals for the integrated marketing communications program follow the company's overall marketing strategy and how these goals determine and are determined by the promotional budget.

Unfortunately, many companies have difficulty with the most critical step in the promotional planning process—setting realistic objectives that will guide the development of the IMC program. Complex marketing situations, conflicting perspectives regarding what advertising and other promotional mix elements are expected to accomplish, and uncertainty over resources make the setting of marketing communications objectives "a job of creating order out of chaos."[1] While the task of setting objectives can be complex and difficult, it must be done properly, because specific goals and objectives are the foundation on which all other promotional decisions are made. Budgeting for advertising and other promotional areas, as well as creative and media strategies and tactics, evolve from these objectives. They also provide a standard against which performance can be measured.

Setting specific objectives should be an integral part of the planning process. However, many companies either fail to use specific marketing communications objectives or

set ones that are inadequate for guiding the development of the promotional plan or measuring its effectiveness. Many marketers are uncertain as to what integrated marketing communications should be expected to contribute to the marketing program. The goal of their company's advertising and promotional program is simple: to generate sales. They fail to recognize the specific tasks that advertising and other promotional mix variables must perform in preparing customers to buy a particular product or service.

As we know, advertising and promotion are not the only marketing activities involved in generating sales. Moreover, it is not always possible or necessary to measure the effects of advertising in terms of sales. For example, the Toyota ad in Exhibit 7-1 is designed to promote the company's concern for the environment.

Consider the State Farm ad shown in Exhibit 7-2. What objectives (other than generating sales) might the company have for this ad? How might its effectiveness be measured?

This chapter examines the nature and purpose of objectives and the role they play in guiding the development, implementation, and evaluation of an IMC program. Attention is given to the various types of objectives appropriate for different situations. We will also examine the budget-setting process and the interdependence of objective setting and budgeting.

The Value of Objectives

Perhaps one reason many companies fail to set specific objectives for their integrated marketing communications programs is that they don't recognize the value of doing so. Another may be disagreement as to what the specific objectives should be. Advertising and promotional objectives are needed for several reasons, including the functions they serve in communications, planning and decision making, and measurement and evaluation.

Communications

Specific objectives for the IMC program facilitate coordination of the various groups working on the campaign. Many people are involved in the planning and development

Exhibit 7-1 The objective of this ad is to demonstrate Toyota's concern for the environment

Exhibit 7-2 State Farm's objectives for this ad may be other than sales

of an integrated marketing communications program on the client side as well as in the various promotional agencies. The advertising and promotional program must be coordinated within the company, inside the ad agency, and between the two. Any other parties involved in the promotional campaign, such as public relations and/or sales promotion firms, research specialists, or media buying services, must also know what the company hopes to accomplish through its marketing communications program. Many problems can be avoided if all parties have written, approved objectives to guide their actions and serve as a common base for discussing issues related to the promotional program.

Planning and Decision Making

Specific promotional objectives also guide development of the integrated marketing communications plan. All phases of a firm's promotional strategy should be based on the established objectives, including budgeting, creative, and media decisions as well as supportive programs such as direct marketing, public relations/publicity, sales promotion, and/or reseller support.

Meaningful objectives can also be a useful guide for decision making. Promotional planners are often faced with a number of strategic and tactical options in terms of choosing creative options, selecting media, and allocating the budget among various elements of the promotional mix. Choices should be made based on how well a particular strategy matches the firm's promotional objectives.

Measurement and Evaluation of Results

An important reason for setting specific objectives is that they provide a benchmark against which the success or failure of the promotional campaign can be measured. Without specific objectives, it is extremely difficult to determine what the firm's advertising and promotion efforts accomplished. One characteristic of good objectives is that they are *measurable;* they specify a method and criteria for determining how well the promotional program is working. By setting specific and meaningful objectives, the promotional planner provides a measure(s) that can be used to evaluate the effectiveness of the marketing communications program. Most organizations are concerned about the return on their promotional investment, and comparing actual performance against measurable objectives is the best way to determine if the return justifies the expense.

Determining Promotional Objectives

Integrated marketing communications objectives should be based on a thorough situation analysis that identifies the marketing and promotional issues facing the company or a brand. The situation analysis is the foundation on which marketing objectives are determined and the marketing plan is developed. Promotional objectives evolve from the company's overall marketing plan and are rooted in its marketing objectives. Advertising and promotion objectives are not the same as marketing objectives (although many firms tend to treat them as synonymous).

Marketing versus Communications Objectives

Marketing objectives are generally stated in the firm's marketing plan and are statements of what is to be accomplished by the overall marketing program within a given time period. Marketing objectives are usually defined in terms of specific, measurable outcomes such as sales volume, market share, profits, or return on investment. Good marketing objectives are *quantifiable;* they delineate the target market and note the time frame for accomplishing the goal (often one year). For example, a copy machine company may have as its marketing objective "to increase sales by 10 percent in the small-business segment of the market during the next 12 months." To be effective, objectives must also be *realistic* and *attainable.*

A company with a very high market share may seek to increase its sales volume by stimulating growth in the product category. It might accomplish this by increasing consumption by current users or encouraging nonusers to use the product. Some firms

IMC INTERNATIONAL PERSPECTIVE 7-1

Video Games Attempt to Go Mainstream in the United States and Europe

In a market where many advertisers are slashing their budgets, the video game industry is taking just the opposite approach. The industry has unleashed a billion-dollar bombardment of IMC communications designed to make Mario the plumber and Munch the Gabit household names as common as Harry Potter or Britney Spears.

The objective of the marketing blitz is to transform the video game from a niche market to as common an activity as watching television or going to the movies. Sony (PlayStation2), Nintendo (GameCube), and Microsoft (Xbox) have all recently redesigned their video games in an attempt to penetrate as many living rooms as possible while ushering in the next generation of digital entertainment.

While the immediate objective is to sell units, the industry's long-term goal is to change the image of the products from a teenage game to family entertainment. The products have become much more sophisticated and have the added capabilities of playing DVD movies and CDs and connecting to the Internet. And, while growing the market is one goal, Sony and Nintendo are also attempting to protect their market shares in the $20 billion market from newcomer Microsoft.

The IMC programs will be as innovative as the products themselves. Traditional advertising media will play a minimal role, while ad messages on soda bottles, in fast-food restaurants, and on college campuses will be commonplace. High-tech trucks and vans equipped with games will tour the United States to allow trial. Nintendo will host Gamecube parties throughout the country, while Sony will employ Britney Spears and Snoop Dog at its events. Not to be outdone, Microsoft is taking its rigs on the road to 40 cities to throw "Xbox Bashes." In all, the companies will use multiple print ads, street marketing teams, college marketing teams, events, sponsorships, TV ads, and the Internet.

The budgets are outrageous as well! Consider that Microsoft ($500 million worldwide) and Nintendo and Sony ($250 million each in North America, and Nintendo at total of $475 million worldwide) will spend five times as much in 2002 as Coke did in 2001 to advertise Coke and Diet Coke. Sega spent over $10 million in the first quarter alone!

Meanwhile, the blitz is hitting Europe as well. The first advertising by Microsoft broke during the Olympic Games, followed by a larger TV campaign with the product launch date in March. A direct-marketing campaign followed, using a database supported by the playmore.com website (fondly referred to as the company's "brand experience" website) as well as 7,000 prelaunch demo units in department stores. Additional brand advertising will also follow the introduction of individual game releases.

The battle for brand share will be intense—maybe more intense than the games themselves. For example, Microsoft has already dubbed its positioning as "positive and inclusive," as opposed to what it calls PlayStation2's "dark and exclusive" strategy. Then again, maybe PlayStation knows something. As noted by one industry observer, "The industry has more casualties than successes."

Sources: Ravi Chandiramani, "Microsoft Xbox Adopts 'Positive' Brand Positioning," *Marketing*, Jan. 24, 2002, p. 1; Kenneth Hein, "Videogame Manufacturers See 0 Ceiling on Selling Season," *Brandweek*, Mar. 18, 2002, p. 13; Alex Pham and Greg Johnson, "Console Industry Taking the Game to a Different Level—Mainstream," *Los Angeles Times*, Sept. 10, 2001, p. C1.

have as their marketing objectives expanding distribution and sales of their product in certain market areas. Companies often have secondary marketing objectives that are related to actions they must take to solve specific problems and thus achieve their primary objectives. IMC International Perspective 7-1 provides an example of how companies invest to pursue multiple objectives.

Once the marketing communications manager has reviewed the marketing plan, he or she should understand where the company hopes to go with its marketing program,

how it intends to get there, and the role advertising and promotion will play. Marketing goals defined in terms of sales, profit, or market share increases are usually not appropriate promotional objectives. They are objectives for the entire marketing program, and achieving them depends on the proper coordination and execution of all the marketing-mix elements, including not just promotion but product planning and production, pricing, and distribution.

Integrated marketing communications objectives are statements of what various aspects of the IMC program will accomplish. They should be based on the particular communications tasks required to deliver the appropriate messages to the target audience. Managers must be able to translate general marketing goals into communications goals and specific promotional objectives. Some guidance in doing this may be available from the marketing plan, as the situation analysis should provide important information on

- The market segments the firm wants to target and the target audience (demographics, psychographics, and purchase motives).
- The product and its main features, advantages, benefits, uses, and applications.
- The company's and competitors' brands (sales and market share in various segments, positioning, competitive strategies, promotional expenditures, creative and media strategies, and tactics).
- Ideas on how the brand should be positioned and specific behavioral responses being sought (trial, repurchase, brand switching, and increased usage).

Sometimes companies do not have a formal marketing plan, and the information needed may not be readily available. In this case, the promotional planner must attempt to gather as much information as possible about the product and its markets from sources both inside and outside the company.

After reviewing all the information, the promotional planner should see how integrated marketing communications fits into the marketing program and what the firm hopes to achieve through advertising and other promotional elements. The next step is to set objectives in terms of specific communications goals or tasks.

Many promotional planners approach promotion from a communications perspective and believe the objective of advertising and other promotional mix elements is usually to communicate information or a selling message about a product or service. Other managers argue that sales or some related measure, such as market share, is the only meaningful goal for advertising and promotion and should be the basis for setting objectives. These two perspectives have been the topic of considerable debate and are worth examining further.

Sales versus Communications Objectives

Sales-Oriented Objectives

To many managers, the only meaningful objective for their promotional program is sales. They take the position that the basic reason a firm spends money on advertising and promotion is to sell its product or service. Promotional spending represents an investment of a firm's scarce resources that requires an economic justification. Rational managers generally compare investment options on a common financial basis, such as return on investment (ROI). As we'll discuss later in this chapter, determining the specific return on advertising and promotional dollars is often quite difficult (as seen in the chapter introduction). However, many managers believe that monies spent on advertising and other forms of promotion should produce measurable results, such as increasing sales volume by a certain percentage or dollar amount or increasing the brand's market share. They believe objectives (as well as the success or failure of the campaign) should be based on the achievement of sales results. For example, two of the largest three oral care manufacturers (Unilever and Colgate-Palmolive) recently joined Procter & Gamble in the marketing of at-home tooth-whitening kits (Exhibit 7-3). Unilever spent $20 million on Mentadent and Colgate allocated $60 million on Simply White in their product launches. Colgate's objective was to get $100 million in sales in the first year (the total category sales are estimated at $300 million and growing). Mentadent focused on in-

store efforts, promotions, ads in beauty magazines, and professional outreach programs to gain its share of the market.[2]

As a result, they have increased their efforts to make agencies more accountable for their performances. In turn, some agencies have developed their own tools to attempt to provide more ROI information in regard to how their integrated communications programs are performing. Grey Global Group, Interpublic Group, and J. Walter Thompson are just a few of the agencies that are boasting of their ability to measure their client's ROIs. McCann-Erickson's World Group Fusion 2.0 system has been adopted by many of its clients including General Motors, Microsoft, and Pfizer.[3]

Some managers prefer sales-oriented objectives to make the individuals involved in advertising and promotion think in terms of how the promotional program will influence sales. Or they may confuse marketing objectives with advertising and promotional objectives. For example, in recent years the major U.S. cereal manufacturers have focused on goals designed to stimulate sales. When cereal sales dropped in the mid-1990s, Post Cereals and General Mills both slashed their prices in an attempt to increase sales. Kellogg immediately followed suit. Much of the money used to fund the price cuts came from decreases in advertising and promotions spending. By the end of 1998 an estimated $1.5 billion had been cut from advertising budgets. Yet sales continued to fall, profits dropped, and still no brand-share gains were recorded. In 2002—a full six years after the initial cuts—cereal sales remain stagnant. Interestingly, the few bright spots came from heavily advertised brands. Kellogg's Smart Start and Special K brands showed sales increases of 72 and 22 percent, respectively, in the first quarter of 2002, when their advertising budgets were significantly increased.[4] For Kellogg and Post the goal was to increase sales and market share versus store brands. This goal not only became the basis of the marketing plan but carried over as the primary objective of the promotional program. The success of the advertising and promotional campaign is judged only by attainment of these goals.

Exhibit 7-3 Competition in the tooth-whitening market led to this advertisement for Whitestrips

Problems with Sales Objectives Given Kellogg's and Post's failures to reverse their sales declines, does this mean the advertising and promotional program was ineffective? Or does it mean the price cuts didn't work? It might help to compare this situation to a football game and think of advertising as a quarterback. The quarterback is one of the most important players on the team but can be effective only with support from the other players. If the team loses, is it fair to blame the loss entirely on the quarterback? Of course not. Just as the quarterback is but one of the players on the football team, promotion is but one element of the marketing program, and there are many other reasons why the targeted sales level was not reached. The quarterback can lead his team to victory only if the linemen block, the receivers catch his passes, and the running backs help the offense establish a balanced attack of running and passing. Even if the quarterback plays an outstanding game, the team can still lose if the defense gives up too many points.

In the business world, poor sales results can be due to any of the other marketing-mix variables, including product design or quality, packaging, distribution, or pricing. Advertising can make consumers aware of and interested in the brand, but it can't make them buy it, particularly if it is not readily available or is priced higher than a competing brand. As shown in Figure 7-1, sales are a function of many factors, not just advertising and promotion. There is an adage in marketing that states, "Nothing will kill a poor product faster than good advertising." Taken with the other factors shown in Figure 7-1, this adage demonstrates that all the marketing elements must work together if a successful plan is to be implemented.

Another problem with sales objectives is that the effects of advertising often occur over an extended period. Many experts recognize that advertising has a lagged or **carryover effect;** monies spent on advertising do not necessarily have an immediate impact on sales.[5] Advertising may create awareness, interest, and/or favorable attitudes toward a brand, but these feelings will not result in an actual purchase until the

Figure 7-1 Factors influencing sales

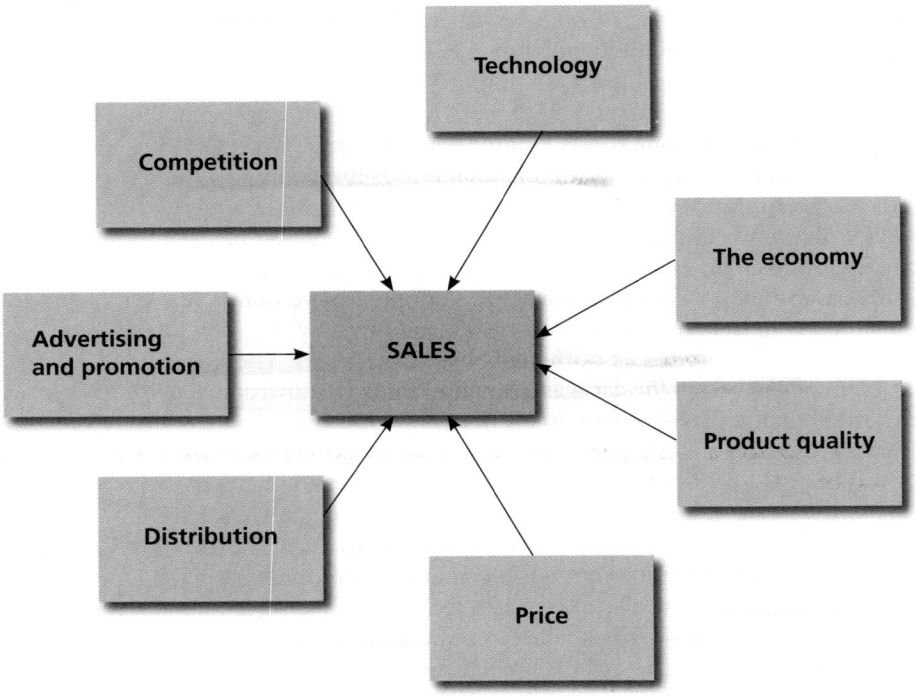

consumer enters the market for the product, which may occur later. A review of econometric studies that examined the duration of cumulative advertising effects found that for mature, frequently purchased, low-priced products, advertising's effect on sales lasts up to nine months.[6] Models have been developed to account for the carryover effect of advertising and to help determine the long-term effect of advertising on sales.[7] The carryover effect adds to the difficulty of determining the precise relationship between advertising and sales.

Another problem with sales objectives is that they offer little guidance to those responsible for planning and developing the promotional program. The creative and media people working on the account need some direction as to the nature of the advertising message the company hopes to communicate, the intended audience, and the particular effect or response sought. As you will see shortly, communications objectives are recommended because they provide operational guidelines for those involved in planning, developing, and executing the advertising and promotional program.

Where Sales Objectives Are Appropriate

While there can be many problems in attempting to use sales as objectives for a promotional campaign, there are situations where sales objectives are appropriate. Certain types of promotion efforts are direct action in nature; they attempt to induce an immediate behavioral response from the prospective customer. A major objective of most sales promotion programs is to generate short-term increases in sales. The "ads" in Exhibit 7-4 were part of BMW Group's non-traditional integrated marketing campaign that simultaneously relaunched the MINI brand, introduced two new models; the MINI Cooper and MINI Cooper S and established a new automotive segment (MINI is the smallest car on the American road) to the American public. Over 5.3 million Classic Mini's were sold worldwide from 1959–2000 but only 10,000 Classic Minis were sold in the US from 1960–1967. Over the years, MINI became a British automotive icon, with milkmen, rock stars and royalty alike behind the wheel. Since the SUV dominated the American marketplace, the spirit of the MINI brand values and

Exhibit 7-4 MINI USA used a non-traditional, integrated campaign to relaunch the MINI brand in the US market

extremely low brand awareness necessitated the development of a non-traditional campaign that would uniquely position the MINI brand and break through the cluttered automotive advertising environment. In the pre-launch phase, MINIs were stacked on top of SUVs that toured the country to bring attention to the brand. Then, seats were removed from sports stadiums in Oakland, CA and New Orleans, and MINIs were put on display at Major League Baseball and NFL football games. At these events, wallet cards were handed out encouraging interested parties to visit the MINIUSA.com website to create their own customized MINI and sign up to become a "MINI Insider." For launch, traditional media (magazine and out-of-home) was used in non-traditional ways and complemented by extensive public relations activities. The campaign yielded over 115,000 "MINI Insider" registrants on the website, and record click-through rates on outbound email campaigns. Thousands of MINIs were pre-ordered even before the car was available in dealer showrooms, putting MINI well on track to reach its sales goal of 20,000 units.[8]

Direct-response advertising is one type of advertising that evaluates its effectiveness on the basis of sales. Merchandise is advertised in material mailed to customers, in newspapers and magazines, through the Internet, or on television. The consumer purchases the merchandise by mail, on the Net, or by calling a toll-free number. The direct-response advertiser generally sets objectives and measures success in terms of the sales response generated by the ad. For example, objectives for and the evaluation of a direct-response ad on TV are based on the number of orders received each time a station broadcasts the commercial. Because advertising is really the only form of communication and promotion used in this situation and response is generally immediate, setting objectives in terms of sales is appropriate. The SkyTel interactive messaging system shown in Exhibit 7-5 is an example of a product sold through direct-response advertising.

Retail advertising, which accounts for a significant percentage of all advertising expenditures, is another area where the advertiser often seeks a direct response, particularly when sales or special events are being promoted. The ad for Mattress Gallery's special purchase sale shown in Exhibit 7-6 is designed to attract consumers to stores during the sales period (and to generate sales volume). Mattress Gallery's management can determine the effectiveness of its promotional effort by analyzing store traffic and sales volume during sale days and comparing them to figures for nonsale days. But retailers may also allocate advertising and promotional dollars to image-building

Exhibit 7-5 Sales results are an appropriate objective for direct-response advertising

Exhibit 7-6 Retail ads often seek sales objectives

campaigns designed to create and enhance favorable perceptions of their stores. In this case, sales-oriented objectives would not be appropriate; the effectiveness of the campaign would be based on its ability to create or change consumers' image of the store.

Sales-oriented objectives are also used when advertising plays a dominant role in a firm's marketing program and other factors are relatively stable. For example, many packaged-goods companies compete in mature markets with established channels of distribution, stable competitive prices and promotional budgets, and products of similar quality. They view advertising and sales promotion as the key determinants of a brand's sales or market share, so it may be possible to isolate the effects of these promotional mix variables.[9] Many companies have accumulated enough market knowledge with their advertising, sales promotion, and direct-marketing programs to have considerable insight into the sales levels that should result from their promotional efforts. Referring to the cereal companies, mentioned earlier, Jeff Montie, president of Kellogg's Morning Foods Division, now believes that it takes at least $20 million to "do it right" in promoting a cereal brand.[10] Thus, many companies believe it is reasonable to set objectives and evaluate the success of their promotional efforts in terms of sales results. Established brands are often repositioned (as discussed in Chapter 2) with the goal of improving their sales or relative market share.

Advertising and promotional programs tend to be evaluated in terms of sales, particularly when expectations are not being met. Marketing and brand managers under pressure to show sales results often take a short-term perspective in evaluating advertising and sales promotion programs. They are often looking for a quick fix for declining sales or loss of market share. They ignore the pitfalls of making direct links between advertising and sales, and campaigns, as well as ad agencies, may be changed if sales expectations are not being met. As discussed in Chapter 3, many companies want their agencies to accept incentive-based compensation systems tied to sales performance. Thus, while sales may not be an appropriate objective in many advertising and promotional situations, managers are inclined to keep a close eye on sales and market share figures and make changes in the promotional program when these numbers become stagnant.

Exhibit 7-7 Hitachi creates an image of speed and reliability

Communications Objectives

Some marketers do recognize the problems associated with sales-oriented objectives. They recognize that the primary role of an IMC program is to communicate and that planning should be based on communications objectives. Advertising and other promotional efforts are designed to achieve such communications as brand knowledge and interest, favorable attitudes and image, and purchase intentions. Consumers are not expected to respond immediately; rather, advertisers realize they must provide relevant information and create favorable predispositions toward the brand before purchase behavior will occur.

For example, the ad for Hitachi in Exhibit 7-7 is designed to inform consumers of the speed and reliability of the company's products and technologies. While there is no call for immediate action, the ad creates favorable impressions about the company by creating a distinct image. Consumers will consider it when they enter the market for products in this category.

Advocates of communications-based objectives generally use some form of the hierarchical models discussed in Chapter 5 when setting advertising and promotion objectives. In all these models, consumers pass through three successive stages: cognitive, affective, and conative. As consumers proceed through the three stages, they move closer to making a purchase. Figure 7-2 shows the

Related behavioral dimensions	Movement toward purchase	Example of types of promotion or advertising relevant to various steps
Conative The realm of motives. Ads stimulate or direct desires.	**Purchase**	Point-of-purchase Retail store ads Deals "Last-chance" offers Price appeals Testimonials
	Conviction	
Affective The realm of emotions. Ads change attitudes and feelings.	**Preference**	Competitive ads Argumentative copy
	Liking	"Image" copy Status, glamour appeals
Cognitive The realm of thoughts. Ads provide information and facts.	**Knowledge**	Announcements Descriptive copy Classified ads Slogans Jingles Skywriting
	Awareness	Teaser campaigns

Figure 7-2 Effect of advertising on consumers: movement from awareness to action

various steps in the Lavidge and Steiner hierarchy of effects model as the consumer moves from awareness to purchase, along with examples of types of promotion or advertising relevant to each step.

Communications Effects Pyramid Advertising and promotion perform communications tasks in the same way that a pyramid is built, by first accomplishing lower-level objectives such as awareness and knowledge or comprehension.[11] Subsequent tasks involve moving consumers who are aware of or knowledgeable about the product or service to higher levels in the pyramid (Figure 7-3). The initial stages, at the base of the pyramid, are easier to accomplish than those toward the top, such as trial and repurchase or regular use. Thus, the percentage of prospective customers will decline as they move up the pyramid. Figure 7-4 shows how a company introducing a new brand of shampoo targeted at 18- to 34-year-old females might set its IMC objectives using the communications effects pyramid.

The communications pyramid can also be used to determine promotional objectives for an established brand. The promotional planner must determine where the target audience lies with respect to the various blocks in the pyramid. If awareness levels for a brand and knowledge of its features and benefits are low, the communications objective should be to increase them. If these blocks of the pyramid are already in place, but liking or preference is low, the advertising goal may be to change the target markets' image of the brand and move consumers through to purchase.

Problems with Communications Objectives Not all marketing and advertising managers accept communications objectives; some say it is too difficult to

Figure 7-3
Communications effects pyramid

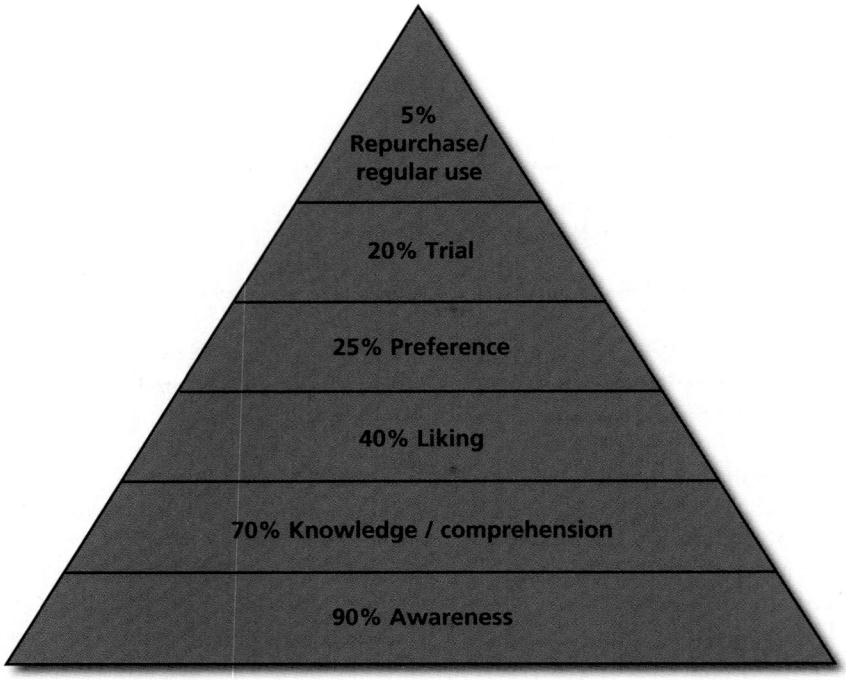

translate a sales goal into a specific communications objective. But at some point a sales goal must be transformed into a communications objective. If the marketing plan for an established brand has as an objective of increasing sales by 10 percent, the promotional planner will eventually have to think in terms of the message that will be communicated to the target audience to achieve this. Possible objectives include the following:

- Increasing the percentage of consumers in the target market who associate specific features, benefits, or advantages with our brand.
- Increasing the number of consumers in the target audience who prefer our product over the competition's.
- Encouraging current users of the product to use it more frequently or in more situations.
- Encouraging consumers who have never used our brand to try it.

Figure 7-4 Setting objectives using the communications effects pyramid

Product: Backstage Shampoo

Time period: Six months

Objective 1: Create awareness among 90 percent of target audience. Use repetitive advertising in newspapers, magazines, TV and radio programs. Simple message.

Objective 2: Create interest in the brand among 70 percent of target audience. Communicate information about the features and benefits of the brand—i.e., that it contains no soap and improves the texture of the hair. Use more copy in ads to convey benefits.

Objective 3: Create positive feelings about the brand among 40 percent and preference among 25 percent of the target audience. Create favorable attitudes by conveying information, promotions, sampling, etc. Refer consumer to website for more information, beauty tips, etc.

Objective 4: Obtain trial among 20 percent of the target audience. Use sampling and cents-off coupons along with advertising and promotions. Offer coupons through website.

Objective 5: Develop and maintain regular use of Backstage Shampoo among 5 percent of the target audience. Use continued-reinforcement advertising, fewer coupons and promotions. Increase communications efforts to professionals.

In some situations, promotional planners may gain insight into communications objectives' relationship to sales from industry research. Evalucom, Inc., conducted a study of commercials for new products. Some succeeded in stimulating anticipated levels of sales; others did not. Figure 7-5 shows four factors the study identified that affect whether a commercial for a new product is successful in generating sales.

In attempting to translate sales goals into specific communications objectives, promotional planners often are not sure what constitutes adequate levels of awareness, knowledge, liking, preference, or conviction. There are no formulas to provide this information. The promotional manager will have to use his or her personal experience and that of the brand or product managers, as well as the marketing history of this and similar brands. Average scores on various communications measures for this and similar products should be considered, along with the levels achieved by competitors' products. This information can be related to the amount of money and time spent building these levels as well as the resulting sales or market share figures.

At some point, sales-oriented objectives must be translated into what the company hopes to communicate and to whom it hopes to communicate it. For example, in the highly competitive office supply industry Boise Cascade has been around for over 35 years. In a market where differentiation is difficult to achieve due to the fact that many companies make the same products at about equal prices, Boise lacked personality. The company needed to change the consumers' focus from price to the advantages provided by its knowledge and experience in the industry. After identifying the target market as women 18 to 54 with a high school diploma, the company combined with its agency to develop a "personality test" that customers and potential customers could take to learn more about their personalities and interactive styles. In addition, participants could learn more about the styles of coworkers, relatives, and so on, to improve communications. The "You've Got to Have Personality" campaign was designed in an attempt to have participants learn more about themselves as well as Boise Cascade. Initially using advertising, direct mail, the Internet, and sales promotions, the program was later extended to include trade shows and other promotions. The results were obvious—a 30 percent increase in web traffic and a 250 percent jump in visitors to the company's online magazine. Most important, recognition of the Boise name increased, a personality was established, and sales of the products promoted in the "Personality" flyer increased 15.8 percent over the previous year.[12]

Many marketing and promotional managers recognize the value of setting specific communications objectives and their important role as operational guidelines to the planning, execution, and evaluation of the promotional program. Communications objectives are the criteria used in the DAGMAR approach to setting advertising goals and objectives, which has become one of the most influential approaches to the advertising planning process.

- **Communicating that something is different about the product.** Successful introductory commercials communicated some point of difference for the new product.
- **Positioning the brand difference in relation to the product category.** Successful commercials positioned their brand's difference within a specific product category. For example, a new breakfast product was positioned as the "crispiest cereal" and a new beverage as the "smoothest soft drink."
- **Communicating that the product difference is beneficial to consumers.** Nearly all of the successful commercials linked a benefit directly to the new product's difference.
- **Supporting the idea that something about the product is different and/or beneficial to consumers.** All the successful commercials communicated support for the product's difference claim or its relevance to consumers. Support took the form of demonstrations of performance, information supporting a uniqueness claim, endorsements, or testimonials.

Figure 7-5 Factors related to success of advertising for new products

DAGMAR: An Approach to Setting Objectives

In 1961, Russell Colley prepared a report for the Association of National Advertisers titled *Defining Advertising Goals for Measured Advertising Results* (DAGMAR).[13] In it, Colley developed a model for setting advertising objectives and measuring the results of an ad campaign. The major thesis of the **DAGMAR** model is that communications effects are the logical basis for advertising goals and objectives against which success or failure should be measured. Colley's rationale for communications-based objectives was as follows:

> Advertising's job, purely and simply, is to communicate to a defined audience information and a frame of mind that stimulates action. Advertising succeeds or fails depending on how well it communicates the desired information and attitudes to the right people at the right time and at the right cost.[14]

Under the DAGMAR approach, an advertising goal involves a **communications task** that is specific and measurable. A communications task, as opposed to a marketing task, can be performed by, and attributed to, advertising rather than to a combination of several marketing factors. Colley proposed that the communications task be based on a hierarchical model of the communications process with four stages:

- *Awareness*—making the consumer aware of the existence of the brand or company.
- *Comprehension*—developing an understanding of what the product is and what it will do for the consumer.
- *Conviction*—developing a mental disposition in the consumer to buy the product.
- *Action*—getting the consumer to purchase the product.

As discussed earlier, other hierarchical models of advertising effects can be used as a basis for analyzing the communications response process. Some advertising theorists prefer the Lavidge and Steiner hierarchy of effects model, since it is more specific and provides a better way to establish and measure results.[15]

While the hierarchical model of advertising effects was the basic model of the communications response process used in DAGMAR, Colley also studied other specific tasks that advertising might be expected to perform in leading to the ultimate objective of a sale. He developed a checklist of 52 advertising tasks to characterize the contribution of advertising and serve as a starting point for establishing objectives.

Characteristics of Objectives

A second major contribution of DAGMAR to the advertising planning process was its definition of what constitutes a good objective. Colley argued that advertising objectives should be stated in terms of concrete and measurable communications tasks, specify a target audience, indicate a benchmark starting point and the degree of change sought, and specify a time period for accomplishing the objective(s).

Concrete, Measurable Tasks The communications task specified in the objective should be a precise statement of what appeal or message the advertiser wants to communicate to the target audience. Advertisers generally use a copy platform to describe their basic message. The objective or copy platform statement should be specific and clear enough to guide the creative specialists who develop the advertising message. For example, Foster's Beer, after a successful introduction, saw sales decline significantly. Knowing that to reverse the downward trend something significant had to be done, Fosters developed an entirely new positioning campaign with the following objectives:

- Strengthen the brand's image
- Maximize brand presence
- Broaden the market base beyond traditional import beer drinkers
- Increase sales

Exhibit 7-8 Foster's Beer delivers a very successful new campaign

Using a variety of tools including billboards, videos, point-of-sale promotions, and spot television (Exhibit 7-8), the program doubled its unaided awareness scores, tripled trial, and increased brand awareness by 40 percent. In addition, beer sales doubled in test markets, and overall beer sales increased by 12.1 percent in the first year of the campaign.[16]

According to DAGMAR, the objective must also be measurable. There must be a way to determine whether the intended message has been communicated properly. For example Midwest Express measured its communications objective by asking airline travelers whether they thought Midwest's airfares were higher than those of competing airlines.

Target Audience Another important characteristic of good objectives is a well-defined target audience. The primary target audience for a company's product or service is described in the situation analysis. It may be based on descriptive variables such as geography, demographics, and psychographics (on which advertising media selection decisions are based) as well as on behavioral variables such as usage rate or benefits sought. Figure 7-6 demonstrates the objective-setting process involved in the launch of the new Subaru Outback. Notice how specifically the target audience was defined.

Target Market:	Male, 35–55, married, household income $55,000+, active lifestyle
Positioning:	Carlike qualities without sacrificing SUV qualities
Objectives:	Convince SUV buyers to consider the Outback rather than SUV under consideration; generate high awareness, generate high numbers of showroom visits, avoid discounts, generate high sales volume, attract at least 50% of sales from those intending to buy Ford, Chevy, or Jeep
Budget:	$17 million
Media:	Advertising:
	TV: Prime-time programs, local news and sports
	Cable TV: National Geographic Explorer, Discovery, Learning Channel
	Print: *Backpacker, Outside, National Geographic, Smithsonian*
	Support Media: Outdoor and POP
	Public Relations: Press kits and PR campaign
	Direct Marketing: Prospective buyers; dealers
Results:	Recall increased from 33 to 38% in first 60 days; 50% by completion of campaign
	Dealer traffic increased by 15 to 20%
	Sales were highest in 9 years—four times projections; 55% from non-Subaru owners; top three models traded in: Jeep Grand Cherokee, Ford Explorer, Chevy Blazer

Figure 7-6 Subaru Outback Objective Setting

Benchmark and Degree of Change Sought To set objectives, one must know the target audience's present status concerning response hierarchy variables such as awareness, knowledge, image, attitudes, and intentions and then determine the degree to which consumers must be changed by the advertising campaign. Determining the target market's present position regarding the various response stages requires **benchmark measures.** Often a marketing research study must be conducted to determine prevailing levels of the response hierarchy. In the case of a new product or service, the starting conditions are generally at or near zero for all the variables, so no initial research is needed.

Establishing benchmark measures gives the promotional planner a basis for determining what communications tasks need to be accomplished and for specifying particular objectives. For example, a preliminary study for a brand may reveal that awareness is high but consumer perceptions and attitudes are negative. The objective for the advertising campaign must then be to change the target audience's perceptions of and attitudes toward the brand. In the case of Outback, the objectives were to generate high levels of awareness, given that existing levels were so low.

Quantitative benchmarks are not only valuable in establishing communications goals and objectives but essential for determining whether the campaign was successful. Objectives provide the standard against which the success or failure of a campaign is measured. An ad campaign that results in a 90 percent awareness level for a brand among its target audience cannot really be judged effective unless one knows what percentage of the consumers were aware of the brand before the campaign began. A 70 percent precampaign awareness level would lead to a different interpretation of the campaign's success than would a 30 percent level.

Specified Time Period A final consideration in setting advertising objectives is specifying the time period in which they must be accomplished. Appropriate time periods can range from a few days to a year or more. Most ad campaigns specify time periods from a few months to a year, depending on the situation facing the advertiser and the type of response being sought. For example, awareness levels for a brand can be created or increased fairly quickly through an intensive media schedule of widespread, repetitive advertising to the target audience. Repositioning of a product requires a change in consumers' perceptions and takes much more time. The repositioning of Marlboro cigarettes from a feminine brand to one with a masculine image, for instance, took several years.

Assessment of DAGMAR

The DAGMAR approach to setting objectives has had considerable influence on the advertising planning process. Many promotional planners use this model as a basis for setting objectives and assessing the effectiveness of their promotional campaigns. DAGMAR also focused advertisers' attention on the value of using communications-based rather than sales-based objectives to measure advertising effectiveness and encouraged the measurement of stages in the response hierarchy to assess a campaign's impact. Colley's work has led to improvements in the advertising and promotional planning process by providing a better understanding of the goals and objectives toward which planners' efforts should be directed. This usually results in less subjectivity and leads to better communication and relationships between client and agency.

Criticisms of DAGMAR While DAGMAR has contributed to the advertising planning process, it has not been totally accepted by everyone in the advertising field. A number of problems have led to questions regarding its value as a planning tool:[17]

- *Problems with the response hierarchy.* A major criticism of the DAGMAR approach is its reliance on the hierarchy of effects model. The fact that consumers do not always go through this sequence of communications effects before making a purchase has been recognized, and alternative response models have been developed.[18] DAGMAR MOD II recognizes that the appropriate response model depends on the situation and

emphasizes identifying the sequence of decision-making steps that apply in a buying situation.[19]

- *Sales objectives.* Another objection to DAGMAR comes from those who argue that the only relevant measure of advertising objectives is sales. They have little tolerance for ad campaigns that achieve communications objectives but fail to increase sales. Advertising is seen as effective only if it induces consumers to make a purchase.[20] The problems with this logic were addressed in our discussion of communications objectives.
- *Practicality and costs.* Another criticism of DAGMAR concerns the difficulties involved in implementing it. Money must be spent on research to establish quantitative benchmarks and measure changes in the response hierarchy. This is costly and time-consuming and can lead to considerable disagreement over method, criteria, measures, and so forth. Many critics argue that DAGMAR is practical only for large companies with big advertising and research budgets. Many firms do not want to spend the money needed to use DAGMAR effectively.
- *Inhibition of creativity.* A final criticism of DAGMAR is that it inhibits advertising creativity by imposing too much structure on the people responsible for developing the advertising. Many creative personnel think the DAGMAR approach is too concerned with quantitative assessment of a campaign's impact on awareness, brandname recall, or specific persuasion measures. The emphasis is on passing the numbers test rather than developing a message that is truly creative and contributes to brand equity.

Problems in Setting Objectives

Although the DAGMAR model suggests a logical process for advertising and promotion planning, most advertisers and their agencies fail to follow these basic principles. They fail to set specific objectives for their campaigns and/or do not have the proper evidence to determine the success of their promotional programs. A classic study conducted by Stewart H. Britt examined problems with how advertisers set objectives and measure their accomplishment.[21] The study showed that most advertising agencies did not state appropriate objectives for determining success and thus could not demonstrate whether a supposedly successful campaign was really a success. Even though these campaigns may have been doing something right, they generally did not know what it was.

Although this study was conducted in 1969, the same problems exist in advertising today. A more recent study examined the advertising practices of business-to-business marketers to determine whether their ads used advertising objectives that met Colley's four DAGMAR criteria.[22] Entries from the annual Business/Professional Advertising Association Gold Key Awards competition, which solicits the best marketing communications efforts from business-to-business advertisers, were evaluated with respect to their campaigns' objectives and summaries of results. Most of these advertisers did not set concrete advertising objectives, specify objective tasks, measure results in terms of stages of a hierarchy of effects, or match objectives to evaluation measures. The authors concluded: "Advertising practitioners have only partially adopted the concepts and standards of objective setting and evaluation set forth 25 years ago."[23]

Improving Promotional Planners' Use of Objectives

As we have seen, it is important that advertisers and their agencies pay close attention to the objectives they set for their campaigns. They should strive to set specific and measurable objectives that not only guide promotional planning and decision making but also can be used as a standard for evaluating performance. Unfortunately, many companies do not set appropriate objectives for their integrated marketing communications programs.

Many companies fail to set appropriate objectives because top management has only an abstract idea of what the firm's IMC program is supposed to be doing. In a study by the American Business Press that measured the attitudes of chairs, presidents, and other senior managers of business-to-business advertising companies, more than half of the 427 respondents said they did not know whether their advertising was

working and less than 10 percent thought it was working well.[24] This study showed overwhelmingly that top management did not even know what the company's advertising was supposed to do, much less how to measure it.

Few firms will set objectives that meet all the criteria set forth in DAGMAR. However, promotional planners should set objectives that are specific and measurable and go beyond basic sales goals. Even if specific communications response elements are not always measured, meeting the other criteria will sharpen the focus and improve the quality of the IMC planning process.

Setting Objectives for the IMC Program

One reason so much attention is given to advertising objectives is that for many companies advertising has traditionally been the major way of communicating with target audiences. Other promotional mix elements such as sales promotion, direct marketing, and publicity are used intermittently to support and complement the advertising program.

Another reason is that traditional advertising-based views of marketing communications planning, such as DAGMAR, have dominated the field for so long. These approaches are based on a hierarchical response model and consider how marketers can develop and disseminate advertising messages to move consumers along an effects path. This approach, shown in Figure 7-7, is what professor Don Schultz calls *inside-out planning*. He says, "It focuses on what the marketer wants to say, when the marketer wants to say it, about things the marketer believes are important about his or her brand, and in the media forms the marketer wants to use."[25]

Schultz advocates an *outside-in planning* process for IMC that starts with the customer and builds backward to the brand. This means that promotional planners study the various media customers and prospects use, when the marketer's messages might be most relevant to customers, and when they are likely to be most receptive to the message.

A similar approach is suggested by Professor Tom Duncan, who argues that IMC should use **zero-based communications planning,** which involves determining what tasks need to be done and which marketing communications functions should be used and to what extent.[26] This approach focuses on the task to be done and searches for the best ideas and media to accomplish it. Duncan notes that as with a traditional advertising campaign, the basis of an IMC campaign is a big idea. However, in IMC the big idea can be public relations, direct response, packaging, or sales promotion. Duncan suggests that an effective IMC program should lead with the marketing communications function that most effectively addresses the company's main problem or opportunity and should use a promotional mix that draws on the strengths of whichever communications functions relate best to the particular situation.

Many of the considerations for determining advertising objectives are relevant to setting goals for other elements of the integrated marketing communications program.

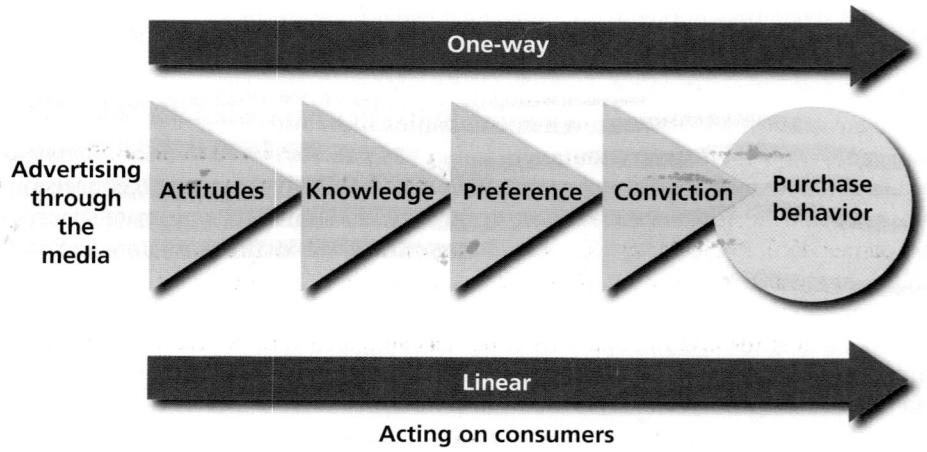

Figure 7-7 Traditional advertising-based view of marketing communications

The promotional planner should determine what role various sales promotion techniques, publicity and public relations, direct marketing, and personal selling will play in the overall marketing program and how they will interact with advertising as well as with one another.

For example, the marketing communications program for the San Diego Zoological Society has a number of objectives. First, it must provide funding for the society's programs and maintain a large and powerful base of supporters for financial and political strength. The program must educate the public about the society's various programs and maintain a favorable image on a local, regional, national, and even international level. A major objective of the IMC program is drawing visitors to the two attractions (Exhibit 7-9).

Exhibit 7-9 The San Diego Zoo attempts to attract visitors through advertising

To achieve these objectives, the San Diego Zoological Society and its advertising agency developed an IMC program. As can be seen in Figure 7-8, this program employed a variety of integrated marketing communication tools. When setting objectives for these promotional elements, planners must consider what the firm hopes to communicate through the use of this element, among what target audience, and during what time period. As with advertising, results should be measured and evaluated against the original objectives, and attempts should be made to isolate the effects of each promotional element. Objectives for marketing communications elements other than advertising are discussed more thoroughly in Part Five of the text.

Establishing and Allocating the Promotional Budget

If you take a minute to look back at Figure 1-4 on page 26, you will see that while the arrows from the review of the marketing plan and the promotional situation analysis to analysis of the communications process are *unidirectional,* the flow between the communications analysis and budget determination is a *two-way interaction.* What this means is that while establishing objectives is an important part of the planning process, the limitations of the budget are important too. No organization has an unlimited budget, so objectives must be set with the budget in mind.

Often when we think of promotional expenditures of firms, we think only about the huge amounts being spent. We don't usually take the time to think about how these monies are being allocated and about the recipients of these dollars. The budgeting decisions have a significant impact not only on the firm itself but also on numerous others involved either directly or indirectly. The remainder of this chapter provides insight into some underlying theory with respect to budget setting, discusses how companies budget for promotional efforts, and demonstrates the inherent strengths and weaknesses associated with these approaches. Essentially, we focus on two primary budgeting decisions: establishing a budget amount and allocating the budget.

Establishing the Budget

The size of a firm's advertising and promotions budget can vary from a few thousand dollars to more than a billion. When companies like Ford, Procter & Gamble, and General Motors spend over 2 billion dollars per year to promote their products, they expect such expenditures to accomplish their stated objectives. The budget decision is no less critical to a firm spending only a few thousand dollars; its ultimate success or failure may depend on the monies spent. One of the most critical decisions facing the marketing manager is how much to spend on the promotional effort.

Unfortunately, many managers fail to realize the value of advertising and promotion. They treat the communications budget as an expense rather than an investment. Instead of viewing the dollars spent as contributing to additional sales and market share, they see budget expenses as cutting into profits. As a result, when times get tough, the advertising and promotional budget is the first to be cut—even though there

Figure 7-8 The San Diego Zoo sets objectives for various promotional elements

Advertising

Objectives: Drive attendance to Zoo and Wild Animal Park. Uphold image and educate target audience and inform them of new attractions and special events and promotions.

Audience: Members and nonmembers of Zoological Society. Households in primary and secondary geographic markets consisting of San Diego County and 5 other counties in southern California. Tertiary markets of 7 western states. Tourist and group sales markets.

Timing: As allowed and determined by budget. Mostly timed to coincide with promotional efforts.

Tools/media: Television, radio, newspaper, magazines, direct mail, outdoor, tourist media (television and magazine).

Sales Promotions

Objectives: Use price, product, and other variables to drive attendance when it might not otherwise come.

Audience: Targeted, depending on co-op partner, mostly to southern California market.

Timing: To fit needs of Zoo and Wild Animal Park and cosponsoring partner.

Tools/media: Coupons, sweepstakes, tours, broadcast tradeouts, direct mail: statement stuffers, fliers, postcards.

Public Relations

Objectives: Inform, educate, create, and maintain image for Zoological Society and major attractions; reinforce advertising message.

Audience: From local to international, depending on subject, scope, and timing.

Timing: Ongoing, although often timed to coincide with promotions and other special events. Spur-of-the-moment animal news and information such as acquisitions, births, etc.

Tools/media: Coverage by major news media, articles in local, regional, national and international newspapers, magazines and other publications such as visitors' guides, tour books and guides, appearances by Zoo spokesperson Joanne Embery on talk shows (such as "The Tonight Show").

Cause Marketing/Corporate Sponsorships/Events Underwriting

Objectives: To provide funding for Zoological Society programs and promote special programs and events done in cooperation with corporate sponsor. Must be win-win business partnership for Society and partner.

Audience: Supporters of both the Zoological Society and the corporate or product/service partner.

Timing: Coincides with needs of both partners, and seasonal attendance generation needs of Zoo and Wild Animal Park.

Tools: May involve advertising, publicity, discount co-op promotions, ticket trades, hospitality centers. Exposure is directly proportional to amount of underwriting by corporate sponsor, both in scope and duration.

Direct Marketing

Objectives: Maintain large powerful base of supporters for financial and political strength.

Audience: Local, regional, national and international. Includes children's program (Koala Club), seniors (60+), couples, single memberships, and incremental donor levels.

Timing: Ongoing, year-round promotion of memberships.

Tools: Direct mail and on-grounds visibility.

Group Sales

Objectives: Maximize group traffic and revenue by selling group tours to Zoo and Wild Animal Park.

Audience: Conventions, incentive groups, bus tours, associations, youth, scouts, schools, camps, seniors, clubs, military, organizations, domestic and foreign travel groups.

Timing: Targeted to drive attendance in peak seasons or at most probable times such as convention season.

Tools: Travel and tourism trade shows, telemarketing, direct mail, trade publication advertising.

Internet

Objectives: Provide information regarding the zoo, programs, memberships and public relations activities.

Audience: All audiences interested in acquiring more information about the zoo.

Timing: Ongoing, updated frequently over time.

Tools: Website, including videos, shop zoo and zoo calendar.

is strong evidence that exactly the opposite should occur, as Exhibit 7-10 argues. Moreover, the decision is not a one-time responsibility. A new budget is formulated every year, each time a new product is introduced, or when either internal or external factors necessitate a change to maintain competitiveness.

While it is one of the most critical decisions, budgeting has perhaps been the most resistant to change. A comparison of advertising and promotional texts over the past 10 years would reveal the same methods for establishing budgets. The theoretical basis for this process remains rooted in economic theory and marginal analysis. (Advertisers also use an approach based on **contribution margin**—the difference between the total revenue generated by a brand and its total variable costs. But, as Robert Steiner says, *marginal analysis* and *contribution margin* are essentially synonymous terms.)[27] We begin our discussion of budgeting with an examination of these theoretical approaches.

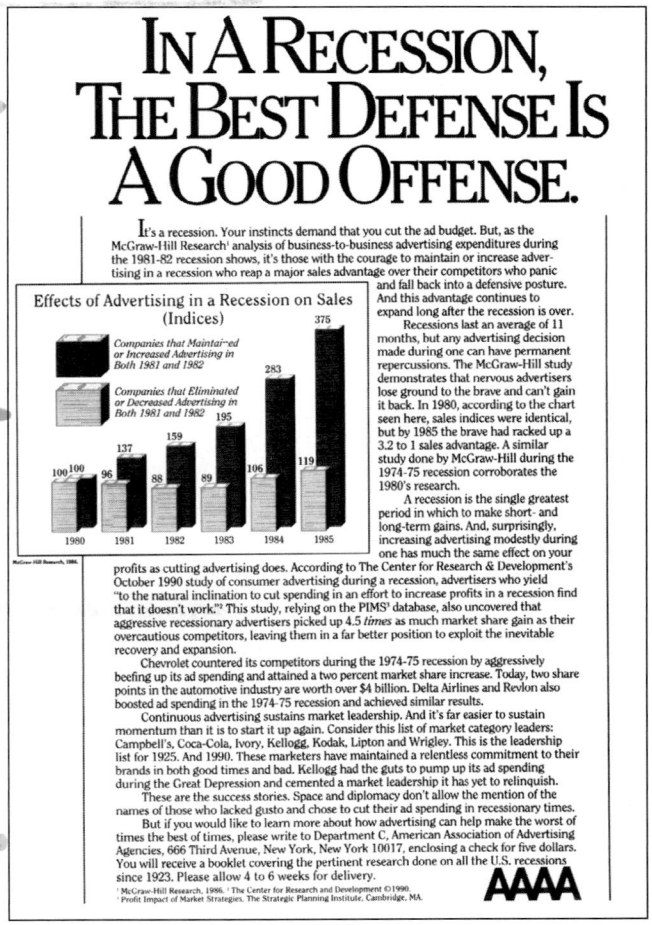

IN A RECESSION, THE BEST DEFENSE IS A GOOD OFFENSE.

It's a recession. Your instincts demand that you cut the ad budget. But, as the McGraw-Hill Research[1] analysis of business-to-business advertising expenditures during the 1981-82 recession shows, it's those with the courage to maintain or increase advertising in a recession who reap a major sales advantage over their competitors who panic and fall back into a defensive posture. And this advantage continues to expand long after the recession is over.

Recessions last an average of 11 months, but any advertising decision made during one can have permanent repercussions. The McGraw-Hill study demonstrates that nervous advertisers lose ground to the brave and can't gain it back. In 1980, according to the chart seen here, sales indices were identical, but by 1985 the brave had racked up a 3.2 to 1 sales advantage. A similar study done by McGraw-Hill during the 1974-75 recession corroborates the 1980's research.

Effects of Advertising in a Recession on Sales (Indices)

Companies that Maintained or Increased Advertising in Both 1981 and 1982

Companies that Eliminated or Decreased Advertising in Both 1981 and 1982

100 100 96 137 88 159 89 195 106 283 119 375

1980 1981 1982 1983 1984 1985

McGraw-Hill Research, 1986.

A recession is the single greatest period in which to make short- and long-term gains. And, surprisingly, increasing advertising modestly during one has much the same effect on your profits as cutting advertising does. According to The Center for Research & Development's October 1990 study of consumer advertising during a recession, advertisers who yield "to the natural inclination to cut spending in an effort to increase profits in a recession find that it doesn't work."[2] This study, relying on the PIMS[3] database, also uncovered that aggressive recessionary advertisers picked up 4.5 *times* as much market share gain as their overcautious competitors, leaving them in a far better position to exploit the inevitable recovery and expansion.

Chevrolet countered its competitors during the 1974-75 recession by aggressively beefing up its ad spending and attained a two percent market share increase. Today, two share points in the automotive industry are worth over $4 billion. Delta Airlines and Revlon also boosted ad spending in the 1974-75 recession and achieved similar results.

Continuous advertising sustains market leadership. And it's far easier to sustain momentum than it is to start it up again. Consider this list of market category leaders: Campbell's, Coca-Cola, Ivory, Kellogg, Kodak, Lipton and Wrigley. This is the leadership list for 1925. And 1990. These marketers have maintained a relentless commitment to their brands in both good times and bad. Kellogg had the guts to pump up its ad spending during the Great Depression and cemented a market leadership it has yet to relinquish.

These are the success stories. Space and diplomacy don't allow the mention of the names of those who lacked gusto and chose to cut their ad spending in recessionary times.

But if you would like to learn more about how advertising can help make the worst of times the best of times, please write to Department C, American Association of Advertising Agencies, 666 Third Avenue, New York, New York 10017, enclosing a check for five dollars. You will receive a booklet covering the pertinent research done on all the U.S. recessions since 1923. Please allow 4 to 6 weeks for delivery.

[1] McGraw-Hill Research, 1986. [2] The Center for Research and Development ©1990.
[3] Profit Impact of Market Strategies. The Strategic Planning Institute, Cambridge, MA.

AAAA

Exhibit 7-10 The AAAA promotes the continued use of advertising in a recession

Theoretical Issues in Budget Setting

Most of the models used to establish advertising budgets can be categorized as taking an economic or a sales response perspective.

Marginal Analysis Figure 7-9 graphically represents the concept of **marginal analysis.** As advertising/promotional expenditures increase, sales and gross margins also increase to a point, but then they level off. Profits are shown to be a result of the gross margin minus advertising expenditures. Using this theory to establish its budget, a firm would continue to spend advertising/promotional dollars as long as the marginal revenues created by these expenditures exceeded the incremental advertising/promotional costs. As shown on the graph, the optimal expenditure level is the point where marginal costs equal the marginal revenues they generate (point *A*). If the sum of the advertising/promotional expenditures exceeded the revenues they generated, one would conclude the appropriations were too high and scale down the budget. If revenues were higher, a higher budget might be in order. (We will see later in this chapter that this approach can also be applied to the allocation decision.)

While marginal analysis seems logical intuitively, certain weaknesses limit its usefulness. These weaknesses include the assumptions that (1) sales are a direct result of advertising and promotional expenditures and this effect can be measured and (2) advertising and promotion are solely responsible for sales. Let us examine each of these assumptions in more detail.

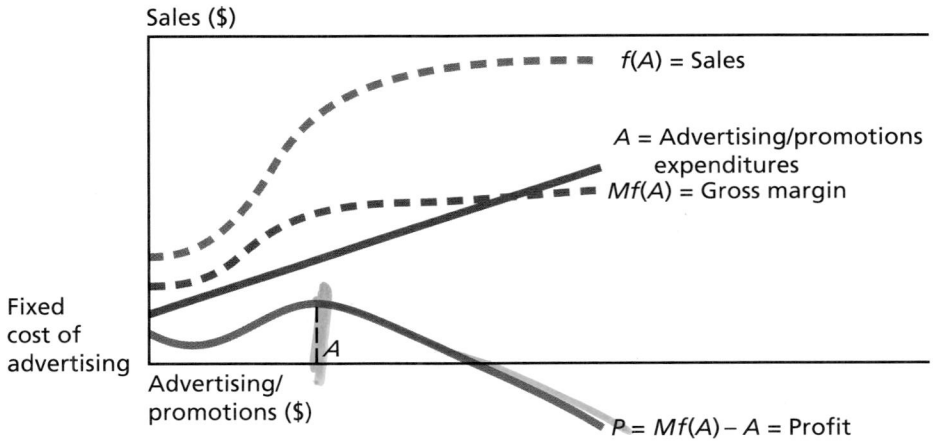

Figure 7-9 Marginal analysis

1. *Assumption that sales are a direct measure of advertising and promotions efforts.* Earlier in this chapter we discussed the fact that the advertiser needs to set communications objectives that contribute to accomplishing overall marketing objectives but at the same time are separate. One reason for this strategy is that it is often difficult, if not impossible, to demonstrate the effects of advertising and promotions on sales. In studies using sales as a direct measure, it has been almost impossible to establish the contribution of advertising and promotion. As noted by Frank Bass, "There is no more difficult, complex, or controversial problem in marketing than measuring the influence of advertising on sales."[28] In the words of David Aaker and James Carman, "Looking for the relationship between advertising and sales is somewhat worse than looking for a needle in a haystack."[29] Thus, to try to show that the size of the budget will directly affect sales of the product is misleading. A more logical approach would be to examine the impact of various budgets on the attainment of communications objectives.

As we saw in the discussion of communications objectives, sales are not the only goal of the promotional effort. Awareness, interest, attitude change, and other communications objectives are often sought, and while the bottom line may be to sell the product, these objectives may serve as the basis on which the promotional program is developed.

2. *Assumption that sales are determined solely by advertising and promotion.* This assumption ignores the remaining elements of the marketing mix—price, product, and distribution—which do contribute to a company's success. Environmental factors may also affect the promotional program, leading the marketing manager to assume the advertising was or was not effective when some other factor may have helped or hindered the accomplishment of the desired objectives.

Overall, you can see that while the economic approach to the budgeting process is a logical one, the difficulties associated with determining the effects of the promotional effort on sales and revenues limit its applicability. Marginal analysis is seldom used as a basis for budgeting (except for direct-response advertising).

Sales Response Models You may have wondered why the sales curve in Figure 7-9 shows sales leveling off even though advertising and promotions efforts continue to increase. The relationship between advertising and sales has been the topic of much research and discussion designed to determine the shape of the response curve.

Almost all advertisers subscribe to one of two models of the advertising/sales response function: the concave-downward function or the S-shaped response curve.

- *The concave-downward function.* After reviewing more than 100 studies of the effects of advertising on sales, Julian Simon and Johan Arndt concluded that the effects of advertising budgets follow the microeconomic law of diminishing returns.[30] That is, as the amount of advertising increases, its incremental value decreases. The logic is that those with the greatest potential to buy will likely act on the first (or earliest) exposures, while those less likely to buy are not likely to change as a result of the advertising. For those who may be potential buyers, each additional ad will supply little or no new information that will affect their decision. Thus, according to the **concave-downward function model,** the effects of advertising quickly begin to diminish, as shown in Figure 7-10A. Budgeting under this model suggests that fewer advertising dollars may be needed to create the optimal influence on sales.

- *The S-shaped response function.* Many advertising managers assume the **S-shaped response curve** (Figure 7-10B), which projects an S-shaped response function to the budget outlay (again measured in sales). Initial outlays of the advertising budget have little impact (as indicated by the essentially flat sales curve in range A). After a certain budget level has been reached (the beginning of range B), advertising and promotional efforts begin to have an effect, as additional increments of expenditures result in increased sales. This incremental gain continues only to a point, however, because at the beginning of range C additional expenditures begin to return little or nothing in the way of sales. This model suggests a small advertising budget is likely to have no impact beyond the sales that may have been generated through other means

Figure 7-10 Advertising sales/response functions

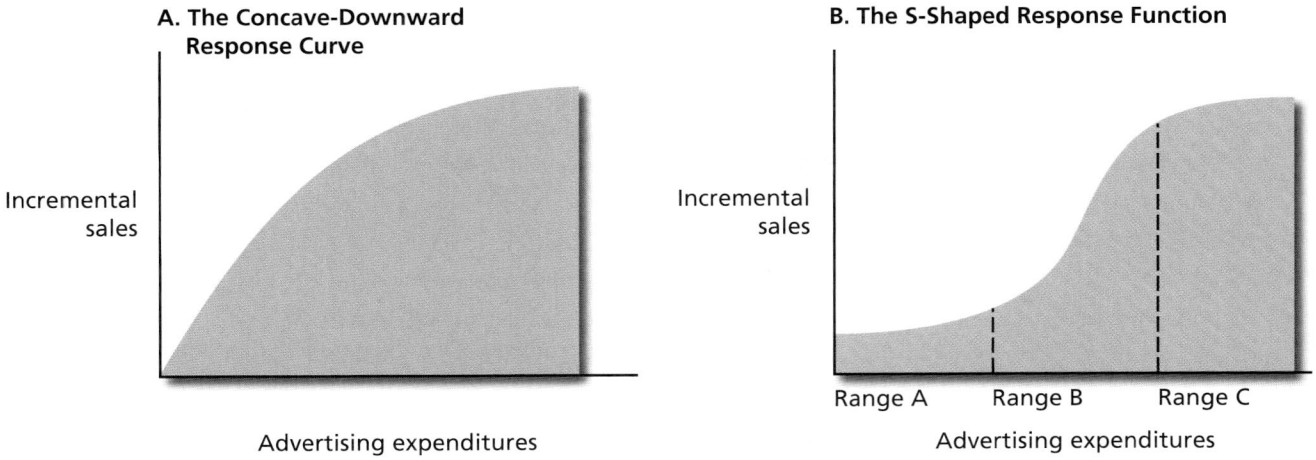

(for example, word of mouth). At the other extreme, more does not necessarily mean better: Additional dollars spent beyond range B have no additional impact on sales and for the most part can be considered wasted. As with marginal analysis, one would attempt to operate at that point on the curve in area B where the maximum return for the money is attained.

Weaknesses in these sales response models render them of limited use to practitioners for direct applications. Many of the problems seen earlier—the use of sales as a dependent variable, measurement problems, and so on—limit the usefulness of these models. At the same time, keep in mind the purpose of discussing such models. Even though marginal analysis and the sales response curves may not apply directly, they give managers some insight into a theoretical basis of how the budgeting process should work. Some empirical evidence indicates the models may have validity. One study, based on industry experience, has provided support for the S-shaped response curve; the results indicate that a minimum amount of advertising dollars must be spent before there is a noticeable effect on sales.[31]

The studies discussed in earlier chapters on learning and the hierarchy of effects also demonstrate the importance of repetition on gaining awareness and on subsequent higher-order objectives such as adoption. Thus, while these models may not provide a tool for setting the advertising and promotional budget directly, we can use them to guide our appropriations strategy from a theoretical basis. As you will see later in this chapter, such a theoretical basis has advantages over many of the methods currently being used for budget setting and allocation.

Exhibit 7-11 A strong basis for differentiation could show a noticeable effect of advertising on sales

Additional Factors in Budget Setting

While the theoretical bases just discussed should be considered in establishing the budget appropriation, a number of other issues must also be considered. A weakness in attempting to use sales as a *direct* measure of response to advertising is that various situational factors may have an effect. In one comprehensive study, 20 variables were shown to affect the advertising/sales ratio. Figure 7-11 lists these factors and their relationships.[32] For a product characterized by emotional buying motives, hidden product qualities, and/or a strong basis for differentiation, advertising would have a noticeable impact on sales (see Exhibit 7-11). Products characterized as large-dollar purchases and those in the maturity or decline stages of the product would be less likely to benefit. The study showed that other factors involving the market, customer, costs, and strategies employed have different effects.

The results of this study are interesting but limited, since they relate primarily to the percentage of sales dollars allocated to advertising and the factors influencing these ratios. As we will see later in this chapter,

Figure 7-11 Factors influencing advertising budgets

Factor	Relationship of Advertising/Sales	Factor	Relationship of Advertising/Sales
Product Factors		***Customer Factors***	
Basis for differentiation	+	Industrial products users	—
Hidden product qualities	+	Concentration of users	+
Emotional buying motives	+	***Strategy Factors***	
Durability	—	Regional markets	—
Large dollar purchase	—	Early stage of brand life cycle	+
Purchase frequency	Curvilinear	High margins in channels	—
Market Factors		Long channels of distribution	+
Stage of product life cycle:		High prices	+
Introductory	+	High quality	+
Growth	+	***Cost Factors***	
Maturity	—	High profit margins	+
Decline	—		
Inelastic demand	+		
Market share	—		
Competition:			
Active	+		
Concentrated	+		
Pioneer in market	—		

Note: + relationship means the factor leads to a positive effect of advertising on sales; — relationship indicates little or no effect of advertising on sales.

the percentage-of-sales method of budgeting has inherent weaknesses in that the advertising and sales effects may be reversed. So we cannot be sure whether the situation actually led to the advertising/sales relationship or vice versa. Thus, while these factors should be considered in the budget appropriation decision, they should not be the sole determinants of where and when to increase or decrease expenditures.

The *Advertising Age* Editorial Sounding Board consists of 92 executives of the top 200 advertising companies in the United States (representing the client side) and 130 executives of the 200 largest advertising agencies and 11 advertising consultants (representing the agency side). A survey of the board yielded the factors shown in Figure 7-12 that are important in budget setting.

Overall, the responses of these two groups reflect in part their perceptions as to factors of importance in how budgets are set. To understand the differences in the relative importance of these factors, it is important to understand the approaches currently employed in budget setting. The next section examines these approaches.

Figure 7-12 Factors considered in budget setting

Changes in advertising strategy and/or creative approach	51%
Competitive activity and/or spending levels	47
Profit contribution goal or other financial target	43
Level of previous year's spending, with adjustment	17
Senior management dollar allocation or set limit	11
Volume share projections	8
Projections/assumptions on media cost increases	25
Modifications in media strategy and/or buying techniques	17

Budgeting Approaches

The theoretical approaches to establishing the promotional budget are seldom employed. In smaller firms, they may never be used. Instead, a number of methods developed through practice and experience are implemented. This section reviews some of the more traditional methods of setting budgets and the relative advantages and disadvantages of each. First, you must understand two things: (1) Many firms employ more than one method, and (2) budgeting approaches vary according to the size and sophistication of the firm.

Top-Down Approaches

The approaches discussed in this section may be referred to as **top-down approaches** because a budgetary amount is established (usually at an executive level) and then the monies are passed down to the various departments (as shown in Figure 7-13). These budgets are essentially predetermined and have no true theoretical basis. Top-down methods include the affordable method, arbitrary allocation, percentage of sales, competitive parity, and return on investment (ROI).

The Affordable Method In the **affordable method** (often referred to as the "all-you-can-afford method"), the firm determines the amount to be spent in various areas such as production and operations. Then it allocates what's left to advertising and promotion, considering this to be the amount it can afford. The task to be performed by the advertising/promotions function is not considered, and the likelihood of under- or overspending is high, as no guidelines for measuring the effects of various budgets are established.

Strange as it may seem, this approach is common among small firms. Unfortunately, it is also used in large firms, particularly those that are not marketing-driven and do not understand the role of advertising and promotion. For example, many high-tech firms focus on new product development and engineering and assume that the product, if good enough, will sell itself. In these companies, little money may be left for performing the advertising and promotions tasks.

The logic for this approach stems from "We can't be hurt with this method" thinking. That is, if we know what we can afford and we do not exceed it, we will not get into financial problems. While this may be true in a strictly accounting sense, it does not reflect sound managerial decision making from a marketing perspective. Often this method does not allocate enough money to get the product off the ground and into the market. In terms of the S-shaped sales response model, the firm is operating in range A. Or the firm may be spending more than necessary, operating in range C. When the

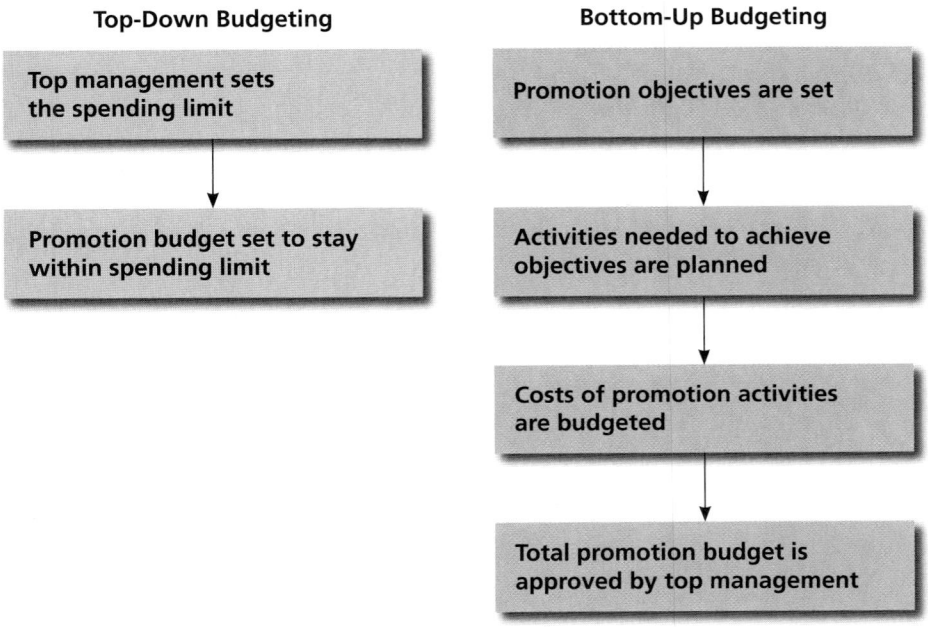

Figure 7-13 Top-down versus bottom-up approaches to budget setting

market gets tough and sales and/or profits begin to fall, this method is likely to lead to budget cuts at a time when the budget should be increased.

Arbitrary Allocation Perhaps an even weaker method than the affordable method for establishing a budget is **arbitrary allocation,** in which virtually no theoretical basis is considered and the budgetary amount is often set by fiat. That is, the budget is determined by management solely on the basis of what is felt to be necessary. In a discussion of how managers set advertising budgets, Melvin Salveson reported that these decisions may reflect "as much upon the managers' psychological profile as they do economic criteria."[33] While Salveson was referring to larger corporations, the approach is no less common in small firms and nonprofit organizations.

The arbitrary allocation approach has no obvious advantages. No systematic thinking has occurred, no objectives have been budgeted for, and the concept and purpose of advertising and promotion have been largely ignored. Other than the fact that the manager believes some monies must be spent on advertising and promotion and then picks a number, there is no good explanation why this approach continues to be used. Yet budgets continue to be set this way, and our purpose in discussing this method is to point out only that it is used—not recommended.

Percentage of Sales Perhaps the most commonly used method for budget setting (particularly in large firms) is the **percentage-of-sales method,** in which the advertising and promotions budget is based on sales of the product. Management determines the amount by either (1) taking a percentage of the sales dollars or (2) assigning a fixed amount of the unit product cost to promotion and multiplying this amount by the number of units sold. These two methods are shown in Figure 7-14.

A variation on the percentage-of-sales method uses a percentage of projected future sales as a base. This method also uses either a straight percentage of projected sales or a unit cost projection. In the straight-percentage method, sales are projected for the coming year based on the marketing manager's estimates. The budget is a percentage of these sales, often an industry standard percentage like those presented in Figure 7-15.

One advantage of using future sales as a base is that the budget is not based on last year's sales. As the market changes, management must factor the effect of these changes on sales into next year's forecast rather than relying on past data. The resulting budget is more likely to reflect current conditions and be more appropriate.

Figure 7-15 reveals that the percentage allocated varies from one industry to the next. Some firms budget a very small percentage (for example, 0.7 percent in lumber and wood products), and others spend a much higher proportional amount (12.0 percent in the games and toy industry). Actual dollar amounts spent vary markedly according to the company's total sales figure. Thus, a smaller percentage of sales in the construction machinery industry may actually result in significantly more advertising dollars being spent.

Proponents of the percentage-of-sales method cite a number of advantages. It is financially safe and keeps ad spending within reasonable limits, as it bases spending on the past year's sales or what the firm expects to sell in the upcoming year. Thus,

Figure 7-14 Alternative methods for computing percentage of sales for Eve Cologne

Method 1: Straight Percentage of Sales		
2002	Total dollar sales	$1,000,000
	Straight % of sales at 10%	$100,000
2003	Advertising budget	$100,000
Method 2: Percentage of Unit Cost		
2002	Cost per bottle to manufacturer	$4.00
	Unit cost allocated to advertising	1.00
2003	Forecasted sales, 100,000 units	
2003	Advertising budget (100,000 × $1)	$100,000

Figure 7-15 2001 advertising-to-sales ratios for the 200 largest ad-spending industries

Industry	SIC Code	Ad Dollars: As % of Sales	Ad Dollars: As % of Margin	Annual Ad Growth Rate	Industry	SIC Code	Ad Dollars: As % of Sales	Ad Dollars: As % of Margin	Annual Ad Growth Rate
Accident & health insurance	6321	0.9%	10.6%	11.3%	Drugs and proprietary-whsl	5122	2.6%	28.9%	11.6%
Advertising	7310	4.5	10.6	30.8	Eating and drinking places	5810	3.8	27.9	5.7
Agricultural chemicals	2870	8.1	25.8	16.6	Eating places	5812	4.2	16.4	6.6
Agriculture production—crops	100	2.1	8.2	3.0	Educational services	6200	4.2	10.2	9.3
Air courier services	4513	1.5	12.2	56.7	Elec meas & test instruments	3825	2.9	6.1	7.2
Air transport, scheduled	4512	1.2	7.8	2.7	Electr, oth elec eq, ex cmp	3600	1.3	5.3	–5.7
Air cond., heating, refrig. equipment	3585	1.4	5.3	6.1	Electric housewares and fans	3634	6.4	18.3	6.9
Amusement & recreation svcs	7900	5.1	20.9	23.1	Electric lighting, wiring eq	3640	1.9	5.0	1.5
Apparel & other finished products	2300	5.5	15.3	1.6	Electrical indi apparatus	3620	2.3	6.7	8.0
Apparel and accessory stores	5600	6.3	14.2	9.6	Electromedical apparatus	3845	1.3	2.1	10.1
Auto and home supply stores	5531	1.1	2.7	8.1	Electronic comp, accessories	3670	2.2	5.4	1.6
Auto dealers, gas stations	5500	1.7	10.1	29.6	Electronic computers	3571	1.5	4.4	10.5
Auto rent & lease, no drivers	7510	2.7	6.0	14.4	Engines and turbines	3510	2.4	8.2	9.5
Bakery products	2050	1.4	2.7	5.0	Engr, acct, research, mgmt. rel svcs	8700	1.7	5.7	22.2
Beverage	2080	7.4	12.1	–6.4	Equip rental & leasing, nec	7359	2.0	3.4	9.4
Biological pds, except diagnostics	2836	2.4	5.2	10.2	Fabricated plate work	3443	2.7	13.8	12.9
Blankbooks, binders, bookbind	2780	4.2	7.1	–0.4	Fabricated rubber products, nec	3060	1.8	5.8	11.7
Bldg matl, hardwr, garden-retl	5200	2.6	6.8	5.9	Family clothing stores	5651	3.7	10.0	14.1
Books: pubg, pubg & printing	2731	8.5	19.0	5.4	Farm machinery and equipment	3523	1.1	3.8	4.6
Btld & can soft drinks, water	2086	5.3	10.9	11.7	Food and kindred products	2000	10.2	24.0	–0.4
Business services, nec	7389	0.5	1.6	5.6	Food stores	5400	4.0	12.6	15.2
Cable and other pay TV svcs	4841	1.3	2.8	–1.6	Footwear, except rubber	3140	4.5	11.2	10.1
Can, frozn, presrv fruit & veg	2030	4.7	10.7	5.0	Furniture stores	5712	6.9	17.4	9.4
Catalog, mail-order houses	5961	8.4	27.8	10.6	Games, toys, chld. veh, except dolls	3944	12.0	21.1	4.3
Chemicals & allied products	2800	1.9	4.4	1.7	General indi mach & equip, nec	3569	0.9	2.3	13.9
Cigarettes	2111	3.9	6.8	–8.7	Grain mill products	2040	7.5	15.0	–5.6
Cmp and cmp software stores	5734	1.1	7.2	–2.2	Greeting cards	2771	3.5	5.1	1.5
Cmp integrated sys design	7373	0.7	2.4	7.6	Groceries & related products-whsl	5140	2.2	14.7	5.5
Cmp processing, data prep svc	7374	1.1	2.4	3.2	Grocery stores	5411	1.1	3.8	8.6
Cmp programming, data process	7370	6.8	16.7	5.3	Hardwr, plumb, heat equip-whsl	5070	4.1	27.5	9.6
Communications equip, nec	3669	1.3	3.4	5.3	Health services	8000	8.7	21.1	20.8
Communications services, nec	4899	3.4	6.0	29.4	Heating equip, plumbing fixture	3430	6.6	15.4	–11.8
Computer & office equipment	3570	1.6	5.3	1.8	Help supply services	7363	0.8	3.8	19.5
Computer communication equip	3576	2.7	4.5	15.1	Hobby, toy and games shops	5945	3.0	11.3	1.0
Computer peripheral equip. nec	3577	2.2	4.6	7.7	Home furniture & equip store	5700	3.0	7.3	10.3
Computer storage devices	3572	1.8	6.1	12.7	Hospital & medical svc plans	6324	0.4	2.6	10.2
Computers & software-whsl	5045	0.3	3.8	13.1	Hotels and motels	7011	2.7	11.4	–1.8
Construction machinery & equip	3531	0.5	1.4	7.9	Household appliances	3630	3.0	10.3	6.0
Construction-special trade	1700	3.2	8.4	10.6	Household audio & video equip	3651	4.2	12.3	8.8
Convenience stores	5412	1.2	3.0	–5.3	Household furniture	2510	7.6	24.0	12.6
Convrt papr, paprbrd, except boxes	2670	3.8	8.0	4.8	Ice cream & frozen desserts	2024	2.0	7.6	–6.6
Cookies and crackers	2052	3.5	6.2	10.0	In vitro, in vivo diagnostics	2835	1.1	2.6	–6.9
Cutlery, hand tools, gen hrdwr	3420	11.8	24.1	10.6	Indi inorganic chemicals	2810	1.1	2.6	3.2
Dairy products	2020	0.9	34.5	20.7	Indi trucks, tractors, trailers	3537	1.7	7.0	6.6
Dental equipment & supplies	3843	1.6	2.9	9.1	Industrial measurement instr	3823	0.8	1.8	7.7
Department stores	5311	3.7	13.0	5.3	Industrial organic chemicals	2860	1.1	3.2	–3.1
Distilled and blended liquor	2085	4.3	33.1	10.8	Investment advice	6282	5.4	16.1	10.5
Dolls and stuffed toys	3942	15.2	29.5	11.2	Jewelry stores	5944	4.6	10.3	9.4
Drawng, insulatng nonfer wire	3357	0.8	2.0	2.2	Knit outerwear mills	2253	2.9	10.4	3.5
Drug & proprietary stores	5912	0.9	3.2	18.2	Knitting mills	2250	3.6	12.5	–2.5

Figure 7-15 Concluded

Industry	SIC Code	Ad Dollars: As % of Sales	Ad Dollars: As % of Margin	Annual Ad Growth Rate
Lab analytical instruments	3826	1.7%	3.2%	11.6%
Leather and leather products	3100	8.8	15.5	12.2
Lumber & oth bldg matl-retl	5211	0.7	2.3	8.4
Malt beverages	2082	7.5	16.2	–1.5
Management services	8741	1.0	6.6	10.0
Manifold business forms	2761	9.7	26.5	7.5
Meat-packing plants	2011	7.8	26.0	7.2
Membership sport & rec clubs	7997	5.6	13.5	–2.5
Men's, boys' frnsh, work clthng	2320	3.0	7.0	11.6
Metal forgings and stampings	3460	1.7	8.1	47.5
Metalworking machinery & equip	3540	4.5	11.5	1.7
Millwork, veneer, plywood	2430	3.5	9.9	12.8
Misc amusement & rec service	7990	3.7	8.9	18.0
Misc business services	7380	1.3	2.4	12.4
Misc durable goods-whsl	5090	3.5	14.5	25.6
Misc elec machy, equip, supplies	3690	4.2	12.3	4.4
Misc fabricated textile products	2390	1.0	3.8	14.4
Misc food preps, kindred products	2090	3.0	7.7	17.8
Misc furniture and fixtures	2590	2.3	6.4	10.2
Misc general mdse stores	5399	4.5	19.5	–4.5
Misc manufacturing industries	3990	4.2	7.9	9.7
Misc nondurable goods-whsl	5190	0.5	2.3	–17.9
Misc shopping goods stores	5940	3.2	11.0	12.7
Misc transportation equip	3790	5.3	17.3	3.0
Miscellaneous publishing	2741	27.1	41.0	18.2
Miscellaneous retail	5900	0.7	2.3	0.4
Mortgage bankers & loan corr	6162	4.9	10.5	16.7
Motion pict, videotape prodtn	7812	8.0	25.4	2.8
Motion pict, videotape distr	7822	5.6	14.3	–1.3
Motion picture theaters	7830	2.8	15.8	10.4
Motor veh supply, new pts-whsl	5013	0.4	1.5	–1.7
Motor vehicle part, accessory	3714	0.9	3.3	10.9
Motor vehicles & car bodies	3711	2.7	10.9	6.8
Motorcycles, bicycles & parts	3751	1.7	4.9	9.6
Motors and generators	3621	0.9	3.2	6.4
Newspaper: pubg, pubg & print	2711	2.2	5.0	2.5
Office furniture, except wood	2522	1.0	2.5	16.2
Operative builders	1531	1.0	8.1	11.9
Ophthalmic goods	3851	7.8	11.4	16.4
Ordnance and accessories	3480	2.1	7.2	2.2
Ortho, prosth, surg appl, supply	3842	2.1	3.8	4.1
Paints, varnishes, lacquers	2851	3.1	7.3	11.1
Paper & paper products-whsl	5110	0.4	1.9	12.1
Paper mills	2621	1.8	4.3	–1.4
Patent owners and lessors	6794	7.5	11.8	–34.3
Pens, pencils, oth artist matl	3950	8.1	19.3	–0.2
Perfume, cosmetic, toilet prep	2844	11.9	19.0	4.8
Periodical: pubg, pubg & print	2721	6.0	12.6	6.5
Personal credit institutions	6141	2.5	5.0	25.3
Personal services	7200	2.4	7.1	6.1
Petroleum refining	2911	0.7%	3.4%	2.8%
Pharmaceutical preparation	2834	5.8	8.2	3.1
Phone comm except radiotelephone	4813	3.0	6.5	9.9
Phono records, audiotape, disk	3652	13.4	37.8	15.1
Photographic equip & supply	3861	4.3	8.7	–1.5
Plastics products, nec	3089	5.1	15.0	5.7
Plastics, resins, elastomers	2821	0.5	1.8	–31.1
Poultry slaughter & process	2015	3.4	18.4	9.4
Prefab wood bldgs, components	2452	1.8	6.1	22.3
Prepackaged software	7372	3.7	5.1	12.2
Prof & coml eq & supply-whsl	5040	1.3	3.8	8.7
Racing, incl track operations	7948	2.5	5.8	14.0
Radio broadcasting stations	4832	6.3	18.6	31.1
Radio, TV broadcast, comm equip	3663	0.4	1.2	8.1
Radio, TV, cons electr stores	5731	3.9	15.5	6.8
Radiotelephone communication	4812	4.6	8.4	21.9
Real estate dealers	6532	3.9	5.4	17.2
Real estate investment trust	6798	3.8	12.2	30.6
Record and tape stores	5735	1.4	3.7	7.0
Refrig & service ind machine	3580	2.0	6.4	12.9
Retail stores, nec	5990	3.7	9.9	15.1
Rubber and plastics footwear	3021	10.4	27.8	12.5
Scrap & waste materials-whsl	5093	4.7	48.5	28.1
Security brokers & dealers	6211	1.1	1.8	9.1
Semiconductor, related device	3674	3.2	5.6	14.9
Shoe stores	5661	3.0	7.8	8.4
Soap, detergent, toilet preps	2840	10.7	21.9	4.4
Spec outpatient facility, nec	8093	0.9	2.7	17.6
Special clean, polish props	2842	12.8	22.1	7.9
Special industry machinery	3550	2.1	6.0	9.6
Special industry machy, nec	3559	1.2	2.9	2.7
Sporting & athletic gds, nec	3949	5.6	14.8	13.9
Steel works & blast furnaces	3312	1.9	21.0	17.0
Structural clay products	3250	2.7	5.9	10.2
Subdivide, dev, except cemetery	6552	6.9	20.2	8.8
Sugar & confectionery prods	2060	12.7	32.6	3.8
Surgical, med instr, apparatus	3841	1.7	2.6	12.2
Tele & telegraph apparatus	3661	1.0	2.8	–2.2
TV broadcast station	4833	5.6	13.8	12.8
Tires and inner tubes	3011	1.8	5.8	2.0
Tobacco products	2100	3.9	5.7	7.2
Trucking, courier svc, except air	4210	0.6	9.9	10.7
Variety stores	5331	1.1	5.0	4.7
Watches, clocks and parts	3873	13.7	23.3	17.4
Water transportation	4400	7.3	18.5	15.6
Wine, brandy & brandy spirits	2084	11.3	19.2	10.5
Wmns, miss, chld, infnt undgrmt	2340	5.4	15.0	9.4
Women's clothing stores	5621	4.7	12.3	6.8
Women's, misses, jrs outerwear	2330	3.7	12.6	7.5
Wood hshld furn, except upholsrd	2511	3.5	11.6	7.4

there will be sufficient monies to cover this budget, with increases in sales leading to budget increases and sales decreases resulting in advertising decreases. The percentage-of-sales method is simple, straightforward, and easy to implement. Regardless of which basis—past or future sales—is employed, the calculations used to arrive at a budget are not difficult. Finally, this budgeting approach is generally stable. While the budget may vary with increases and decreases in sales, as long as these changes are not drastic the manager will have a reasonable idea of the parameters of the budget.

At the same time, the percentage-of-sales method has some serious disadvantages, including the basic premise on which the budget is established: sales. Letting the level of sales determine the amount of advertising and promotions dollars to be spent reverses the cause-and-effect relationship between advertising and sales. It treats advertising as an expense associated with making a sale rather than an investment. As shown in Figure 7-16, companies that consider promotional expenditures an investment reap the rewards.

A second problem with this approach was actually cited as an advantage earlier: stability. Proponents say that if all firms use a similar percentage, that will bring stability to the marketplace. But what happens if someone varies from this standard percentage? The problem is that this method does not allow for changes in strategy either internally or from competitors. An aggressive firm may wish to allocate more monies to the advertising and promotions budget, a strategy that is not possible with a percentage-of-sales method unless the manager is willing to deviate from industry standards.

The percentage-of-sales method of budgeting may result in severe misappropriation of funds. If advertising and promotion have a role to perform in marketing a product, then allocating more monies to advertising will, as shown in the S-shaped curve, generate incremental sales (to a point). If products with low sales have smaller promotion budgets, this will hinder sales progress. At the other extreme, very successful products may have excess budgets, some of which may be better appropriated elsewhere.

The percentage-of-sales method is also difficult to employ for new product introductions. If no sales histories are available, there is no basis for establishing the budget. Projections of future sales may be difficult, particularly if the product is highly innovative and/or has fluctuating sales patterns.

Finally, if the budget is contingent on sales, decreases in sales will lead to decreases in budgets when they most need to be increased. Continuing to cut the advertising and promotion budgets may just add impetus to the downward sales trend. On the other hand,

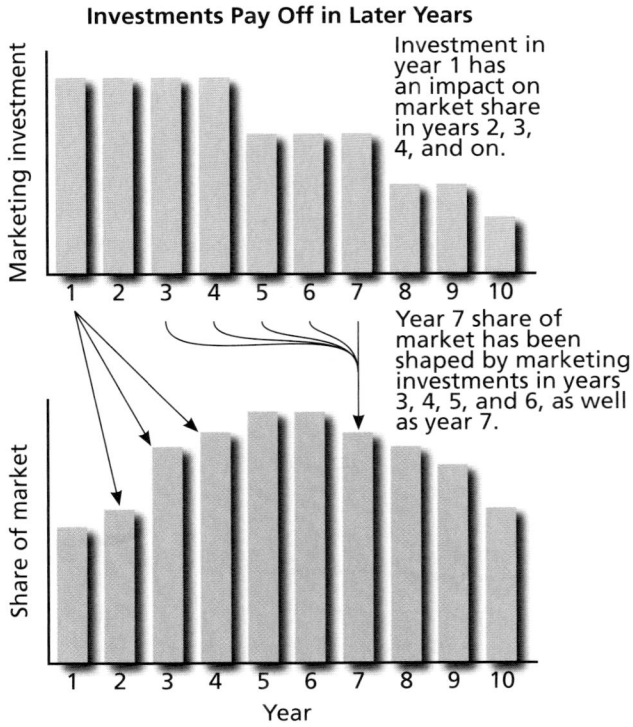

Figure 7-16 Investments pay off in later years

some of the more successful companies have allocated additional funds during hard times or downturns in the cycle of sales. Companies that maintain or increase their ad expenditures during recessions achieve increased visibility and higher growth in both sales and market share (compared to those that reduce advertising outlays). For example, Sunkist can attribute at least some of its success in maintaining its strong image to the fact that it has maintained consistent levels of advertising expenditures over 80 years, despite recessions.[34] IMC Perspective 7-2 discusses this issue in more detail.

While the percentage-of-future-sales method has been proposed as a remedy for some of the problems discussed here, the reality is that problems with forecasting, cyclical growth, and uncontrollable factors limit its effectiveness.

Competitive Parity If you asked marketing managers if they ever set their advertising and promotions budgets on the basis of what their competitors allocate, they would probably deny it. Yet if you examined the advertising expenditures of these companies, both as a percentage of sales and in respect to the media where they are allocated, you would see little variation in the percentage-of-sales figures for firms within a given industry. Such results do not happen by chance alone. Companies that provide competitive advertising information, trade associations, and other advertising industry periodicals are sources for competitors' expenditures. Larger corporations often subscribe to services such as Competitive Media Reporting, which estimates the top 1,000 companies' advertising in 10 media and in total. Smaller companies often use a **clipping service,** which clips competitors' ads from local print media, allowing the company to work backward to determine the cumulative costs of the ads placed.

In the **competitive parity method,** managers establish budget amounts by matching the competition's percentage-of-sales expenditures. The argument is that setting budgets in this fashion takes advantage of the collective wisdom of the industry. It also takes the competition into consideration, which leads to stability in the marketplace by minimizing marketing warfare. If companies know that competitors are unlikely to match their increases in promotional spending, they are less likely to take an aggressive posture to attempt to gain market share. This minimizes unusual or unrealistic ad expenditures.

The competitive parity method has a number of disadvantages, however. For one, it ignores the fact that advertising and promotions are designed to accomplish specific objectives by addressing certain problems and opportunities. Second, it assumes that because firms have similar expenditures, their programs will be equally effective. This assumption ignores the contributions of creative executions and/or media allocations, as well as the success or failure of various promotions. Further, it ignores possible advantages of the firm itself; some companies simply make better products than others.

Also, there is no guarantee that competitors will continue to pursue their existing strategies. Since competitive parity figures are determined by examination of competitors' previous years' promotional expenditures (short of corporate espionage), changes in market emphasis and/or spending may not be recognized until the competition has already established an advantage. Further, there is no guarantee that a competitor will not increase or decrease its own expenditures, regardless of what other companies do. Finally, competitive parity may not avoid promotional wars. Coke versus Pepsi and Anheuser-Busch versus Miller have been notorious for their spending wars, each responding to the other's increased outlays.

In summary, few firms employ the competitive parity method as a sole means of establishing the promotional budget. This method is typically used in conjunction with the percentage-of-sales or other methods. It is never wise to ignore the competition; managers must always be aware of what competitors are doing. But they should not just emulate them in setting goals and developing strategies.

Return on Investment (ROI) In the percentage-of-sales method, sales dictate the level of advertising appropriations. But advertising causes sales. In the marginal analysis and S-shaped curve approaches, incremental investments in advertising and promotions lead to increases in sales. The key word here is *investment.* In the **ROI budgeting method,** advertising and promotions are considered investments, like plant and equipment. Thus, the budgetary appropriation (investment) leads to certain

IMC PERSPECTIVE 7-2

Cutting Budgets When Times Get Tough—Wise Strategy or Potential Pitfall?

A downturn in the U.S. economy led a number of companies to slash their advertising budgets significantly in 2001 and 2002. Even the top spenders cut deeply, with GM cutting the budget by 24 percent and the top 10 overall spending 7 percent less on the average. The companies seemed to be saying that since sales are down, advertising expenditures should go down. But is this the right thing to do? A lot of companies don't think so.

For example, not all of the top 10 advertisers slashed budgets (though 7 of them did). Some like AOL and AT&T actually increased expenditures. For these companies, the downturn is viewed as an opportunity rather than a threat. They take a "spend now, win later" approach, viewing such expenditures as an investment rather than a cost. Take Monster.com as an example. While many dot-coms announced advertising cuts for 2002, Monster indicated that it would maintain its advertising expenditures and number of ads constant. Not only that, but it announced that it would spend additional promotional dollars in other areas. In the first quarter of 2001 Monster invested $37.4 million in measured media, as opposed to $28.7 in the same period for 2000. The same amount was budgeted for 2002. In addition, Monster paid more than $10 million to be part of the Winter Olympics in Salt Lake City. The company is also negotiating for advertising on the 2003 Super Bowl. Monster has also kept its print budget the same, though it is increasing expenditures online.

What does Monster know that others do not? The goal of the new Monster campaign is to raise brand awareness. The company believes that in a time when the economy is down and layoffs may occur, a job placement firm has a golden opportunity to gain by increased investing. Jim Dietz, president of Andover Franchising, Inc., agrees with this philosophy. As Dietz notes, "Pink slips can help us. When downsizing is in the headlines, more folks are willing to look at making an investment in themselves." Andover has increased its expenditures, as well as its media options. Primarily an online advertiser, its 2002 plan included print ads in *Entrepreneur* and *Franchise Times* magazines.

To encourage advertisers to consider ad dollars as an investment rather than an expense, the American Advertising Federation (AAF) has initiated a "Great Brands" campaign, debuting with two 15-second TV spots and a number of print ads encouraging marketers not to neglect market spending during the slump. Wally Snyder, CEO of the AAF, notes: "The companies behind leading global brands . . . recognize that advertising dollars translate into increased market share." The first two companies featured in the campaign are Intel and Coca-Cola.

Thus, while some companies cut, others increase expenditures in a down economy. Much of the reason for this is rooted in the underlying philosophy as to what advertising is all about—an investment or a cost of doing business.

Sources: Erin Strout, "Spend Now, Win Later," *Sales & Marketing Management,* April 2002, pp. 65-66; Hillary Chura, "Monster.com Beefs Up Ad Plans," www.Adage.com, Dec. 3, 2001, pp. 1-2; Vanessa O'Connell, "Ad Spending in All Media Is Slashed 5.2%," *The Wall Street Journal,* June 8, 2001, p. B6.

returns. Like other aspects of the firm's efforts, advertising and promotion are expected to earn a certain return.

While the ROI method looks good on paper, the reality is that it is rarely possible to assess the returns provided by the promotional effort—at least as long as sales continue to be the basis for evaluation. Thus, while managers are certain to ask how much return they are getting for such expenditures, the question remains unanswered and as shown in the chapter introduction, depends on the criteria used to determine effectiveness. ROI remains a difficult method to employ.

Summary of Top-Down Budgeting Methods You are probably asking yourself why we even discussed these budgeting methods if they are not recommended for use or have severe disadvantages that limit their effectiveness. But you must understand the various methods used in order to recognize their limitations, especially since these flawed methods are commonly employed by marketers throughout the United States, Europe, and Canada, as demonstrated in the results of a number of research studies shown in Figure 7-17. Tradition and top management's desire for control are probably the major reasons why top-down methods continue to be popular.

As shown in Figure 7-17, the use of percentage-of-sales methods remained high over the periods included, particularly the method based on anticipated sales. Unfortunately, the affordable method appeared to be on the increase. On the decrease are two methods not yet discussed: quantitative models and the objective and task method. Let us now turn our discussion to these methods as well as one other, payout planning.

Build-Up Approaches The major flaw associated with the top-down methods is that these judgmental approaches lead to predetermined budget appropriations often not linked to objectives and the strategies designed to accomplish them. A more effective budgeting strategy would be to consider the firm's communications objectives and budget what is deemed necessary to attain these goals. As noted earlier, the promotional planning model shows the budget decision as an interactive process, with the communications objectives on one hand and the promotional mix alternatives on the other. The idea is to budget so these promotional mix strategies can be implemented to achieve the stated objectives.

Objective and Task Method It is important that objective setting and budgeting go hand in hand rather than sequentially. It is difficult to establish a budget without spe-

Figure 7-17 Comparison of methods for budgeting

Study	San Augustine and Foley (1975)	Patti and Blasko (1981)	Lancaster and Stern (1983)	Blasko and Patti (1984)	Hung and West (1991)
Population	Large Consumer/ Industrial Advertisers	Large Consumer/ Services Advertisers	Large Consumer Advertisers	Large Industrial Advertisers	Large & Medium Advertisers in U.K., U.S., & Canada
Sample	50/50	54	60	64	100
Methods					
Quantitative models	2/4	51	20	3	NA
Objective and task	6/10	63	80	74	61
Percent anticipated sales	50/28	53	53	16	32
Unit anticipated sales	8/10	22	28	NA	9
Percent past year's sales	14/16	20	20	23	10
Unit past year's sales	6/4	NA	15	2	NA
Affordable	30/26	20	13	33	41
Arbitrary	12/34	4	NA	13	NA
Competitive parity	NA	24	33	21	25
Previous budget	NA	NA	3	NA	NA
Share of voice	NA	NA	5	NA	NA
Others	26/10	NA	12	NA	NA

Note: Figures exceed 100% due to multiple responses. NA = No answer.

cific objectives in mind, and setting objectives without regard to how much money is available makes no sense. For example, a company may wish to create awareness among *X* percent of its target market. A minimal budget amount will be required to accomplish this goal, and the firm must be willing to spend this amount.

The **objective and task method** of budget setting uses a **buildup approach** consisting of three steps: (1) defining the communications objectives to be accomplished, (2) determining the specific strategies and tasks needed to attain them, and (3) estimating the costs associated with performance of these strategies and tasks. The total budget is based on the accumulation of these costs.

Implementing the objective and task approach is somewhat more involved. The manager must monitor this process throughout and change strategies depending on how well objectives are attained. As shown in Figure 7-18, this process involves several steps:

1. *Isolate objectives.* When the promotional planning model is presented, a company will have two sets of objectives to accomplish—the marketing objectives for the product and the communications objectives. After the former are established, the task involves determining what specific communications objectives will be designed to accomplish these goals. Communications objectives must be specific, attainable, and measurable, as well as time limited.
2. *Determine tasks required.* A number of elements are involved in the strategic plan designed to attain the objectives established. (These strategies constitute the remaining chapters in this text.) These tasks may include advertising in various media, sales promotions, and/or other elements of the promotional mix, each with its own role to perform.
3. *Estimate required expenditures.* Buildup analysis requires determining the estimated costs associated with the tasks developed in the previous step. For example, it involves costs for developing awareness through advertising, trial through sampling, and so forth.
4. *Monitor.* As you will see in Chapter 19 on measuring effectiveness, there are ways to determine how well one is attaining established objectives. Performance should be monitored and evaluated in light of the budget appropriated.
5. *Reevaluate objectives.* Once specific objectives have been attained, monies may be better spent on new goals. Thus, if one has achieved the level of consumer awareness sought, the budget should be altered to stress a higher-order objective such as evaluation or trial.

The major advantage of the objective and task method is that the budget is driven by the objectives to be attained. The managers closest to the marketing effort will have specific strategies and input into the budget-setting process.

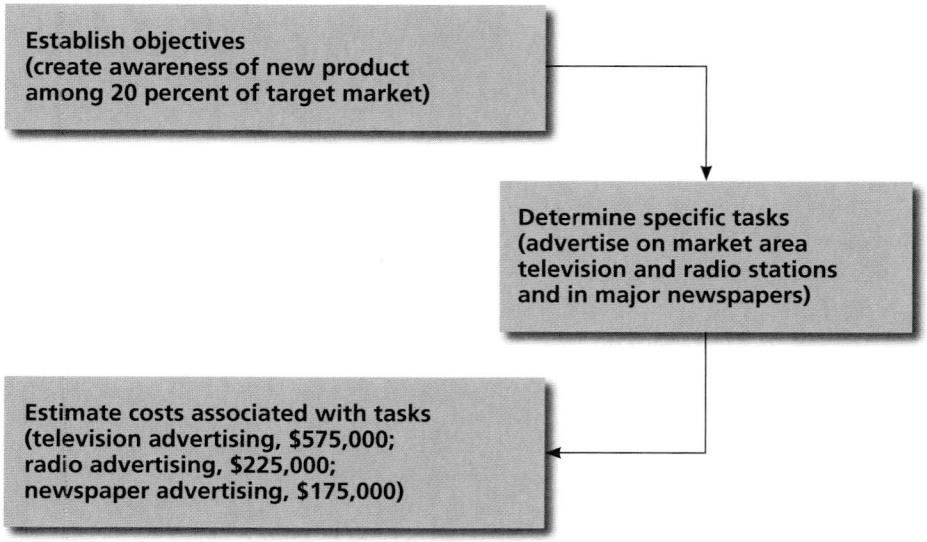

Figure 7-18 The objective and task method

The major disadvantage of this method is the difficulty of determining which tasks will be required and the costs associated with each. For example, specifically what tasks are needed to attain awareness among 50 percent of the target market? How much will it cost to perform these tasks? While these decisions are easier to determine for certain objectives—for example, estimating the costs of sampling required to stimulate trial in a defined market area—it is not always possible to know exactly what is required and/or how much it will cost to complete the job. This process is easier if there is past experience to use as a guide, with either the existing product or a similar one in the same product category. But it is especially difficult for new product introductions. As a result, budget setting using this method is not as easy to perform or as stable as some of the methods discussed earlier. Given this disadvantage, many marketing managers have stayed with those top-down approaches for setting the total expenditure amount.

The objective and task method offers advantages over methods discussed earlier but is more difficult to implement when there is no track record for the product. The following section addresses the problem of budgeting for new product introductions.

Payout Planning The first months of a new product's introduction typically require heavier-than-normal advertising and promotion appropriations to stimulate higher levels of awareness and subsequent trial. After studying more than 40 years of Nielsen figures, James O. Peckham estimated that the average share of advertising to sales ratio necessary to launch a new product successfully is approximately 1.5:2.0.[35] This means that a new entry should be spending at approximately twice the desired market share, as shown in the two examples in Figure 7-19. For example, in the food industry,

Figure 7-19 Share of advertising/sales relationship (two-year summary)

A. New Brands of Food Products

Brand	Average share of advertising	Attained share of sales	Ratio of share of advertising to share of sales
101	34%	12.6%	2.7
102	16	10.0	1.6
103	8	7.6	1.1
104	4	2.6	1.5
105	3	2.1	1.4

B. New Brands of Toiletry Products

Brand	Average share of advertising	Attained share of sales	Ratio of share of advertising to share of sales
401	30%	19.5%	1.5
402	25	16.5	1.5
403	20	16.2	1.2
404	12	9.4	1.3
405	16	8.7	1.8
406	19	7.3	2.6
407	14	7.2	1.9
408	10	6.0	1.7
409	7	6.0	1.2
410	6	5.9	1.0
411	10	5.9	1.7
412	6	5.2	1.2

brand 101 gained a 12.6 percent market share by spending 34 percent of the total advertising dollars in this category. Likewise, brand 401 in the toiletry industry had a 30 percent share of advertising dollars to gain 19.5 percent of sales.

To determine how much to spend, marketers often develop a **payout plan** that determines the investment value of the advertising and promotion appropriation. The basic idea is to project the revenues the product will generate, as well as the costs it will incur, over two to three years. Based on an expected rate of return, the payout plan will assist in determining how much advertising and promotions expenditure will be necessary when the return might be expected. A three-year payout plan is shown in Figure 7-20. The product would lose money in year 1, almost break even in year 2, and finally begin to show substantial profits by the end of year 3.

The advertising and promotion figures are highest in year 1 and decline in years 2 and 3. This appropriation is consistent with Peckham's findings and reflects the additional outlays needed to make as rapid an impact as possible. (Keep in mind that shelf space is limited, and store owners are not likely to wait around for a product to become successful.) The budget also reflects the firm's guidelines for new product expenditures, since companies generally have established deadlines by which the product must begin to show a profit. Finally, keep in mind that building market share may be more difficult than maintaining it—thus the substantial dropoff in expenditures in later years.

While the payout plan is not always perfect, it does guide the manager in establishing the budget. When used in conjunction with the objective and task method, it provides a much more logical approach to budget setting than the top-down approaches previously discussed. Yet on the basis of the studies reported on in Figure 7-17, payout planning does not seem to be a widely employed method.

Quantitative Models Attempts to apply *quantitative models* to budgeting have met with limited success. For the most part, these methods employ **computer simulation models** involving statistical techniques such as multiple regression analysis to determine the relative contribution of the advertising budget to sales. Because of problems associated with these methods, their acceptance has been limited, as demonstrated in the figures reported earlier in Figure 7-17. Quantitative models have yet to reach their potential. As computers continue to find their way into the advertising domain, better models may be forthcoming. Specific discussion of these models is beyond the scope of this text, however. Such methods do have merit but may need more refinement before achieving widespread success.

Summary of Budgeting Methods

There is no universally accepted method of setting a budget figure. Weaknesses in each method may make it unfeasible or inappropriate. As Figure 7-17 shows, the use of the objective and task method continues to stay high, whereas less sophisticated methods vary. More advertisers are also employing the payout planning approach.

In a more recent study of how managers make decisions regarding advertising and promotion budgeting decisions, George Low and Jakki Mohr interviewed 21 managers in eight consumer-product firms. Their research focused on the decision processes and procedures used to set spending levels on the factors that influence the allocation of advertising and promotion dollars.

	Year 1	Year 2	Year 3
Product sales	15.0	35.50	60.75
Profit contribution (@ $0.50/case)	7.5	17.75	30.38
Advertising/promotions	15.0	10.50	8.50
Profit (loss)	(7.5)	7.25	21.88
Cumulative profit (loss)	(7.5)	(0.25)	21.63

Figure 7-20 Example of three-year payout plan ($ millions)

Figure 7-21 How advertising and promotions budgets are set

The Nature of the Decision Process

- Managers develop overall marketing objectives for the brand.
- Financial projections are made on the basis of the objectives and forecasts.
- Advertising and promotions budgets are set on the basis of quantitative models and managerial judgment.
- The budget is presented to senior management, which approves and adjusts the budgets.
- The plan is implemented (changes are often made during implementation).
- The plan is evaluated by comparing the achieved results with objectives.

Factors Affecting Budget Allocations

- The extent to which risk taking is encouraged and/or tolerated.
- Sophistication regarding the use of marketing information.
- Managerial judgment.
- Use of quantitative tools.
- Brand differentiation strategies.
- Brand equity.
- The strength of the creative message.
- Retailer power.
- Short- versus long-term focus.
- Top-down influences.
- Political sales force influences.
- Historical inertia.
- Ad hoc changes.

On the basis of their results (shown in Figure 7-21), the authors concluded that the budget-setting process is still a perplexing issue to many managers and that institutional pressures led to a greater proportion of dollars being spent on sales promotions than managers would have preferred. In addition, the authors concluded that to successfully develop and implement the budget, managers must (1) employ a comprehensive strategy to guide the process, avoiding the piecemeal approach often employed, (2) develop a strategic planning framework that employs an integrated marketing communications philosophy, (3) build in contingency plans, (4) focus on long-term objectives, and (5) consistently evaluate the effectiveness of programs.[36]

By using these approaches in combination with the percentage-of-sales methods, these advertisers are likely to arrive at a more useful, accurate budget. For example, many firms now start the budgeting process by establishing the objectives they need to accomplish and then limit the budget by applying a percentage-of-sales or another method to decide whether or not it is affordable. Competitors' budgets may also influence this decision.

Allocating the Budget

Once the budget has been appropriated, the next step is to allocate it. The allocation decision involves determining which markets, products, and/or promotional elements will receive which amounts of the funds appropriated.

Allocating to IMC Elements

As noted earlier, advertisers have begun to shift some of their budget dollars away from traditional advertising media and into sales promotions targeted at both the consumer and the trade. Direct marketing, the Internet, and other promotional tools are also receiving increased attention and competing for more of the promotional budget. Figure 7-22 reports the results of a survey conducted on 197 marketing executives, asking how they would allocate their dollars if the budget were

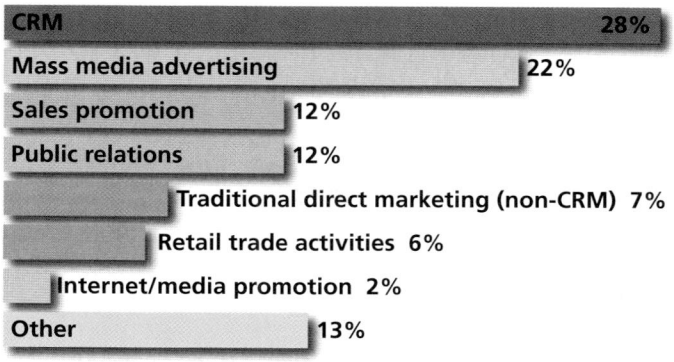

Figure 7-22 How U.S. marketers would invest the majority of their marketing dollars if budget were not an issue, May 2002 (as a percent of respondents)

not an issue. While no comparative figures were available from previous years, you can see how the monies would be spread around. Figure 7-23, from a different source, shows how some of these dollars were allocated. The advantage of more target selectivity has led to an increased emphasis on direct marketing, while a variety of new media have given marketers new ways to reach prospective customers. Rapidly rising media costs, the ability of sales promotions to motivate trial, maturing of the product and/or brand, and the need for more aggressive promotional tools have also led to shifts in strategy.[37] (We will discuss consumer and trade promotions and the reasons for some of these changes in Chapter 16.)

Some marketers have also used the allocation decision to stretch their advertising dollar and get more impact from the same amount of money. For example, General Motors recently reevaluated its advertising and promotional expenditures and made significant shifts in allocations by both media and product.[38] Other companies have reevaluated as well, including Procter & Gamble, Apple Computer, and Dow Chemical.

Client/Agency Policies Another factor that may influence budget allocation is the individual policy of the company or the advertising agency. The agency may discourage the allocation of monies to sales promotion, preferring to spend them on the

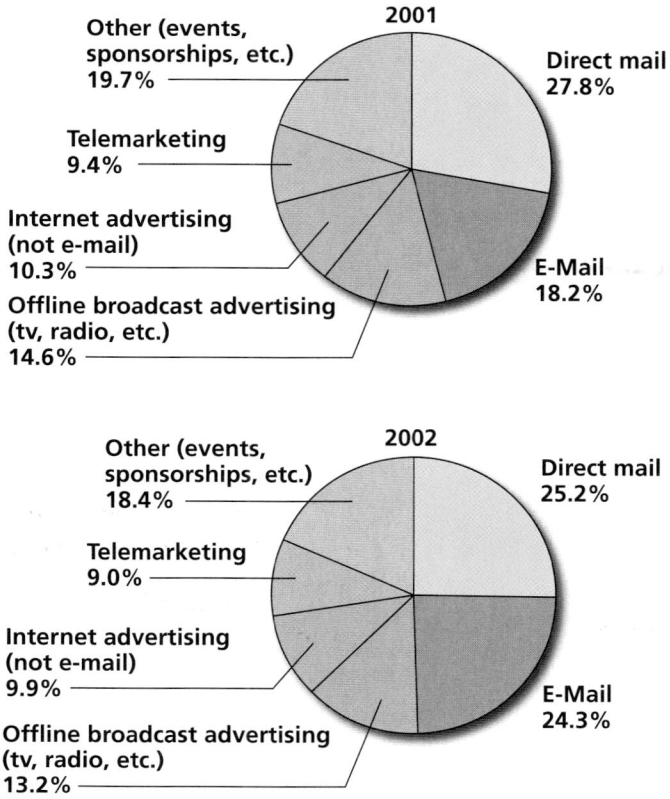

Figure 7-23 U.S. marketing budgets, by marketing vehicle, 2001 and 2002 (as percent of overall budget)

advertising area. The agency position is that promotional monies are harder to track in terms of effectiveness and may be used improperly if not under its control. (In many cases commissions are not made on this area, and this fact may contribute to the agency's reluctance.)[39]

The orientation of the agency or the firm may also directly influence where monies are spent. Many ad agencies are managed by officers who have ascended through the creative ranks and are inclined to emphasize the creative budget. Others may have preferences for specific media. For example, BBDO Worldwide, one of the largest advertising agencies in the United States, has positioned itself as an expert in cable TV programming and often spends more client money in this medium. McCann-Erickson is spending more monies on the Internet. Both the agency and the client may favor certain aspects of the promotional program, perhaps on the basis of past successes, that will substantially influence where dollars are spent.

Market Size While the budget should be allocated according to the specific promotional tools needed to accomplish the stated objectives, the *size* of the market will affect the decision. In smaller markets, it is often easier and less expensive to reach the target market. Too much of an expenditure in these markets will lead to saturation and a lack of effective spending. In larger markets, the target group may be more dispersed and thus more expensive to reach. Think about the cost of purchasing media in Chicago or New York City versus a smaller market like Columbus, Ohio, or Birmingham, Alabama. The former would be much more costly and would require a higher budget appropriation.

Market Potential For a variety of reasons, some markets hold more potential than others. Marketers of snow skis would find greater returns on their expenditures in Denver, Colorado, than in Fort Lauderdale, Florida. Imported Mexican beers sell better in the border states (Texas, Arizona, California) than in the Midwest. A disproportionate number of imported cars are sold in California and New England. When particular markets hold higher potential, the marketing manager may decide to allocate additional monies to them. (Keep in mind that just because a market does not have high sales does not mean it should be ignored. The key is *potential*—and a market with low sales but high potential may be a candidate for additional appropriations.)

There are several methods for estimating marketing potential. Many marketers conduct research studies to forecast demand and/or use secondary sources of information such as those provided by government agencies or syndicated services like Dun & Bradstreet, A. C. Nielsen, and Audits and Surveys. One source for consumer goods information is the *Survey of Buying Power,* published annually by *Sales & Marketing Management* magazine. The survey contains population, income, and retail sales data for states, counties, metropolitan statistical areas, and cities in the United States and Canada with populations of 40,000 or more.

Market Share Goals Two studies in the *Harvard Business Review* discussed advertising spending with the goal of maintaining and increasing market share.[40] John Jones compared the brand's share of market with its share of advertising voice (the total value of the main media exposure in the product category). Jones classified the brands as "profit taking brands, or underspenders" and "investment brands, those whose share of voice is clearly above their share of market." His study indicated that for those brands with small market shares, profit takers are in the minority; however, as the brands increase their market share, nearly three out of five have a proportionately smaller share of voice.

Jones noted that three factors can be cited to explain this change. First, new brands generally receive higher-than-average advertising support. Second, older, more mature brands are often "milked"—that is, when they reach the maturity stage, advertising support is reduced. Third, there's an advertising economy of scale whereby advertising works harder for well-established brands, so a lower expenditure is required. Jones concluded that for larger brands, it may be possible to reduce advertising expenditures and still maintain market share. Smaller brands, on the other hand, have to continue to maintain a large share of voice.

James Schroer addressed the advertising budget in a situation where the marketer wishes to increase market share. His analysis suggests that marketers should:

- Segment markets, focusing on those markets where competition is weak and/or underspending instead of on a national advertising effort.
- Determine their competitors' cost positions (how long the competition can continue to spend at the current or increased rate).
- Resist the lure of short-term profits that result from ad budget cuts.
- Consider niching strategies as opposed to long-term wars.

Figure 7-24 shows Schroer's suggestions for spending priorities in various markets.

Economies of Scale in Advertising Some studies have presented evidence that firms and/or brands maintaining a large share of the market have an advantage over smaller competitors and thus can spend less money on advertising and realize a better return.[41] Larger advertisers can maintain advertising shares that are smaller than their market shares because they get better advertising rates, have declining average costs of production, and accrue the advantages of advertising several products jointly. In addition, they are likely to enjoy more favorable time and space positions, cooperation of middlepeople, and favorable publicity. These advantages are known as **economies of scale.**

Reviewing the studies in support of this position and then conducting research over a variety of small package products, Kent Lancaster found that this situation did not hold true and that in fact larger brand share products might actually be at a disadvantage.[42] His results indicated that leading brands spend an average of 2.5 percentage points more than their brand share on advertising. More specifically, his study concluded:

1. There is no evidence that larger firms can support their brands with lower relative advertising costs than smaller firms.
2. There is no evidence that the leading brand in a product group enjoys lower advertising costs per sales dollar than do other brands.
3. There is no evidence of a static relationship between advertising costs per dollar of sales and the size of the advertiser.

The results of this and other studies suggest there really are no economies of scale to be accrued from the size of the firm or the market share of the brand.[43]

Organizational Characteristics In a review of the literature on how allocation decisions are made between advertising and sales promotion, George Low and Jakki Mohr concluded that organizational factors play an important role in determining how communications dollars are spent.[44] The authors note that the following factors influence the allocation decision. These factors vary from one organization to another, and each influences the relative amounts assigned to advertising and promotion:

- The organization's structure—centralized versus decentralized, formalization, and complexity.
- Power and politics in the organizational hierarchy.
- The use of expert opinions (for example, consultants).

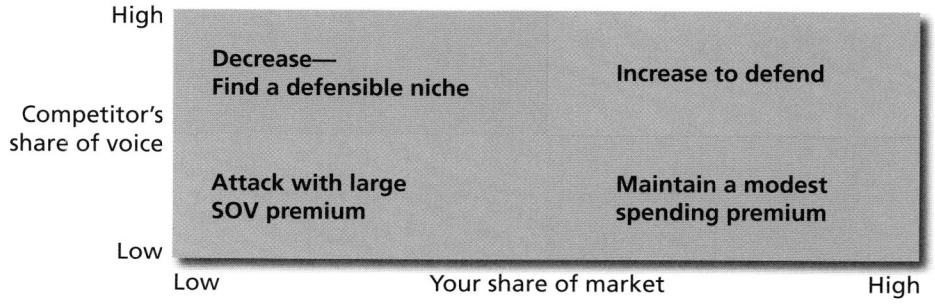

Figure 7-24 The share of voice (SOV) effect and ad spending: priorities in individual markets

- Characteristics of the decision maker (preferences and experience).
- Approval and negotiation channels.
- Pressure on senior managers to arrive at the optimal budget.

One example of how these factors might influence allocations relates to the level of interaction between marketing and other functional departments, such as accounting and operations. The authors note that the relative importance of advertising versus sales promotion might vary from department to department. Accountants, being dollars-and-cents minded, would argue for the sales impact of promotions, while operations would argue against sales promotions because the sudden surges in demand that might result would throw off production schedules. The marketing department might be influenced by the thinking of either of these groups in making its decision.

The use of outside consultants to provide expert opinions might also affect the allocation decision. Trade journals, academic journals, and even books might also be valuable inputs into the decision maker's thinking. In sum, it seems obvious that many factors must be taken into account in the budget allocation decision. Market size and potential, specific objectives sought, and previous company and/or agency policies and preferences all influence this decision.

Summary

This chapter has examined the role of objectives in the planning and evaluation of the IMC program and how firms budget in an attempt to achieve these objectives. Specific objectives are needed to guide the development of the promotional program, as well as to provide a benchmark against which performance can be measured and evaluated. Objectives serve important functions as communications devices, as a guide to planning the IMC program and deciding on various alternatives, and for measurement and evaluation.

Objectives for IMC evolve from the organization's overall marketing plan and are based on the roles various promotional mix elements play in the marketing program. Many managers use sales or a related measure such as market share as the basis for setting objectives. However, many promotional planners believe the role of advertising and other promotional mix elements is to communicate because of the various problems associated with sales-based objectives. They use communications-based objectives like those in the response hierarchy as the basis for setting goals.

Much of the emphasis in setting objectives has been on traditional advertising-based views of marketing communications. However, many companies are moving toward zero-based communications planning, which focuses on what tasks need to be done, which marketing communication functions should be used, and to what extent. Many of the principles used in setting advertising objectives can be applied to other elements in the promotional mix.

As you have probably concluded, the budget decision is not typically based on supporting experiences or strong theoretical foundations. Nor is it one of the more soundly established elements of the promotional program. The budgeting methods used now have some major problems. Economic models are limited, often try to demonstrate the effects on sales directly, and ignore other elements of the marketing mix. Some of the methods discussed have no theoretical basis and ignore the roles advertising and promotion are meant to perform.

One possible way to improve the budget appropriation is to tie the measures of effectiveness to communications objectives rather than to the broader-based marketing objectives. Using the objective and task approach with communications objectives may not be the ultimate solution to the budgeting problem, but it is an improvement over the top-down methods. Marketers often find it advantageous to employ a combination of methods.

As with determining the budget, managers must consider a number of factors when allocating advertising and promotions dollars. Market size and potential, agency policies, and the preferences of management itself may influence the allocation decision.

Key Terms

marketing objectives, 196
integrated marketing communications objectives, 198
carryover effect, 199
DAGMAR, 206
communications task, 206
benchmark measures, 208
zero-based communications planning, 210
contribution margin, 213
marginal analysis, 213
concave-downward function model, 214
S-shaped response curve, 214
top-down approaches, 217
affordable method, 217
arbitrary allocation, 218
percentage-of-sales method, 218
clipping service, 222
competitive parity method, 222
ROI budgeting method, 222
objective and task method, 225
buildup approach, 225
payout plan, 227
computer simulation models, 227
economies of scale, 231

Discussion Questions

1. The lead-in to the chapter discusses the fact that the companies that spend the most on advertising do not necessarily achieve the highest brand value for their products. Sometimes, those who spend very little are able to achieve this objective. Explain what factors may lead to these results. Provide examples.

2. Some marketers feel that the cereal companies have focused too much on sales objectives, creating a situation in which price cutting and couponing have become essential to selling the product. Do you think that these companies may be able to reverse this situation? Describe some of the options available to the cereal manufacturers.

3. Figure 7-1 notes the numerous factors that influence sales. Provide examples of products and/or services that have been directly influenced by each of these factors.

4. What is DAGMAR? Explain how marketers might use DAGMAR in establishing objectives. What are some of the problems associated with the use of DAGMAR?

5. Discuss the two sales response models described in the text. Explain the differences between the two models. Provide examples of types of products that might follow each of these response curves.

6. Critics of the percentage-of-sales method of budget setting contend that this method "reverses the advertising and sales relationship" and that it "treats advertising as an expense rather than an investment." Explain what these arguments mean and discuss their merits.

7. In meeting with your new boss, he informs you that the only goal of advertising and promotion is to generate sales. Present your argument as to why communications objectives must also be considered.

8. Discuss some of the reasons managers continue to set budgets using "top-down" budgeting methods.

9. What are some of the organizational characteristics that influence the budgeting decision? Give examples of each.

10. In Figure 7-21, Low and Mohr list a number of factors that affect the budget allocation decision. Describe and provide examples of each.

Creative Strategy: Planning and Development

8

Chapter Objectives

1. To discuss what is meant by advertising creativity and examine the role of creative strategy in advertising.
2. To examine creative strategy development and the roles of various client and agency personnel involved in it.
3. To consider the process that guides the creation of advertising messages and the research inputs into the stages of the creative process.
4. To examine various approaches used for determining major selling ideas that form the basis of an advertising campaign.

Nike Targets Women

Perhaps no company in the world has been as successful in capitalizing on the fitness boom of the past few decades as Nike. Since its inception

Nike has been a leader in the high-performance athletic-shoe market and has become one of the world's great brand names. The company ran past all its competitors to become the largest seller of athletic footwear and apparel in the world, with sales of nearly $10 billion in 2002. The Nike ethos of pure, brash performance is captured in the "Just Do It" slogan, which has become a catchphrase for the sports world and has been personified in advertising featuring some of the world's greatest athletes.

Nike is the overall leader in the $15.6 billion market for athletic shoes and apparel in the United States. However, the industry has been stagnant for years, and Nike, along with its competitors, is looking for new growth opportunities and areas where the company can gain market share and attract first-time customers. One of the areas Nike is targeting is the women's market, which has been experiencing strong sales growth but has been the company's Achilles' heel. Women's athletic footwear accounts for one-third of the total industry sales and apparel for more than 50 percent, but women's products account for only 20 percent of Nike's revenue. Although the company has been selling shoes and apparel to women for years, Nike has been better known as a brand catering to male athletes and building its image around superstars such as Michael Jordan, Pete Sampras, Lance Armstrong, and Tiger Woods. These efforts have resulted in Nike's dominance of the male market, where the company has a 50 percent market share.

For much of its 30-year history, Nike has been about men and either treated women like men or didn't give them much attention. However, sometimes Nike did get it right in communicating with women. In 1995 the company ran a campaign titled "If You Let Me Play" that struck a responsive chord with many women. The campaign featured ads showing female athletes talking about how sports could change women's lives, from reducing teen pregnancy to increasing the chances of getting a college education. The campaign, along with subsequent ads featuring top female athletes such as sprinter Marion Jones, helped make Nike the market leader, but it was focused primarily on the high-performance segment of the female market.

In 2001 Nike launched a new strategic initiative termed "Nike Goddess," which is a companywide, grassroots effort that has the goal of changing how the company does business with women. The

new strategy appeals to a broader segment of the female market and is designed to take advantage of the differences between women and men in how they conceive of sport, how they shop for clothing and shoes, and even how they view celebrity athletes. Nike wants to appeal more to women's desire for an active lifestyle than to any image they have of themselves as hard-core athletes.

Nike began its new women's movement by spending time listening to women and learning how they balance their lives, what they like to wear, where and how they shop, and what moves them. Nike designers and researchers spent time scouring trendy workout spots like London's Third Space to pick up on new fitness trends. One key insight that emerged from the research is that for most women, high performance isn't about sports; it's about fitness fitting in with their active lifestyles. Nike stepped up its product development and introduced flashier shoe designs such as the Air Max Craze, which has a strap for a heel and a zipper over the lace. Another new line, the Air Visi Havoc, features materials not normally seen on a playing field, such as a faux snakeskin look, baby-blue satin, and red mesh.

Nike Goddess also includes new ways to reach women and communicate better with them. A new ad campaign takes a different look at women and sports and veers away from Nike's traditional strategy of relying on big-name endorsers and producing product lines named after them. Jackie Thomas, Nike's U.S. brand marketing director for women, notes: "Women love that Nike is aggressive, that it is competitive. The difference between women and men is that women don't treat athletes like heroes. No woman thinks that she'll be able to run like Marion Jones because she wears shoes that are named after her." Rather than dwell on superstars, the new advertising campaign consists of print and TV ads that show ordinary women taking part in sport—from a swimmer to a young fencer to the "Yogini," a yoga instructor who stands on her hands on a hardwood floor and arches her back until her feet touch her head.

Nike has also launched a new website for women: nikegoddess.com. The site offers profiles of both famous athletes and everyday women who are trying to meet the challenges of balancing their hectic lives. It includes product information, health and fitness tips, city profiles to help women find fitness and fun when they are traveling, links to other sites, and online shopping for Nike products. Nike also launched *NikeGoddess,* the company's first "magalog" (a cross between a magazine and a catalog), to help roll out the name and communicate with today's active women.

One analyst noted that for many years, even within Nike there was a "general sense that it's by guys for guys." However, if Nike is to continue to grow, a company built on brash ads and male athletic fantasies is going to have to connect with female customers as well. The goal for the Nike Goddess initiative is to double Nike's sales to women by mid-decade. This will require that Nike change the way it sells to, designs for, and communicates with women. However, it appears that Nike is rising to the challenge. And lest anyone forget, Nike is named after a woman—the Greek goddess of victory.

Sources: Fara Warner, "Nike's Women's Movement," *Fast Company,* August 2002, pp. 70–75; Edward Wong, "Nike Trying New Strategies for Women," *The New York Times,* June 19, 2001, p. C1; Hillary Cassidy, "Hail the Goddess," *Brandweek,* Feb. 5, 2001, p. 42.

One of the most important components of an integrated marketing communications program is the advertising message. While the fundamental role of an advertising message is to communicate information, it does much more. The commercials we watch on TV or hear on radio and the print ads we see in magazines and newspapers are a source of entertainment, motivation, fascination, fantasy, and sometimes irrita-

tion as well as information. Ads and commercials appeal to, and often create or shape, consumers' problems, desires, and goals. From the marketer's perspective, the advertising message is a way to tell consumers how the product or service can solve a problem or help satisfy desires or achieve goals. Advertising can also be used to create images or associations and position a brand in the consumer's mind as well as transform the experience of buying and/or using a product or service. Many consumers who have never driven or even ridden in a BMW perceive it as "the ultimate driving machine" (Exhibit 8-1). Many people feel good about sending Hallmark greeting cards because they have internalized the company's advertising theme, "when you care enough to send the very best."

One need only watch an evening of commercials or peruse a few magazines to realize there are a myriad of ways to convey an advertising message. Underlying all of these messages, however, are a **creative strategy** that determines what the advertising message will say or communicate and **creative tactics** for how the message strategy will be executed. In this chapter, we focus on advertising creative strategy. We consider what is meant by creativity, particularly as it relates to advertising, and examine a well-known approach to creativity in advertising.

Exhibit 8-1 Excellent advertising helps create an image for BMW automobiles as "the ultimate driving machine"

We also examine the creative strategy development process and various approaches to determining the *big idea* that will be used as the central theme of the advertising campaign and translated into attention-getting, distinctive, and memorable messages. Creative specialists are finding it more and more difficult to come up with big ideas that will break through the clutter and still satisfy the concerns of their risk-averse clients. Yet their clients are continually challenging them to find the creative message that will strike a responsive chord with their target audience.

Some of you may not be directly involved in the design and creation of ads; you may choose to work in another agency department or on the client side of the business. However, because creative strategy is often so crucial to the success of the firm's promotional effort, everyone involved in the promotional process should understand the creative strategy and tactics that underlie the development of advertising campaigns and messages, as well as the creative options available to the advertiser. Also, individuals on the client side as well as agency people outside the creative department must work with the creative specialists in developing the advertising campaign, implementing it, and evaluating its effectiveness. Thus, marketing and product managers, account representatives, researchers, and media personnel must appreciate the creative process and develop a productive relationship with creative personnel.

The Importance of Creativity in Advertising

For many students, as well as many advertising and marketing practitioners, the most interesting aspect of advertising is the creative side. We have all at one time or another been intrigued by an ad and admired the creative insight that went into it. A great ad is a joy to behold and often an epic to create, as the cost of producing a TV commercial can exceed $1 million. Many companies see this as money well spent. They realize that the manner in which the advertising message is developed and executed is often critical to the success of the promotional program, which in turn can influence the effectiveness of the entire marketing program. Procter & Gamble, Levi Strauss, Nissan, General Motors, Coca-Cola, PepsiCo, Nike, McDonald's, and many other companies spend millions of dollars each year to produce advertising messages and hundreds of millions more to purchase media time and space to run them. While these companies make excellent products, they realize creative advertising is also an important part of their marketing success.

Good creative strategy and execution can often be central to determining the success of a product or service or reversing the fortunes of a struggling brand. Conversely, an

Figure 8-1 Burger King advertising themes and agencies

- "We Do It Like You Do It" (1987–1989)
  Agency: NW Ayer
- "Sometimes you gotta break the rules" (1989–1991)
- "Your way. Right away" (1991–1992)
- "BK Tee Vee: I Love This Place" (1992–1994)
  Agency: D'Arcy Masius Benton & Bowles
- "Back to Basics" (1994)
  Agency: UniWorld Group, Inc.
- "Get Your Burger's Worth" (1994–1996)
- "It Just Tastes Better" (1996–1998)
- "Go the Distance—When You Have It Your Way It Just Tastes Better" (1999)
- "Got the Urge" (2000)
  Agency: Lowe Lintas & Partners
- "The Whopper Says" (2001–2002)
  Agency: McCann-Erickson
- "At Burger King, You Got It" (2002–)
  Agency: Amoeba

advertising campaign that is poorly conceived or executed can be a liability. Many companies have solid marketing and promotional plans and spend substantial amounts of money on advertising, yet have difficulty coming up with a creative campaign that will differentiate them from their competitors. For example, Burger King has changed its advertising theme 11 times in the past 15 years and changed agencies 6 times in search of a campaign that would give the chain a strong identity in the fast-food market (Figure 8-1). During many of these campaigns, market share dropped and franchises were unhappy with the company's inability to come up with an effective campaign.[1] In July 2002, Burger King was sold by parent company Diageo to an investment consortium led by Texas Pacific Group.[2] The company also added an additional agency, Deutsch, to its roster to handle the advertising for its value menu and some local franchisee associations. It will be interesting to see if the agencies can develop an effective campaign to reposition Burger King in the fast-food market (and how long it will be before the company changes agencies once again).

Just because an ad or commercial is creative or popular does not mean it will increase sales or revive a declining brand. Many ads have won awards for creativity but failed to increase sales. In some instances, the failure to generate sales has cost the agency the account. For example, many advertising people believe some of the best ads of all time were those done for Alka-Seltzer in the 1960s and 70s, including the classic "Mama Mia! That's a spicy meatball!" and "I can't believe I ate the whole thing." While the commercials won numerous creative awards, Alka-Seltzer sales still declined and the agencies lost the account.[3] In the late 90s, Nissan asked its agency to change the popular "Enjoy the ride" campaign that was widely praised for its amusing, creative executions but was not helping increase sales.[4] Nissan dealers complained that the ads did not focus enough attention on the product, and in some cases comparisons with the competition were used. However, in late 2002 Nissan launched a new advertising campaign using "Shift" as the umbrella tagline.[5] The new campaign uses a combination of emotional and product-focused ads that are designed to strengthen Nissan's brand image while showing its revitalized product line, which includes the new 350Z sports car (Exhibit 8-2).

Many advertising and marketing people have become ambivalent toward, and in some cases even critical of, advertising awards.[6] They argue that agency creative people are often more concerned with creating ads that win awards than ones that sell their clients' products. Other advertising people believe awards are a good way to recognize

Exhibit 8-2 In Nissan's new ads, the cars are once again the stars

creativity that often does result in effective advertising. Global Perspective 8-1 discusses how the emphasis on creative awards has shifted to the international arena with awards like the Cannes Lions.

As we saw in Chapter 7, the success of an ad campaign cannot always be judged in terms of sales. However, many advertising and marketing personnel, particularly those on the client side, believe advertising must ultimately lead the consumer to purchase the product or service. Finding a balance between creative advertising and effective advertising is difficult. To better understand this dilemma, we turn to the issue of creativity and its role in advertising.

Advertising Creativity

What Is Creativity?

Creativity is probably one of the most commonly used terms in advertising. Ads are often called creative. The people who develop ads and commercials are known as creative types. And advertising agencies develop reputations for their creativity. Perhaps so much attention is focused on the concept of creativity because many people view the specific challenge given to those who develop an advertising message as being creative. It is their job to turn all of the information regarding product features and benefits, marketing plans, consumer research, and communication objectives into a creative concept that will bring the advertising message to life. This begs the question: What is meant by *creativity* in advertising?

Different Perspectives on Advertising Creativity

Perspectives on what constitutes creativity in advertising differ. At one extreme are people who argue that advertising is creative only if it sells the product. An advertising message's or campaign's impact on sales counts more than whether it is innovative or wins awards. At the other end of the continuum are those who judge the creativity of an ad in terms of its artistic or aesthetic value and originality. They contend creative ads can break through the competitive clutter, grab the consumer's attention, and have some impact.

As you might expect, perspectives on advertising creativity often depend on one's role. A study by Elizabeth Hirschman examined the perceptions of various individuals involved in the creation and production of TV commercials, including management types (brand managers and account executives) and creatives (art director, copywriter, commercial director, and producer).[7] She found that product managers and account executives view ads as promotional tools whose primary purpose is to communicate favorable impressions to the marketplace. They believe a commercial should be evaluated in terms of whether it fulfills the client's marketing and communicative objectives.

GLOBAL PERSPECTIVE 8-1

Cannes Festival Becomes the Olympic Games of Advertising

For many years the most coveted prize for creativity in advertising was a Clio Award. However, the Clios lost much of their prestige after financial problems resulted in cancellation of the 1992 awards ceremony. And even though they still sponsor an annual awards competition, the Clios have never regained their former status as the advertising industry's premier award for creative excellence. There are a number of other popular and well-recognized U.S.-based advertising award competitions that recognize outstanding creative work. These include the Kelley Awards given by the Magazine Publishers of America, the Best Awards sponsored by *Advertising Age,* the One Show sponsored by the One Club for Art & Copy, and the Effies, which are given each year by the New York American Marketing Association.

While these contests remain very popular in the United States, on a global level the Cannes Lions International Advertising Festival is now widely considered the most prestigious advertising award competition. Inspired by the movie industry's more famous Cannes Film Festival, the Cannes Lions Festival is considered by many to be the "Olympics of Advertising." The Cannes competition receives entries from agencies around the world hoping to win Lions (the name of the awards) in each of the major categories—television, press and poster (print and outdoor ads), cyber (online marketing and ads for websites), media planning and buying, and direct marketing (which was added in 2002).

Agencies from the U.S. generally focus their entries on the TV part of the competition, where they fare much better than in the print and poster category, which is usually dominated by agencies from the United Kingdom whose style of advertising is considered more popular among the Cannes jury. Such was the case in the 2002 Cannes competition, as U.S. agencies failed to win any Gold Lions in the print and poster competition. However, while U.K. agencies won the most Gold Lion Awards for film, U.S. agencies dominated the category, winning 4 Gold Lions, 3 Silver Lions, and 13 Bronzes. For the third consecutive year, a U.S. agency won the Grand Prix Award for the world's best TV commercial, as Wieden & Kennedy took home the honors for the "Tag" spot it created for Nike. The commercial features an inventive game of tag set to a techno beat as young adults play the kid's game and chase each other around the streets, office buildings, and subways of a major city. A young man wearing Nike sneakers runs and hides from the other urbanites during the commercial, which ends with the simple one-word message "Play." The Nike spot narrowly beat out an eye-popping commercial created for Microsoft's Xbox; called "Champagne," it showed a newborn being shot out of a window, aging rapidly, and landing in a grave. The theme: Life is short, play more. The spot was created by Microsoft's European agency, Bartle Bogle Hegarty, based in London.

One of the other big winners at the 2002 competition was the campaign for BMW Films from Fallon Worldwide, of Minneapolis. The campaign (discussed in the opening vignette to Chapter 3) won a Grand Prix in the cyber category and in many ways dominated the festival. The Cannes jury had problems deciding how to categorize the breakthrough campaign, which combined a website, short films, and movie trailers in ways no one in the industry had seen before. The president of the cyber-category jury noted: "BMWFilms is probably the most innovative and important marketing program in the last year. This work has made people stop and pause and reconsider what they are doing."

While many advertising people in the United States are critical of creative awards, the Cannes competition attracted over 5,000 entries in 2002 from 61 countries, so someone must think they are important. And don't try to downplay their importance in advertising-crazy countries like Brazil and Argentina, where agency creative directors are treated like rock stars, or in Europe, where agency leaders are seen as titans of industry, on par with top CEOs. Agencies like Saatchi & Saatchi, of London, which was selected as the Agency of the Year, know that the prestige of a Cannes Lion Award enhances their image and helps attract new business.

Sources: Laurel Wentz and Stefano Hatfield, "Nike 'Tag' Bags Grand Prix," *Advertising Age,* June 24, 2002, pp. 1, 76–77; Michael McCarthy, "Nike's 'Tag' Ad Runs Away with Top Honors at Cannes," *USA Today,* June 24, 2002, p. 7B.

The perspective of those on the creative side was much more self-serving, as Hirschman noted:

> In direct contrast to this client orientation, the art director, copywriter, and commercial director viewed the advertisement as a communication vehicle for promoting their own aesthetic viewpoints and personal career objectives. Both the copywriter and art director made this point explicitly, noting that a desirable commercial from their standpoint was one which communicated their unique creative talents and thereby permitted them to obtain "better" jobs at an increased salary.[8]

In her interviews, Hirschman also found that brand managers were much more risk-averse and wanted a more conservative commercial than the creative people, who wanted to maximize the impact of the message.

What constitutes creativity in advertising is probably somewhere between the two extremes. To break through the clutter and make an impression on the target audience, an ad often must be unique and entertaining. As noted in Chapter 5, research has shown that a major determinant of whether a commercial will be successful in changing brand preferences is its "likability," or the viewer's overall reaction.[9] TV commercials and print ads that are well designed and executed and generate emotional responses can create positive feelings that are transferred to the product or service being advertised. Many creative people believe this type of advertising can come about only if they are given considerable latitude in developing advertising messages. But ads that are creative only for the sake of being creative often fail to communicate a relevant or meaningful message that will lead consumers to purchase the product or service.

Everyone involved in planning and developing an advertising campaign must understand the importance of balancing the "it's not creative unless it sells" perspective with the novelty/uniqueness and impact position. Marketing and brand managers or account executives must recognize that imposing too many sales- and marketing-oriented communications objectives on the creative team can result in mediocre advertising, which is often ineffective in today's competitive, cluttered media environment. At the same time, the creative specialists must recognize that the goal of advertising is to assist in selling the product or service and good advertising must communicate in a manner that helps the client achieve this goal.

Advertising creativity is the ability to generate fresh, unique, and appropriate ideas that can be used as solutions to communications problems. To be *appropriate* and effective, a creative idea must be relevant to the target audience. Many ad agencies recognize the importance of developing advertising that is creative and different yet communicates relevant information to the target audience. Figure 8-2 shows the perspective on creativity that the former D'Arcy, Masius Benton & Bowles agency developed to guide its creative efforts and help achieve superior creativity consistently. The agency views a creative advertising message as one that is built around a creative core or power idea and uses excellent design and execution to communicate information that interests the target audience. It has used these principles in doing outstanding creative work for Procter & Gamble's Charmin and Pampers brands, Norelco, and many other popular brands for many years.

Advertising creativity is not the exclusive domain of those who work on the creative side of advertising. The nature of the business requires creative thinking from everyone involved in the promotional planning process. Agency people, such as account executives, media planners, researchers, and attorneys, as well as those on the client side, such as marketing and brand managers, must all seek creative solutions to problems encountered in planning, developing, and executing an advertising campaign. An excellent example of creative synergy between the media and creative departments of an agency, as well as with the client, is seen in the TBWA/Chiat/Day agency and its relationship with Absolut vodka. As discussed in Chapter 1, the creative strategy for the brand plays off the distinctive shape of its bottle and depicts it with visual puns and witty headlines that play off the Absolut name. The agency and client recognized they could carry the advertising campaign further by tailoring the print ads for the magazines or regions where they appear. Absolut's media schedule includes over 100 magazines, among them various consumer and business publications. The

Figure 8-2 D'Arcy, Masius Benton & Bowles's universal advertising standards

1. *Does this advertising position the product simply and with unmistakable clarity?*

   The target audience for the advertised product or service must be able to see and sense in a flash *what* the product is for, *whom* it is for, and *why* they should be interested in it.

   Creating this clear vision of how the product or service fits into their lives is the first job of advertising. Without a simple, clear, focused positioning, no creative work can begin.

2. *Does this advertising bolt the brand to a clinching benefit?*

   Our advertising should be built on the most compelling and persuasive consumer benefit—not some unique-but-insignificant peripheral feature.

   Before you worry about how to say it, you must be sure you are saying *the right thing.* If you don't know what the most compelling benefit is, you've got to find out before you do anything else.

3. *Does this advertising contain a Power Idea?*

   The Power Idea is the vehicle that transforms the strategy into a dynamic, creative communications concept. It is the core creative idea that sets the stage for brilliant executions to come. The ideal Power Idea should:

   - Be describable in a simple word, phrase, or sentence without reference to any final execution.
   - Be likely to attract the prospect's attention.
   - Revolve around the clinching benefit.
   - Allow you to brand the advertising.
   - Make it easy for the prospect to vividly experience our client's product or service.

4. *Does this advertising design in Brand Personality?*

   The great brands tend to have something in common: the extra edge of having a Brand Personality. This is something beyond merely identifying what the brand does for the consumer; all brands *do* something, but the great brands also *are* something.

   A brand can be whatever its designers want it to be—and it can be so from day one.

5. *Is this advertising unexpected?*

   Why should our clients pay good money to wind up with advertising that looks and sounds like everybody else's in the category? They shouldn't.

   We must dare to be different, because sameness is suicide. We can't be outstanding unless we first stand out.

   The thing is not to *emulate* the competition but to *annihilate* them.

6. *Is this advertising single-minded?*

   If you have determined the right thing to say and have created a way to say it uncommonly well, why waste time saying anything else?

   If we want people to remember one big thing from a given piece of advertising, let's not make it more difficult than it already is in an overcommunicated world.

   The advertising should be all about that one big thing.

7. *Does this advertising reward the prospect?*

   Let's give our audience something that makes it easy—even pleasurable—for our message to penetrate: a tear, a smile, a laugh. An emotional stimulus is that special something that makes them want to see the advertising again and again.

8. *Is this advertising visually arresting?*

   Great advertising you remember—and can play back in your mind—is unusual to look at: compelling, riveting, a nourishing feast for the eyes. If you need a reason to strive for arresting work, go no further than Webster: "Catching or holding the attention, thought, or feelings. Gripping. Striking. Interesting."

9. *Does this advertising exhibit painstaking craftsmanship?*

   You want writing that is really written. Visuals that are designed. Music that is composed.

   Lighting, casting, wardrobe, direction—all the components of the art of advertising are every bit as important as the science of it. It is a sin to nickel-and-dime a great advertising idea to death.

   Why settle for good, when there's great? We should go for the absolute best in concept, design, and execution.

   This is our craft—the work should sparkle.

   "Our creative standards are not a gimmick," Steve emphasizes. "They're not even revolutionary. Instead, they are an explicit articulation of a fundamental refocusing on our company's only reason for being.

   "D'Arcy's universal advertising standards are the operating link between our vision today—and its coming reality."

creative and media departments work together selecting magazines and deciding on the ads that will appeal to the readers of each publication. The creative department is often asked to create media-specific ads to run in a particular publication. Exhibit 8-3 shows an Absolut ad that was developed specifically for *Los Angeles Magazine.*

Exhibit 8-3 Absolut vodka creates ads specifically for the publications in which they appear, such as this one for *Los Angeles Magazine*

Planning Creative Strategy

The Creative Challenge

Those who work on the creative side of advertising often face a real challenge. They must take all the research, creative briefs, strategy statements, communications objectives, and other input and transform them into an advertising message. Their job is to write copy, design layouts and illustrations, or produce commercials that effectively communicate the central theme on which the campaign is based. Rather than simply stating the features or benefits of a product or service, they must put the advertising message into a form that will engage the audience's interest and make the ads memorable.[10]

The job of the creative team is challenging because every marketing situation is different and each campaign or advertisement may require a different creative approach. Numerous guidelines have been developed for creating effective advertising,[11] but there is no magic formula. As copywriter Hank Sneiden notes in his book *Advertising Pure and Simple:*

> Rules lead to dull stereotyped advertising, and they stifle creativity, inspiration, initiative, and progress. The only hard and fast rule that I know of in advertising is that there are no rules. No formulas. No right way. Given the same problem, a dozen creative talents would solve it a dozen different ways. If there were a sure-fire formula for successful advertising, everyone would use it. Then there'd be no need for creative people. We would simply program robots to create our ads and commercials and they'd sell loads of product—to other robots.[12]

Taking Creative Risks

Many creative people follow proven formulas when creating ads because they are safe. Clients often feel uncomfortable with advertising that is too different. Bill Tragos, former chair of TBWA, the advertising agency noted for its excellent creative work for Absolut vodka, Evian, and many other clients, says, "Very few clients realize that the reason that their work is so bad is that they are the ones who commandeered it and directed it to be that way. I think that at least 50 percent of an agency's successful work resides in the client."[13]

Many creative people say it is important for clients to take some risks if they want breakthrough advertising that gets noticed. One agency that has been successful in getting its clients to take risks is Wieden & Kennedy, best known for its excellent creative work for companies such as Nike, Microsoft, and ESPN. The agency's founders believe a key element in its success has been a steadfast belief in taking risks when most agencies and their clients have been retrenching and becoming more conservative.[14] The agency can develop great advertising partly because clients like Nike are willing to take risks and go along with the agency's priority system, which places the creative work first and the client–agency relationship second. The agency has even terminated relationships with large clients like Gallo when they interfered too much with the creative process.

An example of a company that has begun taking more creative risks with its advertising is Wrigley. For many years the company, which has long dominated the market for chewing gum, was very conservative with its advertising and relied on more traditional, attribute-focused messages. However, in recent years Wrigley has taken a more dynamic approach to its marketing by introducing new products and using an edgier creative approach in its ads.[15] For example, advertising for the company's Big Red brand used the tried and true "Kiss a Little Longer" campaign, featuring smooching couples, for many years. However, in 2000 Wrigley decided to develop a new image for the brand

Exhibit 8-4 Wrigley's takes more of a creative risk with its new ads

and began using a new campaign that focuses on the product's bold cinnamon taste and little "wisdoms" regarding fresh breath (Exhibit 8-4).

Not all companies or agencies agree that advertising has to be risky to be effective, however. Many marketing managers are more comfortable with advertising that simply communicates product or service features and benefits and gives the consumer a reason to buy. They see their ad campaigns as multimillion-dollar investments whose goal is to sell the product rather than finance the whims of their agency's creative staff. They argue that some creative people have lost sight of advertising's bottom line: Does it sell? IMC Perspective 8-2 discusses the ongoing debate over the artsy, image-oriented approach to advertising taken by many creative types versus the more hard-sell approach that many clients prefer.

The issue of how much latitude creative people should be given and how much risk the client should be willing to take is open to considerable debate. However, clients and agency personnel generally agree that the ability to develop novel yet appropriate approaches to communicating with the customer makes the creative specialist valuable—and often hard to find.

Creative Personnel

The image of the creative advertising person perpetuated in novels, movies, and TV shows is often one of a freewheeling, freethinking, eccentric personality. The educational background of creative personnel is often in nonbusiness areas such as art, literature, music, humanities, or journalism, so their interests and perspectives tend to differ from those of managers with a business education or background. Creative people tend to be more abstract and less structured, organized, or conventional in their approach to a problem, relying on intuition more often than logic. For example, Arthur Kover conducted a study of advertising copywriters and found that they work without guidance from any formal theories of communication. However, those interviewed in his study did have similar informal, implicit theories that guide them in creating ads. These theories are based on finding ways to break through the ad clutter, open the consciousness of consumers, and connect with them to deliver the message.[16]

Advertising creatives are sometimes stereotyped as odd, perhaps because they dress differently and do not always work the conventional 9-to-5 schedule. Of course, from the perspective of the creatives, it is the marketing or brand managers and account executives (the "suits") who are strange. In many agencies, you can't tell the creative personnel from the executives by their dress or demeanor. Yet the differences between creative and managerial personalities and perspectives must be recognized and tolerated so that creative people can do their best work and all those involved in the advertising process can cooperate.

Most agencies thrive on creativity, for it is the major component in the product they produce. Thus, they must create an environment that fosters the development of creative thinking and creative advertising. Clients must also understand the differences between the perspectives of the creative personnel and marketing and product managers. While the client has ultimate approval of the advertising, the opinions of creative specialists must be respected when advertising ideas and content are evaluated. (Evaluation of the creative's ideas and work is discussed in more detail in Chapter 9.)

The Creative Process

Some advertising people say creativity in advertising is best viewed as a process and creative success is most likely when some organized approach is followed. This does not mean there is an infallible blueprint to follow to create effective advertising; as we saw earlier, many advertising people reject attempts to standardize creativity or develop rules. However, most do follow a process when developing an ad.

One of the most popular approaches to creativity in advertising was developed by James Webb Young, a former creative vice president at the J. Walter Thompson agency. Young said, "The production of ideas is just as definite a process as the production of Fords; the production of ideas, too, runs an assembly line; in this production the mind follows an operative technique which can be learned and controlled; and

IMC PERSPECTIVE 8-2

The Perpetual Debate: Creative versus Hard-Sell Advertising

For decades there has been a perpetual battle over the role of advertising in the marketing process. The war for the soul of advertising has been endlessly fought between those who believe ads should move people and those who just want to move product. On one side are the "suits" or "rationalists," who argue that advertising must sell the product or service and that the more selling points or information in the ad, the better its chance of moving the consumer to purchase. On the other side are the "poets" or proponents of creativity, who argue that advertising has to build an emotional bond between consumers and brands or companies that goes beyond product advertising. The debate over the effectiveness of creative or artsy advertising is not new. The rationalists have taken great delight in pointing to long lists of creative and award-winning campaigns over the years that have failed in the marketplace, such as the humorous commercials for Alka-Seltzer from the 1960s and 70s and the Joe Isuzu spokes-liar ads from the late 80s. They also point to the recent dot-com explosion that brought with it a lot of creative and award-winning ads but proved that great advertising alone cannot make consumers buy a product or service they really do not want or need.

There are many examples of creative campaigns that moved consumers' emotions but were terminated because they failed to move the sales needle and they put accounts and reputations on the line. In 1998 Levi Strauss & Co. terminated Foote, Cone & Belding, of San Francisco, from its Levi's jean account after 67 years because of declining sales, even though the agency had consistently earned rave reviews and awards for its creative work. The company moved its account to TBWA/Chiat/Day, which won accolades for its creative work on campaigns such as "Opt for the Original" and "Make Them Your Own." However, the popularity of Levi's among young people plummeted 74 percent from 1996 to 2001, with only 8 percent citing the brand as their favorite jean, down from 31 percent in 1996. In early 2002 Levi Strauss parted company with TBWA/Chiat/Day and moved its business to Bartle Bogle Hegarty, the agency that has handled advertising for Levi's in Europe for a number of years.

Another company that had differences of opinion with its agency over artsy versus more hard-sell advertising is Norwegian Cruise Lines. The company's marketing director, Nina Cohen, felt that the sensual "It's different out here" campaign produced by Goodby, Silverstein & Partners in the mid-90s was gorgeous but irrelevant. She said, "Every frame of those ads was frameable, but we're not in the framing business." Cohen added that "while there are some creative icons out there who feel they have some higher voice to answer to, as clients, we're the ones you have to answer to." However, the agency's co-creative director, Jeff Goodby, considered his agency's creative work for Norwegian both beautiful and effective and argues that the impact of creative and entertaining advertising on sales isn't always quantifiable for good reason. He notes: "It's where the magic happens in advertising, and you can never predict that. It's dangerous to be suspicious of that." Many of the "poets" on the creative side agree with Goodby and like to cite the teaching of legendary adman Bill Bernbach, who preached that persuasion is an art, not a science, and that its success is dependent on a complex mix of intangible human qualities that can be neither measured nor predicted.

Most of the "poets" who support advertising that connects on an emotional level insist that selling product is as much a priority for them as it is for those on the rational side of the debate. One top agency executive notes, "We've proven that this kind of advertising works; otherwise we wouldn't be in business, us or the agencies that practice the craft at this level." However, Brent Bouchez, founder of Bouchez Kent and Company and a creative director for 20 years, argues that the poets are losing sight of the fact that advertising is

about selling things and that being really creative in advertising means solving problems and building interesting brands that people want to buy. He notes: "It's time we stopped teaching young creative people to consider it a victory if the logo in an ad is hard to find, or if the product doesn't appear in the commercial at all. It's time we stopped using "break through the clutter" as an excuse to say nothing about what it is we're selling or why you should buy it."

It is unlikely there will ever be peace between the warring factions as long as there are "rationalists" and "poets" who make a point of arguing over which approach works best. Steve Hayden, vice-chairman of Ogilvy Worldwide, says, "It's the ad industry's reflection of the essential Platonic/Aristotelian split in the world, pitting two groups of people against each other who usually can't agree which end is up." However, Nina Cohen, who has worked on both the agency and the client side of the business, is bewildered by the intense opinions held by people on each side and asks, "Aren't we all here to do the same thing?" meaning to build brands and business. While the answer is, of course, yes, the debate over how to do it is likely to continue.

Sources: Alice Z. Cuneo, "Bartle Bogle Tapped to Cure Levi's Blues," *Advertising Age,* Jan. 14, 2002, p. 6; Brent Bouchez, "Trophies Are Meaningless," *Advertising Age,* July 30, 2001; Anthony Vagnoni, "Creative Differences," *Advertising Age,* Nov. 17, 1997, pp. 1, 28, 30

that its effective use is just as much a matter of practice in the technique as in the effective use of any tool."[17] Young's model of the creative process contains five steps:

1. *Immersion.* Gathering raw material and information through background research and immersing yourself in the problem.
2. *Digestion.* Taking the information, working it over, and wrestling with it in the mind.
3. *Incubation.* Putting the problems out of your conscious mind and turning the information over to the subconscious to do the work.
4. *Illumination.* The birth of an idea—the "Eureka! I have it!" phenomenon.
5. *Reality or verification.* Studying the idea to see if it still looks good or solves the problem; then shaping the idea to practical usefulness.

Young's process of creativity is similar to a four-step approach outlined much earlier by English sociologist Graham Wallas:

1. *Preparation.* Gathering background information needed to solve the problem through research and study.
2. *Incubation.* Getting away and letting ideas develop.
3. *Illumination.* Seeing the light or solution.
4. *Verification.* Refining and polishing the idea and seeing if it is an appropriate solution.

Models of the creative process are valuable to those working in the creative area of advertising, since they offer an organized way to approach an advertising problem. Preparation or gathering of background information is the first step in the creative process. As we saw in earlier chapters, the advertiser and agency start by developing a thorough understanding of the product or service, the target market, and the competition. They also focus on the role of advertising in the marketing and promotional program.

These models do not say much about how this information will be synthesized and used by the creative specialist because this part of the process is unique to the individual. In many ways, it's what sets apart the great creative minds and strategists in advertising. However, many agencies are now using a process called *account planning* to gather information and help creative specialists as they go through the creative process of developing advertising.

Account Planning

To facilitate the creative process, many agencies now use **account planning,** which is a process that involves conducting research and gathering all relevant information about a client's product or service, brand, and consumers in the target audience. Account planning began in Great Britain during the 1960s and 70s and has spread to agencies in the United States as well as throughout Europe and Asia. The concept has

become very popular in recent years as many agencies have seen the successful campaigns developed by agencies that are strong advocates of account planning.[18] One such agency is Goodby, Silverstein & Partners, which has used account planning to develop highly successful campaigns for clients such as Polaroid, Hewlett-Packard, Sega, and Nike, as well as the popular "Got milk?" ads for the California Milk Processor Board.

Jon Steel, vice president and director of account planning at the agency's San Francisco office, has written an excellent book on the process titled *Truth, Lies & Advertising: The Art of Account Planning.*[19] He notes that the account planner's job is to provide the key decision makers with all the information they require to make an intelligent decision. According to Steel, "Planners may have to work very hard to influence the way that the advertising turns out, carefully laying out a strategic foundation with the client, handing over tidbits of information to creative people when, in their judgment, that information will have the greatest impact, giving feedback on ideas, and hopefully adding some ideas of their own."

Account planning plays an important role during creative strategy development by driving the process from the customers' point of view. Planners will work with the client as well as other agency personnel, such as the creative team and media specialists. They discuss how the knowledge and information they have gathered can be used in the development of the creative strategy as well as other aspects of the advertising campaign. Account planners are usually responsible for all the research (both qualitative and quantitative) conducted during the creative strategy development process. In the following section we examine how various types of research and information can provide input to the creative process of advertising. This information can be gathered by account planners or others whose job it is to provide input to the process.

Inputs to the Creative Process: Preparation, Incubation, Illumination

Background Research

Only the most foolish creative person or team would approach an assignment without first learning as much as possible about the client's product or service, the target market, the competition, and any other relevant background information. The creative specialist should also be knowledgeable about general trends, conditions, and developments in the marketplace, as well as research on specific advertising approaches or techniques that might be effective. The creative specialist can acquire background information in numerous ways. Some informal fact-finding techniques have been noted by Sandra Moriarty:

- Reading anything related to the product or market—books, trade publications, general interest articles, research reports, and the like.
- Asking everyone involved with the product for information—designers, engineers, salespeople, and consumers.
- Listening to what people are talking about. Visits to stores, malls, restaurants, and even the agency cafeteria can be informative. Listening to the client can be particularly valuable, since he or she often knows the product and market best.
- Using the product or service and becoming familiar with it. The more you use a product, the more you know and can say about it.
- Working in and learning about the client's business to understand better the people you're trying to reach.[20]

To assist in the preparation, incubation, and illumination stages, many agencies provide creative people with both general and product-specific preplanning input. **General preplanning input** can include books, periodicals, trade publications, scholarly journals, pictures, and clipping services, which gather and organize magazine and newspaper articles on the product, the market, and the competition, including the latter's ads. This input can also come from research studies conducted by the client, the agency, the media, or other sources.

Another useful general preplanning input concerns trends, developments, and happenings in the marketplace. Information is available from a variety of sources,

Exhibit 8-5 Advertising industry publications are excellent sources of information on market trends

including local, state, and federal governments, secondary research suppliers, and various industry trade associations, as well as advertising and media organizations. For example, advertising industry groups like the American Association of Advertising Agencies and media organizations like the National Association of Broadcasters (NAB) and Magazine Publishers of America (MPA) publish research reports and newsletters that provide information on market trends and developments and how they might affect consumers. Those involved in developing creative strategy can also gather relevant and timely information by reading publications like *Adweek, Advertising Age, BrandWeek,* and *The Wall Street Journal* (Exhibit 8-5).

Product/Service-Specific Research In addition to getting general background research and preplanning input, creative people receive **product/service-specific preplanning input.** This information generally comes in the form of specific studies conducted on the product or service, the target audience, or a combination of the two. Quantitative and qualitative consumer research such as attitude studies, market structure and positioning studies such as perceptual mapping and lifestyle research, focus group interviews, and demographic and psychographic profiles of users of a particular product, service, or brand are examples of product-specific preplanning input.

Many product- or service-specific studies helpful to the creative team are conducted by the client or the agency. A number of years ago, the BBDO ad agency developed an approach called **problem detection**[21] for finding ideas around which creative strategies could be based. This research technique involves asking consumers familiar with a product (or service) to generate an exhaustive list of things that bother them or problems they encounter when using it. The consumers rate these problems in order of importance and evaluate various brands in terms of their association with each problem. A problem detection study can provide valuable input for product improvements, reformulations, or new products. It can also give the creative people ideas regarding attributes or features to emphasize and guidelines for positioning new or existing brands.

Some agencies conduct psychographic studies annually and construct detailed psychographic or lifestyle profiles of product or service users. DDB Needham conducts a large-scale psychographic study each year using a sample of 4,000 U.S. adults. The agency's Life Style Study provides its creative teams with a better understanding of the target audience for whom they are developing ads.

For example, information from its Life Style Study was used by DDB Needham's creative department in developing an advertising campaign for Westin a few years ago. The agency's Life Style Study showed that the younger business travelers the luxury hotel chain was targeting are highly confident, intelligent, assertive, and classy and considered themselves to be "winners." Rather than using the traditional images that feature buildings and golf courses, the creative team decided to "brand the users" by playing to their ego and reinforcing their strong self-image. The ad campaign used the tagline "Who is he/she sleeping with? Westin. Choose your travel partner wisely" (Exhibit 8-6).

Recently a number of advertising agencies have been conducting branding research to help better identify clients' customers and how they connect to their brands. Agencies use this research to determine how a brand is perceived among consumers, and these insights, in turn, are used to develop more effective advertising campaigns.[22] IMC Perspective 8-3 discusses how some of the

Exhibit 8-6 DDB Needham's Life Style Study provided valuable input in the development of this campaign for Westin

IMC PERSPECTIVE 8-3

Advertising Agencies Find Ways to Build Stronger Brands

Branding has become more important than ever to companies competing in today's marketplace. At a time when battered investors, customers, and even employees are questioning whom they can trust, the ability of a familiar brand to deliver proven value has become extremely important. A belief in the power of brands has spread beyond the traditional consumer-goods marketers, and branding has become a very important part of the marketing strategy for companies in almost every industry. Purveyors of products ranging from Gillette razors to BMW automobiles to Starbucks coffee have been able to use their strong brands to keep growing without succumbing to the pricing pressure of an intense promotional environment. However, many of the traditional big-brand companies are striving to reinvent themselves and to restore value to their venerable brands. And as they do so, many are looking to their advertising agencies to help them determine the best way to build strong brands and connect with their customers.

Advertising agencies often conduct research studies for their clients, using techniques such as surveys, focus groups, and ethnographic studies to help them better understand their customers and determine the best way to communicate with them. However, in recent years a number of agencies have been conducting branding research and developing proprietary models to help better identify clients' customers and determine how they connect to their brands.

DDB Worldwide provides clients with branding insights through its *Brand Capital Study,* which amasses information on more than 500 brands ranging from Wal-Mart to Yahoo and from Budweiser to Michelin. The proprietary branding research is based on a global marketing study consisting of quantitative surveys conducted among 14,000 consumers in 14 countries. The surveys consist of a battery of questions focusing on consumer attitudes, interests, desired self-image, values, and product use as well as various subjects and issues including family, religion, politics, advertising, and brands. The agency uses the information from the Brand Capital Study to compare the desired self-images and lifestyles of consumers who love a brand with those who have a less strong connection. The study also measures *brand magnetism,* which is the brand's ability to strengthen its connection with consumers and is based on four factors: high quality, leadership in the category, growth in popularity, and uniqueness in the category. According to the agency's worldwide brand planning director, the success of a product or brand is tied to how it is perceived in popular culture: "In category after category, around the world, the evidence is clear. As a brand's breadth of connection with consumers increases, its depth of connection increases exponentially." DDB describes this phenomenon of each consumer's feelings about a brand being directly affected by other consumer's feelings as "brand contagion."

Young & Rubicam is another agency that has developed a proprietary tool for building and managing brands, a tool it refers to as the *Brand Asset Valuator.* The agency has invested over $70 million and conducted over 120 studies in building a comprehensive global database of consumer perceptions of brands. This tool views brands as developing through a very specific progression of four consumer perceptions, including differentiation, relevance, esteem, and knowledge. Differentiation measures the strength of the brand's meaning, while relevance measures the personal appropriateness of the brand to consumers. These two measures together form *brand strength,* which is viewed as an important indicator of future performance and potential. Esteem is the extent to which consumers like a brand and hold it in high regard, while knowledge represents awareness of the brand and what it stands for and is the culmination of brand-building efforts. Esteem and knowledge form *brand stature,* which is a more traditional measure of the status of a brand and its current performance, which is a strong strategic indicator of the health of a brand. The Brand Asset Valuator uses measures of these four factors to identify core issues for the brand and to evaluate current brand performance and potential.

The Leo Burnett agency relies on its *Brand Belief System* to guide its global brand-building philosophy and practice. This system focuses on the development of the brand–believer bond, which is at the core of the relationship between a brand and its believers, and considers four fundamental questions. The first question involves the category and asks, Where does the brand truly belong? The second involves the content and asks, How will the brand inspire belief? The third question considers the culture and asks, What shapes belief in the brand? The final question involves the customer and asks, With whom and how will the brand belong? Leo Burnett uses a set of proprietary research tools to provide information that can be used as part of the Brand Belief System and provide the agency with a basis for brand analysis and planning.

Nearly all the major agencies are conducting branding research and/or developing models or systems

that they can use to gain better insight into consumers and develop more effective campaigns for their clients. The importance of building and maintaining strong brands is likely to become even greater in the future. This will put even more pressure on agencies to develop new and better tools and techniques that can be used to guide their clients' advertising campaigns.

Sources: Kathryn Kranhold, "Agencies Beefing Up on Brand Research," *The Wall Street Journal,* Mar. 9, 2000, p. B14; Brand Asset Valuator White Paper, www.yr.com; "DDB Worldwide Explores What Makes Big Brands Big," www.ddb.com, March 2000.

major agencies are conducting branding research and developing models to determine how consumers connect with their client's brands.

Qualitative Research Input Many agencies, particularly larger ones with strong research departments, have their own research programs and specific techniques they use to assist in the development of creative strategy and provide input to the creative process. In addition to the various quantitative research studies, qualitative research techniques such as in-depth interviews or focus groups can provide the creative team with valuable insight at the early stages of the creative process. **Focus groups** are a research method whereby consumers (usually 10 to 12 people) from the target market are led through a discussion regarding a particular topic. Focus groups give insight as to why and how consumers use a product or service, what is important to them in choosing a particular brand, what they like and don't like about various products or services, and any special needs they might have that aren't being satisfied. A focus group session might also include a discussion of types of ad appeals to use or evaluate the advertising of various companies.

Focus group interviews bring the creative people and others involved in creative strategy development into contact with the customers. Listening to a focus group gives copywriters, art directors, and other creative specialists a better sense of who the target audience is, what the audience is like, and who the creatives need to write, design, or direct to in creating an advertising message. Focus groups can also be used to evaluate the viability of different creative approaches under consideration and suggest the best direction to pursue.[23]

Another form of qualitative input that has become popular among advertising agencies is **ethnographic research,** which involves observing consumers in their natural environment.[24] Some agencies send anthropologists or trained researchers into the field to study and observe consumers in their homes, at work, or at play. For example, the Ogilvy & Mather agency has a research unit called the Discovery Group which moves into consumers' homes, follows consumers in their leisure pursuits, or trails them as they move through their daily lives.[25] For Ogilvy client Miller beer, Discovery staffers traveled around the country filming Miller drinkers, as well as those drinking competitive brands. They used the tapes to study group dynamics and how the dynamics changed while people were drinking. The agency used the insights gained from the study to help develop a new advertising campaign for Miller Lite beer, which will be discussed later in the chapter. Many marketing and agency researchers prefer ethnographic research over the use of focus groups, as the latter technique has a number of limitations. Strong personalities can often wield undue influence in focus groups, and participants often will not admit, or may not even recognize, their behavior patterns and motivations. However, ethnographic studies can cost more to conduct and are more difficult to administer.

Generally, creative people are open to any research or information that will help them understand the client's target market better and assist in generating creative ideas. The advertising industry is recognizing the importance of using research to guide the creative process. The Advertising Research Foundation recently initiated the David Ogilvy Awards, named after the advertising legend who founded Ogilvy & Mather. These awards are presented to teams of advertising agencies, client companies, and research companies in recognition of research that has been used successfully to determine the strategy and effectiveness of ad campaigns. For example, the California Milk Processor Board, which is a past winner of the David Ogilvy Award, has used both quantitative and qualitative research in developing the popular "Got

Exhibit 8-7 Research helped in the development of the popular "got milk?" campaign

milk?" advertising campaign. Focus groups and survey research studies were conducted to help understand companion foods that are consumed with milk and how consumers react to the effect of "milk deprivation," which is the key idea behind the humorous ads in the campaign.[26] (Exhibit 8-7)

Inputs to the Creative Process: Verification, Revision

The verification and revision stage of the creative process evaluates ideas generated during the illumination stage, rejects inappropriate ones, refines and polishes those that remain, and gives them final expression. Techniques used at this stage include directed focus groups to evaluate creative concepts, ideas, or themes; message communication studies; portfolio tests; and evaluation measures such as viewer reaction profiles.

At this stage of the creative process, members of the target audience may be asked to evaluate rough creative layouts and to indicate what meaning they get from the ad, what they think of its execution, or how they react to a slogan or theme. The creative team can gain insight into how a TV commercial might communicate its message by having members of the target market evaluate the ad in storyboard form. A **storyboard** is a series of drawings used to present the visual plan or layout of a proposed commercial. It contains a series of sketches of key frames or scenes along with the copy or audio portion for each scene (Exhibit 8-8).

Testing a commercial in storyboard form can be difficult because storyboards are too abstract for many consumers to understand. To make the creative layout more realistic and easier to evaluate, the agency may produce an **animatic,** a videotape of the storyboard along with an audio soundtrack. Storyboards and animatics are useful for research purposes as well as for presenting the creative idea to other agency personnel or to the client for discussion and approval.

At this stage of the process, the creative team is attempting to find the best creative approach or execution style before moving ahead with the campaign themes and going into actual production of the ad. The verification/revision process may include more formal, extensive pretesting of the ad before a final decision is made. Pretesting and related procedures are examined in detail in Chapter 19.

Creative Strategy Development

Advertising Campaigns

Most ads are part of a series of messages that make up an IMC or **advertising campaign,** which is a set of interrelated and coordinated marketing communication activities that center on a single theme or idea that appears in different media across a specified time period. Determining the unifying theme around which the campaign will be built is a critical part of the creative process, as it sets the tone for the individual ads and other forms of marketing communications that will be used. A **campaign theme** should be a strong idea, as it is the central message that will be communicated in all the advertising and other promotional activities.

Exhibit 8-8 Marketers can gain insight into consumers' reactions to a commercial by showing them a storyboard

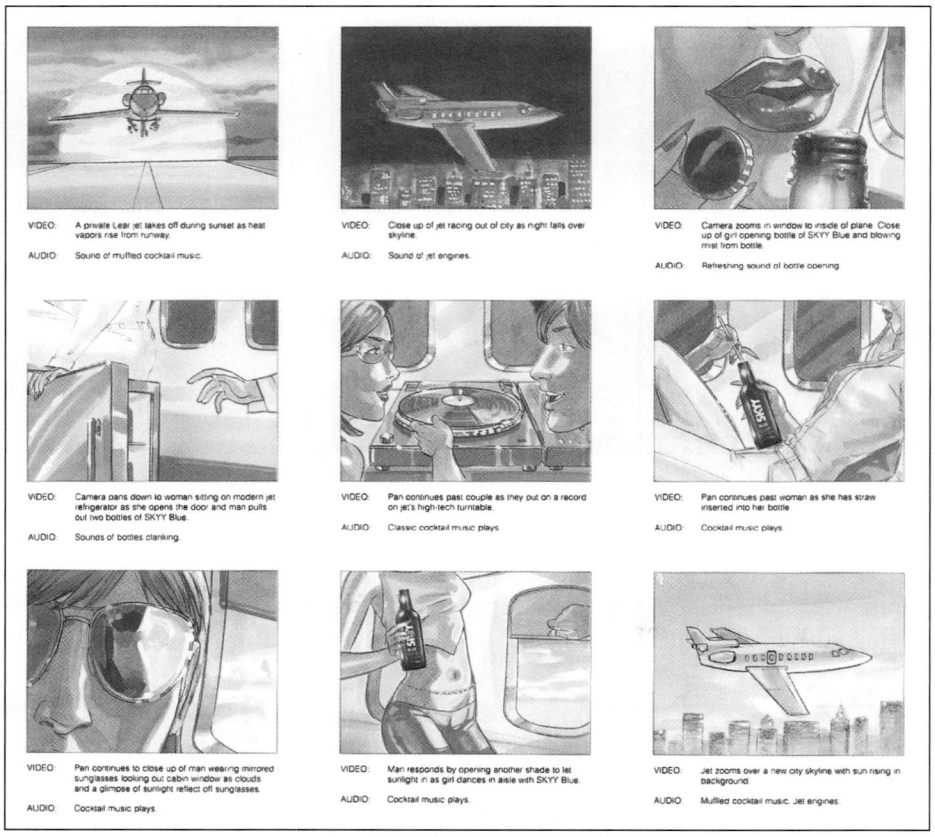

Advertising campaign plans are short-term in nature and, like marketing and IMC plans, are done on an annual basis. However, the campaign themes are usually developed with the intention of being used for a longer time period. Unfortunately, many campaign themes last only a short time, usually because they are ineffective or market conditions and/or competitive developments in the marketplace change. IMC Perspective 8-4 discusses the problems the Miller Brewing Co. has had in trying to find an effective ad campaign for its Miller Lite brand.

While some marketers change their campaign themes often, a successful campaign theme may last for years. Philip Morris has been using the "Marlboro country" campaign for over 40 years, General Mills has positioned Wheaties cereal as the "Breakfast of Champions" for decades, and BMW has used the "ultimate driving machine" theme since 1974. Even though BMW has changed agencies several times over the past three decades, the classic tagline has been retained. Figure 8-3 lists the top 10 advertising slogans of the past century, as selected by *Advertising Age*.

Figure 8-3 Top 10 advertising slogans of the century

Company or Brand	Campaign Theme
1. DeBeers	Diamonds are forever
2. Nike	Just do it
3. Coca-Cola	The pause that refreshes
4. Miller Lite	Tastes great, less filling
5. Avis	We try harder
6. Maxwell House	Good to the last drop
7. Wheaties	Breakfast of champions
8. Clairol	Does she . . . or doesn't she
9. Morton Salt	When it rains it pours
10. Wendy's	Where's the beef?

IMC PERSPECTIVE 8-4

Miller Lite Searches for the Right Campaign Theme

One of the most memorable and successful advertising campaigns of all times was the "Tastes Great, Less Filling" theme for Miller Lite beer, which began in 1974. The campaign used humorous commercials featuring famous (and not-so-famous) ex-athletes and other celebrities arguing over whether the brand's main appeal was its great taste or the fact that it contained fewer calories than regular beer and was less filling. The campaign ran for 17 years and helped make Miller Lite the second-best-selling beer in the United States for many years, as well as making light beer a legitimate segment of the beer market.

In the late 80s, Miller began taking the campaign in a new direction, and the ads began moving away from the use of ex-athletes. Although the tagline was still being used, the executions started using rock bands, old movie and party scenes, the Miller Lite girls, and other images in order to appeal to a broader and younger market. Miller Lite was also facing strong competition in the light-beer market from other brands such as Bud Light and Coors Light. Despite not entering the market until 1982, Anheuser-Busch had developed Bud Light into a strong brand and Coors Light had replaced the flagship brand as the company's best-selling product. By the early 90s, Miller Lite was continuing to lose market share and the company decided to drop the "Tastes great, Less Filling" campaign. What followed was a six-year odyssey of advertising flip-flops that included adolescent humor and far-out wit to chase young male beer drinkers. Spots featuring cowboys singing good-bye to their beer on the way to the bathroom didn't help sell a lot of Miller Lite.

In early 1999 Miller dusted off the 24-year-old formula of having people debate the merits of the brand. The new ad theme, "The Great Taste of a True Pilsner Beer," pitted celebrities against one another in mock arguments over whether Miller Lite tastes great because its smooth or because of its choice hops. Miller marketing people felt the celebrity-bickering approach would work a second time because the new campaign was different from the original ads. In the new campaign there was no more talk about "less filling," since this claim had lost its uniqueness as other light beers appeared. The ads focused on Miller Lite's taste and ingredients, which is what the company felt really mattered to beer drinkers. This campaign lasted less than a year: Miller switched agencies as well as ad themes and revived the 30-year-old "Miller Time" tagline that was used in the 1970s for the Miller High Life brand. The new ads, from the Ogilvy & Mather agency, modified the theme to "Grab a Miller Lite. It's Miller Time" and featured guys bonding over beer, sexy women, and humorous vignettes. They showed friends doing things and enjoying their time together and focused on the ritual and camaraderie of having a beer. The agency's creative director noted: "When we get down to the heart and soul of the brand, it's always been about the occasion and the time guys spend together—the banter and the real talk."

In 2002 the agency took the bonding concept in a slightly different direction with a new campaign for Miller Lite featuring ads that focus on real consumer insights and storytelling. The commercials open with a flashback to an embarrassing moment and end showing the embarrassed person telling the story. For example, one of the ads begins with a couple in a car, each with something he or she wants to discuss. The young man talks first, telling the woman he doesn't want to marry her. She then tells him that she won millions in the lottery. The commercial ends with the man telling the story to friends while playing pool and, afterward, one of the friends sneaking off to phone the woman for a date. Each ad closes with the slogan "Life is best told over a great-tasting Miller Lite at a place called Miller Time." Print executions also focus on the theme of friends getting together to enjoy a Miller Lite.

The new Miller Lite ads have been received very favorably by Miller beer distributors and by consumers. Some critics have argued that, with the storyteller ads, Miller has created one of its most popular campaigns since "Tastes Great, Less Filling." A Miller executive notes: "This whole storytelling metaphor is very powerful. Consumers tell us, 'This is how I drink beer with my friends.'" Of course, the company hopes that the new ads ensure that Miller Lite is the brand consumers are drinking when they get together with their friends.

Sources: Michael McCarthy, "Miller Turns to Classic Strategy," *USA TODAY*, Aug. 5, 2002, p. 2B; Sally Beatty, "Philip Morris Taps Old Formula to Help Boost Miller Lite Brand," *The Wall Street Journal*, Mar. 15, 1999, p. B5.

Like any other area of the marketing and promotional process, the creative aspect of advertising and the development of the campaign theme is guided by specific goals and objectives. A creative strategy that focuses on what must be communicated will guide the selection of the campaign theme and the development of all messages used in the ad campaign. The creative strategy is based on several factors, including identification of the target audience; the basic problem, issue, or opportunity the advertising must address; the major selling idea or key benefit the message needs to communicate; and any supportive information that needs to be included in the ad. Once these factors are determined, a creative strategy statement should describe the message appeal and execution style that will be used. Many ad agencies outline these elements in a document known as the copy or creative platform.

Copy Platform

The written **copy platform** specifies the basic elements of the creative strategy. Different agencies may call this document a *creative platform* or *work plan, creative brief, creative blueprint,* or *creative contract.* The account representative or manager assigned to the account usually prepares the copy platform. In larger agencies, an individual from research or the strategic account planning department may write it. People from the agency team or group assigned to the account, including creative personnel as well as representatives from media and research, have input. The advertising manager and/or the marketing and brand managers from the client side ultimately approve the copy platform. Figure 8-4 shows a sample copy-platform outline that can be used to guide the creative process. Just as there are different names for the copy platform, there are variations in the outline and format used and in the level of detail included.

Several components of the copy platform were discussed in previous chapters. For example, Chapter 7 examined the DAGMAR model and showed how the setting of advertising objectives requires specifying a well-defined target audience and developing a communication task statement that spells out what message must be communicated to this audience. Determining what problem the product or service will solve or what issue must be addressed in the ad helps in establishing communication objectives for the campaign to accomplish. For example, in developing a campaign for Polaroid a few years ago, Goodby, Silverstein & Partners was faced with the challenge of redefining the relevancy of instant photography and bringing Polaroid cameras out of the closet and back into everyday use. Working with Polaroid's marketing personnel, the agency came up with the idea of focusing on an instant picture as a solution to a problem, an instant tool or "catalyst" to make something happen. The advertising message is designed to give people ideas about how to use their forgotten Polaroid cameras.

Two critical components of the copy platform are the development of the major selling idea and creative strategy development. These two steps are often the responsibility of the creative team or specialist and form the basis of the advertising campaign theme. For Polaroid, the major selling idea was "the picture is only the beginning," and the resulting campaign theme built around this idea was "See what develops." The creative strategy was to have each ad in the campaign tell a story in which a Polaroid camera sets off a chain reaction. For example, one of the TV commercials featured a harried architect in a meeting telling his wife on the phone that he can't possibly come

Figure 8-4 Copy platform outline

1. Basic problem or issue the advertising must address.
2. Advertising and communications objectives.
3. Target audience.
4. Major selling idea or key benefits to communicate.
5. Creative strategy statement (campaign theme, appeal, and execution technique to be used).
6. Supporting information and requirements.

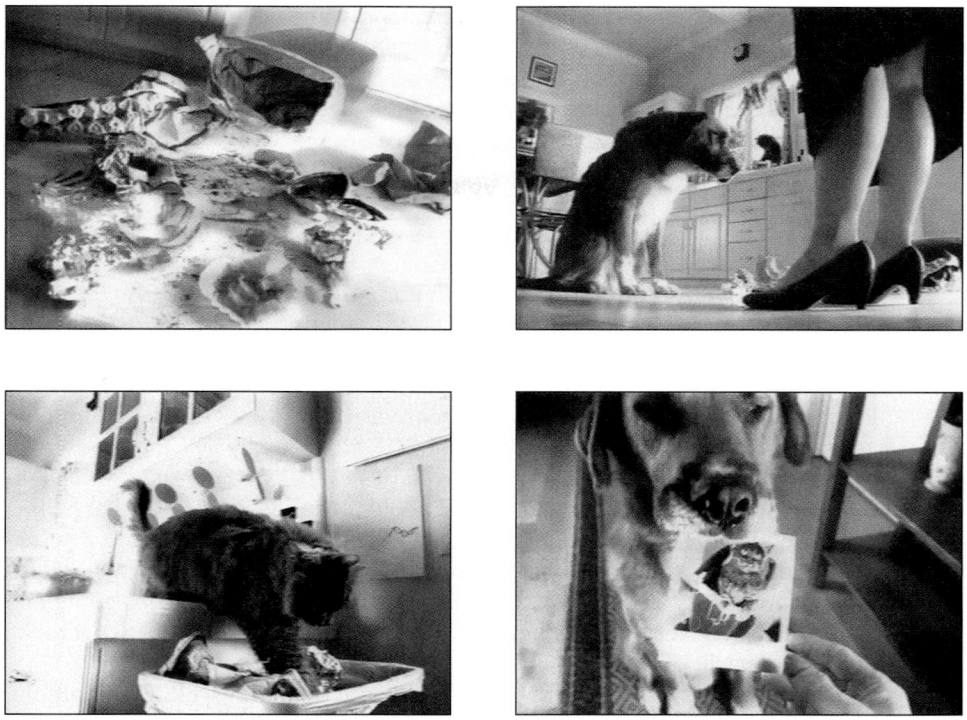

Exhibit 8-9 The major selling idea behind this Polaroid commercial is that the picture is only the beginning of the story

home for lunch. But in a sultry voice she tells him to look in his briefcase, saying "I left you something this morning." He pulls out a Polaroid photo, his eyes widen, and he says, "I'll be there in 10 minutes." Another humorous spot from the campaign shows a dog, wrongfully being scolded for upsetting the trash while an evil-looking cat sneers from the other side of the kitchen. The owner leaves, and the cat goes for the trash once again. However, this time the dog takes a Polaroid snapshot of the cat, astride the trash with a chicken bone in its mouth, and then patiently waits, incriminating photo in mouth, as the door opens and the owner returns. "Oh dear," we hear as the picture fades (Exhibit 8-9).

Many copy platforms also include supporting information and requirements (brand identifications, disclaimers, and the like) that should appear in any advertising message. This information may be important in ensuring uniformity across various executions of the ads used in a campaign or in meeting any legal requirements. One of the major challenges for the creative team is determining the major selling idea that will be used as the basis of the campaign. We examine below some approaches often used for determining the major selling idea and campaign theme.

The Search for the Major Selling Idea

An important part of creative strategy is determining the central theme that will become the **major selling idea** of the ad campaign. As A. Jerome Jeweler states in his book *Creative Strategy in Advertising:*

> The major selling idea should emerge as the strongest singular thing you can say about your product or service. This should be the claim with the broadest and most meaningful appeal to your target audience. Once you determine this message, be certain you can live with it; be sure it stands strong enough to remain the central issue in every ad and commercial in the campaign.[27]

Some advertising experts argue that for an ad campaign to be effective it must contain a big idea that attracts the consumer's attention, gets a reaction, and sets the advertiser's product or service apart from the competition's. Well-known adman John O'Toole describes the *big idea* as "that flash of insight that synthesizes the purpose of the strategy, joins the product benefit with consumer desire in a fresh, involving way, brings the subject to life, and makes the reader or audience stop, look, and listen."[28]

Exhibit 8-10 United Technologies "punks" ad is an excellent example of a big idea in business-to-business advertising

Of course, the real challenge to the creative team is coming up with the big idea to use in the ad. Many products and services offer virtually nothing unique, and it can be difficult to find something interesting to say about them. The late David Ogilvy, generally considered one of the most creative advertising copywriters ever to work in the business, has stated:

> I doubt if more than one campaign in a hundred contains a big idea. I am supposed to be one of the more fertile inventors of big ideas, but in my long career as a copywriter I have not had more than 20, if that.[29]

While really great ideas in advertising are difficult to come by, there are many big ideas that became the basis of very creative, successful advertising campaigns. Classic examples include "We try harder," which positioned Avis as the underdog car-rental company that provided better service than Hertz; the "Pepsi generation" theme and subsequent variations like "the taste of a new generation" and "GenerationNext"; the "Be all you can be" theme used in recruitment ads for the U.S. Army; and Wendy's "Where's the beef?" which featured the late, gravelly voiced Clara Peller delivering the classic line that helped make the fast-food chain a household name. More recent big ideas that have resulted in effective advertising campaigns include the "Intel inside" campaign for Intel microprocessors that go in personal computers; Nike's "Just do it"; the "It keeps going and going" theme for Energizer batteries, featuring the pink bunny; and the "Like a rock" theme for Chevrolet trucks.

Big ideas are important in business-to-business advertising as well. For example, United Technologies Corp., a company that provides high-technology products to aerospace and building-systems industries throughout the world, recently began a major advertising campaign to increase awareness of the firm and its various subsidiaries. One of the first advertisements in the campaign was the eye-catching ad shown in Exhibit 8-10, which uses the headline "the punks who killed heavy metal," with the headline atop of what vaguely looks like a movie blood splotch. The copy explains that the punks are actually scientists (notice the white pocket protectors) from the company's research center and touts their role in developing metal foams—materials much lighter than traditional metals—that will help make a variety of UTC products, from helicopters to jet engines to elevators, lighter and more economical to operate. The ad was very effective in cutting through the clutter of corporate advertising in publications such as the *Wall Street Journal, Barron's* and *BusinessWeek.*

It is difficult to pinpoint the inspiration for a big idea or to teach advertising people how to find one. However, several approaches can guide the creative team's search for a major selling idea and offer solutions for developing effective advertising. Some of the best-known approaches follow:

- Using a unique selling proposition.
- Creating a brand image.
- Finding the inherent drama.
- Positioning.

Unique Selling Proposition

The concept of the **unique selling proposition (USP)** was developed by Rosser Reeves, former chair of the Ted Bates agency, and is described in his influential book *Reality in Advertising.* Reeves noted three characteristics of unique selling propositions:

1. Each advertisement must make a proposition to the consumer. Not just words, not just product puffery, not just show-window advertising. Each advertisement must say to each reader: "Buy this product and you will get this benefit."

2. The proposition must be one that the competition either cannot or does not offer. It must be unique either in the brand or in the claim.

3. The proposition must be strong enough to move the mass millions, that is, pull over new customers to your brand.[30]

Reeves said the attribute claim or benefit that forms the basis of the USP should dominate the ad and be emphasized through repetitive advertising. An example of advertising based on a USP is the campaign for Colgate's new Total toothpaste (Exhibit 8-11).The brand's unique ingredients make it the only toothpaste that provides long-lasting protection and has been proved effective in fighting cavities between brushings.

For Reeves's approach to work, there must be a truly unique product or service attribute, benefit, or inherent advantage that can be used in the claim. The approach may require considerable research on the product and consumers, not only to determine the USP but also to document the claim. As we shall see in Chapter 21, the Federal Trade Commission objects to advertisers' making claims of superiority or uniqueness without providing supporting data. Also, some companies have sued their competitors for making unsubstantiated uniqueness claims.[31]

Advertisers must also consider whether the unique selling proposition affords them a *sustainable competitive advantage* that competitors cannot easily copy. In the packaged-goods field in particular, companies quickly match a brand feature for feature, so advertising based on USPs becomes obsolete. For example, a few years ago Procter & Gamble invented a combination shampoo and conditioner to rejuvenate its struggling Pert brand. The reformulated brand was called Pert Plus and its market share rose from 2 to 12 percent, making it the leading shampoo. But competing brands like Revlon and Suave quickly launched their own two-in-one formula products.[32]

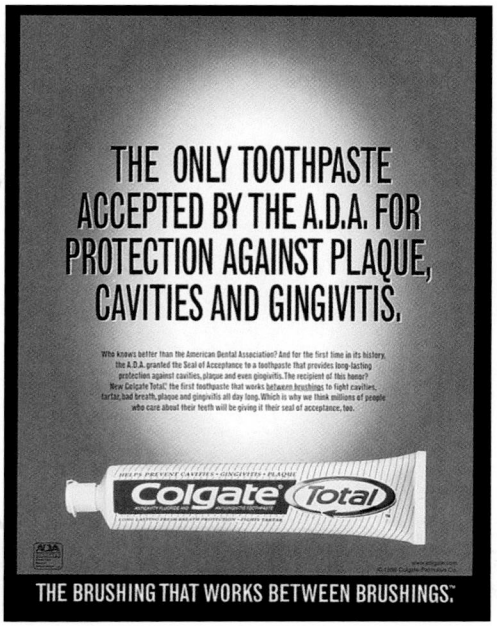

Exhibit 8-11 This Colgate Total ad uses a unique selling proposition

Creating a Brand Image In many product and service categories, competing brands are so similar that it is very difficult to find or create a unique attribute or benefit to use as the major selling idea. Many of the packaged-goods products that account for most of the advertising dollars spent in the United States are difficult to differentiate on a functional or performance basis. The creative strategy used to sell these products is based on the development of a strong, memorable identity for the brand through **image advertising.**

David Ogilvy popularized the idea of brand image in his famous book *Confessions of an Advertising Man.* Ogilvy said that with image advertising, "every advertisement should be thought of as a contribution to the complex symbol which is the brand image." He argued that the image or personality of the brand is particularly important when brands are similar:

> The greater the similarity between brands, the less part reason plays in brand selection. There isn't any significant difference between the various brands of whiskey, or cigarettes, or beer. They are all about the same. And so are the cake mixes and the detergents and the margarines. The manufacturer who dedicates his advertising to building the most sharply defined personality for his brand will get the largest share of the market at the highest profit. By the same token, the manufacturers who will find themselves up the creek are those shortsighted opportunists who siphon off their advertising funds for promotions.[33]

Image advertising has become increasingly popular and is used as the main selling idea for a variety of products and services, including soft drinks, liquor, cigarettes, cars, airlines, financial services, perfume/colognes, and clothing. Many consumers wear designer jeans or Ralph Lauren polo shirts or drink certain brands of beer or soft drinks because of the image of these brands. The key to successful image advertising is developing an image that will appeal to product users. For example, the sports apparel company No Fear uses this type of advertising to create a unique image for the brand as representing the outer limits of human performance. Ads like the one in Exhibit 8-12 have helped create this image for No Fear.

Exhibit 8-12 Advertising for No Fear creates a unique image for the brand as representing the outer limits of human performance

Exhibit 8-13 This Hallmark commercial uses an inherent-drama approach

LEO BURNETT COMPANY, INC.
AS FILMED AND RECORDED (4/96) "Report Card" 2:00
HALLMARK CARDS, INC.
HMHF6359

1. (MUSIC: UNDER THROUGHOUT)

2. MAXX: Hi, Mom, I'm home!
MOM: Hi. Is your coat on the floor?
MAXX: No...

3. MAXX: Can I go over to Lee's house?
MOM: Do you have any homework?
MAXX: Yeah.
MOM: After you finish it you can go.

4. MAXX: Cool.
MOM: Did you turn in your milk money?
MAXX: Yeah.

5. Hey--who moved my lunar module?

6. MOM: Maxx, what's this?
MAXX: Did Amy move my lunar module?
MOM: Maxx?

7. MAXX: It's something from Mrs. Bennett.
MOM: What'd she give you a card for?
MAXX: Cause I was nice to somebody.

8. MOM: Who were you nice to?
MAXX: Scott.
MOM: Who's Scott?

9. MAXX: The boy who comes to school just once in a while cause he's sick.
MOM: Was he at the school play?
MAXX: Nope, can we get an armadillo?

10. MOM: How were you nice to him?

11. MAXX: Well, Mrs. Bennett always has me sit next to him. Scott can't go out for recess and stuff so I stay in and play Yahtzee with him.

12. MOM: I didn't know you were doing that.
MAXX: I like him. It's no big deal. Could I see your card?

13. MAXX: Sure. MOM: (READING): "You didn't have to do what you did. And that's what made it so special." Maxx? Do you know what this means?

14. MAXX: Kinda.
MOM: It means you should be very proud of yourself. I know I am.

15. MAXX: Mom?
MOM: Yeah?
MAXX: You're squooshing me.

Finding the Inherent Drama Another approach to determining the major selling idea is finding the **inherent drama** or characteristic of the product that makes the consumer purchase it. The inherent drama approach expresses the advertising philosophy of Leo Burnett, founder of the Leo Burnett agency in Chicago. Burnett said inherent-drama "is often hard to find but it is always there, and once found it is the most interesting and believable of all advertising appeals."[34] He believed advertising should be based on a foundation of consumer benefits with an emphasis on the dramatic element in expressing those benefits.

Burnett advocated a down-home type of advertising that presents the message in a warm and realistic way. Some of the more famous ads developed by his agency using the inherent-drama approach are for McDonald's, Maytag appliances, Kellogg cereals, and Hallmark cards. Notice how the Hallmark commercial shown in Exhibit 8-13 uses this approach to deliver a poignant message.

Positioning The concept of *positioning* as a basis for advertising strategy was introduced by Jack Trout and Al Ries in the early 1970s and has become a popular basis of creative development.[35] The basic idea is that advertising is used to establish or "position" the product or service in a particular place in the consumer's mind. Positioning is done for companies as well as for brands. For example, the ad shown in Exhibit 8-14 is part of a campaign designed to reinforce 3M's image and position as an innovative company.

Exhibit 8-14 This ad positions 3M as an innovative company

Trout and Ries originally described positioning as the image consumers had of the brand in relation to competing brands in the product or service category, but the concept has been expanded beyond direct competitive positioning. As discussed in Chapter 2, products can be positioned on the basis of product attributes, price/quality, usage or application, product users, or product class. Any of these can spark a major selling idea that becomes the basis of the creative strategy and results in the brand's occupying a particular place in the minds of the target audience. Since positioning can be done on the basis of a distinctive attribute, the positioning and unique selling proposition approaches can overlap. Positioning approaches have been used as the foundation for a number of successful creative strategies.

Positioning is often the basis of a firm's creative strategy when it has multiple brands competing in the same market. For example, the two top-selling brands of motor oil, Pennzoil and Quaker State, were merged into the same company when the two companies merged a few years ago. The Pennzoil–Quaker State Co. creates separate identities for the two brands by positioning them differently.[36] Pennzoil is positioned as a brand that stands for protection, while Quaker State uses a performance positioning. Advertising for Pennzoil uses the "we're driving protection" tagline, while Quaker State ads use the "stay tuned" theme. (Exhibit 8-15)

The USP, brand image, inherent-drama, and positioning approaches are often used as the basis of the creative strategy for ad campaigns. These creative styles have become associated with some of the most successful creative minds in advertising and their agencies.[37] However, many other creative approaches are available.

Some of the more contemporary advertising visionaries who have had a major influence on modern-day advertising include Hal Riney of Hal Riney & Partners, Lee Clow and Jay Chiat of TBWA/Chiat/Day, Dan Wieden of Wieden & Kennedy, and Jeff Goodby and Rich Silverstein of Goodby, Silverstein & Partners. In describing today's creative leaders, Anthony Vagnoni of *Advertising Age* writes: "The modern creative kings don't write books, rarely give interviews or lay out their theories on advertising. They've endorsed no set of rules, professed no simple maxims like Mr. Ogilvy's

Exhibit 8-15 Advertising for Pennzoil and Quaker State positions the brands differently

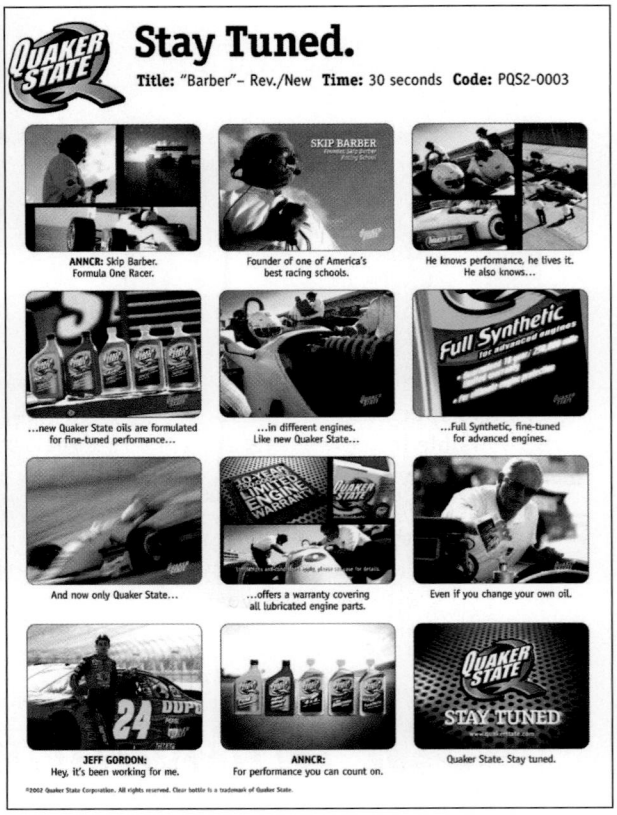

famous 'When you don't have anything to say, sing it.' If pronouncements and books are out the window, what's replaced them is a conscious desire to lift the intelligence level of advertising. Today's leaders see advertising as an uplifting social force, as a way to inspire and entertain."[38]

Goodby and Silverstein note: "Advertising works best when it sneaks into people's lives, when it doesn't look or feel like advertising. It's about treating people at their best, as opposed to dealing with them at their lowest common denominator." They describe their creative formula as doing intelligent work that the public likes to see and that, at the same time, has a sales pitch.[39] Lee Clow says: "No rule book will tell you how to target the masses anymore. The best of us understand the sociocultural realities of people and how they interact with the media. If we didn't, we couldn't make the kinds of messages that people would be able to connect with."[40]

Specific agencies are by no means limited to any one creative approach. For example, the famous "Marlboro country" campaign, a classic example of image advertising, was developed by Leo Burnett Co. Many different agencies have followed the unique selling proposition approach advocated by Rosser Reeves at Ted Bates. The challenge to the creative specialist or team is to find a major selling idea—whether it is based on a unique selling proposition, brand image, inherent drama, position in the market, or some other approach—and use it as a guide in developing an effective creative strategy.

Summary

The creative development and execution of the advertising message are a crucial part of a firm's integrated marketing communications program and are often the key to the success of a marketing campaign. Marketers generally turn to ad agencies to develop, prepare, and implement their creative strategy since these agencies are specialists in the creative function of advertising. The creative specialist or team is responsible for developing an effective way to communicate the marketer's message to the customer. Other individuals on both the client and the agency sides work with the creative specialists to develop the creative strategy, implement it, and evaluate its effectiveness.

The challenge facing the writers, artists, and others who develop ads is to be creative and come up with fresh, unique, and appropriate ideas that can be used as solutions to communications problems. Creativity in advertising is a process of several stages, including preparation, incubation, illumination, verification, and revision. Various sources of information are available to help the creative specialists determine the best campaign theme, appeal, or execution style.

Creative strategy development is guided by specific goals and objectives and is based on a number of factors, including the target audience, the basic problem the advertising must address, the objectives the message seeks to accomplish, and the major selling idea or key benefit the advertiser wants to communicate. These factors are generally stated in a copy platform, which is a work plan used to guide development of the ad campaign. An important part of creative strategy is determining the major selling idea that will become the central theme of the campaign. There are several approaches to doing this, including using a unique selling proposition, creating a brand image, looking for inherent drama in the brand, and positioning.

Key Terms

creative strategy, 237
creative tactics, 237
advertising creativity, 241
account planning, 246
general preplanning input, 247
product/service-specific preplanning input, 248
problem detection, 248
focus groups, 250
ethnographic research, 250
storyboard, 251
animatic, 251
advertising campaign, 251
campaign theme, 251
copy platform, 254
major selling idea, 255
unique selling proposition (USP), 256
image advertising, 257
inherent drama, 258

Discussion Questions

1. The opening vignette discusses Nike's strategic initiative to improve the way the company does business with women which includes finding new ways to reach and communicate with them. Evaluate the efforts of Nike to reach women from an integrated marketing communications perspective. Do you feel Nike will be successful in its efforts to communicate with women?

2. Explain what is meant by creative strategy and creative tactics in advertising. Find an example of an advertising campaign and evaluate the creative strategy and tactics used in the ads.

3. Figure 8-1 lists the various advertising campaign themes used by Burger King over the past 15 years. Why do you think the company has had such a difficult time finding an effective advertising theme and changed campaigns and agencies so many times? Find an example of a current Burger King ad and evaluate the advertising theme being used.

4. What is your opinion of advertising awards, such as the Cannes Lions, that are based solely on creativity? If you were a marketer, would you take these creative awards into consideration in your agency evaluation process? Why or why not?

5. Find an example of an advertising campaign for a company or brand that you feel is very good and evaluate it using the universal advertising standards of the D'Arcy Benton & Bowles agency that are shown in Figure 8-2. Discuss how the advertising reflects these standards.

6. IMC Perspective 8-2 discusses the debate over creative versus hard-sell advertising. Discuss the arguments for and against each perspective. Which do you support? Who should be responsible for judging the creativity of an ad—clients or agency creative personnel?

7. What are the various stages of the creative process? Do you agree with the notion that advertising creativity can or should follow a definitive process?

8. Assume that you have been hired as an account planner by an advertising agency and assigned to work on the advertising campaign for a new brand of bottled water. Describe the various types of general and product-specific preplanning input you might provide to the creative team.

9. What are the differences between focus group research and ethnographic research? Discuss how each research method could be used to provide qualitative research input that could be used in the creative process.

10. IMC Perspective 8-4 discusses the problems Miller Lite has had in developing a successful advertising campaign. Evaluate the various campaign themes that have been used for Miller Lite in recent years and discuss why they have not been effective. Evaluate the current campaign being used for the brand.

11. Find an example of an ad or campaign that you think reflects one of the approaches used to develop a major selling idea such as unique selling proposition, brand image, inherent drama, or positioning. Discuss how the major selling idea is reflected in this ad or campaign.

Creative Strategy: Implementation and Evaluation

Chapter Objectives

1. To analyze various types of appeals that can be used in the development and implementation of an advertising message.
2. To analyze the various creative execution styles that advertisers can use and the advertising situations where they are most appropriate.
3. To analyze various tactical issues involved in the creation of print advertising and TV commercials.
4. To consider how clients evaluate the creative work of their agencies and discuss guidelines for the evaluation and approval process.

Reaching for the Skyy

The last five years have been heady times for vodka as the product category has experienced strong growth and one wave of chic new brands has been followed by another. Consumption of vodka has increased steadily since 1998, and the vodka category is double the size of the next distilled-spirits segment, rum. Ironically, a bland-tasting product that was best known for helping Russians make it through a cold, bleak winter has become a status symbol for many trendy 20- and 30-somethings in America. Marketers have been trying to capitalize on the growing popularity of vodka, and the growth of the "cocktail culture" that has brought more young adults to the spirits market, by creating a distinct image for their brands and getting consumers to think of them as cutting edge, edgy, and hip. While a myriad of new vodka brands have been introduced in recent years, none has been as successful at attracting the attention of consumers as Skyy. The brand has overtaken Stolichnaya as the number-two super-premium vodka in the United States, trailing only Absolut.

A blend of orange, lemon, lime, grapefruit and tangerine

Skyy was founded in 1992 by Maurice Kanbar, who developed it as a premium brand for older connoisseurs, like himself, desirous of the perfect martini. Kanbar developed a four-stage distillations process that extracts many of the congers, which are natural impurities that remain in alcohol after distillations and may contribute to headaches, and created what he believed to be the purest of vodkas. The Skyy name came to him one day when he was looking out the window of his San Francisco apartment and viewing a brilliant blue sky. The additional "y" in the brand name was simply an addition to make the name less common and develop a trademark, while the cobalt-blue bottle was selected to connote a distinctive, daring product.

Much of Skyy's initial growth was driven by word of mouth. The company was successful in getting its eye-catching blue bottle into swanky Hollywood parties and nightclubs known for attracting a hip crowd. Skyy quickly generated a buzz on the nightclub circuit, where word spread that its quadruple-distilled formula reduced the likelihood of hangovers. The company also spent much of its limited marketing budget on sponsoring independent film festivals and producing artsy short films that were shown at these events. Skyy commissioned these short films by well-known independent film directors as part of its commitment to the independent film industry, which is one of Kanbar's passions. The directors are not asked to create an advertisement for Skyy, although each film does include "a cocktail moment." The Oscar-winning director of the film *Europa* has directed one of the films, and supermodel Claudia Schiffer has costarred with Skyy in another cocktail moment. The company uses the Internet to feature these films as a way of expanding its presence on the Web and also shows them as part of the festivals and movie premieres that it sponsors.

Advertising has also become an important part of Skyy's brand-building efforts. When the

Lambesis agency took over the account in 1998, the challenge was to create a brand image that would generate buzz among young adults and create awareness and trial in a category already dominated by strong brands such as Absolut and Stolichnaya. The agency realized that it would be critical to establish an emotional connection with young adults, who were beginning to develop their brand loyalties, and set out to create image-based advertising that would distinguish the brand from competitors' more product-focused ads.

The "Skyy Cinema" campaign was launched in 1998 and targets 21- to 34-year-old urban, metro-consumers. To establish Skyy's brand platform, identifiable cinematic cocktail moments were created for the advertising. The high-impact ads do not contain any copy but, rather, rely on stylish, seductive visuals that set up various *noir*-inspired story lines but leave the actual scenarios up to the mind of the viewer. Chad Farmer, the creative director for Lambesis, notes that all the ads establish Skyy's distinctive cobalt-blue bottle as the "star" and have made it an iconic symbol while showcasing the brand as a catalyst for a great cocktail moment. To create a buzz about the campaign, a media plan was developed to reach style-conscious trendsetters through avant-garde publications such as *Paper* and *Interview.* As the buzz developed, more mainstream magazines were added to the media mix, such as *Details, Spin, Vogue, Rolling Stone, InStyle, Movieline,* and *Entertainment Weekly,* along with outdoor ads in key influential markets.

Skyy's former brand manager, Teresa Zepeda, notes that Skyy is all about style, innovation, and quality. She notes: "We have to be disciplined and be focused, and make an impact speaking to our target rather than speaking to every consumer just a little bit." Skyy has achieved its tremendous growth despite spending only a fraction of the media dollars of its big-spending competitors such as Absolut and Stolichnaya. Zepeda adds, "We look bigger than we actually are and that is the strength of our creative and focus behind the brand." Actually Skyy is becoming quite big: Its sales have jumped from 3,000 cases in 1993 to more than 1.3 million cases in 2002. The liquor trade has recognized Skyy as the "fasting-growth spirit of the decade," and it has received *Impact* magazine's Hot Brand Award in the spirits category for six consecutive years. It appears the skyy may be the limit for this hot brand.

Sources: Kenneth Hein, "Strategy: Skyy Sets the Stage in Sultry Cinematic Scenes," *Adweek,* June 17, 2002; Melinda Fulmer, "Skyy Vodka Shoots for the Hip," *Los Angeles Times,* Apr. 17, 1999, pp. C1, 3; Theresa Howard, "Marketers of the Next Generation: Teresa Zepeda," *Brandweek,* Nov. 8, 1999, pp. 18–21.

In Chapter 8, we discussed the importance of advertising creativity and examined the various steps in the creative process. We focused on determining what the advertising message should communicate. This chapter focuses on *how* the message will be executed. It examines various appeals and execution styles that can be used to develop the ad and tactical issues involved in the design and production of effective advertising messages. We conclude by presenting some guidelines clients can use to evaluate the creative work of their agencies.

Appeals and Execution Styles

The **advertising appeal** refers to the approach used to attract the attention of consumers and/or to influence their feelings toward the product, service, or cause. An advertising appeal can also be viewed as "something that moves people, speaks to their wants or needs, and excites their interest."[1] The **creative execution style** is the way a particular appeal is turned into an advertising message presented to the consumer. According to William Weilbacher:

> The appeal can be said to form the underlying content of the advertisement, and the execution the way in which that content is presented. Advertising appeals and executions are usually independent of each other; that is, a particular appeal can be executed in a variety of ways and a particular means of execution can be applied to a variety of advertising appeals. Advertising

appeals tend to adapt themselves to all media, whereas some kinds of executional devices are more adaptable to some media than others.[2]

Advertising Appeals

Hundreds of different appeals can be used as the basis for advertising messages. At the broadest level, these approaches are generally broken into two categories: informational/rational appeals and emotional appeals. In this section, we focus on ways to use rational and emotional appeals as part of a creative strategy. We also consider how rational and emotional appeals can be combined in developing the advertising message.

Informational/Rational Appeals

Informational/rational appeals focus on the consumer's practical, functional, or utilitarian need for the product or service and emphasize features of a product or service and/or the benefits or reasons for owning or using a particular brand. The content of these messages emphasizes facts, learning, and the logic of persuasion.[3] Rational-based appeals tend to be informative, and advertisers using them generally attempt to convince consumers that their product or service has a particular attribute(s) or provides a specific benefit that satisfies their needs. Their objective is to persuade the target audience to buy the brand because it is the best available or does a better job of meeting consumers' needs. For example, the Nordica ad shown in Exhibit 9-1 uses a rational appeal to explain the features and benefits of its Beast Synergy System ski collection.

Many rational motives can be used as the basis for advertising appeals, including comfort, convenience, economy, health, and sensory benefits such as touch, taste, and smell. Other rational motives or purchase criteria commonly used in advertising include quality, dependability, durability, efficiency, efficacy, and performance. The particular features, benefits, or evaluative criteria that are important to consumers and can serve as the basis of an informational/rational appeal vary from one product or service category to another as well as among various market segments.

Weilbacher identified several types of advertising appeals that fall under the category of rational approaches, among them feature, competitive advantage, favorable price, news, and product/service popularity appeals.

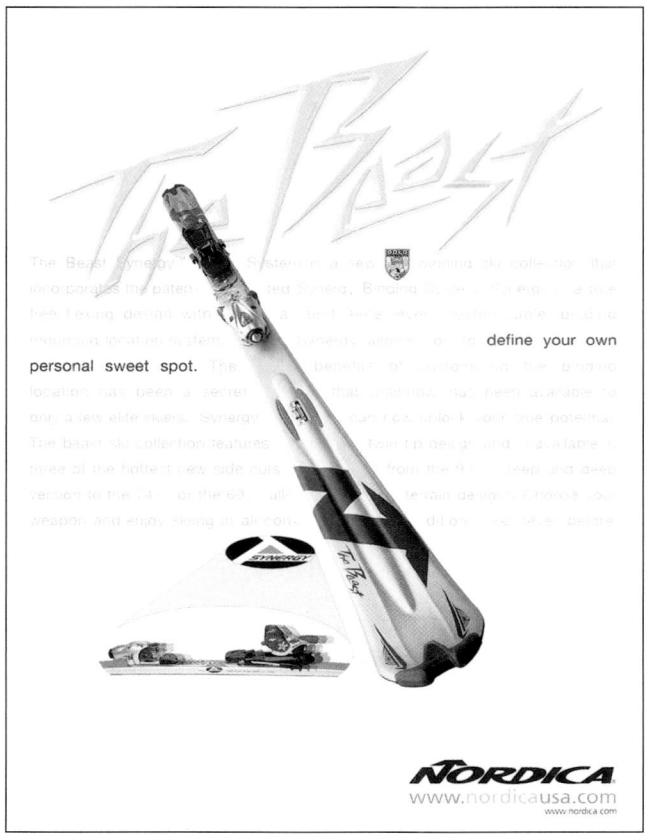

Exhibit 9-1 Nordica uses a rational appeal to advertise the features of its skis and bindings

Exhibit 9-2
DaimlerChrysler uses a feature appeal ad to promote its new Jeep® Grand Cherokee Overland

Ads that use a *feature appeal* focus on the dominant traits of the product or service. These ads tend to be highly informative and present the customer with a number of important product attributes or features that will lead to favorable attitudes and can be used as the basis for a rational purchase decision. Technical and high-involvement products such as automobiles often use this type of advertising appeal. Notice how the ad shown in Exhibit 9-2 focuses on the various features of the new Jeep Grand Cherokee Overland.

When a *competitive advantage appeal* is used, the advertiser makes either a direct or an indirect comparison to another brand (or brands) and usually claims superiority on one or more attributes. This type of appeal was discussed in Chapter 6 under "Comparative Advertising."

A *favorable price appeal* makes the price offer the dominant point of the message. Price appeal advertising is used most often by retailers to announce sales, special offers, or low everyday prices. Price appeal ads are often used by national advertisers during recessionary times. Many fast-food chains have made price an important part of their marketing strategy through promotional deals and "value menus" or lower overall prices, and their advertising strategy is designed to communicate this. Many other types of advertisers use price appeals as well, such as airlines and car-rental companies.

News appeals are those in which some type of news or announcement about the product, service, or company dominates the ad. This type of appeal can be used for a new product or service or to inform consumers of significant modifications or improvements. This appeal works best when a company has important news it wants to communicate to its target market. The Quaker Oatmeal ad shown in Exhibit 9-3, which announced the news from the Food and Drug Administration regarding the health benefits of eating oatmeal, is an example of a news appeal.

Product/service popularity appeals stress the popularity of a product or service by pointing out the number of consumers who use the brand, the number who have

Exhibit 9-3 Quaker Oatmeal uses a news appeal to promote the health benefits of oatmeal

Exhibit 9-4 This ad promotes the popularity of Excedrin among doctors

Exhibit 9-5 Nutri-Grain appeals to consumers' self-esteem and respect in this clever ad

switched to it, the number of experts who recommend it, or its leadership position in the market. The main point of this advertising appeal is that the wide use of the brand proves its quality or value and other customers should consider using it. The Excedrin ad in Exhibit 9-4 uses this type of advertising appeal.

Emotional Appeals

Emotional appeals relate to the customers' social and/or psychological needs for purchasing a product or service. Many consumers' motives for their purchase decisions are emotional, and their feelings about a brand can be more important than knowledge of its features or attributes. Advertisers for many products and services view rational, information-based appeals as dull. Many advertisers believe appeals to consumers' emotions work better at selling brands that do not differ markedly from competing brands, since rational differentiation of them is difficult.[4]

Many feelings or needs can serve as the basis for advertising appeals designed to influence consumers on an emotional level, as shown in Figure 9-1. These appeals are based on the psychological states or feelings directed to the self (such as pleasure or excitement), as well as those with a more social orientation (such as status or recognition). The ad for Kellogg's Nutri-Grain cereal bars shown in Exhibit 9-5 appeals to

Personal States or Feelings		Social-Based Feelings
Safety	Arousal/stimulation	Recognition
Security	Sorrow/grief	Status
Fear	Pride	Respect
Love	Achievement/accomplishment	Involvement
Affection	Self-esteem	Embarrassment
Happiness	Actualization	Affiliation/belonging
Joy	Pleasure	Rejection
Nostalgia	Ambition	Acceptance
Sentiment	Comfort	Approval
Excitement		

Figure 9-1 Bases for emotional appeals

emotional motives such as self-esteem and respect by using a clever visual image to suggest what might happen to women who eat pastry in the morning. The "Respect yourself" campaign has been very effective in positioning Nutri-Grain as a healthy alternative for those who don't take time to eat breakfast.

Advertisers can use emotional appeals in many ways in their creative strategy. Kamp and Macinnis note that commercials often rely on the concept of *emotional integration,* whereby they portray the characters in the ad as experiencing an emotional benefit or outcome from using a product or service.[5] Ads using humor, sex, and other appeals that are very entertaining, arousing, upbeat, and/or exciting can affect the emotions of consumers and put them in a favorable frame of mind. Many TV advertisers use poignant ads that bring a lump to viewers' throats. Hallmark, AT&T, Kodak, and Oscar Mayer often create commercials that evoke feelings of warmth, nostalgia, and/or sentiment. IMC Perspective 9-1 discusses how many marketers have been using nostalgic appeals by bringing back some of their classic advertising characters and commercials as well as using television stars from the 80s in their ads.

Marketers use emotional appeals in hopes that the positive feeling they evoke will transfer to the brand and/or company. Research shows that positive mood states and feelings created by advertising can have a favorable effect on consumers' evaluations of a brand.[6] Studies also show that emotional advertising is better remembered than nonemotional messages.[7]

McDonald's changed its advertising strategy recently and is putting more emotion in its commercials to evoke a feel-good connection with consumers. The company's senior vice president of marketing explained the change by stating, "Over the last couple of years, we had been very good on the humor side but we really hadn't done a lot to reach and touch people with heartwarming or wholesome or romantic or heart-tugging emotions."[8] McDonald's feels the emotional ads take advantage of the chain's unique bond with consumers, which is a significant point of differentiation in the highly competitive fast-food business.

Another reason for using emotional appeals is to influence consumers' interpretations of their product usage experience. One way of doing this is through what is known as transformational advertising. A **transformational ad** is defined as "one which associates the experience of using (consuming) the advertised brand with a unique set of psychological characteristics which would not typically be associated with the brand experience to the same degree without exposure to the advertisement."[9]

Transformational ads create feelings, images, meanings, and beliefs about the product or service that may be activated when consumers use it, transforming their interpretation of the usage experience. Christopher Puto and William Wells note that a transformational ad has two characteristics:

1. It must make the experience of using the product richer, warmer, more exciting, and/or more enjoyable than that obtained solely from an objective description of the advertised brand.
2. It must connect the experience of the advertisement so tightly with the experience of using the brand that consumers cannot remember the brand without recalling the experience generated by the advertisement.[10]

Transformational advertising can differentiate a product or service by making the consumption experience more enjoyable. The "reach out and touch someone" campaign used by AT&T for many years to encourage consumers to keep in touch with family and friends by phone is an example of the successful use of transformational advertising. McDonald's has also used transformational advertising very effectively to position itself as the fast-food chain where parents (or grandparents) can enjoy a warm, happy experience with their children. Norwegian Cruise Lines used transformational advertising to create a unique image of the cruise experience and differentiate itself from competitors with its "As far from the everyday as a ship can take you. That's the Norwegian Way" campaign. The goal of the campaign was to demonstrate how Norwegian provides each guest with a unique reprieve from the mundane routines of everyday life. Both the dramatic visuals and ad copy depicted the vast array of

IMC PERSPECTIVE 9-1

Everything Old Is New Again

Advertising generally prides itself on being ahead of the curve and helping to create and define popular culture rather than trying to revisit it. However, recently many advertisers have been bringing back some of their classic advertising characters and commercials rather than looking for new creative ides. The D'Arcy Masius Benton & Bowles agency brought back the original "Mr. Whipple," the stern grocer known for his famous request, "Please don't squeeze the Charmin," in commercials for the brand. The ads, which ran over a period of 18 months, resulted in an onslaught of e-mails and letters from consumers indicating their fondness for the iconic character. The Quaker company brought back the classic "Mikey" commercial for Life cereal, which first aired in 1972 and ran for 12 years. The spot features a cute three-year-old boy who hates everything but likes the taste of Life cereal when he tries it. The director of account planning at the FCB agency noted that the commercial was successful because people had a warm and fuzzy feeling about Mikey, and it is still relevant today.

Other popular advertising characters from the past have resurfaced recently. Isuzu brought back Joe Isuzu, the sleazy pitchman with a creepy smile who satirizes the clichés of car ads, to hawk its Rodeo SUV after he had been off the air for 11 years. Several animated characters have also returned to the airways, including the Jolly Green Giant for Green Giant vegetables and Charlie the Tuna for Starkist. Music and fashion from the 1980s are also back in vogue, so advertisers are bringing back some of the decade's iconic TV stars to appear in their commercials. Alien puppet ALF, whose show was popular in the late 80s, appears in ads for discount phone service 10-10-220, while Mr. T, from the hit show *The A-Team,* endorses 1-800-COLLECT. Robin Leach, who hosted the celebrity-watching show *Lifestyles of the Rich and Famous,* appears in ads for Courtyard by Marriott hotels. Robert Thompson, director of Syracuse University's Center for the Study of Popular Television, says that there's usually a two-decade break between a TV show and the resurrection of its stars.

Astute marketers recognize they cannot rely solely on the recognition and nostalgia generated by past ads and simply bring back the same thing. Thus, advertisers are seeking to avoid the inherent risks associated with retrospective marketing, primarily by contemporizing the classic elements of their ads to make them relevant to current consumers, especially young people. For example, Pepsi created an extravagant commercial featuring pop star Brittany Spears taking a trip through generations of Pepsi advertising and revisiting jingles while dressed in period garb. Although the commercial has a nostalgic tone, it also has a modern, forward-looking ending as it transitions to the current image for the brand. Fruit of the Loom recently brought back the "fruit guys," four obnoxious little men who dress up as pieces of fruit and appear in humorous commercials for the brand of underwear. However, the new ads indirectly poke fun at the four middle-aged fruit guys from the old days.

Reviving time-tested advertising characters, spokespeople, and commercials has long been a popular advertising tactic among marketers, particularly during uncertain times, such as the post-September 11 era. Experts note that new creative ideas are often put aside for the reassuringly familiar. One brand identity consultant notes: "When we feel less secure, with less control over our daily lives, we reach out in brands to connect with a time when things felt better, more comfortable. It's about finding security, what we can trust." However, marketers recognize that they must recalibrate the familiar if they want to make their ads relevant to the modern-day consumer.

Sources: Vanessa O'Connell, "Ad Campaign Again Bears Fruit Guys." *The Wall Street Journal,* July 19, 2002, p. B2; Stuart Elliott, "Ads from the Past with Modern Touches," *The New York Times,* Sept. 9, 2002, p. C8; Julia Cosgrove, "Listen Up Sucka, the '80s Are Back," *BusinessWeek,* Aug. 5, 2002, p. 16.

Exhibit 9-6 Norwegian Cruise Lines used transformational advertising to create a unique image of the cruise experience

experiences and activities to be enjoyed during one individual day on a Norwegian Cruise Line's voyage (Exhibit 9-6).

Combining Rational and Emotional Appeals In many advertising situations, the decision facing the creative specialist is not whether to choose an emotional or a rational appeal but, rather, determining how to combine the two approaches. As noted copywriters David Ogilvy and Joel Raphaelson have stated:

> Few purchases of any kind are made for entirely rational reasons. Even a purely functional product such as laundry detergent may offer what is now called an emotional benefit—say, the satisfaction of seeing one's children in bright, clean clothes. In some product categories the rational element is small. These include soft drinks, beer, cosmetics, certain personal care products, and most old-fashioned products. And who hasn't experienced the surge of joy that accompanies the purchase of a new car?[11]

Consumer purchase decisions are often made on the basis of both emotional and rational motives, and attention must be given to both elements in developing effective advertising. Exhibit 9-7 shows a very clever ad that uses the Freudian concepts of id and superego to suggest that there are both emotional and rational reasons for purchasing the Lexus SC 400 coupe.

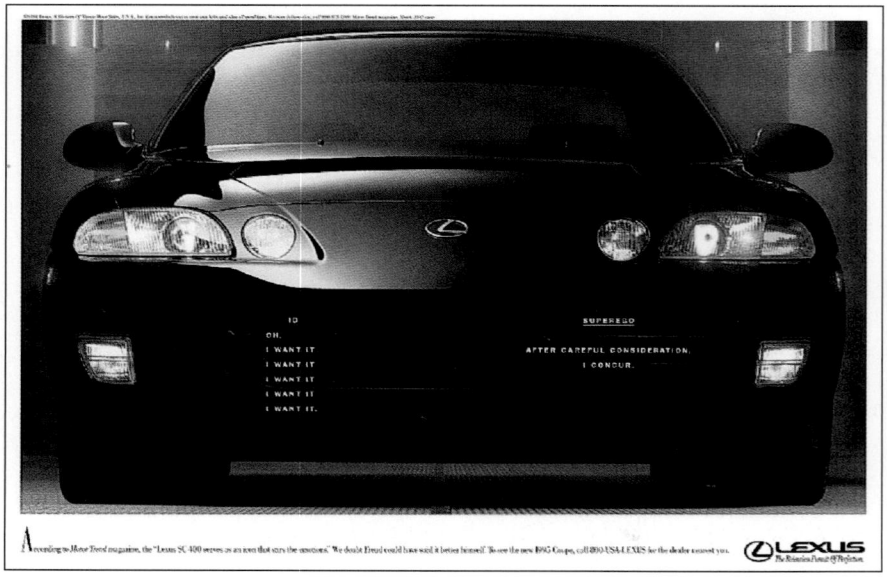

Exhibit 9-7 Lexus addresses both rational and emotional appeals in this clever ad

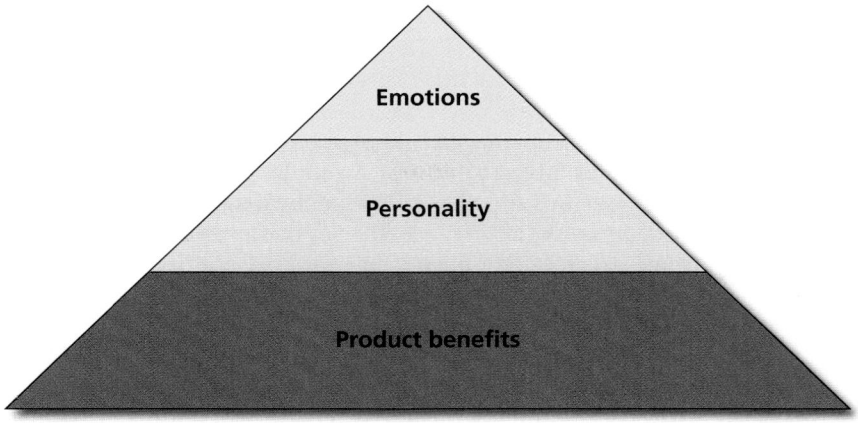

Figure 9-2 Levels of relationships with brands

Advertising researchers and agencies have given considerable thought to the relationship between rational and emotional motives in consumer decision making and how advertising influences both. McCann-Erickson Worldwide, in conjunction with advertising professor Michael Ray, developed a proprietary research technique known as *emotional bonding*. This technique evaluates how consumers feel about brands and the nature of any emotional rapport they have with a brand compared to the ideal emotional state they associate with the product category.[12]

The basic concept of emotional bonding is that consumers develop three levels of relationships with brands, as shown in Figure 9-2. The most basic relationship indicates how consumers *think* about brands in respect to product benefits. This occurs, for the most part, through a rational learning process and can be measured by how well advertising communicates product information. Consumers at this stage are not very brand loyal, and brand switching is common.

At the next stage, the consumer assigns a *personality* to a brand. For example, a brand may be thought of as self-assured, aggressive, and adventurous, as opposed to compliant and timid. The consumer's judgment of the brand has moved beyond its attributes or delivery of product/service benefits. In most instances, consumers judge the personality of a brand on the basis of an assessment of overt or covert cues found in its advertising.

McCann-Erickson researchers believe the strongest relationship that develops between a brand and the consumer is based on feelings or emotional attachments to the brand. Consumers develop *emotional bonds* with certain brands, which result in positive psychological movement toward them. The marketer's goal is to develop the greatest emotional linkage between its brand and the consumer. McCann-Erickson believes advertising can develop and enrich emotional bonding between consumers and brands. McCann and its subsidiary agencies use emotional bonding research to provide strategic input into the creative process and determine how well advertising is communicating with consumers. McCann-Erickson used emotional bonding research as the basis for its award-winning "Priceless" campaign for MasterCard International. When the agency took over the account a few years ago, MasterCard was perceived as an ordinary credit card you keep in your wallet. The challenge was to create an emotional bond between consumers and MasterCard without losing the brand's functional appeal. McCann-Erickson developed a sentimental campaign that uses ads that take the sum total of an experience and declare that it has no price tag. Each commercial and print ad ends with the theme "There are some things money can't buy. For everything else there's MasterCard" (Exhibit 9-8).

Exhibit 9-8 MasterCard's "Priceless" campaign creates an emotional bond with consumers

Exhibit 9-9 Altoids uses reminder advertising to build brand awareness

Additional Types of Appeals

Not every ad fits neatly into the categories of rational or emotional appeals. For example, ads for some brands can be classified as **reminder advertising,** which has the objective of building brand awareness and/or keeping the brand name in front of consumers. Well-known brands and market leaders often use reminder advertising. For example, Altoids breath mints runs reminder ads to build national brand awareness and communicate its quirky "curiously strong" message to consumers (Exhibit 9-9). Products and services that have a seasonal pattern to their consumption also use reminder advertising, particularly around the appropriate period. For example, marketers of candy products often increase their media budgets and run reminder advertising around Halloween, Valentine's Day, Christmas, and Easter.

Advertisers introducing a new product often use **teaser advertising,** which is designed to build curiosity, interest, and/or excitement about a product or brand by talking about it but not actually showing it. Teasers, or *mystery ads* as they are sometimes called, are also used by marketers to draw attention to upcoming advertising campaigns and generate interest and publicity for them. For example, Lee Jeans used teaser ads as part of its successful "Can't bust 'em" campaign for its new Dungarees line that features the Buddy Lee doll (Exhibit 9-10). The denim-dressed doll, which was used in Lee's promotional displays from the 1920s through the 50s, was brought back and billed as a "Man of Action." Lee's agency, Fallon McElligott, introduced Buddy with a "phantom campaign" designed to intrigue influential trendsetters among the 17- to 22-year-old target market. Posters of Buddy Lee, unidentified and unbranded, were wild-posted in "cool" areas of 15 markets to generate curiosity. The agency then produced a six-minute film, *The Buddy Lee Story,* that was run on "graveyard cable," 2 A.M. slots on Comedy Central and other cable channels. Again, the product was never mentioned, but the film did associate Buddy with the Lee Company and its "Can't bust 'em" spirit.

The goal of the teaser campaign was to let the trendsetters discover Buddy and spread the news about him. The teaser campaign was successful in generating word of mouth and helped accelerate the popularity of the brand as subsequent advertising featuring Buddy hawking the Dungarees line was introduced. The campaign helped make initial sales of the Dungarees line four times higher than anticipated and resulted in a 3 percent increase in market share for Lee even though overall denim sales were flat.[13]

Teaser ads are often used for new movies or TV shows and for major product launches. They are especially popular among automotive advertisers for introducing a new model or announcing significant changes in a vehicle. For example, Porsche used

Exhibit 9-10 Lee Jeans used a successful teaser campaign featuring Buddy Lee to help introduce its Dungarees line

teaser ads to generate interest in and excitement for the Cayenne SUV when it was introduced to the U.S. market (Exhibit 9-11). The ads used the theme "The next Porsche" and were part of an integrated campaign that included a website telling the story of the new Cayenne, from development through testing to its unveiling in fall 2002.

Teaser campaigns can generate interest in a new product, but advertisers must be careful not to extend them too long or they will lose their effectiveness.[14] Many advertising experts thought the teaser campaign used by Infiniti to introduce its cars to the U.S. market in 1989 ran too long and created confusion among consumers.[15] As one advertising executive says, "Contrary to what we think, consumers don't hold seminars about advertising. You have to give consumers enough information about the product in teaser ads to make them feel they're in on the joke."[16]

Many ads are not designed to sell a product or service but rather to enhance the image of the company or meet other corporate goals such as soliciting investment or recruiting employees. These are generally referred to as corporate image advertising and are discussed in detail in Chapter 17.

Exhibit 9-11 Porsche used teaser ads to create interest in the new Cayenne SUV

Advertising Execution

Once the specific advertising appeal that will be used as the basis for the advertising message has been determined, the creative specialist or team begins its execution. *Creative execution* is the way an advertising appeal is presented. While it is obviously important for an ad to have a meaningful appeal or message to communicate to the consumer, the manner in which the ad is executed is also important.

One of the best-known advocates of the importance of creative execution in advertising was William Bernbach, founder of the Doyle Dane Bernbach agency. In his famous book on the advertising industry, *Madison Avenue,* Martin Mayer notes Bernbach's reply to David Ogilvy's rule for copywriters that "what you say in advertising is more important than how you say it." Bernbach replied, "Execution can become content, it can be just as important as what you say. A sick guy can utter some words and nothing happens; a healthy vital guy says them and they rock the world."[17] Bernbach was one of the revolutionaries of his time who changed advertising creativity on a fundamental level by redefining how headlines and visuals were used, how art directors and copywriters worked together, and how advertising could be used to arouse feelings and emotions. IMC Perspective 9-2 discusses how many in advertising thought the dot-com ad boom that occurred a few years ago would drive a new creative revolution in advertising.

An advertising message can be presented or executed in numerous ways:

- Straight sell or factual message
- Scientific/technical evidence
- Demonstration
- Comparison
- Testimonial
- Slice of life
- Animation
- Personality symbol
- Fantasy
- Dramatization
- Humor
- Combinations

We now examine these formats and considerations involved in their use.

Exhibit 9-12 Castrol uses a straight-sell execution style in this ad

Straight Sell or Factual Message

One of the most basic types of creative executions is the straight sell or factual message. This type of ad relies on a straightforward presentation of information concerning the product or service. This execution is often used with informational/rational appeals, where the focus of the message is the product or service and its specific attributes and/or benefits.

Straight-sell executions are commonly used in print ads. A picture of the product or service occupies part of the ad, and the factual copy takes up the rest of the space. (See the ad for Castrol Syntec motor oil in Exhibit 9-12.)

IMC PERSPECTIVE 9-2

Dot-com Advertising Fails to Inspire a New Creative Revolution

"I'm always hoping that one day some young man will come into my office and say, 'Your 96 rules for creating good ads are for the birds. They're all based on research that is out of date and irrelevant. Here are 96 new rules based on new research. Throw yours out the window . . . You're an old dodo, living in the past. Moreover, I have written a new dogma, a new dialectic, and I am the prophet of the future.'"

This appeal for someone to lead a new creative revolution in advertising was written by legendary adman David Ogilvy in his classic book *The Art of Writing Advertising,* which was published in 1965. In the 60s revolutionaries such as Ogilvy, Bill Bernbach, Leo Burnett, and Rosser Reeves turned advertising creativity on its head. The creative director of a major agency describes the state of advertising creativity before these revolutionaries came along as follows: "It was the Dark Ages, manufacturers shouting out the factory window. There was no emotional connection. It was basically what the client wanted you to say. The creative revolution was about finding a way to talk to people. It was like finding perspective."

The creative revolution that occurred during the 60s was in many ways inspired by the emergence of television as a dominant medium for advertising. Now the Internet is the new technology invading homes in the United States as well as other countries, and many felt it would be the catalyst for a new creative revolution in advertising. Madison Avenue had never seen a boom as explosive, spectacular, and sudden as the "great dot-com ad boom" of the late 90s that continued on into the new millennium. Ads for Internet companies such as portals and e-commerce sites were everywhere. And as these companies competed for consumers' attention and a piece of their mind-set, many were producing a new type of advertising whose style was as daring and unconventional as the entrepreneurs who built the online companies.

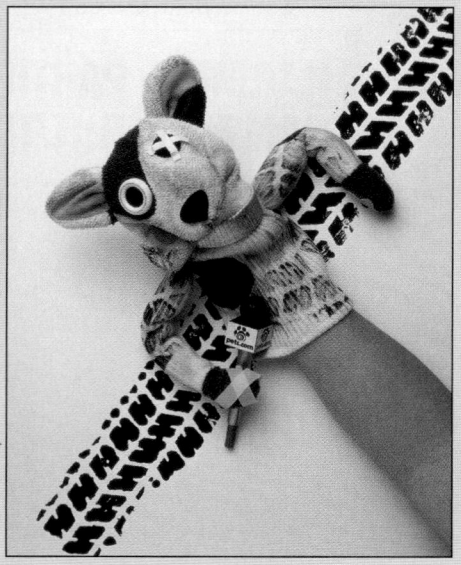

Among the most creative and popular of the ads for the dot-com companies were the campaign created for the online trading firm Ameritrade that featured Stuart, the young, ponytailed, red-headed day trader; ads featuring Socks, the fast-talking dog sock puppet for Pets.com; ads with sci-fi celebrity William Shatner singing off key for Priceline.com; and commercials for the online financial services company E*Trade featuring a chimpanzee. There were also numerous dot-com ads that pushed the limits of good taste to get attention and build awareness. Commercials for online retailer Outpost.com included a spot showing gerbils being shot out of cannon into a backboard, and another featured a marching band on a football field forming the words *outpost.com* and then being attacked by a pack of wolves. Beyond.com, an online retailer of software and computer-related products, helped pioneer the crazy dot-com advertising genre with its "Naked Man" campaign that featured a fictitious character shopping for software at home *au naturel.*

Many of the ads for online companies were creative and fun to watch. However, critics argued that most of the ads were ineffective at communicating a meaningful message for the companies and much of the $3 billion per year that was being spent on dot-com advertising was wasted. All of the dot-coms wanted their advertising to be the funniest or most outrageous. However, in the end it all started to look the same and became boring. The end of the great dot-com ad boom was perhaps best signified by an award-winning commercial for E*Trade that ran during the 2001 Super Bowl. The ad was a spoof of a 1971 "Keep America Beautiful" spot from the Ad Council and showed the E-Trade chimp riding on horseback into a deserted town replete with lots of dot-com businesses that had gone bust. After picking up a tattered sock puppet, the simian sheds a tear—just as the American Indian did in the much admired public service announcement years ago. E*Trade was one of the survivors of the dot-com shakeout and recently began a new campaign promoting the

change of its name to E*Trade Financial and poking fun at the excesses of the dot-com era.

Many in the advertising community believe that the next creative revolution in advertising will come not from ads for Internet companies but from the medium itself. They feel that the skill set of the creativity community will really be unleashed as technological limitations that handcuff web creativity, such as bandwidth problems, are solved and the Internet converges with other traditional media such a television and print. As discussed earlier, advertisers such as BMW, Skyy vodka, and Levi Strauss are taking advertising in a new direction by creating short films that can be viewed and/or downloaded from their websites. This hybrid of advertising and entertainment is referred to in the ad world as "branded content." The agency for Nike created a campaign with cliff-hanger commercials whose endings could be found only on the Nike website. A new creative revolution may indeed be under way. However, this time it may involve more than ads showing gerbils being shot out of cannons.

Source: Suzanne Vranica, "Dot-Com TV Ads Make a Comeback," *The Wall Street Journal,* Apr. 10, 2002, p. B5; Suein L. Hwang and Kathryn Kranhold, "Where Have All the Gerbils Gone?" *The Wall Street Journal,* March 30, 2000, p. B1; Eleftheria Parpis, "You Say You Want a Revolution," *Adweek,* Dec. 13, 1999, pp. 29–36.

They are also used in TV advertising, with an announcer generally delivering the sales message while the product/service is shown on the screen. Ads for high-involvement consumer products as well as industrial and other business-to-business products generally use this format.

Scientific/Technical Evidence In a variation of the straight sell, scientific or technical evidence is presented in the ad. Advertisers often cite technical information, results of scientific or laboratory studies, or endorsements by scientific bodies or agencies to support their advertising claims. For example, an endorsement from the American Council on Dental Therapeutics on how fluoride helps prevent cavities was the basis of the campaign that made Crest the leading brand on the market. The ad for Dermasil Pharmaceutical Dry Skin Treatment shown in Exhibit 9-13 uses this execution style to emphasize the breakthrough from Vaseline Research.

Demonstration Demonstration advertising is designed to illustrate the key advantages of the product/service by showing it in actual use or in some staged situation. Demonstration executions can be very effective in convincing consumers of a product's utility or quality and of the benefits of owning or using the brand. TV is particularly well suited for demonstration executions, since the benefits or advantages of the product can be shown right on the screen. Although perhaps a little less dramatic than TV, demonstration ads can also work in print, as shown in the ad for Du Pont's Teflon Bakeware Liners (Exhibit 9-14).

Comparison Brand comparisons can also be the basis for the advertising execution. The comparison execution approach is increasingly popular among advertisers, since it offers a direct way of communicating a brand's particular advantage over its competitors or positioning a new or lesser-known brand with industry leaders. Comparison executions are often used to execute competitive advantage appeals, as discussed earlier.

Testimonial Many advertisers prefer to have their messages presented by way of a testimonial, where a person praises the product or service on the basis of his or her personal experience with it. Testimonial executions can have ordinary satisfied customers discuss their own experiences with the brand and the benefits of using it. This approach can be very effective when the person delivering the testimonial is someone with whom the target audience can identify or who has an interesting story to tell. The testimonial must be based on actual use of the product or service to avoid legal problems, and the spokesperson must be credible.

Apple Computer made effective use of testimonials as part of its "Switch" campaign, which features computer users from various walks of

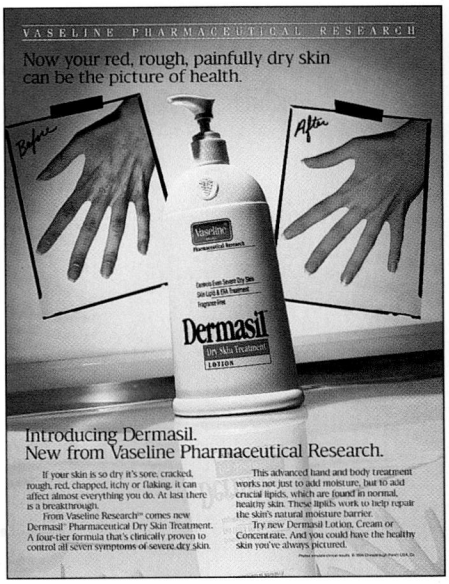

Exhibit 9-13 This Dermasil ad cites a scientific study

Exhibit 9-14 This ad demonstrates the benefits of Du Pont's Teflon Bakeware Liners

life discussing why they switched from Windows-based machines to Macintoshes (Exhibit 9-15). The people giving the testimonials in the ads are from various walks of life, including a writer, publisher, programmer, and Windows network administrator, and were chosen from a group of some 10,000 former PC users who wrote the company to proclaim their love for Apple. As part of the campaign Apple created a website that includes testimonials from PC users who switched to Macs and provides more detailed information for those considering switching.

A related execution technique is the *endorsement,* where a well-known or respected individual such as a celebrity or expert in the product or service area speaks on behalf of the company or the brand. When endorsers promote a company or its products or services, the message is not necessarily based on their personal experiences.

Exhibit 9-15 Apple's "Switch" campaign makes effective use of testimonials

Slice of Life A widely used advertising format, particularly for packaged-goods products, is the slice-of-life execution, which is generally based on a problem/solution approach. This type of ad portrays a problem or conflict that consumers might face in their daily lives. The ad then shows how the advertiser's product or service can resolve the problem.

Slice-of-life executions are often criticized for being unrealistic and irritating to watch because they are often used to remind consumers of problems of a personal nature, such as dandruff, bad breath, body odor, and laundry problems. Often these ads come across as contrived, silly, phony, or even offensive to consumers. However, many advertisers still prefer this style because they believe it is effective at presenting a situation to which most consumers can relate and at registering the product feature or benefit that helps sell the brand.

For many years, Procter & Gamble was known for its reliance on slice-of-life advertising executions. In 1980, two-thirds of the company's com-

Exhibit 9-16 AT&T uses a slice-of-life execution to advertise its wireless services

mercials used either the slice-of-life or testimonial format. However, P&G has begun using humor, animation, and other less traditional execution styles and now relies less on slice-of-life or testimonials.[18]

Slice-of-life or problem/solution execution approaches are not limited to consumer-product advertising. Many business-to-business marketers use this type of advertising to demonstrate how their products and services can be used to solve business problems. For example, AT&T used this approach in executing the "It's all within your reach" campaign that promoted a broad array of the company's offerings. The ads in the campaign used emotionally charged moments to demonstrate how AT&T understands and helps individuals reach their goals by offering the most relevant solutions to the challenges of working and living in today's fast-paced world and managing one's personal life and business pressures.

An award-winning commercial from the campaign was a spot called "Beaches," which focused on a working mother and her very busy life (Exhibit 9-16). The ad addressed the problem facing many working parents: They would like to spend more time with their children but need to go to work and kids don't always understand why. This situation, and the frustration often associated with it, is captured in the ad when the little girl says to her mother, "Mom, when can I be a client?" Thanks to AT&T Wireless Services, the mother is able to take the kids to the beach and still conduct her important conference call as scheduled.[19]

Some business-to-business marketers use a variation of the problem/solution execution that is sometimes referred to as *slice-of-death advertising*.[20] This execution style is used in conjunction with a fear appeal, as the focus is on the negative consequences that result when businesspeople make the wrong decision in choosing a supplier or service provider. For example, FedEx has used this type of advertising for nearly three decades through humorous, but to-the-point, commercials that show what might happen when important packages and documents aren't received on time.

Animation An advertising execution approach that has become popular in recent years is animation. With this technique, animated scenes are drawn by artists or created on the computer, and cartoons, puppets, or other types of fictional characters may be used. Cartoon animation is especially popular for commercials targeted at children.

Animated cartoon characters have also been used successfully by the Leo Burnett agency in campaigns for Green Giant vegetables (the Jolly Green Giant) and Keebler cookies (the Keebler elves). Another successful example of animation execution was the ad campaign developed for the California Raisin Advisory Board. A technique called Claymation was used to create the dancing raisin characters used in these ads.

The use of animation as an execution style may increase as creative specialists discover the possibilities of computer-generated graphics and other technological innovations.[21] Exhibit 9-17 shows an ad for Stagg Chili that uses computer-generated graphics and animation.

Exhibit 9-17 This ad for Stagg Chili uses computer-generated graphics and animation

Some advertisers have begun using Roger Rabbit-style ads that mix animation with real people. Nike has used this technique to develop several creative, entertaining commercials. One featured Michael Jordan and Bugs Bunny trouncing a foursome of bullies on the basketball court and was the inspiration for the movie *Space Jam.* The agency for Star-Kist tuna also used this technique when the H. J. Heinz Company recently brought its animated Charlie the Tuna character out of retirement to appear in commercials for the brand. While the old "Sorry Charlie" commercials portrayed Charlie as not being good enough for Star-Kist, the new ads used him in a different way, such as giving a courtroom address arguing that not all tunas are created equal and asking for jurors to judge for themselves (Exhibit 9-18).

Exhibit 9-18 This Star-Kist commercial mixes an animated character with real people.

Personality Symbol Another type of advertising execution involves developing a central character or personality symbol that can deliver the advertising message and with which the product or service can be identified. This character can be a person, like Mr. Whipple, who asked shoppers, "Please don't squeeze the Charmin," or the Maytag repairman, who sits anxiously by the phone but is never needed because the company's appliances are so reliable.

Personality figures can also be built around animated characters and animals. As discussed in Chapter 5, visual image personalities (VIPs) such as Morris the Cat and Tony the Tiger have been used for decades to promote 9-Lives cat food and Kellogg's Frosted Flakes, respectively. Recently, commercials featuring the AFLAC duck have made him a popular personality symbol and mascot for the insurance company and have helped build awareness and interest. The humorous spots show the quirky duck in all sorts of odd places—lounging in a sauna, conking his head on the ice at a skating rink, and fighting for the attention of a couple on a roller coaster—as he desperately tries to raise a flap about the supplemental insurance provider (Exhibit 9-19).

Anheuser-Busch created popular personality symbols in the talking lizards, Frank and Louie, who appeared in ads for Budweiser beer for five years. However, the company had to deal with complaints from some consumer groups who argue that the animated characters were popular among children and might encourage underage drinking. The company strongly denied that it was using the characters to target minors and argued that the ads did not have any effect on children or encourage underage drinking.[22] Actually the controversy over the Budweiser lizards has been mild compared to the furor that was created by R. J. Reynolds' use of Old Joe Camel, the cartoon character used in ads for Camel cigarettes for many years. Critics argued that Camel ads featuring the "smooth character" were more effective at marketing the brand to minors than to adults. The controversy surrounding the campaign eventually led to a settlement between the federal government and the tobacco industry that bans the use of cartoon characters in tobacco advertising.[23]

Fantasy An execution technique that is popular for emotional types of appeals such as image advertising is fantasy. Fantasy executions are particularly well suited for television, as the commercial can become a 30-second escape for the viewer into another lifestyle. The product or service becomes a central part of the situation created by the advertiser. Cosmetics ads often use fantasy appeals to create images and symbols that become associated with the brand.

Dramatization Another execution technique particularly well suited to television is dramatization, where the focus is on telling a short story with the product or

Exhibit 9-19 The AFLAC duck has become a popular mascot and personality symbol for the company

service as the star. Dramatization is somewhat akin to slice-of-life execution in that it often relies on the problem/solution approach, but it uses more excitement and suspense in telling the story. The purpose of using drama is to draw the viewer into the action it portrays. Advocates of drama note that when it is successful, the audience becomes lost in the story and experiences the concerns and feelings of the characters.[24] According to Sandra Moriarty, there are five basic steps in a dramatic commercial:

> First is exposition, where the stage is set for the upcoming action. Next comes conflict, which is a technique for identifying the problem. The middle of the dramatic form is a period of rising action where the story builds, the conflict intensifies, the suspense thickens. The fourth step is the climax, where the problem is solved. The last part of a drama is the resolution, where the wrap-up is presented. In advertising that includes product identification and call to action.[25]

The real challenge facing the creative team is how to encompass all these elements in a 30-second commercial. A good example of the dramatization execution technique is the ad for Zerex antifreeze in Exhibit 9-20, which shows a woman's sense of relief when her car starts at the airport on a cold winter night. The ad concludes with a strong identification slogan, "The temperature never drops below Zerex," that connects the brand name to its product benefit.

Humor Like comparisons, humor was discussed in Chapter 6 as a type of advertising appeal, but this technique can also be used as a way of presenting other advertising appeals. Humorous executions are particularly well suited to television or radio, although some print ads attempt to use this style. The pros and cons of using humor as an executional technique are similar to those associated with its use as an advertising appeal.

Combinations Many of the execution techniques can be combined to present the advertising message. For example, animation is often used to create personality symbols or present a fantasy. Slice-of-life ads are often used to demonstrate a product or service. Comparisons are sometimes made using a humorous approach. FedEx uses

Exhibit 9-20 This Zerex ad uses a dramatization execution

humorous executions of the slice-of-death genre depicting businesspeople experiencing dire consequences when they use another delivery service and an important document doesn't arrive on time. It is the responsibility of the creative specialist(s) to determine whether more than one execution style should be used in creating the ad.

Creative Tactics

Our discussion thus far has focused on the development of creative strategy and various appeals and execution styles that can be used for the advertising message. Once the creative approach, type of appeal, and execution style have been determined, attention turns to creating the actual advertisement. The design and production of advertising messages involve a number of activities, among them writing copy, developing illustrations and other visual elements of the ad, and bringing all of the pieces together to create an effective message. In this section, we examine the verbal and visual elements of an ad and discuss tactical considerations in creating print ads and TV commercials.

Creative Tactics for Print Advertising

The basic components of a print ad are the headline, the body copy, the visual or illustrations, and the layout (the way they all fit together). The headline and body copy portions of the ad are the responsibility of the copywriters; artists, often working under the direction of an art director, are responsible for the visual presentation. Art directors also work with the copywriters to develop a layout, or arrangement of the various components of the ad: headlines, subheads, body copy, illustrations, captions, logos, and the like. We briefly examine the three components of a print ad and how they are coordinated.

Headlines

The **headline** is the words in the leading position of the ad—the words that will be read first or are positioned to draw the most attention.[26] Headlines are usually set in larger type and are often set apart from the body copy or text portion of the ad to give them prominence. Most advertising people consider the headline the most important part of a print ad.

The most important function of a headline is attracting readers' attention and interesting them in the rest of the message. While the visual portion of an ad is obviously important, the headline often shoulders most of the responsibility of attracting readers' attention. Research has shown the headline is generally the first thing people look at in a print ad, followed by the illustration. Only 20 percent of readers go beyond the headline and read the body copy.[27] So in addition to attracting attention, the headline must give the reader good reason to read the copy portion of the ad, which contains more detailed and persuasive information about the product or service. To do this, the headline must put forth the main theme, appeal, or proposition of the ad in a few words. Some print ads contain little if any body copy, so the headline must work with the illustration to communicate the entire advertising message.

Headlines also perform a segmentation function by engaging the attention and interest of consumers who are most likely to buy a particular product or service. Advertisers begin the segmentation process by choosing to advertise in certain types of publications (e.g., a travel, general-interest, or fashion magazine). An effective headline goes even further in selecting good prospects for the product by addressing their specific needs, wants, or interests. For example, the headline in the ad for RCA's LYRA personal digital player shown in Exhibit 9-21 catches the attention of consumers who want the latest technology in audio products.

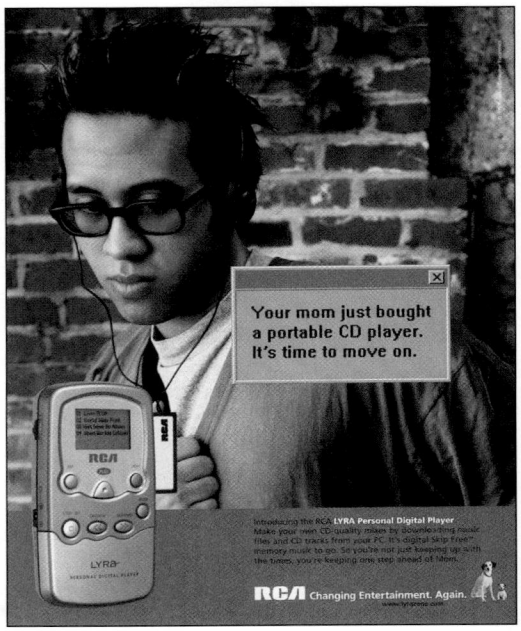

Exhibit 9-21 The headline of this ad catches the attention of young consumers

Types of Headlines There are numerous headline possibilities. The type used depends on several factors, including the creative strategy, the particular advertising situation (e.g., product type, media vehicle(s) being used, timeliness), and its relationship to other components of the ad, such as the illustration or body copy. Headlines can be categorized as direct and indirect. **Direct headlines** are

straightforward and informative in terms of the message they are presenting and the target audience they are directed toward. Common types of direct headlines include those offering a specific benefit, making a promise, or announcing a reason the reader should be interested in the product or service.

Indirect headlines are not straightforward about identifying the product or service or getting to the point. But they are often more effective at attracting readers' attention and interest because they provoke curiosity and lure readers into the body copy to learn an answer or get an explanation. Techniques for writing indirect headlines include using questions, provocations, how-to statements, and challenges.

Indirect headlines rely on their ability to generate curiosity or intrigue so as to motivate readers to become involved with the ad and read the body copy to find out the point of the message. This can be risky if the headline is not provocative enough to get the readers' interest. Advertisers deal with this problem by using a visual appeal that helps attract attention and offers another reason for reading more of the message. For example, the ad for the Lexus GS sports sedan shown in Exhibit 9-22 uses a question as the headline that invites consumers to read the copy to learn more about the features of the car and decide how to categorize it. The visual portion of the ad supports the positioning theme by showing the GS 430 being driven on a windy road.

Subheads While many ads have only one headline, it is also common to see print ads containing the main head and one or more secondary heads, or **subheads.** Subheads are usually smaller than the main headline but larger than the body copy. They may appear above or below the main headline or within the body copy. The Cambridge SoundWorks ad shown in Exhibit 9-23 uses subheads within the body copy.

Subheads are often used to enhance the readability of the message by breaking up large amounts of body copy and highlighting key sales points. Their content reinforces the headline and advertising slogan or theme.

Exhibit 9-22 This ad uses a question-style headline and strong visual image that motivate consumers to read the copy

Exhibit 9-23 This ad uses subheads to make the copy easier to read

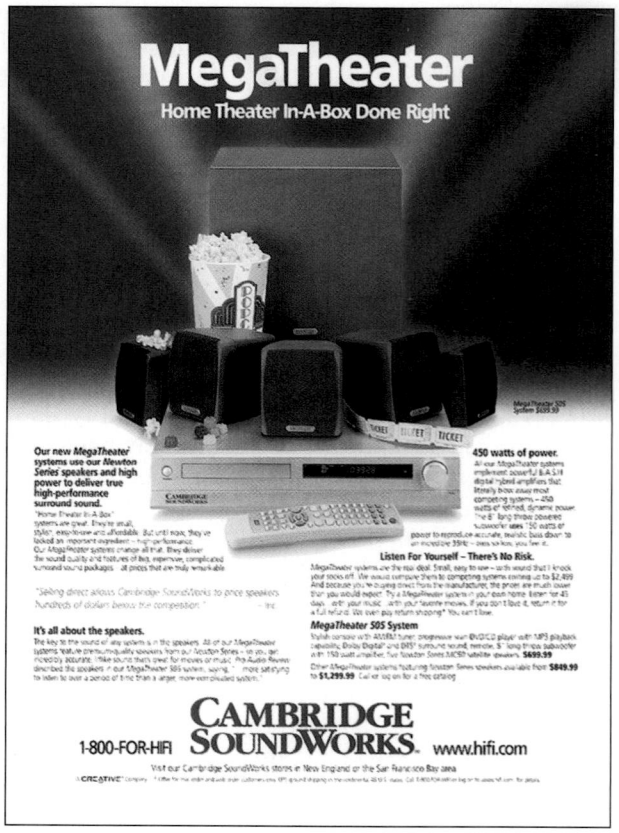

Body Copy The main text portion of a print ad is referred to as the **body copy** (or sometimes just *copy*). While the body copy is usually the heart of the advertising message, getting the target audience to read it is often difficult. The copywriter faces a dilemma: The body copy must be long enough to communicate the advertiser's message yet short enough to hold readers' interest.

Body copy content often flows from the points made in the headline or various subheads, but the specific content depends on the type of advertising appeal and/or execution style being used. For example, straight-sell copy that presents relevant information, product features and benefits, or competitive advantages is often used with the various types of rational appeals discussed earlier in the chapter. Emotional appeals often use narrative copy that tells a story or provides an interesting account of a problem or situation involving the product.

Advertising body copy can be written to go along with various types of creative appeals and executions—comparisons, price appeals, demonstrations, humor, dramatizations, and the like. Copywriters choose a copy style that is appropriate for the type of appeal being used and effective for executing the creative strategy and communicating the advertiser's message to the target audience.

Visual Elements The third major component of a print ad is the visual element. The illustration is often a dominant part of a print ad and plays an important role in determining its effectiveness. The visual portion of an ad must attract attention, communicate an idea or image, and work in a synergistic fashion with the headline and body copy to produce an effective message. In some print ads, the visual portion of the ad is essentially the message and thus must convey a strong and meaningful image. For example, the award-winning ad for Sims Snowboards shown in Exhibit 9-24 uses a powerful visual image. In a scene reminiscent of the protestor blocking military vehicles in Beijing's Tiananmen Square during the 1989 student uprising, a snowboarder stands in the path of snow-grooming machines (which pack the snow, to the distress of snowboarders). The single line of copy, "In a courageous act of solidarity, a lone snowboarder stands up for freedom," reinforces the message presented by the visual image.

Many decisions have to be made regarding the visual portion of the ad: what identification marks should be included (brand name, company or trade name, trademarks, logos); whether to use photos or hand-drawn or painted illustrations; what colors to use (or even perhaps black and white or just a splash of color); and what the focus of the visual should be.

Layout While each individual component of a print ad is important, the key factor is how these elements are blended into a finished advertisement. A **layout** is the physical arrangement of the various parts of the ad, including the headline, subheads, body

Exhibit 9-24 This ad for Sims Snowboards uses a strong visual image and a layout that resembles a newspaper page

copy, illustrations, and any identifying marks. The layout shows where each part of the ad will be placed and gives guidelines to the people working on the ad. For example, the layout helps the copywriter determine how much space he or she has to work with and how much copy should be written. The layout can also guide the art director in determining the size and type of photos. In the ad for Sims Snowboards shown in Exhibit 9-24, the layout is designed to make the ad look like it was reprinted from a newspaper page. Notice how this theme is carried through in the copy, which reads like a newspaper photo caption and ends with "Story on 2C." Layouts are often done in rough form and presented to the client so that the advertiser can visualize what the ad will look like before giving preliminary approval. The agency should get client approval of the layout before moving on to the more costly stages of print production.

Creative Tactics for Television

As consumers, we see so many TV commercials that it's easy to take for granted the time, effort, and money that go into making them. Creating and producing commercials that break through the clutter on TV and communicate effectively is a detailed, expensive process. On a cost-per-minute basis, commercials are the most expensive productions seen on television.

TV is a unique and powerful advertising medium because it contains the elements of sight, sound, and motion, which can be combined to create a variety of advertising appeals and executions. Unlike print, the viewer does not control the rate at which the message is presented, so there is no opportunity to review points of interest or reread things that are not communicated clearly. As with any form of advertising, one of the first goals in creating TV commercials is to get the viewers' attention and then maintain it. This can be particularly challenging because of the clutter and because people often view TV commercials while doing other things (reading a book or magazine, talking).

Like print ads, TV commercials have several components. The video and audio must work together to create the right impact and communicate the advertiser's message.

Video

The video elements of a commercial are what is seen on the TV screen. The visual portion generally dominates the commercial, so it must attract viewers' attention and communicate an idea, message, and/or image. A number of visual elements may have to be coordinated to produce a successful ad. Decisions have to be made regarding the product, the presenter, action sequences, demonstrations, and the like, as well as the setting(s), the talent or characters who will appear in the commercial, and such other factors as lighting, graphics, color, and identifying symbols.

Audio

The audio portion of a commercial includes voices, music, and sound effects. Voices are used in different ways in commercials. They may be heard through the direct presentation of a spokesperson or as a conversation among various people appearing in the commercial. A common method for presenting the audio portion of a commercial is through a **voice-over,** where the message is delivered or action on the screen is narrated or described by an announcer who is not visible. A trend among major advertisers is to have celebrities with distinctive voices do the voiceovers for their commercials.[28] Actor Richard Dreyfuss does the voiceovers in some Honda commercials, Jeff Goldblum does Apple Computers, and mega-stars such as Ben Affleck, Renee Zelwegger, and Ashley Judd have done Diet Coke commercials.

Music is also an important part of many TV commercials and can play a variety of roles.[29] In many commercials, the music provides a pleasant background or helps create the appropriate mood. Advertisers often use **needledrop,** which Linda Scott describes as follows:

> Needledrop is an occupational term common to advertising agencies and the music industry. It refers to music that is prefabricated, multipurpose, and highly conventional. It is, in that sense, the musical equivalent of stock photos, clip art, or canned copy. Needledrop is an inexpensive substitute for original music; paid for on a one-time basis, it is dropped into a commercial or film when a particular normative effect is desired.[30]

In some commercials, music is much more central to the advertising message. It can be used to get attention, break through the advertising clutter, communicate a key

selling point, help establish an image or position, or add feeling.[31] For example, music can work through a classical conditioning process to create positive emotions that become associated with the advertised product or service. Music can also create a positive mood that makes the consumer more receptive toward the advertising message.[32]

Because music can play such an important role in the creative strategy, many companies have paid large sums for the rights to use popular songs in their commercials. There are two kinds of works to which companies negotiate rights when licensing music for use in commercials. The *musical composition* includes the music notes and the words, while the *master recording* includes the voice(s) of the original artist.[33] The latter is usually much more expensive to buy, so advertisers will often negotiate for the rights to use the music and have it performed by someone with a similar voice. Rights to music can be held by various parties, such as the original artist, the artist's estate, or a music publishing company. For example, the rights to songs done by the late reggae star Bob Marley are held by his estate, while the rights to songs by the Beatles are controlled by a music publishing company. Nortel Networks licensed the composition rights to use the classic Beatles song "Come Together" (which it had performed by a different artist) and used the music as the central theme in the global advertising campaign the company ran recently.[34] While it is less expensive to rerecord the music, some advertisers are willing to pay millions of dollars to use the voices of the original artists in their commercials. IMC Perspective 9-3 discusses how companies such as Cadillac, Chevrolet Trucks, Microsoft, and Mitsubishi have made songs an important part of their commercials in recent years.

Another important musical element in both TV and radio commercials is **jingles,** catchy songs about a product or service that usually carry the advertising theme and a simple message. For example, Doublemint gum has used the well-known "Double your pleasure, double your fun with Doublemint, Doublemint gum" for years. The jingle is very memorable and serves as a good reminder of the product's minty flavor. Oscar Mayer has used the popular jingles for some of its products, such as the bologna song ("My bologna has a first name/ It's O-S-C-A-R") and the Oscar Mayer wiener song ("I'd love to be an Oscar Mayer wiener"), as the basis of integrated marketing programs. The company's fleet of wienermobiles travel the country as part of the Oscar Mayer Talent Search, where local auditions are held in search of children who will continue the 30-year tradition of singing the catchy bologna and wiener jingles.[35]

Jingles can be used by themselves as the basis for a musical commercial. Diet Coke brought back its old slogan "Just for the taste of it," set it to a luxurious musical score, and made it the basis of a multimillion-dollar ad campaign. In some commercials, jingles are used more as a form of product identification and appear at the end of the message. Jingles are often composed by companies that specialize in writing commercial music for advertising. These jingle houses work with the creative team to determine the role music will play in the commercial and the message that needs to be communicated. Figure 9-3 shows the 10 jingles selected by *Advertising Age* as the best of the past century.

Jingle	Company or Brand
1. You deserve a break today	McDonald's
2. Be all that you can be	U.S. Army
3. Pepsi Cola Hits the Spot	Pepsi Cola
4. M'm, M'm Good	Campbell's Soup
5. See the USA in your Chevrolet	Chevrolet
6. I wish I was an Oscar Mayer Wiener	Oscar Mayer
7. Double your pleasure, double your fun	Wrigley's Doublemint gum
8. Winston tastes good like a cigarette should	Winston
9. It's the Real Thing	Coca-Cola
10. Brylcreem—A little dab'll do ya	Brylcreem

Figure 9-3 Top 10 jingles of the century

IMC PERSPECTIVE 9-3

Advertisers Marry Music with Their Products

While music has always been an important part of television commercials, more and more advertisers are using popular songs in their ads that resonate with consumers and help keep their products and services top-of-mind. Songs from artists and rock groups such as Madonna, Sting, Bob Seger, Led Zeppelin, the Rolling Stones, and the Beatles serve as the backdrop in commercials for just about everything, including cars, beer, fast food, computers, and insurance. Nike pioneered the commercial use of music from major artists in 1987 when it featured the original recording of the classic Beatle's song "Revolution" in ads for its shoes. Cadillac recently struck a multimillion-dollar deal with Led Zeppelin to use the legendary band's song "Rock and Roll" in its commercials. Service companies are also using popular songs as part of their ads as well. Tax preparation firm H&R Block recently used the words and music to the Beatle's tune "Tax Man," while AllState Insurance uses the famous group's "When I'm 64" to help sell life insurance.

There are a number of reasons why companies are paying large sums of money to use popular songs in their commercials. Music plays an important role in setting the tone for a commercial and can be used for entertainment, to target an audience, and/or to create an emotional or nostalgic connection with the viewer. When advertisers marry the right song with the right product, they can strike a responsive chord with consumers, which gets them to attend to the commercial and can help differentiate the company or brand. For example, ads for Chevrolet trucks began using Bob Seger's hit song "Like a Rock" in 1991, and the agency made it the tagline for one of the most successful and long-lasting campaigns in automotive advertising. The manager for Chevy trucks says, "It is not just a marketing campaign. It captures the soul of the brand. It is how to build a truck, it is how to run a company."

Other companies have also used the lyrics of a song to help deliver their advertising message. Microsoft paid a reported $12 million to the Rolling Stones for the use of its song "Start Me Up," which was featured in ads for its Windows 95 operating system. Six years later the company used the song from another megastar when it tapped Madonna for a multimillion deal to use the Material Girl's Grammy Award–winning song "Ray of Light" to introduce its new XP software. The creative director at McCann-Erickson, in San Francisco, which created the ad campaign, noted that the lyrics of the song were exactly what the agency was looking for to use in commercials for a technology product like the XP software. The upbeat electric song uses phrases like "faster then the speeding light she's flying." He also noted that the agency wanted music from an artist with some weight and star power and Madonna fit the bill because she still remains relevant and cool without being trendy.

For many years, many popular singers and rock groups would not allow their songs to be used in commercials. However, artists have learned that the benefits, exposure, and money often far outweigh an

outdated concern over the stigma of selling out to the advertising world. As it becomes more difficult to get airtime or become part of a radio station's playlist, many artists are finding that the exposure from commercials can actually help sell their music. For example, Sting sold the rights to his song "Desert Rose" to Jaguar for a commercial in March 2000. The song, which did not fit well with radio playlists, lingered on *Billboard's* top 100 list but didn't become a hit until the commercial started airing. "Start the Commotion" by the Wiseguys was released in 1999 but didn't hit *Billboard's* top 40 list until it was featured in a commercial for the Mitsubishi Eclipse two years later. A newly commissioned recording of "Ooh La La," originally performed by the Faces in 1973, is a key part of a Mitsubishi Galant commercial, and sales of the song have more than doubled since the ad debuted.

While more companies than ever are using music in their ads, an important issue for all of them is using it effectively and making sure the song fits with the advertiser's message. For example, Mitsubishi has made music a key element of its commercials, which usually show a group of young, fun adults in the car bopping to the beat or singing to the tunes of songs such as "Start the Commotion" or "One Week" by the Barenaked Ladies. An executive for the Deutsch agency, which creates the ads, notes that the message the ads want to communicate, without actually saying it, is that "Cool people drive cool cars," and this campaign is about unspoken coolness. Apparently consumers are getting the message from the music as the coolness created by the ads has helped increase awareness of the Mitsubishi brand and its appeal to younger car buyers.

Watching television commercials these days is almost like turning the radio dial as more songs, from every kind of era and every kind of artist, can be heard during the commercial breaks. And as more artists open to the idea of having their music used in ads, it is likely we will hear our favorite songs as part of the pitch for a variety of products and services.

Sources: Donna De Marc, "TV Ads Go Pop," *Washington Times,* May 12, 2002, p. A1; Jean Halliday, "Caddy Goes 'Rock and Roll,'" *Advertising Age,* Feb. 4, 2002, p. 3; Joe Urschel, "Three Words That Evolved into a Corporate Hymn," *USA Today,* Feb. 19, 1996. p. 6B.

Planning and Production of TV Commercials One of the first decisions that has to be made in planning a TV commercial is the type of appeal and execution style that will be used. Television is well suited to both rational and emotional advertising appeals or combinations of the two. Various execution styles used with rational appeals, such as a straight sell or announcement, demonstration, testimonial, or comparison, work well on TV.

Advertisers recognize that they need to do more than talk about, demonstrate, or compare their products or services. Their commercials have to break through the clutter and grab viewers' attention; they must often appeal to emotional, as well as rational, buying motives. Television is essentially an entertainment medium, and many advertisers recognize that their commercials are most successful when they entertain as well as inform. Many of the most popular advertising campaigns are characterized by commercials with strong entertainment value, like the "Whassup?" campaign for Budweiser, the humorous "Got milk" ads, musical spots for the Gap, and the many stylish and engaging Nike ads. Some of the most popular commercials recently have been those created for Volkswagen's "Drivers wanted" campaign, which explores drivers' life experiences with their VWs[36] (Exhibit 9-25). TV is particularly well suited to drama; no other advertising medium can touch emotions as well. Various emotional appeals such as humor, fear, and fantasy work well on TV, as do dramatizations and slice-of-life executions.

Planning the Commercial The various elements of a TV commercial are brought together in a **script,** a written version of a commercial that provides a detailed description of its video and audio content. The script shows the various audio components of the commercial—the copy to be spoken by voices, the music, and sound effects. The video portion of the script provides the visual plan of the commercial—camera actions and angles, scenes, transitions, and other important descriptions. The script also shows how the video corresponds to the audio portion of the commercial.

Once the basic script has been conceived, the writer and art director get together to produce a storyboard, a series of drawings used to present the visual plan or layout of a proposed commercial. The storyboard contains still drawings of the video scenes and

Exhibit 9-25
Volkswagen's award-winning commercials are some of the most popular in recent years

descriptions of the audio that accompanies each scene. Like layouts for print ads, storyboards provide those involved in the production and approval of the commercial with a good approximation of what the final commercial will look like. In some cases an animatic (a videotape of the storyboard along with the soundtrack) may be produced if a more finished form of the commercial is needed for client presentations or pretesting.

Production Once the storyboard or animatic of the commercial is approved, it is ready to move to the production phase, which involves three stages:

1. *Preproduction*—all the work and activities that occur before the actual shooting/recording of the commercial.
2. *Production*—the period during which the commercial is filmed or videotaped and recorded.
3. *Postproduction*—activities and work that occur after the commercial has been filmed and recorded.

The various activities of each phase are shown in Figure 9-4. Before the final production process begins, the client must usually review and approve the creative strategy and the various tactics that will be used in creating the advertising message.

Figure 9-4 The three phases of production for commercials

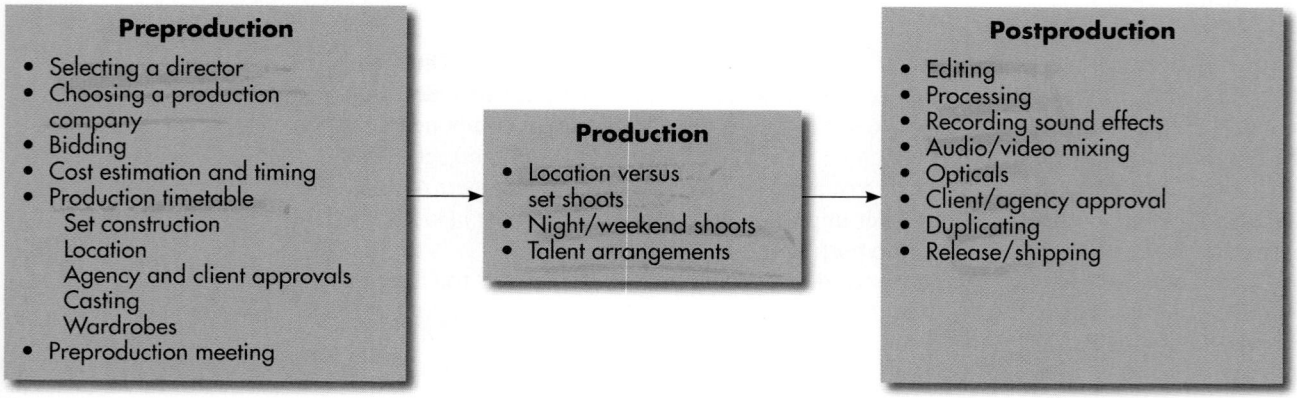

Client Evaluation and Approval of Creative Work

While the creative specialists have much responsibility for determining the advertising appeal and execution style to be used in a campaign, the client must evaluate and approve the creative approach before any ads are produced. A number of people on the client side may be involved in evaluating the creative work of the agency, including the advertising or communications manager, product or brand managers, marketing director or vice president, representatives from the legal department, and sometimes even the president or chief executive officer (CEO) of the company or the board of directors.

The amount of input each of these individuals has in the creative evaluation and approval process varies depending on the company's policies, the importance of the product to the company, the role of advertising in the marketing program, and the advertising approach being recommended. For example, the Chiat/Day agency had to convince Apple's board of directors to air the famous "1984" commercial used to introduce the Macintosh personal computer. Apple's board thought the commercial, which was based on the concept of Big Brother from George Orwell's classic novel *1984,* was too controversial and might be detrimental to its image, particularly in the business market. The spot used stark images of Orwell's dystopia, and a dramatic scene of a young woman throwing a mallet through a movie screen to destroy a controlling force, purportedly symbolizing its major competitor IBM (Exhibit 9-26). The agency convinced Apple's board to run the commercial during the 1984 Super Bowl, which is the only time it ever appeared as a commercial on TV, and the impact was tremendous. The spot was the focus of attention in the media and was the talk of the marketing and advertising industries. A few years ago, *TV Guide* named the "1984" spot the greatest television commercial of all time.

Earlier in this chapter, we noted that Procter & Gamble has been moving away from testimonials and slice-of-life advertising executions to somewhat riskier and more lively forms of advertising. But the company remains conservative and has been slow to adopt the avant-garde ads used by many of its competitors. Agencies that do the advertising for various P&G brands recognize that quirky executions that challenge the company's subdued corporate culture are not likely to be approved.[37] As discussed in the previous chapter, Wrigley was always very conservative in its advertising for its various brands of gum. However, since Bill Wrigley, Jr. took over the company in 1999 following the death of his more traditional father, the company has allowed its ad agency to take more creative risks and use more edgy advertising.[38]

In many cases, top management is involved in selecting an ad agency and must approve the theme and creative strategy for the campaign. Evaluation and approval of the individual ads proposed by the agency often rest with the advertising and product managers who are primarily responsible for the brand. The account executive and a member of the creative team present the creative concept to the client's advertising and product and/or marketing managers for their approval before beginning production. A careful evaluation should be made before the ad actually enters production, since this stage requires considerable time and money as suppliers are hired to perform the various functions required to produce the actual ad.

The client's evaluation of the print layout or commercial storyboard can be difficult, since the advertising or brand manager is generally not a creative expert and must

Exhibit 9-26 Apple's famous "1984" commercial almost never made it to television

be careful not to reject viable creative approaches or accept ideas that will result in inferior advertising. However, personnel on the client side can use the guidelines discussed next to judge the efficacy of creative approaches suggested by the agency.

Guidelines for Evaluating Creative Output

Advertisers use numerous criteria to evaluate the creative approach suggested by the ad agency. In some instances, the client may want to have the rough layout or storyboard pretested to get quantitative information to assist in the evaluation. However, the evaluation process is usually more subjective; the advertising or brand manager relies on qualitative considerations. Basic criteria for evaluating creative approaches are discussed next:

- *Is the creative approach consistent with the brand's marketing and advertising objectives?* One of the most important factors the client must consider is whether the creative appeal and execution style recommended by the agency are consistent with the marketing strategy for the brand and the role advertising and promotion have been assigned in the overall marketing program. This means the creative approach must be compatible with the image of the brand and the way it is positioned in the marketplace and should contribute to the marketing and advertising objectives. IMC Perspective 9-4 discusses how Savin Corporation has changed its advertising creative approach several times in recent years as its marketing strategy has changed.
- *Is the creative approach consistent with the creative strategy and objectives? Does it communicate what it is supposed to?* The advertising appeal and execution must meet the communications objectives laid out in the copy platform, and the ad must say what the advertising strategy calls for it to say. Creative specialists can lose sight of what the advertising message is supposed to be and come up with an approach that fails to execute the advertising strategy. Individuals responsible for approving the ad should ask the creative specialists to explain how the appeal or execution style adheres to the creative strategy and helps meet communications objectives.
- *Is the creative approach appropriate for the target audience?* Generally, much time has been spent defining, locating, and attempting to understand the target audience for the advertiser's product or service. Careful consideration should be given to whether the ad appeal or execution recommended will appeal to, be understood by, and communicate effectively with the target audience. This involves studying all elements of the ad and how the audience will respond to them. Advertisers do not want to approve advertising that they believe will receive a negative reaction from the target audience. For example, it has been suggested that advertising targeted to older consumers should use models who are 10 years younger than the average age of the target audience, since most people feel younger than their chronological age.[39] Advertisers also face a considerable challenge developing ads for the teen market because teenagers' styles, fashions, language, and values change so rapidly. They may find they are using an advertising approach, a spokesperson, or even an expression that is no longer popular among teens.
- *Does the creative approach communicate a clear and convincing message to the customer?* Most ads are supposed to communicate a message that will help sell the brand. Many ads fail to communicate a clear and convincing message that motivates consumers to use a brand. While creativity is important in advertising, it is also important that the advertising communicate information attributes, features and benefits, and/or images that give consumers a reason to buy the brand.
- *Does the creative execution keep from overwhelming the message?* A common criticism of advertising, and TV commercials in particular, is that so much emphasis is placed on creative execution that the advertiser's message gets overshadowed. Many creative, entertaining commercials have failed to register the brand name and/or selling points effectively.

For example, a few years ago the agency for North American Philips Lighting Corp. developed an award-winning campaign that focused on the humorous results when lightbulbs fail at just the wrong time. The spots included a woman who appears to accidentally vacuum up her screeching cat after a lightbulb blows out and an elderly

IMC PERSPECTIVE 9-4

Savin Advertising Connects with Customers

In the late 1970s and early 80s Savin Corp. used a very effective comparative advertising campaign to overtake Xerox and become the top brand of office copiers in America. With the help of small, inexpensive copiers made by Ricoh Corporation of Japan but sold in the United States under the Savin brand, the company caught Xerox off guard by running advertising comparing its products directly against the market leader. However, a decision to manufacture the copiers in-house at a new factory in Binghamton, New York, caused a severe financial crisis that ultimately led to Savin's filing for bankruptcy protection in 1992. A year after emerging from bankruptcy proceedings in 1994, Savin agreed to be acquired by Ricoh. Since being acquired, Savin is getting back to what it did best: marketing copiers made by Ricoh under its own name primarily through its own network of dealers that sell directly to companies. And creative advertising has been an important part of its strategy for gaining market share by positioning Savin as a feisty and committed company with the best products, service, and support, as well as willingness to take on the competition.

Savin's first campaign after being purchased by Ricoh was launched in 1996 and used the tagline "We're going to win you over." The goal of the campaign was to build awareness of and add value to the brand name and to place Savin on the "considered list" of the middle managers who influence or make the copier purchase decisions for their company. A year later Savin launched the second phase of the campaign, which focused on document management and product line attributes, and the tagline evolved into "We've got what it takes to win you over." The first two phases of the campaign leveraged Savin's renewed focus on people, products, and programs and positioned the company as faster and easier to do business with. However, the market was changing rapidly with the emergence of digital technology that offered improved output quality in black and white and color as well as network connectivity.

The merging of printing and copying functionality changed the marketing focus, as more companies were offering products with similar benefits to the same customers. However, the target audience within companies was shifting. The traditional copier buyer, such as an office manager, was no longer the only person involved in the purchase decision or was losing power to information technology (IT) departments. Moreover, Savin's competitors such as Xerox, Canon, and Hewlet-Packard were seen as the safe choice, and there was still a need to position the company as a viable player in the digital office equipment market.

In 1998 Savin launched the "Alternative to Xerox" campaign. The comparative ads piggybacked off Xerox's efforts to promote new digital copiers and mocked Xerox for wanting to be the "biggest" document company. Savin's ads positioned the company as the "fastest, most responsive and easy to work with name in the business." Savin's CEO, Jim Ivy, noted: "Going toe to toe with Xerox is part of our history. People remember Savin going after Xerox." And since there was a need to reach both existing copier buyers and new customers in the IT space, Savin felt the ad campaign would ring a bell with them. When the comparative campaign began in mid-1998, Savin had a small 2.9 percent share of the U.S. office-copier market, placing it a lowly eleventh out of 14 brands, while Xerox led the industry with a 16.4 percent market share. However, in 1998 and 1999 Savin's growth in sales outpaced that of all major providers of document output systems, and the company nearly doubled its digital sales.

While Savin's comparative campaign was very successful, by 2000 market conditions had changed, causing the company to reconsider its creative strategy. Negative press reports about financial, sales, and marketing issues at Xerox raised concern about using the company as a reference point in Savin advertising and positioning itself as an alternative to the troubled competitor. Also, with the growth of the Internet, intranets, e-mail, and fax machines, the office environment was changing from a "print and distribute" approach to more of a "distribute and print" process. Thus in 2001 Savin decided to take its advertising in a different direction to position the company as an attractive player in the digital office equipment market with its "Think Inside the Box" campaign. The objective of the new creative strategy is to convince decision makers that Savin provides both the advanced digital imaging solutions they need and the customer-focused attitude they want to support all of

their network printing and copying requirements. A softening of media costs due to the advertising recession opened the opportunity for Savin to use television advertising for the first time in recent years as part of the campaign, and three 15-second spots were created. The shift to TV makes it possible to broaden awareness of Savin, maximize impact, and generate excitement among its dealer partners. However, creativity was important to enable the spots to break through the clutter, which they have done successfully. Savin is enjoying almost double-digit growth in a category that has experienced a 2 percent annual decline in recent years.

Companies have been responding very favorably to Savin's easy-to-do-business-with philosophy and its ability to provide solutions to all of their printing and copying needs. They also have been responding well to Savin's advertising, which has helped build awareness of the company and position it as a major player in the digital office equipment market.

Sources: Personal correspondence with Louise Stix, Manager of Corporate Communications and Creative Services, Savin Corporation; Raju Narisetti, "Savin Hopes Campaign Will Boost Image," *The Wall Street Journal,* May 19, 1998, p. B10; "Savin Corp. Having Award-Winning Year," *Business Wire,* June 8, 1999.

couple using Philips Pastel bulbs to create a romantic mood (Exhibit 9-27). While the purpose of the campaign was to help Philips make inroads into General Electric's dominance in the lightbulb market, many consumers did not notice the Philips brand name. A survey showed that many viewers thought the ads were for GE lightbulbs. Surveys taken a year later by the agency that created the campaign showed that brand

Exhibit 9-27 Some advertising experts think these Philips Lighting commercials may have been too creative and overwhelmed the message

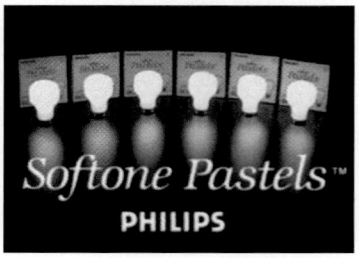

(Partial overhead of living room. Man reads paper. Wife walks in with Pastel bulbs, goes straight to lamp).
ANNCR: For a change of mood,
(Wife turns off lamp, as husband ignores her).
ANNCR: Change to Philips Softone Pastel lightbulbs.
(Woman switches on lamp. It now gives a warm peach hue to the whole room).
MUSIC. (Piano riff) (Shot over piano as man sings).

MAN: I'm in the mood for love. Simply because . . .
(Woman slides into frame with bottle of champagne).
MAN: (Singing) you're near me. (Suddenly, the cork pops out and flies at the man).
MAN: Funny but when you're
SFX: Cork pop. (Cork hits man on forehead, leaving a little impression).
SFX: Bop! (He's stunned into silence for a brief moment. He launches back into the song with great enthusiasm).

MAN: near me.
(Woman puts bottle in bucket at left of piano and slides next to him).
MAN: I'm in the mood for love.
ANNCR: Make everything seem more beautiful . . .
(All the colors are represented. Each bulb lights up in sequence from left to right. "Philips" clicks on) . . .
ANNCR: With new Softone Pastels. It's time to change your bulb to Philips.

CAREER PROFILE

Louise Stix

Manager of Corporate Communications and Creative Services, Savin Corporation

I graduated from Lake Forest College in Illinois with a degree in Art History. My first position out of college was as an Assistant Curator of the art collection at First Chicago Corporation, a large bank, where I observed many aspects of business and decided that a career in marketing was preferable to that of a museum curator. I first learned consumer package goods marketing disciplines as a product manager at American Can and then at Cadbury Schweppes. However, the allure of the advertising business was too great to resist and my experience as a brand manager was attractive to agencies like BBDO who were looking for this type of experience in their account management personnel. As an account executive at BBDO, New York, I worked on major brands such as GE Lighting, Black & Decker DustBuster, Wisk and others. While there I learned about advertising strategy, creative development and production. My expertise was attractive to public relations firms with package goods clients and I decided to round out my expertise by joining a PR firm where I worked on Colgate Oral Care products.

"It is exciting to see creative ideas come to life and to take something from an idea to execution in the marketplace and see how it works."

I returned to the corporate side in my present position at Savin Corporation where I draw on all of my experience in marketing, advertising and public relations to run the equivalent of a communications agency within a company. My department is responsible for most of the internal and external communications for Savin, and our primary focus is developing and implementing integrated marketing communications programs. We handle Savin's public relations, websites, e-communications, print and electronic product collateral, and, of course, advertising. This is where the fun comes in. It is exciting to see creative ideas come to life and to take something from an idea to execution in the marketplace and see how it works.

I work with copywriters, art directors, web designers, producers, printers, designers, photographers and other communication specialists. I also work closely with Savin's top management and our agency to develop a strategic communications plan that we can execute across many of the customer touch-points that are available. We extend our marketing communication strategy includes beyond advertising to our web site, direct marketing, electronic mail and other collateral.

My career has been evolutionary in terms of the areas I have worked in, what I have learned, and what has taken place in communications the past 25 years. Every day brings new challenges and opportunities. It is important to be adaptable and never stop learning. When I began working in advertising, network television, magazines, newspapers, radio and out-of-home were the media options. All of the cable TV networks, different radio formats, the 11,000+ magazines, the Internet, and digital technology did not exist. Who could have ever imagined that the television commercials for Savin's new "Think Inside the Box" campaign could be produced entirely through computer technology and that the only "shoot" we had was a one-hour digital session to film the machine in the closing frames! The myriad of media options now available require creative thinking and a well-planned IMC program if a company wants to communicate effectively.

In addition to working at Savin, I am also an adjunct professor at Norwalk Community College where I teach Principles of Advertising and Introduction to Business. I am in the unique position of being able to "practice what I preach" and "preach what I practice." I don't think there is a more interesting and dynamic field in which to work and teach. I hope you all have the opportunity to enjoy it as much as I have.

awareness and sales had increased considerably, but some advertising people still think the ads were so creative and entertaining that they overwhelmed the message.[40]

With the increasing amount of clutter in most advertising media, it may be necessary to use a novel creative approach to gain the viewer's or reader's attention. However, the creative execution cannot overwhelm the message. Clients must walk a fine line: Make sure the sales message is not lost, but be careful not to stifle the efforts of the creative specialists and force them into producing dull, boring advertising.

- *Is the creative approach appropriate for the media environment in which it is likely to be seen?* Each media vehicle has its own specific climate that results from the nature of its editorial content, the type of reader or viewer it attracts, and the nature of the ads it contains. Consideration should be given to how well the ad fits into the media environment in which it will be shown. For example, the Super Bowl has become a showcase for commercials. People who care very little about advertising know how much a 30-second commercial costs and pay as much attention to the ads as to the game itself, so many advertisers feel compelled to develop new ads for the Super Bowl or to save new commercials for the game.
- *Is the ad truthful and tasteful?* Marketers also have to consider whether an ad is truthful, as well as whether it might offend consumers. For example, the Just For Feet athletic footwear chain ran a commercial on the 1999 Super Bowl that featured a Kenyan runner who was tracked like an animal by white mercenaries, drugged unconscious, and fit with a pair of running shoes—which goes against centuries of Kenyan tradition. The spot led to charges of neocolonialism and racism from outraged consumers and the media and created a major public relations problem for the company. Just For Feet had to pull the spot after running it only one time and ended up suing its ad agency.[41] The ultimate responsibility for determining whether an ad deceives or offends the target audience lies with the client. It is the job of the advertising or brand manager to evaluate the approach suggested by the creative specialists against company standards. The firm's legal department may be asked to review the ad to determine whether the creative appeal, message content, or execution could cause any problems for the company. It is much better to catch any potential legal problems before the ad is shown to the public.

The advertising manager, brand manager, or other personnel on the client side can use these basic guidelines in reviewing, evaluating, and approving the ideas offered by the creative specialists. There may be other factors specific to the firm's advertising and marketing situation. Also, there may be situations where it is acceptable to deviate from the standards the firm usually uses in judging creative output. As we shall see in Chapter 19, the client may want to move beyond these subjective criteria and use more sophisticated pretesting methods to determine the effectiveness of a particular approach suggested by the creative specialist or team.

Summary

In this chapter, we examined how the advertising message is implemented and executed. Once the creative strategy that will guide the ad campaign has been determined, attention turns to the specific type of advertising appeal and execution format to carry out the creative plan. The appeal is the central message used in the ad to elicit some response from consumers or influence their feelings. Appeals can be broken into two broad categories, rational and emotional. Rational appeals focus on consumers' practical, functional, or utilitarian need for the product or service; emotional appeals relate to social and/or psychological reasons for purchasing a product or service. Numerous types of appeals are available to advertisers within each category.

The creative execution style is the way the advertising appeal is presented in the message. A number of common execution techniques were examined in the chapter, along with considerations for their use. Attention was also

given to tactical issues involved in creating print and TV advertising. The components of a print ad include headlines, body copy, illustrations, and layout. We also examined the video and audio components of TV commercials and various considerations involved in the planning and production of commercials.

Creative specialists are responsible for determining the advertising appeal and execution style as well as the tactical aspects of creating ads. However, the client must review, evaluate, and approve the creative approach before any ads are produced or run. A number of criteria can be used by advertising, product, or brand managers and others involved in the promotional process to evaluate the advertising messages before approving final production.

Key Terms

advertising appeal, 266
creative execution style, 266
informational/rational appeals, 267
emotional appeals, 269
transformational ad, 270
reminder advertising, 274
teaser advertising, 274
headline, 283
direct headlines, 283
indirect headlines, 284
subheads, 284
body copy, 285
layout, 285
voice-over, 286
needledrop, 286
jingles, 287
script, 287

Discussion Questions

1. The opening vignette to the chapter discusses the strong growth Skyy vodka has experienced over the past decade. Discuss how advertising and other forms of marketing communication have contributed to the success of Skyy.

2. Discuss the difference between an advertising appeal and a creative execution style. Find several ads and analyze the particular appeal and execution style used in each.

3. What are the differences between informational/rational and emotional advertising appeals and the factors that would lead to the use of one over the other. Find examples of advertising campaigns that use each type of appeal and discuss the reasons why it is used by the advertiser.

4. IMC Perspective 9-1 discusses how a number of companies have been bringing back classic advertising characters, spokespeople and/or commercials. Why do you think companies are doing this? Discuss the pros and cons of this strategy.

5. What is meant by emotional bonding? Discuss how this concept can be used in developing an advertising campaign for a brand.

6. Discuss how teaser advertising might be used to introduce a new product or brand or to reposition an existing brand. What factors should marketers take into consideration when using a teaser campaign?

7. IMC Perspective 9-2 discusses how advertising for online companies failed to inspire a new creative revolution in advertising. Do you think Internet and dot.com companies relied too much on developing outrageous advertising? Might some of these companies been more successful if they had used more traditional advertising approaches?

8. What is meant by slice-of-death advertising? Discuss some of the reasons business-to-business marketers might use this technique.

9. AFLAC, which is a provider of supplemental insurance, has been very successful in making a duck a popular personality symbol for the company in its advertising. Discuss why an insurance company would develop an advertising campaign featuring a duck.

10. Discuss the role of headlines and subheads in print advertisements. Find examples of print ads that use various types of direct and indirect headlines.

11. Discuss the role of music in advertising. Why might companies such as General Motors and Microsoft pay large sums of money to use popular songs in their commercials?

Media Planning and Strategy

10

Chapter Objectives

1. To understand the key terminology used in media planning.
2. To know how a media plan is developed.
3. To know the process of developing and implementing media strategies.
4. To be familiar with sources of media information and characteristics of media.

DSL, VOD, TiVo and PVR: They All Add Up to Convergence—Or Do They?

While you are probably already familiar with terms like *PIP* (picture in a picture), *DVD,* and *PDA* (personal digital assistant), you may not know about *DSL* (digital subscriber lines), *VOD*

(video on demand), and *PVR*s (personal video recorders). You may have heard of these technologies, but do you really know what they do? Media and entertainment people think they know about all of these things, but whether they do or not is open to debate.

The recent buzz in these industries is about *convergence* and how it is going to change the media landscape. The advent of digital television, mobile phones, and the Internet has led to the belief that the traditional means of watching television will be a thing of the past, with viewers now "multitasking," that is, using more than one medium at once (e.g., surfing on the Internet while watching television). Such technologies will empower consumers to control their own streams of information, entertainment, and content, where and when they want them. Should this be the case, media planning in the future will have to change demonstratively to keep pace. The new technologies may alter the communications landscape forever.

Consider the changes that may occur as a result of interactive television. Rather than being just a box that provides viewing entertainment, the television is being transformed into an interactive tool that allows the viewer to play games, access movies on demand, surf the Web, and make purchases. Microsoft is betting that in the future most of us will access the Internet through our television sets rather than on our PCs.

A recent study conducted by the Nielsen Interactive Group claimed that 30 percent of Internet users now have Internet access in the same room as their TV sets. Further, the study showed that 67 percent of active Internet users are on the Net at the same time that they are watching television. What this means—according to Nielsen and others—is that the likelihood of watching television commercials will decrease and advertising revenues to this medium will also go down. What it also means is that opportunities will exist to reach consumers through other media like the Internet and cell phones. To a degree, consumers will almost never be out of the reach of a commercial message, and advertisers will have the opportunity to send their messages through a variety of platforms.

Take Nissan, for example. The company's launch of a new 4 × 4 in Britain employed interactive TV to provide specifications, additional information, and requests for brochures and test drives, all at the click of a button. Virgin Mobile, another British company, used iTV to ask potential customers what annoyed them about their

existing providers. The responses were used to establish a database and tailor Virgin's services more specifically to customer needs. In the United States, Sony Pictures Entertainment and Real Networks have developed 10-minute, "longer-format advertisements" to provide more information than 30-second commercials. The companies debuted the ads to the 420,000 TiVo subscribers in the summer of 2002, in an attempt to test the concept while getting consumers to choose to actually view ad content. Another company is experimenting with PIP technology to send commercials without interrupting the TV program. These examples demonstrate previously unforeseen uses of interactive media, and they are considered to be only the beginning of numerous new communications methods.

Not everyone is ready to embrace the new technologies just yet, however. Some experts feel the industries know much more about the technologies than they do about how to use them. Other observers feel that consumers are not as excited about these capabilities as the providers think they are. The Nielsen study cited earlier demonstrated that of the 67 percent of viewers who were multitasking by using the Internet while they watched TV, more than 90 percent were pursuing unrelated tasks (e.g., not co-using two media for the same content and/or program). Studies in Britain indicate that most of the early programming developed for iTV was not around four years later and was not what consumers wanted. Other studies have shown that for the majority of consumers, television is an entertainment medium that they want to watch as "couch potatoes," not interact with. David Poltrack, head of research at CBS, notes that "TV is something you do when you don't want to do anything." Jeff Zucker, head of entertainment at NBC, agrees, noting: "The majority of people want to sit back and just passively enjoy TV." Add the cost of building the enormous infrastructure associated with interactive TV, and you will see that the interactive future is a long time away. Are the TV industry experts just fooling themselves? At least one study conducted by the Statistical Research Corporation says they are not. In the study, conducted in the summer of 2001, 72 percent of respondents said they are *not* interested in interactive TV. Maybe media planning won't be so hard after all?

Sources: Tobi Elkin, "TiVo Inks Pacts for Long-Form TV Ads," *Advertising Age,* June 17, 2002, p. 1; Paul Knight, "Let's Not Miss a Chance to Make iTV a Big Winner," *Marketing,* Feb. 21, 2002, p. 20; Ian Darby, "How the Ad Industry Has Learnt to Stop Worrying and Love TiVo," campaign, May 17, 2002, p. 16; "Survey: Entertain Me," *The Economist,* Apr. 13, 2002, pp. 4–6; "Interactive Television a Dud," *Inman News Features,* Aug. 31, 2001, p. 1.

The discussion in this chapter's opening vignette describes just one of the many changes taking place in the media environment. Perhaps at no other time in history have so many changes taken place that significantly alter the media decision process. As a result, media planning has become more complex than ever before. As you will see in the following chapters, these changes offer the marketer opportunities not previously available, but they also require in-depth knowledge of all the alternatives. Integrated marketing communications programs are no longer a luxury; they are a necessity. Media planners must now consider new options as well as recognize the changes that are occurring in traditional sources. New and evolving media contribute to the already difficult task of media planning. Planning when, where, and how the advertising message will be delivered is a complex and involved process. The primary objective of the media plan is to develop a framework that will deliver the message to the target audience in the most efficient, cost-effective manner possible—that will communicate what the product, brand, and/or service can do.

This chapter presents the various methods of message delivery available to marketers, examines some key considerations in making media decisions, and discusses the development of media strategies and plans. Later chapters will explore the relative advantages and disadvantages of the various media and examine each in more detail.

An Overview of Media Planning

The media planning process is not an easy one. Options include mass media such as television, newspapers, radio, and magazines (and the choices available within each of these categories) as well as out-of-the-home media such as outdoor advertising, transit advertising, and electronic billboards. A variety of support media such as direct marketing, interactive media, promotional products advertising, and in-store point-of-purchase options must also be considered. The Internet and interactive media such as those described in the chapter lead-in increase the complexity of this process.

While at first glance the choices among these alternatives might seem relatively straightforward, this is rarely the case. Part of the reason media selection becomes so involved is the nature of the media themselves. TV combines both sight and sound, an advantage not offered by other media. Magazines can convey more information and may keep the message available to the potential buyer for a much longer time. Newspapers also offer their own advantages, as do outdoor, direct media, and each of the others. The Internet offers many of the advantages of other media but is also limited in its capabilities. The characteristics of each alternative must be considered, along with many other factors. This process becomes even more complicated when the manager has to choose between alternatives within the same medium—for example, between *Time* and *Newsweek* or between *Alias* and *Friends.*

The potential for achieving effective communications through a well-designed media strategy warrants the added attention. The power of an effective media strategy was demonstrated by PC Flowers, at one time the smallest of the 25,000 members in the Florists' Transworld Delivery Association. The company then started to advertise its services on the Internet. Within four months, PC Flowers moved into the top 10; now it consistently ranks as one of the top two FTD members in the world.[1] Likewise, an online advertising and e-mail campaign with a budget of only $300,000 was effective enough to get 12,000 new members to sign up for British Air's frequent-flyer program (40 percent more than its goal) in only two weeks.[2]

The product and/or service being advertised affects the media planning process. As demonstrated in Figure 10-1, firms have found some media more useful than others in conveying their messages to specific target audiences. For example, GM and Procter & Gamble tend to rely more heavily on broadcast media, while others like JCPenney and Federated Department Stores (not shown) place more emphasis on print media. The result is placement of advertising dollars in these preferred media—and significantly different media strategies.

Some Basic Terms and Concepts

Before beginning our discussion of media planning, we review some basic terms and concepts used in the media planning and strategy process.

Media planning is the series of decisions involved in delivering the promotional message to the prospective purchasers and/or users of the product or brand. Media planning is a process, which means a number of decisions are made, each of which may be altered or abandoned as the plan develops.

The media plan is the guide for media selection. It requires development of specific **media objectives** and specific **media strategies** (plans of action) designed to attain these objectives. Once the decisions have been made and the objectives and strategies formulated, this information is organized into the media plan.

The **medium** is the general category of available delivery systems, which includes broadcast media (like TV and radio), print media (like newspapers and magazines), direct mail, outdoor advertising, and other support media. The **media vehicle** is the specific carrier within a medium category. For example, *Time* and *Newsweek* are print vehicles; *20/20* and *60 Minutes* are broadcast vehicles. As you will see in later chapters, each vehicle has its own characteristics as well as its own relative advantages and disadvantages. Specific decisions must be made as to the value of each in delivering the message.

Reach is a measure of the number of different audience members exposed at least once to a media vehicle in a given period of time. **Coverage** refers to the potential audience that might receive the message through a vehicle. Coverage relates to potential

Figure 10-1 Leading National Advertisers, ranked by total U.S. advertising spending, 2001—$ millions

Rank				Total U.S. Ad Spending		Estimated	Measured	Consumer						Yellow
2001	2000	Advertiser	Headquarters	2001	% CHG	Unmeasured	Media	Magazine	Newspaper	Outdoor	TV	Radio	Internet	Pages
1	1	General Motors Corp.	Detroit	$3,374.4	–14.5	$1,167.6	$2,206.9	$402.6	$225.6	$25.7	$1,452.9	$35.8	$44.3	$20.0
2	2	Procter & Gamble Co.	Cincinnati	2,540.6	–2.8	838.4	1,702.2	522.0	10.3	10.2	1,117.6	31.2	10.9	0.0
3	3	Ford Motor Co.	Dearborn, Mich.	2,408.2	2.7	1,138.4	1,269.8	304.7	210.5	14.0	681.0	20.9	14.0	24.7
4	6	PepsiCo	Purchase, N.Y.	2,210.4	4.5	1,536.3	674.2	76.9	6.7	7.3	570.3	7.1	6.0	0.0
5	4	Pfizer	New York	2,189.5	–3.0	1,384.8	804.6	169.5	12.5	0.1	591.9	27.8	2.8	0.0
6	5	DaimlerChrysler	Auburn Hills, Mich./ Stuttgart, Germany	1,985.3	–8.2	585.7	1,399.6	267.3	161.4	16.2	913.8	18.2	8.7	14.0
7	9	AOL Time Warner	New York	1,885.3	6.2	320.5	1,564.8	310.0	266.3	27.4	892.3	41.6	27.2	0.0
8	7	Philip Morris Cos.	New York	1,815.7	–7.7	490.2	1,325.5	461.0	6.3	41.5	784.7	23.6	8.3	0.0
9	8	Walt Disney Co.	Burbank, Calif.	1,757.3	–3.4	702.9	1,054.4	143.9	211.4	25.5	618.4	43.8	11.5	0.0
10	10	Johnson & Johnson	New Brunswick, N.J.	1,618.1	1.0	736.2	881.8	217.2	0.7	0.8	655.2	4.0	3.9	0.0

audience; reach refers to the actual audience delivered. (The importance of this distinction will become clearer later in this chapter.) Finally, **frequency** refers to the number of times the receiver is exposed to the media vehicle in a specified period.

The Media Plan

The media plan determines the best way to get the advertiser's message to the market. In a basic sense, the goal of the media plan is to find that combination of media that enables the marketer to communicate the message in the most effective manner to the largest number of potential customers at the lowest cost.

The activities involved in developing the media plan and the purposes of each are presented in Figure 10-2. As you can see, a number of decisions must be made throughout this process. As the plan evolves, events may occur that necessitate changes. Many advertisers find it necessary to alter and update their objectives and strategies frequently.

Problems in Media Planning

Unfortunately, the media strategy decision has not become a standardized task. A number of problems contribute to the difficulty of establishing the plan and reduce its effectiveness. These problems include insufficient information, inconsistent terminologies, time pressures, and difficulty measuring effectiveness.

Insufficient Information

While a great deal of information about markets and the media exists, media planners often require more than is available. Some data are just not measured, either because they cannot be or because measuring them would be too expensive. For example, continuous measures of radio listenership exist, but only periodic listenership studies are reported due to sample size and cost constraints. There are problems with some measures of audience size in TV and print as well, as demonstrated by IMC Perspective 10-1.

The timing of measurements is also a problem; some audience measures are taken only at specific times of the year. (For example, **sweeps periods** in February, May, July, and November are used for measuring TV audiences and setting advertising rates.) This information is then generalized to succeeding months, so future planning decisions must be made on past data that may not reflect current behaviors. Think about planning for TV advertising for the fall season. There are no data on the audiences of new shows, and audience information taken on existing programs during the summer may not indicate how these programs will do in the fall because summer viewership is generally much lower. While the advertisers can review these programs before they air, they do not have actual audience figures.

The lack of information is even more of a problem for small advertisers, who may not be able to afford to purchase the information they require. As a result, their decisions are based on limited or out-of-date data that were provided by the media themselves, or no data at all.

Inconsistent Terminologies

Problems arise because the cost bases used by different media often vary and the standards of measurement used to establish these costs are not always consistent. For example, print media may present cost data in terms of the cost to reach a thousand people (cost per thousand, or CPM), broadcast media use the cost per ratings point (CPRP), and outdoor media use the number of showings. Audience information that is used as a basis for these costs has also been collected by different methods. Finally, terms that actually mean something different (such as *reach* and *coverage*) may be used synonymously, adding to the confusion.

Time Pressures

It seems that advertisers are always in a hurry—sometimes because they need to be; other times because they think they need to be. Actions by a competitor—for example, the cutting of airfares by one carrier—require immediate response. But sometimes a false sense of urgency dictates time pressures. In either situation, media selection decisions may be made without proper planning and analyses of the markets and/or media.

Figure 10-2 Activities involved in developing the media plan

The situation analysis

Purpose: To understand the marketing problem. An analysis is made of a company and its competitors on the basis of:

1. Size and share of the total market.
2. Sales history, costs, and profits.
3. Distribution practices.
4. Methods of selling.
5. Use of advertising.
6. Identification of prospects.
7. Nature of the product.

The marketing strategy plan

Purpose: To plan activities that will solve one or more of the marketing problems. Includes the determination of:

1. Marketing objectives.
2. Product and spending strategy.
3. Distribution strategy.
4. Which elements of the marketing mix are to be used.
5. Identification of "best" market segments.

The creative strategy plan

Purpose: To determine what to communicate through advertisements. Includes the determination of:

1. How product can meet consumer needs.
2. How product will be positioned in advertisements.
3. Copy themes.
4. Specific objectives of each advertisement.
5. Number and sizes of advertisements.

Setting media objectives

Purpose: To translate marketing objectives and strategies into goals that media can accomplish.

Determining media strategy

Purpose: To translate media goals into general guidelines that will control the planner's selection and use of media. The best strategy alternatives should be selected.

Selecting broad media classes

Purpose: To determine which broad class of media best fulfills the criteria. Involves comparison and selection of broad media classes such as newspapers, magazines, radio, television, and others. The analysis is called intermedia comparisons. Audience size is one of the major factors used in comparing the various media classes.

Selecting media within classes

Purpose: To compare and select the best media within broad classes, again using predetermined criteria. Involves making decisions about the following:

1. If magazines were recommended, then which magazines?
2. If television was recommended, then
   a. Broadcast or cable television?
   b. Network or spot television?
   c. If network, which program(s)?
   d. If spot, which markets?
3. If radio or newspapers were recommended, then
   a. Which markets shall be used?
   b. What criteria shall buyers use in making purchases of local media?

Media use decisions—broadcast

1. What kind of sponsorship (sole, shared, participating, or other)?
2. What levels of reach and frequency will be required?
3. Scheduling: On which days and months are commercials to appear?
4. Placement of spots: In programs or between programs?

Media use decisions—print

1. Number of ads to appear and on which days and months.
2. Placements of ads: Any preferred position within media?
3. Special treatment: Gatefolds, bleeds, color, etc.
4. Desired reach or frequency levels.

Media use decisions—other media

1. Billboards
   a. Location of markets and plan of distribution.
   b. Kinds of outdoor boards to be used.
2. Direct mail or other media: Decisions peculiar to those media.

IMC PERSPECTIVE 10-1

Media Companies Expand and Improve Their Services

Advertising costs are determined by how many people can be reached through the medium. In print media, such costs are based on circulation and readership figures; in broadcast, the basis is ratings. As in any industry, firms compete directly to provide advertisers with these audience numbers. Because so many billions of dollars are spent on advertising each year, the figures the services provide are critical. One would expect that competing firms' information would be valid and consistent. Those in the magazine and newspaper industries believe that it isn't, and they are unhappy about it.

The two primary providers of information on magazine readership are Mediamark Research Inc. (MRI) and Simmons Market Research Bureau (SMRB). Because of the importance media buyers place on the figures, they have become crucial to individual publications. As the vice president of one top ad agency noted, "If the readership numbers shift just a hair, there is a big shift in the number of ad pages." Yet MRI's and SMRB's numbers rarely agree, causing many to question their validity.

In the late 1990s both MRI and SMRB came under attack. *USA Today* and *The Wall Street Journal* were unhappy with MRI, while Hearst, Times Mirror, and Condé Nast were dissatisfied with SMRB. The issues involved the research methodologies of the two companies. The Magazine Publishers of America research committee noticed what appeared to be illogical numbers in the SMRB research materials. Like MRI, SMRB said it would change its research methods—to those previously employed by MRI.

In 2002, SMRB announced another improvement based on internal research that indicated usage of color logo representations improved reporting accuracy. As a result, color magazine logos replaced black-and-white images in an attempt to improve attention and the ability to differentiate between potentially confusing titles.

MRI also responded and made significant changes of its own. One such change was the addition of diary data to the existing methodology. Borrowing from Nielsen Media Research—the TV audience measurement counterpart—approximately 12,000 respondents were asked to maintain diaries recording their magazine reading habits on a day-to-day basis. MRI claimed that the study would allow magazines to present more coherent and precise quantitative readership measures showing exactly when readership takes place and how magazine audiences grow. The company also added 35 questions from the VALS program to help agencies and publishers identify consumer groups that have the greatest affinity with their products.

MRI also announced a partnership with Nielsen to share data to produce a "share-of-voice" report that combines national TV ratings with magazine readership. The new report allows media planners to compare ad schedules in national TV, cable, and 200 magazines based on audience delivery, expressed in gross rating points and cost-per-thousand figures.

You would figure that this would make everyone happy, right? Well, not exactly. Recently media buyers have criticized MRI's reporting of Sunday magazines that appear in newspapers, arguing that MRI overestimates the readership. The MRI method uses newspaper circulation figures and assumes that everyone who reads the Sunday paper reads the magazine section as well. Magazine competitors contend that this gives *Parade* and *USA Weekend* an unfair advantage.

To add validity to the MRI numbers, *Parade* announced that it was undertaking its own five-month study to ensure the accuracy of the MRI figures. Who's next?

Sources: Tony Case, "By the Numbers," *Mediaweek,* Feb. 4, 2002, p. 32; Katy Bachman, "Data Upgrades," *Mediaweek,* Mar. 25, 2002, p. 41; "Mediamark Probes Consumer Psyche," *Mediaweek,* Feb. 26, 2001, p. 48; Jon Fine, "MRI Arms Magazines with Diary Data," *Advertising Age,* Oct. 23, 2000, p. 4.

Difficulty Measuring Effectiveness Because it is so hard to measure the effectiveness of advertising and promotions in general, it is also difficult to determine the relative effectiveness of various media or media vehicles. While progress is being made in this regard, the media planner may have little more than an estimate of or a good guess at the impact of these alternatives.

Because of these problems, not all media decisions are quantitatively determined. Sometimes managers have to assume the image of a medium in a market with which they are not familiar, anticipate the impact of recent events, or make judgments without full knowledge of all the available alternatives.

While these problems complicate the media decision process, they do not render it an entirely subjective exercise. The remainder of this chapter explores in more detail how media strategies are developed and ways to increase their effectiveness.

Figure 10-3 Developing the media plan

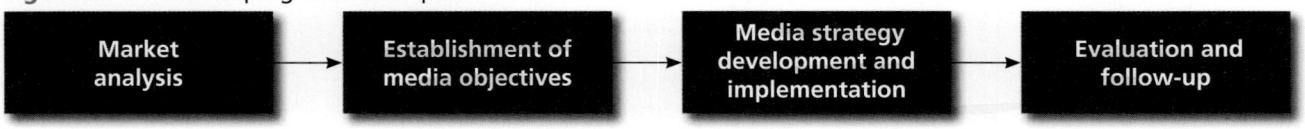

Developing the Media Plan

The promotional planning model in Chapter 1 discussed the process of identifying target markets, establishing objectives, and formulating strategies for attaining them. The development of the media plan and strategies follows a similar path, except that the focus is more specifically keyed to determining the best way to deliver the message. The process, shown in Figure 10-3, involves a series of stages: (1) market analysis, (2) establishment of media objectives, (3) media strategy development and implementation, and (4) evaluation and follow-up. Each of these is discussed in turn, with specific examples. Appendix B to this chapter is an actual media plan, which we refer to throughout the remainder of the chapter to exemplify each phase further.

Market Analysis and Target Market Identification

The situation analysis stage of the overall promotional planning process involves a complete review of internal and external factors, competitive strategies, and the like. In the development of a media strategy, a market analysis is again performed, although this time the focus is on the media and delivering the message. The key questions at this stage are these: To whom shall we advertise (who is the target market)? What internal and external factors may influence the media plan? Where (geographically) and when should we focus our efforts?

To Whom Shall We Advertise?

While a number of target markets might be derived from the situation analysis, to decide which specific groups to go after, the media planner may work with the client, account representative, marketing department, and creative directors. A variety of factors can assist media planners in this decision. Some will require primary research, whereas others will be available from published (secondary) sources.

The Simmons Market Research Bureau (SMRB) provides secondary information: syndicated data on audience size and composition for approximately 100 publications, as well as broadcast exposure and data on usage of over 800 consumer products and services. This information comes in the form of raw numbers, percentages, and indexes. As seen in Figure 10-4, information is given on (1) the number of adults in the United States by each category under consideration; (2) the number of users; (3) the percentage of users falling into each category (for example, the percentage who are female); (4) the percentage of each category that uses the product (for example, the percentage of all females using); (5) an index number; and (6) the same information classified by heavy, medium, and light users. Both Simmons and its major competitor, Mediamark Research Inc. (MRI), also provide lifestyle information and media usage characteristics of the population.

Media planners are often more concerned with the percentage figures and index numbers than with the raw numbers. This is largely due to the fact that they may have their own data from other sources, both primary and secondary; the numbers provided may not be specific enough for their needs; or they question the numbers provided because of the methods by which they were collected. (See IMC Perspective 10-1.) The total (raw) numbers provided by Simmons and MRI are used in combination with the media planner's own figures.

On the other hand, the **index number** is considered a good indicator of the potential of the market. This number is derived from the formula

$$\text{Index} = \frac{\text{Percentage of users in a demographic segment}}{\text{Percentage of population in the same segment}} \times 100$$

An index number over 100 means use of the product is proportionately greater in that segment than in one that is average (100) or less than 100. For example, the MRI

		Filter Sample '(000)	Total Sample 21452 202447 *Regular Cola (Not Diet)-Drink?* *YES*	*Heavy Users*	*Medium Users*	*Light Users*
	Sample		13820	415	2521	9802
	'(000)		141102	5610.93	28022.6	97006
	Vertical		100.00%	100.00%	100.00%	100.00%
	Horizontal		69.70%	2.77%	13.84%	47.92%
	Index		100	100	100	100
SEX: MALE	Sample	9538	6634	235	1324	4666
	'(000)	97199.5	71224.6	3238.06	15000.3	48607.6
	Vertical	48.01%	50.48%	57.71%	53.53%	50.11%
	Horizontal	100.00%	73.28%	3.33%	15.43%	50.01%
	Index	100	105	120	111	104
SEX: FEMALE	Sample	11914	7186	180	1197	5136
	'(000)	105248	69877.4	2372.87	13022.4	48398.4
	Vertical	51.99%	49.52%	42.29%	46.47%	49.89%
	Horizontal	100.00%	66.39%	2.26%	12.37%	45.99%
	Index	100	95	81	89	96
AGE: 18–24	Sample	2017	1550	97	388	968
	'(000)	26148.3	20700.6	1522.87	4904.96	13146.1
	Vertical	12.92%	14.67%	27.14%	17.50%	13.55%
	Horizontal	100.00%	79.17%	5.82%	18.76%	50.28%
	Index	100	114	210	136	105
AGE: 25–34	Sample	2918	2176	67	446	1501
	'(000)	38580.7	30089.7	1430.86	6509.51	19703.8
	Vertical	19.06%	21.33%	25.50%	23.23%	20.31%
	Horizontal	100.00%	77.99%	3.71%	16.87%	51.07%
	Index	100	112	134	122	107
AGE: 35–44	Sample	4547	3042	79	564	2162
	'(000)	45760.3	32541.8	805.978	6585.31	22802.8
	Vertical	22.60%	23.06%	14.36%	23.50%	23.51%
	Horizontal	100.00%	71.11%	1.76%	14.39%	49.83%
	Index	100	102	64	104	104
AGE: 45–54	Sample	4722	2979	80	547	2132
	'(000)	36552.8	24895.1	976.554	5069.16	17142.1
	Vertical	18.06%	17.64%	17.40%	18.09%	17.67%
	Horizontal	100.00%	68.11%	2.67%	13.87%	46.90%
	Index	100	98	96	100	98
AGE: 55–64	Sample	3110	1907	45	318	1390
	'(000)	22980.8	14994.6	469.025	2617.5	10849.2
	Vertical	11.35%	10.63%	8.20%	9.34%	11.18%
	Horizontal	100.00%	65.25%	2.00%	11.39%	47.21%
	Index 100	94	72	82	99	
AGE: 65+	Sample	4138	2166	47	258	1649
	'(000)	32424.2	17880.1	414.636	2336.19	13362
	Vertical	16.02%	12.67%	7.39%	8.34%	13.77%
	Horizontal	100.00%	55.14%	1.28%	7.21%	41.21%
	Index	100	79	46	52	86
AGE: 18–34	Sample	4935	3726	164	834	2468
	'000)	64729	50790.4	2953.74	11414.5	32849.9
	Vertical	31.97%	36.00%	52.64%	40.73%	33.86%
	Horizontal	100.00%	78.47%	4.56%	17.63%	50.75%
	Index	100	113	165	127	106
AGE: 18–49	Sample	11918	8336	287	1671	5764
	'(000)	129634	96569.7	4349.01	20484.1	64875.3
	Vertical	64.03%	68.44%	77.51%	73.10%	66.88%
	Horizontal	100.00%	74.49%	3.36%	15.80%	50.05%
	Index	100	107	121	114	104
AGE: 35–49	Sample	6983	4610	123	837	3295
	'(000)	64905.3	45779.4	1395.28	9069.66	32025.4
	Vertical	32.06%	32.44%	24.87%	32.37%	33.01%
	Horizontal	100.00%	70.53%	2.15%	13.97%	49.34%
	Index	100	101	78	101	103
AGE: 25–54	Sample	12187	8197	226	1557	5795
	'(000)	120894	87526.6	3213.4	18164	59648.7
	Vertical	59.72%	62.03%	57.27%	64.82%	61.49%
	Horizontal	100.00%	72.40%	2.66%	15.03%	49.34%
	Index	100	104	96	109	103
AGE: 50+	Sample	9534	5484	128	850	4038
	'(000)	72812.9	44532.3	1261.92	7538.5	32130.7
	Vertical	35.97%	31.56%	22.49%	26.90%	33.12%
	Horizontal	100.00%	61.16%	1.73%	10.35%	44.13%
	Index	100	88	63	75	92
HIGH SCHOOL - 12 YEARS (GRADUATED)	Sample	6330	4334	156	828	3067
	'(000)	69022.9	50021.6	2343.45	10345.5	33973.3
	Vertical	34.09%	35.45%	41.77%	36.92%	35.02%
	Horizontal	100.00%	72.47%	3.40%	14.99%	49.22%
	Index	100	104	123	108	103
COLLEGE-4 YEARS (GRADUATED)	Sample	3494	2145	37	345	1569
	'(000)	25136.4	16638.5	281.425	2964.29	12050.7
	Vertical	12.42%	11.79%	5.02%	10.58%	12.42%
	Horizontal	100.00%	66.19%	1.12%	11.79%	47.94%
	Index	100	95	40	85	100
DID NOT GRADUATE HIGH SCHOOL	Sample	2196	1527	78	325	1021
	'(000)	32884.4	24128.2	1528.37	5285.51	15608.2
	Vertical	16.24%	17.10%	27.24%	18.86%	16.09%
	Horizontal	100.00%	73.37%	4.65%	16.07%	47.46%
	Index	100	105	168	116	99
ATTENDED COLLEGE (1–3 YEARS)	Sample	4915	3201	84	574	2297
	'(000)	42788.9	29502.1	970.031	5565.53	20926
	Vertical	21.14%	20.91%	17.29%	19.86%	21.57%
	Horizontal	100.00%	68.95%	2.27%	13.01%	48.91%
	Index	100	99	82	94	102
Employed Male	Sample	6863	4962	173	1020	3477
	'(000)	69831.6	53300.2	2421.39	11075.3	36505.1
	Vertical	34.49%	37.77%	43.16%	39.52%	37.63%
	Horizontal	100.00%	76.33%	3.47%	15.86%	52.28%
	Index	100	110	125	115	109

Figure 10-4 Market research profile of cola users

data in Figure 10-5 show that people in the age groups 45–54, 35–44, and 25–34, respectively, are more likely to purchase cellular phones than those in the other age segments, as are those with a household income of $40,000 or more. Most occupation groups are users, though executives/managers and professionals are more likely to be. College graduates also have a high index. Depending on their overall strategy, mar-

Figure 10-5 Cellular phones purchased in the past year—MRI report

3.1% of all adults purchased a cellular phone in the past year. Of this group, women account for 51.1%; 36.4% graduated from college; 26.0% are age 25 to 34; and 15.1% have $50,000 to $59,999 household income. Members of this group are 62% more likely than average adults to have purchased a cellular phone in the past year.

Base: All adults	Population (000) 5,863 Percent of Target	Percent of Base 3.1% Index
Men	48.9	102
Women	51.1	98
Household heads	54.3	89
Homemakers	58.9	95
Graduated college	36.4	176
Attended college	29.8	112
Graduated high school	26.7	79
Did not graduate high school	7.2	38
18–24	11.9	92
25–34	26.0	117
35–44	27.7	128
45–54	20.5	132
55–64	9.2	82
65 or over	4.6	28
18–34	37.9	108
18–49	78.1	119
25–54	74.3	125
Employed full-time	74.8	137
Employed part-time	10.8	112
Sole wage earner	15.3	87
Not employed	14.4	40
Professional	16.1	166
Executive/admin/managerial	15.5	172
Clerical/sales/technical	26.6	141
Precision/crafts/repair	9.4	132
Other employed	18.0	92
H/D income $75,000 or more	38.5	239
H/D income $60,000–$74,999	15.7	162
H/D income $50,000–$59,999	15.1	162
H/D income $40,000–$49,999	13.5	119
H/D income $30,000–$39,999	8.5	62
H/D income $20,000–$29,999	5.0	33
H/D income $10,000–19,999	3.2	22
H/D income less than $10,000	0.4	4

Age Segment	Population in Segment (%)	Product Use in Segment (%)	Index
18–24	15.1	18.0	119
25–34	25.1	25.0	100
35–44	20.6	21.0	102
45+	39.3	36.0	91

Figure 10-6 How high indexes can be misleading

keters may wish to use this information to determine which groups are now using the product and target them or to identify a group that is currently using the product less and attempt to develop that segment.

While the index is helpful, it should not be used alone. Percentages and product usage figures are also needed to get an accurate picture of the market. Just because the index for a particular segment of the population is very high, that doesn't always mean it is an attractive segment to target. The high index may be a result of a low denominator (a very small proportion of the population in this segment). In Figure 10-6, the 18- to 24-year-old age segment has the highest index, but it also has both the lowest product usage and the lowest population percentage. A marketer who relied solely on the index would be ignoring a full 82 percent of product users.

Keep in mind that while Simmons and MRI provide demographic, geographic, and psychographic information, other factors may be more useful in defining specific markets.

What Internal and External Factors Are Operating?

Media strategies are influenced by both internal and external factors operating at any given time. *Internal factors* may involve the size of the media budget, managerial and administrative capabilities, or the organization of the agency, as demonstrated in Figure 10-7. *External factors* may include the economy (the rising costs of media),

Figure 10-7 Organizing the media buying department

While various firms and ad agencies have different ways of organizing the media buying department, three seem to be the most common. The first form employs a product/media focus, the second places more emphasis on the market itself, and the third organizes around media classes alone:

- **Form 1** In this organizational arrangement, the media buyers and assistant media buyers are responsible for a product or group of products and/or brands. Their media planner both plans and buys for these products/brands in whichever geographic areas they are marketed. For example, if the agency is responsible for the advertising of Hart skis, the media planners determine the appropriate media in each area for placing the ads for these skis. The logic underlying this approach is that the planner knows the product and will identify the best media and vehicles for promoting it.
- **Form 2** In this approach, the market is the focal point of attention. Media planners become "experts" in a particular market area and are responsible for planning and buying for all products/brands the firm and/or agency markets in those areas. For example, a planner may be responsible for the Memphis, Tennessee, market. If the agency has more than one client who wishes to market in this area, media selection for all of the brands/products is the responsibility of the same person. The logic is that his or her knowledge of the media and vehicles in the area allows for a more informed media choice. The nonquantitative characteristics of the media get more attention under this approach.
- **Form 3** Organizing around a specific class of media—for example, print or broadcast—is a third alternative. The purchasing and development unit handles all the agency print or broadcast business. Members of the media department become specialists who are brought in very early in the promotional planning process. Planners perform only planning functions, while buyers are responsible for all purchases. The buying function itself may be specialized with specific responsibilities for specialty advertising, national buys, local buys, and so on. Knowledge of the media and the audience each serves is considered a major benefit. Also, people who handle all the media buys can negotiate better deals.

As to which strategy works best, who's to say? Each has been in use for some time. The second approach requires that the agency be big enough and have enough clients to support the geographic assignment. The third alternative seems to be the most common design.

changes in technology (the availability of new media), competitive factors, and the like. While some of this information may require primary research, much information is available through secondary sources, including magazines, syndicated services, and even the daily newspaper.

One service's competitive information was shown in Figure 10-1. The Competitive Media Reporting Service provides media spending figures for various brands competing in the same market. Competitive information is also available from many other sources, as shown in Appendix A to this chapter.

Where to Promote?

The question of where to promote relates to geographic considerations. As noted in Chapter 7, companies often find that sales are stronger in one area of the country or the world than another and may allocate advertising expenditures according to the market potential of an area (see Figure 10-8). For years, Whirlpool has had a much greater brand share of the appliance market in the East and Midwest than in the Southeast and West. The question is, where will the ad dollars be more wisely spent? Should Whirlpool allocate additional promotional monies to those markets where the brand is already the leader to maintain market share, or does more potential exist in those markets where the firm is not doing as well and there is more room to grow? Perhaps the best answer is that the firm should spend advertising and promotion dollars where they will be the most effective—that is, in those markets where they will achieve the desired objectives. Unfortunately, as we have seen so often, it is not always possible to measure directly the impact of promotional efforts. At the same time, certain tactics can assist the planner in making this determination.

Using Indexes to Determine Where to Promote

In addition to the indexes from Simmons and MRI, three other indexes may also be useful:

1. The **survey of buying power index,** published annually by *Sales & Marketing Management* magazine, is conducted for every major metropolitan market in the United States and is based on a number of factors, including population, effective buying income, and total retail sales in the area. Each of these factors is individually weighted to drive a buying power index that charts the potential of a particular metro area, county, or city relative to the United States as a whole. The resulting index gives media planners insight into the relative value of that market, as shown in Figure 10-9. When used in combination with other market information, the survey of buying power index helps the marketer determine which geographic areas to target.

2. The **brand development Index (BDI)** helps marketers factor the rate of product usage by geographic area into the decision process.

$$\text{BDI} = \frac{\text{Percentage of brand to total U.S. sales in the market}}{\text{Percentage of total U.S. population in the market}} \times 100$$

Figure 10-8 Companies allocation of media dollars—U.S. and international

		Media Spending (millions)								
Rank	Advertiser	Outside U.S.	U.S.	World-wide	Africa	Asia	Europe	Latin America	Middle East	Canada
1	Unilever	$2,967	$698	$3,664	$24	$931	$1,713	$291	$7	$0
2	Procter & Gamble	$2,610	1,542	4,152	7	589	1,513	397	41	61
3	Nestlé	1,560	327	1,886	7	404	985	163	1	0
4	Toyota	1,345	790	2,135	6	905	365	0	13	55
5	Volkswagen	1,290	424	1,714	4	14	1,101	150	0	20

Figure 10-9 Survey of buying power index

Metro Area / County	Population					Effective Buying Income				Retail Sales				Buying Power Index	
	1/1/01 Total Pop. (000s)	1/1/06 Total Pop. (000s)	% Change 2001–2006	1/1/06 Total Hshlds. (000s)	% Change 2001–2006	2005 Total EBI ($000)	% Change 2000–2005	Average Household EBI ($) 2000	Average Household EBI ($) 2005	2006 Total Retail Sales ($000)	% Change 2001–2006	Retail Sales Per Household ($) 2001	Retail Sales Per Household ($) 2006	2001	2006
OREGON															
CORVALLIS	78.7	81.1	3.0	30.9	4.4	1,854,799	30.6	47,993	60,026	992,224	31.9	25,423	32,111	.0253	.0263
BENTON	78.7	81.1	3.0	30.9	4.4	1,854,799	30.6	47.993	60,026	992,224	31.9	25,423	32,111	.0253	.0263
EUGENE-SPRINGFIELD	**326.0**	**343.0**	**5.2**	**137.7**	**6.4**	**6,555,563**	**25.9**	**40,234**	**47,608**	**5,760,107**	**20.8**	**36,864**	**41,831**	**.1118**	**.1124**
LANE	326.0	343.0	5.2	137.7	6.4	6,555,563	25.9	40,234	47,608	5,760,107	20.8	36,864	41,831	.1118	.1124
MEDFORD-ASHLAND	183.9	198.5	7.9	80.2	9.4	3,698,500	28.2	39,366	46,116	5,323,418	36.8	53,074	66,377	.0725	.0769
JACKSON	183.9	198.5	7.9	80.2	9.4	3,698,500	28.2	39,366	46,116	5,323,418	36.8	53,074	66,377	.0725	.0769
PORTLAND-VANCOUVER	**1,948.3**	**2,125.2**	**9.1**	**835.6**	**9.9**	**52,817,163**	**35.6**	**51,205**	**63,209**	**36,596,371**	**26.1**	**38,160**	**43,797**	**.7474**	**.7940**
CLACKAMAS	342.9	372.6	8.7	141.7	9.8	10,102,780	35.8	57,611	71,297	4,621,412	12.8	31,730	32,614	.1288	.1343
COLUMBIA	44.0	48.9	11.1	18.4	12.2	973,958	34.4	44,179	52,933	421,167	36.4	18,823	22,890	.0126	.0136
MULTNOMAH	666.2	688.8	3.4	287.1	3.9	15,876,995	26.6	45,390	55,301	16,090,416	32.2	44,054	56,045	.2665	.2751
WASHINGTON	455.4	507.4	11.4	198.4	12.6	14,049,490	40.1	56,921	70,814	9,554,319	19.0	46,041	48,661	.1945	.2076
YAMHILL	86.5	97.3	12.5	33.8	14.2	1,949,382	36.9	48,097	57,674	960,790	15.2	28,169	28,426	.0265	.0281
CLAPK, WASH	353.3	410.2	16.1	156.2	17.4	9,864,558	45.3	51,050	63,153	4,848,267	38.4	26,332	31,039	.1185	.1353
PORTLAND-SALEM CONSOLIDATED AREA	**2,300.7**	**2,507.5**	**9.0**	**979.9**	**9.9**	**60,054,928**	**35.0**	**49,892**	**61,287**	**42,004,281**	**26.1**	**37,370**	**42,866**	**.8604**	**.9116**
SALEM	**352.4**	**382.3**	**8.5**	**144.3**	**10.1**	**7,237,765**	**30.6**	**42,276**	**50,158**	**5,407,910**	**25.8**	**32,784**	**37,477**	**.1130**	**.1176**
MARION	289.1	312.2	8.0	118.1	9.7	5,934,535	30.2	42,308	50,250	5,193,924	26.5	38,135	43,979	.0976	.1014
POLK	63.3	70.1	10.7	26.2	12.0	1,303,230	32.2	42,130	49,742	213,986	12.2	8,153	8,167	.0154	.0162
TOTAL METRO COUNTIES	**2,536.0**	**2,719.9**	**7.3**	**1,072.5**	**8.2**	**62,299.232**	**32.0**	**47,640**	**58,088**	**49,231,763**	**25.5**	**39,590**	**45,904**	**.9515**	**.9919**
TOTAL STATE	**3,464.9**	**3,702.3**	**6.9**	**1,465.3**	**8.0**	**78,533,444**	**30.3**	**44,416**	**53,595**	**62,519,210**	**24.5**	**37,014**	**42,666**	**1.2320**	**1.2726**

Source: *Sales & Marketing Management,* September 2001.

The BDI compares the percentage of the brand's total U.S. sales in a given market area with the percentage of the total population in the market to determine the sales potential for that brand in that market area. An example of this calculation is shown in Figure 10-10. The higher the index number, the more market potential exists. In this case, the index number indicates this market has high potential for brand development (see Appendix B for targeted cities).

3. The **category development index (CDI)** is computed in the same manner as the BDI, except it uses information regarding the product category (as opposed to the brand) in the numerator:

$$\text{CDI} = \frac{\text{Percentage of product category total sales in market}}{\text{Percentage of total U.S. population in market}} \times 100$$

The CDI provides information on the potential for development of the total product category rather than specific brands. When this information is combined with the BDI, a much more insightful promotional strategy may be developed. For example, consider the market potential for coffee in the United States. One might first look at how well the product category does in a specific market area. In Utah and Idaho, for example, the category potential is low (see Figure 10-11). The marketer analyzes the BDI to find how the brand is doing relative to other brands in this area. This information can then be used in determining how well a particular product category and a particular brand are performing and figuring what media weight (or quantity of advertising) would be required to gain additional market share, as shown in Figure 10-12.

While these indexes provide important insights into the market potential for the firm's products and/or brands, this information is supplemental to the overall strategy

$$\text{BDI} = \frac{\text{Percentage of brand sales in South Atlantic region}}{\text{Percentage of U.S. population in South Atlantic region}} \times 100$$

$$= \frac{50\%}{16\%} \times 100$$

$$= 312$$

Figure 10-10 Calculating BDI

Figure 10-11 Using CDI and BDI to determine market potential

$$\text{CDI} = \frac{\text{Percentage of product category sales in Utah/Idaho}}{\text{Percentage of total U.S. population in Utah/Idaho}} \times 100$$

$$= \frac{1\%}{1\%} \times 100$$

$$= 100$$

$$\text{BDI} = \frac{\text{Percentage of total brand sales in Utah/Idaho}}{\text{Percentage of total U.S. population in Utah/Idaho}} \times 100$$

$$= \frac{2\%}{1\%} \times 100$$

$$= 200$$

Figure 10-12 Using BDI and CDI indexes

	High BDI	Low BDI
High CDI	High market share Good market potential	Low market share Good market potential
Low CDI	High market share Monitor for sales decline	Low market share Poor market potential

High BDI and high CDI	This market usually represents good sales potential for both the product category and the brand.
High BDI and low CDI	The category is not selling well, but the brand is; probably a good market to advertise in but should be monitored for declining sales.
Low BDI and high CDI	The product category shows high potential but the brand is not doing well; the reasons should be determined.
Low BDI and low CDI	Both the product category and the brand are doing poorly; not likely to be a good place for advertising.

determined earlier in the promotional decision-making process. In fact, much of this information may have already been provided to the media planner. Since it may be used more specifically to determine the media weights to assign to each area, this decision ultimately affects the budget allocated to each area as well as other factors such as reach, frequency, and scheduling.

Establishing Media Objectives

Just as the situation analysis leads to establishment of marketing and communications objectives, the media situation analysis should lead to determination of specific media objectives. The media objectives are not ends in themselves. Rather, they are designed to lead to the attainment of communications and marketing objectives. Media objectives are the goals for the media program and should be limited to those that can be accomplished through media strategies. An example of media objectives is this: Create awareness in the target market through the following:

- Use broadcast media to provide coverage of 80 percent of the target market over a six-month period.
- Reach 60 percent of the target audience at least three times over the same six-month period.
- Concentrate heaviest advertising in winter and spring, with lighter emphasis in summer and fall.

Developing and Implementing Media Strategies

Having determined what is to be accomplished, media planners consider how to achieve these objectives. That is, they develop and implement media strategies, which evolve directly from the actions required to meet objectives and involve the criteria in Figure 10-13.

Figure 10-13 Criteria considered in the development of media plans

- The media mix
- Target market coverage
- Geographic coverage
- Scheduling
- Reach versus frequency
- Creative aspects and mood
- Flexibility
- Budget considerations

The Media Mix

A wide variety of media and media vehicles are available to advertisers. While it is possible that only one medium and/or vehicle might be employed, it is much more likely that a number of alternatives will be used. The objectives sought, the characteristics of the product or service, the size of the budget, and individual preferences are just some of the factors that determine what combination of media will be used.

As an example, consider a promotional situation in which a product requires a visual demonstration to be communicated effectively. In this case, TV may be the most effective medium. If the promotional strategy calls for coupons to stimulate trial, print media may be necessary. For in-depth information, the Internet may be best.

By employing a media mix, advertisers can add more versatility to their media strategies, since each medium contributes its own distinct advantages (as demonstrated in later chapters). By combining media, marketers can increase coverage, reach, and frequency levels while improving the likelihood of achieving overall communications and marketing goals.

Target Market Coverage

The media planner determines which target markets should receive the most media emphasis. (In the media plan for Bumble Bee Tuna in Appendix B, this was determined to be women 25–54 and geographic markets.) Developing media strategies involves matching the most appropriate media to this market by asking, "Through which media and media vehicles can I best get my message to prospective buyers?" The issue here is to get coverage of the market, as shown in Figure 10-14. The optimal goal is full market coverage, shown in the second pie chart. But this is a very optimistic scenario. More realistically, conditions shown in the third and fourth charts are most likely to occur. In the third chart, the coverage of the media does not allow for coverage of the entire market, leaving some potential customers without exposure to the message. In the fourth chart, the marketer is faced with a problem of overexposure (also called **waste coverage**), in which the media coverage exceeds the targeted audience. If media coverage reaches people who are not sought as buyers and are not potential users, then it is wasted. (This term is used for coverage that reaches people who are not potential buyers and/or users. Consumers may not be part of the intended target market but may still be considered as potential—for example, those who buy the product as a gift for someone else.)

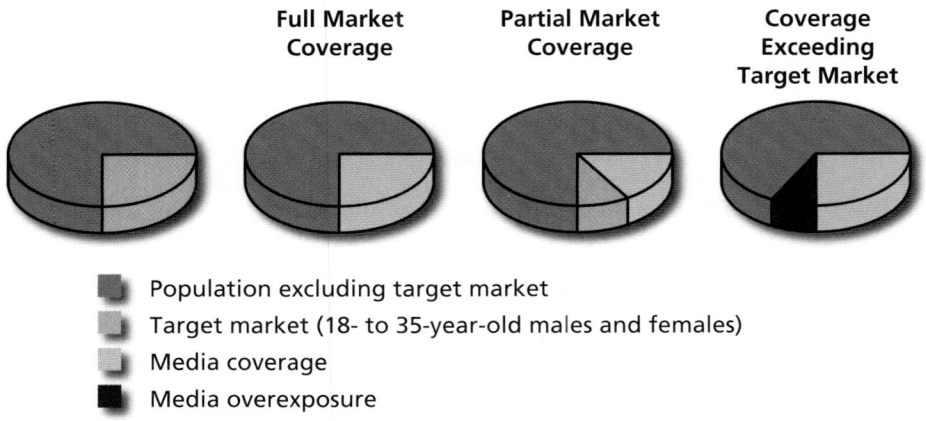

Figure 10-14 Marketing coverage possibilities

The goal of the media planner is to extend media coverage to as many of the members of the target audience as possible while minimizing the amount of waste coverage. The situation usually involves trade-offs. Sometimes one has to live with less coverage than desired; other times, the most effective media expose people not sought. In this instance, waste coverage is justified because the media employed are likely to be the most effective means of delivery available and the cost of the waste coverage is exceeded by the value gained from their use.

When watching football games on TV, you may have noticed commercials for stock brokerage firms such as Charles Schwab, Merrill Lynch, and E Trade. Not all viewers are candidates for stock market services, but a very high percentage of potential customers can be reached with this strategy. So football programs are considered a good media buy because the ability to generate market coverage outweighs the disadvantages of high waste coverage.

Figure 10-15 shows how information provided by Simmons can be used to match media to target markets. It profiles magazines read and TV shows watched by people who do aerobics. (You can practice using index numbers here.) From Figure 10-15, you can see that *Shape, Self,* and *Seventeen* magazines would likely be wise selections for aerobics ads, whereas *Road and Track,* or *Sports Afield,* would be less likely to lead to the desired exposures.

Geographic Coverage

Snow skiing is much more popular in some areas of the country than in others. It would not be the wisest of strategies to promote skis in those areas where interest is not high, unless you could generate an increase in interest. It may be possible to promote an interest in skiing in the Southeast, but a notable increase in sales of ski equipment is not very likely, given the market's distance from snow. The objective of weighting certain geographic areas more than others makes sense, and the strategy of exerting more promotional efforts and dollars in those areas follows naturally. (The Bumble Bee media plan emphasizes 5 primary and 6 secondary cities.)

Scheduling

Obviously, companies would like to keep their advertising in front of consumers at all times as a constant reminder of the product and/or brand name. In reality, this is not possible for a variety of reasons (not the least of which is the budget). Nor is it necessary. The primary objective of *scheduling* is to time promotional efforts so that they will coincide with the highest potential buying times. For some products these times are not easy to identify; for others they are very obvious. Three scheduling methods available to the media planner—continuity, flighting, and pulsing—are shown in Figure 10-16.

Continuity refers to a continuous pattern of advertising, which may mean every day, every week, or every month. The key is that a regular (continuous) pattern is developed without gaps or nonadvertising periods. Such strategies might be used for advertising for food products, laundry detergents, or other products consumed on an ongoing basis without regard for seasonality.

A second method, **flighting,** employs a less regular schedule, with intermittent periods of advertising and nonadvertising. At some time periods there are heavier promotional expenditures, and at others there may be no advertising. Many banks, for example, spend no money on advertising in the summer but maintain advertising throughout the rest of the year. Snow skis are advertised heavily between October and April; less in May, August, and September; and not at all in June and July.

Pulsing is actually a combination of the first two methods. In a pulsing strategy, continuity is maintained, but at certain times promotional efforts are stepped up. In the beer industry, advertising continues throughout the year but may increase at holiday periods such as Labor Day or the Fourth of July. The scheduling strategy depends on the objectives, buying cycles, and budget, among other factors. There are certain advantages and disadvantages to each scheduling method, as shown in Figure 10-17. (Notice that in the Bumble Bee media plan in Appendix B, flighting is recommended for all markets.) One very recent and comprehensive study (acclaimed by many in the

	Filter Sample '(000)	Total Sample 20,936 204,894	SPORTS-PLAYED/ PARTICIPATED LAST 12 MOS: AEROBICS
	Sample		2619
	'(000)		24786.5
	Vertical		100.00%
	Horizontal		12.10%
	Index		100
MAGAZINES - READ/LOOK INTO LAST 6 MOS: REDBOOK	Sample	1564	345
	'(000)	14665.1	3395.09
	Vertical	7.16%	13.70%
	Horizontal	100.00%	23.15%
	Index	100	191
MAGAZINES - READ/LOOK INTO LAST 6 MOS: ROAD & TRACK	Sample	770	84
	'(000)	8536.71	940.121
	Vertical	4.17%	3.79%
	Horizontal	100.00%	11.01%
	Index	100	91
MAGAZINES - READ/LOOK INTO LAST 6 MOS: ROLLING STONE	Sample	1392	294
	'(000)	16281.6	3280.79
	Vertical	7.95%	13.24%
	Horizontal	100.00%	20.15%
	Index	100	167
MAGAZINES - READ/LOOK INTO LAST 6 MOS: SCIENTIFIC AMERICAN	Sample	550	88
	'(000)	4512.03	770.294
	Vertical	2.20%	3.11%
	Horizontal	100.00%	17.07%
	Index	100	141
MAGAZINES - READ/LOOK INTO LAST 6 MOS: SELF	Sample	854	296
	'(000)	7859.25	2747.37
	Vertical	3.84%	11.08%
	Horizontal	100.00%	34.96%
	Index	100	289
MAGAZINES - READ/LOOK INTO LAST 6 MOS: SEVENTEEN	Sample	904	237
	'(000)	10984.9	2824.24
	Vertical	5.36%	11.39%
	Horizontal	100.00%	25.71%
	Index	100	213
MAGAZINES - READ/LOOK INTO LAST 6 MOS: SHAPE	Sample	787	307
	'(000)	7707.39	2925.69
	Vertical	3.76%	11.80%
	Horizontal	100.00%	37.96%
	Index	100	314
MAGAZINES - READ/LOOK INTO LAST 6 MOS: SKI MAGAZINE	Sample	301	56
	'(000)	2497.3	413.07
	Vertical	1.22%	1.67%
	Horizontal	100.00%	16.54%
	Index	100	137
MAGAZINES - READ/LOOK INTO LAST 6 MOS: SMITHSONIAN	Sample	1348	186
	'(000)	10116.6	1452.75
	Vertical	4.94%	5.86%
	Horizontal	100.00%	14.36%
	Index	100	119
MAGAZINES - READ/LOOK INTO LAST 6 MOS: SOAP OPERA DIGEST	Sample	1036	201
	'(000)	11571.8	2138.36
	Vertical	5.65%	8.63%
	Horizontal	100.00%	18.48%
	Index	100	153
MAGAZINES - READ/LOOK INTO LAST 6 MOS: SOUTHERN LIVING	Sample	2121	346
	'(000)	17598	2779.82
	Vertical	8.59%	11.22%
	Horizontal	100.00%	15.80%
	Index	100	131
MAGAZINES - READ/LOOK INTO LAST 6 MOS: THE SPORTING NEWS	Sample	504	77
	'(000)	5457.05	907.028
	Vertical	2.66%	3.66%
	Horizontal	100.00%	16.62%
	Index	100	137
MAGAZINES - READ/LOOK INTO LAST 6 MOS: SPORTS AFIELD	Sample	586	59
	'(000)	6483.66	738.638
	Vertical	3.16%	2.98%
	Horizontal	100.00%	11.39%
	Index	100	94
MAGAZINES - READ/LOOK INTO LAST 6 MOS: SPORTS ILLUSTRATED	Sample	3023	369
	'(000)	31309.9	4047.81
	Vertical	15.28%	16.33%
	Horizontal	100.00%	12.93%
	Index	100	107
MAGAZINES - READ/LOOK INTO LAST 6 MOS: STAR	Sample	941	143
	'(000)	10171.3	1500.63
	Vertical	4.96%	6.05%
	Horizontal	100.00%	14.75%
	Index	100	122
MAGAZINES - READ/LOOK INTO LAST 6 MOS: SUNSET	Sample	743	130
	'(000)	6776.34	1168.59
	Vertical	3.31%	4.72%
	Horizontal	100.00%	17.25%
	Index	100	143
MAGAZINES - READ/LOOK INTO LAST 6 MOS: TENNIS	Sample	307	63
	'(000)	2750.2	582.462
	Vertical	1.34%	2.35%
	Horizontal	100.00%	21.18%
	Index	100	175
MAGAZINES - READ/LOOK INTO LAST 6 MOS: TRAVEL & LEISURE	Sample	758	140
	'(000)	5688.04	1071.52
	Vertical	2.78%	4.32%
	Horizontal	100.00%	18.84%
	Index	100	156
MAGAZINES - READ/LOOK INTO LAST 6 MOS: TV GUIDE	Sample	2939	429
	'(000)	30103.8	4294.41
	Vertical	14.69%	17.33%
	Horizontal	100.00%	14.27%
	Index	100	118
MAGAZINES - READ/LOOK INTO LAST 6 MOS: US WEEKLY	Sample	759	155
	'(000)	7397.39	1622.07
	Vertical	3.61%	6.54%
	Horizontal	100.00%	21.93%
	Index	100	181
MAGAZINES - READ/LOOK INTO LAST 6 MOS: USA WEEKEND	Sample	6086	806
	'(000)	59393.8	7280.44
	Vertical	28.99%	29.37%
	Horizontal	100.00%	12.26%
	Index	100	101

Figure 10-15 SMRB profile of aerobics participants magazine readership

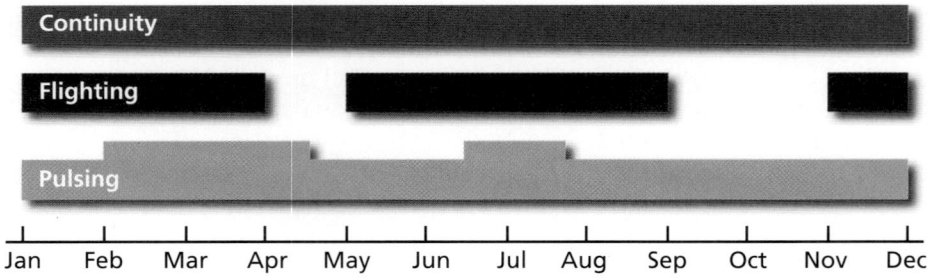

Figure 10-16 Three methods of promotional scheduling

TV research community as "the most comprehensive study ever to shed light on scheduling") indicates that continuity is more effective than flighting. On the basis of the idea that it is important to get exposure to the message as close as possible to when the consumer is going to make the purchase, the study concludes that advertisers should continue weekly schedules as long as possible.[3] The key here may be the "as long as possible" qualification. Given a significant budget, continuity may be more of an option than it is for those with more limited budgets.

Reach versus Frequency

Since advertisers have a variety of objectives and face budget constraints, they usually must trade off reach and frequency. They must decide whether to have the message be seen or heard by more people (reach) or by fewer people more often (frequency).

How Much Reach Is Necessary?

Thinking back to the hierarchies discussed in Chapter 5, you will recall that the first stage of each model requires awareness of the product and/or brand. The more people are aware, the more are likely to move to each subsequent stage. Achieving awareness requires reach—that is, exposing potential buyers to the message. New brands or products need a very high level of reach, since the objective is to make all potential buyers aware of the new entry. High reach is also

Figure 10-17
Characteristics of scheduling methods

	Continuity
Advantages	Serves as a constant reminder to the consumer Covers the entire buying cycle Allows for media priorities (quantity discounts, preferred locations, etc.)
Disadvantages	Higher costs Potential for overexposure Limited media allocation possible

	Flighting
Advantages	Cost efficiency of advertising only during purchase cycles May allow for inclusion of more than one medium or vehicle with limited budgets
Disadvantages	Weighting may offer more exposure and advantage over competitors Increased likelihood of wearout Lack of awareness, interest, retention of promotional message during nonscheduled times Vulnerability to competitive efforts during nonscheduled periods

	Pulsing
Advantages	All of the same as the previous two methods
Disadvantages	Not required for seasonal products (or other cyclical products)

desired at later stages of the hierarchy. For example, at the trial stage of the adoption hierarchy, a promotional strategy might use cents-off coupons or free samples. An objective of the marketer is to reach a larger number of people with these samples, in an attempt to make them learn of the product, try it, and develop favorable attitudes toward it. (In turn, these attitudes may lead to purchase.)

The problem arises because there is no known way of determining how much reach is required to achieve levels of awareness, attitude change, or buying intentions, nor can we be sure an ad placed in a vehicle will actually reach the intended audience. (There has been some research on the first problem, which will be discussed in the section below on effective reach.)

If you buy advertising time on *60 Minutes,* will everyone who is tuned to the program see the ad? No. Many viewers will leave the room, be distracted during the commercial, and so on, as shown in Figure 10-18 (which also provides a good example of the difference between reach and coverage). If I expose everyone in my target group to the message once, will this be sufficient to create a 100 percent level of awareness? The answer again is no. This leads to the next question: What frequency of exposure is necessary for the ad to be seen and to have an impact?

What Frequency Level Is Needed? With respect to media planning, *frequency* carries a slightly different meaning. (Remember when we said one of the problems in media planning is that terms often take on different meanings?) Here frequency is the number of times one is exposed to the media vehicle, not necessarily to the ad itself. While one study has estimated the actual audience for a commercial may be as much as 30 percent lower than that for the program, not all researchers agree.[4] Figure 10-18 demonstrates that depending on the program, this number may range from 12 to 40 percent.

Most advertisers do agree that a 1:1 exposure ratio does not exist. So while your ad may be placed in a certain vehicle, the fact that a consumer has been exposed to that vehicle does not ensure that your ad has been seen. As a result, the frequency level expressed in the media plan overstates the actual level of exposure to the ad. This overstatement has led some media buyers to refer to the reach of the media vehicle as "opportunities to see" an ad rather than actual exposure to it.

Because the advertiser has no sure way of knowing whether exposure to a vehicle results in exposure to the ad, the media and advertisers have adopted a compromise: One exposure to the vehicle constitutes reach, given that this exposure must occur for

Figure 10-18 Who's still there to watch the ads?

How many viewers actually watch a commercial? R. D. Percy & Co. reports that its advanced people meters, equipped with heat sensors that detect viewers present, indicate that spots retain, on average, 82 percent of the average-minute ratings for the quarter hour. During early morning news programs, "commercial efficiency" (as Percy calls it) is lower because so many people are bustling about, out of the room (blue), but the rate rises at night.

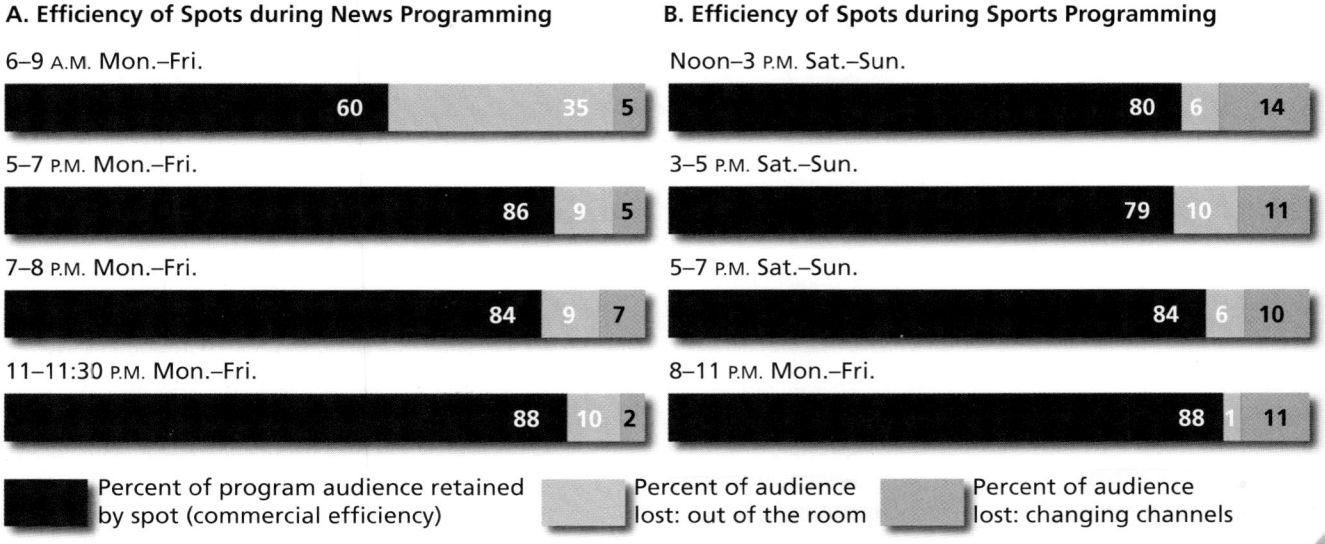

the viewer even to have an opportunity to see the ad. Thus, the exposure figure is used to calculate reach and frequency levels. But this compromise does not help determine the frequency required to make an impact. The creativity of the ad, the involvement of the receiver, noise, and many other intervening factors confound any attempts to make a precise determination.

At this point, you may be thinking, "If nobody knows this stuff, how do they make these decisions?" That's a good question, and the truth is that the decisions are not always made on hard data. Says Joseph Ostrow, executive vice president/director of communications services with Young and Rubicam, "Establishing frequency goals for an advertising campaign is a mix of art and science but with a definite bias toward art."[5] Let us first examine the process involved in setting reach and frequency objectives and then discuss the logic of each.

Establishing Reach and Frequency Objectives

It is possible to be exposed to more than one media vehicle with an ad, resulting in repetition (frequency). If one ad is placed on one TV show one time, the number of people exposed is the reach. If the ad is placed on two shows, the total number exposed once is **unduplicated reach.** Some people will see the ad twice. The reach of the two shows, as depicted in Figure 10-19, includes a number of people who were reached by both shows (C). This overlap is referred to as **duplicated reach.**

Both unduplicated and duplicated reach figures are important. Unduplicated reach indicates potential new exposures, while duplicated reach provides an estimate of frequency. Most media buys include both forms of reach. Let us consider an example.

A measure of potential reach in the broadcast industry is the TV (or radio) **program rating.** This number is expressed as a percentage. For an estimate of the total number of homes reached, multiply this percentage times the number of homes with TV sets. For example, if there are 102.2 million homes with TV sets in the United States and the program has a rating of 30, then the calculation is 0.30 times 102.2, or 30.66 million homes. (We go into much more detail on ratings and other broadcast terms in Chapter 11.)

Using Gross Ratings Points

The media buyer typically uses a numerical indicator to know how many potential audience members may be exposed to a series of commercials. A summary measure that combines the program rating and the average number of times the home is reached during this period (frequency of exposure) is a commonly used reference point known as **gross ratings points (GRPs):**

$$\text{GRP} = \text{Reach} \times \text{Frequency}$$

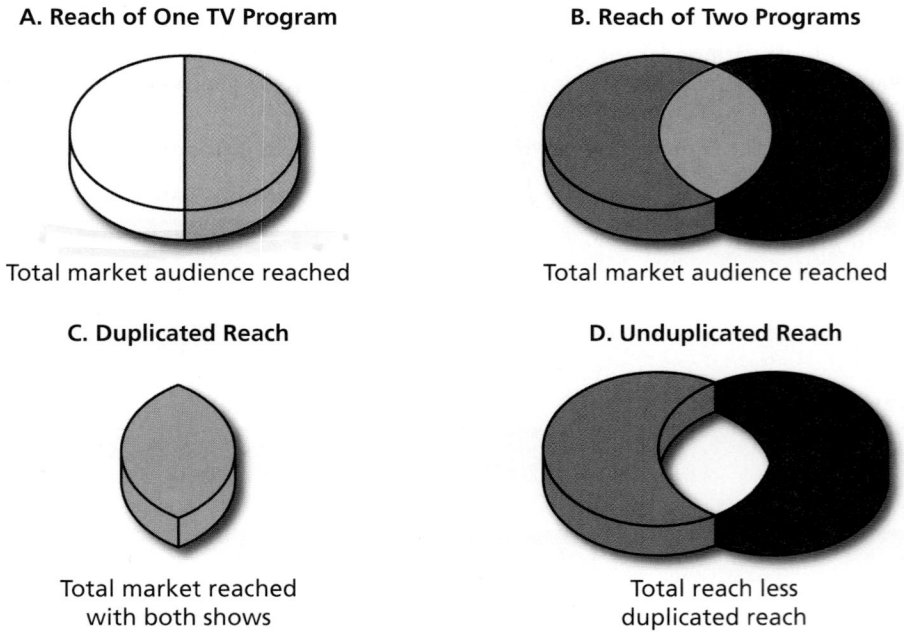

Figure 10-19
Representation of reach and frequency

GRPs are based on the total audience the media schedule may reach; they use a duplicated reach estimate. **Target ratings points (TRPs)** refer to the number of people in the primary target audience the media buy will reach—and the number of times. Unlike GRP, TRP does not include waste coverage.

Given that GRPs do not measure actual reach, the advertiser must ask: How many GRPs are needed to attain a certain reach? How do these GRPs translate into effective reach? For example, how many GRPs must one purchase to attain an unduplicated reach of 50 percent, and what frequency of exposure will this schedule deliver? The following example may help you to understand how this process works.

First you must know what these ratings points represent. A purchase of 100 GRPs could mean 100 percent of the market is exposed once or 50 percent of the market is exposed twice or 25 percent of the market is exposed four times, and so on. As you can see, this information must be more specific for the marketer to use it effectively. To know how many GRPs are necessary, the manager needs to know how many members of the intended audience the schedule actually reaches. The graph in Figure 10-20 helps make this determination.

In Figure 10-20, a purchase of 100 TRPs on one network would yield an estimated reach of 32 percent of the total households in the target market. This figure would climb to 37.2 percent if two networks were used and 44.5 percent with three. Working backward through the formula for GRPs, the estimate of frequency of exposure—3.125, 2.688, and 2.247, respectively—demonstrates the trade-off between reach and frequency.

As an example of a media buy, Denny's purchased 1,300 GRPs in a 10-week period to introduce a new Grand Slam promotion. This purchase employed TV spots in 28 markets and was estimated to reach 40 percent of the target audience an average of 17 times. To determine if this was a wise media buy, we need to know whether this was an effective reach figure. Certainly, reaching 40 percent of the target market is attractive. But why was the frequency level so high? And was it likely to be effective? In other words, does this level of GRPs affect awareness, attitudes, and purchase intentions?

A number of researchers have explored this issue. David Berger, vice president and director of research at Foote, Cone & Belding, has determined that 2,500 GRPs are likely to lead to roughly a 70 percent probability of high awareness, 1,000 to 2,500 would yield about a 33 percent probability, and less than 1,000 would probably result in almost no awareness.[6] David Olson obtained similar results and further showed that as awareness increased, trial of the product would also increase, although at a significantly slower rate.[7] In both cases, it was evident that high numbers of GRPs were required to make an impact.

Figure 10-21 summarizes the effects that can be expected at different levels of exposure, on the basis of research in this area. A number of factors may be operating, and direct relationships may be difficult to establish.[8] In addition to the results shown in Figure 10-21, Joseph Ostrow has shown that while the number of repetitions increases awareness rapidly, it has much less impact on attitudinal and behavioral responses.[9]

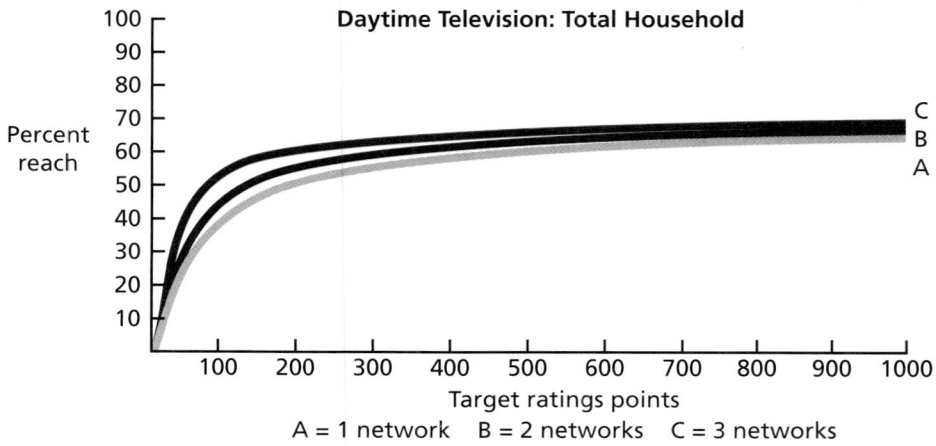

Figure 10-20 Estimates of reach for network TRPs

Figure 10-21 The effects of reach and frequency

1. One exposure of an ad to a target group within a purchase cycle has little or no effect in most circumstances.
2. Since one exposure is usually ineffective, the central goal of productive media planning should be to enhance frequency rather than reach.
3. The evidence suggests strongly that an exposure frequency of two within a purchase cycle is an effective level.
4. Beyond three exposures within a brand purchase cycle or over a period of four or even eight weeks, increasing frequency continues to build advertising effectiveness at a decreasing rate but with no evidence of decline.
5. Although there are general principles with respect to frequency of exposure and its relationship to advertising effectiveness, differential effects by brand are equally important.
6. Nothing we have seen suggests that frequency response principles or generalizations vary by medium.
7. The data strongly suggest that wearout is not a function of too much frequency; it is more of a creative or copy problem.

You can imagine how expensive it was for Denny's to purchase 1,300 gross ratings points on TV. Now that you have additional information, we will ask again, "Was this a good buy?"

Determining Effective Reach

Since marketers have budget constraints, they must decide whether to increase reach at the expense of frequency or increase the frequency of exposure but to a smaller audience. A number of factors influence this decision. For example, a new product or brand introduction will attempt to maximize reach, particularly unduplicated reach, to create awareness in as many people as possible as quickly as possible. At the same time, for a high-involvement product or one whose benefits are not obvious, a certain level of frequency is needed to achieve effective reach.

Effective reach represents the percentage of a vehicle's audience reached at each effective frequency increment. This concept is based on the assumption that one exposure to an ad may not be enough to convey the desired message. As we saw earlier, no one knows the exact number of exposures necessary for an ad to make an impact, although advertisers have settled on three as the minimum. Effective reach (exposure) is shown in the shaded area in Figure 10-22 in the range of 3 to 10 exposures. Fewer than 3 exposures is considered insufficient reach, while more than 10 is considered overexposure and thus ineffective reach. This exposure level is no guarantee of effec-

Figure 10-22 Graph of effective reach

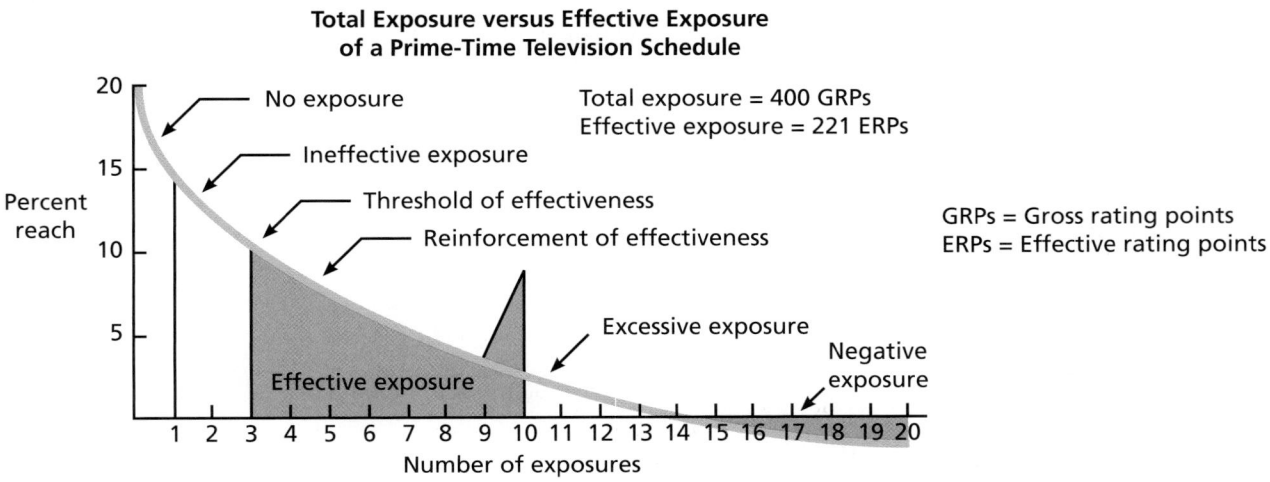

tive communication; different messages may require more or fewer exposures. For example, Jack Myers, president of Myers Reports, argues that the three-exposure theory was valid in the 1970s when consumers were exposed to approximately 1,000 ads per day. Now that they are exposed to 3,000 to 5,000 per day, three exposures may not be enough. Adding in the fragmentation of television, the proliferation of magazines, and the advent of a variety of alternative media leads Myers to believe that 12 exposures may be the *minimum* level of frequency required. Also, Jim Surmanek, vice president of International Communications Group, contends that the complexity of the message, message length, and recency of exposure also impact this figure.[10]

Since they do not know how many times the viewer will actually be exposed, advertisers typically purchase GRPs that lead to more than three exposures to increase the likelihood of effective reach and frequency.

Determining effective reach is further complicated by the fact that when calculating GRPs, advertisers use a figure that they call **average frequency,** or the average number of times the target audience reached by a media schedule is exposed to the vehicle over a specified period. The problem with this figure is revealed in the following scenario:

Consider a media buy in which:

50 percent of audience is reached 1 time.

30 percent of audience is reached 5 times.

20 percent of audience is reached 10 times.

Average frequency = 4

In this media buy, the average frequency is 4, which is slightly more than the number established as effective. Yet a full 50 percent of the audience receives only one exposure. Thus, the average-frequency number can be misleading, and using it to calculate GRPs might result in underexposing the audience.

Although GRPs have their problems, they can provide useful information to the marketer. A certain level of GRPs is necessary to achieve awareness, and increases in GRPs are likely to lead to more exposures and/or more repetitions—both of which are necessary to have an effect on higher-order objectives. Perhaps the best advice for purchasing GRPs is offered by Ostrow, who recommends the following strategies:[11]

1. Instead of using average frequency, the marketer should decide what minimum frequency goal is needed to reach the advertising objectives effectively and then maximize reach at that frequency level.
2. To determine effective frequency, one must consider marketing factors, message factors, and media factors. (See Figure 10-23.)

In summary, the reach-versus-frequency decision, while critical, is very difficult to make. A number of factors must be considered, and concrete rules do not always apply. The decision is often more of an art than a science.

Creative Aspects and Mood

The context of the medium in which the ad is placed may also affect viewers' perceptions. A specific creative strategy may require certain media. Because TV provides both sight and sound, it may be more effective in generating emotions than other media; magazines may create different perceptions from newspapers. In developing a media strategy, marketers must consider both creativity and mood factors. Let us examine each in more detail.

Creative Aspects

It is possible to increase the success of a product significantly through a strong creative campaign. But to implement this creativity, you must employ a medium that will support such a strategy. For example, the campaign for 212 cologne shown in Chapter 4 used print media to communicate the message effectively. Kodak and Hallmark, among many others, have effectively used TV to create emotional appeals. In some situations, the media strategy to be pursued may be the driving force behind the creative strategy, as the media and creative departments work closely together to achieve the greatest impact with the audience of the specific media.

Figure 10-23 Factors important in determining frequency levels

Marketing Factors

- *Brand history.* Is the brand new or established? New brands generally require higher frequency levels.
- *Brand share.* An inverse relationship exists between brand share and frequency. The higher the brand share, the lower the frequency level required.
- *Brand loyalty.* An inverse relationship exists between loyalty and frequency. The higher the loyalty, the lower the frequency level required.
- *Purchase cycles.* Shorter purchasing cycles require higher frequency levels to maintain top-of-mind awareness.
- *Usage cycle.* Products used daily or more often need to be replaced quickly, so a higher level of frequency is desired.
- *Competitive share of voice.* Higher frequency levels are required when a lot of competitive noise exists and when the goal is to meet or beat competitors.
- *Target group.* The ability of the target group to learn and to retain messages has a direct effect on frequency.

Message or Creative Factors

- *Message complexity.* The simpler the message, the less frequency required.
- *Message uniqueness.* The more unique the message, the lower the frequency level required.
- *New versus continuing campaigns.* New campaigns require higher levels of frequency to register the message.
- *Image versus product sell.* Creating an image requires higher levels of frequency than does a specific product sell.
- *Message variation.* A single message requires less frequency; a variety of messages requires more.
- *Wearout.* Higher frequency may lead to wearout. This effect must be tracked and used to evaluate frequency levels.
- *Advertising units.* Larger units of advertising require less frequency than smaller ones to get the message across.

Media Factors

- *Clutter.* The more advertising that appears in the media used, the more frequency is needed to break through the clutter.
- *Editorial environment.* The more consistent the ad is with the editorial environment, the less frequency is needed.
- *Attentiveness.* The higher the level of attention achieved by the media vehicle, the less frequency is required. Low-attention-getting media require more repetitions.
- *Scheduling.* Continuous scheduling requires less frequency than does flighting or pulsing.
- *Number of media used.* The fewer media used, the lower the level of frequency required.
- *Repeat exposures.* Media that allow for more repeat exposures (for example, monthly magazines) require less frequency.

Mood Certain media enhance the creativity of a message because they create a mood that carries over to the communication. For example, think about the moods created by the following magazines: *Gourmet, Skiing, Travel,* and *House Beautiful.* Each of these special-interest vehicles puts the reader in a particular mood. The promotion of fine wines, ski boots, luggage, and home products is enhanced by this mood. What different images might be created for your product if you advertised it in the following media?

The New York Times versus the *National Enquirer*

Architectural Digest versus *Reader's Digest*

A highly rated prime-time TV show versus an old rerun

Television versus the Internet

The message may require a specific medium and a certain media vehicle to achieve its objectives. Likewise, certain media and vehicles have images that may carry over to the perceptions of messages placed within them.

Flexibility

An effective media strategy requires a degree of flexibility. Because of the rapidly changing marketing environment, strategies may need to be modified. If the plan has not built in some flexibility, opportunities may be lost and/or the company may not be able to address new threats. Flexibility may be needed to address the following:

1. *Market opportunities.* Sometimes a market opportunity arises that the advertiser wishes to take advantage of. For example, the development of a new advertising medium may offer an opportunity that was not previously available.
2. *Market threats.* Internal or external factors may pose a threat to the firm, and a change in media strategy is dictated. For example, a competitor may alter its media strategy to gain an edge. Failure to respond to this challenge could create problems for the firm.
3. *Availability of media.* Sometimes a desired medium (or vehicle) is not available to the marketer. Perhaps the medium does not reach a particular target segment or has no time or space available. There are still some geographic areas that certain media do not reach. Even when the media are available, limited advertising time or space may have already been sold or cutoff dates for entry may have passed. Alternative vehicles or media must then be considered.
4. *Changes in media or media vehicles.* A change in the medium or in a particular vehicle may require a change in the media strategy. For example, the advent of cable TV opened up new opportunities for message delivery, as will the introduction of interactive media. The Internet has led many consumer companies to adopt this medium, while for business-to-business marketers the Web has almost become a requirement to succeed. Likewise, a drop in ratings or a change in editorial format may lead the advertiser to use different programs or print alternatives.

Fluctuations in these factors mean the media strategy must be developed with enough flexibility to allow the manager to adapt to specific market situations.

Budget Considerations

One of the more important decisions in the development of media strategy is cost estimating. The value of any strategy can be determined by how well it delivers the message to the audience with the lowest cost and the least waste. We have already explored a number of factors, such as reach, frequency, and availability that affect this decision. The marketer tries to arrive at the optimal delivery by balancing cost with each of these. (Again, the Bumble Bee plan in Appendix B demonstrates how this issue is addressed.) As the following discussion shows, understanding cost figures may not be as easy as it seems.

Advertising and promotional costs can be categorized in two ways. The **absolute cost** of the medium or vehicle is the actual total cost required to place the message. For example, a full-page four-color ad in *Newsweek* magazine costs about $183,000. **Relative cost** refers to the relationship between the price paid for advertising time or space and the size of the audience delivered; it is used to compare media vehicles. Relative costs are important because the manager must try to optimize audience delivery within budget constraints. Since a number of alternatives are available for delivering the message, the advertiser must evaluate the relative costs associated with these choices. The way media costs are provided and problems in comparing these costs across media often make such evaluations difficult.

Determining Relative Costs of Media

To evaluate alternatives, advertisers must compare the relative costs of media as well as vehicles within these media. Unfortunately, the broadcast, print, and out-of-home media do not always provide the

same cost breakdowns, nor necessarily do vehicles within the print media. Following are the cost bases used:

1. **Cost per thousand (CPM).** For years the magazine industry has provided cost breakdowns on the basis of cost per thousand people reached. The formula for this computation is

$$\text{CPM} = \frac{\text{Cost of ad space (absolute cost)}}{\text{Circulation}} \times 1{,}000$$

Figure 10-24 provides an example of this computation for two vehicles in the same medium—*Time* and *Newsweek*—and shows that (all other things being equal) *Time* is a more cost-effective buy, even though its absolute cost is higher. (We will come back to "all other things being equal" in a moment.)

2. **Cost per ratings point (CPRP).** The broadcast media provide a different comparative cost figure, referred to as cost per ratings point or *cost per point (CPP),* based on the following formula:

$$\text{CPRP} = \frac{\text{Cost of commercial time}}{\text{Program rating}}$$

An example of this calculation for a spot ad in a local TV market is shown in Figure 10-25. It indicates that *Survivor* would be more cost-effective than *CSI.*

3. **Daily inch rate.** For newspapers, cost effectiveness is based on the daily inch rate, which is the cost per column inch of the paper. Like magazines, newspapers now use the cost-per-thousand formula discussed earlier to determine relative costs. As shown in Figure 10-26, the *Detroit News* costs significantly more to advertise in than does the *Chicago Tribune* (again, all other things being equal).

As you can see, it is difficult to make comparisons across various media. What is the broadcast equivalent of cost per thousand or the column inch rate? In an attempt to standardize relative costing procedures, the broadcast and newspaper media have begun to provide costs per thousand, using the following formulas:

$$\text{Television: } \frac{\text{Cost of 1 unit of time} \times 1{,}000}{\text{Program rating}} \qquad \text{Newspapers: } \frac{\text{Cost of ad space} \times 1{,}000}{\text{Circulation}}$$

Figure 10-24 Cost per thousand computations: *Time* versus *Newsweek*

	Time	*Newsweek*
Per-page cost	$202,000	$183,000
Circulation	4.0 million	3.1 million
Calculation of CPM	$\frac{202{,}000 \times 1{,}000}{4{,}000{,}000}$	$\frac{183{,}000 \times 1{,}000}{3{,}100{,}000}$
CPM	$50.5	$59.03

Figure 10-25 Comparison of cost per ratings point: *CSI versus Survivor* in a local TV market

	CSI	*Survivor*
Cost per spot ad	$9,000	$8,000
Rating	20	19
Reach (households)	195,140	185,383
Calculation	$9,000/20	$8,000/19
CPRP (CPP)	$450	$421

	Detroit News	*Chicago Tribune*
Cost per page	$43,680	$20,450
Cost per inch	453	490
Circulation	626,450	653,000
Calculation	$\text{CPM} = \frac{\text{Page cost} \times 1{,}000}{\text{Circulation}}$	
	$= \frac{\$43{,}680 \times 1{,}000}{626{,}450}$	$\frac{\$20{,}450 \times 1{,}000}{653{,}000}$
	$69.72	$31.32

Figure 10-26
Comparative costs in newspaper advertising

While the comparison of media on a cost-per-thousand basis is important, intermedia comparisons can be misleading. The ability of TV to provide both sight and sound, the longevity of magazines, and other characteristics of each medium make direct comparisons difficult. The media planner should use the cost-per-thousand numbers but must also consider the specific characteristics of each medium and each media vehicle in the decision.

The cost per thousand may overestimate or underestimate the actual cost effectiveness. Consider a situation where some waste coverage is inevitable. The circulation (using the *Time* magazine figures to demonstrate our point) exceeds the target market. If the people reached by this message are not potential buyers of the product, then having to pay to reach them results in too low a cost per thousand, as shown in scenario A of Figure 10-27. We must use the potential reach to the target market—the destination sought—rather than the overall circulation figure. A medium with a much higher cost per thousand may be a wiser buy if it is reaching more potential receivers. (Most media buyers rely on **target CPM (TCPM),** which calculates CPMs based on the target audience, not the overall audience.)

Scenario A: Overestimation of Efficiency

Target market	18–49
Magazine circulation	4,000,000
Circulation to target market	65% (2,600,000)
Cost per page	$202,000

$$\text{CPM} = \frac{\$202{,}000 \times 1{,}000}{4{,}000{,}000} = \$50.5$$

$$\text{CPM (actual target audience)} = \frac{\$202{,}000 \times 1{,}000}{2{,}600{,}000} = \$77.69$$

Scenario B: Underestimation of Efficiency

Target market	All age groups, male and female
Magazine circulation	4,000,000
Cost per page	$202,000
Pass-along rate	3* (33% of households)

$$\text{CPM (based on readers per copy)} = \frac{\text{Page cost} \times 1{,}000}{\text{Circulation} + 3(1{,}320{,}000)} = \frac{202{,}000 \times 1{,}000}{7{,}960{,}000}$$

$$= \$25.37$$

*Assuming pass-along was valid.

Figure 10-27 Cost per thousand estimates

CPM may also underestimate cost efficiency. Magazine advertising space sellers have argued for years that because more than one person may read an issue, the actual reach is underestimated. They want to use the number of **readers per copy** as the true circulation. This would include a **pass-along rate,** estimating the number of people who read the magazine without buying it. Scenario B in Figure 10-27 shows how this underestimates cost efficiency. Consider a family in which a father, mother, and two teenagers read each issue of *Time.* Assume such families constitute 33 percent of *Time*'s circulation base. While the circulation figure includes only one magazine, in reality there are four potential exposures in these households, increasing the total reach to 7.96 million.

While the number of readers per copy makes intuitive sense, it has the potential to be extremely inaccurate. The actual number of times the magazine changes hands is difficult to determine. How many people in a fraternity read each issue of *Sports Illustrated* or *Maxim* that is delivered? How many people in a sorority or on a dorm floor read each issue of *Cosmopolitan* or *Vanity Fair?* How many of either group read each issue of *BusinessWeek?* While research is conducted to make these determinations, pass-along estimates are very subjective and using them to estimate reach is speculative. These figures are regularly provided by the media, but managers are selective about using them. At the same time, the art of media buying enters, for many magazines' managers have a good idea how much greater the reach is than their circulation figures provided.

In addition to the potential for over- or underestimation of cost efficiencies, CPMs are limited in that they make only *quantitative* estimates of the value of media. While they may be good for comparing very similar vehicles (such as *Time* and *Newsweek*), they are less valuable in making intermedia comparisons, for example, CPM for magazines versus Internet banner ads. We have already noted some differences among media that preclude direct comparisons.

You can see that the development of a media strategy involves many factors. Ostrow may be right when he calls this process an art rather than a science, as so much of it requires going beyond the numbers. IMC Perspective 10-2 demonstrates how involved successful media plans can be.

Evaluation and Follow-Up

All plans require some evaluation to assess their performance. The media plan is no exception.

In outlining the planning process, we stated that objectives are established and strategies developed for them. Having implemented these strategies, marketers need to know whether or not they were successful. Measures of effectiveness must consider two factors: (1) How well did these strategies achieve the media objectives? (2) How well did this media plan contribute to attaining the overall marketing and communications objectives? If the strategies were successful, they should be used in future plans. If not, their flaws should be analyzed.

The problem with measuring the effectiveness of media strategies is probably obvious to you at this point. At the outset of this chapter, we suggested the planning process was limited by problems with measurements and lack of consistent terminology (among others). While these problems limit the degree to which we can assess the relative effectiveness of various strategies, it is not impossible to make such determinations. Sometimes it is possible to show that a plan has worked. Even if the evaluation procedure is not foolproof, it is better than no attempt.

Computers in Media Planning

Attempts to improve on the media buying process through the use of computers have received a great deal of attention. While advanced planning models have been around since at least 1963, for the most part these models have met with limited success. Programs based on linear programming, simulation, and iteration have been adopted by a number of agencies, but there remains a great deal of skepticism regarding their practicality.[12]

Computers have been used, however, to automate each of the four steps involved in planning and strategy development. While the art of media strategy has not been mechanized, advances in the quantitative side have significantly improved managers'

IMC PERSPECTIVE 10-2

The Best Media Plans

Loosen up a little™

Each year *Adweek* selects the best media plans of the year. The selection is made by a number of top executives of advertising and media agencies, with category winners including "Best media plan spending more than $25 million," ". . . between $10 and $25 million," ". . . between $1 and 10 million," and ". . . less than $1 million." In addition, there are winners in specific categories such as "best use of cable TV," "best use of outdoor," "best use of new media," and so on. While we would like to report on all of them, space permits only a few. However, this sampling will demonstrate what successful plans include.

- *Spending more than $25 million*—Dunkin' Donuts (Hill Holliday Agency): Dunkin' Donuts has over 3,500 franchises in over 120 markets, with multiple products and varying advertising budgets. Trying to find a positioning statement that serves everyone is no easy task. Hill Holliday's creative "Loosen Up"—designed to help consumers overcome guilt associated with eating donuts—required a very unique media strategy to communicate. To be effective for all franchisees, a "modular" strategy was developed from which individual locations could pick and choose what would work best given their needs and budgets. For example, sponsorships were created for early morning shows such as the *Today* show. Drive-time and in-office radio spots were purchased, as was space on the Captivate Network, which places advertisements on screens in high-rise elevators. Local TV spots at prime time and late fringe were included on shows like *Friends, Everybody Loves Raymond,* and the *Letterman* and *Jay Leno* shows. A 20-foot-high inflatable coffee cup was hung over the Massachusetts Pike in downtown Boston, and mobile billboards were common around Dunkin' Donuts sites. While no endorsement deals were made, the brand was able to receive the cooperation of radio and TV personalities while effectively communicating the "have fun" message through a "have fun" media strategy.
- *Spending between $10 and $25 million*—Baskin-Robbins (Initiative Media): Changing lifestyles, supermarket sales of ice cream, and a limited media investment restricted for years to spot TV and radio led to flat sales for the ice-cream purveyor and its franchisees. Armed with what the agency considered to be "a ton of proprietary research," the agency realized that the target audience included both children and adults and that the strategy had to change in respect to communications with consumers, field organizations, and promotional partners. Baskin-Robbins first teamed up with DreamWorks to promote the animated film *Shrek.* Movie signage appeared in stores, a "Free Scoop Night" promotion was initiated, and new products that tied in with the movie were developed. Initiative Media's plan was to leverage this success through media buys. TV spots were placed on Nick, Nick at Nite, Fox Family, Hallmark, and the Discovery channel, among others. Oprah, Jack Hanna, and Home Improvement also received shorter (10-second) spots. Cable included the Hallmark channel, VH1, and the TV Guide channel. Most of the ads were accompanied with sales promotions like "Flava of the Week," "Birthday Scoops," and others.
- *Spending less than $1 million*—Archipelago (Fallon Minneapolis): Archipelago's goal was to attract stock traders away from traditional brokers to online trading. A $245,000 budget employing street protests, pennies, and other nontraditional media was allocated to reach the traders—most of whom were unhappy with their current means of trading. Fallon developed a creative strategy that capitalized on this dissatisfaction with the campaign slogan "Don't Get Pennied," which referred to the New York Stock Exchange's switch to expressing stock transactions to the penny rather than in increments of 6.25 cents—a practice that many traders perceived to be to their disadvantage. The agency actually organized demonstrations along Wall Street and in Boston's Post Office Square—where many traders had offices. An armored truck drove past the traders' offices playing the Beatle's "Penny Lane," and out-of-work actors took to the streets chanting "A penny saved is a penny earned. Choose Archipelago and don't get burned." Direct-mail pieces including advertising specialties and a roll of pennies followed, as did handouts in Boston subway stations and wallscapes in specified Manhattan communities. A full-page ad was placed in regional editions of *The Wall Street Journal.* The website was also altered to reflect the "Don't Get Pennied" campaign.

As these plans clearly demonstrate, a variety of media are now employed to get one's message across. They also demonstrate that effective plans don't have to cost millions and millions of dollars—but don't tell that to the media people!

Sources: Kate Macarthur, "Dunkin' Donuts Tries New Tag," Advertising Age, Aug. 12, 2002, p. 8; Eric Schmuckler and Todd Shields, "Media Plan of the Year," *Adweek,* June 17, 2002, pp. SR 1-16; "Green Giant Produces Big Sales for Baskin-Robbins," *Potentials,* July 2002, p. 13.

decision-making capabilities while saving substantial time and effort. Let us briefly examine some of these methods.

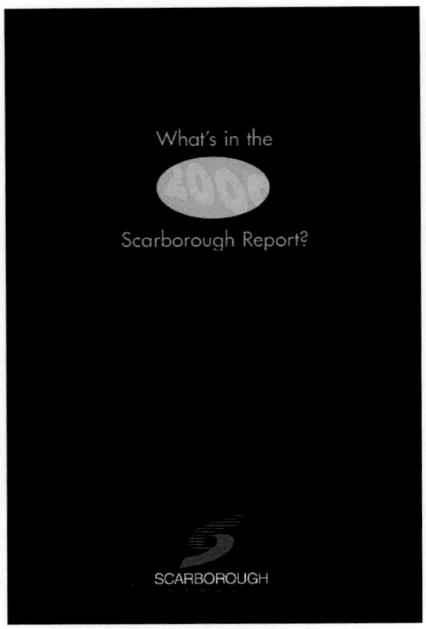

Exhibit 10-1 Scarborough Reports provide valuable information to media planners

Computers in Market Analysis

Earlier in this chapter, we provided examples of Simmons and MRI data. In Chapter 2, we reviewed the information in Prizm and VALS, as well as other such systems. All these data can be accessed either through an interactive system or on the agency's own PC. For example, MRI offers its clients interactive capabilities with its mainframe or its MEMRI software database that can be used on a PC to cross-tabulate media and demographic data, estimate reach and frequency, and rank costs, in addition to numerous other applications. The databases can also interface with Prizm and VALS data. Simmons also allows access to Prizm, VALS, and others.

Other market analysis programs are also available. Nelson and Scarborough provide demographic, geographic, psychographic, and product and media use information that can be used for media planning (Exhibit 10-1). Census tract information and socioeconomic data are also accessible. These systems are linked to Nielsen data for scheduling and targeting to specific groups.

Analyses of these data can help planners determine which markets and which groups should be targeted for advertising and promotions. By using this information along with other data, the marketer can also define media objectives.

Computers in Media Strategy Development

In the section on strategy development, we discussed the need to make decisions regarding coverage, scheduling, costs, and the trade-off between reach and frequency, among others. Of primary benefit to media planners are the programs that assist in development of these strategies. While there are far too many of these programs to review here, we will provide a small sampling to demonstrate our point.

Reach and Frequency Analyses on the Computer

Figure 10-28 demonstrates how software programs are being used to determine reach and frequency levels and assist in deciding which alternative is best. The Telmar program computes

Figure 10-28 Telmar media plan for a local bank

Media Mix (A 25–54)	Reach Frequency (%/X)	3+ Level (%)	1st Quarter Weekly Cost
TV (125)	84/4.5	51	$21,480
TV (125) R (125)	91/8.2	71	29,450
TV (125) R (150)*	92/9.0	73	31,045
TV (150)	86/5.2	57	25,660
TV (150) R (125)	92/9.0	73	33,625
TV (150) R (150)	92/9.8	74	35,220
TV (175)	89/5.9	61	29,930
TV (175) R (125)	93/9.7	75	37,900
TV (175) R (150)	93/10.5	76	39,490
TV (200)	90/6.7	65	34,255
TV (200) R (125)	93/10.5	76	42,225
TV (200) R (150)	93/11.3	78	43,820

Note: Based on a three-week flight.
*Recommended.

various media mixes for TV and radio at different TRPs, with reach and frequency estimates, the number of people reached three or more times, and the costs. The program has determined that a mix of 125 TRPs on TV and 150 TRPs on radio would result in the best buy. Keep in mind that this recommendation considers only the most efficient combination of quantifiable factors and does not allow for the art of media buying.

Figure 10-28 shows just one of the many examples of how computer programs are being used in media strategy development. Other computer-based media planning programs are available; the following list is just a small sample:

- *ADplus* provides for media planning, reach and frequency analysis, media mix information, budgeting, and more.
- *Adware* provides Arbitron and Nielsen information, calculates media costs, projects GRPs, and more.
- *DSI (Datatrak Systems, Inc.)* provides integrated systems for a full range of agency functions, from media and production to planning, buying, billing, and traffic. Software programs include Spot Media Datatrak, Network Media Datatrak, Print Media Datatrak, and Print Analysis Datatrak.
- *IMS* offers a fully integrated suite of software that performs market analysis, target identification, print and broadcast planning, and more. It also provides access to over 600 databases, including syndicated and proprietary, media and marketing, consumer, trade, domestic, and international data.
- *Media Plan, Inc.,* offers multimedia planning, reach and frequency, and flowchart tools. Software includes Manas (flowchart), MultiReach, and MediaPlan RollUp.
- *Media Control by Control G Software* has a Print Media Control Module and Broadcast Media Control. The software packages help to manage media planning by controlling deadlines, station and spot mix, contract usage, and much more.
- *Strata Marketing, Inc.* provides Windows-based TV and radio prebuy and postbuy software systems. Programs include StrataView Radio, StrataView TV, StrataView Buy Management System, and Q-View.
- *Tapscan* uses syndicated data useful in radio media planning, including ratings data and reach and frequency analysis.
- *MRI+* contains MRI research, rate card data, and ABC and BPA figures for 5,700 consumer and trade magazines.
- *Telmar* allows planners to analyze media data, devise media plans, and create flowcharts. It is linked to major syndicated data services.
- *TVscan* provides information like Tapscan's for TV.
- *TV Conquest* combines Nielsen, Donnelley, and Simmons data to provide demographic, product usage, and ratings information.

In addition to these, media models have been developed to show the effects of media selection on advertising responses:

1. *Evaluation models* are exposure distribution models that estimate the reach and frequency of media vehicles on the basis of probability theories.
2. *Allocation models* are comprehensive models used to optimize advertising budget allocation.
3. *Interaction models* consider the interaction effects between copy and media selection in predicting advertising effects.

Unfortunately, these models also have weaknesses that limit their adoption.[13]

The one area where computers have not yet provided a direct benefit is in the evaluation stage of the media plan. While these programs do generate what they consider to be optimal TRP, GRP, and media mixes and allow for pre- and postbuy analyses, the true test is what happens when the plan is implemented. We reserve our discussion of the evaluation process for Chapter 19, on measuring effectiveness.

Figure 10-29
Optimization

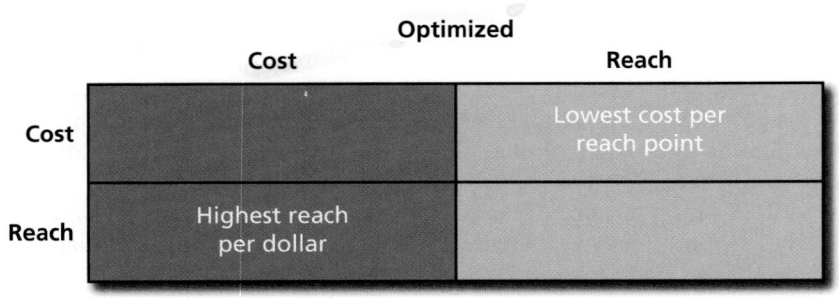

Optimizers In recent years the U.S. market has been introduced to computer programs designed to maximize the reach of the media buy or minimize the cost. These programs, known as **optimizers,** were developed in the United Kingdom and brought to the United States and linked to Nielsen data. Originally cost-prohibitive, programs

Figure 10-30 Media characteristics

Media	Advantages	Disadvantages
Television	Mass coverage High reach Impact of sight, sound, and motion High prestige Low cost per exposure Attention getting Favorable image	Low selectivity Short message life High absolute cost High production costs Clutter
Radio	Local coverage Low cost High frequency Flexible Low production costs Well-segmented audiences	Audio only Clutter Low attention getting Fleeting message
Magazines	Segmentation potential Quality reproduction High information content Longevity Multiple readers	Long lead time for ad placement Visual only Lack of flexibility
Newspapers	High coverage Low cost Short lead time for placing ads Ads can be placed in interest sections Timely (current ads) Reader controls exposure Can be used for coupons	Short life Clutter Low attention-getting capabilities Poor reproduction quality Selective reader exposure
Outdoor	Location specific High repetition Easily noticed	Short exposure time requires short ad Poor image Local restrictions
Direct mail	High selectivity Reader controls exposure High information content Opportunities for repeat exposures	High cost/contact Poor image (junk mail) Clutter
Internet and interactive media	User selects product information User attention and involvement Interactive relationship Direct selling potential Flexible message platform	Limited creative capabilities Websnarl (crowded access) Technology limitations Few valid measurement techniques Limited reach

such as SuperMidas, Xpert, and Spot-On have now become affordable to most agencies and buyers.

Optimizers use cost, reach, and target points to provide the media buyer with either the highest reach or the lowest cost available on the basis of Nielsen respondent data, not a formula. As shown in Figure 10-29, the buyer specifies whether he or she wants to achieve highest reach or lowest cost. One is specified, the second is optimized, and the result (target points) is a function of the two. As an example, the buyer may dictate a specified budget, and the program will yield the optimal reach. Alternatively, one may start with a defined reach goal, and the budget will be optimized.

Optimizers have met with both great acceptance and criticism in the television industry. Supporters believe that these programs will provide the long-sought solution to optimizing reach and cost trade-offs. They cite the success of optimizers in Britain to support their position. Others are not so sure. Erwin Ephron of Ephron, Papazian & Ephron advertising in New York notes that the programs may be more suited to the controlled markets of the United Kingdom than those of the United States. He cautions that optimization should not be considered a substitute for media planning and that the programs base all decisions on CPMs rather than taking into consideration the value of viewers reached. Given the short time optimizers have been used in the United States, it is difficult to determine their value at this point.[14]

Characteristics of Media

To this point, we have discussed the elements involved in the development of media strategy. One of the most basic elements in this process is the matching of media to markets. In the following chapters, you will see that each medium has its own characteristics that make it better or worse for attaining specific objectives. First, Figure 10-30 provides an overall comparison of media and some of the characteristics by which they are evaluated. This is a very general comparison, and the various media options must be analyzed for each situation. Nevertheless, it is a good starting point and serves as a lead-in to subsequent chapters.

Summary

This chapter has presented an overview of the determination of media objectives, development of the media strategy, and formalization of objectives and strategy in the form of a media plan. Sources of media information, characteristics of media, and an actual plan were also provided.

The media strategy must be designed to supplement and support the overall marketing and communications objectives. The objectives of this plan are designed to deliver the message the program has developed.

The basic task involved in the development of media strategy is to determine the best matching of media to the target market, given the constraints of the budget. The media planner attempts to balance reach and frequency and to deliver the message to the intended audience with a minimum of waste coverage. At the same time, a number of additional factors affect the media decision. Media strategy development has been called more of an art than a science because while many quantitative data are available, the planner also relies on creativity and nonquantifiable factors.

This chapter discussed many factors, including developing a proper media mix, determining target market and geographic coverage, scheduling, and balancing reach and frequency. Creative aspects, budget considerations, the need for flexibility in the schedule, and the use of computers in the media planning process were also considered.

The chapter also introduced a number of resources available to the media planner. A summary chart of advantages and disadvantages of various media was provided, as was an example of a media plan.

Key Terms

media planning, 301
media objectives, 301
media strategies, 301
medium, 301
media vehicle, 301
reach, 301
coverage, 301
frequency, 303
sweeps periods, 303
index number, 306
survey of buying power index, 310
brand development index (BDI), 310
category development index (CDI), 311
waste coverage, 313
continuity, 314
flighting, 314
pulsing, 314
unduplicated reach, 318
duplicated reach, 318
program rating, 318
gross ratings points (GRPs), 318
target ratings points (TRPs), 319
effective reach, 320
average frequency, 321
absolute cost, 323
relative cost, 323
cost per thousand (CPM), 324
cost per ratings point (CPRP), 324
daily inch rate, 324
target CPM (TCPM), 325
readers per copy, 326
pass-along rate, 326
optimizers, 330

Discussion Questions

1. Describe the three methods of promotional scheduling. Give examples of products and/or services that might employ each method.

2. The text notes that one problem in media planning is that ratings information is gathered during sweeps periods. Explain what sweeps periods are, and why this might pose a problem.

3. Figure 10-30 notes some of the advantages and disadvantages associated with various media options. Referring to Figure 10-30, provide examples of products and/or services that might most benefit from the use of each medium.

4. Describe what is meant by waste coverage. The decision must often be made between waste coverage and undercoverage. Give examples when the marketer might have to choose between the two, and when it may be acceptable to live with waste coverage.

5. Figure 10-4 provides a profile of the cola user. Using the indices, describe the profile of the cola user. Now describe the profile of the heavy cola user.

6. The text lists both internal and external factors that might impact the media strategy. Provide examples of each and discuss how they might impact the media plan.

7. Using the BDI and CDI indices, explain the least desirable market situation for marketers. Provide an example. Then do the same for the most desirable situation.

8. Discuss the role of optimizers in media planning.

9. Media planning involves a trade-off between reach and frequency. Explain what this means and give examples of when reach should be emphasized over frequency and vice versa.

10. One long-time advertising agency executive noted that buying media is both an art and a science, with a leaning toward art. Explain what this means and provide examples.

Appendixes

APPENDIX A
Sources of Media Information

APPENDIX B
Media Plan for Bumble Bee Tuna

Appendix A

Sources of Media Information

Cross-reference guide to advertising media sources

	General Information	Competitive Activities	Market Information (Geographic)	Audience Information (Target Groups)	Advertising Rates
Nonmedia information (general marketing)	1, 10, 15, 16, 20, 21, 22	1	10, 11, 15, 16, 18, 19, 21, 24	15, 16, 20	
Multimedia or intermedia	1, 15, 16, 20	1, 13	18	2, 24	2
Daily newspapers	9			5, 9, 15, 16, 20	2, 23
Weekly newspapers	9				23
Consumer magazines	3, 14	13	3	3, 15, 16, 20	2, 23
Farm publications				5, 25	2, 23
Business publications			6, 8	6, 25	2, 23
Network television		7, 13		15, 16, 17, 20	2
Spot television		7, 13		15, 16, 17, 20	2, 23
Network radio		7		12, 15, 16, 17, 20, 26	2
Spot radio				4, 5, 12, 17, 20	2, 23

1. *Advertising Age*
2. Advertising agency media estimating guides
3. Magazine Publishers Association (MPA)
4. Arbitron Ratings Company
5. Audit Bureau of Circulations (ABC)
6. Business/Professional Advertising Association (B/PAA) Media Data
7. Broadcast Advertisers Reports (BAR)
8. Business Publications Audit of Circulation (BPA)
9. Newspaper Association of America (NAA)
10. *State and Metropolitan Area Data Book*
11. *Editor & Publisher Market Guide*
12. Survey of World Advertising Expenditures, Stach/Inra/Hooper
13. Competitive Media Reporting
14. Magazine Publishers Association of America (MPA)
15. Mediamark Research, Inc. (MRI)
16. Mendelsohn Media Research, Inc. (MMR)
17. Nielsen Media Research Company
18. Prizm
19. *Sales & Marketing Management Survey of Buying Power*
20. Simmons Market Research Bureau: *Study of Media and Markets*
21. *Standard Directory of Advertisers*
22. *Standard Directory of Advertising Agencies*
23. Standard Rate and Data Service
24. Telmar
25. Verified Audit Circulation Corporation (VAC)

Appendix B

Media Plan for Bumble Bee Tuna

Bumble Bee Tuna
Media Plan
Phillips-Ramsey

Communications Objectives

- Increase expansion strategies into 11 markets, with primary emphasis on 5 key markets (Group A) and 6 secondary markets (Group B).
- Develop media strategies to create high awareness in new product intro markets.
- Develop media strategies to sustain achieved awareness levels.

Media Overview

Media Objectives

- Achieve the following combined TV/Print minimum average four-week TRP levels:
  - Bumble Bee Introduction 700
  - Sustaining #1 200
  - New Product Introduction 400
  - Sustaining #2 200
- As budget permits, incorporate the following expansion strategies:
  1. Run the complete TV plan—24 weeks—in all five markets.
  2. Beef up the New Product Introduction to 500 TRPs/four weeks.
  3. Increase the Sustaining #2 levels to 250 TRPs/four weeks.

Market Groups

- Top five: 45% category white meat (WM) volume and 51% Bumble Bee (BB) white meat (WM) volume.
- Remaining six: 18% category WM volume and 17% BB WM volume.

Media Details

Television

- Schedule length: On-air weeks total 24 in all Top Five markets.
- Weight levels: TRPs vary by campaign period in order to achieve the combined TV/Print Media Objectives.

Print

- Regional editions of publications selected for ad flexibility and CPM.
- Will provide May–December continuity coverage in all eleven markets.

Out-of-Home: New York

- Subway posters: 1,000+ per month for 5 months.
- Bus shelters: 60+ per month for 3 months.

Media Plan Summary

Markets

	Group A	Group B	Combined
# markets	5	6	11
% BB WM volume	51.0	17.4	68.4
% category WM volume	44.7	17.8	62.5
% U.S. TV HH	14.2	11.9	26.1

Media Strategy

Develop a media mix, where required and affordable, as follows:

- **Television:** Deliver designated weekly TRP levels over a maximum of three periods: 2nd Q, 3rd Q, and 4th Q, depending upon market importance and TV costs.
- **Out-of-home:** Bus shelters/subway signs in NY; posters in selective markets.
- **Magazine:** Regional editions rather than local-market editions due to lower cost and CPMs.

Select the media emphasis by market based on:

1. High BB and category WM volume.
2. BB strength vis-a-vis the category and competitors.
3. Opportunity for BB share increase.
4. Targeted media availability and cost.
5. Total available media budget.

Note: *All* markets receive magazine ad support.

Local Media Selection Rationale

New York:	Protect highest volume = TV in 2nd and 3rd Qtrs; shelters and subway signs.
Boston:	Share-increase opportunity = TV in all three Qtrs; posters in 2nd Q.
Miami:	BB dominant in share = TV in 2nd Q; posters in 2nd Q.
Hartford:	BB strongest, protect share = TV in 2nd and 3rd Qtrs.
Philadelphia:	Share-increase opportunity = TV in all three Qtrs.
Tampa:	Protect share = TV in 2nd and 3rd Qtrs.
Detroit:	Share-increase opportunity = TV in all three Qtrs.
Baltimore:	Strong BB share = Media too costly [print only].
Washington:	BB highest share = Media too costly [print only].
Los Angeles:	Share-increase opportunity in #3 category market = TV in 3rd Q.
Albany:	Mid-range share, volume potential law = Print only.

Market BDIs

Market	% BB WM Volume		% Category WM			WM: BDIs			% U.S. TV HH	
	Per mkt	Cume	Per mkt	Cume	WM: CDI	BB	COS	SK	Per mkt	Cume
New York	26.8	26.8	20.2	20.2	297	395	260	256	6.9	6.9
Boston	7.7	34.5	10.4	30.6	372	275	349	246	2.22	9.12
Miami	7.6	42.1	4.4	35	236	407	111	182	1.42	10.54
Hartford/ New Haven	3.8	45.9	3.4	38.4	300	315	219	247	0.94	11.48
Philadelphia	5.1	51	6.3	44.7	199	160	215	202	2.72	142

BB: Bumble Bee
COS: Chicken of the Sea
SK: Starkist

IMS Model Summary Report

Target: women 25–54

Media/ Calculations	A	B	C	D
Better Homes & Gardens	0	2	2	1
Parade	3	0	0	0
People	2	2	2	1
USA Weekend	2	3	0	1
Family Circle	0	3	2	1
Total inserts	7	10	6	4
Gross rating points	223	241	156	99
Reach percent	77.6	75.1	65.8	63.1
Effective reach percent 3+	45.8	41.7	24.0	7.7
Average frequency	2.88	3.21	2.37	1.57
Median frequency	2.77	2.80	2.09	1.39

Schedule Key:
A = Qtr. AMJ
B = Qtr. JAS
C = Qtr. OND
D = "Avg." 4-week

Combined Media Delivery: TV + Print

Average 4-week

GRPs	Reach %	Avg Freq	Eff Rch 3+ %
405	86.3%	4.69	50.1%

Source: 1997 MRI Fall. © MRI All Rights Reserved.

Market Mate—TV Market Report (March 12, 1998)

Report demo: Females 25–54 Schedule: A (4 weeks) Budget $(000): 0.0

	Bumble Bee Introduction: May				
Market	Total GRPs	Reach %	Avg Freq	Gr Imps (000)	3+ Reach %
Boston	700	62.7	11.16	9181	44.6
Hartford & New Haven	700	64.6	10.83	3834	48.2
Miami–Ft. Lauderdale	700	68.0	10.30	5427	48.7
New York	700	65.1	10.75	30473	45.5
Philadelphia	700	54.7	10.83	11237	45.2

Report demo: Females 25–54 Schedule: B (4 weeks) Budget $(000): 0.0

	Sustaining Period: June/July/Aug				
Market	Total GRPs	Reach %	Avg Freq	Gr Imps (000)	3+ Reach %
Boston	200	47.5	4.21	2623	24.3
Hartford & New Haven	200	48.8	4.10	1096	24.8
Miami–Ft. Lauderdale	200	49.7	4.02	1551	25.1
New York	200	47.6	4.20	8707	24.4
Philadelphia	200	48.5	4.13	3211	24.7

Report demo: Females 25–54 Schedule: C (4 weeks) Budget $(000): 0.0

	"New Product" Introduction: Aug/Sept				
Market	Total GRPs	Reach %	Avg Freq	Gr Imps (000)	3+ Reach %
Boston	400	56.3	7.11	5246	35.8
Hartford & New Haven	400	58.0	6.90	2191	36.9
Miami–Ft. Lauderdale	400	59.5	6.72	3101	37.7
New York	400	56.6	7.07	17413	36.0
Philadelphia	400	52.0	7.70	6421	33.3

Report demo: Females 25–54 Schedule: D (4 weeks) Budget $(000): 0.0

	Sustaining Period: Sept/Oct/Nov/Dec				
Market	Total GRPs	Reach %	Avg Freq	Gr Imps (000)	3+ Reach %
Boston	200	46.0	4.34	2623	23.8
Hartford & New Haven	200	48.8	4.10	1096	24.8
Miami–Ft. Lauderdale	200	51.9	3.85	1551	25.8
New York	200	51.0	3.83	8707	25.5
Philadelphia	200	48.3	4.14	3211	24.7

Market Mate—TV Schedule Comparison Report (March 12, 1998)

Market: BOSTON
Report demo: Females 25–54
Pop (000): 1311.6

Calculation	A	B	C	D
GRPs	700	200	400	200
Reach %	62.7	47.5	56.3	48.0
Avg Freq	11.16	4.21	7.11	4.34
Gr Imps (000)	9181	2623	5246	2823
Eff Reach % 3+	44.6	24.3	35.8	23.8

Market: HARTFORD & NEW HAVEN
Report demo: Females 25–54
Pop (000): 547.7

Calculation	A	B	C	D
GRPs	700	200	400	200
Reach %	64.6	48.8	58.0	48.8
Avg Freq	10.83	4.10	6.90	4.10
Gr Imps (000)	3834	1095	2191	1096
Eff Reach % 3+	46.2	24.8	35.9	24.8

Market: MIAMI–FT. LAUDERDALE
Report Demo: Females 25–54
Pop (000): 775.3

Calculation	A	B	C	D
GRPs	700	200	400	200
Reach %	68.0	49.7	59.5	51.9
Avg Freq	10.30	4.02	6.72	3.85
Gr Imps (000)	5427	1551	3101	1551
Eff Reach % 3+	48.7	25.1	37.7	25.8

Market: NEW YORK
Report demo: Females 25–54
Pop (000): 4363.3

Calculation	A	B	C	D
GRPs	700	200	400	200
Reach %	65.1	47.6	56.6	51.0
Avg Freq	10.75	4.20	7.07	3.93
Gr Imps (000)	30473	8707	17413	8707
Eff Reach % 3+	48.5	24.4	38.0	25.5

Market: PHILADELPHIA
Report Demo: Females 25–54
Pop (000): 1605.3

Calculation	A	B	C	D
GRPs	700	200	400	200
Reach %	64.7	48.5	52.0	48.3
Avg Freq	10.83	4.13	7.70	4.14
Gr Imps (000)	11237	3211	6421	3211
Eff Reach % 3+	46.2	24.7	33.3	24.7

Average Four-Week TV Delivery
A = Bumble Bee Intro: May
B = Sustaining Period: June/July/August
C = New Product Intro: August/Sept
D = Sustaining Period: Sept/Oct/Nov/Dec

Media Plans by Market

	Apr				May					Jun				Jul				Aug					Sep				Oct				Nov					Dec			
	28	8	13	20	27	4	11	18	28	1	8	18	22	28	6	13	26	27	9	10	17	24	31	7	14	21	28	5	12	19	26	2	9	14	23	30	7	14	21
TV :30 TRPs						165	135	100	100		30	30		30	28		25	25			110	110	75	75		55	80		80	80		40	40		50	60		30	30
TV :18 TRPs								55	65		70	20		20	20		25	28					25	26		30	30		30	30		40	48		50	60		30	30
						Bumble Bee Intro															New Product Intro																		
New York TV																																							
Subway Posters																																							
Bus Shelters																																							
Print																																							
Boston TV																																							
Print																																							
Miami TV																																							
Print																																							
Hartford TV																																							
Print																																							
Philadelphia TV																																							
Print																																							

Avg. 4 week delivery	Intro	Sustaining	Intro	Sustaining
TRPs	794	214	406	346
Net reach %	88.2	81.5	87.0	72.8
Average frequency	7.10	2.56	5.80	3.37
3+ reach %	62%	38.6	53.8	33%

TV Plan

	Apr				May					Jun				Jul				Aug					Sep				Oct				Nov					Dec			
	28	8	13	20	27	4	11	18	28	1	8	18	22	28	6	13	26	27	9	10	17	24	31	7	14	21	28	5	12	19	26	2	9	14	23	30	7	14	21
						Bumble Bee Intro															New Product Intro																		
:30 TRPs						155	155	160	160		30	30		30	28		25	25			110	110	75	75		55	80		80	80		40	40		50	60		30	30
:18 TRPs								55	65		70	20		20	20		25	28					25	26		30	30		30	30		40	48		50	60		30	30
New York																																							
Boston																																							
Miami																																							
Hartford																																							
Philadelphia																																							

Regional Print Plan—All Markets

	Apr				May					Jun				Jul				Aug					Sep				Oct				Nov					Dec				First Key Dates	
	28	8	13	20	27	4	11	18	28	1	8	18	22	28	6	13	26	27	9	10	17	24	31	7	14	21	28	5	12	19	26	2	9	14	23	30	7	14	21	Issue	Closing
Parade									X			X			X																									May 24	Apr 10
USA Weekend							X			X				X			X					X																		May 17	Apr 10
People								→				→						→		→								→		→											May 18	Mar 30
Better Homes & Gardens														→	→	→	→	→	→	→	→	→					→	→	→	→	→	→	→	→	→						July	Apr 16
Family Circle													→	→	→	→	→	→	→	→	→	→				→	→	→				→	→								June 23	Mar 20

Market Media Plan: New York

TV info:
- 6.90% U.S. TV households
- 7.45% U.S. women 25–54

Food sales:
- 73% by chains

Top chains:
- A&P, Grand Union, Pathmark, Waldbaum, Edwards, King Kullen, Acme, Food Emporium, ShopRite

Brand data:
- 26.8% BB WM volume
- WM CDI = 297
- BB BDI = 395
- COS BDI = 260
- SK BDI = 255

Local Media Plans

Television

19 weeks on-air.

	2nd Q	3rd Q	4th Q	Total
$(000) by Q:	269.0	247.2	-0-	516.2

"Political Protection Period" = Aug. 1–Sept. 14

Out-of-Home

1,140 subway signs @ $24K/month* × 6 months.
107 bus shelters @ $100K/month** × 3 months.
*NY metro. **NY metro, Long Is., Westchester.

	2nd Q	3rd Q	4th Q	Total
$(000) by Q:	372.0	72.0	-0-	444.0

Magazine

	# inserts
Parade	3
USA Weekend	5
People	6
Better Homes & Gardens	4
Family Circle	5

Market Media Plan: Boston

TV info:
- 2.22% U.S. TV households
- 2.27% U.S. women 25–54

Food sales:
- 77% by chains

Top chains:
- Stop & Shop, Demoulas, Shaws, Star, Shop N Save

Brand data:
- 7.7% BB WM volume
- WM CDI = 372
- BB BDI = 275
- COS BDI = 349
- SK BDI = 246

Local Media Plans

Television

Full 26 weeks on-air.

	2nd Q	3rd Q	4th Q	Total
$(000) by Q:	125.7	115.9	68.0	309.6

"Political Protection Periods" = Aug. 1–Sept. 14 [state].
Sept. 4–Nov. 2 [federal].

Out-of-Home

70 posters @ $51K/month × 3 months.

	2nd Q	3rd Q	4th Q	Total
$(000) by Q:	153.0	-0-	-0-	153.0

Magazine

	# inserts
Parade	3
USA Weekend	5
People	6
Better Homes & Gardens	4
Family Circle	5

Market Media Plan: Miami

TV info:
- 1.42% U.S. TV households
- 1.37% U.S. women 25–54

Food sales:
- 73% by chains

Top chains:
- Publix, Winn Dixie, Sedanos

Brand data:
- 7.6% BB WM volume
- WM CDI = 236
- BB BDI = 407
- COS BDI = 111
- SK BDI = 182

Local Media Plans

Television

9 weeks on-air.

	2nd Q	3rd Q	4th Q	Total
$(000) by Q:	112.8	-0-	-0-	112.8

Out-of-Home

55 posters @ $40K/month × 4 months.

	2nd Q	3rd Q	4th Q	Total
$(000) by Q:	120.0	40.0	-0-	160.0

Magazine

	# inserts
Parade	3
People	6
Better Homes & Gardens	4
Family Circle	5

[*USA Weekend* dropped due to minimal coverage at high cost.]

Market Media Plan: Hartford/ New Haven

TV info:
- .94% U.S. TV households
- .93% U.S. women 25–54

Food sales:
- 61% by chains

Top chains:
- Stop & Shop, Waldbaums, Big Y, Shaws

Brand data:
- 3.8% BB WM volume
- WM CDI = 300
- BB BDI = 315
- COS BDI = 219
- SK BDI = 247

Local Media Plans

Television

19 weeks on-air.

	2nd Q	3rd Q	4th Q	Total
$(000) by Q:	56.6	53.1	-0-	109.7

"Political Protection Period" = Aug. 1–Sept. 14.

Out-of-Home

[not recommended].

	2nd Q	3rd Q	4th Q	Total
$(000) by Q:				-0-

Magazine

	# inserts
Parade	3
USA Weekend	5
People	6
Better Homes & Gardens	4
Family Circle	5

Market Media Plan: Philadelphia

TV info:
2.72% U.S. TV households
2.74% U.S. women 25–54

Food sales:
69% by chains

Top chains:
Acme, Super Fresh, Pathmark, Genuardi, Food Lion, Giant Martins

Brand data:
5.1% BB WM volume
WM CDI = 199
BB BDI = 160
COS BDI = 215
SK BDI = 202

Local Media Plans

Television

Full 26 weeks on-air.

	2nd Q	3rd Q	4th Q	Total
$(000) by Q:	167.6	156.8	90.6	415.0

"Political Protection Periods" = Aug. 1–Sept. 14 [state].
Sept. 4–Nov. 2 [federal].

Out-of-Home

[not recommended].

	2nd Q	3rd Q	4th Q	Total
$(000) by Q:				-0-

Magazine

	# inserts
Parade	3
USA Weekend	5
People	6
Better Homes & Gardens	4
Family Circle	5

Evaluation of Broadcast Media

11

Chapter Objectives

1. To examine the structure of the television and radio industries and the role of each medium in the advertising program.
2. To consider the advantages and limitations of TV and radio as advertising media.
3. To explain how advertising time is purchased for the broadcast media, how audiences are measured, and how rates are determined.
4. To consider future trends in TV and radio and how they will influence the use of these media in advertising.

PVRs May Change the Future of Television Advertising

How much would you be willing to pay to never have to watch another TV commercial, be able to automatically record shows with your favorite actor, or record more than one show at a time?

How about being able to leave the room in the middle of an exciting football game to answer the door or go to the bathroom and, when you return, being able to resume watching the game from the point where you left off? These capabilities are no longer the dreams of TV viewers. They are now realities thanks to new consumer electronic devices called *personal video recorders,* or *PVR*s (also called *digital video recorders*), which hit the market a few years ago. And while they may be the answer to TV viewers' dreams, many argue that PVRs may be the television and advertising industries' worst nightmare.

Two companies, TiVo Inc. and SONICblue, Inc., are marketing PVRs, which are better known by the brand names TiVo and ReplayTV. The devices digitally record television shows and save them on a massive multigigabyte internal hard drive that can hold 10 to 30 hours of programming. Using a phone line, the PVRs download program schedules that pop up on the screen, and, with some simple programming through a remote control, consumers can click on shows they want to watch rather than punching in times and channels. The devices also allow users to create "channels" based on their own search criteria, such as types of shows or names of entertainers. The TiVo device even makes recommendations based on how users have rated other programs.

PVRs also allow users to rewind or pause in the middle of a live broadcast while it keeps recording, resume watching from the point where they stopped, and then skip ahead to catch up to the live broadcast. And among the devices' most anticipated, and controversial, features are buttons that allow users to skip past commercials at superhigh speeds. SONICblue recently announced plans to market a new version of ReplayTV with features that will automatically skip commercials in recorded programs. Both TiVo and SONICblue hope that these features, along with the ease of using the devices, will win over consumers, many of whom have given up trying to master their VCRs. If consumers do embrace the new technology, the result will be TV on demand, which will have a dramatic impact on television advertising.

Television shows have always been shown in time slots, with viewers watching whatever is on at that particular time. Advertisers are used to this world of synchronous viewing and buy ad time based on Nielsen ratings, which measure how many people are watching a show at a given moment. However, the digital PVRs make it very easy for TV viewers to watch shows at any time they choose. Watching TV will be more like surfing the Web than viewing a movie. This may reduce the influence of the Nielsen ratings and

bring the one-to-one world of the Internet to television. PVRs will also make it much easier for content providers to push programming directly to end-users, potentially on a pay-per-view, commercial-free basis.

The PVR companies note that rather than fearing their new technology, advertisers should be embracing it, since the marriage of TV and the Internet will make possible interactive advertising and give viewers the ability to purchase products directly from the television screen. PVR companies could take certain commercials out of a program and replace them with ads that are of more interest to specific types of TV viewers or ads that include contests or other incentives that will encourage consumers not to skip them. Moreover, both companies argue that they are not out to kill the television networks, because their business relies on the programming the networks provide. Without commercials, there would be no money to pay for new programming, which would mean the supply of new shows could end unless other means of funding were found.

Both TiVo and SONICblue have been marketing their PVRs and personal television service very heavily, although TiVo is the brand that has become practically synonymous with the product category. However, as of late 2002, only 1 percent of the nation's 106 million TV households owned a PVR, and the new technology has not had a major impact on television advertising's traditional business model. Nevertheless, market tracking firm Forrester Research predicts that PVRs will be in nearly 50 million households by 2007. A senior analyst for the company notes that TV as we know it is going to die in the next five years. Instead of being on a network schedule, it's going to become demand-driven as consumers will use PVRs or this capability will be supplied by cable and satellite TV companies. Consumers will be able to watch what they want and when they want, and this will clearly change how they relate to advertisers.

Not everyone agrees with these predictions: Many argue that television is a passive medium and viewing habits will not change easily. A TiVo senior vice president notes: "There's tremendous inertia associated with watching TV. There's no other human behavior that's as entrenched. We've been watching TV the same way our whole lives." However, as prices of the devices come down and they become easier to use, there is a strong chance that sales will take off. Thus, many marketers view the PVR as a very serious threat to TV advertising and are searching for ways around the problem. TiVo is encouraging marketers to experiment with extended-form ads and other types of "advertainment" that can be shown to its subscribers. The company feels that viewers may choose to watch advertising if the content is as compelling as the programming.

It appears that changes are well under way that may revolutionize the way we watch television and threaten to make the traditional TV advertising business model obsolete. In the future, TV viewers may not have to sit through all those ads for paper towels, toothpaste, and automobiles. On the other hand, would TV really be as much fun without the commercials?

Sources: Jefferson Graham, "PVRs Change the Broadcast Picture," *USA Today,* Aug. 13, 2002, pp. D1, 2; Scott Kirsner, "Can TiVo Go Prime Time?" *Fast Company,* August 2002, pp. 82–88; Tobi Elkin, "TiVo Signs Sony, Realplayer for Long-Play Ads," *Advertising Age,* June 17, 2002, pp. 1, 41.

The emergence of new products such as personal video recorders is very important because they will have a profound impact on television, which is our primary form of entertainment as well as the quintessential advertising medium. TV has virtually saturated households throughout the United States and most other countries and has become a mainstay in the lives of most people. The average American household watches over seven hours of TV a day, and the tube has become the predominant source of news and entertainment for many people. Nearly 90 percent of the TV

households in the United States have a VCR, and many people have entertainment centers with big-screen TVs, VCRs, and stereos. On any given evening during the prime-time hours of 8 to 11 P.M., more than 100 million people are watching TV. Popular shows like *CSI: Miami* and *Everybody Loves Raymond* may have more than 30 million viewers. The large numbers of people who watch television are important to the TV networks and stations because they can sell time on these programs to marketers who want to reach that audience with their advertising messages. Moreover, the qualities that make TV a great medium for news and entertainment also encourage creative ads that can have a strong impact on customers.

Radio is also an integral part of our lives. Many of us wake up to clock radios in the morning and rely on radio programs to inform and/or entertain us while we drive to work or school. For many people, radio is a constant companion in their cars, at home, even at work. The average American listens to the radio more than three hours each day.[1] Like TV viewers, radio listeners are an important audience for marketers.

In this chapter, we examine the broadcast media of TV and radio, including the general characteristics of each as well as their specific advantages and disadvantages. We examine how advertisers use TV and radio as part of their advertising and media strategies, how they buy TV and radio time, and how audiences are measured and evaluated for each medium. We also examine the factors that are changing the role of TV and radio as advertising media.

Television

It has often been said that television is the ideal advertising medium. Its ability to combine visual images, sound, motion, and color presents the advertiser with the opportunity to develop the most creative and imaginative appeals of any medium. However, TV does have certain problems that limit or even prevent its use by many advertisers.

Advantages of Television

TV has numerous advantages over other media, including creativity and impact, coverage and cost effectiveness, captivity and attention, and selectivity and flexibility.

Creativity and Impact Perhaps the greatest advantage of TV is the opportunity it provides for presenting the advertising message. The interaction of sight and sound offers tremendous creative flexibility and makes possible dramatic, lifelike representations of products and services. TV commercials can be used to convey a mood or image for a brand as well as to develop emotional or entertaining appeals that help make a dull product appear interesting.

Television is also an excellent medium for demonstrating a product or service. For example, print ads are effective for showing a car and communicating information regarding its features, but only a TV commercial can put you in the driver's seat and give you the sense of actually driving, as shown by the Porsche commercial in Exhibit 11-1.

Exhibit 11-1 This TV commercial helps viewers feel the sensation of driving a sports car

Coverage and Cost Effectiveness Television advertising makes it possible to reach large audiences. Nearly everyone, regardless of age, sex, income, or educational level, watches at least some TV. Most people do so on a regular basis. According to Nielsen Media Research estimates, nearly 270 million people age 2 or older live in the nation's 106.7 million TV households, nearly 76 percent of whom are 18 or older.[2]

Marketers selling products and services that appeal to broad target audiences find that TV lets them reach mass markets, often very cost efficiently. The average prime-time TV show reaches 7 million homes; a top-rated show like *ER* may reach nearly 15 million homes and perhaps twice that many viewers. In 2002, the average cost per thousand (CPM) homes reached was around $14 for network evening shows and $4 for daytime weekly shows.[3]

Because of its ability to reach large audiences in a cost-efficient manner, TV is a popular medium among companies selling mass-consumption products. Companies with widespread distribution and availability of their products and services use TV to reach the mass market and deliver their advertising messages at a very low cost per thousand. Television has become indispensable to large consumer packaged-goods companies, carmakers, and major retailers. Companies like General Motors and Ford spend nearly two-thirds of their media budgets on various forms of TV—network, spot, cable, and syndicated programs—while PepsiCo and Coca-Cola spend more than 80 percent. Figure 11-1 shows the top 10 network television advertisers and their expenditures.

Captivity and Attention Television is basically intrusive in that commercials impose themselves on viewers as they watch their favorite programs. Unless we make a special effort to avoid commercials, most of us are exposed to thousands of them each year. The increase in viewing options and the penetration of VCRs, DVDs, PVRs, remote controls, and other automatic devices have made it easier for TV viewers to avoid commercial messages. Studies of consumers' viewing habits found that as much as a third of program audiences may be lost during commercial breaks.[4] However, the remaining viewers are likely to devote some attention to many advertising messages. As discussed in Chapter 5, the low-involvement nature of consumer learning and response processes may mean TV ads have an effect on consumers simply through heavy repetition and exposure to catchy slogans and jingles.

Selectivity and Flexibility Television has often been criticized for being a nonselective medium, since it is difficult to reach a precisely defined market segment through the use of TV advertising. But some selectivity is possible due to variations in the composition of audiences as a result of program content, broadcast time, and geographic coverage. For example, Saturday morning TV caters to children; Saturday and Sunday afternoon programs are geared to the sports-oriented male; and weekday daytime shows appeal heavily to homemakers.

Figure 11-1 Top 10 network TV advertisers, 2001

Rank	Company	Measured TV Advertising (millions)
1	General Motors Corp.	$661.8
2	Procter & Gamble Co.	596.5
3	Johnson & Johnson	430.4
4	Philip Morris Cos.	416.7
5	AOL Time Warner	359.4
6	Pfizer	343.8
7	GlaxoSmithKline	335.4
8	PepsiCo.	334.8
9	Walt Disney Co.	311.4
10	Ford Motor Co.	305.1

Exhibit 11-2 Court TV promotes its ability to reach an important demographic segment

With the growth of cable TV, advertisers refine their coverage further by appealing to groups with specific interests such as sports, news, history, the arts, or music, as well as specific demographic groups. Exhibit 11-2 shows an ad promoting Court TV and its ability to reach the 18-to-49 market.

Advertisers can also adjust their media strategies to take advantage of different geographic markets through local or spot ads in specific market areas. Ads can be scheduled to run repeatedly or to take advantage of special occasions. For example, companies such as Anheuser-Busch and Gillette are often major sponsors during baseball's World Series, which allows them to advertise heavily to men who constitute the primary market for their products.

Limitations of Television

Although television is unsurpassed from a creative perspective, the medium has several disadvantages that limit or preclude its use by many advertisers. These problems include high costs, the lack of selectivity, the fleeting nature of a television message, commercial clutter, limited viewer attention, and distrust of TV ads.

Costs Despite the efficiency of TV in reaching large audiences, it is an expensive medium in which to advertise. The high cost of TV stems not only from the expense of buying airtime but also from the costs of producing a quality commercial. Production costs for a national brand 30-second spot average over $300,000 and can reach over a million for more elaborate commercials.[5] Many advertisers such as Burger King, Coca-Cola, and others develop commercials specifically for certain ethnic markets such as African-Americans and Hispanics.[6] More advertisers are using media-driven creative strategies that require production of a variety of commercials, which drive up their costs. Even local ads can be expensive to produce and often are not of high quality. The high costs of producing and airing commercials often price small- and medium-size advertisers out of the market. IMC Perspective 11-1 discusses the most

IMC PERSPECTIVE 11-1

The Super Bowl Is Not the Only Big Advertising Game in Town

The Super Bowl has long been considered the premier event for television advertising. Despite the high costs of advertising on the Super Bowl, many companies think it is well worth the money. They point out that the big game is usually the most watched program of the year and delivers more than 100 million viewers. Advertisers also note that the Super Bowl is one occasion where as much attention is paid to the commercials as to the program. Many consumers actually wait to see the new ads that often debut during the telecast, and the spots often receive a considerable amount of hype and publicity prior to as well as after the game.

While the Super Bowl remains the showcase for advertising, many companies are opting for other alternatives rather than paying more than $2 million to run a 30-second ad on the big game. Marketing executives are running the numbers and concluding that there are more cost-effective alternatives to television's highest-rated, but also highest-priced, event. Some of the largest advertisers are opting for other major telecasts such as the Academy Awards, the Grammies, the Golden Globes, and other events that deliver younger, more sophisticated viewers for less money. Others are choosing to spread their media budgets over long-term commitments instead of spending them on an expensive one-night stand. For example, Electronic Data Systems (EDS) launched its popular "Cat Herder" commercial on the 2000 Super Bowl and followed with the "Running of the Squirrels" spot on the 2001 game. However, EDS decided to pass on the 2002 Super Bowl and directed its agency to create a series of commercials that aired 58 times over the 17 days of the Winter Olympics. An EDS executive noted: "The Olympic Games provide 17 days to sell the EDS story, and give us a better chance to make an impact."

There is also a growing sentiment that the Super Bowl has turned into an expensive beauty pageant for big agencies that want to see their creative work on display rather than being a bona fide opportunity for launching new products. The chairman of Sterling Group, an independent branding firm, notes: "The Super Bowl has been the altar of branding and everybody prayed to the Super Bowl god." However, many companies are cutting back on their new product launches or are not launching them during the time period that coincides with the game. In addition, some companies that have long been Super Bowl advertisers are being run by new CEOs or marketing executives who are less interested than their predecessors in advertising on the big game and are looking at other high-profile media events.

The annual event that has become one of the most popular alternatives to the Super Bowl among major advertisers is the Academy Awards show, which airs in late March or early April. The show is traditionally among the most watched events on television, attracting more than 40 million viewers, and the going rate for a 30-second spot has been around $1.1 million to $1.4 million in recent years. Media buyers point out that the Academy Awards program is a good opportunity to attract women viewers, which has earned it the sobriquet "Super Bowl for Women." Many marketers also like to be a part of the excitement and pageantry that surrounds the event. For example, JCPenney's director of strategic marketing has stated that the Academy Awards event "is a place where fashion, culture and style converge and we want to be part of that." The Grammy Awards program is another annual event that has become popular among advertisers, particularly those trying to reach a younger audience.

While a number of marketers are opting for these alternative events to showcase their ads, others are investing their marketing budgets in events that give them several weeks or even months of exposure. For example, Cingular Wireless gained nationwide recognition by running four spots on the 2001 Super Bowl but passed on the 2002 game in favor of events that would give it exposure and impact over a longer term, such as NASCAR racing and tie-ins with movies such as *Spider Man.* The company's vice president of advertising and communications noted: "We are trying to invest our money in those things that give us several weeks—if not months—of mileage."

The Super Bowl is likely to remain advertising's premier event, particularly for companies with large bud-

gets that are willing to spend millions for a 30-second spot. Moreover, National Football League marketing executives have also been making some defensive moves to broaden the game's appeal and to allow more companies to participate in the hoopla surrounding the game. To attract younger viewers, the Super Bowl's half-time show has featured popular rock groups such as U2, whose music has been included in the NFL's promotional ads. The league is also creating new opportunities for advertisers that choose not to pay television's highest commercial prices, such as those for Friday or Saturday televised events, including concerts and pregame shows. The networks have also produced special shows that air on Super Bowl weekend. For example, in 2002 CBS created a special program, which aired the night before the big game, to provide advertisers with an opportunity to be part of the Super Bowl hype. You guessed it: The show was a special look back at the best Super Bowl ads of all time.

Sources: Vanessa O'Connell, "Super Bowl Gets Competition," *The Wall Street Journal,* Jan. 28, 2002, pp. B1, 3; Suzanne Varanica, "Ad Time for Academy Awards Is Sold Out," *The Wall Street Journal,* Mar. 7, 2002, p. B8.

expensive TV program of all, the Super Bowl, and how its high cost is causing some advertisers to look for alternatives to advertising on the big game.

Lack of Selectivity Some selectivity is available in television through variations in programs and cable TV. But advertisers who are seeking a very specific, often small, target audience find the coverage of TV often extends beyond their market, reducing its cost effectiveness (as discussed in Chapter 10). Geographic selectivity can be a problem for local advertisers such as retailers, since a station bases its rates on the total market area it reaches. For example, stations in Pittsburgh, Pennsylvania, reach viewers in western and central Pennsylvania, eastern Ohio, northern West Virginia, and even parts of Maryland. The small company whose market is limited to the immediate Pittsburgh area may find TV an inefficient media buy, since the stations cover a larger geographic area than the merchant's trade area.

Audience selectivity is improving as advertisers target certain groups of consumers through the type of program or day and/or time when they choose to advertise. However, TV still does not offer as much audience selectivity as radio, magazines, newspapers, or direct mail for reaching precise segments of the market.

Fleeting Message TV commercials usually last only 30 seconds or less and leave nothing tangible for the viewer to examine or consider. Commercials have become shorter and shorter as the demand for a limited amount of broadcast time has intensified and advertisers try to get more impressions from their media budgets. Thirty-second commercials became the norm in the mid-1970s, and in September 1986, the three major networks began accepting 15-second spots across their full schedules (except during children's viewing time). Since 1987, these shorter spots have been accounting for about a third of all network commercials and 9 percent of nonnetwork commercial activity. Thirty-second spots remain the dominant commercial length, accounting for nearly 60 percent of network spots and over 80 percent of nonnetwork ads.[7]

An important factor in the decline in commercial length has been the spiraling inflation in media costs over the past decade. With the average cost of a prime-time spot reaching over $100,000, many advertisers see shorter commercials as the only way to keep their media costs in line. A 15-second spot typically sells for half the price of a 30-second spot. By using 15- or even 10-second commercials, advertisers think they can run additional spots to reinforce the message or reach a larger audience. Many advertisers believe shorter commercials can deliver a message just as effectively as longer spots for much less money.

Several years ago, many advertising people predicted 15-second spots would become the dominant commercial unit. However, the growth in the use of 15-second commercials peaked at 38 percent in 1989 and has recently declined to around 32 percent. The decline may be due to several factors, including creative considerations, lower prices for network time, and a desire by the networks to restrict clutter.[8]

Clutter The problems of fleeting messages and shorter commercials are compounded by the fact that the advertiser's message is only one of many spots and other nonprogramming material seen during a commercial break, so it may have trouble being noticed. One of advertisers' greatest concerns with TV advertising is the potential decline in effectiveness because of such *clutter.*

The next time you watch TV, count the number of commercials, promotions for the news or upcoming programs, or public service announcements that appear during a station break and you will appreciate why clutter is a major concern. A recent study sponsored by the advertising industry found that commercial clutter on television during 2001 reached an all-time high in three dayparts—early morning, daytime, and local news.[9] Nonprogramming time was up to 18:02 minutes per hour in the early morning daypart, 20:57 minutes in daytime, and 17:10 minutes during local news. Network prime time was the least cluttered daypart as the four major networks averaged 16:08 minutes of nonprogram content per hour. With all of these messages competing for our attention, it is easy to understand why the viewer comes away confused or even annoyed and unable to remember or properly identify the product or service advertised.

One cause of clutter is the use of shorter commercials and **split-30s,** 30-second spots in which the advertiser promotes two different products with separate messages. Clutter also results when the networks and individual stations run promotional announcements for their shows, make more time available for commercials, and redistribute time to popular programs. For many years, the amount of time available for commercials was restricted by the Code Authority of the National Association of Broadcasters to 9.5 minutes per hour during prime time and 12 minutes during nonprime time. The Justice Department suspended the code in 1982 on the grounds that it violated antitrust law. At first the networks did not alter their time standards, but in recent years they have increased the number of commercial minutes in their schedules. The networks argue that they must increase commercial inventory or raise their already steep rates. Advertisers and agencies have been pressuring the networks to cut back on the commercials and other sources of clutter.

Limited Viewer Attention When advertisers buy time on a TV program, they are not purchasing guaranteed exposure but rather the opportunity to communicate a message to large numbers of consumers. But there is increasing evidence that the size of the viewing audience shrinks during a commercial break. People leave the room to go to the bathroom or to get something to eat or drink, or they are distracted in some other way during commercials.

Getting consumers to pay attention to commercials has become an even greater challenge in recent years. The increased presence of VCRs and remote controls has led to the problems of zipping and zapping. **Zipping** occurs when customers fast-forward through commercials as they play back a previously recorded program. A study by Nielsen Media Research found that while 80 percent of recorded shows are actually played back, viewers zip past more than half of the commercials.[10] Another study found that most viewers fully or partially zipped commercials when watching a prerecorded program.[11]

Zapping refers to changing channels to avoid commercials. Over three-quarters of homes in the United States now have television sets with remote controls, which enable viewers to switch channels easily. An observational study conducted by John Cronin found as much as a third of program audiences may be lost to electronic zapping when commercials appear.[12] A Nielsen study found that most commercial zapping occurs at the beginning and, to a lesser extent, the end of a program. Zapping at these points is likely to occur because commercial breaks are so long and predictable. Zapping has also been fueled by the emergence of 24-hour continuous-format programming on cable channels such as CNN, MTV, and ESPN. Viewers can switch over for a few news headlines, sports scores, or a music video and then switch back to the program. Research shows that young adults zap more than older adults and that men are more likely to zap than women.[13]

How to inhibit zapping? The networks use certain tactics to hold viewers' attention, such as previews of the next week's show or short closing scenes at the end of a program. Some programs start with action sequences before the opening credits and commercials. A few years ago, Anheuser-Busch began using the Bud Frame, in which the ad frames live coverage of a sporting event. Some advertisers believe that producing

different executions of a campaign theme is one way to maintain viewers' attention. Others think the ultimate way to zap-proof commercials is to produce creative advertising messages that will attract and hold viewers' attention. However, this is easier said than done, as many consumers just do not want to watch commercials. As more viewers gain access to remote controls and the number of channels increases, the zapping problem is likely to continue.

A recent study on zapping among viewers of the five major commercial channels in the Netherlands was conducted by Lex van Meurs.[14] He found that during commercial breaks, 29 percent of the audience stopped watching television or switched away to another channel. This loss of viewers was partially compensated for by an average increase of 7 percent of new viewers who zapped in from another channel. The study also found that people stop viewing TV during a commercial break because they have a reason to stop watching television altogether or they want to find out what is being shown on other channels. The number of people zapping in and out during breaks was not caused by the type of products being advertised or by specific characteristics of the commercials. Another recent study, by Alan Tse and Ruby Lee, found that zapping during commercial breaks was very prevalent among TV viewers in Hong Kong and that zappers recalled fewer of the brands advertised than did nonzappers. They also found that most of the brands that were recalled by zappers were placed near the end of the commercial break, which is when viewers would be likely to be returning to a program.[15]

Advances in technology are likely to continue to lead to changes in television viewing habits, which will impact the number of consumers who watch TV commercials. As discussed in the opening vignette to this chapter, personal video recorders (PVRs) are likely to have a major impact on the way consumers watch TV and their likelihood of viewing commercials. If estimates regarding the penetration rates of PVRs prove to be true, this technology will become a major threat to television's traditional advertising-based business model.[16]

Distrust and Negative Evaluation To many critics of advertising, TV commercials personify everything that is wrong with the industry. Critics often single out TV commercials because of their pervasiveness and the intrusive nature of the medium. Consumers are seen as defenseless against the barrage of TV ads, since they cannot control the transmission of the message and what appears on their screens. Viewers dislike TV advertising when they believe it is offensive, uninformative, or shown too frequently or when they do not like its content.[17] Studies have shown that of the various forms of advertising, distrust is generally the highest for TV commercials.[18] Also, concern has been raised about the effects of TV advertising on specific groups, such as children or the elderly.[19]

Buying Television Time

A number of options are available to advertisers that choose to use TV as part of their media mix. They can purchase time in a variety of program formats that appeal to various types and sizes of audiences. They can purchase time on a national, regional, or local basis. Or they can sponsor an entire program, participate in the sponsorship, or use spot announcements during or between programs.

The purchase of TV advertising time is a highly specialized phase of the advertising business, particularly for large companies spending huge sums of money. Large advertisers that do a lot of TV advertising generally use agency media specialists or specialized media buying services to arrange the media schedule and purchase TV time. Decisions have to be made regarding national or network versus local or spot purchases, selection of specific stations, sponsorship versus participation, different classes of time, and appropriate programs. Local advertisers may not have to deal with the first decision, but they do face all the others.

Network versus Spot

A basic decision for all advertisers is allocating their TV media budgets to network versus local or spot announcements. Most national advertisers use network schedules to provide national coverage and supplement this with regional or local spot purchases to reach markets where additional coverage is desired.

Exhibit 11-3 UPN is one of the newest television networks

Network Advertising A common way advertisers disseminate their messages is by purchasing airtime from a **television network.** A network assembles a series of affiliated local TV stations, or **affiliates,** to which it supplies programming and services. These affiliates, most of which are independently owned, contractually agree to preempt time during specified hours for programming provided by the networks and to carry the national advertising within the program. The networks share the advertising revenue they receive during these time periods with the affiliates. The affiliates are also free to sell commercial time in nonnetwork periods and during station breaks in the preempted periods to both national and local advertisers.

The three traditional major networks are NBC, ABC, and CBS. The Fox Broadcasting Co. broadcasts its programs over a group of affiliated independent stations and has become the fourth major network. A number of Fox's prime-time programs, such as *Malcom in the Middle* and *24,* have become very popular, particularly among the 18-to-49 age group that is often targeted by advertisers. Fox has also become a major player in sports programming with its contracts to broadcast sporting events such as NFL football and Major League Baseball.

Two additional competitors in network television have emerged over the past five years. WB is a network that was originally financed by Time Warner and, following the merger with AOL, is now part of the AOL–Time Warner media conglomerate. WB reaches a national audience through its affiliates, and its programming includes comedy, drama, and talk shows such as *Whose Line Is It Anyway?* and *Third Watch.* The other new network is United Paramount Network (UPN), which has more than 100 affiliates and now has five nights a week of prime-time programming that includes shows such as *Buffy the Vampire Slayer, Star Trek: Enterprise,* and *WWE Smackdown* (Exhibit 11-3). In addition to WB, UPN, and the four major networks, there are also now three Spanish-language networks in the United States. Diversity Perspective 11-2 discusses how these Spanish-language television networks are becoming increasingly popular among advertisers and explains the battle being waged between Univision and Telemundo for Hispanic viewers.

The networks have affiliates throughout the nation for almost complete national coverage. When an advertiser purchases airtime from one of these four national networks, the commercial is transmitted across the nation through the affiliate station network. Network advertising truly represents a mass medium, as the advertiser can broadcast its message simultaneously throughout the country.

A major advantage of network advertising is the simplification of the purchase process. The advertiser has to deal with only one party or media representative to air a commercial nationwide. The networks also offer the most popular programs and generally control prime-time programming. Advertisers interested in reaching huge nationwide audiences generally buy network time during the prime viewing hours of 8 to 11 P.M. eastern time.

The major drawback is the high cost of network time, particularly on the four major networks. Figure 11-2 shows cost estimates for a 30-second spot on the networks' prime-time shows during the fall 2002 television season.[20] Many of the popular prime-time shows charge $200,000 or more for a 30-second spot; the highest-rated shows, like *Friends* and *ER,* can command nearly half a million dollars. Thus, only advertisers with large budgets can afford to use network advertising on a regular basis.

Availability of time can also be a problem as more advertisers turn to network advertising to reach mass markets. Traditionally, most prime-time commercial spots, particularly on the popular shows, are sold during the **up-front market,** a buying period that occurs before the TV season begins. Advertisers hoping to use prime-time network advertising must plan their media schedules and often purchase TV time as much as a year in advance. Demands from large clients who are heavy TV advertisers force the biggest agencies to participate in the up-front market. However, TV time is also purchased during the **scatter market** that runs through the TV season. Some key incentives for buying up front, such as cancellation options and lower prices, are becoming more available in the quarterly scatter market. Network TV can also be purchased on a

DIVERSITY PERSPECTIVE 11-2

Spanish-Speaking TV Stations Go *Mano a Mano*

The television industry has grown accustomed to fierce battles among the major networks for viewers, as ABC, CBS, NBC, and Fox have always gone head-to-head with one another. However, the fiercest battle being waged right now in the television industry is the struggle between the two largest Spanish-language television networks in the United States—Univision and Telemundo. The two companies are fighting to lure the eyeballs of the 35 million Hispanics in the United States, a market segment that is projected to grow by 15 percent by 2010. According to Nielsen Media Research estimates, there are nearly 9 million Hispanic-American television households in the United States and about one-third of them speak no English at home. Language usage has an important impact on their choice of TV programs, and a substantial share of viewing in these homes goes to Spanish-language television. Moreover, Hispanics tend to be younger, have larger families, and watch nearly 10 hours of TV a day, which is about 2 hours more than non-Hispanics watch.

Univision, which is based in Los Angeles, dominates the Hispanic market in the United States, as it commands over 70 percent of the audience watching Spanish-language TV. The company has 26 television stations and 32 broadcast affiliates; it also owns Galavision, which is available to 25 million cable subscribers; 50 percent of Disa Records, the world's second-largest Spanish-language record label; and Univision Online, which recently set up a marketing pact with America Online. In 2002 Univision launched the bilingual network TeleFutura, which has captured 8 percent of the estimated 3 million prime-time Hispanic TV viewers, and purchased Hispanic Broadcasting, the largest chain of Hispanic radio operations in the United States, with 55 stations. Programming on Univision's core network is full of *novelas* or soap operas produced by Mexico's Grupo Televisa; the shows are very popular among Hispanics of Mexican descent, who make up nearly two-thirds of the Latino population in the United States. Its programming also includes soccer matches, variety, news, and music shows.

Univision's big rival is Telemundo, based in Hialeah, Florida, which was purchased by General Electric Co.'s NBC network in late 2001. Telemundo has seen its ratings rise for the past three years with programming that includes *novelas* in prime time and sports, movies, and comedies on the weekend. In 2002 Telemundo entered into a three-year deal to broadcast NBA and WNBA games in Spanish. Since it is part of NBC, Telemundo can promote its shows heavily on the network, which will also give it the Spanish-TV rights to other programs such as the Billboard Latin Music Awards, the Olympics, and Miss Universe contests.

A major part of the war between Univision and Telemundo is being waged in battles for programming. Two months after NBC announced its Telemundo deal, Univision rewrote deals with its two largest suppliers, Televisa and Venezuela's Venesision, so that it would have exclusive rights to their programming. Univision also signed an agreement with the Brazilian producers of Telemundo's hottest show, *Betty La Fea* ("Betty the Ugly"), which gives it the rights to the show's sequel. Univision is also counting on Telefutura to help it reach a different audience—the 60 percent of Hispanics in the United States who are tuned to English-language channels. To pull in this audience, Telefutura will air sports and movies popular with men against the prime-time soaps on Univision and Telemundo. Univision is even advertising the new network in

English, placing radio spots on general-market stations to promote Telefutura among bilingual Hispanics in New York and Los Angeles.

Univision and Telemundo are fighting over the fastest-growing media market in the United States: Ad spending on Hispanic television is growing nearly 10 percent a year, while advertising revenues in mainstream network television have shown little or no increases. A major reason for this growth is that major advertisers such as Sears, Kmart, Miller Brewing Co., Ford, McDonald's, and many others recognize the importance of the Hispanic market and are developing commercials specifically for this market. These companies also recognize that Spanish-language TV networks are the best means of reaching this fast-growing market with their television spots. Univision already has surpassed the major networks in several big-city markets, as its stations in Los Angeles, New York, Miami, Houston, and Dallas had higher prime-time ratings in the coveted 18-to-34 age category than did their ABC, CBS, NBC, and Fox counterparts during a recent ratings period.

While Univision and Telemundo are likely to continue their battle for Hispanic TV viewers, it appears there is plenty of room for both networks to continue to grow. However, they are likely to face competition from other media companies, such as ESPN. Owned by Disney, ESPN is launching a 24-hour, Spanish-language sports cable network in late 2003. The ESPN Deportes' programming will include Major League and Latin American baseball, NBA games, volleyball, soccer, and a Spanish version of ESPN's signature show, *Sportscenter.*

Sources: Barry Jackson, "ESPN to Launch Spanish-Language Network," *The Miami Herald,* Sept. 25, 2002, p. 1; Ronald Grover and Aixa M. Pascual, "*Mana a Mano* in Hispanic TV," *BusinessWeek,* Sept. 9, 2002, p. 122; Eduardo Porter, "Univision Seeks a Bigger Pie for Spanish TV," *The Wall Street Journal,* Jan. 14, 2002, pp. B1, 3.

Figure 11-2 What TV shows cost: estimated price of a 30-second spot on the major networks: Fall 2002

SUNDAY 7 p.m. (ET) | 8 p.m. | 9 p.m. | 10 p.m.

abc	Wonderful World of Disney $107,127				Alias $144,890	The Practice $180,106
CBS	60 Minutes $90,000		Bram and Alice $87,133	Becker $107,115	CBS Sunday Movie $79,471	
NBC	Dateline $63,950		American Dreams $108,288		Law & Order: Criminal Intent $124,889	Boomtown $114,729
FOX	Futurama $90,100	Oliver Beene $122,780	Simpsons $248,300	King of the Hill $212,500	Malcolm $196,725	The Grubbs $113,817	No programming
WB	Gilmore Girls: Beginnings $51,295		Charmed $48,672		Angel $55,609	No programming

MONDAY 8 p.m. | 9 p.m. | 10 p.m.

abc	Drew Carey $84,377	Whose Line $64,594	Monday Night Football $298,000		
CBS	King/Queens $168,425	Yes, Dear $165,801	Raymond $301,640	Standing $186,100	CSI: Miami $164,870
NBC	Fear Factor $100,833		Third Watch $126,270		Crossing Jordan $122,960
FOX	Boston Public $146,887		Girls Club $178,400		No programming
WB	7th Heaven $83,752		Everwood $72,204		No programming
UPN	The Parkers $39,267	One on One $40,456	Girlfriends $39,300	Half & Half $38,006	No programming

TUESDAY 8 p.m. | 9 p.m. | 10 p.m.

abc	8 Simple $144,438	Jim $137,750	Bonnie $121,222	Less/Perfect $141,679	NYPD Blue $157,249
CBS	JAG $97,355		The Guardian $82,239		Judging Amy $118,857
NBC	In-Laws $96,500	Shoot Me $115,575	Frasier $252,067	Hidden Hills $172,854	Dateline NBC $106,817
FOX	'70s Show $164,950	Grounded $136,215	24 $184,550		No programming
WB	Gilmore Girls $82,287		Smallville $111,439		No programming
UPN	Buffy the Vampire Slayer $59,032		Haunted $28,400		No programming

WED. 8 p.m. | 9 p.m. | 10 p.m.

abc	My Wife $156,257	G. Lopez $136,594	The Bachelor II $136,334		MDs $102,019
CBS	60 Minutes II $68,322		Amazing Race $96,112		Presidio Med $61,457
NBC	Ed $99,733		West Wing $282,248		Law & Order $266,220
FOX	Bernie Mac $166,375	Cedric $117,213	Fastlane $133,271		No programming
WB	Dawson's Creek $69,657		Birds of Prey $57,420		No programming
UPN	Enterprise $71,383		Twilight Zone $28,613		No programming

THURSDAY 8 p.m. | 9 p.m. | 10 p.m.

abc	Dinotopia $60,038		Push, Nevada $95,812		Primetime $82,199
CBS	Survivor $418,750		CSI $280,043		Without a Trace $115,298
NBC	Friends $455,700	Scrubs $294,667	Will & Grace $376,617	Good Morn'g $279,813	ER $438,514
FOX	30 Secs* $50,125	The Marks* $64,750	Septuplets* $85,500		No programming
WB	FamilyAffair $27,537	Do Over $33,430	J. Kennedy $35,964	Off Centre $40,379	No programming
UPN	WWE Smackdown $30,500				No programming

FRIDAY 8 p.m. | 9 p.m. | 10 p.m.

abc	Funniest Home Videos $63,460		That Was Then $65,369		20/20 $72,118
CBS	48 Hours $37,840		Hack $49,320		RHD/LA $43,620
NBC	Providence $96,160		Dateline $79,608		Law & Order: SVU $114,320
FOX	Firefly $81,000		John Doe $102,350		No programming
WB	What I Like $49,766	Sabrina $45,112	Reba $48,856	Tucson $46,865	No programming
UPN	UPN Movie Friday $12,871				No programming

SATURDAY 8 p.m. | 9 p.m. | 10 p.m.

abc	ABC Big Picture Show $63,069				
CBS	Touched by an Angel $42,342		The District $64,580		The Agency $55,228
NBC	NBC Saturday Movie $61,892				
FOX	Cops $55,917	Cops $61,892	AMW: America Fights Back $61,780		No programming

regional basis, so an advertiser's message can be aired in certain sections of the country with one media purchase.

Spot and Local Advertising

Spot advertising refers to commercials shown on local TV stations, with time negotiated and purchased directly from the individual stations. All nonnetwork advertising done by a national advertiser is known as **national spot advertising;** airtime sold to local firms such as retailers, restaurants, banks, and auto dealers is known as **local advertising.** Local advertisers want media whose coverage is limited to the geographic markets in which they do business. This may be difficult to accomplish with TV, but many local businesses are large enough to make efficient use of TV advertising.

Spot advertising offers the national advertiser flexibility in adjusting to local market conditions. The advertiser can concentrate commercials in areas where market potential is greatest or where additional support is needed. This appeals to advertisers with uneven distribution or limited advertising budgets, as well as those interested in test marketing or introducing a product in limited market areas. National advertisers often use spot television advertising through local retailers or dealers as part of their cooperative advertising programs and to provide local dealer support.

A major problem for national advertisers is that spot advertising can be more difficult to acquire, since the time must be purchased from a number of local stations. Moreover, there are more variations in the pricing policies and discount structure of individual stations than of the networks. However, this problem has been reduced somewhat by the use of **station reps,** individuals who act as sales representatives for a number of local stations in dealings with national advertisers.

Spot ads are subject to more commercial clutter, since local stations can sell time on network-originated shows only during station breaks between programs, except when network advertisers have not purchased all the available time. Viewership generally declines during station breaks, as people may leave the room, zap to another channel, attend to other tasks, or stop watching TV.

While spot advertising is mostly confined to station breaks between programs on network-originated shows, local stations sell time on their own programs, which consist of news, movies, syndicated shows, or locally originated programs. Most cities have independent stations that spot advertisers use. Local advertisers find the independent stations attractive because they generally have lower rates than the major network affiliates.

The decision facing most national advertisers is how to combine network and spot advertising to make effective use of their TV advertising budget. Another factor that makes spot advertising attractive to national advertisers is the growth in syndication.

Syndication

Advertisers may also reach TV viewers by advertising on **syndicated programs,** shows that are sold or distributed on a station-by-station, market-by-market basis. A syndicator seeks to sell its program to one station in every market. There are several types of syndicated programming. *Off-network syndication* refers to reruns of network shows that are bought by individual stations. Shows that are popular in off-network syndication include *Seinfeld, Everybody Loves Raymond,* and *Friends.* The FCC prime-time access rule forbids large-market network affiliates from carrying these shows from 7 to 8 P.M., but independent stations are not affected by this restriction. A show must have a minimum number of episodes before it is eligible for syndication, and there are limits on network involvement in the financing or production of syndicated shows.

Off-network syndication shows are very important to local stations because they provide quality programming with an established audience. The syndication market is also very important to the studios that produce programs and sell them to the networks. Most prime-time network shows initially lose money for the studios, since the licensing fee paid by the networks does not cover production costs. Over four years (the time it takes to produce the 88 episodes needed to break into syndication), half-hour situation comedies often run up a deficit of millions, and losses on a one-hour drama show are even higher. However, the producers recoup their money when they sell the show to syndication.

First-run syndication refers to shows produced specifically for the syndication market. The first-run syndication market is made up of a variety of shows, including some that did not make it as network shows. Examples of popular first-run syndication shows include talk shows such as *Live with Regis & Kelly* and *The Jerry Springer Show,* entertainment shows such as *Inside Edition* and *Entertainment Tonight,* and dramas such as *VIP.*

Advertiser-supported or *barter syndication* is the practice of selling shows to stations in return for a portion of the commercial time in the show, rather than (or in addition to) cash. The commercial time from all stations carrying the show is packaged into national units and sold to national advertisers. The station sells the remaining time to local and spot advertisers. Both off-network and first-run syndicated programs are offered through barter syndication. Usually, more than half of the advertising time is presold, and the remainder is available for sale by the local advertiser. Barter syndication allows national advertisers to participate in the syndication market with the convenience of a network-type media buy, while local stations get free programming and can sell the remainder of the time to local or spot advertisers. Recently, the straight barter deal has given way to more barter/cash arrangements, where the station pays for a program at a reduced rate and accepts a number of preplaced bartered ads. Top-rated barter syndicated programs include *Wheel of Fortune, Jeopardy,* and *The Oprah Winfrey Show.*

Syndication now accounts for more than a third of the national broadcast audience and has become a very big business, generating ad revenue comparable to any of the big-three networks. Syndicated shows have become more popular than network shows in certain dayparts, such as daytime, early prime time, and late fringe. In some markets, syndicated shows like *Wheel of Fortune* draw a larger audience than the network news.

Many national advertisers use syndicated shows to broaden their reach, save money, and target certain audiences. For example, off-network syndication shows such as *Friends, Seinfeld,* and *X-Files* are popular with advertisers because they reach the highly sought after, and often difficult to reach, young-adult audience (age 18 to 34) and are about 15 to 20 percent lower on a cost-per-thousand basis than network shows.[21] Figure 11-3 shows the top 10 syndicated programs in 2002.

Syndication has certain disadvantages, such as more commercial time and thus more clutter. The audience for syndicated shows is often older and more rural, and syndicators do not supply as much research information as the networks do. Syndication also creates more problems for media buyers, since a syndicated show may not be seen in a particular market or may be aired during an undesirable time period. Thus, media buyers have to look at each market and check airtimes and other factors to put together a syndication schedule.

Methods of Buying Time

In addition to deciding whether to use network versus spot advertising, advertisers must decide whether to sponsor an entire program, participate in a program, or use spot announcements between programs. Sponsorship of a program and participations

Figure 11-3 Top 10 regularly scheduled syndicated programs 2001–2002 Season

Rank	Program	Rating (%)
1	Wheel of Fortune	9.5
2	Jeopardy	8.0
3	Friends	6.9
4	Seinfeld	6.3
5	Entertainment Tonight	6.1
6	ESPN NFL Regular Season	5.9
7	Judge Judy	5.8
8	Oprah Winfrey Show	5.8
9	Everybody Loves Raymond	5.6
10	Seinfeld (weekend)	5.0

Source: Nielsen Media Research.

are available on either a network or a local market basis, whereas spot announcements are available only from local stations.

Sponsorship Under a **sponsorship** arrangement, an advertiser assumes responsibility for the production and usually the content of the program as well as the advertising that appears within it. In the early days of TV, most programs were produced and sponsored by corporations and were identified by their name, for example, *Texaco Star Theater* and *The Colgate Comedy Hour.* Today most shows are produced by either the networks or independent production companies that sell them to a network.

Some companies are becoming more involved in the production business. For example, Procter & Gamble, which has been producing soap operas since 1950, entered into an agreement with Paramount Television Groups to develop shows for network TV and first-run syndication. A consortium of nine major advertisers—AT&T, Campbell Soup, General Motors, Coca-Cola, Sears, McDonald's, Clorox, Coors, and Reebok—joined Television Production Partners, a new venture to develop movies, specials, and limited-run series. Each company chooses which programs it wants to be involved with and takes a portion of the commercial spots.[22]

Several major companies have been sponsoring special programs for many years, such as the Kraft Masterpiece Theater and Hallmark Hall of Fame dramatic series. In 1994 Hallmark acquired RHI Entertainment Inc., the company that produces its wholesome Hall of Fame productions as well as TV miniseries and movies. Sole sponsorship of programs is usually limited to specials and has been declining. However, some companies, including Ford, AT&T, General Electric, IBM, and Chrysler, do still use program sponsorships occasionally.

A company might choose to sponsor a program for several reasons. Sponsorship allows the firm to capitalize on the prestige of a high-quality program, enhancing the image of the company and its products. For example, the Ford Motor Company received a great deal of favorable publicity when it sponsored the commercial-free television debut of the Holocaust movie *Schindler's List.* Companies also sponsor programs to gain more control over the shows carrying their commercials. For example, Wendy's International has been involved in sponsorship of family-oriented programs.

Another reason is that the sponsor has control over the number, placement, and content of its commercials. Commercials can be of any length as long as the total amount of commercial time does not exceed network or station regulations. Advertisers introducing a new product line often sponsor a program and run commercials that are several minutes long to introduce and explain the product. IBM used this strategy to introduce new generations of products. While these factors make sponsorship attractive to some companies, the high costs of sole sponsorship limit this option to large firms. Most commercial time is purchased through other methods, such as participations.

Participations Most advertisers either cannot afford the costs of sponsorship or want greater flexibility than sole sponsorship permits. Nearly 90 percent of network advertising time is sold as **participations,** with several advertisers buying commercial time or spots on a particular program. An advertiser can participate in a certain program once or several times on a regular or irregular basis. Participating advertisers have no financial responsibility for production of the program; this is assumed by the network or individual station that sells and controls the commercial time.

There are several advantages to participations. First, the advertiser has no long-term commitment to a program, and expenditures can be adjusted to buy whatever number of participation spots fits within the budget. This is particularly important to small advertisers with a limited budget. The second advantage is that the TV budget can be spread over a number of programs, thereby providing for greater reach in the media schedule.

The disadvantage of participations is that the advertiser has little control over the placement of ads, and there may also be problems with availability. Preference is given to advertisers willing to commit to numerous spots, and the firm trying to buy single spots in more than one program may find that time is unavailable in certain shows, especially during prime time.

Spot Announcements As discussed earlier, spot announcements are bought from the local stations and generally appear during time periods adjacent to network programs (hence the term **adjacencies**), rather than within them. Spot announcements are most often used by purely local advertisers but are also bought by companies with no network schedule (because of spotty or limited distribution) and by large advertisers that use both network and spot advertising.

Selecting Time Periods and Programs

Another consideration in buying TV time is selecting the right period and program for the advertiser's commercial messages. The cost of TV advertising time varies depending on the time of day and the particular program, since audience size varies as a function of these two factors. TV time periods are divided into **dayparts,** which are specific segments of a broadcast day.

The time segments that make up the programming day vary from station to station. However, a typical classification of dayparts for a weekday is shown in Figure 11-4. The various daypart segments attract different audiences in both size and nature, so advertising rates vary accordingly. Prime time draws the largest audiences, with 8:30 to 9 P.M. being the most watched half-hour time period and Sunday the most popular night for television. Since firms that advertise during prime time must pay premium rates, this daypart is dominated by the large national advertisers.

The various dayparts are important to advertisers since they attract different demographic groups. For example, daytime TV generally attracts women; early morning attracts women and children. The late-fringe (late-night) daypart period has become popular among advertisers trying to reach young adults who tune in to *The Late Show with David Letterman* on CBS and NBC's *The Tonight Show with Jay Leno.* Audience size and demographic composition also vary depending on the type of program. Situation comedies attract the largest prime-time audiences, with women 18 to 34 comprising the greatest segment of the audience. Feature films rank second, followed by general drama shows. Women 55 and older are the largest audience segment for these programs.

Cable Television

The Growth of Cable Perhaps the most significant development in the broadcast media has been the expansion of **cable television.** Cable, or CATV (community antenna television), which delivers TV signals through fiber or coaxial wire rather than the airways, was developed to provide reception to remote areas that couldn't receive broadcast signals. Cable then expanded to metropolitan areas and grew rapidly due to the improved reception and wider selection of stations it offered subscribers. Cable has experienced substantial growth during the past two decades. In 1975, only 13 percent of TV households had cable. By 2002, cable penetration reached 68 percent of the nation's 106 million households.[23] Cable programming also reaches another 10 percent of U.S. homes through alternative delivery systems such as direct broadcast satellite (DBS).

Cable subscribers pay a monthly fee for which they receive an average of more than 60 channels, including the local network affiliates and independent stations, various

Figure 11-4 Common television dayparts

Morning	7:00 A.M.–9:00 A.M., Monday through Friday
Daytime	9:00 A.M.–4:30 P.M., Monday through Friday
Early fringe	4:30 P.M.–7:30 P.M., Monday through Friday
Prime-time access	7:30 P.M.–8:00 P.M., Sunday through Saturday
Prime time	8:00 P.M.–11:00 P.M., Monday through Saturday, and 7:00 P.M.–11:00 P.M., Sunday
Late news	11:00–11:30 P.M., Monday through Friday
Late fringe	11:30–1:00 A.M., Monday through Friday

cable networks, superstations, and local cable system channels. Cable networks and channels have a dual revenue stream; they are supported by both subscriber fees and ad revenue. Cable operators also offer programming that is not supported by commercial sponsorship and is available only to households willing to pay a fee beyond the monthly subscription charge. These premium channels include HBO, Showtime, and The Movie Channel.

Cable TV broadens the program options available to the viewer as well as the advertiser by offering specialty channels, including all-news, pop music, country music, sports, weather, educational, and cultural channels as well as children's programming. Figure 11-5 shows the most popular cable channels along with the types of programming they carry. Many cable systems also carry **superstations,** independent

Figure 11-5 Major cable networks

Network	Type of Programming
ABC Family	Family/general/original
A&E Network	Biographies/dramas/movies/documentaries
American Movie Classics	Movies/documentaries
Animal Planet	Wildlife and nature documentaries/adventure/children's entertainment
BBC America	Drama/comedy/news/arts and lifestyle documentaries
BET Networks	Entertainment/information for African Americans
BET Jazz	Jazz music/documentaries/concerts
Cartoon Network	Cartoons
CMT: Country Music Television	Country music video/concert/specials
CNBC	Financial and business news/interviews and discussions
CNN	News/information
CNN en Espanol	News/information (Spanish language)
CNN Headline News	News/information
CNN fn	Financial and business news
CNN Sports Illustrated	Sports
Comedy Central	Comedy programs/original
Court TV	Court/legal
Discovery Channel	Family/health/technology/science
Discovery Health Channel	Health/medical
E! Entertainment Television	Entertainment/celebrities/pop culture
ESPN	Sports/specials/events
ESPN 2	Sports
ESPN Sports Classics	Sports history/biographies
ESPN Deportes	Sports (Spanish language)
ESPNEWS	Sports news
Food Network	Food/cooking/entertainment
FOX News Channel	News/information
FOX Sports Net	Sports
FX Networks	Entertainment/original programs
Galavision	Programming/entertainment for Hispanics
Game Show Network	Game shows
Golf Channel	Golf
History Channel	Historical documentaries/movies
Home & Garden Television	Decorating/gardening
Lifetime Television	News/information/women's interests
MSNBC	News/information
MTV: Music Television	Music/videos/documentaries
National Geographic Channel	Adventure/exploration/science/culture
Nickelodeon/Nick at Nite	Youth interest/cartoons/comedy/game shows
Oxygen	Movies/news/comedy/women's interests
SCI FI Channel	Science fiction
TBS	Entertainment/movies/sports
TLC (Learning Channel)	Science/history/adventure/behavior
TNN: The National Network	Pop culture/movies/sports/drama
TNT	Movies/general entertainment/sports
Travel Channel	Travel information
USA Network	Entertainment/movies/sports
VH1	Music videos/movies/concerts/documentaries
Weather Channel	Weather
WGN	Entertainment/sports/movies

local stations that send their signals nationally via satellite to cable operators to make their programs available to subscribers. Programming on superstations such as TBS and WGN generally consists of sports, movies, and reruns of network shows (Exhibit 11-4). The superstations do carry national advertising and are a relatively inexpensive option for cable households across the country.

Cable has had a considerable influence on the nature of television as an advertising medium. First, the expanded viewing options have led to considerable audience fragmentation. Much of the growth in cable audiences has come at the expense of the three major networks. Cable channels now have about 40 percent of the prime-time viewing audience, while the total share of the three networks has declined to around 50 percent. Many cable stations have become very popular among consumers, leading advertisers to reevaluate their media plans and the prices they are willing to pay for network and spot commercials on network affiliate stations. The networks, recognizing the growing popularity of cable, have become involved with the cable industry. ABC purchased ESPN, while NBC started two cable channels in the early 90s—the Consumer News and Business Channel (CNBC) and Sports Channel America—and in 1996 entered in a joint venture with Microsoft to launch MSNBC, a 24-hour news channel.[24]

Advertising on Cable Cable advertising revenues have increased steadily since the mid-1980s and exceeded $12 billion in 2002. Much of this growth has come from advertising on the national cable networks such as CNN, ESPN, USA, and MTV.

Exhibit 11-4 WGN is one of the top superstations

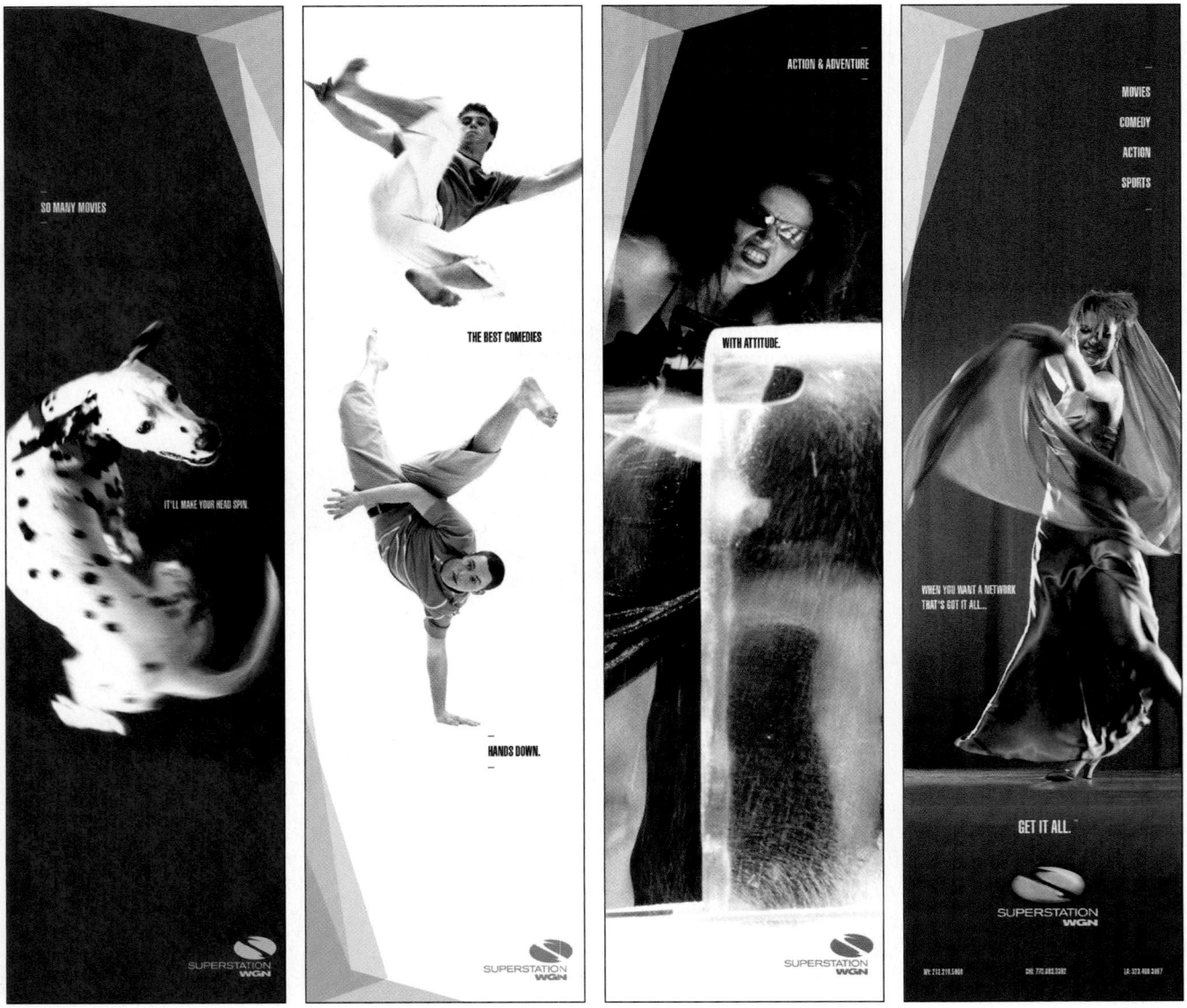

However, many national advertisers have been shifting some of their advertising budgets to spot cable and purchasing through local operators as well as the national cable networks. Over the past four years, spot cable revenues have averaged 20 percent annual growth, reaching nearly $33 billion in 2002.

Like broadcast TV, cable time can be purchased on a national, regional, or local (spot) level. Many large marketers advertise on cable networks to reach large numbers of viewers across the country with a single media buy. Regional advertising on cable is available primarily through sports and news channels that cover a certain geographic area.

Many national advertisers are turning to spot advertising on local cable systems to reach specific geographic markets. Spot cable affords them more precision in reaching specific markets, and they can save money by using a number of small, targeted media purchases rather than making one network buy. The growth in spot cable advertising is also being facilitated by the use of **interconnects,** where a number of cable systems in a geographic area are joined for advertising purposes. These interconnects increase the size of the audience an advertiser can reach with a spot cable buy. For example, Chicago Cable Interconnect reaches more than 1.7 million subscribers in the greater Chicago metropolitan area; the ADLINK Digital Interconnect delivers 3 million cable subscribers in Los Angeles and four surrounding counties. New York Interconnect reaches 3.6 million households in the largest market area in the country and offers advertisers 31 different cable networks (Exhibit 11-5). More sophisticated interconnect systems are developing that will pool large numbers of cable systems and allow spot advertisers to reach more viewers. These new systems will also allow local advertisers to make more selective cable buys, since they can purchase the entire interconnect or one of several zones within the system.

Exhibit 11-5 New York Interconnect promotes its targeting potential to advertisers

While spot cable is becoming very popular among national advertisers, it has some of the same problems as spot advertising on broadcast TV. The purchasing process is very complicated and time-consuming; media buyers must contact hundreds of cable systems to put together a media schedule consisting of spot cable buys. Local cable systems also do not provide advertisers with strong support or much information on demographics, lifestyle, or viewership patterns.

Advantages of Cable

Cable TV has experienced tremendous growth as an advertising medium because it has some important advantages. A primary one is selectivity. Cable subscribers tend to be younger, more affluent, and better educated than nonsubscribers and have greater purchasing power. Moreover, the specialized programming on the various cable networks reaches very specific target markets.

Many advertisers have turned to cable because of the opportunities it offers for **narrowcasting,** or reaching very specialized markets. For example, MTV is used by advertisers in the United States and many other countries to reach teenagers and young adults. CNBC is now the worldwide leader in business news and reaches a highly educated and affluent audience (Exhibit 11-6). ESPN has become synonymous with sports and is very popular among advertisers who want to target men of all ages. As discussed in IMC Perspective 11-3, ESPN has become more than just a 24-hour sports channel and is changing its strategy to attract a broader audience.

Exhibit 11-6 CNBC has become the leader in business news and has a very affluent viewing audience

Advertisers are also interested in cable because of its low cost and flexibility. Advertising rates on cable programs are much lower than those for the shows on the major networks. Advertising time on network shows can cost two to three times as much on a cost-per-thousand basis in some time periods.[25] Spot advertising is also considerably cheaper on most cable stations, while local cable is the most affordable television advertising vehicle available. This makes TV a much more viable media option for smaller advertisers with limited budgets and those interested in targeting their commercials to a well-defined target audience. Also,

IMC PERSPECTIVE 11-3

ESPN—More "E" and Less "S"?

For many years, TV sports programming consisted primarily of football, baseball, and to a lesser extent basketball shown primarily on weekends on network television. When ESPN, the first cable network devoted entirely to sports programming, was launched in 1979, the critics declared that "all the good sports are already on the three networks." They ridiculed the network for broadcasting sports such as stock-car racing, which was described as "two hours of left turns." However, no one is laughing at ESPN today. It is one of the top cable networks, reaching 86 million homes in the United States—10 million more than its closest competitor. Its signature show, *SportsCenter*—a one-hour sports news show that is aired numerous times throughout the day and night—is emblematic of the entire network and has helped position ESPN as the place for the ultimate sports fan, not just another cable channel showing sports. An award-winning advertising campaign consisting of humorous spots that purport to give viewers a behind-the-scenes look at *SportsCenter* has helped contribute to the popularity and image of the show and create a brand identity that has carried over to the entire network.

ESPN (which originally was an acronym for "Entertainment and Sports Program Network") is much more than the number-one cable network. It is an entire brand that has become synonymous with sports in America as well as many other countries. It has expanded beyond its stalwart network, as the ESPN franchise now includes six other U.S. channels, a radio network, a popular website, *ESPN The Magazine,* and eight ESPN Zone restaurants. Its latest venture is an interactive channel on DirecTV that allows viewers to grab news with a flick of the remote, and its wireless unit is charging users for scores and news it delivers to cell phones, personal digital assistants, and even scrolling screens on billboards and atop taxicabs.

In addition to being very popular among sports fans, ESPN has become one of Madison Avenue's favorites, as the network is particularly good at delivering large numbers of young, male sports fans, a group that is difficult to reach but highly coveted by marketers. However, ESPN now finds itself among cable TV's once-hot but maturing brands such as MTV and CNN. Its prime-time viewership among the coveted audience of males 18 to 49 was down by 14 percent in the past year. Its main rival, Fox Sports net, which puts more emphasis on local and regional sports, is up by 12 percent among the same demographic group. The ratings slide isn't the only problem facing the company. ESPN charges cable and satellite operators $1.50 per subscriber per month for its programming, and its contracts call for 20 percent-a-year increases. These fees are among the highest in the cable industry and have created long-simmering resentment from many cable and satellite operators. They also argue that ESPN's parent company, the Walt Disney Co., uses the sports network aggressively in negotiations to make cable operators carry Disney's other, less watched channels.

ESPN management has recognized that the 23-year-old sports network needs to make some changes to sustain its growth and continue as the preeminent sports network. In early 2002 ESPN, along with the ABC television network, which is also owned by Disney, outbid NBC for the rights to televise National Basketball Association games. The $2.4 billion deal marks the first time a cable player has grabbed a major sports contract from the broadcast networks. Although expensive, ABC and ESPN feel the deal will work financially because they will be able to broadcast as many as 75 regular-season games, mostly on ESPN and ESPN 2, and sell more ads.

ESPN is also making a major change in its strategy by entering another new arena: original programming, which includes variety shows, made-for-TV movies, reality shows, and game shows. The first movie produced by ESPN was *A Season on the Brink: A Year with Bob Knight and the Indiana Hoosiers,* based on the book by John Feinstein, which aired in March 2002. Later that year the network launched a late-night sports variety show hosted by actor Jay Mohr and a new reality game show, *Beg, Borrow and Deal,* which follows players as they head across the country in a

marathon of athletic events. Another reality show is planned called *The Life,* which is based on a feature in *ESPN The Magazine* and will show viewers how rich and famous athletes manage to spend all that money.

Analysts explain these recent moves by noting that the Walt Disney Company didn't just buy a 24-hour sports cable network when it bought ESPN as part of a package deal for ABC/Capital Cities back in 1995. Disney bought a valuable brand, out of which it wants to squeeze as much value as possible. The ESPN-produced programs will have secondary markets on other channels owned by Disney, and they may also help expand the viewing audience beyond the core sports junkie. However, some media experts argue that ESPN is taking a big risk and may alienate its core viewers in an effort to get higher ratings. ESPN's success may ultimately depend on how elastic the brand is to viewers and how far the network can stretch the definition of "sports coverage." It will be interesting to see what happens as the "E" in ESPN steps forward.

Sources: Tom Lowry, "ESPN's Full-Court Press," *BusinessWeek,* Feb. 11, 2002, pp. 60–61; Joseph Guinto "Against the Grain," *Southwest Airlines Spirit,* Feb. 2002, pp. 67–70.

cable advertisers generally do not have to make the large up-front commitments, which may be as much as a year in advance, the networks require.

The low costs of cable make it a very popular advertising medium among local advertisers. Car dealers, furniture stores, restaurants, and many other merchants are switching advertising spending from traditional media such as radio, newspapers, and even magazines to take advantage of the low rates of local cable channels. Local cable advertising is one of the fastest-growing segments of the advertising market, and cable systems are increasing the percentage of revenue they earn from local advertising.

Limitations of Cable While cable has become increasingly popular among national, regional, and local advertisers, it still has a number of drawbacks. One major problem is that cable is overshadowed by the major networks, as households with basic cable service still watch considerably more network and syndicated programming than cable shows. This stems from the fact that cable generally has less desirable programming than broadcast TV.

Another drawback of cable is audience fragmentation. Although cable's share of the TV viewing audience has increased significantly, the viewers are spread out among the large number of channels available to cable subscribers. The number of viewers who watch any one cable channel is generally quite low. Even MTV, ESPN, and CNN have prime-time ratings of only about 1 or 2. The large number of cable stations has fragmented audiences and made buying procedures more difficult, since numerous stations must be contacted to reach the majority of the cable audience in a market. There are also problems with the quality and availability of local ratings for cable stations as well as research on audience characteristics.

Cable also still lacks total penetration, especially in the major markets. As of 2002, cable penetration was 74 percent in the New York City designated market area and 65 percent in Los Angeles and Chicago. While cable programming now penetrates 78 percent of all U.S. television households, this still means that nearly a quarter of the market cannot be reached by advertising on cable.

The Future of Cable Cable TV should continue to experience strong growth as its audience share increases and advertisers spend more money to reach cable viewers. However, the cable industry faces several challenges: increases in the number of channels, leading to fragmentation of the audience, changes in government regulations, and competition in the programming distribution business from other telecommunications companies and direct broadcast satellite services. Advances in technology such as digital video compression and fiber optics, coupled with massive investments in system upgrades, are making it possible for cable operators to offer more channels and thus subject existing cable channels to greater competition. In 2002, over 42 million U.S. homes could receive at least 54 channels. An average 95 percent of cable subscribers could receive 30 channels or more. Increases in the number of channels available lead to further fragmentation of the cable audience and make it more difficult for cable networks to charge the ad rates needed to finance original programming. Some

of the growth in cable channels will come from **multiplexing,** or transmitting multiple channels from one network. Several major cable networks, including ESPN, VH1, and the Discovery Channel, own several channels.

The cable industry has also been affected by changes in government regulation. In the early 90s, concerns over poor service and high rates led to a revolt against the cable industry. As a result, Congress passed legislation in 1993 that rolled back the provisions of the Cable Television Act of 1984, allowed local governments to regulate basic cable rates, and forced cable operators to pay licensing fees for local broadcast programming they used to retransmit for free. The Telecommunications Act of 1996 allows local phone companies to offer cable service. However, as part of this act, federal regulation of the cable industry expired on April 1, 1999, and cable rates are now deregulated.[26]

One of the biggest threats facing the cable industry is competition from **direct broadcast satellite (DBS) services,** which use a system whereby TV and radio programs are sent directly from a satellite to homes equipped with a small dish. DBS companies such as DirecTV and EchoStar now have nearly 10 million subscribers, many of whom have come to them at the expense of cable companies. DBS companies have been aggressively marketing their service, superior picture quality, and greater channel choice as subscribers receive as many as 200 channels that include news, music, and sports in crisp, digital video and CD-quality sound. A major competitive restriction to DBS services was removed in late 1999 when the federal government passed legislation allowing satellite TV companies to carry local broadcast signals in most major markets.[27]

The future of cable as an advertising medium will ultimately depend on the size and quality of the audiences cable stations can reach with their programs. This in turn will depend on cable's ability to offer programs that attract viewers and subscribers. Cable's image as a stepchild in program development and acquisition has changed. Cable networks such as VH1, E!, TBS, and others have been creating original films, documentaries, and other programs that draw significant ratings. Networks like A&E, the Discovery Channel, and the Learning Channel provide outstanding cultural and educational programming. IMC Perspective 11-4 discusses how MTV recently created one of the most popular entertainment shows ever shown on cable—*The Osbournes.*

Cable TV will continue to be a popular source of sports programming and is very important to advertisers interested in reaching the male market. There are over 11 regional cable sports networks, and with companies such as Fox Sports, advertisers can buy multiple regions with one media buy. Cable networks are also paying large sums for the rights to sports programming. Deals by ESPN for exclusive Sunday night coverage of National Football League and Major League Baseball games, along with its new six-year deal to broadcast National Basketball Association games, have proved that cable networks can compete with the major networks in a sports bidding war.[28]

As cable penetration increases, its programming improves, and more advertisers discover its efficiency and ability to reach targeted market segments, cable's popularity as an advertising medium should continue to grow. Many agencies have developed specialists to examine the use of cable in their clients' media schedules. Cable networks are also looking to international markets as a source of future growth. Both ESPN and MTV have expanded into South America, Europe, and Asia, while TV viewers throughout the world tune to CNN International for news (Exhibit 11-7).

Exhibit 11-7 CNN International is the authoritative source for news throughout the world

Measuring the TV Audience

One of the most important considerations in TV advertising is the size and composition of the viewing audience. Audience measurement is critical to advertisers as well as to the networks and stations. Advertisers want to know the size and characteristics of the audience they are reaching when they purchase time on a particular program. And since the rates they pay are a function of audience size, advertisers want to be sure audience measurements are accurate.

IMC PERSPECTIVE 11-4

The Osbournes Gives New Meaning to Reality TV

In recent years reality shows have become some of the most popular programs on television. Shows such as *Survivor, Fear Factor, The Bachelor, Temptation Island,* and *American Idol: The Search for a Superstar* have been among the most popular of the reality genre and have spawned a slew of copycats. However, many of these shows might never have come about had not the path been blazed nearly a decade earlier by MTV's real-life soap opera *The Real World,* which has been running for 11 years and remains a staple of the music channel's lineup. The series single-handedly created the 24/7, "soap-u-mentary" style of most contemporary reality series.

A decade later MTV has created yet another hit reality show, *The Osbournes,* which is a no-holds-barred look at the real life of aging British rock star Ozzy Osbourne and his family as they go about their daily routine. They show has been described as a bizarre, unscripted, profanity-laced family comedy that gives new meaning to "reality TV." Osbourne plays himself—a tattoo-covered hellion-turned-slipper-wearing dad with world-weary teenagers and a wife who is also his manager. The show is set in Osbourne's Beverly Hills mansion, which is furnished in a style that might be termed "kinky robber baron": plush couches, antique carpets, crucifixes galore, totems of the occult, and a menagerie of rebellious house pets.

The Osbournes premiered in spring 2002 and, after only 10 episodes, became a bona fide pop cultural sensation, as well as MTV's top-rated series ever and one of the most watched entertainment shows on cable. Nearly 8 million people have been tuning in to the show when it airs, and they aren't just MTV's core audience of 12- to 24-year-olds. *The Osbournes* appeals to a broader demographic of 18- to 34-year-olds and beyond and spans generations in many households, as teens often find themselves laughing at the family's antics with their baby-boomer parents. Television critics attribute the show's success to the quirky, unscripted approach of the show and the characters, who include Ozzy, his wife Sharon, his kids Jack and Kelly, Melinda the nanny, the band, the pets, the assistants, the roadies, and the security guards. MTV president Van Toffler notes: "I'm not sure we could ever find a family as unique, as unpredictable and as twisted as the Osbournes are."

The success of the show has made Ozzy Osbourne very popular. He has been invited to play for Queen Elizabeth II, he has received a six-figure book contract, and his concert tours have been sold out wherever the band plays. The Viacom network has also benefited from the success of the show, as its ratings success has made it a smash hit for MTV's advertising department. Media executives report that some 30-second commercials in the show have gone for close to $100,000, which is a record for a regular nonsports cable series. MTV can show each episode worldwide up to 100 times, and it can raise advertising rates as the show's popularity increases.

As might be expected, the success of *The Osbournes* has resulted in other networks' trying to one-up one another with oddball reality shows. E! Entertainment Television launched a similar reality show in August 2002 featuring buxom model/actress Anna Nicole Smith, while MTV began exploring projects that would provide behind-the-scenes looks at other entertainers and celebrities, such as rapper "P. Diddy" Combs. VH1 turned its cameras on singer Liza Minnelli and her husband, David Getz, in *Liza and David.*

Some television critics feel that it is only a matter of time until viewers become tired of reality shows. However, MTV executives must not agree with this prediction, as the network has signed *The Osbournes* to a two-year deal. MTV is also coming up with ways to keep the show popular, such as shooting some episodes in England. One writer notes that the attraction of *The Osbournes* is simple: famous people doing ordinary things. It will be interesting to see how long people want to watch Ozzy continue to do simple things such as curse and yell "Sharon."

Sources: Megan Larson, "Strange Brew," *Mediaweek,* Sept. 16, 2002, pp. 26–27; David Calvo and Geoff Boucher, "Surreality TV Triumphs: 'Osbournes' Is Renewed," *Los Angeles Times,* May 30, 2002, pp. A1, 23; Wayne Friedman, "'Osbournes' Hits Peak Cable Program Pricing," *Advertising Age,* May 13, 2002, pp. 1, 75.

Audience size and composition are also important to the network or station, since they determine the amount it can charge for commercial time. Shows are frequently canceled because they fail to attract enough viewers to make their commercial time attractive to potential advertisers. Determining audience size is not an exact science and has been the subject of considerable controversy through the years. In this section, we examine how audiences are measured and how advertisers use this information in planning their media schedules.

Audience Measures

The size and composition of television audiences are measured by ratings services. The sole source of network TV and local audience information is the A. C. Nielsen Co. For many years local audience information was also available from the Arbitron Co., but Arbitron exited the local TV ratings business at the end of 1993 due to steep financial losses.[29] Nielsen gathers viewership information from a sample of TV homes and then projects this information to the total viewing area. The techniques used to gather audience measurement information include diaries, electronic meters or recorders, and personal interviews. Nielsen provides various types of information that can be used to measure and evaluate a station's audience. These measures are important to media planners as they weigh the value of buying commercial time on a program.

Television Households The number of households in the market that own a TV is sometimes referred to as the *universe estimate (UE).* Nielsen estimates that 106.7 million U.S. households owned at least one TV set as of August 2002. Since over 98 percent of U.S. households own a TV set, **television households** generally correspond to the number of households in a given market.[30]

Program Rating Probably the best known of all audience measurement figures is the **program rating,** the percentage of TV households in an area that are tuned to a specific program during a specific time period. The program rating is calculated by dividing the number of households tuned to a particular show by the total number of households in the area. For example, if 14 million households (HH) watched *ER,* the national rating would be 11.9, calculated as follows:

$$\text{Rating} = \frac{\text{HH tuned to show}}{\text{Total U.S. HH}} = \frac{14{,}000{,}000}{106{,}700{,}000} = 13.1$$

A **ratings point** represents 1 percent of all the television households in a particular area tuned to a specific program. On a national level, 1 ratings point represents 1,067,000 households. Thus, if a top-rated program like *ER* averages a rating of 12, it would reach 12.8 million households each week ($12 \times 1{,}067{,}000$).

The program rating is the key number to the stations, since the amount of money they can charge for commercial time is based on it. Ratings points are very important to the networks as well as to individual stations. A 1 percent change in a program's ratings over the course of a viewing season can gain or lose millions of dollars in advertising revenue. Advertisers also follow ratings closely, since they are the key measure for audience size and commercial rates.

Households Using Television The percentage of homes in a given area where TV is being watched during a specific time period is called **households using television (HUT).** This figure, sometimes referred to as *sets in use,* is always expressed as a percentage. For example, if 70 million of the U.S. TV households have their sets turned on at 10 P.M. on a Thursday night, the HUT figure is 65.6 percent (70 million out of 106.7 million). Television usage varies widely depending on the time of day and season of the year.

Share of Audience Another important audience measurement figure is the **share of audience,** which is the percentage of households using TV in a specified time period that are tuned to a specific program. This figure considers variations in the number of sets in use and the total size of the potential audience, since it is based only on those households that have their sets turned on. Audience share is calculated by dividing the

number of households (HH) tuned to a show by the number of households using television (HUT). Thus, if 70 million U.S. households had their sets turned on during the 10 P.M. time slot when *ER* is shown, the share of audience would be 20, calculated as follows:

$$\text{Share} = \frac{\text{HH tuned to show}}{\text{U.S. households using TV}} = \frac{14{,}000{,}000}{70{,}000{,}000} = 20$$

Audience share is always higher than the program rating unless all the households have their sets turned on (in which case they would be equal). Share figures are important since they reveal how well a program does with the available viewing audience. For example, late at night the size of the viewing audience drops substantially, so the best way to assess the popularity of a late-night program is to examine the share of the available audience it attracts relative to competing programs.

Ratings services also provide an audience statistic known as **total audience,** the total number of homes viewing any five-minute part of a telecast. This number can be broken down to provide audience composition figures that are based on the distribution of the audience into demographic categories.

Network Audience Information

Nielsen Television Index The source of national and network TV audience information is the Nielsen Media Research, which provides daily and weekly estimates of TV viewing and national sponsored network and major cable program audiences. For more than 50 years, Nielsen provided this information using a two-pronged system consisting of a national sample of metered households along with a separate sample of diary households. In the metered households, an electronic measurement device known as the **audimeter** (audience meter) was hooked up to the TV set to continuously measure the channels to which the set was tuned. Network viewing for the country (the famous Nielsen ratings) was based on the results provided by audimeters placed in a national sample of homes carefully selected to represent the population of U.S. households. The metered households were supported by a separate panel of households that recorded viewing information in diaries. Since the audimeter could measure only the channel to which the set was tuned, the diary panel was used to gather demographic data on the viewing audience.

For many years, the television and advertising industries expressed concern over the audimeter/diary system. The information from diaries was not available to the network and advertising analysts for several weeks, and studies indicated the method was overstating the size of some key demographic audiences. Cooperation rates among diary keepers declined, and often the person who kept a household's diary did not note what other family members watched when he or she wasn't home. The complex new video environment and explosion in viewing options also made it difficult for diary keepers to maintain accurate viewing records.

As a result of these problems, and in response to competitive pressure from an audience measurement company from England, AGB, in 1987 Nielsen made the people meter the sole basis of its national rating system and eliminated the use of the diary panel.

The People Meter The **people meter** is an electronic measuring device that incorporates the technology of the old-style audimeter in a system that records not only what is being watched but also by whom in 6,000 households. The actual device is a small box with eight buttons—six for the family and two for visitors—that can be placed on the top of the TV set (Exhibit 11-8). A remote control unit permits electronic entries from anywhere in the room. Each member of the sample household is assigned a button that indicates his or her presence as a viewer. The device is also equipped with a sonar sensor to remind viewers entering or leaving the room to log in or out on the meter.

Exhibit 11-8 Nielsen uses the people meter to measure national TV audiences

The viewership information the people meter collects from the household is stored in the home system until it is retrieved by Nielsen's computers. Data collected include when the set is turned on, which channel is viewed, when the channel is changed, and when the set is off, in addition to

LOCAL 8 KFMBTV

Sweep News- May '02

KFMB Flexes its Muscle in Early News

KFMB has the #1 Local Newscasts at 4pm, 6pm and 6:30pm!

Station	Program	Rtg/Shr
KFMB	Local 8 News at 4pm	4.1/10
KNSD	KNSD News at 4:30pm	2.3/5
KFMB	Local 8 News at 6pm	5.1/10
KNSD	KNSD News at 6pm	3.6/7
KFMB	Local 8 News at 6:30pm	5.6/11
KGTV	10 News Live at 6:30pm	4.9/10

Source: NSI, May '02

KFMB TV Research, JT, 5/24/02

Exhibit 11-9 KFMB promotes its dominance of the sweeps rating period for local news

who is viewing. The demographic characteristics of the viewers are also in the system, and viewership can be matched to these traits. Nielsen's operation center processes all this information each week for release to the TV and advertising industries. Nielsen uses a sample of metered households in 55 markets across the country to provide overnight viewing results.

Local Audience Information

Information on local audiences is important to both local advertisers and firms making national spot buys. Nielsen Media Research measures TV station audiences in 210 local markets known as **designated market areas (DMAs).** DMAs are nonoverlapping areas used for planning, buying, and evaluating TV audiences and are generally a group of counties in which stations located in a metropolitan or central area achieve the largest audience share. Nielsen Media Research reports information on viewing by time periods and programs and includes audience size and estimates of viewing over a range of demographic categories for each DMA.

Nielsen measures viewing audiences in every television market at least four times a year. The major markets are covered six times a year. The ratings periods when all 210 DMAs are surveyed are known as **sweeps.** The networks and local stations use numbers gathered during the sweeps rating periods in selling TV time. Exhibit 11-9 shows how KFMB, the CBS affiliate in San Diego, promotes its dominance of the sweeps ratings for local news.

However, as discussed in IMC Perspective 11-5, many advertising professionals believe the audience estimates gathered during the sweeps are overestimated because of special programming and promotions that occur during these periods.

Developments in Audience Measurement

For years the advertising industry has been calling for changes in the way TV viewing audiences are measured, at both the national and local levels. Many people believe people meters are only the first step in improving the way audiences are measured. While the people meter is seen as an improvement over the diary method, it still requires cooperation on an ongoing basis from people in the metered homes. Viewers in the Nielsen households, including young children, must punch a preassigned number on the remote control device each time they start or stop watching. Media researchers argue that kids forget and adults tire of the task over the two years they are in the Nielsen sample. Nielsen has been trying to develop passive measurement systems that require less involvement by people in metered homes and can produce more accurate measures of the viewing audience. However, such a system does not appear to be forthcoming in the near future.

Much of the concern over the Nielsen measurements involves the diary system used to measure viewing in the 210 local markets. This system requires that every 15 minutes viewers write down station call letters, channel numbers, programs, and who is watching. Many homes do not return completed diaries, and many of those that are returned are often not filled out correctly. Nielsen executives acknowledge the problems with its measurement system for local markets and is trying to correct them. The company is testing new diaries, sending out more of them, and working to improve the response rates.[31] Nielsen is also considering switching to a continuous measurement system for local markets rather than relying solely on the sweeps measurement system.[32] (See IMC Perspective 11-5.)

Recently a number of advertisers and ad agencies increased their criticism of Nielsen's local diary system, saying the handwritten method used to measure viewing audiences and gather demographic data in local audiences is antiquated. They argue that people meters are a far more accurate measurement system and should be used in local markets as well as on a national level. Nielsen has begun exploring the possibility of expanding the use of people meters to local markets. However, issues such as who will bear the cost of installing the people meters and how they would add to the cost of Nielsen's services are still major factors that have to be addressed.[33] As of October 2002 Nielsen began using people meters in the Boston area, making the nation's sixth-largest TV market the first to use the device for local audience measurement.[34]

IMC PERSPECTIVE 11-5

Is It Time to Do Away with Sweeps Ratings?

The cornerstone of selling local television time is the sweeps ratings periods, which are held in February, May, November, and, to a lesser extent, August by Nielsen Media Research to determine what stations and shows are being watched in all 210 U.S. television markets. The term *sweeps* dates back to the 1950s, when Nielsen began mailing diaries to households and reporting the results, first with the East Coast markets before sweeping across the country. As TV networks gradually took control of programming, they needed better demographic numbers to calculate how much they could charge for commercials on specific shows. Local stations could not afford to measure TV viewing audiences year-round, as the networks do, so they settled on the four month-long sweeps ratings periods.

The numbers gathered during the sweeps periods are used as guideposts in the buying and selling of TV commercial time during the rest of the year and are extremely important to local stations. However, many people in the advertising industry are enraged over the tactics used by networks and their local affiliates to bolster their ratings during sweeps periods, such as special programming, contests, games, and other non-typical promotions. They argue that the extraordinary programming and promotion efforts inflate the ratings taken during these periods and that they are not indicative of audience sizes for the other 36 weeks of the year, when networks run their regular programming and promotions are not used to boost local viewing audiences.

Advertisers and their agencies have become accustomed to the usual tactics used to beef up program schedules during the sweeps months, from blockbuster network programming to lurid sensationalism in local newscasts. Many local stations follow the accepted practice of producing and heavily promoting sex and scandal stories to lure viewers to their newscasts. For example, a Miami station ran an investigation into female college students who work as strippers to pay their tuition. Of much greater concern, however, is the blatant use of ratings grabbers such as big-prize sweepstakes, contests, and giveaways during sweeps periods. Nielsen Media Research has expressed concern over the number of unusual sweeps-period station promotions—most often giveaway contests on local newscasts. For example, a Houston station conducted a watch-and-win contest offering $2,000 each day to viewers of its 5 P.M., 6 P.M. and 10 P.M. newscasts. Nielsen's research has confirmed that giveaway promotions increase a station's audience share but that it generally drops back to precontest levels when the promotion ends.

Nielsen Media Research is working with the advertising industry to solve the sweeps problems. It provides red flags in its printed reports if stations use special promotions to bump up their ratings. Nielsen also recently dropped a San Diego TV station from its sweeps measurement period when it discovered that the station tried to pump up its ratings by sending promotional tapes to Nielsen's local panel members. However, the advertising industry argues that the only real solution to the problem is to increase the number of weeks Nielsen measures local audiences rather than relying on the artificially hyped numbers from sweeps periods. However, Nielsen argues that a continuous measurement system like that used for the network ratings would be very expensive and the TV and advertising industry would have to be willing to pay a higher price for local ratings information. Nielsen's director of communications notes: "In a perfect world, putting people meters in all the markets is what we'd want to do. But there's not enough advertising dollars in the smaller markets to make it worth their while."

Nielsen may also be getting some resistance from the local stations that have grown accustomed to getting higher ad rates year-round based on the inflated sweeps numbers. In the top 20 television markets, as much as half of a station's revenue comes from commercial time sold during the four or five hours of local newscasts aired each day, and a 30-second spot may sell for $2,500 to $3,000. Local stations are limited in the amount of airtime they can sell during network programs, so they concentrate on local newscasts to increase ad revenue. Ironically, however, some media researchers argue that sweeps don't always help boost a local station's ratings. They note that many viewers are loyal to local station news teams while others see through all of the sensational stories and promotional gimmicks.

Despite the many drawbacks of the system, many local stations continue to support sweeps for three main reasons: habit, fear, and money. However, nearly everyone in the advertising industry argues that some type of overhaul of the sweeps system is needed. The chair of the media research committee for the American Association of Advertising Agencies notes: "Sweeps are a travesty. Advertisers buy time on stations 365 days a year, yet we have no idea what ratings are for most of the year when there aren't those hyped, big-event programs." She speaks for many in the advertising industry when she concludes, "Sweeps should be done away with." It will be interesting to see if the television industry takes action to solve the sweeps problem or just continues to sweep it under the rug.

Sources: Michael J. Weis, "Sweeps," *American Demographics,* May 2001, pp. 43–49; Allen Banks, "Close the Book on Sweeps," *Advertising Age,* Mar. 15, 1999.

Nielsen has been battling with the networks, local TV stations, and ad agencies for years over the accuracy of its numbers. Many in the industry suspect that Nielsen is not moving fast enough to improve its audience measurement systems because it has a virtual monopoly in both the national and the local ratings business. They would like to see some competition.

The major networks, advertisers, and agencies have explored alternatives to Nielsen Media Research. One such recent effort was a system developed by Statistical Research Inc. (SRI) called *Smart-TV,* which was initially funded by the three major networks and big advertisers such as Procter & Gamble, AT&T, and General Motors. SRI claimed its Smart-TV system had many advantages over Nielsen's people meter and tested the system in Philadelphia in 1998. However, in May 1999 SRI canceled a national rollout of the new measurement system due to a lack of funding.[35] The latest effort to develop a TV audience measurement system that challenges Nielsen comes from a joint venture involving shopping network QVC and its majority owner, cable system operator Comcast.[36] The new service is called *TargetTV* and relies on digital set-top boxes to monitor viewer behavior by recording clickstream data in increments as small as five seconds in order to track channel surfing. The service was launched in 60,000 homes in Philadelphia in late 2000 and has moved into several other markets. The system has several drawbacks, however, as it is limited to households with set-top boxes and does not account for noncable TV users or those with analog cable boxes. It is not likely that the TargetTV service will mount a serious challenge to Nielsen anytime soon.

Another alternative to Nielsen is the *portable people meter (PPM)* system, which is being tested by Arbitron Inc.[37] The pager-size device detects an inaudible code embedded in the audio signal of a TV program, radio show, or Internet streaming audio. At the end of the day, users of the device drop it into a bay station, which then sends the ratings information to Arbitron's central database. Arbitron maintains that the PPM is superior to traditional set-top meters because it captures audience behavior year-round, it tracks media use outside the home, and it tracks all different types of media. The company began field tests of the system in Philadelphia in 2002 and plans to expand into as many as 100 markets by 2008. Arbitron has skirted potential opposition to the system from Nielsen by giving its one-time rival the option to develop PPM technology if it goes into commercial production.

Many advertising professionals hope that a focus of new technology for measuring viewing audiences will be on developing rating systems for commercials, not just for programs. The Nielsen system measures the audiences for the programs surrounding the commercials rather than the commercials themselves. But with new technologies such as personal video recorders, as well as zipping, zapping, people leaving the room, and people being distracted from the TV during commercial breaks, there is a need to develop accurate ratings of more than just program audience viewing. Nielsen has announced that it can now monitor the TiVo personal video recorder behavior of all the U.S. TV households it monitors.[38] However, the impending arrival of convergence technology also means that people may soon routinely watch television shows on their computers, personal digital assistants, and other wireless devices such as cell phones, which will add to the problem of accurately measuring TV viewing.

For over 50 years consumers passively received TV programming and commercials. This is changing rapidly, however, as the major cable operators, telecommunications companies, and others bring various entertainment, information, and interactive services into homes via television. Researchers argue that the Nielsen system is being overwhelmed by the explosion in the number of TV sets, delivery systems, and program options available. These developments must be carefully monitored by advertisers and media planners as well as by people in the TV industry, as they can have a profound impact on audience size and composition and on the way advertisers use and pay for the use of TV as an advertising medium. Improvements in measurement technology are needed to accommodate these developments.

Media experts also argue that consideration must be given to measuring media involvement and determining when consumers are most tuned into television programs and open to receiving advertisements and other types of marketing messages.[39] Current audience measurement methods are often criticized for only reporting the

sizes of viewing audiences and not distinguishing among them in terms of the intensity of their relationships with television programs. These limitations have prompted researchers to investigate the qualitative distinctions among viewers who may all be counted as "watching" a TV program but have very different levels of attention, attitudes, and even behaviors related to the show. Researchers Cristel Russell, Andrew Norman, and Susan Heckler have introduced the concept of audience *connectedness* to capture the fact that some television viewers build relationships, loyalty, and connections with certain TV shows, with the characters portrayed in these programs, and with fellow audience members.[40] These connected viewers are very different from viewers who are less involved with a program. They may be more attentive to advertising and product placements and more likely to engage in behaviors such as visiting a program's website or purchasing brands that are associated with the show.

Radio

Television has often been referred to as the ideal advertising medium, and to many people it personifies the glamour and excitement of the industry. Radio, on the other hand, has been called the Rodney Dangerfield of media because it gets no respect from many advertisers. Dominated by network programming and national advertisers before the growth of TV, radio has evolved into a primarily local advertising medium. Network advertising generally accounts for less than 5 percent of radio's revenue. Radio has also become a medium characterized by highly specialized programming appealing to very narrow segments of the population.

The importance of radio is best demonstrated by the numbers. There are more than 11,000 radio stations in this country, including 4,784 commercial AM stations and 5,766 commercial FM stations. There are over 576 million radios in use in the United States, an average of 5.6 per household. Radio reaches 77 percent of all Americans over the age of 12 each day and has grown into a ubiquitous background to many activities, among them reading, driving, running, working, and socializing. The average American listens to radio 3 hours every weekday and nearly 5 hours every weekend.[41] The pervasiveness of this medium has not gone unnoticed by advertisers; radio advertising revenue grew from $8.8 billion in 1990 to over $18 billion in 2001 (Exhibit 11-10).

Radio has survived and flourished as an advertising medium because it offers advertisers certain advantages for communicating messages to their potential customers. However, radio has inherent limitations that affect its role in the advertiser's media strategy.

Advantages of Radio

Radio has many advantages over other media, including cost and efficiency, selectivity, flexibility, mental imagery, and integrated marketing opportunities.

Cost and Efficiency

One of the main strengths of radio as an advertising medium is its low cost. Radio commercials are very inexpensive to produce. They require only a script of the commercial to be read by the radio announcer or a copy of a prerecorded message that can be broadcast by the station. The cost for radio time is also low. A minute on network radio may cost only $5,000, which translates into a cost per thousand of only $3 to $4. Local advertising on radio stations costs about $6 per thousand households, compared to more than $20 for local TV advertising. The low relative costs of radio make it one of the most efficient of all advertising media, and the low absolute cost means the budget needed for an effective radio campaign is often lower than that for other media.

The low cost of radio means advertisers can build more reach and frequency into their media schedule within a certain budget. They can use different stations to broaden the reach of their messages and multiple spots to ensure adequate frequency. For example, a number of Internet start-ups have been heavy users of radio in their efforts to build brand awareness. Companies such as More.com, which sells

Exhibit 11-10 Radio is a very important advertising medium

drugstore items on the Internet, see radio as a fast and relatively inexpensive way to get their names known. Radio commercials can be produced more quickly than TV spots, and the companies can run them more often.[42] Many national advertisers also recognize the cost efficiency of radio and use it as part of their media strategy.

Selectivity Another major advantage of radio is the high degree of audience selectivity available through the various program formats and geographic coverage of the numerous stations. Radio lets companies focus their advertising on specialized audiences such as certain demographic and lifestyle groups. Most areas have radio stations with formats such as adult contemporary, easy listening, classical music, country, news/talk shows, jazz, and all news, to name a few. Figure 11-6 shows the percentage of the radio listening audience captured by various radio formats for different age groups. For example, among 12- to 17-year-olds and 18- to 24-year olds, the most popular radio format is contemporary hits, while those between the ages of 45 and 54 prefer news/talk. Elusive consumers like teenagers, college students, and working adults can be reached more easily through radio than most other media.

Radio can reach consumers other media can't. Light television viewers spend considerably more time with radio than with TV and are generally an upscale market in terms of income and education level. Light readers of magazines and newspapers also spend more time listening to radio. Radio has become a popular way to reach specific non-English-speaking ethnic markets. Los Angeles, New York City, Dallas, and Miami have several radio stations that broadcast in Spanish and reach these areas' large Hispanic markets. As mass marketing gives way to market segmentation and regional marketing, radio will continue to grow in importance.

Flexibility Radio is probably the most flexible of all the advertising media because it has a very short closing period, which means advertisers can change their message almost up to the time it goes on the air. Radio commercials can usually be produced and scheduled on very short notice. Radio advertisers can easily adjust their messages to local market conditions and marketing situations.

Mental Imagery A potential advantage of radio that is often overlooked is that it encourages listeners to use their imagination when processing a commercial message. While the creative options of radio are limited, many advertisers take advantage of the absence of a visual element to let consumers create their own picture of what is happening in a radio message.

Radio may also reinforce television messages through a technique called **image transfer,** where the images of a TV commercial are implanted into a radio spot.[43] First the marketer establishes the video image of a TV commercial. Then it uses a similar, or even the same, audio portion (spoken words and/or jingle) as the basis for the radio counterpart. The idea is that when consumers hear the radio message, they will make the connection to the TV commercial, reinforcing its video images. Image transfer offers advertisers a way to make radio and TV ads work together synergistically. This promotional piece put out by the Radio Advertising Bureau shows how the image transfer process works (Exhibit 11-11).

Exhibit 11-11 The Radio Advertising Bureau promotes the concept of imagery transfer

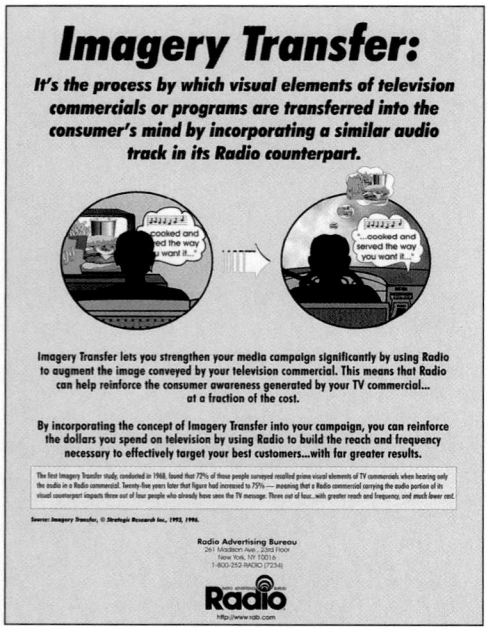

Integrated Marketing Opportunities Radio provides marketers with a variety of integrated marketing opportunities. Radio stations become an integral part of many communities, and the deejays and program hosts may become popular figures. Advertisers often use radio stations and personalities to enhance their involvement with a local market and to gain influence with local retailers. Radio also works very effectively in conjunction with place-based/point-of-purchase promotions. Retailers often use on-site radio broadcasts combined with special sales or promotions to attract consumers to their stores and get them to make a purchase. Live radio broadcasts are also used in conjunction with event marketing. For example, Banana Boat Suncare often sponsors live

Figure 11-6 Radio format audience shares by age group

Format	12–17 Share (%)	Format	18–24 Share (%)
Contemporary hits radio (CHR)	43.7	Contemporary hits radio (CHR)	26.2
Urban	16.3	Urban	13.5
Alternative	10.5	Adult contemporary (AC)	12.1
Adult contemporary (AC)	6.9	Alternative	10.2
Hispanic	4.7	Hispanic	9.2
Country	4.3	Country	6.3
Oldies	2.6	News/talk	4.1
Album rock (AOR)	2.1	Classic rock	4.0
News/talk/information	1.8	Album rock (AOR)	3.9
Classic rock	1.6	Oldies	3.9
Religious	1.6	Religious	1.3
Remaining formats	3.5	NAC/smooth jazz	0.8
		Remaining formats	4.5

Format	24–35 Share (%)	Format	35–44 Share (%)
Adult contemporary (AC)	15.8	Adult contemporary (AC)	17.6
Contemporary hits radio (CHR)	14.3	News/talk/information	14.7
Urban	11.0	Urban	9.5
News/talk/information	10.4	Contemporary hits radio (CHR)	8.3
Hispanic	9.8	Country	8.3
Alternative	8.5	Classic rock	8.0
Country	7.2	Oldies	7.9
Oldies	5.4	Hispanic	7.8
Classic rock	5.0	Alternative	4.5
Album rock (AOR)	4.8	Album rock (AOR)	4.1
Religious	2.1	NAC/smooth jazz	3.3
NAC/smooth jazz	1.6	Religious	2.9
Classical	0.5	Classical	0.8
Remaining formats	3.6	Remaining formats	2.3

Format	45–54 Share (%)	Format	55–64 Share (%)
News/talk/information	20.5	News/talk/information	28.1
Adult contemporary (AC)	17.5	Adult contemporary (AC)	15.2
Oldies	13.7	Country	12.6
Country	9.2	Oldies	12.3
Alternative	7.2	Hispanic	5.9
Urban	6.0	Urban	5.7
Hispanic	5.6	NAC/smooth jazz	4.5
Classic rock	5.6	Adult standards	3.9
NAC/smooth jazz	5.1	Classical	3.2
Contemporary hits radio (CHR)	4.4	Religious	3.1
Religious	2.9	Contemporary hits radio (CHR)	1.9
Album rock (AOR)	1.9	Classic rock	1.7
Classical	1.6	Alternative	0.8
Adult standards	1.0	Album rock (AOR)	0.6
Remaining formats	3.4	Remaining formats	0.5

Note: Read as the contemporary hits radio (CHR) format captures a 43.7% share of radio listening among persons 12 to 17 years old.
Source: Radio Advertising Bureau, *Radio Marketing Guide & Fact Book for Advertisers,* 2002–2003, p. 36.

Exhibit 11-12 Banana Boat uses live radio broadcasts to promote its sun-care products

broadcast promotions at beaches, sporting events, and festivals, setting up product booths for sampling and giveaways (Exhibit 11-12).

Limitations of Radio

Several factors limit the effectiveness of radio as an advertising medium, among them creative limitations, fragmentation, chaotic buying procedures, limited research data, limited listener attention, and clutter. The media planner must consider them in determining the role the medium will play in the advertising program.

Creative Limitations A major drawback of radio as an advertising medium is the absence of a visual image. The radio advertiser cannot show the product, demonstrate it, or use any type of visual appeal or information. A radio commercial is, like a TV ad, a short-lived and fleeting message that is externally paced and does not allow the receiver to control the rate at which it is processed. Because of these creative limitations many companies tend to ignore radio, and agencies often assign junior people to the development of radio commercials.

Fragmentation Another problem with radio is the high level of audience fragmentation due to the large number of stations. The percentage of the market tuned to any particular station is usually very small. The top-rated radio station in many major metropolitan areas with a number of AM and FM stations may attract less than 10 percent of the total listening audience. Advertisers that want a broad reach in their radio advertising media schedule have to buy time on a number of stations to cover even a local market. IMC Perspective 11-6 discusses how the fragmentation of radio audiences may become even greater with the emergence of satellite radio. This new technology is now available for automobiles from companies such as XM Satellite Radio.

Chaotic Buying Procedures It should be readily apparent how chaotic the media planning and purchasing process can become for the advertiser that wants to use radio on a nationwide spot basis. Acquiring information and evaluating and contracting for time with even a fraction of the 10,500 commercial stations that operate across the country can be very difficult and time-consuming. This problem has diminished somewhat in recent years as the number of radio networks and of syndicated programs offering a package of several hundred stations increases.

Limited Research Data Audience research data on radio are often limited, particularly compared with TV, magazines, or newspapers. Most radio stations are small operations and lack the revenue to support detailed studies of their audiences. And most users of radio are local companies that cannot support research on radio

IMC PERSPECTIVE 11-6

XM Hopes to Reinvent the Radio

When *Fortune* magazine named its Product of the Year in 2001, the winner was a new technology that many feel may revolutionize the way we listen to radio when we drive. The magazine's rationale for its selection stated: "Of all the new technologies of 2001, XM Satellite Radio is way, way, way above the rest. It's the first major advance in radio since FM emerged in the 1960s, and the best thing to happen to mobile music since the dashboard CD player." After spending more than a billion dollars for programming and satellite operating expenses, as well as catchy TV commercials featuring celebrities such as David Bowie, B. B. King, and Snoop Dogg, XM Satellite Radio hit the airways in November 2001, claiming that it will do for radio what cable did for television.

XM radio uses "Rock" and "Roll," its two Boeing 702 satellites stationed over the East and West Coasts, to beam 100 audio channels from the stratosphere to subscribers' cars. While subscribers to satellite radio still get regular broadcast stations via their car antennas, they get 100 XM channels, about a third of which are commercial-free. Subscribers get 71 channels of music, including 7 for hip-hop, soul, and R&B; 5 for jazz and blues; 5 for Latin music; and 3 for classical and opera. Each decade from the 40s to the 90s gets its own XM channel, featuring not just music but period commercials and interviews with personalities from the era. XM rounds out the lineup with news, sports, talk, and children's programming. The 12 news channels include Fox News and CNN; CNBC, CNNfn, and Bloomberg News for business junkies; and CNET for the technofile. Commercial-free news is available on C-SPAN or BBC World Service. XM offerings also include radio versions of network fare from ESPN, MTV, VH1, the Discovery Channel, and BET.

Many industry observers note that there is a tremendous opportunity for satellite radio. There has been consolidation in the radio industry, which has led to repetitious, cookie-cutter formats in markets across the country. To pay for the huge radio conglomerates they have built, moguls must increase the commercial load, which means less programming and more frustrated listeners. XM's chief programmer, Lee Abrams, notes that the company hopes to have the same creative effect as the FM revolution of the late 60s and 70s, which brought major changes to the radio scene. FM's superior sound and lack of commercial clutter triggered a huge audience shift away from AM radio. However, Abrams argues that FM has sprouted a potbelly and gone gray at the temples and become the stodgy establishment, complacent and vulnerable to a hard-charging rival such as XM. "Right now, we live in a

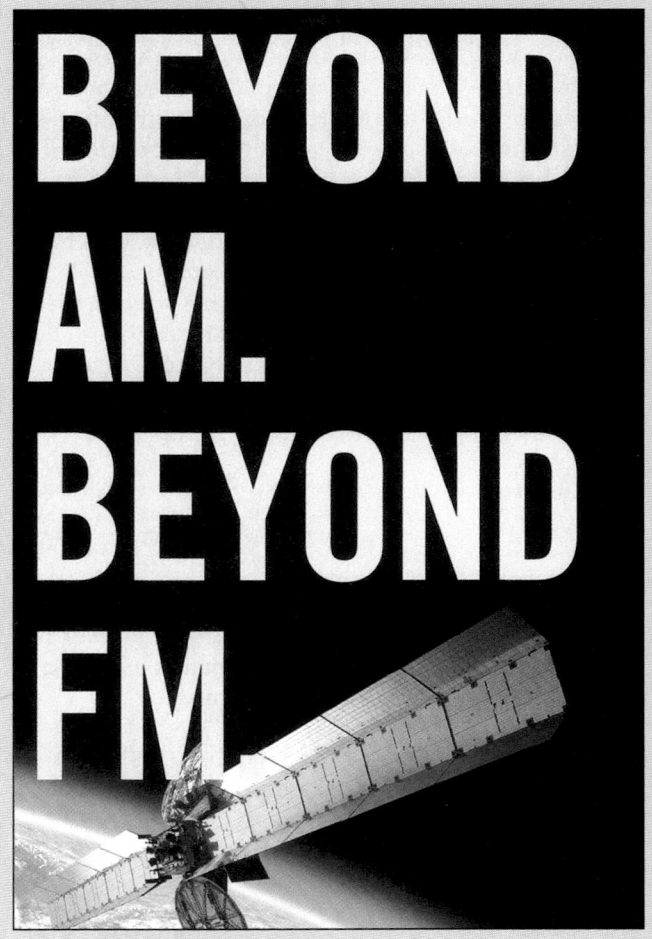

very vanilla age, radio-wise," says Abrams. "Except for talk radio, it's stay in the middle, don't upset anybody, and play the big hits everybody's comfortable with. We're 180 degrees from that. We want to challenge people."

If XM is going to be successful in taking on the radio establishment, it is going to have to overcome a number of challenges itself. One of the major challenges facing the company is getting consumers to pay anywhere from $300 to nearly $1,000 for satellite-radio-ready receivers, antennas, and installation charges and then pay an additional $10 per month for the XM service. The company's strategy is to first win the battle for the dashboard, where consumers spend more than $2 billion each year to install about 11 million after-market car radios. An additional 17 million radios are installed annually in new vehicles, and XM has been working the automakers to get them to make satellite radio an option for buyers when purchasing vehicles. XM officials claim that the company can

make a profit with 4 million subscribers, which is less than 3 percent of the nation's 200 million registered vehicles.

In addition to competing with one other satellite company, Sirius Satellite Radio, XM will face a torrent of competition from traditional radio. In 2000, the Federal Communications Commission authorized low-powered radio—a service that could create up to 1,000 new stations. Although their signals will not travel very far, they will spawn a great deal of content. The FCC also plans to auction up to 350 now-dormant FM stations and set a standard for the AM and FM stations to switch to new digital technology, which will allow broadcasters to offer better-quality sound as well as new programs and services. Some experts argue that local broadcasters have an advantage over the new satellite technology since they can offer traffic reports, local sports information, and community talk shows that appeal to rush-hour motorists.

XM acknowledges that for people who don't spend a lot of time in their cars or local drivers who have a short commute, satellite radio may be more than they need. The natural audience for satellite radio will be the true car potatoes—salespeople, suburban-sprawl commuters, or long-haul drivers such as truckers (who have their own channel on XM, Open Road). Another market may be the real music junkies who want the listening options and superior sound quality offered by satellite radio.

It is too early to tell whether satellite radio will revolutionize our radio listening habits or become the CB-radio fad of the new millennium. Consumers may not want to be faced with another monthly bill for XM or Sirius when they are used to getting radio for free. However, remember that there was a time when many experts predicted that people would never pay for cable television. Stay tuned.

Sources: Jube Shiver, Jr., "Satellite Radio Aiming High," *Los Angeles Times,* Feb. 4, 2002, pp. C1, 6; Chris Tucker, "Sky-High Fidelity," *Southwest Airlines Spirit,* Feb. 2002, pp. 76–85; "Product of the Year," *Fortune,* Dec. 24, 2001, p. 170.

listenership in their markets. Thus, media planners do not have as much audience information available to guide them in their purchase of radio time as they do with other media.

Limited Listener Attention Another problem that plagues radio is that it is difficult to retain listener attention to commercials. Radio programming, particularly music, is often the background to some other activity and may not receive the listeners' full attention. Thus they may miss all or some of the commercials. One environment where radio has a more captive audience is in cars. But getting listeners to pay attention to commercials can still be difficult. Most people preprogram their car radio and change stations during commercial breaks. A study by Avery Abernethy found large differences between exposure to radio programs versus advertising for listeners in cars. They were exposed to only half of the advertising broadcast and changed stations frequently to avoid commercials.[44] Another factor that is detracting from radio listening in motor vehicles is the rapid growth of cellular phones. A recent study found that half of commuters surveyed who own a cell phone reported listening to less radio than they did a year earlier.[45]

Clutter Clutter is just as much a problem with radio as with other advertising media. Most radio stations carry an average of nearly 10 minutes of commercials every hour. During the popular morning and evening rush hours, the amount of commercial time may exceed 12 minutes. Also contributing to the clutter problem is the practice of some stations to offer "commercial-free" blocks of music to attract listeners. This practice results in more commercials being aired in a short time period and may also result in listeners switching to another station rather than listening through a long block of ads. Advertisers must create commercials that break through the clutter or use heavy repetition to make sure their messages reach consumers. In a study of radio listeners conducted by Edison Research, perceptions of increased ad clutter were cited by participants as a reason for spending less time listening to radio.[46]

Another factor that may contribute to the problem of commercial clutter on radio is a new technological system called *Cash,* developed by the Prime Image Company.[47] The machine momentarily stores the broadcast of a live show, creating an imperceptible delay. When the rebroadcast airs seconds later, the Cash system has reduced the pauses between words and shortened long syllables in order to add more space for

Exhibit 11-13 Rush Limbaugh's talk radio show is syndicated nationally

commercials. This allows stations to add up to six minutes of extra airtime per hour, which may mean as many as 12 more 30-second commercials. Unlike the case with previous systems that compressed broadcasts and replayed them at a faster pace, listeners cannot recognize the effect. However, they are very likely to recognize the increased number of commercials, which will only compound the clutter problem.

Buying Radio Time

The purchase of radio time is similar to that of television, as advertisers can make either network, spot, or local buys. Since these options were reviewed in the section on buying TV time, they are discussed here only briefly.

Network Radio Advertising time on radio can be purchased on a network basis using one of the national networks. There are currently three major national radio networks, Westwood One, ABC, and Premiere. There are also more than 100 regional radio networks across the country. Using networks minimizes the amount of negotiation and administrative work needed to get national or regional coverage, and the costs are lower than those for individual stations. However, the number of affiliated stations on the network roster and the types of audiences they reach can vary considerably, so the use of network radio reduces advertisers' flexibility in selecting stations.

An important trend in radio is the increasing number of radio networks and syndicated programs that offer advertisers a package of several hundred stations. For example, conservative Rush Limbaugh's radio show is syndicated nationally and is carried by more than 500 stations, reaching more than 11 million people weekly (Exhibit 11-13). Syndication reduces audience fragmentation and purchasing problems and increases radio's appeal to national advertisers.

Spot Radio National advertisers can also use spot radio to purchase airtime on individual stations in various markets. The purchase of spot radio provides greater flexibility in selecting markets, individual stations, and airtime and adjusting the message for local market conditions. Spot radio accounts for about 20 percent of radio time sold. Figure 11-7 shows the top 20 advertisers by brand and how they allocate their radio budgets between network and spot radio.

Local Radio By far the heaviest users of radio are local advertisers; nearly 79 percent of radio advertising time is purchased from individual stations by local companies. Auto dealers, retailers, restaurants, and financial institutions are among the heaviest users of local radio advertising. But a number of radio advertisers are switching to local cable TV because the rates are comparable and there is the added advantage of TV's visual impact.

Time Classifications

As with television, the broadcast day for radio is divided into various time periods or dayparts, as shown in Figure 11-8. The size of the radio listening audience varies widely across the dayparts, and advertising rates follow accordingly. The largest radio

Figure 11-7 Radio's top 20 national network and spot advertisers

Rank	National Brand Advertiser	Total*	Network*	National Spot*
1	Verizon Wireless–Wireless Service	$52.1	$ 4.8	$47.3
2	Cingular Wireless Service	41.7	—	41.7
3	Home Depot Home Center	39.5	—	39.5
4	AT&T Wireless Store	22.4	—	22.4
5	Autozone Parts Store	21.6	18.8	2.8
6	SBC Communications Internet Services	19.8	—	19.8
7	Burger King Restaurant	19.7	0.2	19.5
8	Radio Shack Electronics Stores	17.4	11.5	5.9
9	Wells Fargo Bank Consumer Services	16.8	—	16.8
10	Dish Network Satellite System	16.7	8.0	8.7
11	Dodge Dealer Assn.—various autos and trucks	16.7	—	16.7
12	Kohl's Dept. Stores—multiple products	16.0	—	16.0
13	Hyundai Dealer Assn.—various autos and trucks	15.7	—	15.7
14	Fox TV Network Entertainment Div.	15.7	—	15.7
15	Audi Dealer Assn.—various autos	15.7	—	15.7
16	Denny's Restaurants	15.5	—	15.5
17	Jared's Jewelers	14.9	—	14.9
18	Epson Printers	14.3	9.2	5.1
19	State Farm Insurance—various	14.2	10.9	3.3
20	Nextel Cellular Service	13.9	—	13.9

*All revenue figures are in millions of dollars.
Source: *Radio Marketing Guide & Fact Book for Advertisers, 2002–2003,* p. 27.

audiences (and thus the highest rates) occur during the early morning and late afternoon drive times. Radio rates also vary according to the number of spots or type of audience plan purchased, the supply and demand of time available in the local market, and the ratings of the individual station. Rate information is available directly from the stations and is summarized in Standard Rate and Data Service's (SRDS's) Spot Radio Rates and Data for both local stations and radio networks. Some stations issue rate cards like the one shown in Figure 11-9. But many stations do not adhere strictly to rate cards and the rates published in SRDS. Their rates are negotiable and depend on factors such as availability, time period, and number of spots purchased.

Figure 11-8 Dayparts for radio

Morning drive time	6:00–10:00 A.M.
Daytime	10:00 A.M.–3:00 P.M.
Afternoon/evening drive time	3:00–7:00 P.M.
Nighttime	7:00 P.M.–12:00 A.M.
All night	12:00–6:00 A.M.

Rate Card

XHTZ-FM (JAMMIN' Z-90)

RATE CARD (96-4)

GRID	I	II	III	IV	DAY/DAYPART
AAA	350	300	250	200	M-F 3P-8P SAT 10A-8P
AA	300	250	200	150	M-F 5:30A-10A SUN 10A-8P
A	275	225	175	125	M-F 10A-3P M-SUN 8P-12A
B	200	150	100	50	SA/SU 5:30A-10A
C	275	225	175	125	R.O.S.

- ALL RATES APPLY TO :30 OR :60 SECOND COMMERCIAL ANNOUNCEMENTS.

XHTZ 90.3 FM • 1229 Third Avenue • Chula Vista, California 91911 • FAX (619) 426-3690 • (619) 585-9090

Figure 11-9 Sample radio rate card

Audience Information

One problem with radio is the lack of audience information. Because there are so many radio stations and thus many small, fragmented audiences, the stations cannot support the expense of detailed audience measurement. Also, owing to the nature of radio as incidental or background entertainment, it is difficult to develop precise measures of who listens at various time periods and for how long. The major radio ratings services are owned by Arbitron which provides audience information for local stations and network audiences.

Arbitron

Arbitron covers 286 local radio markets with one to four ratings reports per year. Arbitron has a sample of representative listeners in each market maintain a diary of their radio listening for seven days. Audience estimates for the market are based on these diary records and reported by time period and selected demographics in the Arbitron Radio Market Report, to which clients subscribe. Figure 11-10 provides a sample page from the Arbitron ratings report for people in the 18-to-49 age target audience across the various dayparts. The three basic estimates in the Arbitron report are

- Person estimates—the estimated number of people listening.
- Rating—the percentage of listeners in the survey area population.
- Share—the percentage of the total estimated listening audience.

These three estimates are further defined by using quarter-hour and cume figures. The **average quarter-hour (AQH)** figure expresses the average number of people estimated to have listened to a station for a minimum of five minutes during any quarter-hour in a time period. For example, station KCBQ has an average quarter-hour listenership of 2,500 during the weekday 6 to 10 A.M. daypart. This means that any weekday, for any 15-minute period during this time period, an average of 2,500 people between the ages of 18 and 49 are tuned to this station. This figure helps to determine the audience and cost of a spot schedule within a particular time period.

Cume stands for "cumulative audience," the estimated total number of different people who listened to a station for at least five minutes in a quarter-hour period within a reported daypart. In Figure 11-10, the cumulative audience of people 18 to 49 for

Figure 11-10 Partial sample page from Arbitron radio ratings report

	Target Audience, Persons 18–49							
	Monday–Friday 6–10 A.M.				Monday–Friday 10 A.M.–3 P.M.			
	AQH (00)	CUME (00)	AQH RTG	AQH SHR	AQH (00)	CUME (00)	AQH RTG	AQH SHR
KCBQ								
METRO	25	263	.2	.8	40	365	.3	1.3
TSA	25	263			40	365		
KCBQ-FM								
METRO	101	684	.7	3.1	117	768	.9	3.7
TSA	101	684			117	768		
KCEO								
METRO	11	110	.1	.3	8	81	.1	.3
TSA	11	110			8	81		
KFMB								
METRO	171	790	1.3	5.3	106	678	.8	3.3
TSA	171	790			106	678		

station KCBQ during the weekday morning daypart is 26,300. Cume estimates the reach potential of a radio station.

The **average quarter-hour rating (AQH RTG)** expresses the estimated number of listeners as a percentage of the survey area population. The **average quarter-hour share (AQH SHR)** is the percentage of the total listening audience tuned to each station. It shows the share of listeners each station captures out of the total listening audience in the survey area. The average quarter-hour rating of station KCBQ during the weekday 6 to 10 A.M. daypart is 0.2, while the average quarter-hour share is 0.8.

Arbitron is conducting market trials of its portable people meter (PPM) device, which was discussed earlier in the chapter, for use in measuring radio audiences. The radio industry and advertisers have always had concerns over the use of Arbitron's diary method. Many view the new PPM technology as a more valid audience measurement system.[48]

Arbitron also recently began measuring listenership to webcasts. Arbitron Webcast Ratings is an audience measurement service that measures Internet audio and video tuning across all webcasting sources. However, this service is still in a pilot testing phase.[49] Arbitron's research has found that 30 percent of online users have listened to Internet radio stations and the number continues to grow. This will make the measurement of radio listening over the Internet a very important area in the future.

RADAR Another rating service that is now owned by Arbitron is RADAR (Radio's All-Dimension Audience Research) studies, which are sponsored by the major radio networks. Audience estimates are collected twice a year on the basis of 12,000 daily telephone interviews covering seven days of radio listening behavior. Each listener is called daily for a week and asked about radio usage from the day before until that moment. RADAR provides network audience measures, along with estimates of audience and various segments. The audience estimates are time-period measurements for the various dayparts. RADAR also provides estimates of network audiences for all commercials and commercials within various programs.

As with TV, media planners must use the audience measurement information to evaluate the value of various radio stations in reaching the advertiser's target audience and their relative cost. The media buyer responsible for the purchase of radio time works with information on target audience coverage, rates, time schedules, and availability to optimize the advertiser's radio media budget.

	Target Audience, Persons 18–49											
	Monday–Friday 3–7 P.M.				Monday–Friday 7 P.M.–Mid.				Weekend 10 A.M.–7 P.M.			
	AQH (00)	CUME (00)	AQH RTG	AQH SHR	AQH (00)	CUME (00)	AQH RTG	AQH SHR	AQH (00)	CUME (00)	AQH RTG	AQH SHR
KCBQ												
METRO	36	340	.3	1.4	6	138		.5	51	356	.4	2.4
TSA	36	340			6	138			51	356		
KCBQ-FM												
METRO	83	736	.6	3.2	23	354	.2	2.1	67	616	.5	3.2
TSA	83	736			23	354			67	616		
KCEO												
METRO	10	95	.1	.4		8			1	8		
TSA	10	95				8			1	8		
KFMB												
METRO	141	1092	1.0	5.4	87	827	.6	7.9	92	567	.7	4.4
TSA	141	1092			87	827			92	567		

Summary

Television and radio, or the broadcast media, are the most pervasive media in most consumers' daily lives and offer advertisers the opportunity to reach vast audiences. Both broadcast media are time- rather than space-oriented and organized similarly in that they use a system of affiliated stations belonging to a network, as well as individual stations, to broadcast their programs and commercial messages. Advertising on radio or TV can be done on national or regional network programs or purchased in spots from local stations.

TV has grown faster than any other advertising medium in history and has become the leading medium for national advertisers. No other medium offers its creative capabilities; the combination of sight, sound, and movement give the advertiser a vast number of options for presenting a commercial message with high impact. Television also offers advertisers mass coverage at a low relative cost. Variations in programming and audience composition, along with the growth of cable, are helping TV offer more audience selectivity to advertisers. While television is often viewed as the ultimate advertising medium, it has several limitations, including the high cost of producing and airing commercials, a lack of selectivity relative to other media, the fleeting nature of the message, and the problem of commercial clutter. The latter two problems have been compounded in recent years by the trend toward shorter commercials.

Information regarding the size and composition of national and local TV audiences is provided by the A. C. Nielsen Co. The amount of money networks or stations can charge for commercial time on their programs is based on its audience measurement figures. This information is also important to media planners, as it is used to determine the combination of shows needed to attain specific levels of reach and frequency with the advertiser's target market.

Future trends in television include the continued growth of cable, competition to local cable operators from direct broadcast satellite systems, and a resulting increase in channels available to television households. Changes are also likely to occur in the measurement of viewing audiences—for example, continuous measurement of audiences.

The role of radio as an entertainment and advertising medium has changed with the rapid growth of television. Radio has evolved into a primarily local advertising medium that offers highly specialized programming appealing to narrow segments of the market. Radio offers advertisers the opportunity to build high

reach and frequency into their media schedules and to reach selective audiences at a very efficient cost. It also offers opportunities for integrated marketing programs such as place-based promotions and event sponsorships.

The major drawback of radio is its creative limitations owing to the absence of a visual image. The short and fleeting nature of the radio commercial, the highly fragmented nature of the radio audience, and clutter are also problems.

As with TV, the rate structure for radio advertising time varies with the size of the audience delivered. The primary sources of audience information are Arbitron for local radio and its RADAR studies for network audiences.

Key Terms

split-30s, 356
zipping, 356
zapping, 356
television network, 358
affiliates, 358
up-front market, 358
scatter market, 358
spot advertising, 361
national spot advertising, 361
local advertising, 361
station reps, 361
syndicated programs, 361
sponsorship, 363
participations, 363
adjacencies, 364
dayparts, 364
cable television, 364
superstations, 365
interconnects, 367
narrowcasting, 367
multiplexing, 370
direct broadcast satellite (DBS) services, 370
television households, 372
program rating, 372
ratings point, 372
households using television (HUT), 372
share of audience, 372
total audience, 373
audimeter, 373
people meter, 373
designated market areas (DMAs), 374
sweeps, 374
image transfer, 378
average quarter-hour (AQH) figure, 385
cume, 385
average quarter-hour (AQH RTG) rating, 386
average quarter-hour (AQH SHR) share, 386

Discussion Questions

1. The opening vignette to the chapter discusses how personal video recorders (PVRs) being marketed by companies such as TiVo and SONICblue are becoming more popular. Discuss how these products are impacting the way people watch television. What are the implications for television's traditional advertising business model?

2. Discuss the advantages of television as an advertising medium and the importance of these factors to major advertisers such as automobile companies or packaged-goods marketers.

3. IMC Perspective 11-1 discusses how some major companies are no longer advertising on the Super Bowl. Discuss the pros and cons of advertising during the Super Bowl. Do you feel that paying more than $2 million for a 30-second spot on the big game is a good investment? Why or why not?

4. Explain what is meant by zipping and zapping and how they affect television viewing behavior. Discuss some of the ways advertisers can deal with the zapping problem.

5. Discuss how the growth of Spanish-language television networks in the United States such as Univision and Telemundo is likely to affect the media strategy of marketers targeting the Hispanic market.

6. IMC Perspective 11-3 discusses how ESPN is changing its strategy and adding more entertainment programs such as variety shows, reality shows, and original movies. Discuss the reasons ESPN is making these changes in its programming. Do you think these changes will be successful in increasing the viewing audience for ESPN?

7. Discuss the various reasons reality programs such as *The Osbournes, Survivor, The Bachelorette,* and *American Idol* have become so popular. How is the growing popularity of these shows impacting the television viewing audience?

8. Evaluate the use of sweeps ratings periods as a method for measuring local television viewing audiences. Do you think sweeps ratings provide reliable and valid estimates of local television viewing audiences? How might they be improved?

9. Discuss the advantages and disadvantages of advertising on radio. Discuss how radio advertising might be used by national versus local advertisers.

10. IMC Perspective 11-6 discusses how companies such as XM and Sirius are trying to market satellite radio. Discuss how satellite radio might impact traditional radio and the business model for radio advertising if it is successful. Do you think satellite radio will be successful? Why or why not?

11. Discuss how the concept of image transfer can be used in radio advertising. Find an example of a radio campaign that is using this concept and evaluate it.

Evaluation of Print Media

Chapter Objectives

1. To examine the structure of the magazine and newspaper industries and the role of each medium in the advertising program.
2. To analyze the advantages and limitations of magazines and newspapers as advertising media.
3. To examine the various types of magazines and newspapers and the value of each as an advertising medium.
4. To discuss how advertising space is purchased in magazines and newspapers, how readership is measured, and how rates are determined.
5. To consider future developments in magazines and newspapers and how these trends will influence their use as advertising media.

Rolling Stone Reinvents Itself

For more than three decades *Rolling Stone* magazine has been considered the bible of music and popular culture. The magazine's founder and publisher, Jan Wenner, was able to build *Rolling Stone* into a publishing empire because he was one of the first magazine moguls to recognize that rock 'n' roll was the language of choice for the baby-boom generation. Wenner also had the insight and daring to move the magazine beyond music into movies, politics, and other significant cultural issues. *Rolling Stone* took its readers to the bloody streets outside the 1968 Democratic convention in Chicago, to Woodstock, and to the Vietnam war. It also led its readers into the minds of some of the greatest performing artists of the time, such as John Lennon, Bob Dylan, and Mick Jagger, with long, penetrating interviews by Wenner himself. The magazine attracted some of the finest writers in the country and featured the work of gifted photographers such as Annie Leibovitz. It was an honor for writers to be published in the magazine and for musicians to be on the cover.

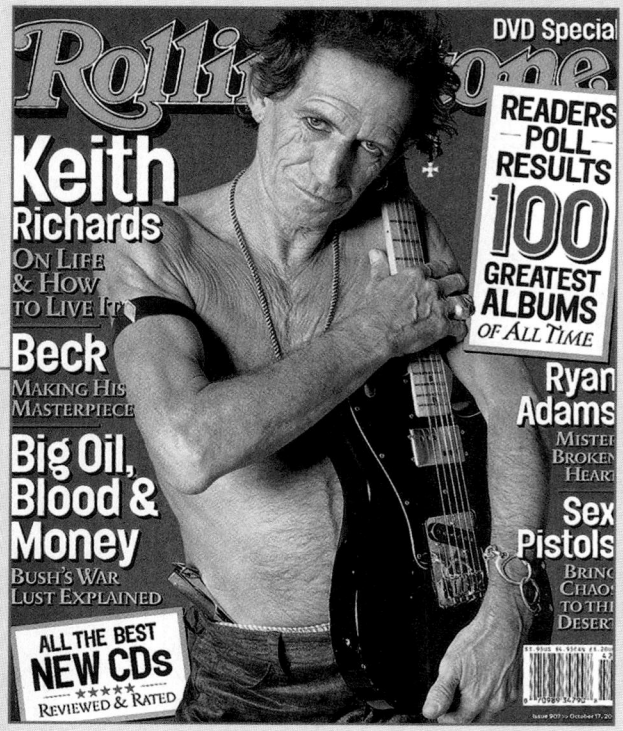

Rolling Stone dominated the music/pop cultural space for more than two decades. However, in the late 80s and early 90s the music scene began to change with the emergence of new genres such as alternative rock, metal, rap, and hip-hop. Critics note that *Rolling Stone*'s music focus began to blur and it fell behind in its coverage of new artists and musical trends, a situation that created an opportunity for new publications. One of the major competitors to emerge was *Spin* magazine, which was started in 1986 by Bob Guccione, Jr., who moved the magazine aggressively into alternative rock and metal in the early 90s. Guccione notes that he modeled the magazine after *Rolling Stone:* "My model for *Spin* was *Rolling Stone* of the 70s, which meant something to me when I was a young man. My romanticism was to parallel what *Rolling Stone* meant to me when I was 18 and have *Spin* be that to today's people who are 18." In addition to *Spin, Rolling Stone* is now being encroached upon by other direct competitors such as *Vibe, Blender,* and *Alternative Press* as well as publications targeting the young male audience, ranging from *ESPN The Magazine* to "lad mags" such as *Maxim, Stuff,* and *FHM.*

Rolling Stone must find a way to make the magazine essential again in a publishing world that has been inspired by it and has long been chipping away at its relevance. Jan Wenner says: "Maybe there is a generational change. Maybe there is a larger significance. But *Rolling Stone* has got to be as relevant today as it was 25 or 30 years ago." *Rolling Stone* is taking steps not only to remain relevant but to recapture its position as a cutting-edge publication that is the bible of

music and popular culture. The magazine has undergone a major redesign and changes to update its image and make it appealing to a younger audience. The new *Rolling Stone* has shorter articles, brighter colors, and less serious news content. The Rock 'n' Roll section has been expanded, with new subsections like "rock feuds," which highlights rock-star whining in convenient sound-byte form. The Reviews section has been broadened to regularly feature movies, books, DVDs, video games, and music gadgets. The New Releases section has been expanded to include more CD reviews in each issue and compete with *Blender*'s exhaustive review section. The redesigned *Rolling Stone* uses more sidebars and navigational aids like toolbars that emblazon department titles across the pages it runs.

The CEO of another publishing company equates the challenge facing *Rolling Stone* with that facing Levi's jeans, noting: "They are both iconic brands in their own sectors, but the biggest challenge is to make sure folks don't perceive Levi's as my father's jeans and *Rolling Stone* as my father's magazine." In the late 80s *Rolling Stone* ran its now famous "Perception/reality" campaign, which was successful in repositioning the publication and changing advertisers' image of the type of person who reads the magazine. The goal of the campaign was to convince advertisers that *Rolling Stone* was not a "hippie magazine" read only by those stuck in the 60s but rather that it reached a well-educated and affluent audience and reflected the changing attitudes, ideas, and lifestyles of people who were changing the world. The challenge facing *Rolling Stone* this time is different, as it must now convince a new generation of young people that it is still relevant to them.

Sources: "It's Over 30; Can Rolling Stone Be Trusted?" *Los Angeles Times,* Sept. 7, 2002, pp. F1, 5; Jon Fine, *Rolling Stone* Reinvents Itself," *Advertising Age,* Aug. 26, 2002, pp. 1, 19.

Magazines and newspapers have been advertising media for more than two centuries; for many years, they were the only major media available to advertisers. With the growth of the broadcast media, particularly television, reading habits declined. More consumers turned to TV viewing not only as their primary source of entertainment but also for news and information. But despite the competition from the broadcast media, newspapers and magazines have remained important media vehicles to both consumers and advertisers.

Thousands of magazines are published in the United States and throughout the world. They appeal to nearly every specific consumer interest and lifestyle, as well as to thousands of businesses and occupations. By becoming a highly specialized medium that reaches specific target audiences, the magazine industry has prospered. Newspapers are still the primary advertising medium in terms of both ad revenue and number of advertisers. Newspapers are particularly important as a local advertising medium for hundreds of thousands of retail businesses and are often used by large national advertisers as well.

Magazines and newspapers are an important part of our lives. For many consumers, newspapers are their primary source of product information. They would not think of going shopping without checking to see who is having a sale or clipping coupons from the weekly food section or Sunday inserts. Many people read a number of different magazines each week or month to become better informed or simply entertained. Individuals employed in various occupations rely on business magazines to keep them current about trends and developments in their industries as well as in business in general.

While most of us are very involved with the print media, it is important to keep in mind that few newspapers or magazines could survive without the support of advertising revenue. Consumer magazines generate an average of 47 percent of their revenues from advertising; business publications receive nearly 73 percent. Newspapers generate 70 percent of their total revenue from advertising. In many cities, the number of daily newspapers has declined because they could not attract enough advertising rev-

enue to support their operations. The print media must be able to attract large numbers of readers or a very specialized audience to be of interest to advertisers.

The Role of Magazines and Newspapers

The role of magazines and newspapers in the advertiser's media plan differs from that of the broadcast media because they allow the presentation of detailed information that can be processed at the reader's own pace. The print media are not intrusive like radio and TV, and they generally require some effort on the part of the reader for the advertising message to have an impact. For this reason, newspapers and magazines are often referred to as *high-involvement media.*[1] Over 80 percent of U.S. households subscribe to or purchase magazines, while the average household buys six different magazines each year.[2]

Newspapers are received in nearly two-thirds of American households daily. Most magazines, however, reach a very selective audience. Like radio, they can be valuable in reaching specific types of consumers and market segments. While both magazines and newspapers are print media, the advantages and disadvantages of the two are quite different, as are the types of advertising each attracts. This chapter focuses on these two major forms of print media. It examines the specific advantages and limitations of each, along with factors that are important in determining when and how to use newspapers and magazines in the media plan.

Magazines

Over the past several decades, magazines have grown rapidly to serve the educational, informational, and entertainment needs of a wide range of readers in both the consumer and business markets. Magazines are the most specialized of all advertising media. While some magazines—such as *Reader's Digest, Time,* and *TV Guide*—are general mass-appeal publications, most are targeted to a very specific audience. There is a magazine designed to appeal to nearly every type of consumer in terms of demographics, lifestyle, activities, interests, or fascination. Numerous magazines are targeted toward specific businesses and industries as well as toward individuals engaged in various professions (Exhibit 12-1).

The wide variety makes magazines an appealing medium to a vast number of advertisers. Although TV accounts for the largest dollar amount of advertising expenditures among national advertisers, more companies advertise in magazines than in any other medium. Users of magazines range from large consumer-product companies such as Procter & Gamble and General Motors, which spend over $400 million a year on magazine advertising, to a small company advertising scuba equipment in *Skin Diver* magazine.

Classifications of Magazines

To gain some perspective on the various types of magazines available and the advertisers that use them, consider the way magazines are generally classified. Standard Rate and Data Service (SRDS), the primary reference source on periodicals for media planners, divides magazines into three broad categories based on the audience to which they are directed: consumer, farm, and business publications. Each category is then further classified according to the magazine's editorial content and audience appeal.

Consumer Magazines Consumer magazines are bought by the general public for information and/or entertainment. SRDS divides 2,700 domestic consumer magazines into 75 classifications, among them general editorial, sports, travel, and women's. Another way of classifying consumer magazines is by distribution: They can be sold through subscription or circulation, store distribution, or both. *Time* and *Newsweek* are sold both through subscription and in stores; *Woman's World* is sold only through stores. *People* magazine was originally sold only through stores but then added subscription sales as it gained in popularity. Figure 12-1 shows the top 10 magazines in terms of subscriptions and single-copy sales, respectively. Magazines can also be classified by frequency; weekly, monthly, and bimonthly are the most common.

Exhibit 12-1 Magazines targeted to a specific industry or profession

Figure 12-1 Top magazines by subscriptions and single-copy sales

By Subscriptions		By Single-Copy Sales	
1. *NRTA/AARP Bulletin*	21,712,410	1. *Cosmopolitan*	2,043,873
2. *AARP Modern Maturity*	17,538,189	2. *Family Circle*	1,607,143
3. *Reader's Digest*	11,527,098	3. *Woman's World*	1,575,731
4. *TV Guide*	8,103,380	4. *National Enquirer*	1,467,702
5. *Better Homes and Gardens*	7,268,408	5. *Woman's Day*	1,419,322
6. *National Geographic*	6,630,182	6. *People Weekly*	1,392,465
7. *Time*	3,948,602	7. *First For Women*	1,392,465
8. *My Generation*	3,843,250	8. *Star*	1,194,676
9. *Ladies' Home Journal*	3,746,271	9. *Glamour*	1,007,390
10. *Good Housekeeping*	3,707,740	10. *Good Housekeeping*	1,001,224

Note: Figures are averages for first six months of 2002 based on Audit Bureau of Circulation statements.
Source; Magazine Publishers of America, fact sheet, www.magazine.org.

Consumer magazines represent the major portion of the magazine industry, accounting for nearly two-thirds of all advertising dollars spent in magazines. Consumer magazines are best suited to marketers interested in reaching general consumers of products and services as well as to companies trying to reach a specific target market. The most frequently advertised categories in consumer magazines are automotive, direct response, toiletries and cosmetics, computers, office equipment and stationery, and business and consumer services. Marketers of tobacco products spend much of their media budget in magazines, since they are prohibited from advertising in the broadcast media.

While large national advertisers tend to dominate consumer magazine advertising in terms of expenditures, the more than 2,000 consumer magazines are also important to smaller companies selling products that appeal to specialized markets. Special-interest magazines assemble consumers with similar lifestyles or interests and offer marketers an efficient way to reach these people with little wasted coverage or circulation. For example, a manufacturer of ski or snowboarding equipment such as Nordica, Rossignol, or Salomon might find *Powder* the best vehicle for advertising to skiers or snowboarders.

Not only are these specialty magazines of value to firms interested in reaching a specific market segment, but their editorial content often creates a very favorable advertising environment for relevant products and services. For example, avid skiers and snowboarders cannot wait for the first snowfall after reading the season's first issues of *Snowboarding* or *Powder* magazine and may be quite receptive to the ads they carry for skiing and snowboarding products and destination ski resorts (Exhibit 12-2).

Exhibit 12-2
Snowboarding magazine is an excellent medium for reaching the serious snowboarder

Farm Publications The second major SRDS category consists of all the magazines directed to farmers and their families. About 300 publications are tailored to nearly every possible type of farming or agricultural interest. Standard Rate and Data Service breaks farm publications into 9 classifications, ranging from general-interest magazines aimed at all types of farmers (e.g., *Farm Journal, Successful Farming, Progressive Farmer*) to those in specialized agricultural areas such as poultry (*Gobbles*), hog farming (*National Hog Farmer*), or cattle raising (*Beef*—see Exhibit 12-3). A number of farm publications are directed at farmers in specific states or regions, such as *Nebraska Farmer* or *Montana Farmer Stockman.* Farm publications are not classified with business publications because historically farms were not perceived as businesses.

Business Publications Business publications are those magazines or trade journals published for specific businesses, industries, or occupations. Standard Rate and Data Service breaks down over 9,300 U.S. magazines and trade journals into more than 180 market classifications. The major classifications include:

1. Magazines directed at specific professional groups, such as *National Law Review* for lawyers and *Architectural Forum* for architects.
2. Industrial magazines directed at businesspeople in various manufacturing and production industries—for example, *Iron and Steelmaker, Chemical Week,* and *Industrial Engineering.*
3. Trade magazines targeted to wholesalers, dealers, distributors, and retailers, among them *Progressive Grocer, Drug Store News, Women's Wear Daily,* and *Restaurant Business.*
4. General business magazines aimed at executives in all areas of business, such as *Forbes, Fortune,* and *BusinessWeek.* (General business publications are also included in SRDS's consumer publications edition.)
5. Health care publications targeted to various areas including dental, medical and surgical, nursing, biotechnological sciences, and hospital administration.

Exhibit 12-3 *Beef* magazine is read by many cattle ranchers

The numerous business publications reach specific types of professional people with particular interests and give them important information relevant to their industry, occupation, and/or careers. Business publications are important to advertisers because they provide an efficient way of reaching the specific types of individuals who constitute their target market. Much marketing occurs at the trade and business-to-business level, where one company sells its products or services directly to another.

Advantages of Magazines

Magazines have a number of characteristics that make them attractive as an advertising medium. Strengths of magazines include their selectivity, excellent reproduction quality, creative flexibility, permanence, prestige, readers' high receptivity and involvement, and services they offer to advertisers.

Selectivity One of the main advantages of using magazines as an advertising medium is their **selectivity,** or ability to reach a specific target audience. Magazines are the most selective of all media except direct mail. Most magazines are published for special-interest groups. The thousands of magazines published in the United States reach all types of consumers and businesses and allow advertisers to target their advertising to segments of the population who buy their products. For example, *Modern Photography* is targeted toward camera buffs, *Stereo Review* reaches those with an avid interest in music, and *Ebony* focuses on the upscale African-American market. Many new magazines are introduced each year targeting new interests and trends. According to Samir Husni, who has been tracking magazine launches since 1985, the category with the greatest number of new magazines during the past 15 years is sports.[3] Nearly 1,000 new titles have been introduced into the crowded sports magazine field, with many of these launches occurring in recent years. Many of the new magazines are targeted at nontraditional sports, such as skateboarding, snowboarding, wrestling, and weight lifting. For example, *Muscle & Fitness Hers* is a new magazine that targets women who are into serious fitness training and weight

Exhibit 12-4 *Muscle & Fitness Hers* is one of the many magazines launched in the sports category in recent years

lifting (Exhibit 12-4). Weider Publications launched the magazine in response to the recent dramatic increase in strength training by women.[4]

In addition to providing selectivity based on interests, magazines can provide advertisers with high demographic and geographic selectivity. *Demographic selectivity,* or the ability to reach specific demographic groups, is available in two ways. First, most magazines are, as a result of editorial content, aimed at fairly well defined demographic segments. *Ladies' Home Journal, Ms., Self,* and *Cosmopolitan* are read predominantly by women; *Esquire, Playboy,* and *Sports Illustrated* are read mostly by men. Older consumers can be reached through publications like *Modern Maturity.* IMC Perspective 12-1 discusses how publishers have been introducing new magazines targeted at teens in an effort to reach this elusive, but important, market segment.

A second way magazines offer demographic selectivity is through special editions. Even magazines that appeal to broader audiences, such as *Reader's Digest, Time,* or *Newsweek,* can provide a high degree of demographic selectivity through their special demographic editions. Most of the top consumer magazines publish different editions targeted at different demographic markets.

Geographic selectivity lets an advertiser focus ads in certain cities or regions. One way to achieve geographic selectivity is by using a magazine that is targeted toward a particular area. Magazines devoted to regional interests include *Yankee* (New England), *Southern Living* (South), *Sunset* (West), and *Texas Monthly* (guess where?), among many others. One of the more successful media developments of recent years has been the growth of city magazines in most major American cities. *Los Angeles Magazine, Philadelphia,* and *Boston,* to name a few, provide residents of these areas with articles concerning lifestyle, events, and the like, in these cities and their surrounding metropolitan areas (Exhibit 12-5). City and regional magazines make it possible for advertisers to focus on specific local markets that may be of interest to them. These publications also have a readership profile that appeals to marketers of upscale brands: high income, college educated, loyal, and influential in their communities.

Another way to achieve geographic selectivity in magazines is through purchasing ad space in specific geographic editions of national or regional magazines. A number of publications divide their circulation into groupings based on regions or major metropolitan areas and offer advertisers the option of concentrating their ads in these editions. For example, *Newsweek* breaks the United States into 11 geographic areas and

Exhibit 12-5 City magazines offer advertisers high geographic selectivity

IMC PERSPECTIVE 12-1

Magazines Seek the Most Elusive Readers of All—Young Males

Teenagers are one of the fastest-growing market segments in America. There are nearly 31 million teenagers in the United States, and according to Teenage Research Unlimited (TRU), a market research firm that specializes in teens, they spend more than $155 billion a year. While their numbers and purchasing power make them a very attractive segment for marketers, teens are very difficult to reach—particularly through magazines. Teenagers spend a lot more time listening to radio, watching TV, and surfing the Internet than reading magazines. And while teenagers in general are an elusive segment for advertisers, young males are a particularly difficult audience to capture.

According to TRU, 80 percent of girls between the ages of 12 and 19 read a magazine for pleasure every week compared to only 65 percent of boys. The Big Five teen magazines—*Seventeen, YM, Teen, Teen People,* and *CosmoGirl*—all target girls. Only *Teen People* manages to pull in a sizable male audience, as male teens account for around 20 percent of its readers. Conventional wisdom in the magazine industry says that teenage males are too antsy to cozy up with a magazine for any length of time. And when they do, they tend to read publications such as *Sports Illustrated, ESPN The Magazine,* or niche titles catering to specific interests such as extreme sports or video gaming. Publishers also note that teen guys are so worried about being teased by friends for needing advice on things such as muscle building or snagging girls that they balk at picking up magazines that deal with these topics. And today, no matter how racy the content, it's difficult for a magazine to compete with the raw subject matter available on the Internet and many cable TV channels.

While few magazines have been successful in reaching the elusive teenage male segment on a large scale, publishers continue to look for the right formula to do so. After years of watching girl-oriented magazines dominate the teen-glossies market, a number of publishers are trying to lure teenage boys. For example, Rodale Inc. created a spin-off of its *Men's Health* magazine for teen guys called *MH-18.* The new magazine's content was similar to the girl's magazine *Seventeen* as it included boyish lifestyle fare: workout plans, girl-kissing tips, and ways to boost grades. When *MH-18* was launched in August 2000, the editor acknowledged that it was a risky venture as he was not sure how teen guys would respond to the new magazine. It did not take long for him to get an answer: *MH-18* lasted only one year before being shuttered by the publisher.

While *MH-18* was unsuccessful with a fairly tame editorial mix, another publisher, TransWorld Media, is taking a different approach with its publication

Stance, which debuted in early 2000. The new publication takes its cover-shot and content cues from adult magazines such as *Gear, Maxim, Stuff,* and *FHM. Stance*'s publisher says that the magazine is a combination of the things teenage boys want to look at: girls, action sports, video games, cars, and music. *Stance* steers clear of grooming articles and girl-getting pointers, focusing more on cool stuff to buy such as computers and video game players and exotic things to do such as snowboarding in Austria. The magazine has been very successful in attracting readers as well as a variety of advertisers.

Marketers will be keeping a close watch on *Stance* and other new magazines that target the elusive teen male market. Advertisers would love to see magazines that can attract teenage boys succeed so that they can better target this important market segment. Publishers have already proved that they can attract teenage girls. Now if they can only get the guys to pick up a magazine!

Sources: Jon Fine, "Rodale Names Steve Murphy New CEO," *Advertising Age,* Jan. 14, 2002, p. 7; Larry Dobrow, "Sounding Boards," *Advertising Age,* June 25, 2001, pp. S1, 8; Erin White, "Teen Mags for Guys Not Dolls," *The Wall Street Journal,* Aug. 10, 2000, pp. B1, 4.

Exhibit 12-6 Geographic editions of *Newsweek* magazine

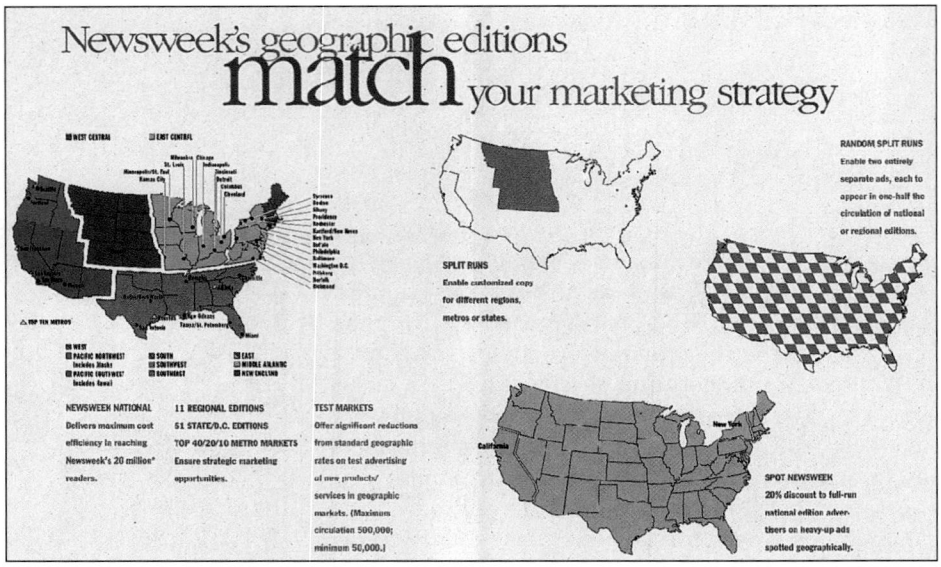

offers regional editions for each, as shown in Exhibit 12-6. *Newsweek* also offers advertisers their choice of editions directed to the top 40, 20, or 10 metropolitan areas. Many magazines allow advertisers to combine regional or metropolitan editions to best match the geographic market of interest to them.

Standard Rate and Data Service lists over 350 consumer magazines offering geographic and/or demographic editions. Regional advertisers can purchase space in editions that reach only areas where they have distribution, yet still enjoy the prestige of advertising in a major national magazine. National advertisers can use the geographic editions to focus their advertising on areas with the greatest potential or those needing more promotional support. They can also use regional editions to test-market products or alternative promotional campaigns in various regions of the country.

Ads in regional editions can also list the names of retailers or distributors in various markets, thus encouraging greater local support from the trade. The trend toward regional marketing is increasing the importance of having regional media available to marketers. The availability of regional and demographic editions can also reduce the cost per thousand for reaching desired audiences.

Reproduction Quality One of the most valued attributes of magazine advertising is the reproduction quality of the ads. Magazines are generally printed on high-quality paper stock and use printing processes that provide excellent reproduction in black and white or color. Since magazines are a visual medium where illustrations are often a dominant part of an ad, this is a very important property. The reproduction quality of most magazines is far superior to that offered by the other major print medium of newspapers, particularly when color is needed. The use of color has become a virtual necessity in most product categories, and more than two-thirds of all magazine ads now use color.

Creative Flexibility In addition to their excellent reproduction capabilities, magazines also offer advertisers a great deal of flexibility in terms of the type, size, and placement of the advertising material. Some magazines offer (often at extra charge) a variety of special options that can enhance the creative appeal of the ad and increase attention and readership. Examples include gatefolds, bleed pages, inserts, and creative space buys.

Gatefolds enable an advertiser to make a striking presentation by using a third page that folds out and gives the ad an extra-large spread. Gatefolds are often found at the inside cover of large consumer magazines or on some inside pages. Advertisers use gatefolds to make a very strong impression, especially on special occasions such as the introduction of a new product or brand. For example, automobile advertisers often use gatefolds to introduce new versions of their cars each model year. Not all magazines offer gatefolds, however, and they must be reserved well in advance and are sold at a premium.

Bleed pages are those where the advertisement extends all the way to the end of the page, with no margin of white space around the ad. Bleeds give the ad an impression

of being larger and make a more dramatic impact. Many magazines charge an extra 10 to 20 percent for bleeds.

In addition to gatefolds and bleed pages, creative options available through magazines include unusual page sizes and shapes. Some advertisers have grabbed readers' attention by developing three-dimensional pop-up ads that jump off the page. Exhibit 12-7 shows a pop-up ad that Nabisco used in several trade magazines to promote its Reduced Fat cracker and cookie products.

Various other *inserts* are used in many magazines. These include return cards, recipe booklets, coupons, records, and even product samples. Cosmetic companies use scratch-and-sniff inserts to introduce new fragrances, and some companies use them to promote deodorants, laundry detergents, or other products whose scent is important. Inserts are also used in conjunction with direct-response ads and as part of sales promotion strategies.

Exhibit 12-7 Nabisco used a pop-up ad to get the attention of trade magazine readers

Scented ads, pop-ups, singing ads, and other techniques are ways to break through the clutter in magazines and capture consumers' attention. However, there recently has been some backlash against various types of *printaculars.* Critics argue that they alter the appearance and feel of a magazine and the reader's relationship to it. Advertisers do not want to run regular ads that have to compete against heavy inserts, pop-ups, talking ads, or other distractions. Some advertisers and agencies are even asking publishers to notify them when they plan to run any spectacular inserts so that they can decide whether to pull their regular ads from the issue.[5]

Creative space buys are another option of magazines. Some magazines let advertisers purchase space units in certain combinations to increase the impact of their media budget. For example, WD-40, an all-purpose lubrication product, uses half- or quarter-page ads on consecutive pages of several magazines, mentioning a different use for the product on each page, as shown in Exhibit 12-8. This strategy gives the company greater impact for its media dollars and is helpful in promoting the product's variety of uses.

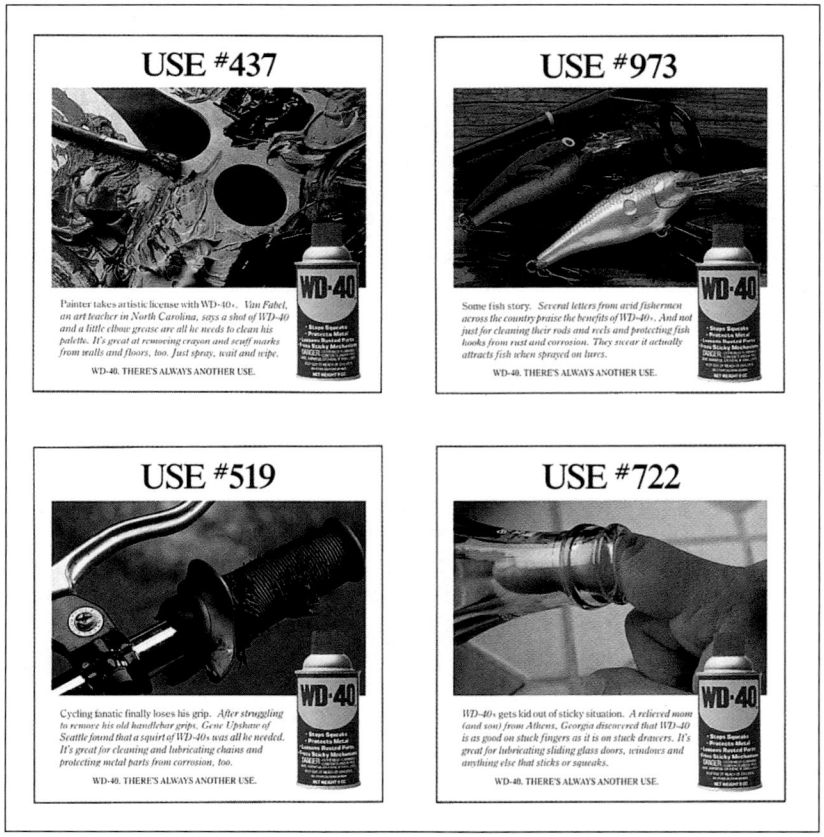

Exhibit 12-8 WD-40 uses quarter-page ads to get greater impact from its media budget

Permanence Another distinctive advantage offered by magazines is their long life span. TV and radio are characterized by fleeting messages that have a very short life span; newspapers are generally discarded soon after being read. Magazines, however, are generally read over several days and are often kept for reference. They are retained in the home longer than any other medium and are generally referred to on several occasions. A study of magazine audiences found that readers devote nearly an hour over a period of two or three days to reading an average magazine.[6] Studies have also found that nearly 75 percent of consumers retain magazines for future reference.[7] One benefit of the longer life of magazines is that reading occurs at a less hurried pace and there is more opportunity to examine ads in considerable detail. This means ads can use longer and more detailed copy, which can be very important for high-involvement and complex products or services. The permanence of magazines also means readers can be exposed to ads on multiple occasions and can pass magazines along to other readers.

Prestige Another positive feature of magazine advertising is the prestige the product or service may gain from advertising in publications with a favorable image. Companies whose products rely heavily on perceived quality, reputation, and/or image often buy space in prestigious publications with high-quality editorial content whose consumers have a high level of interest in the advertising pages. For example, *Esquire* and *GQ* cover men's fashions in a very favorable environment, and a clothing manufacturer may advertise its products in these magazines to enhance the prestige of its lines. *Architectural Digest* provides an impressive editorial environment that includes high-quality photography and artwork. The magazine's upscale readers are likely to have a favorable image of the publication that may transfer to the products advertised on its pages. *Good Housekeeping* provides a unique consumer's refund or replacement policy for products that bear the limited warranty seal or advertise in the magazine. This can increase a consumer's confidence in a particular brand and reduce the amount of perceived risk associated with a purchase.

While most media planners recognize that the environment created by a publication is important, it can be difficult to determine the image a magazine provides. Subjective estimates based on media planners' experience are often used to assess a magazine's prestige, as are objective measures such as reader opinion surveys.[8]

Consumer Receptivity and Involvement With the exception of newspapers, consumers are more receptive to advertising in magazines than in any other medium. Magazines are generally purchased because the information they contain interests the reader, and ads provide additional information that may be of value in making a purchase decision. The Study of Media Involvement conducted for the Magazine Publishers of America (MPA) found that magazines are the medium turned to most by consumers for knowledge, information, and usable ideas (see Figure 12-2). The study found that magazines are consumers' primary source of information for a variety of products and services, including automobiles, beauty and grooming, clothing and fashion, financial planning, and personal and business travel.[9] The MPA cites consumer involvement as a reason for the success of magazine advertising in its "Magazine Plans That Work" campaign. This campaign consists of a series of ads promoting the results achieved by advertisers who have made magazines the lead media vehicle or part of their media mix plan (Exhibit 12-9).

In addition to their relevance, magazine ads are likely to be received favorably by consumers because, unlike broadcast ads, they are nonintrusive and can easily be ignored. Studies show that the majority of magazine readers welcome ads; only a small percentage have negative attitudes toward magazine advertising.[10] Some magazines, such as bridal or fashion publications, are purchased as much for their advertising as for their editorial content. MPA-sponsored studies have shown that magazine readers are more likely to attend to and recall ads than are TV viewers.

Exhibit 12-9 The MPA has been promoting the value of magazines in successful marketing and brand-building programs with a series of ads such as the one shown

The Study of Media Involvement, conducted by Beta Research, an independent research firm, reports that magazines are the medium turned to most by consumers for knowledge, information, and usable ideas. In fact, 95 percent of U.S. adults cite magazines as their premier source of insight and ideas. This is also true when consumers seek information about specific topics affecting their lives—ranging from automobiles to fashion to personal finance.

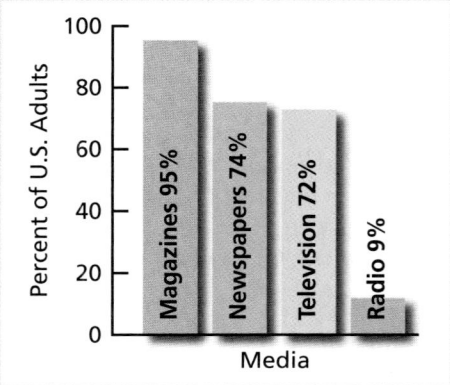

Note: Based on net of 12 measured product categories, multiple responses.

Figure 12-2 Magazines are the premier source of consumer knowledge

Area of Interest	Percent of Adults Referring to: Magazines	TV	Newspapers	Radio
Automobiles	39%	21%	29%	1%
Beauty and grooming	63	20	5	0
Clothing and fashion	58	18	15	0
Computers: hardware and software	54	14	11	0
Food	50	19	22	1
Fitness and exercise	49	36	6	1
Financial planning	45	11	31	2
Home repair/decorating	69	13	11	0
Sports: equipment/performance	49	24	7	1
Travel: personal and business	42	16	29	2

Services A final advantage of magazines is the special services some publications offer advertisers. Some magazines have merchandising staffs that call on trade intermediaries like retailers to let them know a product is being advertised in their publication and to encourage them to display or promote the item. Another service offered by magazines (usually the larger ones) is research studies that they conduct on consumers. These studies may deal with general consumer trends, changing purchase patterns, and media usage or may be relevant to a specific product or industry.

An important service offered by some magazines is **split runs,** where two or more versions of an ad are printed in alternate copies of a particular issue of a magazine. This service is used to conduct a split-run test, which allows the advertiser to determine which ad generates the most responses or inquiries, providing some evidence as to their effectiveness.

Disadvantages of Magazines

Although the advantages offered by magazines are considerable, they have certain drawbacks too. These include the costs of advertising, their limited reach and frequency, the long lead time required in placing an ad, and the problem of clutter and heavy advertising competition.

Costs The costs of advertising in magazines vary according to the size of the audience they reach and their selectivity. Advertising in large mass-circulation magazines like *TV Guide, Time,* or *Reader's Digest* can be very expensive. For example, a full-page, four-color ad in *Time* magazine's national edition (circulation 4.2 million) cost

$202,000 in 2002. Popular positions such as the back cover cost even more. By contrast, a full-page, four-color ad in *Tennis* (circulation 710,000) cost $64,000.

Like any medium, magazines must be considered not only from an absolute cost perspective but also in terms of relative costs. Most magazines emphasize their effectiveness in reaching specific target audiences at a low cost per thousand. Also, an increasing number of magazines are offering demographic and geographic editions, which helps lower their costs. Media planners generally focus on the relative costs of a publication in reaching their target audience. However, they may recommend a magazine with a high cost per thousand because of its ability to reach a small, specialized market segment. Of course, advertisers with limited budgets will be interested in the absolute costs of space in a magazine and the costs of producing quality ads for these publications.

Limited Reach and Frequency Magazines are generally not as effective as other media in offering reach and frequency. While nearly 90 percent of adults in the United States read one or more consumer magazines each month, the percentage of adults reading any individual publication tends to be much smaller, so magazines have a thin penetration of households. For example, *Reader's Digest* has the third-highest circulation of any magazine, at 12.2 million, but this represents only 11 percent of the 106 million households in the United States.

As shown in Figure 12-3, only 37 magazines had a paid circulation over 2 million in 2002. Thus, advertisers seeking broad reach must make media buys in a number of magazines, which means more negotiations and transactions. For a broad-reach strategy, magazines are used in conjunction with other media. Since most magazines are monthly or at best weekly publications, the opportunity for building frequency through the use of the same publication is limited. Using multiple ads in the same issue of a publication is an inefficient way to build frequency. Most advertisers try to achieve frequency by adding other magazines with similar audiences to the media schedule.

Long Lead Time Another drawback of magazines is the long lead time needed to place an ad. Most major publications have a 30- to 90-day lead time, which means space must be purchased and the ad must be prepared well in advance of the actual publication date. No changes in the art or copy of the ad can be made after the closing date. This long lead time means magazine ads cannot be as timely as other media, such as radio or newspapers, in responding to current events or changing market conditions.

Clutter and Competition While the problem of advertising clutter is generally discussed in reference to the broadcast media, magazines also have this drawback. The clutter problem for magazines is something of a paradox: The more successful a magazine becomes, the more advertising pages it attracts, and this leads to greater clutter. In fact, magazines generally gauge their success in terms of the number of advertising pages they sell.

Magazine publishers do attempt to control the clutter problem by maintaining a reasonable balance of editorial pages to advertising. According to the Magazine Publishers of America, the average consumer magazine contains 45 percent advertising and 55 percent editorial.[11] However, many magazines contain ads on more than half of their pages. This clutter makes it difficult for an advertiser to gain readers' attention and draw them into the ad. Thus, many print ads use strong visual images, catchy headlines, or some of the creative techniques discussed earlier to grab the interest of magazine readers. Some advertisers create their own custom magazines to sidestep the advertising clutter problem as well as to have control over editorial content. A number of companies have also been publishing their own magazines to build relationships with their customers. For example, Farmer's Insurance sends its customers a magazine called *The Friendly Review* that contains useful articles on a variety of topics. Swedish retailer IKEA has partnered with John Brown Contract Publishing to custom-publish a magazine titled *space*.[12] *space* is both a showcase for IKEA merchandise and a magazine that contains informative articles about home furnishings, modern design, and

Figure 12-3 Top 50 magazines in average paid circulation

Rank	Publication	Total Paid Circulation	Rank	Publication	Total Paid Circulation
1	*NRTA/AARP Bulletin*	21,712,410	26	*Southern Living*	2,546,471
2	*AARP Modern Maturity*	17,538,189	27	*Glamour*	2,509,566
3	*Reader's Digest*	12,212,040	28	*Seventeen*	2,431,943
4	*TV Guide*	9,072,609	29	*Redbook*	2,380,410
5	*Better Homes and Gardens*	7,602,575	30	*Martha Stewart Living*	2,323,129
6	*National Geographic*	6,890,852	31	*O, The Oprah Magazine*	2,275,599
7	*Good Housekeeping*	4,708,964	32	*YM*	2,262,574
8	*Family Circle*	4,671,052	33	*AAA Going Places*	2,191,629
9	*Woman's Day*	4,167,933	34	*Parents*	2,092,443
10	*Time—The Weekly Newsmagazine*	4,114,137	35	*Smithsonian*	2,040,294
			36	*Parenting Magazine*	2,039,462
11	*Ladies' Home Journal*	4,101,280	37	*U.S. News & World Report*	2,018,621
12	*My Generation*	3,846,955	38	*Money*	1,945,265
13	*People Weekly*	3,617,127	39	*Ebony*	1,884,739
14	*Rosie*	3,503,993	40	*National Enquirer*	1,801,598
15	*Westways*	3,328,280	41	*Country Living*	1,711,449
16	*Home & Away*	3,313,966	42	*Shape*	1,692,690
17	*Sports Illustrated*	3,252,896	43	*Woman's World*	1,668,482
18	*Newsweek*	3,248,097	44	*In Style*	1,660,193
19	*Playboy*	3,217,269	45	*Men's Health*	1,659,594
20	*Prevention*	3,131,814	46	*Teen People*	1,651,723
21	*Cosmopolitan*	2,963,351	47	*VFW Magazine*	1,645,944
22	*Guideposts*	2,747,626	48	*Entertainment Weekly*	1,635,623
23	*Via Magazine*	2,655,203	49	*Cooking Light*	1,603,680
24	*American Legion Magazine*	2,644,518	50	*Golf Digest*	1,578,248
25	*Maxim*	2,569,172			

Note: Figures are averages for first six months of 2002 based on Audit Bureau of Circulation statements.
Source: Magazine Publishers of America, fact sheet, www.magazine.org.

lifestyle trends. *space* is sold at IKEA stores, and on newsstands, throughout North America. Custom-published magazines have also become very popular among tobacco companies, such as Philip Morris, which direct-mail them to their customer base.[13] IMC Perspective 12-2 discusses how a number of companies are now publishing "admazines" to better communicate with their customers.

Clutter is not as serious an issue for the print media as for radio or TV, since consumers tend to be more receptive and tolerant of print advertising. They can also control their exposure to a magazine ad simply by turning the page.

Magazine Circulation and Readership

Two of the most important considerations in deciding whether to use a magazine in the advertising media plan are the size and characteristics of the audience it reaches. Media buyers evaluate magazines on the basis of their ability to deliver the advertiser's message to as many people as possible in the target audience. To do this, they must consider the circulation of the publication as well as its total readership and match these figures against the audience they are attempting to reach.

IMC PERSPECTIVE 12-2

Companies Create "Admazines" to Connect with Customers

Advertising clutter is a problem in most media, and magazines are no exception. The average consumer magazine has ads on nearly half of its pages, and in some publications the percentage is even higher. Some companies are dealing with the clutter problem by publishing their own custom magazines. Custom publications started more than 10 years ago; some of the latest include *No Boundaries,* a quarterly publication from Ford that is sent to owners of the company's sport utility vehicles; *Everyday Pictures,* which is published by Kodak; *Nikegoddess,* which is an important part of Nike's efforts to reach women; and *Mary Beth's Beanies & More,* a bright bimonthly that quickly sold out its 100,000-copy premier issue, which cost $5. Marketers spend nearly $1.5 billion a year producing their own magazines, according to the Custom Publishing Council, and more companies are entering the fray.

Custom publications offer marketers a way of dealing with the clutter problem, but there are also other reasons why companies with big brand names are publishing their own "admazines." Marketers have total control of the editorial and advertising content of these publications and view them as a way of providing valuable information to their customers that can help with retention and loyalty. Kodak's new custom magazine, *Everyday Pictures,* is sized to fit in supermarket checkout racks and provides the average person with tips on how to take better pictures. A Kodak consumer-imaging-product manager notes: "There was nothing in the photography category that spoke to the average soccer mom."

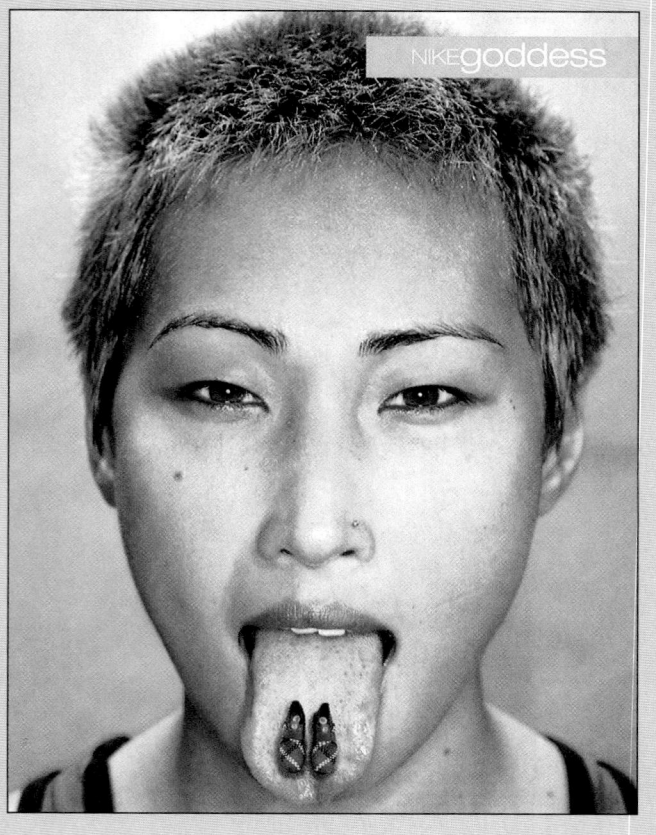

Ford feels that its new publication, *No Boundaries,* can play an important role in creating owner loyalty. The magazine contains seasonal outdoor-adventure and travel stories and provides owners of Ford SUVs, such as Explorers, Expeditions, and Excursions, with the opportunity to purchase gear and clothing brands. Ford's advertising agency, J. Walter Thompson, suggested the customer magazine because "it can take us to places where advertising would never let us" in developing owner loyalty. The magazine also complements Ford's move into television programming, which will include a TV program with the same name.

Nike's new custom publication, *Nikegoddess,* is sent to select subscribers of women's magazines such as *Sports Illustrated for Women, In Style, Self,* and *Teen People* and is also available at the company's Nike Town stores and retailers such as Nordstrom and Finish Line. The quarterly publication is part of the company's effort to communicate better with women and showcases Nike's women's products as well as providing lifestyle fitness and sports information. In early 2002 Nike launched another custom publication, *Brand Jordan,* in partnership with Hearst Custom Publishing. Nike plans to publish the magazine four times a year and will use it primarily to promote the company's new Jordan brand.

Many in the publishing industry feel that the number of custom publications will increase in the future. Publishers are interested in doing deals with major companies and brands to lessen the financial risk of launching a new magazine, and marketers see such publications as another means of communicating with their customers and connecting them to their brands. As new technology makes it easier for companies to build databases and track their customers, many are looking to custom magazines as a way of communicating with their most valued customers and building long-term relationships with them.

Sources: Aileen Jacobson, "Magazines with a Message: Companies Are Turning to Custom Publications to Build Goodwill—and Sales," *Newsday,* Feb. 13, 2002, p. B6; Theresa Howard, "They Look Like Magazines, but They're Really Ads," *USA Today,* Aug. 13, 2001, p. B4.

Circulation

Circulation figures represent the number of individuals who receive a publication through either subscription or store purchase. The number of copies distributed to these original subscribers or purchasers is known as *primary circulation* and is the basis for the magazine's rate structure. Circulation fluctuates from issue to issue, particularly for magazines that rely heavily on retail or newsstand sales. Many publications base their rates on *guaranteed circulation* and give advertisers a rebate if the number of delivered magazines falls below the guarantee. To minimize rebating, most guaranteed circulation figures are conservative; that is, they are set safely below the average actual delivered circulation. Advertisers are not charged for any excess circulation.

Many publishers became unhappy with the guaranteed circulation concept, since it requires them to provide refunds if guarantees are not met but results in a bonus for advertisers when circulation exceeds the guarantee. Thus, many publications have gone to a circulation rate base system. Rates are based on a set average circulation that is nearly always below the actual circulation delivered by a given issue but carries no guarantee. However, circulation is unlikely to fall below the rate base, since this would reflect negatively on the publication and make it difficult to attract advertisers at prevailing rates.

Circulation Verification Given that circulation figures are the basis for a magazine's advertising rates and one of the primary considerations in selecting a publication, the credibility of circulation figures is important. Most major publications are audited by one of the circulation verification services. Consumer magazines and farm publications are audited by the Audit Bureau of Circulations (ABC), which was organized in 1914 and is sponsored by advertisers, agencies, and publishers. ABC collects and evaluates information regarding the subscriptions and sales of magazines and newspapers to verify their circulation figures. Only publications with 70 percent or more paid circulation are eligible for verification audits by ABC. In 2002 the ABC approved new guidelines for counting magazine circulation and sales. The changes did away with the long-standing "50 percent rule," in which copies that sold for less than half of the basic price of a magazine could not be counted as paid circulation. Under the new rules copies sold at any price may be counted, but the magazine must disclose sales and prices in its circulation statements.[14] Certain business publications are audited by the Business Publications Audit (BPA) of Circulation. Many of these are published on a **controlled-circulation basis,** meaning copies are sent (usually free) to individuals the publisher believes can influence the company's purchases.

Circulation verification services provide media planners with reliable figures regarding the size and distribution of a magazine's circulation that help them evaluate its worth as a media vehicle. The ABC statement also provides other important information. It shows how a magazine is distributed by state and size, as well as percentage of the circulation sold at less than full value and percentage arrears (how many subscriptions are being given away). Many advertisers believe that subscribers who pay for a magazine are more likely to read it than are those who get it at a discount or for free.

Media buyers are generally skeptical about publications whose circulation figures are not audited by one of the verification services, and some companies will not advertise in unaudited publications. Circulation data, along with the auditing source, are available from Standard Rate and Data Service or from the publication itself. Exhibit 12-10 shows a sample magazine publisher's statement, which is subject to audit by Audit Bureau of Circulations.

Readership and Total Audience

Advertisers are often interested in the number of people a publication reaches as a result of secondary, or pass-along, readership. **Pass-along readership** can occur when the primary subscriber or purchaser gives a magazine to another person or when the publication is read in doctors' waiting rooms or beauty salons, on airplanes, and so forth.

Advertisers generally attach greater value to the primary in-home reader than the pass-along reader or out-of-home reader, as the former generally spends more time with the publication, picks it up more often, and receives greater satisfaction from it. Thus, this reader is more likely to be attentive and responsive to ads. However, the

Exhibit 12-10 Example of an Audit Bureau of Circulations publisher's statement

MAGAZINE
PUBLISHER'S STATEMENT
Subject to Audit

Audit Bureau of Circulations
900 N. Meacham Road Schaumburg, IL 60173-4968
P: 847.605.0909 • F: 847.605.0483
URL: www.accessabc.com

Prototype Magazine

For the six months ended June 30, 2002

Field Served: Health Industry.

Established:	1990	ABC Member since:	1992
Frequency:	10 times/year	ABC Member Number:	04-0000-0

Published by XYZ Publications, Inc.
123 Any Lane • Anytown, IL 60000
P: 000.000.0000 • F: 000.000.000 • URL: www.prototype.com

AVERAGE CIRCULATION

1 Total Average Paid Circulation: 805,237

		% of Total	
Subscriptions:	657,209	81.6	
Association, See Par. 9(c) - Non-deductible	100,000	12.4	
Total Subscriptions:	757,209		
Single Copy Sales:	48,028	6.0	
Total Paid	805,237	100.0	
Paid Advertising Rate Base:			800,000
% Above/Below Rate Base (+/–)			0.7

PRICES

2A AVERAGE PRICE
Represents the price of individual subscriptions sold during the 12 month period ending December 31, 2001

Average subscription price:	Net	Gross
Per Copy	$1.58	$2.10 (optional)
Annualized	$15.80	$21.00 (optional)
Single copy cover price		$3.95
Publisher's suggested 1 year price		$24.95

2B SUPPLEMENTAL ANALYSIS OF PRICE
Gross individual subscriptions sold in the six month period ended June 30, 2002 at below 35% of average net price.

1 yr. $4.50. See Par. 9(d) 38,000
Total ..... 38,000 (6.9% of total new and renewal subscriptions for the six-month period)

ANALYSIS OF TOTAL NEW AND RENEWAL SUBSCRIPTIONS

3 Total gross individual subscriptions (new and renewal) sold in the six month period ended June 30, 2002

A. DURATION		%
(a) One to six months (1 to 5 issues)	21,537	5.0
(b) Seven to eleven months (6 to 9 issues)	8,535	1.9
(c) Twelve months (10 issues)	270,330	63.3
(d) Thirteen to twenty-four months	71,149	16.7
(e) Twenty-five months and more	57,059	13.4
Total Subscriptions Sold in Period	427,003	100.0

B. USE OF PREMIUMS		
(a) Ordered without premium	427,000	100.0
(b) Ordered with material reprinted from this publication	None	
(c) Ordered with other premiums	None	
Total Subscriptions Sold in Period	427,003	100.0

C. CHANNELS		%
(a) Ordered by mail and/or direct request (may include direct mail, renewal mail, insert cards, television, direct mail agents, Internet and e-mail, etc.)	273,389	64.0
(b) Ordered through salespeople:		
1. Catalog agencies and individual agents - includes institutional and library subscriptions	4,597	1.1
2. Publisher's own and independent salespeople - includes sales through both direct personal contact and telemarketing efforts for consumer, trade and public place subscriptions	116,853	27.4
3. Members of schools, churches, fraternal and similar organizations - includes fund-raising programs directed to individuals	12,161	2.8
(c) Association members. See Par. 9(c)	20,000	4.7
Total Subscriptions Sold in Period	427,000	100.0

This publication also has Web Site Activity audited by ABC:

www. ABC Interactive™ June 1 - 30, 2002 Latest Data Available

	Total	Daily	Mon. to Fri.	Sat. & Sun.
Page Impressions	356,550	8,948	10,741	4,540
Unique Users	4,728,001	197,434	178,248	160,291

7/26/2002

ANALYSIS OF AVERAGE CIRCULATION

4A PAID BY ISSUE

Issue	Subscriptions	Single Copy Sales	Total Paid
Jan.	759,381	46,228	805,609
Feb.	758,848	46,601	805,449
Mar.	756,100	48,436	804,536
Apr.	753,899	51,602	805,501
May/June	757,818	47,273	805,091

4B SUPPLEMENTAL ANALYSIS OF AVERAGE PAID CIRCULATION

The following averages, as reported below, are included in Par. 1 and annotated here per applicable rules. See Par. 9 for full explanation.

Subscriptions:

Club/Membership (1). See Par. 9(f)	90,000
Public Place/Sponsored Sales (1). See Par. 9(g)	100,000

(1) This average exceeds 10% of average subscription circulation as reported in Par. 1.

AVERAGE CIRCULATION of Regional Metro and Demographic Editions

5

Edition & Number of Issues	Paid
South (5)	130,000
Northeast (5)	170,000

POST EXPIRATION COPIES

6 (a) Average number of copies served on subscriptions not more than three months after expiration. 3,750 0.4%

GEOGRAPHIC DATA for the April, 2002 Issue

7A ANALYSIS BY ABCD COUNTY SIZE

Paid circulation of this issue was 0.0% greater than the total average paid circulation.

County Size	% of Households	Paid Circulation	% of Total Circulation	Index (% of Circulation/ % of Households)
A	40	364,174	46.8	117
B	30	240,133	30.6	103
C	15	103,535	13.3	89
D	15	70,598	9.1	61

County Size Group Definitions by the A.C. Nielsen Company- Data for the conterminous 48 states.

Page 2 of 4 - Prototype Magazine (04-0000-0)
Copyright © Audit Bureau of Circulations. All rights reserved.

value of pass-along readers should not be discounted. They can greatly expand a magazine's readership. *People* magazine commissioned a media research study to determine that its out-of-home audience spends as much time reading the publication as do its primary in-home readers.

You can calculate the **total audience,** or **readership,** of a magazine by multiplying the readers per copy (the total number of primary and pass-along readers) by the circulation of an average issue. For example, a magazine that has a circulation of 1 million and 3.5 readers per copy has a total audience of 3.5 million. However, rate structures are generally based on the more verifiable primary circulation figures, and many media planners devalue pass-along readers by as much as 50 percent. Total readership estimates are reported by major syndicated magazine research services (discussed next), but media buyers view these numbers with suspicion.

Exhibit 12-11 Information about magazines is available from SRDS

SRDS - 98.006 Record Number 4 October 23, 2002; 14:20; 2

ESPN

A Burda Media Magazine, Inc. Publication
See Advertising Front Cover.
See Our Ad Second Cover.

ABC

CAUTION
NEW RATES EFFECTIVE
January 1, 2003
SEE FUTURE RATES AT THE END OF
THIS LISTING.

Effective 1-1-02 Continued 10-02

September, 2002

5. BLACK/WHITE RATES

	1 X	3 X	6 X	12 X
1 page	92,000	86,080	80,400	69,985
2/3 page	69,000	64,560	60,300	52,490
1/2 page	60,400	51,370	46,230	40,255
1/3 page (v)	47,400	44,345	39,930	31,485
1/3 page (sq)	47,400	44,345	39,930	31,485
6. COLOR RATES	1 X	3 X	6 X	12 X
1 page	92,000	86,080	80,400	69,985
2/3 page	69,000	64,560	60,300	52,490
1/2 page	60,400	51,370	46,230	40,255
1/3 page (v)	47,400	44,345	39,930	31,485
1/3 page (sq)	47,400	44,345	39,930	31,485
4-Color	125,000	116,900	109,200	95,000
2nd cover	102,000	102,000	102,000	102,000
3rd cover	102,000	102,000	102,000	102,000
4th cover	125,000	117,000	109,200	95,000
7. COVERS	1 X	3 X	6 X	12 X
4-Color	125,000	116,900	109,200	95,000
2nd cover	102,000	102,000	102,000	102,000
3rd cover	102,000	102,000	102,000	102,000
4th cover	125,000	117,000	109,200	95,000
8. INSERTS	1 X	3 X	6 X	12 X
1 page	92,000	86,080	80,400	69,985
2/3 page	69,000	64,560	60,300	52,490
1/2 page	60,400	51,370	46,230	40,255
1/3 page (v)	47,400	44,345	39,930	31,485
1/3 page (sq)	47,400	44,345	39,930	31,485
4-Color	125,000	116,900	109,200	95,000
2nd cover	102,000	102,000	102,000	102,000
3rd cover	102,000	102,000	102,000	102,000
4th cover	125,000	117,000	109,200	95,000

9. GUIDE
No charge.

10. MECHANICAL REQUIREMENTS
Ads are SWOP Print Media Production Source.
Printing Process: Offset Full Run, Gloss.
Binding: Saddle.
Binding Method: Saddle Stitched.
Cover Available: 4-color process; GAS/SWOP; Metallic, Varnish, 4-color process.

NON-BLEED
STANDARD AD PAGE DIMENSIONS

	Trim	Bleed	Live
Spread	16 X 10	16 X 10	14 X 8.5
1/2 V	8 X 10	8 X 10	7 X 9.5
1/2 H	16 X 5	16 X 5	14 X 4.5
1/4 V	8 X 5	8 X 5	7 X 4.5

11. ISSUE AND CLOSING DATES
Published 9 times.

	On sale	Closing
Dec 2002	10/1	8/30
Oct 14/02	10/1	8/13
Nov 11/02	11/1	9/10
Nov 25/02	11/15	10/25
Dec 9/02	11/15	10/25
Dec 23/02	12/1	11/8
Jan 6/03	12/15	11/26
Jan 20/03	1/1	12/6
Feb 3/03	1/15	12/26
Feb 17/03	1/15	1/3
Mar 3/03	2/1	1/10
Mar 17/03	2/15	1/31
Mar 31/03	2/15	1/31
Apr 14/03	3/1	2/14
Apr 28/03	3/15	2/28
May 12/03	4/1	3/14
May 26/03	3/15	4/25
Jun 9/03	4/15	4/25
Jun 23/03	4/15	4/25
Jul 7/03	5/1	5/9
Jul 21/03	5/15	5/30
Aug 4/03	6/1	5/30
Aug 18/03	6/15	6/27
Sep 1/03	7/1	7/8
Sep 15/03	7/15	7/29
Sep 29/03	7/15	7/29
Oct 13/03	8/1	8/12
Oct 27/03	8/15	8/26
Nov 10/03	9/1	9/9
Nov 24/03	9/15	9/30
Dec 8/03	9/15	9/30
Dec 22/03	10/1	10/7

12. CIRCULATION
Established 1990. Totals: rate 1,700,000 (as of 06-30)
Statistics from: Audit Bureau of Circulations
A.B.C. 6-30-02 (6 mos. ave.-Magazine Form)
Total Average Paid Circulation: 1,700,000 (Rate)
Average Non-Analyzed Non-Paid Circulation (not incl. above): 0
Average Non-Analyzed Non-Paid Circulation (not incl. above): 0
Qualified Recipients: 0
DEPARTMENT DISTRIBUTION: Rate (Rate) 1,700,000
Sex: Male 50 Female 50 Age: 18-24 10 25-34 20 35-44 20 45-54 20 55-64 15 65 & Over 15 Median Age 35 Median Income $ 45,000
Ethnic: Caucasian 75 Black 10 Hispanic 10 Other 5
Occupation: Prof/Tech 20 Clerical 10 Sales 10 Mgr/Adm 20 Craftsmen 10 Other 30
Advertising rate base: 1,700,000
Effective date rate base: 2-01
Circulation Guarantee: Effective with January 1, 2003 issue, guarantee is set at 1,600,000
Circulation Verification Method: Audit Bureau of Circulations

FUTURE RATES
ADVERTISING RATES

Effective 1-1-03 Continued 10-02

5. BLACK/WHITE RATES

	1 X	3 X	6 X	12 X
1 page	95,000	89,300	83,000	72,500
2/3 page	71,500	66,900	62,500	54,400
1/2 page	62,500	53,200	47,900	41,700
1/3 page (v)	49,100	45,900	41,400	32,600
1/3 page (sq)	49,100	45,900	41,400	32,600
6. COLOR RATES	1 X	3 X	6 X	12 X
1 page	95,000	89,300	83,000	72,500
2/3 page	71,500	66,900	62,500	54,400
1/2 page	62,500	53,200	47,900	41,700
1/3 page (v)	49,100	45,900	41,400	32,600
1/3 page (sq)	49,100	45,900	41,400	32,600
4-Color	129,000	120,900	113,200	98,500
2nd cover	105,500	105,500	105,500	105,500
3rd cover	105,500	105,500	105,500	105,500
4th cover	129,000	121,000	113,200	98,500
7. COVERS	1 X	3 X	6 X	12 X
4-Color	129,000	120,900	113,200	98,500
2nd cover	105,500	105,500	105,500	105,500
3rd cover	105,500	105,500	105,500	105,500
4th cover	129,000	121,000	113,200	98,500

Access the SRDS Consumer Magazine Advertising Source - online at www.srds.com

While circulation and total audience size are important in selecting a media vehicle, the media planner is also interested in the match between the magazine's readers and the advertiser's

Audience Information and Research for Magazines

A very valuable source for information on magazines is the Standard Rate and Data Service (SRDS), whose print and online service provides complete planning information on domestic and international consumer magazines as well as business and health care trade publications. The SRDS proprietary database contains standardized ad rates, circulation figures, dates, general requirements, contact information, and links to online media kits, websites, and audit statements that provide additional information on readership and positioning. Exhibit 12-11 shows an example of the type of information that is available about magazines from SRDS.

CAREER PROFILE

Greg Hancock

Sales Representative for *Rolling Stone* Magazine

I chose the University of Southern California to get my undergraduate degree because they had one of the top-rated Business Entrepreneurship programs, which I felt would prepare me to own my own business. However, after graduating I realized it takes a lot of money and experience to start up a new business. I lacked both, so I searched for a job to learn sales, marketing and advertising. These are important skills, no matter what industry you work in.

Using my social network, I found a friend of a friend that sold advertising for magazines. I offered to take her for lunch to learn more about her job. Following lunch, she introduced me to her boss, the owner of the James G. Elliott Company, a Los Angeles Rep Firm (a Rep Firm is sometimes used by a magazine to sell their advertising rather than using an in-house sales team). They had an entry-level position available, but unfortunately "entry-level" in the ad sales industry meant at least a couple of years of experience. Most people selling advertising get their start by working at an ad agency. They learn the industry, and then move into sales. Although I did not have enough experience, I just kept calling. I told Jim Elliott, "Give me three months to prove myself and if you don't like me you don't have to pay me!" It turns out persistence was more important than experience and they offered me the job.

"My job requires a lot of hard work but it is also a lot of fun."

I worked for the rep firm for four years, selling ads for more than 11 different magazines—many you've probably never heard of including *Sporting Goods Dealer, North American Hunter,* and *Attache* (the US Airways in-flight magazine). As my knowledge and selling skills improved, I was allowed to work on magazines with larger circulation such as *Popular Science.* Larger circulation means higher ad cost, which means higher commissions. Each magazine exposed me to a different group of clients and it wasn't long before I started getting calls from other magazines to work for them. After a 6-month stint at *Shape* magazine, I received a call from *Rolling Stone.* I had finally made it to one of the most recognizable and highly respected magazines in the industry.

Since 1967 *Rolling Stone* has been the largest music magazine in the US and arguably one of the most influential voices in matters of pop culture. With an audience of over 11,000,000 readers every two weeks, we reach an outstanding audience for advertisers to deliver their message. I'm responsible for over $7 million dollars of advertising every year coming from a list of hundreds of potential advertisers including: Toyota, Honda, and Nissan; high tech companies like Apple Computers and Symantec; and fashion accounts like Guess and Skechers. The pressure is high, the workload is heavy, but the perks are outstanding. Sales is not just about selling a product, it's also about building relationships and friendships. We do this by entertaining our cients—lunches and dinners in the best restaurants, drinks at the coolest clubs, and of course, great seats to the hottest concerts.

Ultimately the sale of an ad comes down to the research we show the buyers regarding our readers. They want to know as much as possible about the reader of *Rolling Stone* including their demographic and psychographic profiles and how well our readers match the target market the advertiser wants to reach. Research is the key and it is best learned by working for an advertising agency first.

My job requires a lot of hard work but it is also a lot of fun and there are many things about it that suit me very well. I like to be in charge, I need flexibility, and I like to be paid well for what I do. So here are my words of advice for those of you who want to pursue a career in business: You can try to climb the corporate ladder quickly by skipping steps, but at some point, you'll need to know what steps you skipped or you'll end up falling back down faster than you went up! In the words of the Talking Heads, "And you may find yourself in a beautiful house, with a beautiful wife. And you may ask yourself—Well, how did I get here?"

target audience. Information on readers is available from several sources, including the publication's own research and syndicated studies. Most magazines provide media planners with reports detailing readers' demographics, financial profile, lifestyle, and product usage characteristics. The larger the publication, the more detailed and comprehensive the information it usually can supply about its readers.

Syndicated research studies are also available. For consumer magazines, primary sources of information are Simmons Market Research Bureau's *Study of Media and Markets* and the studies of Mediamark Research Inc. (MRI). These studies provide a broad range of information on the audiences of major national and regional magazines, including demographics, lifestyle characteristics, and product purchase and usage data. Most large ad agencies and media buying services also conduct ongoing research on the media habits of consumers. All this information helps determine the value of various magazines in reaching particular types of product users.

Audience information is generally more limited for business publications than for consumer magazines. The widely dispersed readership and nature of business publication readers make audience research more difficult. Media planners generally rely on information provided by the publication or by sources such as Standard Rate and Data Service. SRDS's Business Publication Advertising Source provides the titles of individuals who receive the publication and the type of industry in which they work. This information can be of value in understanding the audiences reached by various business magazines.

Purchasing Magazine Advertising Space

Cost Elements Magazine rates are primarily a function of circulation. Other variables include the size of the ad, its position in the publication, the particular editions (geographic, demographic) chosen, any special mechanical or production requirements, and the number and frequency of insertions.

Advertising space is generally sold on the basis of space units such as full page, half page, and quarter page, although some publications quote rates on the basis of column inches. The larger the ad, the greater the cost. However, many advertisers use full-page ads since they result in more attention and readership. Studies have found that full-page ads generated 30 percent more readership than half-page ads.[15]

Ads can be produced or run using black and white, black and white plus one color, or four colors. The more color used in the ad, the greater the expense because of the increased printing costs. On average, a four-color ad costs 30 percent more than a black-and-white ad. Advertisers generally prefer color ads because they have greater visual impact and are superior for attracting and holding attention.[16] Roper Starch Worldwide analyzed the effect of various factors on the readership of magazine ads. The "noted" scores (the percentage of readers who remember seeing the ad in a publication they read) are anywhere from 6 to 59 percent higher for a four-color full-page ad than for a black-and-white ad, depending on the product category. "Read-most" scores (the percentage who say they read more than half of the copy of an ad) are also higher for four-color versus black-and-white ads, by about 25 percent on average.[17] Other studies have examined the impact of size and color and found that a four-color spread (two facing pages) outperforms a one-page color ad by 30 percent and a black-and-white spread by 35 percent in terms of ad recall.[18] Ads requiring special mechanical production such as bleed pages or inserts may also cost extra.

Rates for magazine ad space can also vary according to the number of times an ad runs and the amount of money spent during a specific period. The more often an advertiser contracts to run an ad, the lower are the space charges. Volume discounts are based on the total space purchased within a contract year, measured in dollars. Advertisers can also save money by purchasing advertising in magazine combinations, or networks.

Magazine networks offer the advertiser the opportunity to buy space in a group of publications as a package deal. The publisher usually has a variety of magazines that reach audiences with similar characteristics. Networks can also be publishers of a group of magazines with diversified audiences or independent networks that sell space in groups of magazines published by different companies. For example, the News Network sells space in a group of news-oriented publications such as *Time, Newsweek,*

and *U.S. News & World Report.* The Ivy League Network is a consortium of alumni magazines of Ivy League schools and one non-Ivy, Stanford University. Advertisers can purchase ad space and reach the well-educated, affluent alumni of all eight schools with one media purchase through the network (Exhibit 12-12).

Exhibit 12-12 Advertisers can reach alumni of Ivy League schools through the Ivy League Network

The Future for Magazines

Like other major advertising media, magazines are strongly impacted by the economy and the increases and decreases in ad spending that occur with changes in economic situations. The past several years have been very difficult for the magazine industry; many publications experienced reductions in revenue as advertisers cut back on spending due to the recession.[19] Many publications saw their number of advertising pages decline and found it difficult to raise their rates to offset the reduction in ad pages. And while advertising revenue has been decreasing, publishers' other major revenue stream, circulation, has also been declining. A number of magazines, such as *Working Woman* and *Industry Standard,* could not survive these reductions in revenue and ceased publication.[20] Several computer/Internet magazines were impacted by the reductions in ad spending by dot-com and computer companies and went out of business, including *Family PC* and *Yahoo! Internet Life.*

While the health of the economy has a major impact on the magazine industry, there are a number of other important issues facing the industry. The costs of paper and ink continue to rise, and the industry has had to weather several significant increases in postal rates in recent years, which have had a major impact on their cost structure.[21] Magazines are also facing strong competition from other media such as television, the Internet, and direct mail; and, as discussed in IMC Perspective 12-3, they are being asked to demonstrate that they can build brand awareness and help increase sales. Publishers are looking at a number of ways to improve their position—including stronger editorial platforms, better circulation management, cross-magazine and media deals, database marketing, technological advances, and electronic delivery methods—to make advertising in magazines more appealing to marketers.

Exhibit 12-13 *Fast Company* has been successful as a new type of business magazine

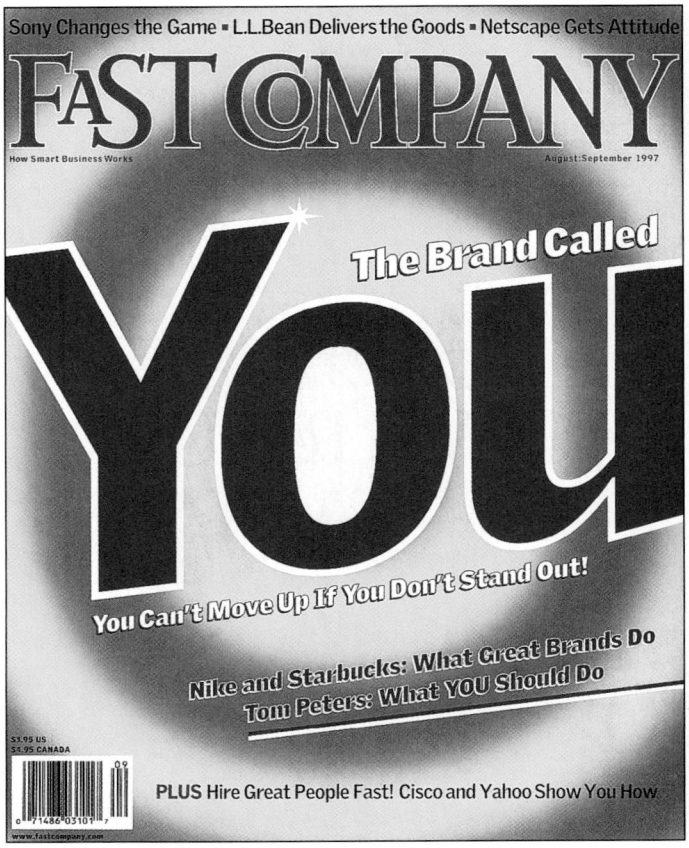

Stronger Editorial Platforms

Magazines with strong editorial platforms that appeal to the interests, lifestyles, and changing demographics of consumers as well as business and market trends in the new millennium are in the best position to attract readers and advertisers. For example, *Fast Company* has been successful by developing a different type of business magazine that provides readers with information and ideas for succeeding in the modern workplace (See Exhibit 12-13). Publications such as *Maxim, FHM,* and *Stuff* have been very successful at targeting a group described as "adultescents," 18- to 34-year-old males who cling to the trappings of youth culture.[22]

Circulation Management

One of the major challenges facing magazine publishers is trying to increase or even maintain their circulation bases. Circulation is the second major source of revenue for most publications, and publishers must carefully manage the costs of attracting and maintaining additional readers or subscribers. The cost of acquiring subscriptions has increased dramatically over the past decade. At the same time, there has been a decline in

IMC PERSPECTIVE 12-3

Proving That Magazine Ads Work

For years magazine publishers focused most of their attention on selling ads in their magazines and devoted less attention to proving the ads were effective. At many magazines, efforts at measuring effectiveness were often limited to tracking consumer response to 800 numbers that appeared in print ads. However, the carefree days are over as many new advertising media have emerged, such as niche-oriented cable TV networks, narrowly targeted radio stations, and the Internet. Moreover, there are more than twice as many magazines competing for media dollars as there were a decade ago. With so many media options available, marketers now want tangible proof that magazine advertising is effective and can build brand awareness, help position a brand, or actually deliver sales.

Magazines have typically promised advertisers *exposure* or access to a well-defined audience such as fashion-conscious young women, sports-obsessed men, or automotive buffs. However, advertisers want evidence of more than exposure. They want proof that seeing an ad for Calvin Klein jeans in *Cosmo* makes readers more likely to spend $80 to buy them or that placing an ad for a Volkswagen Jetta in *Rolling Stone* helps the brand stick in consumers' minds long enough to influence their next auto purchase. The executive vice president of Conde Naste Publications, Inc., which publishes popular titles such as *Vogue, GQ, Glamour,* and *Vanity Fair,* says: "Twenty years ago, our only obligation to advertisers was to gather people who would see the ad. Now we must prove the ad actually does something. Sometimes, that's possible; sometimes it's not."

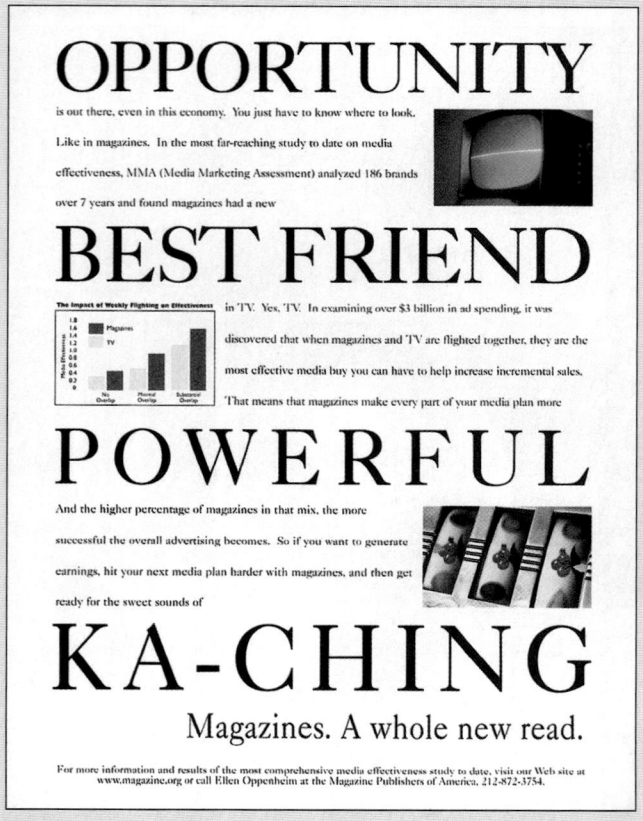

Magazines increasingly have to compete against media that can provide evidence that their ads do indeed do something. For example, the Internet can show accountability instantly because consumers' movements and purchases can be tracked through their mouse clicks. And with new digital technology, television sets will soon become transactional tools, allowing consumers to order information and goods right from their sofas with a remote control. Magazines can ill afford to wait any longer to prove that they work.

The magazine industry is taking steps to address the accountability issue. The industry's lead trade group, Magazine Publishers of America (MPA), recently spent half a million dollars investigating ways to prove magazine effectiveness. One of the group's studies found that boosting ad spending in magazines increased short-term sales of products and also generated more sales over time. Sales increased among magazine-exposed households for 8 of the 10 brands measured. Individual magazines are also trying to prove how advertising in their pages can help build a brand or move the sales needle. Another phase of the study found a significant relationship between advertising awareness and purchase intention. Moreover, awareness attributed to a combination of both television and magazines was most strongly related to positive changes in purchase intention. This "media multiplier" effect occurs because the heavy magazine reader is traditionally a light TV viewer and magazines deliver a new audience when added to a heavy TV schedule and can also help build frequency.

Consumers' loyalty to magazines and their willingness to spend uninterrupted, focused time with them has always been a powerful selling point for the medium. Now, however, magazines must prove that their connection with readers will generate sales for the companies that advertise in them. As Chris Miller, the MPA's head of marketing, notes: "One of the most important questions for this industry is the bottom-line question—does it drive sales?"

Source: Wendy Bounds, "Magazines Seek to Demonstrate Efficacy of Ads," *The Wall Street Journal,* Apr. 12, 1999, pp. B1, 3. Magazine Publishers of America, "Documenting the Effectiveness of Magazines in the Media Mix," www.magazine.org.

the prices consumers pay for subscriptions. In 1990 the average magazine subscription rate was $26.90. In 2001 it was $25.30. Thus, publishers have to pay more to maintain their rate bases (the circulation level guaranteed to advertisers), but they make less money on each subscription sold.

Publishers are also facing a drop in sweepstakes-generated circulation as a result of the controversy that developed over consumer confidence in the sweepstakes-related subscription offers. Agents such as Publishers Clearing House and American Family Enterprises have been going through changes, both self-imposed and externally dictated, that have greatly reduced the number of subscriptions they generate for publishers.[23] To compensate for losses from sweepstakes agents, publishers are looking to other methods of generating subscribers, such as making subscriptions available through websites, offering free trial copies online, conducting special promotions, or using other agents such as school-related subscription services.[24]

Many magazines are also focusing more attention on managing their circulation bases. For many years, magazines focused on increasing their circulation under the assumption that higher circulation meant higher advertising rates. However, publishers are now realizing that the cost of attracting and maintaining the last 10 to 15 percent of their circulation base is often greater than the additional revenue generated, since these subscribers require numerous direct-mail solicitations, premium offers, or discount subscriptions.

A number of magazines have reduced their circulation base in recent years. Many publishers believe they can pass on price increases more easily to their core readers or subscribers and offer advertisers a more loyal and focused audience. Many advertisers welcome the improvement in circulation management. They would rather reach a few hundred thousand fewer subscribers than pay for inefficient circulation and be hit with advertising rate increases each year. Many magazines are also using the monies saved on the circulation side to improve the editorial content of their publications, which should attract more readers—and advertisers.

Cross-Magazine and Media Deals

Another important development involves the way ad space is sold; there will be more cross- or multimagazine and cross-media ad packages. **Multimagazine deals** involve two or more publishers offering their magazines to an advertiser as one package. For example, *Newsweek* offers cross-magazine deals with several other publishers, including Meredith and Times Mirror. Many magazines are also making **cross-media advertising** deals that include several different media opportunities from a single company or a partnership of media providers. For example, with the merger of America Online (AOL) and Time Warner, the new company offers advertisers the opportunity for cross-media deals whereby they can advertise in magazines owned by the media conglomerate, such as *Time, Sports Illustrated, People,* and *Fortune;* on its TV stations, such as CNN, TNT, TBS, and the WB Network; and through AOL and other websites.[25]

Database Marketing

Many advertisers are increasingly turning to magazines as a cost-efficient way of reaching specialized audiences. As marketers continue to move toward greater market segmentation, market niche strategies, and regional marketing, they are making greater use of magazines because of their high selectivity and ability to avoid wasted coverage or circulation. Magazines are using advances in technology and *database marketing* to divide their audiences on the basis of demographics, psychographics, or regions and to deliver more personalized advertising messages. Database marketing lets advertisers personalize their advertising by merging their own databases with those of a magazine. By selectively accessing information from a magazine's database, advertisers can choose from an array of information on consumers, such as product usage or purchase intention data. Marketers will increasingly advertise in magazines that are targeted specifically to narrow groups of subscribers.[26]

Advances in Technology

Two important technological developments are making it possible for advertisers to deliver personalized messages to tightly targeted audiences: selective binding technology and ink-jet imaging. **Selective binding** is a

Exhibit 12-14 *Newsweek* promotes the value of ink-jet imaging

computerized production process that allows the creation of hundreds of copies of a magazine in one continuous sequence. Selective binding enables magazines to target and address specific groups within a magazine's circulation base. They can then send different editorial or advertising messages to various groups of subscribers within the same issue of a publication. **Ink-jet imaging** reproduces a message by projecting ink onto paper rather than using mechanical plates. This process makes it possible to personalize an advertising message. Many publishers believe selective binding and ink-jet imaging will let advertisers target their messages more finely and let magazines compete more effectively with direct mail and other direct-marketing vehicles. Exhibit 12-14 shows how *Newsweek* promotes the capabilities of ink-jet imaging for targeting advertising messages.

Publishers are also developing new technologies that will enhance the creative opportunities available to magazine advertisers. Advertisers use a variety of techniques in print ads to capture readers' attention, including sound, scents, moving images, and pop-up ads. Current technologies are being refined and made more cost effective, and a number of new technologies will be incorporated into print ads soon. These include anaglyphic images (three-dimensional materials that are viewed with colored glasses); lenticular (color) images printed on finely corrugated plastic that seem to move when tilted; and pressure- or heat-sensitive inks that change color on contact. These new technologies give advertisers ways to break through the advertising clutter. However, these new print technologies can be very costly. Moreover, many advertisers and agencies are concerned that ads that use these new technologies may do so at the expense of other ads in the magazine, so they may pressure publishers to control their use. Some creative people have also expressed concern that these new technologies are gimmicks being substituted for creative advertising ideas.[27]

Online Delivery Methods Many magazines are keeping pace with the digital revolution and the continuing consumer interest in technology by making their publications available online. There are more than 300 magazines with online versions, and many more are becoming available each month. Online versions of magazines such as *BusinessWeek* offer the many advantages of the Internet to publishers and subscribers (Exhibit 12-15). They also provide advertisers with the opportunity for sponsorships as well as banner ads and promotions on the online versions of the magazines. However, it remains to be seen whether people will want their magazines delivered online

Exhibit 12-15 Magazines such as *BusinessWeek* are now available online

or prefer to read them in more traditional form. As the presence of magazines online grows, the industry will also have to address important issues regarding audience measurement and how to determine consumers' exposure to and interactions with online advertising. Advertising on the Internet is discussed in Chapter 15.

Newspapers

Newspapers, the second major form of print media, are the largest of all advertising media in terms of total dollar volume. In 2002 an estimated $44 billion was spent on newspaper advertising, or about 22 percent of the total advertising expenditures in the United States. Newspapers are an especially important advertising medium to local advertisers, particularly retailers. However, newspapers are also valuable to national advertisers. Many of the advertising dollars spent by local retailers are actually provided by national advertisers through cooperative advertising programs (discussed in Chapter 16). Newspapers vary in terms of their characteristics and their role as an advertising medium.

Types of Newspapers

The traditional role of newspapers has been to deliver prompt, detailed coverage of news as well as to supply other information and features that appeal to readers. The vast majority of newspapers are daily publications serving a local community. However, weekly, national, and special-audience newspapers have special characteristics that can be valuable to advertisers.

Daily Newspapers Daily newspapers, which are published each weekday, are found in cities and larger towns across the country. Many areas have more than one daily paper. Daily newspapers are read by nearly 60 percent of adults each weekday and by 68 percent on Sundays.[28] They provide detailed coverage of news, events, and issues concerning the local area as well as business, sports, and other relevant information and entertainment. Daily newspapers can further be classified as morning, evening, or Sunday publications. In 2002 there were 1,468 daily newspapers in the United States; of these, 48 percent were evening papers and 52 percent morning. There were also 913 Sunday newspapers, most of which were published by daily newspapers.

Weekly Newspapers Most weekly newspapers originate in small towns or suburbs where the volume of news and advertising cannot support a daily newspaper. These papers focus primarily on news, sports, and events relevant to the local area and usually ignore national and world news, sports, and financial and business news. There are nearly 8,000 weekly newspapers published in the United States, and they have an average circulation of close to 6,000. Weeklies appeal primarily to local advertisers because of their geographic focus and lower absolute cost. Most national advertisers avoid weekly newspapers because of their duplicate circulation with daily or Sunday papers in the large metropolitan areas and problems in contracting for and placing ads in these publications. However, the contracting and scheduling problems associated with these papers have been reduced by the emergence of syndicates that publish them in a number of areas and sell ad space in all of their local newspapers through one office.

National Newspapers Newspapers in the United States with national circulation include *USA Today, The Wall Street Journal,* and *The Christian Science Monitor.* All three are daily publications and have editorial content with a nationwide appeal. *USA Today,* which positions itself as "the nation's newspaper," has the largest circulation of any newspaper in the country, at 2.3 million copies a day. *The Wall Street Journal* sells over 1.8 million copies a day and is an excellent means of reaching businesspeople. National newspapers appeal primarily to large national advertisers and to regional advertisers that use specific geographic editions of these publications. For example, *The Wall Street Journal* has three geographic editions covering 18 regions in which ads can be placed, while *USA Today* offers advertisers the opportunity to run ads in its national edition or any of 25 regionals.

Exhibit 12-16 The *New York Times* promotes its classification as a national newspaper

Recently the *New York Times* was classified as a national newspaper rather than a regional publication by Competitive Media Reporting, which has developed a new policy on how it defines national newspapers.[29] This policy states that a paper must publish at least five times a week and have no more than 67 percent of its distribution in any one area. More than 33 percent of its display advertising must come from national advertising categories, and more than 50 percent of its advertising must come from national advertisers. Designation as a national newspaper is important to major newspapers in attracting national advertisers.[30] Exhibit 12-16 shows an ad run by the *New York Times* informing advertisers of its classification as a national newspaper. IMC Perspective 12-4 discusses the battle among the *Times, The Wall Street Journal,* and *USA Today* to be the leading national newspaper.

Special-Audience Newspapers A variety of papers offer specialized editorial content and are published for particular groups, including labor unions, professional organizations, industries, and hobbyists. Many people working in advertising read *Advertising Age,* while those in the marketing area read *Marketing News.* Specialized newspapers are also published in areas with large foreign-language-speaking ethnic groups, among them Polish, Chinese, Hispanics, Vietnamese, and Filipinos. In the United States, there are newspapers printed in more than 40 languages.

Newspapers targeted at various religious groups compose another large class of special-interest papers. For example, more than 140 Catholic newspapers are published across the United States. Another type of special-audience newspaper is one most of you probably read regularly during the school year, the college newspaper. More than 1,300 colleges and universities publish newspapers that offer advertisers an excellent medium for reaching college students (Exhibit 12-17).

Newspaper Supplements Although not a category of newspapers per se, many papers include magazine-type supplements, primarily in their Sunday editions. Sunday supplements have been part of most newspapers for many years and come in various forms. One type is the syndicated Sunday magazine, such as *Parade* or *USA*

THE DAILY COLLEGIAN

FRIDAY Feb. 4, 2000 — WEATHER Page 2 — TODAY: Cloudy with flurries

Vol. 100 No. 124 26 pages — PUBLISHED INDEPENDENTLY BY STUDENTS AT PENN STATE — 30 cents off campus ©2000 Collegian Inc.

Students plan protest of post office changes

By Heather Cook

The recent sign removal from the University Park Post Office, which received attention from the Undergraduate Student Government and Penn State President Graham Spanier, has inspired at least one student to plan a protest of the action.

John Lawrence (senior-marketing) sent out e-mails to friends after visiting the University Park Post Office once the signs had been removed. He e-mail detailed a plan to rally outside the post office at 4 p.m. today, and then march to State College post office, around with signs and chants.

"I had seen the note 'Improved' post office and it really made me mad, students here are pretty apathetic — we don't get excited about much of anything except football, and that's only when we're winning," Lawrence said. "I think we need to show a little more activism."

Eric Halle Sen. Bryan McKinney, who heard about the planned rally through a friend, used the e-mail addresses on an unrelated mass mailing he received to send information to other students.

McKinney's letter detailed the plan to meet near the University Park Post Office and added each student should bring a letter addressed to the district post office in Erie. McKinney intends to have students hand their letters to Mike "the Mailman" Hore

Lawrence, who hadn't included the idea about letters in his original e-mail, said anything students want to do is OK, as long as it remains legal and peaceful.

"Bring letters, bring signs and bring frisbees," Lawrence said. "There is no demo on my behalf for anything that is illegal or shady in any way."

Kelly Hough (junior-religious studies) also will be standing outside the post office at 4 p.m. today with petitions that she has been circulating. She said she hopes to gather more signatures to send to the district post office in Erie.

"I'm still encouraging people to send letters to Erie, as well," Hough added.

Though many students have been circulating e-mails around campus asking friends to email postal officials in protest of the sign removal, Tim Delio, retail manager of the Erie District post office, said she has only received two letters addressed to her.

Delio added she has not spoken to State College Postmaster Linda Bartram since Monday, but at the point Delio's views on the issue have not changed, despite polarity in support of the post office.

"Some of the articles state that there are petitions that have been there for years and years," Delio said. "Stuff like that should be put in the student union ... why are they at a post office?"

Despite the support that many students have shown for those sending the letters, others were upset by the mass mailings.

McKinney, who received a warning from the Center for Academic Computing after a student complained about the e-mail he sent, said he had tried to make his letter official and even included his phone number and USG title.

"I probably should have thought about what I was doing," McKinney said. "I was just trying to help."

Barbara Copland, associate director of Judicial Affairs, said though students are free to send e-mails to lists of people they know, spamming is never a good idea.

"This is a worthy cause, but it's (spam) strategy not permitted in the system," Copland said

Ads keep students looking for answers

By Sarah Carol and Alissa Wismouse

Do you agree with Adam?

Students might find it hard to answer this question, given that the campus-wide advertising campaign has not yet revealed anything about Adam or his message.

Although studentboards and bulletin boards are filled with the teaser and rumors abound, no purpose has not been officially revealed.

"On Monday, we're going to reveal more about the campaign," said Bruce Henderson, director of Penn State's Campus Crusade for Christ.

The club promises Monday's revelation will be as big as this week's campaign.

"The point of the campaign is to build anticipation," CCPE member Gini Stopper (senior-communications disorders) said, adding CCPE, the organization sponsoring the advertisements, wants people to want to know more.

They insist students will learn much more about Adam sometime next week.

"People are supposed to find out who

which entailed an affirmation of Christian beliefs, and paying $5. In the final phase of the campaign, "Dave" revealed his identity — Dave Guilfoyle, a religious studies and history sophomore at the university.

Despite the hoopla surrounding the campaign, there has

Students hand dissenting opinions on the numerous "Adam" signs in buildings across campus.

Exhibit 12-17 College newspapers such as *The Daily Collegian* are an excellent way to reach students

IMC PERSPECTIVE 12-4

The Battle to Be the Nation's Newspaper

It's been more than 20 years since the Gannett Company, one of the nation's leading newspaper publishers, caught the attention of the media world with its decision to publish a daily national newspaper called *USA Today.* The new paper was launched in September 1982 amid considerable skepticism by the media community as well as the advertising industry. Some critics called it the "fast-food of journalism" and nicknamed it "McPaper" for its light approach to the news and its lack of in-depth news coverage.

While *USA Today* lost an estimated $600 million in its first decade, Gannett stuck to its long-term plan. People became increasingly interested in a full-color, upscale national newspaper that offered particularly thorough coverage of areas such as sports, entertainment, and business news. More important, Gannett found a segment of upscale newspaper readers few had noticed before—the business traveler. Airline deregulation had made flying more affordable and spurred a surge in business travel. And when they were on the road, businesspeople wanted a way to catch up with national and business news as well as sports. The paper found its target readers with a novel distribution strategy—it followed them around by selling large numbers of papers in airports and through hotel chains that provided the paper as a service to their guests. Nearly half of *USA Today*'s readers pick up their copies of the paper in these venues. National advertisers noticed the growing popularity of *USA Today,* and the paper became profitable by 1993.

USA Today has become the newspaper with the largest readership in the country. Boasting a circulation of 2.2 million on Monday through Thursday and 2.6 million for its Friday weekend edition, *USA Today* dubs itself "the nation's newspaper." However, there are two other papers that want that title as well—*The Wall Street Journal* and the *New York Times,* which are the second and third most widely circulated newspapers in America. *USA Today*'s pursuit of the business traveler has placed it in direct competition with *The Wall Street Journal.* Though the *Journal* has been a national newspaper since the 1940s, it had traditionally positioned itself as a paper for businesspeople rather than general readers. However, as the interests of its readership expanded, the *Journal* has been forced to follow suit. The paper has added several new sections in recent years and expanded beyond its roots with "Weekend Journal," its Friday arts and culture supplement.

In 2002 the *Journal* underwent a major redesign in an effort to attract a more diverse base of readers and advertisers. The changes included the first redesign since 1944 of the paper's front page, which now has color. The new *Journal* also sports more white space, with more room around the columns, and presents advertisers with greater flexibility in ad sizing and placement. One problem facing *The Wall Street Journal* is its image as a business paper, which makes it difficult to attract readers with more general interests. Its circulation has remained relatively flat at 1.8 million, and its business focus leaves it dependent on a few advertising categories such as business to business, finance, and technology.

USA Today's other major competitor is the *New York Times,* whose entry into the national newspaper sweepstakes is more recent. The *Times* has published a national edition since 1980, and journalistically it has long viewed itself as a national newspaper. Until recently, however, the *Times* did not have a way to circulate copies widely on a national level, so few out-of-town readers could get the paper in a timely manner. To remedy this, the *Times* has completely overhauled its distribution network: Home delivery is now available in 217 U.S. markets and a distribution deal was signed with Starbucks to sell the paper in more than 2,000 of its stores. By going national, the *Times* escaped the sharp decline in circulation that most large daily newspapers have experienced over the past decade. The paper now has a circulation of 1.2 million (1.6 million on Sundays), and although most of its readers are still on the East Coast, the paper's appeal to national advertisers has grown.

The competition among the three publications to be the leading national newspaper is likely to continue, although *USA Today* is clearly the leader. Its sports coverage remains unmatched, and the paper now runs longer stories and more coverage of hard news. The paper also has the advantage of being part of the Gannett empire, which owns 94 daily newspapers, 300 nondailies, 22 television stations, and numerous websites. Every morning, anchors on the 22 Gannett TV stations spend 10 minutes summarizing that morning's *USA Today.* The paper's president argues that it is no longer just a newspaper but, rather, a platform that feeds content to other media such as television and the Internet. It appears that *USA Today* is best positioned to remain the front-runner in the race to be "the nation's newspaper."

Sources: Ira Teinowitz, *USA Today:* No Longer a Newspaper," *Advertising Age,* Sept. 2, 2002, p. 18; Nicholas Stein, "Deadline U.S.A.," *Fortune,* July 8, 2002, pp. 78–83; Jon Fine, "'WSJ' Targets More Ads, Young Readers," *Advertising Age,* Mar. 25, 2002, p. 3.

Weekend, distributed in hundreds of papers throughout the country. *Parade* has a circulation of over 35 million; *USA Weekend* is carried by more than 350 newspapers with a combined circulation of over 22 million. These publications are similar to national magazines and carry both national and regional advertising.

Some large newspapers publish local Sunday supplements distributed by the parent paper. These supplements contain stories of more local interest, and both local and national advertisers buy ad space. The *New York Times Sunday Magazine* is the best-known local supplement. The *Washington Post, San Francisco Examiner,* and *Los Angeles Times* have their own Sunday magazines.

In some areas, papers have begun carrying regional supplements as well as specialized weekday supplements that cover specific topics such as food, sports, or entertainment. Supplements are valuable to advertisers that want to use the newspaper yet get four-color reproduction quality in their ads.

Types of Newspaper Advertising

The ads appearing in newspapers can also be divided into different categories. The major types of newspaper advertising are display and classified. Other special types of ads and preprinted inserts also appear in newspapers.

Display Advertising

Display advertising is found throughout the newspaper and generally uses illustrations, headlines, white space, and other visual devices in addition to the copy text. Display ads account for approximately 70 percent of the advertising revenue of the average newspaper. The two types of display advertising in newspapers are local and national (general).

Local advertising refers to ads placed by local organizations, businesses, and individuals who want to communicate with consumers in the market area served by the newspaper. Supermarkets and department stores are among the leading local display advertisers, along with numerous other retailers and service operations such as banks and travel agents. Local advertising is sometimes referred to as retail advertising because retailers account for 85 percent of local display ads.

National or *general advertising* refers to newspaper display advertising done by marketers of branded products or services that are sold on a national or regional level. These ads are designed to create and maintain demand for a company's product or service and to complement the efforts of local retailers that stock and promote the advertiser's products. Major retail chains, automakers, and airlines are heavy users of newspaper advertising.

Exhibit 12-18 Newspaper inserts are used to reach target markets

Classified Advertising

Classified advertising also provides newspapers with a substantial amount of revenue. These ads are arranged under subheads according to the product, service, or offering being advertised. Employment, real estate, and automotive are the three major categories of classified advertising. While most classified ads are just text set in small type, some newspapers also accept classified display advertising. These ads are run in the classified section of the paper but use illustrations, larger type sizes, white space, borders, and even color to stand out.

Special Ads and Inserts

Special advertisements in newspapers include a variety of government and financial reports and notices and public notices of changes in business and personal relationships. Other types of advertising in newspapers include political or special-interest ads promoting a particular candidate, issue, or cause. **Preprinted inserts** are another type of advertising distributed through newspapers. These ads do not appear in the paper itself; they are printed by the advertiser and then taken to the newspaper to be inserted before delivery. Many retailers use inserts such as circulars, catalogs, or brochures in specific circulation zones to reach shoppers in their particular trade areas. Exhibit 12-18 shows how the *San Diego Union-Tribune* promotes its insert distribution service to advertisers.

Advantages of Newspapers

Newspapers have a number of characteristics that make them popular among both local and national advertisers. These include their extensive penetration of local markets, flexibility, geographic selectivity, reader involvement, and special services.

Extensive Penetration One of the primary advantages of newspapers is the high degree of market coverage, or penetration, they offer an advertiser. In most areas, 50 percent or more of households read a daily newspaper, and the reach figure may exceed 70 percent among households with higher incomes and education levels. Most areas are served by one or two daily newspapers, and often the same company owns both, publishing a morning and an evening edition. By making one space buy, the advertiser can achieve a high level of overall reach in a particular market.

The extensive penetration of newspapers makes them a truly mass medium and provides advertisers with an excellent opportunity for reaching all segments of the population with their message. Also, since many newspapers are published and read daily, the advertiser can build a high level of frequency into the media schedule.

Flexibility Another advantage of newspapers is the flexibility they offer advertisers. First, they are flexible in terms of requirements for producing and running the ads. Newspaper ads can be written, laid out, and prepared in a matter of hours. For most dailies, the closing time by which the ad must be received is usually only 24 hours before publication (although closing dates for special ads, such as those using color, and Sunday supplements are longer). The short production time and closing dates make newspapers an excellent medium for responding to current events or presenting timely information to consumers. For example, Chevrolet Trucks ran a newspaper ad congratulating major league baseball star Cal Ripken, Jr. the day after he got his 3,000th career hit. Ripken is a spokesperson for the Chevy Truck line, and the newspaper ad was a very timely salute to his reaching this great milestone (Exhibit 12-19).

A second dimension of newspapers' flexibility stems from the creative options they make available to advertisers. Newspaper ads can be produced and run in various

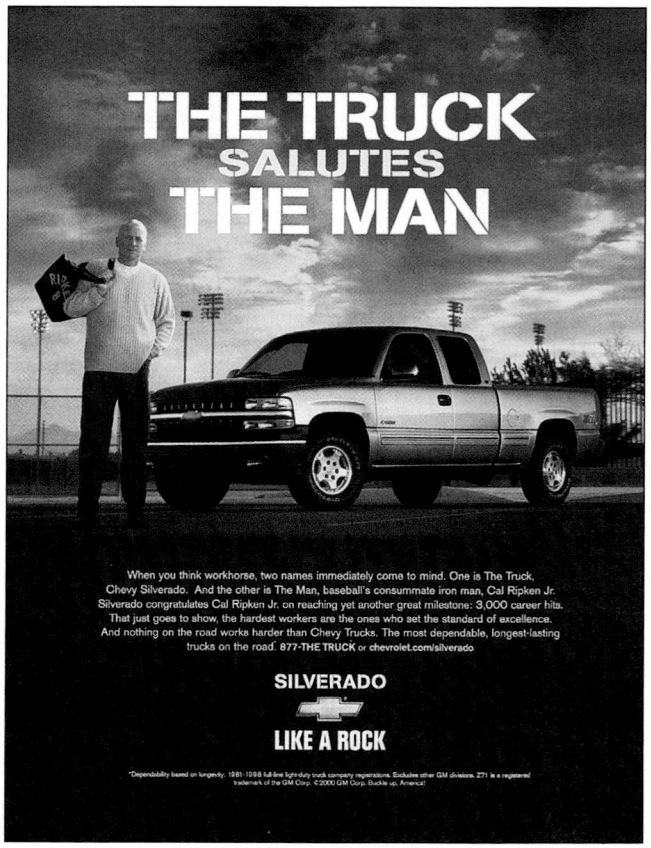

Exhibit 12-19 Chevy Trucks used a newspaper ad for a timely salute to Cal Ripken

sizes, shapes, and formats; they can use color or special inserts to gain the interest of readers. Ads can be run in Sunday magazines or other supplements, and a variety of scheduling options are possible, depending on the advertiser's purpose.

Geographic Selectivity Newspapers generally offer advertisers more geographic or territorial selectivity than any other medium except direct mail. Advertisers can vary their coverage by choosing a paper—or combination of papers—that reaches the areas with the greatest sales potential. National advertisers take advantage of the geographic selectivity of newspapers to concentrate their advertising in specific areas they can't reach with other media or to take advantage of strong sales potential in a particular area. For example, BMW, Mercedes, and Volvo use heavy newspaper media schedules in California and New York/New Jersey to capitalize on the high sales potential for luxury import cars in these markets.

A number of companies, including General Motors, AT&T, and Campbell, use newspapers in their regional marketing strategies. Newspaper advertising lets them feature products on a market-by-market basis, respond and adapt campaigns to local market conditions, and tie into more retailer promotions, fostering more support from the trade.

Local advertisers like retailers are interested in geographic selectivity or flexibility within a specific market or trade area. Their media goal is to concentrate their advertising on the areas where most of their customers are. Many newspapers now offer advertisers various geographic areas or zones for this purpose. For example, the *Chicago Tribune* offers advertisers a number of different circulation area zones as shown in Exhibit 12-20.

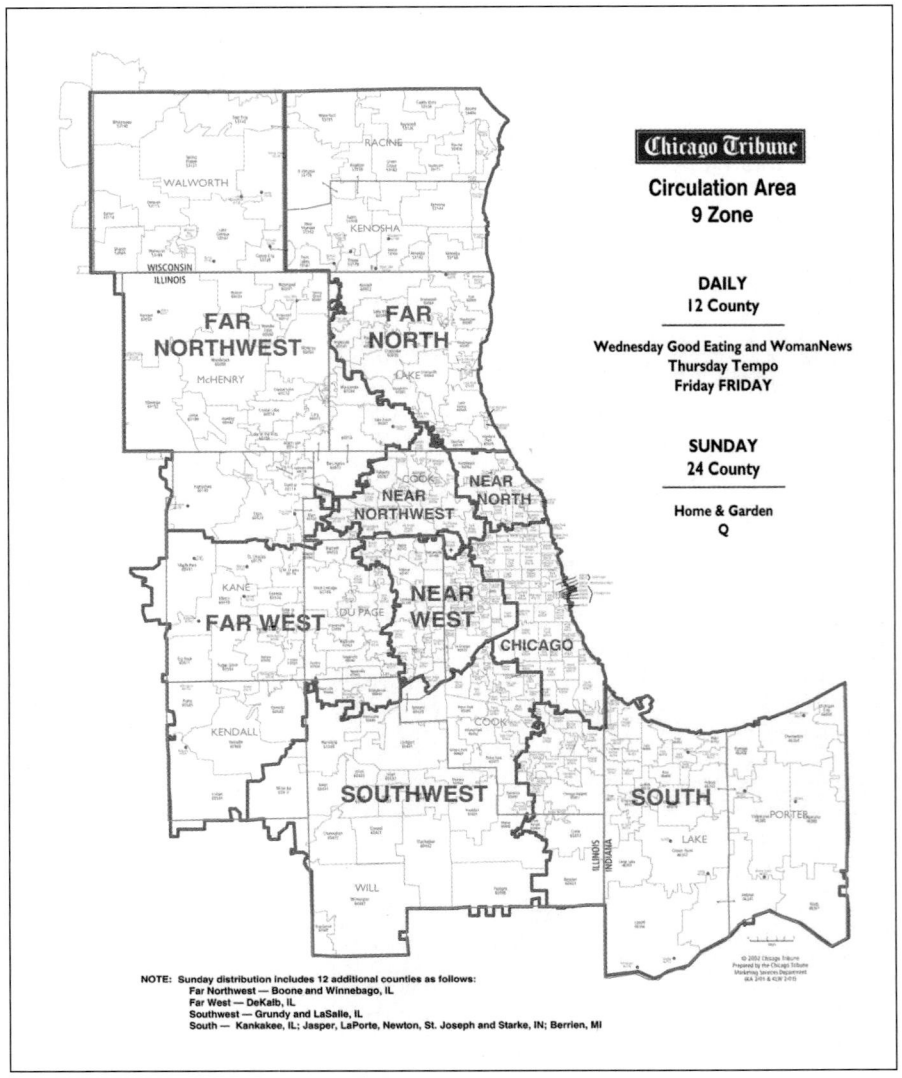

Exhibit 12-20 The *Chicago Tribune* offers advertisers combinations of different circulation area zones

Reader Involvement and Acceptance Another important feature of newspapers is consumers' level of acceptance and involvement with papers and the ads they contain. The typical daily newspaper reader spends time each day reading the weekday newspaper and even more time reading the Sunday paper. Most consumers rely heavily on newspapers not only for news, information, and entertainment but also for assistance with consumption decisions.

Many consumers actually purchase a newspaper *because* of the advertising it contains. Consumers use retail ads to determine product prices and availability and to see who is having a sale. One aspect of newspapers that is helpful to advertisers is readers' knowledge about particular sections of the paper. Most of us know that ads for automotive products and sporting goods are generally found in the sports section, while ads for financial services are found in the business section. The weekly food section in many newspapers is popular for recipe and menu ideas as well as for the grocery store ads and coupons offered by many stores and companies. Exhibit 12-21 shows how the *San Diego Union-Tribune* promotes various sections of the paper to potential advertisers.

The value of newspaper advertising as a source of information has been shown in several studies. One study found that consumers look forward to ads in newspapers more than in other media. In another study, 80 percent of consumers said newspaper

MEDIA SNAPSHOT SAN DIEGO MARKETBOOK 2002

daily paper

THE SAN DIEGO UNION-TRIBUNE DAILY READERSHIP: 883,690

MAIN NEWS
The San Diego Union-Tribune is read by more San Diegans than any other newspaper — that's 884,000 consumers daily.

LOCAL NEWS
Six targeted editions cover the county completely, from the North Coastal cities to the South Bay and all points in between.

SPORTS
Award-winning coverage and nationally ranked professional sports teams make the Sports section a prime pick.

SPORTS EXTRA — MONDAY
Recaps of the weekend's big games, results, trades, news and more. An in-depth vehicle to reach San Diego sports lovers.

BUSINESS
From the work week to Wall Street, Business covers national, regional and local news, plus stock and financial information.

BUSINESS / PERSONAL TECHNOLOGY — MONDAY
Local business news-makers, hot technology, computer tidbits and the latest in mergers.

QUEST — WEDNESDAY
Science and technology get front-page space in this special edition of Currents for readers of all ages and interests.

RELIGION & ETHICS — FRIDAY
Movie listings and reviews are always found here in Currents, but every Friday the cover story focuses on religion and ethics.

FAMILY — SATURDAY
San Diego families find advice and resources in this Saturday edition devoted to family activities and problem-solving.

CLASSIFIEDS
Where the locals go to buy, sell, trade, find a date or a roommate. Daily and special sections cover all your needs.

FOOD — WEDNESDAY
Those who love to eat and cook turn to Food weekly for recipes, coupons and the newest trends in food and restaurants.

NIGHT&DAY — THURSDAY
This popular entertainment tab covers the latest in arts, dining and leisure. Reach 884,000 San Diegans looking for excitement.

CHANGE OF ADDRESS — SATURDAY
This full-color advertorial section is designed for San Diego's new-home builders to showcase their homes and communities.

WHEELS — SATURDAY
Your road to hot prospects. Reach 53% of San Diegans who plan to purchase a new or used vehicle in the next 12 months.

Sources: February 2001 - January 2002 San Diego Scarborough Report.

Exhibit 12-21 Ads can be run in various sections of most newspapers

Exhibit 12-22 Newspaper publishers are often an excellent source for information on local markets

ads were most helpful to them in doing their weekly shopping. Newspaper advertising has also been rated the most believable form of advertising in numerous studies.

Services Offered The special services newspapers offer can be valuable to advertisers. For example, many newspapers offer merchandising services and programs to manufacturers that make the trade aware of ads being run for the company's product and help convince local retailers they should stock, display, and promote the item.

Many newspapers are also excellent sources of local market information through their knowledge of market conditions and research like readership studies and consumer surveys. For example, the publisher of the *San Diego Union-Tribune,* the major daily newspaper in San Diego, provides information on the local market through reports such as the "San Diego Market Close-Up" (Exhibit 12-22).

Newspapers can also assist small companies through free copywriting and art services. Small advertisers without an agency or advertising department often rely on the newspaper to help them write and produce their ads.

Limitations of Newspapers

While newspapers have many advantages, like all media they also have disadvantages that media planners must consider. The limitations of newspapers include their reproduction problems, short life span, lack of selectivity, and clutter.

Poor Reproduction One of the greatest limitations of newspapers as an advertising medium is their poor reproduction quality. The coarse paper stock used for newspapers, the absence of color, and the lack of time papers have available to achieve high-quality reproduction limits the quality of most newspaper ads. Newspapers have improved their reproduction quality in recent years, and color reproduction has become more available. Also, advertisers desiring high-quality color in newspaper ads can turn to such alternatives as freestanding inserts or Sunday supplements. However, these are more costly and may not be desirable to many advertisers. As a general rule, if the visual appearance of the product is important, the advertiser will not rely on newspaper ads. Ads for food products and fashions generally use magazines to capitalize on their superior reproduction quality and color.

Short Life Span Unlike magazines, which may be retained around the house for several weeks, a daily newspaper is generally kept less than a day. So an ad is unlikely to have any impact beyond the day of publication, and repeat exposure is very unlikely. Compounding this problem are the short amount of time many consumers spend with the newspaper and the possibility they may not even open certain sections of the paper. Media planners can offset these problems somewhat by using high frequency in the newspaper schedule and advertising in a section where consumers who are in the market for a particular product or service are likely to look. Figure 12-4 shows readership figures for various sections of newspapers by gender and ethnic background.

Lack of Selectivity While newspapers can offer advertisers geographic selectivity, they are not a selective medium in terms of demographics or lifestyle characteristics. Most newspapers reach broad and very diverse groups of consumers, which makes it difficult for marketers to focus on narrowly defined market segments. For example, manufacturers of fishing rods and reels will find newspapers very inefficient because of the wasted circulation that results from reaching all the newspaper readers who don't fish. Thus, they are more likely to use special-interest magazines such as *Field & Stream* or *Fishing World.* Any newspaper ads for their products will be done through cooperative plans whereby retailers share the costs or spread them over a number of sporting goods featured in the ad.

Figure 12-4 U.S. daily newspaper pages or sections usually read

Section Readership	Percentage of Weekday Audience					
	Adults	Men	Women	White	African-American	Spanish/Hispanic*
Business/finance	59	66	53	61	50	48
Classified	53	55	52	53	58	54
Comics	58	59	57	59	53	52
Entertainment (movies, theater, etc.)	65	61	70	66	64	63
Food or cooking	55	46	63	56	49	45
Main news	88	87	89	89	83	81
Sports	61	74	46	61	58	59
TV/radio listings	52	52	52	53	50	45

*Defined as "of Spanish or Hispanic origin or descent."
Source: Newspaper Association of America, "Facts about Newspapers 2002," www.naa.org.

Clutter Newspapers, like most other advertising media, suffer from clutter. Because 64 percent of the average daily newspaper in the United States is devoted to advertising, the advertiser's message must compete with numerous other ads for consumers' attention and interest. Moreover, the creative options in newspapers are limited by the fact that most ads are black and white. Thus, it can be difficult for a newspaper advertiser to break through the clutter without using costly measures such as large space buys or color. Some advertisers use creative techniques like *island ads*—ads surrounded by editorial material. Island ads are found in the middle of the stock market quotes on the financial pages of many newspapers. Exhibit 12-23 shows an island ad for Cathay Pacific Airways that targets business travelers to Hong Kong and other Asian destinations.

The Newspaper Audience

As with any medium, the media planner must understand the nature and size of the audience reached by a newspaper in considering its value in the media plan. Since newspapers as a class of media do an excellent job of penetrating their market, the typical daily newspaper gives advertisers the opportunity to reach most of the households in a market. But, while local advertisers aim to cover a particular market or trade area, national advertisers want to reach broad regions or even the entire country. They must purchase space in a number of papers to achieve the desired level of coverage.

The basic sources of information concerning the audience size of newspapers come from the circulation figures available through rate cards, publishers' statements, or Standard Rate and Data Service's *Newspaper Rates and Data.* Circulation figures for many newspapers are verified by the Audit Bureau of Circulation which was discussed earlier. Advertisers that use a number of papers in their media plan generally find SRDS the most convenient source.

Newspaper circulation figures are generally broken down into three categories: the city zone, the retail trading zone, and all other areas. The **city zone** is a market area composed of the city where the paper is published and contiguous areas similar in character to the city. The **retail trading zone** is the market outside the city zone whose residents regularly trade with merchants within the city zone. The "all other" category covers all circulation not included in the city or retail trade zone.

Sometimes circulation figures are provided only for the primary market, which is the city and retail trade zones combined, and the other area. Both local and national advertisers consider the circulation patterns across the various categories in evaluating and selecting newspapers.

Exhibit 12-23 Island ads are a way to break through the clutter in newspaper advertising

National advertisers often buy newspaper space on the basis of the size of the market area they cover. For example, General Motors might decide to purchase advertising in the top 10 markets, the top 50 markets, the top 100 markets, and so on. A national advertiser gets different levels of market coverage depending on the number of market areas purchased.

Audience Information

Circulation figures provide the media planner with the basic data for assessing the value of newspapers and their ability to cover various market areas. However, the media planner also wants to match the characteristics of a newspaper's readers with those of the advertiser's target audience. Data on newspaper audience size and characteristics are available from studies conducted by the papers as well as from commercial research services. As for magazines, a very valuable source for information on newspapers is the Standard Rate and Data Service (SRDS), whose print and online service provides complete planning information on daily papers, newspaper groups, ethnic newspapers, college newspapers, comics, and newspaper-distributed magazines. The SRDS data contain standardized ad rates, circulation figures, dates, general requirements, contact information, and other valuable information for media.

Companies such as Simmons Market Research Bureau and Mediamark Research Inc. provide syndicated research studies on lifestyles, media behavior, and product/brand preferences that include information on newspapers. These studies can be valuable for comparing newspapers with other media vehicles.

Many newspapers commission their own audience studies to provide current and potential advertisers with information on readership and characteristics of readers such as demographics, shopping habits, and lifestyles. These studies are often designed to promote the effectiveness of the newspaper in reaching various types of consumers. Since they are sponsored by the paper itself, many advertisers are skeptical of their results. Careful attention must be given to the research methods used and conclusions drawn by these studies.

Purchasing Newspaper Space

Advertisers are faced with a number of options and pricing structures when purchasing newspaper space. The cost of advertising space depends not only on the newspaper's circulation but also on factors such as premium charges for color or special sections as well as discounts available. The purchase process and the rates paid for newspaper space differ for general and local advertisers.

General versus Local Rates

Newspapers have different rate structures for general or national advertisers and local or retail advertisers. **General advertising rates** apply to display advertisers outside the newspaper's designated market area (DMA) and to any classification deemed by the publisher to be "general" in nature. This includes ads run by national advertisers such as automotive, tobacco, packaged-goods, and pharmaceutical companies. **Retail** or **local advertising rates** apply to advertisers that conduct business or sell goods or services within the DMA. The rates paid by general advertisers are, on average, 75 percent higher than those paid by local advertisers. Newspaper publishers claim the rate differential is justified for several reasons. First, they argue it costs more to handle general advertising since ad agencies get a 15 percent commission and commissions must also be paid to the independent sales reps who solicit nonlocal advertising. Second, they note that general advertising is less dependable than local advertising; general advertisers usually don't use newspapers on a continual basis like local advertisers do. Finally, newspaper publishers contend that demand for general advertising is inelastic—it will not increase if rates are lowered or decrease if rates are raised. This means there is no incentive to lower the national advertisers' rates.

National advertisers do not view these arguments as valid justification for the rate differential. They argue that the costs are not greater for handling national advertising than for local business and that many national advertisers use newspapers on a regular basis. Since they use an agency to prepare their ads, national advertisers are less

Exhibit 12-24 The Newspaper National Network encourages national advertisers to run their ads in newspapers

likely to request special services. The large and costly staff maintained by many newspapers to assist in the design and preparation of advertising is used mostly by local advertisers.

The differential rate structure for national versus local advertising has been the source of considerable controversy. Some newspapers are making efforts to narrow the rate differential, as is the Newspaper Association of America (NAA). In 1993, the NAA created the Newspaper National Network (NNN) to target national advertisers in six low-use categories: automotive, cosmetics and toiletries, food, household products, liquor and beverages, and drugs and remedies.[31] The network's goal is to attract more advertising dollars from national advertisers in these categories by promoting the strategic use of newspapers and facilitating the purchase of newspaper space with their one order/one bill model. Exhibit 12-24 shows an ad encouraging national advertisers to place their ads in newspapers through the NNN.

Many marketers sidestep the national advertiser label and the higher rates by channeling their newspaper ads through special category plans, cooperative advertising deals with retailers, and local dealers and distributors that pay local rates. However, the rate differential does keep many national advertisers from making newspapers a larger part of their media mix.

Newspaper Rates

Traditionally, newspaper space for national advertisers has been sold by the agate line. The problem is that newspapers use columns of varying width. Some have six columns per page, while others have eight or nine, which affects the size, shape, and costs of an ad. This results in a complicated production and buying process for national advertisers purchasing space in a number of newspapers.

To address this problem and make newspapers more comparable to other media that sell space and time in standard units, the newspaper industry switched to **standard advertising units (SAUs)** in 1984. All newspapers under this system use column widths $2^1/_{16}$ inches wide, with tabloid-size papers five columns wide and standard or

Figure 12-5 The standard advertising unit system

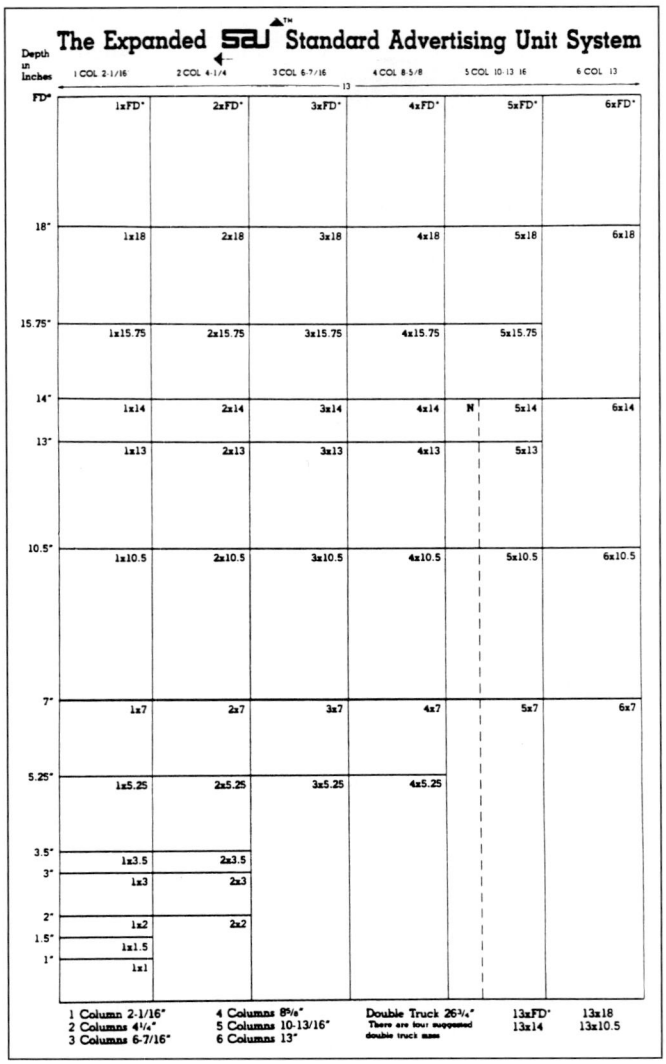

broadcast papers six columns. The column inch is the unit of measurement to create the 57 standard units or format sizes shown in Figure 12-5.

A national advertiser can prepare one ad in a particular SAU, and it will fit every newspaper in the country that accepts SAUs. Rates are quoted on that basis. Since over 1,400 (about 90 percent) of daily newspapers use the SAU system, the purchase and production process has been simplified tremendously for national advertisers.

Newspaper rates for local advertisers continue to be based on the column inch, which is 1 inch deep by 1 column wide. Advertising rates for local advertisers are quoted per column inch, and media planners calculate total space costs by multiplying the ad's number of column inches by the cost per inch.

Rate Structures

While the column inch and SAU are used to determine basic newspaper advertising rates, the media planner must consider other options and factors. Many newspapers charge **flat rates,** which means they offer no discount for quantity or repeated space buys. Others have an **open-rate structure,** which means various discounts are available. These discounts are generally based on frequency or bulk purchases of space and depend on the number of column inches purchased in a year.

Newspaper space rates also vary with an advertiser's special requests, such as preferred position or color. The basic rates quoted by a newspaper are **run of paper (ROP),** which means the paper can place the ad on any page or in any position it desires. While most newspapers try to place an ad in a requested position, the advertiser can ensure a specific section and/or position on a page by paying a higher **pre-**

ferred position rate. Color advertising is also available in many newspapers on an ROP basis or through preprinted inserts or Sunday supplements.

Advertisers can also buy newspaper space based on **combination rates,** where they get a discount for using several newspapers as a group. Typically, a combination rate occurs when a publisher owns both a morning and an evening newspaper in a market and offers a reduced single rate for running the same ad in both newspapers, generally within a 24-hour period. Combination discounts are also available when the advertiser buys space in several newspapers owned by the publisher in a number of markets or in multiple newspapers affiliated in a syndicate or newspaper group. Exhibit 12-25 shows an ad promoting the three newspapers published by the *Miami Herald* in the south Florida market.

The Future for Newspapers

Newspapers remain the largest advertising medium in terms of total advertising volume. Newspapers' largest advertising category is retail, and consolidation among department stores and grocery chains is likely to lead to a slight decline in ad volume. National advertising in newspapers is growing as major advertisers such as Procter & Gamble, Kraft, Nestlé, and General Motors use the medium more. However, newspapers have fallen behind TV and magazines as a medium for national advertisers; they accounted for only 4.5 percent of the estimated $144 billion spent by national advertisers in 2002.

Newspapers' major strength lies in their role as a medium that can be used effectively by local advertisers on a continual basis. It is unlikely that newspapers' importance to local advertisers will change in the near future. However, there are a number of problems and issues newspapers must address to maintain their strong position as a dominant local advertising medium and to gain more national advertising. These include competition from other advertising media, maintaining and managing circulation, cross-media opportunities, and declining readership.

Competition from Other Media

The newspaper industry's battle to increase its share of national advertising volume has been difficult. In addition to the

Exhibit 12-25
Marketers can advertise in the three newspapers published by the *Miami Herald*

problems of reproduction quality and rate differentials, newspapers face competition from other media for both national and local advertisers' budgets. The newspaper industry is particularly concerned about the *bypass,* or loss of advertisers to direct marketing and telemarketing.

To deal with this problem, many newspapers will have to gear up to compete as direct marketers. Many papers are already building databases by collecting information from readers that potential advertisers can use to target specific groups or for direct marketing. Newspapers already have a distribution system that can reach nearly every household in a market every day. It is likely that many newspapers will find ways to make their extensive databases and distribution systems available to marketers that want to target consumers with direct-marketing efforts. By supplementing newspaper advertising with direct mail, marketers can be encouraged to invest more of their advertising dollars with newspaper publishers.

The intermedia battle that newspapers find themselves involved in is no longer limited to national advertising. Many companies are investigating the Internet as a marketing tool and a place to invest advertising dollars that might otherwise go to newspapers. Local radio and TV stations (particularly cable stations), as well as the expanding number of Yellow Pages publishers, are aggressively pursuing local advertisers. Newspapers will have to fight harder to retain those advertisers. Many newspapers have expanded their marketing capabilities and are making efforts to develop and sustain relationships with their advertisers. Some have created sophisticated databases and direct-mail capabilities, which they offer as value-added services. Others are increasing their marketing research departments, preparing comprehensive market studies for major customers, and, in some cases, serving as media advisors and marketing partners.[32]

Circulation The newspaper industry has been struggling for years to reverse declining circulation. While most of the major newspapers in the United States have been able to maintain their circulation, the rest of the industry has been experiencing a decline.[33] Like magazines, many newspapers are taking a closer look at their circulation and analyzing whether the cost of getting additional circulation is justified by the advertising revenue it generates. Many papers are raising newsstand and home delivery rates and circulation revenue is accounting for more of their total revenue.

Several major metropolitan newspapers have found that advertisers use newspapers to reach consumers within specific geographic areas and do not want to pay for readers in outlying areas. Thus, some papers are eliminating what has been called "ego circulation" and focusing more on regional editions in their immediate trade area.

Cross-Media Buys Another area where newspapers may be following the lead of magazines is cross-newspaper and media buys. Newspapers within, as well as across, various regions are banding together to offer national advertisers a package of newspapers so they won't have to purchase space in individual papers. A number of newspaper networks are being formed to help newspapers compete for more of the media expenditures of national advertisers.

Cross-media buys involving newspapers with other media vehicles are also likely to become more prevalent. For example, the *Washington Post* has been involved in a cross-media deal with *Newsweek,* while large companies that own newspapers, magazines, and broadcast media are also offering cross-media packages to advertisers (Exhibit 12-26).

Attracting and Retaining Readers The growth of newspapers as an advertising medium may be limited by the reduced popularity of the medium itself. Newspaper readership has been on a steady decline for the past two decades. The percentage of the adult population reading a newspaper on the average weekday has declined from 78 percent in 1970 to 54 percent today. The percentage of U.S. households receiving a daily newspaper has declined from 77 percent in 1980 to 60 percent. The decline in newspaper readership can be attributed to several factors, including the fast-paced, time-poor lifestyle of the modern dual-income household and the continued growth, popularity, and viewing options of TV.

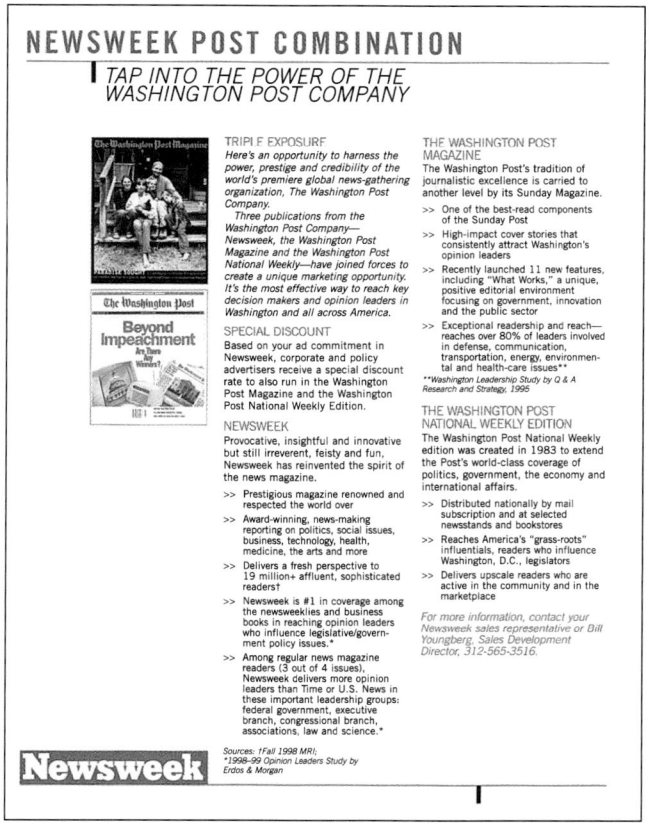

NEWSWEEK POST COMBINATION

TAP INTO THE POWER OF THE WASHINGTON POST COMPANY

The Washington Post Magazine

The Washington Post
Beyond Impeachment
Are There Any Winners?

TRIPLE EXPOSURE

Here's an opportunity to harness the power, prestige and credibility of the world's premiere global news-gathering organization, The Washington Post Company.

Three publications from the Washington Post Company—Newsweek, the Washington Post Magazine and the Washington Post National Weekly—have joined forces to create a unique marketing opportunity. It's the most effective way to reach key decision makers and opinion leaders in Washington and all across America.

SPECIAL DISCOUNT

Based on your ad commitment in Newsweek, corporate and policy advertisers receive a special discount rate to also run in the Washington Post Magazine and the Washington Post National Weekly Edition.

NEWSWEEK

Provocative, insightful and innovative but still irreverent, feisty and fun, Newsweek has reinvented the spirit of the news magazine.

>> Prestigious magazine renowned and respected the world over
>> Award-winning, news-making reporting on politics, social issues, business, technology, health, medicine, the arts and more
>> Delivers a fresh perspective to 19 million+ affluent, sophisticated readers†
>> Newsweek is #1 in coverage among the newsweeklies and business books in reaching opinion leaders who influence legislative/government policy issues.*
>> Among regular news magazine readers (3 out of 4 issues), Newsweek delivers more opinion leaders than Time or U.S. News in these important leadership groups: federal government, executive branch, congressional branch, associations, law and science.*

THE WASHINGTON POST MAGAZINE

The Washington Post's tradition of journalistic excellence is carried to another level by its Sunday Magazine.

>> One of the best-read components of the Sunday Post
>> High-impact cover stories that consistently attract Washington's opinion leaders
>> Recently launched 11 new features, including "What Works," a unique, positive editorial environment focusing on government, innovation and the public sector
>> Exceptional readership and reach—reaches over 80% of leaders involved in defense, communication, transportation, energy, environmental and health-care issues**

***Washington Leadership Study by Q & A Research and Strategy, 1995*

THE WASHINGTON POST NATIONAL WEEKLY EDITION

The Washington Post National Weekly edition was created in 1983 to extend the Post's world-class coverage of politics, government, the economy and international affairs.

>> Distributed nationally by mail subscription and at selected newsstands and bookstores
>> Reaches America's "grass-roots" influentials, readers who influence Washington, D.C., legislators
>> Delivers upscale readers who are active in the community and in the marketplace

For more information, contact your Newsweek sales representative or Bill Youngberg, Sales Development Director, 312-565-3516.

Newsweek

*Sources: †Fall 1998 MRI; *1998–99 Opinion Leaders Study by Erdos & Morgan*

Exhibit 12-26 *Newsweek* and the *Washington Post* offer advertisers a cross-media opportunity

A number of newspapers have been redesigned to be more interesting and easier and faster to read. Changes include the increased use of color and graphics as well as expanded coverage of sports and entertainment. Some papers have begun providing short summaries of articles in each section of the paper so readers can skim them and decide what they want to read.

Of particular concern to publishers is the decline in newspaper readership among important market segments such as women and young adults. Surveys show that the percentage of women who read a newspaper on a typical day declined from 67 percent in 1981 to 51 percent in 2001.[34] Newspapers and advertisers are concerned because women are far more likely than men to make buying decisions. Many newspapers are introducing new women's sections and revising old ones to make them more appealing to modern women. This means including articles on such issues as health, parenting, and careers—for example, how women with children and jobs manage their time.

Newspapers are also concerned about where their future readers will come from, since many young people are heavy TV viewers and also are spending more and more time surfing the Internet. However, a recent study found that newspaper readership is high among teens, and many papers are making special efforts to attract teenagers in hopes they will become and remain regular readers. The newspaper industry is also taking steps to maintain readership among young people. For example, the Newspaper Association of America (NAA) developed an advertising campaign using the theme "It all starts with newspapers" that encourages young people to read the newspaper every day.[35] The ads ask parents to "encourage your child to read a newspaper every day" and feature celebrities such as musician Jon Bon Jovi, basketball star Grant Hill, and actress Meryl Streep promoting newspapers as literacy tools. Exhibit 12-27 shows one of the ads from that campaign, featuring Jackie Chan, the popular action-movie star, reading *The Tuxedo Times.* The ad was run to coincide with the release of Chan's action-comedy film *The Tuxedo.*

The newspaper industry faces a major challenge. To increase circulation and readership and continue to attract advertising revenue, it must make newspapers

Exhibit 12-27 This ad is part of a campaign encouraging young people to read newspapers

more interesting to readers by targeting specific groups and expanding services to encourage advertisers to continue using newspapers. The newspaper industry launched a comprehensive program to address some of these issues. Called the Newspaper Readership Initiative, this program seeks to reverse the decline in newspaper readership and circulation and make newspapers a part of every advertiser's media plan.[36]

The growth of the Internet and online services is another factor that may erode newspaper readership. As penetration of the Internet into households increases, newspapers and magazines are among the most threatened of the major media. A survey conducted for *Advertising Age* found that consumers with home Internet access are less likely to use magazines or newspapers as a primary information source when shopping for a car, financial services, travel, or fashion. The study also found that consumers from teens to seniors are comfortable with the idea of using the Internet in the future to read books, magazines, and newspapers.[37]

Newspaper publishers are addressing this threat by making their papers available online. Nearly every major newspaper has established a website, and many publishers now make their papers available online. The number of U.S. newspapers available online increased from less than 100 in 1995 to more than 1,300 in 2002. Many papers are also developing innovative programs for advertisers to attract their online advertising dollars. Networks are forming to help local newspapers go online and to facilitate the sale and purchase of banner ads and sponsorships. But as with magazines, audience measurement and user involvement are making it difficult for newspapers to attract advertisers and are issues that must be addressed.

Summary

Magazines and newspapers, the two major forms of print media, play an important role in the media plans and strategy of many advertisers. Magazines are a very selective medium and are very valuable for reaching specific types of customers and market segments. The three broad categories of magazines are consumer, farm, and business publications. Each of these categories can be further classified according to the publication's editorial content and audience appeal.

In addition to their selectivity, the advantages of magazines include their excellent reproduction quality, creative flexibility, long life, prestige, and readers' high receptivity to magazine advertising, as well as the services they offer to advertisers. Disadvantages of magazines include their high cost, limited reach and frequency, long lead time, and the advertising clutter in most publications.

Advertising space rates in magazines vary according to a number of factors, among them the size of the ad, position in the publication, particular editions purchased, use of color, and number and frequency of insertions. Rates for magazines are compared on the basis of the cost per thousand, although other factors such as the editorial content of the publication and its ability to reach specific target audiences must also be considered.

Newspapers represent the largest advertising medium in terms of total volume, receiving nearly a fourth of all advertising dollars. Newspapers are a very important medium to local advertisers, especially retailers. They are also used by national advertisers, although the differential rate structure for national versus local advertisers is a source of controversy. Newspapers are a broad-based medium that reaches a large percentage of households in a particular area. Newspapers' other advantages include flexibility, geographic selectivity, reader involvement, and special services. Drawbacks of newspapers include their lack of high-quality ad reproduction, short life span, lack of audience selectivity, and clutter.

Trends toward market segmentation and regional marketing are prompting many advertisers to make more use of newspapers and magazines. However, both magazines and newspapers face increasing competition from such other media as radio, cable TV, direct marketing, and the Internet. Both magazines and newspapers are working to improve the quality of their circulation bases, offer database marketing services, and initiate cross-media deals. Rising costs and declining readership are problems for many magazines and newspapers. Both magazines and newspapers are making their publications available online, but problems with audience measurement and interactions with ads are important issues that must be resolved.

Key Terms

selectivity, 395
gatefolds, 398
bleed pages, 398
split runs, 401
controlled-circulation basis, 405
pass-along readership, 405
total audience/readership, 406
magazine networks, 408
multimagazine deals, 411
cross-media advertising, 411
selective binding, 411
ink-jet imaging, 412
display advertising, 416
classified advertising, 416
preprinted inserts, 416
city zone, 421
retail trading zone, 421
general advertising rates, 422
retail advertising rates, 422
standard advertising units (SAUs), 423
flat rates, 424
open-rate structure, 424
run of paper (ROP), 424
preferred position rate, 425
combination rates, 425

Discussion Questions

1. The vignette at the beginning of the chapter discusses how *Rolling Stone* magazine is undergoing major changes to update its image and make it more appealing to a younger audience. Evaluate the changes being made by *Rolling Stone* to reposition itself and the challenges the magazine faces in trying to compete against other magazines that are targeting young adults.

2. Discuss the role of newspapers and magazines in the development and implementation of an integrated marketing communications program. What advantages are offered by each medium?

3. What is meant by selectivity with regard to the purchase of advertising media? Discuss the various ways magazines offer selectivity to advertisers.

4. Choose a specific target market that an advertiser might want to reach. Discuss how magazines and/or newspapers might be used to reach this particular market in a cost effective manner.

5. IMC Perspective 12-1 discusses the challenges marketers targeting products and services to the young male market face in trying to reach this segment. Why do you think teenage males are such a difficult market to reach with magazines? Do you think a magazine such as *Stance* will be successful in appealing to the teen male market?

6. Discuss why many companies such as Nike, Kodak, Ford, Ikea and others are choosing to publish their own custom magazines. Do you think these custom publications are an effective way to reach their customers?

7. If you were purchasing magazine advertising space for a manufacturer of golf clubs such as Taylor-Made or Calloway, what factors would you consider? Would your selection of magazines be limited to golf publications? Why or why not?

8. Discuss how the use of newspapers as an advertising medium would differ for national versus local advertisers. Find examples of newspaper advertising used by a national and a local advertiser and evaluate the type of ad used by each.

9. Discuss the reasons why *USA Today* has become the leading national newspaper. What challenges do other national newspapers such as *The Wall Street Journal* and the *New York Times* face in trying to compete against *USA Today* for national advertising?

10. Why has newspaper readership in the United States been declining over the past decade? Do you think campaigns such as the Newspaper Association of America's "It all starts with newspapers" can help reverse the decline in newspaper readership among young people?

Support Media

Chapter Objectives

1. To recognize the various support media available to the marketer in developing an IMC program.
2. To develop an understanding of the advantages and disadvantages of support media.
3. To know how audiences for support media are measured.

Stealth Marketing Goes Mainstream

The next time you see a campus opinion leader or Hollywood star driving a certain type of car, drinking a soda, or talking about the merits of some product or service, realize that he or she may be being paid to promote the item. While not a completely new idea, the use of nonconventional methods of getting products promoted appears to almost be becoming conventional. Referred to by a variety of titles including *stealth marketing, ambush marketing,* and *guerrilla marketing,* these "under-the-radar" methods attempt to get exposure for products or services in a number of ways at the lowest cost. For smaller companies stealth marketing may be the only form of communications they can afford, so this means of communication is a necessity. But now many of the larger advertisers have also adopted the approach.

One of the more popular brands in Britain is Colman's Mustard. Founded 188 years ago, Colman's has successfully employed under-the-radar tactics since the 1920s, when its advertising agency initiated the idea of a fictitious "mustard club." The campaign started with the agent himself pasting stickers on buses that read, "Has father joined the mustard club?" The campaign caught on very quickly with Brits and eventually expanded into an integrated campaign that included a club members' newsletter, card games, and badges (500,000 badges were distributed in 1933 alone!). The success of the campaign led Colman's to be the top-selling mustard by 1938, and it has remained a brand leader ever since, although it is now owned by Unilever.

In the United States, a number of brands that have become successful through more conventional advertising approaches are also attempting to capitalize on the stealth approach. For example, Revlon paid ABC to include its cosmetics as part of the plot on the soap opera *All My Children.* Calvin Klein's $45 million launch of the men's cologne Crave will include street sampling, "seeding"—having designated opinion leaders be seen with and talk about the brand—and sand sculptures of the logo on beaches on both coasts. Sony Ericsson hired troupes of actors to pose as tourists in New York City and Los Angeles to ask passers-by to take their picture with the company's new combination cell-phone camera. Procter & Gamble sent elaborate Porta Potties to state fairs to promote Charmin toilet paper, and *Elle* magazine (among others) has hired individuals to log on to Internet chat rooms and talk about its product. And this is just a sampling!

Like many other things, however, overuse creates problems. Many consumers and businesspeople consider the practice of stealth marketing

deceptive, arguing that such practices attempt to trick the consumer. Some have even fought back. One such group is the Federation Internationale de Football Association (FIFA), the governing body of international soccer ("football" to most of the world). During the 2002 World Cup the agency took on the role of policing unauthorized promotions at the games in South Korea. Pushed by Coca-Cola, Adidas, and Philips Electronics—all of whom paid $35 million to $40 million to be official sponsors, the "cops" clamped down on competitors that attempted to gain exposure to the estimated 40 billion TV viewers through stealth methods. One such effort—according to FIFA, but denied by the company—was that by Samsung. At one game more than 100 Chinese spectators were adorned in bright red hats with a logo of South Korea's Samsung electronics prominently emblazoned on them. The police made them remove the hats prior to entering the stadium, as Samsung just happens to be a competitor of sponsor Philips Electronics. At another game, more than thirty 10-meter-long banners were confiscated, each trying to promote companies ranging from electronics to car-repair shops.

While some success was achieved at the World Cup games, the reality is that stealth methods are on the rise and are almost impossible to stop. And not everyone believes that they should be stopped. As noted by Salim Ahmed of *Marketing,* a London business magazine, stealth may be the only future marketing has—at least for some companies.

Sources: Daniel Eisenberg, "It's an Ad, Ad, Ad, Ad World," *Time Magazine,* Sept. 2, 2002, pp. 38–41; Gabriel Kahn, "Stop That Logo!" *The Wall Street Journal Europe,* June 21–23, 2002, p. N1; "Colman's Mustard," *Marketing,* Aug. 1, 2002, p. G19; Salim Ahmed, "Stealth May Be the Only Future Marketing Has," *Marketing,* Nov. 2, 2000, p. 32.

The stealth marketing techniques discussed in the lead-in to this chapter reflect the many different ways (some unconventional) that companies and organizations get their messages out. Ads have also appeared on manhole covers, inside rest-room stalls, on lettuce wrappers in grocery stores, on hubcaps, on cell phones, and even on beepers. In this chapter, we review a number of support media, some that are new to the marketplace and others that have been around a while. We discuss the relative advantages and disadvantages, cost information, and audience measurement of each. We refer to them as **support media** because the media described in the previous chapters dominate the media strategies of large advertisers, particularly national advertisers. Support media are used to reach those people in the target market the primary media may not have reached and to reinforce, or support, their messages.

You may be surprised at how many different ways there are to deliver the message and how often you are exposed to them. Let's begin by examining the scope of the support media industry and some of the many alternatives available to marketers.

The Scope of the Support Media Industry

Support media are referred to by several titles, among them **alternative media, nonmeasured media,** and **nontraditional media.** These terms describe a vast variety of channels used to deliver communications and to promote products and services. In this chapter we will discuss many of these media (though, as you might imagine, it would be impossible for us to discuss them all).

Many advertisers, as well as the top 100 advertising agencies, have increased their use of nontraditional support media, and as new alternatives are developed, this use will continue to grow. Figures for nontraditional media do not include some of the most popular support media, such as out-of-home advertising, specialty advertising, and advertising in the Yellow Pages. Let us examine some of these in more detail.

Out-of-Home Media

Out-of-home advertising encompasses many advertising forms, including outdoor (billboards and signs), transit (both inside and outside the vehicle), skywriting, and a variety of other media. While outdoor advertising is used most often, as shown in Figure 13-1, the others are also increasing in use.

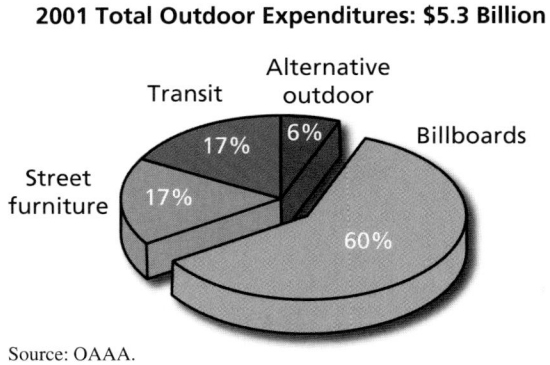

Source: OAAA.

Figure 13-1 Estimated gross billings by media category show that outdoor ads are still the most popular.

Outdoor Advertising

Outdoor advertising has probably existed since the days of cave dwellers. Both the Egyptians and the Greeks used it as early as 5,000 years ago. Outdoor is certainly one of the more pervasive communication forms, particularly if you live in an urban or suburban area.

Even though outdoor accounts for only about 2.3 percent of all advertising expenditures and the number of billboards has decreased, the medium has grown steadily in terms of dollars billed. In 1982, approximately $888 million was spent in this area; in 2001, expenditures reached $5.3 billion.[1] As the medium was once dominated by tobacco advertisers (25 percent of its $1.5 billion revenue came from cigarette advertising in 1991), there were concerns in the industry when an agreement was reached with 46 states in November 1998 to ban all cigarette ads. Increased expenditures from automotive, retail, and financial companies and from new advertisers such as the dot-coms have more than made up for the losses. Companies like McDonald's, Miller, and AT&T are some of the top spenders in this medium. As shown in Figure 13-2, outdoor continues to be used by a broad client base, a demonstration of its continued acceptance in the

Figure 13-2 Outdoor advertising expenditures ranked by percent of total 2001 revenues

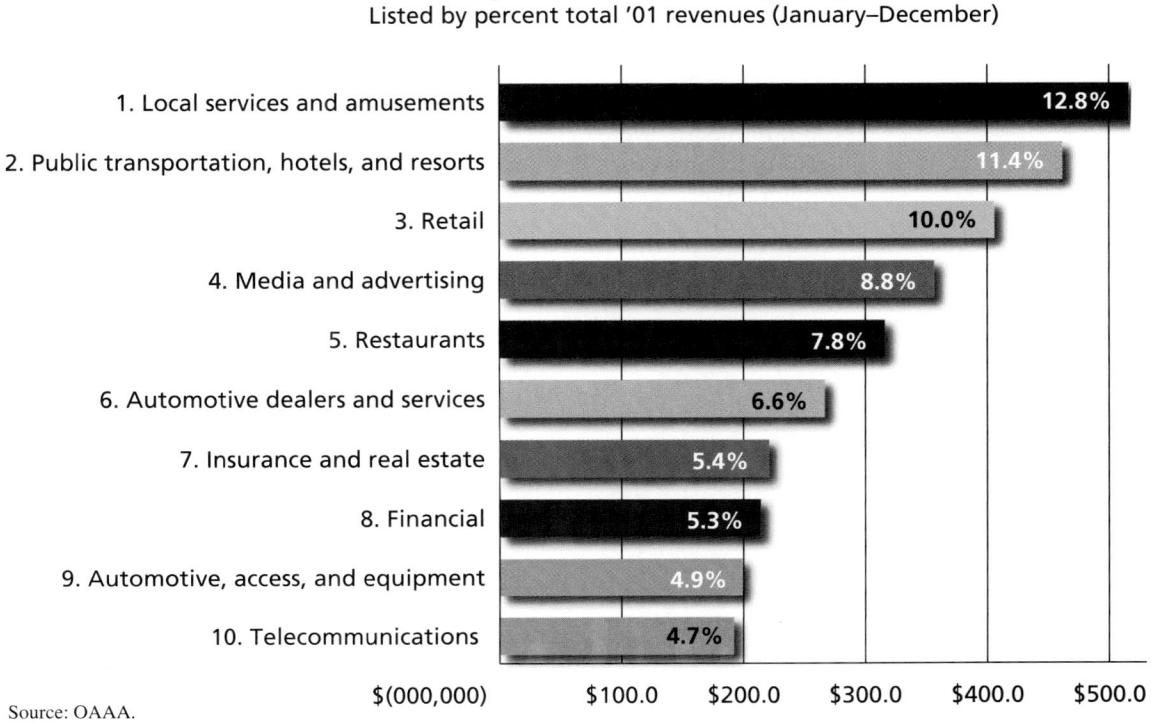

Source: OAAA.

Exhibit 13-1 Outdoor advertising goes beyond two dimensions

industry. The increase in the number of women in the work force has led to more advertising of products targeted to this segment, and the increases in the number of vehicles on the road and the number of miles driven have led to increased expenditures by gas companies and food and lodging providers.

A major reason for the continued success of outdoor is its ability to remain innovative through technology. As Exhibit 13-1 shows, billboards are no longer limited to standard sizes and two dimensions; 3-D forms and extensions are now used to attract attention. Electronic billboards and inflatables, like the one in Exhibit 13-2 that was used to promote Power Rangers, have also opened new markets. You probably have been exposed to either signboards or electronic billboards at sports stadiums, in supermarkets, in the campus bookstore and dining halls, in shopping malls, on the freeways, or on the sides of buildings, from neon signs on skyscrapers in New York City to Mail Pouch Tobacco signs painted on the sides of barns in the Midwest. This is truly a pervasive medium (Exhibit 13-3).

Outdoor advertising does have its critics. Ever since Lady Bird Johnson tried to rid the interstate highways of billboard advertising during her husband's presidency with the Highway Beautification Act of 1965, there has been controversy regarding its use. As previously noted, legislation has passed in 46 states banning the advertising of cigarettes on billboards. In addition, a number of cities and states have considered extending the ban to alcoholic beverages.[2] Consumers themselves seem to have mixed emotions about the medium. In a Maritz AmeriPoll asking consumers about their opinions of billboards, 62 percent of the respondents said they thought billboards should not be banned, while 52 percent said they should be strictly regulated. When asked if billboards were entertaining, 80 percent of those surveyed said no, and when asked if billboards could be beautiful, only 27 percent said yes.[3]

Media buyers have not completely adopted outdoor, partially because of image problems and because of the belief that it is difficult to buy. (Approximately 80 per-

Exhibit 13-2 Inflatables bring new meaning to outdoor advertising

cent of outdoor advertising is purchased by local merchants and companies.) Let us examine some of the advantages and disadvantages of the medium in more detail.

Advantages and Disadvantages of Outdoor Advertising

Outdoor advertising offers a number of advantages:

1. *Wide coverage of local markets.* With proper placement, a broad base of exposure is possible in local markets, with both day and night presence. A 100 GRP **showing** (the percentage of duplicated audience exposed to an outdoor poster daily) could yield exposure to an equivalent of 100 percent of the marketplace daily, or 3,000 GRPs over a month. This level of coverage is likely to yield high levels of reach.

2. *Frequency.* Because purchase cycles are typically for 30-day periods, consumers are usually exposed a number of times, resulting in high levels of frequency.

3. *Geographic flexibility.* Outdoor can be placed along highways, near stores, or on mobile billboards, almost anywhere that laws permit. Local, regional, or even national markets may be covered.

4. *Creativity.* As shown in Exhibit 13-1, outdoor ads can be very creative. Large print, colors, and other elements attract attention.

5. *Ability to create awareness.* Because of its impact (and the need for a simple message), outdoor can lead to a high level of awareness.

6. *Efficiency.* Outdoor usually has a very competitive CPM when compared to other media. The average CPM of outdoor is approximately one-half of radio and far less than that of TV, magazines, and newspapers.

7. *Effectiveness.* Outdoor advertising can often lead to sales, as demonstrated in Figure 13-3. In a study reported by BBDO advertising, 35 percent of consumers surveyed said they had called a phone number they saw on an out-of-home ad.[4] A study reported by Mukesh Bhargava and Naveen Donthu showed that outdoor advertising can have a significant effect on sales, particularly when combined with a promotion.[5]

8. *Production capabilities.* Modern technologies have reduced production times for outdoor advertising to allow for rapid turnaround time.

At the same time, however, there are limitations to outdoor, many of them related to its advantages:

1. *Waste coverage.* While it is possible to reach very specific audiences, in many cases the purchase of outdoor results in a high degree of waste coverage. It is not likely that everyone driving past a billboard is part of the target market.

2. *Limited message capabilities.* Because of the speed with which most people pass by outdoor ads, exposure time is short, so messages are limited to a few words and/or an illustration. Lengthy appeals are not likely to be effective.

Bright lights, big cities

The most expensive and desirable locations for out-of-home advertising, based on an informal poll of more than a dozen top outdoor media company executives, agency media buyers and Wall Street observers, conducted by *Advertising Age*.

Location	Price/month
Times Square New York City	$50,000-$150,000
Sunset Strip Los Angeles	$30,000-$100,000
Lincoln Tunnel New York City/Weehawken, N.J.	$25,000-$60,000
Long Island Expressway (outside Midtown Tunnel) Long Island City, N.Y.	$25,000-$60,000
Union Square San Francisco	$20,000-$50,000
101N Freeway (toward Bay Bridge) San Francisco	$20,000-$40,000
Kennedy Expressway Chicago	$20,000-$30,000
Eisenhower Expressway Chicago	$15,000-$30,000
I-95 (at Biscayne heading toward South Beach) Miami	$10,000-$20,000
I-94 Detroit	$10,000-$20,000
Southwest Freeway (outside Galleria) Houston	$10,000-$20,000
Intersection of Stemmons & LBJ freeways Dallas	$10,000-$20,000
West side of L.A. (Hollywood, Santa Monica)	$10,000-$15,000

Exhibit 13-3 Most desirable out-of-home advertising locations

Brand	Outdoor Used	Results
Sunsplash Amusement Park	25 GRP billboards	6,000 new customers in first 14 days
Bennett Infiniti	25 GRP billboards in upscale markets	Moved from #35 to #3 in sales in state; sales increased from 8 to 30 per month
Altoids	30 sheet posters; transit, bus panels; kiosks	Sales increased 50%; sales increased 5 to 1 in advertised vs. nonadvertised markets

Figure 13-3 Higher sales from outdoor advertising

3. *Wearout.* Because of the high frequency of exposures, outdoor may lead to a quick wearout. People are likely to get tired of seeing the same ad every day.

4. *Cost.* Because of the decreasing signage available and the higher cost associated with inflatables, outdoor advertising can be expensive in both an absolute and a relative sense.

5. *Measurement problems.* One of the more difficult problems of outdoor advertising lies in the accuracy of measuring reach, frequency, and other effects. (As you will see in the measurement discussion, this problem is currently being addressed, though it has not been resolved.)

6. *Image problems.* Outdoor advertising has suffered some image problems as well as some disregard among consumers.

In sum, outdoor advertising has both advantages and disadvantages for marketers. Some of these problems can be avoided with other forms of out-of-home advertising.

Additional Out-of-Home Media

Several other forms of outdoor advertising are also available. As you read about them, keep in mind the advantages and disadvantages of outdoor in general mentioned earlier and consider whether these alternatives have the same advantages and/or provide a possible solution to the disadvantages.

Aerial Advertising

Airplanes pulling banners, skywriting (in letters as high as 1,200 feet), and blimps all constitute another form of outdoor advertising available to the marketer: **aerial advertising.** Generally these media are not expensive in absolute terms and can be useful for reaching specific target markets. For example, Coppertone has often used skywriting over beach areas to promote its tanning lotions, beer companies (among others) commonly employ aerial advertising at sporting events, and local advertisers promote special events, sales, and the like. Exhibit 13-4 shows one of the many products, services, and/or events that have used this medium. Perhaps one of the more interesting examples of aerial advertising is that shown in Exhibit 13-5. Pizza Hut paid about $1 million to have a 30-foot version of its new logo on an unmanned Russian Proton rocket. The logo was visible for only a few seconds, but Pizza Hut felt the exposure was well worth the investment. (The company also put pizza on the Space Shuttle for those assembling the orbiting space platform.)

Mobile Billboards

Another outdoor medium is **mobile billboards** (see Exhibit 13-6). Some companies paint Volkswagen Beetles with ads called Beetleboards;

Exhibit 13-4 A variety of companies use blimps as an advertising medium

Exhibit 13-5 Pizza Hut takes aerial advertising to new heights

Exhibit 13-6 An interesting and unusual example of a mobile billboard

Trucks often serve as mobile billboards

others paint trucks and vans. Still others put ads on small billboards, mount them on trailers, and drive around and/or park in the geographic areas being targeted (Exhibit 13-6). Costs depend on the area and the mobile board company's fees, though even small and large organizations have found the medium affordable. One small company in California found that its five mobile cars account for 25 percent of its earnings, and a study conducted jointly by 3M and the American Trucking Association estimated that one truck traveling about 60,000 miles a year would create about 10 million viewer impressions of the ad placed on it.[6] In a study employing tracking methodology, the Traffic Audit Bureau (TAB) estimated that three trucks with a Seiko watch ad on them were seen by an average of 121,755 people per day in the Chicago area.[7] America Online, Lexus, Wolfgang Puck, and numerous dot-com companies are some of the advertisers that have used this medium.

In-Store Media

Advertisers spend an estimated $17 billion to promote their products in supermarkets and other stores with untypical media like displays, banners, and shelf signs. These point-of-purchase materials include video displays on shopping carts, kiosks that provide recipes and beauty tips, and coupons at counters and cash registers, LED (light-emitting diode) boards, and ads that broadcast over in-house screens. At one time, Miller Brewing Co. used 30 to 40 agencies to provide these services (it now uses 10). Figure 13-4 lists a few of the many **in-store media** options.

Much of the attraction of point-of-purchase media is based on figures from the Point of Purchase Advertising Institute (POPAI) that state approximately two-thirds of consumers' purchase decisions are made in the store; some impulse categories demonstrate an 80 percent rate.[8] Many advertisers are spending more of their dollars where decisions are made now that they can reach consumers at the point of purchase, providing additional product information while reducing their own efforts.

Miscellaneous Outdoor Media

As shown in Figure 13-5, there are numerous outdoor media available, adding to the pervasiveness of this medium. The next time you are out, take a few moments to observe how many different forms of outdoor advertising you are exposed to.

Audience Measurement in Out-of-Home Media

A number of sources of audience measurement and other information are available:

- Competitive Media Reports (formerly BAR/LNA) provides information on expenditures on outdoor media by major advertisers.
- Simmons Market Research Bureau conducts research annually for the Institute of Outdoor Advertising, providing demographic data, exposures, and the like. Mediamark Research Inc. (MRI) provides similar data.

Figure 13-4 In-store media options

Company/Program	Medium
ActMedia	
Act Now	Co-op couponing/sampling
Aisle Vision	Ad posters inserted in stores' directory signs
Carts	Ad placed on frame inside/outside shopping cart
Impact	Customized in-store promotion events
Instant Coupon Machine	Coupon dispensers mounted in shelf channels
Act Radio	Live format in-store radio network
Shelf Take-One	Two-sided take-one offers in plastic see-thru cartridges placed at shelf
Shelf Talk	Plastic frames on shelf near product
Addvantage Media Group	Shopping cart calculators
Advanced Promotion Technologies	
Vision System	Scanner-driven, card-based promotion system using audio/video at checkout
Alpine Promotions	"Adsticks" dividers that separate food at grocery store checkout
Audits and Surveys Worldwide	Tracks in-store sales using scanner data
Catalina Marketing	
Checkout Coupon	Scanner-driven coupon program that generates coupons at checkout
Checkout Message	Targeted ad messages delivered at checkout
Save Now	Instant electronic discounts
Donnelly Marketing	
Convert	Solo/customized promotion events
In-Store Advertising	Two-sided LED display units that hang above five high-traffic areas
Innova Marketing	In-store actresses and actors providing product demonstrations
Time In-Store	In-store couponing
Valassis In-Store	In-store couponing
SPAR Marketing Force	In-store demos and customized events
Media One, Inc.	
SuperAd	Backlit ads placed in checkout lanes
Stratmar Systems	
Field Services	In-store demos and customized events
StratMedia	Shopping cart ad program
Supermarket Communications Systems	
Good Neighbor Direct	Bulletin board distribution center

- Standard Rate & Data Service provides a sourcebook on rate information, production requirements, closing dates, and so on.
- Eight-Sheet Outdoor Advertising Association provides a buyers' guide containing facts and figures regarding outdoor advertising.
- Shelter Advertising Association provides a buyers' guide containing facts and figures regarding shelter advertising.

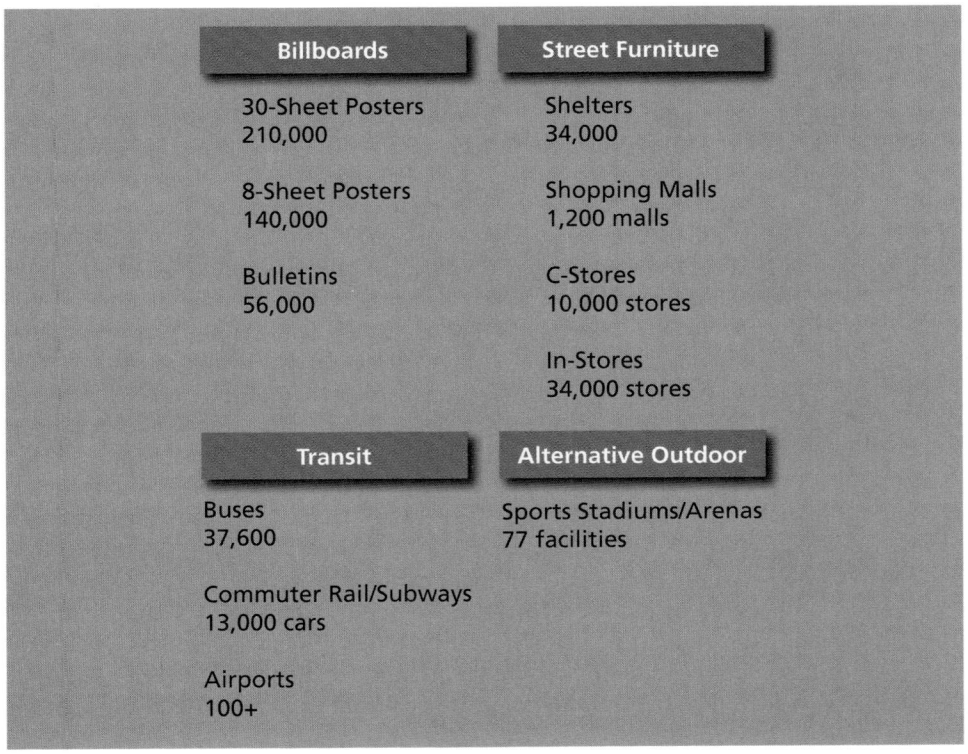

Figure 13-5 Out-of-home advertising faces/vehicles

- Audience Measurement by Market for Outdoor (AMMO) audience estimates are provided by Marketmath, Inc., for outdoor showings in over 500 markets. Published annually, the reports are based on a series of local market travel studies and circulation audits and provide demographic characteristics of audiences.
- The Institute of Outdoor Advertising is a trade organization of the outdoor advertising industry. It gathers cost data and statistical information for outdoor advertising space purchases.
- Harris-Donovan Media Systems employs a mathematical model using data supplied by the Traffic Audit Bureau and segmented by time period and billboard size. The data provide audience figures in the top 50 metropolitan areas and are available to subscribers on any IBM-compatible computer.
- The Point of Purchase Advertising Institute is a trade organization of point-of-purchase advertisers collecting statistical and other market information on POP advertising.
- The Outdoor Advertising Association of America (OAAA) is the primary trade association of the industry. It assists members with research, creative ideas, and more effective use of the medium and has a website at www.oaa.org.
- The Media Market Guide (MMG) provides physical dimensions, population characteristics, and media opportunities for the top 100 media markets.
- The Traffic Audit Bureau (TAB) is the auditing arm of the industry. TAB conducts traffic counts on which the published rates are based.
- The Traffic Audit Bureau for Media Measurement provides data regarding exposures to a variety of out-of-home media, including bus shelters, aerial banners, in-store media, and billboards. This organization was formed in response to complaints that current methodologies might overstate the reach provided by these media.
- Scarborough publishes local market studies providing demographic data, product usage, and outdoor media usage.
- Computer packages like Telmar, Donnelly, TAPSCAN, and IMS also provide information comparing outdoor with other media.

One of the weaknesses associated with outdoor advertising is audience measurement. Space rates are usually based on the number of desired showings, as shown in

Figure 13-6 Posting space rates, Memphis market (per-month basis)

18+ Pop. (000)	GRP	Total Faces	4-Week Circulation (000)	4-Week Rate per Face	Total 4-Week Rate	CPM
898.3	100	65	26,098.8	$800	$52,000	$1.99
853.3	95	62	24,925.6	847	52,514	2.11
808.4	90	58	23,276.4	847	49,126	2.11
763.5	85	55	22,103.2	847	46,585	2.11
718.6	80	52	20,930.0	847	44,044	2.10
673.7	75	49	19,756.8	847	41,503	2.10
628.8	70	45	18,107.6	882	39,690	2.19

Note: Memphis-Memphis, 30-sheet poster, general market.

Figure 13-6. For example, a 100 GRP showing would theoretically provide coverage to the entire 18-plus market. In Memphis, this would mean coverage of approximately 26 million people for a monthly rate of $52,000. Along with rate information, the companies offering outdoor billboards provide reach and frequency estimates—but there is no valid way to verify that the showings are performing as promised. The buyer is somewhat at the mercy of the selling agent.

In response to criticism, the industry has implemented a gross ratings point system similar to that used in the television industry. While the system has helped, problems associated with the use of GRPs (discussed earlier in this text) limit the usefulness of this information. Many experts think the new service provided by Harris Media Systems is a significant improvement over the AMMO system, resulting in more credible information.[9]

Transit Advertising

Another form of out-of-home advertising is **transit advertising.** While similar to outdoor in the sense that it uses billboards and electronic messages, transit is targeted at the millions of people who are exposed to commercial transportation facilities, including buses, taxis, commuter trains, elevators, trolleys, airplanes, and subways.

Transit advertising has been around for a long time, but recent years have seen a renewed interest in this medium. Due in part to the increased number of women in the work force (they can be reached on their way to work more easily than at home), audience segmentation, and the rising cost of TV advertising, yearly transit ad spending increased from $43 million in 1972 to over $900 million in 2001.[10] Much of this spending has come from packaged-goods companies such as Colgate, Nestlé, Kraft–General Foods, America Online, and Lycos, which like transit's lower costs and improved frequency of exposures. Other retailers, movie studios, and business-to-business companies have also increased expenditures in this area (Exhibit 13-7).

Exhibit 13-7 The FBI uses outdoor to recruit

Types of Transit Advertising

There are actually three forms of transit advertising: (1) inside cards, (2) outside posters, and (3) station, platform, or terminal posters.

Inside Cards If you have ever ridden a commuter bus, you have probably noticed the **inside cards** placed above the seats and luggage area advertising restaurants, TV or radio stations, or a myriad of other products and services. An innovation is the electronic message boards that carry current advertising information. The ability to change the message and the visibility provide the advertiser with a more attention-getting medium.

Transit cards can be controversial. For example, in the New York subway system, many of the ads for chewing gum, soup, and Smokey the Bear have given way to public service announcements about AIDS, unwanted pregnancies, rape, and infant mortality. While subway riders may agree that such issues are important, many of them complain that the ads are depressing and intrusive.

Exhibit 13-8 Electronic outside posters often appear on taxicabs

Outside Posters Advertisers use various forms of outdoor transit posters to promote products and services. These **outside posters** may appear on the sides, backs, and/or roofs of buses, taxis, trains, and subway and trolley cars.

The increasing sophistication of this medium is demonstrated by a new technology, developed by Vert, Inc., a small company in Boston, that transforms ads on top of taxicabs into real-time animated electronic billboards. Available in New York and Boston, a web server that communicates with a global positioning satellite (GPS) is built into the taxi-top screen. The GPS determines the taxi's location and sends it to the local server, which then delivers the relevant ads for a particular area. A taxi traveling through a Hispanic community can have a message in Spanish, stock quotes could appear in the financial district, and so on. The ads appear in color in a format similar to banner ads, at 10 times the brightness of a TV screen. Space is sold in blocks of time, with cost dependent on the neighborhood, usually ranging from $1 to $5 CPM.[11] (See Exhibit 13-8.)

Station, Platform, and Terminal Posters Floor displays, island showcases, electronic signs, and other forms of advertising that appear in train or subway stations, airline terminals, and the like are all forms of transit advertising. As Exhibit 13-9 shows, **terminal posters** can be very attractive and attention-getting. Bus shelters often provide the advertiser with expanded coverage where other outdoor boards may be restricted. Gannett Transit recently introduced electronic signs on subway platforms in New York.

Exhibit 13-9 Terminal posters can be used to attract attention

Advantages and Disadvantages of Transit Advertising

Advantages of using transit advertising include the following:

1. *Exposure.* Long length of exposure to an ad is one major advantage of indoor forms. The average ride on mass transit is 45 minutes, allowing for plenty of exposure time.[12] As with airline tickets, the audience is essentially a captive one, with nowhere else to go and nothing much to do. As a result, riders are likely to read the ads—more than once. A second form of exposure transit advertising provides is the absolute number of people exposed. About 9 million people ride mass transit every week, and over 9.4 billion rides were taken in 2001, providing a substantial number of potential viewers.[13]

2. *Frequency.* Because our daily routines are standard, those who ride buses, subways, and the like are exposed to the ads repeatedly. If you rode the same subway to work and back every day, in one month you would have the opportunity to see the ad 20 to 40 times. The locations of station and shelter signs also afford high frequency of exposure.

3. *Timeliness.* Many shoppers get to stores on mass transit. An ad promoting a product or service at a particular shopping area could be a very timely communication.

4. *Geographic selectivity.* For local advertisers in particular, transit advertising provides an opportunity to reach a very select segment of the population. A purchase of a location in a certain neighborhood will lead to exposure to people of specific ethnic backgrounds, demographic characteristics, and so on.

5. *Cost.* Transit advertising tends to be one of the least expensive media in terms of both absolute and relative costs. An ad on the side of a bus can be purchased for a very reasonable CPM.

Some disadvantages are also associated with transit:

1. *Image factors.* To many advertisers, transit advertising does not carry the image they would like to represent their products or services. Some advertisers may think having their name on the side of a bus or on a bus stop bench does not reflect well on the firm.

2. *Reach.* While an advantage of transit advertising is the ability to provide exposure to a large number of people, this audience may have certain lifestyles and/or behavioral characteristics that are not true of the target market as a whole. For example, in rural or suburban areas, mass transit is limited or nonexistent, so the medium is not very effective for reaching these people.

3. *Waste coverage.* While geographic selectivity may be an advantage, not everyone who rides a transportation vehicle or is exposed to transit advertising is a potential customer. For products that do not have specific geographic segments, this form of advertising incurs a good deal of waste coverage.

Another problem is that the same bus may not run the same route every day. To save wear and tear on the vehicles, some companies alternate city routes (with much stop and go) with longer suburban routes. Thus, a bus may go downtown one day and reach the desired target group but spend the next day in the suburbs, where there may be little market potential.

4. *Copy and creative limitations.* It may be very difficult to place colorful, attractive ads on cards or benches. And while much copy can be provided on inside cards, on the outside of buses and taxis the message is fleeting and short copy points are necessary.

5. *Mood of the audience.* Sitting or standing on a crowded subway may not be conducive to reading advertising, let alone experiencing the mood the advertiser would like to create. Controversial ad messages may contribute to this less than positive feeling. Likewise, hurrying through an airport may create anxieties that limit the effectiveness of the ads placed there.

In summary, an advantage for one product or service advertiser may be a disadvantage for another. Transit advertising can be an effective medium, but one must understand its strengths and weaknesses to use it properly.

Audience Measurement in Transit Advertising

As with outdoor advertising, the cost basis for transit is the number of showings. In transit advertising, a 100 showing means one ad appears on or in each vehicle in the system; a showing of 50 means half of the vehicles carry the ad. If you are placing such ads on taxicabs, it may be impossible to determine who is being exposed to them.

Rate information comes from the sellers of transit advertising, and audience information is very limited. So much of the information marketers need to purchase transit ads does not come from purely objective sources.

Promotional Products Marketing

According to the Promotional Products Association International (PPA), **promotional products marketing** is "the advertising or promotional medium or method that uses promotional products, such as ad specialties, premiums, business gifts, awards, prizes, or commemoratives." Promotional products marketing is the more up-to-date name for what used to be called specialty advertising. **Specialty advertising** has now been provided with a new definition:

> A medium of advertising, sales promotion, and motivational communication employing imprinted, useful, or decorative products called advertising specialties, a subset of promotional products.
>
> Unlike premiums, with which they are sometimes confused (called advertising specialties), these articles are always distributed free—recipients don't have to earn the specialty by making a purchase or contribution.[14]

As you can see from these descriptions, specialty advertising is often considered both an advertising and a sales promotion medium. In our discussion, we treat it as a supportive advertising medium in the IMC program (Exhibit 13-10).

There are over 15,000 *advertising specialty* items, including ballpoint pens, coffee mugs, key rings, calendars, T-shirts, and matchbooks. Unconventional specialties such as plant holders, wall plaques, and gloves with the advertiser's name printed on them are also used to promote a company or its product; so are glassware, trophies, awards, and vinyl products. In fact, advertisers spend over $16.5 billion per year on specialty advertising items. The increased use of this medium makes it the fastest-growing of all advertising or sales promotion media.[15]

If you stop reading for a moment and look around your desk (or bed or beach blanket), you'll probably find some specialty advertising item nearby. It may be the pen you are using, a matchbook, or even a book cover with the campus bookstore name on it. (Figure 13-7 shows the percentage of sales by product category.) Specialty items are used for many promotional purposes: to thank a customer for patronage, keep the name of the company in front of consumers, introduce new products, or reinforce the name of an existing company, product, or service. Advertising specialties are often used to support other forms of product promotions.

Advantages and Disadvantages of Promotional Products Marketing

Like any other advertising medium, promotional products marketing offers the marketer both advantages and disadvantages. Advantages include the following:

1. *Selectivity.* Because specialty advertising items are generally distributed directly to target customers, the medium offers a high degree of selectivity. The communication is distributed to the desired recipient, reducing waste coverage.

2. *Flexibility.* As the variety of specialty items in Figure 13-7 demonstrates, this medium offers a high degree of flexibility. A message as simple as a logo or as long as is necessary can be distributed through a number of means. Both small and large companies can employ this medium, limited only by their own creativity.

3. *Frequency.* Most forms of specialty advertising are designed for retention. Key chains, calendars, and pens remain with the potential customer

Exhibit 13-10
Promotional products can be a valuable contributor to the IMC program

Figure 13-7 Sales of promotional products by category (numbers in parentheses indicate sales by product category)

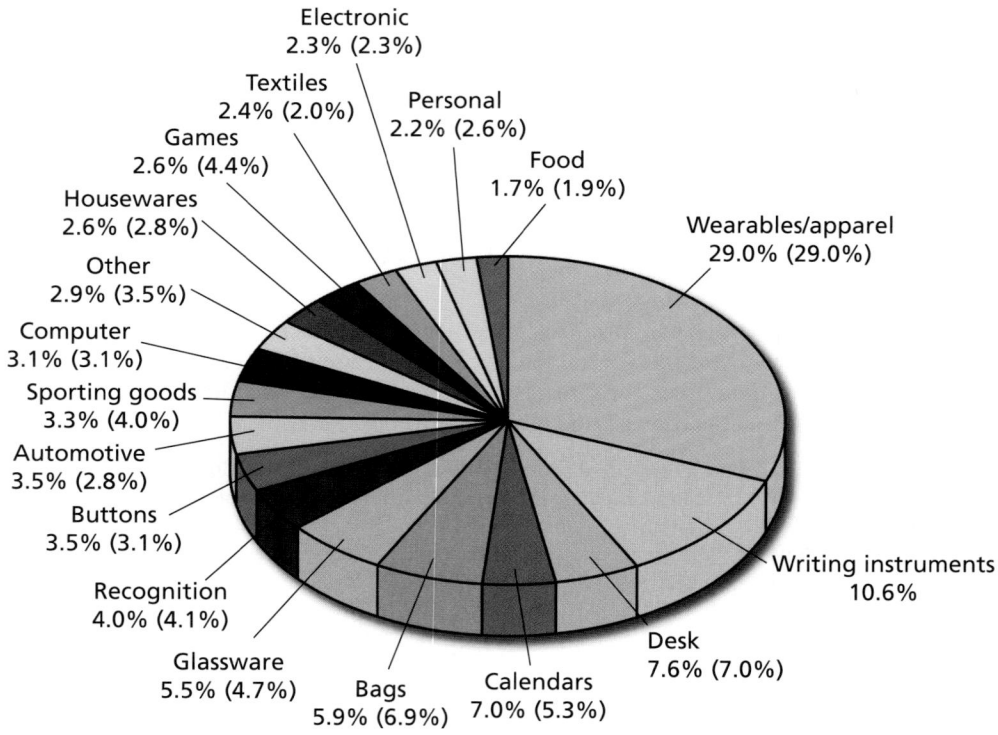

Product Category	Items Included
Wearables	T-shirts, golf shirts, aprons, uniforms, blazers, headwear, jackets, neckwear, footwear, etc.
Writing instruments	Pens, pencils, markers, highlighters, etc.
Desk/office/business accessories	Briefcases, folders, desk pen sets, calculators, cubed paper, etc.
Bags	Totebags, shopping bags, satchels, gift bags, drawstring bags, cosmetic bags, etc.
Calendars	Wall and wallet calendars, desk diaries, pocket secretaries, etc.
Glassware/ceramics	China, crystal, mugs, figurines, etc.
Games/toys/playing cards/inflatables	Kites, balls, puzzles, stuffed animals, etc.
Recognition awards/trophies/jewelry/clocks and watches	Plaques, certificates, etc.
Sporting goods/leisure products/travel accessories	Picnic/party products, camping equipment, barbecue items, bar products, plastic cups, binoculars, luggage, passport cases, etc.
Computer products	Mouse pads, monitor frames, disk carriers, wrist pads, software, etc.
Buttons/badges/ribbons/stickers/magnets	Decals, transfers, signs, banners, etc.
Housewares/tools	Measuring devices, kitchen products, picture frames, household decorations, ornaments, tool kits, first-aid kits, furniture, flashlights, cutlery, weather instruments, etc.
Automotive accessories	Key tags, bumper strips, road maps, floor mats, window shades, etc.
Personal/pocket-purse products	Pocket knives, grooming aids, lighters, matches, sunglasses, wallets, etc.
Electronic devices and accessories	Radios, TVs, videotapes, music CDs, phone cards, etc.
Textiles	Flags, towels, umbrellas, pennants, throws, blankets, etc.
Food gifts	Candy, nuts, gourmet meat, spices, etc.
Other	No examples reported

for a long time, providing repeat exposures to the advertising message at no additional cost.

4. *Cost.* Some specialty items are rather expensive (for example, leather goods), but most are affordable to almost any size organization. While they are costly on a CPM basis when compared with other media, the high number of repeat exposures drives down the relative cost per exposure of this advertising medium.

5. *Goodwill.* Promotional products are perhaps the only medium that generates goodwill in the receiver. Because people like to receive gifts and many of the products are functional (key chains, calendars, etc.), consumers are grateful to receive them. In a recent study of users of promotional products, goodwill was cited as the number-one reason for use.

6. *Supplementing other media.* A major advantage of promotional products marketing is its ability to supplement other media. Because of its low cost and repeat exposures, the simplest message can reinforce the appeal or information provided through other forms. Figure 13-8 demonstrates how promotional products have been used to supplement other IMC strategies.

Promotional products have also been used to support trade shows, motivate dealers, recognize employees, and promote consumer and sales force contests.

Disadvantages of promotional products marketing include the following:

1. *Image.* While most forms of specialty advertising are received as friendly reminders of the store or company name, the firm must be careful choosing the specialty item. The company image may be cheapened by a chintzy or poorly designed advertising form.

2. *Saturation.* With so many organizations now using this advertising medium, the marketplace may become saturated. While you can always use another ballpoint pen or book of matches, the value to the receiver declines if replacement is too easy, and the likelihood that you will retain the item or even notice the message is reduced. The more unusual the specialty, the more value it is likely to have to the receiver.

3. *Lead time.* The lead time required to put together a promotional products message is significantly longer than that for most other media.

Even with its disadvantages, promotional products marketing can be an effective medium.

Audience Measurement in Promotional Products Marketing

Owing to the nature of the industry, specialty advertising has no established ongoing audience measurement system. Research has been conducted in an attempt to determine the impact of this medium, however, including the following reports.

Figure 13-8 The Impact of promotional products in an IMC program

Combining Promotional Products with:	Effect
Advertising	Including direct mail with a promotional product increased response to a print ad to 4.2%, versus 2.3% with direct mail only and .7% with an ad only.
Personal selling	Customers receiving a promotional product expressed more goodwill toward the company than did those receiving a letter. They rated the company more positively in 52% of the cases and rated the salespeople more proficient (34%) and more capable (16%). Business-to-business customers receiving a promotional product were 14% more likely to provide leads, while salespersons who gave gifts to customers received 22% more leads than those who did not.
Trade shows	Responses to invitations to visit a booth were higher when a promotional product was enclosed.
Direct	Responses to direct-mail sales pieces were 1.9% with only a letter but 3.3% with a promotional product (75% higher). Other studies have shown increases of 50 to 66%.

A study by Schreiber and Associates indicated 39 percent of people receiving advertising specialties could recall the name of the company as long as six months later, and a study conducted by A. C. Nielsen found that 31 percent of respondents were still using at least one specialty they had received a year or more earlier.[16]

A study by Gould/Pace University found the inclusion of a specialty item in a direct-mail piece generated a greater response rate and 321 percent greater dollar purchases per sale than mail pieces without such items.[17] Studies at Baylor University showed that including an ad specialty item in a thank-you letter can improve customers' attitudes toward a company's sales reps by as much as 34 percent and toward the company itself by as much as 52 percent.[18] Finally, Richard Manville Research reported the average household had almost four calendars; if they had not been given such items free, two-thirds of the respondents said they would purchase one, an indication of the desirability of this particular specialty item.[19]

The Promotional Products Association International (www.ppai.org) is the trade organization of the field. The PPAI helps marketers develop and use specialty advertising forms. It also provides promotional and public relations support for specialty advertising and disseminates statistical and educational information.

Yellow Pages Advertising

When we think of advertising media, many of us overlook one of the most popular forms in existence—the **Yellow Pages.** While most of us use the Yellow Pages frequently, we tend to forget they are advertising. Over 200 publishers produce more than 6,500 Yellow Pages throughout the United States, generating $13.6 billion in advertising expenditures. This makes the Yellow Pages the fifth-largest medium (just behind radio).[20]

More than 90 percent of the industry's ad revenues are accounted for by nine big operators: the seven regional Bell companies, the Donnelley Directory, and GTE Directories.[21] Local advertisers constitute the bulk of the ads in these directories (about 90 percent), though national advertisers such as U-Haul, Sears, and General Motors use them as well.[22]

Interestingly, there are several forms of Yellow Pages. (Because AT&T never copyrighted the term, any publisher can use it.) They include the following:

- *Specialized directories.* Directories are targeted at select markets such as Hispanics, blacks, Asians, and women. Also included in this category are toll-free directories, Christian directories, and many others.
- *Audiotex.* The "talking Yellow Pages" offer oral information on advertisers.
- *Interactive.* Consumers search the database for specific types of information. Advertisers can update their listings frequently.
- *Internet directories.* A number of websites provide some form of Internet-based Yellow Pages (see www.kelseygroup.com). These directories include national directories which provide a nationwide database of business listings; local and regional directories, which provide information on a local or regional basis; and "shared" directories, in which local companies join together to form a national database.
- *Other services.* Some Yellow Pages directories offer coupons and freestanding inserts. In Orange County, California, telephone subscribers received samples of Golden Grahams and Cinnamon Toast Crunch cereals when their Yellow Pages were delivered.

Exhibit 13-11 The Yellow Pages are the final link in the buying cycle

The Yellow Pages are often referred to as a **directional medium** because the ads do not create awareness or demand for products or

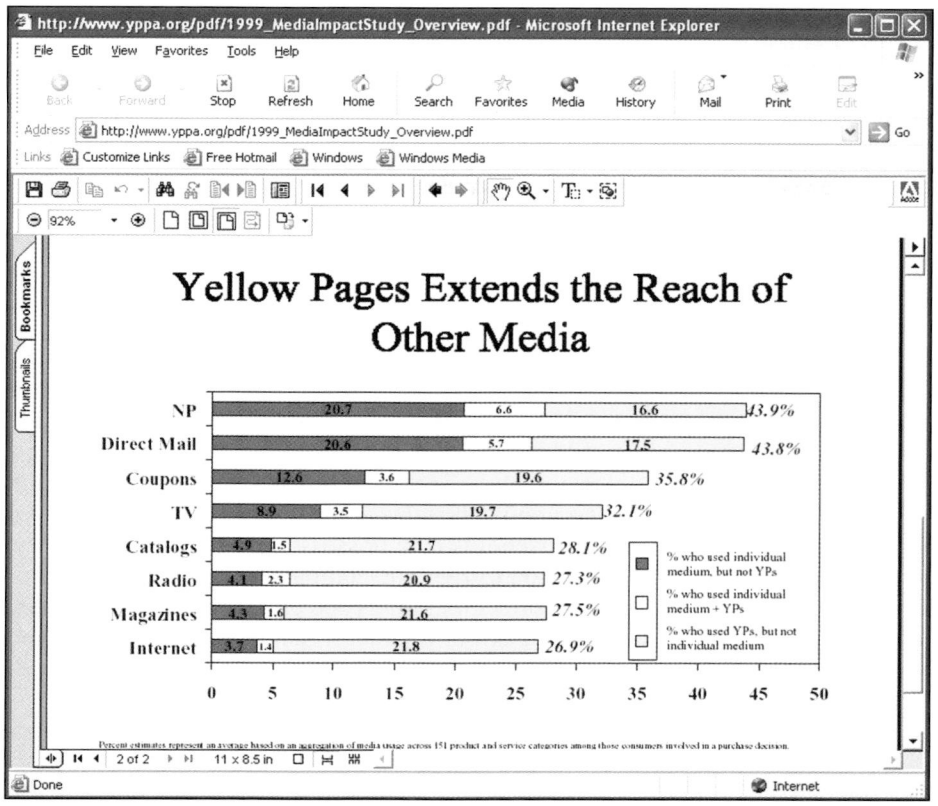

Figure 13-9 The Yellow Pages extend the reach of other media

Note: Percent estimates represent an average based on an aggregation of media usage across 151 product and service categories among those consumers involved in a purchase decision.

services; rather, once consumers have decided to buy, the Yellow Pages point them in the direction where their purchases can be made.[23] The Yellow Pages are thus considered the final link in the buying cycle, as shown in Exhibit 13-11. As shown in Figure 13-9, the Yellow Pages can extend the reach of other IMC media.

Advantages and Disadvantages of Yellow Pages The Yellow Pages offer the following advantages to advertisers:

1. *Wide availability.* A variety of directories are published. According to the Yellow Pages Publishers Association, consumers refer to the Yellow Pages more than 19.4 billion times yearly.[24]

2. *Action orientation.* Consumers use the Yellow Pages when they are considering, or have decided to take, action.

3. *Costs.* Ad space and production costs are relatively low compared to other media.

4. *Frequency.* Because of their longevity (Yellow Pages are published yearly), consumers return to the directories time and again. The average adult refers to the Yellow Pages about 1.4 times a week, and 56 percent of U.S. households use the Yellow Pages weekly, and 76 percent monthly.[25]

5. *Nonintrusiveness.* Because consumers choose to use the Yellow Pages, they are not considered an intrusion. Studies show that most consumers rate the Yellow Pages very favorably.[26] Among users, 79 percent agree that the Yellow Pages are an important source of information, and 76 percent report that the books are helpful for learning about new products.

Disadvantages of the Yellow Pages include the following:

1. *Market fragmentation.* Since Yellow Pages are essentially local media, they tend to be very localized. Add to this the increasing number of specialized directories, and the net result is a very specific offering.

2. *Timeliness.* Because Yellow Pages are printed only once a year, they become outdated. Companies may relocate, go out of business, or change phone numbers in the period between editions.

3. *Lack of creativity.* While the Yellow Pages are somewhat flexible, their creative aspects are limited.

4. *Lead times.* Printing schedules require that ads be placed a long time before the publications appear. It is impossible to get an ad in after the deadline, and advertisers need to wait a long time before the next edition.

5. *Clutter.* A recent study by Avery Abernethy indicates that the Yellow Pages (like other media) experience problems with clutter.

6. *Size requirements.* Response to Yellow Pages ads is directly tied to the size of the ad. A study by Abernethy and Laband indicates that for large directories a minimum of one-half page may be required just to get noticed.[27]

Audience Measurement in the Yellow Pages

Two forms of audience measurement are employed in the Yellow Pages industry. As with other print media, *circulation* is counted as the number of either individuals or households possessing a particular directory. But Yellow Pages advertisers have resisted the use of circulation figures for evaluating audience size, arguing that this number represents only *potential* exposures to an ad.[28] Given that households may possess more than one directory, advertisers argued for a figure based on *usage.* The National Yellow Pages Monitor (NYPM) now provides Yellow Pages directory ratings and usage behavior by market. Using a diary method similar to that used for broadcast media, this ratings method allows advertisers to determine both the absolute and relative costs of advertising in different directories (see Figure 13-10). Statistical Research Inc. (SRI) conducts national studies to measure Yellow Pages usage. Simmons and MRI provide demographic and usage information.

The trade association for the Yellow Pages, the Yellow Pages Integrated Media Association (www.yellowpagesima.org and www.yppa.org), provides industry information, rates, educational materials, and assistance to advertisers and potential advertisers. The YPPA also disseminates educational and statistical information.

Other Media

There are numerous other nontraditional ways to promote products. Some are reviewed here.

Advertising in Movie Theaters

Another method of delivering the message that is increasing quickly (to the dismay of many) is the use of movie theaters to promote products and/or services. Commercials shown before the film and previews, with both local and national sponsorships, have replaced cartoons. In addition, ads in theater lobbies, at kiosks, and on popcorn tubs and drink cups are used. For example, Coca-Cola Co. has frequently advertised the Coke Classic brand in movie theaters. PepsiCo, Sears, Gap, and Target have also employed this medium, as have numerous other companies. McDonald's, Clairol, and Toyota are prime users. At least one study has estimated that more than one-half of all theaters show ads before the films (Figure 13-11). The growth rate has averaged 20 percent a year sine 1992, resulting in a $400 million industry by 2001.[29] On videos, companies place ads before the movies as well as on the cartons they come in. Pepsi

Figure 13-10 The Yellow Pages use a usage rating system

CPM Based on Directory Circulation

Directory	Circulation	Cost for a Full-Page Ad	CPM
A	509,000	$28,000	$55.01
B	505,000	21,000	41.58

CPM Based on Directory Usage (Ratings)

Directory	Total References per Year	Share of References	Cost for a Full-Page Ad	CPM
A	58,400,000	76.9%	$28,000	.48
B	17,500,000	23.1	21,000	1.20

Cinema	Number of Screens	Number of Theaters	Commercial Time
Regal Cinema	4,449	424	3 minutes
AMC Entertainment Inc.	2,736	197	2 minutes
Loews Cineplex Entertainment	2,726	359	3 minutes
Carmike Cinemas Inc.	2,445	350	3 minutes
Cinemark USA Inc.	2,227	192	3 minutes
United Artists Theatres	1,858	257	3 minutes
National Amusements	1,076	102	No limit
General Cinema Theatres	1,060	133	3 minutes
Hoyts Cinema Corp.	967	113	3 minutes
Century Theatres	700	75	No rolling stock ads
Edwards Theatres Circuit	690	59	No rolling stock ads

Source: National Association of Theatre Owners, individual cinema circuits.

Figure 13-11 The Show Before the Show: Movie theaters are screening commercials, along with previews, before the main attraction.

advertises on the video of *Casper.* Disney often promotes its upcoming movies as well as Disney World (10 minutes of advertising preceded *The Lion King* on video).[30] (If you have ever rented a Disney movie, you are well aware of this!) The Canadian government has shown "stay in school" spots, knowing that the movies are a good way to reach 12- to 17-year-olds. Dozens of other advertisers have also used this medium, including Sega, AT&T, and DeBeers.

Consumer reaction to ads in movie theaters is mixed. A number of studies have shown that most people think these ads are annoying or very annoying. But in an *Advertising Age*/Gallup national sample of moviegoers, 35 percent were against a ban on ads in movie theaters and another 21 percent were unsure whether such a ban should be enacted.[31] The survey was taken after Walt Disney Co. announced it would stop showing its movies in any theater that runs on-screen advertising along with the films. While advertisers were infuriated, Disney claimed its surveys showed that customers were extremely irritated by such ads and as a result might quit coming to the theaters.[32] (Disney still bans ads, and some movie chains refuse to accept them as well.)

Adam Snyder, writing in *Brandweek* magazine, believes that pushing movies is acceptable but beyond that consumers are likely to react negatively.[33] Nevertheless, Blake Thomas, marketing vice president for MGM/UA Home Entertainment, claims, "We could conceivably sell as much air time as we want, since advertisers cannot resist the temptation of reaching tens of millions of viewers."[34]

Advantages of Movie Theater Advertising

Movies provide a number of advantages to advertisers, including the following:

1. *Exposure.* The number of people attending movies is substantial: over 1.49 billion tickets were sold in 2001.[35] Ticket sales are over $7.7 billion per year, and attendance continues to climb.[36]

2. *Mood.* If viewers like the movie, the mood can carry over to the product advertised.

3. *Cost.* The cost of advertising in a theater varies from one setting to the next. However, it is low in terms of both absolute and relative costs per exposure.

4. *Recall.* Research indicates that the next day about 83 percent of viewers can recall the ads they saw in a movie theater. This compares with a 20 percent recall rate for television.[37]

5. *Clutter.* Lack of clutter is another advantage offered by advertising in movie theaters. Most theaters limit the number of ads.

6. *Proximity.* Since many theaters are located in or adjacent to shopping malls, potential customers are "right next door." (Of moviegoers, 73 percent combine the activity with dining out, 69% percent with shopping.)

7. *Segmentation.* A key advantage of movie advertising is the ability to target specific demographic segments. The profile of the moviegoer is above-average in education and affluent. The movie titles and ratings enable advertisements to reach specific groups.

Disadvantages of Movie Theater Advertising

Some of the disadvantages associated with movie theaters as advertising media follow:

1. *Irritation.* Perhaps the major disadvantage is that many people do not wish to see advertising in these media. A number of studies suggest these ads may create a high degree of annoyance.[38] This dissatisfaction may carry over to the product itself, to the movies, or to the theaters. Mike Stimler, president of the specialty video label Water Bearer Films, says, "People boo in movie theaters when they see product advertising."[39] Anne-Marie Marcus, vice president of sales for Screen Vision, contends that the furor has died down, though the T. J. Maxx retail chain says it is unlikely to use this form of advertising again.[40]

2. *Cost.* While the cost of advertising in local theaters has been cited as an advantage because of the low rates charged, ads exposed nationally are often as much as 20 percent higher than an equal exposure on television. CPMs also tend to be higher than in other media.

While only two disadvantages of theater advertising have been mentioned, the first is a strong one. Many people who have paid to see a movie perceive advertising as an intrusion. In a study by Michael Belch and Don Sciglimpaglia, many moviegoers stated that not only would they not buy the product advertised, but they would consider boycotting it. So advertisers should be cautious in their use of this medium. If they want to use movies, they might consider an alternative—placing products in the movies.

Product Placements in Movies and on TV

An increasingly common way to promote a product or service is by showing the actual product or an ad for it as part of a movie or TV show. While such **product placement** does not constitute a major segment of the advertising and promotions business, it has proved effective for some companies and has taken on increased importance with advertisers' concerns over viewers' ability to avoid watching commercials. (Note: Like specialty advertising, product placement is sometimes considered a promotion rather than an advertising form. This distinction is not a critical one, and we have decided to treat product placement as a form of advertising.)

Exhibit 13-12 Many companies use movies to promote their products

A number of companies pay to have their products used in movies and music videos. For example, in the movie *Austin Powers,* the villain Dr. Evil's spacecraft was in the shape of a "Big Boy" from the Big Boy restaurant chain. In *Austin Powers III,* Taco Bell, Jaguar, and Starbucks were just a few of the many product placements to appear. Essentially, this form is advertising without an advertising medium. Often, the audience doesn't realize a product promotion is going on (See Exhibit 13-12). Viewers tend to see brand names in films as lending realism to the story. Yet the impact on the buying public is real. For example, when Reese's Pieces were used in the movie *E.T.,* sales rose 70 percent and the candies were added to the concessions of 800 movie theaters where they had previously not been sold.[41] Sales of Ray-Ban Wayfarer sunglasses tripled after Tom Cruise wore them in the movie *Risky Business,* and Ray-Ban Aviator sales increased 40 percent after he wore

them in *Top Gun.* After he wore Oakleys in *Mission Impossible II,* sales increased 80 percent.[42]

The move to place products on TV programs has also been on the increase, since 1988, when CBS broke its long-standing tradition of not mentioning brand names in its programs. The use of product placements has become commonplace, as demonstrated in IMC Perspective 13-1, and is also on the increase in foreign markets

Advantages of Product Placements

A number of advantages of product tie-ins have been suggested:

1. *Exposure.* A large number of people see movies each year (over 1.4 billion admissions per year). The average film is estimated to have a life span of three and one-half years (with 75 million exposures), and most of the moviegoers are very attentive audience members. When this is combined with the increasing home video rental market and network and cable TV (for example, HBO, Showtime, the Movie Channel), the potential exposure for a product placed in a movie or on television is enormous. And this form of exposure is not subject to zapping, at least not in the theater.

High exposure numbers are also offered for TV tie-ins, based on the ratings and the possibility to direct the ad to a defined target market.

2. *Frequency.* Depending on how the product is used in the movie (or program), there may be ample opportunity for repeated exposures (many, for those who like to watch a program or movie more than once). For example, if you are a regular watcher of the CBS program *Survivor,* you will be exposed to the products placed therein a number of times.

3. *Support for other media.* Product placements may support other promotional tools. A trend in the movie industry is to have the client that is placing the product cross-promote the product and movie tie-in in multiple media venues as well as through the Internet and sales promotions.

4. *Source association.* In Chapter 6, we discussed the advantages of source identification. When consumers see their favorite movie star wearing Oakleys, drinking Starbucks coffee, or driving a Mercedes, this association may lead to a favorable product image. Most of those involved in the business of product placements believe that association with the proper source is critical to success.

5. *Cost.* While the cost of placing a product may range from free samples to $1 million, the latter is an extreme. The CPM for this form of advertising can be very low, owing to the high volume of exposures it generates.

6. *Recall.* A number of firms have measured the impact of product placements on next-day recall. Results ranged from Johnson's Baby Shampoo registering 20 percent to Kellogg's Corn Flakes registering 67 percent (in the movie Raising Arizona). Average recall is approximately 38 percent. Again, these scores are better than those reported for TV viewing. A study provided by Pola Gupta and Kenneth Lord showed that prominently displayed placements led to strong recall.[43]

7. *Bypassing regulations.* In the United States as well as many foreign countries, some products are not permitted to advertise on television or to specific market segments. Product placements have allowed the cigarette and liquor industries to have their products exposed, circumventing these restrictions.

8. *Acceptance.* A study by Pola Gupta and Stephen Gould indicated that viewers are accepting of product placements and in general evaluate them positively, though some products (alcohol, guns, cigarettes) are perceived as less acceptable.[44]

Disadvantages of Product Placements

Some disadvantages are also associated with product placements:

1. *High absolute cost.* While the CPM may be very low for product placement in movies, the absolute cost of placing the product may be very high, pricing some advertisers out of the market. Although only a small percentage of placements are paid for directly, the increased demand by the studios for cross-promotions drives costs up considerably.

IMC PERSPECTIVE 13-1

Product Placements Invade New Media

Can you think of the last time you watched a movie and didn't see a product placement—that is, a branded product displayed in the scene? While product placements have been around for quite some time, there has been a tremendous increase in their usage in the past few years. And now, they are invading television programs as well.

Exactly when product placements originated is hard to determine, but most marketers agree that the frequency of their use increased significantly with the placement of Reese's Pieces in the movie *E.T.* over 20 years ago. Since that time, placements have become so common that some advertisers are concerned that the novelty of the brand exposures has worn off, leading them to be less effective, or—even worse—that they are so common and so obvious that viewers are getting turned off by them. The recent *James Bond* and *Austin Powers* movies have so many placements in them that one has to wonder if such movies are created just to promote products.

But instead of cutting back on placements, the advertising industry has now turned to other mediums to get its products shown. For example, the novel *The Bulgari Connection,* by Fay Weldon, was actually so-named (at least in part) because an "undisclosed sum" of money was paid to the author by the Italian Bulgari jewelry company. Television has also seen a marked increase in the number of placements. Junior Mints, Calvin Klein, Kenny Roger's Roasted Chicken, and numerous cereals are just a few of the many brands that have appeared in *Seinfeld,* with many other products appearing in other shows as well. Budweiser, Mountain Dew, and Doritos have all been in *Survivor,* Pottery Barn was integrated into the plot in *Friends,* and Procter & Gamble products are all over *Sex and the City.* When Unilever launched Cheese Creations sauces, a major promotional effort was expended on radio DJ parties to get the jockeys talking about the products on the air. Nivea did the same thing with its wrinkle-control cream targeted to women, P&G did it with its Downy Wrinkle Releaser spray, and so has Compaq computers. Jeep Wrangler and Liberty are prominently displayed throughout Tony Hawk's Pro Skater 3 video game, which is extremely popular with males in their 20s.

Is it possible that product placements have gone too far—maybe even bordering on deception? A number of critics think so, arguing that the lines have blurred between content and promotions. They cite the new TV show *No Boundaries,* a reality-based show in which the contestants drive Ford Boundaries. Ford, whose campaign slogan is "No Boundaries," helped pay for the show's production costs. Gary Ruskin, executive director of Commercial Alert, a nonprofit advertising watchdog group, notes that today's movies are "being corrupted by commercialization that has mushroomed beyond mere product placement to include script doctoring and related sins." Ruskin goes on to note: "In movies like *Minority Report,* you have a bunch of ads with a couple of scenes thrown in, with artistic concerns taking a back seat." He is particularly perturbed by a film to be released under the title *Food Fight,* which features brands as characters such as Mr. Clean, Mr. Pringle, and Twinkie the Kid. Even some people in the product placement industry itself are concerned that viewers will see the placements as commercial, infringing on their pleasure of watching.

Others are not so concerned, however. Citing the growth of TiVo, the increase in commercial zipping and zapping, and the increasing number of advertisers vying for more time through regular television commercials, they argue that this may be the only way to have one's product or brand shown in the future. Those assuming this position suggest that you will see even more placements in even more media in the future. So the next time you turn on HBO to get away from the commercials on network TV, pay attention. Who knows, you may see a product placement on *Sex and the City* (Jabra cell-phone earpieces) or on *The Sopranos* (Gateway computers)—and maybe you'll notice and maybe you won't. Either way, the placement may still work, as some research indicates that products that you do not actually notice may have a greater impact than those that you do.

Sources: Jennifer Davies, "Where Do Films Start, Ads Stop?" *San Diego Union-Tribune,* Aug. 3, 2002, p. C1; T. L. Stanley, "Brand X: Ready on . . .," *Brandweek,* May 13, 2002, pp. 34-40; Joann Muller, "Chrysler's Wink-Wink, Nudge-Nudge Campaign," *BusinessWeek,* Dec. 17, 2001, p. 114; Betsy Spethmann, "Hot Air," *Promo Magazine,* September 2001, pp. 37-40; Laura Shanahan, "Designated Shopper," *Brandweek,* Sept. 24, 2001, p. 38.

2. *Time of exposure.* While the way some products are exposed to the audience has an impact, there is no guarantee viewers will notice the product. Some product placements are more conspicuous than others. When the product is not featured prominently, the advertiser runs the risk of not being seen (although, of course, the same risk is present in all forms of media advertising).

3. *Limited appeal.* The appeal that can be made in this media form is limited. There is no potential for discussing product benefits or providing detailed information. Rather, appeals are limited to source association, use, and enjoyment. The endorsement of the product is indirect, and the flexibility for product demonstration is subject to its use in the film.

4. *Lack of control.* In many movies, the advertiser has no say over when and how often the product will be shown. Many companies have found that their placements in movies did not work as well as expected. Fabergé developed an entire Christmas campaign around its Brut cologne and its movie placement, only to find the movie was delayed until February.

5. *Public reaction.* Many TV viewers and moviegoers are incensed at the idea of placing ads in programs or movies. These viewers want to maintain the barrier between program content and commercials. If the placement is too intrusive, they may develop negative attitudes toward the brand. The increased use of placements has led many consumers to be annoyed by what they consider to be crass commercialization. The FTC has explored options for limiting placements without consumer notification.

6. *Competition.* The appeal of product placements has led to increased competition to get one's product placed. Movie production houses continue to increase demands for key placements.

7. *Negative placements.* Some products may appear in movie scenes that are disliked by the audience or create a less than favorable mood. For example, in the movie Missing, a very good, loyal father takes comfort in a bottle of Coke, while a Pepsi machine appears in a stadium where torturing and murders take place—not a good placement for Pepsi.

Audience Measurement for Product Placements

To date, no audience measurement is available except from the providers. Potential advertisers often have to make decisions based on their own creative insights or rely on the credibility of the source. However, at least two studies have demonstrated the potential effectiveness of product placements.

In addition to the studies reported earlier, research by Eva Steortz showed that viewers had an average recall for placements of 38 percent.[45] And Damon Darlin has provided evidence that an aura of glamour is added to products associated with celebrities.[46] Research companies like PR Data Systems (mentioned earlier) compare the amount of time a product is exposed in the program/movie to the cost of an equivalent ad spot to measure value. (As you will see in Chapter 19, however, we have problems with this measure of effectiveness.)

In-Flight Advertising

Another rapidly growing medium is **in-flight advertising.** As the number of flying passengers increases, so too does the attractiveness of this medium. In-flight advertising includes three forms:

- *In-flight magazines.* Free magazines (like the one shown in Exhibit 13-13) published by the airlines are offered on almost every plane in the air. United Airlines

Exhibit 13-13 In-flight magazines are available on most carriers

distributes over 1 million of its *Hemispheres* magazines each month and estimates potential exposures at 1.7 million.[47]

• *In-flight videos.* In-flight videos have been common on international flights for some time and are now being used on domestic flights. Commercials were not originally included in these videos. Now about $18 million in commercials is booked on flights per year ($12 million on international flights).[48] While not all airlines offer in-flight commercials, companies like Japan Air Lines, Delta, American, and British Airways are participating. Some of these commercial messages are as long as three minutes. For example, SKY-TV has features on United, TWA, and US Airways, with a bonus feature on broadcast.com included (Exhibit 13-14). American's *CBS Eye on American* is broadcast in English and Spanish.

• *In-flight radio.* USA Today's in-flight radio is run by the same people responsible for publishing its newspaper.

• *In-flight catalogs.* Twenty domestic airlines (as well as Amtrak) now offer in-flight shopping catalogs, with more than 90 percent of passengers having access. The catalogs usually range from 160 to 180 pages and include products offered by Sharper Image, Magellan's, Lego, and Hammacher Schlemmer, among many others.[49]

Advantages and Disadvantages of In-Flight Advertising

Advantages of in-flight advertising include the following:

1. *A desirable audience.* The average traveler is 45 years old and has a household income over $83,700. Both business and tourist travelers tend to be upscale, an attractive audience to companies targeting these groups. Many of these passengers hold top management positions in their firms. *Hemispheres* reaches over 4 percent of business professionals and estimates that almost 71 percent of the magazine's readership are professionals. Other demographics are favorable as well (see Figure 13-12).[50]

2. *A captive audience.* As noted in the discussion about ticket covers, the audience in an airplane cannot leave the room. Particularly on long flights, many passengers are willing (and even happy) to have in-flight magazines to read, news to listen to, and even commercials to watch.

3. *Cost.* The cost of in-flight commercials is lower than that of business print media. A 30-second commercial on United Airlines that offers exposure to 3,500,000 passengers costs approximately $27,500. A four-color spread in *Forbes* and *Fortune* would cost double that amount. A full-page ad in *American Way* costs from $16,474 to $19,154 depending on the number of placements.[51] The SKY-TV videos mentioned earlier cost less than a half-page ad in *The Wall Street Journal.*

Exhibit 13-14 United Airlines' passengers can watch SKY-TV in flight

	(000)	Percent Coverage	Percent Composition	Index	Rank
Upwardly Employed					
Base: Adults					
Target market: Professional/managerial					
Harvard Business Review	370	1.4	76.9	141	1
Attache	868	3.2	75.2	137	2
ABA Journal	356	1.3	74.0	135	3
Robb Report	233	0.9	71.9	131	4
Cigar Aficionado	548	2.0	71.7	131	5
Hemispheres	1133	4.1	70.9	130	6
Corporate Influentials					
Base: Adults					
Target market: Top management					
Departures	203	2.3	42.6	242	1
Harvard Business Review	201	2.3	41.8	237	2
Robb Report	124	1.4	38.3	217	3
The Wall Street Journal	1754	19.9	35.5	201	4
Hemispheres	541	6.1	33.9	192	5
ABA Journal	160	1.8	33.3	189	6
Business Travelers					
Base: Adults					
Target market: Spent 7+ nights in hotels for business during the past year					
Hemispheres	1108	7.3	69.4	227	1
Attache	780	5.1	67.5	221	2
American Way 2-issue	1649	10.8	65.4	214	3
SW Airlines Spirit	965	6.3	64.2	211	4
Sky Magazine	1574	10.3	64.2	210	5
NW Air World Traveler	785	5.1	63.1	207	6

Figure 13-12 In-flight media reach a desirable target audience

4. *Segmentation capabilities.* In-flight allows the advertiser to reach specific demographic groups, as well as travelers to a specific destination. For example, Martell cognac targeted only first-class passengers on JAL's New York to Tokyo route. American Airlines' *Celebrated Living* readers have a median income of $174,500, with 42 percent having a net worth of more than $1 million.[52]

Disadvantages of in-flight advertising include the following:

1. *Irritation.* Many consumers are not pleased with the idea of ads in general and believe they are already too intrusive. In-flight commercials are just one more place, they think, where advertisers are intruding.

2. *Limited availability.* Many airlines limit the amount of time they allow for in-flight commercials. Japan Air Lines, for example, allows a mere 220 seconds per flight.

3. *Lack of attention.* Many passengers may decide to tune out the ads, not purchase the headsets required to get the volume, or simply ignore the commercials.

4. *Wearout.* Given projections for significant increases in the number of in-flight ads being shown, airline passengers may soon be inundated by these commercials.

Miscellaneous Other Media

As noted earlier in this chapter, the variety of advertising support media continues to increase, and discussing or even mentioning all is beyond the scope of this text. However, the following are provided just to demonstrate a few of the many options:

- *Place-based media.* The idea of bringing the advertising medium to the consumers wherever they may be underlies the strategy behind place-based media. TV monitors and magazine racks have appeared in classrooms, doctors' offices, and health clubs, among a variety of other locations. After an initial introduction and failure by Whittle Communications, Promedia now owns Channel One; Cass Communications offers place-based media options for the college market. Place-based media have become a profitable venture and an attractive alternative for media buyers. Many advertisers, like Vans, Paramount Pictures, and Disney, support and use this medium in the classroom, arguing that both the sponsor and the "cash-strapped" schools benefit. But some observers, like the Consumers Union and consumer advocate Ralph Nader, denounce it as "crass commercialism."[53]

- *Kiosks.* The growth of interactive kiosks was briefly mentioned in Chapter 10. Advertisers pay rates ranging from $1,000 to $2,500 a month for signage and interactive ads on kiosks that are placed in malls, movie theaters, and other high-traffic areas. Additional charges may accrue for more complex interactive programs. Companies like Ameritech and North Communications have increased their involvement in this medium. Intel has deployed over 1,000 kiosks in computer stores to give consumers immediate access to the Internet.[54] Kmart estimates that 20 percent of its sales comes from its in-store kiosks.

- *Others.* Just a few other examples of the use of support media: Coca-Cola has installed 1,000 feet of light boxes in the Atlanta subway to show motion picture ads for Dasani; Motorola is advertising on pagers; Muzak, a provider of background music, has teamed with Tyme ATMs to broadcast ads at bank ATM sites; ads now appear on luggage conveyors at some airports, on hubcaps, in elevators, on fruit, and on gasoline pumps (visual and talking). There are many other examples, as is well demonstrated in IMC Perspective 13-2 and Exhibit 13-15 (at least he earned something from the fight!).

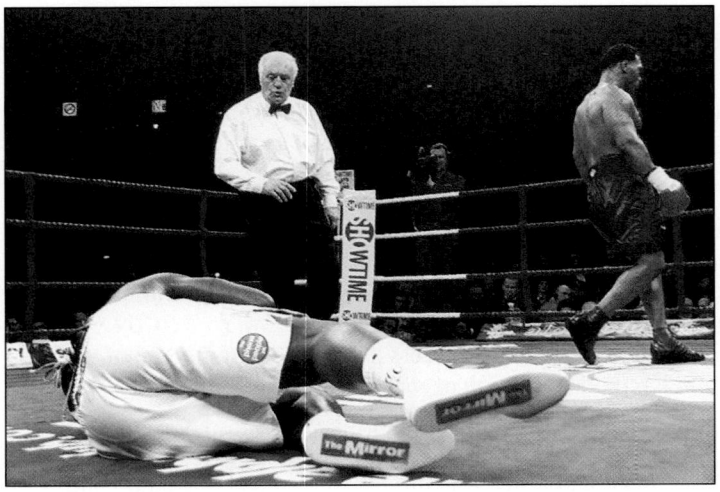

Exhibit 13-15 Ads often appear in the strangest places

IMC PERSPECTIVE 13-2

How Can They Change the Ads on the Backstops between Innings?—It's "Virtually" Possible

Next time you watch a Major League Baseball game, watch the advertisements appearing on the backstop behind the batter. At the top of the inning, you will see an ad for one company—let's say Yahoo.com—between innings you may see one for Office Depot, and at the bottom of the inning you may see Toyota's message. Or perhaps you were watching a college football game on ESPN and you saw different ads between the goalposts every time an extra point or field goal was kicked. Did you ever wonder how they could change those ads so quickly? Actually they don't. What you are seeing is a new technology called *virtual advertising,* in which the ads are digitally entered onto your screen. While you are seeing the ads on your screen, people at the stadium are seeing a blank wall.

Virtual advertising has been around for a few years, with the San Francisco Giants baseball team being the first to test the medium in the summer of 1996. The San Diego Padres, Philadelphia Phillies, and Seattle Mariners have used it. Fox Sports has used virtually advertising on a regional basis, and ESPN has placed virtual ads on its Sunday night football games aired nationally. The new advertising form is catching on so quickly that the San Diego Padres sold out all their virtual spots for the baseball season, and a number of other teams are expected to begin to offer them in the future.

In virtual advertising, ad messages are inserted into a TV picture so that they appear to be part of the stadium scene. The advertiser can pay the same price for the virtual placement as it would for a 30-second spot on the same game telecast. The cost can range from as low as $8,000 to as much as $25,000 on an ESPN national telecast. In baseball, the ads last as long as the half inning—typically 4 to 8 minutes. Other sports events using virtual advertising include football, arena football, and tennis. Exposure times, of course, are calculated differently for each sport.

Advertisers like the new virtual capabilities for a number of reasons. First, the ads are shown while the event is still active, rather than during commercial slots, increasing the likelihood of viewer attention. Second, the format allows for a large number of companies to participate (the three mentioned above all appeared in a single Padres game), and since the ads are digitally created, there are few production difficulties and little inventory to contend with. The same game shown in two different markets can carry different ads for each market.

Before you begin to think that this technology is limited to sports, consider this: In an episode of the prime-time entertainment show *Seven Days,* virtual product placements appeared for the first time in such programming. After the program had been produced and put on the air, Princeton Video Image created the placements in a syndicated rerun, with a Wells Fargo bank sign, Kenneth Cole shopping bags, and bottles of Coca-Cola and Evian appearing on the screen. The products, bags, and signs never existed in the actual episode. The Mexican TV network Televisia is also inserting visual product placements in entertainment shows in Mexico. Televisia charges $1,000 per insertion. The potential seems endless, as almost any product can be placed in a syndicated show, in almost any scene—creating a bonanza for advertisers.

Not everyone is so happy about the new technology, however. Some industry experts are concerned that the potential for virtual advertising and product placements may lead to oversaturation, becoming offensive and in poor taste. They note that product placement buyers will seek prominent placements, at key parts of the program, and that actors and actresses will become

unknowing (and even unwilling) endorsers. (Imagine Sydney Bristow of *Alias* carrying a purse even though she never actually had one in the performance!) Equally important, they contend, is the potential for crass commercialism, with ads and placements getting in the way of program content—again irritating the viewer. Finally, and no less important, what about the actual sponsor or advertiser in a commercial break of the program? If Pepsi buys a regular ad on the program, and Coke, or even Evian, is allowed to appear as a product placement, what impact does that have on Pepsi's commercial? If General Motors sponsors college football games, and a virtual ad for Toyota appears every time a field goal or extra point is kicked, is that fair? FIFA, the governing body of international soccer (football), doesn't think so: After a match in Greece showed a giant spray can of deodorant hovering above the field, FIFA issued guidelines designed to limit the use of virtual placements. Viewers watching CBS's evening news broadcast from Times Square saw a billboard advertising CBS news, but it really wasn't there—it was a placement.

At this point, virtual advertising and product placements are in the infancy stage. But who knows how quickly the medium will catch on? The next time you watch *I Love Lucy,* Lucy may be drinking a Diet Coke, while Ricky takes Viagra. Or the UCLA placekicker—whose team is sponsored by Adidas—may be kicking into a Nike ad. The Turner Broadcasting System (TBS) has recently struck a deal to insert virtual advertising in its syndicated programming of *Law and Order.* The inserts will likely include ads on the coffee cups police officers drink from and on the soda machine in the police station. Who knows how things will change?

Sources: Stuart Elliott, "A Video Process Allows the Insertion of Brand-Name Products in TV Shows Already on Film," *New York Times,* Mar. 29, 1999, p. 11; John Consoli, "Virtual Ads Set to Pitch," *Mediaweek,* Mar. 22, 1999, mediaweek.com; "Virtual Ads, Real Problems," *Advertising Age,* Mar. 24, 1999, p. 30; "Virtual Signage Breaks into Prime Time," *Mediaweek,* Mar. 29, 1999, mediaweek.com; David Goetel, "TBS Tries Virtual Advertising," *Advertising Age,* May 21, 2001, p. 8; "Virtual Advertising," *Economist,* Jan. 15, 2000, p. 68.

Summary

This chapter introduced you to the vast number of support media available to marketers. These media, also referred to as nontraditional or alternative media, are just a few of the many ways advertisers attempt to reach their target markets. We have barely scratched the surface here. Support media include out-of-home advertising (outdoor, in-store, and transit), promotional products, product placements in movies and on TV, and in-flight advertising, among many others.

Support media offer a variety of advantages. Cost, ability to reach the target market, and flexibility are just a few of those cited in this chapter. In addition, many of the media discussed here have effectively demonstrated the power of their specific medium to get results.

But each of these support media has disadvantages. Perhaps the major weakness with most is the lack of audience measurement and verification. Unlike many of the media discussed earlier in this text, most nontraditional media do not provide audience measurement figures. So the advertiser is forced to make decisions without hard data or based on information provided by the media.

As the number and variety of support media continue to grow, it is likely the major weaknesses will be overcome. When that occurs, these media may no longer be considered nontraditional or alternative.

Key Terms

support media, 432
alternative media, 432
nonmeasured media, 432
nontraditional media, 432
out-of-home advertising, 432
showing, 435
aerial advertising, 436
mobile billboards, 436
in-store media, 437
transit advertising, 440
inside cards, 441
outside posters, 441
terminal posters, 441
promotional products marketing, 443
specialty advertising, 443
Yellow Pages, 446
directional medium, 446
product placement, 450
in-flight advertising, 453

Discussion Questions

1. Transit advertising takes a variety of forms, and many advertisers may be reluctant to use these media. Discuss some of the various forms of transit advertising and their relative advantages and disadvantages. Give examples of which products and/or services might effectively utilize this medium.

2. Describe what is meant by "stealth marketing." Give examples of products and/or services that you know have employed this strategy. Then describe some of the characteristics of companies that might most benefit from stealth marketing.

3. There seems to be a growing interest among marketers to engage in the use of product placements. These marketers are attracted by the success experienced by prior product placements. Give examples of product placements that you have seen. Then discuss what factors impact the success or lack of success of product placements.

4. Advertising in movie theaters is on the increase. A variety of reasons as to why this medium may be effective are offered in the chapter. Discuss the reasons why movie theater advertising may be advantageous. Then discuss some of the reasons why it might not be as successful as planned.

5. As advertisers engage in stealth marketing tactics, many companies are taking action to prohibit such activities. Ethical issues are raised on both sides—one side claiming free speech, while the other argues that such activities are unfair to paying advertisers, sponsors, etc. Discuss the positions of each side. Which do you favor?

6. Some advertisers claim that virtual ads are bad for the advertising industry in general. Explain some of the reasons why they feel this way. Are these reasons valid?

7. What are promotional products? List some of the advantages and disadvantages of this medium. Provide examples where the use of this medium would be appropriate.

8. Discuss some of the merits of in-flight advertising. What types of products might most effectively use this medium?

9. Support media have also been called alternative media, nonmeasured media, and nontraditional media. Why has the medium been assigned these titles?

10. Explain how various support media might be used as part of an IMC program. Take any three of the media discussed in the chapter and explain how they might be used in an IMC program for automobiles, cellular telephones, and Internet services.

Direct Marketing

Chapter Objectives

1. To recognize the area of direct marketing as a communications tool.
2. To know the strategies and tactics involved in direct marketing.
3. To demonstrate the use of direct-marketing media.
4. To determine the scope and effectiveness of direct marketing.

What Do Ab Rockers, Ginsu Knives, Mercedes, and Kitchen Appliances Have in Common?

If you don't know the answer to the above question, perhaps a few more hints will help. What if we added Monsters, Excite@Home, and the Indy Races to the list? That's right, all of the above are sponsors of infomercials—an advertising form that has long been considered appropriate only for Ronco Vegematics, Whopper Choppers, and Dione Warwick's *Psychic Friends.*

The infomercial, or—as those in the industry like to refer to it—long-form advertisement, is a 30- to 60-minute television segment designed to provide the viewer with a great deal of information and detail about a product or service. In effect, infomercials are long commercials designed to provide information as well as to sell. You will usually see long-form ads late at night, in the wee hours of the morning, or at any time when the advertising rates are at their lowest. As a result, this ad form has long been the domain of smaller, direct-response companies. But all that is changing.

The new infomercials are no longer low-budget productions that attempt only to sell, sell, sell. And low-audience spots are no longer their only medium. Mercedes-Benz recently aired an infomercial for its E320 on national cable networks. The long-form ad, titled "The Mark of Passion," was very expensive looking and plugged the Starmark used-car program through archival footage and testimonials from very satisfied owners. Excite's objective was to provide information on its complex products and services and to demonstrate the advantages of broadband. Monster.com's "Monster Show" included a number of specific features, such as the "Learn to Love Monday Morning Quiz," which measures satisfaction with one's current employer. While the infomercials had a sales component, other measures of success were also employed. Mercedes's ads directed the viewers to learn more about the Starmark program by calling a toll-free number or logging on to the Starmark website (70 percent of the viewers used the website). Once there, information was collected for the development of a database and for mailings with additional information. Monster tracked activity on various aspects of the website.

But why use an infomercial for household appliances? Can't they just be sold through regular advertising and retail outlets? And, at an average price of $369.95 per appliance, isn't that a bit expensive for this medium? No and no says Brian Maynard, director of integrated marketing for KitchenAid, a 90-year-old company out of Benton Harbor, Michigan. The highly competitive market requires different thinking and different

ways to drive sales. The initial infomercial—which was designed to drive retail and break even on direct response—exceeded expectations by 60 to 70 percent. But, once again, it was not your typical infomercial. Set in a very expensive kitchen, the infomercial was portrayed to be more like a cooking show than a commercial. Well-known chefs, and two hosts from PBS cooking shows, were brought in, and additional IMC tools were employed. Traditional ads air between the two segments of the long-form ad. The company's website was enhanced to stimulate selling, and sales promotions featuring "free gifts" of aprons, spatulas, and bowl covers were included. Buyers also received three free issues of *Food & Wine.* And let's not forget the website's recipe page—with instructions written in "KitchenAid-ese." For consumers reluctant to purchase on their first visit, direct-mail pieces were sent. The results speak for themselves: 45 percent of the company's mixers are now sold through the website. Retail sales are up, and many of the viewers already own mixers but come to buy attachments.

And now about those Indy races. The Indy races include a circuit of 12 races plus the Indianapolis 500. Given that the races are not as well known as the NASCAR series, the goal of the infomercial was to educate racing fans on the Indy races' strengths relative to NASCAR. Included are shots from inside the race cars, interviews with drivers like Al Unser Jr., and testimonials from fans. Besides an overall increase in sales, attendance has been up by 15 percent at every track in areas where the infomercials have run preceding the races. And you thought infomercials were only for Tummy Tuckers.

Sources: Charles Wesley Orton; "KitchenAid Shares Its Recipe for DRTV," *Response,* January 2002, pp. 26–30; Bernard Stamler, "Indy Racing Uses Infomercial to Lure Viewers to the Track," New York Times.com, Aug. 8, 2001, pp. 1–2; Evantheia Schibsted, "Ab Rockers, Ginshu Knives, E320s," *Business 2.0,* May 29, 2001, pp. 46–49.

As marketers continue to explore options for delivering their messages, the media landscape is itself changing. The addition of new options like the Internet and interactive media is one change that has occurred. Another is the variety of innovations taking place in regard to existing media and the companies using them. Earlier in this text we discussed the changing role of support media such as product placements and movie theater advertising. The examples in this chapter's lead-in demonstrate one of the changes occurring in the direct-marketing area, specifically in regard to infomercials. But it is important to realize that the infomercial is only one of the tools used by direct marketers.

Direct Marketing

While most companies continue to rely primarily on the other promotional mix elements to move their products and services through intermediaries, an increasing number are going directly to the consumer. These companies believe that while the traditional promotional mix tools such as advertising, sales promotion, and personal selling are effective in creating brand image, conveying information, and/or creating awareness, going direct with these same tools can generate an immediate behavioral response. Direct marketing is a valuable tool in the integrated communications program, though it seeks somewhat different objectives.

In this chapter, we discuss direct marketing and its role as a communications tool. Direct marketing is one of the fastest-growing forms of promotion in terms of dollar expenditures, and for many marketers it is rapidly becoming the medium of choice for reaching consumers. Stan Rapp and Thomas Collins, in their book *Maximarketing,* propose that direct marketing be the driving force behind the overall marketing program.[1] Recently, others have agreed. Ropp and Collins present a nine-step model that includes creating a database, reaching prospects, developing the sale, and developing the relationship. We begin by defining direct marketing and then examine direct-marketing media and their use in the overall communications strategy. The section concludes with a basis for evaluating the direct-marketing program and a discussion of the advantages and disadvantages of this marketing tool.

Defining Direct Marketing

As noted in Chapter 1, **direct marketing** is a system of marketing by which organizations communicate directly with target customers to generate a response or transaction. This response may take the form of an inquiry, a purchase, or even a vote. In his *Dictionary of Marketing Terms,* Peter Bennett defines direct marketing as:

> the total of activities by which the seller, in effecting the exchange of goods and services with the buyer, directs efforts to a target audience using one or more media (direct selling, direct mail, telemarketing, direct-action advertising, catalogue selling, cable TV selling, etc.) for the purpose of soliciting a response by phone, mail, or personal visit from a prospect or customer.[2]

First we must distinguish between direct marketing and direct-marketing media. As you can see in Figure 14-1, direct marketing is an aspect of total marketing—that is, it involves marketing research, segmentation, evaluation, and the like, just as our planning model in Chapter 1 did. Direct marketing uses a set of **direct-response media,** including direct mail, telemarketing, interactive TV, print, the Internet, and other media. These media are the tools by which direct marketers implement the communications process.

The purchases of products and services through direct-response advertising currently exceed $2 trillion and are projected to reach $2.8 trillion by the year 2006.[3] Firms that use this marketing method range from major retailers such as the Gap, Restoration Hardware, and Victoria's Secret to publishing companies to computer retailers to financial services. Business-to-business and industrial marketers have also significantly increased their direct-marketing efforts, with an estimated $1.3 trillion in sales forecast by 2004.[4]

The Growth of Direct Marketing

Direct marketing has been around since the invention of the printing press in the 15th century. Ben Franklin was a very successful direct marketer in the early 1700s, and Warren Sears and Montgomery Ward (you may have heard of these guys) were using this medium in the 1880s.

The major impetus behind the growth of direct marketing may have been the development and expansion of the U.S. Postal Service, which made catalogs available to both urban and rural dwellers. Catalogs revolutionized America's buying habits; consumers could now shop without ever leaving their homes.

But catalogs alone do not account for the rapid growth of direct marketing. A number of factors in American society have led to the increased attractiveness of this medium for both buyer and seller:

- *Consumer credit cards.* There are now over 1 billion credit cards—bank, oil company, retail, and so on—in circulation in the United States. This makes it feasible for consumers to purchase both low- and high-ticket items through direct-response channels and assures sellers that they will be paid. It is estimated that over $1.23 trillion was charged on credit cards in the year 2001.[5] Of course, not all of this was through direct marketing, but a high percentage of direct purchases do use this method of payment, and companies such as American Express, Diners Club, MasterCard, and Visa are among the heaviest direct advertisers.
- *Direct-marketing syndicates.* Companies specializing in list development, statement inserts, catalogs, and sweepstakes have opened many new opportunities to marketers. The number of these companies continues to expand, creating even more new users.
- *The changing structure of American society and the market.* One of the major factors contributing to the success of direct marketing is that so many Americans are now "money-rich and time-poor."[6] The rapid increase in dual-income families has meant more income. (It is estimated that by 2008 women will make up about 48 percent of the labor force.)[7] At the same time, the increased popularity of physical fitness, do-it-yourself crafts and repairs, and home entertainment have reduced the time available for shopping and have increased the attractiveness of direct purchases.
- *Technological advances.* The rapid technological advancement of the electronic media and of computers has made it easier for consumers to shop and for marketers to be successful in reaching the desired target markets. Well over 110 million television

Figure 14-1 Direct marketing flowchart

Direct Marketing...*An Aspect of Total Marketing*

Direct Marketing is an interactive system of marketing that uses one or more advertising media to effect a measurable response and/or transaction at any location, with this activity stored on database.

DIRECT MARKETING FLOW CHART

Martin Baier, Henry R. Hoke Jr., Robert Stone

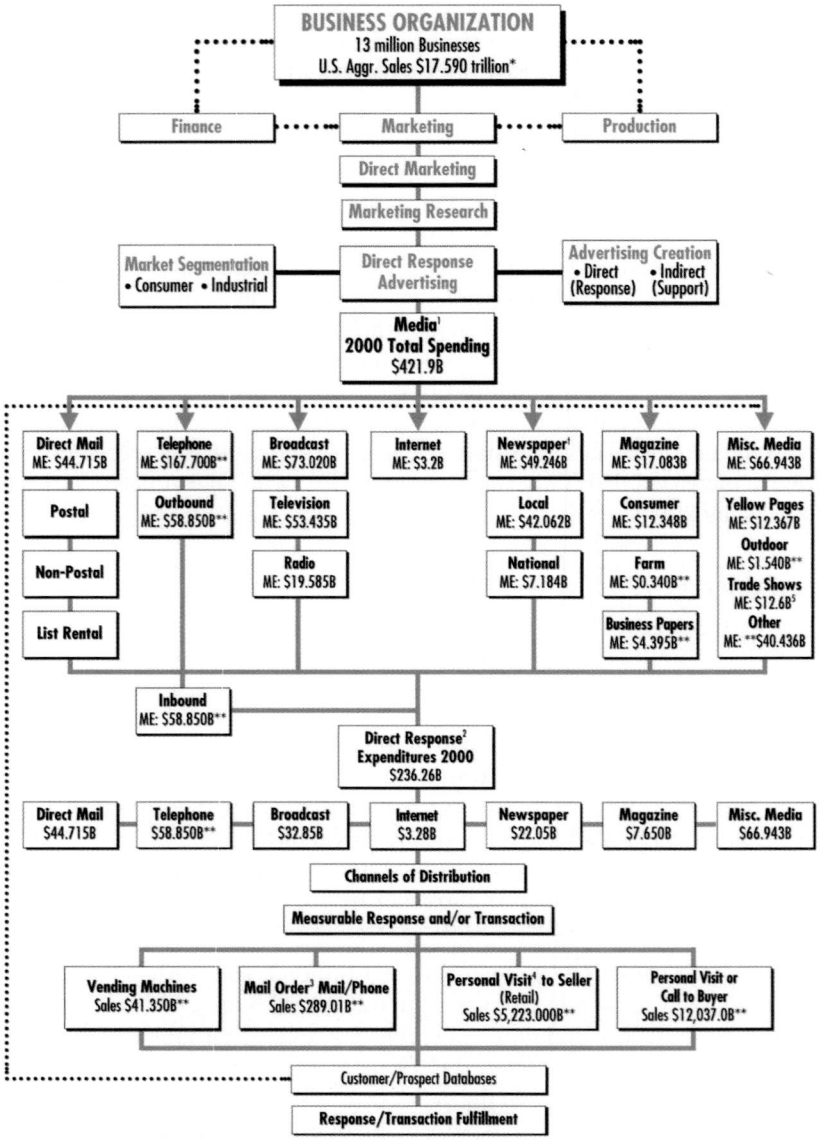

* 1998 U.S. Business Census ** Numbers refer to 1998 levels. [1] Newspaper includes supplements

[1]U.S. Census, Robert J. Coen (Universal McCann).

[2]Direct Response Expenditures are calculated as a percentage of total expenditures in each medium: Direct Mail (100%), Telephone (50%), Broadcast (45%), Yellow Pages (100%), Newspaper (45%), Magazine (45%), Misc. (100%), Internet (100%).

[3]The Mail Order Sales Figure excludes $69.810 billion** of charitable mail order contributions which are not included in the $17.590 trillion of U.S. Aggregate Sales.

[4]Personal visit to seller (retail) includes $2.213 trillion of Consumer Product Sales at retail plus 90% of Consumer Services Sales; 10% of Consumer Services Sales are conducted by salespeople visiting the buyer.

[5]*Business Marketing*, May 1999. Figure based on companies with sales/revenues of $50 million and up.

ME: Media Expenditures

Total advertising for 2000 was $421.9 billion. It is estimated that $236.26 billion of the $421.9 billion, or 56% of this volume, is direct response advertising. A growing percentage of Broadcast, Newspaper, Magazine and Internet advertising dollars can be categorized as direct response advertising. The percentage continues to grow rapidly as marketers learn the efficiency of measuring advertising performance.

Permission granted for reproduction with appropriate acknowledgment of source: *Direct Marketing* magazine, 224 Seventh Street, Garden City, New York 11530-5771.

homes receive home shopping programs, and home channel purchases are projected to reach $15.6 billion by 2006.[8]

- *Miscellaneous factors.* A number of other factors have contributed to the increased effectiveness of direct marketing, including changing values, more sophisticated marketing techniques, and the industry's improved image. These factors will also ensure the success of direct marketing in the future. The variety of companies employing direct marketing demonstrates its potential.

While some organizations rely on direct marketing solely to generate consumer response, in many others direct marketing is an integral part of the IMC program. They use direct marketing to achieve other than sales goals and integrate it with other program elements. We first examine the role of direct marketing in the IMC program and then consider its more *traditional* role.

The Role of Direct Marketing in the IMC Program

Long the stepchild of the promotional mix, direct marketing is now becoming an important component in the integrated marketing programs of many organizations. In fact, direct-marketing activities support and are supported by other elements of the promotional mix.

Combining Direct Marketing with Advertising

Obviously, direct marketing is in itself a form of advertising. Whether through mail, print, or TV, the direct-response offer is an ad. It usually contains a toll-free or 900 number or a form that requests mailing information. Sometimes the ad supports the direct-selling effort. For example, Victoria's Secret runs image ads to support its store and catalog sales. Both Marlboro and Benson & Hedges advertise their cigarettes, achieving a carryover effect of their image to their direct-response merchandise catalogs. Direct-response ads or infomercials are also referred to in retail outlet displays. Sometimes an advertisement will be sent through direct mail. CBS has tied into a Blockbuster video mailer to advertise its new fall lineup and offer a sneak-preview CD.

Combining Direct Marketing with Public Relations

As you will see later in this text, public relations activities often employ direct-response techniques. Private companies may use telemarketing activities to solicit funds for charities or cosponsor charities that use these and other direct-response techniques to solicit funds. Likewise, corporations and/or organizations engaging in public relations activities may include toll-free numbers or website URLs in their ads or promotional materials. Direct mail has also been shown to be effective in recruiting job candidates.[9]

Combining Direct Marketing with Personal Selling

Telemarketing and direct selling are two methods of personal selling (others will be discussed in Chapter 18). Nonprofit organizations like charities often use telemarketing to solicit funds. As you will see, for-profit companies are also using telemarketing with much greater frequency to screen and qualify prospects (which reduces selling costs) and to generate leads. Direct-mail pieces are often used to invite prospective customers to visit auto showrooms to test-drive new cars; the salesperson then assumes responsibility for the selling effort. The GM and BMW examples cited earlier in this text demonstrate effective use of this approach.

Combining Direct Marketing with Sales Promotions

How many times have you received a direct-mail piece notifying you of a sales promotion or event or inviting you to participate in a contest or sweepstakes? Ski shops regularly mail announcements of special end-of-season sales. Airlines send out mailers or e-mails announcing promotional airfares. Nordstom and other retail outlets call their existing customers to notify them of special sales promotions. Each of these is an example of a company using direct-marketing tools to inform customers of sales promotions. In turn, the sales promotion event may support the direct-marketing effort. Databases are often built from the names and addresses acquired from a promotion, and direct mail and/or telemarketing calls follow.

CAREER PROFILE

Melissa L. Fisher

Vice President, Marketing and Communications Cox Target Media, Inc.

I've always been envious of graduates from prestigious schools such as Northwestern, Wharton or Harvard, who land the ultimate marketing job and work on the mega brands. My story is different. I went to schools that gave me scholarships and work-study opportunities, participated in a number of internships and chose entry-level jobs that would give me vast experiences.

I graduated from Houghton College with a BS in business administration and a minor in music. I interned with the Buffalo Chamber of Commerce working on the "I Love New York" campaign, had a summer internship in Nashville to learn about the music industry, and filled in as the art director in the college's PR dept. I volunteered for the campus activity council and worked with a student chapter of the American Marketing Association.

After graduation, I moved back home and worked at the local credit and collections company for a year. I attended Regent University's School of Business. I received a partial scholarship but my meager finances motivated me to complete my master's degree in under a year. After I graduated, a local company recruited me to work in research and development. In a few months, I was promoted to Director of R&D and Marketing, directing all facets of product research, development and marketing. I worked with product suppliers, laboratories, nutritionists, chemists, printers, advertising agencies, media planners, research development firms, FDA/trademark/patent attorneys, and media service bureaus. Working there was a crash course in management, business law and marketing. I resigned when the company was sold and relocated to Dallas, Texas.

My next job was as a manager at Sentara Health Systems Inc., a large healthcare and hospital system. I was responsible for daily operations and patient flow of their Oncology, Urgent Care, Rehabilitation and Emergency departments. I did well at that job, but it was not my dream vocation. I missed marketing, and left Sentara to accept a position at CableRep, the advertising sales wing of COX Communications, the local cable company. I was hired as a Promotions Coordinator but was promoted to Marketing Manager within the first year.

I went from an event coordinator and planner to having full responsibility for marketing, promotional, and strategic development. My efforts to build revenue streams—commercial spots in over 40 networks, local origination programs, direct mail coupons, video production, resort programming and COX Interactive Media Internet ad sales—were so successful, that we broke all earnings records several times over and I won several awards.

"I think the best part of working in marketing is that there is continual change and challenges."

I am now the Vice President of Marketing and Communications at Cox Target Media. I joined CTM in 2000 to create unified sales tools for disparate national sales teams representing eight direct marketing product lines. In 2001, CTM consolidated several of its product lines including Cox Direct, Cox Sampling, Carol Wright and Valpak Direct Marketing Systems, Inc. I was selected to lead the consolidation and direction of CTM's marketing and communications functions, a role requiring me to unify various departments to more effectively market the company's signature products: Valpak and Valpak.com. Valpak envelopes deliver over 15 billion coupons and advertising offers to consumers each year. I was responsible for Valpak's 2002 rebranding program and its national advertising campaign. I also led Valpak's effort to develop new national promotional partnerships with such media companies as CBS, 20th Century Fox, Warner Bros. and Paramount Pictures.

I think the best part of working in marketing is that there is continual change and challenges. Every day is different and you are always dealing with interesting problems and issues. And, most important, I enjoy every minute of it.

Combining Direct Marketing with Support Media Adding a promotional product to a direct mailer has proved to increase response rates. One company included a promotional product in half of its 10,000 mailers and not in the other half. The former generated 65 percent more orders. 3M used a promotional product as an incentive for people responding to a direct-mail offer. The incentive generated a 23 percent response rate versus only 9 percent for the regular mailer.

To successfully implement direct-marketing programs, companies must make a number of decisions. As in other marketing programs, they must determine (1) what the program's objectives will be; (2) which markets to target (through the use of a list or marketing database); (3) what direct-marketing strategies will be employed; and (4) how to evaluate the effectiveness of the program.

Direct-Marketing Objectives

The direct marketer usually seeks a direct response. The objectives of the program are normally behaviors—for example, test drives, votes, contributions, and/or sales. A typical objective is defined through a set response, perhaps a 2 to 3 percent response rate.

Not all direct marketing seeks a behavioral response, however. Many organizations use direct marketing to build an image, maintain customer satisfaction, and inform and/or educate customers in an attempt to lead to future actions. Exhibit 14-1 shows how the city of San Diego uses direct mail to encourage tourism.

Exhibit 14-1 San Diego encourages visits through direct mail

Developing a Database

As we have discussed throughout this text, market segmentation and targeting are critical components of any promotional program. Direct-marketing programs employ these principles even more than others, since the success of a direct-marketing program is in large part tied to the ability to do *one-to-one marketing*. To segment and target their markets, direct marketers use a **database,** a listing of customers and/or potential customers. Research by the U.S. Postal Service showed that 65 percent of the companies surveyed rely on their internal databases for marketing purposes.[10] This database is a tool for **database marketing**—the use of specific information about individual customers and/or prospects to implement more effective and efficient marketing communications.[11]

Figure 14-2 demonstrates how database marketing works. As you can see, the database marketing effort must be an integral part of the overall IMC program. At the

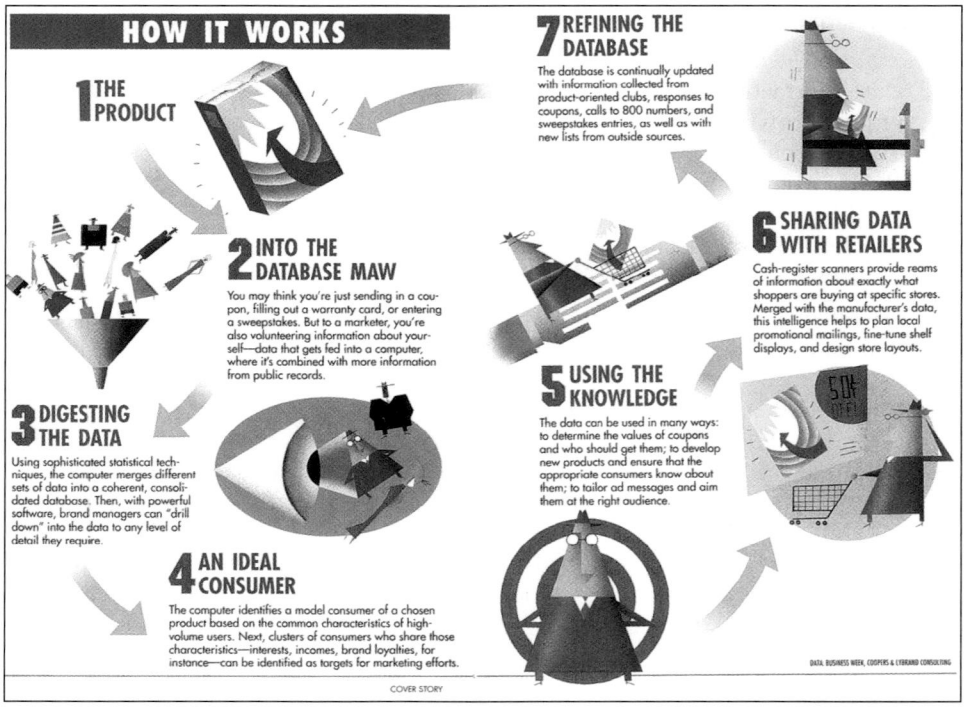

Figure 14-2 How database marketing works

Figure 14-3 Contents for a comprehensive database

Consumer Database	Business-to-Business Database
Name	Name of company/contact/decision maker(s)
Address/Zip code	Title of contact
Telephone number	Telephone number
Length of residence	Source of order/inquiry or referral
Age	Credit history
Gender	Industrial classification
Marital status	Size of business
Family data (number of children, etc.)	Revenues
Education	Number of employees
Income	Time in business
Occupation	Headquarters location
Transaction history	Multiple locations
Promotion history	Purchase history
Inquiring history	Promotion history
Unique identifier	Inquiry history
	Unique identifier

very least, this list contains names, addresses, and Zip codes; more sophisticated databases include information on demographics and psychographics, purchase transactions and payments, personal facts, neighborhood data, and even credit histories (see Figure 14-3). This database serves as the foundation from which the direct-marketing programs evolve. Databases are used to perform the following functions:[12]

- *Improving the selection of market segments.* Some consumers are more likely to be potential purchasers, users, voters, and so on than others. By analyzing the characteristics of the database, a marketer can target a greater potential audience. For example, catalog companies have become very specialized. Companies such as Lands' End, Lilly's Kids, and Johnson & Murphy have culled their lists and become much more efficient, targeting only those who are most likely to purchase their products.
- *Stimulate repeat purchases.* Once a purchase has been made, the customer's name and other information are entered into the database. These people are proven direct-marketing users who offer high potential for repurchase. Magazines, for example, routinely send out renewal letters and/or call subscribers before the expiration date. Blockbuster Entertainment helps its video-rental customers select movies, locate additional Blockbuster stores, and review their membership. Companies from window cleaners to carpet cleaners to car dealers build a base of customers and contact them when they are "due" to repurchase.
- *Cross-sell.* Customers who demonstrate a specific interest also constitute strong potential for other products of the same nature. For example, the National Geographic Society has successfully sold globes, maps, videos, travel magazines, and an assortment of other products to subscribers who obviously have an interest in geography and/or travel. Likewise, Victoria's Secret has expanded its clothing lines primarily through sales to existing customers, and Kraft–GF has successfully cross-sold products in its varied food line. Upon responding to the direct-mail piece sent by Hertz (Exhibit 14-2), you are asked for your permission for Hertz to provide your name to its parent company, Ford, and others, and to allow Hertz to send you information on other products and services. Notice how many cross-selling offers are contained in the Blockbuster piece in Exhibit 14-3.
- *Customer relationship management.* Customer relationship management (CRM), which is described in more detail in Chapter 16, requires that the marketer develop

Exhibit 14-2 Hertz seeks permission to use receivers' names

and maintain a significant amount of information about its clients. The aim of CRM is to establish a relationship with one's customers through affinities, personalized communications, and product/service offerings. For CRM to work effectively, a database is required. While CRM relies on technology specifically designed for managing customer relationships, there are overlapping characteristics of CRM and database marketing. Suffice it to say at this point that many of the techniques employed in database marketing are necessary to develop an effective CRM program.

Numerous other companies have established comprehensive databases on existing and potential customers both in the United States and internationally. IMC Perspective 14-1 provides additional examples. Database marketing has become so ubiquitous that many people are concerned about invasion of privacy. Direct marketers are concerned as well. The Direct Marketing Association (DMA), the trade association for direct marketers, has asked its members to adhere to ethical rules of conduct in their marketing efforts. It points out that if the industry does not police itself, the government will.

Sources of Database Information There are many sources of information for direct-marketing databases:

- *The U.S. Census Bureau.* Census data provide information on almost every household in the United States. Data include household size, demographics, income, and other information.

Exhibit 14-3 Blockbuster uses mailers to cross promote

IMC PERSPECTIVE 14-1

Database Marketers Cross Over Industries

Many marketers subscribe to the notion that one's current customers are also one's best potential customers. Now more and more companies from a variety of industries are taking that rule to heart—or should we say to their databases?

These days, it seems that every time we make a purchase we are asked to give our life histories. Buy something from Radio Shack, and the salesclerk will ask you for your Zip code and, if you are willing to spend the time, for much additional information, including your name, address, phone number, and e-mail address. Other companies collect the same information through warranty cards, credit card applications, or online registrations on the Internet.

But then what? Why do companies want this information? For many companies, the database constitutes the basis for all other IMC activities. Consider the following examples:

- *Petco.* Over 62 percent of households in the United States have at least one pet, creating a gold mine of opportunities for the $26 billion pet supply industry. Historically dominated by large brands like Alpo, Kal Kan, and Purina, the majority of sales have been through supermarkets. Now specialty pet stores like PetsMart and Petco want some of this action, and they are getting it, due in part to successful database marketing. While Petco is price-competitive, the company's marketing success can be attributed to strong customer service and direct marketing, which in turn guides its other IMC efforts. Petco was the first to introduce a customer loyalty program—PALS ("Petco Animal Lovers Save")—which now has over 17 million card members. The information provided by members allows the specialty store to effectively personalize direct-marketing efforts and gain an understanding of its customers' needs. This information is used to provide customers with highly targeted in-store discounts and promotional offers. Advertising plays an important role in creating awareness of Petco programs, and the company frequently advertises through monthly circular ads in Sunday newspapers. Radio and cable TV spots are also employed, as is localized public relations (each store gets involved in activities in its trade area). All these approaches consistently remind the pet food customer of the advantages of being a PALS member.
- *Wrigley.* How do you create a database of gum chewers? Ask Wrigley. The long-time purveyor of chewing gum recently launched its "Get your code and go" summer movie promotion for PlenTPaks of Winterfresh gum by dropping 8.8 million packs into stores bearing splash graphics for the promotion. Consumers were directed to the Internet site www.winterfresh.com to sign in (and, of course, provide information about themselves) and to enter a code found on the inside wrapper to earn points. Point totals were tracked, with 5 points automatically triggering a free-ticket voucher valid at participating theaters. The promotional campaign was supported by TV ads promoting the gum's flavor. The objectives of the movie promo were to provide Wrigley with more data on who is chewing its gum and to initiate the development of a loyalty program.
- *General Motors.* GM, the largest automobile company in the United States, has apparently discovered yet another way to successfully market its cars. Using national TV and print to promote the "Overdrive" corporate umbrella theme, GM used information provided by more than 1 million GM cardholders who registered at gmcard.com to target direct mailers to those cardholders who indicated that they might currently be in the market for a new car or truck. The mailer offered cardholders monetary incentives for new-vehicle purchases that could total as much as $3,500 over seven years. New cardholders were also being attracted through GM's sponsorship of country singer Kenny Chesney's 50-stop concert tour. Those who agreed to fill out an application received a free CD featuring Chesney and four other artists and the chance to win an opportunity to meet the singer. Did it work? Within two weeks of the mailing, GM recorded four of its top 10 new-vehicle sales days in the history of the credit card. And you thought such companies just wanted mailing information!

Sources: Jean Halliday, "GM Plays Cards Right," *Advertising Age,* May 27, 2002, p. 45; Mike Beime, "Wrigley Gum Entices Info via Internet," *Brandweek,* July 15, 2002, p. 4.

- *The U.S. Postal Service.* Postal Zip codes and the extended four-digit code provide information on both household and business locations.
- *List services.* Many providers of lists are available. The accuracy and timeliness of the lists vary.
- *Standard Rate and Data Service.* SRDS provides information regarding both consumer and business lists. Published in two volumes, *Direct Mail List Rates and Data* contains over 50,000 list selections in hundreds of classifications.
- *Simmons Market Research Bureau.* SMRB conducts an annual study of customers who buy at home via mail or telephone (see Figure 14-4). It compiles information on total orders placed, types of products purchased, demographics, and purchase satisfaction, among others.
- *Direct Marketing Association.* The direct marketers' trade organization promotes direct marketing and provides statistical information on direct-marketing use. The DMA's *Fact Book of Direct Marketing* contains information regarding use, attitudes toward direct marketing, rules and regulations, and so forth.

Consumer-goods manufacturers, banks, credit bureaus, retailers, charitable organizations, and other business operations also sell lists and other selected information. Companies can build their own databases through completed warranty cards, surveys, and so on.

Determining the Effectiveness of the Database

While many companies maintain a database, many do not use them effectively. Collecting names and information is not enough; the list must be kept current, purged of old and/or inactive customers, and updated frequently. The more information about customers that can be contained in the database, the more effective it will be. The Postal Service recommends an **RFM scoring method** for this purpose.[13] *RFM* stands for the recency, frequency, and monetary transactions between the company and the customer. More specifically, data need to be entered each time there is a transaction so the company can track how recently purchases have been made, how often they are made, and what amounts of money are being spent. In addition, tracking which products and/or services are used increases the ability to conduct the activities previously mentioned (on page 467). By analyzing the database on a regular basis, the company or organization can identify trends and buying patterns that will help it establish a better relationship with its customers by more effectively meeting their needs.

Direct-Marketing Strategies and Media

As with all other communications programs discussed in this text, marketers must decide the message to be conveyed, the size of the budget, and so on. Perhaps the major difference between direct-marketing programs and other promotional mix programs regards the use of media.

As shown in Figure 14-1, direct marketing employs a number of media, including direct mail, telemarketing, direct-response broadcasting, the Internet, and print. Each medium is used to perform specific functions, although they all generally follow a one- or two-step approach.

In the **one-step approach,** the medium is used directly to obtain an order. You've probably seen TV commercials for products like wrench sets, workout equipment, or magazine subscriptions in which the viewer is urged to phone a toll-free number to place an order immediately. Usually these ads accept credit cards or cash on delivery and give an address. Their goal is to generate an immediate sale when the ad is shown.

The **two-step approach** may involve the use of more than one medium. The first effort is designed to screen, or qualify, potential buyers. The second effort generates the response. For example, many companies use telemarketing to screen on the basis of interest, and then follow up to interested parties with more information designed to achieve an order or use personal selling to close the sale.

Direct Mail

Direct mail is often called "junk mail"—the unsolicited mail you receive. More advertising dollars continue to be spent in direct mail than in almost any

Figure 14-4 SMRB provides information on consumers who ordered merchandise by mail or phone

	Total US 000	Ordered by Mail or Phone A 000	B % Down	C Across %	D Index
Total adults	185,822	97,715	100.0	52.6	100
Males	88,956	42,488	43.5	47.8	91
Females	96,866	55,227	56.5	57.0	108
Principal shoppers	112,018	60,697	62.1	54.2	103
18–24	23,965	9,846	10.1	41.1	78
25–34	42,832	22,434	23.0	52.4	100
35–44	39,908	23,902	24.5	59.9	114
45–54	27,327	16,047	16.4	58.7	112
55–64	21,238	10,939	11.2	51.5	98
65 or older	30,552	14,547	14.9	47.6	91
18–34	66,798	32,280	33.0	48.3	92
18–49	121,918	65,339	66.9	53.6	102
25–54	110,067	62,383	63.8	56.7	108
35–49	55,120	33,059	33.8	60.0	114
50 or older	63,905	32,376	33.1	50.7	96
Graduated college	36,463	23,374	23.9	64.1	122
Attended college	44,294	24,904	25.5	56.2	107
Graduated high school	66,741	34,408	35.2	51.6	98
Did not graduate high school	38,324	15,028	15.4	39.2	75
Employed males	65,500	32,228	33.0	49.2	94
Employed females	55,910	34,804	35.6	62.3	118
Employed full-time	110,363	60,402	61.8	54.7	104
Employed part-time	11,047	6,630	6.8	60.0	114
Not employed	64,412	30,682	31.4	47.6	91
Professional/manager	31,718	19,851	20.3	62.6	119
Technical/clerical/sales	37,895	22,703	23.2	59.9	114
Precision/craft	13,954	6,930	7.1	49.7	94
Other employed	37,843	17,548	18.0	46.4	88
Single	41,284	17,744	18.2	43.0	82
Married	109,023	62,594	64.1	57.4	109
Divorced/separated/widowed	35,515	17,376	17.8	48.9	93
Parents	62,342	35,701	36.5	57.3	109
White	158,841	87,327	89.4	55.0	105
Black	21,122	7,896	8.1	37.4	71
Other	5,859	2,492	2.6	42.5	81
Household income					
$75,000 or more	24,165	14,731	15.1	61.0	116
$60,000 or more	40,979	24,220	24.8	59.1	112
$50,000 or more	57,996	34,185	35.0	58.9	112
$40,000 or more	80,078	47,018	48.1	58.7	112
$30,000 or more	106,838	62,069	63.5	58.1	110
$30,000–$39,000	26,759	15,051	15.4	56.2	107
$20,000–$29,000	30,669	15,147	15.5	49.4	94
$10,000–$19,999	29,083	13,069	13.4	44.9	85
Under $10,000	19,232	7,430	7.6	38.6	73

Exhibit 14-4 Porsche targets direct mail to upscale audiences

other advertising medium—an estimated $46.5 billion in 2001.[14] Mail-order sales exceeded $582 billion in 2001 ($359 billion in the consumer market).[15] Direct mail is not restricted to small companies seeking our business. Respected large companies such as General Electric, American Express, and Citicorp have increased their expenditures in this area, as have many others. Sales through direct mail in the business-to-business market are expected to reach over $345 billion by the year 2006.[16]

Many advertisers shied away from direct mail in the past, fearful of the image it might create or harboring the belief that direct mail was useful only for low-cost products. But this is no longer the case. For example, Porsche Cars North America, Inc., uses direct mail to target high-income, upscale consumers who are most likely to purchase its expensive sports cars (Exhibit 14-4). In one example, Porsche developed a direct-mail piece that was sent to a precisely defined target market: physicians in specialties with the highest income levels. This list was screened to match the demographics of Porsche buyers and narrowed further to specific geographic areas. The direct-mail piece was an X ray of a Porsche 911 Carrera 4 written in the language of the medical audience. This creative campaign generated one of the highest response rates of any mailing Porsche has done in recent years.[17] The materials shown in Exhibit 14-5 are just some of the ones sent by Mercedes to introduce its new sports utility vehicle. The *Express* retail chain and *Vogue* magazine teamed up to offer the store's credit card holders a one-year subscription to the magazine, to be charged to their credit cards.

Keys to the success of direct mail are the **mailing list,** which constitutes the database from which names are generated, and the ability to segment markets. Lists have become more current and more selective, eliminating waste coverage. Segmentation on the basis of geography (usually through Zip codes), demographics, and lifestyles

Exhibit 14-5 Mercedes used direct mail to introduce its new SUV

Exhibit 14-6 VNU provides lists for purchase

has led to increased effectiveness. The most commonly used lists are of individuals who have already purchased direct-mail products.

The importance of the list has led to a business of its own. It has been estimated that there are over 38 billion names on lists, and many companies have found it profitable to sell the names of purchasers of their products and/or services to list firms. Companies like A. B. Zeller and VNU Business Media (Exhibit 14-6) provide such lists on a national level, and in most metropolitan areas there are firms providing the same service locally.

While direct mail continues to be a favorite medium of many advertisers, and projections are that the market will continue to grow, this medium has been seriously threatened by the Internet. Between 1996 and 2001 direct-mail expenditures rose at the rate of 6.15 percent per year while Internet expenditures increased at the rate of 95 percent.[18] Interestingly, the Internet is both a threat and an opportunity, as Internet companies have increased their expenditures in direct mail to drive potential customers to their sites. For example, AOL frequently mails disks with free time to induce trial of its Internet service. Nevertheless, the direct-mail business has experienced lower response rates from customers than in the past and has seen many advertisers shift dollars from this medium to the Net.[19] Many companies, particularly in the business-to-business market, have shifted from print to online catalogs, and legal problems have also hurt the industry.

Catalogs Major participants in the direct-marketing business include catalog companies. The number of catalogs mailed and the number of catalog shoppers have increased significantly since 1984, with sales growing by an average of 11.4 percent each year between 1996 and 2001. Catalog sales are expected to reach $16.3 billion in 2006.[20]

Many companies use catalogs in conjunction with their more traditional sales and promotional strategies. For example, companies like Pottery Barn, Nordstrom, and JCPenney sell directly through catalogs but also use them to inform consumers of product offerings available in the stores. Some companies (for example, Fingerhut and Alloy) rely solely on catalog sales. Others that started out exclusively as catalog com-

panies have branched into retail outlets, among them The Sharper Image, Lands' End, and Banana Republic. L.L. Bean recently opened a superstore on the East Coast. As you can see by the following examples, the products being offered through this medium have reached new heights as well:

- The 2002 Neiman Marcus Christmas catalog was used to introduce the 2004 Cadillac XLR—MFRP $85,000. Cadillac produced only 101 of the "Neiman-Marcus XLRs—99 for sale through the catalog, 2 for charity. They sold out in 14 minutes! (Exhibit 14-7)
- Victoria's Secret featured a $1 million Miracle Bra in its Christmas catalog. Modeled by supermodel Claudia Schiffer, the bra contained over 100 carats of real diamonds as well as hundreds of semiprecious stones.
- Saks' Holding Co., a division of Saks Fifth Avenue, offered a pair of Mercedes-Benz convertibles in a catalog, with bidding to start at $50,000.
- Hammacher Schlemmer featured a $43,000 taxicab and a $34,000 train set in its Christmas catalog.
- The Sharper Image offered a $375,000 silver saddle in its catalog (though it didn't sell any).

Exhibit 14-7 Neiman-Marcus is one of many successful catalog companies

In addition to the traditional hard copies, catalogs are now available on the Internet for both consumer and business-to-business customers. In some instances in the consumer market the catalog merchandise is available in retail stores as well. In others, the catalog and retail divisions are treated as separate entities. For example, if you purchase through the Eddie Bauer catalog, you can exchange or return the merchandise to the retail stores. Victoria's Secret products must be returned to the catalog department. At the Gap, the catalog is used to supplement the inventory in stock, and phone orders for different sizes and so on can be made from the store and shipped for free.

Broadcast Media The success of direct marketing in the broadcast industry has been truly remarkable; over 77 percent of the U.S. population report that they have viewed a direct-response appeal on TV.[21] Direct-response TV is estimated to have generated more than $79.3 billion in sales in 2002—with projections of $108.2 billion by 2006. However, forecasts are for slower growth in the next few years, averaging 8.8 percent through 2007.[22]

Two broadcast media are available to direct marketers: television and radio. While radio was used quite extensively in the 1950s, its use and effectiveness have dwindled substantially in recent years. Thus, the majority of direct-marketing broadcast advertising now occurs on TV, which receives the bulk of our attention here. It should be pointed out, however, that the two-step approach is still very common on the radio, particularly with local companies.

Direct marketing in the broadcast industry involves both direct-response advertising and support advertising. In **direct-response advertising,** the product or service is offered and a sales response is solicited, through either the one- or two-step approach previously discussed. Examples include ads for magazine subscriptions, CDs and tapes, and tips on football or basketball betting. Toll-free phone numbers are included so that the receiver can immediately call to order. **Support advertising** is designed to do exactly that—support other forms of advertising. Ads for Publishers Clearing House or *Reader's Digest* or other companies telling you to look in your mailbox for a sweepstakes entry are examples of support advertising.

Direct-response TV encompasses a number of media, including direct-response TV spots like those just mentioned, infomercials, and home shopping shows (teleshopping). And as noted in Chapter 10, Internet TV has recently been introduced.

Infomercials The lower cost of commercials on cable and satellite channels has led advertisers to a new form of advertising. An **infomercial** is a long commercial that ranges from 30 to 60 minutes. Many infomercials are produced by the advertisers and

Exhibit 14-8 A variety of companies use infomercials to sell their products

are designed to be viewed as regular TV shows. Consumers dial a toll-free or 900 number to place an order. Programs such as "Liquid Luster," "Amazing Discoveries," and "Stainerator" (the so-called miracle-product shows) were the most common form of infomercial in the 1980s. While this form of show is still popular, the infomercial industry has been adopted by many big, mainstream marketers, as noted in the lead-in to this chapter (see Exhibits 14-8 and 14-9).

As to their effectiveness, studies indicate that infomercials get watched and sell products. Figure 14-5 shows the demographics of TV shoppers. This profile is consistent with research conducted by Naveen Donthu and David Gilliland profiling infomercial viewers and buyers. These studies demonstrate that this advertising medium is indeed effective with a broad demographic base, not significantly different from the infomercial nonshopper in age, education, income, or gender. Infomercial sales in the year 2002 were expected to exceed $20 billion, three times the amount spent in 1995.[23] Retail stores are benefiting from infomercials as well, as brand awareness leads to increased in-store purchases. For example, a $500,000 print campaign combined with an infomercial for the George Foreman Grill led to more sales at retail stores than through Direct TV.[24]

However, some people are not sold on the idea of ads disguised as programs. For example, infomercials disguised as "ultrahip" TV shows have been targeted at teenagers, raising fears that kids under the age of 13 will be susceptible to their lure. Consumer complaints are on the rise, and the FTC has already levied fines for deceptive endorsements against infomercial sponsors. Four consumer groups (the Consumer Federation of America, Center for the Study of Commercialism, Center for Media Education, and Telecommunications Research and Action Center) have asked the FCC to require all infomercials to display a symbol that indicates a "paid ad" or "sponsored by" so that viewers won't confuse them with regular programming.

TV Advertorials

In 1999, Peugot took its first step into TV programming by developing a series of **advertorials** to show the public its entire model range. Peugeot is the first auto manufacturer to use TV advertorials. The company developed eight 5-minute films positioning the autos as "The Drive of Your Life" while providing comprehensive information on test drives, technical specifications, and demonstrations. In addition, the auto company developed advertorials for its website, with each advertorial targeted to different target audiences.[25]

Teleshopping

The development of toll-free telephone numbers, combined with the widespread use of credit cards, has led to a dramatic increase in the number of people who shop via their TV sets. Jewelry, kitchenware, fitness products, insurance,

Figure 14-5 Here's who's watching (and buying from) infomercials

	Survey				
	U.S. Census	2001	2000	1999	1998
Female purchaser	n/a	79%	84%	84%	84%
Caucasian	69%	73	76	80	84
Married	52	61	68	63	77
White collar/technical	n/a	41	33	37	57
Homeowner	66	76	73	72	87
Income:					
$26,000–$35,000	12	13	13	15	8
$36,000–$55,000	22	27	27	27	10
$56,000 or more	46	34	42	34	62

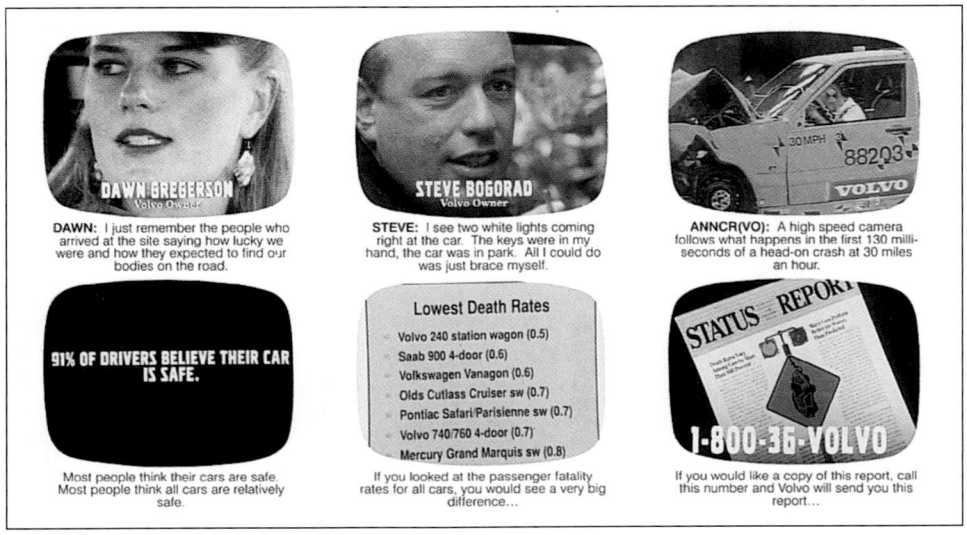

Exhibit 14-9 Volvo uses an infomercial to attract buyers

compact discs, and a variety of items are now promoted (and sold) this way. The major shopping channel in the United States (QVC) accounted for over $3.9 billion worth of sales in 2002, reaching over 84 million households and fielding more than 130 million calls.[26] Industry studies project a 5 percent growth rate, to $15.6 billion, by 2006.[27] QVC is pursuing international markets (including the United Kingdom, Canada, and Latin America) to follow up on its successes in Germany and Japan, partnerships (United signed on as official airline of the "Quest for America's Best" program), and sponsorships (for example, Geoff Bodine on the NASCAR circuit).

Print Media Magazines and newspapers are difficult media to use for direct marketing. Because these ads have to compete with the clutter of other ads and because the space is relatively expensive, response rates and profits may be lower than in other media. This does not mean these media are not used (as evidenced by the fact that expenditures totaled over $9.8 billion in 2001.)[28] Exhibit 14-10 shows a direct ad that appeared in a magazine. You can find many more in specific interest areas like financial newspapers or sports, sex, or hobby magazines.

Telemarketing If you have a telephone, you probably do not have to be told about the rapid increase in the use of **telemarketing,** or sales by telephone. Both profit and charitable organizations have employed this medium effectively in both one- and two-step approaches. Combined telemarketing sales (consumer and business-to-business) totaled over $661 billion in 2001—with $274.2 billion in the consumer market.[29] Telemarketing is a very big industry and still growing. Consider these facts:

- Over 6.3 million people are now employed in the telemarketing industry.[30]
- Telemarketing accounts for 45.2 percent of all b-to-b marketing sales.[31]
- Marketers spend an estimated $76.2 billion a year on outbound telemarketing calls.[32]

Business-to-business marketers like Adobe Systems, Kaiser Permanente, and Hewlett-Packard are just a few of the many companies that use this direct-marketing medium effectively. B-to-b sales are expected to reach $588 billion by 2006.[33]

As telemarketing continues to expand in scope, a new dimension referred to as **audiotex** or **telemedia** has evolved. Tom Eisenhart defines telemedia as the "use of telephone and voice information services (900, 800, and 976 numbers) to market, advertise, promote, entertain, and inform."[34] Many telemedia programs are interactive. While many people

Exhibit 14-10 A direct-response print ad

Figure 14-6 The use of 800, 900, and 976 numbers in marketing

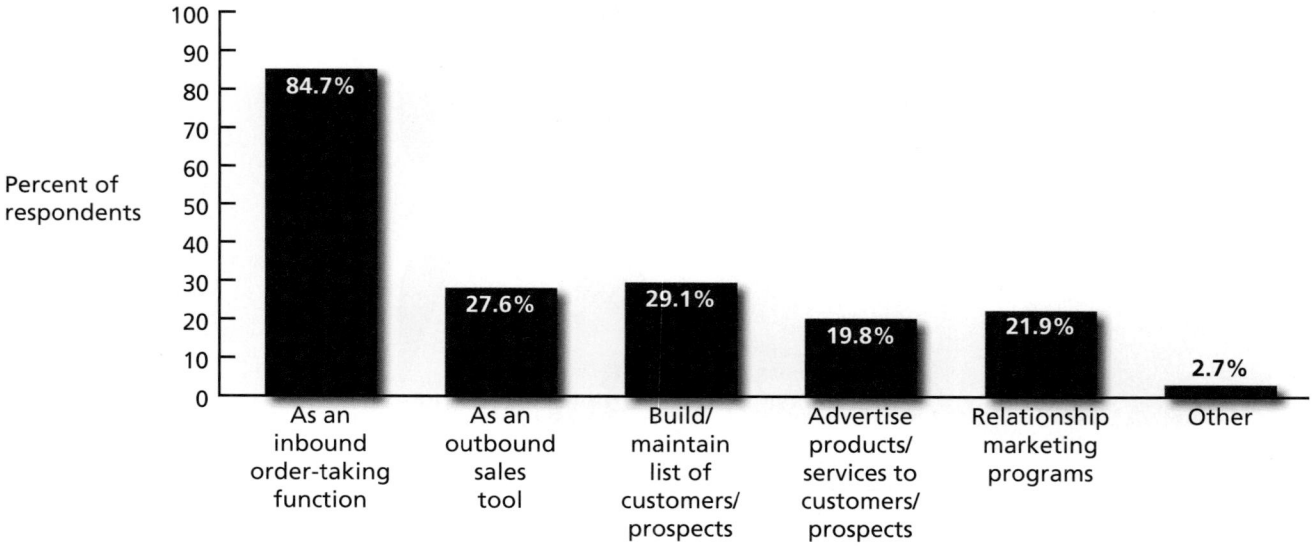

Note: *Direct* forecast survey was conducted by Jacobson Consulting Applications. The firms mailed a four-page questionnaire to direct-marketing executives on an *n*th name basis from *Direct's* circulation list. There were 565 responses.

still think of 900 and 976 numbers as rip-offs or "sex, lies, and phone lines," over 7,000 programs are carried on 900 numbers alone, including Tele-Lawyer, a legal information services organization; Bally's Health & Tennis Corp., the nation's largest health-club chain; and NutraSweet. Figure 14-6 shows more specifically how 800, 976 and 900 numbers are used as marketing tools.[35]

Problems associated with telemarketing include its potential for fraud and deception and its potential for annoyance. (Doesn't it seem as if every time you sit down to dinner you receive a phone call from someone trying to sell you something or asking for a donation?)

Those in the telemarketing and telemedia industry have responded to public criticisms. Dial-a-Porn and its ilk hold a diminishing share of 800, 900, and 976 offerings. As more and more large companies use telemedia, its tarnished image will likely brighten up.

Electronic Teleshopping

Unlike infomercials and home shopping channels, which have relied on broadcast or cable TV, **electronic teleshopping** is an online shopping and information retrieval service accessed through personal computers. While we will discuss e-commerce in detail in the next chapter, it is important to reiterate that Internet shopping is a direct-response medium that traditional direct marketers are adding to their businesses as well. For example, QVC, the home shopping channel, has started iQVC, an Internet home shopping channel that complements its cable TV channel and adds incremental sales (the cable channel drives customers to the website). The company was one of the first "Web department stores" to turn a profit. QVC's Internet shopping channel did $400 million in sales in 2002.[36] Other direct marketers have met with less success, finding out the hard way that selling on the Internet requires different strategies. One such company, K-Tel, Inc., a highly successful direct-response TV marketer (Top 40 music, Veg-o-matic), has had much less success in adapting its traditional methods to the Web.[37]

Direct Selling

An additional element of the direct-marketing program is **direct selling,** the direct, personal presentation, demonstration, and sales of products and services to consumers in their homes. Avon, Cutco, Mary Kay Inc., and Tupperware are some of the best-known direct-selling companies in the United States and are now extending these programs overseas (Exhibit 14-11). Close to 11 million people engage in direct selling throughout the world; 99 percent of them are independent contractors (not employees of the firm they represent). These 11 million generate approximately $25.57 billion in sales.[38]

Exhibit 14-11 Cutco uses direct selling successfully in marketing their knives

The three forms of direct selling are

1. *Repetitive person-to-person selling.* The salesperson visits the buyer's home, job site, or other location to sell frequently purchased products or services (for example, Amway).
2. *Nonrepetitive person-to-person selling.* The salesperson visits the buyer's home, job site, or other location to sell infrequently purchased products or services (for example, Encyclopaedia Britannica).
3. *Party plans.* The salesperson offers products or services to groups of people through home or office parties and demonstrations (for example, Tupperware and PartyLite Gifts).

While a number of products and services are sold through direct selling, home and family care products (33.7 percent) and personal care products (26.4 percent) are the most popular. The "typical" direct-selling representative is female (73 percent), married (76 percent), and between 35 and 44 years of age (Figure 14-7). For most of the

Figure 14-7 2002 direct sales force demographics

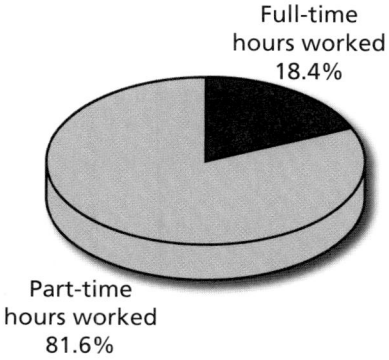

Demographics of Direct Salespeople	
Independent contractors	99.8%
Married	76
Female	73
Age: 35–54	54
Less than 30 hours per week	83.1

Source: From DSA's 2002 National Salesforce Survey.

representatives, direct selling is not a full-time job but an opportunity to earn additional income and a way to get the product at a discount for themselves. Over half of those employed in this industry spend less than 10 hours a week selling, and 81.6 percent spend less than 30 hours a week.

Evaluating the Effectiveness of Direct Marketing

Because they generate a direct response, measuring the effectiveness of direct-marketing programs is not difficult. Using the **cost per order (CPO),** advertisers can evaluate the relative effectiveness of an ad in only a few minutes based on the number of calls generated. By running the same ad on different stations, a direct marketer can determine the relative effectiveness of the medium itself. For example, if the advertiser targets a $5 return per order and a broadcast commercial (production and print) costs $2,500, the ad is considered effective if it generates 500 orders. Similar measures have been developed for print and direct-mail ads.

For direct-marketing programs that do not have an objective of generating a behavioral response, traditional measures of effectiveness can be applied. (We discuss these measures in Chapter 19.)

Advantages and Disadvantages of Direct Marketing

Many of the advantages of direct marketing have already been presented. A review of these and some additions follow:

1. *Selective reach.* Direct marketing lets the advertiser reach a large number of people and reduces or eliminates waste coverage. Intensive coverage may be obtained through broadcast advertising or through the mail. While not everyone drives on highways where there are billboards or pays attention to TV commercials, virtually everyone receives mail. A good list allows for minimal waste, as only those consumers with the highest potential are targeted. For example, a political candidate can direct a message at a very select group of people (those living in a certain Zip code or members of the Sierra Club, say); a music club can target recent purchasers of CD players.

2. *Segmentation capabilities.* Marketers can purchase lists of recent product purchasers, car buyers, bank-card holders, and so on. These lists may allow segmentation on the basis of geographic area, occupation, demographics, and job title, to mention a few. Combining this information with the geocoding capabilities of Prizm or VALS (discussed in Chapter 2), marketers can develop effective segmentation strategies.

3. *Frequency.* Depending on the medium used, it may be possible to build frequency levels. The program vehicles used for direct-response TV advertising are usually the most inexpensive available, so the marketer can afford to purchase repeat times. Frequency may not be so easily accomplished through the mail, since consumers may be annoyed to receive the same mail repeatedly.

4. *Flexibility.* Direct marketing can take on a variety of creative forms. For example, the Discovery Network sent 17-inch TV sets to media buyers through the mail. The only message accompanying the TV sets was one on the cord that said "Plug me in" and another on a videotape that read "Play me." Upon doing so, the recipient was greeted with a seven-minute promotional video. Direct-mail pieces also allow for detailed copy that provides a great deal of information. The targeted mailing of videotapes containing product information has increased dramatically, as companies have found this a very effective way to provide potential buyers with product information.

5. *Timing.* While many media require long-range planning and have long closing dates, direct-response advertising can be much more timely. Direct mail, for example, can be put together very quickly and distributed to the target population. TV programs typically used for direct-response advertising are older, less sought programs that are

likely to appear on the station's list of available spots. Another common strategy is to purchase available time at the last possible moment to get the best price.

6. *Personalization.* No other advertising medium can personalize the message as well as direct media. Parents with children at different age levels can be approached, with their child's name included in the appeal. Car owners are mailed letters congratulating them on their new purchase and offering accessories. Computer purchasers are sent software solicitations. Graduating college students receive very personalized information that recognizes their specific needs and offers solutions (such as credit cards).

7. *Costs.* While the CPM for direct mail may be very high on an absolute and a relative basis, its ability to specifically target the audience and eliminate waste coverage reduces the actual CPM. The ads used on TV are often among the lowest-priced available, and a video can be delivered for less than $1 (including postage).

A second factor contributing to the cost effectiveness of direct-response advertising is the cost per customer purchasing. Because of the low cost of media, each sale generated is very inexpensive.

8. *Measures of effectiveness.* No other medium can measure the effectiveness of its advertising efforts as well as direct response. Feedback is often immediate and always accurate.

Disadvantages of direct marketing include the following:

1. *Image factors.* As we noted earlier, the mail segment of this industry is often referred to as junk mail. Many people believe unsolicited mail promotes junk products, and others dislike being solicited. Even some senders of direct mail, including Motorola, GM, and Air Products & Chemicals, say they throw out most of the junk mail they receive. This problem is particularly relevant given the increased volume of mail being sent. (One study estimates the typical American receives 14 pieces of junk mail per week.)[39] Another predicts that by 2007 consumers will receive over 3,900 junk e-mails per year.[40] In 2002 over 205.7 billion pieces of mail were sent in the United States alone.[41]

Likewise, direct-response ads on TV are often low-budget ads for lower-priced products, which contributes to the image that something less than the best products are marketed in this way. (Some of this image is being overcome by the home shopping channels, which promote some very expensive products.) Telemarketing is found to be irritating to many consumers, as is "spam" or Internet junk mail. As you can see in Ethical Perspective 14-2, other factors have also created image problems for the direct-marketing industry.

2. *Accuracy.* One of the advantages cited for direct mail and telemarketing was targeting potential customers specifically. But the effectiveness of these methods depends on the accuracy of the lists used. People move, change occupations, and so on, and if the lists are not kept current, selectivity will decrease. Computerization has greatly improved the currency of lists and reduced the incidence of bad names; however, the ability to generate lists is becoming a problem.[42]

3. *Content support.* In our discussion of media strategy objectives in Chapter 10, we said the ability of magazines to create mood contributes to the overall effectiveness of the ads they carry. In direct-response advertising, mood creation is limited to the surrounding program and/or editorial content. Direct mail and online services are unlikely to create a desirable mood.

4. *Rising costs.* As postal rates increase, direct-mail profits are immediately and directly impacted.

ETHICAL PERSPECTIVE 14-2

Scam Artists Know No Boundaries

As direct-marketing scam artists get more sophisticated, they have expanded their efforts beyond the United States and into foreign countries. Apparently—like legitimate marketers—they have discovered market potential in these new markets.

One such market is Canada. Driven by the strength of the dollar (one U.S. dollar is worth about one-and-a-half Canadian dollars), Canada's lenient stance on white-collar crime, and the problems with getting lawbreakers back into the United States to face trial, Canada has become a virtual haven for telemarketing scam artists preying on Canadian and U.S. citizens as well as the elderly in England and Australia. With all due respect to both Canadian and U.S. officials, it is not as though the scammers operate at will. Both countries have increased their efforts against scammers, but the sophistication of the telemarketing rings make it hard to catch them.

The rings use a maze of business names, bank accounts, and mail drops. They are highly mobile, moving monthly or even weekly, and know how to throw authorities off track. Their primary target audiences are the elderly, the financially desperate, persons seeking a lucrative investment, and/or those just hoping to get rich quick.

One such scheme is the sweepstakes-winner scam. Working from lists, the telemarketers phone and tell the unwary receivers that they may already have won a lottery or sweepstakes but they must pay a fee ranging from a few hundred dollars to thousands of dollars to cover taxes or currency exchanges to collect. Once they pay, they are told they may have won an even larger prize, and more fees are collected. Some scammers pose as FBI or IRS agents. Others prey on the emotions of victims—particularly those with children in poor physical or financial health. All are good at what they do.

Another scam artist very good at what she does—or shall we say, did—is Miss Cleo. The flamboyant Caribbean clairvoyant scammed consumers out of millions of dollars with false promises of free psychic readings. Miss Cleo was actually a fictitious name established by two Florida firms, Psychic Readers Network, Inc., and Access Resources Services, Inc., that used TV ads, infomercials, and direct mailings to lure in customers. The ads featured the Caribbean-accented voice of a woman saying "Call me now" and promised free psychic readings if people called an 800 number. Once they did, they were referred to a 900 number for a "free" three-minute reading. After the three minutes the customer would be billed at $4.99 a minute, and operators did everything they could to get them past the free time—including putting them on hold! Over 6 million people called the hot line, averaging $60 per call, for a total of $360 million before the scam was busted. A settlement was awarded in December 2002.

A London-based company was forced by the FTC to suspend operations for selling false domain names ending in ".USA"—the names were useless. Shortly after the September 11, 2001, terrorist attacks, the promotion used e-mails to encourage consumers to be patriotic and register for USA domain names. The FTC believes the company made over $1 million from the scams.

While these are just some of the many scams being run, no one knows how many more are operating on a daily basis or how many people are being cheated. The only things that are known is that the scammers are a very tiny minority of the direct marketers out there and that legitimate telemarketers are as unhappy about the scams as are consumers and the authorities. After all, they are getting scammed too.

Sources: Myron Levin, "Canada Scam Artists Have a Global Reach," *Los Angeles Times,* July 7, 2002, p. C4; Myron Levin, "Psychic Hotline Accused of Caller Scam," *Los Angeles Times,* Feb. 1, 2002, p. C1; Christopher Saunders, "Courts Silence '.USA' Marketer," *Advertising Report,* Mar. 12, 2002, pp. 1–2.

Summary

This chapter introduced you to the rapidly growing field of direct marketing, which involves a variety of methods and media beyond direct mail and telemarketing. The versatility of direct marketing offers many different types of companies and organizations a powerful promotional and selling tool.

Direct marketing continues to outpace other advertising and promotional areas in growth; many of the Fortune 500 companies now use sophisticated direct-marketing strategies. Database marketing has become a critical component of many marketing programs.

Advantages of direct marketing include its selective reach, segmentation, frequency, flexibility, and timing. Personalized and custom messages, low costs, and the ability to measure program effectiveness are also advantages of direct-marketing programs.

At the same time, a number of disadvantages are associated with the use of direct marketing. Image problems, the proliferating sale and use of databases (some of them based on inaccurate lists), lack of content support, and the intrusive nature of the medium make some marketers hesitant to use direct-marketing tools. However, self-policing of the industry and involvement by large, sophisticated companies have led to significant improvements. As a result, the use of direct marketing will continue to increase.

Key Terms

direct marketing, 463
direct-response media, 463
database, 467
database marketing, 467
RFM scoring method, 471
one-step approach, 471
two-step approach, 471
mailing list, 473
direct-response advertising, 475
support advertising, 475
infomercial, 475
advertorial, 477
telemarketing, 477
audiotex, 477
telemedia, 477
electronic teleshopping, 478
direct selling, 478
cost per order (CPO), 480

Discussion Questions

1. Many marketers felt that the Internet would hurt the direct mail catalog industry. In fact, this has not been the case. Explain some of the similar characteristics of catalog shopping and shopping on the Internet. Then explain why you feel the mail catalog business has not been hurt.

2. What is the difference between direct marketing and direct selling? Describe the various forms of direct selling and some of the characteristics of the industry that make it unique.

3. What are the characteristics of the infomercial watcher? In viewing this profile, does it surprise you? Explain why or why not.

4. Explain why companies like those cited in the lead in to Chapter 14 have been successful in adopting direct marketing techniques. Describe the conditions that contribute to the successful implementation of direct marketing programs.

5. Identify some of the factors that have contributed to the growth of direct marketing. Do you see these factors being as relevant today? Discuss why or why not, and the impact they will have on direct marketing in the future.

6. The catalog has become an important part of the shopping lives of many consumers. Describe different groups that you think might find catalogs useful in the consumer market, and explain what aspects of catalogs would attract them to this medium.

7. Most of the methods for measuring effectiveness of direct marketing have to do with behaviors like sales, cost per order, etc. Explain how the adoption model discussed in Chapter 5 might also be employed to measure effectiveness.

8. One of the disadvantages associated with direct-marketing media is the high cost per exposure. Some marketers feel that this cost is not really as much of a disadvantage as is claimed. Argue for or against this position.

9. Why have companies like Volvo, Cadillac, and General Motors increased their use of infomercials? Is this a wise strategy?

10. Give an example of how companies might use direct marketing as part of an IMC program. Provide examples of both consumer and business marketers.

The Internet and Interactive Media

15

Chapter Objectives

1. To understand the different ways the Internet is used to communicate.
2. To know the advantages and disadvantages of the Internet and interactive media.
3. To know the role of the Internet and interactive media in an IMC program.
4. To understand how to evaluate the effectiveness of communications through the Internet.

The Internet: Powerful IMC Tool or Just Another Medium?

The rise and fall of the World Wide Web (WWW) brings to mind images of riding a roller-coaster. First there was the very rapid growth of the medium and the dot-com boom. Next came the

dot-com bust and rapid downhill spending by marketers. Now the predictions are that the Net is slowly climbing back up. It appears that the ups and downs of this medium have many marketers confused about how to use the Internet.

Part of the problem regarding how best to use the Internet can be attributed to the infancy of this medium and to differing opinions as to what role the Internet should assume. Direct marketers, for example, argue that the Internet is just another direct-marketing medium—albeit one with great sales potential. Others take a much broader perspective, viewing the Internet as an important IMC tool capable of supporting and enhancing other program elements. They see the Internet as a medium whose role is central to the effectiveness of the IMC program.

One of the proponents of the latter perspective is David A. Aaker, a University of California–Berkeley professor and the author of numerous articles and books on branding. Aaker argues that one of the ways to improve the ROI of brand marketing is to "increase the synergies and impact among the firm's individual brand-building programs so that the whole is greater than the sum of its parts." Aaker's view of the Internet is not that it is just another medium but that it is the "integrator" of the IMC program—the "glue" that holds the IMC program together. Proper integration of the Internet into the IMC program, he argues, requires that it is used creatively and as a component of the overall brand-building process. He feels that the Internet can be used to amplify other IMC elements.

One of the problems with the Internet, however, has been the inability of marketers to implement what Aaker has suggested. For years, companies have struggled with how to use the Net for branding purposes. The literature is full of articles on this problem, and many are of the notion that marketers aren't quite there yet. They cite the fact that there are not many powerful success stories to support the branding efforts.

At the same time, there are numerous examples of Internet success stories that go beyond direct marketing and support the position of proponents of a more enhanced role for the medium. Aaker cites numerous examples of effective branding and integration programs involving PepsiCo, Oscar Mayer, Valvoline, FedEx, and Procter & Gamble among others. Since it declared bankruptcy in 2002, Kmart has also relied more heavily on the Net to reclaim its brand image, emphasizing tighter cross-integration of IMC components through its "Stuff of Life" campaign. Its website now carries exactly the same logo,

type fonts, and imagery as every other component, including TV and print.

While the above list reflects the success experienced by large companies with large communications budgets, one shouldn't be deceived into thinking that integration is the domain of only those with large expenditure capabilities. The issue is not so much the amount of money spent but how it is spent, and there are plenty of success stories among smaller companies with less money but good strategies. Crate & Barrel, Godiva, and Sharper Image are just a few of the companies that have enhanced their brands through effective merchandising on the Web while still maintaining the selling component. Territory Ahead, akademiks, and fubu have created strong brand images among their target audiences with limited budgets and a strong Internet premise.

The capability of the Internet to tie together various elements of the IMC program may take the medium back to the top again. Let's just hope that its lack of integration doesn't take it back down.

Sources: David A. Aaker, "Fast Brand Building in Slow-Growth Markets," *strategy+business,* Third Quarter 2002, pp. 48–57; Mary Wagner, "Richard Blunck Has Kmart.com Ready for Success—the Rest Is Up to Kmart," *Internet Retailer,* September 2002, pp. 18–21; Mary Wagner, "On the Web, Merchandising No Longer Follows Rules Developed in Other Channels," *Internet Retailer,* September 2002, pp. 22–25.

Anyone who has followed the Internet industry over the last decade has seen an amazing series of events. Moving from a medium with almost no presence in the marketing environment to one that was the center of attention, the Internet experienced a boom that unfortunately became a bust. What some marketers thought would be the "be all and end all" of communications has now become a puzzle waiting to be solved, as many marketers have yet to discover what role the Internet will assume in their communications program.

What the lead-in to this chapter illustrates, however, is that some companies have apparently solved the puzzle and have effectively integrated the Internet into their marketing communications programs. As you will see in this chapter, others have been successful as well, particularly when they view the Internet as a component of the integrated marketing communications program and not as the only tool required for success.

In this chapter we will discuss the Internet and interactive media, marketers' objectives for using these media, and ways to measure their effectiveness. As you will see, the Internet and interactive media are valuable components of the integrated marketing communications program and, like other components, are most effective when used in conjunction with other program elements. We will begin our discussion with the Internet.

Defining the Internet

Before beginning our discussion, it may be useful to establish some common ground. While all of us are familiar with the Internet, the degree to which we are familiar varies. Understanding the material presented in this chapter will be easier if you are familiar with the terms used in the discussion.

The **Internet** is a worldwide means of exchanging information and communicating through a series of interconnected computers. It was started as a U.S. Defense Department project, but it is now accessible to anyone with a computer and a modem. While the most popular component of the Internet is the **World Wide Web (WWW),** there are other features as well, as shown in Figure 15-1. For marketers, a number of these features offer potential, but it is the Web that has developed as the commercial component. For that reason, the following discussion will focus on using the Web as a communications and sales tool. Before reading further, however, please take a few minutes to examine Figure 15-2, to familiarize yourself with some of the terms that we will be using. In reality, there are many more words that have been added to our language as a result of the growth of the Internet (you can actually purchase a dictionary of Internet terms), but space permits only a small inclusion here. Thus, we have stayed away from the technical jargon, concentrating primarily on marketing communications terms. If you are not familiar with terms like *URL, backbone, browser,* and so on, you may wish to consult another source before continuing.

Figure 15-1 Features of the Internet

Feature	Use
Electronic mail (e-mail)	Allows users to send electronic mail anywhere in the world
Usenet	Discussion groups, newsgroups, and electronic bulletin boards, similar to those offered by online services
Telnet	Online databases, library catalogs, and electronic journals at hundreds of colleges and public libraries
File transfer protocol (ftp) or hypertext transfer protocol (http)	The ability to transfer files from one mainframe computer to another
Client server	Allows for the transfer of files from one mainframe computer to another
Gopher	A document retrieval system used to search for information
Wide Area Information Server (WAIS)	Enables one to use keywords in specific databases and retrieve full text information
World Wide Web (WWW)	Does much the same thing as gopher and WAIS, but combines sound, graphic images, video, and hypertext on a single page; the commercial arm of the Internet

Figure 15-2 Internet terminology

Term	Definition
Ad clicks	Number of times users click on an ad banner.
Ad click rate	Often referred to as "click-through," the percentage of ad views that result in an ad click.
Ad views (impressions)	Number of times an ad banner is downloaded (and presumably seen by viewers).
Banner	An ad on a Web page that may be "hot-linked" to the advertiser's site.
Button	An advertisement smaller than a traditional banner ad. Buttons are usually square in shape and located down the left or right side of the site; sometimes referred to as "tiles."
CPC	Cost per click—a marketing formula used to price ad banners. Some advertisers pay on the basis of the number of clicks a specific ad banner gets.
CPM	Cost per thousand for a site.
Domain name	The unique name of an Internet site. There are six domains widely used in the U.S.: .com (commercial), .edu (education), .net (network operations), .gov (U.S. government), .mil (U.S. military), and .org (organization). Additional two letter domains specify a country, for example, .sp for Spain.
Hit	Each instance in which a server sends a file to a browser. Hits are used to measure the traffic on a site.
Interstitial	An advertisement that appears in a window on your screen while you are waiting for a Web page to load.
Link	An electronic connection between two websites.
Opt-in-e-mail	List of Internet users who have voluntarily signed up to receive commercial e-mail about topics of interest.
Page views	Number of times a user requests a page that contains a particular ad; used to indicate the number of times an ad was potentially seen, or "gross impressions."
Rich media	Advanced technology used in Internet ads, such as streaming video, which allows interaction and special effects.
Sponsorships	The sponsoring of a site's content by an advertiser.
Unique users	Number of different individuals who visit a site within a specific time period.
Valid hits	Number of hits that deliver all the information to a user (excludes error messages, redirects, etc.)
Visits	A sequence of requests made by one user at one site.

Figure 15-3 Internet users worldwide, by region, 2000–2004 (in millions)

	2000*	2001	2002	2003	2004	CAGR** 2000–2004
North America†	108.1	133.4	152.0	169.3	184.5	14.3%
Europe	100.9	139.3	170.7	196.2	221.1	21.7
Asia-Pacific	123.3	145.9	168.0	205.0	232.1	17.1
Latin America	15.8	22.0	32.0	43.4	60.6	39.9
Africa	4.1	5.3	7.2	9.0	10.9	27.7
Total	352.2	445.9	529.9	622.9	709.1	19.1

**eMarketer*'s year 2000 baseline is from the International Telecommunication Union's estimate of Internet users age 2 years and older, who have accessed the Internet within the previous 30 days.
**Compound annual growth rate.
†North America includes the United States and Canada; Mexico is included in Latin America.

Developing an Internet Program

As with other media discussed earlier in this text, using the Internet requires the development of a plan. This plan should consider target audiences (users of the Net), specific objectives and strategies, and methods for measuring effectiveness.

Web Participants

The Web, like all other media, has both customers (users) and those trying to reach these users (advertisers, sponsors, e-commerce). As with other media, target markets include consumers and the business-to-business (b-to-b) markets. Let's start our discussion with the users—the target markets.

Users: Consumer Market

In 1995, there were an estimated 14.9 million users on the Net. By mid-2002, there were an estimated 150 million, with 64.3 percent of all U.S. households now accessing the medium.[1] The rapid adoption continues internationally as well, with an estimated 445.9 million users worldwide.[2] (See Figure 15-3.) As shown in Figure 15-4, the adoption curve of the Internet greatly outpaces that of

Figure 15-4 Adoption curves for various media—the Web is ramping fast

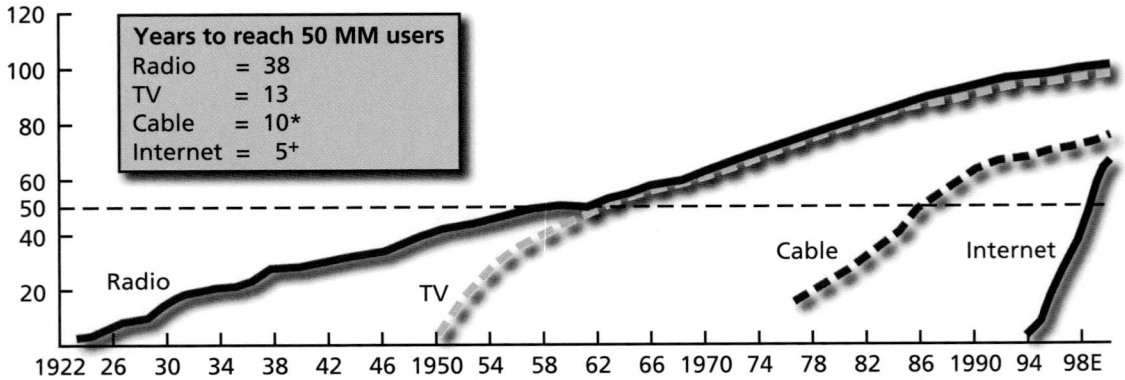

* The launch of HBO in 1976 was used to estimate the beginning of cable as an entertainment/advertising medium. Though cable technology was developed in the late 1940s, its initial use was primarily for the improvement of reception in remote areas. It was not until HBO began to distribute its pay-TV movie service via satellite in 1976 that the medium became a distinct content and advertising alternate to broadcast television.
+ Morgan Stanley Technology Research Estimate

any other medium. A number of reasons have been offered to explain this rapid adoption. A long period of economic prosperity, Internet innovation, heavy investments by companies, and (as noted in the previous chapter) changing lifestyles of the American consumer (consumers are now "money rich and time poor") have all contributed.

The demographic profile of Internet users has changed as well. Whereas in 1996, the Web was clearly a male-dominated medium (82 percent male versus 18 percent female), Internet users are now much more consistent with the profile of the overall U.S. population (Figure 15-5), although persons with more education and more income tend to be online slightly more than others. The use of the Internet for shopping, searching for information about products and services, and buying is predicted to continue to show growth, as indicated in Figure 15-6. Whether the increase in Internet usage and e-commerce will slow or continue to grow at its current pace, it will account for a substantial amount of consumer spending, as can be seen in Figure 15-6.

Users: Business to Business The consumer market figures may seem astronomical enough, but they pale in comparison to the figures on business-to-business marketing. While some consumer companies feel that a website is not a critical component of their communications mix, most business marketers consider a good site a necessity. The number of businesses online is expected to rise to 8.3 million by 2004, with over 100 million business-to-business decision makers online.[3] The revenue generated by these business sites is much higher than that generated in the consumer market—with projections of $6.2 trillion by the year 2004 (yes, that is a *t!*).[4] Businesses in the computer and electronics, shipping and warehousing, and utilities industries expect that by 2004 they will conduct over 70 percent of their transactions over the Internet. (So-called heavy industries like aerospace and defense are expected to transact less than 50 percent through this medium.)

	Adults Online	All Adults
Age:		
18–29	28%	22
30–39	23	22
40–49	23	20
50–64	24	18
65+	5	16
Gender:		
Men	49	48
Women	51	52
Race/Ethnicity:		
White	76	76
Black	12	12
Hispanic	9	10
Education:		
High school or less	37	52
Some college	31	26
College grad/post grad	32	22
Household Income:		
$25,000 or less	18	25
$25,001–$50,000	25	29
$50,001 and over	46	32

Figure 15-5 Profile of U.S. online population, February–March 2002

Figure 15-6 U.S. consumer online buying and shopping grid, 2000–2004 (in millions and percent penetration)

	2000	2001	2002	2003	2004
Shoppers:					
Internet users aged 14+	73.0%	77.0%	79.0%	81.0%	82.0%
Shoppers aged 14+	63.2	83.2	97.5	111.6	123.2
Buyers:					
Internet users aged 14+	48.5%	53.2%	55.8%	58.3%	59.9%
Buyers aged 14+	42.0	57.5	68.9	80.3	90.0
Average annual purchase per online buyer	$969.02	$880.67	$1,089.21	$1,248.48	$1,400.47
Total U.S. B2C e-commerce revenues (incl. online travel)*	$40,700	$50,600	$75,000	$100,300	$126,000

**eMarketer* benchmarks its B2C retail revenue figures against U.S. Department of Commerce data, for which the last period measured was Q4 2001; the travel component was formulated based on aggregated data.

Business-to-business marketers use the Internet in a variety of ways. Hewlett-Packard has budgeted over $100 million to target b-to-b users of its equipment.[5] Cisco and Dell use the Web to track and distribute sales leads in real time, while others like Scientific International train their sales representatives and host sales meetings via the Web as well as sell.[6] Cisco estimates that it saves $1 million per month by having sales meetings on the Web.[7] One of the main benefits for business-to-business marketers is the ability to acquire information about products and services. In today's Internet world, a company can immediately pull up the product and service offerings of a provider, without having to make a phone call or wait for a salesperson to visit. In turn, the same company can reach thousands of potential customers that it would not have been possible to reach without a website—at a significantly reduced cost.

Web Objectives

When major corporations first began to conduct business on the Internet, they put up websites primarily for information purposes. Companies like United Airlines and Maytag had sites that were really not much more than online catalogs designed for information purposes only. The role of the website quickly changed, however; sites have become much more creative, promoting brand images, positioning, and offering promotions, product information, and even products and services for sale. With the introduction of Java in 1995, it became possible to create fancier graphics, audio, and animation online. This resulted in marketers' utilizing the Internet in an entirely new way, moving beyond the purely informational role. As you will see, the objective of disseminating information still remains, but additional communications and sales objectives are now being pursued.

Developing and Maintaining a Website

Before we discuss marketers' Web objectives in detail, it is important that you understand the role of the **website**—the place where information is made available to users of the Internet by the provider. Developing and maintaining a successful website requires significant time and effort. To attract visitors to the site and have them return to it requires a combination of creativity, effective marketing, and continual updating of the site. In addition, other media must be integrated with the website, as noted in the introduction to this chapter.

Exhibit 15-1 Hot Hot Hot founders demonstrate what makes a website work

GOOD FORM

Hot Hot Hot's founders show what makes for a Web site that works:

On the Web, you're instantaneously a global company. So we tried to use colorful graphics that people would understand even if they didn't get all the English. We kept the icons simple—fire coming out of the little guy's mouth means the sauce is really hot. The icon strips take a little longer to download, but they're also pictures of the product listings by category, and the buttons you push to get there. Keeping the graphics horizontal and using only a few colors means they download faster.

Dividing our products into categories—with an icon you can activate for each category—presents the information in a way that's easy for the user to sort through. It would take too long to look through one list of all 125 products on the Web.

Customers' comfort level is very important with on-line ordering—especially when you don't have encryption. We send an electronic-mail confirmation of each order. Maybe 1% of the orders are corrected or canceled by customers at that point.

Netscape: HotHotHot!

HOTHOTHOT

The Net's Coolest Hot Shop

We have one of the largest collections of international hot sauces for you to discover; best of all it's here, online and always available.

GIFTS OF FIRE

Sauces organized by:

HEAT LEVEL

ORIGIN

INGREDIENTS

NAME

Our featured sauce this month is Hot Buns at the Beach.

Check out our latest issue: selected articles from Chile Pepper Magazine.

Be sure to check out our What's New page and our Customer of the Month.

To order a sauce, select Select—we'll keep track of your order for you!

Also, if you ever have any questions or comments, just select

Copyright (c) 1994 Presence and Lobo Enterprises

At a lot of sites, you can get lost; there's no visual continuity. It needs to be simple to move around in, like a catalog, where it's easy to flip back to page two if you want. So there's a graphic on each page to keep the continuity going—like the heat level appearing again at the top of this page. You know you're still in the same catalog. And the icons at the bottom make it easy to get back to where you were.

Hypertext links are what people use to navigate the Web, jumping from page to page by clicking on the highlighted text. You can add hypertext links to external sites as much as you want. But then you're sending people *away* from your site instead of involving them in your catalog. The one or two external links we use are specifically related to our product, rather than just a cool site users might want to see. Internally, we'd like customers to be able to use a hypertext link to go directly to the order form from anywhere in our site. This is one change we'll be making.

Netscape: Hot Level

HEAT LEVEL

Select the icon below to see sauces organized by their heat level.

(for more explanation about our heat scale, please see our Frequently Asked Questions list)

FIERY

EXTRA HOT

HOT

MEDIUM

One of our most Frequently Asked Questions is "What is your hottest sauce?" Well, although there are many contenders for the throne, Dave's clearly stands out. Take a look at it, taste it, and see what we mean.

HEAT ORIGIN INGREDIENTS NAME HOME

Copyright (c) 1994 Presence and Lobo Enterprises

It's important to keep people coming back to the site and to involve them. People were sending us stories about their hot sauces, so we had a contest to pick the best ones and ran those to encourage people to come back. We get lots of requests to carry certain products, and those pay off. The gift pack of four sauces was a customer's idea, and now it's one of our top five best-selling items.

Exhibit 15-1 demonstrates what makes a website work. Making a site work and having one work successfully are not the same thing, however, and whether a site is effective is determined by what it is that management hopes to achieve through the site. As already noted, some sites are offered for informational purposes only (this tends to be more common in the business-to-business market than the consumer market), while others approach the market much more aggressively. For example, Kimberly-Clark Corporation, the manufacturer of Huggies brand (diapers, Pull-Ups training pants, and Little Swimmers swim pants) has been extremely successful in its Internet marketing efforts. The Huggies homepage (Exhibit 15-2) goes well beyond providing information. The site has additional objectives, such as developing a relationship with parents, establishing a brand image for the products, and supporting sales. Part of the site is

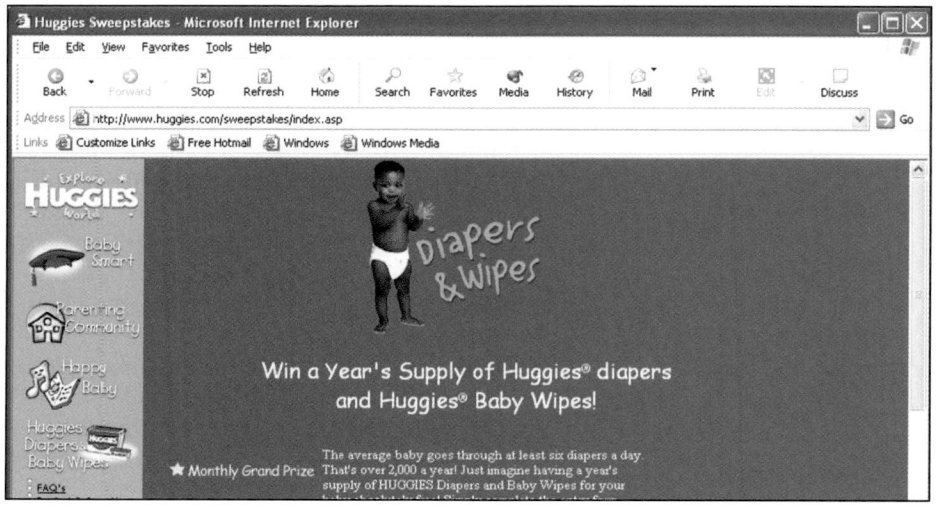

Exhibit 15-2 Huggies homepage

designed to develop one-on-one relationships by offering a free sample to anyone who sends in his or her name, address, and e-mail address. Thousands of people have responded to the offer, providing Kimberly-Clark with an enormous database useful for future marketing efforts. Another part targets parents visiting other websites such as CTW.org (Children's Television Workshop—producer of *Sesame Street*), Women.com, iVillage.com, and BabyZone.com. In addition, anyone typing in the keywords *diapers* or *infant care* on the portal AltaVista is greeted with a Huggies banner ad. To bring visitors to the site, Huggies provides tips on baby care, chats with other parents, access to other baby links, and additional information about Huggies products. Finally, to support sales, the site directs customers to the nearest retail store that sells Huggies brands.

As the Huggies example demonstrates, a website can be an effective tool for the marketer. Depending on the nature of one's business and one's marketing objectives for the Internet, a website can range from being a very simple source of information about the company and its products to being a powerful tool for developing a brand image, sampling, and even generating sales. Following are some of the objectives sought by those marketing on the Internet.

Communications Objectives

Unlike other media discussed thus far in the text, the Internet is actually a hybrid of media. In part, it is a communications medium, allowing companies to create awareness, provide information, and influence attitudes, as well as pursue other communications objectives. But for some it is also a direct-response medium, allowing the user to both purchase and sell products through e-commerce. Thus, we will discuss two sets of objectives pursued by companies that use the Internet. Let's first look at some of the communications objectives these companies want to achieve.

Create Awareness

Advertising on the Web can be useful in creating awareness of an organization as well as its specific product and service offerings. For small companies with limited budgets, the Web offers the opportunity to create awareness well beyond what might be achieved through traditional media. For example, a company in Los Angeles that distributed paper to business-to-business firms in the local market now conducts 80 percent of its business internationally as a result of posting its website. While a valuable tool for creating awareness—particularly for smaller companies that may have limited advertising budgets—the Internet is not likely to be the most effective of the IMC elements for achieving this objective. Advertising may be more useful for this purpose, given its larger reach.

Generate Interest

A visit to CocaCola.com or Snapple.com will demonstrate how companies attempt to use the Web to generate interest in their sites as well as their products and services. On the Coca-Cola site, visitors can find a number of activities to generate and maintain their interests. For example, there is "Coke Music," a click upon which will take you on a musical tour and allow you to create your own demo, take a quiz, and chat with others about music. If your interest is football, you can visit Coke Football Town to see where the Coke football tour is in your state. If your interests tend more to philanthropic events, you can explore the Coke Youth Partnership. While on the site, you can also learn about Coca-Cola products, the company itself, or visit the Coca-Cola Store to purchase Coca-Cola clothing, clocks, and other products. Snapple, in its attempt to attract visitors and hold their interests, has created Snappleton, a make-believe town with many places to visit while learning about Snapple products (Exhibit 15-3). The objectives of these sites is simple: Create interest that will bring visitors back to learn more about the products.

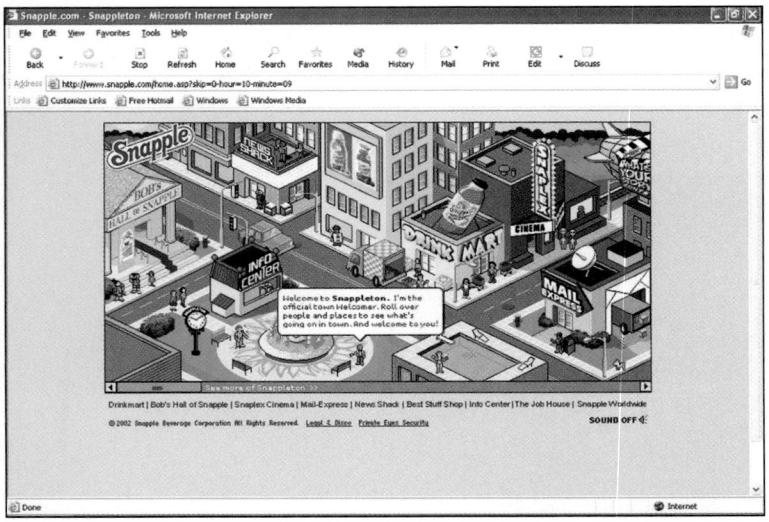

Exhibit 15-3 Snapple creates interest through their website

Disseminate Information One of the primary objectives for using the Web is to provide in-depth information about a company's products and services. In business-to-business markets, having a website has become a necessity, as more and more buyers expect that a company will have a site providing them with detailed information about its offerings. In the government sector, contracts are often put out to bid on the Internet. Information regarding requirements, specifications, submission dates, and so on, is disseminated much quicker, to more potential candidates, and at a much lower cost via the Net than it is through other media. For many consumer companies, their websites serve as a means of communicating more information about their products and services. The Huggies site discussed earlier shows how a website can facilitate this objective, while the Cheerios box shown in Exhibit 15-4 demonstrates how General Mills uses its package to refer users to its site for additional information.

Exhibit 15-4 Cheerios uses its package to send users to its homepage

Create an Image Many websites are designed to reflect the image a company wants to portray (Exhibit 15-5). For example, when you have a few minutes to spare, check out the consumer sites at www.fubu.com and www.akademiks.com or the business-to-business site at www.sharp.com (Exhibit 15-6). All of these are excellent examples of websites used for image building. Interestingly, one of the difficulties traditional marketers have experienced is that of creating a brand image on the Internet. While some of these companies have been successful, others have not fared as well and have come to realize that branding and image-creating strategies must be specifically adapted to this medium.

Create a Strong Brand As David Aaker pointed out in the introduction to this chapter, the Internet—as part of an integrated marketing communications program—can be a useful tool for branding. Unfortunately, many companies have not yet figured out how to successfully brand through the Internet. A review of the literature over the past five years will lead to a number of articles discussing this very topic and the difficulties in achieving this objective. While space does not permit an in-depth review, let's discuss just a few of the many reasons why companies attempting to create branding through the Internet may not be achieving their goals.

Branding Is a Complicated Process While creating a strong brand is not easy in any communications effort, some marketers feel that it may be even more difficult to do on the Internet. As noted by Karen Benezra, editor of *Brandweek* magazine,

Exhibit 15-5 Sean John uses the Web to establish an image

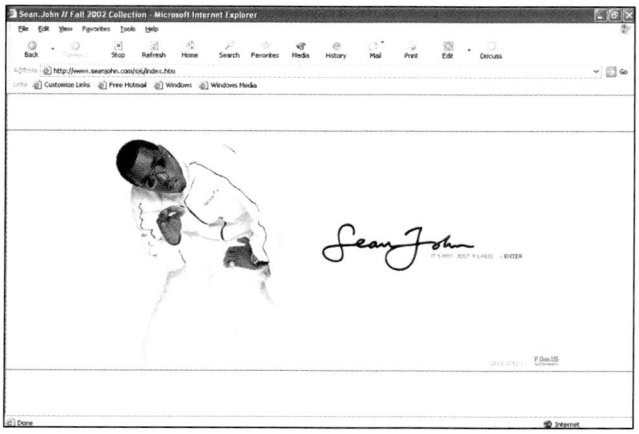

Exhibit 15-6 Sharp uses the Web to enhance its image

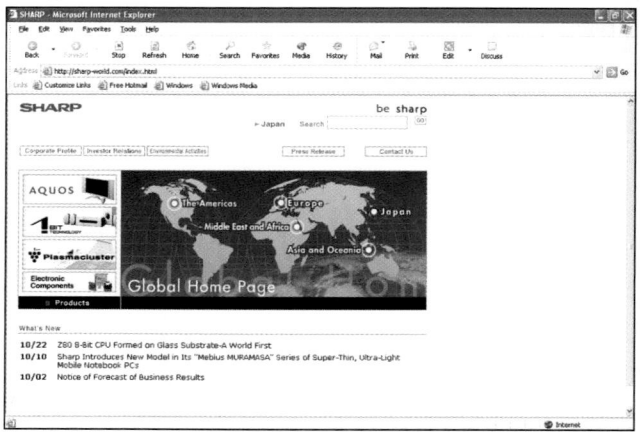

many companies—dot-coms as well as traditional—have spent millions of dollars trying to brand by advertising on the Internet, with only lukewarm success. One reason behind this problem, Benezra notes, is the lack of a clear understanding of the role the Web should assume in the branding process. New or less well known brands may have to assume different strategies than those used by more established brands such as Volvo, BMW, or The Gap. Another reason is that many marketers mistakenly believe that simply creating awareness or attention will lead to a strong brand. Finally, notes Benezra, it takes a long time to establish a brand relationship with a customer, and the Internet hasn't been around long enough to prove its branding capabilities.[8]

Branding and Direct Response May Be Counterobjectives Noting the similarities between the Internet and other direct-response media like catalogs or interactive TV, some marketers feel that the Internet is best suited to be a direct-response medium. They contend that direct marketing requires a very targeted effort, searching for high-probability buyers. Branding, on the other hand, is much less targeted and reaches out to numerous audiences. According to Erwin Ephron of *Advertising Age,* the Internet is somewhere in between, and trying to achieve both objectives at the same time has led to unsuccessful branding efforts.[9]

The Costs Are Too High Successful branding does not take place overnight. Unfortunately, many marketers aren't willing, or feel that they can't afford, to wait. Such marketers may view the Internet as a "quick fix" that will allow them to instantly establish their brands. When they discover that the Internet is not able to provide instant identity, they may quickly return to their focus on ROI or the bottom line. Cutting advertising and brand identity efforts on the Internet will immediately reflect cost savings and a return to business as normal.[10]

The above are just a few of many reasons that can be offered as to why branding on the Internet has been less successful than many hoped. We believe that the Internet—as part of an integrated marketing communications program—can be used for branding purposes, as well as for other objectives. IMC Perspective 15-1 provides just a few examples of companies that have used this medium effectively, by integrating media.

Stimulate Trial

Many marketers have found the Internet to be an effective medium for stimulating trial of their products or services. Some websites offer electronic coupons in an attempt to stimulate trial of their products. Others offer samples, promotions, and sweepstakes designed to encourage trial.

E-Commerce

The Internet also offers the opportunity to sell directly to customers in both the consumer market and the business-to-business market. This direct selling of goods and services has been labeled **e-commerce.** Many of the sites already mentioned in this chapter have a sales component—either as a primary or secondary goal.

Many companies maintain their existing "brick and mortar" stores while also selling through the Internet. Consumer-targeted companies like Eddie Bauer, The Gap, and Barnes and Noble are a few examples. Sears allows online visitors to Sears.com to choose from 4 million parts and carries schematics of 90,000 items. The items carry the same prices as they do in the stores and can be picked up at and returned to the stores as well.[11] Circuit City has a similar program. Others like Amazon.com, eBay.com, and E-toys.com maintain Internet sites only (Exhibit 15-7).

We will discuss more about e-commerce and strategies employed in this area a little later in the chapter. Before we do, let's have a look at how the Internet can be used as part of an IMC program.

Exhibit 15-7 eBay is a very popular Internet site

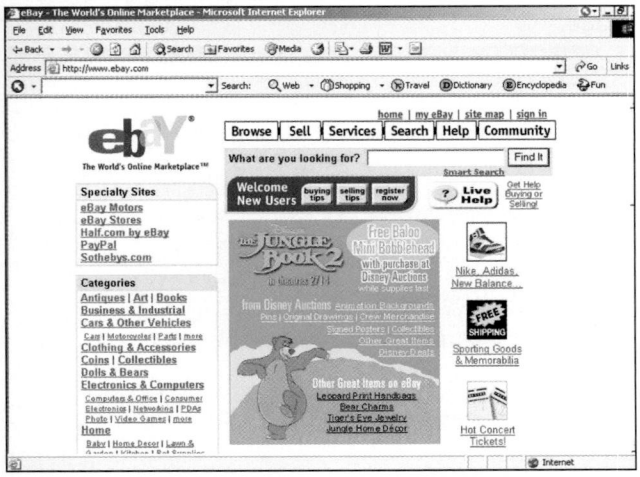

IMC PERSPECTIVE 15-1

Integrating the Internet—TV Commercials Hit the Web

As the Internet moves beyond being a direct-response medium, assuming additional marketing objectives such as branding, the format of the communications are changing as well. Knowing that banner ads and interstitials may not be doing the job, electronic marketers are turning to an old reliable—the TV commercial. Only now, the TV commercial is on the Web. As the technology on the Internet improves, more and more marketers have taken their commercials to the Web hoping to attract viewers' attention and interest. Traditional advertisers and their agencies like the idea, because they are used to dealing with commercials and the costs are lower than those for TV. While the idea of delivering commercials via websites is not new—now defunct PointCast and Excite@Home have done it for a few years—the poor quality led many advertisers to shy away from the medium. But all that is changing.

Take Apple Computers as an example. With its latest "Switch" campaign, designed to attract Windows users to the Macintosh camp, Apple has taken the integration of TV and the Web to a new level. Eight 30-second TV spots created by TBWA/Chiat/Day and directed by Errol Morris (director of the movie *The Thin Blue Line*) feature regular people talking about their switch from Windows to Macintosh—and, of course, about how happy they are for having done so. The $75 million ad campaign has been integrated with a new Apple website (apple.com/switch) by directing viewers to the site for more information. That's nothing new. But once at the site, consumers can actually view the TV commercials (the IMC program also includes print). The commercials appear in the same quality as they would on TV, and they have become a big hit—in one case creating a new crush named Ellen Feiss, whose homework was eaten by a PC.

Apple is not the only one integrating TV and the Internet in this manner. PepsiCo featured a Britney Spears spot on its site nearly a year before Apple added its commercials, and Universal Pictures used its website to promote its movie *A Beautiful Mind.* A video ad for the movie *Collateral Damage* was shown on the *Los Angeles Times* website, the city of New York ran commercials to promote New York City on the *New York Times* website, and the New York Stock Exchange ran digital ads on the website of *The Wall Street Journal.* Automobile companies like Toyota and Volvo have also run spots, as has Porsche in the introduction of its new SUV, the Cayenne. The CBS MarketWatch site estimated that as many as 75 percent of the campaigns run on its site in 2002 would include commercials.

But the real question is, "Will consumers watch the commercials?" Skeptics argue that consumers are watching fewer commercials on television and are probably less likely to watch commercials on their computers. Amicada, one of the companies offering the technology to deliver high-quality commercials, thinks they will watch them—particularly if other traditional methods are also employed. Amicada suggests a permission-based program coupled with incentives (gaining points for watching) and access to premium content and entertaining video content such as music videos or movie previews that would include the ads. Viewers would get credit only when they viewed the entire commercial, which would be tracked using Internet technology. Advertisers would pay only for the commercials watched—$1 for each CPCV (Amicada's equivalent of CPM). While some advertisers are not sold on the CPCV concept (Greg Smith of Carat Interactive, in New York, considers it arm twisting), they do seem to like the permission-based and pay-for-performance aspects. With a number of large companies now showing commercials on TV and the Internet, can others be far behind?

Sources: Mylene Mangalindan, "Now TV Ads Are in Reruns on Web Sites," *The Wall Street Journal,* Feb. 11, 2002, p. B5; Aaron Baar, "Porsche SUV Entry Teases with Web, Print Effort," adweek.com, Apr. 29, 2002, pp. 1-2; Thom Weidlich, "Online Spots—a New Generation," *Advertising Age,* July 30, 2001, p. S10; John Schwartz, "Out-of-It Eyebrow Lift Gives Apple a Superstar," *New York Times,* Aug. 19, 2002, p. 3; Theresa Howard, "PC Users Make the Switch in Mac Ads; Apple Launches $75M Campaign to Nab Some of Microsoft's Market," *USA Today,* June 11, 2002, p. B2.

The Internet and Integrated Marketing Communications

Up to this point, we have mentioned the need for using the Internet as part of an IMC program. In this section, we discuss how the Web can be used with other program elements.

Exhibit 15-8 Banner ad formats

Advertising

Advertising on the Internet

Like broadcast or print, the Internet is an advertising medium. Companies and organizations working to promote their products and services must consider this medium as they would television, magazines, outdoor, and so on. Advertising on the Internet employs a variety of forms, as shown in Figure 15-7.

Banners The most common form of advertising on the Web is **banner ads.** Banner ads may be used for creating awareness or recognition or for direct-marketing objectives. Banner ads may take on a variety of forms, as shown in Exhibit 15-8, as well as a number of names such as *side panels, skyscrapers,* or *verticals.* Initially banner ads constituted the vast majority of advertising on the Net, but studies indicating their questionable effectiveness have led to a decline in usage. Reports on click-through rates vary, but most studies indicate a less than 1 percent response rate.[12] A few studies have shown an increase in response rates in recent years. These findings may lead to increased use of this method of advertising in the future.[13]

Sponsorships Another common form of advertising is **sponsorships.** There are two types of sponsorships. *Regular sponsorships* occur when a company pays to sponsor a section of a site, for example, Clairol's sponsorship of a page on GirlsOn.com and Intuit's Turbo Tax sponsorship of a page on Netscape's financial section. A more involved agreement is the **content sponsorship,** in which the sponsor not only provides dollars in return for name association but participates in providing the content itself. In some cases, the site is responsible for providing content and having it approved by the sponsor; in other instances, the sponsor may contribute all or part of the content. Due in part to the lack of effectiveness of banner ads, sponsorships have been increasing in popularity. Notice the number of partners on the iVillage site in Exhibit 15-9—each of which provides content.

Pop-Ups/Pop-Unders When you access the Internet, have you ever seen a small window appear on Netscape advertising AOL's "Instant Messenger"? Such windows

Exhibit 15-9 iVillage has numerous Internet partners

Figure 15-7 Way Beyond the Banner. New online ad formats are whirling, shaking, popping, and tilting all over the Web.

Ad Format	Cost* (CPM)	Effective-ness	Annoyance Factor	Pros	Cons	Check It Out
Banner Standard rectangular ad still found atop most webpages	$6–$60	•	•	Much, much cheaper than ever before, and clickthrough rates have rebounded	Average clickthrough rate: just 0.75%	Any commercial website
Floating ad or *shoshkele* Animated object, like a car that races across your screen	$25–$35	••••	••••	Can be amusing and attention-getting	They work only with the latest Web browsers	www.unitedvirtualities.com
Interstitial or *superstitial* Full page ad, often with video or animation	$30–45	••••	••••	Unavoidable; can accommodate movie trailers and TV spots	Web users complain that ads take over the screen	www.unicast.com
Large rectangle Oversize ad placed in the center of the page	$10–$85	••	•••	Ideal for news outlets, where readers don't want to leave website	Average clickthrough rate: 1% to 1.5%	www.news.com
Pop-under Ad opens in a win-down under the webpage	$2–$5	••	••••	Low cost; intrusive	72.4% of people close the ads without reading them	www.latimes.com
Pop-up Ad opens in a window on top of the webpage	$10–$75	•••	•••••	Highly intrusive	Highly intrusive	www.hollywood.com
Skyscraper Vertical banner	$5–$75	••	••	In tests, raise brand awareness 7%	On small screens, reader's can't see ads	www.americangreetings.com
Superbanner Twice as wide as a standard banner	$6–$35	••	•••	20% higher clickthrough than banners	0.9%? That's still pretty low	www.yahoo.com
Surround session Users are served ads from one advertiser during their entire visit to a site	$90–$115	••••	••	Raise brand awareness 11%, nearly three times more than banner ads do	Costly	www.nytimes.com
Text ad No-frills, text-only ad that appears alongside search results	$20–$80	•••••	•	Average clickthrough: 2% on Google	No graphics	www.google.com

*Prices are measured in cost per 1,000 impressions (CPM) and are based on ranges found in published rate cards; negotiated rates may be much lower.
Adapted from: Bus. 2.0 June 2002, p. 120.

are known as **pop-ups,** and they often appear when you access a certain site. Pop-ups are usually larger than a banner ad but smaller than a full screen.

Pop-unders are ads that appear underneath the web page and become visible only when the user leaves the site. For example, if you ever visited a travel website, you probably were hit with a pop-under ad for Orbitz—one of the heaviest users of this form of web advertising. Go to the *Los Angeles Times* website, and when you leave, you will almost certainly see an example of this form of advertising.

While some companies like Orbitz believe that pop-ups and pop-unders are effective forms of advertising, others disagree. Consumer complaints have led Google.com, iVillage.com, and Earthlink (among others) to no longer accept these advertising forms. (According to iVillage, its research indicates that as many as 90 percent of its users dislike such ads.) Nevertheless, indications are that despite the annoying qualities of pop-ups and pop-unders, more and more websites are offering this type of advertising.

Interstitials **Interstitials** are ads that appear on your screen while you are waiting for a site's content to download. Although some advertisers believe that interstitials are irritating and more of a nuisance than a benefit, a study conducted by Grey Advertising found that only 15 percent of those surveyed felt that the ads were irritating (versus 9 percent for banner ads) and that 47 percent liked the ads (versus 38 percent for banners). Perhaps more importantly, while ad recall of banner ads was approximately 51 percent, recall of interstitials was much higher, at 76 percent. Recently, Acura introduced its Integra Type R model using an interstitial. Coca-Cola, TriStar, and Macy's commonly employ this ad form.

Push Technologies **Push technologies,** or **webcasting** technologies, allow companies to "push" a message to consumers rather than waiting for them to find it. Push technologies dispatch web pages and news updates and may have sound and video geared to specific audiences and even individuals. For example, a manager whose job responsibilities involve corporate finance might log on to his or her computer and find new stories are automatically there on the economy, stock updates, or a summary of a speech by Alan Greenspan. Companies provide screen savers that automatically "hook" the viewer to their sites for sports, news, weather reports, and/or other information that the viewer has specified. Users can use **personalization**—that is, they can personalize their sites to request the kinds of specific information they are most interested in viewing. For example, if you are into college sports, you can have updates sent to you through sites providing college sports information. The service is paid for by advertisers who flash their messages on the screen.

Links While considered by some as not a type of advertising, **links** serve many of the same purposes as are served by the types discussed above. For example, a visitor to one site may click on a link that provides additional information and/or related materials at another site. At the bottom of the homepage at women.com are a number of links to magazines, including *Cosmopolitan* and *Good Housekeeping* among others. Clicking on one of these takes you to the magazine's site and usually a pop-up for a subscription to the magazine appears.

Other forms of advertising, such as ads placed in chat rooms, are also available. Given the limited use of many of these alternatives, we suggest the reader consult additional resources for more information.

Exhibit 15-10 Pepsi uses sales promotions on the Web

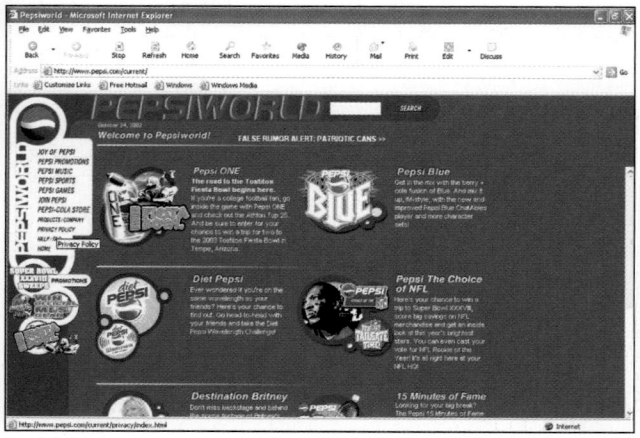

Sales Promotion on the Internet

Companies have found the Internet to be a very effective medium for disseminating sales promotions. As noted earlier, Huggies ties in the use of sales promotions with its website. Other examples such as GMC's special financing offers, Pontiac Vibe's announcements of events, and PepsiCo's use of sweepstakes and contests (Exhibit 15-10) are just a few of many. Levis has used

the net for a variety of promotions including contests, Internet films and Super Bowl tie-ins.

Personal Selling on the Internet

The Internet has been both a benefit and a detriment to many of those involved in personal selling—particularly those in the business-to-business market. For some, the Internet has been a threat that might take away job opportunities. Companies have found that they can remain effective—even increase effectiveness—by building a strong Web presence. The high-cost and poor-reach disadvantages of personal selling are allowing these companies to reduce new hires and even cut back on their existing sales forces.

On the positive side, websites have been used quite effectively to enhance and support the selling effort. As noted earlier, the Web has become a primary source of information for millions of customers in the consumer and business-to-business markets. Visitors to websites can gain volumes of information about a company's products and services. In return, the visitors become a valuable resource for leads that both internal and external salespersons can follow up, and they become part of a prospect database. Not only can potential customers learn about the company's offerings, but the selling organization can serve and qualify prospects more cost-effectively.

The Web can also be used to stimulate trial. For many companies, personal salespersons can reach only a fraction of the potential customer base. Through trial demonstrations and/or samples offered online, customers can determine if the offering satisfies their needs and if so request a personal sales call. In such cases both parties benefit from time and cost savings.

Some companies have used the Internet to improve their one-on-one relationships with customers. By providing more information in a more timely and efficient manner, a company enables customers to learn more about what it has to offer. This increases the opportunity for cross-selling and customer retention. For example, Neoforma.com links hospitals and medical supply vendors with listings of 300,000 medical products, with pages describing separate product categories.[14] For those interested in medical products, the site has become a one-stop shopping center (Exhibit 15-11). In addition, by providing a website, companies can improve their response times to inquiries as well as complaints, thereby improving customer service.

In a well-designed IMC program, the Internet and personal selling are designed to be complementary tools—working together to increase sales. It appears that more and more companies are coming to this realization.

Public Relations on the Internet

As with other media, the Internet is a useful medium for conducting public relations activities. Many sites devote a portion of their content to public relations activities, including the provision of information about the company, its philanthropic activities, annual reports, and so on. Shel Holtz, in his book *Public Relations on the Internet,* notes that the public relations industry has been slow to adopt the Internet. Some of the more traditional public relations organizations do not use the Net at all, while most others use it primarily as a tool for disseminating information. Holtz notes that the Web offers a number of opportunities to public relations practitioners, including: (1) the development of media relations websites, (2) the ability to provide customized information dissemination, and (3) the development of positive e-mail relationships.

One example of the use of public relations on the Internet is provided by Chrysler. Working with reporters, Chrysler developed a one-stop information source for the media (the public could also use the site, but reporters would have to register to use the "newsroom"). News stories and other forms of content, photo images, and cross-references to other sites or media were included on the site,

Exhibit 15-11 Neoforma sells products on the net

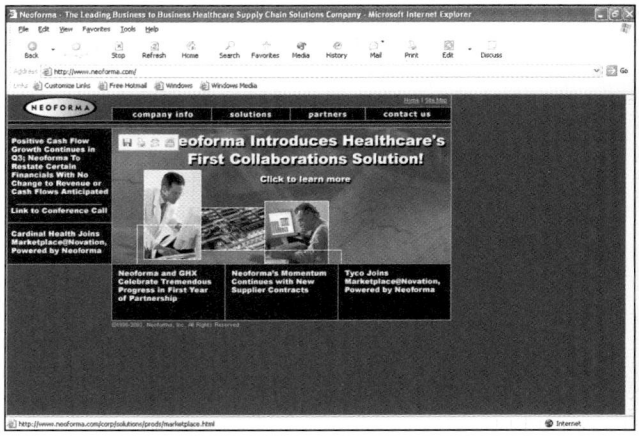

Exhibit 15-12 Chrysler provides public relations information on its site

as were press kits and a calendar of upcoming events (Exhibit 15-12). The objective of the site was to improve relations with the press, and Chrysler was quite effective in doing so. In addition, Chrysler's newsroom contains many of the articles written about the corporation, including awards won and philanthropic efforts such as its $10 million support for children of the victims of the September 11 terrorist attack.

Other examples of effective use of public relations activities on the Internet are also available, as you will see in the chapter on public relations. The Web is a useful medium for conducting public relations activities, and its use for this function is on the increase.

At the same time, many philanthropic and nonprofit organizations have found the Internet to be a useful way to generate funds. Several sites have developed to perform the functions that are required in traditional fund-raising programs. For example, Ben and Jerry's uses its website to express concerns about dioxin and forced child labor as well as its support for the Red Cross and other charities. Other sites have been formed to handle public relations activities for charitable organizations, provide information regarding the causes the charity supports, collect contributions, and so on. In an example of integrating the Internet with public relations and television, Youth AIDS has initiated a Public Service campaign featuring artists like Alicia Keyes, Destiny's Child, and others to direct 15- to 24-year-olds to its website www.youthAIDS.org to learn more about the disease and contribute to the cause.

Direct Marketing on the Internet

Our discussion of direct marketing and the Internet will approach the topic from two perspectives: the use of direct-marketing tools for communications objectives (as discussed in Chapter 14), and e-commerce. As we stated previously, many direct-marketing tools like direct mail, infomercials, and the like, have been adapted to the Internet, as you will see. At the same time, e-commerce—selling directly to the consumer via the Internet—has become an industry of its own.

Direct Mail

Direct mail on the Internet (e-mail) is essentially an electronic version of regular mail. Like regular mail it is highly targeted, relies heavily on lists, and attempts to reach consumers with specific needs through targeted messages. As we discussed earlier under personalization, consumers can opt to have specific types of e-mail sent to them and other types not sent. For example, if you permit, The *New York Times* will e-mail you information about specific promotions, articles that will appear, books on sale, and other items that you might purchase from it.

Sometimes users may also receive less targeted and unwanted e-mails. The electronic equivalent of junk mail, these messages are referred to as **SPAM.** (One e-mail-filtering company estimates that as many as 25 percent of all e-mails are SPAM.)[15] U.S. companies spent $927 million on e-mail ads in 2001, up 87 percent from

2000.[16] Because of the high volumes of SPAM that have been sent, and the fact that many consumers consider it a nuisance, the U.S. government has passed laws regulating its use.

Catalog-oriented companies like Lands' End have also increased their use of electronic media. Lands' End sells more apparel online than any other retailer ($327 million in 2001); online sales constitute 21 percent of its total revenues. Interestingly, unlike many other e-mail marketers, the company does not use SPAM. It sends messages only to those who have agreed to receive them—an indication that junk mailing may not be necessary to be successful.[17] (See Exhibit 15-13.) The company recently aired television commercials to promote the ease and efficiency of using its online catalog, and sent customers in its existing database direct-mail pieces informing them of the same. In turn, many e-marketing companies now send out print catalogs to promote their sites.

While many consumers don't like SPAM or other forms of e-mail, studies have shown the effectiveness of e-mails. A study by Abacus indicated that in 2001 the value of online transactions increased by 47 percent while that of off-line catalogs remained the same. According to the study, the number of persons who received a catalog off-line and then ordered online increased by 7 percent.[18]

Exhibit 15-13 Lands' End is an effective Internet user

Infomercials Yes, even the infomercial has discovered the Net. The same people who brought you "Amazing Discoveries" infomercials on television now produce infomercials for the Internet (and they are not alone). One such infomercial, by iMall, a company based in Provo, Utah, runs marketing seminars on how to make money on the Internet. Other companies are expected to follow. Does this mean we will soon see FlowBees on the Web?

E-Commerce E-commerce, or direct sales on the Internet, has truly taken off. Online spending for the fourth quarter was expected to reach $19.6 billion, a 23 percent gain over 2001.[19]

While more and more consumers buy online, consumer sales are only about one-fifth of those by business-to-business marketers. B-to-b sales are expected to be over $6 trillion by 2004.[20] Many business-to-business companies like Applied Industrial Technologies, National SemiConductor, and Xerox have also found success in the world of e-commerce.

Home Shopping Channels In the direct-marketing chapter, we mentioned that QVC has taken its home shopping TV channel to the Internet in the form of iQVC. HSN also has an Internet shopping channel. In fall 2002, buy.com (the Internet-only company) announced that it would be initiating a new shopping channel on television.

Measuring Effectiveness of the Internet

Companies measuring the effectiveness of the Internet employ a variety of methods, most of which can be done electronically. As you will see in a moment, a number of companies provide Internet measures as part of a package; that is, they provide audience measurement information (demographics, psychographics, etc.) as "up-front' information, as well as some of the effectiveness measures described below. First, we will discuss some of the measures used to determine the effectiveness of a website. Then, we will discuss some of the companies providing these measures.

Audience Measures and Measures of Effectiveness

You will see that while the Internet industry has developed its own measures of effectiveness, there are some problems with these measures that must be considered when employing them. In an attempt to respond to criticism of the audience metrics employed, as well as to standardize some of the measures used to gauge effectiveness

Figure 15-8 IAB Guidelines for Internet measurement

Ad impression. This is a measurement of responses from an ad delivery system to an ad request from the user's browser.

Click. This measure includes three forms: click-through, in-unit click and mouse-over. A *click-through* occurs when the viewer clicks on the ad to have information sent to him or her. The *in-unit click* and the *mouse-over* are ad interactions without the content being sent to the viewer.

Visit. A *visit* is defined as "one or more text and/or graphics downloads from a site qualifying as at least one page, without 30 consecutive minutes of inactivity, which can be reasonably attributed to a single browser for a single session." The browser must "pull" text or graphic content to be considered a visit.

Unique measurement (browsers, visitors, and users). This is the number of actual individual people, within a designated reporting timeframe, with activity consisting of one or more visits to a site or the delivery of pushed content. A unique user can be either (1) an actual individual who accesses a site (*unique visitor*) or (2) an actual individual who is pushed content and/or ads such as e-mail, newsletters, interstitials, and pop-up or pop-under ads. Each individual is counted only once in the unique-user or visitor measure for the reporting period. When no attempt is made to estimate the number of unique users based on the number of unique cookies received, the measure should be referred to as *unique browsers.*

Page impression. This is a measurement of the responses from a web server to a page request from the user's browser. Pagelike items should be counted as follows:

- Pop-ups—ad impressions
- Interstitials—ad impressions
- Pop-unders—ad impressions
- HTML newsletters (if opened)—page impressions (if ad only—ad impressions)
- Auto-refreshed pages—page impressions
- Frames—page impressions

of the Internet, the Internet Advertising Bureau (IAB)—the largest and most influential trade group—combined with eight prominent Web publishers and two technology firms (in total representing nearly two-thirds of all industry revenue) to conduct research on these methods. In 2002 their report was completed, and the group created voluntary guidelines intended to make uniform the various incompatible systems that evaluate effectiveness of Internet advertisements. The guidelines included five measures that would allow for independent auditing and verification (Figure 15-8). It is believed that the adoption of these guidelines, along with objective auditing, will make the Internet a more attractive medium for many of those who advertise in traditional media. Figure 15-9 shows the frequency of use of these measures among the research agencies participating.

The measures suggested do not include a commonly employed method referred to as *hits*—the number of times that a specific component of a site is requested. Hits could include 100 people making one request each or one person making 100 requests. As a measure of communication effectiveness, hits have generally been considered a weak metric. Thus, while some may still track hits, many companies have abandoned this measure or place little emphasis on it.

Information on users is typically collected robotically by a **cookie,** an electronic device attached to your file (usually without your knowing it) that collects information on where you visit, how many times you visit, where you click, and the like. Due in part to weaknesses in previously employed measures and advertisers' desire for additional information, a number of other measures are now being employed, including the ones discussed below.

Online Measuring A joint venture between IntelliQuest and Millward Brown has led to a research tool employing online measuring that collects information regard-

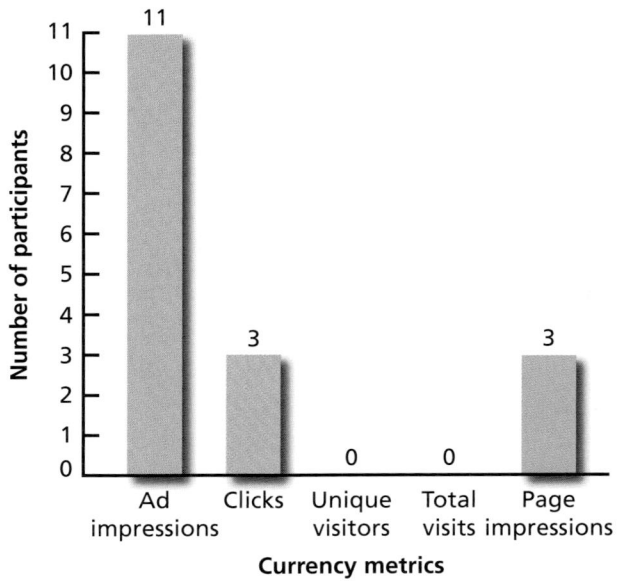

Figure 15-9 Use of metrics by participating companies

ing demographics, psychographics, location of Web access, media usage, and buying habits. Clients can determine who saw their ads, determine reach, and ascertain whether the right target audience was reached. Advertisers can test the impact of their messages, receiving a report detailing impressions and clicks by time of day and day of the week.

In another joint venture, Amazon.com paid $250 million in stock to acquire Alexa, a little-known service. The service tracks what sites are on the Internet and where, as well as who, goes to them. The appeal of Alexa is that it goes beyond "cookies," which don't track a user's other Web visits. Alexa collects data on all Web activity by any user who signs up for it. Measures as to how much traffic a site gets, whether users like the site, and where they go next are all reported. The database is already twice the size of all the printed matter in the Library of Congress.[21]

Recall and Retention Ipsos-ASI performs 20,000 continuous daily interviews with Web users to determine recall and whether viewers remember the ads they see, as well as whether there is a "halo-effect" among ads.

Surveys Survey research, conducted both online and through traditional methods, is employed to determine everything from site usage to attitudes toward a site. Brand Optics tracks responses of Internet users to ads, e-mails, and other communications using cookies and surveys to track effectiveness.

Sales Of course, for the e-commerce marketers, a prime indicator of effectiveness is the number of sales generated. Adding information regarding demographics, user behaviors, and so on, can increase the effectiveness of this measure.

Tracking Some companies now offer more traditional tracking measures. For example, Dynamic Logic, Inc., provides information such as brand awareness, ad recall, message association, and purchase intent.

The above measures reveal that the Internet has its own set of criteria for measuring effectiveness and is also borrowing from traditional measures—for example, brand recall is becoming a major area of focus.[22] In 2002 the Association of Advertising Agencies and the Association of National Advertisers announced a system called *Advertising Digital Identification (Ad-Id).* Ad-Id assigns advertising across all media a specific media code to facilitate cross-media buys. The goal of the coalition is to develop cross-media standards employing reach/frequency comparisons that include

the Internet. Many of the companies that provide research information in traditional media (Nielsen, Ipsos-ASI) are now extending their reach into the Internet world. Others (MediaMetrics, Forrester) have developed measures specifically for online users. Academics are also beginning to publish articles related to measuring effectiveness on the Internet. Studies on consumers' attitudes toward a site, response variations in e-mail surveys, and similarities between brick-and-mortar retailing and e-commerce are just a few of the many articles being published in academic journals to advance the measurement of the Internet.[23]

Unfortunately, not all of the methods used to measure Internet activity and effectiveness are accurate. We discuss some of these later in this chapter, under disadvantages of the Internet.

Sources of Measurement Data

The number of sources available that provide information about the Internet is enormous. Below we provide a partial list just to give you some indication of the types of information available. Most of the companies listed are the largest and/or most cited sources, and the list is by no means intended to be exhaustive:

- *Arbitron.* Arbitron provides demographic, media usage, and lifestyle data on users of the Internet as well as other interactive media.
- *MRI* and *SMRB.* Both of these companies (discussed in Chapter 10) now provide information regarding viewership profiles for the Internet and other interactive media. Nielsen offers similar data.
- *Audit Bureau of Circulations.* This print agency is developing a product called WebFacts to certify Web counts.
- *Interactive Advertising Bureau (IAB).* A trade organization of the Internet, IAB provides information on statistics, usage, and strategies regarding the Internet.
- *eMarketer.* This company publishes comparative data from various research sources and explains the different methods used to arrive at the projections. It also publishes its own projections.
- *Nielsen Net Ratings.* Nielsen provides audience information and analyses based on click-by-click Internet behavior through a meter installed on users' computers at home and work.
- *Jupiter MediaMetrics, Inc.* Previously separate companies, Jupiter, PC Meter, and MediaMetrics have joined to provide statistics and website information, including data on users, projections, trends, and so on.
- *Business 2.0* and *Fast Company.* These business-to-business magazines target persons interested in the Internet, from both a technological and a business perspective, with emphasis on the latter.
- *Internet Advertising Report and office.com.* Both these organizations provide an online newsletter containing information on trends, statistics, and other articles of interest to Internet users. The latter focuses on the business community.

Advantages and Disadvantages of the Internet

A number of advantages of the Internet can be cited:

1. *Target marketing.* A major advantage of the Web is the ability to target very specific groups of individuals with a minimum of waste coverage. For those in the business-to-business market, the Internet resembles a combination trade magazine and trade show, as only those most interested in the products and/or services a site has to offer will visit the site (others have little or no reason to do so). In the consumer market, through personalization and other targeting techniques, sites are becoming more tailored to meet one's needs and wants.

2. *Message tailoring.* As a result of precise targeting, messages can be designed to appeal to the specific needs and wants of the target audience. The interactive capabili-

ties of the Net make it possible to carry on one-to-one marketing with increased success in both the business and the consumer markets.

3. *Interactive capabilities.* Because the Internet is interactive, it provides strong potential for increasing customer involvement and satisfaction and almost immediate feedback for buyers and sellers. A recent study indicated that as many as 47 percent of Internet users multitask.[24] As multitasking increases, the interactive capabilities of the Internet will make this medium even more attractive.

4. *Information access.* Perhaps the greatest advantage of the Internet is its availability as an information source. Internet users can find a plethora of information about almost any topic of their choosing merely by conducting a search through one of the search engines. Once they have visited a particular site, users can garner a wealth of information regarding product specifications, costs, purchase information, and so on. Links will direct them to even more information if it is desired.

5. *Sales potential.* The numbers provided earlier in this chapter demonstrate the incredible sales numbers being generated in both the business-to-business and the consumer segments. Forecasts are for continued growth in the future.

6. *Creativity.* Creatively designed sites can enhance a company's image, lead to repeat visits, and positively position the company or organization in the consumer's mind. Visit some of the sites mentioned earlier to see what we mean.

7. *Exposure.* For many smaller companies, with limited budgets, the World Wide Web enables them to gain exposure to potential customers that heretofore would have been impossible. For a fraction of the investment that would be required using traditional media, companies can gain national and even international exposure in a timely manner.

8. *Speed.* For those requesting information on a company, its products, and/or its service offerings, the Internet is the quickest means of acquiring this information.

9. *Complement to IMC.* The Net both complements and is complemented by other IMC media. As such, it serves as a vital link in the integrative process.

While it is a potentially effective medium, the Internet also has its disadvantages:

1. *Measurement problems.* One of the greatest disadvantages of the Internet is the lack of reliability of the research numbers generated. A quick review of forecasts, audience profiles, and other statistics offered by research providers will demonstrate a great deal of variance—leading to a serious lack of validity and reliability. One company mentioned earlier, eMarketer, has attempted to reconcile such differences and explain the reasoning for the discrepancies (differences in methodologies employed), but the problem still exists. One of the industry's largest and most cited trade publications has written an exposé of a heavily cited Internet research company, referring to the numbers it provides as "scary."[25] Others have stressed concerns over the fact that most site's figures are not audited, which may lead to rampant cheating in respect to the numbers reported.[26] The recent actions taken by the IAB to standardize metrics will help in reducing some of this problem. But due to difficulties involved in both measuring and forecasting in this medium, it remains necessary to proceed with caution when using these numbers.

2. *Websnarl.* At times, downloading information from the Net takes a long time. When there are a number of users, the time increases and some sites may be inaccessible due to too many visitors. For many users who expect speed, this is a major disadvantage. Broadband is helping to reduce this problem.

3. *Clutter.* As the number of ads proliferates, the likelihood of one ad's being noticed drops accordingly. The result is that some ads may not get noticed, and some consumers may become irritated by the clutter. Some studies already show that banner ads may be losing effectiveness for this very reason.

4. *Potential for deception.* The Center for Media Education has referred to the Web as "a web of deceit" in regard to attempts of advertisers to target children with subtle advertising messages. The Center, among others, has asked the government to regulate the Internet. In addition, data collection without consumers' knowledge and

permission, hackers, and credit card theft are a number of problems confronting the Internet.

5. *Privacy.* Like their direct-marketing counterparts, Internet marketers must be careful not to impinge upon the privacy of users. The IAB has issued a policy on privacy that it asks companies to abide by (see www.iab.net).

6. *Limited production quality.* Although it is improving, net advertising does not offer the capabilities of many competitive media from a production standpoint. While the advent of advanced technologies and rich media is narrowing the gap, the Net still lags behind some traditional media in this area.

7. *Poor reach.* While the Internet numbers are growing in leaps and bounds, its reach is still far behind that of television. As a result, as discussed earlier, Internet companies have turned to traditional media to achieve reach and awareness goals. In addition, statistics show that only a small percentage of sites on the Internet are captured by search engines and that the top 50 sites listed account for 95 percent of the sites visited.[27]

8. *Irritation.* Numerous studies have reported on the irritating aspects of some Web tactics. These studies have shown consumers' discontent with clutter,[28] e-mail SPAM,[29] and pop-ups and pop-unders.[30] These irritating aspects will deter visitors from coming to the sites.[31] Ethical Perspective 15-2 expands on this issue.

Overall, the Internet offers marketers some very definite advantages over traditional media. At the same time, disadvantages and limitations render this medium as less than a one-stop solution. However, as part of an IMC program, the Internet is a very valuable tool.

Additional Interactive Media

While the Internet has captured most of the attention of marketers, additional interactive media are also available and can be used as a contributor to an IMC program. Interactive CD-ROMs, kiosks, and interactive phones have been used by marketers to provide information to their audiences. Agency executives stated that the most important capability of these media was their ability to be linked with traditional marketing projects.

One of the more attention getting and promising of the new interactive media is interactive TV. **Interactive TV,** or *iTV,* allows the viewer of a television program to interact with the progam and/or the ads. Many marketers are betting on the fact that future computer users will access the Internet through their television sets. As noted earlier, multitasking will allow television viewers to watch an event—for example, a football game—and pull up information on players, history of the matchups between the teams, and other statistics without ever leaving the couch or the game. ABC promotes "enhanced TV" on its college football bowl games. (The numbers will appear in a window.) Or suppose you are watching the TV show *Friends* and like the sweater Rachel is wearing. You simply drag your mouse over to Rachel and click on her sweater, and a window will appear providing you with information regarding colors, materials, sizes, and costs. You may then ask to see other garments to mix and match with the sweater. You may then be asked if you wish to order and what shipping arrangements you prefer. If you have previously ordered, you are done, as your information has been stored in a database. If not, this first time you will be asked for personal information, including credit card number. You have ordered without leaving the couch or missing a minute of programming.

Wink-enhanced advertisements allow advertisers to communicate directly with Wink-subscribed viewers (4 million as of 2002) during a traditional 30- or 60-second spot. By clicking on an icon, advertisers can pose questions, offer samples, solicit contest entries, or even make a sale (Exhibit 15-14). For example, one Wink-enabled Ford ad asked viewers if they would like a Ford Outfitters catalog. If they wanted it, they were asked to select a model (Excursion, Expedition, or Explorer) and then to specify their interest in a two-door, four-door, or sport Track edition. Direct-mail pieces were then sent to respondents. Glaxo-SmithKline ran a similar ad allowing viewers to request information on its migraine medicine Imitrex. The company's six-month response goal was achieved in one week.[32]

ETHICAL PERSPECTIVE 15-2

Effective Marketing or Deception and Invasion of Privacy?

The direct-marketing industry has taken its share of criticism from consumers and government agencies for a long time. Critics of direct marketing cite junk mail, telemarketing, and the selling of names contained in a database as just some of the reasons for their discontent. While it is a very effective medium for marketers, the mention of direct marketing conjures up negative connotations to many consumers. Now, it appears that the Internet may be taking a similar track.

Consider this: Estimates indicate that over 31 billion commercial e-mails were sent in 2002. Approximately one-third of these were automated mailings, including stock price alerts, newsletters, or sales/marketing messages. By the year 2006, the number of e-mails sent annually is expected to exceed 60 billion, with over 50 percent being commercial in nature. As noted by Mark Levitt, vice president of IDC Collaborative Computing Services and co-author of the estimates study, "Like water flowing out of a hose, e-mail has the potential to fill our inboxes and workdays, overwhelming our abilities to navigate through the growing currents of content." A study conducted by Ferris Research estimated that SPAM cost U.S. corporations $8.9 billion in lost worker productivity in 2002. Other studies have shown that 59 percent of consumers can differentiate between legitimate e-mail and SPAM and are becoming more and more annoyed with the latter. Click-through rates on e-mails are also dropping. Permission-based online marketers have already experienced the negative impact of increased e-mails and expect to see response rates continue to decline. Many are already exploring other options.

But e-mails are not the only problem. How many times have you visited a site only to be immediately confronted with an ad (pop-up) or exited a site and had to close one or more advertisements that you didn't want to see (pop-unders)? How many times have you been unable to close them, no matter how often you tried? How many times have you tried to "unsubscribe" to a site yet not been removed from its list? While these practices irritate consumers, many Internet marketers continue to conduct business in this manner, arguing that clicking off does not require a great deal of effort, or that consumers accept this as part of the Internet experience, or offering other unfounded excuses.

And now a new form of Internet deception has surfaced. The website of the *New York Times* recently refused to accept ads from Sony Electronics that the *Times* claims "blur the lines between advertising and editorial content." The ads—which appear in the form of journalistic articles—are written by freelance writers and are designed to appear as content on popular websites. The articles are accompanied by sidebars that link readers to SonyStyle.com for more information. The "advertorials" provide only a small subhead that reads "feature by Sony." Sony is spending $10 million on 60 stories to appear on 40 different content sites including People.com, InStyle.com, NationalGeographic.com and others such as AOL and AOL Music. While Sony contends the articles are just a new means of presenting content, and sees nothing wrong with the practice, the *Times* refused to accept the argument, noting that "advertorial content must be clearly labeled to distinguish it from editorial content." Time, Inc., saw no problem with the content.

Like legitimate direct marketers, many marketers on the Internet are being hurt by the irritating and/or deceptive practices of others in their industry. But what can they do? A number of suggestions have been offered. First, the industry must police itself. The actions of the *New York Times* and of sites that refuse to accept pop-ups and pop-unders are one example. Second, trade organizations such as the Interactive Advertising Bureau (IAB) must take a more active role. Establishing and adhering to privacy guidelines is a good first step that individual companies can take on their own—for example, pursuing permission-based practices. The questionable practices discussed above—and numerous others not mentioned—are considered by many consumers to be, at best, an invasion of their privacy. A lack of action may lead to more drastic measures, as the direct-marketing industry can attest to—not the least of which is government action. It would be best for the Internet industry to regulate itself before it is too late.

Sources: Brian Morrissey, "SPAM Cost Corporate America $9B Last Year," www.internetnews.com, Jan. 6, 2003, pp. 1-2; Tobi Elkin, "New York Times Web Site Refuses Sony Ads," www.adage.com, July 22, 2002, pp. 1-3; _____, "Study: E-Mail to Double by 2006," www.internetnews.com, Sept. 27, 2002, pp. 1-2; _____, "Sifting through Spam and E-Mail Marketing," *eMarketer Daily,* Sept. 24, 2002, pp. 1-2.

Many marketers believe that the rapid adoption of iTV is just around the corner. Others feel that it is a very large corner, given that the promise of iTV has not been fulfilled, even though the technology has been around for quite some time. (A number of test markets have proved to be unsuccessful and have been abandoned.) While numbers vary (*eMarketer* estimates that 20 percent of households will have iTV in 2002 and 50 percent by 2005; others predict less), the fact remains that over 75 percent of consumers still need to be convinced that they should interact with their TV sets. A study indicated that 72 percent of U.S. viewers had no interest in interactive services.[33] Another study, conducted in 2002 in Europe—where iTV has been more rapidly adopted than in the United States—found that 94 percent of interactive customers haven't purchased anything through their TVs, 35 percent are not interested in doing so, and 40 percent can't figure it out.[34]

Nevertheless, some companies have demonstrated successful interactive campaigns. Volvo sponsored a two-week interactive television campaign during the NCAA basketball tournament in March 2002 and another on the Bravo cable television network later in the year. The company stated that it was "surprised" at the number of inquiries the campaign generated, and it considered the campaign a big success.[35] Another car dealer, Toyota, will run an integrated campaign using print, TV, and outdoor, as well as interactive and online ads, to introduce its new 4Runner. The campaign will be designed to drive viewers to a portal sight to gain more information, while providing Toyota with a database of interested parties.[36]

While interactive TV sounds like the future, so far the results have not been as encouraging as marketers had hoped for. Two of the test markets for the concept have proved to be failures, and the major content providers like General Electric (NBC) and Walt Disney Company (ABC) have expressed less interest in the concept than had been expected. Microsoft's WebTV (now MSN TV) has seen limited growth since 2000,[37] and OpenTV—although it has grown—is still of relatively small size.[38] It may just be that when viewers are watching TV, they just want to watch TV—we will wait to see.

Wireless

A rapidly growing interactive medium capturing the attention of marketers is **wireless** communication. While still in its early stages, some companies are already sending advertisements, coupons, and direct-response offers through cell phones and PDAs. By 2002 an estimated $53 million was being spent on mobile ads in Europe, with estimates that the United States would surpass that amount by 2006. Some applications already integrate global positioning satellite (GPS) technologies, changing the messages sent based on the geographic location of the user. Companies have already begun to use product placements in games as well as to offer special promotions. While just beginning, wireless is already an integrated medium.

Exhibit 15-14 Interactive television has been slow to catch on

Summary

This chapter introduced you to the Internet and interactive media. It explained some of the objectives for these media and how they can be used in an IMC program.

The discussion of the Internet focused on understanding the key terms used in the industry, the objectives sought when using the Internet, and Internet communications strategies. In addition, the role of the Internet in an IMC program was discussed, with an explanation of how all the IMC program elements can be used with the Internet. Advantages of the Internet—including the ability to target markets, interactive capabilities, and relationship building—were discussed. In addition, disadvantages—including high costs, unreliable measurements and statistics, and relatively low reach (compared to that of traditional media)—were reviewed. Sources of Internet measurement data were also provided.

The Internet has been the most rapidly adopted medium of our time. It holds great potential for both business-to-business and consumer marketers. However, contrary to popular belief, the Internet is not a stand-alone medium. Its role in an integrated marketing communications program strengthens the overall program as well as the effectiveness of the Internet itself.

Interactive media have not yet fulfilled their promise. While still in its infancy, the medium has not received the acceptance and use expected. Test market indications are that the medium still needs improvements—particularly in content—before reaching mass acceptance. Wireless is starting to experience growth.

Key Terms

Internet, 486
World Wide Web (WWW), 486
website, 490
e-commerce, 494
banner ads, 496
sponsorships, 496
content sponsorship, 496
pop-ups, 496
pop-unders, 496
interstitials, 498
push technologies, 498
webcasting, 498
personalization, 498
links, 498
SPAM, 500
cookie, 502
interactive TV, 506
wireless, 508

Discussion Questions

1. One of the problems slowing the rate of adoption of the Internet as an advertising medium is the fact that this medium has been slow to adopt traditional advertising metrics. Discuss why this has been the case, and what must be done to overcome this problem.

2. Interactive television has not been adopted by consumers as rapidly as was expected. Give some reasons for this slower than expected adoption rate, and what *iTV* must do to overcome these problems.

3. What is meant by wireless? Provide examples of companies that currently are employing this communications medium. For what type of companies might wireless best be suited?

4. The IAB recently provided guidelines for metrics for use by those in the Internet industry. Explain what these guidelines entailed and why they are important.

5. Provide examples of companies with which you are familiar that have successfully integrated the Internet into their communications programs. Explain the role of the Internet in these IMC programs.

6. The Internet is growing at an extremely rapid pace. At the same time there are indications that this growth will slow. Discuss some factors that may lead to decreased growth of the use of this medium.

7. Discuss the objectives marketers may be seeking in their use of the Internet. Which is the Internet best suited for?

8. Explain the different forms that advertisers might use to advertise on the Internet. Discuss some of the advantages and disadvantages associated with each.

9. A number of Internet marketers have been criticized as engaging in unethical practices. Discuss some of the practices that might be considered unethical. What should be done to curtail these practices?

10. What is interactive TV? Explain how interactive television differs from traditional television. Give an example of how a company might employ this medium.

Sales Promotion

16

Chapter Objectives

1. To understand the role of sales promotion in a company's integrated marketing communications program and to examine why it is increasingly important.
2. To examine the various objectives of sales promotion programs.
3. To examine the types of consumer- and trade-oriented sales promotion tools and the factors to consider in using them.
4. To understand how sales promotion is coordinated with advertising.
5. To consider potential problems and abuse by companies in their use of sales promotion.

Sales Promotion Has an Interesting History as Well

Advertising has a long and fascinating history and has had a major impact, both good and bad, on our culture. Advertising has entertained, moved, and motivated consumers for more than

a century, and many of the images created by advertisers have become cultural icons—Ronald McDonald, the Marlboro Man, Tony the Tiger, and the Energizer Bunny, to name just a few. Much has been written about the history of advertising and how it reflects society and its whole range of activities. However, sales promotion also has a very rich and interesting history: Marketers have developed and used a variety of techniques over the past century to give consumers an extra incentive to use their products and services. Many of the sales promotion offers that motivate consumers today and have become part of their everyday lives have been around for nearly a century or more.

The oldest, most widely used, and most effective sales promotion tool is the cents-off coupon. Coupons have been around since 1895 when the C.W. Post Co. first began using the penny-off coupon to help sell its new Grape Nuts cereal brand. Procter & Gamble began using coupons in 1920, and its first ones were metal coins that were good for discounts or buy-one-get-one-free deals. Those were soon replaced by cheaper, more convenient paper versions, which have been around ever since. Another classic promotional tool is the premium offer, which dates back to 1912 when Cracker Jack began offering "a prize in every box." Ovaltine developed one of the first interactive premiums in 1930, when it gave away decoder rings that were needed to decode secret messages broadcast in *Little Orphan Annie* radio shows in the 30s. The promotion was brought back 20 years later as television became the new mass medium and the rings were used to decode messages in *Texas Rangers* TV shows. Perhaps no company has used premium offers as effectively as McDonald's, which launched its Happy Meals in 1979 and has been using them ever since. Happy Meals account for a significant portion of McDonald's sales and have made the company the world's largest toy manufacturer.

Marketers also have a long history of taking their promotional programs to the customer. The first Oscar Mayer Wienermobile hit the streets in 1936, when the nephew of the company's founder had the idea of introducing a 13-foot-long hot dog on wheels. Soon it was seen driving the streets of Chicago, promoting Oscar Mayer "German Style Wieners." Seven updates and 66 years later, there is now a fleet of eight Wienermobiles that cruise the highways of America and other countries playing 21 versions of the famous Wiener Jingle and helping to promote the brand. Pepsi is another company that took a promotional program on the road, with its launch of

the famous "Pepsi Challenge" in 1975, which was one of the most successful promotions ever used to attract users of a competing brand. Pepsi took on its archrival and industry leader Coca-Cola in a hard-hitting promotion that challenged consumers to taste the two brands in blind taste tests. Pepsi ran the challenge promotion for nearly a decade and relaunched it again in 2000 as it began cruising for a new generation.

Contests and sweepstakes also have an interesting history. Pillsbury launched its first Bake-Off Contest in 1949, when the company's advertising agency created the contest to celebrate the company's 80th birthday and invited homemakers to share their treasured recipes. The response was so great that Pillsbury decided to hold the contest again in subsequent years, and the Bake-Off has become an institution as well as the nation's most prestigious cooking competition. Many of the winning recipes in each year's competition have become part of the repertoire of home cooks and have led to innovative new products from Pillsbury.

McDonald's has taken another institution, the world-famous Monopoly board game, and turned it into a long-running and immensely popular contest. The first McDonald's Monopoly game contest was in 1987, and its collect-and-win format and big prizes generated tremendous interest and excitement and was very effective at generating repeat business. McDonald's began running the game annually in 1991, tweaking it each year by adding new partners and prizes and making the game more complex with new iterations such as the Pick Your Prize twist. However, in 2001 the game had the most surprising twist of all: The FBI used it to collect evidence against an embezzlement ring that had been stealing high-value game pieces throughout the years. It remains to be seen if McDonald's will try to bring back the popular game.

Another promotional program of historical significance is the American Airlines AAdvantage frequent-flier program, which was launched in 1981. The program created a new currency and has set the gold standard for loyalty marketing as it now has nearly 44 million members. American also has a steady stream of partners that offer AAdvantage miles as an incentive to encourage consumers to purchase their products and services. Loyalty programs have also become very prevalent in many other industries such as hospitality, rental cars, and retailing.

Many of the marketers discussed here are promotional pioneers, as they have found creative ways to provide consumers with an extra incentive to purchase their brands. The success of these promotions has had a major impact on consumers throughout the years and also has resulted in similar programs being developed by competitors. Such promotions show that advertising is not the only IMC tool with a rich and interesting history.

Sources: "A Look at 16 Campaigns That Helped Redefine Promotion Marketing," *Promo,* March 2002, pp. 58–70; www.bakeoff.com/history.

As discussed in the opening vignette, marketers have come to recognize that advertising alone is not always enough to move their products off store shelves and into the hands of consumers. Companies also use sales promotion methods targeted at both consumers and the wholesalers and retailers that distribute their products to stimulate demand. Most companies' integrated marketing communications programs include consumer and trade promotions that are coordinated with advertising, direct marketing, and publicity/public relations campaigns as well as sales force efforts.

This chapter focuses on the role of sales promotion in a firm's IMC program. We examine how marketers use both consumer- and trade-oriented promotions to influence the purchase behavior of consumers as well as wholesalers and retailers. We explore the objectives of sales promotion programs and the various types of sales promotion tools that can be used at both the consumer and trade level. We also consider how sales promotion can be integrated with other elements of the promotional mix and look at problems that can arise when marketers become overly dependent on consumer and trade promotions, especially the latter.

Direct Inducement

The Scope and Role of Sales Promotion

Sales promotion has been defined as "a direct inducement that offers an extra value or incentive for the product to the sales force, distributors, or the ultimate consumer with the primary objective of creating an immediate sale."[1] Keep in mind several important aspects of sales promotion as you read this chapter.

First, sales promotion involves some type of inducement that provides an *extra incentive* to buy. This incentive is usually the key element in a promotional program; it may be a coupon or price reduction, the opportunity to enter a contest or sweepstakes, a money-back refund or rebate, or an extra amount of a product. The incentive may also be a free sample of the product, given in hopes of generating a future purchase, or a premium that serves as a reminder of the brand and reinforces its image, such as the miniature race car premium offer that ties into Tide's NASCAR sponsorship (Exhibit 16-1). Most sales promotion offers attempt to add some value to the product or service. While advertising appeals to the mind and emotions to give the consumer a reason to buy, sales promotion appeals more to the pocketbook and provides an incentive for purchasing a brand.

Extra Incentive to Buy

Sales promotion can also provide an inducement to marketing intermediaries such as wholesalers and retailers. A trade allowance or discount gives retailers a financial incentive to stock and promote a manufacturer's products. A trade contest directed toward wholesalers or retail personnel gives them extra incentive to perform certain tasks or meet sales goals.

A second point is that sales promotion is essentially an *acceleration tool*, designed to speed up the selling process and maximize sales volume.[2] By providing an extra incentive, sales promotion techniques can motivate consumers to purchase a larger quantity of a brand or shorten the purchase cycle of the trade or consumers by encouraging them to take more immediate action.

Companies also use limited-time offers such as price-off deals to retailers or a coupon with an expiration date to accelerate the purchase process.[3] Sales promotion attempts to maximize sales volume by motivating customers who have not responded to advertising. The ideal sales promotion program generates sales that would not be achieved by other means. However, as we shall see later, many sales promotion offers end up being used by current users of a brand rather than attracting new users.

A final point regarding sales promotion activities is that they can be *targeted to different parties* in the marketing channel. As shown in Figure 16-1, sales promotion can be broken into two major categories: consumer-oriented and trade-oriented promotions. Activities involved in **consumer-oriented sales promotion** include sampling, couponing, premiums, contests and sweepstakes, refunds and rebates, bonus packs, price-offs, frequency programs, and event marketing. These promotions are directed at consumers, the end purchasers of goods and services, and are designed to induce them to purchase the marketer's brand.

As discussed in Chapter 2, consumer-oriented promotions are part of a promotional pull strategy; they work along with advertising to encourage consumers to purchase a particular brand and thus create demand for it. Consumer promotions are also used by retailers to encourage consumers to shop in their particular stores. Many grocery stores use their own coupons or sponsor contests and other promotions to increase store patronage.

Trade-oriented sales promotion includes dealer contests and incentives, trade allowances, point-of-purchase displays, sales training programs, trade shows, cooperative advertising, and other programs designed to motivate distributors and retailers to carry a product and make an extra effort to push it to their customers. Many marketing programs include both trade- and consumer-oriented promotions, since motivating both groups maximizes the effectiveness of the promotional program.

Exhibit 16-1 Procter & Gamble offers a premium offer to provide extra incentive to purchase Tide and Downy

Figure 16-1 Types of sales promotion activities

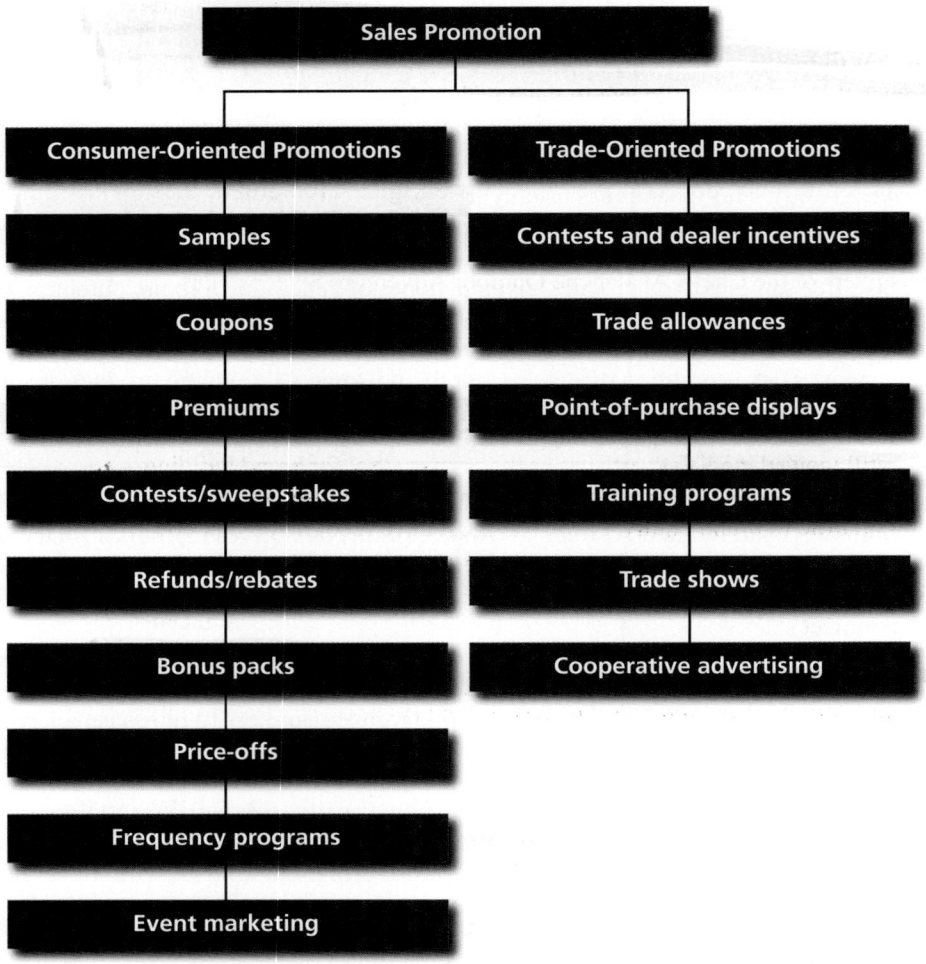

The Growth of Sales Promotion

While sales promotion has been part of the marketing process for a long time, its role and importance in a company's integrated marketing communications program have increased dramatically over the past decade. Consumer sales promotion–related spending increased from $56 billion in 1991 to nearly $100 billion in 2001.[4] Marketers also spend an estimated $150 billion each year on promotions targeted at retailers and wholesalers. Consumer packaged goods firms continue to be the core users of sales promotion programs and tools. However, sales promotion activity is also increasing in other categories, including health care, computer hardware and software, consumer electronics, and service industries.

Not only has the total amount of money spent on sales promotion increased, but the percentage of marketers' budgets allocated to promotion has grown as well. For many years advertising was the major component in the promotional mix of most consumer-product companies. Until the 1980s, nearly half of marketers' promotional dollars was spent on advertising campaigns designed to create or reinforce brand awareness and build long-term loyalty. However by the mid- to late 80s, a fundamental change had occurred in the way most consumer-product companies were marketing their products. The proportion of the marketing budget allocated to sales promotion rose sharply, while the amount spent on media advertising declined. The increase in spending on sales promotion at the expense of media advertising continued throughout the decade of the 90s and into the new millennium. Currently, estimates are that marketers spend between 60 and 75 percent of their promotional budgets on sales promotion, with the remainder being allocated to media advertising.[5]

Allocation of marketing budgets among consumer promotions, trade promotions, and media advertising varies by industry and company. For example, trade promotion

accounts for nearly 50 percent of the budget for consumer packaged-goods companies, with 27 percent going to consumer promotion and 24 percent to media advertising.[6] Moreover, a significant amount of the monies that marketers allocate to media advertising is spent on ads that deliver promotional messages regarding contests, games, sweepstakes, and rebate offers.[7] Surveys have shown that marketers devote about 17 percent of their ad budgets to promotional messages.[8] Promotional messages are also used to help attract attention to image-building ads. For example, the ad shown in Exhibit 16-2 delivers a message informing consumers of the Chevy Avalanche Outdoor Adventure Sweepstakes.

Exhibit 16-2
Advertisements are often used to deliver messages about promotions such as sweepstakes

Reasons for the Increase in Sales Promotion

The reallocation of the marketing budget concerned many marketers who still viewed media advertising as the primary tool for brand building and saw sales promotion programs as little more than gimmicks that contributed little to brand equity. However, most have recognized that consumers may love certain brands but often want an extra incentive to buy them. Marketers also know they must partner effectively with trade accounts, and this often means providing them with an additional incentive to stock and promote their brands and participate in various promotional programs.

A major reason for the increase in spending on sales promotion is that the promotion industry has matured over the past several decades. Increased sophistication and a more strategic role and focus have elevated the discipline and its role in the IMC program of many companies.[9] In the past, sales promotion specialists would be brought in after key strategic branding decisions were made. Promotional agencies were viewed primarily as tacticians whose role was to develop a promotional program such as a contest or sweepstakes or a coupon or sampling program that could create a short-term increase in sales. However, many companies are now making promotional specialists part of their strategic brand-building team, a move that puts sales promotion on par with media advertising. Promotional agencies have expanded their integrated marketing capabilities as well as their expertise in branding and helping their clients build relationships with their customers. For example, Exhibit 16-3 shows an ad for DVC Worldwide, one of the leading promotion agencies, that touts the agency's expertise in strategy and brand building.

Exhibit 16-3 DVC Worldwide touts its expertise in branding

There are also a number of other factors that have led to the increase in the importance of sales promotion and the shift in marketing dollars from media advertising to consumer and trade promotions. Among them are the growing power of retailers, declining brand loyalty, increased promotional sensitivity, brand proliferation, fragmentation of the consumer market, the short-term focus of many marketers, increased accountability, competition, and clutter.

The Growing Power of Retailers

One reason for the increase in sales promotion is the power shift in the marketplace from manufacturers to retailers. For many years, manufacturers of national brands had the power and influence; retailers were just passive distributors of their products. Consumer-product manufacturers created consumer demand for their brands by using heavy advertising and some consumer-oriented promotions, such as samples, coupons, and premiums, and exerted pressure on retailers to carry the products. Retailers did

very little research and sales analysis; they relied on manufacturers for information regarding the sales performance of individual brands.

In recent years, however, several developments have helped to transfer power from the manufacturers to the retailers. With the advent of optical checkout scanners and sophisticated in-store computer systems, retailers gained access to data concerning how quickly products turn over, which sales promotions are working, and which products make money.[10] Retailers use this information to analyze sales of manufacturers' products and then demand discounts and other promotional support from manufacturers of lagging brands. Companies that fail to comply with retailers' demands for more trade support often have their shelf space reduced or even their product dropped.

Used to Promo money

Another factor that has increased the power of retailers is the consolidation of the grocery store industry, which has resulted in larger chains with greater buying power and clout. These large chains have become accustomed to trade promotions and can pressure manufacturers to provide deals, discounts, and allowances. Consolidation has also given large retailers more money for advancing already strong private label initiatives, and sales promotion is the next step in the marketing evolution of private label brands. Private label brands in various packaged-good categories such as foods, drugs, and health and beauty care products are giving national brands more competition for retail shelf space and increasing their own marketing, including the use of traditional sales promotion tools. Well-marketed private label products are forcing national brand leaders, as well as second-tier brands, to develop more innovative promotional programs and to be more price-competitive.[11]

↑ Private Label

Declining Brand Loyalty Another major reason for the increase in sales promotion is that consumers have become less brand loyal and are purchasing more on the basis of price, value, and convenience. Some consumers are always willing to buy their preferred brand at full price without any type of promotional offer. However, many consumers are loyal coupon users and/or are conditioned to look for deals when they shop. They may switch back and forth among a set of brands they view as essentially equal. These brands are all perceived as being satisfactory and interchangeable, and consumers purchase whatever brand is on special or for which they have a coupon.

Increased Promotional Sensitivity Marketers are making greater use of sales promotion in their marketing programs because consumers respond favorably to the incentives it provides. A major research project completed by Promotion Decisions, Inc., tracked the purchase behavior of over 33,000 consumers and their response to both consumer and trade promotions. The results showed that 42 percent of the total unit volume of the 12 packaged-good products analyzed was purchased with some type of incentive while 58 percent was purchased at full price. Coupons were particularly popular among consumers, as 24 percent of the sales volume involved the use of a coupon.[12]

Consumer has Time limitations TO Shop.

An obvious reason for consumers' increased sensitivity to sales promotion offers is that they save money. Another reason is that many purchase decisions are made at the point of purchase by consumers who are increasingly time-sensitive and facing too many choices. Some studies have found that up to 70 percent of purchase decisions are made in the store, where people are very likely to respond to promotional deals.[13] Buying a brand that is on special or being displayed can simplify the decision-making process and solve the problem of overchoice. Professor Leigh McAlister has described this process:

> As consumers go down the supermarket aisle they spend 3 to 10 seconds in each product category. They often don't know the regular price of the chosen product. However, they do have a sense of whether or not that product is on promotion. As they go down the aisle, they are trying to pensively fill their baskets with good products without tiresome calculations. They see a "good deal" and it goes in the cart.[14]

Brand Proliferation A major aspect of many firms' marketing strategies over the past decade has been the development of new products. Consumer-product companies are launching nearly 30,000 new products each year, according to the research firm Marketing Intelligence Service (compared with only 2,689 in 1980).[15] The market has become saturated with new brands, which often lack any significant advantages that can be used as the basis of an advertising campaign. Thus, companies increasingly depend

on sales promotion to encourage consumers to try these brands. In Chapter 4, we saw how sales promotion techniques can be used as part of the shaping process to lead the consumer from initial trial to repeat purchase at full price. Marketers are relying more on samples, coupons, rebates, premiums, and other innovative promotional tools to achieve trial usage of their new brands and encourage repeat purchase (Exhibit 16-4).

Promotions are also important in getting retailers to allocate some of their precious shelf space to new brands. The competition for shelf space for new products in stores is enormous. Supermarkets carry an average of 30,000 products (compared with 13,067 in 1982). Retailers favor new brands with strong sales promotion support that will bring in more customers and boost their sales and profits. Many retailers require special discounts or allowances from manufacturers just to handle a new product. These slotting fees or allowances, which are discussed later in the chapter, can make it expensive for a manufacturer to introduce a new product.

Exhibit 16-4 Sales promotion tools such as coupons are often used to encourage trial of a new brand

Fragmentation of the Consumer Market As the consumer market becomes more fragmented and traditional mass-media–based advertising less effective, marketers are turning to more segmented, highly targeted approaches. Many companies are tailoring their promotional efforts to specific regional markets. Sales promotion tools have become one of the primary vehicles for doing this, through programs tied into local flavor, themes, or events. For example, fast-food restaurants and take-out pizza chains such as Domino's spent a high percentage of their marketing budget on local tie-ins and promotions designed to build traffic and generate sales from their trade areas.[16]

A number of marketers are also using sales promotion techniques to target ethnic markets. For example, Sears targets the Hispanic market by hosting grassroots events at stores and tie-ins with local festivals. Sears also develops other promotions targeted specifically at the Hispanic community. For example, the "Los Heroes De Mi Vida" contest shown in Exhibit 16-5 invited young people of Hispanic heritage to submit an essay to honor a person who has had a positive influence on their lives. Diversity Perspective 16-1 discusses how a number of companies are using sales promotion tools to target the African-American market.

Marketers are also shifting more of their promotional efforts to direct marketing, which often includes some form of sales promotion incentive. Many marketers use information they get from premium offers, trackable coupons, rebates, and sweepstakes

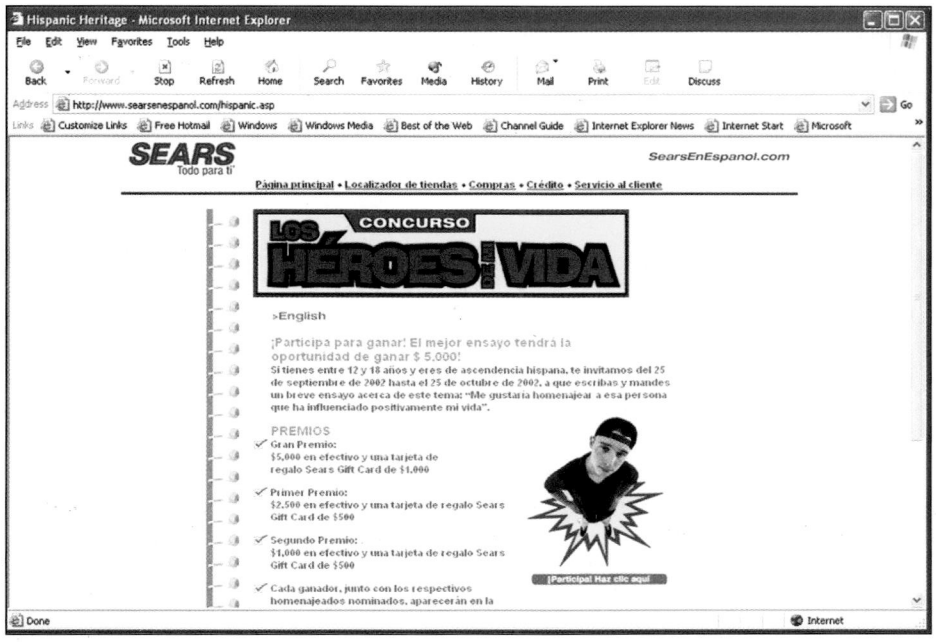

Exhibit 16-5 Sears targets the Hispanic market with this promotion

DIVERSITY PERSPECTIVE 16-1

Using Sales Promotion to Target African-Americans

The African-American market has become very important to many marketers as this segment accounts for two-thirds of the money spent by minorities in the United States and commands an estimated $572 billion in purchasing power. African-Americans represent about 13 percent (36.4 million) of the U.S. population, and nearly half belong to the middle class. According to the most recent U.S. census, 5.3 million of the 12.8 million African-American households earn more than $35,000 annually; nearly 14 million now live in the suburbs, and 10 percent of those suburban dwellers earn more than $100,000 annually.

Traditionally, marketers have targeted African-Americans and other ethnic markets by running ads in the various TV, radio, and print media that reach these markets. However, many marketers are discovering that sales promotion techniques are often more effective ways to reach these markets and can be very valuable in developing relationships with them. For example, American Airlines has developed several programs to entrench its brand in the African-American community. One of these programs is called "Comfort Zone," an effort whose name played on two themes: the literal comfort of the extra leg room in American cabins, and the figurative level of satisfaction African-Americans have with the airline. The program centered on Comfort Zone parties in American's five hub markets. Urban radio stations held call-in contests giving away passes to the parties, which featured raffles awarding trips and cruises. American followed the campaign by sponsoring Sisters in the Spirit, a national gospel tour, and also teamed with Coca-Cola for a sweepstakes giving away trips to Hawaii that were advertised in various African-American magazines including *Ebony* and *Black Enterprise.*

Other companies are using ongoing promotional programs to reach the African-American market. For example, Volvo Cars North America has launched its largest minority-targeted promotion ever, a Buckle Up for Safety campaign run in conjunction with the Edward Davis Education Foundation and the National Highway Traffic Safety Administration. The goal of the campaign is to promote seat belt usage within the African-American and Hispanic communities—particularly among young adults—and to reinforce the proper use of car and booster seats for infants and children.

Mott's Inc. has expanded its annual Hawaiian Punch Black History "Our Words! Our Art!" contest from 8 to 16 markets. The month-long promotion asks students to share what they have learned about African-American historical figures. First- and second-graders submit artwork, while fourth- through sixth-graders

write essays. Forty-five winners, selected by the National Association of Black School Educators, win family trips to Disney World. Burger King also has developed a connection with the African-American community by celebrating its heritage. The company sponsors Black History month through a campaign called "Everyday Heroes" that recognizes the achievements of more obscure figures such as chess grand master Morris Ashley and Brigadier General Ronald Coleman. The chain distributed more than 10 million special calendars through its restaurants during the 2002 promotion. African-Americans and Hispanics account for 30 percent of Burger King's overall sales.

Marketers are also using sales promotion tools in conjunction with cause-related marketing to connect with African-Americans. For example, Kraft Foods recently partnered with Motown Records on *Women of the Times,* a 10-song CD featuring African-American singers such as Erykah Badu and Patti LaBelle that was sold through point-of-purchase displays in grocery stores. The CD could be purchased for $2.99 with three Kraft proofs of purchase, and the company donated 25 cents of each purchase to the United Negro College Fund.

Sales promotion is becoming an integral part of marketer efforts to reach the African-American market and build a genuine connection with this important segment. As DiversityInc.com notes, "The African-American market is positioned to make or break profits for many leading U.S. companies." Many companies are hoping that their promotional efforts will help them fully entrench their brands in the African-American community.

Sources: Matthew Kinsman, "Equal Opportunities," *Promo,* February 2002, pp. 14–16; Lafayette Jones, "A Sign of the Times," *Promo,* February 2002, pp. 16–17.

to build databases for future direct-marketing efforts. As marketers continue to shift from media advertising to direct marketing, promotional offers will probably be used even more to help build databases. The technology is already in place to enable marketers to communicate individually with target consumers and transform mass promotional tools into ways of doing one-to-one marketing.[17]

Short-Term Focus Many businesspeople believe the increase in sales promotion is motivated by marketing plans and reward systems geared to short-term performance and the immediate generation of sales volume. Some think the packaged-goods brand management system has contributed to marketers' increased dependence on sales promotion. Brand managers use sales promotions routinely, not only to introduce new products or defend against the competition but also to meet quarterly or yearly sales and market share goals. The sales force, too, may have short-term quotas or goals to meet and may also receive requests from retailers and wholesalers for promotions. Thus, reps may pressure marketing or brand managers to use promotions to help them move the products into the retailers' stores.

Many managers view consumer and trade promotions as the most dependable way to generate short-term sales, particularly when they are price-related. The reliance on sales promotion is particularly high in mature and slow-growth markets, where it is difficult to stimulate consumer demand through advertising. This has led to concern that managers have become too dependent on the quick sales fix that can result from a promotion and that the brand franchise may be eroded by too many deals.

Increased Accountability In addition to pressuring their marketing or brand managers and sales force to produce short-term results, many companies are demanding to know what they are getting for their promotional expenditures. Results from sales promotion programs are generally easier to measure than those from advertising. Many companies are demanding measurable, accountable ways to relate promotional expenditures to sales and profitability. For example, Kraft Foods uses computerized sales information from checkout scanners in determining compensation for marketing personnel. Part of the pay managers receive depends on the sales a promotion generates relative to its costs.[18]

Managers who are being held accountable to produce results often use price discounts or coupons, since they produce a quick and easily measured jump in sales. It takes longer for an ad campaign to show some impact and the effects are more difficult to measure. Marketers are also feeling pressure from the trade as powerful retailers demand sales performance from their brands. Real-time data available from computerized checkout scanners make it possible for retailers to monitor promotions and track the results they generate on a daily basis.

Competition Another factor that led to the increase in sales promotion is manufacturers' reliance on trade and consumer promotions to gain or maintain competitive advantage. The markets for many products are mature and stagnant, and it is increasingly difficult to boost sales through advertising. Exciting, breakthrough creative ideas are difficult to come by, and consumers' attention to mass-media advertising continues to decline. Rather than allocating large amounts of money to run dull ads, many marketers have turned to sales promotion.

Many companies are tailoring their trade promotions to key retail accounts and developing strategic alliances with retailers that include both trade and consumer promotional programs. A major development in recent years is **account-specific marketing** (also referred to as *comarketing*), whereby a manufacturer collaborates with an individual retailer to create a customized promotion that accomplishes mutual objectives. For example, Coppertone's promotion agency created an account-specific promotion for "Spot the Dog Scavenger Hunt" that was based on the iconic Little Miss Coppertone losing her dog in a Wal-Mart store (Exhibit 16-6). The in-store scavenger hunt involved having consumers find clues throughout the store, fill in a game piece, and receive a prize. The game piece promoted Coppertone's rub-free adult and children's spray and included a $2 Wal-Mart–specific rebate coupon. The promotion resulted in a 6 percent increase in Coppertone sales during the promotion.

Exhibit 16-6 Coppertone developed an account-specific promotion for Wal-Mart

Estimates are that marketers will soon be spending more than half of their promotion budgets on account-specific marketing. A number of companies are developing promotional programs for major retail accounts such as supermarket chains, mass merchandisers, and convenience stores.[19]

Retailers may use a promotional deal with one company as leverage to seek an equal or better deal with its competitors. Consumer and trade promotions are easily matched by competitors, and many marketers find themselves in a promotional trap where they must continue using promotions or be at a competitive disadvantage. (We discuss this problem in more detail later in the chapter.)

Clutter A promotional offer in an ad can break through the clutter that is prevalent in most media today. A premium offer may help attract consumers' attention to an ad, as will a contest or sweepstakes. Some studies have shown that readership scores are higher for print ads with coupons than for ads without them.[20] However, more recent studies by Starch INRA Hooper suggest that magazine ads with coupons do not generate higher readership.[21] A recent study found that promotional messages are very prevalent in both magazine and newspaper ads, particularly the latter. Sweepstakes, games, and contests were prevalent in magazine ads, while coupons and sales offers were used the most in newspaper advertising.[22]

Combining an AD with a Coupon is very effective

Concerns about the Increased Role of Sales Promotion

How allocation of funds to promo effect Brand Equity

Many factors have contributed to the increased use of sales promotion by consumer-product manufacturers. Marketing and advertising executives are concerned about how this shift in the allocation of the promotional budget affects brand equity. As noted in Chapter 2, *brand equity,* or consumer franchise, is an intangible asset of added value or goodwill that results from consumers' favorable image, impressions of differentiation, and/or strength of attachment to a brand.

Some critics argue that sales promotion increases come at the expense of brand equity and every dollar that goes into promotion rather than advertising devalues the brand.[23] They say trade promotions in particular contribute to the destruction of brand franchises and equity as they encourage consumers to purchase primarily on the basis of price.

Proponents of advertising argue that marketers must maintain strong franchises if they want to differentiate their brands and charge a premium price for them. They say advertising is still the most effective way to build the long-term franchise of a brand. It informs consumers of a brand's features and benefits, creates an image, and helps build and maintain brand loyalty. However, many marketers are not investing in their brands as they take monies away from media advertising to fund short-term promotions.

Marketing experts generally agree that advertising plays an important role in building and maintaining a brand's image and position, which are core components of its equity. Many are concerned that if the trend toward spending more on sales promotion at the expense of media advertising continues, brands may lose the equity that advertising helped create and be forced to compete primarily on the basis of price. Many of these concerns are justified, but not all sales promotion activities detract from the value of a brand. It is important to distinguish between consumer franchise-building and nonfranchise-building promotions.

Consumer Franchise-Building versus Nonfranchise-Building Promotions

Sales promotion activities that communicate distinctive brand attributes and contribute to the development and reinforcement of brand identity are **consumer franchise-building (CFB) promotions.**[24] Consumer sales promotion efforts cannot make consumers loyal to a brand that is of little value or does not provide them with a specific benefit. But they can make consumers aware of a brand and, by communicating its specific features and benefits, contribute to the development of a favorable brand image. Consumer franchise-building promotions are designed to build long-term brand prefer-

Exhibit 16-7 This promotion agency ad stresses the importance of using trade promotions to build brand equity

ence and help the company achieve the ultimate goal of full-price purchases that do not depend on a promotional offer.

For years, franchise or image building was viewed as the exclusive realm of advertising, and sales promotion was used only to generate short-term sales increases. But now marketers are recognizing the image-building potential of sales promotion and paying attention to its CFB value. Surveys have found that nearly 90 percent of senior marketing executives believe consumer promotions can help build brand equity while nearly 60 percent think trade promotions can contribute.[25] Marketers recognize that the value of sales promotion extends well beyond quick-fix tactics such as price-off deals. Most sales promotion agencies recognize the importance of developing consumer and trade promotions that can help build brand equity. For example, Exhibit 16-7 shows an ad for Ryan Partnership that stresses how the agency develops trade promotions that help build brand equity.

Companies can use sales promotion techniques in a number of ways to contribute to franchise building. Rather than using a one-time offer, many companies are developing frequency programs that encourage repeat purchases and long-term patronage. Many credit cards have loyalty programs where consumers earn bonus points every time they use their card to charge a purchase. These points can then be redeemed for various items. Most airlines and many hotel chains offer frequent-flyer or guest programs to encourage repeat patronage. Many retail stores have also begun using frequency programs to build loyalty and encourage repeat purchases.[26]

Companies can also use sales promotion to contribute to franchise building by developing an offer consistent with the image of the brand. An example of a successful consumer brand-building promotion is the Search for 2000 Uses Sweepstakes promotion for WD-40, shown in Exhibit 16-8. The WD-40 Company positions its brand as the leading multipurpose problem solver that cleans, protects, penetrates, lubricates, and displaces moisture like no other product on earth. The marketing strategy for WD-40 is to continually promote the myriad of uses for the product. The Search for 2000 Uses Sweepstakes, which was launched to coincide with the new millennium, asked consumers to suggest their use for WD-40 in order to be entered for a chance to win various prizes such as WD-40 can radios, T-shirts, and baseball caps and a grand prize of $10,000 in company stock. The sweepstakes

Exhibit 16-8 WD-40's Search for 2000 Uses Sweepstakes is an excellent example of a consumer brand-building promotion

reinforced WD-40's image as a multipurpose problem solver and also encouraged consumers to visit the company's website to enter their uses.

Nonfranchise-building (non-FB) promotions are designed to accelerate the purchase decision process and generate an immediate increase in sales. These activities do not communicate information about a brand's unique features or the benefits of using it, so they do not contribute to the building of brand identity and image. Price-off deals, bonus packs, and rebates or refunds are examples of non-FB sales promotion techniques. Trade promotions receive the most criticism for being nonfranchise building—for good reason. First, many of the promotional discounts and allowances given to the trade are never passed on to consumers. Most trade promotions that are forwarded through the channels reach consumers in the form of lower prices or special deals and lead them to buy on the basis of price rather than brand equity.

Many specialists in the promotional area stress the need for marketers to use sales promotion tools to build a franchise and create long-term continuity in their promotional programs. Whereas non-FB promotions merely borrow customers from other brands, well-planned CFB activities can convert consumers to loyal customers. Short-term non-FB promotions have their place in a firm's promotional mix, particularly when competitive developments call for them. But their limitations must be recognized when a long-term marketing strategy for a brand is developed.

Consumer-Oriented Sales Promotion

In this section, we examine the various sales promotion tools and techniques marketers can use to influence consumers. We study the consumer-oriented promotions shown in Figure 16-1 and discuss their advantages and limitations. First, we consider some objectives marketers have for sales promotion programs targeted to the consumer market.

Objectives of Consumer-Oriented Sales Promotion

As the use of sales promotion techniques continues to increase, companies must consider what they hope to accomplish through their consumer promotions and how they interact with other promotional activities such as advertising, direct marketing, and personal selling. When marketers implement sales promotion programs without considering their long-term cumulative effect on the brand's image and position in the marketplace, they often do little more than create short-term spikes in the sales curve.

Not all sales promotion activities are designed to achieve the same objectives. As with any promotional mix element, marketers must plan consumer promotions by conducting a situation analysis and determining sales promotion's specific role in the integrated marketing communications program. They must decide what the promotion is designed to accomplish and to whom it should be targeted. Setting clearly defined objectives and measurable goals for their sales promotion programs forces managers to think beyond the short-term sales fix (although this can be one goal).

While the basic goal of most consumer-oriented sales promotion programs is to induce purchase of a brand, the marketer may have a number of different objectives for both new and established brands—for example, obtaining trial and repurchase, increasing consumption of an established brand, defending current customers, targeting a specific market segment, or enhancing advertising and marketing efforts.

Obtaining Trial and Repurchase

One of the most important uses of sales promotion techniques is to encourage consumers to try a new product or service. While thousands of new products are introduced to the market every year, as many as 90 percent of them fail within the first year. Many of these failures are due to the fact that the new product or brand lacks the promotional support needed either to encourage initial trial by enough consumers or to induce enough of those trying the brand to repurchase it. Many new brands are merely new versions of an existing product without unique benefits, so advertising alone cannot induce trial. Sales promotion tools have become an important part of new brand introduction strategies; the level of initial trial can be increased through techniques such as sampling, couponing, and refund offers.

The success of a new brand depends not only on getting initial trial but also on inducing a reasonable percentage of people who try the brand to repurchase it and

establish ongoing purchase patterns. Promotional incentives such as coupons or refund offers are often included with a sample to encourage repeat purchase after trial. For example, when Lever Brothers introduced its Lever 2000 brand of bar soap, it distributed millions of free samples along with a 75-cent coupon. The samples allowed consumers to try the new soap, while the coupon provided an incentive to purchase it.

Increasing Consumption of an Established Brand Many marketing managers are responsible for established brands competing in mature markets, against established competitors, where consumer purchase patterns are often well set. Awareness of an established brand is generally high as a result of cumulative advertising effects, and many consumers have probably tried the brand. These factors can create a challenging situation for the brand manager. Sales promotion can generate some new interest in an established brand to help increase sales or defend market share against competitors.

Marketers attempt to increase sales for an established brand in several ways, and sales promotion can play an important role in each. One way to increase product consumption is by identifying new uses for the brand. Sales promotion tools like recipe books or calendars that show various ways of using the product often can accomplish this. One of the best examples of a brand that has found new uses is Arm & Hammer baking soda. Exhibit 16-9 shows a clever freestanding insert (FSI) that promotes the brand's new fridge-freezer pack, which absorbs more odors in refrigerators and freezers.

Exhibit 16-9 Arm & Hammer used this FSI to promote a specific use for the product

Another strategy for increasing sales of an established brand is to use promotions that attract nonusers of the product category or users of a competing brand. Attracting nonusers of the product category can be very difficult, as consumers may not see a need for the product. Sales promotions can appeal to nonusers by providing them with an extra incentive to try the product, but a more common strategy for increasing sales of an established brand is to attract consumers who use a competing brand. This can be done by giving them an incentive to switch, such as a coupon, premium offer, bonus pack, or price deal. Marketers can also get users of a competitor to try their brand through sampling or other types of promotional programs.

One of the most successful promotions ever used to attract users of a competing brand was the Pepsi Challenge. In this campaign, Pepsi took on its archrival, industry leader Coca-Cola, in a hard-hitting comparative promotion that challenged consumers to taste the two brands in blind taste tests (Exhibit 16-10). The Pepsi Challenge promotion included national and local advertising, couponing, and trade support as part of a fully integrated promotional program. The campaign was used from 1975 to the early 80s and was instrumental in helping Pepsi move ahead of Coke to become the market share leader in supermarket sales. In response Coke launched a variety of counterattacks, including the controversial decision to change its formula and launch New Coke in 1986. Pepsi brought back the promotion in 2000 to recruit a new generation of brand

Exhibit 16-10 The Pepsi Challenge was a very successful promotion for attracting users of a competing brand

ANNCR: All across America people are taking the Pepsi Challenge. In California here's what they are saying.
TRACY KUERBIS: Pepsi really is the better drink.
DAVE JOHNSON: I've proven to myself now that I like Pepsi better.

ANNCR: Nationwide more people prefer the taste of Pepsi over Coca-Cola.
CHERIE BOOTH: I think today's test was very honest.
DAVE: Pepsi has a better product and that's probably why they are running a test like this because it's obvious how many people over here have picked Pepsi.

SUZANNE MACK: Being able to compare the two, I'd pick Pepsi.
CHERIE: If someone offered me either or, I choose the Pepsi.
ANNCR: What will you say? Take the Pepsi Challenge and find out.

switchers. Taste tests comparing Pepsi and Pepsi ONE with Coca-Cola products were conducted in more than 30 cities. This latest version of the challenge also included a cross promotion designed to further engage young consumers in Pepsi products. Consumers taking the Pepsi Challenge had their photos taken and posted online at pepsi.com, generating awareness of and traffic to Pepsi's website.

Defending Current Customers With more new brands entering the market every day and competitors attempting to take away their customers through aggressive advertising and sales promotion efforts, many companies are turning to sales promotion programs to hold present customers and defend their market share. A company can use sales promotion techniques in several ways to retain its current customer base. One way is to load them with the product, taking them out of the market for a certain time. Special price promotions, coupons, or bonus packs can encourage consumers to stock up on the brand. This not only keeps them using the company's brand but also reduces the likelihood they will switch brands in response to a competitor's promotion.

Targeting a Specific Market Segment Most companies focus their marketing efforts on specific market segments and are always looking for ways to reach their target audiences. Many marketers are finding that sales promotion tools such as contests and sweepstakes, events, coupons, and samplings are very effective ways to reach specific geographic, demographic, psychographic, and ethnic markets. Sales promotion programs can also be targeted to specific user-status groups such as nonusers or light versus heavy users.

Contests have become a popular sales promotion tool for targeting specific market segments. For example, Perdue Farms, Inc., the country's fourth-largest poultry producer, developed a contest to support its Fun Shapes line of breaded chicken nuggets among its core target of women between the ages of 25 and 49 and its secondary market of children ages 2 to 12. The Fun Shapes line is a series of different and uniquely shaped nuggets including basketball, baseball, tic-tac-toe, dinosaur, and space-theme designs. Its promotion agency, DVC, developed a contest known as the Perdue "Masterpieces in Chicken" that invited children to design the nugget shape they would most like to see Perdue add to its line of fun shapes (Exhibit 16-11). The grand-prize winner was designated "Artist of the Year" and received an all-expense paid family trip to Paris for a guided tour of the Louvre and passes to Euro-Disney. The winning design was also made into a shape by Perdue and introduced into its line in 2000. The program received thousands of entries and in the weeks during and after the promotion, sales volume increased by 10 percent.

Exhibit 16-11 Perdue Farms' "Masterpieces in Chicken" contest was targeted at mothers and their children

Enhancing Integrated Marketing Communications and Building Brand Equity A final objective for consumer-oriented promotions is to enhance or support the integrated marketing communications effort for a brand or company. Building brand equity and image has traditionally been done through advertising. However, sales promotion techniques such as contests or sweepstakes and premium offers are often used to draw attention to an ad, increase involvement with the message and product/service, and help build relationships with consumers. For example, one of the objectives of Perdue Farms' "Masterpiece in Chicken" promotion was to increase consumers' involvement level by encouraging them to interact with the brand. The promotion contributed to brand equity by using a contest that was fun and relevant to both mothers and children.

IMC Perspective 16-2 discusses how a number of marketers are recognizing the value of contests as a way of building and/or maintaining brand equity.

IMC PERSPECTIVE 16-2

Using Contests to Build Brand Equity

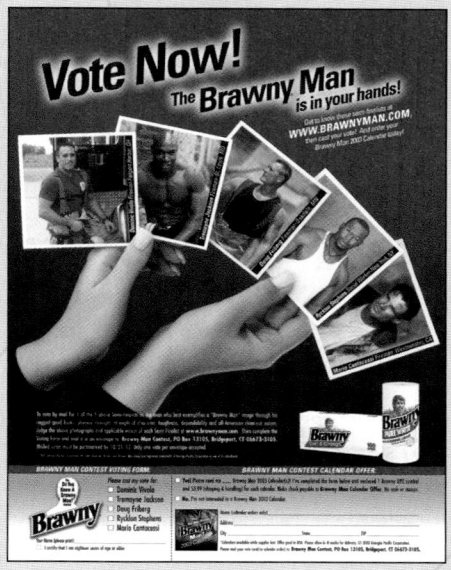

Building and/or maintaining brand equity has become an important goal for marketers as they develop their sales promotion strategies. Companies are asking their promotion agencies to think strategically and develop promotional programs that can do more than just generate short-term sales. They want promotions that require consumers to become more involved with their brands and offer a means of presenting the brand essence in an engaging way. Many marketers are recognizing that a well-designed and -executed contest can be a very effective way to engage consumers and differentiate their brands. Contests are experiencing resurgence as marketers focus less on awareness and more on ways to engender consumer interaction and get their branding messages across.

One of the reasons for the growing popularity of contests is that they can be used to get consumers to think about a brand and how they can relate to it. Some companies are using contests rather than sweepstakes as the latter are seen as less involving and less motivating. Because of the additional work involved in participating, contests attract brand loyalists who are not just entering to win a big prize. The right type of contest can also transcend its role as a promotional tool and help build the brand franchise. For example, the Pillsbury Bake-Off, which has been around since 1949, requires participants to whip up their favorite dishes featuring Pillsbury ingredients. The contest has been adapted to fit the times, and now includes an "Easy Cook Night" for contemporary on-the-go eating habits and a $1 million grand prize. The final round brings 100 chefs together for a televised bake-off, and thousands of recipe books are distributed annually. Eighty percent of the female entrants now have careers, and 10 percent of the entries in recent years have come from men. The director of corporate promotion and marketing for Pillsbury notes, "Prizes are certainly part of the incentive, but the real motivation is the fundamental desire for recognition."

Contests can also be helpful in rejuvenating struggling brands by creating interest and excitement that can get consumers to become involved with them. When the Georgia-Pacific Corp. acquired the Brawny paper-towel business a few years ago, it inherited a declining brand. As part of its effort to rebuild the brand, the company wanted to leverage the Brawny Man icon as well as gain insight into the modern-day woman's opinions as to what makes a man brawny. In the summer of 2002 Georgia-Pacific conducted the "Do You Know a Brawny Man™?" promotion, which included a contest asking women to send in photos and 150-word descriptions explaining why their guys are as rugged as the product. More than 40,000 entry forms were downloaded from the Brawnyman.com website, and over 4,000 people wrote to the company to nominate someone to be the Brawny Man. Five finalists were selected, and consumers were able to vote online and through the mail to choose a winner, whose picture appeared on the package for a few weeks. Information gathered from the entrants was used by the Brawny marketing team to develop a permanent Brawny Man image to replace the smiling lumberjack, who was long overdue for a makeover.

Marketers feel that contests can often provide them with insight into consumers who use their brands. Campbell Soup Co. has run a "What Do You Do With Your Pace?" recipe contest for several years as a way of understanding how its customers actually use the salsa brand. The contest averages about 12,000 entries and has produced some interesting tidbits into how consumers use the product. A recent grand-prize winner submitted a recipe for banana bread that included salsa as an ingredient. Thales Navigation, manufacturer of the Magellan GPS navigation system, ran a contest requiring entrants to write an essay about their off-road adventures. The winner was sponsored in the Jaos Adventure Road Rally, an annual high-tech scavenger hunt that sends participants into the Nevada desert looking for cues with GPS devices.

More marketers are realizing that contests can get consumers to think more about a product than about the prize they might win. As the brand manager for Brawny paper towels notes: "For the winner, the contest provides 15 minutes of fame. For the consumer, it provides a better opportunity to relate to the brand than just seeing it as they walk down the aisle."

Sources: Evan Perez and Chad Terhune, "Today, 'Brawny' Men Help with the Kids and the Housework," *The Wall Street Journal,* Oct. 4, 2002, p. B2; Matthew Kinsman, "May the Best Brand Win," *Promo,* August 2002, pp. 45–47.

Consumer-Oriented Sales Promotion Techniques

Sampling

Marketers use various sales promotion techniques to meet the objectives just discussed. Figure 16-2 shows the extent to which these consumer promotions are used by packaged-goods companies.

Sampling involves a variety of procedures whereby consumers are given some quantity of a product for no charge to induce trial. Sampling is generally considered the most effective way to generate trial, although it is also the most expensive. As a sales promotion technique, sampling is often used to introduce a new product or brand to the market. However, as Figure 16-2 shows, sampling is also used for established products as well. Some companies do not use sampling for established products, reasoning that samples may not induce satisfied users of a competing brand to switch and may just go to the firm's current customers, who would buy the product anyway. This may not be true when significant changes (new and improved) are made in a brand.

Manufacturers of packaged-goods products such as food, health care items, cosmetics, and toiletries are heavy users of sampling since their products meet the three criteria for an effective sampling program:

1. The products are of relatively low unit value, so samples do not cost too much.
2. The products are divisible, which means they can be broken into small sample sizes that are adequate for demonstrating the brand's features and benefits to the user.
3. The purchase cycle is relatively short, so the consumer will consider an immediate purchase or will not forget about the brand before the next purchase occasion.

Benefits and Limitations of Sampling

Samples are an excellent way to induce trial as they provide consumers with a risk-free way to try new products. A

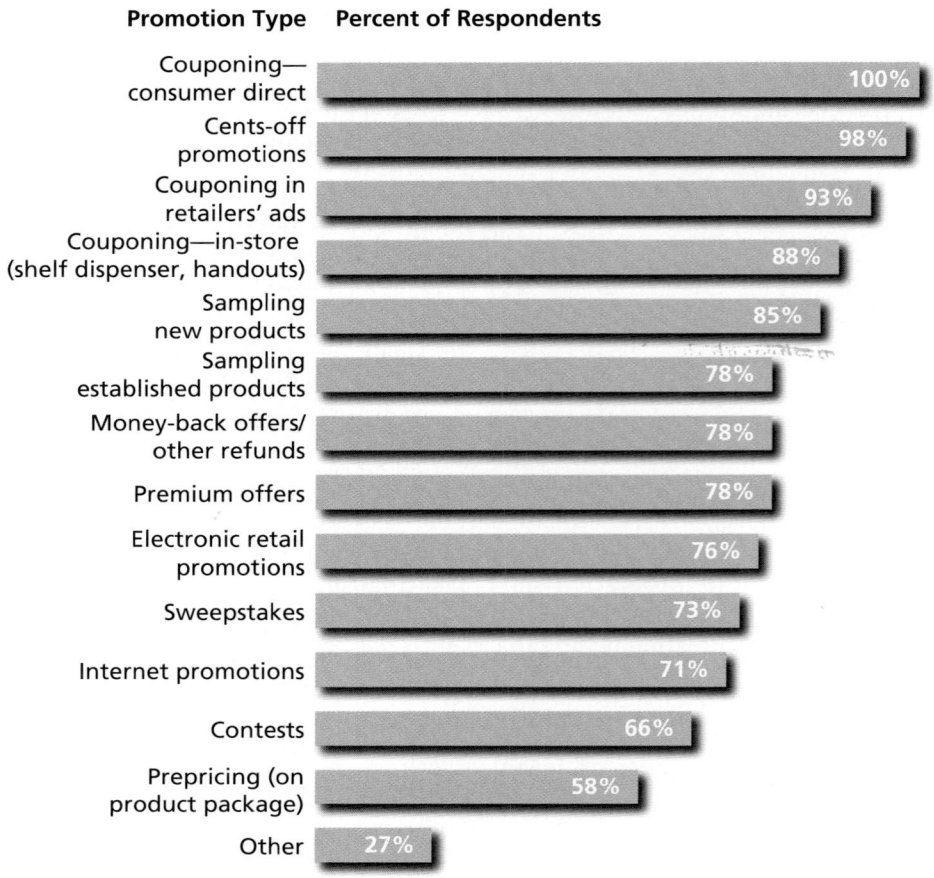

Figure 16-2 Types of consumer promotions used by packaged-goods manufacturers

major study conducted by the Promotion Marketing Association in 2002 found that the vast majority of consumers receiving a sample either use it right away or save it to use sometime later.[27] Sampling generates much higher trial rates than advertising or other sales promotion techniques.

Getting people to try a product leads to a second benefit of sampling: Consumers experience the brand directly, gaining a greater appreciation for its benefits. This can be particularly important when a product's features and benefits are difficult to describe through advertising. Many foods, beverages, and cosmetics have subtle features that are most appreciated when experienced directly. Nearly 70 percent of the respondents in the PMA survey indicated they have purchased a product they did not normally use after trying a free sample. The study also found that samples are even more likely to lead to purchase when they are accompanied by a coupon.

While samples are an effective way to induce trial, the brand must have some unique or superior benefits for a sampling program to be worthwhile. Otherwise, the sampled consumers revert back to other brands and do not become repeat purchasers. The costs of a sampling program can be recovered only if it gets a number of consumers to become regular users of the brand at full retail price.

Another possible limitation to sampling is that the benefits of some products are difficult to gauge immediately, and the learning period required to appreciate the brand may require supplying the consumer with larger amounts of the brand than are affordable. An example would be an expensive skin cream that is promoted as preventing or reducing wrinkles but has to be used for an extended period before any effects are seen.

Sampling Methods One basic decision the sales promotion or brand manager must make is how the sample will be distributed. The sampling method chosen is important not only in terms of costs but also because it influences the type of consumer who receives the sample. The best sampling method gets the product to the best prospects for trial and subsequent repurchase. Some basic distribution methods include door-to-door, direct-mail, in-store, and on-package approaches.

Door-to-door sampling, in which the product is delivered directly to the prospect's residence, is used when it is important to control where the sample is delivered. This distribution method is very expensive because of labor costs, but it can be cost-effective if the marketer has information that helps define the target market and/or if the prospects are located in a well-defined geographic area. Some companies have samples delivered directly to consumers' homes by including them with newspapers. Sunday papers have become an increasingly attractive way of mass distributing samples. However, there are also a number of newspapers that can now distribute a sample into a subscriber segment as small as 250 households with little increase in costs to marketers. Many newspapers distribute samples through polybags which are plastic bags that serve as covers for the paper and deliver a promotional message along with the sample.(Exhibit 16-12).

Sampling through the mail is common for small, lightweight, nonperishable products. A major advantage of this method is that the marketer has control over where and when the product will be distributed and can target the sample to specific market areas. Many marketers are using information from geodemographic target marketing programs such as Claritas's Prizm or Microvision to better target their sample mailings. The main drawbacks to mail sampling are postal restrictions and increasing postal rates.

In-store sampling is increasingly popular, especially for food products. The marketer hires temporary demonstrators who set up a table or booth, prepare small samples of the product, and pass them out to shoppers. The in-store sampling approach can be very effective for food products, since consumers get to taste the item and the demonstrator can give them more information about the product while it is being sampled. Demonstrators may also give consumers a cents-off coupon for the sampled item to encourage immediate trial purchase. While this sampling method can be very effective, it can also be expensive and requires a great deal of planning, as well as the cooperation of retailers.

Exhibit 16-12 Polybags are used by many newspapers to distribute samples

Exhibit 16-13 Armor All uses on-package samples for related products

On-package sampling, where a sample of a product is attached to another item, is another common sampling method (see Exhibit 16-13). This procedure can be very cost-effective, particularly for multiproduct firms that attach a sample of a new product to an existing brand's package. A drawback is that since the sample is distributed only to consumers who purchase the item to which it is attached, the sample will not reach nonusers of the carrier brand. Marketers can expand this sampling method by attaching the sample to multiple carrier brands and including samples with products not made by their company.

Event sampling has become one of the fastest-growing and most popular ways of distributing samples. Many marketers are using sampling programs that are part of integrated marketing programs that feature events, media tie-ins, and other activities that provide consumers with a total sense of a brand rather than just a few tastes of a food or beverage or a trial size of a packaged-goods product. Event sampling can take place in stores as well as at a variety of other venues such as concerts, sporting events, and other places.

Other Methods of Sampling

The four sampling methods just discussed are the most common, but several other methods are also used. Marketers may insert packets in magazines or newspapers (particularly Sunday supplements). Some tobacco and cereal companies send samples to consumers who call toll-free numbers to request them or mail in sample request forms. As discussed in Chapter 14, these sampling methods are becoming popular because they can help marketers build a database for direct marketing.

Many companies also use specialized sample distribution services such as Advo Inc. and D. L. Blair. These firms help the company identify consumers who are nonusers of a product or users of a competing brand and develop appropriate procedures for distributing a sample to them. Many college students receive sample packs at the beginning of the semester that contain trial sizes of such products as mouthwash, toothpaste, headache remedies, and deodorant.

The Internet is yet another way companies are making it possible for consumers to sample their products, and it is adding a whole new level of targeting to the mix by giving consumers the opportunity to choose the samples they want. Catalina Marketing's ValuPage.com sampling and distribution service now has over one million members. The Sunflower Group's SiteLinkPlus program offers companies a fulfillment service from their brand or corporate websites for samples, coupons, and premiums (Exhibit 16-14). The service asks consumers qualifying questions on brand loyalty, product usage, and lifestyles that can be used by marketers to target their samples and other promotional offers more effectively.

Some companies cut back on their sampling programs in recent years because they felt they were too expensive, wasteful, and fraught with distribution problems. However, several factors have led to a resurgence in sampling recently. First, big companies like Advo and Time Warner have entered the sampling business, which creates more competition and helps keep sampling costs down. Also, a combination of technology and creativity is driving new sampling methods that let marketers target more

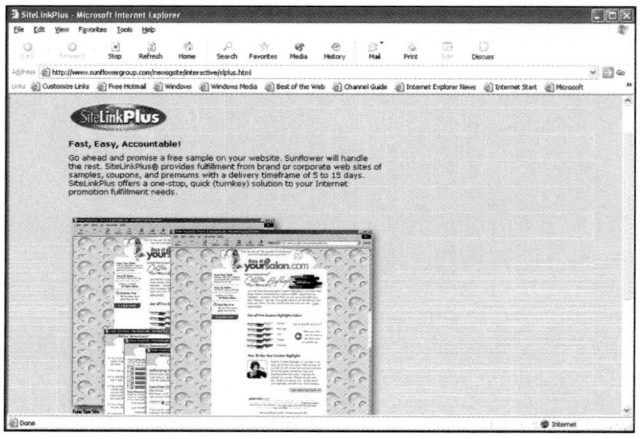

Exhibit 16-14 The Sunflower Group's SiteLinkPlus provides companies with a fulfillment service for samples

efficiently. Yet another factor may be the everyday low-pricing strategies that have prompted companies such as Procter & Gamble to move away from coupons and other price promotions in favor of samples. Many marketers are finding that sampling meets the complementary goals of introducing consumers to their products and getting retailers to support their promotional programs.

Couponing

The oldest, most widely used, and most effective sales promotion tool is the cents-off coupon. Coupons have been around since 1895, when the C. W. Post Co. started using the penny-off coupon to sell its new Grape-Nuts cereal. In recent years, coupons have become increasingly popular with consumers, which may explain their explosive growth among manufacturers and retailers that use them as sales promotion incentives. As Figure 16-2 showed, coupons are the most popular sales promotion technique as they are used by nearly all the packaged-goods firms.

Coupon distribution rose dramatically over the past 30 years. The number of coupons distributed by consumer packaged-goods marketers increased from 16 billion in 1968 to a peak of 310 billion in 1994. Since 1994 coupon distribution has been declining, and it dropped to 239 billion in 2001. According to NCH Promotional Services, a company that tracks coupon distribution and redemption patterns, nearly 80 percent of consumers in the United States use coupons and nearly 25 percent say they always use them when they shop. The average face value of coupons distributed increased from 21 cents in 1981 to 83 cents in 2001. The average face value of the 4 billion coupons that were redeemed in 2001 was 74 cents.[28]

Adding additional fuel to the coupon explosion of the past several decades has been the vast number of coupons distributed through retailers that are not even included in these figures. In most markets, a number of grocery stores make manufacturers' coupons even more attractive to consumers by doubling the face value.

Advantages and Limitations of Coupons

Coupons have a number of advantages that make them popular sales promotion tools for both new and established products. First, coupons make it possible to offer a price reduction only to those consumers who are price-sensitive. Such consumers generally purchase *because* of coupons, while those who are not as concerned about price buy the brand at full value. Coupons also make it possible to reduce the retail price of a product without relying on retailers for cooperation, which can often be a problem. Coupons are generally regarded as second only to sampling as a promotional technique for generating trial. Since a coupon lowers the price of a product, it reduces the consumer's perceived risk associated with trial of a new brand. Coupons can encourage repurchase after initial trial. Many new products include a cents-off coupon inside the package to encourage repeat purchase.

Coupons can also be useful promotional devices for established products. They can encourage nonusers to try a brand, encourage repeat purchase among current users, and get users to try a new, improved version of a brand. Coupons may also help coax users of a product to trade up to more expensive brands. The product category where coupons are used most is disposable diapers, followed by cereal, detergent, and deodorant. Some of the product categories where coupons are used the least are carbonated beverages, candy, and gum.

But there are a number of problems with coupons. First, it can be difficult to estimate how many consumers will use a coupon and when. Response to a coupon is rarely immediate; it typically takes anywhere from two to six months to redeem one. A study of coupon redemption patterns by Inman and McAlister found that many coupons are redeemed just before the expiration date rather than in the period following the initial coupon drop.[29] Many marketers are attempting to expedite redemption by shortening the time period before expiration. The average length of time from issue date to expiration date for coupons in 2001 was 3.2 months, for grocery products. However, coupons remain less effective than sampling for inducing initial product trial in a short period.

A problem associated with using coupons to attract new users to an established brand is that it is difficult to prevent the coupons from being used by consumers who

already use the brand. For example, General Foods decided to reduce its use of coupons for Maxwell House coffee when research revealed the coupons were being redeemed primarily by current users. Rather than attracting new users, coupons can end up reducing the company's profit margins among consumers who would probably purchase the product anyway.

Other problems with coupons include low redemption rates and high costs. Couponing program expenses include the face value of the coupon redeemed plus costs for production, distribution, and handling of the coupons. Figure 16-3 shows the calculations used to determine the costs of a couponing program using an FSI (free-standing insert) in the Sunday newspaper and a coupon with an average face value of 74 cents. As can be seen from these figures, the cost of a couponing program can be very high. Former Procter & Gamble chairman Durk Jager, who led efforts to rein in the company's use of coupons in the late 90s, has argued that they are extremely inefficient. He contends that it may cost as much as $50 to move a case of goods with coupons that may generate only $10 to $12 in gross profit.[30] Marketers should track coupon costs very carefully to ensure their use is economically feasible.

Another problem with coupon promotions is misredemption, or the cashing of a coupon without purchase of the brand. Coupon misredemption or fraud occurs in a number of ways, including:

- Redemption of coupons by consumers for a product or size not specified on the coupon.
- Redemption of coupons by salesclerks in exchange for cash.
- Gathering and redemption of coupons by store managers or owners without the accompanying sale of the product.
- Gathering or printing of coupons by criminals who sell them to unethical merchants, who in turn redeem them.

Estimates of coupon misredemption costs are as high as $500 million.[31] Many manufacturers hold firm in their policy to not pay retailers for questionable amounts or suspicious types of coupon submissions. However, some companies are less aggressive, and this affects their profit margins. Marketers must allow a certain percentage for misredemption when estimating the costs of a couponing program. Ways to identify and control coupon misredemption, such as improved coding, are being developed, but it still remains a problem.

Figure 16-3 Calculating couponing costs

Cost per Coupon Redeemed: An Illustration	
1. Distribution cost 55,000,000 circulation × $6.25/M	$343,750
2. Redemptions at 1.8%	990,000
3. Redemption cost 990,000 redemptions × $.74 face value	$732,600
4. Retailer handling cost and processor fees 990,000 redemptions × $.10	$99,000
5. Total program cost Items 1 + 3 + 4	$1,175,350
6. Cost per coupon redeemed Cost divided by redemption	$1.19
7. Actual product sold on redemption (misredemption estimated at 20%) 990,000 × 80%	792,000
8. Cost per product moved Program cost divided by amount of product sold	$1.48

Coupon Distribution Coupons can be disseminated to consumers by a number of means, including freestanding inserts in Sunday newspapers, direct mail, newspapers (either in individual ads or as a group of coupons in a cooperative format), magazines, and packages. Distribution through newspaper *freestanding inserts* is by far the most popular method for delivering coupons to consumers, accounting for 84 percent of all coupons distributed in 2001. This growth has come at the expense of vehicles such as manufacturers' ads in newspapers (newspaper ROP), newspaper co-op ads, and magazines.

There are a number of reasons why FSIs are the most popular way of delivering coupons, including their high-quality four-color graphics, competitive distribution costs, national same-day circulation, market selectivity, and the fact that they can be competition-free due to category exclusivity (by FSI company). Prices for a full-page FSI are currently about $6 to $7 per thousand, which makes FSI promotions very efficient and affordable. Because of their consumer popularity and predictable distribution, coupons distributed in FSIs are also a strong selling point with the retail trade.

The increased distribution of coupons through FSIs has, however, led to a clutter problem. Consumers are being bombarded with too many coupons, and although each FSI publisher offers product exclusivity in its insert, this advantage may be negated when there are three inserts in a Sunday paper. Redemption rates of FSI coupons have declined from 4 percent to only 1.3 percent and even lower for some products (Figure 16-4). These problems are leading many marketers to look at ways of delivering coupons that will result in less clutter and higher redemption rates, such as direct mail.

Direct mail accounts for about 2.1 percent of all coupons distributed. Most are sent by local retailers or through co-op mailings where a packet of coupons for many different products is sent to a household. These couponing programs include Metromail's Red Letter Day, Advo System's Super Coups, and Cox Target Media's Valpak. IMC Perspective 16-3 discusses how Cox Target Media recently redesigned the familiar Valpak blue envelope that delivers billions of coupons each year and created an advertising campaign to improve the image of the direct-mail piece.

Direct-mail couponing has several advantages. First, the mailing can be sent to a broad audience or targeted to specific geographic or demographic markets such as teenagers, senior citizens, Hispanics, and other market segments. Firms that mail their

Media	Grocery Products	Health and Beauty Products
FSI	1.3%	0.8%
Newspaper	0.8	0.4
Magazine	1.0	0.6
Direct mail	3.2	3.5
Regular in-pack	6.3	2.6
Regular on-pack	8.4	13.7
In-pack cross-ruff	4.7	8.4
On-pack cross-ruff	5.8	6.2
Instant on-pack	18.1	40.8
Instant on-pack cross-ruff	5.3	4.9
Handout electronically dispensed	7.2	4.8
On-shelf distributed	8.3	5.8
All other handouts in store	3.3	4.4
All other handouts away from store	4.0	4.2

Source: NCH Marketing Services, 2002 Trend Report.

Figure 16-4 Coupon redemption rates by media type

IMC PERSPECTIVE 16-3

Getting Consumers to Love the Valpak Blue Envelope

Cox Target Media provides direct-marketing services and solutions to advertisers who want to reach specific target audiences. Its first branded product, the Valpak blue envelope, has been mailed to consumers for over 35 years and is currently distributed to more than 50 million homes and businesses throughout the United States, Canada, Puerto Rico, and the United Kingdom. Every year, 500 Valpak mailings deliver over 15 billion coupons and advertising offers to consumers in highly recognizable light blue envelopes. Valpak is sold through a network of over 220 independent franchisees and has a varied reputation that depends on the quality of the local business owner and content mix. As a direct-mail product, Valpak relies on consumers to open the envelope and examine the contents to spur increased redemptions of the coupons and other promotional offers for its clients' products.

In 2001 Cox Target Media conducted extensive research to determine the overall awareness, growth potential, and consumer perception of the blue envelope. The research showed that Valpak's blue envelope was perceived as a locally mailed product and that its dated design, which had not changed in 15 years, was a turn-off to image-conscious national advertisers. Cox wanted to attract new advertisers as users of its service and leverage relationships with its existing clients, and it recognized that these problems had to be addressed. In 2002 Cox redesigned the blue envelope and launched an extensive advertising campaign to reposition Valpak with the consumer. The new design includes an updated Valpak logo as well as a Valpak.com logo to send shoppers online, splashy graphics and re-energized blue colors to refresh the envelope, and lively color photos that change with the seasons.

Cox also created the Valpak "Loves" advertising campaign with the goal of upscaling the Valpak image in the mind of consumers and potential advertisers. The campaign was designed to connect the contents of the blue envelope with the activities and objects that are already central to the end users' lives. Four television commercials and four complementary print ads were created featuring consumers who closely profile the demographics of people who already take advantage of the coupons and other savings offers found within Valpak. They are everyday, yet upscale, people who enjoy everyday pleasures like improving their homes or engaging in a family outing. The ads also highlight the categories of content and savings that Cox's research indicated consumers want to find inside the blue envelope. The tagline used in all of the commercials and print ads is "There's something in it for you," which reinforces the benefits consumers receive from the offers contained in the Valpak envelope.

The four TV commercials created for the campaign ran on national spot television in 92 Nielsen Designated Market Area territories. Valpak franchise owners were also invited to supplement the national spot placement by purchasing additional time on local stations. Two of the commercials were adapted to 10- and 20-second formats to accommodate the inclusion of local advertiser's logos or information or local Valpak mailing-date information. For the national print campaign, Valpak ads were run in a selection of women's aspirational magazines including *Martha Stewart Living* and *Oprah* as well as service publications such as *Woman's Day, Redbook,* and *Good Housekeeping.*

The "Loves" campaign has been successful in improving both consumer and advertiser perceptions of the quality associated with the Valpak brand and the contents of the blue envelope. Valpak has always been perceived as the best, as well as the best known, of all the cooperative direct-mail marketing vehicles. The repositioning campaign has helped Cox attract a number of high-profile, national advertisers as promotional partners, including 20th Century Fox Studios, CBS, H&R Block, and Burger King. It has also been successful in getting consumers to think twice before tossing out the ubiquitous blue envelopes that appear in their mailboxes. They know there truly is "something in it" for them.

Source: Melissa Fisher, vice president of marketing and communication, Cox Target Media.

own coupons can be quite selective about recipients. Another important advantage of direct-mail couponing is a redemption rate of over 3 percent, much higher than for FSIs. Direct-mail couponing can also be combined with a sample, which makes it a very effective way to gain the attention of consumers.

The major disadvantage of direct-mail coupon delivery is the expense relative to other distribution methods. The cost per thousand for distributing coupons through co-op mailings ranges from $10 to $15, and more targeted promotions can cost $20 to $25 or even more. Also, the higher redemption rate of mail-delivered coupons may result from the fact that many recipients are already users of the brand who take advantage of the coupons sent directly to them.

The use of *newspapers* and *magazines* as couponing vehicles has declined dramatically since the introduction of FSIs. In 2001 only 1.3 percent of coupons were distributed via newspapers. The advantages of newspapers as a couponing vehicle include market selectivity, shorter lead times with timing to the day, cooperative advertising opportunities that can lead to cost efficiencies, and promotional tie-ins with retailers. Other advantages of newspaper-delivered coupons are the broad exposure and consumer receptivity. Many consumers actively search the newspaper for coupons, especially on Sundays or "food day" (when grocery stores advertise their specials). This enhances the likelihood of the consumer at least noticing the coupon. Problems with newspapers as couponing vehicles include higher distribution costs, poor reproduction quality, clutter, and declining readership of newspapers; all contribute to low redemption rates.

The use of magazines as a couponing vehicle has also declined steadily since the introduction of FSIs. Magazines now account for only about 2 percent of the total number of coupons distributed each year. Distribution of coupons through magazines can take advantage of the selectivity of the publication to reach specific target audiences, along with enhanced production capabilities and extended copy life in the home. However, the cost of distributing coupons through magazines is very high and redemption rates are low (just under 1 percent).

Placing coupons either *inside* or on the *outside* of the *package* is a distribution method that accounted for about 3 percent of the coupons distributed in 2001. The in/on-package coupon has virtually no distribution costs and a much higher redemption rate than other couponing methods, averaging between 3 and nearly 14 percent. An in/on-pack coupon that is redeemable for the next purchase of the same brand is known as a **bounce-back coupon.** This type of coupon gives consumers an inducement to repurchase the brand.

Bounce-back coupons are often used with product samples to encourage the consumer to purchase the product after sampling. They may be included in or on the package during the early phases of a brand's life cycle to encourage repeat purchase, or they may be a defensive maneuver for a mature brand that is facing competitive pressure and wants to retain its current users. The main limitation of bounce-back coupons is that they go only to purchasers of the brand and thus do not attract nonusers. A bounce-back coupon placed on the package for Kellogg's Eggo brand waffles is shown in Exhibit 16-15.

Another type of in/on-pack coupon is the **cross-ruff coupon,** which is redeemable on the purchase of a different product, usually one made by the same company but occasionally through a tie-in with another manufacturer. Cross-ruff coupons have a redemption rate of 4 to 8 percent and can be effective in encouraging consumers to try other products or brands. Companies with wide product lines, such as cereal manufacturers, often use these coupons.

Yet another type of package coupon is the **instant coupon,** which is attached to the outside of the package so the consumer can rip it off and redeem it immediately at the time of purchase. Instant coupons have the highest redemption levels of all types of coupons, averaging around 18 percent for grocery products and jumping to over 40 percent for health and beauty items. However, the redemption level is

Exhibit 16-15 Kellogg's uses an on-package coupon to encourage repurchase

much lower for instant cross-ruff coupons, as it averages around 5 percent. Instant coupons give consumers an immediate point-of-purchase incentive, and can be selectively placed in terms of promotion timing and market region. Some companies prefer instant coupons to price-off deals because the latter require more cooperation from retailers and can be more expensive, since every package must be reduced in price.

Another distribution method that has experienced strong growth over the past 10 years or so is **in-store couponing,** which includes all co-op couponing programs distributed in a retail store environment. This medium now accounts for around 8 percent of total coupon distribution. Coupons are distributed to consumers in stores in several ways, including tear-off pads, handouts in the store (sometimes as part of a sampling demonstration), on-shelf dispensers, and electronic dispensers.

Most of the coupons distributed in stores are through ActMedia's Instant Coupon Machine. This coupon dispenser is mounted on the shelf in front of the product being promoted. It has blinking red lights to draw consumers' attention to the savings opportunity. These in-store coupons have several advantages: They can reach consumers when they are ready to make a purchase, increase brand awareness on the shelf, generate impulse buying, and encourage product trial. They also provide category exclusivity. In-store couponing removes the need for consumers to clip coupons from FSIs or print ads and then remember to bring them to the store. Redemption rates for coupons distributed by the Instant Coupon Machine are very high, averaging about 6 to 8 percent.

Another popular way to distribute in-store coupons is through electronic devices such as kiosks or at the checkout counter. Some electronically dispensed coupons, such as Catalina Marketing Corp.'s Checkout Coupon, are tied to scanner data at each grocery store checkout. When the specified product, such as a competitive brand, is purchased, the consumer receives a coupon at the checkout for the company's brand (Exhibit 16-16). Companies also use this system to link purchases of products that are related. For example, a consumer who purchases a caffeine-free cola might be issued a coupon for a decaffeinated coffee.

Major advantages of electronically dispensed checkout coupons are that they are cost-effective and can be targeted to specific categories of consumers, such as users of competitive or complementary products. Since 65 to 85 percent of a manufacturer's coupons are used by current customers, marketers want to target their coupons to users of competitive brands. Redemption rates are also high for electronically dispensed coupons, averaging around 5 to 7 percent.

Exhibit 16-16 Catalina Marketing promotes its checkout coupons

Couponing Trends

Over the past four years the number of coupons distributed has declined by nearly 20 percent. While the average American household is still being barraged with nearly 3,000 coupons per year, many marketers have cut back on their use of coupons because of concerns over costs and effectiveness. Critics argue that coupons cost too much to print, distribute, and process and that they don't benefit enough consumers. Consumers redeemed less than 2 percent of the 239 billion coupons distributed in 2001. Former Procter & Gamble CEO Durk Jager echoed the sentiment of many consumer-product companies when he said, "Who can argue for a practice that fails 98 percent of the time?"[32]

Despite the growing sentiment among major marketers that coupons are inefficient and costly, very few companies, including Procter & Gamble, are likely to abandon them entirely.[33] Although most coupons never get used, consumers use some of them and have come to expect them. More than 80 percent of consumers use coupons and nearly one-quarter say they use them every time they shop. With so many consumers eager for coupons, marketers will continue to accommodate them. However, companies as well as the coupon industry are looking for ways to improve on their use.

Marketers are continually searching for more effective couponing techniques. General Mills, Kellogg, and Post replaced brand-specific coupons with universal coupons good for any of their cereal brands. For example, to make its couponing spending more efficient, Post began using universal coupons worth $1.50 off two boxes (matching the average cereal-coupon discount of 75 cents) and cut coupon distribution in half. Even though Post

dropped only half as many coupons, redemption rates reached 6 percent, far exceeding the FSI average of less than 2 percent.[34]

Some marketers are broadening their use of account-specific direct-mail couponing, in which coupons are cobranded with individual retailers but can be used by consumers at any retail store. Procter & Gamble began using account-specific couponing with Tide detergent and has broadened the program to include mailings for a number of other brands.[35]

Some marketers and retailers are looking to the Internet as a medium for distributing coupons. Several companies now offer online couponing services. Catalina Marketing started Valupage.com as a way for marketers to reach consumers at home with promotions traditionally offered in-store, including coupons. Consumers can log on to the website, type in their Zip code and choose from a list of participating grocery stores in their area and download manufacturer- and retailer-sponsored coupons. A number of retailers, particularly supermarkets, are also using the Internet to distribute coupons to encourage consumers to shop at their stores. Cox Target Media also offers consumers the opportunity to access coupons online, through Valpak.com. The website makes the same coupons and offers available to consumers that come in the Valpak direct-mail envelope (Exhibit 16-17).

Premiums

Premiums are a sales promotion device used by many marketers. A **premium** is an offer of an item of merchandise or service either free or at a low price that is an extra incentive for purchasers. Many marketers are eliminating toys and gimmicks in favor of value-added premiums that reflect the quality of the product and are consistent with its image and positioning in the market. Marketers spend over $4 billion a year on value-added premium incentives targeted at the consumer market. The two basic types of offers are the free premium and the self-liquidating premium.

Free Premiums

Free premiums are usually small gifts or merchandise included in the product package or sent to consumers who mail in a request along with a proof of purchase. In/on-package free premiums include toys, balls, trading cards, or other items included in cereal packages, as well as samples of one product included with another. Surveys have shown that in/on-package premiums are consumers' favorite type of promotion.[36]

Package-carried premiums have high impulse value and can provide an extra incentive to buy the product. However, several problems are associated with their use. First,

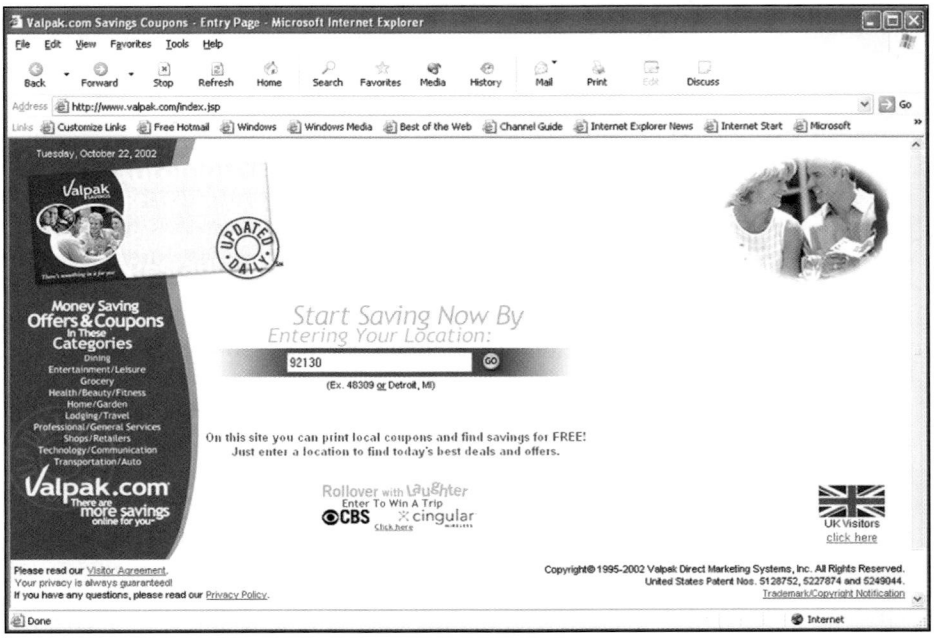

Exhibit 16-17 Coupons are now available online

Exhibit 16-18 McDonald's Happy Meals use toys to help attract children

there is the cost factor, which results from the premium itself as well as from extra packaging that may be needed. Finding desirable premiums at reasonable costs can be difficult, particularly for adult markets, and using a poor premium may do more harm than good.

Another problem with these premiums is possible restrictions from regulatory agencies such as the Federal Trade Commission and the Food and Drug Administration or from industry codes regarding the type of premium used. The National Association of Broadcasters has strict guidelines regarding the advertising of premium offers to children. There is concern that premium offers will entice children to request a brand to get the promoted item and then never consume the product. The networks' policy on children's advertising is that a premium offer cannot exceed 15 seconds of a 30-second spot, and the emphasis must be on the product, not the premium.

Since most free mail-in premium offers require the consumer to send in more than one proof of purchase, they encourage repeat purchase and reward brand loyalty. But a major drawback of mail-in premiums is that they do not offer immediate reinforcement or reward to the purchaser, so they may not provide enough incentive to purchase the brand. Few consumers take advantage of mail-in premium offers; the average redemption rate is only 2 to 4 percent.[37]

Free premiums have become very popular in the restaurant industry, particularly among fast-food chains such as McDonald's and Burger King, which use premium offers in their kids' meals to attract children.[38] McDonald's has become the world's largest toymaker on a unit basis, commissioning about 750 million toys per year for its Happy Meals (Exhibit 16-18). Many of the premium offers used by the fast-food giants have cross-promotional tie-ins with popular movies and can be very effective at generating incremental sales. McDonald's gained a major competitive advantage in the movie tie-in premium wars in 1996 when it signed an agreement with Disney giving McDonald's exclusive rights to promotional tie-ins with Disney movies for 10 years.[39]

One of the fastest-growing types of incentive offers being used by marketers is airline miles, which have literally become a promotional currency. U.S. airlines make more than an estimated $2 billion each year selling miles to other marketers. Consumers are now choosing credit-card services, phone services, hotels, and many other products and services on the basis of mileage premiums for major frequent-flyer programs such as American Airlines' AAdvantage program or United Airlines' Mileage Plus program. Exhibit 16-19 shows a trade ad run by American Airlines promoting the value of AAdvantage miles as a promotional incentive that companies can offer their customers to help generate sales.

Exhibit 16-19 American Airlines promotes the value of AAdvantage miles as a purchase incentive

Self-Liquidating Premiums

Self-liquidating premiums require the consumer to pay some or all of the cost of the premium plus handling and mailing costs. The marketer usually purchases items used as self-liquidating premiums in large quantities and offers them to consumers at lower-than-retail prices. The goal is not to make a profit on the premium item but rather just to cover costs and offer a value to the consumer.

In addition to cost savings, self-liquidating premiums offer several advantages to marketers. Offering values to consumers through the premium products can create interest in the brand and goodwill that enhances the brand's image. These premiums can also encourage trade support and gain in-store displays for the brand and the premium offer. Self-liquidating premiums are often tied directly to the advertising campaign, so they extend the advertising message and contribute to consumer franchise building for a brand. For example, Philip Morris

offers Western wear, outdoor items, and other types of Marlboro gear through its Marlboro Country catalog, which reinforces the cigarette brand's positioning theme.

Self-liquidating premium offers have the same basic limitation as mail-in premiums: a very low redemption rate. Fewer than 10 percent of U.S. households have ever sent for a premium, and fewer than 1 percent of self-liquidating offers are actually redeemed.[40] Low redemption rates can leave the marketer with a large supply of items with a logo or some other brand identification that makes them hard to dispose of. Thus, it is important to test consumers' reaction to a premium incentive and determine whether they perceive the offer as a value. Another option is to use premiums with no brand identification, but that detracts from their consumer franchise-building value.

Contests and Sweepstakes

Contests and sweepstakes are an increasingly popular consumer-oriented promotion. Marketers spent nearly $2 billion on these promotions in 2001. These promotions seem to have an appeal and glamour that tools like cents-off coupons lack. Contests and sweepstakes are exciting because, as one expert has noted, many consumers have a "pot of gold at the end of the rainbow mentality" and think they can win the big prizes being offered.[41] The lure of sweepstakes and promotions has also been influenced by the "instant-millionaire syndrome" that has derived from huge cash prizes given by many state lotteries in recent years. Marketers are attracted to contests and sweepstakes as a way of generating attention and interest among a large number of consumers.

There are differences between contests and sweepstakes. A **contest** is a promotion where consumers compete for prizes or money on the basis of skills or ability. The company determines winners by judging the entries or ascertaining which entry comes closest to some predetermined criteria (e.g., picking the winning teams and total number of points in the Super Bowl or NCAA basketball tournament). Contests usually provide a purchase incentive by requiring a proof of purchase to enter or an entry form that is available from a dealer or advertisement. Some contests require consumers to read an ad or package or visit a store display to gather information needed to enter. Marketers must be careful not to make their contests too difficult to enter, as doing so might discourage participation among key prospects in the target audience.

A **sweepstakes** is a promotion where winners are determined purely by chance; it cannot require a proof of purchase as a condition for entry. Entrants need only submit their names for the prize drawing. While there is often an official entry form, handwritten entries must also be permitted. One form of sweepstakes is a **game,** which also has a chance element or odds of winning. Scratch-off cards with instant winners are a popular promotional tool. Some games occur over a longer period and require more involvement by consumers. Promotions where consumers must collect game pieces are popular among retailers and fast-food chains as a way to build store traffic and repeat purchases.

Because they are easier to enter, sweepstakes attract more entries than contests. They are also easier and less expensive to administer, since every entry does not have to be checked or judged. Choosing the winning entry in a sweepstakes requires only the random selection of a winner from the pool of entries or generation of a number to match those held by sweepstakes entrants. Experts note that the costs of mounting a sweepstakes are also very predictable. Companies can buy insurance to indemnify them and protect against the expense of awarding a big prize. In general, sweepstakes present marketers with a fixed cost, which is a major advantage when budgeting for a promotion.

Contests and sweepstakes can get the consumer involved with a brand by making the promotion product relevant. For example, contests that ask consumers to suggest a name for a product or to submit recipes that use the brand can increase involvement levels. Nabisco developed an "Open a box, make up a snack," promotional contest for its three top cracker brands—Ritz, Triscuit, and Wheat Thins. Consumers sent in their favorite recipes, which were then made available on a dedicated website and at a toll-free number. Marketers can use contests and sweepstakes to build brand equity by connecting the prizes to the lifestyle, needs, or interests of the target audience.

Exhibit 16-20 The Suzuki Heisman Sweepstakes ties into the popularity of college football's top award

Sweepstakes and games can also be used to generate excitement and involvement with a popular and timely event and/or as a way to get consumers to visit a company's website. For example, Suzuki sponsored a sweepstakes that was tied to its sponsorship of the 2002 Heisman Trophy, which is the award given each year to the top college football player (Exhibit 16-20). One official vote was placed in the selection of the winner of the Heisman Trophy based on the results of the voting. Each person who voted was also entered into the Suzuki Heisman Sweepstakes. The contest was an effective way of associating Suzuki with this prestigious award and encouraging consumers to visit the website, where they would learn more about the company's vehicles.

Problems with Contests and Sweepstakes While the use of contests and sweepstakes continues to increase, there are some problems associated with these types of promotions. Many sweepstakes and/or contest promotions do little to contribute to consumer franchise building for a product or service and may even detract from it. The sweepstakes or contest often becomes the dominant focus rather than the brand, and little is accomplished other than giving away substantial amounts of money and/or prizes. Many promotional experts question the effectiveness of contests and sweepstakes. Some companies have cut back or even stopped using them because of concern over their effectiveness and fears that consumers might become dependent on them.[42] The sweepstakes industry also received a considerable amount of negative publicity recently. Lawsuits were filed by a number of states against American Family Publishing for misleading consumers regarding their odds of winning large cash prizes in AFP's annual magazine subscription solicitation sweepstakes.[43]

Numerous legal considerations affect the design and administration of contests and sweepstakes.[44] These promotions are regulated by several federal agencies, and each of the 50 states has its own rules. The regulation of contests and sweepstakes has helped clean up the abuses that plagued the industry in the late 1960s and has improved consumers' perceptions of these promotions. But companies must still be careful in designing a contest or sweepstakes and awarding prizes. Most firms use consultants that specialize in the design and administration of contests and sweepstakes to avoid any legal problems, but they may still run into problems with promotions, as discussed in IMC Perspective 16-4.

A final problem with contests and sweepstakes is participation by professionals or hobbyists who submit many entries but have no intention of purchasing the product or

IMC PERSPECTIVE 16-4

McDonald's and Others Learn the Perils of Promotions

Contests, sweepstakes, and premium offers are often used by marketers to give consumers an extra incentive to purchase their products. However, when these promotions don't go as planned, they can embarrass a company or even create legal problems. A number of high-profile companies known for their marketing excellence have experienced problems with promotions over the years. Kraft Food and PepsiCo encountered problems resulting from printing errors and computer glitches, while more recently McDonald's was the victim of a conspiracy to steal high-value game pieces from its long-running Monopoly game promotion. These botched promotions were embarrassing for the companies and resulted in the loss of goodwill as well as money.

Kraft was one of the first to learn how expensive it can be when a promotion goes awry. In 1989, a printing error resulted in the printing of too many winning game pieces for a match-and-win game promotion. Kraft canceled the promotion but still had to spend nearly $4 million to compensate the winners—versus the $36,000 budgeted for prizes. The snafu gave birth to the "Kraft clause," a disclaimer stating that a marketer reserves the right to cancel a promotion if there are problems and hold a random drawing if there are more winners than prizes.

A few years later, PepsiCo had a major problem when a bottle-cap promotion offering a grand prize of 1 million pesos (about $36,000) went wrong in the Philippines. Due to a computer glitch, the winning number appeared on more than 500,000 bottle caps, which would have made the company liable for more than $18 billion in prize money. When the error was discovered, Pepsi announced that there was a problem and quickly offered to pay $19 for each winning cap, which ended up costing the company nearly $10 million. The furor caused by the botched promotion prompted anti-Pepsi rallies, death threats against Pepsi executives, and attacks on Pepsi trucks and bottling plants.

McDonald's also ran into a major problem with a promotion when winning game pieces were embezzled from its popular Monopoly game promotion. McDonald's ran its first Monopoly game promotion in 1987 and began running it annually in 1991. The company was able to run the game so long because it worked on many different levels. Consumers knew how to play the game, its big prizes generated excitement and interest, and its format—which required participants to collect all the Monopoly board game pieces to win—drove repeat traffic into the restaurants. McDonald's also spent large amounts of money on ads promoting the game and kept refining it with new iterations such as a Pick Your Prize twist. However, in August 2001 the Federal Bureau of Investigation arrested eight people for embezzling winning game pieces from the Monopoly game as well as the company's "Who Wants to Be a Millionaire" sweepstakes in order to divert nearly $24 million worth of prizes to co-conspirators.

The conspiracy is believed to have begun as early as 1995, and the FBI investigation, which was conducted with McDonald's cooperation, lasted two years before the arrests were made. Fifty-one people were indicted in the case, nearly all of whom either pleaded guilty or were convicted following trial. Among those pleading guilty was the director of security for McDonald's promotional agency, Simon Marketing, who stole the winning tickets and conspired with the others to distribute them to a network of recruiters who solicited individuals to falsely claim they were legitimate game winners.

Following the arrests McDonald's immediately fired Simon Marketing, as did several other of the agency's clients, including Kraft Foods and Philip Morris Co. To win back consumer confidence, McDonald's ran a five-day instant giveaway promotion over the Labor Day weekend in which consumers could win 55 cash prizes ranging from $1,000 to $1 million. The company also created an independent task force comprised of antifraud and game security experts to review procedures for future promotions.

The promotion scandal that rocked McDonald's sent shock waves through the industry and threatened to undermine consumer trust in contests and sweepstakes in general. Marketers are now more carefully reviewing their contests and sweepstakes as well as the companies that manage them. However, most industry experts maintain that McDonald's was a rare victim in an industry conducted honestly and legitimately and policed by many private and public watchdogs. While marketers will continue to use contests, sweepstakes, and games, they will be taking extra precautions to safeguard them to avoid the problems Kraft, PepsiCo, and McDonald's encountered.

Sources: Kate McArthur, "Guilty Verdict for Four in McDonald's Sweepstakes Scandal," AdAge.com, Sept. 3, 2002; Kate McArthur, "McSwindle," *Advertising Age,* Aug. 27, 2002, pp. 1, 22; Cara Beardi, "Scandal May Impact Other Sweepstakes," *Advertising Age,* Aug. 27, 2002, p. 22; Betsy Spethmann, "The Perils of Promotion," *Promo,* November 1996, pp. 22, 134.

Exhibit 16-21 Intuit uses a rebate offer to promote its Quicken software products

service. Because most states make it illegal to require a purchase as a qualification for a sweepstakes entry, consumers can enter as many times as they wish. Professional players sometimes enter one sweepstakes several times, depending on the nature of the prizes and the number of entries the promotion attracts. Newsletters are even available that inform them of all the contests and sweepstakes being held, the entry dates, estimated probabilities of winning for various numbers of entries, how to enter, and solutions to any puzzles or other information that might be needed. The presence of these professional entrants not only defeats the purpose of the promotion but may also discourage entries from consumers who think their chances of winning are limited.

Refunds and Rebates

Refunds (also known as *rebates*) are offers by the manufacturer to return a portion of the product purchase price, usually after the consumer supplies some proof of purchase. Consumers are generally very responsive to rebate offers, particularly as the size of the savings increases. Rebates are used by makers of all types of products, ranging from packaged goods to major appliances, cars, and computer software. Exhibit 16-21 shows an ad promoting a $30 rebate on Intuit's popular tax and financial software products, TurboTax and Quicken.

Packaged-goods marketers often use refund offers to induce trial of a new product or encourage users of another brand to switch. Consumers may perceive the savings offered through a cash refund as an immediate value that lowers the cost of the item, even though those savings are realized only if the consumer redeems the refund or rebate offer. Redemption rates for refund offers typically range from 1 to 3 percent for print and point-of-purchase offers and 5 percent for in/on-package offers.

Refund offers can also encourage repeat purchase. Many offers require consumers to send in multiple proofs of purchase. The size of the refund offer may even increase as the number of purchases gets larger. Some packaged-goods companies are switching away from cash refund offers to coupons or cash/coupon combinations. Using coupons in the refund offer enhances the likelihood of repeat purchase of the brand.

Rebates have become a widely used form of promotion for consumer durables. Products such as cameras, sporting goods, appliances, televisions, audio and video equipment, computers, and cars frequently use rebate offers to appeal to price-conscious consumers. The use of rebates for expensive items like cars was begun by Chrysler Corp. in 1981 to boost sales and generate cash for the struggling company. Rebates are now common not only in the auto industry and other durable products but for packaged-goods products as well.

Evaluating Refunds and Rebates

Rebates can help create new users and encourage brand switching or repeat purchase behavior, or they can be a way to offer a temporary price reduction. The rebate may be perceived as an immediate savings even though many consumers do not follow through on the offer. This perception can influence purchase even if the consumer fails to realize the savings, so the marketer can reduce price for much less than if it used a direct price-off deal.

Some problems are associated with refunds and rebates. Many consumers are not motivated by a refund offer because of the delay and the effort required to obtain the savings. They do not want to be bothered saving cash register receipts and proofs of purchase, filling out forms, and mailing in the offer.[45] A study of consumer perceptions found a negative relationship between the use of rebates and the perceived difficulties associated with the redemption process.[46] The study also found that consumers perceive manufacturers as offering rebates to sell products that are not faring well. Nonusers of rebates were particularly likely to perceive the redemption process as too complicated and to suspect manufacturers' motives. This implies that companies using rebates must simplify the redemption process and use other promotional elements such as advertising to retain consumer confidence in the brand.

When small refunds are being offered, marketers may find other promotional incentives such as coupons or bonus packs more effective. They must be careful not to overuse rebate offers and confuse consumers about the real price and value of a product or service. Also, consumers can become dependent on rebates and delay their purchases or purchase only brands for which a rebate is available. Many retailers have become disenchanted with rebates and the burden and expense of administering them.[47]

Bonus Packs

Bonus packs offer the consumer an extra amount of a product at the regular price by providing larger containers or extra units (Exhibit 16-22). Bonus packs result in a lower cost per unit for the consumer and provide extra value as well as more product for the money. There are several advantages to bonus pack promotions. First, they give marketers a direct way to provide extra value without having to get involved with complicated coupons or refund offers. The additional value of a bonus pack is generally obvious to the consumer and can have a strong impact on the purchase decision at the time of purchase.

Bonus packs can also be an effective defensive maneuver against a competitor's promotion or introduction of a new brand. By loading current users with large amounts of its product, a marketer can often remove these consumers from the market and make them less susceptible to a competitor's promotional efforts. Bonus packs may result in larger purchase orders and favorable display space in the store if relationships with retailers are good. They do, however, usually require additional shelf space without providing any extra profit margins for the retailer, so the marketer can encounter problems with bonus packs if trade relationships are not good. Another problem is that bonus packs may appeal primarily to current users who probably would have purchased the brand anyway or to promotion-sensitive consumers who may not become loyal to the brand.

Exhibit 16-22 Bonus packs provide more value for consumers

Price-Off Deals

Another consumer-oriented promotion technique is the direct **price-off deal,** which reduces the price of the brand. Price-off reductions are typically offered right on the package through specially marked price packs, as shown in Exhibit 16-23. Typically, price-offs range from 10 to 25 percent off the regular price, with the reduction coming out of the manufacturer's profit margin, not the retailer's. Keeping the retailer's margin during a price-off promotion maintains its support and cooperation.

Marketers use price-off promotions for several reasons. First, since price-offs are controlled by the manufacturer, it can make sure the promotional discount reaches the consumer rather than being kept by the trade. Like bonus packs, price-off deals usually present a readily apparent value to shoppers, especially when they have a reference price point for the brand and thus recognize the value of the discount.[48] So price-offs can be a strong influence at the point of purchase when price comparisons are being made. Price-off promotions can also encourage consumers to purchase larger quantities, preempting competitors' promotions and leading to greater trade support.

Price-off promotions may not be favorably received by retailers, since they can create pricing and inventory problems. Most retailers will not accept packages with a specific price shown, so the familiar *X* amount off the regular price must be used. Also, like bonus packs, price-off deals appeal primarily to regular users instead of attracting nonusers. Finally, the Federal Trade Commission has regulations regarding the conditions that price-off labels must meet and the frequency and timing of their use.

Exhibit 16-23 Examples of price-off packages

Frequency Programs

One of the fastest-growing areas of sales promotion is the use of **frequency programs** (also referred to as *continuity* or *loyalty programs*). American Airlines was one of the first major companies to use loyalty programs when it introduced its AAdvantage frequent-flyer program in 1981. Since then frequency programs have become commonplace in a number of product and service categories, particularly travel and hospitality, as well as among retailers. Virtually every airline, car rental company, and hotel chain has some type of frequency program. American Airlines has nearly 44 million

members in its AAdvantage program, while Marriott International has enlisted more than 18 million business travelers into its Rewards program.

Many packaged-goods companies are also developing frequency programs. Pillsbury, Nestlé, Kraft, and others have recently introduced continuity programs that offer consumers the opportunity to accumulate points for continuing to purchase their brands; the points can be redeemed for gifts and prizes. For example, Kellogg launched a frequency program called "Eet and Ern" that targets younger consumers. The program allows them to find a 10-character code on the inside of specially-marked packages of Kellogg products, enter the code at the EetandErn.com website, and receive a downloadable reward (Exhibit 16-24). They can also participate in other special promotions including contests, sweepstakes, special offers, games and other activities. The frequency program has been very effective and has helped Kellogg increase its sales despite the overall decline in cereal industry sales.[49]

Frequency programs have become particularly popular among grocery stores.[50] Nearly 7,000 supermarkets now have loyalty programs that offer members discounts, a chance to accumulate points that can be redeemed for rewards, newsletters, and other special services. Loyalty programs are also used by a variety of other retailers, including department stores, home centers, bookstores, and even local bagel shops.

There are a number of reasons why frequency programs have become so popular. Marketers view these programs as a way of encouraging consumers to use their products or services on a continual basis and as a way of developing strong customer loyalty. Many companies are also realizing the importance of customer retention and understand that the key to retaining and growing market share is building relationships with loyal customers. Frequency programs also provide marketers with the opportunity to develop databases containing valuable information on their customers that can be used to better understand their needs, interests, and characteristics as well as to identify and track a company's most valuable customers. These databases can also be used to target specific programs and offers to customers to increase the amount they purchase and/or to build stronger relationships with them.

As frequency programs become more common, marketers will be challenged to find ways to use them as a means of differentiating their product, service, business, or retail store. It has been argued that many of the loyalty programs developed by packaged-goods marketers are really short-term promotions that overreward regular users and do little to develop long-term loyalty.[51] Marketers must find ways to make them true loyalty programs rather than just frequent-buyer programs. This will require the careful management of databases to identify and track valuable customers and their purchase history and the strategic use of targeted loyalty promotions.

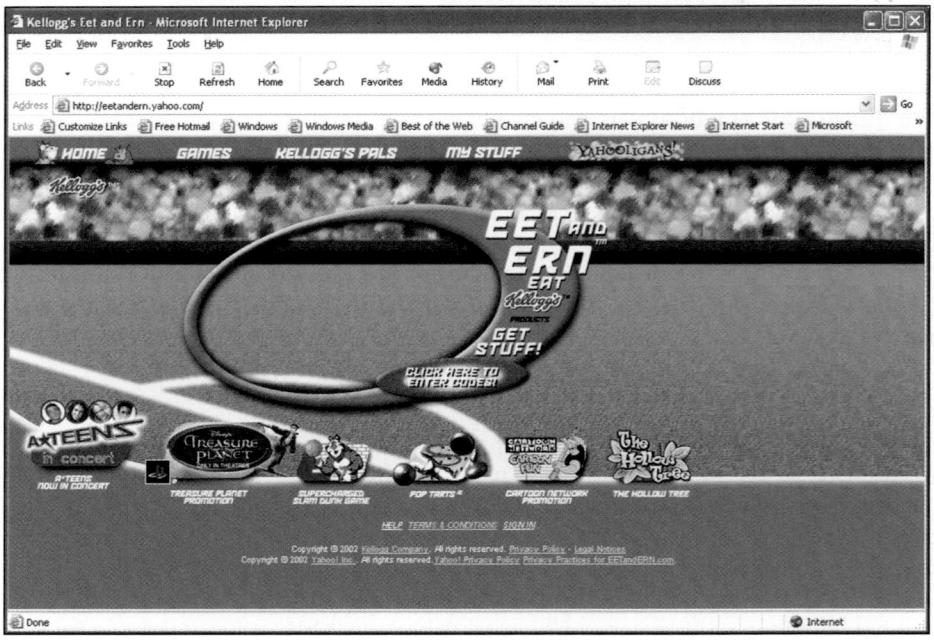

Exhibit 16-24 Kellogg's Eet & Ern loyalty program targets younger consumers

Event Marketing

Another type of consumer-oriented promotion that has become very popular in recent years is the use of event marketing. It is important to make a distinction between *event marketing* and *event sponsorships,* as the two terms are often used interchangeably yet they refer to different activities. **Event marketing** is a type of promotion where a company or brand is linked to an event or where a themed activity is developed for the purpose of creating experiences for consumers and promoting a product or service. Marketers often do event marketing by associating their product with some popular activity such as a sporting event, concert, fair, or festival. However, marketers also create their own events to use for promotional purposes. For example, RC Cola staged events to launch RC Edge Maximum Power, a new soda targeted at teens that contains Indian ginseng and taurine in addition to caffeine. RC put together a 25-market tour that included radio tie-ins and "Edgy" events such as white-water rafting and skydiving at which samples of the product were distributed (Exhibit 16-25). The comarketing promotion Coppertone created for Wal-Mart, which was discussed earlier in the chapter, is an example of an in-store event marketing activity.

An **event sponsorship** is an integrated marketing communications activity where a company develops actual sponsorship relations with a particular event and provides financial support in return for the right to display a brand name, logo, or advertising message and be identified as a supporter of the event. Event marketing often takes place as part of a company's sponsorship of activities such as concerts, the arts, social causes, and sporting events. Decisions and objectives for event sponsorships are often part of an organization's public relations activities and are discussed in the next chapter.

Event marketing has become very popular in recent years as marketers develop integrated marketing programs including a variety of promotional tools that create experiences for consumers in an effort to associate their brands with certain lifestyles and activities. Marketers use events to distribute samples as well as information about their products and services or to actually let consumers experience the product.

Summary of Consumer-Oriented Promotions and Marketer Objectives

The discussion of the various sales promotion techniques shows that marketers use these tools to accomplish a variety of objectives. As noted at the beginning of the chapter, sales promotion techniques provide consumers with an *extra incentive or reward* for engaging in a certain form of behavior such as purchasing a brand. For some types of sales promotion tools the incentive the consumer receives is immediate, while for others the reward is delayed and is not realized immediately. Marketers often

Exhibit 16-25 RC Cola used event marketing to introduce Edge Maximum Power

Figure 16-5 Consumer-oriented sales promotion tools for various marketing objectives

Consumer Reward Incentive	Marketing Objective: Induce trial	Marketing Objective: Customer retention/loading	Marketing Objective: Support IMC program/ build brand equity
Immediate	• Sampling • Instant coupons • In-store coupons • In-store rebates	• Price-off deals • Bonus packs • In- and on-package free premiums • Loyalty programs	• Events • In- and on-package free premiums
Delayed	• Media- and mail-delivered coupons • Mail-in refunds and rebates • Free mail-in premiums • Scanner- and Internet-delivered coupons	• In- and on-package coupons • Mail-in refunds and rebates • Loyalty programs	• Self-liquidating premiums • Free mail-in premiums • Contests and sweepstakes • Loyalty programs

evaluate sales promotion tools in terms of their ability to accomplish specific objectives and consider whether the impact of the promotion will be immediate or delayed. The chart in Figure 16-5 outlines which sales promotion tools can be used to accomplish various objectives of marketers and identifies whether the extra incentive or reward is immediate or delayed.[52]

It should be noted that in Figure 16-3 some of the sales promotion techniques are listed more than once because they can be used to accomplish more than one objective. For example, loyalty programs can be used to retain customers by providing both immediate and delayed rewards. Shoppers who belong to loyalty programs sponsored by supermarkets and receive discounts every time they make a purchase are receiving immediate rewards that are designed to retain them as customers. Some loyalty promotions such as frequency programs used by airlines, car rental companies, and hotels offer delayed rewards by requiring that users accumulate points to reach a certain level or status before the points can be redeemed. Loyalty programs can also be used by marketers to help build brand equity. For example, when an airline or car rental company sends its frequent users upgrade certificates, the practice helps build relationships with these customers and thus contributes to brand equity.

While marketers use consumer-oriented sales promotions to provide current and/or potential customers with an extra incentive, they also use these promotions as part of their marketing program to leverage trade support. Retailers are more likely to stock a brand, purchase extra quantities, or provide additional support such as end-aisle displays when they know a manufacturer is running a promotion during a designated period. The development of promotional programs targeted toward the trade is a very important part of the marketing process and is discussed in the next section.

Trade-Oriented Sales Promotion

Objectives of Trade-Oriented Sales Promotion

Like consumer-oriented promotions, sales promotion programs targeted to the trade should be based on well-defined objectives and measurable goals and a consideration of what the marketer wants to accomplish. Typical objectives for promotions targeted to marketing intermediaries such as wholesalers and retailers include obtaining distribution and support for new products, maintaining support for established brands, encouraging retailers to display established brands, and building retail inventories.

Obtain Distribution for New Products

Trade promotions are often used to encourage retailers to give shelf space to new products. Manufacturers recognize that only a limited amount of shelf space is available in supermarkets, drugstores, and other major retail outlets. Thus, they provide retailers with financial incentives to

stock new products. For example, Lever Brothers used heavy sampling and high-value coupons in the successful introduction of Lever 2000 bar soap. However, in addition to these consumer promotions, the company used discounts to the trade to encourage retailers to stock and promote the new brand.

While trade discounts or other special price deals are used to encourage retailers and wholesalers to stock a new brand, marketers may use other types of promotions to get them to push the brand. Merchandising allowances can get retailers to display a new product in high-traffic areas of stores, while incentive programs or contests can encourage wholesale or retail store personnel to push a new brand.

Maintain Trade Support for Established Brands

Trade promotions are often designed to maintain distribution and trade support for established brands. Brands that are in the mature phase of their product life cycle are vulnerable to losing wholesale and/or retail distribution, particularly if they are not differentiated or face competition from new products. Trade deals induce wholesalers and retailers to continue to carry weaker products because the discounts increase their profit margins. Brands with a smaller market share often rely heavily on trade promotions, since they lack the funds required to differentiate themselves from competitors through media advertising.

Even if a brand has a strong market position, trade promotions may be used as part of an overall marketing strategy. For example, Heinz has relied heavily on trade promotions to hold its market share position for many of its brands. Many consumer packaged-goods companies count on trade promotions to maintain retail distribution and support.

Encourage Retailers to Display Established Brands

Another objective of trade-oriented promotions is to encourage retailers to display and promote an established brand. Marketers recognize that many purchase decisions are made in the store and promotional displays are an excellent way of generating sales. An important goal is to obtain retail store displays of a product away from its regular shelf location. A typical supermarket has approximately 50 display areas at the ends of aisles, near checkout counters, and elsewhere. Marketers want to have their products displayed in these areas to increase the probability shoppers will come into contact with them. Even a single display can increase a brand's sales significantly during a promotion.

Manufacturers often use multifaceted promotional programs to encourage retailers to promote their products at the retail level. For example, Exhibit 16-26 shows a brochure that Chicken of the Sea International provided to retailers showing the various promotions the company planned to use during the year for its Chicken of the Sea

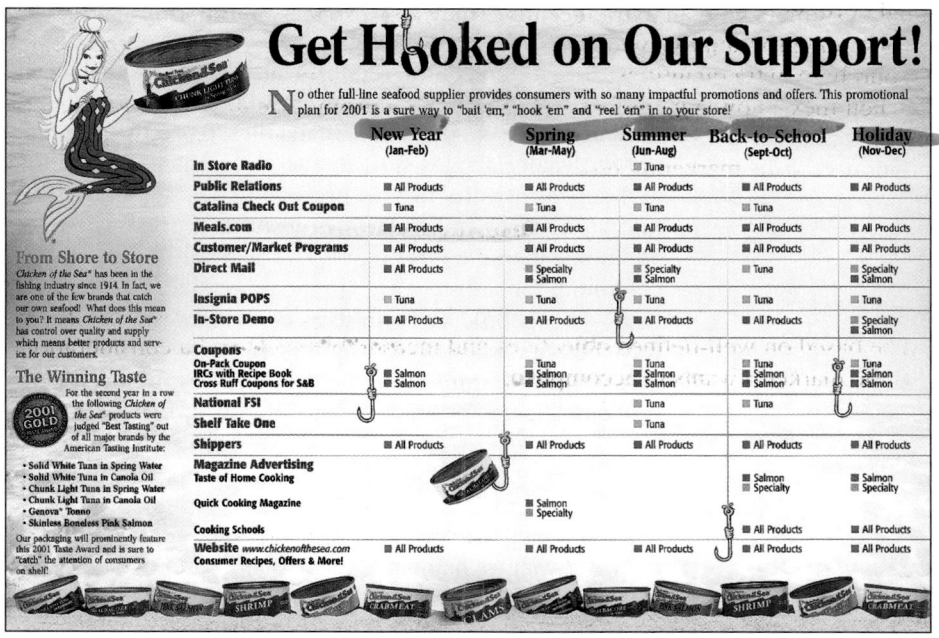

Get Hooked on Our Support!

No other full-line seafood supplier provides consumers with so many impactful promotions and offers. This promotional plan for 2001 is a sure way to "bait 'em," "hook 'em" and "reel 'em" in to your store!

	New Year (Jan-Feb)	Spring (Mar-May)	Summer (Jun-Aug)	Back-to-School (Sept-Oct)	Holiday (Nov-Dec)
In Store Radio			Tuna		
Public Relations	All Products	All Products	All Products	All Products	All Products
Catalina Check Out Coupon	Tuna	Tuna	Tuna	Tuna	
Meals.com	All Products	All Products	All Products	All Products	All Products
Customer/Market Programs	All Products	All Products	All Products	All Products	All Products
Direct Mail	All Products	Specialty Salmon	Specialty Salmon	Tuna	Specialty Salmon
Insignia POPS	Tuna	Tuna	Tuna	Tuna	Tuna
In-Store Demo	All Products	All Products	All Products	All Products	Specialty Salmon
Coupons					
On-Pack Coupon		Tuna	Tuna	Tuna	Tuna
IRCs with Recipe Book	Salmon	Salmon	Salmon	Salmon	Salmon
Cross Ruff Coupons for S&B	Salmon	Salmon	Salmon	Salmon	Salmon
National FSI			Tuna	Tuna	
Shelf Take One			Tuna		
Shippers	All Products	All Products	All Products	All Products	All Products
Magazine Advertising					
Taste of Home Cooking				Salmon Specialty	Salmon Specialty
Quick Cooking Magazine		Salmon Specialty			
Cooking Schools				All Products	All Products
Website *www.chickenofthesea.com* **Consumer Recipes, Offers & More!**	All Products	All Products	All Products	All Products	All Products

From Shore to Store

Chicken of the Sea® has been in the fishing industry since 1914. In fact, we are one of the few brands that catch our own seafood! What does this mean to you? It means *Chicken of the Sea*® has control over quality and supply which means better products and service for our customers.

The Winning Taste

For the second year in a row the following *Chicken of the Sea*® products were judged "Best Tasting" out of all major brands by the American Tasting Institute:

- Solid White Tuna in Spring Water
- Solid White Tuna in Canola Oil
- Chunk Light Tuna in Spring Water
- Chunk Light Tuna in Canola Oil
- Genova® Tonno
- Skinless Boneless Pink Salmon

Our packaging will prominently feature this 2001 Taste Award and is sure to "catch" the attention of consumers on shelf!

Exhibit 16-26 This brochure shows retailers the various promotions Chicken of the Sea planned to use for its various products

brand tuna and salmon. The company used a variety of promotional tools to support the brands and increase retailer participation. These included advertising in magazines, local newspapers, FSI and checkout coupons, in-store displays, premium offers, recipe handouts, Web support, contests, and a continuity program.

Build Retail Inventories Manufacturers often use trade promotions to build the inventory levels of retailers or other channel members. There are several reasons manufacturers want to load retailers with their products. First, wholesalers and retailers are more likely to push a product when they have high inventory levels rather than storing it in their warehouses or back rooms. Building channel members' inventories also ensures they will not run out of stock and thus miss sales opportunities.

Some manufacturers of seasonal products offer large promotional discounts so that retailers will stock up on their products before the peak selling season begins. This enables the manufacturer to smooth out seasonal fluctuations in its production schedule and passes on some of the inventory carrying costs to retailers or wholesalers. When retailers stock up on a product before the peak selling season, they often run special promotions and offer discounts to consumers to reduce excess inventories.

Types of Trade-Oriented Promotions

Manufacturers use a variety of trade promotion tools as inducements for wholesalers and retailers. Next we examine some of the most often used types of trade promotions and some factors marketers must consider in using them. These promotions include contests and incentives, trade allowances, displays and point-of-purchase materials, sales training programs, trade shows, and co-op advertising.

Contests and Incentives Manufacturers may develop contests or special incentive programs to stimulate greater selling effort and support from reseller management or sales personnel. Contests or incentive programs can be directed toward managers who work for a wholesaler or distributor as well as toward store or department managers at the retail level. Manufacturers often sponsor contests for resellers and use prizes such as trips or valuable merchandise as rewards for meeting sales quotas or other goals. Exhibit 16-27 shows a contest Chicken of the Sea sponsored for food-service distributors who call on restaurants.

Exhibit 16-27 This contest sponsored by Chicken of the Sea was targeted toward food-service distributors

Contests or special incentives are often targeted at the sales personnel of the wholesalers, distributors/dealers, or retailers. These salespeople are an important link in the distribution chain because they are likely to be very familiar with the market, more frequently in touch with the customer (whether it be another reseller or the ultimate consumer), and more numerous than the manufacturer's own sales organization. Manufacturers often devise incentives or contests for these sales personnel. These programs may involve cash payments made directly to the retailer's or wholesaler's sales staff to encourage them to promote and sell a manufacturer's product. These payments are known as **push money** (pm) or *spiffs*. For example, an appliance manufacturer may pay a $25 spiff to retail sales personnel for selling a certain model or size. In sales contests, salespeople can win trips or valuable merchandise for meeting certain goals established by the manufacturer. As shown in Figure 16-6, these incentives may be tied to product sales, new account placements, or merchandising efforts.

While contests and incentive programs can generate reseller support, they can also be a source of conflict between retail sales personnel and management. Some retailers want to maintain control over the selling activities of their sales staffs. They don't want their salespeople devoting an undue amount of effort to trying to win a con-

- Product or Program Sales
  Awards are tied to the selling of a product, for example:
  - Selling a specified number of cases
  - Selling a specified number of units
  - Selling a specified number of promotional programs
- New Account Placements
  Awards are tied to:
  - The number of new accounts opened
  - The number of new accounts ordering a minimum number of cases or units
  - Promotional programs placed in new accounts
- Merchandising Efforts
  Awards are tied to:
  - Establishing promotional programs (such as theme programs)
  - Placing display racks, counter displays, and the like

Figure 16-6 Three forms of promotion targeted to reseller salespeople

test or receive incentives offered by the manufacturer. Nor do they want their people becoming too aggressive in pushing products that serve their own interests instead of the product or model that is best for the customer.

Many retailers refuse to let their employees participate in manufacturer-sponsored contests or to accept incentive payments. Retailers that do allow them often have strict guidelines and require management approval of the program.

Trade Allowances

Probably the most common trade promotion is some form of **trade allowance,** a discount or deal offered to retailers or wholesalers to encourage them to stock, promote, or display the manufacturer's products. Types of allowances offered to retailers include buying allowances, promotional or display allowances, and slotting allowances.

Buying Allowances A buying allowance is a deal or discount offered to resellers in the form of a price reduction on merchandise ordered during a fixed period. These discounts are often in the form of an **off-invoice allowance,** which means a certain per-case amount or percentage is deducted from the invoice. A buying allowance can also take the form of *free goods;* the reseller gets extra cases with the purchase of specific amounts (for example, 1 free case with every 10 cases purchased).

Buying allowances are used for several reasons. They are easy to implement and are well accepted, and sometimes expected, by the trade. They are also an effective way to encourage resellers to buy the manufacturer's product, since they will want to take advantage of the discounts being offered during the allowance period. Manufacturers offer trade discounts expecting wholesalers and retailers to pass the price reduction through to consumers, resulting in greater sales. However, as discussed shortly, this is often not the case.

Promotional Allowances Manufacturers often give retailers allowances or discounts for performing certain promotional or merchandising activities in support of their brands. These merchandising allowances can be given for providing special displays away from the product's regular shelf position, running in-store promotional programs, or including the product in an ad. The manufacturer generally has guidelines or a contract specifying the activity to be performed to qualify for the promotional allowance. The allowance is usually a fixed amount per case or a percentage deduction from the list price for merchandise ordered during the promotional period.

Slotting Allowances In recent years, retailers have been demanding a special allowance for agreeing to handle a new product. *Slotting allowances,* also called

CAREER PROFILE

John Boyle

Marketing Analyst, Chicken of the Sea International

Choosing a major is an important decision for undergraduate students. This decision determines the nature of one's college experience and, ultimately, one's career path. I decided to major in marketing as an undergraduate at San Diego State University because I felt this degree would provide me with a number of exciting career opportunities. I also chose marketing because I was intrigued by the way marketers analyze consumers to understand their purchase behavior and the strategies they develop to compete against one another.

After finishing my Bachelor's Degree I decided to continue my education and pursue an MBA, as I wanted to study marketing in more depth. While pursuing my MBA, I had the opportunity to take courses in areas such as advertising and promotion, consumer behavior, marketing research and strategic marketing, all of which prepared me quite well for an entry level position in the field. My educational experience at SDSU was gratifying, and focusing on marketing turned out to be an excellent decision.

"It's very exciting to deal with real world marketing problems every day."

I went to work for Chicken of the Sea International (COSI) after finishing my MBA degree. Since joining COSI I have been working as a Marketing Analyst and have had the opportunity to provide input into decisions that directly affect the direction of the company. I work closely with brand managers on a daily basis and, together, we make marketing decisions for a diverse product line. Chicken of the Sea sells a variety of products ranging from canned tuna to salmon as well as the new pouch pack versions of these products.

An important part of my job as a marketing analyst is to procure, organize, analyze, and disseminate information which provides the foundation for strategic, as well as tactical decisions. I work with many areas of the business, but most closely with marketing communications which includes our advertising, sales promotion and online marketing functions. Sales promotion is a particularly important element of our IMC program because of its ability to directly influence customer behavior. While advertising is used to build the image of our brands over time, we use various types of promotions to elicit a direct response and drive short-term sales. Sales promotions are focused on getting consumers to take action, whether it be redeeming a coupon for one of our products or getting them to save product labels and submit them in exchange for a free movie ticket. Our sales promotion programs are also targeted toward the retailers as we have a variety of programs that are designed to encourage them to stock and promote our products.

Measuring the effectiveness of sales promotions is a challenging but vital component of our promotion program. Technological advances in our industry have greatly enhanced our ability to evaluate promotions. For example, we have access to a variety of rich external data sources including point-of-sale data generated by super-market scanners, consumer panel data, and retailer loyalty card information. Internal data sources such as coupon redemption databases and factory shipments are also valuable. Consumer click-stream data from online grocery retailing websites is a promising new frontier in the area of sales promotion evaluation.

Designing effective sales promotions is a challenging but important task. We constantly ask ourselves the obvious questions: What worked, what didn't, and why? Was the price discount large enough, or was there a competitive promotion being run simultaneously? Perhaps the contest prize value should be increased, or maybe the retailer didn't pass the entire trade discount on to consumers.

It's very exciting to deal with real world marketing problems every day and to use a variety of concepts I studied in business school to develop innovative ways to solve them. The payoff comes from seeing the results and knowing what I do has made a difference.

stocking allowances, introductory allowances, or *street money,* are fees retailers charge for providing a slot or position to accommodate the new product. Retailers justify these fees by pointing out the costs associated with taking on so many new products each year, such as redesigning store shelves, entering the product into their computers, finding warehouse space, and briefing store employees on the new product.[53] They also note they are assuming some risk, since so many new product introductions fail.

Slotting fees can range from a few hundred dollars per store to $50,000 or more for an entire retail chain. Manufacturers that want to get their products on the shelves nationally can face several million dollars in slotting fees. Many marketers believe slotting allowances are a form of blackmail or bribery and say some 70 percent of these fees go directly to retailers' bottom lines.

Retailers can continue charging slotting fees because of their power and the limited availability of shelf space in supermarkets relative to the large numbers of products introduced each year. Some retailers have even been demanding **failure fees** if a new product does not hit a minimum sales level within a certain time. The fee is charged to cover the costs associated with stocking, maintaining inventories, and then pulling the product.[54] Large manufacturers with popular brands are less likely to pay slotting fees than smaller companies that lack leverage in negotiating with retailers.

In late 1999 the Senate Committee on Small Business began taking action against the practice of using slotting fees in the grocery, drugstore, and computer software industries because of the fees' negative impact on small business.[55] The committee recommended that the Federal Trade Commission and Small Business Administration take steps to limit the use of slotting fees because they are anticompetitive. A recent study by Paul Bloom, Gregory Gundlach, and Joseph Cannon examined the views of manufacturers, wholesalers, and grocery retailers regarding the use of slotting fees. Their findings suggest that slotting fees shift the risk of new product introductions from retailers to manufacturers and help apportion the supply and demand of new products. They also found that slotting fees lead to higher retail prices, are applied in a discriminatory fashion, and place small marketers at a disadvantage.[56]

Problems with Trade Allowances Many companies are concerned about the abuse of trade allowances by wholesalers, retailers, and distributors. Marketers give retailers these trade allowances so that the savings will be passed through to consumers in the form of lower prices, but companies such as Procter & Gamble claim that only 30 percent of trade promotion discounts actually reach consumers because 35 percent is lost in inefficiencies and another 35 percent is pocketed by retailers and wholesalers. Moreover, many marketers believe that the trade is taking advantage of their promotional deals and misusing promotional funds.

For example, many retailers and wholesalers engage in a practice known as **forward buying,** where they stock up on a product at the lower deal or off-invoice price and resell it to consumers after the marketer's promotional period ends. Another common practice is **diverting,** where a retailer or wholesaler takes advantage of the promotional deal and then sells some of the product purchased at the low price to a store outside its area or to a middleperson who resells it to other stores.

Forward buying and diverting are widespread practices. Industry studies show that nearly 40 percent of wholesalers' and retailers' profits come from these activities. In addition to not passing discounts on to consumers, forward buying and diverting create other problems for manufacturers. They lead to huge swings in demand that cause production scheduling problems and leave manufacturers and retailers always building toward or drawing down from a promotional surge. Marketers also worry that the system leads to frequent price specials, so consumers learn to make purchases on the basis of what's on sale rather than developing any loyalty to their brands.

The problems created by retailers' abuse led Procter & Gamble, one of the country's most powerful consumer-product marketers, to adopt **everyday low pricing (EDLP),** which lowers the list price of over 60 percent of its product line by 10 to 25 percent while cutting promotional allowances to the trade. The price cuts leave the overall cost of the product to retailers about the same as it would have been with the various trade allowance discounts.

P&G argues that EDLP eliminates problems such as deal buying, leads to regular low prices at the retail level, and helps build brand loyalty among consumers. Yet the EDLP strategy has caused great controversy in the trade, which depends heavily on promotions to attract consumers. Some retailers took P&G products off the shelf; others cut their ads and displays of the company's brands. Retailers prefer to operate on a *high/low strategy* of frequent price specials and argue that EDLP puts them at a disadvantage against the warehouse stores and mass merchandisers that already use everyday low pricing. They also say that some products, such as those that are bought on impulse, thrive on promotions and don't lend themselves to EDLP. Retailers rely on promotions like end-of-aisle displays and price discounts to create excitement and generate incremental sales and profits from products like soft drinks, cookies, and candy.[57]

Critics of EDLP also note that while the strategy may work well for market leaders whose brands enjoy high loyalty, it is not effective for marketers trying to build market share or prop up lagging products. Moreover, many consumers are still motivated more by promotional deals and specials than by advertising claims from retailers promoting everyday low prices.

Despite the criticism, P&G says EDLP is paying off and volume has grown faster in its brands that have switched to the pricing strategy. P&G extended its use of everyday low pricing to international markets, including the United Kingdom and Italy.[58] P&G continues to make changes in the way sales promotions are being used by packaged-goods marketers. The company has taken steps in recent years to simplify its promotional programs by cutting back on many types of promotions including bonus packs, premiums, coupons, and cents-off packs. P&G has long been a bellwether for the packaged-goods industry and its changes with regard to the use of consumer and trade promotions are likely to create a ripple effect among other marketers.[59]

Displays and Point-of-Purchase Materials The next time you are in a store, take a moment to examine the various promotional materials used to display and sell products. Point-of-purchase (POP) displays are an important promotional tool because they can help a manufacturer obtain more effective in-store merchandising of products. Companies in the United States spend more than $15 billion a year on point-of-purchase materials, including end-of-aisle displays, banners, posters, shelf cards, motion pieces, and stand-up racks, among others. Point-of-purchase displays are very important to marketers since many consumers make their purchase decisions in the store. In fact, some studies estimate that nearly two-thirds of a consumer's buying decisions are made in a retail store. Thus, it is very important for marketers to get the attention of consumers, as well as to communicate a sales or promotional message, through POP displays.

A recent measurement study from Point-of-Purchase Advertising International (an industry trade association) and the Advertising Research Foundation estimates that the cost-per-thousand-impressions figure for POPs is $6 to $8 for supermarket displays.[60] The CPM figure is based on findings that a grocery store display makes an average of 2,300 to 8,000 impressions per week, depending on store size and volume. Although this study has shown that POP displays are very effective at reaching consumers, difficulties in getting retail stores to comply with requests for displays often makes it difficult for marketers to use them.[61] Moreover, many retailers are decreasing the amount of signage and displays they will accept as well as the messages they can communicate. Also, as account-specific promotions become more popular, some retailers are requiring customized POP materials. For example, 7-Eleven has taken over the responsibility for the production of all POP materials from vendors—who must still pay for them. The goal is to give 7-Eleven complete control over its in-store environment.

Despite these challenges, marketers recognize that point-of-purchase displays are an important part of their promotional programs. Many continue to develop innovative methods to display their products efficiently, make them stand out in the retail environment, and communicate a sales message to consumers. It should be noted that the importance of creative POP displays is not limited to grocery or convenience stores. Point-of-purchase displays are also important to companies that distribute their prod-

ucts through other types of retail outlets, such as home improvement, consumer electronic, and sporting goods stores. For example, Exhibit 16-28 shows an award-winning POP display for Wilson Sporting Goods Co. that was designed to keep the company's high-end baseball gloves off the shelves and separate from other gloves. The gloves needed a product-specific display that would promote them as the "Official Glove of Major League Baseball" and also maximize space while merchandising more product.

Many manufacturers help retailers use shelf space more efficiently through **planograms,** which are configurations of products that occupy a shelf section in a store. Some manufacturers are developing computer-based programs that allow retailers to input information from their scanner data and determine the best shelf layouts by experimenting with product movement, space utilization, profit yields, and other factors.[62]

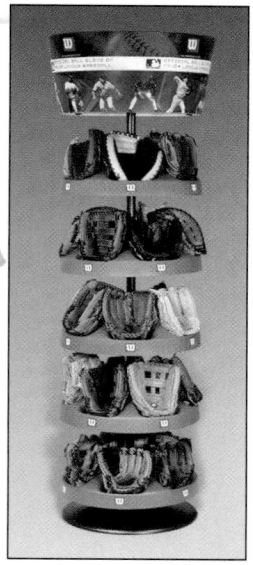

Exhibit 16-28 This award-winning point-of-purchase display plays an important role in the merchandising of Wilson baseball gloves

Sales Training Programs Another form of manufacturer-sponsored promotional assistance is sales training programs for reseller personnel. Many products sold at the retail level require knowledgeable salespeople who can provide consumers with information about the features, benefits, and advantages of various brands and models. Cosmetics, appliances, computers, consumer electronics, and sporting equipment are examples of products for which consumers often rely on well-informed retail sales personnel for assistance.

Manufacturers provide sales training assistance to retail salespeople in a number of ways. They may conduct classes or training sessions that retail personnel can attend to increase their knowledge of a product or a product line. These training sessions present information and ideas on how to sell the manufacturer's product and may also include motivational components. Sales training classes for retail personnel are often sponsored by companies selling high-ticket items or complex products such as personal computers, cars, or ski equipment.

Another way manufacturers provide sales training assistance to retail employees is through their own sales force. Sales reps educate retail personnel about their product line and provide selling tips and other relevant information. The reps can provide ongoing sales training as they come into contact with retail sales staff on a regular basis and can update them on changes in the product line, market developments, competitive information, and the like.

Manufacturers also give resellers detailed sales manuals, product brochures, reference manuals, and other material. Many companies provide videocassettes for retail sales personnel that include product information, product-use demonstrations, and ideas on how to sell their product. These selling aids can often be used to provide information to customers as well.

Trade Shows Another important promotional activity targeted to resellers is the **trade show,** a forum where manufacturers can display their products to current as well as prospective buyers. According to the Trade Show Bureau, nearly 100 million people attend the 5,000 trade shows each year in the United States and Canada, and the number of exhibiting companies exceeds 1.3 million. In many industries, trade shows are a major opportunity to display one's product lines and interact with customers. They are often attended by important management personnel from large retail chains as well as by distributors and other reseller representatives.

A number of promotional functions can be performed at trade shows, including demonstrating products, identifying new prospects, gathering customer and competitive information, and even writing orders for a product. Trade shows are particularly valuable for introducing new products, because resellers are often looking for new merchandise to stock. Shows can also be a source of valuable leads to follow up on through sales calls or direct marketing. The social aspect of trade shows is also important. Many companies use them to entertain key customers and to develop and maintain relationships with the trade. A recent academic study demonstrated that trade shows generate product awareness and interest and can have a measurable economic return.[63]

Cooperative Advertising The final form of trade-oriented promotion we examine is **cooperative advertising,** where the cost of advertising is shared by more than one party. There are three types of cooperative advertising. Although the first two are not trade-oriented promotion, we should recognize their objectives and purpose.

Horizontal cooperative advertising is advertising sponsored in common by a group of retailers or other organizations providing products or services to the market. For example, automobile dealers who are located near one another in an auto park or along the same street often allocate some of their ad budgets to a cooperative advertising fund. Ads are run promoting the location of the dealerships and encouraging car buyers to take advantage of their close proximity when shopping for a new automobile.

Ingredient-sponsored cooperative advertising is supported by raw materials manufacturers; its objective is to help establish end products that include the company's materials and/or ingredients. Companies that often use this type of advertising include Du Pont, which promotes the use of its materials such as Teflon, Thinsulate, and Kevlar in a variety of consumer and industrial products, and NutraSweet, whose artificial sweetener is an ingredient in many food products and beverages. Perhaps the best-known, and most successful, example of this type of cooperative advertising is the "Intel Inside" program, sponsored by Intel Corporation, which is discussed in IMC Perspective 16-5.

The most common form of cooperative advertising is the trade-oriented form, **vertical cooperative advertising,** in which a manufacturer pays for a portion of the advertising a retailer runs to promote the manufacturer's product and its availability in the retailer's place of business. Manufacturers generally share the cost of advertising run by the retailer on a percentage basis (usually 50/50) up to a certain limit.

The amount of cooperative advertising the manufacturer pays for is usually based on a percentage of dollar purchases. If a retailer purchases $100,000 of product from a manufacturer, it may receive 3 percent, or $3,000, in cooperative advertising money. Large retail chains often combine their co-op budgets across all of their stores, which gives them a larger sum to work with and more media options.

Cooperative advertising can take on several forms. Retailers may advertise a manufacturer's product in, say, a newspaper ad featuring a number of different products, and the individual manufacturers reimburse the retailer for their portion of the ad. Or the ad may be prepared by the manufacturer and placed in the local media by the retailer. Exhibit 16-29 shows a cooperative ad format for New Balance athletic shoes that retailers in various market areas can use by simply inserting their store name and location.

Once a cooperative ad is run, the retailer requests reimbursement from the manufacturer for its percentage of the media costs. Manufacturers usually have specific

Exhibit 16-29 This New Balance ad is an example of vertical cooperative advertising

IMC PERSPECTIVE 16-5

Intel Inside: The Co-op Program That Changed the Computer Industry

If you were to ask most owners of personal computers what is inside their PCs, chances are they would respond by saying, "an Intel." And there's a good reason why. Over the past decade consumers have been exposed to hundreds of millions of dollars' worth of ads for personal computers each year that carry the "Intel Inside" logo. The logo has become ubiquitous in PC ads as a result of a landmark cooperative advertising program that is lauded as the most powerful ever and the definitive model for successful "ingredient" branding.

In 1989 Intel was the first computer chip manufacturer to advertise directly to consumers. Its goal was to persuade PC users to upgrade to Intel's 386SX chip from the 286. Known as the "Red X" campaign, the ads depicted the number 286 with a bold, spray-painted X over it. In 1990 Intel selected a new agency, Dahlin Smith White, Salt Lake City, which created the now-famous tagline "Intel. The Computer Inside." The goal of the campaign was to build awareness and position Intel as the real brains of the computer. In early 1991 Intel began pitching the program to PC makers, and IBM, creator of the first Intel-powered personal computer, became the first computer maker to use the logo. Intel then began talking to PC makers about the creation of a co-op fund in which Intel would take 5 percent of the purchase price of processors and put it in a pool to create funds for advertising. The "Intel Inside" co-op program was officially launched in July 1991 and works as follows: In return for showing the logo in print ads and on the PCs, a computer maker can get back 5 percent of what it pays Intel for chips, with the money to be applied to ads paid for jointly by the PC vendor and Intel. More than 150 computer makers signed on to the program and began using the "Intel Inside" logo in their ads.

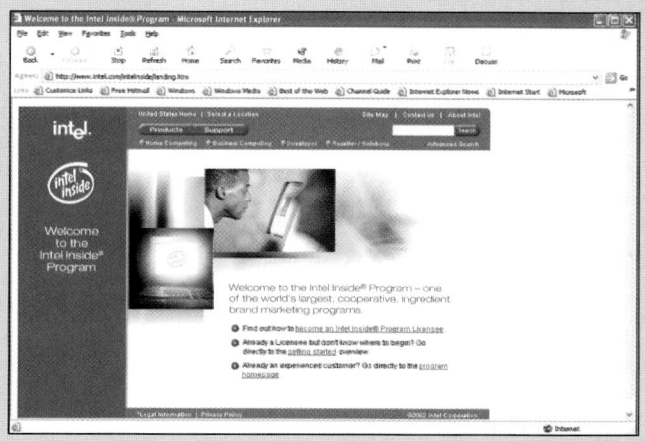

As the program began, Intel started playing up the logo in its own print ads as well. In November 1991 it moved the campaign to television with the classic "Power Source" spot, which magically took viewers on a whirlwind tour of the inside of a computer to show how the Intel chip streamlined upgrading of a PC. In 1993 Intel introduced the Pentium processor brand with a national TV campaign. However, the company was putting the bulk of its advertising budget into the "Intel Inside" co-op program. In 1995 Intel expanded the co-op program to include TV, radio, and in-flight ads. The move led to a boom in PC ads on television featuring the Intel auditory signature at the end of each commercial. In 1997 Intel expanded the co-op program to include Internet ads and provided incentives to PC makers to place ads on media-rich websites. Intel has also extended the co-op program into retail promotions as well.

Since the co-op program began, Intel has pumped into it an estimated $4 billion, and this has been an awfully smart investment. Intel's share of the microprocessor market has grown from 56 percent in 1989 to nearly 80 percent in 2002, and the company's revenue has gone from $3 billion to nearly $30 billion. Nearly 90 percent of the more than 17,000 PC print ads run in the United States carry the "Intel Inside" logo. The program has influenced a generation of PC users and propelled growth of the entire computer industry.

According to positioning expert Al Ries, "Intel Inside" will go down in history as one of the more magnificent campaigns of the century. He notes, "It's brilliant, and, in a sense, it pre-empted the branding of personal computers." Branding guru Jack Trout notes, "They took an old idea—ingredient branding—which Du Pont pioneered, and took it into technology." Trout was an early believer in the program; he told *Advertising Age* in a 1991 interview that conceptually it was a good idea, although Intel would need consistent advertising over time for the logo to have much meaning.

Intel's advertising has been consistent over the past decade as its various ad campaigns have strengthened its brand image and demonstrated the power of various generations of Intel Pentium processors. These campaigns have featured the "Bunny People," who were a takeoff on the workers who wear so-called bunny suits to keep chip labs sterile, as well as the Blue Man Group performance artists. In late 2002, Intel launched a new global brand campaign called "Yes" that is designed to connect with young adults and showcase the benefits of a digital lifestyle. The commercials capture today's digital lifestyle by showing

people using their computers for digital photography, CD-burning, instant messaging, and movie-making. The ads play off the famous tagline by showing people burning CDs and then cutting to the copy line "Intel Inside your music" or by showing how a digital photo can be used followed by the line "Intel Inside your photos." The commercials end with the line "Can a better computer really change your life? Yes."

In its early stages the Intel Inside program encountered criticism, as many advertising and computer marketing executives were skeptical about Intel's ability to differentiate its chips. The head of one agency noted: "Most people who buy computers don't even know that chip is there. They care about the performance of the computer. It really doesn't matter what the chip is." Well, some may still not know exactly what a microprocessor chip does, but apparently it does matter if there is an "Intel Inside."

Sources: Tobi Elkin, "Intel Goes for a New Overall Branding Look," *Advertising Age*, Sept. 1, 2002, pp. 3, 43. Tobi Elkin, "Co-op Crossroads," *Advertising Age*, Nov. 15, 1999, pp. 1, 24, 26.

requirements the ad must meet to qualify for co-op reimbursement, such as size, use of trademarks, content, and format. Verification that the ad was run is also required, in the form of a tearsheet (print) or an affidavit from the radio or TV station (broadcast) and an invoice.

As with other types of trade promotions, manufacturers have been increasing their cooperative advertising expenditures in recent years. Some companies have been moving money out of national advertising into cooperative advertising because they believe they can have greater impact with ad campaigns in local markets. There is also a trend toward more cooperative advertising programs initiated by retailers, which approach manufacturers with catalogs, promotional events they are planning, or advertising programs they have developed in conjunction with local media and ask them to pay a percentage of the cost. Manufacturers often go along with these requests, particularly when the retailer is large and powerful.[64]

Coordinating Sales Promotion and Advertising

Those involved in the promotional process must recognize that sales promotion techniques usually work best in conjunction with advertising and that the effectiveness of an ad campaign can be enhanced by consumer-oriented sales promotion efforts. Rather than separate activities competing for a firm's promotional budget, advertising and sales promotion should be viewed as complementary tools. When properly planned and executed to work together, advertising and sales promotion can have a *synergistic effect* much greater than that of either promotional mix element alone.

Proper coordination of advertising and sales promotion is essential for the firm to take advantage of the opportunities offered by each tool and get the most out of its promotional budget. Successful integration of advertising and sales promotion requires decisions concerning not only the allocation of the budget to each area but also the coordination of the ad and sales promotion themes, the timing of the various promotional activities, and the target audience reached.

Budget Allocation

While many companies are spending more money on sales promotion than on media advertising, it is difficult to say just what percentage of a firm's overall promotional budget should be allocated to advertising versus consumer- and trade-oriented promotions. This allocation depends on a number of factors, including the specific promotional objectives of the campaign, the market and competitive situation, and the brand's stage in its life cycle.

Consider, for example, how allocation of the promotional budget may vary according to a brand's stage in the product life cycle. In the introductory stage, a large amount of the budget may be allocated to sales promotion techniques such as sampling and couponing to induce trial. In the growth stage, however, promotional dollars may be used primarily for advertising to stress brand differences and keep the brand name in consumers' minds.

When a brand moves to the maturity stage, advertising is primarily a reminder to keep consumers aware of the brand. Consumer-oriented sales promotions such as coupons, price-offs, premiums, and bonus packs may be needed periodically to maintain consumer loyalty, attract new users, and protect against competition. Trade-oriented promotions are needed to maintain shelf space and accommodate retailers' demands for better margins as well as encourage them to promote the brand. A study on the synergistic effects of advertising and promotion examined a brand in the mature phase of its life cycle and found that 80 percent of its sales at this stage were due to sales promotions. When a brand enters the decline stage of the product life cycle, most of the promotional support will probably be removed and expenditures on sales promotion are unlikely.

Coordination of Ad and Promotion Themes

To integrate the advertising and sales promotion programs successfully, the theme of consumer promotions should be tied in with the advertising and positioning theme wherever possible. Sales promotion tools should attempt to communicate a brand's unique attributes or benefits and to reinforce the sales message or campaign theme. In this way, the sales promotion effort contributes to the consumer franchise-building effort for the brand.

At the same time, media advertising should be used to draw attention to a sales promotion program such as a contest, sweepstakes, or event or to a special promotion offer such as a price reduction or rebate program. An example of this is the ad shown in Exhibit 16-30 for WD-40, which promotes the Search for 2000 Uses Sweepstakes that was discussed earlier and shown in Exhibit 16-8. Note how both the magazine ad and the sweepstakes promotion integrate the variety-of-uses positioning theme used for WD-40.

Media Support and Timing

Media support for a sales promotion program is critical and should be coordinated with the media program for the ad campaign. Media advertising is often needed to deliver such sales promotion materials as coupons, sweepstakes, contest entry forms, premium offers, and even samples. It is also needed to inform consumers of a promotional offer as well as to create awareness, interest, and favorable attitudes toward the brand.

By using advertising in conjunction with a sales promotion program, marketers can make consumers aware of the brand and its benefits and increase their responsiveness to the promotion. Consumers are more likely to redeem a coupon or respond to a price-off deal for a brand they are familiar with than one they know nothing about.

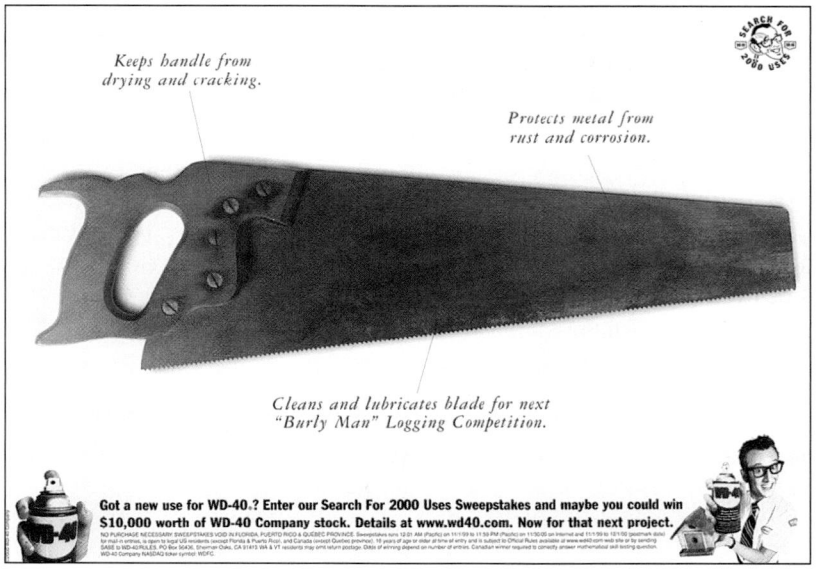

Exhibit 16-30 This WD-40 ad promotes the 2000 Uses Sweepstakes and is consistent with the positioning theme used for the brand

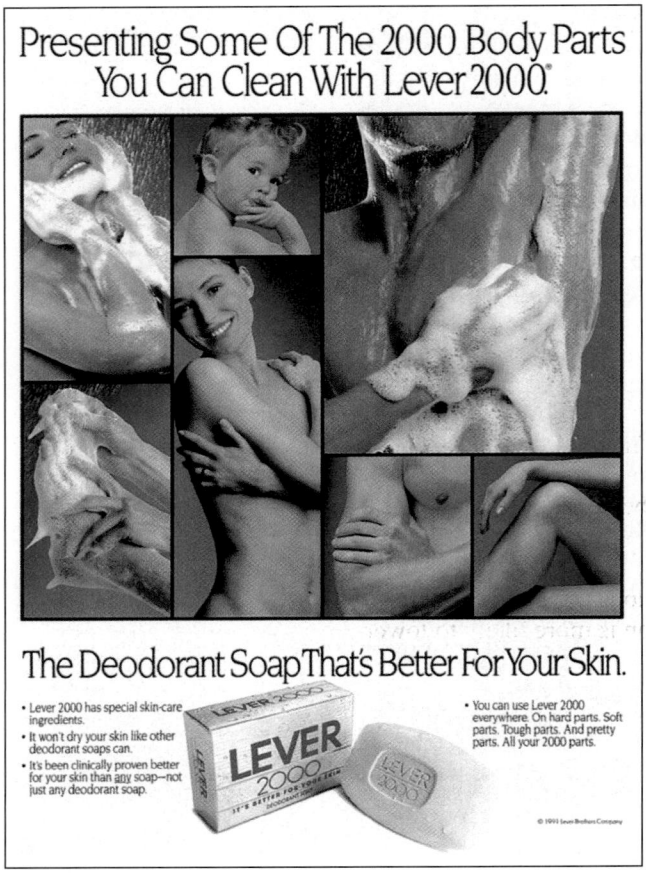

Exhibit 16-31 Creative advertising was coordinated with sales promotion in the successful introduction of Lever 2000 soap

Moreover, product trial created through sales promotion techniques such as sampling or high-value couponing is more likely to result in long-term use of the brand when accompanied by advertising.[65]

Using a promotion without prior or concurrent advertising can limit its effectiveness and risk damaging the brand's image. If consumers perceive the brand as being promotion dependent or of lesser quality, they are not likely to develop favorable attitudes and long-term loyalty. Conversely, the effectiveness of an ad can be enhanced by a coupon, a premium offer, or an opportunity to enter a sweepstakes or contest.

An example of the effective coordination of advertising and sales promotion is the introductory campaign Lever Brothers developed for its Lever 2000 bar soap. As noted earlier in the chapter, Lever Brothers used high-value coupons, sent samples to half of U.S. households, and offered discounts to retailers as part of its introductory marketing blitz. These sales promotion efforts were accompanied by heavy advertising in print and TV with the tagline "Presenting some of the 2000 body parts you can clean with Lever 2000" (Exhibit 16-31).

Sales promotion was important in inducing trial for Lever 2000 and continued after introduction in the form of couponing. But it was the strong positioning created through effective advertising that converted consumers to regular users. Repeat sales of the brand were at about 40 percent even after heavy discounting ended. Just six months after its introduction, Lever 2000 became the number-two deodorant soap in dollar volume, with an estimated 8.4 percent of the $1.5 billion bar-soap market.[66]

To coordinate their advertising and sales promotion programs more effectively, many companies are getting their sales promotion agencies more involved in the advertising and promotional planning process. Rather than hiring agencies to develop individual, nonfranchise-building types of promotions with short-term goals and tactics, many firms are having their sales promotion and advertising agencies work together to develop integrated promotional strategies and programs. Figure 16-7 shows how the role of sales promotion agencies is changing.

Figure 16-7 The shifting role of the promotion agency

Traditional	New and Improved
1. Primarily used to develop short-term tactics or concepts.	1. Used to develop long- and short-term promotional strategies as well as tactics.
2. Hired/compensated on a project-by-project basis.	2. Contracted on annual retainer, following formal agency reviews.
3. Many promotion agencies used a mix—each one hired for best task and/or specialty.	3. One or two exclusive promotion agencies for each division or brand group.
4. One or two contact people from agency.	4. Full team or core group on the account.
5. Promotion agency never equal to ad agency—doesn't work up front in annual planning process.	5. Promotion agency works on equal basis with ad agency—sits at planning table up front.
6. Not directly accountable for results.	6. Very much accountable—goes through a rigorous evaluation process.

Sales Promotion Abuse

The increasing use of sales promotion in marketing programs is more than a passing fad. It is a fundamental change in strategic decisions about how companies market their products and services. The value of this increased emphasis on sales promotion has been questioned by several writers, particularly with regard to the lack of adequate planning and management of sales promotion programs.[67]

Are marketers becoming too dependent on this element of the marketing program? Consumer and trade promotions can be a very effective tool for generating short-term increases in sales, and many brand managers would rather use a promotion to produce immediate sales than invest in advertising and build the brand's image over an extended time. As the director of sales promotion services at one large ad agency noted: "There's a great temptation for quick sales fixes through promotions. It's a lot easier to offer the consumer an immediate price savings than to differentiate your product from a competitor's."[68]

Overuse of sales promotion can be detrimental to a brand in several ways. A brand that is constantly promoted may lose perceived value. Consumers often end up purchasing a brand because it is on sale, they get a premium, or they have a coupon, rather than basing their decision on a favorable attitude they have developed. When the extra promotional incentive is not available, they switch to another brand. A study by Priya Raghubir and Kim Corfman examined whether price promotions affect pretrial evaluations of a brand.[69] They found that offering a price promotion is more likely to lower a brand's evaluation when the brand has not been promoted previously compared to when it has been frequently promoted; that price promotions are used as a source of information about a brand to a greater extent when the evaluator is not an expert but does have some product or industry knowledge; and that promotions are more likely to result in negative evaluations when they are uncommon in the industry. The findings from this study suggest that marketers must be careful in the use of price promotions as they may inhibit trial of a brand in certain situations.

Alan Sawyer and Peter Dickson have used the concept of *attribution theory* to examine how sales promotion may affect consumer attitude formation.[70] According to this theory, people acquire attitudes by observing their own behavior and considering why they acted in a certain manner. Consumers who consistently purchase a brand because of a coupon or price-off deal may attribute their behavior to the external promotional incentive rather than to a favorable attitude toward the brand. By contrast, when no external incentive is available, consumers are more likely to attribute their purchase behavior to favorable underlying feelings about the brand.

Another potential problem with consumer-oriented promotions is that a **sales promotion trap** or spiral can result when several competitors use promotions extensively.[71] Often a firm begins using sales promotions to differentiate its product or service from the competition. If the promotion is successful and leads to a differential advantage (or even appears to do so), competitors may quickly copy it. When all the competitors are using sales promotions, this not only lowers profit margins for each firm but also makes it difficult for any one firm to hop off the promotional bandwagon.[72] This dilemma is shown in Figure 16-8.

A number of industries have fallen into this promotional trap. In the cosmetics industry, gift-with-purchase and purchase-with-purchase promotional offers were

	Our Firm	
All Other Firms	**Cut back promotions**	**Maintain promotions**
Cut back promotions	Higher profits for all	Market share goes to our firm
Maintain promotions	Market share goes to all other firms	Market share stays constant; profits stay low

Figure 16-8 The sales promotion trap

Exhibit 16-32 Dell's sweepstakes started a promotional battle in the personal computer industry

developed as a tactic for getting buyers to sample new products. But they have become a common, and costly, way of doing business.[73] In many areas of the country, supermarkets have gotten into the trap of doubling or even tripling manufacturers' coupons, which cuts into their already small profit margins. Fast-food chains have also fallen into the trap with promotions featuring popular menu items, such as Burger King's Whopper for 99 cents. The sales promotion war spread to yet another industry recently when Dell Computer began using sales promotion offers to help sell its personal computers. Dell's Trip-a-Day Giveaway offered consumers a chance to win a vacation worth up to $50,000 (Exhibit 16-32). Competitors quickly matched Dell's promotion: Compaq and Hewlett Packard developed their own sweepstakes and also began using rebates. Gateway gave away free printers and scanners with certain PCs, and Apple offered no-payment financing. Industry analysts have expressed concern over the impact the promotional war will have on these companies as profit margins in the PC industry are already very low.[74]

Marketers must consider both the short-term impact of a promotion and its long-term effect on the brand. The ease with which competitors can develop a retaliatory promotion and the likelihood of their doing so should also be considered. Marketers must be careful not to damage the brand franchise with sales promotions or to get the firm involved in a promotional war that erodes the brand's profit margins and threatens its long-term existence. Marketers are often tempted to resort to sales promotions to deal with declining sales and other problems when they should examine such other aspects of the marketing program as channel relations, price, packaging, product quality, or advertising.

Summary

For many years, advertising was the major promotional mix element for most consumer-product companies. Over the past decade, however, marketers have been allocating more of their promotional dollars to sales promotion. There has been a steady increase in the use of sales promotion techniques to influence consumers' purchase behavior. The growing power of retailers, erosion of brand loyalty, increase in consumers' sensitivity to promotions, increase in new product introductions, fragmentation of the consumer market, short-term focus of marketing and brand managers, and increase in advertising clutter are some of the reasons for this increase.

Sales promotions can be characterized as either franchise building or nonfranchise building. The former contribute to the long-term development and reinforcement of brand identity and image; the latter are designed to accelerate the purchase process and generate immediate increases in sales.

Sales promotion techniques can be classified as either trade- or consumer-oriented. A number of consumer-oriented sales promotion techniques were examined in this chapter, including sampling, couponing, premiums, contests and sweepstakes, rebates and refunds, bonus packs, price-off deals, frequency programs, and event marketing. The characteristics of these promotional tools were examined, along with their advantages and limitations. Various trade-oriented promotions were also examined, including trade contests and incentives, trade allowances, displays and point-of-purchase materials, sales training programs, trade shows, and cooperative advertising.

Advertising and sales promotion should be viewed not as separate activities but rather as complementary tools. When planned and executed properly, advertising and sales promotion can produce a synergistic effect that is greater than the response generated from either promotional mix element alone. To accomplish this, marketers must coordinate budgets, advertising and promotional themes, media scheduling and timing, and target audiences.

Sales promotion abuse can result when marketers become too dependent on the use of sales promotion techniques and sacrifice long-term brand position and image for short-term sales increases. Many industries experience sales promotion traps when a number of competitors use promotions extensively and it becomes difficult for any single firm to cut back on promotion without risking a loss in sales. Overuse of sales promotion tools can lower profit margins and threaten the image and even the viability of a brand.

Key Terms

sales promotion, 513
consumer-oriented sales promotion, 513
trade-oriented sales promotion, 513
account-specific marketing, 519
consumer franchise-building (CFB) promotions, 520
nonfranchise-building (non-FB) promotions, 522
sampling, 526
bounce-back coupon, 533
cross-ruff coupon, 533
instant coupon, 533
in-store couponing, 534
premium, 535
self-liquidating premiums, 536
contest, 537
sweepstakes, 537
game, 537
refund, 540
bonus packs, 541
price-off deal, 541
frequency programs, 541
event marketing, 543
event sponsorship, 543
push money, 546
trade allowance, 547
off-invoice allowance, 547
slotting allowance, 547
failure fees, 548
forward buying, 549
diverting, 549
everyday low pricing (EDLP), 549
planograms, 551
trade show, 551
cooperative advertising, 552
horizontal cooperative advertising, 552
ingredient-sponsored cooperative advertising, 552
vertical cooperative advertising, 552
sales promotion trap, 557

Discussion Questions

1. Discuss the role of sales promotion as a part of the promotional mix and how it can be integrated with other marketing communication tools.

2. Discuss how sales promotion can be used as an acceleration tool that can speed up the selling and/or purchasing process and increase a company's sales volume.

3. Discuss the various factors that have led to companies shifting more of their marketing budgets to sales promotion. Discuss the pros and cons of this reallocation of marketers' advertising and promotion budgets.

4. IMC Perspective 16-1 discusses how marketers are using contests as a way of increasing involvement with their products and/or services and building brand equity. Discuss how a contest can be used to increase involvement and contribute to brand equity. Find an example of a contest that you believe contributes to the equity of a brand and explain how it does so.

5. Discuss how samples and coupons can be used to generate trial of a new product or increase consumption of an established brand.

6. Discuss how sales promotion programs can be integrated with a company's online strategy and how the Internet can be used as part of a company's sales promotion efforts.

7. In recent years a number of marketers have questioned the economic feasibility of couponing programs. Discuss the various reasons marketers are questioning the value of coupons. Evaluate the arguments for and against the use of coupons.

8. IMC Perspective 16-4 discusses the problems McDonald's encountered as a result of the conspiracy to embezzle winning game pieces from the company's popular Monopoly game promotion. Do you think McDonald's will ever be able to use the Monopoly game promotion again? Why or why not?

9. What is meant by trade-oriented sales promotion? Discuss the various types of trade promotions and reasons why marketers use them.

10. What is meant by a slotting allowance or fee? Evaluate the arguments for and against retailers charging slotting fees to manufacturers.

11. Describe the various forms of cooperative advertising and the reasons they are used by marketers.

12. What is meant by a sales promotion trap or spiral? Evaluate the promotional war that was begun by Dell Computer when the company began using sales promotion offers to help sell personal computers. What are the options for other personal computer companies in deciding whether to match Dell's promotional offers?

Public Relations, Publicity, and Corporate Advertising

17

Chapter Objectives

1. To recognize the roles of public relations, publicity, and corporate advertising in the promotional mix.
2. To know the difference between public relations and publicity and demonstrate the advantages and disadvantages of each.
3. To understand the reasons for corporate advertising and its advantages and disadvantages.
4. To know the methods for measuring the effects of public relations, publicity, and corporate advertising.

Does the Success of Public Relations Mean the Death of Advertising?

Just about a decade ago, some people involved in the public relations (PR) industry were asking marketers to stay out of their domain. These traditional PR people were arguing that marketing and public relations always have been separate communications functions and that they should forever stay that way. My how things have changed!

Recently, two very well known marketing consultants released a book titled *The Fall of Advertising and the Rise of PR.* The gist of the book is that while advertising is still the most dominant medium used by marketers, declining advertising effectiveness means that this communications tool is no longer effective for introducing and building new brands. The only way to build a brand now, they contend, is through public relations. While this obviously led to book burnings in advertising agencies around the world, what made it worse is that the authors—Al Ries and his daughter Laura Ries—are well known and respected marketers! Al Ries (along with a former coauthor, Jack Trout) is best known for first introducing the concept of positioning. And what could be more marketing than that? But now, say the Rieses, consumers have changed, and the communications program and the way we think about branding must change with it. Consumers now learn about products and brands through means other than advertising—the Rieses contend that some brands including Palm, Starbucks, and the Body Shop have succeeded with no advertising—and advertising has lost credibility. The Rieses contend that companies now must create brand images through publicity and media that consumers rely on for more "objective" information. The role of advertising, they say, is to maintain the brand image. And the Rieses are not the only ones who feel this way. Linda Recupero, vice president of the brand marketing company Burson-Marsteller, in New York—which was responsible for the successful PR launches of Botox and Segway—agrees with the premise that PR is more effective in building a brand in the introduction stage. Executives from large marketing companies like Gillette, Unilever, and Georgia-Pacific have also weighed in on the side of public relations.

But not everyone is buying the death-of-advertising argument yet—including some PR executives. Thomas Harris, a public relations consultant, calls the book "a gross generalization" that overlooks other public relations functions beyond publicity. Harris argues that publicity can be a powerful tool for mature brands—not just introductions—citing the Pillsbury Bake-Off as just one example. Others have taken issue with the Rieses' contention that advertising is now

only useful for promoting mature brands, citing their own examples of successful brand introductions supported heavily by advertising. Many advertising and PR people feel that it is hard to control the message disseminated through PR channels. Heinz's introduction of green ketchup in an EZ Squirt bottle is one such example. While Heinz got $10 million worth of free publicity—three times what was to be spent on advertising—the publicity hijacked the marketing plan when word of the launch leaked out two months before Heinz was ready. Heinz's marketing plan called for the emphasis to be placed on the bottle design, while the publicity focused on the green color of the ketchup. While it all ended up okay, Heinz marketing managers admit they were lucky that the green color didn't turn kids off.

So will public relations replace advertising as the mainstay of the communications budget? Not likely, say Jack Neff and others writing in *Advertising Age.* They note that even with major declines in 2001, advertising spending dwarfed that of PR—$31.74 billion to $4.31 billion—and that PR spending actually declined more than did advertising spending. Rance Crain, also of *Advertising Age,* sees advertising and PR working together as a "one-two" punch, with PR as the relationship builder. Crain notes that "integration seems to be the way of the future," arguing that "whatever the disciplines used, they all must work together to give a unified message to the consumer." While opinions differ, no one seems to be saying that public relations should return to its traditional function. Wonder what those PR people who told marketers to stay away are thinking?

Sources: Rance Crain, "Marketers Look at New Ideas, and PR Becomes the 'Closer,'" *Advertising Age,* July 29, 2002, p. 15; Jack Neff, Cara Dipasqule, and Jean Halliday, "Ries' Thesis: Ads Don't Build Brands, PR Does," *Advertising Age,* July 15, 2002, p. 14; Jack Neff, "Will PR Kill Advertising?" advertisingage.com, July 16, 2002, pp. 1–6.

Regardless of which side you take in the advertising–public relations argument, one thing is clear—the role of public relations in the communications program has changed. While some people may disagree as to the importance and/or power of this program element, few, if any, would contend that it is business as usual.

Publicity, public relations, and corporate advertising all have promotional program elements that may be of great benefit to marketers. They are integral parts of the overall promotional effort that must be managed and coordinated with the other elements of the promotional mix. However, these three tools do not always have the specific objectives of product and service promotion, nor do they always involve the same methods you have become accustomed to as you have read this text. Typically, these activities are designed more to change attitudes toward an organization or issue than to promote specific products or affect behaviors directly (though you will see that this role is changing in some organizations). This chapter explores the roles of public relations, publicity, and corporate advertising, the advantages and disadvantages of each, and the process by which they are employed. Examples of such efforts—both successful and unsuccessful—are also included.

Public Relations

What is public relations? How does it differ from other elements of marketing discussed thus far? Perhaps a good starting point is to define what the term *public relations* has traditionally meant and then to introduce its new role.

The Traditional Definition of PR

A variety of books define **public relations,** but perhaps the most comprehensive definition is that offered by the *Public Relations News* (the weekly newsletter of the industry):

> the management function which evaluates public attitudes, identifies the policies and procedures of an organization with the public interest, and executes a program of action (and communication) to earn public understanding and acceptance.[1]

Public relations is indeed a management function. The term management should be used in its broadest sense; it is not limited to business managements but extends to other types of organizations, including nonprofit institutions.

In this definition, public relations requires a series of stages, including:

1. The determination and evaluation of public attitudes.
2. The identification of policies and procedures of an organization with a public interest.
3. The development and execution of a communications program designed to bring about public understanding and acceptance.

This process does not occur all at once. An effective public relations program continues over months or even years.

Finally, this definition reveals that public relations involves much more than activities designed to sell a product or service. The PR program may involve some of the promotional program elements previously discussed but use them in a different way. For example, press releases may be sent to announce new products or changes in the organization, special events may be organized to create goodwill in the community, and advertising may be used to state the firm's position on a controversial issue.

The New Role of PR

As discussed in the introduction to this chapter, in an increasing number of marketing-oriented companies, new responsibilities have been established for public relations. It takes on a much broader (and more marketing-oriented) perspective, designed to promote the organization as well as its products and/or services.

The way that companies and organizations use public relations might best be viewed as a continuum. On one end of the continuum is the use of PR from a traditional perspective. In this perspective public relations is viewed as a nonmarketing function whose primary responsibility is to maintain mutually beneficial relationships between the organization and its publics. In this case, customers or potential customers are only part of numerous publics—employees, investors, neighbors, special-interest groups, and so on. Marketing and public relations are separate departments; if external agencies are being used, they are separate agencies. At the other end of the continuum, public relations is considered primarily a marketing communications function. All noncustomer relationships are perceived as necessary only in a marketing context.[2] In these organizations, public relations reports to marketing. As the book by the Rieses clearly indicates, for many companies the PR function is moving more and more toward a "new role," which is much closer to a marketing function than a traditional one.

The new role of public relations envisions both strong marketing and strong PR departments. Rather than each department operating independently, the two work closely together, blending their talents to provide the best overall image of the firm and its product or service offerings.

Writing in *Advertising Age,* William N. Curry notes that organizations must use caution in establishing this relationship because PR and marketing are not the same thing, and when one becomes dominant, the balance required to operate at maximum efficiency is lost.[3] He says losing sight of the objectives and functions of public relations in an attempt to achieve marketing goals may be detrimental in the long run. Others take an even stronger view that if public relations and marketing distinctions continue to blur, the independence of the PR function will be lost and it will become much less effective.[4] In fact, as noted by Cutlip, Center, and Broom, marketing and public relations are complementary functions, "with each making unique but complementary contributions to building and maintaining the many relationships essential for organizational survival and growth. To ignore one is to risk failure in the other."[5] This position is consistent with our perception that public relations is an important part of the IMC process, contributing in its own way but also in a way consistent with marketing goals.

Integrating PR into the Promotional Mix

Given the broader responsibilities of public relations, the issue is how to integrate it into the promotional mix. Philip Kotler and William Mindak suggest a number of alternative organizational designs: Either marketing or public relations can be the dominant function; both can be equal but separate functions; or the two can perform the same roles.[6] While each of these designs has its merits, in this text we consider public relations an IMC program element. This means that its broad role must include traditional responsibilities.

Whether public relations takes on a traditional role or a more marketing-oriented one, PR activities are still tied to specific communications objectives. Assessing public attitudes and creating a favorable corporate image are no less important than promoting products or services directly.

Marketing Public Relations (MPR) Functions

Thomas L. Harris has referred to public relations activities designed to support marketing objectives as **marketing public relations (MPR)** functions.[7] Marketing objectives that may be aided by public relations activities include raising awareness, informing and educating, gaining understanding, building trust, giving consumers a reason to buy, and motivating consumer acceptance. MPR adds value to the integrated marketing program in a number of ways:

- *Building marketplace excitement before media advertising breaks.* The announcement of a new product, for example, is an opportunity for the marketer to obtain publicity and dramatize the product, thereby increasing the effectiveness of ads. When Volkswagen reintroduced the Beetle, a great deal of anticipation was created through public relations prior to the availability of the cars.
- *Creating advertising news where there is no product news.* Ads themselves can be the focus of publicity. There seems to be as much hype about the ads on the Super Bowl as there is for the game itself. The "Switch" campaign of Apple Computers has generated much publicity for the ads.
- *Introducing a product with little or no advertising.* This strategy has been implemented successfully by a number of companies, including Hewlett-Packard, Kinetix, Ty, and Crayola. Gillette uses PR as the lead medium in every new product launch.[8]
- *Providing a value-added customer service.* Butterball established a hotline where people can call in to receive personal advice on how to prepare their turkeys. The company handled 25,000 calls during one holiday season. Many companies provide such services on their Internet sites. Chicken of the Sea provides recipes to visitors of its site (which of course suggest using Chicken of the Sea tuna).
- *Building brand-to-customer bonds.* The Pillsbury Bake-Off has led to strong brand loyalty among Pillsbury customers, who compete by submitting baked goods. The winner now receives a $1 million prize!
- *Influencing the influentials*—that is, providing information to opinion leaders.
- *Defending products at risk and giving consumers a reason to buy.* By taking constructive actions to defend or promote a company's products, PR can actually give consumers a reason to buy. Energizer's national education campaign that urges consumers to change the batteries in their fire alarms when they reset their clocks in the fall has resulted in a strong corporate citizen image and increased sales of batteries.

An excellent example of using MPRs in an integrated program is a strategy employed by Victoria's Secret. A spot ad that appeared on the Super Bowl (cost, $1.5 million) announcing a live webcast of the Victoria's Secret fashion show that would appear a few days later generated mountains of publicity. An estimated 5 billion people worldwide were made aware of Victoria's Secret. The rush to view the show led to so many users signing on that servers throughout the world overloaded, causing many to crash—and this led to even more publicity. Combining these two events with in-

store merchandising also paid off, as sales rose by 13 percent. The Web presence produced 600,000 new catalog requests, 1.1 million registrations for e-mail updates, and orders from 136 nations. The company has now increased its television budget, as well as its spending in magazines like *Elle* and *Vogue,* to broaden its integrated approach.[9] Additional successful implementations of MPRs are shown in Figure 17-1.

Harris notes that there are a number of advantages of using MPR:[10]

- It is a cost-effective way to reach the market.
- It is a highly targeted way to conduct public relations.
- It benefits from the endorsement of independent and objective third parties who have no association with the product.
- It achieves credibility.
- It supports advertising programs by making messages more credible.
- It breaks through the clutter.
- It circumvents consumer resistance to sales efforts.

He also notes that there are disadvantages, including the following:

- There is a lack of control over the media.
- It is difficult to tie in slogans and other advertising devices.
- Media time and space are not guaranteed.
- There are no standard effectiveness measures.

One of the major threats expressed by Harris is that MPRs may lead to public relations' becoming subservient to marketing—a concern expressed by many opponents of MPR. However, if employed properly and used in conjunction with other traditional public relations practices as well as IMC elements, MPR can continue to be used effectively.

- *Segway.* The strange-looking motorized transport device was introduced with no advertising, yet it generated an estimated 758 million impressions valued at $70 million to $80 million through free publicity. The company did not plan to advertise until over a year after the introduction.[11] (Exhibit 17-1.)
- *Wonderbra.* With almost no advertising support beyond billboards in major markets, Wonderbra created anticipation for the launch of the first Wonderbra in 1994. Already behind two major competitors, the company relied heavily on public relations coverage and media hype to create awareness and gain attention for the product launch. The same strategy has continued over the years, and Wonderbra has become the number-one push-up bra in the United States.
- *Rockport.* Just another shoe company in the 1980s, Rockport was convinced by its public relations agency to promote the concept of "fitness walking" through a series of MPR initiatives. Rockport became known as the "Walking Shoe Company," achieving a tenfold increase in sales.
- *Arbor Mist Wine.* After several years of researching consumer trends and brand preferences for wine, Canandaigua found that younger women (among others) were dissatisfied with the choices of alcoholic beverages available to them. Positioning the product as "Snapple with an attitude," and as a fun wine, Arbor Mist used wine festivals and wine tastings for local media to achieve its success. By building one-on-one relationships with the media, Arbor Mist's PR team was able to generate significant publicity in New York, Chicago, Miami, and Los Angeles. The company became the first wine ever to ship 1 million cases in less than 100 days.
- *California Kiwifruit Commission.* While the commission has been around since 1935, its public relations efforts have primarily focused on disseminating health and nutritional information about kiwis. Through a more marketing-oriented public relations campaign, the commission was able to increase sales by as much as 300 percent in stores and achieved a 12 percent increase in new users.

Figure 17-1 MPR adds value to the marketing program

Exhibit 17-1 Segway used publicity to launch its new product

The Process of Public Relations

The actual process of conducting public relations and integrating it into the promotional mix involves a series of both traditional and marketing-oriented tasks.

Determining and Evaluating Public Attitudes

You've learned that public relations is concerned with people's attitudes toward the firm or specific issues beyond those directed at a product or service. The first question you may ask is why. Why is the firm so concerned with the public's attitudes?

One reason is that these attitudes may affect sales of the firm's products. A number of companies have experienced sales declines as a result of consumer boycotts. Procter & Gamble, Coors, Nike, and Bumble Bee Seafoods are just a few companies that responded to organized pressures. A string of SUV accidents led to major problems for 102-year-old Bridgestone/Firestone. In response to the problem, Firestone replaced nearly 900,000 tires and implemented a communications program to counter the negative publicity, a program including television commercials, personal visits to dealers, and print advertising such as that shown in Exhibit 17-2. As a result of the campaign, Firestone lost none of its 10,000 independent tire dealers and two years later was on the road to recovery.

Exhibit 17-2 Firestone responds to negative publicity

Making It Right.

You have our word on that.

When you buy tires, you're not just buying rubber and steel... you want the confidence that your tires will get you to your destination—safely. Your safety is our primary concern. We want you to have confidence in the way Firestone tires are made and the way they perform. We'll do whatever it takes, however long it takes, to gain your trust.

We call this our "*Making It Right*" plan. With your satisfaction as our goal, Firestone is expanding warranties and making important enhancements in manufacturing and quality control. In the role of watchdogs, a new team of top technical and quality control managers has been assembled to continuously analyze tire and safety data. They'll act to uncover issues ***before*** they become problems. We believe in our tires. We want to prove to you that you can believe in them as well. ***We'll make it right. It's that simple.***

John Lampe,
CEO, Firestone.

Inflate. Rotate. Evaluate.
How to maintain your tires

Maintaining your tires, including checking air pressure monthly, helps protect them from damage and extends the mileage. Most important, properly inflated tires help ensure the security of you and your family on the road. This free brochure will give you the simple steps to tire safety. Get your copy by visiting our web site or your nearest Firestone retailer.

Firestone
America's Tire Since 1900
www.firestonetire.com

tiresafety.com

Second, no one wants to be perceived as a bad citizen. Corporations exist in communities, and their employees may both work and live there. Negative attitudes carry over to employee morale and may result in a less-than-optimal working environment internally and in the community.

Due to their concerns about public perceptions, many privately held corporations, publicly held companies, utilities, and media survey public attitudes. The reasons for conducting this research are many:

1. *It provides input into the planning process.* Once the firm has determined public attitudes, they become the starting point in the development of programs designed to maintain favorable positions or change unfavorable ones.

2. *It serves as an early warning system.* Once a problem exists, it may require substantial time and money to correct. By conducting research, the firm may be able to identify potential problems and handle them effectively before they become serious issues.

3. *It secures support internally.* If research shows a problem or potential problem exists, it will be much easier for the public relations arm to gain the support it needs to address this problem.

4. *It increases the effectiveness of the communication.* The better it understands a problem, the better the firm can design communications to deal with it.[12]

Establishing a PR Plan

In a survey of 100 top and middle managers in the communications field, over 60 percent said their PR programs involved little more than press releases, press kits for trade shows, and new product announcements.[13] Further, these tools were not designed into a formal public relations effort but rather were used only as needed. In other words, no structured program was evident in well over half of the companies surveyed! As we noted earlier, the public relations process is an ongoing one, requiring formalized policies and procedures for dealing with problems and opportunities. Just as you would not develop an advertising and/or promotions program without a plan, you should not institute public relations efforts haphazardly. Moreover, the PR plan needs to be integrated into the overall marketing communications program. Figure 17-2 provides some questions marketers should ask to determine whether their PR plan is workable.

Cutlip, Center, and Broom suggest a four-step process for developing a public relations plan: (1) define public relations problems; (2) plan and program; (3) take action and communicate; and (4) evaluate the program.[14] The questions in Figure 17-2 and the four-step planning process tie in with the promotional planning process stressed throughout this text.

Developing and Executing the PR Program

Because of the broad role that public relations may be asked to play, the PR program may need to extend beyond promotion. A broader definition of the target market, additional communications objectives, and different messages and delivery systems may be employed. Let us examine this process.

Determining Relevant Target Audiences

The targets of public relations efforts may vary, with different objectives for each. Some may be directly involved in selling the product; others may affect the firm in a different way (e.g., they may be aimed at stockholders or legislators). These audiences may be internal or external to the firm.

Internal audiences may include the employees of the firm, stockholders and investors, members of the local community, suppliers, and current customers. Why are community members and customers of the firm considered internal rather than external? According to John Marston, it's because these groups are already connected with the organization in some way and the firm normally communicates with them in the ordinary routine of work.[15] **External audiences** are those people who are not closely connected with the organization (e.g., the public at large).

1. Does the plan reflect a thorough understanding of the company's business situation?
2. Has the PR program made good use of research and background sources?
3. Does the plan include full analysis of recent editorial coverage?
4. Do the PR people fully understand the product's strengths and weaknesses?
5. Does the PR program describe several cogent, relevant conclusions from the research?
6. Are the program objectives specific and measurable?
7. Does the program clearly describe what the PR activity will be and how it will benefit the company?
8. Does the program describe how its results will be measured?
9. Do the research, objectives, activities, and evaluations tie together?
10. Has the PR department communicated with marketing throughout the development of the program?

Figure 17-2 Ten questions for evaluating public relations plans

Exhibit 17-3 An example of a newsletter used for internal communication

It may be necessary to communicate with these groups on an ongoing basis for a variety of reasons, ranging from ensuring goodwill to introducing new policies, procedures, or even products. A few examples may help.

Employees of the Firm Maintaining morale and showcasing the results of employees' efforts are often prime objectives of the public relations program. Organizational newsletters, notices on bulletin boards, paycheck envelope stuffers, direct mail, and annual reports are some of the methods used to communicate with these groups. Exhibit 17-3 shows one such internal communication used by the Business School at San Diego State University.

Personal methods of communicating may be as formal as an established grievance committee or as informal as an office Christmas party. Other social events, such as corporate bowling teams or picnics, are also used to create goodwill.

Stockholders and Investors You may think an annual report like the one in Exhibit 17-4 just provides stockholders and investors with financial information regarding the firm. While this is one purpose, annual reports are also a communications channel for informing this audience about why the firm is or is not doing well, future plans, and other information that goes beyond numbers.

For example, McDonald's has successfully used annual reports to fend off potential PR problems. One year the report described McDonald's recycling efforts to alleviate consumers' concerns about waste; another report included a 12-page spread on food and nutrition. Other companies use similar strategies, employing shareholders' meetings, video presentations, and other forms of direct mail. General Motors' annual public interest report is sent to shareholders and community members to detail the company's high standards of corporate responsibility. GM also produces a sustainability report to update interested parties on its progress. Companies have used these approaches to generate additional investments, to bring more of their stocks "back home" (i.e., become more locally controlled and managed), and to produce funding to solve specific problems, as well as to promote goodwill.

Community Members People who live and work in the community where a firm is located or doing business are often the target of public relations efforts. Such efforts may involve ads informing the community of activities that the organization is

Exhibit 17-4 Annual reports serve a variety of purposes

Exhibit 17-5 Chevron demonstrates concern for the public

engaged in—for example, reducing air pollution, cleaning up water supplies, or, as shown in Exhibit 17-5, protecting turtles. (As you can see, the community can be defined very broadly.) Demonstrating to people that the organization is a good citizen with their welfare in mind may also be a reason for communicating to these groups.

Suppliers and Customers An organization wishes to maintain *goodwill* with its suppliers as well as its consuming public. If consumers think a company is not socially conscious, they may take their loyalties elsewhere. Suppliers may be inclined to do the same.

Sometimes sponsoring a public relations effort results in direct evidence of success. For example, the "Just say no" to drugs campaign was a boon to companies manufacturing drug testing kits, hospitals offering drug rehabilitation programs, and TV news programs' ratings.[16] Indirect indications of the success of PR efforts may include more customer loyalty, less antagonism, or greater cooperation between the firm and its suppliers or consumers.

Sometimes a public relations effort is targeted to more than one group. For example, San Diego Gas & Electric (SDGE), the public utility company for the San Diego area, has suffered from extreme negative attitudes among its customers due to its high rates. This problem was aggravated when a series of management blunders resulted in even higher rates and SDGE announced plans to build a nuclear plant in one of the lagoons near the ocean, resulting in protests from consumers and environmentalists. Stockholders and potential investors lacked trust, and employee morale was low. (Company cars with the SDGE logo on the doors were vandalized, and drivers were threatened to the point where the identifying logos had to be removed.)

The public relations plan developed to deal with these problems targeted a variety of publics and employed a number of channels. TV spots showed consumers how to save energy, print ads explained the reasons for the energy purchases made by management, and PR programs were developed to foster more community interaction. These programs have led to much more favorable attitudes among all the publics targeted. (At least employees can put the SDGE logo back on their cars.)

Relevant audiences may also include people not directly involved with the firm. The press, educators, civic and business groups, governments, and the financial community can be external audiences.

The Media Perhaps one of the most critical external publics is the media, which determine what you will read in your newspapers or see on TV, and how this news will be presented. Because of the media's power, they should be informed of the firm's actions. Companies issue press releases and communicate through conferences, interviews, and special events. The media are generally receptive to such information as long as it is handled professionally; reporters are always interested in good stories.

LOCAL 8 KFMB TV

COMMUNITY

Answering the Needs of the Community

F.O.R.C.E. 8 "Focus On Resolving Conflict Everyday"
A project of KFMB TV Local 8 and the Safe Schools Unit of the San Diego County Office of Education.
Local 8 is committed to helping prevent violence on school campuses. Under the direction of the Safe Schools Unit, Local 8's Larry Himmel is teaching conflict resolution and leadership development skills to San Diego County middle and high school students. Student participants represent a diverse cross section of the student body. They are learning to resolve their conflicts without violence and build relationships for positive, healthy development. F.O.R.C.E. 8 has mentored thousands of students and is currently booked throughout the 2001-2002 school year. The project has received broadcasting's prestigious PROMAX Gold Medallion award for best Community Service project in the country.

ADOPT 8
A project of KFMB TV Local 8 and San Diego County Adoptions.
Everyday, hundreds of children in San Diego County are waiting to find forever families. That's why we partnered with San Diego County Adoptions to start ADOPT 8. Every week, Local 8's Pamela Davis introduces San Diegans to children who are currently in the county's Foster Care System waiting to be adopted. ADOPT 8 profiles are featured every Wednesday on Local 8 News at Noon and Sundays, on Local 8 at 5PM. The heart-warming profiles also educate San Diegans on the process of adoption in San Diego County. Since ADOPT 8 began last year, more than 50 children in San Diego have been adopted and have found their "forever families."

Buddies for Life
A project of Local 8 and UCSD Cancer Center.
Local 8 is proud to partner with UCSD Cancer Center to win the battle against breast cancer by providing the most comprehensive information on prevention, treatment and support. On the 8th of every month on Local 8 at 4PM and 6PM, Barbara-Lee Edwards provides the latest information on breast health. In addition, we're urging viewers to join Buddies for Life by choosing a "buddy" and logging on to our website. Every month, UCSD Cancer Center will provide a free e-mail reminder service to viewers and their buddies to remind them to schedule breast self-exams and clinical exams.

8's COOL SCHOOL
KFMB TV Local 8 believes in recognizing San Diego's finest schools. Every Friday on Local 8 at 4PM, Education Reporter Graham Ledger salutes 8's Cool School of the Week. 8's Cool School honors innovative schools and educational programs that encourage learning and help shape our children's futures. 8's Cool Schools are selected from letters submitted to Local 8. Since the project began nearly four years ago, hundreds of schools have been featured. Students are taking pride in their schools and in their education. Educators are sharing learning programs featured on 8's Cool School.

Volunteer 8
A project of KFMB TV Local 8 and Volunteer San Diego.
Local 8 and Volunteer San Diego have teamed to create Volunteer 8, hosted by Local 8's Michael Tuck and Kathleen Bade. Volunteer 8's goal is to promote volunteerism and help make San Diego a better place. Volunteer San Diego assists community events, non-profits, and corporations in finding volunteers. Through Volunteer 8, we'll match your interests with thousands of volunteer opportunities countywide. Volunteer 8 stories air monthly on Local 8 at 4PM, profiling the efforts volunteers are making in our community.

Exhibit 17-6 The media employ public relations to enhance their image in the community

In turn, the media are concerned about how the community perceives them. Exhibit 17-6 is a public relations piece distributed by a San Diego TV station that describes a variety of ways the station benefits the community.

Educators A number of organizations provide educators with information regarding their activities. The Direct Marketing Association, the Promotional Products Association, and the Yellow Pages Publishers Association (YPPA), among others, keep educators informed in an attempt to generate goodwill as well as exposure for their causes. These groups and major corporations provide information regarding innovations, state-of-the-art research, and other items of interest (Exhibit 17-7). YPPA provides materials specifically designed for educators.

Educators are a target audience because, like the media, they control the flow of information to certain parties—in this case, people like you. *BusinessWeek, Fortune,* and *Fast Company* magazines attempt to have professors use their magazines in their classes, as does *The Wall Street Journal, The New York Times,* and *Advertising Age,* among others. In addition to selling more magazines, such usage would also lend credibility to the mediums.

Civic and Business Organizations The local Jaycees, Kiwanis, and other nonprofit civic organizations also serve as gatekeepers of information. Companies' financial contributions to these groups, speeches at organization functions, and sponsorships are all designed to create goodwill. Corporate executives' service on the boards of nonprofit organizations also generates positive public relations.

Governments Public relations often attempts to influence government bodies directly at both local and national levels. Successful lobbying may mean immediate success for a product, while regulations detrimental to the firm may cost it millions. Imagine for a moment what FDA approval of NutraSweet meant to Searle or what could happen to the beer and wine industries if TV advertising were banned. The bicycle helmet industry sometimes experiences sales increases of 200 to 400 percent in a state when it passes a helmet law.

After decades of criticism from special-interest groups, the beer industry was forced to take steps to counteract legislation and other forms of government intervention similar to those affecting the cigarette and liquor industries. The beer industry's response was to support its political action committee, called Six-PAC, so that the committee could become more visible and active in its lobbying efforts in Washington, D.C. One of the first moves was to establish a new image for the industry, with a new slogan titled "Family businesses delivering America's beverage." Increased campaign contributions to candidates and pressures to investigate groups the industry felt were "gunning for beer" were also initiated. The lobby's efforts have paid off. While cigarettes and liquor continue to fall under attack and have had excise taxes levied on them, the beer industry remains unscathed and has a much more favorable reputation.[17]

Exhibit 17-7 The Yellow Pages provide information about the medium

Financial Groups In addition to current shareholders, potential shareholders and investors may be relevant target markets. Financial advisors, lending institutions, and others must be kept abreast of new developments as well as financial information, since they

Jonathan Schenker of Ketchum Public Relations, New York, suggests four technological methods to make life easier for the press and to increase the likelihood that the media will use your story:

1. *Telephone press conferences.* Since reporters cannot always get to a press conference, use the telephone to call them for coverage.
2. *In-studio media tours.* Satellite communications providing a story, and a chance to interview, from a central location such as a TV studio save broadcast journalists time and money by eliminating their need to travel.
3. *Multicomponent video news releases (VNR).* A five-component package consisting of a complete script in print and on tape, a video release with a live reporter, a local contact source at which to target the video, and a silent video news release that allows the station to fill in with its own news reporter lend an advantage by saving the media money.
4. *Targeted newswire stories.* When the sender targets the public relations message, reporters are spared the need to read through volumes of news stories to select those of interest to their target audiences.

Figure 17-3 Getting the public relations story told

offer the potential for new sources of funding. Press releases and corporate reports play an important role in providing information to these publics.

Implementing the PR Program

Once the research has been conducted and the target audiences identified, the public relations program must be developed and delivered to the receivers. A number of PR tools are available for this purpose, including press releases, press conferences, exclusives, interviews, and community involvement.

The Press Release One of the most important publics is the press. To be used by the press, information must be factual, true, and of interest to the medium as well as to its audience. As shown in Figure 17-3, the source of the **press release** can do certain things to improve the likelihood that the "news" will be disseminated.

The information in a press release won't be used unless it's of interest to the readers of the medium it's sent to (Exhibit 17-8). For example, financial institutions may issue press releases to business trade media and to the editor of the business section of a general-interest newspaper. Information on the release of a new rock album is of more interest to radio disk jockeys than to TV newscasters; sports news also has its interested audiences.

Exhibit 17-8 A Graco press release

Exhibit 17-9 Reebok announces sponsorship of Shakira

Press Conferences We are all familiar with **press conferences** held by political figures. While used less often by organizations and corporations, this form of delivery can be very effective. The topic must be of major interest to a specific group before it is likely to gain coverage. Usually major accomplishments (such as the awarding of the next Super Bowl or Olympics location), major breakthroughs (such as medical cures), emergencies, or catastrophes warrant a national press conference. On a local level, community events, local developments, and the like may receive coverage. Companies often call press conferences when they have significant news to announce, such as the introduction of a new product or advertising campaign. Sports teams use this tool to attract fan attention and interest when a new star is signed. TV3, a Malaysian broadcast system, held an international press conference to announce its introduction of an interactive TV service. Reebok held a press conference and issued a press release to announce it had signed rock star Shakira to an endorsement agreement. The Grammy Award–winning artist would be featured in Reebok's advertising campaign, and Reebok would sponsor her tour. Print ads, billboards, in-store displays, and consumer promotions were also included as part of the IMC package (Exhibit 17-9).

Exclusives Although most public relations efforts seek a variety of channels for distribution, an alternative strategy is to offer one particular medium exclusive rights to the story if that medium reaches a substantial number of people in the target audience. Offering an **exclusive** may enhance the likelihood of acceptance. As you watch television over the next few weeks, look for the various networks' and local stations' exclusives. Notice how the media actually use these exclusives to promote themselves.

Interviews When you watch TV or read magazines, pay close attention to the personal interviews. Usually someone will raise specific questions, and a spokesperson provided by the firm will answer them. For example, when four people died from eating tainted hamburgers at Jack in the Box restaurants, the company's president gave personal interviews with the press to detail the corrective actions the company would take. Microsoft's president, Steve Ballmer, appeared in a number of personal interviews to present the company's position in a legal case brought against it by the U.S. government. Monica Lewinsky's first TV interview with Barbara Walters of ABC was a major coup for the network, as the ratings were among the highest ever recorded. (The interview just happened to take place during "sweeps"!)

Community Involvement Many corporations enhance their public images through involvement in the local community. This involvement may take many forms, including membership in local organizations like the Kiwanis or Jaycees and contributions to or participation in community events. For example, after Hurricane Floyd created so much damage in the South, a number of companies came to the assistance of those experiencing losses. Retail Alliance provided $1 million in interest-free loans to small businesses. Lowe's stores contributed $5,000 and the Franciscus Company, a Virginia Beach condo developer, donated furnishings from professionally decorated model homes.[18] In addition, a local trade association raised $53,000 for victims in less than one week. A flood in Venezuela, which killed hundreds, brought aid from governments and businesses from around the world. Similar actions were taken after floods in the Midwest by Provident Bank, Parmalat USA (milk donations), and Wal-Mart, among others. The media also devoted free airtime to aid victims by coordinating activities, announcing programs and food drop-off points, and so on. After the September 11 terrorist attacks, corporations from all over the world donated time, money, and other types of assistance in a variety of forms to help victims. The subsequent war in Afghanistan resulted in countries' lending assistance by providing medical supplies, clothing, equipment, and food and shelter to people in that country.

The Internet As mentioned briefly in Chapter 15, the Internet has become a means by which companies and organizations can disseminate public relations information. Just as in the print media, companies have used the Web to establish media relations and government, investor, and community relationships; deal with crises; and even conduct cause marketing. Companies have used their websites to address issues, as well as to provide information about products and services, archive press releases, link to other articles and sites, and provide lists of activities and events. In October 2002, poultry processor Pilgrim's Pride issued a nationwide recall of 27.4 million pounds of cooked sandwich meat—the largest meat recall in U.S. history—after warnings of possible contamination from listeria. While not linked directly to the illness, the company wanted to be sure that its products were not responsible. To assist in providing information to consumers, Pilgrim's Pride called a press conference, issued press releases, and provided information on its website (Exhibit 17-10).[19] Other Internet tools, including e-mails and e-mail newsletters, have also been used effectively.

Shel Holtz notes that while there are many similarities between public relations activities conducted in traditional media and those conducted on the Internet, three main elements account for the differences between the two:

1. The Internet offers a more limited opportunity to gain attention due to short exposure times.
2. The Internet offers the opportunity to build internal links that provide the media with instant access to additional sources of information on the issue.
3. The Internet offers the ability to provide much more substantial information. Print and broadcast materials are confined by time and space limitations, while the Internet can literally provide volumes of information at a fingertip—or click of a mouse.[20]

Holtz also notes that while public relations activities are increasing on the Internet, and will continue to do so, PR people have been some of the slowest to adopt the new technology. However, as more and more media people and PR people gain confidence, the Internet will become a major source of public relations activities.

Other methods of distributing information include photo kits, bylined articles (signed by the firm), speeches, and trade shows. Of course, the specific mode of distribution is determined by the nature of the story and the interest of the media and its publics.

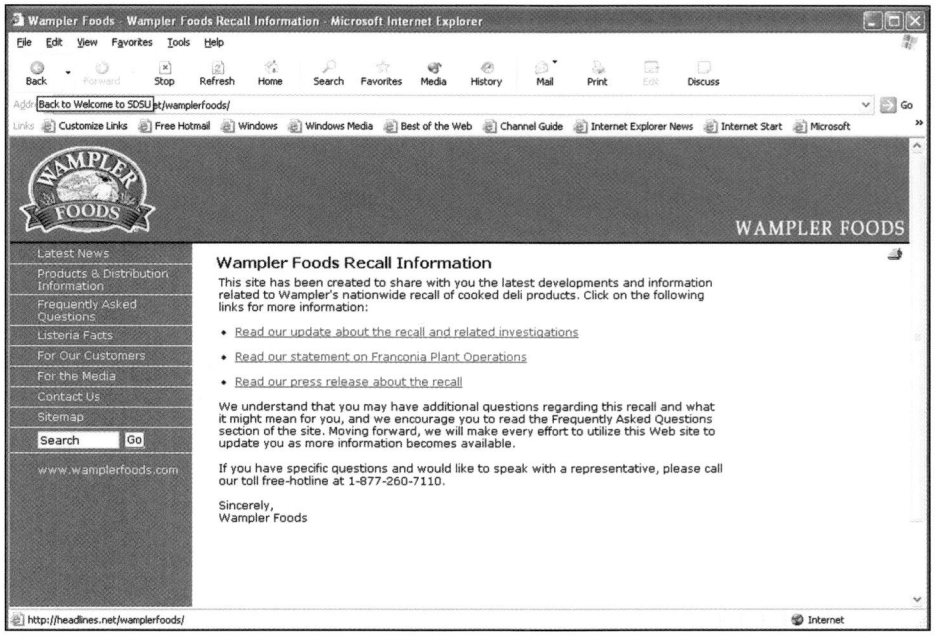

Exhibit 17-10 Pilgrim's Pride responds to negative publicity

Advantages and Disadvantages of PR

Like the other program elements, public relations has both advantages and disadvantages.

Advantages include the following:

1. *Credibility.* Because public relations communications are not perceived in the same light as advertising—that is, the public does not realize the organization either directly or indirectly paid for them—they tend to have more credibility. The fact that the media are not being compensated for providing the information may lead receivers to consider the news more truthful and credible. For example, an article in newspapers or magazines discussing the virtues of aspirin may be perceived as much more credible than an ad for a particular brand of aspirin.

Automotive awards presented in magazines such as *Motor Trend* have long been known to carry clout with potential car buyers. Now marketers have found that even lesser media mean a lot as well. General Motors' Pontiac division played up an award given to Pontiac as "the best domestic sedan" by *MotorWeek* in a 30-minute program carried by about 300 public broadcasting stations. Likewise, Chrysler trumpeted the awards given to its Jeep Cherokee by *4-Wheel & Off Road* magazines.[21] It has become a common practice for car companies to promote their achievements.

News about a product may in itself serve as the subject of an ad. Exhibit 17-11 demonstrates how Olympus used favorable publicity from a variety of sources to promote its digital camera. A number of auto manufacturers have also taken advantage in their ads of high customer satisfaction ratings reported by J. D. Powers & Associates, an independent research firm specializing in automotive research.

2. *Cost.* In both absolute and relative terms, the cost of public relations is very low, especially when the possible effects are considered. While a firm can employ public relations agencies and spend millions of dollars on PR, for smaller companies this form of communication may be the most affordable alternative available.

Exhibit 17-11 Olympus capitalizes on positive publicity in its advertising

Best Consumer Digital Camera
(MacUser EddyAwards, Jan.'97)

Product of the Year
(InfoWorld, Jan.'97)

Stellar
(Windows Sources, Jan.'97)

★★★★
(Computer Life, Feb.'97)

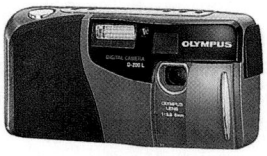

Any questions?

Plenty. How many pictures does the D-200L take?
Up to 80.

You're not sure?
You can shoot in both high-resolution or standard formats. And switch back and forth whenever you want. Even delete the shots you don't want at any time.

How do I know which ones to delete or keep?
You can instantly view the images you just captured.

Where?
On the color LCD screen. One at a time or nine at a time.

What's the resolution?
640 X 480. But you're not buying a pixel taker. It's pictures you're after. And picture quality is where the D-200L really outperforms the competition.

Who says?
InfoWorld, for one: "The image quality far surpassed any of the other digital cameras." And *Windows Sources*: "It delivers the best images we've seen from a consumer-level camera."

What about the lens?
It's a razor sharp, wide angle, macro, Olympus glass lens.

Flash?
With red-eye reduction, fill flash and auto mode.

But does it feel like a camera?
With an optical viewfinder and Olympus design, it follows in the footsteps of the Stylus series, the most successful line of 35mm cameras in the world.

Okay. I take a color shot. Now what?
Download the image into a computer, either Windows™ PC or a Mac® Then go to town.

Talk to me.
Create multiple images from one image. Or combine several. Add and subtract color. Retouch. Crop.

Go on.
E-mail it across the Internet. Put it on a Web page. Store it on disk.

Suppose I want to be creative?
With the included Adobe PhotoDeluxe™ software you can make greeting cards and real estate listings, design layouts, put together mail-order catalogs and newsletters. All in full living color.

Hold it! How much is all of this going to cost me?
$599.

That's it?
That's it.

There must be a science to all this.
And an art.

To learn more about the D-200L and how it completes the ideal home or office imaging system, contact your Olympus Marketing Represenative at 1-800-622-6372. They'll also tell you all about the new Olympus personal storage system and CD writer.

OLYMPUS
THE ART & SCIENCE OF IMAGING™

Visit us at http://www.olympus.com/digital

®and ™ All trademarks and registered trademarks mentioned herein are the property of the respective holders.
The Art and Science of Imaging is a trademark of Olympus America Inc.
InfoWorld & MacUser awards received 1/97. ©1997 Olympus America Inc.

Krispy Kreme, a donut shop, started in 1934 in Winston-Salem. While the one store slowly grew into a 34-state chain over the years, it was really not a popular, well-known national brand. Then with a strong PR program and a subsequent IPO, Krispy Kreme took off. When a new Krispy Kreme shop opens today, press coverage and free publicity almost eliminate the need for advertising.

Many public relations programs require little more than the time and expenses associated with putting the program together and getting it distributed, yet they still accomplish their objectives.

3. *Avoidance of clutter.* Because they are typically perceived as news items, public relations messages are not subject to the clutter of ads. A story regarding a new product introduction or breakthrough is treated as a news item and is likely to receive attention. When Steven Jobs (the founder of Apple Computer) announced his return to Apple, after being with another firm for years, all the networks covered it, as did major newspapers and magazines. Some (like CNN) devoted two- to three-minute segments to the story.

4. *Lead generation.* Information about technological innovations, medical breakthroughs, and the like results almost immediately in a multitude of inquiries. These inquiries may give the firm some quality sales leads.

5. *Ability to reach specific groups.* Because some products appeal to only small market segments, it is not feasible to engage in advertising and/or promotions to reach them. If the firm does not have the financial capabilities to engage in promotional expenditures, the best way to communicate to these groups is through public relations.

6. *Image building.* Effective public relations helps to develop a positive image for the organization. A strong image is insurance against later misfortunes. For example, in 1982, seven people in the Chicago area died after taking Extra Strength Tylenol capsules that had been laced with cyanide (after they reached the store). Within one week of the poisonings, Tylenol's market share fell from 35 to only 6.5 percent. Strong public relations efforts combined with an already strong product and corporate image helped the product rebound (despite the opinions of many experts that it had no chance of recovering). A brand or firm with a lesser image would never have been able to come back. The ad in Exhibit 17-12 demonstrates the power of a strong image. The Firestone tire recall cited earlier is another example. Because of a strong image established over 102 years of doing business, Firestone was able to weather the storm and recover from the incident.

Perhaps the major disadvantage of public relations is the potential for not completing the communications process. While public relations messages can break through the clutter of commercials, the receiver may not make the connection to the source. Many firms' PR efforts are never associated with their sponsors in the public mind.

Public relations may also misfire through mismanagement and a lack of coordination with the marketing department. When marketing and PR departments operate independently, there is a danger of inconsistent communications, redundancies in efforts, and so on.

The key to effective public relations is to establish a good program, worthy of public interest, and manage it properly. To determine if this program is working, the firm must measure the effectiveness of the PR effort.

Measuring the Effectiveness of PR

As with the other promotional program elements, it is important to evaluate the effectiveness of the public relations efforts. In addition to determining the contribution of this program element to attaining communications objectives, the evaluation offers other advantages:

1. It tells management what has been achieved through public relations activities.
2. It provides management with a way to measure public relations achievements quantitatively.
3. It gives management a way to judge the quality of public relations achievements and activities.

Exhibit 17-12 This *Wall Street Journal* ad stresses the value of a strong brand and/or corporate image

WHY A STRONG BRAND IMAGE GIVES YOU AN ALMOST UNFAIR ADVANTAGE.

[**In a world of parity products and services, nothing can tilt things more dramatically in your favor than powerful brand and corporate advertising.**]

A brand or corporate image is not something that can be seen, touched, tasted, defined, or measured. Intangible and abstract, it exists solely as an idea in the mind. Yet it is often a company's most precious asset.

When in the 1980s, corporations laid out billions for the companies that owned brands like Kraft, Jell-O, Del Monte, Maxwell House and Nabisco, it wasn't the products themselves they were after, but the enduring power of warm images, feelings, and impressions associated with the brand names. In fact, when the dust finally settles, it will become clear that the megamergers, takeovers, and leveraged buyouts of that decade were primarily about the acquisition of brands.

Yet despite their enormous value, brands are not immune to neglect, and in the face of a tough economy and strong competition, companies are often tempted to sacrifice brand and corporate advertising for short-term promotion. While such strategies can yield immediate results, over time they can weaken and tarnish the brand.

Studies conducted on the PIMS (Profit Impact on Market Strategy) data base prove that companies that put more money behind (their) image advertising are more likely to be market dominators, ranking first in a category and having sales volume one-and-a-half times greater than the nearest competitor. Moreover, the larger the ratio of brand advertising to promotion, the greater the return on investment (ROI).

AD/PROMOTION RATIO & ROI

Return On Investment

18% — Promo 76% — Adv 24%

27% — Promo 56% — Adv 44%

31% — Promo < 50% — Adv > 50%

Ad/Promotion Ratio

When only a quarter of a company's advertising/promotion budget is spent on brand advertising, the ROI is 18%. When the ratio is increased to 50/50, the return can be over 70% higher.

Backing your brand in good times and bad—keeping that image in front of people—can mean higher profits as well as leadership.

AD/PROMOTION RATIO & MARKET POSITION

Ad/Promo Ratio

31% — Followers

35% — Marginal Leaders

42% — Dominators

Market Position

PROTECTING AND NURTURING A brand is one of advertising's most important jobs. And that means choosing the media for your message with care. For more and more companies, the best environment is The Wall Street Journal. The Journal has always operated on the principle that there is a direct link between the quality of our editorial and the quality of the advertising we attract. Witness the impressive list of corporations appearing in any Journal issue.

In The Myers Marketing & Research survey of The Worldwide Marketing Leadership Panel, The Journal was awarded top honors in five separate categories, including editorial quality and reader involvement—more evidence of The Journal's unmatched stature and prestige.

If you're looking for a publication that can add value to your brand, there's no better brand than ours: The Wall Street Journal.

THE WALL STREET JOURNAL.
THE WORLD'S BUSINESS DAILY. IT WORKS.

© 1991 Dow Jones & Company, Inc. All Rights Reserved. Source: Myers Marketing & Research. 6A292

As shown in Figure 17-4, a number of criteria may be used to measure the effects of PR programs. Raymond Simon suggests additional means for accomplishing this evaluation process, including the following:

- *Personal observation and reaction.* Personal observation and evaluation by one's superiors should occur at all levels of the organization.
- *Matching objectives and results.* Specific objectives designed to attain the overall communications objectives should be related to actions, activities, or media coverage. For example, placing a feature story in a specific number of media is an objective, quantitative, and measurable goal.[22]
- *The team approach.* Harold Mendelsohn suggests that one way to achieve attitude and behavior modification through public information campaigns is the **team approach,** whereby evaluators are actually involved in the campaign.[23] By using research principles and working together, the team develops—and accomplishes—goals.

A system for measuring the effectiveness of the public relations program has been developed by Lotus HAL. The criteria used in the evaluation process follow:

- Total number of impressions over time
- Total number of impressions on the target audience
- Total number of impressions on specific target audiences
- Percentage of positive articles over time
- Percentage of negative articles over time
- Ratio of positive to negative articles
- Percentage of positive/negative articles by subject
- Percentage of positive/negative articles by publication or reporter
- Percentage of positive/negative articles by target audience

Figure 17-4 Criteria for measuring the effectiveness of PR

• *Management by objectives.* Executives and their managers act together to identify goals to be attained and the responsibilities of the managers. These goals are then used as a standard to measure accomplishments.

• *Public opinion and surveys.* Research in the form of public opinion surveys may be used to gather data to evaluate program goal attainment.

• *Audits.* Both internal and external audits may be used. **Internal audits** involve evaluations by superiors or peers within the firm to determine the performance of the employee (or his or her programs). **External audits** are conducted by consultants, the client (in the case of a PR agency), or other parties outside the organization.

A number of other bases for evaluation can be used. Walter Lindenmann says three levels of measures are involved: (1) the basic, which measures the actual PR activities undertaken; (2) the intermediate, which measures audience reception and understanding of the message; and (3) the advanced, which measures the perceptual and behavioral changes that result.[24]

Some organizations may use a combination of measures, depending on their specific needs. For example, Hewlett-Packard uses impression counts, awareness and preference studies, in-house assessments, press clippings counts, and tracking studies.[25]

In summary, the role of public relations in the promotional mix is changing. As PR has become more marketing oriented, the criteria by which the programs are evaluated have also changed. At the same time, nonmarketing activities will continue to be part of the public relations department and part of the basis for evaluation.

Publicity

Publicity refers to the generation of news about a person, product, or service that appears in broadcast or print media. To many marketers, publicity and public relations are synonymous. In fact, publicity is really a subset of the public relations effort.

But there are several major differences. First, publicity is typically a *short-term* strategy, while public relations is a concerted program extending over a period of time. Second, public relations is designed to provide positive information about the firm and is usually controlled by the firm or its agent. Publicity, on the other hand, is not always positive and is not always under the control of, or paid for by, the organization. Both positive and negative publicity often originates from sources other than the firm.

In most organizations, publicity is controlled and disseminated by the public relations department. In this section, we discuss the role publicity plays in the promotional program and some of the ways marketers use and react to these communications.

The Power of Publicity

One of the factors that most sets off publicity from the other program elements is the sheer power this form of communication can generate. Unfortunately for marketers, this power is not always realized in the way they would like it to be. Publicity can make or break a product or even a company.

Earlier we discussed the substantial drop in Tylenol sales after extensive media coverage of the tampering with its products while on store shelves. The Johnson &

Johnson marketing efforts (including a strong public relations emphasis) designed to aid recovery were a model in proficiency that will be studied by students of marketing (in both the classroom and the boardroom) for many years. By January 1983, almost 100 percent of the original brand share had been regained. When Odwalla's brand was threatened by negative publicity resulting from contaminated juice, the company immediately recalled the product, increased safety measures, and paid medical bills for those who had become ill. It also established a website and 800 numbers to make information easily available to concerned customers (Exhibit 17-13). The company has regained 100 percent of its market share as a result of these efforts. Unfortunately, a marketer cannot always capitalize on positive publicity or control the effects of negative publicity so effectively.

Why is publicity so much more powerful than advertising or sales promotion—or even other forms of public relations? First, publicity is highly credible. Unlike advertising and sales promotions, publicity is not usually perceived as being sponsored by the company (in the negative instances, it never is). So consumers perceive this information as more objective and place more confidence in it. In fact, *Consumer Reports,* the medium responsible for one of the examples previously cited, recently ran an ad campaign designed to promote its credibility by noting it does not accept advertising and therefore can be objective in its evaluations.

Publicity information may be perceived as endorsed by the medium in which it appears. For example, publicity regarding a breakthrough in the durability of golf balls will go far to promote them if it is reported by *Golf* magazine. *Car & Driver*'s award for car of the year reflects the magazine's perception of the quality of the auto selected.

Still another reason for publicity's power is its news value and the frequency of exposure it generates. When Krispy Kreme opened a store in Woodbury, Minnesota, anxious consumers camped out overnight waiting for the store to open. Every local television station covered the event—some with live reports from the scene.[26] The free

Exhibit 17-13 Odwalla assures customers of its quality

odwalla

Odwalla Leads The Industry In Quality Assurance

- Dr. Douglas Archer, former Deputy Director at the FDA's Center for Food Safety and Applied Nutrition said, "Odwalla's facility is the best I have seen with regards to systems aimed at assuring product safety."
- Over 90% of Odwalla's capital expenditures in the last two years have gone directly toward improving quality assurance at the plant and throughout our system. We are committed to continuous investment and improvement.
- Odwalla heat treats all of its juices and fruit purees except its fresh squeezed citrus juices. Odwalla's *100% Apple, Pure Pressed Carrot* and citrus mixers are *flash pasteurized* in a process that quickly heats the juice to a temperature high enough to kill harmful bacteria, then cools it immediately to maintain freshness and nutrition.
- Odwalla has implemented the fresh juice industry's first HACCP plan. While the FDA has acknowledged that it may take years for the industry to follow suit, our HACCP plan already exceeds the FDA's recently published food safety objectives.
- Odwalla uses outside, independent laboratory testing, our own microbiology lab and computer analysis to monitor the effectiveness of its safety practices. Also, our *A.M. Sensory Panel* meets daily to taste every batch of juice we make.
- In 1998, Odwalla will source 1500 tons -- 100% of the nation's supply -- of HACCP certified apples from McAfee Apple Gardens. For other suppliers, Odwalla has stringent specifications, including the requirement of a Certificate of Analysis.
- Dr. Ranzell "Nick" Nickelson, one of the nation's top food science and HACCP experts, sits on Odwalla's Board of Directors and chairs the board's committee on quality assurance and nutrition.
- Odwalla cleans and sorts incoming fruit before it even enters the plant. Once inside, the fruit goes through an additional, fully separate line for cleansing, sorting and sanitizing again. Apple, carrot and citrus each has its own line and process which is specifically designed for its unique characteristics.
- Odwalla is the first in the industry to invest in a hyper-sanitized "clean room" where juices are blended and bottled.
- For more information on how we ensure quality control from *Soil to Soul*, please visit www.odwalla.com or call 1-800-odwalla.

publicity (advertising?) is often repeated in other locales where Krispy Kreme opens a shop, and it occurs for other well-hyped products as well.

The bottom line is that publicity is news, and people like to pass on information that has news value. Publicity thus results in a significant amount of free, credible, word-of-mouth information regarding the firm and its products.

The Control and Dissemination of Publicity

In some of the examples cited earlier, the control of publicity was not in the hands of the company. While in some instances it is the firm's own blunder to allow information to leak out, companies like KMart and Martha Stewart could do nothing to stop the media from releasing negative information. When publicity becomes news, it is reported by the media, sometimes despite the efforts of the firm. In these instances, the organization needs to react to the potential threat created by the news. IMC Perspective 17-1 reports on some interesting examples.

A good example of one company's efforts to respond to adverse publicity is shown in Exhibit 17-14. Tree Top's problems began when all the major news media reported that the chemical Alar, used by some growers to regulate the growth of apples, might cause cancer in children. Despite published statements by reliable scientific and medical authorities (including the surgeon general) that Alar does not cause cancer, a few special-interest groups were able to generate an extraordinary amount of adverse publicity, causing concern among consumers and purchasing agents. A few school districts took apples off their menus, and even applesauce and juice were implicated. Tree Top ran the ad in Exhibit 17-14 to state its position and alleviate consumers' fears. It also sent a direct mailing to nutritionists and day care operators. The campaign was successful in assuring consumers of the product's safety and rebuilding their confidence.

In other instances, however, publicity must be managed like any other promotional tool. For example, when Martha Stewart was accused by the SEC (Securities and Exchange Commission) of insider trading, the negative publicity had severe consequences for her company. Sales dropped, stocks plummeted, and advertisers withheld ads waiting to see what would happen.[27]

Publicity can also work for marketers. A number of kids' toys (Pokemon, Power Rangers) achieved significant sales due to high levels of positive publicity and word-of-mouth advertising. Sales of Cabernet Sauvignon increased an average of 45 percent in the month after a CBS *60 Minutes* report that daily moderate consumption of red wine can reduce the risk of heart disease. There are many more examples of the positive impact publicity can have.

Marketers like to have as much control as possible over the time and place where information is released. One way to do this is with the **video news release (VNR),** a publicity piece produced by publicists so that stations can air it as a news story. The videos almost never mention that they are produced by the subject organization, and most news stations don't mention it either. Many pharmaceutical companies like Pfizer, Aventis, and AstraZeneca have used VNRs, as have GNC, Mercedes, Nieman Marcus, and others.

In their efforts to manage publicity and public relations, marketers are continuously learning more about these activities. Courses are offered and books written on how to manage publicity. These books cover how to make a presentation, whom to contact, how to issue a press release, and what to know about each medium addressed, including TV, radio, newspapers, magazines, and direct-response advertising. They discuss such alternative media as news conferences, seminars, events, and personal letters, as well as insights on how to deal with government and other legislative bodies. Because this information is too extensive to include as a

Exhibit 17-14 Tree Top responds to the threat of negative publicity

IMC PERSPECTIVE 17-1

Peace Signs, Bobbleheads, Space Sprouts, and Other PR Blunders

The power of publicity is well known to marketers, who constantly attempt to manage it to create "buzz" about their products and/or services. In success stories like the movie *Blair Witch Project,* The PT Cruiser, and Vespa Scooters, positive publicity played a big part. But what happens when good intentions go wrong? Following are some of the marketing efforts that did not work out so well.

- *McDonald's Bobbleheads.* It seems like everybody is marketing bobbleheads these days. The hot trend of creating the figurine likenesses of people, usually athletes, has been adopted by a variety of companies as well as nonprofits and universities (San Diego State gave away Marshall Faulk bobbleheads). Unfortunately, some of the characters had an excess of lead paint on them, rendering them unsafe for children. McDonald's discovered the problem through its own testing and recalled 100,000 of the likenesses of Chicago Bears players Brian Urlacher and Anthony Thomas. (The figurines were being sold for $5 each in areas just outside Chicago.) The company then alerted the Consumer Products Safety Commission, which issued a recall. McDonald's claimed that the manufacturer—Bobbie Dreams—distributed the products prior to seeing the test results. While no consumers were hurt, you can be sure the relationship between McDonald's and Bobbie Dreams was.
- *Burger King et al.* In 2001, the U.S. Consumer Products Safety Commission ordered four fast-food chains to recall toy premiums that posed a risk to small children. Burger King Corp. and Alcone Marketing Group were forced to recall 2.6 million of the "Hourglass Space Sprout" and "Look for Me Bumblebee" toys after learning that the toys, when broken, released small beads that could cause children to choke if the children put the beads in their mouths. Although no one was hurt, at least 18 incidents were reported. When the problem was discovered, Burger King notified the CPSC and subsequently hired outside safety experts to review future operations.
- *FedEx.* FedEx's well-liked Super Bowl spot which featured the Wizard of Oz munchkins inhaling helium to raise their voices was not so well liked by everyone. The National Inhalant Prevention Coalition, the National PTA, and the Partnership for a Drug Free America banded together to ask FedEx to discontinue airing the spot. The company did so just a few weeks after its initial showing.
- *IBM.* City officials in Chicago and San Francisco threatened to bring lawsuits against IBM because peace symbols, penguins, and hearts were spray-painted on city sidewalks to promote the introduction of IBM's new Linux-based operating system. IBM said the sidewalks were supposed to be painted in biodegradable chalk, instead of the graffiti paint that was used by the contractors. IBM learned about the problem when a painter hired by Ch'rewd Marketing and Promotions was arrested for criminal damage to property, vandalism, and possession of spray paint. Both cities threatened IBM with fines as well as costs associated with cleaning up each of 100-plus paintings. Sun Microsystems, Inc., a competitor of IBM, attempted to turn IBM's gaff into a PR bonanza of its own by offering to clean up the paint to "clean up after IBM."
- *Microsoft.* In the fall of 2002, New York City sent Microsoft a summons for defacing public property when Microsoft logo butterfly decals were pasted on sidewalks, streets and other public properties to announce the launch of MSN 8.0 software.

In each of these cases, and there are many, many more to report, a marketing effort turned into a public relations problem. Fortunately, no one was hurt—except the pride of the companies involved, their pocketbooks, and their contractual relationships.

Sources: Kate MacArthur, "McDonald's Recalls Lead Paint Bobbleheads," Sept. 20, 2002, AdAge.com, p. 1; Margie Mason, "San Francisco and Chicago Officials Rankled by IBM's 'Peace' Ads," www.individual.com, Apr. 30, 2001, pp. 1-2; Thor Olavsrud, "Sun Offers to Clean Up IBM Mess," www.Internetnews.com, Apr. 30, 2001, p. 1; Jeanie Casison, "Toy Story," *Incentive,* October 2001, pp. 10-11.

single chapter in this text, we suggest you peruse one of the many books available on this subject for additional insights.

Advantages and Disadvantages of Publicity

Publicity offers the advantages of credibility, news value, significant word-of-mouth communications, and a perception of being endorsed by the media. Beyond the potential impact of negative publicity, two major problems arise from the use of publicity: timing and accuracy.

Timing Timing of the publicity is not always completely under the control of the marketer. Unless the press thinks the information has very high news value, the timing of the press release is entirely up to the media—if it gets released at all. Thus, the information may be released earlier than desired or too late to make an impact.

Accuracy A major way to get publicity is the press release. Unfortunately, the information sometimes gets lost in translation—that is, it is not always reported the way the provider wishes it to be. As a result, inaccurate information, omissions, or other errors may result. Sometimes when you see a publicity piece that was written on the basis of a press release, you wonder if the two are even about the same topic.

Measuring the Effectiveness of Publicity

The methods for measuring the effects of publicity are essentially the same as those discussed earlier under the broader topic of public relations. Rather than reiterate them here, we thought it would be more interesting to show you an actual example. Figure 17-5 is a model developed by Ketchum Public Relations for tracking the effects of publicity. (I guess we just provided Ketchum with some free publicity.)

Corporate Advertising

One of the more controversial forms of advertising is **corporate advertising.** Actually an extension of the public relations function, corporate advertising does not promote any one specific product or service. Rather, it is designed to promote the firm overall, by enhancing its image, assuming a position on a social issue or cause, or seeking direct involvement in something. Why is corporate advertising controversial? A number of reasons are offered:

1. *Consumers are not interested in this form of advertising.* A Gallup and Robinson study reported in *Advertising Age* found consumers were 35 percent less interested in corporate ads than in product-oriented advertising.[28] This may be because consumers do not understand the reasons behind such ads. Of course, much of this confusion results from ads that are not very good from a communications standpoint.

2. *It's a costly form of self-indulgence.* Firms have been accused of engaging in corporate image advertising only to satisfy the egos of top management. This argument stems from the fact that corporate ads are not easy to write. The message to be communicated is not as precise and specific as one designed to position a product, so the top managers often dictate the content of the ad, and the copy reflects their ideas and images of the corporation.

3. *The firm must be in trouble.* Some critics believe the only time firms engage in corporate advertising is when they are in trouble—either in a financial sense or in the public eye—and are advertising to attempt to remedy the problem. There are a number of forms of corporate advertising, each with its own objectives. These critics argue that these objectives have become important only because the firm has not been managed properly.

4. *Corporate advertising is a waste of money.* Given that the ads do not directly appeal to anyone, are not understood, and do not promote anything specific, critics say the monies could be better spent in other areas. Again, much of this argument has its foundation in the fact that corporate image ads are often intangible. They typically do not ask directly for a purchase; they do not ask for investors. Rather, they present a

Figure 17-5 The Ketchum Effectiveness Yardstick (KEY)—a strategic approach to the measurement of public relations results

At Ketchum, we believe strongly that it is possible to measure public relations effectiveness. We also believe strongly that measuring public relations results can be done in a timely and cost-efficient manner.

Our strategic approach to public relations measurement involves a two-step process:

1. Setting in advance very specific and clearly defined public relations goals and objectives, and,
2. Pinpointing those levels of measurement that are crucial to the organization in determining to what extent those specific public relations goals and objectives have been met.

In the model, there are three levels for measuring PR effectiveness:

- Level #1—the Basic level for measuring public relations OUTPUTS. This measures the amount of exposure an organization receives in the media, the total number of placements, the total number of impressions, and/or the likelihood of having reached specific target audience groups. Research tools often used when conducting Level #1 measurement include content analysis or publicity tracking studies, secondary analysis, segmentation analysis, and basic public opinion polls.
- Level #2—the Intermediate level for measuring public relations OUTGROWTHS. Outgrowths measure whether or not target audience groups actually received the messages directed at them, paid attention to them, understood the messages, and retained those messages in any shape or form. Research tools often used when conducting Level #2 measurement include focus groups; in-depth interviews; telephone, mail, face-to-face, or mall intercept surveys; testing techniques; and recall studies.
- Level #3—the Advanced level for measuring public relations OUTCOMES. This measures opinion, attitude, and/or behavior change to determine if there has been a shift in views and/or how people act when it comes to an organization, its products, or its services. Research tools often used when conducting Level #3 measurement include before-and-after studies, experimental and quasi-experimental research, ethnographic studies, communications audits, and multivariate analyses of data.
- The different levels of measuring public relations impact can be plotted on a yardstick in a hierarchial fashion. Here is a graphic displaying the KETCHUM EFFECTIVENESS YARDSTICK (KEY), which summarizes from left to right these levels of public relations measurement:

Level #1	Level #2	Level #3
Basic—Measuring OUTPUTS	Intermediate—Measuring OUTGROWTHS	Advanced—Measuring OUTCOMES
Media placements Impressions Targeted Audiences	Receptivity Awareness Comprehension Retention	Opinion change Attitude change Behavior change

More detailed information about Ketchum's strategic approach to measuring public relations effectiveness may be obtained by contacting Graham Hueber, Vice President and Director of Research at Ketchum.

position or try to create an image. Because they are not specific, many critics believe their purpose is lost on the audience and these ads are not a wise investment of the firm's resources.

Despite these criticisms and others, corporate advertising has increased in use. It's been estimated that more than 7 percent of all advertising dollars spent are for corporate advertising, meaning billions of dollars are spent on this form of communication.[29]

While corporate advertising has generally been regarded as the domain of companies such as USX, Phillips Petroleum, Aventis, and Deutsche Telekom (that is, companies that primarily sell directly to the consumer market), this is no longer the case. Beatrice Foods, BASF, and Procter & Gamble are just a few consumer-product companies running corporate image ads, and Lucent Technologies, Microsoft, and Pfizer have also increased expenditures in this area.

Since the term *corporate advertising* tends to be used as a catchall for any type of advertising run for the direct benefit of the corporation rather than its products or services, much advertising falls into this category. For purposes of this text (and to attempt to bring some perspective to the term), we use it to describe any type of advertising designed to promote the organization itself rather than its products or services.

Objectives of Corporate Advertising

Corporate advertising may be designed with two goals in mind: (1) creating a positive image for the firm and (2) communicating the organization's views on social, business, and environmental issues. More specific applications include:

- Boosting employee morale and smoothing labor relations.
- Helping newly deregulated industries ease consumer uncertainty and answer investor questions.
- Helping diversified companies establish an identity for the parent firm rather than relying solely on brand names.[30]

As these objectives indicate, corporate advertising is targeted at both internal and external audiences and involves the promotion of the organization as well as its ideas.

Types of Corporate Advertising

Marketers seek attainment of corporate advertising's objectives by implementing image, advocacy, or cause-related advertising. Each form is designed to achieve specific goals.

Image Advertising

One form of corporate advertising is devoted to promoting the organization's overall image. **Image advertising** may accomplish a number of objectives, including creating goodwill both internally and externally, creating a position for the company, and generating resources, both human and financial. A number of methods are used:

1. *General image or positioning ads.* As shown in Exhibit 17-15, ads are often designed to create an image of the firm in the public mind. The exhibit shows how Tyco is attempting to create an image of itself as a market leader and health care expert, not a *toy* company. A number of companies have created new names—for example, Accenture, Verizon, and Allianz—in an attempt to create a new image.

Other companies and organizations have used image advertising to attempt to change an existing image. The American Medical Association (AMA), responding to its less-than-positive image among many Americans who perceived doctors negatively, ran a series of ads portraying doctors in a more sensitive light. It spent over $1.75 million to highlight the caring, sharing, and sensitive side of AMA members.[31] *Penthouse* magazine attempted to change its image with advertisers by running ads in trade magazines that showed *Penthouse* was not just a magazine with pictures of

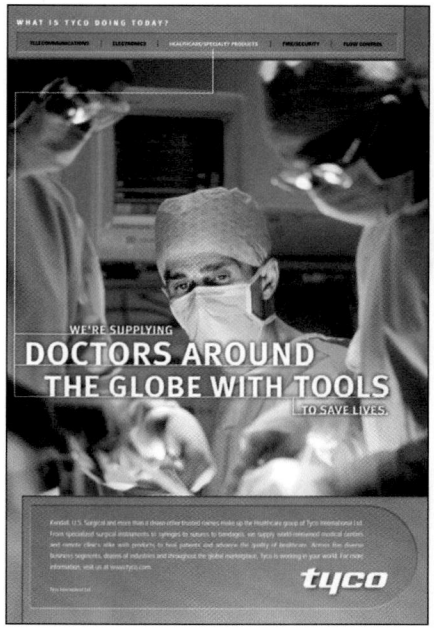

Exhibit 17-15 Tyco uses image advertising to avoid confusion

Exhibit 17-16 The pharmaceutical industry uses image advertising

Exhibit 17-17 KitchenAid supports the fight against breast cancer

nude females. The ad for America's pharmaceutical companies (Exhibit 17-16) casts the industry in a very favorable light. In 2002 Philip Morris Company, Inc., shareholders voted to change the company's name to Altria Group, Inc. Altria is derived from the Latin word meaning to "reach higher." Philip Morris CEO, Geoffrey Bible, said that the name was being changed to reflect the fact that the company was no longer just a cigarette company and that the new name better reflects its diversity. Others contend the move was an attempt to disassociate itself from the negative image of cigarettes.

2. *Sponsorships.* A firm often runs corporate image advertising on TV programs or specials. For example, the Hallmark or IBM specials and documentaries on network TV and Mobil and Gulf Oil program sponsorships on public TV are designed to promote the corporation as a good citizen. By associating itself with high-quality or educational programming, the firm hopes for a carryover effect that benefits its own image.

Other examples of sponsorships include those run by Outback Steak House (LUPUS), Providian Financial (children and youth), McDonald's (UNICEF), and GM (Make-A-Wish). Exhibit 17-17 shows KitchenAid's sponsorship of the fight against breast cancer.

Visa considers sponsorships an important part of its integrated marketing communications. It has sponsored the Olympics, the U.S. decathlon team, U.S. basketball's dream team, the U.S. Gymnastics Federation, the U.S. Open Tennis Championships, and Major League Baseball's All-Star game. According to John Bennett, senior VP for international marketing communications, the sponsorships are designed to fulfill specific business objectives while providing support for the recipients.[32] Figure 17-6 shows a few of the companies that decided an Olympic sponsorship would be good for them.

Figure 17-6 On Board. Some of the U.S. Olympic sponsors

AT&T	Lucent
Bank of America	Marker
Blue Cross	Monster.com
Blue Shield	NuSkin
Budweiser	Office Depot
Delta	Qwest
Gateway	Seiko
General Motors	Sensormatic
Hallmark	Texaco
Home Depot	United
Jet Set	York

3. *Recruiting.* The Mattel piece presented in Exhibit 17-18 is a good example of corporate image advertising designed to attract new employees. If you are interested in working in an innovative and family-oriented company, you might be interested in Mattel.

The Sunday employment section of most major metropolitan newspapers is an excellent place to see this form of corporate image advertising at work. Notice the ads in these papers and consider the images the firms are presenting.

4. *Generating financial support.* Some corporate advertising is designed to generate investments in the corporation. By creating a more favorable image, the firm makes itself attractive to potential stock purchasers and investors. More investments mean more working capital, more monies for research and development, and so on. In this instance, corporate image advertising is almost attempting to make a sale; the product is the firm.

While there is no concrete evidence that corporate image advertising leads directly to increased investment, at least one study shows a correlation between the price of stock and the amount of corporate advertising done.[33] Firms that spend more on corporate advertising also tend to have higher-priced stocks (though a direct relationship is very difficult to substantiate).

This thing called image is not unidimensional. Many factors affect it. Figure 17-7 shows the results of a survey conducted by the Hay Group and *Fortune* magazine on the best corporate reputations in the United States. The most admired firms did not gain their positions merely by publicity and word of mouth (nor, we guess, did the least admired).

Exhibit 17-18 Mattel ad designed to attract new employees

A positive corporate image cannot be created just from a few advertisements. Quality of products and services, innovation, sound financial practices, good corporate citizenship, and wise marketing are just a few of the factors that contribute to overall image. In addition, the type of product marketed and emotional appeal also contribute. The survey mentioned above demonstrated that profits and stock performances had little to do with reputation and that once a reputation is acquired, it has lasting power. A study conducted by Harris Interactive and the Reputation Institute showed that companies are ranked differently on key corporate attributes including emotional appeal, social responsibility, workplace environment, and vision and leadership (among 16

Figure 17-7 *Fortune's* most reputable corporations

Rank	Company	Total Return (%) 2001	Total Return (%) 1996–2001
1	General Electric	–15.1	21.2
2	Southwest Airlines	–17.3	33.7
3	Wal-Mart Stores	9.0	39.1
4	Microsoft	52.7	26.3
5	Berkshire Hathaway	6.5	17.3
6	Home Depot	12.1	36.0
7	Johnson & Johnson	14.0	20.5
8	FedEx	29.8	18.5
9	Citigroup	0.1	28.9
10	Intel	4.9	14.1
	Top ten average	9.7	25.5
	S&P 500	–11.89	10.70

Source: *Fortune,* Mar. 4, 2002.

others).[34] Figure 17-8 shows some of the results of *Business Ethics* magazine's analysis of the 100 best corporate citizens for 2002.

Figure 17-8 The Top 10 *Business Ethics'* list of top 100 corporate citizens

Rank	Company
1	IBM
2	Hewlett-Packard
3	Fannie Mae
4	St Paul Cos
5	Procter & Gamble
6	Motorola Inc.
7	Cummins Engine
8	Herman Miller
9	General Mills, Inc.
10	Avon Products

Source: www.business-ethics.com/100best.htm.

Event Sponsorships As we noted in the last section, corporate sponsorships of charities and causes has become a popular form of public relations. While some companies sponsor specific events and/or causes with primarily traditional public relations objectives in mind, a separate and more marketing-oriented use of sponsorships is also on the increase. Such **event sponsorships** take on a variety of forms, as shown in Figure 17-9. Anything from golf apparel and equipment to concerts, stadiums, and college football bowl games is now a candidate for corporate sponsorship. Sometimes, however, this can prove to be a risky venture, as shown in IMC Perspective 17-2.

Companies spent over $9.5 billion on event sponsorships in 2002, with sports receiving the majority of event sponsorship monies. Among the most popular sporting events for sponsorship are auto racing, golf and tennis tournaments, and running events. Professional sports leagues and teams as well as Olympic teams and competitions also receive large amounts of sponsorship money. Bicycle racing, beach volleyball, skiing, and various water sports are also attracting corporate sponsorship. Traditionally, tobacco, beer, and car companies have been among the largest sports event sponsors. Now a number of other companies have become involved in event sponsorships, including beverage companies, airlines, telecommunications and financial services companies, and high-tech firms.

Many marketers are attracted to event sponsorship because it gets their company and/or product names in front of consumers. By choosing the right events for sponsorship, companies can get visibility among their target market. For example, RJR Nabisco was heavily involved in sponsoring auto racing under its Winston and Camel cigarette brands. The company's market research showed that racing fans fit the demographic profile of users of these brands and consumers would purchase a product that sponsored their favorite sport.[35] For tobacco companies, which are prohibited from advertising on radio and TV, event sponsorship is also a way to have their brand names seen on TV. President Clinton issued an executive order in 1996 that would have prohibited any form of advertising of tobacco sponsorships at sporting events after 1998. The tobacco companies appealed this order in the courts on the grounds that to prohibit advertising a legal product violates free speech.[36] In 2000, the Supreme Court struck down the law, although a settlement did place further restrictions on such sponsorships.[37] A number of international sports are currently considering such bans.[38]

Many companies are attracted to event sponsorships because effective IMC programs can be built around them and promotional tie-ins can be made to local, regional, national, and even international markets. Companies are finding event sponsorships an excellent platform from which to build equity and gain affinity with target audiences as well as a good public relations tool.

Most companies focus their marketing efforts on specific market segments and are always looking for ways to reach these target audiences. Many marketers are finding that sales promotion tools such as event sponsorships, contests and sweepstakes, and

Figure 17-9 Annual sponsorship spending in North America by property ($ millions)

	1996	1997	1998	1999	2002
Sports	$3,540	$3,840	$4,556	$5,100	$6,430
Entertainment tours and attractions	566	650	680	756	865
Festivals, fairs, events	512	558	612	685	834
Causes	485	535	544	630	828
Arts	323	354	408	460	610
Total	$5,426	$5,937	$6,800	$7,631	$9,567

Source: Adapted from *Promo,* June 1, 2002.

IMC PERSPECTIVE 17-2

Naming Stadiums—an Expensive and Risky Business

There was a time when stadiums and arenas were named after their sports teams and/or cities. There were the Boston Gardens in Boston, Tiger Stadium in Detroit, Wimbledon in Wimbledon, and Old Trafford in Old Trafford (where the Manchester United U.K. football team plays). But all of that has changed. Boston Gardens is now the Fleet Center (named after a bank), and stadiums named after companies include Conseco Fieldhouse (home of the Indiana Pacers and named after an insurance company), Reebok Stadium (sports equipment and apparel), Bradford and Bingley Stadium (savings and loan) in the U.K., and ANZ Stadium (bank), North Power Stadium (power company), and Aussie Stadium (Aussie Home Loans) in Australia. Let's not forget Qualcomm Stadium (San Diego), PNB Park (Pittsburgh), and the United Center (Chicago). And the list goes on.

What's behind the name changes? According to Liz Miller, former sports executive, it's "money, money, money"—and a lot of it. Consider the following amounts, which were paid for naming rights: FedEx Field (Washington, D.C., 27 years), $205 million; American Airlines Center (Dallas, Texas, 30 years), $4,195 million; ANZ Stadium (Brisbane, Australia), $27 million ($50 million in Australian dollars); Molson Centre (Montreal, Canada, 20 years) $21 million ($33 million in Canadian dollars); and Eircom Park (Dublin, Ireland, 20 years) $21 million ($23 million in euros). And the prices continue to escalate, as there are apparently more investors than there are stadiums and arenas.

Why would companies be willing to pay that much? One reason is to create the brand awareness and high-profile exposure that come with having one's name associated with a sports franchise. Another is to make an impression on Wall Street, indicating that the company has now become a major force in the market. Every time someone attends the venue or watches a game broadcast from the stadium, he or she sees the company name, argue the buyers—and the payback is well worth it. Consumers remember the names of corporate sponsors, says Jed Pearsall, president of Performance Research, a Rhode Island-based market research firm. And, finally, the ability to interact and network with the cities and their franchises adds value, the buyers say.

Is it really worth it—either to the companies or the franchises themselves? You may remember Enron Field in Houston, named after the now unpopular Enron Corporation. That deal wasn't so good for the franchise or the city of Houston. Savvis Communications (St. Louis), Fruit of the Loom (Miami), and PSINet (Baltimore) are others whose names appeared on stadiums or arenas before they went bankrupt. Then there is the TWA Dome, where the St. Louis Rams play. TWA, bankrupt, was bought out by American Airlines. In such cases, the stadium names don't bode well for the cities, whose teams become associated with the problems, and they are particularly bad for the franchises, which often end up in court with other bankruptcy creditors.

Then there are the public relations and publicity aspects of the deals. As long as things are going well, the move looks like a good one. But a number of problems other than bankruptcy can lead to PR nightmares. For example, in Denver, fans wanted to keep the name Mile High Stadium when a new field was built. They initiated a lawsuit when the naming rights were sold to Invesco for $120 million—bad publicity. Soldier Field in Chicago was named in memory of World War I veterans. When the city council sought naming rights, many people were not very happy (as you might imagine!). When people in Southern California felt that they were being ripped off by their electric company, Southern California Edison, they wondered about the utility's investment in Edison Field. In general, the public often wonders whether companies are spending their monies wisely when they pay such large amounts of money for naming rights. They wonder even more when the same companies go bankrupt.

Consider the case of the Portland, Oregon, triple-A baseball team (whose stadium happens to be called PGE Park). The team gained publicity by having an "Arthur Andersen Appreciation Night" promotion in which there were paper shredding competitions and in-stadium money certificates hidden throughout the stadium. Anyone named Arthur or Andersen got in free, and the first Arthur Andersen received a gift pack and free suite for the game—all a tongue-in-cheek event making fun of Arthur Andersen, Enron's accounting agency. And then, of course, people think about Enron Field.

Sources: Tim Nudd, "Enron Field," *Adweek,* July 15, 2002, p. 34; Greg Johnson, "Some Fumbles in Arena Name Game," *Los Angeles Times,* Apr. 20, 2001, pp. C1-3; brandchannel.com.

sampling are very effective ways to reach specific geographic, demographic, psychographic, and ethnic markets.

Event sponsorship has become a good sales promotion tool for reaching specific target markets. Golf tournaments are a popular event for sponsorship by marketers of luxury automobiles and other upscale products and services. The golf audience is affluent and highly educated, and marketers believe that golfers care passionately about the game, leading them to form emotional attachments to brands they associate with the sport.

Marketers can also turn their sponsorships into effective integrated marketing opportunities. For example, Cadillac is an umbrella sponsor of the Senior PGA Tour, which fits well with its attempt to target age 40-plus professionals with incomes exceeding $60,000. On-site signage and vehicle displays are part of the sponsorship deal. The Team Cadillac golfers, including such notables as Lee Trevino and Arnold Palmer, wear the automaker's logo during tournaments and also help in public relations by giving media interviews and representing Cadillac at tie-in events. In the weeks preceding an event, dealers send out as many as 20,000 direct-mail pieces to owners and prospects inviting them to visit a dealership for a test drive and to pick up tournament tickets and hospitality passes. Response to the direct-mail offerings averages 16 percent. Cadillac also gets automotive advertising exclusivity on the ESPN telecasts and often airs commercials featuring the Team Cadillac members.

Cadillac attributes $250 million in vehicle sales directly to its involvement with the tour since 1990. The dollar figure comes from tracking sales to prospects who respond to Cadillac's direct-marketing programs built around the tournament.[39]

A major issue that continues to face the event sponsorship industry is incomplete research. As marketers become interested in targeted audiences, they will want more evidence that event sponsorship is effective and is a good return on their investment. Measuring the effectiveness of event sponsorships is discussed in Chapter 19.

Exhibit 17-19 Advocacy ads take a position on an issue

Advocacy Advertising

A third major form of corporate advertising addresses social, business, or environmental issues. Such **advocacy advertising** is concerned with propagating ideas and elucidating controversial social issues of public importance in a manner that supports the interests of the sponsor.[40]

While still portraying an image for the company or organization, advocacy advertising does so indirectly, by adopting a position on a particular issue rather than promoting the organization itself. An example is shown in Exhibit 17-19. Advocacy advertising has increased in use over the past few years and has also met with increased criticism. The ads may be sponsored by a firm or by a trade association and are designed to tell readers how the firm operates or management's position on a particular issue.

Sometimes the advertising is a response to negative publicity or to the firm's inability to place an important message through public relations channels. Sometimes the firm just wants to get certain ideas accepted or have society understand its concerns.

Advocacy advertising has been criticized by a number of sources (including consumer advocate Ralph Nader). But as you can see in Exhibit 17-20, this form of communication has been around for a long time. AT&T engaged in issues-oriented advertising way back in 1908 and has continued to employ this form of communication throughout the 20th century. Critics contend that companies with large advertising budgets purchase too much ad space and time and that advocacy ads may be misleading, but the checks and balances of regular product advertising also operate in this area.

For example, an ad run by the seven regional Bell operating companies that addressed the threat of Japanese technologies in the telecommunications industry was perceived by some members of Congress (the group the ads were designed to influence) as Japan-bashing and

★

SHE'S A PARTNER IN A GREAT AMERICAN BUSINESS

She is one of 850,000 owners of Bell System securities. They are typical Americans—some young, some middle age, some old. They live in every part of the nation.

One may be a housewife in Pennsylvania. Another a physician in Oregon—a clerk in Illinois—an engineer in Texas—a merchant in Massachusetts—a miner in Nevada—a stenographer in Missouri—a teacher in California—or a telephone employee in Michigan.

For the most part, Bell System stockholders are men and women who have put aside small sums for saving. More than half of them have held their shares for five years or longer. More than 650,000 of these 850,000 security holders own stock in the American Telephone and Telegraph Company—the parent company of the Bell System. More than 225,000 own five shares or less. Over fifty per cent are women. No one owns as much as one per cent of the stock of A. T. & T. In a very real sense, the Bell System is a democracy in business—owned by the people it serves.

More than 270,000 men and women work for the Bell System. One person out of every 150 in this country owns A. T. & T. securities or stock and bonds of associated companies in the Bell System.

BELL TELEPHONE SYSTEM

Exhibit 17-20 Advocacy ads have been used for years

offensive. When the ad backfired, the campaign was immediately halted and the agency that developed it was fired.[41] The ultimate judge, of course, is always the reader.

Cause-Related Advertising An increasingly popular method of image building is **cause-related marketing,** in which companies link with charities or nonprofit organizations as contributing sponsors. The company benefits from favorable publicity, while the charity receives much-needed funds. Spending on cause-related marketing has increased more than 300 percent since 1990, reaching $828 million in 2002. Proponents of cause marketing say that association with a cause may differentiate one brand or store from another, increase consumer acceptance of price increases, generate favorable publicity, and even win over skeptical officials who may have an impact on the company.[42] Cause-marketing relationships can take a variety of forms. Making outright donations to a nonprofit cause, having companies volunteer for the cause, donating materials or supplies, running public service announcements, or even providing event refreshments are some of the ways companies get involved. Exhibit 17-21 shows Doug Flutie's support for the Doug Flutie, Jr., Foundation's attempts to find a cure for autism.

Wyler's light to Breast Cancer

Exhibit 17-21 Doug Flutie's foundation cause is finding a cure for autism

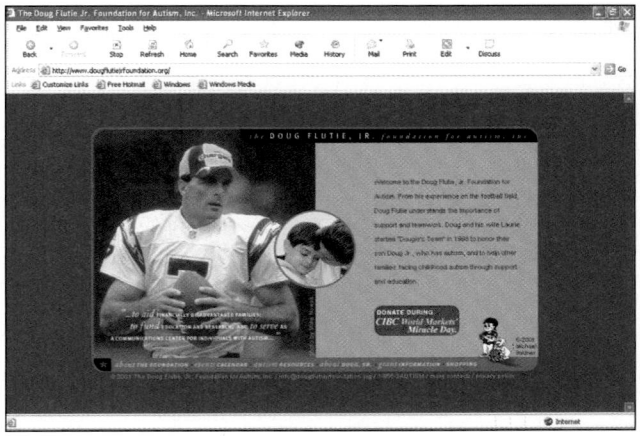

While companies receive public relations benefits from their association with causes, with 80 percent of consumers saying they have a more positive impression of companies that support a cause, they sometimes receive financial rewards as well.[43] Visa's "Reading is Fundamental" campaign led to a 17 percent increase in sales, BMW saw sales increase when it sponsored a program to eradicate breast cancer, and Wendy's International in Denver saw sales increase by more than 33 percent when a portion of purchases was contributed to Denver's Mercy Medical Center.[44]

At the same time, not all cause marketing is a guarantee of success. Cause marketing requires more than just associating with a social issue, and it takes time and

effort. Companies have gotten into trouble by misleading consumers about their relationships, and others wasted money by hooking up with a cause that offered little synergism. One survey showed that over 300 companies had associated themselves with breast cancer concerns, with most becoming lost in sponsorship clutter. Others have simply picked the wrong cause—finding that their customers and potential customers either have little interest in or don't like the cause. In some cases, cause marketing is considered nothing more than shock advertising. Finally, the results of cause-marketing efforts can sometimes be hard to quantify.

Advantages and Disadvantages of Corporate Advertising

A number of reasons for the increased popularity of corporate advertising become evident when you examine the advantages of this form of communication:

1. *It is an excellent vehicle for positioning the firm.* Firms, like products, need to establish an image or position in the marketplace. Corporate image ads are one way to accomplish this objective. A well-positioned product is much more likely to achieve success than is one with a vague or no image. The same holds true of the firm. Stop and think for a moment about the image that comes to mind when you hear the name IBM, Apple, Johnson & Johnson, or Procter & Gamble.

Now what comes to mind when you hear Unisys, USX, or Navistar? How many consumer brands can you name that fall under ConAgra's corporate umbrella? (Swiss Miss, Wesson, La Choy, and many others.) While we are not saying these latter companies are not successful—because they certainly are—we are suggesting their corporate identities (or positions) are not as well entrenched as the identities of those first cited. Companies with strong positive corporate images have an advantage over competitors that may be enhanced when they promote the company overall.

2. *It takes advantage of the benefits derived from public relations.* As the PR efforts of firms have increased, the attention paid to these events by the media has lessened (not because they are of any less value, but because there are more events to cover). The net result is that when a company engages in a public relations effort, there is no guarantee it will receive press coverage and publicity. Corporate image advertising gets the message out, and though consumers may not perceive it as positively as information from an objective source, the fact remains that it can communicate what has been done.

3. *It reaches a select target market.* Corporate image advertising should not be targeted to the general public. It is often targeted to investors and managers of other firms rather than to the general public. It doesn't matter if the general public does not appreciate this form of communication, as long as the target market does. In this respect, this form of advertising may be accomplishing its objectives.

Some of the disadvantages of corporate advertising were alluded to earlier in the chapter. To these criticisms, we can add the following:

1. *Questionable effectiveness.* There is no strong evidence to support the belief that corporate advertising works. Many doubt the data cited earlier that demonstrated a correlation between stock prices and corporate image advertising. A study by Bozell & Jacobs Advertising of 16,000 ads concluded that corporate advertising contributed to only 4 percent of the variability in the company's stock price, compared with a 55 percent effect attributable to financial factors.[45] A second study also casts doubts on earlier studies that concluded that corporate advertising worked.[46]

2. *Constitutionality and/or ethics.* Some critics contend that since larger firms have more money, they can control public opinion unfairly. This point was resolved in the courts in favor of the advertisers. Nevertheless, many consumers still see such advertising as unfair and immediately take a negative view of the sponsor.

A number of valid points have been offered for and against corporate advertising. Two things are certain: (1) No one knows who is right, and (2) the use of this communications form continues to increase.

Measuring the Effectiveness of Corporate Advertising

As you can tell from our discussion of the controversy surrounding corporate advertising, there need to be methods for evaluating whether or not such advertising is effective:

- *Attitude surveys.* One way to determine the effectiveness of corporate advertising is conducting attitude surveys to gain insights into both the public's and investors' reactions to ads. The Phase II study conducted by market research firm Yankelovich, Skelly & White is one of the best-known applications of this measurement method.[47] The firm measured recall and attitudes toward corporate advertisers and found that corporate advertising is more efficient in building recall for a company name than is product advertising alone. Frequent corporate advertisers rated better on virtually all attitude measures than those with low corporate ad budgets.
- *Studies relating corporate advertising and stock prices.* The Bozell & Jacobs study is one of many that have examined the effect of various elements of corporate advertising (position in the magazine, source effects, etc.) on stock prices. These studies have yielded conflicting conclusions, indicating that while the model for such measures seems logical, methodological problems may account for at least some of the discrepancies.
- *Focus group research.* Focus groups have been used to find out what investors want to see in ads and how they react after the ads are developed. As with product-oriented advertising, this method has limitations, although it does allow for some effective measurements.

While the effectiveness of corporate advertising has been measured by some of the methods used to measure product-specific advertising, research in this area has not kept pace with that of the consumer market. (One study reported that only 35 of the Fortune 500 companies ever attempted to measure performance of their annual reports.[48] The most commonly offered reason for this lack of effort is that corporate ads are often the responsibility of those in the highest management positions in the firm, and these parties do not wish to be held accountable. Interestingly, those who should be most concerned with accountability are the most likely to shun this responsibility!

Summary

This chapter examined the role of the promotional elements of public relations, publicity, and corporate advertising. We noted that these areas are all significant to the marketing and communications effort and are usually considered differently from the other promotional elements. The reasons for this special treatment stem from the facts that (1) they are typically not designed to promote a specific product or service and (2) in many instances it is harder for the consumer to make the connection between the communication and its intent.

Public relations was shown to be useful in its traditional responsibilities as well as in a more marketing-oriented role. In many firms, PR is a separate department operating independently of marketing; in others, it is considered a support system. Many large firms have an external public relations agency, just as they have an outside ad agency.

In the case of publicity, another factor enters the equation: lack of control over the communication the public will receive. In public relations and corporate advertising, the organization remains the source and retains much more control. Publicity often takes more of a reactive than a proactive approach, yet it may be more instrumental (or detrimental) to the success of a product or organization than all other forms of promotion combined.

While not all publicity can be managed, the marketer must nevertheless recognize its potential impact. Press releases and the management of information are just two of the factors under the company's control. Proper reaction and a strategy to deal with uncontrollable events are also responsibilities.

Corporate advertising was described as controversial, largely because the source of the message is top management, so the rules for other advertising and promoting forms are often not applied. This

element of communication definitely has its place in the promotional mix. But to be effective, it must be used with each of the other elements, with specific communications objectives in mind.

Finally, we noted that measures of evaluation and control are required for each of these program elements, just as they are for all others in the promotional mix. We presented some methods for taking such measurements and some evidence showing why it is important to use them. As long as the elements of public relations, publicity, and corporate advertising are considered integral components of the overall communications strategy, they must respect the same rules as the other promotional mix elements to ensure success.

Key Terms

public relations, 564
marketing public relations (MPR), 566
internal audiences, 569
external audiences, 569
press release, 573
press conference, 574
exclusive, 574
team approach, 579
internal audits, 579
external audits, 579
publicity, 579
video news release (VNR), 581
corporate advertising, 583
image advertising, 585
event sponsorships, 588
advocacy advertising, 590
cause-related marketing, 590

Discussion Questions

1. The lead-in to the chapter discusses a new book that argues that public relations should replace advertising as the primary means of introducing new products. Explain arguments in favor and opposed to this position. What do you conclude?

2. A number of companies have experienced public relations problems resulting from product recalls, product failures, etc. Describe some of the steps companies can take to minimize the impact of this negative publicity.

3. Describe some of the criteria used by companies to measure effectiveness of the public relations program. Provide examples.

4. Explain why public relations and publicity may have more impact on the consumer than other IMC program elements (for example, advertising, direct marketing, etc.). Provide case examples.

5. The text describes various forms of corporate advertising. Find examples of each type and discuss whether the company has effectively employed this form.

6. Discuss the advantages that the Internet offers for those responsible for conducting public relations activities. Describe how these activities are different than traditional methods.

7. Discuss some of the advantages associated with the use of MPRs. What are some of the disadvantages?

8. Explain why traditional public relations practitioners might be unhappy with the organization's use of MPRs. Take a position as to whether this criticism is justified.

9. List and describe the advantages and disadvantages of the use of public relations in an IMC program. Provide an example of an appropriate use of public relations in this mix.

10. What is a video news release (VNR)? Provide an example of a situation in which a company might employ the use of a VNR. Discuss some of the ethical implications (if any) in using this tool.

Personal Selling

18

Chapter Objectives

1. To understand the role of personal selling in the integrated marketing communications program.
2. To know the advantages and disadvantages of personal selling as a promotional program element.
3. To understand how personal selling is combined with other elements in an IMC program.
4. To know ways to determine the effectiveness of the personal selling effort.

Motivating the Sales Force—Not an Easy Task

Regardless of how good one's advertising, public relations, and other IMC programs are, for many companies, it is the sales force that is called on to close the deal—particularly those in the business-to-business market. As you might imagine, there is always a need for good salespeople, and companies do whatever they can to attract and

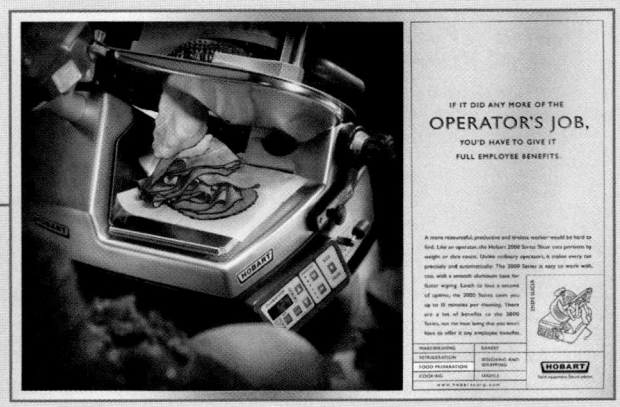

retain them and to motivate them to continue to do good work—regardless of the industry.

As the business environment changes, so too do the needs and wants of the sales force. In the past, when the salesman was the breadwinner, money worked well. By providing the sales force with the opportunity to earn more money by working harder, motivation was easily achieved. But now, times have changed. Dual-worker families, more emphasis on lifestyles, and more opportunities are just some of the factors that are resulting in more diversified salespeople and that explain why money in and of itself doesn't cut it like it used to. So companies have explored a number of options, as seen in the following examples:

- *Jupiter Media Metrix.* As the competition between Jupiter and its number-one rival Forrester Research (both provide Internet research services) intensified, Forrester hung a sign in its headquarters' office inspiring employees to "Beat Jupiter." In response, Jupiter initiated a motivation of its own: leather boxing gloves in the lobby showcase of its New York offices. Each quarter, the sales rep who "scores the biggest knockout" against rival Forrester gets to autograph the gloves.
- *Hobart.* The Ohio-based commercial food manufacturer—whose equipment is in the White House—outfitted the White House cafeteria on the TV show *West Wing* with its equipment. The product placement was well received by the sales force, but to add even more to the punch, the national sales force meeting was held in Hollywood and top-performing salespeople got to tour the set and meet actor Martin Sheen. As noted by Dean Landeche, vice president of marketing for Hobart, "It became the buzz around our campus for quite some time."
- *Guardian Life Insurance.* Among the hardest groups to motivate are the sales forces of insurance companies. As noted by one ex-agent, "The industry is unique in a sense in that we are working with unmotivated buyers—people who have a need for what an agent sells, but do not believe they need to buy it yet. We all deny we are going to die." Keeping salespeople motivated is critical, and companies have taken various approaches. Guardian Life Insurance has created an online "university," available 24 hours a day, to provide its sales force with desired

training. The company also holds regional motivational sales meetings and provides access to outside motivation sources. Sales reps demand, and receive, constantly updated information on "hot topics" to keep them as aware of trends as their increasingly sophisticated clients are.

Other companies have come up with their own incentives, ranging from money to trips to trophies. Mark McMaster, writing in *Sales & Marketing Management* magazine, suggests 51 possibilities, including:

- Have each salesperson bring a joke to the sales meeting.
- Hold a meeting where the only agenda item is popcorn.
- Rent a Porsche Boxster for use by the top performer for the weekend.
- Adopt an animal at the zoo and name it after the top achiever.
- Bring in a comedian for a 7 A.M. sales meeting.

McMaster provides another 46 possibilities, including playing games of tag, providing hotel upgrades, and encouraging practical jokes in the office. Interestingly, none of these include paying more money. Maybe money just doesn't motivate people anymore!

Sources: Mark McMaster, "51 Ways to Motivate Your Sales Force (on Any Budget)," *Sales & Marketing Management,* March 2002, pp. 30–31; Dana James, "Something in Common," *Marketing News,* May 27, 2002, pp. 11–14; Eileen Courter, "Keeping Your Sales Force Happy," *Advisor Today,* October 2001, pp. 50–58; Laurie Luczak, "Sock It to 'Em," *Sales & Marketing Management,* October 2001, pp. 57–64.

The Scope of Personal Selling

The chapter opener demonstrates just a few of the ways organizations attempt to motivate salespeople and illustrates how they are integrating the personal selling function into the overall marketing communications program through the use of product placements, sales promotions, and other IMC tools. The changing marketplace has had a significant impact on how personal selling activities are conducted and how successful firms will compete in the future. In Chapter 1, we stated that while we recognize the importance of personal selling and the role it plays in the overall marketing and promotions effort, it is not emphasized in this text. Personal selling is typically under the control of the sales manager, not the advertising and promotions department. A study conducted by *Sales & Marketing Management* showed that in 46 percent of the companies surveyed, sales and marketing are totally separate departments.[1] But personal selling does make a valuable contribution to the promotional program. As you can see by the introduction to this chapter, additional IMC tools are used in conjunction with personal selling, with the salespeople themselves often the receivers. To develop a promotional plan effectively, a firm must integrate the roles and responsibilities of its sales force into the communications program. Strong cooperation between the departments is also necessary.

This chapter focuses on the role personal selling assumes in the IMC program, the advantages and disadvantages of this program element, and the basis for evaluating its contributions to attaining communications objectives. In addition, we explore how personal selling is combined with other program elements, both to support them and to receive support from them.

Personal selling involves selling through a person-to-person communications process. The emphasis placed on personal selling varies from firm to firm depending on a variety of factors, including the nature of the product or service being marketed, size of the organization, and type of industry. Personal selling often plays the dominant role in industrial firms, while in other firms, such as makers of low-priced consumer nondurable goods, its role is minimized. In many industries, these roles are changing to a more balanced use of promotional program elements. In an integrated marketing communications program, personal selling is a partner with, not a substitute for, the other promotional mix elements.

The Role of Personal Selling in the IMC Program

Manufacturers may promote their products *directly* to consumers through advertising and promotions and/or direct-marketing efforts or *indirectly* through resellers and salespeople. (A sales force may call on customers directly—for example, in the insurance industry or real estate. But this chapter focuses on the personal selling function as it exists in most large corporations or smaller companies—that is, as a link to resellers or dealers in business-to-business transactions.) Depending on the role defined by the organization, the responsibilities and specific tasks of salespeople may differ, but ultimately these tasks are designed to help attain communications and marketing objectives.

Personal selling differs from the other forms of communication presented thus far in that messages flow from a sender (or group of senders) to a receiver (or group of receivers) directly (usually face to face). This *direct* and *interpersonal communication* lets the sender immediately receive and evaluate feedback from the receiver. This communications process, known as **dyadic communication** (between two people or groups), allows for more specific tailoring of the message and more personal communications than do many of the other media discussed. The message can be changed to address the receiver's specific needs and wants.

In some situations, this ability to focus on specific problems is mandatory; a standard communication would not suffice. Consider an industrial buying situation in which the salesperson is an engineer. To promote the company's products and/or services, the salesperson must understand the client's specific needs. This may mean understanding the tensile strength of materials or being able to read blueprints or plans to understand the requirements. Or say a salesperson represents a computer graphics firm. Part of his or her responsibility for making a sale may involve the design of a software program to solve a problem unique to this customer. Mass communications cannot accomplish these tasks. Personal selling plays a critical role not just in industrial settings but in the consumer market as well.

The great entrepreneur Marshall Field said, "The distance between the salesperson and the potential buyer is the most important three feet in business."[2] Personal selling is important in selling to consumers and resellers. Consumer-product companies must secure distribution, motivate resellers to stock and promote the product, and so on.

Why is personal selling so important? Let's examine its role with respect to other promotional program elements.

Determining the Role of Personal Selling

The first questions a manager needs to ask when preparing the promotional program are what the specific responsibilities of personal selling will be and what role it will assume relative to the other promotional mix elements. To determine its role, management should be guided by four questions:

1. What specific information must be exchanged between the firm and potential customers?
2. What are the alternative ways to carry out these communications objectives?
3. How effective is each alternative in carrying out the needed exchange?
4. How cost effective is each alternative?[3]
    - *Determining the information to be exchanged.* In keeping with the objectives established by the communications models in Chapter 5, the salesperson may have a variety of messages to communicate, such as creating awareness of the product or service offering, demonstrating product benefits for evaluation, initiating trial, and/or closing the sale. It may also be necessary to answer questions, counter misconceptions, and discover potentially unmet needs.
    - *Examining promotional mix alternatives.* In previous chapters, we discussed the roles of advertising and sales promotion, direct marketing, and public relations/publicity. Each of these program elements offers specific advantages and disadvantages, and each needs to be considered when the promotional mix is developed. Personal selling is an alternative that offers distinct

Figure 18-1 When the sales force is a major part of the IMC mix

Product or Service	Channels
Complex products requiring customer application assistance (computers, pollution control system, steam turbines)	Channel system relatively short and direct to end users
Major purchase decisions, such as food items purchased by supermarket chains	Product and service training and assistance needed by channel intermediaries
Features and performance of the product requiring personal demonstration and trial by the customer (private aircraft)	Personal selling needed to push product through channel
	Channel intermediaries available to perform personal selling function for supplier with limited resources and experience (brokers or manufacturer's agents)
Price	**Advertising**
Final price is negotiated between buyer and seller (appliances, cars, real estate)	Advertising media do not provide effective link with market targets
Selling price or quality purchased enables an adequate margin to support selling expenses (traditional department store compared to discount house)	Information needed by buyer cannot be provided entirely through advertising and sales promotion (life insurance)
	Number and dispersion of customers will not enable acceptable advertising economies

advantages in some situations but is less appropriate in others, as evidenced in Figure 18-1.

- *Evaluating the relative effectiveness of alternatives.* The effectiveness of each program element must be evaluated based on the target market and the objectives sought. Personal selling is effective in many situations, but other program elements may be more attractive in other cases. For example, advertising may do a better job of repeating messages or reaching a large number of people with one distinct, consistent message.
- *Determining cost effectiveness.* One of the major disadvantages of personal selling is the cost involved. (Cahners Research estimates the average cost per sales call could be as high as $329.)[4] While the cost of a personal sales call may not be prohibitive in industrial settings where a single purchase can be worth millions of dollars, the same cost may be unfeasible in a consumer market. Other media may be able to communicate the required message at a much lower cost.

The Nature of Personal Selling

To integrate the personal selling effort into the overall promotional program, we must understand the nature of this tool. Let us look at how personal selling has evolved over the years and then examine some of its characteristics.

The personal selling task encompasses a variety of responsibilities (some of which we discuss in the next section). Like other aspects of the promotional mix, these responsibilities are constantly changing. As noted by Thomas Wotruba, the personal selling area is constantly evolving as the marketing environment itself evolves.[5] Wotruba identifies five distinct stages of personal selling evolution, shown in Figure 18-2.

1. **Provider stage.** Selling activities are limited to accepting orders for the supplier's available offering and conveying it to the buyer.
2. **Persuader stage.** Selling involves an attempt to persuade market members to buy the supplier's offerings.
3. **Prospector stage.** Activities include seeking out selected buyers who are perceived to have a need for the offering as well as the resources and authority to buy it.

Figure 18-2 The stages in the evolution of selling

Stages and Description	Characteristics of Stages: Customer Needs	Type of Market	Nature and Intensity of Competition	Examples
1. *Provider:* accepts orders and delivers to buyer.	Assumed to exist; not a concern	Sellers'	None	Route salespeople/drivers; some retail salesclerks
2. *Persuader:* attempts to convince anyone to buy available offerings.	Created, awakened	Buyers'	Undifferentiated; slight intensity	Telemarketers for photo studio; many new car dealers
3. *Prospector:* seeks out prospects with need for available offering and resources to buy.	Considered but inferred	Segmented	Differentiated; growing	Car insurance salespeople calling on new car buyers; office supplies sellers calling on small businesses
4. *Problem solver:* matches available offerings to solve customer-stated problems.	Diagnosed, with attention to customer input	Participative	Responsive and counteractive with increasing resources	Communication systems salespeople for a telephone company; architectural services sellers calling on building contractors
5. *Procreator:* creates a unique offering to match the buyer's needs as mutually specified, involving any or all aspects of the seller's total marketing mix.	Mutually defined; matched with tailored offering	Coactive	Focused; growing in breadth of market and service offerings	Materials handling equipment salespeople who design and sell a system to fit a buyer's manufacturing facility

4. **Problem-solver stage.** Selling involves obtaining the participation of buyers to identify their problems, which can be translated into needs, and then presenting a selection from the supplier's offerings that corresponds with those needs and can solve those problems.
5. **Procreator stage.** Selling defines the buyer's problems or needs and their solutions through active buyer-seller collaboration and then creates a market offering uniquely tailored to the customer.

According to Wotruba, firms evolving through these five stages have to assume different market orientations, as well as different organizational designs, staffing, and compensation programs. The different stages require different promotional strategies, each integrated with personal selling to achieve the maximum communications effect.

The New Role of Personal Selling

As previously noted, the business world is going through a very rapid transition as (1) individuals and corporations gain more knowledge and economic power, (2) value is replacing efficiency, and (3) industry boundaries are changing—for example, competitors are joining forces to achieve more buying power.[6] As a result, the role of the sales force will also significantly change, according to Kevin Hoffberg and Kevin Corcoran. Along with retaining their traditional roles, described by Wotruba, salespeople will have to acquire new roles to remain effective. That is, in addition to being information providers, influencers through proximity (i.e., through personal contact), and demonstrators, salespeople will engage in:

- *Surveying*—educating themselves more about their customers' businesses and regularly assessing these businesses and their customers to achieve a position of knowledgeable authority.
- *Mapmaking*—outlining both an account strategy and a solutions strategy (for the customer). This means laying out a plan, discussing it with the customer, and revising it as changes require.

- *Guiding*—bringing incremental value to the customer by identifying problems and opportunities, offering alternative options and solutions, and providing solutions with tangible value.
- *Fire starting*—engaging customers and driving them to commit to a solution.[7]

This new role, say Hoffberg and Corcoran, will create added value and develop a relationship between buyer and seller.

Relationship Marketing

As noted, personal selling is evolving from a focus on persuasive techniques used to sell a product or service to a much more marketing-oriented *partnership* with the customer. This new role requires much broader thinking and expertise on the part of the seller and a more extensive use of the various promotional tools. The modern salesperson is attempting to establish a long-term, symbiotic relationship with clients, working with them as a solutions provider.

Relationship marketing is defined as "an organization's effort to develop a long-term, cost-effective link with individual customers for mutual benefit."[8] Rather than focusing on a short-term sale, the sales rep tries to establish a long-term bond. And rather than just selling, the sales department works with marketing to use techniques like database marketing, message differentiation to different target markets, and tracking of promotional effects to improve the relationship. For example, customer relationship management (CRM) tools have been used by a number of companies. These companies, including Sears, Wells Fargo, Sony, and GM, among others, make extensive uses of their databases on purchase behavior and frequency and duration of customer interactions to estimate profitability at the individual account level. A number of companies now offer software to assist in implementing CRM programs, including Seibel Systems, SAP, and PeopleSoft (Exhibit 18-1). AT&T builds databases of customers with similar profiles, flagging those with the most potential for up-selling. As noted by Copulsky and Wolf, such marketing uses a more personalized form of communication that crosses the previous boundaries between personal selling and the other promotional tools. Relationship building also requires trust, as noted by Pepper and Rodgers; if the customer does not trust the salesperson, there is no relationship and the sale will focus only on price. In a long-term relationship, the buyer and seller collaborate within the context of previous and future transactions.[9]

Adoption of a CRM approach will require sales managers to develop nontraditional sales strategies, according to some observers. Ingram and colleagues note that companies will need to move to a more strategic, less tactical approach, using emerging technologies to support this effort. Bob Donath agrees, noting that traditional communications performance standards—the number of qualified and converted leads generated from a medium—will be less important. Donath notes that a company's reliance on websites and banner ads, as well as ads in print publications, will need to be more strategic, direct marketing will assume a greater role, and the use of more sophisticated CRM programs will be required to be successful.

Exhibit 18-1 PeopleSoft designs software to assist Customer Relationship Management (CRM)

The Costs of Personal Selling

In some industries, personal selling constitutes a substantial portion of the communications effort and may account for most of the promotional budget. This is true because (1) much attention is devoted to this function due to its advantages over other communication methods and (2) it is an expensive form of communication. The average cost per sales call varies by industry, ranging from a low of $276 in the food industry to $354 in electronics. Communication does not come cheap!

When the cost per sales call is compared with the cost per message delivered through other media, these figures seem outrageous. We saw in earlier chapters that these costs could be as low as 3 cents. But taking these numbers at face value may lead to unfair comparisons. In evaluating the costs of personal selling, we must consider the nature of the call, the objectives sought, and whether other program elements could deliver the message as effectively. It may be that the higher costs cannot be avoided.

The costs of personal selling are even higher when you consider that one sales call is not likely to be enough to close a deal. This is particularly true in building and construction; while it may take (on the average) only 3.34 sales calls to close a deal in the building and construction industry, the same close in electronics and computer manufacturing may require 6.5 visits.[10] The industry average is 5.12. As you can see through simple multiplication, the cost per sale is now even more intimidating (though in industrial markets the returns may easily warrant the expense).

Overall, personal selling is an expensive way to communicate. Yet it does usually involve more than just communicating, and the returns (more direct sales) may be greater than those from the other program elements.

Exhibit 18-2 Salespeople may assume multiple responsibilities

Personal Selling Responsibilities

Sales & Marketing Management uses three categories to classify salespeople: **order taking, creative selling,** and **missionary sales**[11] (see Figure 18-3). Of course, not all firms treat each of these responsibilities the same, nor are their salespeople limited to only these tasks (Exhibit 18-2). Personal selling has evolved to include responsibilities beyond these. Job requirements may include (1) locating prospective customers; (2) determining customers' needs and wants that are not being satisfied; (3) recommending a way to satisfy these needs and/or wants; (4) demonstrating the capabilities of the firm and its products for providing this satisfaction; (5) closing the sale and taking the order; and (6) following up and servicing the account. Let's discuss these job classifications and some of the responsibilities assigned to each:

1. *Locating prospective customers.* The process of locating new customers (often referred to as **prospecting**) involves the search for and qualification of prospective

Creative Selling

Creative selling jobs may require the most skill and preparation. In addition to prospecting, the salesperson must assess the situation, determine the needs to be met, present the capabilities for satisfying these needs, and get an order. The salesperson is often the "point person" who has established the initial contact on behalf of the firm and who is primarily responsible for completing the exchange. He or she is, in fact, the order getter. Sales personnel may focus on current customers, encouraging more sales and cross selling, and/or they may seek new customers.

Order Taking

Once the initial sale has taken place, the creative seller may be replaced (not physically!) by an order taker, whose role is much more casual. It may simply involve a straight rebuy—that is, the order does not change much. (A bottled-water delivery person is an example.) When a slight change is considered, the order taker may be involved in a modified rebuy, which may require some creative selling (for example, a salesperson calling on a wholesale food company may have a list of products to sell). If a major purchase decision is required, however, the role of making the sale may again be turned over to the creative seller. Order takers are often classified as *inside* order takers, who work inside the sales office and receive orders by phone, mail, or the Internet, and *field* order takers, who travel to customers to get their orders.

Missionary Sales Reps

The missionary representative is essentially a support role. While performing many of the tasks assumed in creative selling, the missionary rep may not actually take the order. He or she introduces new products, new promotions, and/or new programs, with the actual order to be taken by the company's order taker or by a distributor representing the company's goods. The missionary sales rep may have additional account service responsibilities including customer relationship management. Missionary reps are most often employed in industries where the manufacturer uses a middleperson to distribute the product (for example, food products or pharmaceuticals).

Figure 18-3 Types of sales jobs

customers. Salespeople must follow up on **leads** (those who may become customers) and **prospects** (those who need the product or service). They must also determine whether these prospects are **qualified prospects**—that is, able to make the buying decision and pay for the product. Exhibit 18-3 is an ad for a company that helps sales forces identify qualified leads. Macromedia, a software company in San Francisco, uses an automated lead tracking system to help in this regard. The system gathers all leads, and then with automated scripts and questionnaires the leads are qualified by phone, fax, or Internet. The system then arranges each lead by "grade" and priority status and directs it to the appropriate salesperson. Dell and Cisco, among others, use a Web-based system.

2. *Determining customers' needs and wants.* At this stage, the salesperson gathers more information on the prospect and decides the best way to approach him or her. The rep must determine what the customer needs or wants and make certain the person being approached is capable of making the purchase decision. In some instances the salesperson may have to assist the customer in determining what he or she needs.

3. *Recommending a way to satisfy the customers' needs and wants.* Here the salesperson recommends a possible solution to the problem and/or needs of the potential customer. This may entail providing information the prospect had not considered or identifying alternative solutions that might work. As noted earlier, the salesperson acts as a systems provider.

4. *Demonstrating the capabilities of the firm and its products.* At this stage, the salesperson demonstrates the capabilities of the firm and shows the prospect why that firm is the obvious choice. As you might expect, corporate image (created through advertising and other promotional tools) is important to the salesperson.

5. *Closing the sale.* The key ingredient in any sales presentation is the **close**—getting the prospect's commitment. For many salespeople, this is the most difficult task. Many reps are adept at prospecting, identifying customer needs, and making

Exhibit 18-3 Giltspur offers salespeople expertise on how to qualify leads

presentations, but they are reluctant to ask for the sale. Most managers work with their sales forces to close the sale and help reluctant or uncertain buyers make a decision.

6. *Following up and servicing the account.* The responsibilities of the sales force do not end once the sale has been made. It is much easier to keep existing customers than to attract new ones. Maintaining customer loyalty, generating repeat sales, and getting the opportunity to **cross sell**—that is, sell additional products and services to the same customer—are some of the advantages of keeping customers satisfied through follow-up activities. In a relationship marketing versus selling orientation, follow-up is necessary and expected.

A primary advantage a salesperson offers is the opportunity to assess the situation firsthand and adapt the sales message accordingly (a *direct feedback* network). No other promotional element provides this opportunity. The successful salesperson constantly analyzes the situation, reads the feedback provided by the receiver, and shapes the message to specifically meet the customer's needs.

While you might expect this to be an easy task, it isn't always the case. Sometimes buyers will not or cannot express their needs accurately. Other times, the salesperson must become a problem solver for the client. More and more, salespeople are being asked to assist in the buyers' decision-making process. The more salespeople can become involved in planning and decision making, the more confidence the buyer places in them, and the more bonding the relationship becomes.

Sometimes the true motivation for purchasing is not the one the customer gives. You might expect buyers to base their decisions on rational, objective factors, but this is not always the case. Even in industrial markets (where product specifications may be critical) or reseller markets (where product movements and/or profits are important), many purchase decisions are made on what might be called nonrational criteria (not irrational, but involving factors beyond cost or other product benefits). Since it is generally believed these purchase situations involve less emotion and more rational thinking than many consumer purchases, this is an important insight.

Consider the marketer's dilemma. If a firm provides advertising and promotions that speak only to the rational purchase motives, it may not be able to make the sale. On the other hand, how could an advertiser possibly know all the emotional or nonrational criteria influencing the decision, let alone integrate this information into its messages? The personal sales effort may be the only way to uncover the many motivations for purchasing and address them.

When you review this list of responsibilities, it becomes clear that the salesperson of today is no mere huckster. Figure 18-4 provides a list of the 10 traits that are common to successful salespeople (the list is consistent with other studies conducted),

Figure 18-4 Ten traits of effective salespeople

A *Sales & Marketing Management* survey of 209 salespeople representing 189 companies in 37 industries determined that the following traits characterize top sales performers:

1. *Ego strength:* a healthy self-esteem that allows one to bounce back from rejection.
2. A *sense of urgency:* wanting to get it done now.
3. *Ego drive:* a combination of competitiveness and self-esteem.
4. *Assertiveness:* the ability to be firm, lead the sales process, and get one's point across confidently.
5. *Willingness to take risk:* willing to innovate and take a chance.
6. *Sociable:* outgoing, friendly, talkative, and interested in others.
7. *Abstract reasoning:* ability to understand concepts and ideas.
8. *Skepticism:* a slight lack of trust and suspicion of others.
9. *Creativity:* the ability to think differently.
10. *Empathy:* the ability to place oneself in someone else's shoes.

Figure 18-5 Buyers' likes and dislikes about salespeople

Traits Buyers Consider Most Helpful In Salespeople*	Traits Buyers Consider Most Objectionable In Salespeople*
1. *Knowledgeable.* They want salespeople who know products and policies thoroughly. They value technical support most highly.	1. *Unprepared.* Buyers hate salespeople who waste time by calling without clear purposes, especially on a busy day.
2. *Empathy.* They want salespeople who are interested in them. They want salespeople who listen and learn about them, their problems, and their goals.	2. *Uninformed.* They are vociferous about dealing with salespeople who don't know their products or lines and can't answer simple questions.
3. *Well organized.* They want salespeople who come prepared and do not waste their time. They strongly prefer salespeople who have written objectives.	3. *Aggressive.* They are turned off by "pushy" salespeople who argue and who "care more about their commission than the customer."
4. *Promptness.* They expect quick replies to requests for information, especially when a problem rears its ugly head.	4. *Undependability.* They cite salespeople who do not return calls promptly and who are never there when needed.
5. *Follow-through.* They look for salespeople who will follow through without continuous badgering. This spells personal reliability.	5. *Poor follow-through.* They are disgusted with calling salespeople several times to get information the salespeople promised.
6. *Solutions.* They want salespeople to present innovative solutions to problems. They seek responsiveness and creativity.	6. *Presumptuousness.* Many are offended by salespeople asking for competitors' quotes.
7. *Punctuality.* They expect salespeople to keep appointments promptly and to let them know if they will be late. They will excuse tardiness occasionally, but not frequently.	7. *"Walk-ins."* They list people who call without appointments, with no specific purposes. They also feel invaded by many telemarketers.
8. *Hard work.* They appreciate salespeople who work hard. They are impressed by salespeople who put in long and hard hours.	8. *"Gabbers."* They dislike compulsive talkers who go on and on and don't listen. They describe the "Gift of Gab" as boring. They are tired of hearing the "latest jokes."
9. *Energetic.* They are impressed by a positive attitude, enthusiasm, affability, consistency, and flexibility.	9. *Problem avoiders.* They dislike salespeople who go to pieces in a crisis, those with no clout, and those who are afraid of their principals.
10. *Honesty.* They want specifics instead of generalities. They look for personal integrity.	10. *Lack of personal respect.* They resent salespeople who go to other people in the company without their knowledge.

*In order of greatest number of times mentioned.
Source: Better Repping Survey Report, Berman Information Services, Inc., 2002.

while Figure 18-5 shows the results of one company's survey of buyers' likes and dislikes regarding the sales force.

The importance of personal selling in the integrated marketing communications program should now be clear. This program element provides opportunities that no other form of message delivery does. But while the tasks performed by salespeople offer some distinct advantages to the marketing program, they may also constitute disadvantages, as you will now see.

Advantages and Disadvantages of Personal Selling

The nature of personal selling positions this promotional tool uniquely among those available to marketers. Its advantages include the following:

1. *Allowing for two-way interaction.* The ability to interact with the receiver allows the sender to determine the impact of the message. Problems in comprehension or objections can be resolved and in-depth discussions of certain selling points can be provided immediately. In mass communications this direct feedback is not available and such information cannot be obtained immediately (if at all).

2. *Tailoring of the message.* Because of the direct interaction, messages can be tailored to the receiver. This more precise message content lets the sender address the

consumer's specific concerns, problems, and needs. The sales rep can also determine when to move on to the next selling point, ask for the sale, or close the deal.

3. *Lack of distraction.* In many personal selling situations, a one-to-one presentation is conducted. The likelihood of distractions is minimized and the buyer is generally paying close attention to the sales message. Even when the presentation is made by a group of salespeople or more than one decision maker is present, the setting is less distracting than those in which nonpersonal mass media are used.

4. *Involvement in the decision process.* Through consultative selling and relationship marketing, the seller becomes more of a partner in the buying decision process, acting in conjunction with the buyer to solve problems. This leads the buyer to rely more on the salesperson and his or her products and services. An added benefit may be increasing the involvement of the organization's own employees.

5. *Source of research information.* In a well-integrated marketing/sales department the sales force can be the "eyes and ears" of the firm. Sales reps can collect information on competitors' products and services, promotions, pricing, and so on, firsthand. In addition, they can learn about the buying needs and wants of customers and potential customers.

As you can see, the advantages of personal selling focus primarily on the dyadic communications process, the ability to alter the message, and the opportunity for direct feedback. Sometimes, however, these potential advantages are not always realized. In fact, they may become disadvantages.

Disadvantages associated with personal selling include the following:

1. *Inconsistent messages.* Earlier we stated that the ability to adapt the message to the receiver is a distinct advantage of personal selling. But the lack of a standardized message can become a disadvantage. The message to be communicated is generally designed by the marketing staff with a particular communications objective in mind. Once this message has been determined, it is communicated to all receivers. But the salesperson may alter this message in ways the marketer did not intend. Thus, the marketing staff is at the mercy of the sales force with respect to what exactly is communicated. (Sales communications aids can offset this problem to some degree, as you will see later in this chapter.)

2. *Sales force/management conflict.* Unfortunately, there are situations in even the best companies when one wonders if the sales staff and marketing staff know they work for the same company and for the same goals. Because of failure to communicate, corporate politics, and myriad other reasons, the sales force and marketing may not be working as a team. The marketing staff may not understand the problems faced by the sales staff, or the salespeople may not understand why marketing people do things the way they do. The result is that the sales force may not use materials provided from marketing, marketing may not be responsive to the field's assessment of customer needs, and so forth. The bottom line is that the communications process is not as effective as it could be due to faulty internal communications and/or conflicts.

3. *High cost.* We discussed earlier the high cost of personal selling. As the cost per sales call continues to climb, the marketer may find mass communications a more cost-effective alternative.

4. *Poor reach.* Personal selling cannot reach as many members of the target audience as other elements. Even if money were no object (not a very likely scenario!), the sales force has only so many hours and so many people it can reach in a given time. Further, the frequency with which these accounts are reached is also low.

5. *Potential ethical problems.* Because the manager does not have complete control over the messages the salespeople communicate and because income and advancement are often directly tied to sales, sometimes sales reps bend the rules. They may say and do things they know are not entirely ethical or in the best interest of the firm in order to get a sale. Other, perhaps more serious, problems can also occur. For example, many organizations are concerned about salespersons committing bribery. In a study reported in *Sales & Marketing Management,* 25 percent of managers and/or sales reps reported that they sometimes or often have felt pressured by a client to give the client something worth more than $100 in exchange for their business. Even more scary is that almost

89 percent said that they had offered such gifts in exchange for business.[12] The potential for this problem has led to a renewed emphasis on ethics in the marketplace and has caused as many as 20 percent of companies to use surveillance measures to ensure that their representatives are not engaging in illegal activities.[13]

Combining Personal Selling with Other Promotional Tools

Like the other program elements, personal selling is usually one component of the integrated marketing communications program. Rarely, if ever, is it used alone. Rather, this promotional tool both supports and is supported by other program elements.

Combining Personal Selling and Advertising

With specific market situations and communications objectives, the advantages of advertising make it more effective in the early stages of the response hierarchy (for example, in creating awareness and interest), whereas personal selling is more likely to be used in the later stages (for example, stimulating trial and getting the order). Thus, each may be more or less appropriate depending on the objectives sought. These elements can be combined in the promotional mix to compensate for each other's weaknesses and complement each other.

Consider a new product introduction. Given an adequate budget, the initial objective might be to reach as many people in the target market as quickly and cost effectively as possible. Since the primary objective is awareness and a simple message will suffice, advertising will likely be the most appropriate medium.

Now suppose specific benefits must be communicated that are not very obvious or easy to comprehend, and a product demonstration would be useful. Or consider a situation in which the objective is to ask for the sale and/or to establish a relationship. Here personal selling is a more appropriate tool than advertising. In common marketing situations like these, you can see how well advertising and personal selling work together to attain the objectives sought.

A number of studies bear out this complementary relationship. A study by Theodore Levitt showed that sales reps from well-known companies are better received than those from companies that do not spend advertising dollars to create awareness.[14] (Once they are in the door, however, the buyer expects the salesperson to perform better than those from lesser-known companies.) If a salesperson from a lesser-known company can get in to see the buyer, he or she is as likely to make the sale. But in risky situations, the well-advertised company rep has the advantage. Gateway recently embarked upon a $50 million IMC campaign (Exhibit 18-4) using advertising, direct marketing, sales promotion, and the Internet to create awareness that Gateway is interested in companies' business (Gateway has been perceived by many as being a consumer PC). The campaign is designed to position the company as a solutions provider and to assist and enhance the sales force's efforts.

Exhibit 18-4 Gateway's IMC campaign informs customers that Gateway is in the business-to-business market

Which would you rather have? A company that's simple to do business with or a company that makes business simple?

Why choose?

At Gateway, we believe that customizing technology is a lot more than a simple sales pitch. It's a powerful way to help your business succeed. All you have to do is contact us either by phone, Internet, or through our Gateway Business Solution℠ centers, which offer face-to-face service and the chance to test-drive the latest technology, like the Gateway GP-Series PCs featuring Intel® Pentium® III processors. Then we'll get to know your business, your needs and your budget. Innovative lease options, and client care and enhanced service plans let us craft a technology bundle that truly fits your needs and respects your budget. Call, click or come into your nearest Gateway Country® location. It's the simplest way to get business technology to work for you.

GP-Series Professional Desktop
GP7-450
Intel® Pentium® III Processor 450MHz with 512K Cache
64MB SDRAM (expandable to 384MB)
6.8GB Ultra ATA Hard Drive
EV700 17" Color Monitor (15.9" viewable)
16MB AGP Graphics
17X min/40X max CD-ROM Drive
10/100 Ethernet Network Card
Iomega® Internal ZIP® Drive
Business Audio & Speakers
Microsoft® Windows® 95 or Windows 98
MS® Office 2000 Small Business Software
$1299 or $45/mo.
36 mos. business lease[1]

Gateway
Connect with us.

Complete your solution by choosing from thousands of business hardware accessories and software at gateway.com

CALL 1-800-216-3360 | CLICK www.gateway.com | OR COME IN TO A GATEWAY BUSINESS SOLUTIONS℠ CENTER Gateway Country®

Ad Code: 000050

In other studies, John Morrill found that selling costs were 2 to 28 percent lower if the buyer had received an advertising message before the salesperson's arrival.[15] McGraw-Hill Corp., in a review of 54 studies, concluded the combination of advertising and personal selling is important since "less than 10 percent of industrial decision makers had been called upon by a salesperson from a specific company about a specific product in the previous two months."[16]

The studies suggest that combining advertising and personal selling is likely to improve reach, reduce costs, and increase the probability of a sale (assuming the advertising is effective, a concern reflected in Exhibit 18-5). Unfortunately, many salespeople do not understand the role that advertising plays and the contribution it can make to supporting their sales efforts. Some view the impact advertising makes with skepticism and/or believe that the monies would be better spent on commissions, price reductions, and so on. Ted Pollock, writing in *The American Salesman,* dis-

cusses the fact that advertising contributes to the sales process, and he enumerates 12 ways salespersons can use advertising to help them sell more (Figure 18-6).

Combining Personal Selling and Public Relations

The job descriptions presented earlier demonstrate that personal selling involves much more than just selling products and/or services. The personal selling agent is often the firm's best source of public relations. In their day-to-day duties, salespeople represent the firm and its products. Their personalities, servicing of the account, cooperation, and empathy not only influence sales potential but also reflect on the organizations they represent.

The salesperson may also be used directly in a PR role. Many firms encourage sales reps to participate in community activities like the Jaycees and Little League. Sometimes sales reps, in conjunction with the company, sacrifice time from their daily duties to help people in need. For example, after the Los Angeles earthquake, local companies donated food and their sales forces' time to aid quake victims. Computer salespeople devoted much of their time to getting customers and noncustomers back online. After a catastrophic flood, a beer company in the Northeast had its sales reps distribute water in its cans to flood victims. Coors provided free water in its cans to Pittsburghers when a barge break contaminated the drinking water. These as well as other public relations activities result in goodwill toward both the company and its products while at the same time benefiting society.

Exhibit 18-5 Advertising and personal selling should be designed to work together

Figure 18-6 Twelve ways to use advertising to sell more

1. *Save sales force time.* Sending a reprint of an advertisement ahead of time familiarizes the potential client with the product or service.
2. *Save lengthy explanations.* Sometimes ads can explain much of what the product does and even what it doesn't do, saving time as the salesperson only has to explain what is not already conveyed.
3. *Visual aids.* Ads can add impact to the presentation, reinforcing selling points.
4. *Ego boosters.* Telling prospects that an ad will appear in the media often makes the buyer feel she is important, and that she has inside information. Seeing the ad reinforces this.
5. *Personal refreshers.* Reviewing ad copy will often add insights to the salesperson, or remind him of key points that can be useful in a presentation.
6. *Clues to prospects' interests.* Sometimes prospects call in reference to an ad. By reviewing the ad, the salesperson can gain insights into the benefits the potential customer may be most interested in.
7. *Prove a point.* The printed word adds credibility to salespersons' verbal claims. One medium reinforces the other.
8. *Nudge indecisive prospects.* For indecisive prospects, a review of the ad campaign can often be the closer. If the ad is to include dealers' names, an additional benefit is offered, as the dealer may now directly benefit.
9. *Create preference.* Consistent advertising helps to build brand preference. Keeping customers and prospects aware of advertising creates favorable impressions of the company, the product or service and the salesperson.
10. *Provide follow-ups.* Sending a reprint of an ad after the sales presentation serves as a good reminder, and can be used to focus attention on key benefits offered in the ad and in the presentation. It also demonstrates concern on the part of the salesperson.
11. *Fight lower-priced competitors.* Ads can be used to show support and ward off low priced competitors. The salesperson can explain how the ad will help support the customer's own sales efforts and not have to get into price wars.
12. *Getting the customer into the act.* Asking the customer about the ads and getting his inputs helps cement relationships and provides valuable feedback to one's own organization. Often customers have ideas that may never have been thought of.

Source: Adapted from Ted Pollock, "12 ways to use your advertising to sell more," *American Salesman,* October 2002, pp. 10–15.

Exhibit 18-6 Research and consulting companies offer businesses direct-marketing services

Combining Personal Selling and Direct Marketing

Companies have found that integrating direct marketing, specifically telemarketing, into their field sales operations makes their sales efforts more effective. The cost of a sales call and the cost associated with closing the sale are already very high and on the increase. Many marketers have reduced these costs by combining telemarketing and sales efforts (a typical telesales call costs about 11 cents for each $1 in revenue generated).[17] A number of companies now offer consulting services to help organizations in the sales process including assisting in direct-marketing methods, as shown in Exhibit 18-6.

The telemarketing department is used to screen leads and—after qualifying potential buyers on the basis of interest, credit ratings, and the like—pass them on to the sales force. The net result is a higher percentage of sales closings, less wasted time by the sales force, and a lower average cost per sale. For example, IBM teamed up with Zacson Corp. to open an integrated teleservices center for its Northern California territory. The group handles inquiries, lead generation, and qualification; develops promotional campaigns; distributes PR materials; and does problem solving for IBM clients. The new relationship reduced IBM's customer contact costs by 97 percent, lowered sales visit costs from $500 to $15, and exceeded customer expectations 78 percent of the time.[18]

As shown in Figure 18-7, there has been a rapid growth in the use of the telemarketing/sales combination for other firms as well. They have determined the phone can be used effectively for service and follow-up functions as well as for growth-related activities. Supplementing personal selling efforts with phone calls frees the sales force to spend more time selling.

In addition to selling and supporting the sales efforts, the telemarketing staff provides a public relations dimension. Communicating with buyers more often creates goodwill, improving customer satisfaction and loyalty.

In addition to telemarketing, other forms of direct marketing have been combined successfully with personal selling. Direct mail and e-mail are commonly used methods for supporting sales. For example, many companies send out lead cards to screen prospective customers. The salesperson follows up on those who express a genuine interest, saving valuable time and increasing the potential for a sale. Other uses include database building and mining. Exhibit 18-7 shows an example of a highly used soft-

Figure 18-7 The growth of telemarketing as a sales function: reasons for growth (in percent)

	Telephone Sales and Service*	Field Sales*
Total growth related	58.0	61.8
Overall business growth or expansion	44.7	43.1
Adding product lines	10.2	8.0
Adding territories	3.1	10.7
Total system related	20.8	7.5
Added centralized telemarketing dept.	11.5	1.8
Added/changed computer system	6.2	4.4
Centralized sales and marketing	3.1	1.3
Customer demand	10.5	10.2
Cost efficiencies	1.4	0
Other	2.0	2.2
Can't tell/no response	9.8	18.2

*Figures add to more than 100 percent due to multiple mentions.

ware program available to assist marketers in creating and managing a database.

Combining Personal Selling and Sales Promotion

The program elements of sales promotion and personal selling also support each other. For example, many of the sales promotions targeted to resellers are presented by the sales force, who will ultimately be responsible for removing or replacing them as well.

While trade sales promotions are designed to support the reseller and are often targeted to the ultimate consumer, many other promotional tools are designed to assist the sales staff. Flip charts, leave-behinds, and specialty ads may be designed to assist salespeople in their presentations, serve as reminders, or just create goodwill. The number of materials available may range from just a few to hundreds, depending on the company. (If you ever get the chance, look into the trunk of a consumer-product salesperson's car. You will find everything from pens to calendars to flip charts to samples to lost baseball mitts—all but the last of which are used in the selling effort.) Other forms of sales promotions like contests and sweepstakes are also used, as noted earlier.

Likewise, many sales promotions are targeted at the sales force itself. Incentives such as free trips, cash bonuses, or gifts are often used to stimulate sales efforts. And, as we saw with resellers, contests and sweepstakes may also be used.

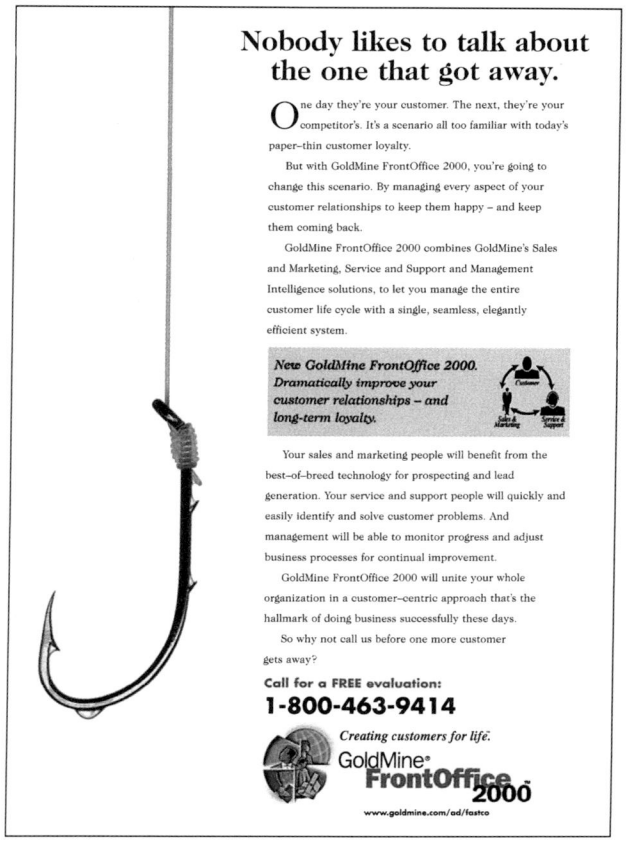

Exhibit 18-7 Goldmine is one of the more popular database management tools

Combining Personal Selling with the Internet

In the Internet chapter, we discussed the increasing use of the Internet as a support to personal selling. As noted, the Internet has been used to provide product information, generate leads, screen prospects, and build and market from databases. While many marketing managers see the Internet taking business away from channel members and direct sales, few are ready to relinquish their sales forces. Even though at least one study predicts that 98 percent of all large companies would be on the Internet by 2002, and that the ROI for direct sales on the Web is five times that for traditional direct marketing, most companies still see the sales force as an integral part of the IMC process—particularly for relationship building.[19] Many managers feel that the Web will be used to fulfill the more mundane tasks of order fulfillment and providing information. This in turn will allow the sales force to be more effective in closing orders, doing close selling, and focusing more attention on high-value and/or new customers. Future salespeople will do what is more profitable for the future—that is, sell and develop relationships, not take orders.

A rapidly growing use of the Internet is that of conducting online meetings in which the sales force and/or clients and potential clients participate. Some companies have found that they can save both time and money by conducting their sales meetings online rather than at a central location. More involved presentations—often referred to as "webinars"—may include a variety of purposes, from conducting job training for employees to making presentations and providing in-depth product information to existing and potential customers. (See Exhibit 18-8.)

It is important that the elements of the promotional program work together, as each has its specific advantages and disadvantages. While personal selling is valuable in accomplishing certain objectives and supporting other promotional tools, it must be supported by the other elements. Ads, sales promotions, and the like may be targeted to the ultimate user, resellers, or the organization's sales force. IMC Perspective 18-1 provides a few examples of companies that have successfully integrated personal selling and other IMC elements.

Exhibit 18-8 The Internet is used to conduct online meetings

IMC PERSPECTIVE 18-1

How Companies Integrate Personal Selling into the IMC Program

For many companies, personal selling has been the primary focus for promoting their goods and services. Other IMC program elements have assumed more of a support role and, in many instances, have not been used effectively by the marketing managers or the sales force. For many companies, all of this is changing—as reflected in the following examples:

• *Xerox—testing ads and sales promotions.* Barbara Basney, director of marketing communications at Xerox's Office Printing Business, is responsible for gathering hundreds of thousands of sales leads for the company's marketing database. Relying heavily on trade shows and direct mail, Basney realized that costs continued to increase but effectiveness did not. In an attempt to try something totally different and innovative, she signed on with the online division of advertising agency Young and Rubicam to test market a program designed specifically to generate leads. Together they launched three direct-response offers: (1) a sweepstakes with information about Xerox's printer and a chance to win a trip to the Winter Olympics in Salt Lake City; (2) a product-information-only banner ad that switches to color; and (3) an interactive game in which the banner ad told visitors to play "Phaser Blast." Each of the offers used links, banners, buttons, and pop-up advertising. The nine-month test exceeded Xerox's expectations, generating 96,000 sales leads in the first four months and 200,000 in the next five months, surpassing the goals established by 117 and 111 percent, respectively—at less than 50 percent of what such results would have cost using traditional methods. What worked? According to Basney, the sweepstakes and product information ad were about equally effective, and the interactive game was the "definite loser."

• *Audi—building a customer relationship program.* Audi's goal was to not have the relationship with the customer end after the sale was made. Operating on the assumption that the company's best potential customers were also its existing customers, the company initiated an online program to maintain contact, while allowing its sales force to concentrate on selling. Based on its television campaign for the new A4 model, Audi offered a downloadable screensaver that frequently broadcasted updated news and information automatically to the consumers' computers. After displaying the screensaver option on its website, Audi sent an e-mail to owners and prospects offering them the opportunity to download it. Over 10,000 people took advantage of the offer. Audi then began to maintain a continuous dialog with the adopters by sending them newsletters and updates. Click-through rates ranged from 25 to 35 percent on various parts of the site—well exceeding the standard rates—and car sales were 25 percent higher than they were the previous year, even in a down economy.

• *ConAgra—introducing a new product.* In a market saturated by ready-to-eat dinners few retailers predicted that Banquet Homestyle Bakes—a meal with the meat already packed in—would have any success. Store owners were reluctant to stock the product and give up valuable shelf space. But the product team was determined that it had a success after three years of research and test marketing. Working closely with the sales team, product managers gathered feedback while providing the sales force with research results and a great consumer story. Sampling (each box weighed 2 to 3 pounds) was supported with a humorous advertising campaign on television and in print, appearing in magazines such as *Good Housekeeping, Parenting, TV Guide,* and *Soap Opera Digest.* Bundling the product discounts with other ConAgra brands including Chef Boyardee and Hunt's Snack Packs helped, as did a contest called "Super

Meals/Super Moms," which included prizes such as maid service, flowers, and spa visits. The contest itself garnered a 77 percent participation rate from wholesalers. Finally, 100 college scholarship offers valued at $10,000 provided a nice public relations touch. How did it work? First-year sales totaled $125 million, the product had the highest repeat purchase rate of any supermarket product introduced in the previous five years, and the introduction was touted as one of the hottest new product introductions of the year by Information Resources Inc.'s "New Product Pacesetters" report.

The above examples are just a few of the many companies that have effectively integrated personal selling into their IMC programs. Each shows how the sales team and marketing can work together to achieve success—what an idea!

Sources: Sonia Reyes, "This One's a Stove Topper," *Brandweek*, Oct. 14, 2002, pp. M30-M33; "Xerox Tests Three Online Sales Lead Generation Tactics—Sweeps vs. Game vs. Product Info," marketingsherpa.com, Sept. 12, 2002, pp. 1-6; Sheree Curry, "E-Marketing Evolution," *Sales & Marketing Management*, June 2002, pp. 32-37.

Evaluating the Personal Selling Effort

Like all other elements of the promotional mix, personal selling must be evaluated on the basis of its contribution to the overall promotional effort. The costs of personal selling are often high, but the returns may be just as high.

Because the sales force is under the supervision of the sales manager, evaluations are typically based on sales criteria. Sales may be analyzed by total sales volume, territories, product line, customer type, or sales rep.[20] Other sales-related criteria such as new account openings and personal traits are also sometimes considered and may be increasing in importance (Figure 18-8).

From a promotional perspective, sales performance is important, as are the contributions of individuals in generating these sales. On the other hand, the promotions manager must evaluate the performance of personal selling as one program element contributing to the overall promotional program. So he or she needs to use different criteria in determining its effectiveness.

Criteria for Evaluating Personal Selling

A number of criteria may be used to evaluate the contribution of the personal selling effort to the promotional program. They include the following.

- *Provision of marketing intelligence*—the ability of the sales force to feed back information regarding competitive programs, customer reactions, market trends, and other factors that may be important in the development of the promotional program.
- *Follow-up activities*—the use and dissemination of promotional brochures and correspondences with new and existing customers, providing feedback on the effectiveness of various promotional programs.
- *Program implementations*—the number of promotional programs implemented; the number of shelf and/or counter displays used, and so forth; the implementation and assessment of cooperative advertising programs.
- *Attainment of communications objectives*—the number of accounts to whom presentations were made (awareness, evaluation), the number of trial offers accepted, and the like. (Specific criteria are often hard to agree on, as evidenced by IMC Perspective 18-2.).

Combining these criteria with those used by the sales department, the promotions manager should be able to accurately assess the effectiveness of the personal selling program. Making these evaluations requires a great deal of cooperation between the departments.

Figure 18-8 Criteria used to evaluate sales forces

Quantitative Measures	
Sales Results	Sales Efforts
Orders	*Sales Calls*
Number of orders obtained	Number made on current customers
Average order size (units or dollars)	Number made on potential new accounts
Batting average (orders ÷ sales calls)	Average time spent per call
Number of orders canceled by customers	Number of sales presentations
Sales Volume	Selling time versus nonselling time
Dollar sales volume	Call frequency ratio per customer type
Unit sales volume	*Selling Expenses*
By customer type	Average per sales call
By product category	As percentage of sales volume
Translated into market share	As percentage of sales quota
Percentage of sales quota achieved	By customer type
Margins	By product category
Gross margin	Direct-selling expense ratios
Net profit	Indirect-selling expense ratios
By customer type	*Customer Service*
By product category	Number of service calls
Customer Accounts	Displays set up
Number of new accounts	Delivery cost per unit sold
Number of lost accounts	Months of inventory held, by customer type
Percentage of accounts sold	Number of customer complaints
Number of overdue accounts	Percentage of goods returned
Dollar amount of accounts receivable	
Collections made of accounts receivable	

Qualitative Measures	
Sales Results	Sales Efforts
Selling Skills	*Sales-related activities*
Knowing the company and its policies	Territory management: sales call preparation, scheduling, routing, and time utilization
Knowing competitors' products and sales strategies	Marketing intelligence: new product ideas, competitive activities, new customer preferences
Use of marketing and technical backup teams	Follow-ups: use of promotional brochures and correspondence with current and potential accounts
Understanding of selling techniques	Customer relations
Customer feedback (positive and negative)	Report preparation and timely submission
Product knowledge	Personal characteristics
Customer knowledge	Cooperation, human relations, enthusiasm, motivation, judgment, care of company property, appearance, self-improvement efforts, patience, punctuality, initiative, resourcefulness, health, sales management potential, ethical and moral behavior
Execution of selling techniques	
Quality of sales presentations	
Communication skills	

IMC PERSPECTIVE 18-2

Measuring the Effectiveness of the Sales Force—Is It Really Just ROI?

Probably for as long as there have been sales forces, managers have sought ways to determine whether they are effective or not. In the past, salespeople were evaluated on the basis of their sales—that is, did they reach their sales quotas? As the role of the sales force changed from being purely concerned with selling to becoming more involved in marketing and more responsible for maintaining customer relationships, managers recognized the need for expanding evaluative criteria beyond just the achievement of sales goals. The evaluation criteria of today are vastly different from those in the past. Sure, sales are still important, but now other measures are gaining in importance as well.

One of the more often discussed measures is ROI (return on investment). More and more top executives are asking their sales managers for accountability—as in "Are we getting the returns we seek from the sales force?" The idea is that by measuring the impact of programs designed to aid the selling process as well as measuring sales closures, the marketing team can be more effective and efficient. Unfortunately, it isn't always that easy. In a survey conducted in 2002 of companies with a marketing budget of $1 million or more, 56 percent indicated they had no system for measuring the ROI on their marketing investments. As noted by David Reibstein of the University of Pennsylvania's Wharton School of Business, "In marketing, benefits like advertising impact aren't easily put into dollar returns. It takes a leap of faith to come up with a number." Marketers know that it is often difficult to separate advertising, promotions, and other communications efforts from the selling effort.

Then what about ranking them? Many of the largest firms in America, including GE, Ford, and Microsoft, rank employees by categorizing them as top 20 percent, bottom 10 percent, and the like, with the top getting highly rewarded and the bottom likely to be let go. Others use A, B, or C grades, with two straight C's constituting grounds for dismissal. Cruel? While Jack Welch, ex-CEO of GE, and Dick Grote, president of Grote Consulting (a performance management company in Texas), don't think so, eight Ford employees did, and they filed a class-action lawsuit claiming discrimination. A study of 17 large companies, conducted by the American Productivity and Quality Center, corroborated the positions of Grote and Welch, concluding that forced rankings were the most effective way to identify and reward core competencies. Whether rankings outweigh discrimination is still to be seen, however, and may have to be decided in the courts rather than the marketing office.

How about sales per employee as a measure of effectiveness? Saleforce.com, for example, uses sales per employee to compare the relative performance of its sales forces. A steady rise in sales per employee is a sign of improving efficiency. Siebel Systems also employees this system, releasing the lowest-performing 10 percent of its employees. Altera, Bea Systems, and Sun Microsystems also use measures of sales generated by employees to determine if they are operating "fat" or "lean." James S. Pepitone, chairman of Pepitone, Berkshire, Piaget Worldwide, a management firm based in Dallas, is not sold on the concept. He considers it a relative metric, arguing that "it only has meaning in comparison to itself" and should be used only as an internal benchmark, and a ballpark figure, confounded by numerous other factors.

Well, then, what about quotas? Perhaps we should go to the old reliable and set sales targets and goals. Many companies are scrapping sales quota systems in favor of compensation packages that promote new behaviors among salespeople (like maintaining customer relationships), arguing that the old system doesn't work anymore. Salespeople have both positive and negative attitudes toward quota dropping. While some feel that it may reduce their sales effectiveness and motivation, others recognize that in today's customer relationship world, providing service and keeping old customers are

as important as finding new ones. They are glad to see the importance of sales quotas diminished.

Then what's a company to do? Many successful companies now use a combination of measures. For example, Siebel Systems—yes, the same company mentioned above—notes that approximately 40 percent of each salesperson's incentive compensation is based on his or her customers' reported satisfaction with service and implementation of products purchased. Nortel, eBay, and AT&T employ similar measures. At JD Edwards, up to 20 percent of a sales rep's earnings are based on two such surveys per year. Many other companies are also moving away from traditional quota-based systems, combining sales goals with less traditional measures such as customer satisfaction, repeat business, profitable revenues, and internal communications. Other measures include prospecting, qualifying, and generating sign-ups to the company's website.

Regardless of what measures are being employed—and there are many more than those mentioned here—the days of the sales quota-based system are on the way out. And no one could be happier than the salespeople themselves.

Sources: Erin Strout, "ROI: More Vital Than Ever," *Sales & Marketing Management,* January 2002, p. 51; Andy Cohen, "Should You Rank Your Salespeople?" *Sales & Marketing Management,* August 2001, p. 13; Kim Cross, "Does Your Team Measure Up?" *Business 2.0,* June 12, 2001, pp. 22-28; Eilene Zimmerman, "Quota Busters," *Sales & Marketing Management,* January 2001, pp. 59-63.

Summary

This chapter discussed the nature of personal selling and the role this program element plays in the promotional mix. The role of personal selling in the IMC program varies depending on the nature of the industry, competition, and market conditions. In many industries (for example, industrial markets) the personal selling component may receive the most attention, while in others (for example, consumer nondurables) it plays a minor role. However, managers in most industries believe the importance of this program element will continue to increase over the next few years.

Personal selling offers the marketer the opportunity for a dyadic communications process (a two-way exchange of information). The salesperson can instantly assess the situation and the effects of the communication and adapt the message if necessary.

While this exchange lets the sales rep tailor the message specifically to the needs and wants of the receiver, its disadvantage is a nonstandardized message, since the final message communicated is under the salesperson's control. In an attempt to develop a standard communication, marketers provide their reps with flip charts, leave-behinds, and other promotional pieces.

Evaluation of the personal selling effort is usually under the control of the sales department, since sales is the most commonly used criterion. The promotions manager must assess the contribution of personal selling with nonsales-oriented criteria as well, integrating this element into the overall IMC program.

Key Terms

personal selling, 598
dyadic communication, 599
provider stage, 600
persuader stage, 600
prospector stage, 600
problem-solver stage, 601
procreator stage, 601
relationship marketing, 602
order taking, 603
creative selling, 603
missionary sales, 603
prospecting, 603
leads, 604
prospects, 604
qualified prospects, 604
close, 604
cross sell, 605

Discussion Questions

1. The lead in to this chapter discusses some of the ways that companies attempt to motivate salespeople without just givng them money. Following upon this, give some examples of how integrating other program elements might also be effective in motivating the sales force.

2. The role of the salesperson has undergone significant changes in recent years. Describe some of these changes, and give examples of the new roles salespeople are being asked to perform.

3. It has been said that the importance of the sales force varies at various stages in the communications hierarchies. Discuss this idea, providing examples to support your position.

4. Organizations are becoming increasingly concerned about dishonesty within their sales organizations. Describe some of the ways that sales people may engage in dishonest activities. What can managers do to avoid such problems?

5. The text describes a number of ways that sales people can use advertising to help them sell more. Discuss these, providing examples of each.

6. One of the advantages of personal selling is the ability for dyadic communication. Explain what this term means. Why is this an advantage over other media?

7. Explain what is meant by "the new role of personal selling." How does this new role differ from what personal selling has involved in the past?

8. Explain why the high costs of personal selling might be warranted. Give a specific example of a situation where this is the case.

9. Explain why the combination of personal selling and advertising may provide benefits that exceed just personal selling alone.

10. Describe some of the criteria used to evaluate qualitative aspects of the effectiveness of the salesperson. How might these be used to support the IMC program?

Measuring the Effectiveness of the Promotional Program

19

Chapter Objectives

1. To understand reasons for measuring promotional program effectiveness.
2. To know the various measures used in assessing promotional program effectiveness.
3. To evaluate alternative methods for measuring promotional program effectiveness.
4. To understand the requirements of proper effectiveness research.

Measuring the Impact of IMC—Bringing It All Together

As marketers continue to allocate dollars to a variety of IMC tools, the question is, How well is the IMC program working? Unfortunately, while numerous efforts have been made to determine effectiveness of specific program elements, only recently have marketers made attempts to examine the interactive effect of communications methods. Here are some of the results of these studies:

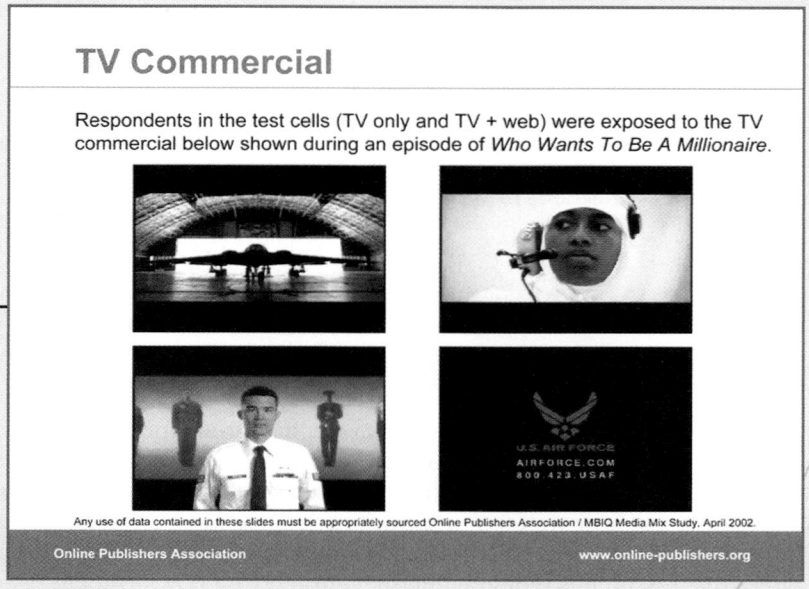

- *Online Publishers Association.* The Online Publishers Association, in partnership with Millward Brown and IntelliQuest, conducted a test to determine how advertising can work in combination with off-line (traditional) advertising. Specifically, the research was designed to test recall and memorability of online advertising and television advertising—alone and in combination. Using an advertisement for the U.S. Air Force, three groups were exposed to the ad by (1) visiting a web page on ESPN.com, (2) watching an episode of *Who Wants to Be a Millionaire,* or (3) watching the TV program and visiting the web page. A control group with no exposure to the ads was also included. The results indicated that:
  - Brand awareness was significantly higher than, and day-after recall was more than double, that of the control group when exposed to online ads.
  - Online advertising is more likely to be seen than TV advertising.
  - Those exposed to both online and TV ads were significantly more likely to recall the TV commercial.

  Overall, the study concluded that there was a synergistic effect when TV and online are used in combination, leading to a 9 percent gain in recall. When the TV and online ads were both used, there was a 48 percent increase in recognition of the online ads, leading to the conclusion that online supports TV commercials and vice versa.
- *MSN online study.* Microsoft joined forces with research company Marketing Evolution, Dynamic Logic, the Advertising Research Foundation, the Interactive Advertising Bureau, and Unilever to examine the impact of online advertising when combined with traditional advertising. Branding metrics such as unaided and aided awareness, brand associations, and purchase intent were measured for Dove and Dove Nutrium Bar soaps, using individual media and a combination of online with TV and print. The results indicated that increasing the frequency of online advertising efficiently improved branding results and that combining online advertising with the more

traditional TV and print media increased the effectiveness of the entire campaign.

- *Differences in media effectiveness.* In an examination of four product categories (automobiles, luxury watches, shampoos, and fast food), it was found that TV was the most used medium for all four product categories and that it was most useful for providing information on low-involvement products while the Internet was more useful for high-involvement products. TV was also shown to be more useful for providing information on affective versus rational decisions. The authors of the study concluded that the Internet should be considered in conjunction with other traditional media alternatives, with its role varying depending on the product category. Further, they noted that there is a need to develop an integrative media plan whereby media executives can determine the relative contribution of various media.

So what do we conclude from these studies? In a nutshell, they confirm the fact that the various elements of an IMC program each make their own contributions to the overall impact of the campaign. They also reveal that a combination of the program elements is likely to have a greater impact than the effect of each element used alone. In other words, the whole really is greater than the sum of its parts.

Sources: Online Publishers Association/MBIQ Media Mix Study, April 2002; Sung-Joon Yoon and Joo-Ho Kim, "Is the Internet More Effective Than Traditional Media? Factors Affecting the Choice of Media," *Journal of Advertising Research,* November–December 2001, pp. 53–60; "Interactive Advertising Bureau, Doubleclick, MSN, and CNET Networks Release Groundbreaking Online Brand Research Findings," www.microsoft.com/press pass, July 1, 2001, pp. 17–18.

As marketers spend their communications dollars in numerous media, the need to determine the effectiveness of these expenditures becomes increasingly important. Both clients and agencies are continually striving to determine whether their communications are working and how well they are working relative to other options. Unfortunately, there seems to be little agreement on the best measures to use. Almost everyone agrees that research is required, but they disagree on how it should be conducted and how the results should be used. At the same time, as can be seen by the lead-in to this chapter, companies and organizations are working together in an attempt to provide answers to these questions.

Measuring the effectiveness of the promotional program is a critical element in the promotional planning process. Research allows the marketing manager to evaluate the performance of specific program elements and provides input into the next period's situation analysis. It is a necessary ingredient to a continuing planning process, yet it is often not carried out.

In this chapter, we discuss some reasons firms should measure the effectiveness of their IMC programs, as well as why many decide not to. We also examine how, when, and where such measurements can be conducted. Most of our attention is devoted to measuring the effects of advertising because much more time and effort have been expended developing evaluation measures in advertising than in the other promotional areas. We will, however, discuss measurement in other areas of the IMC program as well. (In some of these areas, the measures are more directly observable—for example, direct marketing and personal selling.) You'll recall that we addressed the methods used to evaluate many of the other promotional elements in previous chapters.

It is important to understand that in this chapter we are concerned with research that is conducted in an evaluative role—that is, to measure the effectiveness of advertising and promotion and/or to assess various strategies before implementing them. This is not to be confused with research discussed earlier in the text to help develop the promotional program, although the two can (and should) be used together. While evaluative research may occur at various times throughout the promotional process (including the development stage), it is conducted specifically to assess the effects of various strategies. We begin our discussion with the reasons effectiveness should be measured as well as some of the reasons firms do not do so.

Arguments for and Against Measuring Effectiveness

Almost any time one engages in a project or activity, whether for work or fun, some measure of performance occurs. In sports you may compare your golf score against par or your time on a ski course to other skiers' performance. In business, employees are generally given objectives to accomplish, and their job evaluations are based on their ability to achieve these objectives. Advertising and promotion should not be an exception. It is important to determine how well the communications program is working and to measure this performance against some standards.

Reasons to Measure Effectiveness

Assessing the effectiveness of ads both before they are implemented and after the final versions have been completed and fielded offers a number of advantages:

1. *Avoiding costly mistakes.* The top three advertisers in the United States spent over $7.3 billion in advertising and promotion in 2001. The top 10 spent a total of over $21 billion. This is a lot of money to be throwing around without some understanding of how well it is being spent. If the program is not achieving its objectives, the marketing manager needs to know so he or she can stop spending (wasting) money on it.

Just as important as the out-of-pocket costs is the opportunity loss due to poor communications. If the advertising and promotions program is not accomplishing its objectives, not only is the money spent lost but so too is the potential gain that could result from an effective program. Thus, measuring the effects of advertising does not just save money. It also helps the firm maximize its investment. For example, one mass merchant discovered that promoting Tide detergent generated more cross-selling opportunities than did promotions of nonpremium brands like Purex (Exhibit 19-1). At the same time, promotions of motor oil had no cross-selling impact.[1]

2. *Evaluating alternative strategies.* Typically a firm has a number of strategies under consideration. For example, there may be some question as to which medium should be used or whether one message is more effective than another. Or the decision may be between two promotional program elements. For example, should research be spent on sponsorships or on advertising? One retailer found that advertising do-it-yourself products on the radio was effective in rural areas but not in urban locales.[2] Research may be designed to help the manager determine which strategy is most likely to be effective. Companies often test alternate versions of their advertising in different cities to determine which ad communicates most effectively. They may also explore different forms of couponing.

3. *Increasing the efficiency of advertising in general.* You may have heard the expression "can't see the forest for the trees." Sometimes advertisers get so close to the project they lose sight of what they are seeking, and because they know what they are trying to say, they expect their audience will also understand. They may use technical jargon that not everyone is familiar with. Or the creative department may get too creative or too sophisticated and lose the meaning that needs to be communicated. How many times have you seen an ad and asked yourself what it was trying to say, or how often have you seen an ad that you really like, but you can't remember the brand name? Conducting research helps companies develop more efficient and effective communications. An increasing number of clients are demanding accountability for their promotional programs and putting more pressure on the agencies to produce. As IMC Perspective 19-1 demonstrates, effective research can be used for both of these purposes.

4. *Determining if objectives are achieved.* In a well-designed IMC plan, specific objectives are established. If objectives are attained, new ones need to be established in the next planning period. An assessment of how program elements led to the attainment of the goals should take place, and/or reasons for less-than-desired achievements must be determined.

Exhibit 19-1 Tide has been shown to be an effective promotional draw

IMC PERSPECTIVE 19-1

The ARF David Ogilvy Research Awards—No Longer Just Ad Campaign Awards

One of the most prestigious awards an advertiser can receive is the David Ogilvy Award. The award is given by the Advertising Research Foundation (ARF) in honor of researcher-turned-adman David Ogilvy, whose own work always stressed the role of research in developing, evaluating, and improving advertising. To win an Ogilvy Award, the candidate must demonstrate how research was used in developing a program and show marketing success. Awards are given in three areas—(1) services, (2) durables, and (3) packaged goods—and an overall grand-prize winner is announced. Judges come from academia, advertising agencies, companies, and research firms. This year's winners included:

• *Grand Winner: Robert Wood Johnson Foundation—"The Covering Kids Campaign."* In 1997 the federal government allocated money to each state to offer health coverage to children in low-income families. Unfortunately, much of this money went unused. The Robert Wood Johnson Foundation used its own monies to determine why this was the case, as well as to develop a campaign to communicate to parents. The foundation worked with Wirthlin Worldwide, a marketing research company, to determine the motivations, or lack of motivations, for taking advantage of this opportunity. The research demonstrated that financial aid and emotional issues were involved and that while low-income families were concerned with insuring their children, there was a lack of knowledge of the program as well as a number of misperceptions regarding qualifications. In addition, semantics mattered, as many families felt that "insurance" was synonymous with high cost and that if it was free, it was a "handout."

Based on this research, the advertising agency of Greer, Margolis, Mitchell, Burns and Associates developed a "values approach" in which ad messages stated "You could be eligible" and funneled callers directly into the program. The campaign included TV, outdoor, radio, and print ads differentiated for various ethnic groups. An Internet site was also included, as was a toll-free number to call for more assistance.

The results reflected the value of the research, as 8 out of every 10 persons who called the national hotline did so after seeing a Covering Kids ad, and the number of calls doubled during the time the ad campaign ran. Calls to regional toll-free numbers increased by as much as 745 percent!

• *Distinguished Finalist: United States Navy—"An URL in Every Port."* Joining the armed services is not an easy decision. The U.S. Navy had found that its competition included colleges, trade schools, the workforce, and other branches of military services. To compete successfully, the Navy felt that it had to conduct research into the motivations and attitudes of high school students—its primary target audience. Working with advertising agency Campbell-Ewald, the Navy created an extensive research portfolio that included interviews with Navy personnel, recruiters, and decision influencers such as parents and teachers. Focus groups, brand metaphor exercises, and a quantitative survey of teens were all used to explore the values and attitudes of teens. The resulting psychographic profile showed that "Adventurers" (active, fun-oriented outdoor types), "Vocationalists" (concerned about the future and looking for vocational skills to improve their job prospects), and "Independent Skill Seekers" (uncertain about their future, looking for vocational and leadership skills) were most likely to be interested in joining the Navy. However, few of the Generation Y audience knew much, if anything, about the Navy beyond what they had seen in movies. The agency and the Navy knew they had to put something together to assist in the decision process.

A limited budget meant that a wide use of traditional advertising media like TV was impractical. Rather, a "Life Accelerator" web-based program was designed to present the Navy in a nonthreatening

environment as well as one in which teenagers were comfortable (teens are online 50 percent more than adults). The website was supported by an economical media plan designed to drive traffic to the site. Radio (95 percent of teens listen 10 or more hours a week) and other Internet venues received a lot of the resources. TV was used in a more traditional sense—e.g., MTV as well as a direct-response medium to generate leads to be followed up on by Navy personnel.

In the first few months of the campaign, the Life Accelerator had more than 200 million hits, which were in turn referred to recruitment tables. Potential prospects spent 50 percent more time at the site and viewed more pages, and recruitment offices reported an increase in candidates who came in with Life Accelerator pages in hand. Overall, 225,318 leads were generated, 13 percent above the goal. The goal of 53,000 enlistments was easily achieved.

Not all of the Ogilvy Awards are for services or nonprofits (in the chapter we will discuss some winners in the other categories), and not all of the winners employ the same research methods or media strategies. All do, however, use research to guide their strategies, as well as to measure its effectiveness.

What is really interesting is that the Ogilvy Awards, started decades ago as an advertising award in which the ad campaign was based on research, have now become much broader in scope. The above two examples demonstrate that the award is really now more of an IMC award, with an emphasis on the overall campaign—whether or not advertising is a major component.

Sources: "2002 ARF David Ogilvy Research Award Winners," www.arfsite.org, Nov. 4, 2002; "The 2002 ARF David Ogilvy Research Awards," *Journal of Advertising Research,* July-August 2002 (special section).

Reasons Not to Measure Effectiveness

Companies give a number of reasons for not measuring the effectiveness of advertising and promotions strategies:

1. *Cost.* Perhaps the most commonly cited reason for not testing (particularly among smaller firms) is the expense. Good research can be expensive, in terms of both time and money. Many managers decide that time is critical and they must implement the program while the opportunity is available. Many believe the monies spent on research could be better spent on improved production of the ad, additional media buys, and the like.

While the first argument may have some merit, the second does not. Imagine what would happen if a poor campaign were developed or the incentive program did not motivate the target audience. Not only would you be spending money without the desired effects, but the effort could do more harm than good. Spending more money to buy media does not remedy a poor message or substitute for an improper promotional mix. For example, one of the nation's leading brewers watched its test-market sales for a new brand of beer fall short of expectations. The problem, it thought, was an insufficient media buy. The solution, it decided, was to buy all the TV time available that matched its target audience. After two months sales had not improved, and the product was abandoned in the test market. Analysis showed the problem was not in the media but rather in the message, which communicated no reason to buy. Research would have identified the problem, and millions of dollars and a brand might have been saved. The moral: Spending research monies to gain increased exposure to the wrong message is not a sound management decision.

2. *Research problems.* A second reason cited for not measuring effectiveness is that it is difficult to isolate the effects of promotional elements. Each variable in the marketing mix affects the success of a product or service. Because it is often difficult to measure the contribution of each marketing element directly, some managers become frustrated and decide not to test at all. They say, "If I can't determine the specific effects, why spend the money?"

This argument also suffers from weak logic. While we agree that it is not always possible to determine the dollar amount of sales contributed by promotions, research can provide useful results. As demonstrated by the introduction and examples in IMC Perspective 19-1, communications effectiveness can be measured and may carry over to sales or other behaviors.

3. *Disagreement on what to test.* The objectives sought in the promotional program may differ by industry, by stage of the product life cycle, or even for different people

within the firm. The sales manager may want to see the impact of promotions on sales, top management may wish to know the impact on corporate image, and those involved in the creative process may wish to assess recall and/or recognition of the ad. Lack of agreement on what to test often results in no testing.

Again, there is little rationale for this position. With the proper design, many or even all of the above might be measured. Since every promotional element is designed to accomplish its own objectives, research can be used to measure its effectiveness in doing so.

4. *The objections of creative.* It has been argued by many (and denied by others) that the creative department does not want its work to be tested and many agencies are reluctant to submit their work for testing. This is sometimes true. Ad agencies' creative departments argue that tests are not true measures of the creativity and effectiveness of ads; applying measures stifles their creativity; and the more creative the ad, the more likely it is to be successful. They want permission to be creative without the limiting guidelines marketing may impose. The Chiat/Day ad shown in Exhibit 19-2 reflects how many people in the advertising business feel about this subject.

At the same time, the marketing manager is ultimately responsible for the success of the product or brand. Given the substantial sums being allocated to advertising and promotion, it is the manager's right, and responsibility, to know how well a specific program—or a specific ad—will perform in the market. Interestingly, in a study examining the 200 most awarded commercials over a 2-year span, it was shown that 86 percent were deemed effective in achieving their goals, versus only 33 percent for other ads—proving that creative ads are effective.[3]

Exhibit 19-2 Chiat/Day expresses its opinion of recall tests

5. *Time.* A final reason given for not testing is a lack of time. Managers believe they already have too much to do and just can't get around to testing, and they don't want to wait to get the message out because they might miss the window of opportunity.

Planning might be the solution to the first problem. While many managers are overworked and time-poor, research is just too important to skip.

The second argument can also be overcome with proper planning. While timeliness is critical, getting the wrong message out is of little or no value and may even be harmful. There will be occasions where market opportunities require choosing between testing and immediate implementation. But even then some testing may help avoid mistakes or improve effectiveness. For example, after the terrorist attacks on September 11, Motorola developed an ad designed to portray the quality of its mobile phones by showing an FDNY fireman using one. While the ad may have had good intentions, many people felt it was an attempt to capitalize on a tragedy. As a result, much negative publicity was generated. The problem could have been avoided had Motorola pretested consumers' responses to the ad. In most instances, proper planning and scheduling will allow time for research.

Conducting Research to Measure Advertising Effectiveness

What to Test

We now examine how to measure the effects of communications. This section considers what elements to evaluate, as well as where and how such evaluations should occur.

In Chapter 5, we discussed the components of the communications model (source, message, media, receiver) and the importance of each in the promotional program. Marketers need to determine how each is affecting the communications process. Other decisions made in the promotional planning process must also be evaluated.

Source Factors An important question is whether the spokesperson being used is effective and how the target market will respond to him or her. For example, Tiger Woods has proved to be a successful salesperson for Nike and Buick. Or a product spokesperson may be an excellent source initially but, owing to a variety of reasons, may lose impact over time. For example, Britney Spears had been an effective spokesperson for Pepsi, particularly with the teen market. The question was, Will she be able to retain this relationship as she gets older? Apparently Pepsi thought not, as her contract was not renewed. In other instances, changes in the source's attractiveness or likeability or other external factors may lead to changes in source effectiveness. Pepsi pulled a TV sport featuring rapper Ludacris after Fox TV's Bill O'Reilly attacked the violent lyrics in Ludacris's songs.[4]

Message Variables Both the message and the means by which it is communicated are bases for evaluation. For example, in the beer example discussed earlier, the message never provided a reason for consumers to try the new product. In other instances, the message may not be strong enough to pull readers into the ad by attracting their attention or clear enough to help them evaluate the product. Sometimes the message is memorable but doesn't achieve the other goals set by management. One study showed that 7 of the 25 products that scored highest on interest and memorability in Video Storyboard Tests' ad test had flat or declining sales.[5] A number of factors regarding the message and its delivery may have an impact on its effectiveness, including the headline, illustrations, text, and layout.

Many ads are never seen by the public because of the message they convey. For example, an ad in which Susan Anton ate a slice of Pizza Hut pizza was considered too erotic for the company's small-town image. Likewise, an ad created for General Electric in which Uncle Sam got slapped in the face (to demonstrate our growing trade imbalance) was killed by the company's chair.[6]

Media Strategies Media decisions need to be evaluated. Research may be designed to determine which media class (for example, broadcast versus print), subclass (newspaper versus magazines), or specific vehicles (which newspapers or magazines) generate the most effective results. The location within a particular medium

(front page versus back page) and size of ad or length of commercial also merit examination. For example, research has demonstrated that readers pay more attention to larger ads.[7] As shown earlier, a variety of methods have been employed to measure the effectiveness of advertising on the Internet. Similarly, direct-response advertisers on TV have found that some programs are more effective than others. One successful direct marketer found that old TV shows yield more responses than first runs:

> The fifth rerun of "Leave It to Beaver" will generate much more response than will the first run of a prime-time television program. Who cares if you miss something you have seen four times before? But you do care when it's the first time you've seen it.[8]

Another factor is the **vehicle option source effect,** "the differential impact that the advertising exposure will have on the same audience member if the exposure occurs in one media option rather than another."[9] People perceive ads differently depending on their context.[10]

A final factor in media decisions involves scheduling. The evaluation of flighting versus pulsing or continuous schedules is important, particularly given the increasing costs of media time. As discussed in Chapter 10 and IMC Perspective 19-1, there is evidence to support the fact that continuity may lead to a more effective media schedule than does flighting. Likewise, there may be opportunities associated with increasing advertising weights in periods of downward sales cycles or recessions. The manager experimenting with these alternative schedules and/or budget outlays should attempt to measure their differential impact.[11]

Budgeting Decisions A number of studies have examined the effects of budget size on advertising effectiveness and the effects of various ad expenditures on sales. Many companies have also attempted to determine whether increasing their ad budget directly increases sales. This relationship is often hard to determine, perhaps because using sales as an indicator of effectiveness ignores the impact of other marketing mix elements. More definitive conclusions may be possible if other dependent variables, such as the communications objectives stated earlier, are used.

When to Test

Virtually all test measures can be classified according to when they are conducted. **Pretests** are measures taken before the campaign is implemented; **posttests** occur after the ad or commercial has been in the field. A variety of pretests and posttests are available to the marketer, each with its own methodology designed to measure some aspect of the advertising program. Figure 19-1 classifies these testing methods.

Pretesting Pretests may occur at a number of points, from as early on as idea generation to rough execution to testing the final version before implementing it. More than one type of pretest may be used. For example, concept testing (which is discussed later in this chapter) may take place at the earliest development of the ad or commercial, when little more than an idea, basic concept, or positioning statement is under

Figure 19-1 Classification of testing methods

Pretests		
Laboratory Methods		
Consumer juries	Theater tests	Readability tests
Portfolio tests	Rough tests	Comprehension and reaction tests
Physiological measures	Concept tests	
Field Methods		
Dummy advertising vehicles	On-air tests	
Posttests		
Field Methods		
Recall tests	Single-source systems	Recognition tests
Association measures	Inquiry tests	Tracking studies

consideration. Ogilvy Award winner GM used focus groups to derive the concepts to promote its new minivan. In other instances, layouts of the ad campaign that include headlines, some body copy, and rough illustrations are used. For TV commercials, storyboards and animatics may be tested. The GM minivan research also involved the evaluation of six animatics. In these tests specific shortcomings were identified, and the ads were changed to enhance certain executional elements.

The methodologies employed to conduct pretests vary. In focus groups, participants freely discuss the meanings they get from the ads, consider the relative advantages of alternatives, and even suggest improvements or additional themes. In addition to or instead of the focus groups, consumers are asked to evaluate the ad on a series of rating scales. (Different agencies use different measures.) In-home interviews, mall intercept, or laboratory methods may be used to gather the data.

The advantage of pretesting at this stage is that feedback is relatively inexpensive. Any problems with the concept or the way it is to be delivered are identified before large amounts of money are spent in development. Sometimes more than one version of the ad is evaluated to determine which is most likely to be effective.

A study of 4,637 on-air commercials designed to build normative intelligence conducted by MSW Group (formerly McCollum Spielman Worldwide) found that only 19 percent were considered outstanding or really good. Nearly twice as many (34 percent) were failures. On the other hand, of those spots that were pretested before the final form was aired, the share of good to outstanding rose to 37 percent, while the failure rate fell to 9 percent.[12] This is certainly a testimonial to the value of pretesting.

The disadvantage is that mock-ups, storyboards, or animatics may not communicate nearly as effectively as the final product. The mood-enhancing and/or emotional aspects of the message are very difficult to communicate in this format. Another disadvantage is time delays. Many marketers believe being first in the market offers them a distinct advantage over competitors, so they forgo research to save time and ensure this position.

Posttesting

Posttesting is also common among both advertisers and ad agencies (with the exception of testing commercials for wearout). Posttesting is designed to (1) determine if the campaign is accomplishing the objectives sought and (2) serve as input into the next period's situation analysis. An excellent example of using research to guide future advertising strategies is reflected in an experiment conducted by Lowe's, the nation's second-largest home improvement retailer. In a study designed to test 36 different versions of covers for its catalogs (which are sent to between 30 and 40 million homes per year), the company determined that by putting more products on the covers, using real pictures rather than cartoons, and reducing the size of the catalog, the catalogs were more effective. Other tests varying the number of TV spots, newspaper ads, and sports sponsorships led to increases in advertising spending and affirmation of the company's sponsorship of NASCAR auto racing (Exhibit 19-3).[13] A variety of posttest measures are available, most of which involve survey research methods.

Exhibit 19-3 Research affirmed the value of a NASCAR sponsorship for Lowe's

Where to Test

In addition to when to test, decisions must be made as to *where.* These tests may take place in either laboratory or field settings.

Laboratory Tests

In **laboratory tests,** people are brought to a particular location where they are shown ads and/or commercials. The testers either ask questions about them or measure participants' responses by other methods—for example, pupil dilation, eye tracking, or galvanic skin response.

The major advantage of the lab setting is the *control* it affords the researcher. Changes in copy, illustration, formats, colors, and the like can be manipulated inexpensively and the differential impact of each assessed. This makes it much easier for the researcher to isolate the contribution of each factor.

The major disadvantage is the lack of *realism.* Perhaps the greatest effect of this lack of realism is a **testing bias.** When people are

brought into a lab (even if it has been designed to look like a living room), they may scrutinize the ads much more closely than they would at home. A second problem with this lack of realism is that it cannot duplicate the natural viewing situation, complete with the distractions or comforts of home. Looking at ads in a lab setting may not be the same as viewing at home on the couch, with the spouse, kids, dog, cat, and parakeet chirping in the background. (A bit later you will see that some testing techniques have made progress in correcting this deficiency. No, they did not bring in the dogs and the parakeets.) Overall, however, the control offered by this method probably outweighs the disadvantages, which accounts for the frequent use of lab methods.

Field Tests

Field tests are tests of the ad or commercial under natural viewing situations, complete with the realism of noise, distractions, and the comforts of home. Field tests take into account the effects of repetition, program content, and even the presence of competitive messages.

The major disadvantage of field tests is the lack of control. It may be impossible to isolate causes of viewers' evaluations. If atypical events occur during the test, they may bias the results. Competitors may attempt to sabotage the research. And field tests usually take more time and money to conduct, so the results are not available to be acted on quickly. Thus, realism is gained at the expense of other important factors. It is up to the researcher to determine which trade-offs to make.

How to Test

Our discussion of what should be tested, when, and where was general and designed to establish a basic understanding of the overall process as well as some key terms. In this section, we discuss more specifically some of the methods commonly used at each stage. First, however, it is important to establish some criteria by which to judge ads and commercials.

Conducting evaluative research is not easy. Twenty-one of the largest U.S. ad agencies have endorsed a set of principles aimed at "improving the research used in preparing and testing ads, providing a better creative product for clients, and controlling the cost of TV commercials."[14] This set of nine principles, called **PACT (Positioning Advertising Copy Testing),** defines *copy testing* as research "which is undertaken when a decision is to be made about whether advertising should run in the marketplace. Whether this stage utilizes a single test or a combination of tests, its purpose is to aid in the judgment of specific advertising executions."[15] The nine principles of good copy testing are shown in Figure 19-2.

As you can see, advertisers and their clients are concerned about developing *appropriate* testing methods. Adherence to these principles may not make for perfect test-

Figure 19-2 Positioning Advertising Copy Testing (PACT)

1. Provide measurements that are relevant to the objectives of the advertising.
2. Require agreement about how the results will be used in advance of each specific test.
3. Provide multiple measurements (because single measurements are not adequate to assess ad performance).
4. Be based on a model of human response to communications—the reception of a stimulus, the comprehension of the stimulus, and the response to the stimulus.
5. Allow for consideration of whether the advertising stimulus should be exposed more than once.
6. Require that the more finished a piece of copy is, the more soundly it can be evaluated and require, as a minimum, that alternative executions be tested in the same degree of finish.
7. Provide controls to avoid the biasing effects of the exposure context.
8. Take into account basic considerations of sample definition.
9. Demonstrate reliability and validity.

Objective:	Explores consumers' responses to various ad concepts as expressed in words, pictures, or symbols.
Method:	Alternative concepts are exposed to consumers who match the characteristics of the target audience. Reactions and evaluations of each are sought through a variety of methods, including focus groups, direct questioning, and survey completion. Sample sizes vary depending on the number of concepts to be presented and the consensus of responses.
Output:	Qualitative and/or quantitative data evaluating and comparing alternative concepts.

Figure 19-3 Concept testing

ing, but it goes a long way toward improving the state of the art and alleviates at least one of the testing problems cited earlier.

The Testing Process

Testing may occur at various points throughout the development of an ad or a campaign: (1) concept generation research, (2) rough, prefinished art, copy, and/or commercial testing, (3) finished art or commercial pretesting, and (4) market testing of ads or commercials (posttesting).

Concept Generation and Testing

Figure 19-3 describes the process involved in advertising **concept testing,** which is conducted very early in the campaign development process in order to explore the targeted consumer's response to a potential ad or campaign or have the consumer evaluate advertising alternatives. Positioning statements, copy, headlines, and/or illustrations may all be under scrutiny. The material to be evaluated may be just a headline or a rough sketch of the ad. The colors used, typeface, package designs, and even point-of-purchase materials may be evaluated.

One of the more commonly used methods for concept testing is focus groups, which usually consist of 8 to 10 people in the target market for the product. Companies have tested everything from product concepts to advertising concepts using focus groups. For most companies, the focus group is the first step in the research process. The number of focus groups used varies depending on group consensus, strength of response, and/or the degree to which participants like or dislike the concepts. Some companies use 50 or more groups to develop a campaign, although fewer than 10 are usually needed to test a concept sufficiently.

While focus groups continue to be a favorite of marketers, they are often overused. The methodology is attractive in that results are easily obtained, directly observable, and immediate. A variety of issues can be examined, and consumers are free to go into depth in areas they consider important. Also, focus groups don't require quantitative analysis. Unfortunately, many managers are uncertain about research methods that require statistics, and focus groups, being qualitative in nature, don't demand much skill in interpretation. Weaknesses with focus groups are shown in Figure 19-4.

- The results are not quantifiable.
- Sample sizes are too small to generalize to larger populations.
- Group influences may bias participants' responses.
- One or two members of the group may steer the conversation or dominate the discussion.
- Consumers become instant "experts."
- Members may not represent the target market. (Are focus group participants a certain type of person?)
- Results may be taken to be more representative and/or definitive than they really are.

Figure 19-4 Weaknesses associated with focus group research

Clearly, there are appropriate and inappropriate circumstances for employing this methodology.

Another way to gather consumers' opinions of concepts is mall intercepts, where consumers in shopping malls are approached and asked to evaluate rough ads and/or copy. Rather than participating in a group discussion, individuals assess the ads via questionnaires, rating scales, and/or rankings. New technologies allow for concept testing over the Internet, where advertisers can show concepts simultaneously to consumers throughout the United States, garnering feedback and analyzing the results almost instantaneously. While this methodology is gaining acceptance, traditional methods are more commonly used (See Figure 19-5).

Rough Art, Copy, and Commercial Testing

Because of the high cost associated with the production of an ad or commercial (many network commercials cost hundreds of thousands of dollars to produce), advertisers are increasingly spending more monies testing a rendering of the final ad at early stages. Slides of the artwork posted on a screen or animatic and photomatic roughs may be used to test at this stage. (See Figure 19-6 for an explanation of terminology.) Because such tests can be conducted for about $3,000 to $5,000, research at this stage is becoming ever more popular.

But cost is only one factor. The test is of little value if it does not provide relevant, accurate information. Rough tests must indicate how the finished commercial would perform. Some studies have demonstrated that these testing methods are reliable and the results typically correlate well with the finished ad.[16]

Most of the tests conducted at the rough stage involve lab settings, although some on-air field tests are also available. Popular tests include comprehension and reaction tests and consumer juries. Again, the Internet allows field settings to be employed.

1. *Comprehension and reaction tests.* One key concern for the advertiser is whether the ad or commercial conveys the meaning intended. The second concern is the reaction the ad generates. Obviously, the advertiser does not want an ad that evokes a negative reaction or offends someone. **Comprehension and reaction tests** are designed to assess these responses (which makes you wonder why some ads are ever brought to the marketplace).

Tests of comprehension and reaction employ no one standard procedure. Personal interviews, group interviews, and focus groups have all been used for this purpose, and sample sizes vary according to the needs of the client; they typically range from 50 to 200 respondents.

2. *Consumer juries.* This method uses consumers representative of the target market to evaluate the probable success of an ad. **Consumer juries** may be asked to rate a selection of layouts or copy versions presented in pasteups on separate sheets. The

Figure 19-6 Rough testing terminology

A *rough* commercial is an unfinished execution that may fall into three broad categories:

Animatic Rough	*Photomatic Rough*	*Live-Action Rough*
Succession of drawings/cartoons	Succession of photographs	Live motion
Rendered artwork	Real people/scenery	Stand-in/nonunion talent
Still frames	Still frames	Nonunion crew
Simulated movement: Panning/zooming of frame/ rapid sequence	Simulated movements: Panning/zooming of frame/ rapid sequence	Limited props/minimal opticals
		Location settings

A Finished Commercial Uses:

Live motion/animation

Highly paid union talent

Full union crew

Exotic props/studio sets/special effects

Figure 19-5 Testing via the Internet is gaining in popularity

iTest assessments	iTest Product Line					
	iTest Identity (corporate identity, trade names, and trademarks)	**iTest Ad** (TV, radio, print, and Flash email advertising)	**iTest Package** (package designs)	**iTest Product** (product designs)	**iTest Message** (PR and positioning messages)	**iTest Collateral** (promotion and merchandising material)
Quantitative Measures:						
Pre/post brand awareness change	●	●	●	●	●	●
On-shelf visibility			●			
Pick-up power			●			
Correct brand recall	●	●	●	●	●	●
Likability	●	●	●	●	●	●
Persuasion		●	●		●	●
Information completeness			●			●
Brand appropriateness	●	●	●	●	●	●
Brand associations	●	●	●	●	●	●
Competitor associations	●		●	●	●	
Purchase consideration	●	●	●	●		●
Inclination to take desired action					●	
Communication diagnostics	●	●	●	●	●	●
Demographic drivers	●	●	●	●		●
Qualitative Understanding:						
Follow-up phone interviews for expanded understanding of issues and responses	Optional	Optional	Optional	Optional	Optional	Optional

Figure 19-7 Consumer juries

Objective:	Potential viewers (consumers) are asked to evaluate ads and give their reactions to and evaluation of them. When two or more ads are tested, viewers are usually asked to rate or rank order the ads according to their preferences.
Method:	Respondents are asked to view ads and rate them according to either (1) the order of merit method or (2) the paired comparison method. In the former, the respondent is asked to view the ads, then rank them from one to *n* according to their perceived merit. In the latter, ads are compared only two at a time. Each ad is compared to every other ad in the group, and the winner is listed. The best ad is that which wins the most times. Consumer juries typically employ 50 to 100 participants.
Output:	An overall reaction to each ad under construction as well as a rank ordering of the ads based on the viewers' perceptions.

objectives sought and methods employed in consumer juries are shown in Figure 19-7.[17] Sample questions asked of jurists are shown in Figure 19-8.

While the jury method offers the advantages of control and cost effectiveness, serious flaws in the methodology limit its usefulness:

- *The consumer may become a self-appointed expert.* One of the benefits sought from the jury method is the objectivity and involvement in the product or service that the targeted consumer can bring to the evaluation process. Sometimes, however, knowing they are being asked to critique ads, participants try to become more *expert* in their evaluations, paying more attention and being more critical than usual. The result may be a less than objective evaluation or an evaluation on elements other than those intended.
- *The number of ads that can be evaluated is limited.* Whether *order of merit* or *paired comparison* methods are used, the ranking procedure becomes tedious as the number of alternatives increases. Consider the ranking of 10 ads. While the top two and the bottom two may very well reveal differences, those ranked in the middle may not yield much useful information.

  In the paired comparison method, the number of evaluations required is calculated by the formula

  $$\frac{n(n-1)}{2}$$

  If six alternatives are considered, 15 evaluations must be made. As the number of ads increases, the task becomes even more unmanageable.
- *A halo effect is possible.* Sometimes participants rate an ad good on all characteristics because they like a few and overlook specific weaknesses. This tendency, called the **halo effect,** distorts the ratings and defeats the ability to control for specific components. (Of course, the reverse may also occur—rating an ad bad overall due to only a few bad attributes.)
- *Preferences for specific types of advertising may overshadow objectivity.* Ads that involve emotions or pictures may receive higher ratings or rankings than

Figure 19-8 Questions asked in a consumer jury test

1. Which of these ads would you most likely read if you saw it in a magazine?
2. Which of these headlines would interest you the most in reading the ad further?
3. Which ad convinces you most of the quality or superiority of the product?
4. Which layout do you think would be most effective in causing you to buy?
5. Which ad did you like best?
6. Which ad did you find most interesting?

those employing copy, facts, and/or rational criteria. Even though the latter are often more effective in the marketplace, they may be judged less favorably by jurists who prefer emotional appeals.

Some of the problems noted here can be remedied by the use of ratings scales instead of rankings. But ratings are not always valid either. Thus, while consumer juries have been used for years, questions of bias have led researchers to doubt their validity. As a result, a variety of other methods (discussed later in this chapter) are more commonly employed.

Pretesting of Finished Ads

Pretesting finished ads is one of the more commonly employed studies among marketing researchers and their agencies. At this stage, a finished advertisement or commercial is used; since it has not been presented to the market, changes can still be made.

Many researchers believe testing the ad in final form provides better information. Several test procedures are available for print and broadcast ads, including both laboratory and field methodologies.

Print methods include portfolio tests, analyses of readability, and dummy advertising vehicles. Broadcast tests include theater tests and on-air tests. Both print and broadcast may use physiological measures.

Pretesting Finished Print Messages

A number of methods for pretesting finished print ads are available. One is *Diagnostic Research Inc.'s Copytest System,* described in Figure 19-9. The most common of these methods are portfolio tests, readability tests, and dummy advertising vehicles.

Portfolio Tests **Portfolio tests** are a laboratory methodology designed to expose a group of respondents to a portfolio consisting of both control and test ads. Respondents are then asked what information they recall from the ads. The assumption is that the ads that yield the *highest recall* are the most effective.

While portfolio tests offer the opportunity to compare alternative ads directly, a number of weaknesses limit their applicability:

1. Factors other than advertising creativity and/or presentation may affect recall. Interest in the product or product category, the fact that respondents know they are participating in a test, or interviewer instructions (among others) may account for more differences than the ad itself.
2. Recall may not be the best test. Some researchers argue that for certain types of products (those of low involvement) ability to recognize the ad when shown may be a better measure than recall.

One way to determine the validity of the portfolio method is to correlate its results with readership scores once the ad is placed in the field. Whether such validity tests are being conducted or not is not readily known, although the portfolio method remains popular in the industry.

Objective:	Tests recall and readers' impressions of print ads.
Method:	Mall intercepts in two or more cities are used to screen respondents and have them take home "test magazines" for reading. Participants are phoned the next day to determine opinions of the ads, recall of ad contents, and other questions of interest to the sponsor. Approximately 225 people constitute the sample.
Output:	Scores reported include related recall of copy and visual elements, sales messages, and other nonspecific elements. Both quantitative (table) scores and verbatim responses are reported.

Figure 19-9 Diagnostic Research Inc.'s print test

Readability Tests The communications efficiency of the copy in a print ad can be tested without reader interviews. This test uses the **Flesch formula,** named after its developer, Rudolph Flesch, to assess readability of the copy by determining the average number of syllables per 100 words. Human interest appeal of the material, length of sentences, and familiarity with certain words are also considered and correlated with the educational background of target audiences. Test results are compared to previously established norms for various target audiences. The test suggests that copy is best comprehended when sentences are short, words are concrete and familiar, and personal references are drawn.

This method eliminates many of the interviewee biases associated with other tests and avoids gross errors in understanding. The norms offer an attractive standard for comparison.

Disadvantages are also inherent, however. The copy may become too mechanical, and direct input from the receiver is not available. Without this input, contributing elements like creativity cannot be addressed. To be effective, this test should be used only in conjunction with other pretesting methods.

Dummy Advertising Vehicles In an improvement on the portfolio test, ads are placed in "dummy" magazines developed by an agency or research firm. The magazines contain regular editorial features of interest to the reader, as well as the test ads, and are distributed to a *random sample* of homes in predetermined geographic areas. Readers are told the magazine publisher is interested in evaluations of editorial content and asked to read the magazines as they normally would. Then they are interviewed on their reactions to both editorial content and ads. Recall, readership, and interest-generating capabilities of the ad are assessed.

The advantage of this method is that it provides a more natural setting than the portfolio test. Readership occurs in the participant's own home, the test more closely approximates a natural reading situation, and the reader may go back to the magazine, as people typically do.

But the dummy magazine shares the other disadvantages associated with portfolio tests. The testing effect is not eliminated, and product interest may still bias the results. Thus, while this test offers some advantages over the portfolio method, it is not a guaranteed measure of the advertising's impact.

While all the previously described measures are available, the most popular form of pretesting of print ads now involves a series of measures. Companies like Gallup & Robinson and Ipsos-ASI offer copy testing services that have improved upon many of the shortcomings cited above. The tests can be used for rough and/or finished ads and are most commonly conducted in the respondents' homes. For example, Gallup & Robinson's Magazine Impact Research Service (MIRS) uses an at-home, in-magazine context, employing widely dispersed samples, and offers standardized measures as well as a variety of options. Ipsos-ASI's Next*Print methodology also offers multiple measures, as shown in Figure 19-10.

Pretesting Finished Broadcast Ads

A variety of methods for pretesting broadcast ads are available. The most popular are theater tests, on-air tests, and physiological measures.

Figure 19-10 Ipsos-ASI's Next*Print

Objective:	To assist advertisers in copy testing of print advertisements to determine (1) main idea communication, (2) likes and dislikes, (3) believability, (4) ad attribute ratings, (5) overall likeability, and (6) brand attribute ratings.
Method:	Tests are conducted in current issues of newsstand magazines such as *People, Better Homes & Gardens,* and *Newsweek.* The recall measure consists of 150 responses. Diagnostic measures range from 105 to 150 responses. Highly targeted audiences are available through a version known as the Targeted Print Test.
Output:	Standard scores and specific diagnostics.

Theater Tests In the past, one of the most popular laboratory methods for pretesting finished commercials was **theater testing.** In theater tests participants are invited by telephone, mall intercepts, and/or tickets in the mail to view pilots of proposed TV programs. In some instances, the show is actually being tested, but more commonly a standard program is used so audience responses can be compared with normative responses established by previous viewers. Sample sizes range from 250 to 600 participants.

On entering the theater, viewers are told a drawing will be held for gifts and are asked to complete a product preference questionnaire asking which products they would prefer if they win. This form also requests demographic data. Participants may be seated in specific locations in the theater to allow observation by age, sex, and so on. They view the program and commercials, and a form asking for evaluations is distributed. Participants are then asked to complete a second form for a drawing so that changes in product preference can be noted. In addition to product/brand preference, the form may request other information:

1. Interest in and reaction to the commercial.
2. Overall reaction to the commercial as measured by an adjective checklist.
3. Recall of various aspects of the commercial.
4. Interest in the brand under consideration.
5. Continuous (frame-by-frame) reactions throughout the commercial.

The methods of theater testing operations vary, though all measure brand preference changes. For example, many of the services now use videotaped programs with the commercials embedded for viewing in one's office rather than in a theater. Others establish viewing rooms in malls and/or hotel conference rooms. Some do not take all the measures listed here; others ask the consumers to turn dials or push buttons on a keypad to provide the continual responses. An example of one methodology is shown in Figure 19-11.

Those opposed to theater tests cite a number of disadvantages. First, they say the environment is too artificial. The lab setting is bad enough, but asking respondents to turn dials or, as one service does, wiring people for physiological responses takes them too far from a natural viewing situation. Second, the contrived measure of brand preference change seems too phony to believe. Critics contend that participants will see through it and make changes just because they think they are supposed to. Finally, the group effect of having others present and overtly exhibiting their reactions may influence viewers who did not have any reactions themselves.

Proponents argue that theater tests offer distinct advantages. In addition to control, the established norms (averages of commercials' performances) indicate how one's commercial will fare against others in the same product class that were already tested. Further, advocates say the brand preference measure is supported by actual sales results.

Despite the limitations of theater testing, most major consumer-product companies have used it to evaluate their commercials. This method may have shortcomings, but it allows them to identify strong or weak commercials and to compare them to other ads.

Figure 19-11 The AD*VANTAGE/ACT theater methodology

Advertising Control for Television (ACT), a lab procedure of The MSW Group, uses about 400 respondents representing four cities. It measures initial brand preference by asking participants which brands they most recently purchased. Respondents are then divided into groups of 25 to view a 30-minute program with seven commercials inserted in the middle. Four are test commercials; the other three are control commercials with established viewing norms. After viewing the program, respondents are given a recall test of the commercials. After the recall test, a second 30-minute program is shown, with each test commercial shown again. The second measure of brand preference is taken at this time, with persuasion measured by the percentage of viewers who switched preferences from their most recently purchased brand to one shown in the test commercials.

On-Air Tests Some of the firms conducting theater tests also insert the commercials into actual TV programs in certain test markets. Typically, the commercials are in finished form, although the testing of ads earlier in the developmental process is becoming more common. This is referred to as an **on-air test** and often includes single-source ad research (discussed later in this chapter). Information Resources, Ipsos-ASI, MSW Group, and Nielsen are well-known providers of on-air tests.

On-air testing techniques offer all the advantages of field methodologies, as well as all the disadvantages. Further, there are negative aspects to the specific measures taken through the on-air systems. One concern is associated with **day-after recall scores,** the primary measure used in these tests. Lyman Ostlund notes that measurement errors may result from the natural environment—the position of the ad in the series of commercials shown, the adjacent program content, and/or the number of commercials shown.[18] While the testing services believe their methods overcome many of these criticisms, each still uses recall as one of the primary measures of effectiveness. Since recall tests best reflect the degree of attention and interest in an ad, claims that the tests predict the ad's impact on sales may be going too far. (In 28 studies reviewed by Jack Haskins, only 2 demonstrated that factual recall could be related to sales.)[19] Joel Dubow's research indicates that recall is a necessary but not sufficient measure, while research by Jones and Blair was even more demonstrative, noting that "it is unwise to look to recall for an accurate assessment of a commercial's sales effect."[20]

On the plus side, most of the testing services have offered evidence of both validity and reliability for on-air pretesting of commercials. Both Ipsos-ASI and MSW Group claim their pretest and posttest results yield the same recall scores 9 out of 10 times—a strong indication of reliability and a good predictor of the effect the ad is likely to have when shown to the population as a whole.

In summary, on-air pretesting of finished or rough commercials offers some distinct advantages over lab methods and some indications of the ad's likely success. Whether the measures used are as strong an indication as the providers say still remains in question.

Physiological Measures A less common method of pretesting finished commercials involves a laboratory setting in which physiological responses are measured. These measures indicate the receiver's *involuntary* response to the ad, theoretically eliminating biases associated with the voluntary measures reviewed to this point. (Involuntary responses are those over which the individual has no control, such as heartbeat and reflexes.) Physiological measures used to test both print and broadcast ads include pupil dilation, galvanic skin response, eye tracking, and brain waves:

1. *Pupil dilation.* Research in **pupillometrics** is designed to measure dilation and constriction of the pupils of the eyes in response to stimuli. Dilation is associated with action; constriction involves the body's conservation of energy.

Advertisers have used pupillometrics to evaluate product and package design as well as to test ads. Pupil dilation suggests a stronger interest in (or preference for) an ad or implies arousal or attention-getting capabilities. Other attempts to determine the affective (liking or disliking) responses created by ads have met with less success.

Because of high costs and some methodological problems, the use of pupillometrics has waned over the past decade. But it can be useful in evaluating certain aspects of advertising.

2. *Galvanic skin response.* Also known as **electrodermal response,** GSR measures the skin's resistance or conductance to a small amount of current passed between two electrodes. Response to a stimulus activates sweat glands, which in turn increases the conductance of the electrical current. Thus, GSR/EDR activity might reflect a reaction to advertising. In their review of the research in this area, Paul Watson and Robert Gatchel concluded that GSR/EDR (1) is sensitive to affective stimuli, (2) may present a picture of attention, (3) may be useful to measure long-term advertising recall, and (4) is useful in measuring ad effectiveness.[21] In interviews with practitioners and reviews of case studies, Priscilla LaBarbera and Joel Tucciarone also concluded that GSR is an effective measure and is useful for measuring affect, or liking, for ads.[22] While a number of companies have offered skin response measures, this research methodology is not commonly used now, and LaBarbera and Tucciarone believe that it is underused, given its potential.

CAREER PROFILE

John Hallward

President, Global Product Development
Ipsos-ASI Inc, "The Advertising Research Company"

Twenty years ago I applied to consumer packaged good manufacturers such as Procter & Gamble, General Mills, and General Foods. Having studied marketing and finance, I preferred a "marketing" career and wanted to follow the brand management path at P&G in Canada.

On the P&G application they required students to indicate their three most enjoyed courses, and the three least preferred. I mentioned that Market Research was one of my least preferred courses because, most people would agree that market research was a boring science of counting consumers. I just missed the cut.

Later, P&G called and asked if I was interested in a job in the Market Research Department. I took the opportunity to interview. It became apparent that my initial application was on the interviewer's desk. "Tell me about the three least preferred courses" he asked. I provided my honest view of the market research course—this subject was boring, dry, factual and void of real-world input. "Oh" says the Research Manager, "Is my old classmate still teaching that course?"—This turned out to be a humorous start to a friendly interview, and I went on to start my marketing research career at P&G.

"I smile when I think back to my initial thoughts of avoiding marketing research."

The point is that marketing research is not as boring as it might appear! Research offers an exposure to the many aspects of marketing issues than does brand management. The research consultant is exposed to many different projects and problems, across many different brands and categories. In research, one experiences all of the practices of marketing from development of an ad through testing, tracking, product tests, pricing, brand name, and promotion research segmentation and targeting decisions, etc. In research, the emphasis is on "consulting" and adding experienced insight and recommendations, not just collecting data, and it is rarely dull or repetitive.

After a couple of years at P&G, I was offered to be the Market Research manager at Johnson & Johnson. Later I met an individual from the U.K. who had an idea about introducing a unique way of measuring ad effectiveness in North America. We joined together to start our new business. This was the beginning of my entrepreneurial spirit, and my career of a research consultant on the "supplier" side.

Twenty years later, I still enjoy my job immensely. I have also enjoyed being an entrepreneur and growing a business from three to 135 people and 500+ interviewers. I am not sure what other career paths would have exposed me to so much about marketing, with such a quick paced career. I smile when I think back to my initial thoughts of avoiding marketing research.

Today, I have a new challenge. We sold our business to Ipsos, a global research firm operating in over 30 countries. Within Ipsos-ASI, "the advertising research company," I have global responsibility for the development of our advertising and brand equity research tools. This exposes me to the international differences of brand management, with global clients and brands, which makes my career very exciting. It is fulfilling to help direct the brand equity and advertising for the globe's biggest brands. And it is never dull to be able to evolve to different brands, in different categories, for different companies, with different cultural challenges. The information world is growing, and there is room for more research consultants. Give it a thought, and I encourage you to not be so biased by any one university course!

Figure 19-12 Eye movement research

Objective:	Tracks viewers' eye movements to determine what viewers read or view in print ads and where their attention is focused in TV commercials or billboards.
Method:	Fiber optics, digital data processing, and advanced electronics are used to follow eye movements of viewers and/or readers as they process an ad.
Output:	Relationship among what readers see, recall, and comprehend. Scan paths on print ads, billboards, commercials, and print materials. (Can also be used to evaluate package designs.)

3. *Eye tracking.* A methodology that is more commonly employed is **eye tracking** (Figure 19-12), in which viewers are asked to view an ad while a sensor aims a beam of infrared light at the eye. The beam follows the movement of the eye and shows the exact spot on which the viewer is focusing. The continuous reading of responses demonstrates which elements of the ad are attracting attention, how long the viewer is focusing on them, and the sequence in which they are being viewed.

Eye tracking can identify strengths and weaknesses in an ad. For example, attractive models or background action may distract the viewer's attention away from the brand or product being advertised. The advertiser can remedy this distraction before fielding the ad. In other instances, colors or illustrations may attract attention and create viewer interest in the ad.

More recently, eye-tracking has been used to measure the effectiveness of websites and online ads. IMC Perspective 19-2 reports on some of these efforts.

4. *Brain waves.* **Electroencephalographic (EEG) measures** can be taken from the skull to determine electrical frequencies in the brain. These electrical impulses are used in two areas of research, alpha waves and hemispheric lateralization:

- **Alpha activity** refers to the degree of brain activation. People are in an alpha state when they are inactive, resting, or sleeping. The theory is that a person in an alpha state is less likely to be processing information (recall correlates negatively with alpha levels) and that attention and processing require moving from this state. By measuring a subject's alpha level while viewing a commercial, researchers can assess the degree to which attention and processing are likely to occur.
- **Hemispheric lateralization** distinguishes between alpha activity in the left and right sides of the brain. It has been hypothesized that the right side of the brain processes visual stimuli and the left processes verbal stimuli. The right hemisphere is thought to respond more to emotional stimuli, while the left responds to logic. The right determines recognition, while the left is responsible for recall.[23] If these hypotheses are correct, advertisers could design ads to increase learning and memory by creating stimuli to appeal to each hemisphere. However, some researchers believe the brain does not function laterally and an ad cannot be designed to appeal to one side or the other.

While EEG research has engaged the attention of academic researchers, it has been much less successful in attracting the interest of practitioners.

Market Testing of Ads

The fact that the ad and/or campaign has been implemented does not mean there is no longer a need for testing. The pretests were conducted on smaller samples and may in some instances have questionable merit, so the marketer must find out how the ad is doing in the field. In this section, we discuss methods for posttesting an ad. Some of the tests are similar to the pretests discussed in the previous section and are provided by the same companies.

Posttests of Print Ads

A variety of print posttests are available, including inquiry tests, recognition tests, and recall tests.

IMC PERSPECTIVE 19-2

Eye Tracking Branches Out

The use of eye tracking to measure various aspects of the marketing communication program is nothing new. Companies have used this methodology to determine which labels are most likely to catch the consumer's eye in a supermarket and to track how effective various elements of an advertisement are in catching viewers' attention. The technique has also been used to test television commercials, by watching where the viewer's eyes focus and for how long.

Now eye-tracking methodology is being expanded to help companies in new ways. One of these is determining the effectiveness of online advertising. As you would expect, advertisers want to know if their Internet advertising is being noticed.

One measure, of course, is whether or not the viewer clicks on the ad. But this tells only that the ad has been seen (or accidentally clicked on!) but not the impact of various types of ads or the effect of where the ads are placed. As noted by Rice University professor David Lane, who studies the effectiveness of banner ads, "People don't know how effective ads are, and there are so many different ways of advertising. They don't know which ones work best."

Other university researchers have also measured effectiveness through eye tracking. Stanford University researchers used this method to see where people focused while reading online news sites and where and how long they looked at the ads. At the University of Wales in the United Kingdom, ads were sandwiched between flashes of puppies and hairy spiders in an attempt to see what was noticed most.

University researchers are not the only ones interested in determining advertising effectiveness through eye tracking. AT&T is just one of the companies that employ this methodology to determine the impact of their website designs. By tracking the eyes of viewers for 30 minutes, the company was able to document viewing patterns and to uncover exactly what people looked at as they visit home pages. The results were then used to design AT&T's sites to be more user-friendly and to be more effective than competitors' sites. IBM is also using this method to watch what users look at on the screen.

So what do researchers find out by watching our eyes? The Rice study showed that many Internet users largely ignore banner ads. A study at the University of Indiana, which used electrodes to measure heart rate and GSR activity along with eye tracking, produced results that were consistent with those at Rice. The study further indicated that static banner ads elicited no reactions in the additional physiological measures and animated ads elicited a mild response, with both types being less effective than television advertising. The Stanford study showed that viewers' eyes first went to the text on news sites, ignoring graphics and ads, but they later viewed as many as 45 percent of the banners—though only for an average of one second. In essence, the studies concluded that banner ads aren't very effective.

As a result, like AT&T, companies are exploring new ways to make online advertising effective. New forms of ads, new placements, and other creative ideas are being explored to try to catch your eye. Maybe if they just had more creative ads?

Sources: Sharon Machlis, "See Me, Hear Me . . .", *Computerworld,* Aug. 26, 2002, p. 34; Adam Geller, "Online Advertisers Are Looking for Ways to Catch Your Eye," *San Diego Union-Tribune,* Feb. 2, 2001, p. C1; "Eye-Tracking Helps Fine Tune AT&T's Customer Service Site," *Quirks,* July-August 2001, pp. 21-30.

Exhibit 19-4 Reader response cards are popular in business and business markets

TARGET MARKETING Receive the information you need to market smarter instantly! Go to: **www.targetonline.com** and click on free information.

Or...Fill out this card and either FAX your request today: 215-238-5388 or mail. November 2000 • Expires April 2001

Free Subscription

Do you wish to receive (continue to receive) a FREE subscription to TARGET MARKETING? ❑ YES ❑ NO

Signature _____ Date _____

Name (please print) _____ Title _____

Company Name _____

Address _____

City/State/Zip _____

Telephone _____ FAX _____

Email Address: _____

1. TYPE OF BUSINESS AT THIS LOCATION: (Check One)

04 ☐ Catalogers, Mail Order Companies
05 ☐ Retailers, Wholesaler/Distributor
06 ☐ On-line Merchant
03 ☐ Financial Services: Banks, Insurance, Credit Cards, Investment
21 ☐ Fund Raisers: Non-Profit Groups, Charities
33 ☐ High Technology: Internet Services, Computers, Software, Telecommunications, Office Equipment
12 ☐ Manufacturers, Package Goods and Other Business-to-Business Marketers
31 ☐ Non Financial Services Marketers: Associations, Clubs, Educational, Government Agencies, Health Care, Membership Organizations, Personnel Services, Real Estate, Utilities, Communications, Tourism and Travel
13 ☐ Publishers: Magazines, Books, Newsletters, Newspapers, Book & Record Clubs On-line publications
01 ☐ Advertising/DM Agencies, Freelance Creative and Consultants
09 ☐ Mailing List Professionals: Brokers, Compilers, Owners
20 ☐ Other: (Please Specify) _____

2. JOB FUNCTION: (Check One)

10 ☐ Corporate and General Management (Excluding Sales, Marketing and Advertising Management)
02 ☐ Marketing, List and Sales Management
01 ☐ Advertising Promotion and Public Relations Management
08 ☐ Operational, Technical and Telemarketing Management
06 ☐ Circulation Management
11 ☐ Other: (Please Specify) _____

3. MY FIRM'S MARKETING ACTIVITY: (Check All That Apply)

1 ☐ Catalog
2 ☐ Direct Mail
09 ☐ Internet
3 ☐ Telemarketing
10 ☐ Alternate Media
5 ☐ Consumer
6 ☐ Business-to-Business
7 ☐ International
8 ☐ None of the Above

4. IN THE PERFORMANCE OF YOUR JOB, CHECK THE ONE THAT BEST DESCRIBES YOUR PURCHASING AUTHORITY: (Check One)

1 ☐ Authorize/Approve Purchase
2 ☐ Recommend/ Specify Purchase
3 ☐ No Purchasing Authority

Free Information

Circle the free info number for the products and services that interest you

001	002	003	004	005	006	007	008	009	010	011	012
013	014	015	016	017	018	019	020	021	022	023	024
025	026	027	028	029	030	031	032	033	034	035	036
037	038	039	040	041	042	043	044	045	046	047	048
049	050	051	052	053	054	055	056	057	058	059	060
061	062	063	064	065	066	067	068	069	070	071	072
073	074	075	076	077	078	079	080	081	082	083	084
085	086	087	088	089	090	091	092	093	094	095	096
097	098	099	100	101	102	103	104	105	106	107	108
109	110	111	112	113	114	115	116	117	118	119	120
121	122	123	124	125	126	127	128	129	130	131	132
133	134	135	136	137	138	139	140	141	142	143	144
145	146	147	148	149	150	151	152	153	154	155	156
157	158	159	160	161	162	163	164	165	166	167	168
169	170	171	172	173	174	175	176	177	178	179	180

For Information on Product/Service Categories

To request information on any of the following areas of interest, check the appropriate free information number:

501 ☐ Agencies/Consultants/Creative Services
502 ☐ Alternate Media/Delivery
503 ☐ Broadcast Media/Services
504 ☐ Call Center Equipment
505 ☐ Credit/Collection Services
506 ☐ Database Management Systems/ Services/Software
507 ☐ Delivery Services
529 ☐ E-mail Marketing
508 ☐ Envelopes/Order Forms/Labels
509 ☐ Fulfillment Services/Operations
510 ☐ Int'l Call Centers
511 ☐ Int'l Delivery Services
512 ☐ Int'l DM Agencies
525 ☐ International DM Services
530 ☐ Internet Services
513 ☐ Lettershop Services
514 ☐ Lists-Business-to-Business
515 ☐ Lists-Consumer
528 ☐ Lists-E-mail
516 ☐ Lists-International
517 ☐ List Services
518 ☐ Mailing Equipment/Services
520 ☐ Paper
521 ☐ Premiums/Promotional Products
522 ☐ Prepress Equipment/Services
523 ☐ Printers
527 ☐ Printing Systems/Equipment
524 ☐ Telemarketing Services

RS0110

Inquiry Tests Used in both consumer and business-to-business market testing, **inquiry tests** are designed to measure advertising effectiveness on the basis of inquiries generated from ads appearing in various print media, often referred to as "bingo cards." The inquiry may take the form of the number of coupons returned, phone calls generated, or direct inquiries through reader cards. Exhibit 19-4 shows an example of a reader response card, while Figure 19-13 shows that this form is still the most commonly employed response to trade ads. For example, if you called in a response to an ad in a local medium recently, perhaps you were asked how you found out about the company or product or where you saw the ad. This is a very simple measure of the ad's or medium's effectiveness.

More complex methods of measuring effectiveness through inquiries may involve (1) running the ad in successive issues of the same medium, (2) running **split-run tests,** in which variations of the ad appear in different copies of the same newspaper or magazine, and/or (3) running the same ad in different media. Each of these methods yields information on different aspects of the strategy. The first measures the *cumulative* effects of the campaign; the second examines specific elements of the ad or variations on it. The final method measures the effectiveness of the medium rather than the ad itself.

While inquiry tests may yield useful information, weaknesses in this methodology limit its effectiveness. For example, inquiries may not be a true measure of the attention-getting or information-providing aspects of the ad. The reader may be attracted to an ad, read it, and even store the information but not be motivated to inquire at that particular time. Time constraints, lack of a need for the product or service at the time the ad is run, and other factors may limit the number of inquiries. But receiving a small number of inquiries doesn't mean the ad was not effective; attention, attitude change, awareness, and recall of copy points may all have been achieved. At the other extreme, a person with a particular need for the product may respond to any ad for it, regardless of specific qualities of the ad.

Despite the rise in popularity of electronic response mechanisms, the traditional reader service, or "bingo card," remains the most common way to respond to trade publication advertising.

Ad Response Methods Used Frequently or Very Frequently*	
Indirect Methods	
Return reader service cards	41%
Save ads for reference	35
Discuss advertised products with others	30
Pass ads on to others for possible action	26
Direct Methods	
Send back reply cards/coupons	31%
Contact vendors' websites	28
Telephone manufacturers	23
Telephone local distributors/reps	22
Go to magazine websites	21
Stop at vendors' trade show exhibits	20
Discuss products with sales reps	20
Send faxes to vendors	17
Contact distributors' websites	15
Send e-mail messages	10
Mail notes to vendors	6

*The 2,705 respondents could name more than one method.

Figure 19-13 Ad response methods

Major advantages of inquiry tests are that they are inexpensive to implement and they provide some feedback with respect to the general effectiveness of the ad or medium used. But they are usually not very effective for comparing different versions or specific creative aspects of an ad.

Recognition Tests Perhaps the most common posttest of print ads is the **recognition method,** most closely associated with Roper ASW. The *Starch Ad Readership Report* lets the advertiser assess the impact of an ad in a single issue of a magazine, over time, and/or across different magazines (see Figure 19-14). Starch measures over

Objective: Determining recognition of print ads and comparing them to other ads of the same variety or in the same magazine.

Method: Samples are drawn from 20 to 30 urban areas reflecting the geographic circulation of the magazine. Personal interviewers screen readers for qualifications and determine exposure and readership. Samples include a minimum of 200 males and females, as well as specific audiences where required. Participants are asked to go through the magazines, looking at the ads, and provide specific responses.

Output: *Starch Ad Readership Reports* generate three recognition scores:

- Noted score—the percentage of readers who remember seeing the ad.
- Seen-associated score—the percentage of readers who recall seeing or reading any part of the ad identifying the product or brand.
- Read-most score—the percentage of readers who report reading at least half of the copy portion of the ad.

Figure 19-14 The *Starch Ad Readership Report*

Exhibit 19-5 Example of a Starch-scored ad

25,000 ads in more than 400 issues representing more than 100 consumer, farm, and business magazines and newspapers per year and provides a number of measures of the ad's effectiveness. An example of a Starch-scored ad is shown in Exhibit 19-5.

Starch claims that (1) the pulling power of various aspects of the ad can be assessed through the control offered, (2) the effectiveness of competitors' ads can be compared through the norms provided, (3) alternative ad executions can be tested, and (4) readership scores are a useful indication of consumers' *involvement* in the ad or campaign. (The theory is that a reader must read and become involved in the ad before the ad can communicate. To the degree that this readership can be shown, it is a direct indication of effectiveness.)

Of these claims, perhaps the most valid is the ability to judge specific aspects of the ad. Many researchers have criticized other aspects of the Starch recognition method (as well as other recognition measures) on the basis of problems of false claiming, interviewer sensitivities, and unreliable scores:

1. *False claiming.* Research shows that in recognition tests, respondents may claim to have seen an ad when they did not. False claims may be a result of having seen similar ads elsewhere, expecting that such an ad would appear in the medium, or wanting to please the questioner. Interest in the product category also increases reporting of ad readership. Whether this false claiming is deliberate or not, it leads to an overreporting of effectiveness. On the flip side, factors such as interview fatigue may lead to an underreporting bias—that is, respondents not reporting an ad they did see.

2. *Interviewer sensitivities.* Any time research involves interviewers, there is a potential for bias. Respondents may want to impress the interviewer or fear looking unknowledgeable if they continually claim not to recognize an ad. There may also be variances associated with interviewer instructions, recordings, and so on, regardless of the amount of training and sophistication involved.

3. *Reliability of recognition scores.* Starch admits that the reliability and validity of its readership scores increase with the number of insertions tested, which essentially means that to test just one ad on a single exposure may not produce valid or reliable results.

In sum, despite critics, the Starch readership studies continue to dominate the posttesting of print ads. The value provided by norms and the fact that multiple exposures can improve reliability and validity may underlie the decisions to employ this methodology.

Recall Tests There are several tests to measure recall of print ads. Perhaps the best known of these are the Ipsos-ASI Next*Print test and the Gallup & Robinson Magazine Impact Research Service (MIRS) (described in Figure 19-15). These **recall tests** are similar to those discussed in the section on pretesting broadcast ads in that they attempt to measure recall of specific ads.

In addition to having the same interviewer problems as recognition tests, recall tests have other disadvantages. The reader's degree of involvement with the product and/or the distinctiveness of the appeals and visuals may lead to higher-than-accurate recall scores, although in general the method may lead to lower levels of recall than actually exist (an error the advertiser would be happy with). Critics contend the test is not strong enough to reflect recall accurately, so many ads may score as less effective than they really are, and advertisers may abandon or modify them needlessly.

On the plus side, it is thought that recall tests can assess the ad's impact on memory. Proponents of recall tests say the major concern is not the results themselves but how they are interpreted. In one very interesting study of the effects of brand name suggestiveness on recall, Kevin Keller, Susan Heckler, and Michael Houston found that suggestive brand names (those that convey relevant attribute or benefit information about the product) facilitate the initial recall of the brand's benefits but inhibit

Objective:	Tracking recall of advertising (and client's ads) appearing in magazines to assess performance and effectiveness.
Method:	Test magazines are placed in participants' homes and respondents are asked to read the magazine that day. A telephone interview is conducted the second day to assess recall of ads, recall of copy points, and consumers' impressions of the ads. Sample size is 150 people.
Output:	Three measurement scores are provided: • Proven name registration—the percentage of respondents who can accurately recall the ad. • Idea communication—the number of sales points the respondents can recall. • Favorable buying attitude—the extent of favorable purchase reaction to the brand or corporation.

Figure 19-15 Gallup & Robinson Magazine Impact Research Service

recall of subsequently advertised claims. These results would seem to indicate that a suggestive brand name could facilitate initial positioning of the brand but make it more difficult to introduce new attributes at a later time. The authors suggest that these results might be useful in explaining why Jack in the Box has had trouble developing a more adult image and why Old Spice and Oldsmobile have had difficulty with younger audiences.[24]

A very extensive longitudinal study was conducted by the Netherlands Institute of Public Opinion (NIPO) to assess the relationship between recall and recognition. The results indicated that the average correlation between recall and recognition in both newspapers and magazines was very high ($r = .96$ and .95, respectively). The study concluded that recall actually stems from recognition, in that 99 percent of 3,632 cases of recall also had recorded recognition. In addition, likable and interesting ads doubled the recall scores and increased the recall share of recognition. Creative advertising was much more effective for creating perceptions and recall than was the size of the ad.[25]

Posttests of Broadcast Commercials

A variety of methods exist for posttesting broadcast commercials. The most common provide a combination of day-after recall tests, persuasion measures, and diagnostics. Test marketing and tracking studies, including single-source methods, are also employed.

Day-After Recall Tests The most popular method of posttesting employed in the broadcasting industry for decades was the *Burke Day-After Recall test.* While a number of companies offered day-after recall methodologies, the "Burke test" for all intents and purposes became the generic name attached to these tests. While popular, day-after recall tests also had problems, including limited samples, high costs, and security issues (ads shown in test markets could be seen by competitors). In addition, the following disadvantages with recall tests were also suggested:

1. DAR tests may favor unemotional appeals because respondents are asked to verbalize the message. Thinking messages may be easier to recall than emotional communications, so recall scores for emotional ads may be lower.[26] A number of other studies have also indicated that emotional ads may be processed differently from thinking ones; some ad agencies, for example, Leo Burnett and BBDO Worldwide, have gone so far as to develop their own methods of determining emotional response to ads.[27]

2. Program content may influence recall. The programs in which the ad appears may lead to different recall scores for the same brand. The net result is a potential inaccuracy in the recall score and in the norms used to establish comparisons.[28]

3. A prerecruited sample (Gallup & Robinson) may pay increased attention to the program and the ads contained therein because the respondents know they will be tested the next day. This effect would lead to a higher level of recall than really exists.

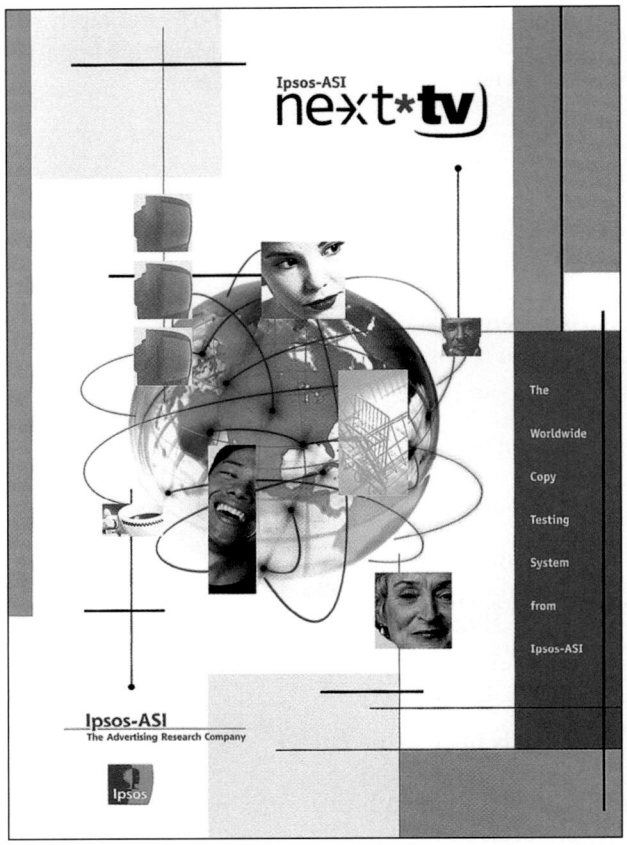

Exhibit 19-6 Ipsos-ASI offers a comprehensive testing measure

The major advantage of day-after recall tests is that they are field tests. The natural setting is supposed to provide a more realistic response profile. These tests are also popular because they provide norms that give advertisers a standard for comparing how well their ads are performing. In addition to recall, a number of different measures of the commercial's effectiveness are now offered, including persuasive measures and diagnostics. (The Burke test itself no longer exists.)

Persuasive Measures As noted earlier in our discussion of pretesting broadcast commercials, a measure of a commercial's persuasive effectiveness is gathered by asking consumers to choose a brand that they would want to win in a drawing and then—after exposure to the ad—ask the question again. In theater settings this is accomplished by announcing a series of prize drawings, with viewers indicating which of the brands they would choose if they won. In field settings, it is accomplished by taking a brand preference measure when the video is delivered and then again the next day. Some of the services offer additional persuasion measures, including purchase-intent and frequency-of-purchase criteria.

Diagnostics In addition to measuring recall and persuasion, copy testing firms also provide diagnostic measures. These measures are designed to garner viewers' evaluations of the ads, as well as how clearly the creative idea is understood and how well the proposition is communicated. Rational and emotional reactions to the ads are also examined. A number of companies offer diagnostic measures, including Diagnostic Research, Inc., Gallup & Robinson, and Millward Brown.

Comprehensive Measures While each of the measures just described provides specific input into the effectiveness of a commercial, many advertisers are interested in more than just one specific input. Thus, some companies provide comprehensive approaches in which each of the three measures just described can be obtained through one testing program. Figure 19-16 describes one such comprehensive program, Ipsos-ASI's Next*TV test (Exhibit 19-6).

Test Marketing Many companies conduct tests designed to measure their advertising effects in specific test markets before releasing them nationally. The markets chosen are

Figure 19-16 Ipsos-ASI's Next*TV

Objectives:	To assist advertisers in copy testing of their commercials through multiple measures to determine (1) the potential of the commercial for impacting sales, (2) how the ad contributes to brand equity, (3) how well it is in line with existing advertising strategies and objectives, and (4) how to optimize effectiveness.
Method:	Consumers are recruited to evaluate a TV program, with ads embedded into the program as they would be on local prime-time television. Consumers view the program on a videotape in their homes to simulate actual field conditions. (The option to use local cable television programs with commercial inserts is also provided.)
Output:	Related recall (day-after recall) scores; persuasion scores, including brand preference shifts, purchase intent and frequency, brand equity differentiation, and relevance and communication; and reaction diagnostics to determine what viewers take away from the ad and how creative elements contribute to or distract from advertising effectiveness.

representative of the target market. For example, a company may test its ads in Portland, Oregon; San Antonio, Texas; or Buffalo, New York, if the demographic and socioeconomic profiles of these cities match the product's market. A variety of factors may be tested, including reactions to the ads (for example, alternative copy points), the effects of various budget sizes, or special offers. The ads run in finished form in the media where they might normally appear, and effectiveness is measured after the ads run.

The advantage of test marketing of ads is realism. Regular viewing environments are used and the testing effects are minimized. A high degree of control can be attained if the test is designed successfully. For example, an extensive test market study was designed and conducted by Seagram and Time, Inc., over three years to measure the effects of advertising frequency on consumers' buying habits. This study demonstrated just how much could be learned from research conducted in a field setting but with some experimental controls. It also showed that proper research can provide strong insights into the impact of ad campaigns. (Many advertising researchers consider this study one of the most conclusive ever conducted in the attempt to demonstrate the effects of advertising on sales.)

The Seagram study also reveals some of the disadvantages associated with test market measures, not the least of which are cost and time. Few firms have the luxury to spend three years and hundreds of thousands of dollars on such a test. In addition, there is always the fear that competitors may discover and intervene in the research process.

A number of companies, including Procter & Gamble and Toyota, have test marketed interactive commercials. Reckitt—the world's largest manufacturer of household cleaning products—and Whirlpool have joined efforts to test *i*TV ads. Customers were offered three different enticements to interact with the campaign: (1) register to win a Whirlpool dishwasher, (2) register for free samples of Finish Dishwater Freshener, or (3) order money-off coupons for Finish Dishwater Tablets. After eight months of testing, Reckitt reported that the target goal of 35,000 responses was exceeded.[29] Sears and Ford are both testing the impact of ads placed on Gemstar—*TV Guide*'s interactive program guide—while Chrysler is experimenting with online gaming to generate leads and stimulate buzz.[30]

Test marketing can provide substantial insight into the effectiveness of advertising if care is taken to minimize the negative aspects of such tests.

Single-Source Tracking Studies Since the 1980s the focus of many research efforts has been on single-source tracking methods. **Single-source tracking methods** track the behaviors of consumers from the television set to the supermarket checkout counter. Participants in a designated area who have cable TV and agree to participate in the studies are given a card (similar to a credit card) that identifies their household and gives the research company their demographics. The households are split into matched groups; one group receives an ad while the other does not, or alternate ads are sent to each. Their purchases are recorded from the bar codes of the products bought. Commercial exposures are then correlated with purchase behaviors.

Earlier we mentioned the use of single-source ad research in pretesting commercials. One study demonstrated that the single-source method can also be used effectively to posttest ads, allowing for a variety of dependent measures and tracking the effects of increased ad budgets and different versions of ad copy—and even ad effects on sales.[31]

A 10-year study conducted by Information Resources' BehaviorScan service demonstrated long-term effects of advertising on sales. The study examined copy, media schedules, ad budgets, and the impact of trade promotions on sales in 10 markets throughout the United States and concluded that advertising can produce sales growth as long as two years after a campaign ends.[32] (The study also concluded that results of copy recall and persuasion tests were unlikely to predict sales reliably.) A number of single-source methods have been used, among them BehaviorScan (Information Resources) and MarketSource. The A. C. Nielsen company's Scantrack is another commonly employed single-source tracking system.

Many advertisers believe these single-source measures will change the way research is conducted due to the advantages of control and the ability to measure directly the ads' effects on sales. A number of major corporations and ad agencies are now employing this method, including Campbell Soup, Colgate-Palmolive, Nestlé, General Foods, P&G,

Exhibit 19-7 Tracking studies provide useful measures

Pepsi-Cola, Leo Burnett, and J. Walter Thompson. After using scanner data to review the advertising/sales relationship for 78 brands, John Jones concluded that single-source data are beginning to fulfill their promise now that more measurements are available.[33]

While single-source testing is a valuable tool, it still has some problems. One researcher says, "Scanner data focus on short-term sales effects, and as a result capture only 10 to 30 percent of what advertising does."[34] Others complain that the data are too complicated to deal with, as an overabundance of information is available. Still another disadvantage is the high cost of collecting single-source data. While the complexity of single-source data resulted in a slow adoption rate, this method of tracking advertising effectiveness became widely adopted in the 1990s by the research companies mentioned earlier (Gallup & Robinson, Millward-Brown, and Ipsos-ASI).

Tracking Print/Broadcast Ads One of the more useful and adaptable forms of posttesting involves tracking the effects of the ad campaign by taking measurements at regular intervals. **Tracking studies** have been used to measure the effects of advertising on awareness, recall, interest, and attitudes toward the ad and/or brand as well as purchase intentions. (Ad tracking may be applied to both print and broadcast ads but is much more common with the latter.) Personal interviews, phone surveys, mall intercepts, and even mail surveys have been used. Sample sizes typically range from 250 to 500 cases per period (usually quarterly or semiannually). Tracking studies yield perhaps the most valuable information available to the marketing manager for assessing current programs and planning for the future. (See Exhibit 19-7.)

The major advantage of tracking studies is that they can be tailored to each specific campaign and/or situation. A standard set of questions can track effects of the campaign over time. The effects of various media can also be determined, although with much less effectiveness. Tracking studies have also been used to measure the differential impact of different budget sizes, the effects of flighting, brand or corporate image, and recall of specific copy points. Finally, when designed properly, as shown in Figure 19-17, tracking studies offer a high degree of reliability and validity.[35]

Some of the problems of recall and recognition measures are inherent in tracking studies, since many other factors may affect both brand and advertising recall. Despite

Figure 19-17 Factors that make or break tracking studies

1. Properly defined objectives
2. Alignment with sales objectives
3. Properly designed measures (e.g., adequate sample size, maximum control over interviewing process, adequate time between tracking periods)
4. Consistency through replication of the sampling plan
5. Random samples
6. Continuous interviewing (that is, not seasonal)
7. Evaluate measures related to behavior (attitudes meet this criterion; recall of ads does not)
8. Critical evaluative questions asked early to eliminate bias
9. Measurement of competitors' performance
10. Skepticism about questions that ask where the advertising was seen or heard (TV always wins)
11. Building of news value into the study
12. "Moving averages" used to spot long-term trends and avoid seasonality
13. Data reported in terms of relationships rather than as isolated facts
14. Integration of key marketplace events with tracking results (e.g., advertising expenditures of self and competitors, promotional activities associated with price changes in ad campaigns, introductions of new brands, government announcements, changes in economic conditions)

these limitations, however, tracking studies are a very effective way to assess the effects of advertising campaigns.

In summary, you can see that each of the testing methods considered in this chapter has its strengths and its limitations. You may wonder: Can we actually test advertising effectiveness? What can be done to ensure a valid, reliable test? The next section of this chapter suggests some answers.

Establishing a Program for Measuring Advertising Effects

There is no surefire way to test advertising effectiveness. However, in response to pressures to determine the contribution of ads to the overall marketing effort, steps are being taken to improve this measurement task. Let's begin by reviewing the major problems with some existing methods and then examine possible improvements.

Problems with Current Research Methods

When current testing methods are compared to the criteria established by PACT (see Figure 19-2), it is clear that some of the principles important to good copy testing can be accomplished readily, whereas others require substantially more effort. For example, principle 6 (providing equivalent test ads) should require a minimum of effort. The researcher can easily control the state of completion of the test communications. Also fairly easy are principles 1 and 2 (providing measurements relative to the objectives sought and determining *a priori* how the results will be used).

We have seen throughout this text that each promotional medium, the message, and the budget all consider the marketing and communications objectives sought. The integrated marketing communications planning model establishes the roles of these elements. So by the time one gets to the measurement phase, the criteria by which these programs will be evaluated should simply fall into place.

Slightly more difficult are principles 3, 5, and 8, although again these factors are largely in the control of the researcher. Principle 3 (providing multiple measurements) may require little more than budgeting to make sure more than one test is conducted. At the most, it may require considering two similar measures to ensure reliability. Likewise, principle 5 (exposing the test ad more than once) can be accomplished with a proper research design. Finally, principle 8 (sample definition) requires little more than sound research methodology; any test should use the target audience to assess an ad's effectiveness. You would not use a sample of nondrinkers to evaluate new liquor commercials.

The most difficult factors to control—and the principles that may best differentiate between good and bad testing procedures—are PACT requirements 4, 7, and 9. Fortunately, however, addressing each of these contributes to the attainment of the others.

The best starting point is principle 4, which states the research should be guided by a model of human response to communications that encompasses reception, comprehension, and behavioral response. It is the best starting point, in our opinion, because it is the principle least addressed by practicing researchers. If you recall, Chapter 5 proposed a number of models that could fulfill this principle's requirements. Yet even though these models have existed for quite some time, few if any common research methods attempt to integrate them into their methodologies. Most current methods do little more than provide recall scores, despite the fact many researchers have shown that recall is a poor measure of effectiveness. Models that do claim to measure such factors as attitude change or brand preference change are often fraught with problems that severely limit their reliability. An effective measure must include some relationship to the communications process.

It might seem at first glance that principle 7 (providing a nonbiasing exposure) would be easy to accomplish. But lab measures, while offering control, are artificial and vulnerable to testing effects. And field measures, while more realistic, often lose control. The Seagram and Time study may have the best of both worlds, but it is too large a task for most firms to undertake. Some of the improvements associated with the single-source systems help to solve this problem. In addition, properly designed ad tracking studies provide truer measures of the impact of the communication. As technology develops and more attention is paid to this principle, we expect to see improvements in methodologies soon.

Last but not least is principle 9, the concern for reliability and validity. Most of the measures discussed are lacking in at least one of these criteria, yet these are two of the most critical distinctions between good and bad research. If a study is properly designed, and by that we mean it addresses principles 1 through 8, it should be both reliable and valid.

Essentials of Effective Testing

Simply put, good tests of advertising effectiveness must address the nine principles established by PACT. One of the easiest ways to accomplish this is by following the decision sequence model in formulating promotional plans.

- *Establish communications objectives.* We have stated that except for a few instances (most specifically direct-response advertising), it is nearly impossible to show the direct impact of advertising on sales. So the marketing objectives established for the promotional program are not good measures of communication effectiveness. For example, it is very difficult (or too expensive) to demonstrate the effect of an ad on brand share or on sales. On the other hand, attainment of communications objectives can be measured and leads to the accomplishment of marketing objectives.
- *Use a consumer response model.* Early in this text we reviewed hierarchy of effects models and cognitive response models, which provide an understanding of the effects of communications and lend themselves to achieving communications goals.
- *Use both pretests and posttests.* From a cost standpoint—both actual cost outlays and opportunity costs—pretesting makes sense. It may mean the difference between success or failure of the campaign or the product. But it should work in conjunction with posttests, which avoid the limitations of pretests, use much larger samples, and take place in more natural settings. Posttesting may be required to determine the true effectiveness of the ad or campaign.
- *Use multiple measures.* Many attempts to measure the effectiveness of advertising focus on one major dependent variable—perhaps sales, recall, or recognition. As noted earlier in this chapter, advertising may have a variety of effects on the consumer, some of which can be measured through traditional methods, others that require updated thinking (recall the discussion on physiological responses). For a true assessment of advertising effectiveness, a number of measures may be required. The Ogilvy Award winners mentioned earlier employed multiple measures to track the effects on communications objectives.
- *Understand and implement proper research.* It is critical to understand research methodology. What constitutes a good design? Is it valid and reliable? Does it measure what we need it to? There is no shortcut to this criterion, and there is no way to avoid it if you truly want to measure the effects of advertising.

A major study sponsored by the Advertising Research Foundation (ARF), involving interviews with 12,000 to 15,000 people, addressed some of these issues.[36] While we do not have the space to analyze this study here, note that the research was designed to evaluate measures of copy tests, compare copy testing procedures, and examine some of the PACT principles. Information on this study has been published in a number of academic and trade journals and by the ARF.

Measuring the Effectiveness of Other Program Elements

Throughout this text, we have discussed how and when promotional program elements should be used, the advantages and disadvantages of each, and so on. In many chapters we have discussed measures of effectiveness used to evaluate these programs. In the final section of this chapter, we add a few measures that were not discussed earlier.

Measuring the Effectiveness of Sales Promotions

Sales promotions are not limited to retailers and resellers of products. Sports marketers have found them a very effective way to attract crowds and have been able to measure their relative effectiveness by the number of fans attending games. Major

Figure 19-18 Measuring the effects of FSIs

A study by Promotion Decisions Inc. examined the actual purchase data of users and nonusers of 27 coupon promotions in its National Shopper Lab (75,000 households) over a period of 18 months. The findings:

- FSI coupons generated significant trial by new and lapsed users of a product (53%).
- Repeat purchase rates were 11.8% higher among coupon redeemers than nonredeemers.
- 64.2% of repeat volume among coupon redeemers was without a coupon.
- There was no significant difference in share of volume between buyers who used coupons and those who did not.
- Coupons returned between 71 and 79% of their cost within 12 weeks.
- Full-page ads provided higher redemption rates, incremental volume, redemption by new users, and a higher number of repeat buyers than half-page ads.
- Consumers who used coupons were brand loyal.

League Baseball teams have seen their attendance increase for those games in which promotions are offered.

A number of organizations measure sales promotions. One firm, MarketSource, provides marketers with a basis for measuring the effectiveness of their sampling programs. While too involved to discuss in detail here, the program calculates a breakeven rate by dividing the sampling investment by the profit for the user. If the conversions exceed the breakeven rate, the sampling program is successful.[37] Promotion Decisions Inc. examines the impact of freestanding inserts (FSIs) (Figure 19-18).

Other measures of sales promotions are also available. Schnucks (St. Louis), Smitty's Super Valu (Phoenix), and Vons (Los Angeles) have all used pretests with effects measured through scanner data. Others have employed this methodology to examine brand and store switching, alternative promotions, price discounts, and merchandising techniques.[38] Other advertisers use awareness tracking studies and count the number of inquiries, coupon redemptions, and sweepstakes entries. They also track sales during promotional and nonpromotional periods while holding other factors constant.

One recent technological development designed to track the effectiveness of sales promotions at the point of sale is offered by Datatec Industries. This automated system, called Shopper Trak, places sensors in the store that track whether a person is coming or going, calculate the shopper's height (to differentiate between adults and children), and gauge traffic patterns. The system helps retailers evaluate the effectiveness of promotions or displays located throughout the store.[39]

Elizabeth Gardener and Minakshi Trivedi offer a communications framework to allow managers to evaluate sales promotion strategies over a given set of specific criteria. Borrowing from advertising applications, and using four communications goals—attention, comprehension (understanding), persuasion, and purchase—the researchers show the impact of four promotional tools and everyday low pricing (EDLP) on each goal (Figure 19-19). In addition, the impact of everyday low pricing,

Figure 19-19 Conceptual framework analysis

		Communication Factors			
		Attention/ Impression	Communication/ Understanding	Persuasion	Purchase
Sales Promotions	FSI coupons	√√	√√√	√√	√√
	On-shelf coupons	√√√	√√√	√√√	√√√
	On-pack promotions	√	√	√√	√
	Bonus packs	√√√	√√	√√	√√
	EDLP	√	√√	√√	√

Note: Promotional tendency to fulfill factor: √√√ = strong; √√ = moderate; √ = weak.

Procter & Gamble's strategy for discontinuing the use of sales promotions, is also discussed in the article.[40]

Measuring the Effectiveness of Nontraditional Media

In Chapter 13, we noted that one of the disadvantages of employing nontraditional media is that it is usually difficult to measure the effectiveness of the programs. But some progress has been made, as shown in these examples:

- *The effects of shopping cart signage.* Earlier we discussed sales increases that occurred when shopping cart signage was used. We have also noted throughout this chapter that while increasing sales is a critical goal, many other factors may contribute to or detract from this measure. (It should be noted that these results are provided by the companies that sell these promotional media.) At least one study has examined the effectiveness of shopping cart signage on data besides sales.[41] This study used personal interviews in grocery stores to measure awareness of, attention to, and influence of this medium. Interestingly, it suggests shopping carts are much less effective than the sign companies claim.
- *The effectiveness of ski-resort-based media.* In Chapter 13, we discussed advertising on ski chair lifts and other areas to attempt to reach selective demographic groups. Now the Traffic Audit Bureau (TAB) is tracking the effectiveness of this form of advertising to give advertisers more reliable criteria on which to base purchase decisions. The TAB data verify ad placements, while the media vendors have employed Simmons Market Research Bureau and Nielsen Media Research to collect ad impressions and advertising recall information.[42] These measures are combined with sales tracking data to evaluate the medium's effectiveness.
- *The effectiveness of other media.* A number of companies provide effectiveness measures to determine the impact of package designs, POP displays, trade show exhibits, and the like. While it is not possible to list them all here, suffice it to say that if one wants to measure the impact of various IMC elements, the resources are available.

Measuring the Effectiveness of Sponsorships

In earlier chapters we discussed the growth in sponsorships and the reasons why organizations have increased their investments in this area. Along with the increased expenditures have come a number of methods for measuring the impact of sponsorships. Essentially, measures of sponsorship effectiveness can be categorized as exposure-based methods or tracking measures:[43]

- *Exposure methods.* Exposure methods can be classified as those that monitor the quantity and nature of the media coverage obtained for the sponsored event and those that estimate direct and indirect audiences. While commonly employed by corporations, scholars have heavily criticized these measures. For example, Pham argues that media coverage is not the objective of sponsorships and should not be considered as a measure of effectiveness. He argues that the measures provide no indication of perceptions, attitude change, or behavioral change and should therefore not be considered as measures of effectiveness.[44]
- *Tracking measures.* These measures are designed to evaluate the awareness, familiarity, and preferences engendered by sponsorship based on surveys. A number of empirical studies have measured recall of sponsors' ads, awareness of and attitudes toward the sponsors and their products, and image effect including brand and corporate images.

A number of companies now measure the effectiveness of sports sponsorships. For example, Joyce Julius & Associates of Ann Arbor, Michigan, assigns a monetary value to the amount of exposure the sponsor receives during the event. It reviews broadcasts and adds up the number of seconds a sponsor's product name or logo can be seen clearly (for example, on signs or shirts). A total of 30 seconds is considered the equivalent of a 30-second commercial. (Such measures are of questionable validity.)

Product	Market	Sales During Event (Dollar or Volume)	Percent Change from Average Sales
Snacks	Louisville	$119,841	+52%
	Salt Lake City	$135,500	+47
	Indianapolis	$347,940	+105
Soap	Atlanta	950 cases	+375
	Minneapolis	880 cases	+867
	Cleveland	972 cases	+238
	Portland, OR	580 cases	+580
	St. Louis	1,616 cases	+1,454
Salad dressing	Atlanta	NA	+175
	Salt Lake City	NA	+143

Figure 19-20 Sales impact of concert sponsorships (average four to six weeks)

Performance Research in Newport, Rhode Island, measures impact on brand awareness and image shifts. PS Productions, a Chicago-based research organization, provides clients with a measure of event sponsorships based on increased sales. PS calculates sales goals based on the cost of the event and the value of extras like donated media, customized displays, ads for key retailers, and tickets given away. An event is a success if it brings in at least that amount in additional sales (Figure 19-20).

While each of these measures has its advantages and disadvantages, we suggest using several in assessing the impact of sponsorships. In addition to those mentioned here, the eight-step process suggested in Figure 19-21 could be used to guide these evaluations.

Measuring the Effectiveness of Other IMC Program Elements

Many of the organizations mentioned in this chapter offer research services to measure the effectiveness of specific promotional program elements. As we noted at the outset of this chapter, the increased use of integrated marketing communications programs has led to more interest in determining the synergistic effects of all program elements. A review of the Ogilvy Award winners from 1993 to date demonstrates the increased integration of additional media (as opposed to specifically the best advertising campaign)

1. Narrowly define objectives with specifics.
2. Establish solid strategies against which programming will be benchmarked and measure your programming and effectiveness against the benchmark.
3. Set measurable and realistic goals; make sure everything you do supports them.
4. Enhance, rather than just change, other marketing variables.
5. Don't pull Marketing Plan 101 off the shelf. Programming should be crafted to reflect the particulars of your company's constituencies and target audiences.
6. Define the scope of your involvement. Will it involve multiple areas within the company? Who internally and externally comprises the team?
7. Think "long term." It takes time to build brand equity. Also, think of leveraging your sponsorship through programming for as long as possible, before and after the event.
8. Build evaluation and a related budget into your overall sponsoring program. Include items such as pre- and post-event attitude surveys, media analysis, and sales results.

Figure 19-21 Eight steps to measuring event sponsorship

Figure 19-22 Heart-wear.com hits, 2002

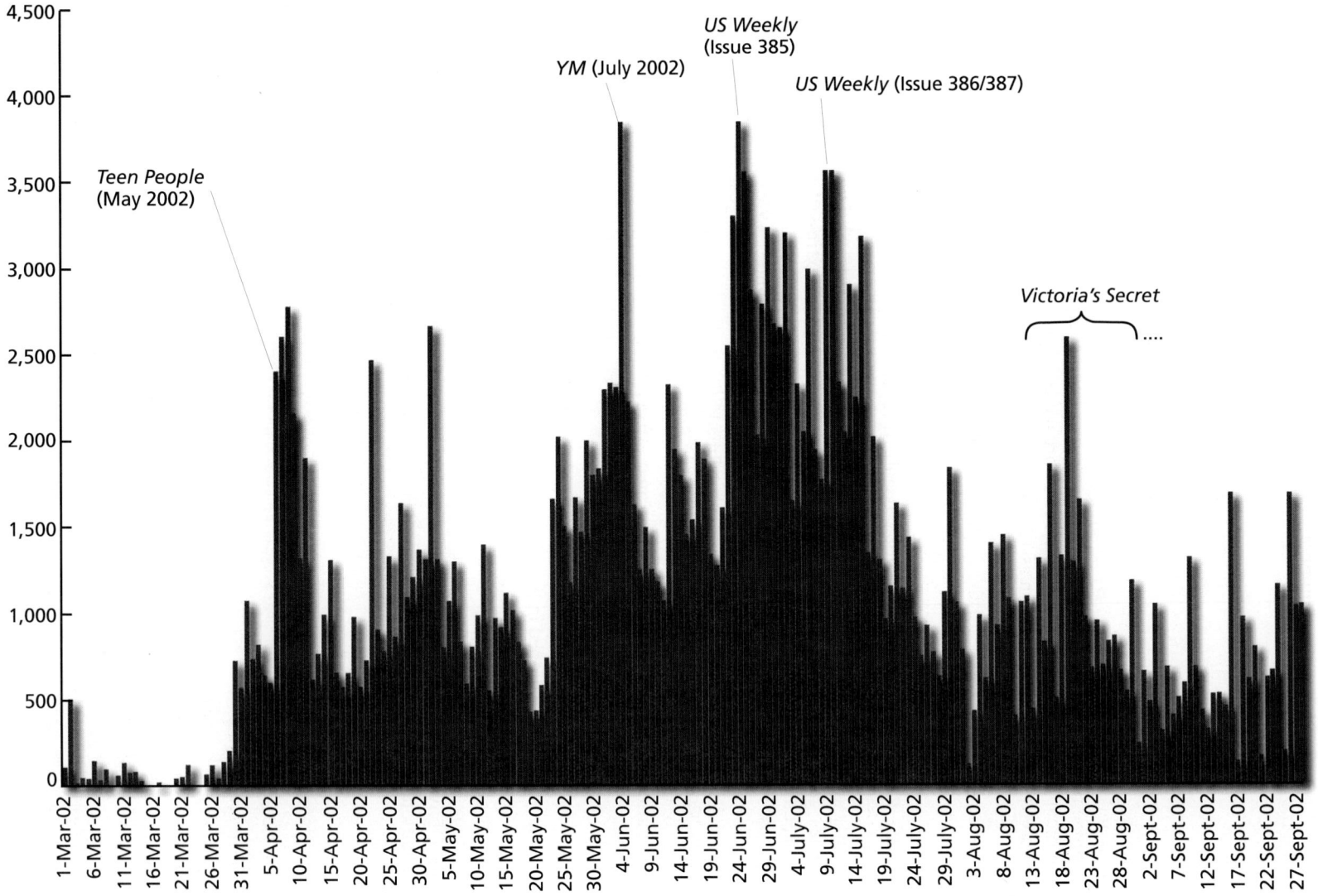

and the value of measuring their contribution to the program's success. Also departing from the specific focus on advertising are the awards given by the London-based *Institute of Practitioners,* which in 2002 opened the competition for the first time to nontraditional media as well as public relations, sales promotions, and other entries.[45]

As noted throughout the chapter, a number of studies have been implemented to determine the combined effects of two or more media as well as their synergistic impact. Before we close, we would like to cite one final example of the impact of a combination of media. This case is particularly interesting because it demonstrates that companies do not have to be as large as Microsoft, spend millions of dollars on communications, or employ large research agencies to measure effectiveness.

Heart-wear, a small jewelry manufacturer with almost no advertising budget, relies to a large degree on word of mouth and its Internet site as the primary means of creating awareness and interest in the brand. By tracking visitors to its site, Heart-wear was able to determine the impact of having its product appear in various publications, thus getting an indication of the value of publicity. In February 2002, Heart-wear page requests ranged from a low of 5 to as high as 726 per day, with an average of 199 (see Figure 19-22). In March, the average number dropped. Then the jewelry was shown in various magazines—not as an ad but with someone wearing the product or just with a small print name mention. As can be seen, the appearances in *Teen People, YM,* and *US Weekly* significantly increased the number of hits to almost 4,000 each time the jewelry appeared. The actual exposures were minimal but still led to significant increases in visits, with lower numbers associated with no exposure periods. The August and September spikes were associated with appearances in *Victoria's Secret* catalog mailings, with each increase correlated with the mailing period. Sales figures also correlated highly with the site visits.

The Heart-wear example is just one more indication of the value of measuring the effectiveness of the impact of various IMC elements. Perhaps just as important, it indicates that the excuse of not measuring due to costs has little or no merit.

All the advertising effectiveness measures discussed here have their inherent strengths and weaknesses. They offer the advertiser some information that may be useful in evaluating the effectiveness of promotional efforts. While not all promotional efforts can be evaluated effectively, progress is being made.

Summary

This chapter introduced you to issues involved in measuring the effects of advertising and promotions. These issues include reasons for testing, reasons companies do not test, and the review and evaluation of various research methodologies. We arrived at a number of conclusions: (1) Advertising research to measure effectiveness is important to the promotional program, (2) not enough companies test their ads, and (3) problems exist with current research methodologies. In addition, we reviewed the criteria for sound research and suggested some ways to accomplish effective studies.

All marketing managers want to know how well their promotional programs are working. This information is critical to planning for the next period, since program adjustments and/or maintenance are based on evaluation of current strategies. Problems often result when the measures taken to determine such effects are inaccurate or improperly used.

This chapter demonstrated that testing must meet a number of criteria (defined by PACT) to be successful. These evaluations should occur both before and after the campaigns are implemented.

A variety of research methods were discussed, many provided by syndicated research firms such as Ipsos-ASI, MSW, Arbitron, and A. C. Nielsen. Many companies have developed their own testing systems. There has been an increase in testing through the Internet.

Single-source research data were discussed. These single-source systems offer strong potential for improving the effectiveness of ad measures in the future, since commercial exposures and reactions may be correlated to actual purchase behaviors.

It is important to recognize that different measures of effectiveness may lead to different results. Depending on the criteria used, one measure may show that an ad or promotion is effective while another states that it is not. This is why clearly defined objectives and the use of multiple measures are critical to determining the true effects of an IMC program.

Key Terms

vehicle option source effect, 626
pretests, 626
posttests, 626
laboratory tests, 627
testing bias, 627
field tests, 628
PACT (Positioning Advertising Copy Testing), 628
concept testing, 629
comprehension and reaction tests, 631
consumer juries, 631
halo effect, 632
portfolio tests, 633
Flesch formula, 634
theater testing, 635
on-air test, 636
day-after recall scores, 636
pupillometrics, 636
electrodermal response, 636
eye tracking, 638
electroencephalographic (EEG) measures, 638
alpha activity, 638
hemispheric lateralization, 638
inquiry tests, 640
split-run tests, 640
recognition method, 641
recall tests, 642
single-source tracking methods, 645
tracking studies, 646

Discussion Questions

1. The chapter lead in discusses a number of studies that indicate that the combined effects of advertising in various media may lead to more effectiveness than just using one medium. Explain why you think this might occur, using some of the examples cited in the chapter.

2. Discuss some of the aspects of the communication program that advertisers may wish to test. Provide some examples.

3. Describe what is meant by focus group testing. What are some of the advantages and disadvantages of this methodology as it relates to advertising testing?

4. IMC perspective 19-2 discusses the research methodology known as eye tracking. Describe this methodology, and provide examples of how marketing researchers might use it to enhance advertising effectiveness.

5. One of the most commonly used forms of measuring advertising effectiveness in the broadcast industry is that of day after recall. Explain this methodology, and some of the advantages and disadvantages associated with its use. Provide examples where possible.

6. Discuss some of the reasons why some companies decide not to measure the effectiveness of their promotional programs. Explain why this may or may not be a good strategy.

7. Discuss the differences between pretesting and posttesting. Give examples of each.

8. What is the difference between a lab test and a field test? When should each be employed?

9. Give examples of the various types of rough testing methodologies. Describe why a company might wish to test at this phase of the process. When might it wish to test only completed ads?

10. Major changes have taken place in the way that theater tests are conducted. Describe some of these changes and the changes in measures that have also occurred in this testing method.

International Advertising and Promotion

20

Chapter Objectives

1. To examine the importance of international marketing and the role of international advertising and promotion.
2. To review the various factors in the international environment and how they influence advertising and promotion decisions.
3. To consider the pros and cons of global versus localized marketing and advertising.
4. To examine the various decision areas of international advertising.
5. To understand the role of other promotional mix elements in the international integrated marketing communications program.

How Many Truly Global Brands Are There?

In his classic 1983 book *The Marketing Imagination,* Harvard marketing professor Theodore Levitt argued that the world was becoming a common marketplace where people have the same basic needs, wants, desires, and tastes no matter where they live. Levitt called on marketers to develop global marketing strategies and true global brands that could be sold under one name around the globe. Many multinational companies heeded the call for globalization, and their ad agencies were given the charge of helping them turn their products into global brands that could be promoted with the same advertising theme and approach worldwide.

A number of consumer-product companies such as PepsiCo, Coca-Cola, Procter & Gamble, and Nestlé have been successful in turning many of their products into global brands. However, while many companies refer to their products as "global brands," precious few consumer packaged-goods brands are really global in scope. According to a recent study by the A. C. Nielsen Company, one of the world's leading market research firms, only 43 consumer-product brands can be considered truly global. To be part of Nielsen's global brand list, a brand was required to have sales of over a billion dollars (U.S.), have at least 5 percent of its sales outside of its home region, and have a geographic presence in all major regions of the world. The study findings are based on data from 30 countries that account for 90 percent of the world's gross domestic product (GDP) and are spread across all the major regions of the world.

The 43 brands on the Nielsen global brand list represent 23 companies and more than $125 billion in annual sales. Brands with major presence in North America dominate the list. PepsiCo had the most brands on the list, with six, while Philip Morris Companies (including Kraft Foods) and Procter & Gamble each had five brands, followed by Coca-Cola with four, and Kimberly-Clark, Gillette, and Mars with two each. The product category with the most global brands was beverages, which is probably not surprising to any global traveler. Nearly one-third of the brands on the list were some type of beverage, including five carbonated beverages, two juice brands, one sports drink, two coffee brands, and three beer brands. Beverage companies are clearly ahead on the globalization curve, both in the number of products and in the level of sales. The total Coca-Cola brand was number one among the beverages, with over $15 billion in sales.

Many of the brands on the global list rely heavily on foreign markets for sales. Coca-Cola generates the most sales outside of its home market, as over 70 percent of its revenue comes from international markets; next are Marlboro cigarettes, Pampers diapers, and Gillette razors and blades, each of which is over 60 percent. All of the global brands on the Nielsen list have their largest markets in North America or the Europe, Middle East, and Africa region. This is not surprising considering that North America accounts for 32 percent of the world's GDP while Europe represents 33 percent.

The Nielsen study shows that despite the efforts of major companies to find new markets for their products and make them more global, there are really not that many truly global brands. Nielsen examined more than 200 brands in this study and while more than half had a global presence, they did not reach the billion-dollar sales figure needed to make the final list. According to Jane Perrin, managing director of global services for A. C. Nielsen, many companies call their brands "global" and Nielsen is trying to set some standards regarding the use of the term. She stresses that there is a difference between a global product or portfolio of brands and a global brand. To meet Nielsen's definition of the latter, consumers should be able to find the same product with the same name around the world.

Many marketers and advertising executives are questioning the criteria used by Nielsen for a brand to achieve global status. One agency executive notes: "Global branding does not mean having the same brand everywhere. It means having an overarching strategy that optimizes brand effectiveness in local, regional, and international markets." He notes that one soap formula sold under different names can achieve global brand status—as long as the marketing efforts are managed centrally.

Many companies aspire to labeling their products "global brands," and marketers are likely to continue to use the term to describe products that are sold in foreign markets. However, A. C. Nielsen hopes that its study will bring some common understanding to what global brand truly is and will ensure that companies rightfully claim the moniker.

Sources: A. C. Nielsen Global Services, "Reaching the Billion Dollar Mark: A Review of Today's Global Brands." September 2001; "AC Nielsen Study Finds 43 Brands Have Billion Dollar Presence," news release, acnielsen.com; Shelly Branch, "AC Nielsen Gives 43 Brands Global Status," *The Wall Street Journal*, Oct. 31, 2001, p. B8.

The primary focus of this book so far has been on integrated marketing communications programs for products and services sold in the U.S. market. Many American companies have traditionally devoted most of their marketing efforts to the domestic market, since they often lack the resources, skills, or incentives to go abroad. This is changing rapidly, however, as U.S. corporations recognize the opportunities that foreign markets offer for new sources of sales and profits as well as the need to market their products internationally. Many companies are striving to develop global brands that can be advertised and promoted the world over.

In this chapter, we look at international advertising and promotion and the various issues marketers must consider in communicating with consumers around the globe. We examine the environment of international marketing and how companies often must adapt their promotional programs to conditions in each country. We review the debate over whether a company should use a global marketing and advertising approach or tailor it specifically for various countries.

We also examine how firms organize for international advertising, select agencies, and consider various decision areas such as research, creative strategy, and media selection. While the focus of this chapter is on international advertising, we also consider other promotional mix elements in international marketing, including sales promotion, personal selling, publicity/public relations, and the Internet. Let's begin by discussing some of the reasons international marketing has become so important to companies.

The Importance of International Markets

One of the major developments in the business world during the decade of the 90s was the globalization of markets. The emergence of a largely borderless world has created a new reality for all types of companies. Today, world trade is driven by global competition among global companies for global consumers.[1] With the development of faster communication, transportation, and financial transactions, time and distance are no longer barriers to global marketing. Products and services developed in one country quickly find their way to other countries where they are finding enthusiastic acceptance. Consumers around the world wear Nike shoes and Calvin Klein jeans, eat at McDonald's, shave with Gillette razors, use Apple and Dell computers, drink Coca-Cola and Pepsi Cola soft drinks and Starbucks coffee, talk on cellular phones made by Nokia and Motorola, and drive cars made by global automakers such as Ford, Honda, and Nissan.[2]

Companies are focusing on international markets for a number of reasons. Many companies in the U.S. and Western Europe recognize that their domestic markets offer them limited opportunities for expansion because of slow population growth, saturated markets, intense competition, and/or an unfavorable marketing environment. For example, U.S. tobacco companies face declining domestic consumption as a result of restrictions on their marketing and advertising efforts and the growing antismoking sentiment in this country. Companies such as R. J. Reynolds and Philip Morris are turning to markets outside the United States such as Asia and South America, where higher percentages of people smoke, nonsmokers are far more tolerant of the habit, opposition is less organized, and consumers are less litigious.[3] Many U.S.-based brewers, among them Anheuser-Busch and Coors, are looking to international markets to sustain growth as beer sales in the United States decline and regulatory pressures increase. However, these brewers are facing strong competition from foreign companies that are also targeting international markets. For example, in 2002 the Miller Brewing Co. was purchased by South African Breweries, whose largest markets are in Asia and Africa. The acquisition gives SAB access to the U.S. beer market while expanding opportunities for Miller brands in global markets.[4]

Many companies must focus on foreign markets to survive. Most European nations are relatively small in size and without foreign markets would not have the economies of scale to compete against larger U.S. and Japanese companies. For example, Swiss-based Nestlé and Netherlands-based Unilever are two of the world's largest consumer-product companies because they have learned how to market their brands to consumers in countries around the world. Two of the world's major marketers of cellular telephones are from Scandinavian countries. Nokia is based in Finland and Ericsson is located in Sweden. Australia's tourist industry is a major part of its economy and relies heavily on visitors from other countries. Australia's major tourist markets experienced dramatic declines in visitors following the global economic downturn in the tourist industry after the terrorist attacks of September 11.[5] Exhibit 20-1 shows an ad used by the Australian Tourist Commission to attract visitors from abroad.

Exhibit 20-1 The Australian Tourist Commission promotes the country as a tourist destination

Companies are also pursuing international markets because of the opportunities they offer for growth and profits. The dramatic economic, social, and political changes around the world in recent years have opened markets in Eastern Europe and China. China's joining of the World Trade Organization in 2001 has provided foreign competitors with access to 1.2 billion potential Chinese consumers, and Western marketers are eager to sell them a variety of products and services.[6] The growing markets of the Far East, Latin America, and other parts of the world present tremendous opportunities to marketers of consumer products and services as well as business-to-business marketers.

Many companies in the United States as well as in other countries have long recognized the importance and potential profitability of international markets.

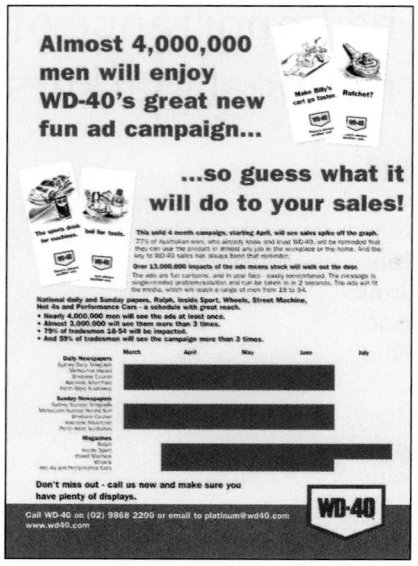

Exhibit 20-2 The WD-40 Co. gets much of its sales growth from foreign markets such as Australia

General Electric, Ford, General Motors, Nissan, Nestlé, and Procter & Gamble have made the world their market and generate much of their sales and profits from abroad. Gillette sells over 800 products in more than 200 countries. Colgate-Palmolive generates almost 70 percent of its nearly $10 billion in sales from outside the United States and Canada.[7] Starbucks sells lattes around the world as its name and image connect with consumers in Europe and Asia as well as North America. The company has coffee shops in 28 countries and operates 1,200 international outlets from Beijing to London. Starbucks plans to double its number of stores worldwide to over 10,000 by 2005.[8] Coca-Cola, Pepsi, Nike, KFC, Dell, McDonald's, and many other U.S. companies and brands are known all over the world.

Many U.S.-based companies have formed joint ventures or strategic alliances with foreign companies to market their products internationally. For example, General Mills and Swiss-based Nestlé entered into a joint venture to create Cereal Partners Worldwide (CPW), taking advantage of General Mills' popular product line and Nestlé's powerful distribution channels in Europe, Asia, Latin America, and Africa. CPW is now the world's second-largest cereal company, operating in 75 international markets, and it generated over $800 million in sales in 2002.[9] Nestlé also has entered into joint ventures with Coca-Cola to have the beverage giant distribute its instant coffee and tea throughout the world. Häagen-Dazs entered into a joint venture in Japan with Suntory Ltd., and its premium ice cream, frozen yogurt, and other brands are now sold throughout Asia.

International markets are important to small and mid-size companies as well as the large multinational corporations. Many of these firms can compete more effectively in foreign markets, where they may face less competition or appeal to specific market segments or where products have not yet reached the maturity stage of their life cycle. For example, the WD-40 Co. has saturated the U.S. market with its lubricant product and now gets much of its sales growth from markets in Europe, Asia, Latin America, and Australia (Exhibit 20-2).

Another reason it is increasingly important for U.S. companies to adopt an international marketing orientation is that imports are taking a larger and larger share of the domestic market for many products. The United States has been running a continuing **balance-of-trade deficit;** the monetary value of our imports exceeds that of our exports. American companies are realizing that we are shifting from being an isolated, self-sufficient, national economy to being part of an interdependent *global economy.* This means U.S. corporations must defend against foreign inroads into the domestic market as well as learn how to market their products and services to other countries.

While many U.S. companies are becoming more aggressive in their pursuit of international markets, they face stiff competition from large multinational corporations from other countries. Some of the world's most formidable marketers are European companies such as Unilever, Nestlé, Siemens, Philips, and Renault, as well as the various Japanese car and electronic manufacturers and packaged-goods companies such as Suntory, Shiseido, and Kao.

The Role of International Advertising and Promotion

Advertising and promotion are important parts of the marketing program of firms competing in the global marketplace. An estimated $236 billion was spent on advertising in the United States in 2002, with much of this money being spent by multinational companies headquartered outside this country.[10] Advertising expenditures outside the United States have increased by nearly 60 percent since 1990, reaching an estimated $214 million in 2002, as global marketers based in the United States, as well as European and Asian countries, increase their worldwide advertising.[11] Figure 20-1 shows the top 10 companies in terms of advertising spending outside the United States.

In addition, estimates are that another $500 billion is spent on sales promotion efforts targeted at consumers, retailers, and wholesalers around the world. The United States is still the world's major advertising market, accounting for slightly more than half of the estimated $450 billion in worldwide ad expenditures. Nearly 90 percent of the money spent on advertising products and services around the world is concentrated

Figure 20-1 Advertising spending outside the United States, top 10 companies, 2000

Rank	Advertiser	Headquarters	Ad Spending (Millions, US$)		
			Outside the U.S.	U.S.	Worldwide
1.	Unilever	London, England/ Rotterdam, Netherlands	$2,967	$ 698	$3,665
2.	Procter & Gamble	Cincinnati, Ohio	2,610	1,542	4,152
3.	Nestlé	Vevey, Switzerland	1,560	327	1,887
4.	Toyota Motor Corp.	Toyota City, Japan	1,345	790	2,135
5.	Volkswagen	Wolfsburg, Germany	1,290	424	1,714
6.	Coca-Cola	Atlanta, Georgia	1,176	403	1,579
7.	Ford Motor Co.	Dearborn, Michigan	1,127	1,196	2,323
8.	General Motors	Detroit, Michigan	1,028	2,951	3,979
9.	PSA Peugeot Citroen	Paris, France	1,004	0	1,004
10.	Fiat	Turin, Italy	988	2	990

Source: adageglobal.com.

in the United States and Canada along with the industrialized countries of Western Europe and the Pacific Rim, including Japan, South Korea, and Australia. However, advertising spending is increasing rapidly in China and in several Latin American countries, such as Mexico and Brazil.[12]

More and more companies recognize that an effective promotional program is important for companies competing in foreign markets. As one international marketing scholar notes:

> Promotion is the most visible as well as the most culture bound of the firm's marketing functions. Marketing includes the whole collection of activities the firm performs in relating to its market, but in other functions the firm relates to the market in a quieter, more passive way. With the promotional function, however, the firm is standing up and speaking out, wanting to be seen and heard.[13]

Many companies have run into difficulties developing and implementing advertising and promotion programs for international markets. Companies that promote their products or services abroad face an unfamiliar marketing environment and customers with different sets of values, customs, consumption patterns, and habits, as well as differing purchase motives and abilities. Languages vary from country to country and even within a country, such as India or Switzerland. Media options are quite limited in many countries, owing to lack of availability or limited effectiveness. These factors demand different creative and media strategies as well as changes in other elements of the advertising and promotional program for foreign markets.

The International Environment

Just as with domestic marketing, companies engaging in international marketing must carefully analyze the major environmental factors of each market in which they compete, including economic, demographic, cultural, and political/legal variables. Figure 20-2 shows some of the factors marketers must consider in each category when analyzing the environment of each country or market. These factors are important in evaluating the potential of each country as well as designing and implementing a marketing and promotional program.

The Economic Environment

A country's economic conditions indicate its present and future potential for consuming, since products and services can be sold only to countries where there is enough income to buy them. This is generally not a problem in developed countries such as the United

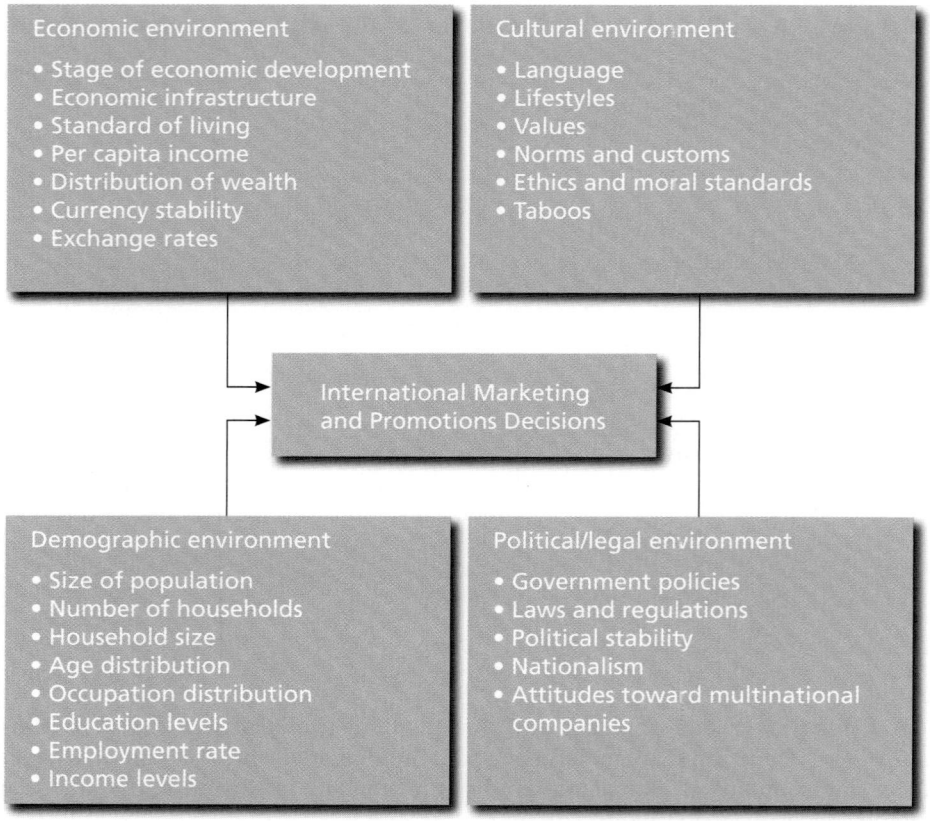

Figure 20-2 Forces in the international marketing environment

States, Canada, Japan, and most of Western Europe, where consumers generally have higher incomes and standards of living. Thus, they can and want to purchase a variety of products and services. Developed countries have the **economic infrastructure** in terms of the communications, transportation, financial, and distribution networks needed to conduct business in these markets effectively. By contrast, many developing countries lack purchasing power and have limited communications networks available to firms that want to promote their products or services to these markets.

For most companies, industrialized nations represent the greatest marketing and advertising opportunities. But most of these countries have stable population bases, and their markets for many products and services are already saturated. Many marketers are turning their attention to parts of the world whose economies and consumer markets are growing. In the early to mid-1990s many marketers began turning their attention to the "four Tigers" of Asia—South Korea, Singapore, Hong Kong, and Taiwan—which were among the fastest-growing markets in the world.[14] However, in 1997 the Asian economic crisis hit, and these countries, as well as other parts of Asia, experienced a severe recession which resulted in major declines in consumer spending. Latin America also has been experiencing a severe economic crisis over the past several years. The economy has been particularly bad in Argentina as a result of government instability and fiscal policies that have resulted in the peso losing 70 percent of its value against the dollar and euro.[15] Advertising spending in Argentina declined from more than $3 billion in 1999 to barely half a billion in 2002. Brazil, which is another major market in Latin America, has also experienced economic problems recently.[16]

The global economic slowdown that began in 2001 has created problems for most multinational companies and has led to reductions in advertising spending in most countries. The economies in many countries are stagnant, making it difficult for companies to meet their growth objectives. However, a number of multinational companies are focusing on markets experiencing stronger economic growth, such as those in China.[17] Many are also turning their attention to third-world countries where consumer markets are slowly emerging. Global Perspective 20-1 discusses the opportunities that these markets present as well as the challenges of marketing to them.

GLOBAL PERSPECTIVE 20-1

Marketing to 4 Billion of the World's Poorest Consumers

Most multinational companies generate the majority of their sales and profits by selling products and services to consumers and businesses in highly developed countries. When they do venture into developing nations such as India or China, they have traditionally focused on urban areas where incomes are higher and communication, transportation, and distribution systems are available to implement their marketing programs. However, many multinational marketers have begun turning their attention to the 4 billion consumers who live in the remote, rural communities of developing countries. These people are yearning for a better way of life and are eager to become consumers for a variety of products.

While this emergent trend has been given various labels such as B2-4B (business-to-4-billion) selling, selling to the "bottom of the pyramid," or selling to pre-markets, a number of companies are recognizing that they can turn a profit while having a positive effect on people not normally considered potential consumers. However, they also realize that it is a tremendous challenge to market to these consumers. Many of the world's poor live in severe poverty, subsisting on less than $1,500 a year, and are illiterate or nearly so. They often live in tiny villages in remote areas that are completely beyond the reach of mass media and common distribution channels. Their access to and ability to use products are determined by the available infrastructure—water, roads, electricity—or lack thereof. Clearly marketers have to package, price, and distribute their products differently as well as find innovative ways to communicate with these consumers.

So how do global marketers such as Procter & Gamble and Unilever sell soap to consumers who use mud to bathe, or how do they market toothpaste to someone who uses wood from a tree to clean his teeth? These companies often start by examining the daily lives of the consumers, including their needs, aspirations, and habits, to better understand what they may want as consumers. In many cases, advertising agencies are following or often leading their clients into these rural areas. For example, the Interpublic Group's Lowe Lintas & Partners recently set up "Linterland," an extension of its integrated marketing communications department, to help clients such as Unilever market to hard-to-reach consumers in Indonesia. Lowe's director of IMC estimates that about 64 percent of Indonesia's population (about 135 million people) lives in rural areas but can afford relatively inexpensive consumer goods such as soft drinks, shampoo, and toothpaste. The director of Linterland Indonesia notes that conventional media are not capable of reaching these rural consumers and so a different form of marketing communications—one that relies on events, road shows, and sampling—is needed to reach them.

Other ad agencies have set up similar operations to reach the vast rural populations in other Asian countries. For example, in India, 75 percent of the population (700 million people) is spread out in 600,000 villages that are virtually untouched by mass media, and they speak more than 360 dialects. WPP Group's Ogilvy and Mather launched its own special unit, Ogilvy Outreach, consisting of 35 teams in four offices that coordinate rural marketing activities across 14 states, using a network of 15,000 field-workers. Ogilvy Outreach has resorted to unusual practices such as painting cows' horns, branding water sources, organizing folk performances, and relying on schoolteachers, village heads and local health workers to relay marketing messages for clients such as Hinustan Lever, Castrol, or Amara Raja batteries. McCann-Erickson Worldwide has developed Group Asia, which specializes in rural event marketing to help its clients reach consumers in remote areas.

The most challenging country for marketers looking beyond urban markets is China, which has nearly 900 million rural consumers who are almost completely untouched by multinational marketers. In addition to the lack of knowledge regarding brands, there are problems of low income and very poor infrastructures. However, many companies are branching out into these rural areas. Word-of-mouth is the supreme marketing tool for reaching consumers in these markets, followed by education and product demonstrations. Marketers also have to adapt their products for these markets by making them available in single-use sachets that cost the equivalent of pennies rather than dollars and can be easily distributed and sold through the small kiosks found in rural villages.

Many developing countries are becoming more stable and open to trade and direct foreign investment, while education levels are also improving. The World Bank has reported that the economic growth rate for developing countries is about twice that of developed nations and is expected to reach nearly 4 percent. While investment in these markets still requires a long-term perspective, many companies are recognizing that the billions of consumers in the third world are eager to become consumers and represent a rich opportunity.

Sources: Dana James, "B2-4B Spells Profits," *Marketing News*, Nov. 5, 2001, pp. 1, 11-14; Normandy Madden, "Marketing in the Field," *Adage Global*, October 2001, p. 8.

The Demographic Environment

Major demographic differences exist among countries as well as within them. Marketers must consider income levels and distribution, age and occupation distributions of the population, household size, education, and employment rates. In some countries, literacy rates are also a factor; people who cannot read will not respond well to print ads. Demographic data can provide insight into the living standards and lifestyles in a particular country to help companies plan ad campaigns.

Demographic information can reveal the market potential of various foreign markets. India's population topped 1 billion in 2000. Only China, with 1.2 billion people, has a larger population.[18] Latin America remains one of the world's largest potential markets, although the meager income of most consumers in the region is still a problem. Brazil, the largest consumer market in South America, now has a population of 200 million and is a growing market for many products and services. More than 50 percent of the Latin American market is younger than age 26, and 30 percent is under 15. Moreover, children are the fastest-growing segment of that market. These numbers have caught the attention of international advertisers such as Mattel, Hasbro, Burger King, and others.[19] Indonesia also has a very young population, with more people under the age of 16 than the United States, and they are very receptive to Western ways and products. For example, Tower Records, a California-based chain of music stores, opened stores in Bangkok that are nearly identical to its U.S. outlets and are very popular with the youth in Thailand.[20]

The Cultural Environment

Another important aspect of the international marketing environment is the culture of each country. Cultural variables marketers must consider include language, customs, tastes, attitudes, lifestyles, values, and ethical/moral standards. Nearly every country exhibits cultural traits that influence not just the needs and wants of consumers but how they go about satisfying them.

Exhibit 20-3 This Heineken ad did not translate well into some languages

Marketers must be sensitive not only in determining what products and services they can sell foreign cultures but also in communicating with them. Advertising is often the most effective way to communicate with potential buyers and create markets in other countries. But it can also be one of the most difficult aspects of the international marketing program because of problems in developing messages that will be understood in various countries.

International advertisers often have problems with language. The advertiser must know not only the native tongue of the country but also its nuances, idioms, and subtleties. International marketers must be aware of the connotations of words and symbols used in their messages and understand how advertising copy and slogans are translated. Marketers often encounter problems in translating their advertising messages and brand names into various languages. The Heineken ad in Exhibit 20-3 is one example. Although this ad worked well in the United States and other English-speaking countries, the line "you don't have to make a great fuss" could not be translated in a meaningful way into many other languages.

Advertisers can encounter problems with the connotative meaning of signs and symbols used in their messages. For example, Pepsodent toothpaste was unsuccessful in Southeast Asia because it promised white teeth

to a culture where black and yellow teeth are symbols of prestige. An American ad campaign using various shades of green was a disaster in Malaysia, where the color symbolizes death and disease.

Problems arising from language diversity and differences in signs and symbols can usually be best solved with the help of local expertise. Marketers should consult local employees or use an ad agency knowledgeable in the local language that can help verify that the advertiser is saying what it wants to say. Many companies turn to agencies that specialize in translating advertising slogans and copy into foreign languages.

Tastes, traditions, and customs are also an important part of cultural considerations. The customs of a society affect what products and services it will buy and how they must be marketed. In France, cosmetics are used heavily by men as well as women, and advertising to the male market is common. There are also cultural differences in grooming and hygiene habits of consumers in various countries. For example, though many U.S. consumers use products like deodorant and shampoo daily, consumers in many other Western countries are not as fanatical about personal hygiene, so consumption of products such as deodorants and mouthwash is much lower than in the United States.

Another aspect of culture that is very important for international marketers to understand is values. **Cultural values** are beliefs and goals shared by members of a society regarding ideal end states of life and modes of conduct. Society shapes consumers' basic values, which affect their behavior and determine how they respond to various situations. For example, cultural values in the United States place a major emphasis on individual activity and initiative, while many Asian societies stress cooperation and conformity to the group. Values and beliefs of a society can also affect its members' attitudes and receptivity toward foreign products and services.[21] Values such as *ethnocentrism,* which refers to the tendency for individuals to view their own group or society as the center of the universe, or nationalism often affect the way consumers in various countries respond to foreign brands or even advertising messages.[22] For many years, consumers in many European countries were reluctant to buy American brands and there was even a backlash against American imagery. In fact, many U.S. companies doing business in Europe were careful not to flaunt their American roots.

One European country, in particular, where American-made products were not well received for many years is France. The French have always been very protective of their culture; for example, they have quotas for French-language shows on TV and music on the radio. As historian Richard Pells notes: "France, like the U.S., has traditionally seen itself as a country with a mission and a country whose culture and civilization is worthy of being exported around the world."[23] However, in recent years many American brands have become popular in France, particularly among younger consumers. For example, the French subsidiary of New Balance, the Boston-based athletic-shoe company, experienced strong sales growth in France when its 576 model shoe became *de rigueur* among the fashion elite (Exhibit 20-4). In recent years, U.S. brands have become popular in many other European countries as well as in Asia. Marketers attribute the rising popularity of many U.S.-made products to the worldwide distribution of American music, films, and TV shows; the growth of the Internet; and the increase in travel to the United States. These factors have made consumers in foreign countries more familiar with American culture, values, and lifestyle.[24]

Japan is one of the more difficult markets for many American advertisers to understand because of its unique values and customs.[25] For example, the Japanese have a very strong commitment to the group; social interdependence and collectivism are as important to them as individualism is to most Americans. Ads stressing individuality and nonconformity have traditionally not done well in Japan, but westernized values have become more prevalent in Japanese advertising in recent years.[26] However, the Japanese dislike ads that confront or disparage the competition and tend to prefer soft rather than hard sells.[27] A recent study found that Japanese and American magazine ads tend to portray teenage girls in different ways and that the differences

Exhibit 20-4 New Balance shoes have become very popular in France

correspond to each country's central concepts of self and society. In many American ads teens are associated with images of independence, rebelliousness, determination, and even defiance that are consistent with the American value of individuality. In contrast, Japanese ads tend to portray a happy, playful, childlike, girlish image that is consistent with the Japanese culture's sense of self, which is more dependent on others.[28] Another recent study examined gender-role portrayals in Japanese magazine advertising and found that some of the previously used hard-line stereotyping of both men and women has softened considerably since the 1980s. Men are not associated as much with stereotypical male traits, while women are shown in more positive ways. The researchers suggest that this may reflect the westernization of the depictions of men and women in Japan.[29]

As advertisers turn their attention to China, more consideration is also being given to understanding the cultural system and values of the world's most populous country. Chinese values are centered around Confucianism, which stresses loyalty and interpersonal relationships. Chinese culture also emphasizes passive acceptance of fate by seeking harmony with nature; inner experiences of meaning and feeling; stability and harmony; close family ties; and tradition.[30] A recent study of advertising appeals used in China found that advertising reflects these traditional Chinese cultural values. Chinese advertisers tend to base their advertising strategies on creating liking for a product through image and emotional appeals rather than information-laden ads. However, the study also found subtle changes in appeals to cultural values used by advertisers, particularly for ads targeting younger consumers. Youth and modernity appeals were found to be prevalent, reflecting the westernization, as well as the modernization, trend in China.[31] Marketing is just beginning to emerge in China, and advertising is a relatively new social phenomenon, so it will be important for marketers to develop a better understanding of Chinese cultural values and their implication for communications strategy.[32]

Religion is another aspect of culture that affects norms, values, and behaviors. For example, in many Arab countries, advertisers must be aware of various taboos resulting from conservative applications of the Islamic religion. Alcohol and pork cannot be advertised. Human nudity is forbidden, as are pictures of anything sacred, such as images of a cross or photographs of Mecca. The faces of women may not be shown in photos, so cosmetics use drawings of women's faces in ads.[33] In conservative Islamic countries, many religious authorities are opposed to advertising on the grounds that it promotes Western icons and culture and the associated non-Islamic consumerism.[34] Procter & Gamble recently took on tradition in Egypt by underwriting a new groundbreaking TV talk show on feminine hygiene called "Frankly Speaking" that tackles some of the most sensitive issues facing women in an Islamic country. The program has the support of the Egyptian government, which has launched its own health education drive. P&G does not promote its products during the show, but the program does contain numerous commercials for its Always brand, which has 85 percent of the disposable sanitary pad market in the country.[35]

The Political/Legal Environment

The political and legal environment in a country is one of the most important factors influencing the advertising and promotional programs of international marketers. Regulations differ owing to economic and national sovereignty considerations, nationalistic and cultural factors, and the goal of protecting consumers not only from false or misleading advertising but, in some cases, from advertising in general. It is difficult to generalize about advertising regulation at the international level, since some countries are increasing government control of advertising while others are decreasing it. Government regulations and restrictions can affect various aspects of a company's advertising program, including:

- The types of products that may be advertised.
- The content or creative approach that may be used.
- The media that all advertisers (or different classes of advertisers) are permitted to employ.

- The amount of advertising a single advertiser may use in total or in a specific medium.
- The use of foreign languages in ads.
- The use of advertising material prepared outside the country.
- The use of local versus international advertising agencies.
- The specific taxes that may be levied against advertising.[36]

A number of countries ban or restrict the advertising of various products. Cigarette advertising is banned in some or all media in numerous countries besides the United States, including Argentina, Canada, France, Italy, Norway, Sweden, and Switzerland. The Australian government limits tobacco advertising to point of purchase. The ban also excludes tobacco companies from sponsoring sporting events. In Malaysia, a government ban on cigarette-related advertising and sponsorship was initiated in 2003 in an effort to curb the rising number of smokers in the country.[37] In China, tobacco and liquor advertising are banned except in hotels for foreigners.

Recently the tobacco industry has been reducing its advertising efforts in markets around the world, including Asia and Eastern Europe, where they have enjoyed much more regulatory freedom. Three of the largest tobacco companies are leading an effort to implement self-imposed restrictions and requirements for their advertising.[38] For example, the tobacco industry agreed to stop all television advertising in Mexico at the end of 2002 as part of a raft of new self-regulatory measures.[39] Many of these restrictions are already being forced on the companies in North America, Western Europe, and North Asia, where governments take a tough stance on tobacco advertising. However, regulations in many other countries, such as Indonesia and the Philippines, are minimal. The industry's self-regulatory efforts are seen as a move to head off a campaign by the World Health Organization for a worldwide ban on all tobacco advertising.

In Europe there has been a longstanding ban on advertising for prescription-drug products, which is designed to keep government-subsidized health care costs under control. The European Union has argued that advertising increases the marketing budgets of drug companies and results in higher prices. The ban prevents prescription-drug companies from mentioning their products even on their websites or in brochures, although some relaxation of these restrictions is being considered by the European Commission for drugs used to treat AIDS, diabetes, and respiratory ailments.[40]

While international marketers are accustomed to restrictions on the advertising of cigarettes, liquor, and pharmaceuticals, they are often surprised by restrictions on other products or services. For example, margarine cannot be advertised in France, nor can restaurant chains. For many years, the French government restricted travel advertising because it encourages the French to spend their francs outside the country.[41]

Many countries restrict the media advertisers can use. In 1999 the European Commission threw out an appeal against Greece's national ban on toy advertising on daytime television. Thus advertisers can advertise toys on TV only during the evening hours.[42] Some of the most stringent advertising regulations in the world are found in Scandinavian countries. Commercial TV advertising did not begin in Sweden until 1992, and both Sweden and Denmark limit the amount of time available for commercials. Advertising aimed at young children has not been legal in Sweden since commercial television was introduced in the country a decade ago. The Swedish government feels that young people are not able to differentiate between advertising and programming and are not capable of understanding the selling intent of commercials.[43] Saudi Arabia opened its national TV system to commercial advertising in 1986, but advertising is not permitted on the state-run radio system. Advertising in magazines and newspapers in the country is subject to government and religious restrictions.[44]

Many governments have rules and regulations that affect the advertising message. For example, comparative advertising is legal and widely used in the United States and Canada but is illegal in some countries such as Korea and Belgium. In Europe, the European Commission has developed a directive to standardize the basic form and content of comparative advertising and develop a uniform policy.[45] Currently, comparative advertising is legal in many European countries, illegal in some, and legal and rarely used in others such as Great Britain. Many Asian and South American countries

Exhibit 20-5 Diet Coke must use a different name in some countries

have also begun to accept comparative ads. However, Brazil's self-regulatory advertising codes are so strict that few advertisers have been able to create a comparative message that has been approved.[46] Many countries restrict the types of claims advertisers can make, the words they can use, and the way products can be represented in ads. In Greece, specific claims for a product, such as "20 percent fewer calories," are not permitted in an advertising message.[47] Copyright and other legal restrictions make it difficult to maintain the same name from market to market. For example, Diet Coke is known as Coca-Cola Light in Germany, France, and many other countries because of legal restrictions prohibiting the word *diet* (Exhibit 20-5).

Government restrictions can influence the use of foreign languages in advertising as well as the production of the ad. Most countries permit the use of foreign languages in print ads and direct mail. However, some do not allow foreign-language commercials on TV or radio or in cinema ads, and some restrict foreign-language ads to media targeted to foreigners in their country.[48] Some countries also restrict the use of foreign-produced ads and foreign talent. For example, with few exceptions, such as travel advertising, all commercials aired on Malaysian television must be made in Malaysia. However, the Asian country is considering changing its rules to allow foreign commercials to air on the new legalized satellite signals into the country.[49]

These restrictions are motivated primarily by economic considerations. Many countries require local production of at least a portion of commercials to build local film industries and create more jobs for local producers of print and audiovisual materials. Nationalistic and cultural factors also contribute to these restrictions, along with a desire to prevent large foreign ad agencies from dominating the advertising business in a country and thus hampering its development. Restrictions affecting the advertising industry took a new twist recently in China when the government began strictly enforcing regulations governing licenses it requires of magazine publishers. Since the new enforcement took effect on January 1, 2000, Western publishers have been required to use a direct translation of the often-obscure name that appears on their license or use no English name at all. Thus, magazines such as *Cosmopolitan, Esquire,* and *Woman's Day* are not able to use their popular names.[50]

In some countries, steps are being taken to ease some of the legal restrictions and other barriers facing international advertisers. For example, the Maastricht Treaty was designed to create a single European market and remove many of the barriers to trade among the 12 member nations of the European Community. One of the goals of this plan was a single advertising law throughout the EC, but when the treaty was ratified in November 1993, many of the advertising directives were not agreed upon—so many advertising regulations are still decided by each country. A directive was passed by the European Commission banning all tobacco advertising, which most of the 15 European Union countries are now implementing. The European Commission may also take steps to restrict alcohol advertising and marketing. Sweden has been leading a Pan-European effort to ban TV advertising targeted at children under the age of 12 that has been gaining support from other members of the European Union.[51] However, marketers, ad agencies, media, and trade associations in several European countries including the United Kingdom and France have begun pushing for self-regulation that would include efforts to help children understand and interpret advertising effectively rather than banning efforts to reach them.[52]

Global versus Localized Advertising

The discussion of differences in the marketing environments of various countries suggests that each market is different and requires a distinct marketing and advertising program. However, in recent years a

great deal of attention has focused on the concept of **global marketing,** where a company uses a common marketing plan for all countries in which it operates, thus selling the product in essentially the same way everywhere in the world. **Global advertising** falls under the umbrella of global marketing as a way to implement this strategy by using the same basic advertising approach in all markets.

The debate over standardization versus localization of marketing and advertising programs began years ago.[53] But the idea of global marketing was popularized by Professor Theodore Levitt, who says the worldwide marketplace has become homogenized and consumers' basic needs, wants, and expectations transcend geographic, national, and cultural boundaries.[54] One writer described Levitt's position on global marketing as follows:

> Levitt's vision of total worldwide standardization is global marketing at the extreme. He argues that, thanks to cheap air travel and new telecommunications technology, consumers the world over are thinking—and shopping—increasingly alike. According to Levitt, the New Republic of Technology homogenizes world tastes, wants, and possibilities into global marketing proportions, which allows for world standardized products.[55]

Not everyone agrees with Levitt's global marketing theory, particularly with respect to advertising. Many argue that products and advertising messages must be designed or at least adapted to meet the differing needs of consumers in different countries.[56] We will consider the arguments for and against global marketing and advertising, as well as situations where it is most appropriate.

Advantages of Global Marketing and Advertising

A global marketing strategy and advertising program offer certain advantages to a company, including the following:

- Economies of scale in production and distribution.
- Lower marketing and advertising costs as a result of reductions in planning and control.
- Lower advertising production costs.
- Abilities to exploit good ideas on a worldwide basis and introduce products quickly into various world markets.
- A consistent international brand and/or company image.
- Simplification of coordination and control of marketing and promotional programs.

Advocates of global marketing and advertising contend that standardized products are possible in all countries if marketers emphasize quality, reliability, and low prices. They say people everywhere want to buy the same products and live the same way. Product standardization results in lower design and production costs as well as greater marketing efficiency, which translates into lower prices for consumers. Product standardization and global marketing also enable companies to roll out products faster into world markets, which is becoming increasingly important as product life cycles become shorter and competition increases.

A number of companies have been very successful using a global advertising approach, including Coca-Cola, Merrill Lynch, Xerox, American Express, and British Airways. Gillette used global advertising in the early 90s to launch its Sensor shaving system, which became one of the most successful products in the company's history. The advertising theme for the global campaign was "The Best a Man Can Get." At the end of the decade Gillette launched the Mach3, its new triple-bladed shaving system, and once again used a global campaign built around the high-tech theme of the product and retaining the same tagline. Prior to the introduction of the new product, Gillette launched the Mach3.com website, which was supported by online advertising to educate prospective customers about the intricacies of the triple-bladed razor. The Web campaign was followed by a $200 million global media blitz that helped make the Mach3 the number-one-selling shaving system after less than a year on the market. Exhibit 20-6 shows an ad for the Mach3 that was used in Spain.

Exhibit 20-6 Gillette used global advertising to launch its new Mach3 shaving system

Problems with Global Advertising

Opponents of the standardized global approach argue that very few products lend themselves to global advertising.[57] Differences in culture, market, and economic development; consumer needs and usage patterns; media availabilities; and legal restrictions make it extremely difficult to develop an effective universal approach to marketing and advertising. Advertising may be particularly difficult to standardize because of cultural differences in circumstances, language, traditions, values, beliefs, lifestyle, music, and so on. Moreover, some experts argue that cultures around the world are becoming more diverse, not less so. Thus, advertising's job of informing and persuading consumers and moving them toward using a particular brand can be done only within a given culture.

Consumer usage patterns and perceptions of a product may vary from one country to another, so advertisers must adjust their marketing and advertising approaches to different problems they may face in different markets. For example, when Nestlé introduced its Nescafé instant coffee brand, the company faced at least five different situations in various parts of the world:

1. In the United States, the idea of instant coffee had great penetration but Nescafé had the minor share.
2. In continental Europe, Nescafé had the major share of the market, but the idea of instant coffee was in the early stages.
3. In the tea-drinking countries, such as the United Kingdom and Japan, tea drinkers had to be converted not just to coffee but to instant coffee.
4. In Latin America, the preferred coffee was a heavy one that could not be duplicated with an instant version.
5. In Scandinavia, Nestlé had to deal with the ingrained custom of keeping a pot of coffee on the stove from early morning until late at night.

Nestlé had to use different advertising strategies for each market; a global campaign would not have been able to address the varying situations adequately. Exhibit

Exhibit 20-7 A. Nescafé instant coffee ad used in Japan B. Nescafé instant coffee ad used in Norway

20-7 shows Nescafé ads used in Japan and Norway. Nestlé encountered yet another challenge when it entered the Israeli market in 1995. *Nescafé* was the generic word for instant coffee as Israelis assumed that it was an abbreviation of the Hebrew word *namess* (dissolving). Israeli consumers were also not very demanding with respect to the quality of their coffee and considered the low-quality powdered coffee, or *nescafé,* produced by a local company, suitable fare. To overcome the generic connotation of Nescafé, all of the advertising presented the Nescafé Classic brand as "Nescafé of Nestlé" and portrayed it as the coffee choice of people all around the world (Exhibit 20-8). The company also relied on taste testing at the points of sale so consumers could experience Nescafé Classic's superior quality. Within one year Nestlé had 30 percent of the instant coffee market in Israel.[58]

Many experts believe that marketing a standardized product the same way all over the world can turn off consumers, alienate employees, and blind a company to diversities in customer needs. For example, when McDonald's expanded to Puerto Rico, it alienated consumers by using American TV ads dubbed in Spanish and then using Hispanic ads that were brought in from New York, which subsequent research showed looked too Mexican.[59]

Parker Pen also encountered problems when it attempted to use global advertising in the mid-1980s. Local managers in its foreign branches resented the home office centralizing the advertising function with one worldwide agency and mandating the type of advertising appeal used in their markets.[60]

Such problems have led some major companies to move away from a completely standardized approach. For example, the Colgate-Palmolive Co. has used global advertising for many of its brands, including the Colgate, Palmolive, Fab, and Ajax product

Exhibit 20-8 Nestlé had to reshape Israel's definition of instant coffee

Exhibit 20-9 Advertising for Colgate toothpaste uses a consistent visual image, but the copy may vary for different markets

lines, and continues to endorse the use of global appeals. Under its current marketing strategy, however, advertising is often modified for a specific country or region, particularly where local creativity can improve the advertising over the global standard. An example of this approach is the advertising used for Colgate toothpaste (see Exhibit 20-9). The globe/smile image is used as the visual in nearly every country where Colgate is marketed, but the copy varies. This ad for the Russian market appeared in the Moscow edition of *Reader's Digest.*

Some marketing experts claim much of the attention to the advantages of global advertising stems from large ad agencies trying to increase business by encouraging clients to use one agency to handle their marketing communications worldwide.[61] Many large multinational companies are indeed consolidating their business with one or a few agencies who have offices around the world and offer international advertising capabilities. However, the consolidations are often driven by the client's increasing emphasis on global markets.[62]

When Is Globalization Appropriate?

While globalization of advertising is viewed by many in the advertising industry as a difficult task, some progress has been made in learning what products and services are best suited to worldwide appeals:[63]

1. Brands or messages that can be adapted for a visual appeal, avoiding the problems of trying to translate words into dozens of languages.
2. Brands that are promoted with image campaigns that play to universal appeals such as sex or wealth.
3. High-tech products and new products coming to the world for the first time, not steeped in the cultural heritage of the country.
4. Products with nationalistic flavor if the country has a reputation in the field.
5. Products that appeal to a market segment with universally similar tastes, interests, needs, and values.

Many companies and brands rely heavily on visual appeals that are easily adapted for use in global advertising campaigns. For example, Boeing launched its first global image campaign in 2000 as part of its effort to be known as more than an airplane manufacturer. While Boeing is the world's leading manufacturer of commercial jets, a series of acquisitions has transformed the company into a major force in markets for military aircraft, rockets, satellites, and broadband communications. Boeing is setting the stage for its future with a global image and branding campaign that uses the tagline "Boeing Forever New Frontiers." The corporate campaign features TV spots as well as print ads, such as the one shown in Exhibit 20-10, that symbolize optimism and future orientation. The commercials use a steady stream of visuals—children with arms outstretched, a young boy releasing a dove, jet planes, and spinning satellites. The goal of the campaign is to leverage Boeing's strong global brand image with customers and aviation, business and government influentials as well as to create excitement among the company's employees regarding the future of the company.

Products such as jewelry, liquor, cosmetics, and cigarettes can be promoted using image advertising, the second category. Marlboro uses its cowboy/western imagery

Exhibit 20-10 Visual appeals work well in global advertising, such as that used by the Boeing company

around the world, and many cosmetic companies use similar image campaigns in different countries.

Levitt, like many advertisers, believes that joy, sentiment, excitement, and many other emotions are universal. Thus, it is common for global advertising campaigns to use emotional and image appeals. One advertising executive said:

> What it all boils down to is that we are all human. We share the gift of emotional response. We feel things. And we feel them in remarkably similar ways. We speak different languages, we observe different customs, but we are wired to each other and to an ultimate power source that transcends us in a way that makes us subject to a common emotional spectrum.[64]

Companies whose products appeal to universal needs, values, and emotions are also recognizing that they can advertise their brands with global campaigns. For example, Calvin Klein, one of the leading fashion and design companies and a brand name recognized around the world, recently launched a global campaign for its Eternity fragrance brand. The ad campaign expands the Eternity ideal of lasting love and intimacy with commercials featuring scenes of family life set to the classic Burt Bacharach song "What the World Needs Now Is Love," which is sung by Aimee Mann. The print advertising depicts life's special moments and features the tagline "Love, Sweet Love" and is designed to resemble photographs pulled from a family album. The campaign features supermodel Christy Turlington as the Eternity woman.

High-tech consumer products such as personal computers, calculators, VCRs, TVs, and audio equipment are in the third category, as are various types of business-to-business products and services such as computer systems. Business-to-business marketers like EDS and Xerox have begun using global advertising campaigns, as have Hewlett-Packard and IBM.

Products in the fourth category are those whose national reputation for quality can be the basis for a global advertising campaign. Examples include Swiss watches, French wine, and German beer or automobiles. As discussed earlier in the chapter, many U.S. companies are taking advantage of the cachet American products have acquired among consumers in Europe and other international markets. For example, Jeep promotes itself as "the American legend" in Europe and Japan. Brown-Forman has been using an American theme for its Jack Daniel's and Southern Comfort liquor brands since it began selling them in foreign markets more than two decades ago.

In the final category for which globalization is appropriate are products and services that can be sold to common market segments around the world, such as those identified by Salah Hassan and Lea Katsansis.[65] One such segment is the world's elite—people who, by reason of their economically privileged position, can pursue a lifestyle that includes fine jewelry, expensive clothing, quality automobiles, and the

like. Marketers of high-quality products such as Bally leather goods, Cartier jewelry, Godiva chocolates, and Louis Vuitton luggage can use global advertising to appeal to the elite market segment around the world. Well-known international brands competing in the luxury goods marketplace often present a singular image of prestige and style to the entire world.

Another segment of global consumers who have similar needs and interests and seek similar features and benefits from products and services is teenagers. There are more than 200 million teens in Europe, Latin America, and the Pacific Rim countries of Asia whose lifestyles are converging with those of the 40 million teens in the United States and Canada to create a vast, free-spending global market.[66] Teens now have intense exposure to television, magazines, movies, music, travel, and global advertising from companies such as Levi Strauss, Benetton, Nike, Coca-Cola, Pepsi, and many others. MTV is now seen in 136 countries. Global Perspective 20-2 discusses how the youth of the world have become an important global market segment for many companies.

Global Products, Local Messages

While the pros and cons of global marketing and advertising continue to be debated, many companies are taking an in-between approach by standardizing their products and basic marketing strategy but localizing their advertising messages. This approach recognizes similar desires, goals, needs, and uses for products and services but tailors advertising to the local cultures and conditions in each market. Some agencies call this approach "Think globally, act locally." Grey Advertising describes it as "global vision with a local touch."[67]

Although some marketers use global ads with little or no modification, most companies adapt their messages to respond to differences in language, market conditions, and other factors. Many global marketers use a strategy called **pattern advertising;** their ads follow a basic approach, but themes, copy, and sometimes even visual elements are adapted to differences in local markets. For example, Unilever's Dove soap uses the same basic advertising and positioning theme globally, but models from Australia, France, Germany, and Italy are used to appeal to women in those countries. The TaylorMade Golf Company uses pattern advertising to promote its golf clubs in different countries. Exhibit 20-11 shows ads for the company's R500 driver used in the United States and Germany.

Another way global marketers adapt their campaigns to local markets is by producing a variety of ads with a similar theme and format and allowing managers in various countries or regions to select those messages they believe will work best in their markets. Some companies are also giving local managers more autonomy in adapting

Exhibit 20-11
TaylorMade uses pattern advertising to promote its golf clubs in various countries

GLOBAL PERSPECTIVE 20-2

Youth Become an Important Global Market Segment

Marketers are continually searching for global consumer market segments to whom products and services can be advertised in a similar fashion all over the world. Many companies are recognizing that the most global segment of all is the youth of the world, as they show amazing similarities in tastes, interests, language, and attitudes. Elissa Moses, author of *The $100 Billion Allowance: Accessing the Global Teen Market,* says: "Pop culture is totally transient. Teens are simultaneously plugged into two cultural channels—local and global. For global (culture), they are a homogeneous target. This includes music, fashion, film, video games and technology." Marketing experts note that there are more similarities than differences among youthful consumers. Teens in the United States as well as Latin America, Europe, Asia, and Australia are surfing the Internet, talking on their cell phones, playing video games, watching MTV, going to the movies, and drinking Coke or Pepsi.

Multinational companies recognize that one of their major marketing challenges is tapping into the billions of dollars being spent by young consumers around the world. Global youth is a very ripe and growing market, as there are over 200 million teens in Europe, Latin America, and the Pacific Rim countries of Asia who are converging with the 40 million in the United States and Canada to create a vast, free-spending global market. U.S.-based companies in particular recognize the importance of marketing to young people in foreign markets. The youthfulness of many other countries is far greater than that of the United States, especially in Asia and South America. Twenty-one percent of the population in the United States is age 14 and under versus 25 percent in China, 33 percent in India, 37 percent in the Philippines, 29 percent in Brazil, and 27 percent in Argentina.

The convergence in the lifestyles, tastes, attitudes, and product preferences of young people is being driven by several factors. Many young people around the globe have a strong interest in U.S. culture and lifestyle, and their hunger for Americana is being fed by their access to satellite television and the Internet. Music, movies, and sports are universal languages for young people, and many marketers capitalize on these interests by having celebrities with global appeal appear in their ads targeting youth. Pepsi ads featuring pop-star Britney Spears are shown around the world, while athletes with global appeal such as Tiger Woods, Lance Armstrong, and Michael Jordan endorse products for Nike and other global marketers.

To tap into the global youth market, companies have to understand young people's common characteristics. For example, Harvard marketing professor Rohit Desphande notes that one of the most important characteristics of young consumers globally is a sense of individualism that goes beyond what their parents' generation felt. He notes that this characteristic is a result of values portrayed in Western music, film, the Internet, and news media. Individualistic values are even prevalent among young people in Asia, where collectivist values have always been the norm. A study of Asian teens conducted by the Roper ASW research firm found that youth between the ages of 13 and 19 ranked values such as individualism, ambition, and freedom much higher than did adults between the ages of 40 and 65.

While many companies are marketing to the similarities of global youth, they must also be mindful of the cultural differences that still exist from one country to the next. For example, while American teens view fast food as a way to eat on the go, youth in other countries favor meals they can savor. Pizza Hut and Kentucky Fried Chicken are considered upscale restaurants in Asia, and many young people consider them very cool places to go and be seen.

Cellular phones are much more prevalent in Europe than in the United States. For example, 65 percent of 10- to 19-year-olds in the United Kingdom have mobile phones versus less than 20 percent in the United States. Instant messaging and text messaging is widely used in Europe and Japan and has made cell phones in those regions very important possessions for teens, while for American youth the technology is seen as a nice-to-have accessory. European teens consume much of the same media as their American counterparts, with TV and the Internet topping the list of their favorites. However, 67 percent of European boys and 47 percent of European girls consider the Internet

"too American" and would rather buy a local product over the Internet than an American one.

Despite these regional variations, most marketers' attraction to the youth market lies in the youngsters' similarities. Many experts still note that it is difficult to find anything different, other than language, among teenagers in Japan, China, France, Brazil, or the United States. It doesn't matter where they live, the youth of the world are an important market segment and represent a tremendous opportunity for marketers.

Sources: Arundhati Parmar, "Global Youth United," *Marketing News,* Oct. 28, 2002, pp. 1, 49; Lisa Bertagnoli, "Continental Spendthrifts," *Marketing News,* Oct. 22, 2001, pp. 1,15; Laurel Wentz, "Japan: The Ultimate Buyers Market," *Advertising Age International,* January 1997, p. 135.

global campaign themes to local markets. For example, when Douglas Daft took over as CEO of the Coca-Cola Co. in late 1999, he noted that global brand management and marketing had distanced the company from the crucial differences that existed from market to market. Daft announced a new strategy that gives managers in various regions and countries around the world more freedom to adapt their marketing and advertising to local conditions.[68] The new approach puts a stronger emphasis on creativity that is tailored to local markets. Coca-Cola first used this new approach when it launched its "Coca-Cola Enjoy" advertising campaign in 2000 (Exhibit 20-12). To ensure that the global theme could be adapted to various regions and countries, local ad agencies were brought into the process early on to develop ads for their markets.[69]

Coca-Cola continued with the "go local" strategy a year later when it developed the "Life Tastes Good" campaign, which celebrates the positive values of the brand in stories of everyday life. Marketing directors from 13 regions around the world helped create 30 TV commercials as well as print ads tailored to their own markets. In countries like Brazil, four different commercials were produced adapted to regional differences and habits regarding the consumption of soft drinks.[70]

Although many marketers are striving to develop global brands, research suggests most are doing so by using a localized approach. A study of international advertising

Exhibit 20-12 The Coca-Cola Co. uses a global advertising theme but local adaptations are used to respond to conditions in various markets

strategies of successful U.S. multinational corporations found that only 9 percent used totally standardized global advertising for all foreign markets, while 37 percent used all localized advertising. The remaining 54 percent used a combination strategy, standardizing portions of their advertising but adapting it for local markets.[71] Marketers said a major risk of the global approach was a lack of communication owing to cultural differences. Another study found that most U.S. consumer durable goods manufacturers used a localized advertising approach—but most used some standardized messages.[72]

A more recent study of international advertising decision makers found that "think globally, act locally" still appears to be the dominant strategy of international advertisers, but with a slight revision: "Think globally, act regionally."[73] Most of the respondents in this survey said their companies' worldwide headquarters play a dominant role in determining their international advertising messages so they are consistent worldwide. However, there is a trend toward giving regional offices the autonomy to adapt the global theme for their local markets.

Most managers believe it is important to adapt components of their advertising messages—such as the language, models, scenic backgrounds, message content, and symbols—to reflect the culture and frame of reference of consumers in various countries. Many companies are making these tactical adjustments to their advertising messages while still pursuing global strategies that will help them project a consistent global image and turn their products and services into global brands.

Decision Areas in International Advertising

Companies developing advertising and promotional programs for international markets must make certain organizational and functional decisions similar to those for domestic markets. These decisions include organization style, agency selection, advertising research, creative strategy and execution, and media strategy and selection.

Organizing for International Advertising

One of the first decisions a company must make when it decides to market its products to other countries is how to organize the international advertising and promotion function. This decision is likely to depend on how the company is organized overall for international marketing and business. Three basic options are centralization at the home office or headquarters, decentralization of decision making to local foreign markets, or a combination of the two.

Centralization Many companies prefer to *centralize* the international advertising and promotion function so that all decisions about agency selection, research, creative strategy and campaign development, media strategy, and budgeting are made at the firm's home office.

Complete centralization is likely when market and media conditions are similar from one country to another, when the company has only one or a few international agencies handling all of its advertising, when the company can use standardized advertising, or when it desires a consistent image worldwide. Centralization may also be best when a company's international business is small and it operates through foreign distributors or licensees who do not become involved in the marketing and promotional process.

Many companies prefer the centralized organizational structure to protect their foreign investments and keep control of the marketing effort and corporate and/or brand image. Centralization can save money, since it reduces the need for staff and administration at the local subsidiary level. As the trend toward globalized marketing and advertising strategies continues, more companies are likely to move more toward centralization of the advertising function to maintain a unified world brand image rather than presenting a different image in each market. Some foreign managers may actually prefer centralized decision making, as it removes them from the burden of advertising and promotional decisions and saves them from defending local decisions to the home office.

However, many marketing and advertising managers in foreign markets oppose centralized control. They say the structure is too rigid and makes it difficult to adapt the advertising and promotional program to local needs and market conditions. As noted earlier, Parker Pen encountered such resistance when it attempted to implement a global advertising strategy.

Decentralization Under a *decentralized* organizational structure, marketing and advertising managers in each market have the authority to make their own advertising and promotional decisions. Local managers can select ad agencies, develop budgets, conduct research, approve creative themes and executions, and select advertising media. Companies using a decentralized approach put a great deal of faith in the judgment and decision-making ability of personnel in local markets. This approach is often used when companies believe local managers know the marketing situation in their countries the best. They may also be more effective and motivated when given responsibility for the advertising and promotional program in their markets. Decentralization also works well in small or unique markets where headquarters' involvement is not worthwhile or advertising must be tailored to the local market.

International fragrance marketer Chanel, Inc., uses a decentralized strategy. Chanel found that many of its fragrance concepts do not work well globally and decided to localize advertising. For example, the U.S. office has the option of using ads created by the House of Chanel in Paris or developing its own campaigns for the U.S. market. Chanel executives in the United States think that the French concept of prestige is not the same as Americans' and the artsy ads created in France do not work well in this country.[74]

Combination While there is an increasing trend toward centralizing the international advertising function, many companies combine the two approaches. The home office, or headquarters, has the most control over advertising policy, guidelines, and operations in all markets. The international advertising manager works closely with local or regional marketing managers and personnel from the international agency (or agencies) and sets advertising and promotional objectives, has budgetary authority, approves all creative themes and executions, and approves media selection decisions, especially when they are made on a regional basis or overlap with other markets.

Advertising managers in regional or local offices submit advertising plans and budgets for their markets, which are reviewed by the international advertising manager. Local managers play a major role in working with the agency to adapt appeals to their particular markets and select media.

The combination approach allows for consistency in a company's international advertising yet permits local input and adaptation of the promotion program. Most consumer-product companies find that local adaptation of advertising is necessary for foreign markets or regions, but they want to maintain control of the overall worldwide image they project. Eastman Kodak, for example, provides central strategy and support to local offices and acts as consultant to them. Although each country is autonomous, the main office controls the quality of advertising and advertising policy. Media buying is done on a local level, but the main office becomes involved in special media opportunities and overall strategy for events such as Olympic sponsorship and regionalized campaigns. Levi's created a centralized vice president of global marketing position to oversee the company's marketing in over 60 countries but still provides a great deal of autonomy to regional marketing directors.

Agency Selection

One of the most important decisions for a firm engaged in international marketing is the choice of an advertising agency. The company has three basic alternatives in selecting an agency to handle its international advertising. First, it can choose a major agency with both domestic and overseas offices. Many large agencies have offices all over the world and have become truly international operations. Some Western agencies have opened offices in Eastern Europe and Russia to create ads for the multinational companies participating in the free-market economies that are developing in these countries. Global Perspective 20-3 discusses how many agencies are moving

GLOBAL PERSPECTIVE 20-3

Shanghai—The Next New York City of the Advertising World

For many years marketers could only dream of selling their products to China's 1.2 billion consumers. But with the end of the cultural revolution in 1979 and its massive modernization drive over the past 25 years, China has become one of the fastest-growing consumer markets in the world. A number of multinational companies—including Coca-Cola, General Motors, Gillette, Procter & Gamble, Unilever, and Nokia—are marketing their products to the world's largest potential mass market. And advertising, once banned as a capitalist scourge, is now encouraged by the Chinese government, which views it as a catalyst that can accelerate China's economic development.

Over the past two decades, many of world's largest marketers, as well as advertising agencies, opened offices in the island enclave of Hong Kong, which is located on China's far southern coast. Hong Kong, which was a British colony for many years before returning to China's control in 1997, provides a well-developed infrastructure; an experienced, English-speaking work force; low taxes; a fair judicial system; and transparent business practices. However, a growing number of major marketers and their agencies are deciding that if they really want to compete in the world's largest consumer market, they need to be more centrally located on the mainland of China. Thus they are abandoning Hong Kong for Shanghai, which is China's largest city, with 15 million people, and is strategically located on China's central coast.

Although Beijing is the nation's capital, Shanghai is a cosmopolitan city and is home to China's largest port, largest industrial base, best shops and restaurants, and most fashionable people, a throwback to the city's heritage as the "Paris of the East" in the 1920s and 1930s. A major reason why companies are moving to Shanghai is that they realize they can no longer treat China, or offices in China, as satellites of Hong Kong. The country has 28 provinces, each of which is a market in its own right, and 34 cities with populations of over 1 million. The major benefits of being located in Shanghai are that it affords an opportunity for greater market intelligence and understanding of consumers.

Among the companies that have moved to Shanghai is Coca-Cola, which relocated its Greater China marketing team from Hong Kong in 2001. The company's regional communications director explained the move by noting: "Only by breathing the same air as our consumers can we get to know them. We used to market to China, now we market to individual markets within China based on the size of their population." Being closer to consumers in China has helped Coca-Cola react more quickly and develop more impactful marketing programs. For example, Coke realized it could create buzz among young Chinese by tapping into their aspirations to own a computer and be more connected with the outside world. During the summer of 2002, the company ran a promotion called "Vibrant Connections" that included the largest webcast in China, sponsored hundreds of road show events that were supported by TV spots by its agency, McCann-Erickson Worldwide, and distributed 7,000 personal computers as prizes.

Many advertising agencies that were previously located in Hong Kong are following their clients to Shanghai as well as Beijing. Executives from major international agency networks, such as Denstu Young & Rubicam Partnerships (DYR) and M&C Saatchi, have followed clients such as Sony and Nestlé to Shanghai. Beijing, which has become China's high-tech center, has also benefited from marketers' desire to be closer to the Chinese market, as telecom companies such as Nokia have moved there.

International agencies are also moving to cities such as Shanghai and Beijing and expanding their mainland resources to attract Chinese companies, as well as multinational clients, since local brands dominate China's advertising business. Only two foreign brands, Procter & Gamble's Safeguard soap and Crest toothpaste, ranked among the 10 most advertised products in China in 2002. The rest were local over-the-counter drugs such as tonics, vitamins, and stomach medicines. However, since China joined the World Trade Organization in 2001, these products, along with national brands such as Legend Computers, Tsingato

beer, and White Rabbit candy, will have to compete against foreign brands in many sectors.

Multinational companies and advertising agencies recognize that the enormous size of the Chinese market, along with its strong economic development and growth, make it important for them to establish a foothold there. They want to begin marketing their products and creating ads when a significant number of China's 1.2 billion consumers can afford the cars, mobile phones, cosmetics, and other products. They know that they need to be close to the action, which means setting up operations in key mainland cities. It is likely that the advertising business in China will come to resemble that in the United States, with Shanghai, like New York, being the key city and Beijing and Hong Kong, like Chicago and Los Angeles, being important centers.

Sources: Normandy Madden, "Shanghai Rises as Asia's Newest Marketing Capital," *Advertising Age*, Oct. 14, 2002, pp. 1, 13; Michael Flagg, "China Remains a Tough Game, but Ad Agencies See Opportunity," *The Wall Street Journal*, May 21, 2000, p. B10.

their offices from Hong Kong to Shanghai to be closer to the world's largest consumer market, on the mainland of China.

Many American companies prefer to use a U.S.-based agency with foreign offices; this gives them greater control and convenience and also facilitates coordination of overseas advertising. Companies often use the same agency to handle international and domestic advertising. As discussed in Chapter 3, the flurry of mergers and acquisitions in the ad agency business in recent years, both in the United States and in other countries, has created large global agencies that can meet the international needs of global marketers. A number of multinational companies have consolidated their advertising with one large agency. The consolidation trend began in 1994 when IBM dismissed 40 agencies around the world and awarded its entire account to Ogilvy & Mather Worldwide.[75] A year later Colgate-Palmolive consolidated all of its global advertising with New York–based Young & Rubicam. The move, which followed the worldwide restructuring of Colgate's manufacturing and distribution system, marked the first time a large multibrand advertiser put all of its billings with one agency.[76]

There are a number of reasons why global marketers consolidate their advertising with one agency. Many companies recognize they must develop a consistent global image for the company and/or its brands and speak with one coordinated marketing voice around the world. For example, IBM officials felt the company had been projecting too many images when its advertising was divided among so many agencies. The consolidation enabled IBM to present a single brand identity throughout the world while taking advantage of one of the world's best-known brand names. Likewise, the H. J. Heinz Company consolidated the advertising for its flagship ketchup brand to help develop a consistent message and image worldwide.

Companies are also consolidating their global advertising in an effort to increase efficiency and gain greater leverage over their agencies. Colgate notes that a major reason for its agency consolidation is to achieve greater cost efficiency. The company has moved into 25 new countries in recent years and increased its advertising and promotional spending in many markets around the globe (Exhibit 20-13). Consolidation has generated savings that can be invested in additional advertising. Consolidation also gives advertisers greater leverage over their agencies. When a major client puts all of its advertising with one agency, that company often becomes the agency's most important account. And, as one IBM executive notes, "You become a magnet for talent and attention."[77]

Advertising executives also noted that a major reason for all of the account consolidation is that agencies now have the ability to communicate and manage globally. Fax machines, e-mail, and airline connections make it much easier to manage accounts around the globe. Of course, placing an entire global advertising account with one agency can be risky. If the agency fails to deliver an effective campaign, the client has no backup agency to make a fast rebound and the search for a new agency can be very time-consuming. Clients who consolidate also face the problem of selling the idea to regional offices, which often previously enjoyed their own local agency relationship.

Exhibit 20-13 Colgate has consolidated all of its global advertising with one agency

However, it appears that more and more companies are willing to take these risks and rely on one agency to handle their advertising around the world.

A second alternative for the international marketer is to choose a domestic agency that, rather than having its own foreign offices or branches, is affiliated with agencies in other countries or belongs to a network of foreign agencies. An agency may acquire an interest in several foreign agencies or become part of an organization of international agencies. The agency can then sell itself as an international agency offering multinational coverage and contacts. For example, many U.S. agencies are expanding into Latin America by forming associations with regional agencies and acquiring partial or full ownership of agencies in various countries. Leo Burnett has majority stakes in agencies in 11 Latin American countries and minority ownership or associations in seven others.[78]

The advantage of this arrangement is that the client can use a domestic-based agency yet still have access to foreign agencies with detailed knowledge of market conditions, media, and so on in each local market. There may be problems with this approach, however. The local agency may have trouble coordinating and controlling independent agencies, and the quality of work may vary among network members. Companies considering this option must ask the local agency about its ability to control the activities of its affiliates and the quality of their work in specific areas such as creative and media.

The third alternative for the international marketer is to select a local agency for each national market in which it sells its products or services. Since local agencies often have the best understanding of the marketing and advertising environment in their country or region, they may be able to develop the most effective advertising.

Some companies like local agencies because they may provide the best talent in each market. In many countries, smaller agencies may, because of their independence, be more willing to take risks and develop the most effective, creative ads. Choosing local agencies also increases the involvement and morale of foreign subsidiary managers by giving them responsibility for managing the promotion function in their markets. Some companies have the subsidiary choose a local agency, since it is often in the best position to evaluate the agency and will work closely with it.

Criteria for Agency Selection

The selection of an agency to handle a company's international advertising depends on how the firm is organized for international marketing and the type of assistance it needs to meet its goals and objectives in foreign

Figure 20-3 Criteria for selecting an agency to handle international advertising

- Ability of agency to cover relevant markets
- Quality of agency work
- Market research, public relations, and other services offered by agency
- Relative roles of company advertising department and agency
- Level of communication and control desired by company
- Ability of agency to coordinate international campaign
- Size of company's international business
- Company's desire for local versus international image
- Company organizational structure for international business and marketing (centralized versus decentralized)
- Company's level of involvement with international operations

markets. Figure 20-3 lists some criteria a company might use in selecting an agency. In a study conducted among marketing directors of European companies, creative capability was ranked the most important factor in selecting an advertising agency network, followed by understanding of the market, understanding of marketing goals, and ability to produce integrated communications. Size of the agency and agency reputation were cited as important criteria by less than 2 percent of the respondents.[79] Another recent study found that most clients choose an agency based on its creative reputation and the creative presentation it had made. However, a large number of clients felt their agencies lacked international expertise and account coordination ability.[80]

Some companies choose a combination of the three alternatives just discussed because their involvement in each market differs, as do the advertising environment and situation in each country. Several experts in international marketing and advertising advocate the use of international agencies by international companies, particularly those firms moving toward global marketing and striving for a consistent corporate or brand image around the world. The trend toward mergers and acquisitions and the formation of mega-agencies with global marketing and advertising capabilities suggests the international agency approach will become the preferred arrangement among large companies.

Advertising Research

Research plays the same important role in the development of international advertising and promotion programs that it does domestically—helping managers make better, more informed decisions. However, many companies do not conduct advertising research in international markets. Probably the main reason for this is the high cost of conducting research in foreign markets, coupled with the limited budgets many firms have for international advertising and promotion. When international markets represent a small percentage of overall sales, investments in research are difficult to justify. Rather than quality marketing information, generalizations based on casual observations of foreign markets have guided the promotional process.

As companies increase their investment in international marketing, they are recognizing the importance of conducting marketing and advertising research to better understand the characteristics and subtleties of consumers in foreign markets. There are a number of areas where research on foreign markets can help firms make better advertising decisions:

- Information on demographic characteristics of markets.
- Information on cultural differences such as norms, lifestyles, and values.
- Information on consumers' product usage, brand attitudes, and media preferences.
- Information on media usage and audience size.
- Copy testing to determine reactions to different types of advertising appeals and executions.
- Research on the effectiveness of advertising and promotional programs in foreign markets.

A great deal of information on international markets is available through secondary sources. One of the most valuable sources of information for companies based in this country is the U.S. Department of Commerce, which works closely with American companies to help them sell their products overseas through its International Trade Administration (ITA) division. The ITA publishes a series of *Overseas Business Reports* that provide valuable information on most major world markets, including economic and marketing data as well as laws and regulations. Information on markets is sometimes available from other countries' government agencies, embassies, or consulates. The ITA also publishes *Export America,* which is a monthly magazine that provides valuable information on foreign markets and issue related to global business. The Central Intelligence Agency (CIA) publishes the *World Fact Book,* which contains information on more than 250 countries in eight categories, including geography, population, economy, government, communications, transportation, military, and transnational issues (Exhibit 20-14). The information includes data on telephones, radios, television sets, and communication-satellite use for nearly every country in the world and is usually updated annually. Circulation figures for the world's newspapers are also published every year.

Exhibit 20-14 The World Fact Book is a valuable source of information on different countries

The *United Nations Statistical Yearbook,* which is published annually, provides demographic and economic data on more than 200 countries. Yearbooks and other reports are also available for regions such as Latin America, Europe, and Asia. Other international organizations that can provide valuable information on world markets include the International Monetary Fund and regional organizations like the Japanese External Trade Organization and the European Union. The World Bank's annual *World Development Reports* has many national statistics including per capita incomes, literacy rates, imports, exports, and a variety of other information.

Information on product and brand attitudes, usage patterns, and media habits is generally more difficult to find, particularly in developing countries. However, more information is becoming available. A. C. Nielsen Worldwide Consumer Panel Services provides marketers with key consumer insights for 18 countries around the world. The company tracks consumer purchases in nearly 125,000 households using scanning technology or, in some markets, more traditional purchase diaries. Information from the panels is useful for understanding purchase behavior and shopping patterns for different segments of the population across various retail outlets. NCH Nù World Marketing Limited now collects information on coupon distribution and redemption patterns in the United States and a number of European countries. Data on media usage in European countries have increased tremendously over the past decade. However, information on TV audiences is still lacking in many countries.

Much of the information advertisers need must be gathered from research generated by the company and/or ad agency. Consumer needs and wants, purchase motives, and usage patterns often vary from one country to another, and research is needed to understand these differences. Some companies and their agencies conduct psychographic research in foreign markets to determine activities, interests, and opinions as well as product usage patterns.

Advertisers should also research consumers' reactions to the advertising appeal and execution style they plan to use in foreign markets. One agency researcher recommends testing the basic premise and/or selling idea to be used in a global campaign first to be sure it is relevant to the target audiences in the markets where it will appear.[81]

Creative Decisions

Another decision facing the international advertiser is determining the appropriate advertising messages for each market. Creative strategy development for international advertising is basically similar in process and procedure to that for domestic advertising. Advertising and communications objectives should be based on the marketing strategy and market conditions in foreign markets. Major selling ideas must be developed and specific appeals and execution styles chosen.

An important factor in the development of creative strategy is the issue of global versus localized advertising. If the standardized approach is taken, the creative team must develop advertising that will transcend cultural differences and communicate effectively in every country. For example, Tropicana Products Inc. uses a global advertising campaign for its pure premium orange juice. Its ads, though tailored a bit for each market, stress the superior, nearly fresh-squeezed taste of its juice over local brands that are often reconstituted from concentrates.

When companies follow a **localized advertising strategy,** the creative team must determine what type of selling idea, ad appeal, and execution style will work in each market. A product may have to be positioned differently in each market depending on consumers' usage patterns and habits. For example, General Foods found that in France, people drink very little orange juice and almost none at breakfast. Thus, when the company decided to market its Tang instant breakfast drink in France, the agency developed ads positioning the brand as a refreshment for any time of day rather than as a substitute for orange juice (the approach used in the United States).

Marketers must also figure out what type of advertising appeal or execution style will be most effective in each market. Emotional appeals such as humor may work well in one country but not in another because of differences in cultural backgrounds and consumer perceptions of what is or is not funny. While humorous appeals are popular in the United States and Britain, they are not used often in Germany, where consumers do not respond favorably to them. German advertising typically uses rational appeals that are text-heavy and contain arguments for a product's superiority.[82] France, Italy, and Brazil are more receptive to sexual appeals and nudity in advertising than are most other societies. The French government recently stepped up its efforts to convince advertisers and their ad agencies to tone down the use of sexual imagery and violence in their advertising.[83] France's Truth in Advertising Commission, which is the main self-regulatory body, has issued new standards regarding the presentation of human beings in advertising. However, several of the French fashion houses such as Dior and Yves Saint Laurent set off a new controversy in 2002 with the use of provocative sexual imagery in ads for their perfumes. YSL was criticized for using full-frontal nudity in a print ad featuring martial-arts-champion-turned-male-model Samuel de Cubber.[84]

International marketers sometimes find they can change consumer purchasing patterns by taking a creative risk. For example, Häagen-Dazs broke through cultural barriers in Britain, where ice cream consumption is only a third as great as in the United States and consumers usually purchase low-grade, low-priced local brands. A sexy advertising campaign showing seminude couples feeding each other the ice cream helped get British consumers to pay premium prices for Häagen-Dazs. The company also used an avant-garde billboard campaign in Japan showing a young couple kissing in public, a near-taboo. The posters were so popular that many were stolen (Exhibit 20-15).

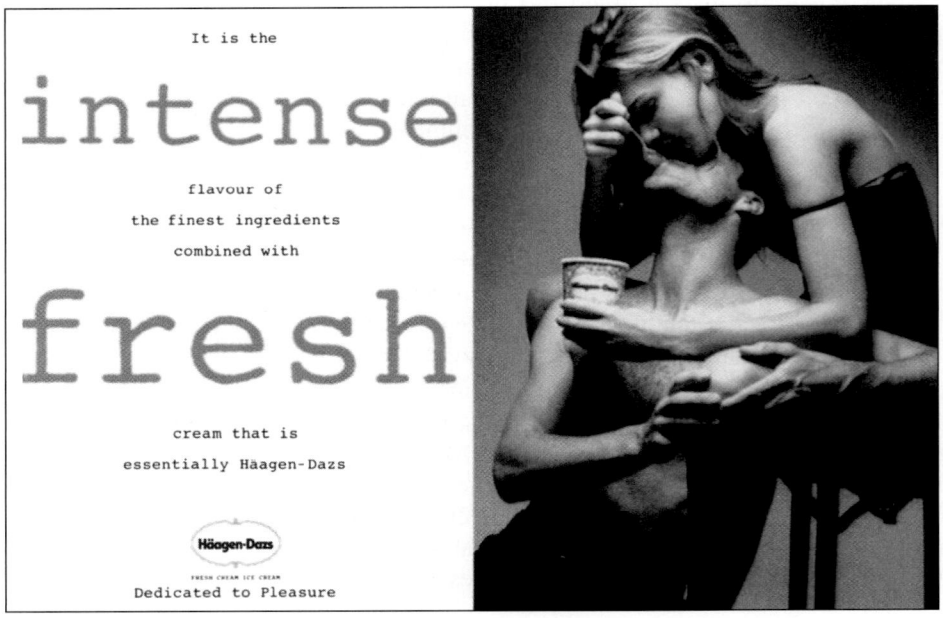

Exhibit 20-15 Häagen-Dazs used sexy ads to get attention in Britain

Media Selection

One of the most challenging areas for international marketers is media strategy and selection. Companies generally find major differences in the media available outside their home markets, and media conditions may vary considerably from one country to another. In less developed countries such as Vietnam, Kenya, and Egypt, most consumers do not have contact with a marketer's advertising and promotion efforts until they enter a store. Packaging and other point-of-purchase elements, rather than media advertising, will have the greatest impact on purchase decisions. On the other hand, advertising bombards consumers in the more affluent countries of Europe, the Pacific Rim, and North America through a variety of print and broadcast as well as interactive media. Media planners face a number of problems in attempting to communicate advertising and promotional messages to consumers in various countries. First, the types of media available are different in different countries. Many homes in developing countries do not have TV sets. For example, in many South and Central African nations (such as Uganda, Tanzania, Kenya, and Zimbabwe), radio is the dominant medium and access to TV sets is very limited.[85] Vietnam's 71 million people own an estimated 7 million radios and 2.5 million television sets, and reported newspaper circulation is only 1.2 million copies. Outdoor advertising reaches the most Vietnamese, followed by point-of-purchase material.[86] Only one in three of the 151 million Russians has access to a television or radio, although Russians are better-educated than people in less developed nations and 26 million newspapers circulate throughout the country each day.

In some countries, TV advertising is not accepted or the amount of commercial time is severely limited. For example, in Germany, TV advertising is limited to 20 minutes a day on each of the government-owned channels (four 5-minute breaks) and banned on Sundays and holidays. Germany's privately-owned television stations, however, are permitted to devote up to 20 percent of their airtime to commercials. In the Netherlands, TV spots are limited to 5 percent of airtime and must be booked up to a year in advance. Programs also do not have fixed time slots for ads, making it impossible to plan commercial buys around desired programs. In some countries the limited number of channels and demand for commercial time result in extremely high levels of advertising clutter.

The number of TV sets is increasing tremendously in India, but there is still controversy over TV advertising. Commercials are restricted to only 10 percent of programming time and must appear at the beginning or end of a program.[87] Australia lifted a ban on cable TV advertising in 1997. However, some cable channels won't accept any advertising, and Australian consumers will not tolerate as much advertising on cable channels as on free TV networks.[88]

The characteristics of media differ from country to country in terms of coverage, cost, quality of reproduction, restrictions, and the like. In some countries, media rates are negotiable or may fluctuate owing to unstable currencies, economic conditions, or government regulations. For example, in China TV stations charge a local rate for Chinese advertisers, a foreign rate, and a joint venture rate.[89] Although its 900 million TV viewers make China the world's largest television market, the medium is strictly controlled by the Communist Party. State-owned China Central Television (CCTV) controls the national networks. Politics frequently intrude into program selection and scheduling: A show might be delayed for several months to coincide with a key political event, or programs from foreign countries may be pulled off the air.[90]

Another problem international advertisers face is obtaining reliable media information such as circulation figures, audience profiles, and costs. Many countries that had only state-owned TV channels are now experiencing a rapid growth in commercial channels, which is providing more market segmentation opportunities. However, reliable audience measurement data are not available, and media buyers often rely on their instincts when purchasing TV time. A number of research companies are developing audience measurement systems for countries in Eastern Europe, Russia, and China. In China, A. C. Nielsen began using PeopleMeters in urban areas such as Shanghai and the southern city of Guangzhou. Television research also is available from China Sofres Media, a joint venture formed by the French company Sofres and the state-owned China Viewers Survey & Consulting Centre. International advertising and television trade groups are also working to develop standardized measurement principles for global TV advertising.[91]

The goal of international advertisers is to select media vehicles that reach their target audience most effectively and efficiently. Media selection is often localized even for a centrally planned, globalized campaign. Local agencies or media buyers generally have more knowledge of local media and better opportunities to negotiate rates, and subsidiary operations can maintain control and adapt to media conditions and options in their market. Media planners have two options: using national or local media or using international media.

Local Media Many advertisers choose the local media of a country to reach its consumers. Print is the most used medium worldwide, since TV commercial time and the number of homes with TV sets are limited in many countries. Many countries have magazines that are circulated nationwide as well as national or regional newspapers that carry advertising directed to a national audience. Most countries also have magazines that appeal to special interests or activities, allowing for targeting in media selection. For example, Exhibit 20-16 shows an ad promoting *President,* which is a magazine that reaches top executives in Japan.

Although restrictions and regulations have limited the development of TV as a dominant advertising medium in many countries, it is a primary medium for obtaining nationwide coverage in most developed countries and offers tremendous creative opportunities. Restrictions on television may be lessening in some countries, and time availability may increase. For example, the number of TV stations and television advertising in Italy have exploded in the past decade since government restrictions against private broadcasting were lifted. Advertising groups are using economic, legal, and political pressure to get more television commercial time from reluctant European governments. The increase in TV channels through direct broadcasting by satellite to many European households (discussed later in this section) is hastening this process.

In addition to print and television, local media available to advertisers include radio, direct mail, billboards, cinema, and transit advertising. These media give international advertisers great flexibility and the opportunity to reach specific market segments and local markets within a country. Most international advertisers rely heavily on national and local media in their media plans for foreign markets.

Exhibit 20-16 *President* magazine targets top Japanese executives

International Media The other way for the international advertiser to reach audiences in various countries is through international media that have multimarket coverage. The primary focus of international media has traditionally been magazines and newspapers. A number of U.S.-based consumer-oriented publications have international editions, including *Time, Newsweek, Reader's Digest,* and *National Geographic* as well as the newspaper *USA Today. Cosmopolitan* publishes 29 international editions that reach over 30 million readers in various countries (Exhibit 20-17). U.S.-based business publications with foreign editions include *BusinessWeek, Fortune, Harvard Business Review,* and *The Wall Street Journal.*

International publications offer advertisers a way to reach large audiences on a regional or worldwide basis. Readers of these publications are usually upscale, high-income individuals who are desirable target markets for many products and services. There are, however, several problems with these international media that can limit their attractiveness to many advertisers. Their reach in any one foreign country may be low, particularly for specific segments of a market. Also, while they deliver desirable audiences to companies selling business or upscale consumer products and services, they do not cover the mass consumer markets or specialized market segments very well. Other U.S.-based publications in foreign markets do offer advertisers ways to reach specific market segments.

While print remains the dominant medium for international advertising, many companies are turning their attention to international commercial TV. Packaged-goods companies in particular, such as Gillette, McDonald's, Pepsi, and Coca-Cola, view TV advertising as the best way to reach mass markets and effectively communicate their advertising messages. Satellite technology has helped spread the growth of TV in other countries and made global television networks a reality. Global Perspective 20-4 discusses how MTV has become the largest global television network in the world.

Exhibit 20-17
Cosmopolitan reaches women around the world with 29 international editions

GLOBAL PERSPECTIVE 20-4

MTV Goes Global—but with a Local Touch

MTV (Music Television) Network was launched in the United States in 1981 as a joint venture between American Express and Warner Communications. Almost from the outset, the pioneering 24-hour music video cable channel put young viewers in a trance, influencing how they looked, talked, and shopped. The outfit that all but invented the rock video has become perhaps the biggest force in the music world. It is also the premiere platform for marketers trying to woo young consumers in 136 countries and 340 million households around the world. Every week nearly 188 million people watch their MTV—and 80 percent of them tune in outside the U.S.

In 1986, Viacom International purchased MTV and a year later launched its first overseas channel in Europe. MTV's first international venture got off to a wobbly start, piping a single feed across Europe, with English-speaking veejays. MTV learned the hard way that, while Europe's youth agreed with the slogan "I want my MTV!" they didn't want a homogeneous version, as their tastes vary by country. Local copycats cropped up and stole MTV's viewers and sponsors, and the network suffered as a result. In 1995 MTV changed its strategy and broke Europe into regional feeds. It now has five feeds on the Continent: one for the United Kingdom and Ireland; another for Germany, Austria, and Switzerland; one for Scandinavia; a broader broadcast for Belgium, Greece, France, and Israel; and one just for Italy alone.

Following its European debut, MTV moved into Latin America in 1990 and launched a pan-regional service in Asia in 1995. Viacom has been pushing MTV ever deeper into markets in Asia, where it now reaches 125 million households and has seven separate channels: Southeast Asia, which is English-language programming for Singapore, Indonesia, Malaysia, Thailand, and the Philippines; separate Mandarin feeds for China and Taiwan; an English-Hindi channel for India; South Korea; and its most recent launch, Japan. MTV Japan originally debuted in 1992 but only lasted until 1998, as its mainly international content did not fare well in a market where Japanese artists dominate the music scene. When MTV relaunched its Japanese channel in 2001, it did so with a local staff from its Tokyo production base that determines all music playlists and features a mixture of Japanese and international content. MTV's coverage is unmatched in reaching Asia's vast ranks of young consumers. Nearly two-thirds of Asia's 3 billion people are under the age of 35. The middle class is expanding and splashy Western-brands products, from Procter & Gamble personal products to Nokia cell phones, are symbols of making it among consumers.

In Europe and Asia, digital and satellite technology have made localization of programming easier and less expensive, as six feeds can be beamed off one satellite transponder. While some of the programming shown in various countries can originate from the United States, MTV channels worldwide air more locally produced and programmed content. However, in most markets, 70 percent of the video fare is local music, as more and more countries have their own popular music and local stars who sing in their own language. For example, in Brazil, MTV first began by playing an equal amount of Brazilian and international music. However, MTV has become more of a Brazilian channel and features more music from local artists as well as programming with stronger cultural, social, and political relevance. Over the past three years, MTV Brazil's audience size has doubled and advertising income has increased by 30 percent. The president of MTV's international networks says: "People root for the home team, culturally and musically. Local repertoire is a worldwide trend. There are fewer global megastars."

Going local offers political benefits as well. MTV must constantly fight the perception that it is trying to take an American version of what is popular and trying to implant it globally. MTV executives note that the company is always trying to fight the stereotype that MTV channels in various countries are importing American culture. Viacom's chairman, Sumner Redstone, denies the charge and says to do so would be a

kind of cultural imperialism. Instead, he says, MTV is "cultivating and nurturing local artists and shows." For example, MTV India produces 21 homegrown shows hosted by local veejays who speak Hinglish, a kind of hip, city-bred blend of Hindi and English. The country also has a very vibrant and rapidly expanding movie and music scene and most of the music on MTV India comes from Hindi movies.

In all, MTV now airs 29 different feeds around the world, all tailored for their respective markets. Localized feeds and programming make it easier to sell commercials overseas, because the advertising budgets of multinational companies tend to be local, rather than regional. MTV's advertising revenues continue to rise as more marketers are recognizing that young people trust MTV and trust what is shown on MTV. Music is a common language that travels, and MTV has a formula that entrances young people around the globe.

Sources: Anne-Marie Crawford, "MTV: Out of Its Teens," *Adage Global,* May 2001, pp. 25-26; Claudia Penteado, "MTV Brazil Wins Success with Local Programming," *Adage Global,* May 2001, p. 29; Brett Pulley and Andrew Tanzer, "Sumner's Gemstone," *Forbes,* Feb. 21, 2000, pp. 106-111.

A major development affecting broadcasting in Europe, Asia, and Latin America is **direct broadcast by satellite (DBS)** to homes and communities equipped with small, low-cost receiving dishes. A number of satellite networks operate in these regions and beam entertainment programming across several countries. For example, media baron Rupert Murdoch's News Corp. owns 40 percent of British Sky Broadcasting (BSkyB), which was formed by the merger of Sky Television and British Satellite Broadcasting and beams over 300 channels to 6 million subscribers in the United Kingdom. Sky also owns and operates 11 channels including Sky One, Sky News, Sky Travel, the Sky Sports channels, and The Sky Movies channels. In 1993 News Corp. purchased Satellite Television Asian Region (STAR TV), which is now the world's largest satellite network, stretching from the Middle East and India to South Korea (Exhibit 20-18). It broadcasts 40 services in eight languages and reaches more than 300 million viewers throughout 53 Asian countries. In India and China alone, it produces over 16,000 hours of original programming each year.[92] In 1996 Star entered into a partnership with two Hong Kong companies to launch the Phoenix Satellite Television Co. Along with airing reruns of popular American shows, the Mandarin-language Phoenix Chinese Channel offers a mix of locally produced sports, news, and talk shows. Phoenix has greater reach in China than any other foreign channel, particularly among upscale, educated viewers in urban areas such as Beijing, Shanghai, and Guangzhou. The favorable demographics make the channel popular among blue-chip advertisers.[93]

The main incentive to the growth of these satellite networks has been the severely limited program choices and advertising opportunities on government-controlled stations in many countries. However, many European and Asian governments are moving to preserve cultural values and protect advertising revenues from going to foreign-based networks. In India, for example, advertising revenue has been shifting to ISkyB, a subsidiary of STAR TV, from Doordarshan, the state-run television network.[94] The Indian government is considering legislation that would regulate foreign satellite channels and advertisers and favor the Doordarshan. India's minister for information and broadcasting says foreign satellite channels are a threat to India's cultural fabric and should be curbed. He cites offensive program content and the amount of nudity on foreign channels as reasons why the Indian government needs to regulate satellite channels. In China, most people are officially barred from receiving foreign satellite broadcasts, but millions do anyway from unauthorized cable operators or through their satellite dishes. In 1999 the government did begin enforcing the ban, particularly in Beijing, but the Phoenix channel remains popular among Chinese viewers who want more options than China's state-run television.[95]

Advances in satellite and communications technology, the expansion of multinational companies with global marketing perspectives, and the development of global ad agencies mean advertisers' use of television as a global medium is likely to increase.

Exhibit 20-18 STAR TV reaches more than 100 million homes across Asia

The Roles of Other Promotional Mix Elements in International Marketing

This chapter has focused on advertising, since it is usually the primary element in the promotional mix of the international marketer. However, as in domestic marketing, promotional programs for foreign markets generally include such other elements as sales promotion, personal selling, public relations, and websites on the Internet. The roles of these other promotional mix elements vary depending on the firm's marketing and promotional strategy in foreign markets.

Sales promotion and public relations can support and enhance advertising efforts; the latter may also be used to create or maintain favorable images for companies in foreign markets. For some firms, personal selling may be the most important promotional element and advertising may play a support role. This final section considers the roles of some of these other promotional mix elements in the international marketing program.

Sales Promotion

Sales promotion activity in international markets is growing due in part to the transfer of promotion concepts and techniques from country to country and in part to the proliferation of media. The growth also stems from the liberalization of trade, the rise of global brands, the spread of cable and satellite TV, and the deregulation and/or privatization of media. Sales promotion and direct-response agencies have been becoming more common, particularly in Europe and more recently in South American, Asian, and Middle Eastern countries. In many less developed countries, spending on sales promotion often exceeds media spending on TV, radio, and print ads.[96]

As we saw in Chapter 16, sales promotion is one of the fastest-growing areas of marketing in the United States. Companies increasingly rely on consumer- and trade-oriented sales promotion to help sell their products in foreign markets as well. Many of the promotional tools that are effective in the United States, such as free samples, premiums, event sponsorships, contests, coupons, and trade promotions, are also used in foreign markets. For example, Häagen-Dazs estimates it gave out more than 5 million free tastings of its ice cream as part of its successful strategy for entering the European market. Since taste is the major benefit of this premium product, sampling was an appropriate sales promotion tool for entering foreign markets. The WD-40 Company uses samples in the United States as well as foreign markets to educate consumers about the versatility of the product and encourage trial. The sample shown in Exhibit 20-19, which uses the front headline "One Can. One Thousand Uses," was translated into 20 different languages. This makes it possible for the distributors in different countries to use a sampling tool in their local languages.

Exhibit 20-19 WD-40 uses product samples in various countries to encourage trial

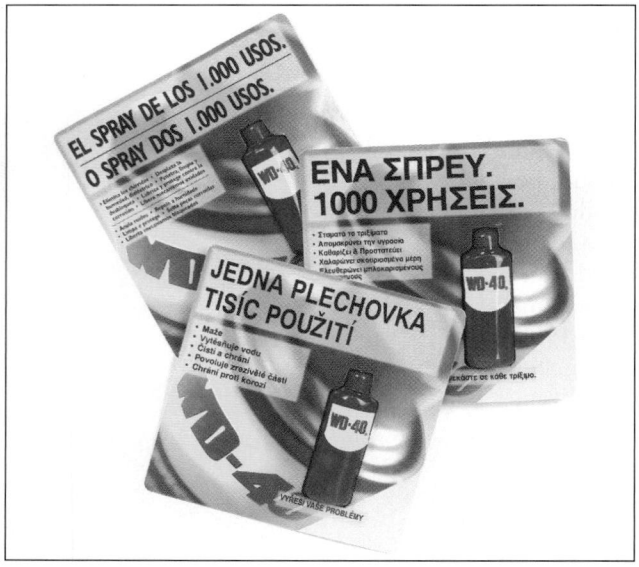

A type of promotion that has become very popular in foreign markets is event sponsorship. Many companies sponsor sporting events, concerts, and other activities in foreign countries to promote their products and enhance corporate image. Sponsorship of sporting events has become a cornerstone of the Coca-Cola Company's promotional efforts. The company is now the largest corporate sports sponsor in the world, spending nearly $1 billion a year on global sports sponsorships. Its programs pervade several different levels, from grassroots sponsorship of youth sports programs to global sponsorship of major sporting events such as the Olympic Games and World Cup soccer.[97] A number of other multinational companies are also involved with sponsorship of sporting events in foreign markets. MasterCard, Canon, and Gillette sponsor Asian soccer teams and tournaments, while Nike sponsors the Brazilian national soccer team that won the 2002 World Cup. Visa was an official sponsor of the Rugby World Cup 2003 in Australia, which is one of the world's most popular sporting events, attracting

more than 3 billion viewers in over 200 countries. Visa used the sponsorship to deliver benefits to member banks, merchants, and cardholders. As part of its sponsorship, Visa provided 10,000 tickets worldwide for cardholders to win when Visa cards were used as part of merchant and company promotions.

Sponsorship of concert tours by popular performers has also become an important part of many companies' global marketing programs. For example, AOL sponsored Madonna's Drowned World Tour and used its sponsorship to run promotions in tour cities to get consumers to sign up for its service. E Trade Financial sponsored the North American leg of the Rolling Stones world tour in 2002–2003, which took the legendary rock group to China and India for the first time.

Unlike advertising, which can be done on a global basis, sales promotions must be adapted to local markets. Kamran Kashani and John Quelch noted several important differences among countries that marketers must consider in developing a sales promotion program.[98] They include the stage of economic development, market maturity, consumer perceptions of promotional tools, trade structure, and legal restrictions and regulations:

- *Economic development.* In highly developed countries such as the United States, Canada, Japan, and Western European nations, marketers can choose from a wide range of promotional tools. But in developing countries they must be careful not to use promotional tools such as in- or on-package premiums that would increase the price of the product beyond the reach of most consumers. Free samples and demonstrations are widely used, effective promotional tools in developing countries. But coupons, which are so popular with consumers in the United States, are rarely used because of problems with distribution and resistance from retailers. In the United States and Britain, most coupons are distributed through newspapers (including FSIs) or magazines. Low literacy rates in some countries make print media an ineffective coupon distribution method, so coupons are delivered door to door, handed out in stores, or placed in or on packages. Figure 20-4 shows the total number of coupons distributed and redeemed in various countries in 2001.
- *Market maturity.* Marketers must also consider the stage of market development for their product or service in various countries when they design sales promotions. To introduce a product to a country, consumer-oriented promotional tools such as sampling, high-value coupons, and cross-promotions with established products and brands are often effective. The competitive dynamics of a foreign market are also

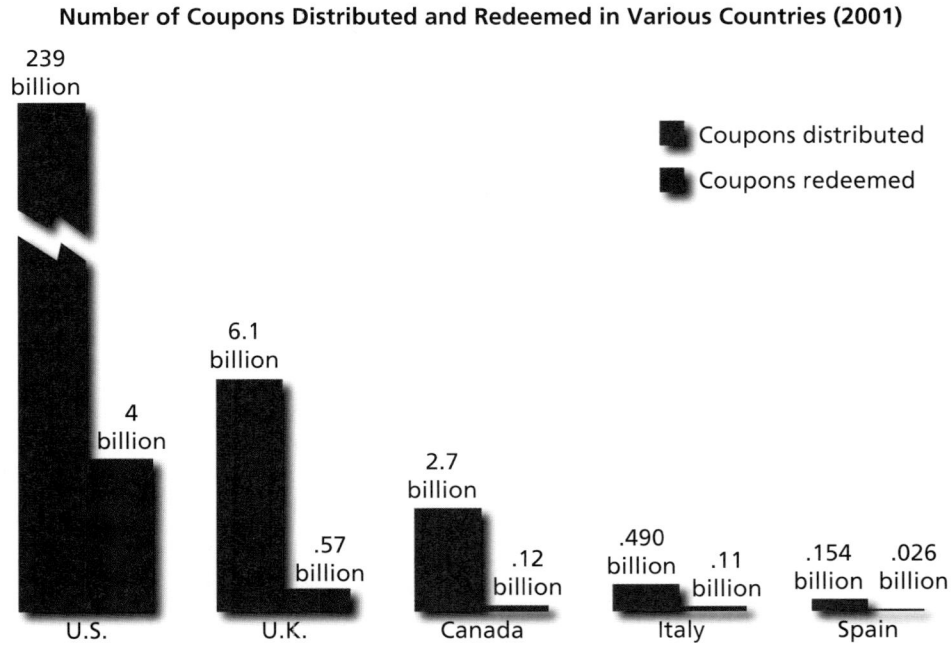

Source: NCH Marketing Services 2002 Trend Report.

Figure 20-4 Number of coupons distributed and redeemed in various countries, 2001

often a function of its stage of development. More competition is likely in well-developed mature markets, which will influence the types of sales promotion tools used. For example, there may be competitive pressure to use trade allowances to maintain distribution or consumer promotions that will maintain customer loyalty, such as bonus packs, price-off deals, or coupons.

- *Consumer perceptions.* An important consideration in the design of sales promotion programs is how they are perceived by consumers as well as the trade. Consumer perceptions of various sales promotion tools vary from market to market. For example, Japanese women are less likely to take advantage of contests, coupons, or other promotions than are women in the United States.[99] Premium offers in particular must be adapted to the tastes of consumers in various markets. A recent study by Huff and Alden examined consumers' opinions toward the use of coupons and sweepstakes in three Asian countries: Taiwan, Malaysia, and Thailand. The study found differences among the three countries with consumers in Taiwan having more negative attitudes and lower levels of use of both sweepstakes and coupons than consumers in Malaysia and Thailand.[100]
- *Trade structure.* In areas with highly concentrated retailing systems, such as northern Europe, the trade situation is becoming much like the United States and Canada as pressure grows for more price-oriented trade and in-store promotions. In southern Europe, the retail industry is highly fragmented and there is less trade pressure for promotions. The willingness and ability of channel members to accommodate sales promotion programs must also be considered. Retailers in many countries do not want to take time to process coupons, post promotional displays, or deal with premiums or packaging that require special handling or storage. In countries like Japan or India, where retailing structures are highly fragmented, stores are too small for point-of-purchase displays or in-store sampling.
- *Regulations.* An important factor affecting the use of sales promotions in foreign countries is the presence of legal restrictions and regulations. Laws affecting sales promotions are generally more restrictive in other countries than in the United States. Some countries ban contests, games, or lotteries, while others restrict the size or amount of a sample, premium, or prize. For example, fair-trade regulations in Japan limit the maximum value of premiums to 10 percent of the retail price; in France the limit is 5 percent. Canada prohibits games of pure chance unless a skill element is used to determine the winner. In Japan the amount of a prize offer is limited to a certain percentage of the product tied to the promotion.[101] In some countries, a free premium must be related to the nature of the product purchased. Many countries have strict rules when it comes to premium offers for children, and some ban them altogether. The appendix at the end of this chapter shows the restrictions on various sales promotion tools in a number of different countries.

Variations in rules and regulations mean marketers must often develop separate consumer sales promotion programs for each country. Many companies have found it difficult to do any promotions throughout Europe because sales promotion rules differ so from one country to another. While the treaty on European Union may result in a more standardized legal environment in Europe, laws regarding sales promotion are still likely to vary. This is why many companies use local agencies or international sales promotion companies to develop sales promotion programs for foreign markets.

Management of Sales Promotion in Foreign Markets Although sales promotion programs of multinational companies have traditionally been managed locally, this is changing somewhat as marketers create global brands. Many global marketers recognize the importance of giving local managers the autonomy to design and execute their own sales promotion programs. However, the ways local promotions influence and contribute to global brand equity must also be considered.

Kashani and Quelch developed a framework for analyzing the role of centralized (headquarters) versus local management in sales promotion decisions based on various stages of globalization (Figure 20-5). This model suggests headquarters' influence will be greatest for global brands and least for local brands. Since global brands

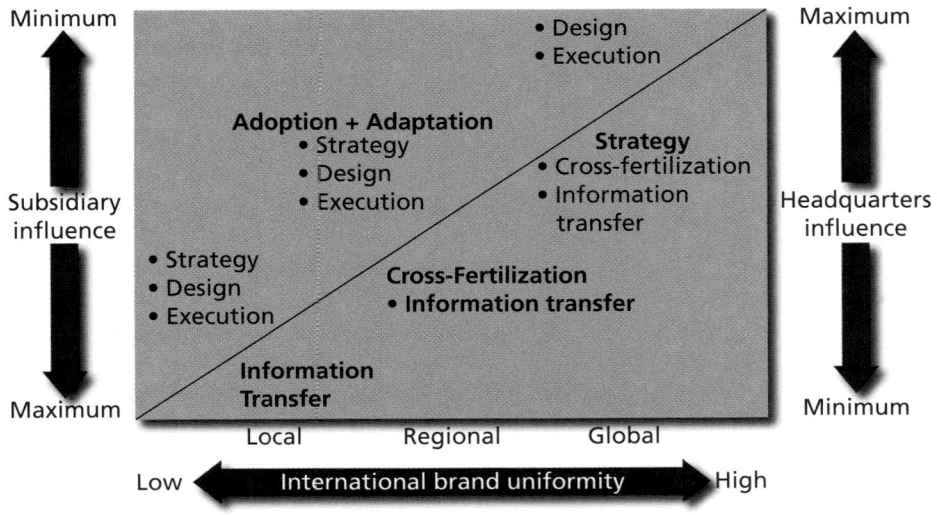

Figure 20-5 Central versus local roles in international sales promotion

require uniformity in marketing communications, the promotional program should be determined at the headquarters level. Decisions regarding overall promotional strategy—including international communications objectives, positioning, allocation of the communications budget to sales promotion versus advertising, and weight of consumer versus trade promotions—are made at the headquarters level.[102]

While the promotional strategy for global brands is determined by global product managers at headquarters, implementation of the programs should be left to local management. It is important to make the promotional strategy broad enough to allow for differences in diverse local markets. Headquarters is also responsible for encouraging the cross-fertilization of ideas and practices among local managers and facilitating the transfer of information. Some companies are now using promotional agencies that have offices around the globe and can coordinate programs in various markets. Exhibit 20-20 shows an ad for DVC Worldwide touting the agency's integrated marketing communications capabilities in local as well as global markets.

Regional brands usually do not require the same level of standardization as global brands, and the promotional strategy can be developed by regional offices and carried out at the local level. However, regional promotions should avoid contradictory brand communications and promotional activities that might upset local activities in nearby markets. The role of national-level brand managers is adoption and adaptation. They determine what promotional ideas to adopt from the region and adapt them to local conditions.

For local brands, decisions regarding promotional strategy, program design, and execution are left to local managers. Of course, local managers may benefit from information about the promotions used in other local markets.

Exhibit 20-20
Promotional agencies such as DVC Worldwide have offices in cities around the world

Personal Selling

As a company's most direct contact with its customers in foreign markets, personal selling is an important part of the marketing and promotional process. Companies selling industrial and high-tech products generally rely heavily on personal selling as the primary method for communicating with their customers, internationally as well as domestically. Consumer-product firms may also use personal selling to call on distributors, wholesalers, or major retailing operations in foreign markets. Due to low wages in many developing countries, some companies hire large sales staffs to perform missionary activities and support selling and advertising efforts. For example, Citibank launched its credit cards in many Asian countries using a multifaceted marketing program that included advertising, direct mail, and personal selling. The company found personal selling a very focused and cost-effective way to

reach prospective credit-card applicants in countries such as India, Malaysia, and Thailand. Citibank captured 40 percent of Thailand's credit-card market, relying primarily on a sales force of 600 part-timers who were paid a fee for each applicant approved.[103]

There are a number of differences in the business environments and cultures of the United States and other countries that impact the personal selling process.[104] First of all, U.S.-based salespeople generally encounter a longer sales cycle in foreign markets than they do domestically, a situation that may be due to several factors such as cultural differences, business practices, and more tenuous economic conditions. In countries such as Italy and Spain, as well as in Latin America, salespeople must spend more time on the social aspects of selling, and this can prolong the sales cycle. There is a tendency toward more conservative business practices in countries such as Germany, where the business culture is older and very ingrained. Germans are more risk-averse and thorough in evaluating business deals. They require strong reassurance and will conduct extensive reviews and ask for multiple references before closing a deal.[105] In the Middle East, price negotiations are common, and buyers often want to feel they extracted some concessions from sellers. Unstable economic conditions in many countries in the Middle East and Latin America can also complicate the selling process, as currency devaluations are common and financing is a major issue that must be addressed.

Because it involves personal contact and communication, personal selling is generally even more culture bound than advertising. So most companies use sales reps from the host country and adapt personal selling activities and sales programs to each market. Management of the sales force is usually decentralized to the local subsidiaries, although the international marketer sets the general sales policy and advises foreign managers on the role personal selling should play in their market, the development of the sales program, and various aspects of sales management.

Public Relations

Many companies involved in international marketing are recognizing the importance of using public relations to support and enhance their marketing and advertising efforts.[106] Public relations activities are needed to deal with local governments, media, trade associations, and the general public, any of which may feel threatened by the presence of a foreign multinational. The job of PR agencies in foreign markets is not only to help the company sell its products or services but also to present the firm as a good corporate citizen concerned about the future of the country.

Companies generally need a favorable image to be successful in foreign markets. Those perceived negatively may face pressure from the media, local governments, or other relevant publics, or even boycotts by consumers. Often, public relations is needed to deal with specific problems a company faces in international markets. For example, NutraSweet had problems getting its low-calorie sweetener into some markets because of strong sugar lobbies in Australia, Canada, and Europe. These lobbies encouraged the foreign press to pick up some unfavorable news about the product from the U.S. media. The company retained Burson-Marsteller, the second-largest PR company in the world, to help design factual ads about the product and to conduct other PR activities to counter the problems and get the facts out about NutraSweet.

Coca-Cola had to deal with a severe public relations crisis in Europe after several hundred Belgians, many of them schoolchildren, became ill after drinking Coke products in the summer of 1999. Several countries banned all Coca-Cola products, while others issued health warnings until the problem, which was traced to bad carbon dioxide in a bottling plant, was resolved. In response to the crisis, Coca-Cola ran full-page newspaper ads from its chairman in the countries where the company had to withdraw its products apologizing for the quality control problem. However, the media criticized the company's chairman, at that time Douglas Ivester, for not stepping forward and becoming involved in the handling of the crisis. In the ads apologizing for the problem Ivester acknowledged, "I should have spoken to you earlier."[107]

Facing a public relations crisis of global dimensions, Coca-Cola retained the European advertising and PR firm Publicis, which had experience in handling crisis management situations for European companies such as Nestlé, Perrier, and Heineken.

Publicis worked closely with executives at Coke's Atlanta headquarters to develop communication strategies and handle contacts with the media. When the ban on Coca-Cola products was lifted in Belgium, Coke and Publicis hired several hundred thousand people to deliver vouchers and coupons for one free family-size bottle of Coke to each of the country's 4.4 million homes. The program was backed by newspaper advertising. In France an existing commercial made by Coke's U.S. agency and adapted for France with the catchline "Today more than ever, we thank you for your loyalty" was aired. In Poland newspaper ads were run guaranteeing the integrity of locally produced Coke products.

Coca-Cola is the world's most valuable brand, and its strong brand equity helped carry the company through the crisis. However, in the process the Coca-Cola Company learned that even the most powerful brand in the world is not immune from a crisis. Global Perspective 20-5 discusses the public relations problems another major American company, McDonald's, has been facing in France in recent years.

The Internet

Worldwide Growth of the Internet

The Internet is coming of age as a global marketing medium and is becoming an important IMC tool for companies around the world, both large and small. Marketers are using the Internet to promote their companies, build their brands, and engage in e-commerce transactions in their own countries as well as across borders. As more homes and offices become connected to the Internet, its importance as an integrated marketing communications tool and way of transacting business will increase tremendously for companies selling consumer products and services as well as business-to-business marketers.

During its formative years the Internet was largely a North American phenomenon. By the end of the 90s, nearly 54 percent of all online users were in North America and English was the language used on three-fourths of all websites and nearly all e-commerce sites, even though it is the primary language of only 8 percent of the world's population. However, this is changing rapidly. As of 2002, the largest number of Internet users still reside in North America, but they account for only one-third of the world's online population. The number of Internet users in Europe and the Asia Pacific region is nearly as large as, and is growing faster than, the number in North America. The United States has the largest number of people online, with an estimated 150 million, followed by Japan with 34 million. However, China has been experiencing very rapid growth of the Internet and now has an estimated 26 million people online versus just over 1 million users only five years earlier.[108] Internet penetration is very high in Scandinavian countries such as Finland and Sweden as well as countries such as South Korea. Most multinational companies are developing websites in a variety of languages as Internet penetration increases and more consumers in various countries go online for information and entertainment.

While the use of the Internet around the globe continues to grow, there is still tremendous variation in consumer usage as well as the level of marketing activity occurring online. In the Asia Pacific region, Internet use is higher in the urban areas of mainland China as well as in Hong Kong. Singapore and Thailand have considerable numbers of upscale users and several domestic service providers. By contrast, in India personal computer penetration is still less than 10 percent, and less than half of the estimated 1 million households with PCs have Internet access. The number of people online is increasing rapidly in Latin America; Internet penetration averages around 13 percent for the entire region but is nearly 20 percent in Peru and Chile.[109] The region is becoming one of the fastest-growing e-commerce markets in the world. However, factors such as unreliable delivery services, low usage of credit cards, security concerns, and customs duties are likely to be daunting obstacles to the growth of e-commerce in the region.[110]

Use of the Internet in International Marketing

The use of the Internet as an IMC tool by companies in various countries is increasing as more marketers learn how to develop and maintain websites and improvements in the systems and technologies needed to support these sites occur. Many multinational companies are developing websites in a number of different languages and making them an important

GLOBAL PERSPECTIVE 20-5

McDonald's Deals with Public Relations Problems in France

One of the challenges facing multinational companies operating in foreign markets is that various groups such as consumers, government, the media, and other relevant publics may feel threatened by their presence. Resentment and concerns over their presence in a country can make public relations problems and crisis situations even more difficult for large multinational companies, as McDonald's has learned from problems it has encountered in France over the past few years.

McDonald's opened its first restaurant in France in 1979 and now has more than 800 outlets across the country. As the company expanded in France, it made efforts to appear as French as possible, dressing up its sandwiches with cheeses and herbs and adapting its menu to better suit the tastes of local consumers. However, in the late 90s McDonald's began receiving negative publicity from ongoing anti-American protests by angry French farmers. The farmers' movement was triggered by a World Trade Organization ruling ordering Europe to accept hormone-fed beef produced in the United States and by sanctions the U.S. government imposed on a host of imported French foods, including Roquefort cheese, truffles, and Dijon mustard. The farmers' protests have included the dumping of tons of animal manure and rotting vegetables at McDonald's restaurants all over France and have attracted mass-media attention in the country.

Additional protests against McDonald's were led by Jose Bove, a French citizen who has been described as a professional militant and is known for headline-grabbing acts of civil disobedience. Bove became a folk hero to many when he led a group that vandalized a partially built McDonald's restaurant in the French town of Millau to protest the U.S. import tax on Roquefort cheese and other European agricultural products. He also lashed out at what he called the global proliferation of "le malbouf," or junk food. A recent book he wrote with fellow farm unionist Francois Dufour, *The World Is Not For Sale: Farmers against Junk Food,* has been translated into eight languages.

Initially McDonald's took a low-key approach to the protests and attacks, declining to press charges for vandalism against its restaurants and placing posters in its restaurants explaining that McDonald's is a major partner of the French agricultural sector. However, in fall 1999 McDonald's France began countering the negative publicity by launching a "Made in France" corporate advertising campaign in 60 regional daily newspapers across the country. The ads inform consumers that while the brand may be American, the products served in France's 750 McDonald's outlets are French in origin. The ads underscore McDonald's policy of buying French products and its role in France's agricultural sector, while thanking consumers who have remained loyal. In response to the farmers' concerns, McDonald's also began substituting locally produced specialties targeted by the U.S. sanctions, such as duck breast and Roquefort cheese, for traditional ingredients in the company's Big Mac and cheeseburger menu items.

French government officials, while deploring violence against McDonald's, have done little, if anything, to improve the company's image in the country. The French prime minister declared that he thought Jose Bove raised valid questions about McDonald's, while the Socialist minister of agriculture publicly referred to the United States as the home of the world's worst food. McDonald's problems in France continued into the new millennium, as an employee in one of the company's restaurants in Brittany was killed in a bombing in April 2000.

McDonald's France executives have asked their compatriots to understand that the company is essentially a French company staffed by industrious employees and to stop using it as a symbol in a fight against U.S. trade sanctions. The company has also pointed to its efforts to ensure that supplies of its products are obtained locally in France and are of high quality. It appears that the company's public relations efforts have been succeeding, as sales in France increased by

more than 9 percent in 2001, making McDonald's French operation the fastest growing in Europe.

While sales have increased, the company's uneasy relationship with the French encountered yet another problem in May 2002 when McDonald's France placed a full-page "advertorial" in the magazine *Femme Actuelle* headlined "McDonald's—Is It Causing Obesity in Children?" The ad was run in response to a report showing that child obesity in France had doubled to 16 percent in 10 years. In the copy of the ad McDonald's France stated that "The number of visits to its outlets should be limited." Forbidding children from eating fast food would be counterproductive. However, there is no reason to eat excessive amounts of junk food, nor go more than once a week to McDonalds." As might be expected, the ad provoked a furious response from McDonald's American corporate headquarters in Chicago, which issued a statement noting that the ad was the opinion of only one consultant and the company does not share this view.

McDonald's can only hope that the latest controversy does not add to its problems in France. To the French, nothing is as symbolic as food, and many have already decided that McDonald's symbolizes globally homogenized tastes and the "McDomination" of its market.

Sources: Marian Burros, "McDonald's France Says Slow Down on the Fast Food," *New York Times*, Oct. 30, 2002, p. C7; David Woodruff, "Just Say No: Jose Bove Has Made a Career as a Professional Agitator; His Latest Target: Globalization," *The Wall Street Journal*, Oct. 1, 2001, p. A1; Larry Speer, "McDonald's Self Defense Is Its French Connection," *Advertising Age*, Sept. 13, 1999, p. 26.

part of their integrated marketing communications programs. Marketers are also using mass-media advertising to drive consumers to their websites and provide them with detailed information about their products and services, encourage them to participate in online promotions, or allow them to make purchases. Exhibit 20-21 shows a page from the Japanese website the Gillette Company developed for its Mach3 shaving system. A number of global business-to-business marketers such as Dell Computer, IBM, Xerox, and Hewlett-Packard are using websites to provide customers with information and conduct business with them.

As the digital revolution continues, marketers will be making greater use of the Internet in their global as well as local IMC programs. However, they will also face some challenges with respect to the way they approach global marketing and branding. As more consumers worldwide have access to the same information and same brands via the World Wide Web, many marketers will have to rethink their strategies of producing the same product under different names and tailoring promotions to local markets. It is predicted that marketers will use more global brands and promotional campaigns to take advantage of the worldwide exposure that will be available through the Internet.

Exhibit 20-21 Gillette developed a Japanese website for its Mach3 razor

Summary

Many U.S. companies are recognizing not only the opportunities but also the necessity of marketing their products and services internationally because of saturated markets and intense competition from both domestic and foreign competitors. Advertising and promotion are important parts of the international marketing program of a multinational corporation. Advertising is generally the most cost-effective way to communicate with buyers and create a market in other countries.

International marketers must carefully analyze the major environmental forces in each market where they compete, including economic, demographic, cultural, and political/ legal factors. These factors are important not only in assessing the potential of each country as a market but also in designing and implementing advertising and promotional programs.

In recent years, much attention has focused on global marketing, where a standard marketing program is used in all markets. Part of global marketing is global advertising, where the same basic advertising approach is used in all markets. Opponents of the global (standardized) approach argue that differences in culture, market and economic conditions, and consumer needs and wants make a universal approach to marketing and advertising impractical. Many companies use an in-between approach, standardizing their basic marketing strategy but localizing advertising messages to fit each market.

There are a number of important decision areas in the development of advertising and promotional programs for international markets. These include organization, agency selection, advertising research, creative strategy and execution, and media strategy and selection.

Sales promotion, personal selling, public relations, and Internet websites are also part of the promotional mix of international marketers. Sales promotion programs usually must be adapted to local markets. Factors to consider include stage of market development, market maturity, consumer perceptions of promotional tools, trade structure, and legal restrictions and regulations. Personal selling is the most important element of some companies' international marketing programs, since it is their main form of contact with foreign customers. PR programs are also important to help international marketers develop and maintain favorable relationships with governments, media, and consumers in foreign countries. The use of the Internet as a marketing tool varies by region. In many countries, there are few Internet users and few local companies with websites. But as the number of consumers online grows, so too does the number of large international marketers using the Internet to support their ad campaigns.

Key Terms

balance-of-trade deficit, 660
economic infrastructure, 662
cultural values, 665
global marketing, 669
global advertising, 669
pattern advertising, 674
localized advertising strategy, 684
direct broadcast by satellite (DBS), 689

Discussion Questions

1. The opening vignette to the chapter discusses the requirements developed by the A. C. Nielsen Company to be on its global brand list. Do you think that a brand should have to meet these criteria in order to achieve global brand status? Why might marketers disagree with the requirements set by A. C. Nielsen?

2. Why are international markets so important to U.S. companies such as Starbucks, McDonald's and Coca-Cola, as well as to European companies such as Nestlé, Unilever, and Nokia? Discuss the role of advertising and other forms of promotion in these companies' international marketing programs.

3. Discuss the importance of the economic environment in a country in evaluating its market potential. How do the economic conditions and factors impact the type of integrated marketing communications program a company can use in a country?

4. Global Perspective 20-1 discusses how many multinational companies have begun focusing more attention on the 4 billion consumers who live in the remote, rural communities of developing countries. Discuss the challenges companies face in marketing their products to the world's poorest consumers. How do they have to

adapt their integrated marketing communication programs in selling to these consumers?

5. What are some of the cultural variables that marketers must consider in developing advertising and promotional programs in a foreign market? Choose one of these cultural variables and discuss how it has created a problem or challenge for a company in developing an advertising and promotional program in a specific country.

6. Discuss the arguments for and against the use of global marketing and advertising. What types of products and services are best suited for global advertising?

7. What is meant by the "think global, act local" approach to global marketing and advertising? Discuss some of the ways marketers can adapt their advertising to local markets.

8. What is meant by a global market segment? Provide an example of a company that has identified a global market segment and advertises its product or service the same way around the world to this market.

9. What are the three basic options a company has for organizing its international advertising and promotion function? Discuss the pros and cons of each.

10. Discuss the problems and challenges international marketers face in developing media strategies for foreign markets.

11. How would the planning and promotional program differ for a global brand versus a regional or local brand?

12. Discuss the role of public relations in the integrated marketing communications program for an international marketer. How would the role of public relations differ from advertising?

APPENDIX C

Promoting Overseas: What's Legal and What's Not

The information contained in this chart has been abbreviated and is for general purposes only. If you're planning to run a promotion in any of these countries, be sure to contact the appropriate legal counsel in each country for more specific details on the restrictions there. You'll find a list of some promotion attorneys in this report, or you can contact www.gala-adlaw.com or one of the featured associations for additional information. Copyright © 1998 PROMO Magazine.

Country	Premiums	Home-Deliv. Coupons	Mail-Deliv. Coupons	Games	Contests
Argentina	Legal	Not in use.	Not in use.	Legal	Legal (if proof of purchase is required, free option must be fixed)
Australia	Legal	Legal, but third parties cannot put together coupon books or coupons from groups of companies.	Legal, but third parties cannot put together coupon books or coupons from groups of companies.	Legal	Legal
Belgium	Legal, but with many restrictions. Value may not exceed 5% of the main product value.	Legal	Legal	Legal, but not when linked with purchase.	Legal, but not when linked with purchase.
Brazil	Legal, very popular.	Legal, but not popular.	Legal, but not popular.	Legal, very popular. If requiring purchase or based on chance, approval from Consumer Defense Dept. required.	Legal, very popular. If requiring purchase or based on chance, approval from Consumer Defense Dept. required.
Chile	Legal	Not in use.	Not in use.	Legal	Legal
Colombia	Legal	Legal	Legal	Legal, but games based on chance or luck require authorization.	Legal, but contests based on chance or luck require authorization.
England	Legal	Legal	Legal	Subject to compliance with Lotteries & Amusements Act.	Subject to compliance with Lotteries & Amusements Act.
Finland	Legal, if gift has very small value or there is an evident material connection between the goods or services offered.	Legal, except coupons having a combined offer or connected to purchase, or containing illegal sweeps or lotteries.	Legal, except coupons having a combined offer or connected to purchase, or containing illegal sweeps or lotteries.	Legal, when based on skill, purchase can be required. When based on chance, free method of entry is required.	Legal, when based on skill, purchase can be required. When based on chance, free method of entry is required.
France	Legal, if gift has a very small value or is identical to the good purchased. Usually not allowed when the premium is free.	Legal, but only when offering discount on same product. Cross coupons forbidden.	Legal, but only when offering discount on same product. Cross coupons forbidden.	Legal, but must be absolutely free and not connected to a purchase.	Legal, but prize promotion must be skill, absolutely free, and not connected to a purchase.
Germany	Buy one get one free not allowed.	Legal, only for product samples. Price-off coupons not allowed.	Legal, only for product samples. Price-off coupons not allowed.	Legal, mechanics must be checked before practiced.	Legal, mechanics must be checked before practiced.

Sweeps	Rebates/ Refunds/	Gift W/ Purchase	Database Marketing	Product Sampling
Legal	Legal	Legal	Legal	Legal
Permit sometimes required. All states require compliance with special laws.	Legal	Legal	Legal, but state privacy laws shortly anticipated.	Legal, except therapeutics.
Usually not allowed.	Legal, but with many restrictions and conditions.	Legal, but with many restrictions and conditions.	Legal	Legal
Legal, very popular. If requiring purchase or based on chance, approval from Consumer Defense Dept. required.	Legal, but not popular.	Legal, popular.	Legal, very popular. Mail must be discontinued at receiver's request.	Legal, very popular.
Legal	All consumers must have the same discount based on volume bought.	Legal	Legal, but consumer can request to have names removed from database.	Legal
Legal, but sweeps based on chance or luck require authorization.	Legal, but not popular.	Legal	Legal	Legal
Subject to compliance with Lotteries & Amusements Act. Free prize draws & instant win must allow free entry.	Legal	Legal	Legal	Legal, but some restrictions on alcohol, tobacco, medicines, solvents, and some food.
Legal, when based on skill, purchase can be required. When based on chance, free method of entry is required.	Legal	Legal, if gift has very small value or there is an evident material connection between the goods or services offered.	Legal, with many restrictions.	Legal, some restrictions.
Legal, but must be absolutely free and not connected to a purchase.	Legal	Legal, if gift has a very small value or is identical to the good purchased. Usually not allowed when the premium is free.	Legal	Legal
Legal, should be checked with lawyer.	Legal, only to 3% maximum.	Usually not allowed. Some small-value giveaways are allowed, lawyers usually can find a way around the law.	Legal, but consumer must consent first.	Usually legal when only samples are used. No regular original retail products.

Country	On-Pack Premiums	On-Pack Coupons	In-Pack Premiums	In-Pack Coupons	Near-Pack Premiums
Argentina	Legal	Not in use.	Legal	Not in use.	Legal
Australia	Legal	Legal, third party trading stamps not a problem.	Legal	Legal	Legal
Belgium	Legal, but with many restrictions.	Legal, but only when offering discount on same product. Cross coupons forbidden.	Legal, but with many restrictions.	Legal, but only when offering discount on same product. Cross coupons forbidden.	Legal, but with many restrictions.
Brazil	Legal, popular.	Legal, but not popular.	Legal, popular.	Legal, but not popular.	Legal, but not popular.
Chile	Legal	Not in use.	Legal	Not in use.	Legal
Colombia	Legal	Legal	Legal	Legal	Legal
England	Legal	Legal	Legal	Legal	Legal
Finland	Legal, if gift has very small value or there is an evident material connection between the goods or services offered. Restriction when directed to children.	Legal, if the good being offered free or at a discount has very small value and there is an evident material connection between the goods or services offered.	Legal, if gift has very small value or there is an evident material connection between the goods or services offered. Restriction when directed to children.	Legal, if the good being offered free or at a discount has very small value and there is an evident material connection between the goods or services offered.	Legal, if gift has very small value or there is an evident material connection between the goods or services offered. Restriction when directed to children.
France	Legal, if gift has a very small value or is identical to the good purchased. Usually not allowed when the premium is free.	Legal, but only when offering discount on same product. Cross coupons forbidden.	Legal, if gift has a very small value or is identical to the good purchased. Usually not allowed when the premium is free.	Legal, but only when offering discount on same product. Cross coupons forbidden.	Legal, if gift has a very small value or is identical to the good purchased. Usually not allowed when the premium is free.
Germany	Usually not allowed.	Retailers cannot make price reductions. Consumers must collect an on-pack code and mail it directly to the manufacturer.	Usually not allowed.	Usually not allowed. Must be checked with lawyer in every case.	Usually not allowed.

Self-Liquid. Premiums	Bonus Packs	Free in the Mail	Continuity/ Loyalty	Phone Cards	Freq. Shop. Cards
Legal	Legal	Not in use.	Legal	Not in use.	Legal
Legal, but exact nature of offer must be revealed (closing date, # of proofs required, etc.).	Legal, but some packaging restrictions.	Legal, except therapeutics, alcohol, cigarettes.	Legal, but many restrictions.	Legal	Legal
Legal, but with many restrictions.	Legal, but with many restrictions.	Legal	Legal	Legal	Legal
Legal, popular.	Legal, very popular.	Legal, but not popular.	Legal, popular.	Legal, but not popular.	Legal, popular.
Legal	Legal	Legal	Legal	Legal	Legal
Legal	Legal	Legal	Legal	Legal	Legal
Legal	Legal	Legal	Legal	Legal	Legal
Not in use.	Legal, as long as offer is not connected to a purchase.	Legal, as long as offer is not connected to a purchase.	Legal	Legal, but not in use.	Legal, as long as offer does not contain illegal benefits.
Legal	Legal	Legal, if gift has a very small value or is identical to the good purchased. Usually not allowed when the premium is free.	Legal	Legal, if gift has a very small value or is identical to the good purchased. Usually not allowed when the premium is free.	Legal
Legal	Legal, but many restrictions. Must be checked with lawyer in every case.	Usually not allowed.	No special refunds except a maximum discount of 3% when paying with cash.	Legal, but can't be combined with purchase.	Legal, members can buy exclusive offers. Advantages such as reduced prices only for members are not allowed.

Country	Premiums	Home-Deliv. Coupons	Mail-Deliv. Coupons	Games	Contests
Holland	Legal	Legal	Legal	Prize value not to exceed US$2,500. Regulations currently under review.	Prize value not to exceed US$2,500. Regulations currently under review.
Hungary	Legal, but only used between trade companies.	Legal, usually used in connection with fragile or large products.	Legal, must contain information as to where the advertiser's office is located.	Legal, must get approval from Gambling Supervision.	Legal, must get approval from Gambling Supervision.
Ireland	Legal	Legal	Legal	Legal, if based on chance free entry required. If winner is determined by skill, purchase can be required.	Legal, if based on chance free entry required. If winner is determined by skill, purchase can be required.
Israel	Legal	Legal, but not popular.	Legal, but not popular.	Legal, but proof of purchase may be required.	Legal, but proof of purchase may be required.
Italy	Legal, 20% tax on prize value. Government notification required.	Legal	Legal	Legal, 45% tax on prize value. Government notification required.	Legal, 45% tax on prize value. Government notification required.
Japan	Legal, but very strict restrictions apply.	Legal	Legal	Legal, but very strict restrictions apply.	Legal
Malaysia	Legal	Legal	Legal	Legal, but prize promotion must be skill, not chance.	Legal, but prize promotion must be skill, not chance.
Mexico	Legal	Legal	Legal	Legal	Legal
New Zealand	Legal	Legal	Legal	Legal	Legal
Poland	Legal	Legal	Legal	Legal, but games of chance restricted by Law on Games of Chance & Mutual Bets.	Legal, but games of chance restricted by Law on Games of Chance & Mutual Bets.
Singapore	Legal	Legal	Legal	Legal, may require permission from authorities.	Legal, may require permission from authorities.
Spain	Legal, but you must ask for permission.	Legal, but you must ask for permission.	Legal, but you must ask for permission.	Legal, you must register with the government.	Legal, you must register with the government.
Sweden	Legal, but exact details of offer must be revealed (closing date, conditions, value, etc.).	Legal, with some restrictions. Illegal to send to persons under age 16. Restrictions when sending to parent of newborns, relatives of deceased persons.	Legal, with some restrictions. Illegal to send to persons under age 16. Restrictions when sending to parent of newborns, relatives of deceased persons.	Legal, but government permit required.	Legal, but promotion must be skill, not chance. Some restrictions to connect to a purchase. Exact details of offer must be revealed (closing date, conditions, value, etc.).
United States	Legal, but all material terms and conditions must be disclosed.	Legal, with restrictions on alcohol, tobacco, drugs.	Legal, with restrictions on alcohol, tobacco, drugs.	Legal, but on-pack games subject to certain restrictions.	Legal, some states prohibit requiring consideration. Bona fide skill must dominate and control final result. Various state disclosure requirements.
Venezuela	Legal, some restrictions when with food. Must register with the government.	Legal, but only in use by very few retailers.	Legal, but only in use by very few retailers.	Legal, must register with the government.	Legal, must register with the government.

Sweeps	Rebates/ Refunds/	Gift W/ Purchase	Database Marketing	Product Sampling
Prize value not to exceed US$2,500. Regulations currently under review.	Rebates—Legal. Refunds—price restrictions.	Legal	Legal, with some restrictions. Consumers can request to have name removed from database.	Legal, except for alcohol, drugs and pharmaceuticals.
Legal, must get approval from Gambling Supervision.	Legal, but only used between trade companies.	Legal, as long as gift has a very small value.	Legal, consumers can request to have names removed from database.	Legal, except for pharmaceuticals, tobacco, alcohol, weapons, or explosives.
Legal, but purchase cannot be required.	Legal	Legal	Legal	Legal, but tobacco prohibited.
Legal, 180 days must be between each sweeps from the same company.	Legal, but not popular.	Legal	Legal, but can't use private data such as credit card, bank, healthcare, etc. info.	Legal
Legal, 45% tax on prize value. Government notification required.	Illegal	Legal, 20% tax on prize value. Government notification required.	Legal, but with use of personal data written permission of consumer required.	Legal
Legal, but very strict restrictions apply.	Legal	Legal, but very strict restrictions apply.	Legal	Legal, except medicine.
Illegal	Legal	Legal	Legal	Legal, except alcohol, cigarette to Muslims.
Legal	Legal	Legal	Legal	Legal
Legal	Legal, with restrictions.	Legal	Legal, but protected by consumer privacy act.	Legal
Legal, but restricted by Law on Games of Chance & Mutual Bets.	Legal, but rebates are not in use.	Legal	Legal, but significantly limited by the Law on Protection of Personal Data.	Legal, except pharmaceuticals, alcoholic beverages.
Legal, with many restrictions, and many require permission from authorities.	Legal	Legal	Legal	Legal
Legal, you must register with the government.	Legal, you must register with the government.	Legal, some restrictions.	Legal, you must register database with data protection agency.	Legal
Legal, but promotion must be skill, not chance. Some restrictions to connect to a purchase. Exact details of offer must be revealed (closing date, conditions, value, etc.).	Legal, but exact details of offer must be revealed (closing date, conditions, value, etc.).	Legal, but exact details of offer must be revealed (closing date, conditions, value, etc.).	Legal, with some restrictions and a permit to maintain a list. The marketing offer must state from where the address was obtained.	Legal
Legal, no consideration. Significant disclosure requirements by states. Some states prohibit everybody wins, direct mail sweeps subject to stringent disclosure requirements.	Legal, must not be coupons.	Legal, but cost of gift may not be built into the cost for purchased product.	Legal, consumers may request to have name removed from industry, state and company lists.	Legal, with restrictions on alcohol, tobacco, drugs and some agricultural products.
Legal, must register with the government.	Legal	Legal, some restrictions with food. Must register with the government.	Legal	Legal, except cigarettes and alcohol to minors. Must register with the government. Some restrictions when with food.

Country	On-Pack Premiums	On-Pack Coupons	In-Pack Premiums	In-Pack Coupons	Near-Pack Premiums
Holland	Legal	Legal	Legal	Legal	Legal
Hungary	Not in use.	Not in use.	Not in use.	Not in use.	Not in use.
Ireland	Legal	Legal	Legal	Legal	Legal
Israel	Legal	Legal, but not popular.	Legal	Legal, but not popular.	Legal
Italy	Legal, 20% tax on prize value. Government notification required.	Legal	Legal, 20% tax on prize value. Government notification required.	Legal, but cross coupons not permitted; 20% tax on redeemed value.	Legal, 20% tax on prize value. Government notification required.
Japan	Legal, but very strict restrictions apply.	Legal	Legal, but very strict restrictions apply.	Legal	Not in use.
Malaysia	Legal	Legal	Legal, must comply with safety requirements.	Legal	Legal
Mexico	Legal	Legal	Legal	Legal	Legal
New Zealand	Legal	Legal	Legal	Legal	Legal
Poland	Legal	Legal, not in use.	Legal	Legal, not in use.	Legal
Singapore	Legal	Legal	Legal	Legal	Legal
Spain	Legal, some restrictions.	Legal, you need permission from data protection agency.	Legal, some restrictions.	Legal, you need permission from data protection agency.	Legal, some restrictions.
Sweden	Legal	Legal	Legal	Legal	Legal
United States	Legal, with restrictions on alcohol, tobacco, drugs. Premium must be appropriate to targeted age group. Certain restrictions apply to premiums directed to children.	Legal, but all material terms must be disclosed. There must be a minimum six month redemption period.	Legal, with restrictions on alcohol, tobacco, drugs. Premium must be appropriate to targeted age group. Certain restrictions apply to premiums directed to children.	Legal, but all material terms must be disclosed. There must be a minimum six month redemption period.	Legal
Venezuela	Legal, must register with the government.	Not in use.	Legal, some sanitary restrictions with food. Must register with the government.	Not in use.	Legal, some restrictions with food. Must register with the government.

Self-Liquid. Premiums	Bonus Packs	Free in the Mail	Continuity/ Loyalty	Phone Cards	Freq. Shop. Cards
Legal	Legal	Legal	Legal, with some restrictions. Must conform with the Privacy Law.	Legal	Legal
Illegal	Not in use.	Legal, except pharmaceuticals, tobacco, alcohol, weapons or explosives.	Not in use.	Legal for use as a surface for advertising, very popular. If used as a credit card, many restrictions.	Legal, not very popular.
Legal	Legal	Legal	Legal	Legal	Legal
Legal	Legal	Legal	Legal	Legal, but not popular.	Legal
Legal, but price of purchase must be more than price of base product alone.	Legal	Legal	Legal, 20% tax on prize value. Government notification required.	Legal, 20% tax on prize value. Government notification required.	Legal, 20% tax on prize value. Government notification required.
Legal, but very strict restrictions apply.	Legal, but very strict restrictions apply.	Legal	Legal, but very strict restrictions apply.	Legal	Legal, but very strict restrictions apply.
Legal	Legal	Legal	Legal	Legal	Legal
Legal	Legal	Legal	Legal	Legal	Legal
Legal	Legal	Legal	Legal	Legal	Legal
Legal	Legal	Not in use.	Legal	Not in use.	Legal
Legal	Legal	Legal	Legal	Legal	Legal
Legal	Legal, some restrictions.	Legal	Legal, you must register database with data protection agency.	Legal	Legal, you must register database with data protection agency.
Legal	Legal	Legal	Legal	Legal	Legal
Legal	Legal	Legal, unordered merchandise considered free gift.	Legal, but all items and conditions must be clearly disclosed and consumer expressly consents to join plan.	Legal, cannot be used to change customers' long distance service without written authorization.	Legal
Legal, some restrictions with food. Must register with the government.	Legal, some restrictions with food. Must register with the government.	Legal, but not very common. Some restrictions when with food. Must register with the government.	—	—	—

Regulation of Advertising and Promotion

Chapter Objectives

1. To examine how advertising is regulated, including the role and function of various regulatory agencies.
2. To examine self-regulation of advertising and evaluate its effectiveness.
3. To consider how advertising is regulated by federal and state government agencies, including the Federal Trade Commission.
4. To examine rules and regulations that affect sales promotion, direct marketing, and marketing on the Internet.

Liquor Advertising Almost Makes It to Network Television

For more than five decades, distilled spirits were not advertised on television or radio because of a self-imposed ban by members of the Distilled Spirits Council of the United States (DISCUS). Council members agreed in 1936 to avoid radio advertising and extended the ban to TV in 1948. But Seagram, the second-largest distiller in the world, ended the U.S. spirits industry's long-standing ban on broadcast advertising in June 1996 by airing commercials for its Crown Royal Canadian Whiskey brand on an affiliate in Corpus Christi, Texas.

Seagram issued a statement explaining that it was ending the liquor industry's decades-old practice of not advertising on TV because DISCUS's voluntary code of good practice placed spirits at a competitive disadvantage to beer and wine, which did not have any such restrictions. Seagram also argued that the ban had become outdated as radio and TV have become more targeted and the company could pinpoint its advertising message to people of legal drinking age.

Initial reactions within the liquor industry were mixed. A number of distillers, eager to turn around the long, slow decline in hard-liquor sales, watched Seagram test the water with its TV ads before rolling out their own commercials. Some held discussions with TV stations but waited for a formal amendment to the DISCUS code of good practice before proceeding. The amendment came on November 7, 1996, when DISCUS members voted unanimously to overturn the self-imposed ban on broadcast ads. The DISCUS president noted that spirits makers wanted to break down the public perception that spirits are stronger or more dangerous than beer and wine and thus deserving of harsher social and political treatment.

After the DISCUS ban was lifted, the four major broadcast TV networks as well as major cable networks such as ESPN and MTV continued to refuse liquor ads, prompting consumer and public interest groups to applaud their actions. In fact, it has been argued that it was really the refusal by TV stations and networks to accept liquor advertising, rather than the DISCUS code, that had kept the ads off the air. However, the major networks cannot control the practices of affiliate stations they do not own, and many affiliates began accepting liquor ads, as did local cable channels and independent broadcast stations. By fall 2001, DISCUS estimated that about

400 local stations and cable channels were permitting or considering spirits ads, although most had restrictions that the ads had to air after 9 P.M.

In December 2001 NBC, which is owned by General Electric Co., made a landmark decision when it announced that it would become the first broadcast network to accept hard-liquor advertising in more than 50 years. NBC decided it was tired of the double standard by which broadcast networks accept beer and wine commercials but not spots for hard liquor and noted that there appeared to be an arbitrary distinction between the ads for the various alcoholic beverage categories. As part of its decision to accept spirits ads, NBC adopted a set of guidelines under which the makers of distilled spirits could advertise in a way similar to beer and wine makers. Under the guidelines, liquor companies had to run four months of so-called social responsibility ads on subjects like designated drivers before general product promotion spots could air. The network would also limit liquor ads to programs for which at least 85 percent of viewers are 21 or older.

NBC was not joined by the three other major broadcast networks—ABC, CBS, and Fox—in its decision to accept liquor commercials. While executives from the other networks stated that they did not think it was the right thing to do, industry experts noted that the networks were also wary of alienating beer companies by accepting ads for hard liquor. While NBC's lead in accepting liquor ads did not generate support from the other networks, it did engender a considerable amount of controversy and criticism from members of Congress, federal regulators, the American Medical Association, and many public advocacy groups. Critics of NBC's decision expressed concern that airing liquor ads on TV would glamorize drinking and encourage children and teenagers to drink.

Facing a widening backlash over its decision, in March 2002 NBC announced that it was dropping its plans to accept liquor advertising. The network's president of standards and practices said: "We promised to do this responsibly and said we would listen to a variety of voices on this subject and have concluded that it would not be appropriate to go forward at this time." NBC's reversal was applauded by groups such as the National Center on Addiction and Substance Abuse and MADD. However, other advocacy groups such as the Center for Science in the Public Interest noted that there still is a need to look at all alcoholic beverage advertising. The center's director expressed concern over the recent introduction of flavored malt beverages known as "alco-pops," which carry the names of liquor brands like Smirnoff, Bacardi, and Jack Daniel's but follow the rules for advertising beer, which are far less restrictive than those for distilled spirits.

The Distilled Spirits Council categorized NBC's reversal as a temporary setback, noting that a few misguided critics, through their attacks on NBC, had been successful in undercutting the effort to bring distilled spirits ads to the major networks. DISCUS chief executive Peter Cressey stated: "Policies on alcohol advertising need to be based on facts, not preconceived notions or misperceptions. There would have been more social responsibility messages about drinking on television than ever before."

NBC's retreat is indicative of the sensitivities that still exist over the issue of airing liquor ads on the major networks. It appears that there are still some advertising frontiers that will be extremely hard to cross, and it may still be some time before hard-liquor commercials appear in TV shows on the major networks. However, industry experts note that liquor ads are becoming more prevalent on broadcast affiliate and independent stations as well as local cable and now reach over two-thirds of U.S. households. They predict that it is only a matter of time before such ads appear on the major networks as well.

Sources: Kate Fitzgerald, "Cable Wrestles with Liquor Ads," *Advertising Age,* June 10, 2002, p. S-16; Stuart Elliott, "Facing Outcry, NBC Ends Plan to Run Liquor Ads," *The New York Times,* Mar. 21, 2002, p. C1; Joe Flint and Shelly Branch, "In Face of Widening Backlash, NBC Gives Up Plan to Run Liquor Ads," *The Wall Street Journal,* Mar. 21, 2002, pp. B1, 3.

Suppose you are the advertising manager for a consumer-product company and have just reviewed a new commercial your agency created. You are very excited about the ad. It presents new claims about your brand's superiority that should help differentiate it from the competition. However, before you approve the commercial you need answers. Are the claims verifiable? Did researchers use proper procedures to collect and analyze the data and present the findings? Do research results support the claims? Were the right people used in the study? Could any conditions have biased the results?

Before approving the commercial, you have it reviewed by your company's legal department and by your agency's attorneys. If both reviews are acceptable, you send the ad to the major networks, which have their censors examine it. They may ask for more information or send the ad back for modification. (No commercial can run without approval from a network's Standards and Practices Department.)

Even after approval and airing, your commercial is still subject to scrutiny from such state and federal regulatory agencies as the state attorney general's office and the Federal Trade Commission. Individual consumers or competitors who find the ad misleading or have other concerns may file a complaint with the National Advertising Division of the Council of Better Business Bureaus. Finally, disparaged competitors may sue if they believe your ad distorts the facts and misleads consumers. If you lose the litigation, your company may have to retract the claims and pay the competitor damages, sometimes running into millions of dollars.

After considering all these regulatory issues, you must ask yourself if the new ad can meet all these challenges and is worth the risk. Maybe you ought to continue with the old approach that made no specific claims and simply said your brand was great.

Regulatory concerns can play a major role in the advertising decision-making process. Advertisers operate in a complex environment of local, state, and federal rules and regulations. Additionally, a number of advertising and business-sponsored associations, consumer groups and organizations, and the media attempt to promote honest, truthful, and tasteful advertising through their own self-regulatory programs and guidelines. The legal and regulatory aspects of advertising are very complex. Many parties are concerned about the nature and content of advertising and its potential to offend, exploit, mislead, and/or deceive consumers.

Advertising has also become increasingly important in product liability litigation involving products that are associated with consumer injuries. In many of these cases the courts have been willing to consider the impact of advertising on behavior of consumers that leads to injury-causing situations. Thus advertisers must avoid certain practices and proactively engage in others to ensure that their ads are comprehended correctly and do not misrepresent their products or services.[1]

Numerous guidelines, rules, regulations, and laws constrain and restrict advertising. These regulations primarily influence individual advertisers, but they can also affect advertising for an entire industry. For example, cigarette advertising was banned from the broadcast media in 1970, and many groups are pushing for a total ban on the advertising of tobacco products.[2] Legislation now being considered would further restrict the advertising of alcoholic beverages, including beer and wine.[3] Advertising is controlled by internal self-regulation and by external state and federal regulatory agencies such as the Federal Trade Commission (FTC), the Federal Communications Commission (FCC), the Food and Drug Administration (FDA), and the U.S. Postal Service. And recently state attorneys general have become more active in advertising regulation. While only government agencies (federal, state, and local) have the force of law, most advertisers also abide by the guidelines and decisions of internal regulatory bodies. In fact, internal regulation from such groups as the media and the National Advertising Review Board probably has more influence on advertisers' day-to-day operations and decision making than government rules and regulations.

Decision makers on both the client and agency side must be knowledgeable about these regulatory groups, including the intent of their efforts, how they operate, and how they influence and affect advertising and other promotional mix elements. In this chapter, we examine the major sources of advertising regulation, including efforts by the industry at voluntary self-regulation and external regulation by government agencies. We also examine regulations involving sales promotion, direct marketing, and marketing on the Internet.

Self-Regulation

For many years, the advertising industry has practiced and promoted voluntary **self-regulation.** Most advertisers, their agencies, and the media recognize the importance of maintaining consumer trust and confidence. Advertisers also see self-regulation as a way to limit government interference, which, they believe, results in more stringent and troublesome regulations. Self-regulation and control of advertising emanate from all segments of the advertising industry, including individual advertisers and their agencies, business and advertising associations, and the media.

Self-Regulation by Advertisers and Agencies

Self-regulation begins with the interaction of client and agency when creative ideas are generated and submitted for consideration. Most companies have specific guidelines, standards, and policies to which their ads must adhere. Recognizing that their ads reflect on the company, advertisers carefully scrutinize all messages to ensure they are consistent with the image the firm wishes to project. Companies also review their ads to be sure any claims made are reasonable and verifiable and do not mislead or deceive consumers. Ads are usually examined by corporate attorneys to avoid potential legal problems and their accompanying time, expense, negative publicity, and embarrassment.

Internal control and regulation also come from advertising agencies. Most have standards regarding the type of advertising they either want or are willing to produce, and they try to avoid ads that might be offensive or misleading. Most agencies will ask their clients to provide verification or support for claims the clients might want to make in their advertising and will make sure that adequate documentation or substantiation is available. However, agencies will also take formal steps to protect themselves from legal and ethical perils through agency-client contracts. For example, many liability issues are handled in these contracts. Agencies generally use information provided by clients for advertising claims, and in standard contracts the agency is protected from suits involving the accuracy of those claims. Contracts will also absolve the agency of responsibility if something goes wrong with the advertised product and consumers suffer damages or injury or other product liability claims arise.[4] However, agencies have been held legally responsible for fraudulent or deceptive claims and in some cases have been fined when their clients were found guilty of engaging in deceptive advertising.[5] Many agencies have a creative review board or panel composed of experienced personnel who examine ads for content and execution as well as for their potential to be perceived as offensive, misleading, and/or deceptive. Most agencies also employ or retain lawyers who review the ads for potential legal problems. Exhibit 21-1 shows an ad for a legal firm specializing in advertising law and intellectual property.

Most marketers and their agencies work closely with one another to develop advertising that adheres to legal and ethical standards. IMC Perspective 21-1 discusses how the former owner of the Just For Feet athletic-shoe chain filed a lawsuit against its

Exhibit 21-1 The Kinney & Lange firm specializes in Intellectual Property Law

IMC PERSPECTIVE 21-1

Just For Feet Sues Its Ad Agency for Malpractice

During the 1999 Super Bowl athletic-shoe retailer Just For Feet ran a commercial that showed a barefoot Kenyan runner fleeing from hunters in a Humvee, who capture and drug him. When he awakes, he finds a pair of running shoes on his feet. The ad was supposed to be part of a brand-building campaign for the retailer that would help move the company away from its "Where the 13th pair is free" positioning theme. However, rather than change the image of the company, the ad created a controversy that resulted in a lawsuit that could have drastically changed the relationships between advertisers and their agencies.

Following the Super Bowl, critics lashed out at the commercial for its racial insensitivity. As a result of the fallout and criticism surrounding the ad, Just For Feet filed a lawsuit against its agency, Saatchi & Saatchi Business Communications, asking for more than $10 million in damages for advertising malpractice. In its lawsuit Just For Feet claimed that the finished spot, called "Kenya," was entirely different from the concept the agency first presented. Moreover, the retailer's CEO claimed in news reports that he was forced into running the spot even though he personally disliked it.

According to the company, the original concept called for a Just For Feet team coming up to a runner whose shoelace had become untied. The team would tie the runner's shoelace and give him water and a towel, the company said. The commercial was one of two that Saatchi had been considering using until immediately before the Super Bowl. A second spot showed a geeky boy playing dodge ball in a school gymnasium when the Just For Feet team comes in and rescues the boy by giving him better shoes. Just For Feet preferred this spot, the lawsuit claims, but one network rejected it, saying it was "mean-spirited and promotes antisocial behavior."

As the Super Bowl approached, Saatchi presented the final "Kenya" spot to its client. Just For Feet said it "expressed strong misgivings and dissatisfaction over the spot," according to the lawsuit, but the agency "then reassured Just For Feet that the commercial would be well received based on Saatchi's expertise and experience with national advertising and marketing, and that having committed to advertise in the Super Bowl it was too late to develop and produce another commercial or to reshoot the dodge ball commercial." Since it had already spent $900,000 on production costs and $2 million for the Super Bowl time slot, Just For Feet said it had no choice but to run the "Kenya" spot.

In addition to its concerns over the creative work, Just For Feet ran into another major problem. The company planned a sweepstakes promotion, the "Just For Feet Third Quarter Super Bowl Win a Hummer Contest." In the weeks leading up to the game, Just For Feet spent $800,000 on promotional teaser spots during the National Football League conference championship games. These spots told viewers to watch the third quarter of the Super Bowl and find out how many times the Just For Feet name was mentioned. Viewers who wanted to participate in the contest could telephone or go to the company's website to enter their answers. However, the spot ran in the fourth quarter of the big game, making the contest's correct answer zero. The website would not accept zero as the answer, so "customers were left with the mistaken impression that Just For Feet was attempting to trick or deceive them," according to the lawsuit. The Super Bowl spot was bought by Zenith media, which is a sibling of Saatchi & Saatchi.

The litigation actually began just as the controversy from the spot was settling down, when Saatchi sued Just For Feet in late February 1999 for failing to pay its $3 million media bill. On March 1, Just For Feet filed its own suit against Saatchi and Fox Broadcasting. The retailer charged Saatchi with breach of guaranty and warranty, misrepresentation, breach of contract, and "professional negligence and malpractice." In the lawsuit the retailer claimed that its favorable reputation had come under attack and that it had been subjected to the entirely unfounded and

unintended public perception that it was a racist or racially insensitive company.

The lawsuit raised a troubling question for the advertising community as to whether ad agencies can be held liable for the ads they produce. In its legal papers Saatchi claimed advertising is a business that has no explicit guidelines and standards and therefore that it cannot have committed malpractice. The agency also noted that the "Kenya" spot was presented to the networks and was not rejected. Many advertising executives have argued that while Saatchi may have used bad judgment in developing the idea for the commercial and carrying it forward, Just For Feet was ultimately responsible because the company approved the spot and should have taken responsibility for it.

In January 2000 Just For Feet declared bankruptcy, and two months later its assets were purchased by Footstar, one of the largest footwear retailers in the United States. Footstar now operates over 90 athletic-footwear superstores under the Just For Feet name. The company hired a new agency, which has developed a campaign to rebuild the image of the stores. However, the former owner of Just For Feet is still pursuing legal action against Saatchi & Saatchi. A ruling in his favor in the landmark case could yet create problems for advertising agencies and have a major impact on their creative limits, as they would have to be careful to avoid making ads that might result in their becoming involved in lawsuits. The outcome of this case could still be very important to the advertising industry.

Sources: Lisa van der Pool, "Just For Feet Makes TV Return," *Adweek*, Feb. 19, 2001, p. 2; Alice Z. Cuneo, "Can an Agency Be Guilty of Malpractice?" *Advertising Age*, Jan. 31, 2000, pp. 24, 25; "Bad Ad Breeds Worse Lawsuit," *Advertising Age*, June 28, 1999, p. 30.

agency for advertising malpractice. If successful, this lawsuit could have redefined the relationships between advertisers and their agencies regarding responsibility for self-regulation of advertising.[6]

Self-Regulation by Trade Associations

Like advertisers and their agencies, many industries have also developed self-regulatory programs. This is particularly true in industries whose advertising is prone to controversy, such as liquor and alcoholic beverages, drugs, and various products marketed to children. Many trade and industry associations develop their own advertising guidelines or codes that member companies are expected to abide by.

The Wine Institute, the U.S. Brewers Association, and the Distilled Spirits Council of the United States all have guidelines that member companies are supposed to follow in advertising alcoholic beverages.[7] Other industry trade associations with advertising guidelines and programs include the Toy Manufacturers Association, the Motion Picture Association of America, the Pharmaceutical Manufacturers Association, and the Proprietary Association (the trade association for nonprescription-drug makers).[8]

Many professions also maintain advertising guidelines through local, state, and national organizations. For years professional associations like the American Medical Association (AMA) and the American Bar Association (ABA) restricted advertising by their members on the basis that such promotional activities lowered members' professional status and led to unethical and fraudulent claims. However, such restrictive codes have been attacked by both government regulatory agencies and consumer groups. They argue that the public has a right to be informed about a professional's services, qualifications, and background and that advertising will improve professional services as consumers become better informed and are better able to shop around.[9]

In 1977, the Supreme Court held that state bar associations' restrictions on advertising are unconstitutional and that attorneys have First Amendment freedom of speech rights to advertise.[10] Many professional associations subsequently removed their restrictions, and advertising by lawyers and other professionals is now common (Exhibit 21-2).[11] In 1982, the Supreme Court upheld an FTC order permitting advertising by dentists and physicians.[12]

Research shows that consumers generally favor increased use of professional advertising. However, professionals continue to have reservations. They worry that advertising has a negative impact on their image, credibility, and dignity and see benefits to consumers as unlikely.[13] Still, advertising by professionals is increasing, particularly among newcomers to medicine, dentistry, and law. Associations such as the AMA and the ABA developed guidelines for members' advertising to help maintain standards and guard against misleading, deceptive, or offensive ads.

Exhibit 21-2 Advertising by lawyers has become more common as the result of a 1977 Supreme Court ruling

The issue of professional advertising, particularly by attorneys, is still hotly debated. Some traditional law firms resist using advertising, particularly on TV, due to concern that it might hurt the profession's image. Many in the legal profession worry that ads soliciting personal injury victims only worsen the public's perception of attorneys. A sizable faction within the American Bar Association blames the legal profession's image problem on sleazy ads. The ABA's Commission on Advertising recently held a series of public hearings on what, if any, restrictive measures to recommend to state ethics panels. Some states, such as Iowa and Florida, already restrict the content of attorney ads and the way they can be delivered. For example, Iowa lawyers are limited to "tombstone" print ads that merely list their name, location, and objective qualifications. And all ads require a disclaimer urging consumers not to base their attorney selection on an advertisement. Florida attorneys cannot use testimonials or endorsements, dramatizations, self-laudatory statements, illustrations, or photos.[14]

Many attorneys are incensed over efforts to restrict their rights to promote themselves because they use advertising to help build their practices. Several cases are currently being litigated, but ultimately the Supreme Court may have to decide just how far states can go in curtailing advertising.

Although industry associations are concerned with the impact and consequences of members' advertising, they have no legal way to enforce their guidelines. They can only rely on peer pressure from members or other nonbinding sanctions to get advertisers to comply.

Self-Regulation by Businesses

A number of self-regulatory mechanisms have been established by the business community in an effort to control advertising practices. The largest and best known is the **Better Business Bureau (BBB),** which promotes fair advertising and selling practices across all industries. The BBB was established in 1916 to handle consumer complaints about local business practices and particularly advertising. Local BBBs are located in most large cities throughout the United States and supported entirely by dues of the more than 100,000 member firms.

Local BBBs receive and investigate complaints from consumers and other companies regarding the advertising and selling tactics of businesses in their area. Each local office has its own operating procedures for handling complaints; generally, the office contacts the violator and, if the complaint proves true, requests that the practice be stopped or changed. If the violator does not respond, negative publicity may be used against the firm or the case may be referred to appropriate government agencies for further action.

While BBBs provide effective control over advertising practices at the local level, the parent organization, the **Council of Better Business Bureaus,** plays a major role at the national level. The council assists new industries in developing advertising codes and standards, and it provides information about advertising regulations and

legal rulings to advertisers, agencies, and the media. The council also plays an important self-regulatory role through its National Advertising Division (NAD) and Children's Advertising Review Unit (CARU). The NAD works closely with the **National Advertising Review Board** (NARB) to sustain truth, accuracy, and decency in national advertising.

The National Advertising Review Council and the NAD/NARB

In 1971 four associations—the American Advertising Federation (AAF), the American Association of Advertising Agencies (AAAA), the Association of National Advertisers (ANA), and the Council of Better Business Bureaus—joined forces to establish the **National Advertising Review Council** (NARC). The NARC's mission is to sustain high standards of truth, accuracy, and social responsibility in national advertising. The council has two operating arms, the National Advertising Division of the Council of Better Business Bureaus and the National Advertising Review Board. The NAD is the first level that investigates the truthfulness and accuracy of an ad. The NAD reviews only national advertisements, those disseminated on a nationwide or broadly regional basis. Product performance claims, superiority claims against competitive products, and all kinds of scientific and technical claims made in national advertising are the types of cases accepted by the NAD. When an advertiser or a challenger disagrees with the NAD's findings, the decision can be appealed to the NARB for additional review. The NAD/NARB has become the advertising industry's primary self-regulatory mechanism.

The NAD's advertising monitoring program is the source of many of the cases it reviews (Figure 21-1). It also reviews complaints from consumers and consumer groups, local BBBs, and competitors. For example, in 2002 the NAD received a complaint from the Center for Science in the Public Interest, a consumer advocacy group, over an ad run by Campbell Soup for the company's V8 vegetable juice that suggested a link between the tomato-based product and a reduced risk of cancer. Though the NAD decided that Campbell provided competent and reliable evidence to support certain claims, it recommended that the company modify language stating "for prostate cancer, a lower risk is apparent when five or more servings (of tomato products) are consumed per week." Campbell agreed to change the wording of the ad.[15] During the 1970s and 80s, many of the complaints to the NAD came from consumers. However, with the increased use of comparative advertising, the majority of the complaints are now coming from marketers that are challenging competitors' comparisons with their brands.[16] For example, BMW filed a complaint with the NAD over a Volvo commercial claiming the Volvo 850 Turbo Sportswagon accelerates faster than a BMW 328I.[17] Procter & Gamble recently filed a challenge with the NAD over a TV commercial from Fort James Corp. that claimed Brawny paper towels were stronger than P&G's Bounty brand. The commercial in question was the popular "Grannies" spot that showed two grandmothers pushing over a refrigerator to make a mess that was more easily cleaned with Brawny paper towels than with Bounty.[18]

The NAD acts as the investigative arm of the NARC. After initiating or receiving a complaint, it determines the issue, collects and evaluates data, and makes the initial decision on whether the advertiser's claims are substantiated. The NAD may ask the

Figure 21-1 Sources of NAD cases and decisions, 2001

Sources	Number	Percent	Decisions	Number	Percent
Competitor challenges	77	66%	Modified/discontinued	71	60%
NAD monitoring	18	15	Administratively closed	13	11
Local BBB challenges	6	5	Substantiated	17	15
Consumer challenges	16	14	Compliance	8	7
Total	117	100%	Referred to government	8	7
			Total	117	100%

advertiser to supply substantiation for the claim in question. If the information provided is considered adequate to support the claim, the case is deemed substantiated. In the Volvo case, the NAD ruled that the company did have test results to support its superior-acceleration claim and the case was considered substantiated. If the substantiation is unsatisfactory, the NAD negotiates with the advertiser to modify or discontinue the advertising. For example, in the case involving Brawny and Bounty paper towels, the NAD found that several performance claims in the Brawny ads were substantiated. However, the NAD also found that the Brawny ads conveyed an overall-superiority claim that could not be supported, and it recommended that Fort James modify the spot or discontinue using it.

If the NAD and the advertiser fail to resolve the controversy, either can appeal to a five-person panel from the National Advertising Review Board. For example, Fort James Corp. chose to appeal the NAD decision regarding its overall-superiority claim for Brawny versus Bounty paper towels to the NARB rather than modify its ad. The NARB is composed of 85 advertising professionals and prominent public-interest/academia members. If the NARB panel agrees with the NAD and rules against the advertiser, the advertiser must discontinue the advertising. If the advertiser refuses to comply, the NARB refers the matter to the appropriate government agency and indicates the fact in its public record. NAD/NARB decisions are released to the press and also are published in its monthly publication, *NAD Case Reports.*

Although the NARB has no power to order an advertiser to modify or stop running an ad and no sanctions it can impose, advertisers who participate in an NAD investigation and NARB appeal rarely refuse to abide by the panel's decision. Most cases do not even make it to the NARB panel. For example, in 2001, of the 117 NAD investigations, 17 ad claims were substantiated, 5 were referred to the government, and 71 were modified or discontinued (Figure 21-1). Of the 71 cases where the advertising claims were modified or discontinued, in only 2 did the advertiser appeal to the NARB for resolution.[19]

The National Advertising Review Council is also involved in the self-regulation of children's advertising through the Children's Advertising Review Unit (CARU) of the Council of Better Business Bureaus. The NARC board sets policy for CARU's self-regulatory program, which is administered by the Council of Better Business Bureaus and funded directly by members of the children's advertising industry. The CARU's activities include the review and evaluation of child-directed advertising in all media, as well as online privacy issues that affect children. The CARU also provides a general advisory service for advertisers and agencies and has developed self-regulatory guidelines for children's advertising (Exhibit 21-3).

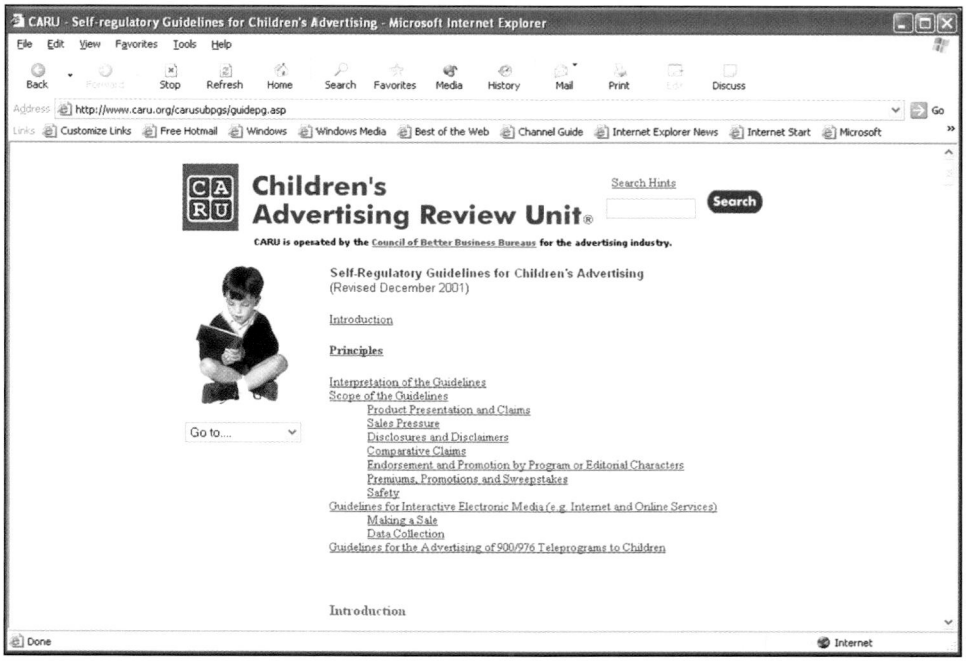

Exhibit 21-3 The Children's Advertising Review Unit provides self-regulatory guidelines for children's advertising

The National Advertising Review Council, working through the NAD/NARB and CARU, has become a valuable and effective self-regulatory body. Cases brought to it are handled at a fraction of the cost (and with much less publicity) than those brought to court and are expedited more quickly than those reviewed by a government agency such as the FTC. The system also works because judgments are made by the advertiser's peers, and most companies feel compelled to comply. Firms may prefer self-regulation rather than government intervention in part because they can challenge competitors' unsubstantiated claims through groups like the NARB.[20]

Advertising Associations Various groups in the advertising industry also favor self-regulation. The two major national organizations, the American Association of Advertising Agencies and the American Advertising Federation, actively monitor and police industry wide advertising practices. The AAAA, which is the major trade association of the ad agency business in the United States, has established standards of practice and its own creative code. It also issues guidelines for specific types of advertising such as comparative messages (Figure 21-2). The AAF consists of advertisers, agencies, media, and numerous advertising clubs. The association has standards for truthful and responsible advertising, is involved in advertising legislation, and actively influences agencies to abide by its code and principles.

Self-Regulation by Media

The media are another important self-regulatory mechanism in the advertising industry. Most media maintain some form of advertising review process and, except for

Figure 21-2 AAAA policy statement and guidelines for comparative advertising

The Board of Directors of the American Association of Advertising Agencies recognizes that when used truthfully and fairly, comparative advertising provides the consumer with needed and useful information.

However, extreme caution should be exercised. The use of comparative advertising, by its very nature, can distort facts and, by implication, convey to the consumer information that misrepresents the truth.

Therefore, the Board believes that comparative advertising should follow certain guidelines:

1. The intent and connotation of the ad should be to inform and never to discredit or unfairly attack competitors, competing products, or services.
2. When a competitive product is named, it should be one that exists in the marketplace as significant competition.
3. The competition should be fairly and properly identified but never in a manner or tone of voice that degrades the competitive product or service.
4. The advertising should compare related or similar properties or ingredients of the product, dimension to dimension, feature to feature.
5. The identification should be for honest comparison purposes and not simply to upgrade by association.
6. If a competitive test is conducted, it should be done by an objective testing source, preferably an independent one, so that there will be no doubt as to the veracity of the test.
7. In all cases the test should be supportive of all claims made in the advertising that are based on the test.
8. The advertising should never use partial results or stress insignificant differences to cause the consumer to draw an improper conclusion.
9. The property being compared should be significant in terms of value or usefulness of the product to the consumer.
10. Comparatives delivered through the use of testimonials should not imply that the testimonial is more than one individual's thought unless that individual represents a sample of the majority viewpoint.

political ads, may reject any they regard as objectionable. Some media exclude advertising for an entire product class; others ban individual ads they think offensive or objectionable. For example, *Reader's Digest* does not accept advertising for tobacco or liquor products. A number of magazines in the United States and other countries refused to run some of Benetton's shock ads on the grounds that their readers would find them offensive or disturbing (Exhibit 21-4).[21]

Newspapers and magazines have their own advertising requirements and restrictions, which often vary depending on the size and nature of the publication. Large, established publications, such as major newspapers or magazines, often have strict standards regarding the type of advertising they accept. Some magazines, such as *Parents* and *Good Housekeeping,* regularly test the products they advertise and offer a "seal of approval" and refunds if the products are later found to be defective. Such policies are designed to enhance the credibility of the publication and increase the reader's confidence in the products it advertises.

Advertising on television and radio has been regulated for years through codes developed by the industry trade association, the National Association of Broadcasters (NAB). Both the radio code (established in 1937) and the television code (1952) provided standards for broadcast advertising for many years. Both codes prohibited the advertising of certain products, such as hard liquor. They also affected the manner in which products could be advertised. However, in 1982, the NAB suspended all of its code provisions after the courts found that portions (dealing with time standards and required length of commercials in the TV code) were in restraint of trade. While the NAB codes are no longer in force, many individual broadcasters, such as the major TV networks, have incorporated major portions of the code provisions into their own standards.[22]

The four major television networks have the most stringent review process of any media. All four networks maintain standards and practices divisions, which carefully review all commercials submitted to the network or individual affiliate stations. Advertisers must submit for review all commercials intended for airing on the network or an affiliate.

A commercial may be submitted for review in the form of a script, storyboard, animatic, or finished commercial (when the advertiser believes there is little chance of objection). A very frustrating, and often expensive, scenario for both an agency and its client occurs when a commercial is approved at the storyboard stage but then is rejected after it is produced. Commercials are rejected for a variety of reasons, including violence, morbid humor, sex, politics, and religion. Network reviewers also consider whether the proposed commercial meets acceptable standards and is appropriate for certain audiences. For example, different standards are used for ads designated for

Exhibit 21-4 A number of magazines refused to run this Benetton ad

Figure 21-3 A sampling of the TV networks' guidelines for children's advertising

Each of the major TV networks has its own set of guidelines for children's advertising, although the basics are very similar. A few rules, such as the requirement of a static "island" shot at the end, are written in stone; others, however, can sometimes be negotiated. Many of the rules below apply specifically to toys. The networks also have special guidelines for kids' food commercials and for kids' commercials that offer premiums.

Must not overglamorize product

No exhortative language, such as "Ask Mom to buy . . ."

No realistic war settings

Generally no celebrity endorsements

Can't use "only" or "just" in regard to price

Show only two toys per child or maximum of six per commercial

Five-second "island" showing product against plain background at end of spot

Animation restricted to one-third of a commercial

Generally no comparative or superiority claims

No costumes or props not available with the toy

No child or toy can appear in animated segments

Three-second establishing shot of toy in relation to child

No shots under one second in length

Must show distance a toy can travel before stopping on its own

prime-time versus late-night spots or for children's versus adults' programs (see Figure 21-3). Although most of these guidelines remain in effect, ABC and NBC loosened their rules on celebrity endorsements.[23]

The four major networks receive nearly 50,000 commercials a year for review; nearly two-thirds are accepted, and only 3 percent are rejected. Most problems with the remaining 30 percent are resolved through negotiation, and the ads are revised and resubmitted.[24] Most commercials run after changes are made. For example, censors initially rejected a humorous "Got milk?" spot that showed children watching an elderly neighbor push a wheelbarrow. Suddenly, the man's arms rip off, presumably because he doesn't drink milk. The spot was eventually approved after it was modified so that the man appears unhurt after losing his limbs and there was no expression of pain (Exhibit 21-5).[25]

Network standards regarding acceptable advertising change constantly. The networks first allowed lingerie advertisers to use live models rather than mannequins in 1987. Advertising for contraceptives is now appearing on some stations. The networks also loosened long-standing restrictions on endorsements and competitive advertising claims.[26] Network standards will continue to change as society's values and attitudes

Exhibit 21-5 This humorous "Got milk?" commercial had to be modified slightly to satisfy network censors

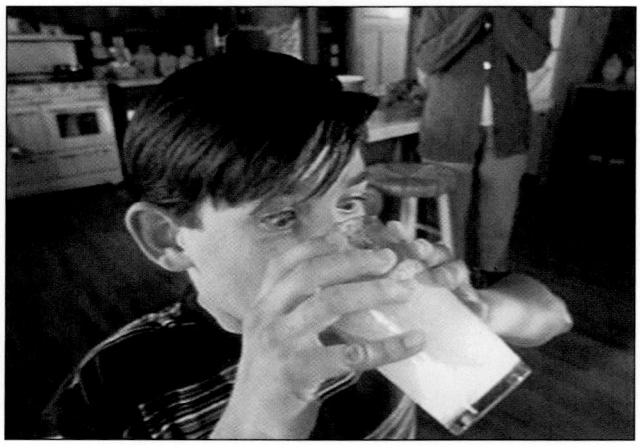

toward certain issues and products change. Also, many advertising people believe these changes are a response to competition from independent and cable stations, which tend to be much less stringent in their standards and practices. However, since television is probably the most carefully scrutinized and frequently criticized of all forms of advertising, the networks must be careful not to offend their viewers and detract from advertising's credibility.

Appraising Self-Regulation

The three major participants in the advertising process—advertisers, agencies, and the media—work individually and collectively to encourage truthful, ethical, and responsible advertising. The advertising industry views self-regulation as an effective mechanism for controlling advertising abuses and avoiding the use of offensive, misleading, or deceptive practices, and it prefers this form of regulation to government intervention. Self-regulation of advertising has been effective and in many instances probably led to the development of more stringent standards and practices than those imposed by or beyond the scope of legislation.

A senior vice president and general counsel at Kraft Foods, while praising the NAD, summarized the feelings of many advertisers toward self-regulation. In his testimonial he stated: "NAD is superior to its competition, which is regulation by the government or regulation by the courts. Accurate, prompt, and inexpensive decisions year in and year out have earned NAD its well-deserved credibility with the industry and with regulators." Federal Trade Commission chairman Timothy Murris has described the NAD as a "model of self-regulation" (Exhibit 21-6).

There are, however, limitations to self-regulation, and the process has been criticized in a number of areas. For example, the NAD may take six months to a year to resolve a complaint, during which time a company often stops using the commercial anyway. Budgeting and staffing constraints may limit the number of cases the NAD/NARB system investigates and the speed with which it resolves them.[27] And some critics believe that self-regulation is self-serving to the advertisers and advertising industry and lacks the power or authority to be a viable alternative to federal or state regulation.

Many do not believe advertising can or should be controlled solely by self-regulation. They argue that regulation by government agencies is necessary to ensure that consumers get accurate information and are not misled or deceived. Moreover, since advertisers do not have to comply with the decisions and recommendations of self-regulatory groups, it is sometimes necessary to turn to the federal and/or state government.

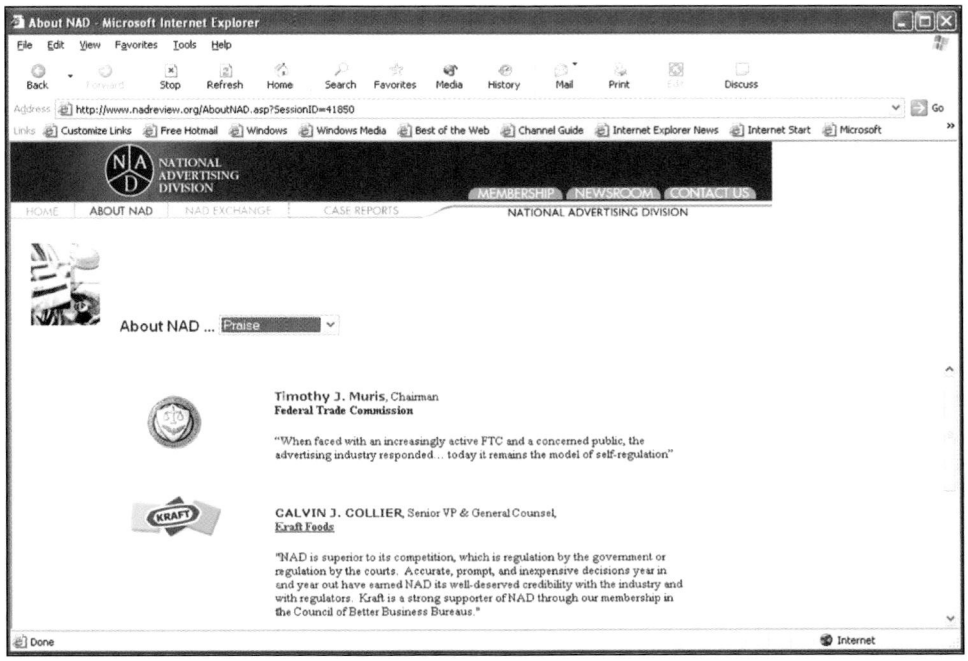

Exhibit 21-6 Praise for the NAD is noted on its website

Federal Regulation of Advertising

Advertising is controlled and regulated through federal, state, and local laws and regulations enforced by various government agencies. The federal government is the most important source of external regulation since many advertising practices come under the jurisdiction of the **Federal Trade Commission.** In addition, depending on the advertiser's industry and product or service, other federal agencies such as the Federal Communications Commission, the Food and Drug Administration, the U.S. Postal Service, and the Bureau of Alcohol, Tobacco, and Firearms may have regulations that affect advertising. We will begin our discussion of federal regulation of advertising by considering the basic rights of marketers to advertise their products and services under the First Amendment.

Advertising and the First Amendment

Freedom of speech or expression, as defined by the First Amendment to the U.S. Constitution, is the most basic federal law governing advertising in the United States. For many years, freedom of speech protection did not include advertising and other forms of speech that promote a commercial transaction. However, the courts have extended First Amendment protection to **commercial speech,** which is speech that promotes a commercial transaction. There have been a number of landmark cases over the past three decades where the federal courts have issued rulings supporting the coverage of commercial speech by the First Amendment.

In a 1976 case, *Virginia State Board of Pharmacy* v. *Virginia Citizens Consumer Council,* the U.S. Supreme Court ruled that states cannot prohibit pharmacists from advertising the prices of prescription drugs, because such advertising contains information that helps the consumer choose between products and because the free flow of information is indispensable.[28] As noted earlier, in 1977 the Supreme Court ruled that state bar associations' restrictions on advertising are unconstitutional and attorneys have a First Amendment right to advertise their services and prices.[29] In another landmark case in 1980, *Central Hudson Gas & Electric Corp.* v. *New York Public Service Commission,* the Supreme Court ruled that commercial speech was entitled to First Amendment protection in some cases. However, the Court ruled that the U.S. Constitution affords less protection to commercial speech than to other constitutionally guaranteed forms of expression. In this case the Court established a four-part test, known as the **Central Hudson Test,** for determining restrictions on commercial speech.[30] In a more recent case, the Supreme Court's 1996 decision in *44 Liquormart, Inc.* v. *Rhode Island* struck down two state statutes designed to support the state's interest in temperance. The first prohibited the advertising of alcoholic beverage prices in Rhode Island except on signs within a store, while the second prohibited the publication or broadcast of alcohol price ads. The Court ruled that the Rhode Island statutes were unlawful because they restricted the constitutional guarantee of freedom of speech, and the decision signaled strong protection for advertisers under the First Amendment.[31]

In the cases regarding advertising, the U.S. Supreme Court has ruled that freedom of expression must be balanced against competing interests. For example, the courts have upheld bans on the advertising of products that are considered harmful, such as tobacco. The Court has also ruled that only truthful commercial speech is protected, not advertising or other forms of promotion that are false, misleading, or deceptive.

In a very recent case involving Nike, the California Supreme Court issued a ruling that is likely to impact corporate image advertising campaigns and the way companies engage in public debate regarding issues that affect them.[32] The California high court ruled that corporations are not protected by the First Amendment when they present as fact statements about their labor policies or company operations in advertisements, press releases, letters to the editor, or public statements. The court ruled that corporations can be found liable for deceptive advertising if they make misleading statements about their operations and conduct. Nike had argued that statements the company made to defend itself against charges involving its labor practices were protected by

constitutional guarantees of free speech. In this case the court did not find Nike guilty of misleading advertising. However, the court did rule that the statements made by the company to defend itself against charges regarding its labor practices in Third World countries were commercial in nature and thus subject to government regulation. This ruling also affects other aspects of marketing communications, such as public relations, since the court ruled that speech can be considered commercial even if it is not in the form of an advertisement. It is expected that Nike will appeal the ruling to the U.S. Supreme Court.[33]

The job of regulating advertising at the federal level and determining whether advertising is truthful or deceptive is a major focus of the Federal Trade Commission. We now turn our attention to federal regulation of advertising and the FTC.

Background on Federal Regulation of Advertising

Federal regulation of advertising originated in 1914 with the passage of the **Federal Trade Commission Act** (FTC Act), which created the FTC, the agency that is today the most active in, and has primary responsibility for, controlling and regulating advertising. The FTC Act was originally intended to help enforce antitrust laws, such as the Sherman and Clayton acts, by helping to restrain unfair methods of competition. The main focus of the first five-member commission was to protect competitors from one another; the issue of false or misleading advertising was not even mentioned. In 1922, the Supreme Court upheld an FTC interpretation that false advertising was an unfair method of competition, but in the 1931 case *FTC* v. *Raladam Co.,* the Court ruled the commission could not prohibit false advertising unless there was evidence of injury to a competitor.[34] This ruling limited the power of the FTC to protect consumers from false or deceptive advertising and led to a consumer movement that resulted in an important amendment to the FTC Act.

In 1938, Congress passed the **Wheeler-Lea Amendment.** It amended section 5 of the FTC Act to read: "Unfair methods of competition in commerce and unfair or deceptive acts or practices in commerce are hereby declared to be unlawful." The amendment empowered the FTC to act if there was evidence of injury to the public; proof of injury to a competitor was not necessary. The Wheeler-Lea Amendment also gave the FTC the power to issue cease-and-desist orders and levy fines on violators. It extended the FTC's jurisdiction over false advertising of foods, drugs, cosmetics, and therapeutic devices. And it gave the FTC access to the injunctive power of the federal courts, initially only for food and drug products but expanded in 1972 to include all products in the event of a threat to the public's health and safety.

In addition to the FTC, numerous other federal agencies are responsible for, or involved in, advertising regulation. The authority of these agencies is limited, however, to a particular product area or service, and they often rely on the FTC to assist in handling false or deceptive advertising cases.

The Federal Trade Commission

The FTC is responsible for protecting both consumers and businesses from anticompetitive behavior and unfair and deceptive practices. The major divisions of the FTC include the bureaus of competition, economics, and consumer protection. The Bureau of Competition seeks to prevent business practices that restrain competition and is responsible for enforcing antitrust laws. The Bureau of Economics helps the FTC evaluate the impact of its actions and provides economic analysis and support to antitrust and consumer protection investigations and rule makings. It also analyzes the impact of government regulation on competition and consumers. The Bureau of Consumer Protection's mandate is to protect consumers against unfair, deceptive, or fraudulent practices. This bureau also investigates and litigates cases involving acts or practices alleged to be deceptive or unfair to consumers. The Division of Advertising Practices of the Bureau of Competition protects consumers from deceptive and unsubstantiated advertising and enforces the provisions of the FTC Act that forbid misrepresentation, unfairness, and deception in general advertising at the national and regional

Exhibit 21-7 The Division of Advertising Practices protects consumers from deceptive and unsubstantiated advertising claims

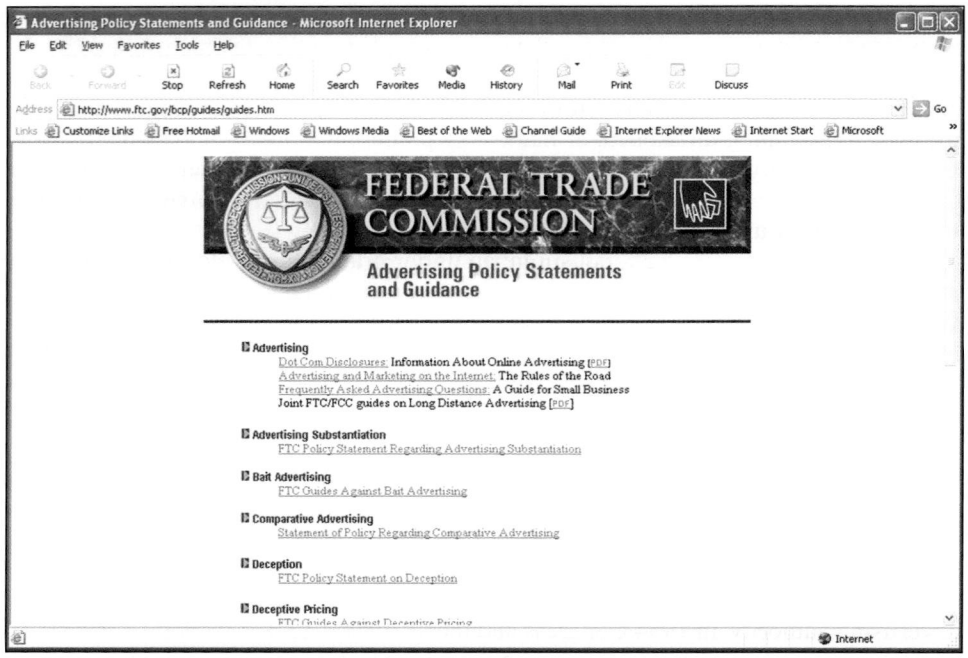

level (Exhibit 21-7). The Division of Marketing Practices of the Bureau of Competition engages in activities that are related to various marketing and warranty practices such as fraudulent telemarketing schemes, 900-number programs, and disclosures relating to franchise and business opportunities.

The FTC has had the power to regulate advertising since passage of the Wheeler-Lea Amendment. However, not until the early 1970s—following criticism of the commission in a book by "Nader's Raiders" and a special report by the American Bar Association citing its lack of action against deceptive promotional practices—did the FTC become active in regulating advertising.[35] The authority of the FTC was increased considerably throughout the 1970s. The Magnuson-Moss Act of 1975, an important piece of legislation, dramatically broadened the FTC's powers and substantially increased its budget. The first section of the act dealt with consumers' rights regarding product warranties; it allowed the commission to require restitution for deceptively written warranties where the consumer lost more than $5. The second section, the FTC Improvements Act, empowered the FTC to establish **trade regulation rules** (TRRs), industrywide rules that define unfair practices before they occur.

During the 1970s, the FTC made enforcement of laws regarding false and misleading advertising a top priority. Several new programs were instituted, budgets were increased, and the commission became a very powerful regulatory agency. However, many of these programs, as well as the expanded powers of the FTC to develop regulations on the basis of "unfairness," became controversial. At the root of this controversy is the fundamental issue of what constitutes unfair advertising.

The Concept of Unfairness

Under section 5 of the FTC Act, the Federal Trade Commission has a mandate to act against unfair or deceptive advertising practices. However, this statute does not define the terms *unfair* and *deceptive,* and the FTC has been criticized for not doing so itself. While the FTC has taken steps to clarify the meaning of *deception,* people have been concerned for years about the vagueness of the term *unfair.*

Controversy over the FTC's authority to regulate unfair advertising practices began in 1978, when the agency relied on this mandate to formulate its controversial "kid vid" rule restricting advertising to children.[36] This interpretation caused widespread concern in the business community that the term *unfair* could be used to encompass anything FTC commissioners might find objectionable. For example, in a 1980 policy statement the FTC noted that "the precise concept of consumer unfairness is one whose precise meaning is not immediately obvious." Consequently, in 1980 Congress

responded by suspending the children's advertising rule and banning the FTC from using unfairness as a legal basis for advertising rulemaking.

The FTC responded to these criticisms in December 1980 by sending Congress a statement containing an interpretation of unfairness. According to FTC policy, the basis for determining **unfairness** is that a trade practice (1) causes substantial physical or economic injury to consumers, (2) could not reasonably be avoided by consumers, and (3) must not be outweighed by countervailing benefits to consumers or competition. The agency also stated that a violation of public policy (such as of other government statutes) could, by itself, constitute an unfair practice or could be used to prove substantial consumer injury. Practices considered unfair are claims made without prior substantiation, claims that might exploit such vulnerable groups as children and the elderly, and instances where consumers cannot make a valid choice because the advertiser omits important information about the product or competing products mentioned in the ad.[37]

The FTC's statement was intended to clarify its interpretation of unfairness and reduce ambiguity over what might constitute unfair practices. However, efforts by the FTC to develop industrywide trade regulation rules that would define unfair practices and have the force and effect of law were limited by Congress in 1980 with the passage of the FTC Improvements Act. Amidst calls to end the stalemate over the FTC's regulation of unfair advertising by having the agency work with Congress to define its advertising authority, in 1994 Congress and the advertising industry agreed on a definition of unfair advertising that is very similar to the FTC's 1980 policy statement discussed earlier. However, the new agreement requires that before the FTC can initiate any industrywide rule, it has to have reason to believe that the unfair or deceptive acts or practices are prevalent.[38]

The FTC does have specific regulatory authority in cases involving deceptive, misleading, or untruthful advertising. The vast majority of advertising cases that the FTC handles concern deception and advertising fraud, which usually involve knowledge of a false claim.

Deceptive Advertising

In most economies, advertising provides consumers with information they can use to make consumption decisions. However, if this information is untrue or misleads the consumer, advertising is not fulfilling its basic function. But what constitutes an untruthful or deceptive ad? Deceptive advertising can take a number of forms, ranging from intentionally false or misleading claims to ads that, although true, leave some consumers with a false or misleading impression.

The issue of deception, including its definition and measurement, receives considerable attention from the FTC and other regulatory agencies. One of the problems regulatory agencies deal with in determining deception is distinguishing between false or misleading messages and those that, rather than relying on verifiable or substantiated objective information about a product, make subjective claims or statements, a practice known as puffery. **Puffery** has been legally defined as "advertising or other sales presentations which praise the item to be sold with subjective opinions, superlatives, or exaggerations, vaguely and generally, stating no specific facts."[39] The use of puffery in advertising is common. For example, Bayer aspirin calls itself the "wonder drug that works wonders," Nestlé claims "Nestlé makes the very best chocolate," Snapple advertises that its beverages are "made from the best stuff on Earth," and BMW uses the tagline "The Ultimate Driving Machine." Superlatives such as *greatest, best,* and *finest* are puffs that are often used.

Puffery has generally been viewed as a form of poetic license or allowable exaggeration. The FTC takes the position that because consumers expect exaggeration or inflated claims in advertising, they recognize puffery and don't believe it. But some studies show that consumers may believe puffery and perceive such claims as true.[40] One study found that consumers could not distinguish between a verifiable fact-based claim and puffery and were just as likely to believe both types of claims.[41] Ivan Preston argues that puffery has a detrimental effect on consumers' purchase decisions by burdening them with untrue beliefs and refers to it as "soft-core deception" that should be illegal.[42]

Advertisers' battle to retain the right to use puffery was supported in the latest revision of the Uniform Commercial Code in 1996. The revision switches the burden of proof to consumers from advertisers in cases pertaining to whether certain claims were meant to be taken as promises. The revision states that the buyer must prove that an affirmation of fact (as opposed to puffery) was made, that the buyer was aware of the advertisement, and that the affirmation of fact became part of the agreement with the seller.[43]

The use of puffery as a defense for advertising claims is periodically challenged in court. IMC Perspective 21-2 discusses a recent legal battle involving Pizza Hut and Papa John's in which the U.S. Supreme Court issued a decision in support of the use of puffery as the basis for a comparative advertising claim.

Since unfair and deceptive acts or practices have never been precisely defined, the FTC is continually developing and refining a working definition in its attempts to regulate advertising. The traditional standard used to determine deception was whether a claim had the "tendency or capacity to deceive." However, this standard was criticized for being vague and all-encompassing.

In 1983 the FTC, under Chair James Miller III, put forth a new working definition of **deception:** "The commission will find deception if there is a misrepresentation, omission, or practice that is likely to mislead the consumer acting reasonably in the circumstances to the consumer's detriment."[44] There are three essential elements to this definition of deception.[45] The first element is that the representation, omission, or practice must be *likely to mislead* the consumer. The FTC defines *misrepresentation* as an express or implied statement contrary to fact, whereas a *misleading omission* occurs when qualifying information necessary to prevent a practice, claim, representation, or reasonable belief from being misleading is not disclosed.

The second element is that the act or practice must be considered from the perspective of *the reasonable consumer.* In determining reasonableness, the FTC considers the group to which the advertising is targeted and whether their interpretation of or reaction to the message is reasonable in light of the circumstances. The standard is flexible and allows the FTC to consider factors such as the age, education level, intellectual capacity, and frame of mind of the particular group to which the message or practice is targeted. For example, advertisements targeted to a particular group, such as children or the elderly, are evaluated with respect to their effect on a reasonable member of that group.

The third key element to the FTC's definition of deception is *materiality.* According to the FTC a "material" misrepresentation or practice is one that is likely to affect a consumer's choice or conduct with regard to a product or service. What this means is that the information, claim, or practice in question is important to consumers and, if acted upon, would be likely to influence their purchase decisions. In some cases the information or claims made in an ad may be false or misleading but would not be regarded as material since reasonable consumers would not make a purchase decision on the basis of this information.

Miller's goal was to help the commission determine which cases were worth pursuing and which were trivial. Miller argued that for an ad to be considered worthy of FTC challenge, it should be seen by a substantial number of consumers, it should lead to significant injury, and the problem should be one that market forces are not likely to remedy. However, the revised definition may put a greater burden on the FTC to prove that deception occurred and that the deception influenced the consumers' decision-making process in a detrimental way.

Determining what constitutes deception is still a gray area. Two of the factors the FTC considers in evaluating an ad for deception are (1) whether there are significant omissions of important information and (2) whether advertisers can substantiate the claims made for the product or service. The FTC has developed several programs to address these issues.

Affirmative Disclosure

An ad can be literally true yet leave the consumer with a false or misleading impression if the claim is true only under certain conditions or circumstances or if there are limitations to what the product can or cannot do. Thus, under its **affirmative disclosure** requirement, the FTC may require advertisers to

IMC PERSPECTIVE 21-2

The Pizza Wars Legal Battle Upholds the Use of Puffery

The use of unsubstantiated superlatives such as *good, better,* and *best* have long been a staple of American advertising. The Federal Trade Commission views the use of these terms, as well as other forms of marketing bravado, as puffery. The FTC defines puffery as "clear hyperbole" and takes the position that consumers would not expect these claims to be documented and would not take them seriously. However, a recent legal battle between Pizza Hut and Papa John's over the latter's use of puffery nearly resulted in a redefining of the limits of advertising claims that would have opened a large can of worms for the entire industry.

In 1997 Papa John's began running ads comparing its product to market leader Pizza Hut and using the tagline "Better ingredients. Better pizza." The battle heated up in 1998 when Papa John's ran a series of ads designed to show just why it believed that better ingredients do indeed make a better pizza. One spot featured Papa John's brash founder, John Schnatter, claiming consumers preferred his chain's tomato sauce because Papa John's uses fresh tomatoes picked from the vine while Pizza Hut uses "remanufactured paste." Another spot explained that Papa John's dough is made with clear filtered water and yeast given several days to work its magic while the "biggest chain" (Pizza Hut) uses whatever comes out of the tap to make frozen dough or dough made the same day.

Pizza Hut responded with what it called a "corrective ad" on the dough issue and, after getting no sympathy from the National Advertising Division of the Council of Better Business Bureaus, filed a lawsuit against Papa John's in 1998 claiming that much of its advertising was false and misleading. The suit was heard in November 1999 and after weeks of testimony in federal court, which included dough experts and sauce demonstrations, a jury sided with Pizza Hut, ruling that Papa John's "Better ingredients. Better pizza" slogan was false and misleading because the chain had failed to prove its sauce and dough were superior. The judge in the case upheld the jury's decision and ruled that the slogan was acceptable puffery until Papa John's began running ads touting its tomato sauce and pizza dough as superior. He held that the slogan then became tainted to the extent that its continued use should be stopped. The judge admonished both sides for the dubious nature of their advertising, but ordered Papa John's to pay Pizza Hut $468,000 in damages and also issued an injunction against the entire "Better ingredients. Better pizza" integrated marketing blitz, including use of the slogan on store signage, pizza boxes, car toppers, menus, napkins, and hats as well as in advertisements.

In January 2000 Papa John's appealed the decision, arguing that the judge had misinterpreted the law as use of the "Better ingredients. Better pizza" slogan was legally acceptable puffery. The court of appeals handed down a complicated ruling that sided with Papa John's on the puffery issue and lifted the injunction. The appellate judges ruled that Papa John's ads were misleading but argued that Pizza Hut had not provided enough evidence that the misrepresentation was "material" and had a negative effect on consumers' purchase behavior. Pizza Hut was outraged by the ruling, arguing that as "evidence" it had produced three different consumer surveys at the original trial, all of which indicated that consumers were wrongly influenced by the Papa John's campaign. However, all three surveys were ignored by the courts on technicalities.

Pizza Hut continued to believe that if the judges felt the advertising was misleading, and their ruling said they did, they should have punished Papa John's. So, in December 2000, Pizza Hut's lawyers decided to appeal the case to the U.S. Supreme Court on the basis that the appeals judges had required an unusually high standard of evidence to prove that consumers had been misled by Papa John's. An attorney for Pizza Hut who argued the case before the Supreme Court stated: "There is no social value in false advertising, and the concept that you turn a blind eye to false advertising simply because of the inability to prove very precise purchasing decisions strikes me as a standard of proof that is extremely high and completely unwarranted." However, in March 2001 the Supreme Court handed down its two-word decision: "Petition

denied." The court of appeals ruling favoring Papa John's was allowed to stand.

Despite being disappointed at losing the case, Pizza Hut's general counsel was philosophical about the ruling, noting that it trapped Papa John's in a curious catch 22: If Pizza Hut won, it could describe Papa John's advertising as false; but if Papa John's won, it would be only because it had successfully argued that its advertising was mere puffery—not to be believed—which is exactly what happened. Papa John's expressed satisfaction with the case and indicated that it was glad the matter was over—and for good reason. The company's financial reports indicated that it had spent at least $7 million to cover the legal costs of the case. Experts noted that it is reasonable to assume that Pizza Hut incurred similar costs.

The advertising industry was also relieved that the Supreme Court had ruled in favor of Papa John's. The case had put many executives on edge, as a ruling against the puffery defense could have prompted other challenges and a redrawing of the blurry line separating so-called puffery and outright false advertising. With this ruling, advertisers are still free to use words such as *good, better,* and *best* and let consumers determine what they really mean.

Sources: Jim Edwards, "Sour Dough: Pizza Hut v. Papa John's," *Brandweek,* May 21, 2001, pp. 26–30; Davan Maharaj and Greg Johnson, "Battle over Pizza Puffery Could Reshape Ad Landscape," *Los Angeles Times,* Apr. 2, 2000, pp. C1, 4; Michael Fumento, "Free-a-the Papa!" *Forbes,* Feb. 21, 2000, p. 53; Louise Kramer, "Jury Finds Papa John's Ads Misled," *Advertising Age,* Nov. 22, 1999, p. 46.

include certain types of information in their ads so that consumers will be aware of all the consequences, conditions, and limitations associated with the use of a product or service. The goal of affirmative disclosure is to give consumers sufficient information to make an informed decision. An ad may be required to define the testing situation, conditions, or criteria used in making a claim. For example, fuel mileage claims in car ads are based on Environmental Protection Agency (EPA) ratings since they offer a uniform standard for making comparisons. Cigarette ads must contain a warning about the health risks associated with smoking.

An example of an affirmative disclosure ruling is the FTC's case against Campbell Soup for making deceptive and unsubstantiated claims. Campbell's ads, run as part of its "Soup is good food" campaign, linked the low-fat and -cholesterol content of its soup with a reduced risk of heart disease. However, the advertising failed to disclose that the soups are high in sodium, which may increase the risk of heart disease. In a consent agreement accepted in 1991, Campbell agreed that, for any soup containing more than 500 milligrams of sodium in an 8-ounce serving, it will disclose the sodium content in any advertising that directly or by implication mentions heart disease in connection with the soup. Campbell also agreed it would not imply a connection between soup and a reduction in heart disease in future advertising.[46]

Another area where the Federal Trade Commission is seeking more specificity from advertisers is in regard to country of origin claims. The FTC has been working with marketers and trade associations to develop a better definition of what the "Made in the USA" label means. The 50-year-old definition used until recently required full manufacturing in the United States, using U.S. labor and parts, with only raw materials from overseas.[47] Many companies argue that in an increasingly global economy, it is becoming very difficult to have 100 percent U.S. content and remain price-competitive. However, the FTC argues that advertising or labeling a product as "Made in the USA" can provide a company with a competitive advantage. For many products some consumers do respond to the claim, as they trust the quality of domestic-made products and/or feel patriotic when they buy American. For example, athletic-shoe maker New Balance is a company that promotes its commitment to domestic manufacturing and the fact that a percentage of its products are made in the United States (Exhibit 21-8).

In December 1998 the FTC issued new guidelines for American-made products. The guidelines spell out what it means by "all or virtually all" in mandating how much U.S. content a product must have to wear a "Made in USA" label or be advertised as such. According to the new FTC guidelines, all significant parts and processing that go into the product must be of U.S. origin and the product should have no or very little foreign content. Companies do not have to receive the approval of the FTC before making a "Made in USA" claim. However, the commission does have the authority to take action against false and unsubstantiated "Made in USA" claims just as it does with other advertising claims.[48]

Exhibit 21-8 New Balance promotes its commitment to U.S. manufacturing

Advertising Substantiation A major area of concern to regulatory agencies is whether advertisers can support or substantiate their claims. For many years, there were no formal requirements concerning substantiation of advertising claims. Many companies made claims without any documentation or support such as laboratory tests and clinical studies. In 1971, the FTC's **advertising substantiation** program required advertisers to have supporting documentation for their claims and to prove the claims are truthful.[49] Broadened in 1972, this program now requires advertisers to substantiate their claims before an ad appears. Substantiation is required for all express or implied claims involving safety, performance, efficacy, quality, or comparative price.

The FTC's substantiation program has had a major effect on the advertising industry, because it shifted the burden of proof from the commission to the advertiser. Before the substantiation program, the FTC had to prove that an advertiser's claims were unfair or deceptive.

Ad substantiation seeks to provide a basis for believing advertising claims so consumers can make rational and informed decisions and companies are deterred from making claims they cannot adequately support. The FTC takes the perspective that it is illegal and unfair to consumers for a firm to make a claim for a product without having a "reasonable basis" for the claim. In their decision to require advertising substantiation, the commissioners made the following statement:

> Given the imbalance of knowledge and resources between a business enterprise and each of its customers, economically it is more rational and imposes far less cost on society, to require a manufacturer to confirm his affirmative product claims rather than impose a burden on each individual consumer to test, investigate, or experiment for himself. The manufacturer has the ability, the know-how, the equipment, the time and resources to undertake such information, by testing or otherwise, . . . the consumer usually does not.[50]

Many advertisers respond negatively to the FTC's advertising substantiation program. They argue it is too expensive to document all their claims and most consumers either won't understand or aren't interested in the technical data. Some advertisers threaten to avoid the substantiation issue by using puffery claims, which do not require substantiation.

Generally, advertisers making claims covered by the substantiation program must have available prior substantiation of all claims. However, in 1984, the FTC issued a new policy statement that suggested after-the-fact substantiation might be acceptable in some cases and it would solicit documentation of claims only from advertisers that are under investigation for deceptive practices.

In a number of cases, the FTC has ordered advertisers to cease making inadequately substantiated claims. In 1993, the FTC took on the weight-loss industry when it filed a

Exhibit 21-9 Weight-loss program marketers are now required to substantiate their claims as a result of an FTC ruling

complaint charging that none of five large, well-known diet program marketers had sufficient evidence to back up claims that their customers achieved their weight-loss goals or maintained the loss (Exhibit 21-9). Three of the companies agreed to publicize the fact that most weight loss is temporary and to disclose how long their customers kept off the weight they lost. The agreement required the companies to substantiate their weight-loss claims with scientific data and to document claims that their customers keep off the weight by monitoring a group of them for two years.[51]

In 1997 the FTC challenged advertising claims made by Abbott Laboratories for its Ensure brand nutritional beverage. The FTC charged that Abbott made false and unsubstantiated claims that many doctors recommend Ensure as a meal supplement and replacement for healthy adults, including those in their 30s and 40s. The agency complaint said Abbott relied on a survey of doctors that wasn't designed to determine *whether* many doctors actually recommended Ensure as a meal replacement for healthy adults. Rather, according to the FTC complaint, the survey asked doctors to assume that they would recommend a supplement for adults who were not ill and then merely select which brand they would suggest. The FTC ruled that Abbott went too far when it suggested that doctors recommend Ensure for healthy, active people, like those pictured in its ads, in order to stay healthy and active. Abbott agreed to settle the charges and stop using endorsements from medical professionals unless it could produce reliable scientific evidence to substantiate the claims.[52]

Recently the FTC has stepped up its action against false and unsubstantiated claims in ads and infomercials. A few years ago, the commission fined the Home Shopping Network $1.1 million for making unsubstantiated advertising claims for two weight-loss products, an acne treatment, and a dietary supplement for menopause and premenstrual syndrome. Under the settlement Home Shopping is enjoined from making product claims about curing and treating diseases without "reliable scientific evidence."

The FTC's Handling of Deceptive Advertising Cases

Consent and Cease-and-Desist Orders Allegations of unfair or deceptive advertising come to the FTC's attention from a variety of sources, including competitors, consumers, other government agencies, or the commission's own monitoring and investigations. Once the FTC decides a complaint is justified and warrants further action, it notifies the offender, who then has 30 days to respond. The advertiser can agree to negotiate a settlement with the FTC by signing a **consent order,** which is an agreement to stop the practice or advertising in question. This agreement is for settlement purposes only and does not constitute an admission of guilt by the advertiser. Most FTC inquiries are settled by consent orders because they save the advertiser the cost and possible adverse publicity that might result if the case went further.

If the advertiser chooses not to sign the consent decree and contests the complaint, a hearing can be requested before an administrative law judge employed by the FTC but not under its influence. The judge's decision may be appealed to the full five-member commission by either side. The commission either affirms or modifies the order or dismisses the case. If the complaint has been upheld by the administrative law judge and the commission, the advertiser can appeal the case to the federal courts.

The appeal process may take some time, during which the FTC may want to stop the advertiser from engaging in the deceptive practice. The Wheeler-Lea Amendment empowers the FTC to issue a **cease-and-desist order,** which requires that the advertiser stop the specified advertising claim within 30 days and prohibits the advertiser from engaging in the objectionable practice until after the hearing is held. Violation of a cease-and-desist order is punishable by a fine of up to $10,000 a day. Figure 21-4 summarizes the FTC complaint procedure.

Corrective Advertising By using consent and cease-and-desist orders, the FTC can usually stop a particular advertising practice it believes is unfair or deceptive. However, even if an advertiser ceases using a deceptive ad, consumers may still

Figure 21-4 FTC complaint procedure

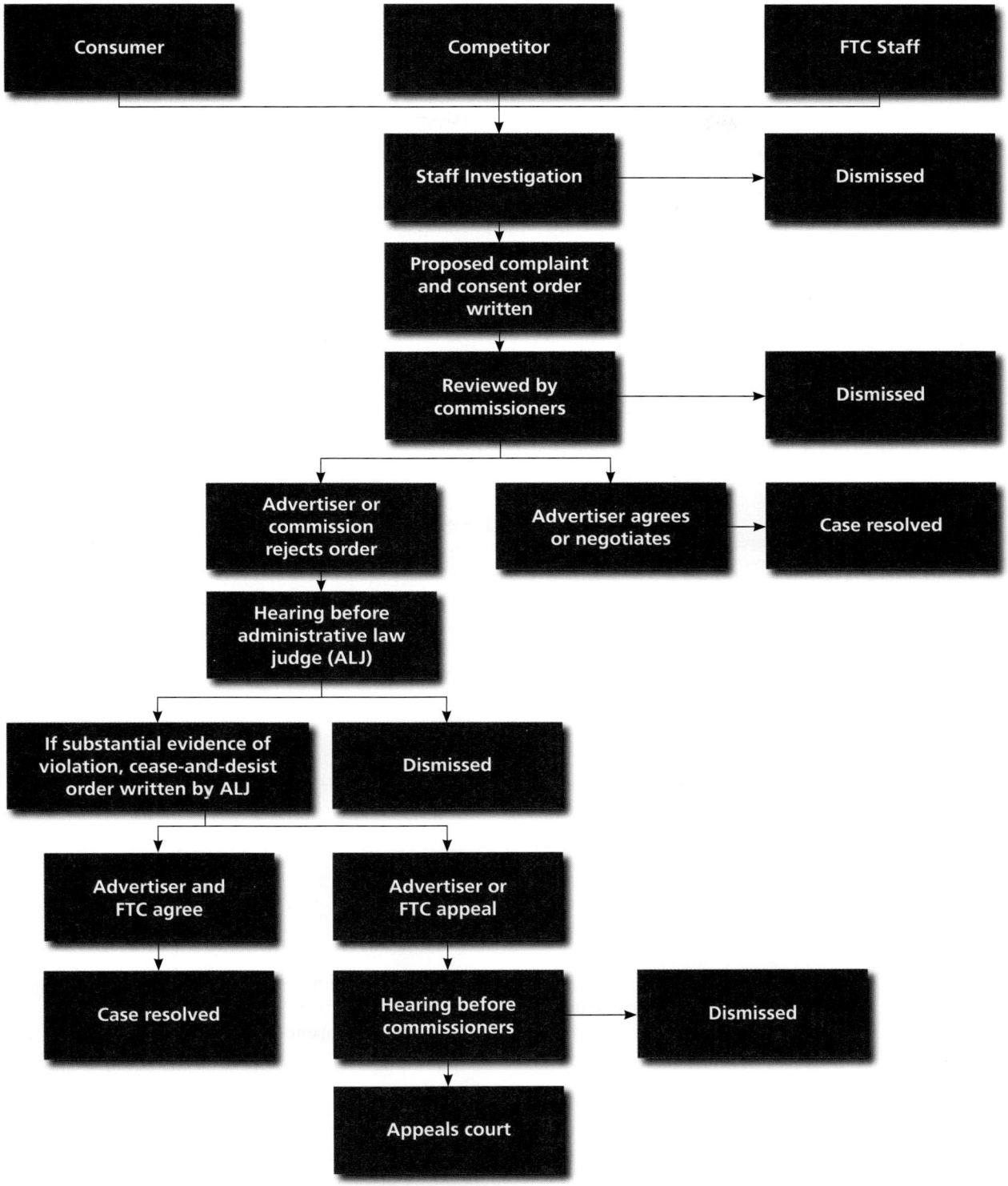

remember some or all of the claim. To address the problem of residual effects, in the 1970s the FTC developed a program known as **corrective advertising.** An advertiser found guilty of deceptive advertising can be required to run additional advertising designed to remedy the deception or misinformation contained in previous ads.

The impetus for corrective advertising was another case involving Campbell Soup, which placed marbles in the bottom of a bowl of vegetable soup to force the solid ingredients to the surface, creating a false impression that the soup contained more vegetables than it really did. (Campbell Soup argued that if the marbles were not used, all the ingredients would settle to the bottom, leaving an impression of

fewer ingredients than actually existed!) While Campbell Soup agreed to stop the practice, a group of law students calling themselves SOUP (Students Opposed to Unfair Practices) argued to the FTC that this would not remedy false impressions created by prior advertising and contended Campbell Soup should be required to run advertising to rectify the problem.[53]

Although the FTC did not order corrective advertising in the Campbell case, it has done so in many cases since then. Profile Bread ran an ad stating each slice contained fewer calories than other brands—but the ad did not mention that slices of Profile bread were thinner than those of other brands. Ocean Spray cranberry juice was found guilty of deceptive advertising because it claimed to have more "food energy" than orange or tomato juice but failed to note it was referring to the technical definition of food energy, which is calories. In each case, the advertisers were ordered to spend 25 percent of their annual media budgets to run corrective ads. The STP Corporation was required to run corrective advertising for claims regarding the ability of its oil additive to reduce oil consumption. Many of the corrective ads run in the STP case appeared in business publications to serve notice to other advertisers that the FTC was enforcing the corrective advertising program. The texts of the corrective messages required in each of these cases are shown in Figure 21-5.

Corrective advertising is probably the most controversial of all the FTC programs.[54] Advertisers argue that corrective advertising infringes on First Amendment rights of freedom of speech. In one of the most publicized corrective advertising cases

Figure 21-5 Examples of corrective advertising messages

Profile Bread

"Hi, [celebrity's name] for Profile Bread. Like all mothers, I'm concerned about nutrition and balanced meals. So, I'd like to clear up any misunderstanding you may have about Profile Bread from its advertising or even its name.

"Does Profile have fewer calories than any other breads? No. Profile has about the same per ounce as other breads. To be exact, Profile has seven fewer calories per slice. That's because Profile is sliced thinner. But eating Profile will not cause you to lose weight. A reduction of seven calories is insignificant. It's total calories and balanced nutrition that count. And Profile can help you achieve a balanced meal because it provides protein and B vitamins as well as other nutrients.

"How does my family feel about Profile? Well, my husband likes Profile toast, the children love Profile sandwiches, and I prefer Profile to any other bread. So you see, at our house, delicious taste makes Profile a family affair."

(To be run in 25 percent of brand's advertising, for one year.)

Ocean Spray

"If you've wondered what some of our earlier advertising meant when we said Ocean Spray Cranberry Juice Cocktail has more food energy than orange juice or tomato juice, let us make it clear: we didn't mean vitamins and minerals. Food energy means calories. Nothing more.

"Food energy is important at breakfast since many of us may not get enough calories, or food energy, to get off to a good start. Ocean Spray Cranberry Juice Cocktail helps because it contains more food energy than most other breakfast drinks.

"And Ocean Spray Cranberry Juice Cocktail gives you and your family Vitamin C plus a great wake-up taste. It's . . . the other breakfast drink."

(To be run in one of every four ads for one year.)

STP

As a result of an investigation by the Federal Trade Commission into certain allegedly inaccurate past advertisements for STP's oil additive, STP Corporation has agreed to a $700,000 settlement. With regard to that settlement, STP is making the following statement:

"It is the policy of STP to support its advertising with objective information and test data. In 1974 and 1975 an independent laboratory ran tests of the company's oil additive which led to claims of reduced oil consumption. However, these tests cannot be relied on to support the oil consumption reduction claim made by STP.

"The FTC has taken the position that, in making the claim, the company violated the terms of a consent order. When STP learned that the test did not support the claim, it stopped advertising containing that claim. New tests have been undertaken to determine the extent to which the oil additive affects oil consumption. Agreement to this settlement does not constitute an admission by STP that the law has been violated. Rather, STP has agreed to resolve the dispute with the FTC to avoid protracted and prohibitively expensive litigation."

ever, involving Listerine mouthwash, Warner-Lambert tested the FTC's legal power to order corrective messages.[55] For more than 50 years Warner-Lambert had advertised that gargling with Listerine helped prevent colds and sore throats or lessened their severity because it killed the germs that caused these illnesses. In 1975, the FTC ruled these claims could not be substantiated and ordered Warner-Lambert to stop making them. In addition, the FTC argued that corrective advertising was needed to rectify the erroneous beliefs that had been created by Warner-Lambert as a result of the large amount of advertising it had run for Listerine over the prior 50 years.

Warner-Lambert argued that the advertising was not misleading and, further, that the FTC did not have the power to order corrective advertising. Warner-Lambert appealed the FTC decision all the way to the Supreme Court, which rejected the argument that corrective advertising violates advertisers' First Amendment rights. The powers of the FTC in the areas of both claim substantiation and corrective advertising were upheld. Warner-Lambert was required to run $10 million worth of corrective ads over a 16-month period stating, "Listerine does not help prevent colds or sore throats or lessen their severity."

Since the Supreme Court ruling in the Listerine case, there have been several other situations where the FTC has ordered corrective advertising on the basis of the "Warner-Lambert test," which considers whether consumers are left with a latent impression that would continue to affect buying decisions and whether corrective ads are needed to remedy the situation.

In a recent case involving Novartis Consumer Health Corp.'s Doan's Pills, the FTC sent a strong message to advertisers and agencies that it will require marketers to run corrective ads to remedy any misleading impressions that were created through unsubstantiated advertising claims.[56] In this case, Novartis was ordered to spend $8 million, or the equivalent of the average annual ad budget for Doan's Pills over an eight-year period, on corrective ads to remedy any impressions that might exist from previous advertising that the brand is more effective than other analgesics for relieving back pain. Novartis is appealing the decision, and this may, like the landmark Listerine mouthwash case, be a major test of the FTC's legal power to order corrective advertising. At issue in the appeal will be not only the FTC's standard for determining whether a latent impression exists but also the question of whether the commission has to prove that advertising created a lingering false impression or whether it can assume that years of advertising would have created the misapprehension.

The Doan's case will have very important implications for the FTC as well as advertisers. A win by the FTC would reaffirm the agency's authority to order corrective advertising and give it greater freedom to use the remedy, but a loss could limit its ability to do so. The case will also have lasting repercussions for advertisers, who are concerned over an FTC commissioner's contention that "corrective advertising is not a drastic remedy" and is an appropriate method for restoring the status quo. Advertisers fear that this may indicate that the FTC will be more willing to apply the punishment in future cases. There is obviously a lot at stake in this case for advertisers. However, the case is also very important to the FTC in the ongoing battle over its authority to require corrective advertising.[57]

Current Status of Federal Regulation by the FTC

By the end of the 1970s, the FTC had become a very powerful and active regulator of advertising. However, Congress was concerned about the FTC's broad interpretation of unfairness, which led to the restrictive legislation of the 1980 FTC Improvements Act. During the 1980s, the FTC became less active and cut back its regulatory efforts, due in large part to the Reagan administration's laissez-faire attitude toward the regulation of business in general. Some feared that the FTC had become too narrow in its regulation of national advertising, forcing companies and consumer groups to seek relief from other sources such as state and federal courts or through self-regulatory groups such as the NAD/NARB.[58]

In 1988–89, an 18-member panel chosen by the American Bar Association undertook a study of the FTC as a 20-year follow-up to the 1969 report used by President Richard Nixon to overhaul the commission. The panel's report expressed strong concern over the FTC's lack of sufficient resources and staff to regulate national advertising effectively and called for more funding.

After more than a decade of relative inactivity, the Federal Trade Commission has once again become active in the regulation of advertising. The commission has shown particular interest in cracking down on misleading advertising in areas such as health, nutrition, weight loss, and environmental claims as well as advertising directed to children and the elderly.[59] The FTC has also become more involved with potential fraud and deception through various other promotional methods such as telemarketing, 900 numbers, infomercials, and the Internet. In addition to monitoring deceptive claims made over the Internet, the FTC has become very involved in privacy issues and the collection of personal information on websites.

Robert Pitofsky, who served as FTC chairman during the Clinton administration, focused the commission's attention on developing new policies, particularly as the growth of the Internet created the need for laws and regulations regarding online privacy and ways of protecting children online. However, under the Bush administration the FTC is focusing its attention on the enforcement of existing regulations, particularly in areas such as telemarketing and Internet privacy.[60] Tim Murris, who took over as FTC chairman in 2001, has expressed concern about marketers that significantly alter privacy policies after consumers log on to their websites. The FTC also plans to eliminate false e-mail advertising and has stepped up its enforcement against senders of deceptive or misleading claims via e-mail.[61] The commission also is scrutinizing the use of testimonial ads more carefully, particularly with respect to the use of a "results not typical" disclosure in situations where the outcomes are more likely to vary substantially than be typical for most consumers.[62]

While the FTC is the major regulator of advertising for products sold in interstate commerce, several other federal agencies and departments also regulate advertising and promotion.

Additional Federal Regulatory Agencies

The Federal Communications Commission The FCC, founded in 1934 to regulate broadcast communication, has jurisdiction over the radio, television, telephone, and telegraph industries. The FCC has the authority to license broadcast stations as well as to remove a license or deny renewal to stations not operating in the public's interest. The FCC's authority over the airways gives it the power to control advertising content and to restrict what products and services can be advertised on radio and TV. The FCC can eliminate obscene and profane programs and/or messages and those it finds in poor taste. While the FCC can purge ads that are deceptive or misleading, it generally works closely with the FTC in the regulation of advertising. For example, in 1999 the Federal Communications Commission and the FTC held a joint workshop and publicly accused long-distance phone marketers of deceiving consumers in their advertising. Officials of both commissions expressed concern over per-minute ads for long distance and so-called dial-around long-distance services. They also warned long-distance marketers that they would take action if steps were not taken to clean up their advertising.[63]

Many of the FCC's rules and regulations for TV and radio stations have been eliminated or modified. The FCC no longer limits the amount of television time that can be devoted to commercials. (But in 1991 the Children's Television Act went into effect. The act limits advertising during children's programming to 10.5 minutes an hour on weekends and 12 minutes an hour on weekdays.)

Under the Reagan administration, the controversial *Fairness Doctrine,* which required broadcasters to provide time for opposing viewpoints on important issues, was repealed on the grounds that it was counterproductive. It was argued that the Fairness Doctrine actually reduced discussion of important issues because a broadcaster might be afraid to take on a paid controversial message in case it might be required to provide equal free exposure for opposing viewpoints. It was under this doctrine that the FCC required stations to run commercials about the harmful effects of smoking before passage of the Public Health Cigarette Smoking Act of 1970, which banned broadcast advertising of cigarettes. Many stations still provide time for opposing viewpoints on controversial issues as part of their public service requirement, not necessarily directly related to fairness.

Several pieces of legislation passed in recent years involve the FCC and have an impact on advertising and promotion. The Cable Television Consumer Protection and Competition Act, passed in 1992, allows the FCC and local governments to regulate basic cable TV rates and forces cable operators to pay licensing fees for local broadcast programming they retransmit for free. One purpose of this bill is to improve the balance between cable rates and rapidly escalating advertising revenue. FCC rules affecting telemarketing will be discussed toward the end of this chapter.

Important issues now facing the FCC are the growth of broadband Internet access and interactive television (ITV), both of which offer new communications opportunities for marketers. Under the Bush administration, the FCC is giving the free markets more rein to expand these new telecommunication technologies.[64] The FCC plans to open more doors for small businesses to get involved in the broadband arena, which is now dominated by large companies. The FCC is also looking for new ways to expand ITV services, which are expected to reach over 18 million U.S. households by 2003 (Exhibit 21-10). ITV enables consumers to request product information or make a purchase without having to dial an 800 number or write down a mail-order address.[65] A major hurdle to the growth of ITV is incompatibility among different service providers' technologies. The FCC plans to develop standard criteria for ITV services that will address the problem of incompatible platforms and help facilitate the growth of this technology.

Exhibit 21-10 The Federal Communications Commission plans to develop standards to encourage the growth of interactive television

The Food and Drug Administration Now under the jurisdiction of the Department of Health and Human Services, the FDA has authority over the labeling, packaging, branding, ingredient listing, and advertising of packaged foods and drug products. The FDA is authorized to require caution and warning labels on potentially hazardous products and also has limited authority over nutritional claims made in food advertising. This agency has the authority to set rules for promoting these products and the power to seize food and drugs on charges of false and misleading advertising.

Like the FTC, the Food and Drug Administration has become a very aggressive regulatory agency in recent years. The FDA has cracked down on a number of commonly used descriptive terms it believes are often abused in the labeling and advertising of food products—for example, *natural, light, no cholesterol,* and *fat free.* The FDA has also become tougher on nutritional claims implied by brand names that might send a misleading message to consumers. For example, Great Foods of America was not permitted to continue using the HeartBeat trademark under which it sold most of its foods. The FDA argued the trademark went too far in implying the foods have special advantages for the heart and overall health.

Many changes in food labeling are a result of the Nutritional Labeling and Education Act, which Congress passed in 1990. Under this law the FDA established legal definitions for a wide range of terms (such as *low fat, light,* and *reduced calories*) and required straightforward labels for all foods beginning in early 1994 (Exhibit 21-11). In its current form the act applies only to food labels, but it may soon affect food advertising as well. The FTC would be asked to ensure that food ads comply with the new FDA standards.

Another regulatory area where the FDA has been heavily involved is the advertising and promotion of tobacco products. In 1996 President Bill Clinton signed an executive order declaring that nicotine is an addictive drug and giving the FDA board jurisdiction to regulate cigarettes and smokeless tobacco. Many of the regulations

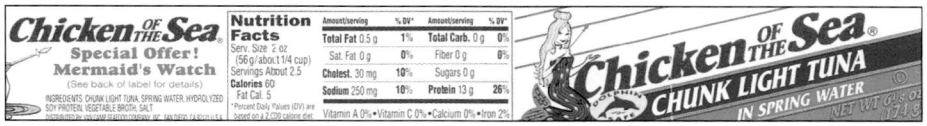

Exhibit 21-11 The Nutritional Labeling and Education Act requires that labels be easy for consumers to understand

resulting from this order were designed to keep teenagers from smoking.[66] However, the tobacco industry immediately appealed the order. While continuing to fight its legal battle with the federal government over the FDA regulations, the tobacco makers did agree to settle lawsuits brought by 46 states against the industry in late 1998 by signing the Master Settlement Agreement. This settlement was considered a better deal for the tobacco industry, as many of the onerous cigarette marketing restrictions contained in the original FDA proposal settlement were missing. The agreement allows large outdoor signs at retailers, whereas the original proposal banned all outdoor ads. The original deal banned all use of humans and cartoons in ads, while the current settlement bans only cartoons and even permits their use on cigarette packs. And while the original proposal eliminated sports sponsorships, the current agreement allows each company to continue one national sponsorship.[67]

An important provision of the Master Settlement Agreement was that the tobacco companies agreed not to target youth (those under the age of 18) in the advertising, promotion, and marketing of tobacco products either directly or indirectly. However, over the past several years there has been considerable debate over whether tobacco companies are complying with the agreement. Much of this debate centers on what is called the 15 percent rule, under which the tobacco companies voluntarily pledged not to advertise in magazines that have more than 15 percent of their readers under the age of 18. Some major tobacco companies such as Philip Morris have stopped advertising in magazines that have a substantial number of youth readers, such as *People, Sports Illustrated, Spin,* and *Rolling Stone.* However, other tobacco companies still advertise in these publications, and it appears that there are still a number of battles to fight in the war over the marketing and advertising of cigarettes.[68]

A number of consumer advocacy groups as well as health departments in many states run ads warning consumers against the dangers of smoking and tobacco-related diseases. For example, the American Legacy Foundation, which was established as part of the 1998 tobacco settlement and is dedicated to reducing tobacco use, has run a number of hard-hitting ads warning consumers of the risk of smoking (Exhibit 21-12).

Another area where the Food and Drug Administration is being asked to become more involved is the advertising of prescription drugs. IMC Perspective 21-3 discusses the tremendous growth in direct-to-consumer drug advertising that has occurred sine the FDA issued new guidelines making it easier for pharmaceutical companies to advertise prescription drugs to consumers.

The U.S. Postal Service Many marketers use the U.S. mail to deliver advertising and promotional messages. The U.S. Postal Service has control over advertising

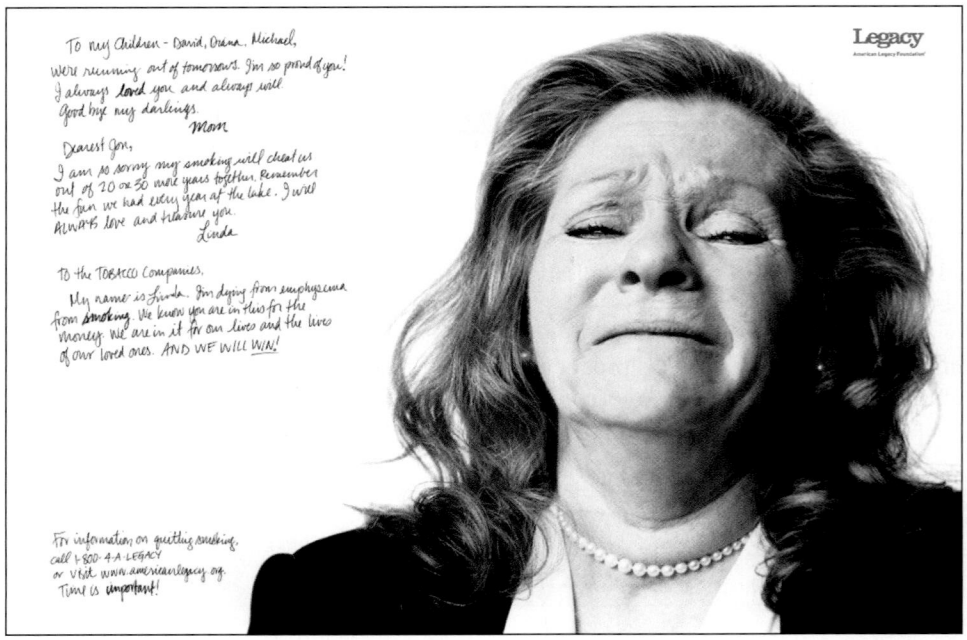

Exhibit 21-12 The American Legacy Foundation was established as part of the Tobacco Settlement Agreement and is dedicated to reducing tobacco use in the United States

IMC PERSPECTIVE 21-3

The Debate over Direct-to-Consumer Drug Advertising

For years, pharmaceutical companies did most of their prescription-drug marketing directly to physicians, either through their sales forces or by advertising in medical journals. However, in 1997 the Food and Drug Administration (FDA) issued new guidelines making it easier for pharmaceutical companies to advertise prescription drugs on television as well as in print media. With the change in guidelines, direct-to-consumer drug advertising has exploded, and pharmaceutical companies are some of the largest consumer advertisers. Brand name prescription drugs such as Prozac, Viagra, and Claritin have become as well known to consumers as brands of soft drinks.

Direct-to-consumer drug advertising spending soared from $859 million in 1997 to $2.8 billion in $2001. In recent years there has been a flurry of ads hawking prescription drugs for a variety of medical problems and conditions, including allergies, heartburn, arthritis, depression, and impotence. Drug companies use celebrities to pitch their products just as effectively as other marketers do. A television commercial for cholesterol drug Zocor features National Football League coach Dan Reeves stating, "Taking care of my cholesterol; it has become an important part of my game plan." Former figure skating champion and Olympic gold medalist Dorothy Hammill talks about experiencing the pain of osteoarthritis in a commercial for Vioxx. Pfizer used former vice president Bob Dole as an advertising spokesperson when it launched Viagra in 1998 and now spends nearly $100 million a year to advertise the male impotence drug. Texas Ranger's baseball star Rafiel Palmeiro appears in ads for the product, stating, "I take batting practice. I take infield practice. I take Viagra."

The pharmaceutical companies note that the increased spending on drug advertising has helped educate consumers about their options and has caused people to see doctors about medications who might not have done so otherwise. However, a number of physician, consumer, and health care groups have expressed concern over the increase in drug advertising for several reasons. A major concern of these groups is whether the ads are accurate and whether they inform consumers of all the risks associated with taking the drugs. Consumer groups have asked the Food and Drug Administration to develop a process for enforcement of the "fair balance" provision, an FDA regulation governing broadcast commercials that requires drug ads to give both the benefits and the risks of taking a medication.

The FDA is charged with the responsibility of ensuring that drug advertising is fair, balanced, and truthful. However, the number of ads submitted annually for FDA scrutiny, including TV spots, magazine ads, Internet sites, and even pamphlets used by sales representatives, has jumped nearly 35 percent over the past five years, from just over 25,000 to more than 34,000. The number of citation letters issue by the FDA to drug companies for ads that might be false, misleading, or otherwise out of compliance has been steadily declining, as only 71 were sent out in 2001. The pharmaceutical companies say that the drop in citations shows that their advertisements are cleaner than before and that the companies are much more knowledgeable about the FDA guidelines than they were in 1997. However, the FDA's director of the Division of Drug Marketing, Advertising and Communication notes that with its limited resources the division cannot investigate all of the ads so it focuses on ads deemed most critical—those that appear on television, make unusual claims, or raise a major public health issue.

Many watchdog organizations such as the Public Citizen's Health Research Group feel that the drug companies' advertising and marketing pitches are not more honest or balanced than they were in the past. They argue that the FDA citations are little more than slaps on the wrist to the powerful drug companies and that the FDA has to be given the authority to levy stiff fines against companies that repeatedly violate its guidelines. Consumer advocates have also argued for stricter regulations on drug ads, noting that while advertisers must include statements about negative side effects or toxicity, it is the dancing couples and happy images that people remember—not the cautionary voiceover.

Another concern over the increase in prescription-drug advertising has been raised by insurance companies as well as employers, who feel that the ads are driving up the costs of health care. These companies

argue that drug advertising is expensive, thus adding to the costs of drugs, and that it also encourages consumers to request the higher-cost brand names rather than less expensive generic alternatives. General Motors, which spent $1.3 billion in 2001 on drugs for employees, has launched a "Generics First" campaign promoting the less expensive alternatives in e-mails, on paycheck stubs, and in corporate newsletters. Health insurer Blue Cross has fired back at the drug companies with its own direct-to-consumer ads promoting generics.

Many experts feel that drug companies will have to pay more attention to the concerns being raised over their rapid increase in advertising spending. However, most drug companies say they have no plans to cut back on their direct-to-consumer advertising as they feel they need to educate consumers on how their products can help them. It may only be a matter of time before Pfizer develops a "Got Viagra?" campaign.

Sources: Christine Bittar, "Creating an Rx Monster," *Brandweek*, July 29, 2002, pp. 22–29; "Reining in Drug Advertising," *The Wall Street Journal*, Mar. 13, 2002, pp. B1, 4; Chris Adams, "FDA Inundated Trying to Assess Drug Ad Pitches," *The Wall Street Journal*, Mar. 14, 2002, pp. B1, 6.

involving the use of the mail and ads that involve lotteries, obscenity, or fraud. The regulation against fraudulent use of the mail has been used to control deceptive advertising by numerous direct-response advertisers. These firms advertise on TV or radio or in magazines and newspapers and use the U.S. mail to receive orders and payment. Many have been prosecuted by the Post Office Department for use of the mail in conjunction with a fraudulent or deceptive offer.

Bureau of Alcohol, Tobacco, and Firearms

The Bureau of Alcohol, Tobacco, and Firearms (BATF) is an agency within the Treasury Department that enforces laws, develops regulations, and is responsible for tax collection for the liquor industry. The BATF regulates and controls the advertising of alcoholic beverages. The agency determines what information can be provided in ads as well as what constitutes false and misleading advertising. It is also responsible for including warning labels on alcohol advertising and banning the use of active athletes in beer commercials. The BATF can impose strong sanctions for violators. As was discussed at the beginning of this chapter, the advertising of alcoholic beverages has become a very controversial issue, with many consumer and public-interest groups calling for a total ban on the advertising of beer, wine, and liquor.

The Lanham Act

While most advertisers rely on self-regulatory mechanisms and the FTC to deal with deceptive or misleading advertising by their competitors, many companies are filing lawsuits against competitors they believe are making false claims. One piece of federal legislation that has become increasingly important in this regard is the Lanham Act. This act was originally written in 1947 as the Lanham Trade-Mark Act to protect words, names, symbols, or other devices adopted to identify and distinguish a manufacturer's products. The **Lanham Act** was amended to encompass false advertising by prohibiting "any false description or representation including words or other symbols tending falsely to describe or represent the same." While the FTC Act did not give individual advertisers the opportunity to sue a competitor for deceptive advertising, civil suits are permitted under the Lanham Act.

More and more companies are using the Lanham Act to sue competitors for their advertising claims, particularly since comparative advertising has become so common. For example, a court ordered Ralston Purina to pay Alpo Petfoods $12 million for damages it caused by making false claims that its Purina Puppy Chow dog food could ameliorate and help prevent joint disease. The court ruled that the claim was based on faulty data and that the company continued the campaign after learning its research was in error. Alpo was awarded the money as compensation for lost revenue and for the costs of advertising it ran in response to the Puppy Chow campaign.[69]

Wilkinson Sword and its advertising agency were found guilty of false advertising and ordered to pay $953,000 in damages to the Gillette Co. Wilkinson had run TV and print ads claiming its Ultra Glide razor and blades produced shaves "six times

smoother" than Gillette's Atra Plus blades. This case marked the first time an agency was held liable for damages in connection with false claims made in a client's advertising.[70] Although the agency was later found not liable, the case served as a sobering reminder to agencies that they can be drawn into litigation over advertising they create for their clients. To deal with this problem, many agencies insist on indemnification clauses in contracts with their clients.

Suing competitors for false claims was made even easier with passage of the Trademark Law Revision Act of 1988. According to this law, anyone is vulnerable to civil action who "misrepresents the nature, characteristics, qualities, or geographical origin of his or her or another person's goods, services, or commercial activities." This wording closed a loophole in the Lanham Act, which prohibited only false claims about one's own goods or services. While many disputes over comparative claims are never contested or are resolved through the NAD, more companies are turning to lawsuits for several reasons: the broad information discovery powers available under federal civil procedure rules, the speed with which a competitor can stop the offending ad through a preliminary injunction, and the possibility of collecting damages.[71] However, companies do not always win their lawsuits. Under the Lanham Act you are required to prove five elements to win a false advertising lawsuit containing a comparative claim.[72] You must prove that:

- False statements have been made about the advertiser's product or your product.
- The ads actually deceived or had the tendency to deceive a substantial segment of the audience.
- The deception was "material" or meaningful and is likely to influence purchasing decisions.
- The falsely advertised products or services are sold in interstate commerce.
- You have been or likely will be injured as a result of the false statements, either by loss of sales or loss of goodwill.

In recent years there has been a significant increase in the use of comparative advertising, and it has resulted in more and more companies' suing one another under the Lanham Act. In the mid-90s the Campbell Soup Co. advertised that its Prego brand of spaghetti sauce was thicker than Van Den Bergh Food's Ragu brand. Van Den Bergh sued to have Campbell's comparative ads for Prego halted but lost the case in district court as well as appeals court. Campbell capitalized on its victory by creating an ad based on it. The ad tweaked Ragu by showing snippets of the comparison ads and then a shot of Prego with a breadstick standing up in the sauce (Exhibit 21-13). The tagline was, "Ragu took us to court. We made our case stand. Just like our breadstick." The two companies finally declared a truce in the spaghetti sauce wars in late 1999.[73]

In 2002 Energizer Holdings filed a suit against Duracell, which is a division of the Gillette Company, over a commercial touting the endurance superiority of the Duracell Coppertop brand over "heavy-duty" competitors. While the ad claim was technically correct, it failed to note that all alkaline batteries outlast so-called heavy-duty batteries, which in industry parlance refers to inexpensive, old-fashioned zinc batteries. Energizer claimed that consumer confusion resulted from the advertisement because consumers thought the commercial was comparing Duracell Coppertop to Energizer alkaline batteries. Gillette agreed to modify the commercial by adding a disclaimer stating "excluding alkaline batteries." However, Energizer plans to pursue the lawsuit and is seeking damages for confusion resulting from the Duracell commercial.[74]

Marketers using comparative ads have to carefully consider whether their messages have the potential to mislead consumers or may overstate their brand's performance relative to that of competitors. A recent study by Michael J. Barone and his colleagues provides a framework for developing measures to assess the misleading effects that may arise from various types of comparative advertising.[75]

Exhibit 21-13
Comparative claims involving the Prego and Ragu brands of spaghetti sauce resulted in a lawsuit

State Regulation

In addition to the various federal rules and regulations, advertisers must also concern themselves with numerous state and local controls. An important early development in state regulation of advertising was the adoption in 44 states of the *Printers Ink* model statutes as a basis for advertising regulation. These statutes were drawn up in 1911 by *Printers Ink,* for many years the major trade publication of the advertising industry. Many states have since modified the original statutes and adopted laws similar to those of the Federal Trade Commission Act for dealing with false and misleading advertising. For example, in California, the Business and Professional Code prohibits "unlawful, unfair, or fraudulent" business practices and "unfair, deceptive, untrue, or misleading advertising."

In addition to recognizing decisions by the federal courts regarding false or deceptive practices, many states have special controls and regulations governing the advertising of specific industries or practices. As the federal government became less involved in the regulation of national advertising during the 1980s, many state attorneys general (AGs) began to enforce state laws regarding false or deceptive advertising. For example, the attorneys general in New York and Texas initiated investigations of Kraft ads claiming the pasteurized cheese used in Cheez Whiz was real cheese.[76] The well-publicized "monster truck" deceptive advertising case involving Volvo and its advertising agency that occurred in the early 90s was initiated by the attorney general's office in the state of Texas.[77]

The **National Association of Attorneys General** (NAAG) moved against a number of national advertisers as a result of inactivity by the FTC during the Reagan administration. In 1987, the NAAG developed enforcement guidelines on airfare advertising that were adopted by more than 40 states. The NAAG has also been involved in other regulatory areas, including car-rental price advertising as well as advertising dealing with nutrition and health claims in food ads. The NAAG's foray into regulating national advertising raises the issue of whether the states working together can create and implement uniform national advertising standards that will, in effect, supersede federal authority. An American Bar Association panel concluded that the Federal Trade Commission is the proper regulator of national advertising and recommended the state AGs focus on practices that harm consumers within a single state.[78] This report also called for cooperation between the FTC and the state attorneys general.

Advertisers are concerned about the trend toward increased regulation of advertising at the state and local levels because it could mean that national advertising campaigns would have to be modified for every state or municipality. Yet the FTC takes the position that businesses that advertise and sell nationwide need a national advertising policy. While the FTC recognizes the need for greater cooperation with the states, the agency believes regulation of national advertising should be its responsibility.[79] Just in case, the advertising industry is still keeping a watchful eye on changes in advertising rules, regulations, and policies at the state and local levels.

Regulation of Other Promotional Areas

So far we've focused on the regulation of advertising. However, other elements of the promotional mix also come under the surveillance of federal, state, and local laws and various self-regulatory bodies. This section examines some of the rules, regulations, and guidelines that affect sales promotion, direct marketing, and marketing on the Internet.

Sales Promotion

Both consumer- and trade-oriented promotions are subject to various regulations. The Federal Trade Commission regulates many areas of sales promotion through the Marketing Practices Division of the Bureau of Consumer Protection. Many promotional practices are also policed by state attorneys general and local regulatory agencies. Various aspects of trade promotion, such as allowances, are regulated by the Robinson-Patman Act, which gives the FTC broad powers to control discriminatory pricing practices.

Contests and Sweepstakes As noted in Chapter 16, numerous legal considerations affect the design and administration of contests and sweepstakes, and these promotions are regulated by a number of federal and state agencies. There are two

important considerations in developing contests (including games) and sweepstakes. First, marketers must be careful to ensure their contest or sweepstakes is not classified as a *lottery,* which is considered a form of gambling and violates the Federal Trade Commission Act and many state and local laws. A promotion is considered a lottery if a prize is offered, if winning a prize depends on chance and not skill, and if the participant is required to give up something of value in order to participate. The latter requirement is referred to as *consideration* and is the basis on which most contests, games, and sweepstakes avoid being considered lotteries. Generally, as long as consumers are not required to make a purchase to enter a contest or sweepstakes, consideration is not considered to be present and the promotion is not considered a lottery.

The second important requirement in the use of contests and sweepstakes is that the marketer provide full disclosure of the promotion. Regulations of the FTC, as well as many state and local governments, require marketers using contests, games, and sweepstakes to make certain all of the details are given clearly and to follow prescribed rules to ensure the fairness of the game.[80] Disclosure requirements include the exact number of prizes to be awarded and the odds of winning, the duration and termination dates of the promotion, and the availability of lists of winners of various prizes (Exhibit 21-14). The FTC also has specific rules governing the way games and contests are conducted, such as requirements that game pieces be randomly distributed, that a game not be terminated before the distribution of all game pieces, and that additional pieces not be added during the course of a game.

Recently a number of states have responded to what they believe is widespread fraud on the part of some contest and sweepstakes operators. In 1995, at least 13 states either passed or tightened prize notification laws, requiring fuller disclosure of rules, odds, and the retail value of prizes. And many of the states are following through with tougher enforcement of these laws. For example, Publishers Clearing House, known for its million-dollar giveaways, agreed to pay $490,000 to 14 states and to change some of its language, better defining terms like "finalist" and "tie breaker." It also began to disclose the odds of winning prizes. More recently the controversy resulting from the lawsuits filed against American Family Publishing for misleading consumers regarding their odds of winning large cash prizes in its annual magazine subscription solicitation sweepstakes has led to investigations and stricter regulation of sweepstakes in a number of states.[81] For example, New York passed a law requiring the odds of winning a sweepstakes "must be conspicuously disclosed in the same type face, size and boldness and adjacent to the most prominent listing of the prizes on the front of the first page of the offer." The state law also prohibits statements that someone is a

Exhibit 21-14 Marketers are required to provide consumers with full details of a contest or sweepstakes

"winner" or that his or her name "has been selected" when no prize has been won. The law carries a fine of $1,000 per incident, which could be $1,000 per letter received by New York residents.[82] Some of the most ambitious legal actions are taking place in individual states, where prosecutors are taking sweepstakes and contest companies to court for misleading and deceptive practices.[83]

Premiums Another sales promotion area subject to various regulations is the use of premiums. A common problem associated with premiums is misrepresentation of their value. Marketers that make a premium offer should list its value as the price at which the merchandise is usually sold on its own. Marketers must also be careful in making premium offers to special audiences such as children. While premium offers for children are legal, their use is controversial; many critics argue that they encourage children to request a product for the premium rather than for its value. The Children's Advertising Review Unit has voluntary guidelines concerning the use of premium offers. These guidelines note that children have difficulty distinguishing a product from a premium. If product advertising contains a premium message, care should be taken that the child's attention is focused primarily on the product. The premium message should be clearly secondary. Conditions of a premium offer should be stated simply and clearly. "Mandatory" statements and disclosures should be stated in terms that can be understood by the child audience.[84] However, a recent study of children's advertising commissioned by CARU found the single most prevalent violation involved devoting virtually an entire commercial message to information about a premium. CARU guidelines state that advertising targeted to children must emphasize the product rather than the premium offer.[85]

Trade Allowances Marketers using various types of trade allowances must be careful not to violate any stipulations of the Robinson-Patman Act, which prohibits price discrimination. Certain sections of the Robinson-Patman Act prohibit a manufacturer from granting wholesalers and retailers various types of promotional allowances and/or payments unless they are made available to all customers on proportionally equal terms.[86] Another form of trade promotion regulated by the Robinson-Patman Act is vertical cooperative advertising. The FTC monitors cooperative advertising programs to ensure that co-op funds are made available to retailers on a proportionally equal basis and that the payments are not used as a disguised form of price discrimination.

As noted in Chapter 16, another trade promotion area where the FTC is becoming involved is the use of slotting fees or allowances paid to retailers for agreeing to handle a new product. In 1999 the Senate Committee on Small Business charged retailers in the grocery, drugstore, and computer software industries with illegally using slotting fees to lock out competitors and prevent consumers from having their choice of the best products. Packaged-goods marketers and retailers have argued that examining slotting fees alone is unfair since they are just part of a wide variety of inducements marketers use to secure the best shelf space. The FTC is investigating the use of slotting fees as anticompetitive weapons that make it difficult for small-size companies to secure retail shelf space.[87] In 2000 the FTC launched its first direct attack on slotting fees when it accused McCormick & Co., the leading spice maker, of offering discriminatory discounts on its products to several grocery chains. McCormick agreed to settle a complaint that the discounts were a way of paying some retailers disproportionately more in slotting fees than others. The FTC charged that the slotting fees were a way for McCormick to gain more shelf space at the expense of smaller rivals. The practice that was deemed illegal by the FTC is a standard way of doing business in the grocery trade as well as other industries, and some legal experts have argued that this case could impact the use of slotting fees in the future.[88]

Direct Marketing As we saw in Chapter 14, direct marketing is growing rapidly. Many consumers now purchase products directly from companies in response to TV and print advertising or direct selling. The Federal Trade Commission enforces laws related to direct marketing, including mail-order offers, the use of 900

telephone numbers, and direct-response TV advertising. The U.S. Postal Service enforces laws dealing with the use of the mail to deliver advertising and promotional messages or receive payments and orders for items advertised in print or broadcast media.

A number of laws govern the use of mail-order selling. The FTC and the Postal Service police direct-response advertising closely to ensure the ads are not deceptive or misleading and do not misrepresent the product or service being offered. Laws also forbid mailing unordered merchandise to consumers, and rules govern the use of "negative option" plans whereby a company proposes to send merchandise to consumers and expects payment unless the consumer sends a notice of rejection or cancellation.[89] FTC rules also encourage direct marketers to ship ordered merchandise promptly. Companies that cannot ship merchandise within the time period stated in the solicitation (or 30 days if no time is stated) must give buyers the option to cancel the order and receive a full refund.[90]

Another area of direct marketing facing increased regulation is telemarketing. With the passage of the Telephone Consumer Protection Act of 1991, marketers who use telephones to contact consumers must follow a complex set of rules developed by the Federal Communications Commission. These rules require telemarketers to maintain an in-house list of residential telephone subscribers who do not want to be called. Consumers who continue to receive unwanted calls can take the telemarketer to state court for damages of up to $500. The rules also ban telemarketing calls to homes before 8:00 A.M. and after 9:00 P.M., automatic dialer calls, and recorded messages to emergency phones, health care facilities, and numbers for which the call recipient may be charged. They also ban unsolicited junk fax ads and require that fax transmissions clearly indicate the sender's name and fax number.[91]

The Federal Trade Commission has also been actively involved with the regulation of advertising that encourages consumers to call telephone numbers with a 900 prefix, whereupon they are automatically billed for the call. While there are many legitimate uses for 900-number technology, it has also been heavily used for sleazy sex operations, contest scams, and other unscrupulous activities.[92] One area of particular concern to the FTC has been ads targeting children and encouraging them to call 900 numbers. In 1993 the FTC issued its 900-Number Rule for advertising directed at children. The rule restricts advertisers from targeting children under the age of 12 with ads containing 900 numbers unless they provide a bona fide educational service. The rule also requires that 900-number ads directed at those under the age of 18 must contain a "clear and conspicuous" disclosure statement that requires the caller to have parental/guardian permission to complete the call. The rule also obligates advertisers to disclose the cost of the call and give the caller the opportunity to hang up without incurring any costs.[93]

The FTC enacted the 900-Number Rule under the provision that it would be reviewed within four years to consider its costs and benefits.[94] This review was undertaken and the rule was retained and revised, although under a new name. The name was changed to the Pay-Per-Call Rule, and in 1998 the rule was revised to give the FTC the authority to broaden its scope and add new provisions. Among other things, the new provisions combat telephone bill cramming, which is the placing of unauthorized charges on consumers' phone bills.[95]

Recently there has been another significant development that has major implications for the telemarketing industry. In mid-2002 the FTC began taking comments on a proposal to develop a national "do-not-call" registry.[96] Under this proposal, consumers could pay a small fee to sign up on a registry that would bar calls from telemarketers. While the Direct Marketing Association has its own do-not-call registry, as do several states, the FTC's registry would be easier to join and would cover a much broader spectrum of telemarketing calls. The development of such a registry is likely to receive strong opposition from the direct-marketing industry. Opponents argue that a do-not-call list would hurt nonprofit organizations as well as have a negative impact on the economy.

The direct-marketing industry is also scrutinized by various self-regulatory groups, such as the Direct Marketing Association and the Direct Selling Association, that have

Exhibit 21-15 The Direct Selling Association has a Code of Ethics for companies engaged in direct selling

DIRECT SELLING ASSOCIATION

CODE OF ETHICS

PREAMBLE

The Direct Selling Association, recognizing that companies engaged in direct selling assume certain responsibilities toward consumers arising out of the personal-contact method of distribution of their products and services, hereby sets forth the basic fair and ethical principles and practices to which member companies of the association will continue to adhere in the conduct of their business.

INTRODUCTION

The Direct Selling Association is the national trade association of the leading firms that manufacture and distribute goods and services sold directly to consumers. The Association's mission is "to protect, serve and promote the effectiveness of member companies and the independent businesspeople marketing their products and to assure the highest level of business ethics and service to consumers." The cornerstone of the Association's commitment to ethical business practices and consumer service is its Code of Ethics. Every member company pledges to abide by the Code's standards and procedures as a condition of admission and continuing membership in the Association. Consumers can rely on the extra protection provided by the Code when they purchase products or services from a salesperson associated with a member company of the Direct Selling Association. For a current list of Association members, contact DSA, 1776 K St., N.W., Washington, DC 20006, (202) 293-5760.

A. CODE OF CONDUCT

1. Deceptive or Unlawful Consumer Practices

No member company of the Association shall engage in any deceptive or unlawful consumer practice.

2. Products or Services

The offer of products or services for sale by member companies of the Association shall be accurate and truthful as to price, grade, quality, make, value, performance, quantity, currency of model, and availability.

3. Terms of Sale

A written order or receipt shall be delivered to the customer at the time of sale, which sets forth in language that is clear and free of ambiguity:

A. All the terms and conditions of sale, with specification of the total amount the customer will be required to pay, including all interest, service charges and fees, and other costs and expenses as required by federal and state law;

B. The name and address of the salesperson or the member firm represented.

4. Warranties and Guarantees

The terms of any warranty or guarantee offered by the seller in connection with the sale shall be furnished to the buyer in a manner that fully conforms to federal and state warranty and guarantee laws and regulations. The manufacturer, distributor and/or seller shall fully and promptly perform in accordance with the terms of all warranties and guarantees offered to consumers.

5. Pyramid Schemes

For the purpose of this Code, pyramid or endless chain schemes shall be considered consumer transactions actionable under this Code. The Code Administrator shall determine whether such pyramid or endless chain schemes constitute a violation of this Code in accordance with applicable federal, state and/or local law or regulation.

specific guidelines and standards member firms are expected to adhere to and abide by. Exhibit 21-15 shows part of the Code of Ethics of the Direct Selling Association.

Marketing on the Internet

The rapid growth of the Internet as a marketing tool is creating a new area of concern for regulators. Currently marketing on the Internet is subject to only limited government regulation, and many consumer and industry groups are concerned that some marketers will use the new medium to get around regulations and restrictions on other promotional areas. Following a Federal Trade Commission hearing in 1996, then chairman Robert Pitofsky issued a plea for voluntary industry codes rather than FTC rules and regulations.[97] He argued that the FTC's legal authority is limited to the areas of unfair or deceptive advertising and promotional practices and that many potential abuses of the Internet may not fall into these categories. Extending the FTC's legal authority would require congressional action. However, the results of the FTC's call for self-regulation of the Internet have been mixed. Two major areas of concern with regard to marketing on the Internet are privacy issues and online marketing to children.

With regard to privacy, several consumer and industry groups have proposed significant restrictions in the way marketers use the World Wide Web to get information from consumers, the types of information they can get, and what they do with this information.[98] The restrictions that have been proposed include:

- Banning unsolicited e-mail that cannot be automatically screened out. The Direct Marketing Association and the Interactive Services Association propose requiring marketers who send unsolicited e-mail messages to use coding that will allow mail systems to automatically remove such messages.

- Disclosing fully and prominently both the marketer's identity and the use for which information is being gathered in every communication.
- Giving consumers the right to bar marketers from selling or sharing any information collected from them as well as to review the personal information collected.

Recently the major privacy issue regarding the Internet that has emerged involves undisclosed profiling whereby Web marketers can profile a user on the basis of name, address, demographics, and online/offline purchasing data. Marketers have suggested that profiling offers them an opportunity to target specific niches and reach consumers with custom-tailored messages. However, the FTC has stated that Internet sites that claim they don't collect information but permit advertisers to surreptitiously profile viewer sites are violating consumer protection laws and are open to a charge of deception.[99] In 1999 DoubleClick, the company that is the leader in selling and managing online advertising as well as tracking Web users, set off a controversy by connecting consumers' names, addresses, and other personal information with information it collects about where consumers go on the Internet. The controversy resulted in the company being investigated by the Federal Trade Commission and lawsuits being filed in some states.[100]

In response to the profiling controversy, companies that collect Internet usage data and information joined together under the banner of the Network Advertising Initiative (NAI) to develop a self-regulatory code.[101] The NAI has developed a set of privacy principles in conjunction with the Federal Trade Commission that provides consumers with explanations of Internet advertising practices and how the practices affect both consumers and the Internet itself. The NAI has also launched a website (www.networkadvertising.org) that provides consumers with information about online advertising practices and gives them the choice to "opt out" of targeted advertising delivered by NAI member companies (Exhibit 21-16). Another industry-driven initiative is the Platform for Privacy Preferences (P3P), which is a new technology that lets consumers screen out websites via operating system software. This technology gives consumers greater control over the collection of information by allowing them to specify their privacy preferences electronically and screen out websites that do not meet these preferences. The privacy debate is likely to escalate, and it is expected that legislation will be introduced to force companies to seek consumers' approval before sharing personal information captured from their websites.

While these proposals are aimed at protecting the privacy rights of adults, one of the biggest concerns is over restricting marketers whose activities or websites are targeted

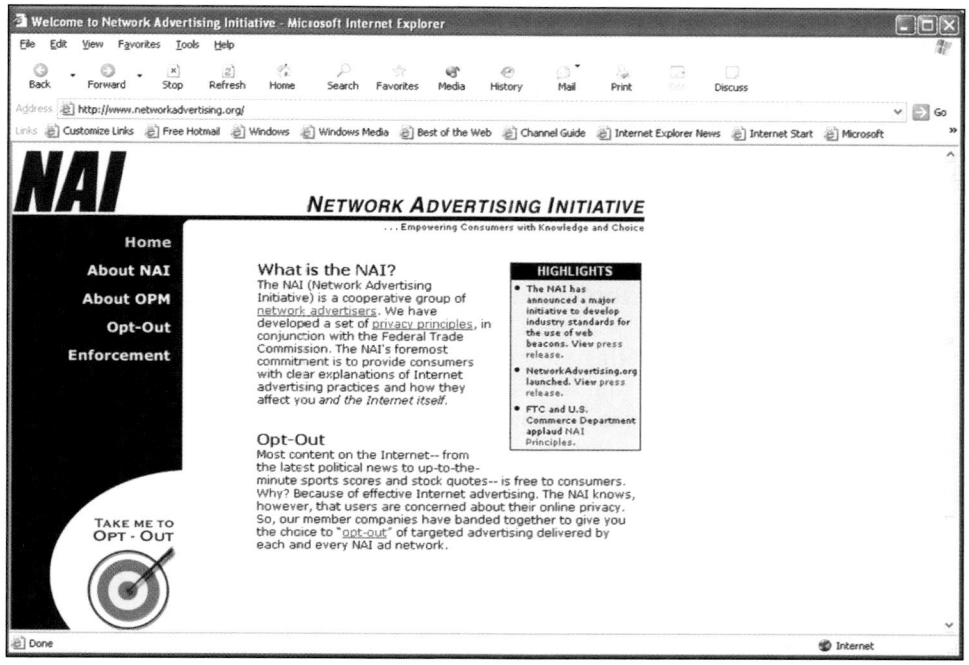

Exhibit 21-16 The Network Advertising Initiative website provides consumers with information about online advertising practices

at children. These concerns over online marketing to children led to the passage of the **Children's Online Privacy Protection Act** of 1998 (COPPA), which the FTC began enforcing in April 2000.[102] This act places tight restrictions on collecting information from children via the Internet and requires that websites directed at children and young teens have a privacy policy posted on their home page and areas of the site where information is collected.

Concerns over consumer privacy have become a major issue among the government and various regulatory agencies such as the FTC.[103] The federal government is currently considering a number of privacy-related laws, many of which would have an impact on marketing and advertising over the Internet. The proposed laws include the Online Privacy Protection Act, which requires the FTC to prescribe regulations to protect the privacy of individuals not covered by COPPA and to provide greater individual control over the collection and use of information.[104]

Another Internet-related area that is receiving more regulatory attention is the use of spam, or unsolicited e-mail.[105] More than 20 states have enacted some type of antispam laws, although they vary in content. For example, California's antispam law prohibits sending unsolicited e-mail unless it includes opt-out instructions and the sender's contact information. Antispam legislation is at the top of the list of the regulatory issues currently being considered by Congress and passage of legislation at the federal level is likely. The Anti-Spamming Act will make it unlawful for anyone to intentionally, and without authorization, transmit bulk unsolicited e-mail without a valid return e-mail address. Laws are also being considered that would outlaw sending unsolicited e-mail after a consumer has sent an unsubscribe message.[106]

As the use of the Internet as a commercial medium increases, the need for ethical standards by marketers and voluntary industry codes and guidelines will become greater. If they fail to respond, stronger intervention by the FTC or other regulatory agencies is likely.

Summary

Regulation and control of advertising stem from internal regulation or self-regulation as well as from external control by federal, state, and local regulatory agencies. For many years the advertising industry has promoted the use of voluntary self-regulation to regulate advertising and limit government interference with and control over advertising. Self-regulation of advertising emanates from all segments of the advertising industry, including advertisers and their agencies, business and advertising associations, and the media.

The NAD/NARB, the primary self-regulatory mechanism for national advertising, has been very effective in achieving its goal of voluntary regulation of advertising. Various media also have their own advertising guidelines. The major television networks maintain the most stringent review process and restrictions.

Traditionally, the federal government has been the most important source of external regulation, with the Federal Trade Commission serving as the major watchdog of advertising in the United States. The FTC protects both consumers and businesses from unfair and deceptive practices and anticompetitive behavior. The FTC became very active in the regulation of advertising during the 1970s when it began several new programs and policies, including affirmative disclosure, advertising substantiation, and corrective advertising. Since 1980 the FTC has not been allowed to implement industry-wide rules that would define unfair advertising practices. However, the advertising industry and Congress are nearing agreement on a definition of unfairness, and this power may be restored to the FTC.

In 1983 the FTC developed a new working definition of deceptive advertising. Recently the FTC has become more active in policing false and deceptive advertising. Under the Lanham Act, many companies are taking the initiative by suing competitors that make false claims. Many states, as well as the National Association of Attorneys General, are also active in exercising their jurisdiction over false and misleading advertising.

A number of laws also govern the use of other promotional mix elements, such as sales promotion and direct marketing. The Federal Trade Commission regulates many areas of sales promotion as well as direct marketing. Various consumer-oriented sales promotion tools such as contests, games, sweepstakes,

and premiums are subject to regulation. Recently many states have become very active in the regulation of contests and sweepstakes. Trade promotion practices, such as the use of promotional allowances and vertical cooperative advertising, are regulated by the Federal Trade Commission under the Robinson-Patman Act. The FTC also enforces laws in a variety of areas that relate to direct marketing and mail-order selling, while the FCC has rules governing telemarketing companies.

Currently there are few specific laws governing marketing practices on the Internet. However, two major areas of concern with regard to marketing on the Internet are privacy and online marketing to children. The Federal Trade Commission has called for voluntary industry codes rather than FTC rules to govern marketers' use of the Internet. Concerns over online marketing to children have led to the passage of the Children's Online Privacy Protection Act, which the FTC began enforcing in early 2000.

Key Terms

self-regulation, 712
Better Business Bureau, 715
Council of Better Business Bureaus, 715
National Advertising Review Board, 716
National Advertising Review Council, 716
Federal Trade Commission, 722
commercial speech, 722
Central Hudson Test, 722
Federal Trade Commission Act, 723
Wheeler-Lea Amendment, 723
trade regulation rules, 724
unfairness, 725
puffery, 725
deception, 726
affirmative disclosure, 726
advertising substantiation, 729
consent order, 730
cease-and-desist order, 730
corrective advertising, 731
Lanham Act, 738
National Association of Attorneys General, 740
Children's Online Privacy Protection Act, 746

Discussion Questions

1. Do you agree with the DISCUS argument that hard liquor is at a competitive advantage against wine and beer if it cannot advertise on television? Evaluate the decisions by NBC to become the first broadcast network to accept liquor advertising and then dropping its plans to do so.

2. Evaluate the controversy discussed in IMC Perspective 21-2 over the "Kenya" commercial from the perspective of both Just For Feet and the Saatchi & Saatchi advertising agency. With whom does the ultimate responsibility for the airing of this commercial lie, the client or the agency?

3. Discuss the role the media play in the self-regulation of advertising. Do you think media self-regulation is an effective way of protecting consumers from offensive or misleading advertising?

4. Do you agree with the decision by the California Supreme Court to view statements about a company's labor policies or operations in ads or press releases as commercial in nature and thus subject to government regulation? Discuss how this ruling might affect various forms of integrated marketing communications used by companies such as Nike.

5. IMC Perspective 21-2 discusses the legal battle between Pizza Hut and Papa John's over the latter's use of the tagline "Better Ingredients. Better Pizza." Which company do you side with in this controversy and why?

6. What is meant by advertising substantiation? Should advertisers be required to substantiate their claims before running an ad or should they be required to provide documentation only if their advertising claims are challenged?

7. Discuss the Lanham Act and how it affects advertising. What elements are necessary to win a false advertising claim under the Lanham Act?

8. IMC Perspective 21-3 discusses the debate over direct-to-consumer advertising. Do you agree with the decision by the Food and Drug Administration to issue new guidelines making it easier for pharmaceutical companies to advertise prescription drugs on television as well as in print media?

9. The Federal Trade Commission is in the process of developing a national "do-not-call" registry. Discuss how this registry will impact the direct marketing industry. What arguments might direct markets use in trying to prevent the implementation of such a program?

10. What are the major areas of concern with regard to marketing on the Internet? Evaluate the steps being taken to address these concerns.

Evaluating the Social, Ethical, and Economic Aspects of Advertising and Promotion

22

Chapter Objectives

1. To consider various perspectives concerning the social, ethical, and economic aspects of advertising and promotion.
2. To evaluate the social criticisms of advertising.
3. To examine the economic role of advertising and its effects on consumer choice, competition, and product costs and prices.

The Brave New World of Advertainment

In 1957 social critic Vance Packard wrote his classic best-seller *The Hidden Persuaders,* in which he purported to reveal all of the secret techniques used by advertisers to dig deeply into the psyches of consumers and manipulate them. When interviewed 40 years later, Packard was still fuming over what he saw coming out of Madison

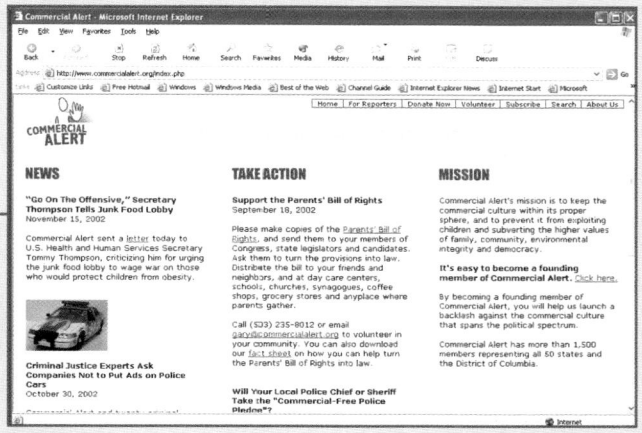

Avenue. Packard was angry not because advertisers had sharpened their brainwashing skills; rather, he was puzzled by modern-day advertising because it seemed to be unrelated to selling anything at all. He noticed that a change had taken place in the way marketers advertise their products, as there is now an obsession with images and feelings and a lack of concrete claims about a product and why anyone should buy it.

Packard was indeed correct in his observation that advertising has changed. However, what he failed to notice was that marketers have actually become less dependent on the traditional forms of mass-media advertising that he felt could be used to manipulate consumers. In the modern-day world of marketing, the debate is less over the ads that consumers see and hear and more about the persuasive messages they receive unknowingly. In recent years marketers have recognized that consumers are tired of the myriad of advertisements and other forms of promotion they are exposed to every day and are becoming very cynical about the sales pitches. To get around this problem, many companies are obliterating the line between marketing communications and entertainment by creating and delivering ads and other messages that appear to be part of popular culture. New-age marketers are redefining the notion of what advertising and other forms of marketing communications are and how they can be used. "Stealth messages" are being woven into our everyday lives, and as consumers we are often unaware of their persuasive intent.

Product placements have been around for years, and branded products are now commonplace in many movies and TV shows. However, the concept of paying to have a product or service promoted covertly has moved into other arenas, often without consumer awareness. Celebrities such as Lauren Bacall, Kathleen Turner, and Rob Lowe have appeared on talk shows and praised prescription drugs without revealing that the drug companies were paying them or making donations to their favorite charities in return for the endorsement. Producers of soap operas and sitcoms and even authors of best-selling books take money to build plots around certain brands of products such as makeup or jewelry. And of course marketers are hiring trendsetters to generate "buzz" for their products on college campuses and in trendy bars and nightclubs as well as other places. Many of the people who recommend products to us are actually pitchpersons in disguise who are being paid to deliver subtle promotional messages.

Critics of these stealth marketing techniques say they are tinkering with our minds. The executive director of the Center for Digital Democracy has called the phenomenon the "brand washing of America." Many advertising industry executives are worried that it could all too easily backfire, making consumers even more wary. Keith Reinhard, chairman of DDB Worldwide, has spoken out against the covert techniques, noting: "I'm against any form of deception. In the end, its bad business." Consumer advocate Ralph Nader has accused marketers of creating "prime-time infomercials" with no line between entertainment and ads. He notes, "What these people on Madison Avenue don't understand is, consumers will reach a saturation point. They'll reach a point where they just tip over and go, 'Yuck.'"

While many marketers realize that they may be alienating consumers with all of these stealth techniques, they argue that they really have no choice. That's because the old approach of relying on 30-second TV spots and other forms of mass-media advertising is becoming less effective. They note that digital video recorders such as TiVo will soon become as common as VCRs and give TV viewers the ability to banish commercials. Some media experts argue that commercial-supported free TV is an endangered species and marketers have to find new ways to reach consumers with their messages. Thus, like it or not, consumers are probably going to see more and more unexpected, and undercover, messages.

Many advertising experts argue that "branded content" is the wave of the future, and there is a growing clamor to reinvent advertising and other forms of marketing communications to be something more akin to entertainment. However, advertising and marketing watchdog groups such as Commercial Alert note that the memories of the movies and TV shows Hollywood is making today are being corrupted by commercialization that has mushroomed beyond mere product placement to include script doctoring and related sins. Gary Ruskin, executive director of Commercial Alert, argues that artistic concerns take a back seat when advertising is integrated into films and TV shows. He has also expressed concern over the effect "advertainment" will have on children who cannot identify or properly process the barrage of advertising messages directed at them, particularly when they are embedded in movies and TV shows.

Many argue that the Brave New World of advertainment and branded content will be exciting and cool. However, critics argue that people would like to have some places in their lives where they are free from ads and efforts to sell them something. Unfortunately, these places are becoming more difficult to find.

Sources: Daniel Eisenberg, "It's an Ad, Ad, Ad, World," *Time,* Sept. 2, 2002, pp. 38–41; Jennifer Davies, "Where Do Films Start, Ads Stop?" *San Diego Union Tribune,* Aug. 8, 2002, pp. C1, 3; Michael McCarthy, "Ads Are Here, There, Everywhere," *USA Today,* June 19, 2001, pp. 1, 2B.

> If I were to name the deadliest subversive force within capitalism, the single greatest source of its waning morality—I would without hesitation name advertising. How else should one identify a force that debases language, drains thought, and undoes dignity?[1]

The primary focus of this text has been on the role of advertising and other promotional variables as marketing activities used to convey information to, and influence the behavior of, consumers. We have been concerned with examining the advertising and promotion function in the context of a business and marketing environment and from a perspective that assumes these activities are appropriate. However, as you can see in this quote from economist Robert Heilbroner, not everyone shares this viewpoint. Advertising and promotion are the most visible of all business activities and are prone to scrutiny by those who are concerned about the methods marketers use to sell their products and services.

Proponents of advertising argue that it is the lifeblood of business—it provides consumers with information about products and services and encourages them to

improve their standard of living. They say advertising produces jobs and helps new firms enter the marketplace. Companies employ people who make the products and provide the services that advertising sells. Free market economic systems are based on competition, which revolves around information, and nothing delivers information better and at less cost than advertising.

Not everyone, however, is sold on the value of advertising. Critics argue that most advertising is more propaganda than information; it creates needs and faults consumers never knew they had. Ads suggest that children won't succeed without a computer, that our bodies should be leaner, our faces younger, and our houses cleaner. They point to the sultry, scantily clad bodies used in ads to sell everything from perfume to beer to power tools and argue that advertising promotes materialism, insecurity, and greed.

One of the reasons advertising and other forms of integrated marketing communications are becoming increasingly criticized is because they are so prevalent. Not only are there more magazine, newspaper, outdoor, TV, and radio ads than ever, but more and more public space is becoming commercialized. Advertising professor David Helm notes: "Between the stickered bananas and the ads over the urinals and the ones on the floor of the supermarkets, we're exposed to 3,000 commercial messages a day. That's one every 15 seconds, assuming we sleep for 8 hours, and I'd guess right now there's someone figuring out how to get us while our eyes are closed."[2]

As marketers intensify their efforts to get the attention of consumers, resentment against their integrated marketing communications efforts is likely to increase. As discussed in the opening vignette, concern is growing that there will be a consumer backlash as integrated marketing efforts move to new heights and marketers become increasingly aggressive. Diane Cook, a former advertising executive who founded the AdCenter at Virginia Commonwealth, says: "The growing practice of placing ads and logos everywhere seems a desperate last attempt to make branding work according to the old rules. As telemarketing, advertising, promotions and the rest continue at a frenzied pace, the value of the messages decrease. The system seems headed for a large implosion."[3]

Because of its high visibility and pervasiveness, along with its persuasive character, advertising has been the subject of a great deal of controversy and criticism. Numerous books are critical of not only advertising's methods and techniques but also its social consequences. Various parties—including scholars, economists, politicians, sociologists, government agencies, social critics, special-interest groups, and consumers—have attacked advertising and other forms of marketing communications for a variety of reasons, including their excessiveness, the way they influence society, the methods they use, their exploitation of consumers, and their effect on our economic system.

Advertising is a very powerful force, and this text would not be complete without a look at the criticisms regarding its social and economic effects as well as some defenses against these charges. We consider the various criticisms of advertising and promotion from an ethical and societal perspective and then appraise the economic effects of advertising.

Advertising and Promotion Ethics

In the previous chapter, we examined the regulatory environment in which advertising and promotion operate. While many laws and regulations determine what advertisers can and cannot do, not every issue is covered by a rule. Marketers must often make decisions regarding appropriate and responsible actions on the basis of ethical considerations rather than on what is legal or within industry guidelines. **Ethics** are moral principles and values that govern the actions and decisions of an individual or group.[4]

A particular action may be within the law and still not be ethical. A good example of this involves target marketing. No laws restrict tobacco companies from targeting advertising and promotion for new brands to African-Americans. However, given the high levels of lung cancer and smoking-related illnesses among the black population, many people would consider this an unethical business practice.

Throughout this text we have presented a number of ethical perspectives to show how various aspects of advertising and promotion often involve ethical considerations.

Ethical issues must be considered in integrated marketing communications decisions. And advertising and promotion are areas where a lapse in ethical standards or judgment can result in actions that are highly visible and often very damaging to a company.

The role of advertising in society is controversial and has sometimes resulted in attempts to restrict or ban advertising and other forms of promotion to certain groups or for certain products. College students are one such group. The level of alcohol consumption and binge drinking by college students has become a serious problem. Alcohol-related problems have proliferated on college campuses in recent years and have resulted in many negative consequences, including death.[5] Several studies have shown that there has been a significant increase in binge drinking among college students and have advocated a ban on alcohol-related advertising and promotion.[6] Many colleges and universities have imposed restrictions on the marketing of alcoholic beverages to their students. These restrictions include banning sponsorships or support of athletic, musical, cultural, or social events by alcoholic-beverage companies and limiting college newspaper advertising to price and product information ads.

A great deal of attention is being focused on the issue of whether alcoholic-beverage companies target not only college students but underage drinkers as well. As noted in Chapter 21, the actions of beer, wine, and liquor marketers are being closely scrutinized in the wake of the distilled-spirits industry's decisions to reverse its long-standing ban on television and radio advertising. Many people feel the industry's push to join beer and wine advertisers on television is testing the public's attitudes and may lead to support for more government restrictions and regulations on alcohol advertising.[7]

A recent study by the Center on Alcohol Marketing and Youth at Georgetown University concluded that underage drinkers are increasingly being targeted by magazine ads for beer and hard liquor.[8] According to the study, magazines that have a significant number of readers under the age of 21, such as *Spin, Vibe, Allure, Maxim,* and *Sports Illustrated,* accounted for nearly one-third of all alcohol advertising in magazines in 2001. The study concluded that despite the Federal Trade Commission's recommendation that the alcohol industry avoid marketing to youth audiences, the advertising practices of the beer and liquor companies fail to follow the commission's guidelines. The study called on the FTC to conduct a new and more rigorous review of the advertising practices of the alcoholic beverage companies.[9]

Exhibit 22-1 This ad is part of a campaign by Anheuser-Busch to encourage parents to talk to their teenagers about the risks of underage drinking

Companies marketing alcoholic beverages such as beer and liquor recognize the need to reduce alcohol abuse and drunken driving, particularly among young people. Many of these companies have developed programs and ads designed to address this problem. For example, Anheuser-Busch has been running a campaign that uses provocative ads such as the one shown in Exhibit 22-1 to encourage parents to talk to their kids about the risks of underage drinking. The company has also teamed up with parents, teachers, community organizations, law enforcement officials, and others to ensure progress in the fight against alcohol abuse.

Criticism often focuses on the actions of specific advertisers. Groups like the National Organization for Women and Women Against Pornography have been critical of advertisers such as Calvin Klein for promoting sexual permissiveness and objectifying women in their ads (Exhibit 22-2). The company was heavily criticized and even boycotted over the controversial "kiddie porn" ads it ran a few years ago featuring intimate snapshots of teenagers in provocative states of undress.[10]

Another company that has received a great deal of criticism for its advertising over the years is Benetton. For nearly two decades the Italian-based clothing company ran numerous "shock" ads containing controversial images such as a black woman nursing a white baby, an AIDS patient and his family moments before his death, and a priest kissing a nun (see Exhibit 21-4). Oliviero Toscani, Benetton's former creative

Exhibit 22-2 Ads by Calvin Klein have been the target of criticism by women's groups and others

director who developed most of these ads, noted that the controversial images were designed to raise public awareness of social issues and position the company as a cutting-edge, socially conscious marketer.[11] The company's most controversial ads, at least in the United States, were those used in its "Death Row" campaign that ran in 2000. The campaign, aimed at drawing attention to the use of capital punishment in the United States, featured ads showing piercing portraits of death-row inmates (Exhibit 22-3).

The campaign created a storm of controversy; the state of Missouri sued Toscani and Benetton for misrepresenting themselves while interviewing four death-row inmates featured in the campaign. Protests from the families of the inmates' victims and threatened boycotts from enraged consumers resulted in Sears Roebuck and Co. dropping the Benetton line. A year later the lawsuit was settled when Benetton agreed to write letters of apology to the four Missouri families whose relatives were murdered by the inmates featured in the ads and to make a donation to the Missouri Crime Victims Compensation Fund.[12]

As you read this chapter, remember that the various perspectives presented reflect judgments of people with different backgrounds, values, and interests. You may see nothing wrong with the ads for cigarettes or beer or sexually suggestive ads. Other students, however, may oppose these actions on moral and ethical grounds. While we attempt to present the arguments on both sides of these controversial issues, you will have to draw your own conclusions as to who is right or wrong.

Exhibit 22-3 Benetton's "Death Row" ads created a major controversy

Social and Ethical Criticisms of Advertising

Much of the controversy over advertising stems from the ways many companies use it as a selling tool and from its impact on society's tastes, values, and lifestyles. Specific techniques used by advertisers are criticized as deceptive or untruthful, offensive or in bad taste, and exploitative of certain groups, such as children. We discuss each of these criticisms, along with advertisers' responses. We then turn our attention to criticisms concerning the influence of advertising on values and lifestyles, as well as charges that it perpetuates stereotyping and that advertisers exert control over the media.

Advertising as Untruthful or Deceptive

One of the major complaints against advertising is that many ads are misleading or untruthful and deceive consumers. A number of studies have shown a general mistrust of advertising among consumers.[13] A study by Banwari Mittal found that consumers felt that less than one-quarter of TV commercials are honest and believable.[14] Sharon Shavitt, Pamela Lowery, and James Haefner conducted a major national survey of over 1,000 adult consumers to determine the general public's current attitudes toward and confidence in advertising. They found that Americans generally do not trust advertising, although they tend to feel more confidence in advertising claims when focused on their actual purchase decisions.[15]

Attempts by industry and government to regulate and control deceptive advertising were discussed in Chapter 21. We noted that advertisers should have a reasonable basis for making a claim about product performance and may be required to provide evidence to support their claims. However, deception can occur more subtly as a result of how consumers perceive the ad and its impact on their beliefs.[16] The difficulty of determining just what constitutes deception, along with the fact that advertisers have the right to use puffery and make subjective claims about their products, tends to complicate the issue. But a concern of many critics is the extent to which advertisers are *deliberately* untruthful or misleading.

Sometimes advertisers have made overtly false or misleading claims or failed to award prizes promoted in a contest or sweepstakes. However, these cases usually involve smaller companies and a tiny portion of the hundreds of billions of dollars spent on advertising and promotion each year. Most advertisers do not design their messages with the intention to mislead or deceive consumers or run sweepstakes with no intention of awarding prizes. Not only are such practices unethical, but the culprits would damage their reputation and risk prosecution by regulatory groups or government agencies. National advertisers in particular invest large sums of money to develop loyalty to, and enhance the image of, their brands. These companies are not likely to risk hard-won consumer trust and confidence by intentionally deceiving consumers.

The problem of untruthful or fraudulent advertising and promotion exists more at the local level and in specific areas such as mail order, telemarketing, and other forms of direct marketing. Yet there have been many cases where large companies were accused of misleading consumers with their ads or promotions. Some companies test the limits of industry and government rules and regulations to make claims that will give their brands an advantage in highly competitive markets.

While many critics of advertising would probably agree that most advertisers are not out to deceive consumers deliberately, they are still concerned that consumers may not be receiving enough information to make an informed choice. They say advertisers usually present only information that is favorable to their position and do not always tell consumers the whole truth about a product or service.

Many believe advertising should be primarily informative in nature and should not be permitted to use puffery or embellished messages. Others argue that advertisers have the right to present the most favorable case for their products and services and should not be restricted to just objective, verifiable information.[17] They note that consumers can protect themselves from being persuaded against their will and that the various industry and government regulations suffice to keep advertisers from misleading consumers. Figure 22-1 shows the advertising principles of the American Advertising Federation, which many advertisers use as a guideline in preparing and evaluating their ads.

Advertising as Offensive or in Bad Taste

Another common criticism of advertising, particularly by consumers, is that ads are offensive, tasteless, irritating, boring, obnoxious, and so on. In the recent study by Shavitt and her colleagues, about half of the respondents reported feeling offended by advertising at least sometimes. A number of other studies have found that consumers feel most advertising insults their intelligence and that many ads are in poor taste.[18]

Sources of Distaste

Consumers can be offended or irritated by advertising in a number of ways. Some object when a product or service like contraceptives or personal hygiene products is advertised at all. Most media did not accept ads for condoms until

1. *Truth.* Advertising shall reveal the truth, and shall reveal significant facts, the omission of which would mislead the public.
2. *Substantiation.* Advertising claims shall be substantiated by evidence in possession of the advertiser and the advertising agency prior to making such claims.
3. *Comparisons.* Advertising shall refrain from making false, misleading, or unsubstantiated statements or claims about a competitor or his products or service.
4. *Bait advertising.* Advertising shall not offer products or services for sale unless such offer constitutes a bona fide effort to sell the advertised products or services and is not a device to switch consumers to other goods or services, usually higher priced.
5. *Guarantees and warranties.* Advertising of guarantees and warranties shall be explicit, with sufficient information to apprise consumers of their principal terms and limitations or, when space or time restrictions preclude such disclosures, the advertisement shall clearly reveal where the full text of the guarantee or warranty can be examined before purchase.
6. *Price claims.* Advertising shall avoid price claims that are false or misleading, or savings claims that do not offer provable savings.
7. *Testimonials.* Advertising containing testimonials shall be limited to those of competent witnesses who are reflecting a real and honest opinion or experience.
8. *Taste and decency.* Advertising shall be free of statements, illustrations, or implications that are offensive to good taste or public decency.

Figure 22-1 Advertising principles of the American Advertising Federation

the AIDS crisis forced them to reconsider their restrictions (Exhibit 22-4). The major TV networks gave their affiliates permission to accept condom advertising in 1987, but the first condom ad did not appear on network TV until 1991, when Fox broadcast a spot.

In 1994 the U.S. Department of Health's Centers for Disease Control and Prevention (CDC) began a new HIV prevention campaign that includes radio and TV commercials urging sexually active people to use latex condoms. The commercials prompted strong protests from conservative and religious groups, which argue that the government should stress abstinence in preventing the spread of AIDS among young people. NBC and ABC agreed to broadcast all the commercials, while CBS said it would air certain spots.[19]

A study of prime-time TV commercials found a strong product class effect with respect to the types of ads consumers perceived as distasteful or irritating. The most irritating commercials were for feminine hygiene products; ads for women's undergarments and hemorrhoid products were close behind.[20] Another study found that consumers are more likely to dislike ads for products they do not use and for brands they would not buy.[21] Ads for personal products have become more common on television and in print, and the public is more accepting of them.[22] However, advertisers must still be careful of how these products are presented and the language and terminology used. There are still many rules, regulations, and taboos advertisers must deal with to have their TV commercials approved by the networks.[23]

Another way advertising can offend consumers is by the type of appeal or the manner of presentation. For example, many people object to appeals that exploit consumer anxieties. Fear appeal ads, especially for products such as deodorants, mouthwash, and dandruff shampoos, are criticized for attempting to create anxiety and using a fear of social rejection to sell these products. Some ads for home computers were also criticized for attempting to make parents think that if their young children couldn't use a computer, they would fail in school.

Sexual Appeals The advertising appeals that have received the most criticism for being in poor taste are those using sexual appeals and/or nudity. These techniques are often used to gain consumers' attention and may not even be appropriate to the product being advertised. Even if the sexual appeal relates to the product, people may be offended by it. Many people object to both nudity in advertising and sexually suggestive ads.

Exhibit 22-4 Many magazines and TV stations now accept ads for condoms

A common criticism of sexual appeals is that they can demean women (or men) by depicting them as sex objects. Ads for cosmetics and lingerie are among the most criticized for their portrayal of women as sex objects (Exhibit 22-5). Some ads have even been criticized for being implicitly suggestive. For example, some women's groups criticized the Airwalk ad shown in Exhibit 22-6, arguing that it showed a submissive and sexually available woman. A critic argued that the ad contained a number of symbolic cues that are sexually suggestive and combine to reinforce an image of the woman's sexual submission to the man.[24]

Critics have been particularly concerned about the use of sexual appeals in the advertising of products such as cigarette, liquor, and beer. Sexual appeals and risqué images have long been used in advertising for alcoholic beverages. In the early 90s an advertising campaign for Old Milwaukee beer featuring the "Swedish Bikini Team," a group of Scandinavian-looking women wearing blue bikinis who appeared out of nowhere in front of groups of beer-drinking men, ignited a major controversy. A number of consumer groups were very critical of the ads, and female employees even sued the Stroh Brewing Co., arguing that the ads contributed to an atmosphere that was conducive to sexual harassment in the workplace.[25]

A number of alcoholic-beverage companies have been criticized more recently for using what many consider raunchy advertising.[26] For example, the Phillips Beverage Co. used several controversial ads to introduce Revelstoke, a spiced Canadian liquor product. One of the ads showed a

Exhibit 22-5 Sexual appeals are often criticized for portraying women as sex objects

Exhibit 22-6 This Airwalk ad was criticized for being suggestive and symbolizing sexual submission

G-stringed lap dancer straddling a seated man in a nightclub. The tagline of the ad read "In Canada, the average paycheck rarely lasts two weeks. It's more like 20 songs." The president of the company noted that he was taking a page from the beer companies that made swimsuits and stilettos standard marketing fare: "It's hard to be in this business and not look at the success of beer advertisers and argue that it doesn't work."[27]

Liquor companies are often criticized not only for their advertising but for some of their other promotional methods as well. For example, in 2002 the Boston Beer Co., which markets the popular Samuel Adams Boston Lager brand, was criticized for its involvement with a "Sex for Sam" radio promotion that encouraged people to have sex in various public places to win a trip to the company's brewery. The promotion was run in conjunction with a talk-radio station whose shock-jocks provided listeners with detailed reports of couples' sexual activity. The controversy resulted in a boycott of the company's products in some bars in Boston, where the company is headquartered. Although the company denied that it was aware of the exact nature of the radio promotion, the chairman of Boston Beer issued a public apology for his company's participation.[28]

Shock Advertising With the increasing clutter in the advertising environment, advertisers continue to use sexual appeals and other techniques that offend many people but catch the attention of consumers and may even generate publicity for their companies. In recent years there has been an increase in what is often referred to as **shock advertising,** in which marketers use nudity, sexual suggestiveness, or other startling images to get consumers' attention. As discussed earlier in the chapter, shock advertising is nothing new; companies such as Benetton and Calvin Klein have been using this tactic in their ads since the 1980s. However, a number of other marketers have been criticized for using shock techniques in their ads as well as in other promotional materials.[29] For example, clothing retailer Abercrombie & Fitch has been criticized numerous times for the content and images used in its quarterly catalogs, which have included sex tips from porn star Jenna Jameson, a spoof interview

Exhibit 22-7 Abercrombie & Fitch's catalogs have been criticized over the use of sex and nudity

with a shopping mall Santa portrayed as a pedophile, and nude photos. The retailer promoted its 2002 Christmas catalog with an advertisement across the plastic covering stating, "Two-hundred and eighty pages of sex and Xmas fun" (Exhibit 22-7).[30] A few years ago officials in four states threatened or pursued legal action against the company, which responded by implementing a policy of carding would-be-buyers of the catalog to ensure they are at least 18 years old.

Another company known for its whimsical, and sometimes controversial, ads is Bijan. The fragrance marketer's ads attracted a great deal of attention a few years ago when it decided to forgo the tall, thin, glamorous supermodels typically used in fragrance ads and use very large, naked women instead. The company's founder, Beverly Hills fashion maven Bijan, defended the ads by stating that they were his homage to artists such as Rubens, who used full-figured models (Exhibit 22-8).

Many advertising experts argue that what underlies the increase in the use of shock advertising is the pressure on marketers and their agencies to do whatever it takes to get their ads noticed. However, critics argue that the more advertisers use the tactic, the more shocking the ads have to be to get attention. How far advertisers can go with these appeals will probably depend on the public's reaction. When consumers think the advertisers have gone too far, they are likely to pressure the advertisers to change their ads and the media to stop accepting them.

Exhibit 22-8 Bijan often uses whimsical and controversial ads

While marketers and ad agencies often acknowledge that their ads push the limits with regard to taste, they also complain about a double standard that exists for advertising versus editorial television program content. The creative director for Abercrombie & Fitch's agency argues that there is a double standard and hypocrisy in the shock advertising debate: "When advertising uses sex, everybody complains—when editorial does it, nobody cares."[31] Advertisers and agency creative directors argue that even the most suggestive commercials are bland compared with the content of many television programs. Ethical Perspective 22-1 discusses the process by which the standards and practices departments of the four major networks review the thousands of commercials they receive each year and try to resolve issues regarding their tastefulness.

Advertising and Children

One of the most controversial topics advertisers must deal with is the issue of advertising to children. TV is a vehicle through which advertisers can reach children easily. Children between the ages of 2 and 11 watch an average of

ETHICAL PERSPECTIVE 22-1

Networks and Advertisers Battle over Tasteful Advertising

Before any commercial airs on network television, it is reviewed by the standards and practices departments of the major networks. There are approximately 30 censors working for the four major broadcast networks who dictate to advertising agencies and their clients what they can and cannot show on national television. The censors review ads often as early as in the storyboard stage and comment on about half of the ads they see, most often with questions about accuracy. However, along with ensuring that product claims are accurate, the censors also concern themselves with the tastefulness of the ads they review. Ads containing sex, violence, adult language, morbid humor, unsafe or antisocial behavior, and controversial political reviews receive very careful scrutiny.

The network clearance departments argue that advertisers and agencies welcome their feedback and that the system is not an adversarial one. However, frustrated marketers and ad agencies often argue that the clearance process is arbitrary and unfair, with an abundance of double standards and unwritten rules. For example, Rich Silverstein, co-chairman of Goodby Silverstein & Partners in San Francisco, notes: "The networks don't play fair about blood, guts and sex. Judgments about the ads depend on who is judging that day. And their standards are a moving target." His agency has been involved in squabbles with the networks over commercials for clients such as E*Trade and the California Milk Advisory Board. The agency has pushed the envelope with censors several times with humorous ads created for the long-running "Got milk?" campaign. For example, one of the spots in the campaign showed a frustrated priest kicking a vending machine when it failed to dispense a carton of milk. Censors cried foul—not because it portrayed the priest in an unflattering light but because it is a misdemeanor to vandalize a vending machine and ads cannot depict criminal actions.

Another issue that is often raised with the networks is whether they have a double standard, holding commercials to a higher standard than they do their own programs. For example, a few years ago the agency for Converse created a commercial featuring "Lupo the Butcher," who gets whacked by his own cleaver as, cursing in Italian, he tries to turn a high-top shoe into a low-cut. ABC deemed the cartoon butcher too bloody, vulgar, and ethnic for mass audiences. The agency tried unsuccessfully to run the ad after making changes that included toning down some of the ad's colorful language. However, ABC later asked the agency and client to feature the spot in its show *The World's Funniest Commercials.* The creative director who worked on the spot notes: "There is definitely a double standard, and it has frustrated me as a creative person that I am limited in what I can use to communicate an idea."

Those who work in the standards and practices departments for the networks do not agree with their critics, arguing that they give agencies ample leeway to communicate their advertising messages. A CBS clearance editor states: "We do not act as censors. We work in a constructive way with advertisers to make sure that we, as carriers of the public trust, present things in the best possible light to viewers." Roland McFarland, who runs the standards and practices department at Fox, argues that his department tries to assist both agencies and television viewers: "We help agencies tailor and craft their ads for the broad-spectrum audience. We are part of the creative process. We know what plays with our audience and what will have more impact."

Advertisers also become frustrated by the lack of consistency in the decisions across the major networks, as commercials accepted by reviewers at one network are not always accepted by other networks. For example, while Fox is known for its irreverent programming, the network has a reputation as "family friendly" and is considered more cautious and conservative than the Big Three. However, the networks argue that inconsistency among standards and practices departments is uncommon and that if one network has problems with a commercial, the others usually will as well.

Advertisers that feel they have been treated unfairly by a network can appeal the decision to the network's sales department, which has the authority to overrule the censors. However, because clearance editors tend to stay in their jobs for years and have

long memories, agencies and clients are leery of this option. Thus, they prefer to negotiate with the clearance editors and often will make changes and modifications in their ads to satisfy the editors' concerns. In some cases, the networks are persuaded to allow an ad to run to gauge the public's reactions. Ads often run subject to viewer complaint—if the network receives negative reactions from viewers, the ad is pulled.

In some cases advertisers give up trying to please the networks and instead seek approval from the network affiliates, which have their own standards and practices departments and usually are easier to please than the network censors. Advertisers also will take their ads to independent broadcasters as well as cable stations, which may be even less stringent in their reviews. The advertising recession that has plagued the industry in recent years has resulted in a decline in demand for TV commercial time, particularly on syndicated programs and cable. Thus it is often easier to get ads accepted on their programs than by the major networks.

The clearance editors at the networks review 50 to 150 commercials a day, sometimes examining revisions of a spot three and four times. While they acknowledge that the process is subjective, they argue that they do their best to serve the sometimes competing interests of advertisers, the viewing audience, and the network affiliates. They argue that they have to please a large number of viewers with very different values and opinions as to what is tasteful and responsible advertising. While they do not feel they are censors, they do think of themselves as protectors of social values.

Sources: Joan Voight and Wendy Melillo, "Rough Cut," *Adweek*, March 11, 2002, pp. 27–29; Joan Voight and Wendy Melillo, "To See or Not to See?" *Adweek*, March 11, 2002, p. 30; Vanessa O'Connell, "Invasion of the Tacky Advertisers," *The Wall Street Journal*, February 20, 2002, pp. B1, 4.

21.5 hours of TV a week and may see between 22,000 and 25,000 commercials a year.[32] Studies show that television is an important source of information for children about products.[33] Concern has also been expressed about marketers' use of other promotional vehicles and techniques such as radio ads, point-of-purchase displays, premiums in packages, and the use of commercial characters as the basis for TV shows.

Critics argue that children, particularly young ones, are especially vulnerable to advertising because they lack the experience and knowledge to understand and evaluate critically the purpose of persuasive advertising appeals. Research has shown that preschool children cannot differentiate between commercials and programs, do not perceive the selling intent of commercials, and cannot distinguish between reality and fantasy.[34] Research has also shown that children need more than a skeptical attitude toward advertising; they must understand how advertising works in order to use their cognitive defenses against it effectively.[35] Because of children's limited ability to interpret the selling intent of a message or identify a commercial, critics charge that advertising to them is inherently unfair and deceptive and should be banned or severely restricted.

At the other extreme are those who argue that advertising is a part of life and children must learn to deal with it in the **consumer socialization process** of acquiring the skills needed to function in the marketplace.[36] They say existing restrictions are adequate for controlling children's advertising. A recent study by Tamara Mangleburg and Terry Bristol provided support for the socialization argument. They found that adolescents developed skeptical attitudes toward advertising that were learned through interactions with socialization agents such as parents, peers, and television. They also found that marketplace knowledge plays an important role in adolescents' skepticism toward advertising. Greater knowledge of the marketplace appears to give teens a basis by which to evaluate ads and makes them more likely to recognize the persuasion techniques used by advertisers.[37]

This issue received a great deal of attention in 1979 when the Federal Trade Commission held hearings on proposed changes in regulations regarding advertising to children. An FTC staff report recommended banning all TV advertising for any product directed to or seen by audiences composed largely of children under age eight because they are too young to understand the selling intent of advertising.[38]

The FTC proposal was debated intensely. The advertising industry and a number of companies argued strongly against it, based on factors including advertisers' right of free speech under the First Amendment to communicate with those consumers who make up their primary target audience.[39] They also said parents should be involved in

helping children interpret advertising and can refuse to purchase products they believe are undesirable for their children.

The FTC proposal was defeated, and changes in the political environment resulted in less emphasis on government regulation of advertising. But parent and consumer groups like the Center for Science in the Public Interest are still putting pressure on advertisers regarding what they see as inappropriate or misleading ads for children. One activist group, Action for Children's Television (ACT), was disbanded in 1992, but first it was instrumental in getting Congress to approve the Children's Television Act in October 1990. The act limits the amount of commercial time in children's programming to 10.5 minutes per hour on weekends and 12 minutes on weekdays.[40]

In 1996 broadcasters, children's advocates, and the federal government reached an agreement requiring TV stations to air three hours of children's educational shows a week.[41] Many believe advertisers will play a major role in implementing the new initiative by providing financial backing for the educational shows—which have long had trouble luring sponsors.[42]

Children are also protected from the potential influences of commercials by network censors and industry self-regulatory groups such as the Council of Better Business Bureaus' Children's Advertising Review Unit (CARU). CARU has strict self-regulatory guidelines regarding the type of appeals, product presentation and claims, disclosures and disclaimers, the use of premiums, safety, and techniques such as special effects and animation. The CARU guidelines for advertising addressed to children under 12 are presented in Figure 22-2.

As we saw in Chapter 21, the major networks also have strict guidelines for ads targeted to children. For example, in network TV ads, only 10 seconds can be devoted to animation and special effects; the final 5 seconds are reserved for displaying all the toys shown in the ad and disclosing whether they are sold separately and whether accessories such as batteries are included. Networks also require 3 seconds of every 30-second cereal ad to portray a balanced breakfast, usually by showing a picture of toast, orange juice, and milk.[43]

While concerns over advertising and other forms of promotion directed at children diminished somewhat over the past decade, the issue has been receiving greater attention recently. Reasons for this growing concern include the increasing viewing options children have as a result of the growth of cable television, an increase in the number of ads encouraging children to call 900 numbers, the increase in the number of toy-based

Five basic principles underlie these guidelines for advertising directed to children:

1. Advertisers should always take into account the level of knowledge, sophistication, and maturity of the audience to which their message is primarily directed. Younger children have a limited capability for evaluating the credibility of what they watch. Advertisers, therefore, have a special responsibility to protect children from their own susceptibilities.
2. Realizing that children are imaginative and that make-believe play constitutes an important part of the growing-up process, advertisers should exercise care not to exploit that imaginative quality of children. Unreasonable expectations of product quality or performance should not be stimulated either directly or indirectly by advertising.
3. Recognizing that advertising may play an important part in educating the child, information should be communicated in a truthful and accurate manner with full recognition by the advertiser that the child may learn practices from advertising that can affect his or her health and well-being.
4. Advertisers are urged to capitalize on the potential of advertising to influence social behavior by developing advertising that, wherever possible, addresses itself to social standards generally regarded as positive and beneficial, such as friendship, kindness, honesty, justice, generosity, and respect for others.
5. Although many influences affect a child's personal and social development, it remains the prime responsibility of the parents to provide guidance for children. Advertisers should contribute to this parent-child relationship in a constructive manner.

Figure 22-2 Children's Advertising Review Unit principles

programs on TV, and general concerns over the content of children's programming, particularly with regard to violence.

The marketing of violent entertainment to minors and the advertising practices and rating systems of the film, music, and electronic game industries are also being monitored very carefully. The issue of what young consumers are watching, listening to, and playing and how much violence that entertainment contains became an area of great concern following the shootings at Columbine High School as well as several other schools. In 2001 legislation was proposed that would have given the FTC authority to take action against companies that violated their own industry's voluntary policies governing the marketing of violent products to minors. However, the bill was suspended following FTC reports that the companies had made improvements.[44]

As discussed in the previous chapter, there is also growing concern over how marketers are using the Internet to communicate with and sell to children. Another area that has received a great deal of attention recently is the use of in-school marketing programs, whereby companies provide equipment or pay money to schools in exchange for the rights to sell their products to students or communicate with them. Ethical Perspective 22-2 discusses the controversy over the commercialization of schools.

Advertising to children will remain a controversial topic. Some groups feel that the government is responsible for protecting children from the potentially harmful effects of advertising and other forms of promotion, while others argue that parents are ultimately responsible for doing so. Various consumer groups have also urged the media, particularly television broadcasters, as well as marketers to assume responsibility for the programs and advertising and promotional messages they offer to children.[45] A study comparing the attitudes of business executives and consumers regarding children's advertising found that marketers of products targeted to children believe advertising to them provides useful information on new products and does not disrupt the parent-child relationship. However, the general public did not have such a favorable opinion. Older consumers and those from households with children had particularly negative attitudes toward children's advertising.[46] A recent survey of 12,500 young people up to 18 years of age was conducted for *Advertising Age* regarding their attitudes toward advertising and various media. The study found that two-thirds of those surveyed believed the main goal of advertising is to make them buy things while only 11 percent felt that its objective is to provide information.[47]

It is important to many companies to communicate directly with children. However, only by being sensitive to the naiveté of children as consumers will they be able to do so freely and avoid potential conflict with those who believe children should be protected from advertising and other forms of promotion.

Social and Cultural Consequences

Concern is often expressed over the impact of advertising on society, particularly on values and lifestyles. While a number of factors influence the cultural values, lifestyles, and behavior of a society, the overwhelming amount of advertising and its prevalence in the mass media lead many critics to argue that advertising plays a major role in influencing and transmitting social values. In his book *Advertising and Social Change,* Ronald Berman says:

> The institutions of family, religion, and education have grown noticeably weaker over each of the past three generations. The world itself seems to have grown more complex. In the absence of traditional authority, advertising has become a kind of social guide. It depicts us in all the myriad situations possible to a life of free choice. It provides ideas about style, morality, behavior.[48]

Mike Hughes, president and creative director of the Martin Agency, notes that advertising has a major impact on society: "Ads help establish what is cool in society; their messages contribute to the public dialogue. Gap ads show white, black and Hispanic kids dancing together. Hilfiger ads showed it's cool for people to get along. Ikea showed a gay couple." He argues that advertising agencies have a social and ethical responsibility to consider the impact of the advertising messages they create for their clients.[49]

ETHICAL PERSPECTIVE 22-2

Marketing to Kids in School—Is It Cool?

In 1990 an entrepreneur named Chris Whittle created a national controversy and gave parents and educators fits because of a plan to put news programming and advertisements in high school classrooms all over America. In return for providing free TV sets for every classroom and a satellite hookup, Whittle's Channel One would be allowed to show a 12-minute daily news program that contained 2 minutes of commercials for products such as acne medicine, electric razors, cereals, and candy. Channel One struggled in its early years, as many schools were reluctant to provide marketers with yet another way of reaching young people with their advertising messages. However, as the demand for upgraded technology in classrooms increased and funds available to pay for it decreased, many school districts became more receptive to Whittle. Today Channel One broadcasts into nearly 12,000 middle, junior, and high schools, and some 8.3 million teenagers see its news show and commercials every school day.

Many educators, consumer activists, and parent groups feared letting Channel One into schools on the grounds that it would open the doors for corporate America to reach students in a place where they are supposed to be learning English and math rather than watching commercials. Marketers recognize that the youth market is a gold mine, as there are nearly 48 million U.S. children in kindergarten through high school and their purchasing power, as well as influence on their parents' purchases, is immense. Moreover, this is the only market segment whose members are held as a captive audience for six to seven hours a day. The concern was that marketers would find all kinds of creative ways to reach a market that was entirely off-limits just a decade ago.

Channel One has clearly helped spawn the new breed of in-school marketers that are taking advantage of the financial squeeze many schools are in and making them offers they find hard to resist. However, not everyone is welcoming the commercialization of America's schools and classrooms. For example, ZapMe Corp., a California-based computer marketing company, had plans to wire America's classrooms by donating 120,000 top-of-the-line computers to 8,000 high schools, along with high-speed, broadband Internet connections. The hitch was that the equipment and access would be supported by banner advertising and the company would get permission to monitor the student's Web browsing habits. ZapMe was launched in 1996 and by the middle of 2000 it had wired 2,300 schools in 45 states, providing approximately 2 million students with Internet access. However, the company's

plan was plagued by political problems as consumer activists and organizations such as Commercial Alert, which is dedicated to protecting communities and children from commercialism, cried foul. Ralph Nader called for parents to "join together to keep ZapMe and other advertisers out of your children's schools." By late 2000 ZapMe announced that it would not add any new schools to its program, and a year later the company abandoned its plans to wire the nation's schools.

High-tech companies are not the only ones finding their way into schools. General Mills' Box Tops for Education program allows schools to earn cash by having students collect box tops from the company's products. Pizza Hut offers a program called Book It, which awards gift certificates to students in elementary schools who complete reading assignments. Since the program's creation in 1985, Pizza Hut has given away about 45 million coupons worth $178 million of pizza to schoolchildren. Individual Pizza Hut franchisees are also free to coordinate additional in-school programs.

The most common in-school marketing agreements are with local soft-drink bottlers, which pay school districts large sums of money for exclusive vending rights. Companies such as Coca-Cola, PepsiCo, and Dr. Pepper/Seven-Up leave the negotiation of these "pouring rights" to their independent bottlers. While the agreements with soft-drink bottlers may generate hundreds of thousands of dollars a year in extra revenue for the schools that have them, they are also highly controversial. The vending machines are targeted because of the lack of nutritional value of soft drinks and concerns over youth obesity. To alleviate these problems, many bottlers offer a variety of beverages in the machines, including fruit juices, juice drinks, and water.

As more schools open their doors to marketers, there is concern that the commercialization of our nation's classrooms has gone too far. Gary Ruskin,

director of Commercial Alert, which is Ralph Nader's consumer advocacy group, says, "Kids are in school to learn to read and write and think, not to learn to desire products." David Walsh, president of the National Institute on Media & Family, is concerned about the increasingly sophisticated advertising in schools. He notes, "Kids are bombarded with commercial messages outside of school. The risk is that they will be treated increasingly as consumers in the one institution where they're supposed to be treated as learners."

The debate is likely to continue over commercialization of classrooms. Many argue that these programs are corrupting young students and contaminating the educational process. They argue that school administrators should not be put in the ethically difficult position of striking deals to make ends meet. However, others argue that the programs are legitimate activities of companies seeking to expand their markets while helping financially strapped schools pay for items that help increase the quality of education.

Sources: Steve Jarvis, "Lesson Plans," *Marketing News,* June 18, 2001, pp. 1, 9, 10; Betsy Schiffman, "ZapMe Kills Computers in the Classroom," www.Forbes.com, Nov. 28, 2000; Peggy J. Faber, "Schools for Sale," *Advertising Age,* Oct. 25, 1999, pp. 22–26; Richard Sale, "Lions among Lambs," *Promo Magazine,* February 1999, pp. 46–51.

While there is general agreement that advertising is an important social influence agent, opinions as to the value of its contribution are often negative. Advertising is criticized for encouraging materialism, manipulating consumers to buy things they do not really need, perpetuating stereotypes, and controlling the media.

Advertising Encourages Materialism

Many critics claim advertising has an adverse effect on consumer values by encouraging **materialism,** a preoccupation with material things rather than intellectual or spiritual concerns. The United States is undoubtedly the most materialistic society in the world, which many critics attribute to advertising that

- Seeks to create needs rather than merely showing how a product or service fulfills them.
- Surrounds consumers with images of the good life and suggests the acquisition of material possessions leads to contentment and happiness and adds to the joy of living.
- Suggests material possessions are symbols of status, success, and accomplishment and/or will lead to greater social acceptance, popularity, sex appeal, and so on.

The ad shown in Exhibit 22-9 for Rolls-Royce automobiles is an example of how advertising can promote materialistic values.

Exhibit 22-9 Rolls-Royce appeals to consumers' materialism

This criticism of advertising assumes that materialism is undesirable and is sought at the expense of other goals. But many believe materialism is an acceptable part of the **Protestant ethic,** which stresses hard work and individual effort and initiative and views the accumulation of material possessions as evidence of success. Others argue that the acquisition of material possessions has positive economic impact by encouraging consumers to keep consuming after their basic needs are met. Many Americans believe economic growth is essential and materialism is both a necessity and an inevitable part of this progress.

Economist John Kenneth Galbraith, often a vocal critic of advertising, describes the role advertising plays in industrialized economies by encouraging consumption:

> Advertising and its related arts thus help develop the kind of man the goals of the industrial system require—one that reliably spends his income and works reliably because he is always in need of more. In the absence of the massive and artful persuasion that accompanies the management of demand, increasing abundance might well have reduced the interest of people in acquiring more goods. Being not pressed by the need for these things, they would have spent less reliably to get more. The consequence—a lower and less reliable propensity to consume—would have been awkward for the industrial system.[50]

It has also been argued that an emphasis on material possessions does not rule out interest in intellectual, spiritual, or cultural values. Defenders of advertising say consumers can be more interested in higher-order goals when basic needs have been met. Raymond Bauer and Stephen Greyser point out that consumers may purchase material things in the pursuit of nonmaterial goals.[51] For example, a person may buy an expensive stereo system to enjoy music rather than simply to impress someone or acquire a material possession.

Even if we assume materialism is undesirable, there is still the question of whether advertising is responsible for creating and encouraging it. While many critics argue that advertising is a major contributing force to materialistic values, others say advertising merely reflects the values of society rather than shaping them.[52] They argue that consumers' values are defined by the society in which they live and are the results of extensive, long-term socialization or acculturation.

The argument that advertising is responsible for creating a materialistic and hedonistic society is addressed by Stephen Fox in his book *The Mirror Makers: A History of American Advertising and Its Creators.* Fox concludes advertising has become a prime scapegoat for our times and merely reflects society. Regarding the effect of advertising on cultural values, he says:

> To blame advertising now for those most basic tendencies in American history is to miss the point. It is too obvious, too easy, a matter of killing the messenger instead of dealing with the bad news. The people who have created modern advertising are not hidden persuaders pushing our buttons in the service of some malevolent purpose. They are just producing an especially visible manifestation, good and bad, of the American way of life.[53]

Exhibit 22-10 The advertising industry argues that advertising reflects society

The ad shown in Exhibit 22-10 was developed by the American Association of Advertising Agencies and suggests that advertising is a reflection of society's tastes and values, not vice versa. The ad was part of a campaign that addressed criticisms of advertising.

Advertising does contribute to our materialism by portraying products and services as symbols of status, success, and achievement and by encouraging consumption. As Richard Pollay says, "While it may be true that advertising reflects cultural values, it does so on a very selective basis, echoing and reinforcing certain attitudes, behaviors, and values far more frequently than others."[54]

Individuals from a variety of backgrounds are concerned over the values they see driving our society. They believe that materialism, greed, and selfishness increasingly dominate American life and that advertising is a major reason for these undesirable values. The extent to which advertising is responsible for materialism and the desirability of such values are deep philosophical issues that will continue to be part of the debate over the societal value and consequences of advertising.

Advertising Makes People Buy Things They Don't Need A common criticism of advertising is that it manipulates consumers into buying things they do not need. Many critics say advertising should just provide information useful in making purchase decisions and should not persuade. They view information advertising (which reports price, performance, and other objective criteria) as desirable but persuasive advertising (which plays on consumers' emotions, anxieties, and psychological needs and desires such as status, self-esteem, and attractiveness) as unacceptable. Persuasive advertising is criticized for fostering discontent among consumers and encouraging them to purchase products and services to solve deeper problems. Critics say advertising exploits consumers and persuades them to buy things they don't need.

Defenders of advertising offer a number of rebuttals to these criticisms. First, they point out that a substantial amount of advertising is essentially informational in nature.[55] Also, it is difficult to separate desirable informational advertising from undesirable persuasive advertising. Shelby Hunt, in examining the *information-persuasion dichotomy,* points out that even advertising that most observers would categorize as very informative is often very persuasive.[56] He says, "If advertising critics really

believe that persuasive advertising should not be permitted, they are actually proposing that no advertising be allowed, since the purpose of all advertising is to persuade."[57]

Defenders of advertising also take issue with the argument that it should be limited to dealing with basic functional needs. In our society, most lower-level needs recognized in Maslow's hierarchy, such as the need for food, clothing, and shelter, are satisfied for most people. It is natural to move from basic needs to higher-order ones such as self-esteem and status or self-actualization. Consumers are free to choose the degree to which they attempt to satisfy their desires, and wise advertisers associate their products and services with the satisfaction of higher-order needs.

Proponents of advertising offer two other defenses against the charge that advertising makes people buy things they do not really need. First, this criticism attributes too much power to advertising and assumes consumers have no ability to defend themselves against it.

Second, it ignores the fact that consumers have the freedom to make their own choices when confronted with persuasive advertising. While they readily admit the persuasive intent of their business, advertisers are quick to note it is extremely difficult to make consumers purchase a product they do not want or for which they do not see a personal benefit. For example, the "green" marketing movement has not gotten consumers to forgo low prices or convenience in favor of products that make environmental claims. The market research firm of Roper ASW conducted an extensive study of 300 green ads that appeared in magazines and found that most were not effective. The study concluded that too many green ads failed to make the connection between what the company is doing for the environment and how this affects individual consumers.[58] Roper ASW conducts an annual "Green Gauge" consumer-marketing poll, which has found that many consumers don't buy green products because they fear they will not work as well as others. And despite all of the environmental claims made by marketers, consumers are more interested in convenience than ideology.[59]

If advertising were as powerful as the critics claim, we would not see products with multimillion-dollar advertising budgets failing in the marketplace. The reality is that consumers do have a choice and they are not being forced to buy. Consumers ignore ads for products and services they do not really need or that fail to interest them (see Exhibit 22-11).

Exhibit 22-11 The AAAA responds to the claim that advertising makes consumers buy things they do not need

Advertising and Stereotyping

Advertising is often accused of creating and perpetuating stereotypes through its portrayal of women, ethnic minorities, and other groups.

Women The portrayal of women in advertising is an issue that has received a great deal of attention through the years.[60] Advertising has received much criticism for stereotyping women and failing to recognize the changing role of women in our society. Critics have argued that advertising often depicts women as preoccupied with beauty, household duties, and motherhood or shows them as decorative objects or sexually provocative figures. The various research studies conducted through the years show a consistent picture of gender stereotyping that has varied little over time. Portrayals of adult women in American television and print advertising have emphasized passivity, deference, lack of intelligence and credibility, and punishment for high levels of efforts. In contrast, men have been portrayed as constructive, powerful, autonomous, and achieving.[61]

Research on gender stereotyping in advertising targeted to children has found a pattern of results similar to that reported for adults. A recent study found sex-role stereotyping in television advertising targeted at children in the United States as well as in Australia.[62] Boys are generally shown as being more knowledgeable, active, aggressive, and instrumental

than girls. Nonverbal behaviors involving dominance and control are associated more with boys than girls. Advertising directed toward children has also been shown to feature more boys than girls, to position boys in more dominant, active roles, and to use male voice-overs more frequently than female ones.[63] A recent study examining race and gender stereotyping of children's advertising on the Turner Cartoon Network found that the primary target for most of the commercials was active, white boys. Girls were portrayed in traditional roles and shown performing limited passive, indoor activities, while boys were shown in the outdoor world engaging in more exciting and active things.[64]

Feminist groups such as the National Organization for Women (NOW) and the Sexual Assault Prevention and Awareness Center argue that advertising that portrays women as sex objects contributes to violence against women. These groups often protest to advertisers and their agencies about ads they find insulting to women and have even called for boycotts against offending advertisers. NOW has also been critical of advertisers for the way they portray women in advertising for clothing, cosmetics, and other products. The organization feels that many of these ads contribute to the epidemic of eating disorders and smoking among women and girls who hope such means will help them control their weight.[65]

While sexism and stereotyping still exist, advertising's portrayal of women is improving in many areas. Many advertisers have begun to recognize the importance of portraying women realistically. The increase in the number of working women has resulted not only in women having more influence in family decision making but also in more single-female households, which mean more independent purchasers.

Researchers Steven Kates and Glenda Shaw-Garlock argue that the transformed social positioning of women in North American society is perhaps the most important social development of this century.[66] They note that as women have crossed the boundary from the domestic sphere to the professional arena, expectations and representations of women have changed as well. For example, a number of magazines, such as *MS* and *Working Woman,* now incorporate and appeal to the sociocultural shifts in women's lives. Many advertisers are now depicting women in a diversity of roles that reflect their changing place in society. In many ads, the stereotypic character traits attributed to women have shifted from weak and dependent to strong and autonomous.[67]

Some advertisers have found that being more sensitive to women customers can influence their purchase behavior. For example, Maidenform ran a campaign critical of negative stereotyping of women that significantly increased sales (Exhibit 22-12).

Exhibit 22-12 Maidenform's campaign lamenting the stereotyping of women resulted in a significant increase in sales

Somehow, women always seem to be portrayed like this.
Or like this.
Like this.

Or like this.
Like this.
Or like this.
While there are many stereotypes of women...

there aren't many women who fit them.
A simple truth known by all women . . . most men . . . and one lingerie company.

Exhibit 22-13 Ikea broke new ground with this ad showing an interracial couple shopping for furniture

Blacks and Hispanics African-Americans and Hispanics have also been the target of stereotyping in advertising. For many years, advertisers virtually ignored all non-white ethnic groups as identifiable subcultures and viable markets. Ads were rarely targeted to these ethnic groups, and the use of blacks and Hispanics as spokespeople, communicators, models, or actors in ads was very limited.[68]

Several studies in the late 1980s and early 90s examined the incidence of minorities in advertising. A study conducted in 1987 found that 11 percent of the people appearing in commercials were African-Americans.[69] Another study conducted two years later found that African-Americans appeared in 26 percent of all ads on network TV that used live models but Hispanics appeared in only 6 percent of the commercials with live models. The researchers also found that TV ads in which blacks appeared were overwhelmingly integrated and the blacks were likely to have played either minor or background roles in the majority of the ads.[70] A study conducted in 1995 found that 17 percent of prime-time network TV ads featured African-Americans as dominant characters and the majority of commercials featured them in minor roles.[71]

Although research suggests that the number of African-Americans shown as dominant characters has not increased dramatically, many advertisers are changing blacks' social and role status in advertising. For example, blacks are increasingly being shown in executive positions in many ads. FedEx said that a commercial featuring a black female executive beating out her white male adversaries in a conference call showdown over a high-stakes business deal was one of its most successful ads in years.[72]

Ads are increasingly likely to be racially integrated. Recently some advertisers have begun breaking the taboo against suggesting interracial attraction. For example, furniture retailer Ikea ran a TV commercial showing an interracial couple shopping for a "daddy chair" and discussing their plans to conceive[73] (Exhibit 22-13). Advertisers are also finding that advertising developed specifically for the African-American market, such as the Head & Shoulders ad shown in Exhibit 22-14 is an effective way of reaching this ethnic market. A recent study by Corliss L. Green found that ads targeting African-Americans through racially targeted media, especially with race-based products, benefit from featuring African-American models with a dominant presence in the ad.[74]

Another minority group that has received attention recently from those researching advertising and stereotyping is Asian-Americans, whose affluence, high education, work ethic, and growth rate has made this group a popular target market. A recent study of prime-time TV

Exhibit 22-14 Many marketers are creating ads specifically for the African-American market

commercials found that Asian male and female models are overrepresented in terms of their proportion of the U.S. population (3.6 percent), appearing in 8.4 percent of the commercials. However, Asian models were more likely than members of other minority groups to appear in background roles, and Asian women were rarely depicted in major roles. The study also found that portrayals of Asian-Americans put more emphasis on the work ethic and less on other aspects of their lives.[75]

There is little question that advertising has been guilty of stereotyping women and ethnic groups in the past and, in some cases, still does so. But as the role of women changes, advertisers are changing their portrayals to remain accurate and appeal to their target audience. Advertisers are also trying to increase the incidence of minority groups in ads while avoiding stereotypes and negative role portrayals. They are being careful to avoid ethnic stereotyping and striving to develop advertising that has specific appeals to various ethnic groups.

Other Groups While the focus here has been on women and ethnic minorities, some other groups feel they are victims of stereotyping by advertisers. Many groups in our society are battling against stereotyping and discrimination, and companies must consider whether their ads might offend them. It is increasingly difficult not to offend some segment of the public. Creative personnel in agencies are feeling restricted as their ideas are squelched out of concern that they might offend someone or be misinterpreted.[76] However, advertisers must be sensitive to the portrayal of specific types of people in their ads, for both ethical and commercial reasons.

One area where significant changes have taken place recently is in advertising targeted to gay consumers. In 1995 Ikea broke new ground with a TV commercial featuring a gay couple shopping for furniture. For years beer companies targeted this market by placing ads in local gay media to support or sponsor AIDS awareness, Gay Pride festivals, and the Gay Games. However, a number of beer companies, including Anheuser-Busch and Miller Brewing Co., now run gay-specific, brand-specific ads in national gay publications.[77]

A number of other companies, including IBM and United Airlines, also now run ads with gay themes, although they generally confine them to magazines and newspapers targeting the gay market. While a TV commercial or print ad with a gay reference occasionally runs in the mainstream media, it usually is so subtle or ambiguous that many heterosexuals do not perceive it as a gay message. However, in 2000 the Gay Financial Network, an online company (gfn.com) with a gay-friendly financial news and information website, became the first gay-oriented company to advertise in major U.S. business news and entertainment publications.[78] The gfn.com ads take a gentle swipe at homophobia in the business world (Exhibit 22-15).

More advertisers are turning to gay themes in their mainstream commercials, though often subtly. However, few run these ads on network television; they limit them to spot TV and local stations in more gay-friendly cities such as New York, Los Angeles, and San Francisco. The Miller Brewing Co. did take a bold step recently by airing a gay-themed commercial on network television. The ad was for Miller Lite beer and showed a gay couple holding hands in a straight bar to the dismay of two women who are interested in them.[79]

Exhibit 22-15 The Gay Financial Network broke barriers by becoming the first gay-oriented company to advertise in the mainstream media

Advertising and the Media The fact that advertising plays such an important role in financing the media has led to concern that advertisers may influence or even control the media. It is well documented that *economic*

censorship occurs, whereby the media avoid certain topics or even present biased news coverage, in acquiescence to advertiser demands.[80] In fact, Professors Lawrence Soley and Robert Craig say, "The assertion that advertisers attempt to influence what the public sees, hears, and reads in the mass media is perhaps the most damning of all criticisms of advertising, but this criticism isn't acknowledged in most advertising textbooks."[81] We will address this important issue in this book by considering arguments on both sides.

Arguments Supporting Advertiser Control Advertising is the primary source of revenue for nearly all the news and entertainment media in the United States. And because advertising pays the bills, newspaper and magazine publishers, as well as TV and radio networks and station executives, must keep their advertisers happy. Some critics charge that the media's dependence on advertisers' support makes them susceptible to various forms of influence, including exerting control over the editorial content of magazines and newspapers; biasing editorial opinions to favor the position of an advertiser; limiting coverage of a controversial story that might reflect negatively on a company; and influencing the program content of television.

Newspapers and magazines receive nearly 70 percent of their revenue from advertising; commercial TV and radio derive virtually all their income from advertisers. Small, financially insecure newspapers, magazines, or broadcast stations are the most susceptible to pressure from advertisers, particularly companies that account for a large amount of the media outlet's advertising revenue. A local newspaper may be reluctant to print an unfavorable story about a car dealer or supermarket chain on whose advertising it depends. For example, a few years ago more than 40 car dealers canceled their ads in the *San Jose Mercury News* when the paper printed an article titled "A Car Buyer's Guide to Sanity." The dealers objected to the tone of the article, which they felt implied consumers should consider car dealers unethical adversaries in the negotiation process.[82] A survey of 147 daily newspapers found that more than 90 percent of editors have been pressured by advertisers and more than one-third of them said advertisers had succeeded in influencing news at their papers.[83]

While larger, more financially stable media should be less susceptible to an advertiser's influence, they may still be reluctant to carry stories detrimental to companies that purchase large amounts of advertising time or space.[84] For example, since cigarette commercials were taken off radio and TV in 1970, tobacco companies have allocated most of their budgets to the print media. The tobacco industry outspends all other national advertisers in newspapers, and cigarettes constitute the second-largest category of magazine advertising (behind transportation). This has led to charges that magazines and newspapers avoid articles on the hazards of smoking to protect this important source of ad revenue.[85] One study found that magazines relying on cigarette advertising are far less likely than others to publish stories about the health hazards associated with smoking.[86]

Individual TV stations and even the major networks also can be influenced by advertisers. Programming decisions are made largely on the basis of what shows will attract the most viewers and thus be most desirable to advertisers. Critics say this often results in lower-quality television as educational, cultural, and informative programming is usually sacrificed for shows that get high ratings and appeal to the mass markets. It is well recognized that advertisers often avoid TV shows that deal with controversial issues. Most advertisers also have contract stipulations allowing them to cancel a media buy if, after prescreening a show, they are uncomfortable with its content or feel sponsorship of it may reflect poorly on their company.

Advertisers have also been accused of pressuring the networks to change their programming. Many advertisers have withdrawn commercials from programs that contain too much sex or violence, often in response to threatened boycotts of their products by consumers if they advertise on these shows. For example, groups such as the American Family Association have been fighting sex and violence in TV programs by calling for boycotts. A number of companies, including Procter & Gamble, Mars Inc., and Kraft Foods, pulled their advertising from certain talk shows, like those of Jerry Springer, because of some of their incendiary topics.[87]

Arguments against Advertiser Control The commercial media's dependence on advertising means advertisers can exert influence on their character, content, and coverage of certain issues. However, media executives offer several reasons why advertisers do not exert undue influence over the media.

First, they point out it is in the best interest of the media not to be influenced too much by advertisers. To retain public confidence, they must report the news fairly and accurately without showing bias or attempting to avoid controversial issues. Media executives point to the vast array of topics they cover and the investigative reporting they often do as evidence of their objectivity. They want to build a large audience for their publications or stations so that they can charge more for advertising space and time.

Media executives also note that an advertiser needs the media more than they need any individual advertiser, particularly when the medium has a large audience or does a good job of reaching a specific market segment. Many publications and stations have a very broad base of advertising support and can afford to lose an advertiser that attempts to exert too much influence. This is particularly true for the larger, more established, financially secure media. For example, a consumer-product company would find it difficult to reach its target audience without network TV and could not afford to boycott a network if it disagreed with a station's editorial policy or program content. Even the local advertiser in a small community may be dependent on the local newspaper, since it may be the most cost-effective media option available.

Most magazine and newspaper publishers insist they do not allow advertiser pressure to influence their editorial content. They argue that they have long regarded the formal separation of their news and business departments as essential to their independence and credibility. This separation is often referred to as "The Wall" and is often spoken of with a mixture of reverence and trepidation.[88] Many magazines and newspapers have traditionally discouraged employees on the publishing side—including advertising, circulation, and other business departments—from interacting with those on the editorial side, who write and edit the articles. This is done by separating editorial and advertising offices, barring the sales force from reading articles before they are printed, and prohibiting editorial employees from participating in advertising sales calls.

Most magazines and newspapers are very concerned over maintaining the concept of The Wall and ensuring that decisions on the writing, editing, and publishing of stories are made on journalistic merit rather than on whether they will attract or repel advertisers. However, the new economics of the publishing industry is making it difficult to maintain the separation: competition from cable TV, direct mail, and the Internet is increasing, and newspaper and magazine readership continues to decline. There have been several well-publicized situations in recent years where major magazines and newspapers were found to have given favorable editorial consideration to an advertiser.[89]

The media in the United States are basically supported by advertising; this means we can enjoy them for free or for a fraction of what they would cost without advertising.[90] The alternative to an advertiser-supported media system is support by users through higher subscription costs for the print media and a fee or pay-per-view system with TV. The ad in Exhibit 22-16, part of a campaign by the International Advertising Association, explains how adver-tising lowers the cost of print media for consumers. Another alternative is government-supported media like those in many other countries, but this runs counter to most people's desire for freedom of the press. Although not perfect, our system of advertising-supported media provides the best option for receiving information and entertainment.

Exhibit 22-16 This ad points out how advertising lowers the cost of newspapers for consumers

Summarizing Social Effects

We have examined a number of issues and have attempted to analyze the arguments for and against them. Many people have reservations about the impact of advertising and promotion on society. The numerous rules, regulations, policies, and guidelines marketers comply with do not cover every

Exhibit 22-17 This ad campaign for the Boys & Girls Clubs is an example of the pro bono work often done by advertising agencies for nonprofit organizations

advertising and promotional situation. Moreover, what one individual views as distasteful or unethical may be acceptable to another.

Negative opinions regarding advertising and other forms of promotion have been around almost as long as the field itself, and it is unlikely they will ever disappear. However, the industry must address the various concerns about the effects of advertising and other forms of promotion on society. Advertising is a very powerful institution, but it will remain so only as long as consumers have faith in the ads they see and hear every day. Many of the problems discussed here can be avoided if individual decision makers make ethics an important element of the IMC planning process.

The primary focus of this discussion of social effects has been on the way advertising is used (or abused) in the marketing of products and services. It is important to note that advertising and other IMC tools, such as direct marketing and public relations, are also used to promote worthy causes and to deal with problems facing society (drunk driving, drug abuse, and the AIDS crisis, among others). For example, IMC Perspective 22-3 discusses how the Partnership for a Drug Free America and now the U.S. government are using advertising to help fight the war against drugs in the United States. Campaigns for nonprofit organizations and worthy causes are often developed pro bono by advertising agencies, and free advertising time and space are donated by the media.

Exhibit 22-17 shows an ad from a very successful public service campaign for the Boys & Girls Clubs of America featuring actor Denzel Washington. The campaign was designed to establish an image to distinguish the Boys & Girls Clubs from other public service groups and to encourage adults to organize clubs.[91]

Economic Effects of Advertising

Advertising plays an important role in a free-market system like ours by making consumers aware of products and services and providing them with information for decision making. Advertising's economic role goes beyond this basic function, however. It is a powerful force that can affect the functioning of our entire economic system (Exhibit 22-18).

Advertising can encourage consumption and foster economic growth. It not only informs customers of available goods and services but also facilitates entry into markets

IMC PERSPECTIVE 22-3

Linking Drug Use with Terrorism

For nearly two decades advertising has been used to address the problem of illicit drug use in the United States. Initially the use of advertising in the war against drugs was waged through the Partnership for a Drug Free America, which is a private, nonprofit coalition of professionals from the communications industry whose collective mission is to reduce the demand for drugs in America through media communication. The partnership was founded in 1986 as the advertising industry's affirmative response to the crack cocaine epidemic in America. Since its founding, more than 600 commercials have been created by advertising agencies that work on these ads on a pro bono basis, donating the time, talent, and services of their creative staffs. More than $2.8 billion in media time also has been donated to the Partnership's national campaign, making it the largest public service ad campaign in history.

In 1997 the U.S. government entered the media war on drugs when the Clinton administration announced a $2 billion federally sponsored five-year campaign to keep kids from using drugs. As part of this effort the U.S. Office of National Drug Control Policy (ONDCP) was created, and the Ogilvy & Mather advertising agency was hired to manage the account and handle the media buying while doing some minor creative work. While the government's drug control office is separate from the Partnership for a Drug Free America, many of the initial ads used in the campaign were pulled from the Partnership's inventory, such as the updated version of the famous "This is your brain on drugs" showing actress Rachel Lee Cook using a frying pan to smash apart a kitchen as she shouts, "This is your brain. This is your brain on heroin."

Over the past five years the Partnership has developed the themes for the drug office ads and selected the ad agencies to produce the ads. The ONDCP has provided nearly $200 million a year in funding for the Partnership's antidrug efforts, primarily to help pay for advertising time and space. However, while the two organizations are supposed to be working together in the battle to combat drug use, they have gone in different directions recently in their approaches to how advertising can best be used to address the problem.

The perspective taken by the Partnership in most of its ads has been to discourage drug use by helping people, particularly children and teenagers, understand the dangers of using them. Many of the ads developed by the Partnership over the past 16 years have focused on resistance techniques that young people can use when confronted with the choice of using drugs, positive alternatives to drug use, and the importance of parental involvement as a way of deterring drug use. However, under its new director, John P. Walters, the ONDCP is taking a different perspective by arguing that the way to deal with the drug problem is to eliminate the flow of drugs at their source. To accomplish this goal, the ONDCP commissioned Ogilvy & Mather to develop an advertising campaign outside the normal channels of the Partnership for a Drug Free America, one linking drug use with the support of terrorism.

The first ads in the campaign ran during the 2002 Super Bowl and took advantage of the public's outrage over the terrorist attacks on the World Trade Center that occurred on September 11, 2001. The commercials featured footage of assault weapons, duct tape, and explosives and implied that the weapons used by terrorists were funded by drug sales in the United States. Some groups were critical of the ads and the government's effort to draw a connection between drug money and terrorism, arguing that it was unfair to blame nonviolent drug users for the actions of terrorists. However, the director of the campaign for the ONDCP described the reaction to the first set of ads as phenomenal, noting that it generated debate on the drug issue.

Eight months after the first ads ran, ONDCP followed with another set of ads that are designed to refute the notion that drug use is a victimless crime by linking drug use to crime and terrorism. The drug office noted that viewers of the initial ads had a difficult time believing that the drug-terrorism link

applied to marijuana purchases. Thus the second set of ads more closely shows the connection between drug use and terrorism. One of the commercials begins with a pretty young woman buying a dime bag of marijuana and ends with a child being shot in drug-warfare crossfire. Another links a marijuana user to various parties in the supply chain and ends with a connection to a drug cartel.

Some critics of the drug-terrorism ads have suggested that they create the false paradigm that terrorism is caused by drugs rather than the illegality of drugs. Groups such as the National Organization for Marijuana Legalization contend that the ads argue more for decriminalization of certain drugs than abstinence. However, the ONDCP feels that the point of the ads is summarized quite well by the onscreen message at the end of each spot: "Drug money supports terrible things. If you buy drugs, you might too."

Sources: Ira Tenowitz, "Ads Linking Drugs, Terrorism Return," *Advertising Age,* Nov. 16, 2002, pp. 1, 45; Vanessa O'Connell, "Drug Czar Says Ad Campaign Has Flopped," *The Wall Street Journal,* May 14, 2002, pp. B1, 10; Ira Tenowitz, "White House Buys Anti-Terror Super Bowl Spots," www.adage.com. Jan. 30, 2002.

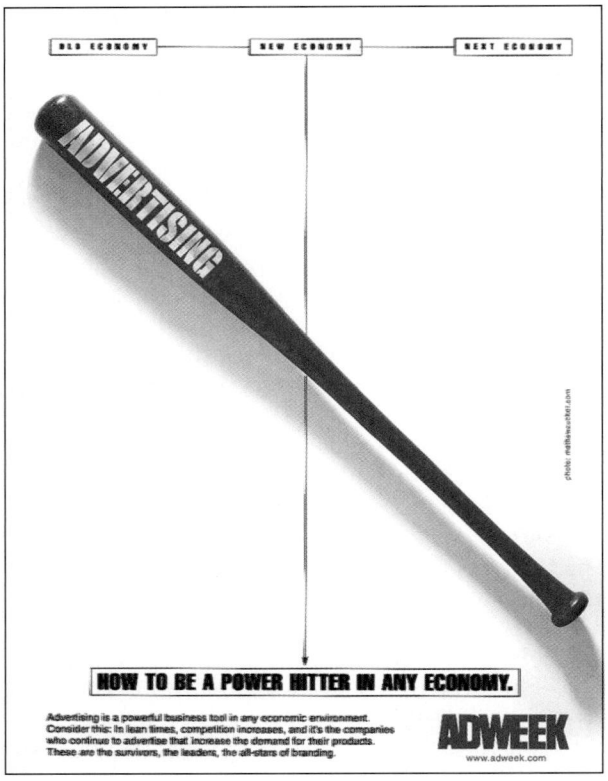

Exhibit 22-18 This ad promotes the economic value of advertising

for a firm or a new product or brand; leads to economies of scale in production, marketing, and distribution, which in turn lead to lower prices; and hastens the acceptance of new products and the rejection of inferior products.

Critics of advertising view it as a detrimental force that not only fails to perform its basic function of information provision adequately but also adds to the cost of products and services and discourages competition and market entry, leading to industrial concentration and higher prices for consumers.

In their analysis of advertising, economists generally take a macroeconomic perspective: they consider the economic impact of advertising on an entire industry or on the economy as a whole rather than its effect on an individual company or brand. Our examination of the economic impact of advertising focuses on these broader macro-level issues. We consider its effects on consumer choice, competition, and product costs and prices.

Effects on Consumer Choice

Some critics say advertising hampers consumer choice, as large advertisers use their power to limit our options to a few well-advertised brands. Economists argue that advertising is used to achieve (1) **differentiation,** whereby the products or services of large advertisers are perceived as unique or better than competitors', and (2) brand loyalty, which enables large national advertisers to gain control of the market, usually at the expense of smaller brands.

Larger companies often end up charging a higher price and achieve a more dominant position in the market than smaller firms that cannot compete against them and their large advertising budgets. When this occurs, advertising not only restricts the choice alternatives to a few well-known, heavily advertised brands but also becomes a substitute for competition based on price or product improvements.

Heavily advertised brands dominate the market in certain product categories, such as soft drinks, beer, and cereals.[92] But advertising generally does not create brand monopolies and reduce the opportunities for new products to be introduced to consumers. In most product categories, a number of different brands are on the store shelves and thousands of new products are introduced every year. The opportunity to advertise gives companies the incentive to develop new brands and improve their existing ones. When a successful new product such as a personal computer is introduced, competitors quickly follow and use advertising to inform consumers about their brand and attempt to convince them it is superior to the original. Companies like

Virgin Atlantic Airways recognize that advertising has been an important part of their success (Exhibit 22-19).

Effects on Competition

One of the most common criticisms economists have about advertising concerns its effects on competition. They argue that power in the hands of large firms with huge advertising budgets creates a **barrier to entry,** which makes it difficult for other firms to enter the market. This results in less competition and higher prices. Economists note that smaller firms already in the market find it difficult to compete against the large advertising budgets of the industry leaders and are often driven out of business. For example, in the U.S. beer industry, the number of national brewers has declined dramatically. In their battle for market share, industry giants Anheuser-Busch and Miller increased their ad budgets substantially and reaped market shares that total over 60 percent. Anheuser-Busch alone spent nearly $700 million on advertising in 2002. However, these companies are spending much less per barrel than smaller firms, making it very difficult for the latter to compete.

Large advertisers clearly enjoy certain competitive advantages. First, there are **economies of scale** in advertising, particularly with respect to factors such as media costs. Firms such as Procter & Gamble and PepsiCo, which spend over $2 billion a year on advertising and promotion, are able to make large media buys at a reduced rate and allocate them to their various products.

"Back in 1983, the world wasn't crying out for another airline to London.

People accepted what was available. But then, they didn't know any better.

As a frequent flyer myself, I always felt being cooped up in a plane could be made more enjoyable. If you had a guest at your house you wouldn't sit him facing a blank wall and put a rubber chicken in his lap, now would you?

So I set out to create an airline people would actually enjoy flying.

I'd give them more space to sit in, more flight attendants to serve them, and more forms of entertainment to...entertain them.

I'd also offer 'Upper Class' passengers the only sleeper seats available in any business class to London. A Sony Video Walkman™ with 25 films to choose from and free chauffeured limousine service to and from each airport. And, of course, gourmet meals and vintage wine in lieu of foul fowl.

Now, having all these niceties would have done me absolutely no good if I kept their existence to myself. So I put every available dollar into getting the word out.

The dollars were hardly momentous at first. But that didn't stop us. We applied some creativity, and over a Memorial day weekend, while everyone crowded the parks and beaches, we introduced Virgin Atlantic Airways to the people of New York. With skywriting.

Virgin is now 7 years old, serving 5 major airports and has the highest transatlantic load factor of any airline.

Print, television and radio messages have replaced skywriting. And more than 40 million advertising dollars later, no one has shed a tear for rubber chickens."

"We spent over 40 million dollars to kill a rubber chicken."

Richard Branson, Chairman, Virgin Atlantic Airways.

AAAA
American Association of Advertising Agencies

If you would like to learn more about the power of advertising, please write to Department D, AAAA, 666 Third Avenue, New York, New York 10017, enclosing a check for five dollars. You will receive our booklet *If Works! How Investment Spending in Advertising Pays Off.* Please allow 4 to 6 weeks for delivery.
Sony Video Walkman® is a trademark of Sony. This advertisement prepared by Korey, Kay & Partners, New York.

Exhibit 22-19 Virgin Atlantic Airways chair Richard Branson acknowledges the importance of advertising

Large advertisers usually sell more of a product or service, which means they may have lower production costs and can allocate more monies to advertising, so they can afford the costly but more efficient media like network television. Their large advertising outlays also give them more opportunity to differentiate their products and develop brand loyalty. To the extent that these factors occur, smaller competitors are at a disadvantage and new competitors are deterred from entering the market.

While advertising may have an anticompetitive effect on a market, there is no clear evidence that advertising alone reduces competition, creates barriers to entry, and thus increases market concentration. Lester Telser noted that high levels of advertising are not always found in industries where firms have a large market share. He found an inverse relationship between intensity of product class advertising and stability of market share for the leading brands.[93] These findings run contrary to many economists' belief that industries controlled by a few firms have high advertising expenditures, resulting in stable brand shares for market leaders.

Defenders of advertising say it is unrealistic to attribute a firm's market dominance and barriers to entry solely to advertising. There are a number of other factors, such as price, product quality, distribution effectiveness, production efficiencies, and competitive strategies. For many years, products such as Coors beer and Hershey chocolate bars were dominant brands even though these companies spent little on advertising. Hershey did not advertise at all until 1970. For 66 years, the company relied on the quality of its products, its favorable reputation and image among consumers, and its extensive channels of distribution to market its brands. Industry leaders often tend to dominate markets because they have superior product quality and the best management and competitive strategies, not simply the biggest advertising budgets.[94]

While market entry against large, established competitors is difficult, companies with a quality product at a reasonable price often find a way to break in. Moreover, they usually find that advertising actually facilitates their market entry by making it possible to communicate the benefits and features of their new product or brand to consumers. For example, South Korea's Daewoo Motor Co. entered the U.S. automotive market in 1998 and has used advertising to create a brand identity for its cars.

Exhibit 22-20 Advertising is very important to companies such as Daewoo Motor America as it enters the U.S. market

Exhibit 22-21 This ad refutes the argument that reducing advertising expenditures will lead to lower prices

Exhibit 22-20 shows an ad for the company's flagship Leganza model, which is positioned as offering "affordable luxury."

Effects on Product Costs and Prices

A major area of debate among economists, advertisers, consumer advocates, and policymakers concerns the effects of advertising on product costs and prices. Critics argue that advertising increases the prices consumers pay for products and services. First, they say the large sums of money spent advertising a brand constitute an expense that must be covered and the consumer ends up paying for it through higher prices. This is a common criticism from consumer advocates. Several studies show that firms with higher relative prices advertise their products more intensely than do those with lower relative prices.[95] As discussed in the previous chapter, concern has been expressed that the tremendous increase in direct-to-consumer drug advertising by pharmaceutical companies in recent years is driving up the cost of prescription drugs. Critics argue that the millions of dollars spent on advertising and other forms of promotion are an expense that must be covered by charging higher prices.[96]

A second way advertising can result in higher prices is by increasing product differentiation and adding to the perceived value of the product in consumers' minds. Paul Farris and Mark Albion note that product differentiation occupies a central position in theories of advertising's economic effects.[97] The fundamental premise is that advertising increases the perceived differences between physically homogeneous products and enables advertised brands to command a premium price without an increase in quality.

Critics of advertising generally point to the differences in prices between national brands and private-label brands that are physically similar, such as aspirin or tea bags, as evidence of the added value created by advertising. They see consumers' willingness to pay more for heavily advertised national brands rather than purchasing the lower-priced, non-advertised brand as wasteful and irrational. The prescription drug industry is again a very good example of this, as critics argue that the increase in advertising is encouraging consumers to request brand-name drugs and steering them away from lower-priced generics.[98] However, consumers do not always buy for rational, functional reasons. The emotional, psychological, and social benefits derived from purchasing a national brand are important to many people. Moreover, say Albion and Farris,

> Unfortunately there seems to be no single way to measure product differentiation, let alone determine how much is excessive or attributable to the effects of advertising . . . Both price insensitivity and brand loyalty could be created by a number of factors such as higher product quality, better packaging, favorable use experience and market position. They are probably related to each other but need not be the result of advertising.[99]

Proponents of advertising offer several other counterarguments to the claim that advertising increases prices. They acknowledge that advertising costs are at least partly paid for by consumers. But advertising may help lower the overall cost of a product more than enough to offset them. For example, advertising may help firms achieve economies of scale in production and distribution by providing information to and stimulating demand among mass markets. These economies of scale help cut the cost of producing and marketing the product, which can lead to lower prices—if the advertiser chooses to pass the cost savings on to the consumer. The ad in Exhibit 22-21, from a campaign sponsored by the American Association of Advertising Agencies, emphasizes this point.

Advertising can also lower prices by making a market more competitive, which usually leads to greater price competition. A study by Lee Benham found that prices of eyeglasses were 25 to 30 percent higher in states that banned eyeglass advertising than in those that permitted it.[100] Robert Steiner analyzed the toy industry and concluded that advertising resulted in lower consumer prices. He argued that curtailment of TV advertising would drive up consumer prices for toys.[101] Finally, advertising is a means to market entry rather than a deterrent and helps stimulate product innovation, which makes markets more competitive and helps keep prices down.

Overall, it is difficult to reach any firm conclusions regarding the relationship between advertising and prices. After an extensive review of this area, Farris and Albion concluded, "The evidence connecting manufacturer advertising to prices is neither complete nor definitive . . . consequently, we cannot say whether advertising is a tool of market efficiency or market power without further research."[102]

Economist James Ferguson argues that advertising cannot increase the cost per unit of quality to consumers because if it did, consumers would not continue to respond positively to advertising.[103] He believes advertising lowers the costs of information about brand qualities, leads to increases in brand quality, and lowers the average price per unit of quality.

Summarizing Economic Effects

Albion and Farris suggest that economists' perspectives can be divided into two principal schools of thought that make different assumptions regarding the influence of advertising on the economy.[104] Figure 22-3 summarizes the main points of the "advertising equals market power" and "advertising equals information" perspectives.

Advertising Equals Market Power

The belief that advertising equals market power reflects traditional economic thinking and views advertising as a way to change consumers' tastes, lower their sensitivity to price, and build brand loyalty among buyers of advertised brands. This results in higher profits and market power for large advertisers, reduces competition in the market, and leads to higher prices and fewer choices for

Figure 22-3 Two schools of thought on advertising's role in the economy

Advertising = Market Power		Advertising = Information
Advertising affects consumer preferences and tastes, changes product attributes, and differentiates the product from competitive offerings.	Advertising	Advertising informs consumers about product attributes but does not change the way they value those attributes.
Consumers become brand loyal and less price sensitive and perceive fewer substitutes for advertised brands.	Consumer buying behavior	Consumers become more price sensitive and buy best "value." Only the relationship between price and quality affects elasticity for a given product.
Potential entrants must overcome established brand loyalty and spend relatively more on advertising.	Barriers to entry	Advertising makes entry possible for new brands because it can communicate product attributes to consumers.
Firms are insulated from market competition and potential rivals; concentration increases, leaving firms with more discretionary power.	Industry structure and market power	Consumers can compare competitive offerings easily and competitive rivalry increases. Efficient firms remain, and as the inefficient leave, new entrants appear; the effect on concentration is ambiguous.
Firms can charge higher prices and are not as likely to compete on quality or price dimensions. Innovation may be reduced.	Market conduct	More informed consumers pressure firms to lower prices and improve quality; new entrants facilitate innovation.
High prices and excessive profits accrue to advertisers and give them even more incentive to advertise their products. Output is restricted compared with conditions of perfect competition.	Market performance	Industry prices decrease. The effect on profits due to increased competition and increased efficiency is ambiguous.

consumers. Proponents of this viewpoint generally have negative attitudes regarding the economic impact of advertising.

Advertising Equals Information The belief that advertising equals information takes a more positive view of advertising's economic effects. This model sees advertising as providing consumers with useful information, increasing their price sensitivity (which moves them toward lower-priced products), and increasing competition in the market. Advertising is viewed as a way to communicate with consumers and tell them about a product and its major features and attributes. More informed and knowledgeable consumers pressure companies to provide high-quality products at lower prices. Efficient firms remain in the market, whereas inefficient firms leave as new entrants appear. Proponents of this model believe the economic effects of advertising are favorable and think it contributes to more efficient and competitive markets.

It is unlikely the debate over the economic effects and value of advertising will be resolved soon. Many economists will continue to take a negative view of advertising and its effects on the functioning of the economy, while advertisers will continue to view it as an efficient way for companies to communicate with their customers and an essential component of our economic system. The International Advertising Association has been running a campaign for several years to convince consumers around the world of the economic value of advertising. Ads like the one shown in Exhibit 22-22 are used in countries such as China and Russia, where consumers are unfamiliar with the concept of advertising. The goal of the campaign is to get consumers in these countries to recognize the role advertising plays in contributing to their economic well-being.[105]

WHEN ADVERTISING DOES ITS JOB, MILLIONS OF PEOPLE KEEP THEIRS.

Good advertising doesn't just inform. It sells. It helps move product and keep businesses in business. Every time an ad arouses a consumer's interest enough to result in a purchase, it keeps a company going strong. And it helps secure the jobs of the people who work there.

Advertising. That's the way it works.

The global partnership of advertisers, agencies and media

Exhibit 22-22 This ad is part of a global campaign by the International Advertising Association to educate consumers about the economic value of advertising

Figure 22-4, excerpts from a speech given by famous adman Leo Burnett, summarizes the perspective of most advertising people on the economic effects of advertising. Many advertising and marketing experts agree that advertising and promotion play an important role in helping to expand consumer demand for new products and services and in helping marketers differentiate their existing brands. IMC Perspective 22-4 discusses a recent campaign developed by the American Advertising Federation to illustrate the economic power and value of advertising.

Figure 22-4 This message describes the positive economic effects of advertising

To me it means that if we believe to any degree whatsoever in the economic system under which we live, in a high standard of living and in high employment, advertising is the most efficient known way of moving goods in practically every product class.

My proof is that millions of businessmen have chosen advertising over and over again in the operations of their business. Some of their decisions may have been wrong, but they must have thought they were right or they wouldn't go back to be stung twice by the same kind of bee.

It's a pretty safe bet that in the next 10 years many Americans will be using products and devices that no one in this room has even heard of. Judging purely by past performance, American advertising can be relied on to make them known and accepted overnight at the lowest possible prices.

Advertising, of course, makes possible our unparalleled variety of magazines, newspapers, business publications, and radio and television stations.

It must be said that without advertising we would have a far different nation, and one that would be much the poorer—not merely in material commodities, but in the life of the spirit.

Leo Burnett

Source: Excerpts from a speech given by Leo Burnett on the American Association of Advertising Agencies' 50th anniversary, April 20, 1967.

IMC PERSPECTIVE 22-4

The AAF Promotes the Value of Advertising

The advertising industry in the United States continually promotes the value of advertising. Major advertising associations, such as the American Association of Advertising Agencies (AAAA) and the American Advertising Federation (AAF), along with trade associations for various media, such as the Magazine Publishers of America, often run campaigns reminding the general public of advertising's contributions to the economy as well as to consumers' social well-being. However, sometimes the industry must also remind advertisers themselves of the value of advertising.

In 1998 a nationwide survey of 1,800 top corporate executives revealed that modern business fails to appreciate the true value of advertising. Although advertising was valued, the survey showed that executives do not truly appreciate its strategic capacity and that the industry's knowledge of consumers was not fully understood. Of the marketers surveyed, 27 percent indicated that advertising would be among the first budget items cut in a sales downturn. Concerned by these results, the American Federation of Advertising, which is the advertising industry's primary trade organization, decided to take action to change the way advertising is viewed by companies. The AAF is a unifying voice for advertising and serves as a home base for advertisers, agencies, media companies, direct marketers, online publishers, and many other specialties that constitute the advertising industry.

The AAF decided that the best way to get marketers to recognize the value of advertising was to practice what it preaches, and thus an integrated marketing communications campaign was developed to redefine advertising in the eyes of corporate executives. The campaign is targeted at the "O's"—CEOs, COOs, CFOs, and CMOs—who are responsible for establishing and maintaining budget levels for advertising. The theme of the campaign is "Advertising: The way great brands get to be great brands," and it cautions corporate America not to neglect brand development. In today's business environment and time of economic challenge, the campaign stresses that advertising is more important than ever and plays a very significant role in building brand equity and profits.

The "Great Brands" campaign broke in October 2000 and initially was run in national newspapers such as *The Wall Street Journal, USA Today,* and *New York Times;* financial magazines such as *Forbes* and *Fortune;* and leading trade magazines such as *Advertising Age, Adweek, Mediaweek, Brandweek,* and *Brand Marketing.* The campaign featured successful brands such as Altoids, Intel, Coca-Cola, Energizer, Budweiser, and Sunkist. In early 2002 the campaign moved to television with the premier of two TV commercials. The 15-second spots feature the Coca-Cola and Intel brands. All media time and space for the campaign are donated; since it began, more than $4 million worth of media coverage has been given to run the ads. The creative work for the campaign is also done on a pro bono basis, by the Carmichael Lynch agency.

The AAF president and CEO, Wally Snyder, notes that the Great Brands campaign is a way to illustrate the economic power of advertising by featuring companies that are synonymous with quality advertising and for which advertising has played a critical role in building brand equity. His goal is to make sure that other marketers get the message regarding the value of advertising.

Sources: "AAF's 'Great Brands' Campaign Moves to Television," press release, AAF News, Jan. 29, 2002; "Advertising. The Way Great Brands Get to Be Great Brands," Great Brands Q&A, www.AAF.org.

Summary

Advertising is a very powerful institution and has been the target of considerable criticism regarding its social and economic impact. The criticism of advertising concerns the specific techniques and methods used as well as its effect on societal values, tastes, lifestyles, and behavior. Critics argue that advertising is deceptive and untruthful; that it is often offensive, irritating, or in poor taste; and that it exploits certain groups, such as children. Many people believe advertising should be informative only and advertisers should not use subjective claims, puffery, embellishment, or persuasive techniques.

Advertising often offends consumers by the type of appeal or manner of presentation used; sexually suggestive ads and nudity receive the most criticism. Advertisers say their ads are consistent with contemporary values and lifestyles and are appropriate for the target audiences they are attempting to reach. Advertising to children is an area of particular concern, since critics argue that children lack the experience, knowledge, and ability to process and evaluate persuasive advertising messages rationally. Although an FTC proposal to severely restrict advertising to children was defeated, it remains an issue.

The pervasiveness of advertising and its prevalence in the mass media have led critics to argue that it plays a major role in influencing and transmitting social values. Advertising has been charged with encouraging materialism, manipulating consumers to buy things they do not really want or need, perpetuating stereotypes through its portrayal of certain groups such as women, minorities, and the elderly, and controlling the media.

Advertising has also been scrutinized with regard to its economic effects. The basic economic role of advertising is to give consumers information that helps them make consumption decisions. Some people view advertising as a detrimental force that has a negative effect on competition, product costs, and consumer prices. Economists' perspectives regarding the effects of advertising follow two basic schools of thought: the advertising equals market power model and the advertising equals information model. Arguments consistent with each perspective were considered in analyzing the economic effects of advertising.

Key Terms

ethics, 751
shock advertising, 757
consumer socialization process, 760
materialism, 764
Protestant ethic, 764
differentiation, 774
barrier to entry, 775
economies of scale, 775

Discussion Questions

1. The opening vignette discusses how "branded content" and "advertainment" are the wave of the future. Discuss what is meant by these two concepts and why they are becoming popular among marketers. Why are many consumer watchdog groups such as Commercial Alert concerned over this trend?

2. Discuss the role of ethics in advertising and promotion. How do ethical considerations differ from legal considerations in developing an integrated marketing communications program?

3. What is meant by shock advertising? Evaluate the arguments for and against the use of shock advertising by marketers.

4. Ethical Perspective 22-1 discusses the clearance process used by the standards and practices departments of the four major television networks. Evaluate the effectiveness of this process from the perspective of the networks as well as advertisers.

5. Ethical Perspective 22-2 discusses how many companies are targeting their promotional programs to schools as a way of reaching the youth market. Do you think companies should allow companies to reach students through programs such as Channel One or by granting "pouring rights" to soft-drink bottlers? Evaluate the arguments for and against these programs.

6. A common criticism of advertising is that it stereotypes women. Discuss the ways this might occur. Do you think the Airwalk ad shown in Exhibit 22-6 is suggestive and symbolizes sexual submission?

7. Discuss the arguments for and against advertiser influence and/or control over the media. How might a newspaper or magazine avoid being influenced by advertisers?

8. IMC Perspective 22-3 discusses the advertising campaign developed by the U.S. Office of National Drug Control Policy linking drug use with the support of terrorism. Do you think these ads are an effective way of dealing with the drug problem? Why or why not?

9. Discuss how advertising can affect product costs and the prices consumers pay for products and services.

10. Discuss the two major perspectives of the economic impact of advertising: "advertising equals market power" versus "advertising equals information."

Glossary of Advertising and Promotion Terms

80/20 rule (2) The principle that 80 percent of sales volume for a product or service is generated by 20 percent of the customers.

5-W's model of communication (5) A model of the communications process that contains five basics elements: who? (source), says what? (message), in what way? (channel), to whom? (receiver), and with what effect? (feedback).

A

AIDA model (5) A model that depicts the successive stages a buyer passes through in the personal selling process including: attention, interest, desire, and action.

ASI Recall Plus Test (18) A day-after recall test of television commercials (formerly known as the Burke Test).

absolute costs (10) The actual total cost of placing an ad in a particular media vehicle.

account executive (3) The individual who serves as the liaison between the advertising agency and the client. The account executive is responsible for managing all of the services the agency provides to the client and representing the agency's point of view to the client.

account specific marketing (16) Development of customized promotional programs for individual retail accounts by marketers.

ad click rate (15) Often referred to as "click-through," this is the percentage of ad views that resulted in an ad click.

ad clicks (15) Number of times users click on a banner ad.

ad execution-related thoughts (5) A type of thought or cognitive response a message recipient has concerning factors related to the execution of the ad such as creativity, usual effects, color, and style.

adjacencies (11) Commercial spots purchased from local television stations that generally appear during the time periods adjacent to network programs.

advertising (1) Any paid form of nonpersonal communication about an organization, product, service, or idea by an identified sponsor.

advertising agency (3) A firm that specializes in the creation, production, and placement of advertising messages and may provide other services that facilitate the marketing communications process.

advertising appeal (9) The basis or approach used in an advertising message to attract the attention or interest of consumers and/or influence their feelings toward the product, service, or cause.

advertising campaign (8) A comprehensive advertising plan that consists of a series of messages in a variety of media that center on a single theme or idea.

advertising creativity (8) The ability to generate fresh, unique, and appropriate ideas that can be used as solutions to communication problems.

Note: Numbers in parentheses after term indicate chapter(s) where term is discussed.

advertising manager (3) The individual in an organization who is responsible for the planning, coordinating, budgeting, and implementing of the advertising program.

advertising specialties (13) Items used as giveaways to serve as a reminder or stimulate remembrance of a company or brand such as calendars, T-shirts, pens, key tags, and the like. Specialties are usually imprinted with a company or brand name and other identifying marks such as an address and phone number.

advertising substantiation (21) A Federal Trade Commission regulatory program that requires advertisers to have documentation to support the claims made in their advertisements.

ad views (impressions) (15) Number of times a banner ad is downloaded (and presumably seen) by viewers.

advocacy advertising (17) Advertising that is concerned with the propagation of ideas and elucidation of social issues of public importance in a manner that supports the position and interest of the sponsor.

aerial advertising (13) A form of outdoor advertising where messages appear in the sky in the form of banners pulled by airplanes, skywriting, and on blimps.

affect referral decision rule (4) A type of decision rule where selections are made on the basis of an overall impression or affective summary evaluation of the various alternatives under consideration.

affiliates (11) Local television stations that are associated with a major network. Affiliates agree to preempt time during specified hours for programming provided by the network and carry the advertising contained in the program.

affiliation (15) A relationship with other websites in which a company can cross-promote and is credited for sales that accrue through their site.

affirmative disclosure (21) A Federal Trade Commission program whereby advertisers may be required to include certain types of information in their advertisements so consumers will be aware of all the consequences, conditions, and limitations associated with the use of the product or service.

affordable method (7) A method of determining the budget for advertising and promotion where all other budget areas are covered and remaining monies are available for allocation.

agate line (12) Unit of newspaper space measurement, 1 column wide by 1/14 inch deep. (Thus, 14 agate lines = 1 column inch.)

agency evaluation process (3) The process by which a company evaluates the performance of its advertising agency. This process includes both financial and qualitative aspects.

alpha activity (19) A measure of the degree of brain activity that can be used to assess an individual's reactions to an advertisement.

alternative media (13) A term commonly used in advertising to describe support media.

animatic (8) A preliminary version of a commercial whereby a videotape of the frames of a storyboard is produced along with an audio soundtrack.

arbitrary allocation (7) A method for determining the budget for advertising and promotion based on arbitrary decisions of executives.

area of dominant influence (ADI) (11) A geographic survey area created and defined by Arbitron. Each county in the nation is assigned to an ADI, which is an exclusive geographic area consisting of all counties in which the home market stations receive a preponderance of viewing.

attitude toward the ad (5) A message recipient's affective feelings of favorability or unfavorability toward an advertisement.

attractiveness (6) A source characteristic that makes him or her appealing to a message recipient. Source attractiveness can be based on similarity, familiarity, or likability.

audimeter (11) An electric measurement device that is hooked to a television set to record when the set is turned on and the channel to which it is tuned.

audiotex (13) The use of telephone and voice information services to market, advertise, promote, entertain, and inform consumers.

average frequency (10) The number of times the average household reached by a media schedule is exposed to a media vehicle over a specified period.

average quarter-hour figure (AQH) (11) The average number of persons listening to a particular station for at least five minutes during a 15-minute period. Used by Arbitron in measuring the size of radio audiences.

average quarter-hour rating (11) The average quarter-hour figure estimate expressed as a percentage of the population being measured. Used by Arbitron in measuring the size of radio audiences.

average quarter-hour share (11) The percentage of the total listening audience tuned to each station as a percentage of the total listening audience in the survey area. Used by Arbitron in measuring the size of radio audiences.

B

balance-of-trade deficit (20) A situation where the monetary value of a country's imports exceeds its exports.

banner (15) An ad on a Web page that may be "hot-linked" to the advertiser's site.

barrier to entry (22) Conditions that make it difficult for a firm to enter the market in a particular industry, such as high advertising budgets.

barter syndication (11) The offering of television programs to local stations free or at a reduced rate but with some of the advertising time presold to national advertisers. The remaining advertising time can be sold to local advertisers.

behavioristic segmentation (2) A method of segmenting a market by dividing customers into groups based on their usage, loyalties, or buying responses to a product or service.

benchmark measures (7) Measures of a target audience's status concerning response hierarchy variables such as awareness, knowledge, image, attitudes, preferences, intentions, or behavior. These measures are taken at the beginning of an advertising or promotional campaign to determine the degree to which a target audience must be changed or moved by a promotional campaign.

benefit segmentation (2) A method of segmenting markets on the basis of the major benefits consumers seek in a product or service.

Better Business Bureau (BBB) (21) An organization established and funded by businesses that operates primarily at the local level to monitor activities of companies and promote fair advertising and selling practices.

big idea (8) A unique or creative idea for an advertisement or campaign that attracts consumers' attention, gets a reaction, and sets the advertiser's product or service apart from the competition.

billings (3) The amount of client money agencies spend on media purchases and other equivalent activities. Billings are often used as a way of measuring the size of advertising agencies.

bleed pages (12) Magazine advertisements where the printed area extends to the edge of the page, eliminating any white margin or border around the ad.

body copy (9) The main text portion of a print ad. Also often referred to as copy.

bonus packs (16) Special packaging that provides consumers with extra quantity of merchandise at no extra charge over the regular price.

bounce-back coupon (16) A coupon offer made to consumers as an inducement to repurchase the brand.

brand development index (BDI) (10) An index that is calculated by taking the percentage of a brand's total sales that occur in a given market as compared to the percentage of the total population in the market.

brand equity (2) The intangible asset of added value or goodwill that results from the favorable image, impressions of differentiation, and/or the strength of consumer attachment of a company name, brand name, or trademark.

brand loyalty (4) Preference by a consumer for a particular brand that results in continual purchase of it.

brand manager (3) The person responsible for the planning, implementation, and control of the marketing program for an individual brand.

broadcast media (12) Media that use the airwaves to transmit their signal and programming. Radio and television are examples of broadcast media.

build-up approach (7) A method of determining the budget for advertising and promotion by determining the specific tasks that have to be performed and estimating the costs of performing them. See objective and task method.

Burke Test (19) A method of posttesting television commercials using a day-after recall test (now known as Ipsos-ASI Recall Test).

business-to-business advertising (19) Advertising used by one business to promote the products and/or services it sells to another business.

buying center (5) A committee or group of individuals in an organization who are responsible for evaluating products and services and making purchase decisions.

C

cable television (11) A form of television where signals are carried to households by wire rather than through the airways.

carryover effect (7) A delayed or lagged effect whereby the impact of advertising on sales can occur during a subsequent time period.

category development index (CDI) (10) An index that is calculated by taking the percentage of a product category's total sales that occur in a given market area as compared to the percentage of the total population in the market.

category extension (2) The strategy of applying an existing brand name to a new product category.

category management (3) An organizational system whereby managers have responsibility for the marketing programs for a particular category or line of products.

cease-and-desist order (21) An action by the Federal Trade Commission that orders a company to stop engaging in a practice that is considered deceptive or misleading until a hearing is held.

central route to persuasion (5) One of two routes to persuasion recognized by the elaboration likelihood model. The central route to persuasion views a message recipient as very active and involved in the communications process and as having the ability and motivation to attend to and process a message.

centralized organizational structure (20) A method of organizing for international advertising and promotion whereby all decisions are made in a company's home office.

centralized system (3) An organizational system whereby advertising along with other marketing activities such as sales, marketing research, and planning are divided along functional lines and are run from one central marketing department.

channel (5) The method or medium by which communication travels from a source or sender to a receiver.

Children's Online Privacy Protection Act of 1998 (21) Federal legislation which places restrictions on information collected from children via the Internet and requires that websites directed at children have a privacy policy posted on their home page and areas of the site where information is collected.

city zone (12) A category used for newspaper circulation figures that refers to a market area composed of the city where the paper is published and contiguous areas similar in character to the city.

classical conditioning (4) A learning process whereby a conditioned stimulus that elicits a response is paired with a neutral stimulus that does not elicit any particular response. Through repeated exposure, the neutral stimulus comes to elicit the same response as the conditioned stimulus.

classified advertising (12) Advertising that runs in newspapers and magazines that generally contains text only and is arranged under subheadings according to the product, service, or offering. Employment, real estate, and automotive ads are the major forms of classified advertising.

clients (3) The organizations with the products, services, or causes to be marketed and for which advertising agencies and other marketing promotional firms provide services.

clipping service (7) A service which clips competitors' advertising from local print media allowing the company to monitor the types of advertising that are running or to estimate their advertising expenditures.

close (18) Obtaining the commitment of the prospect in a personal selling transaction.

clutter (6, 11) The nonprogram material that appears in a broadcast environment, including commercials, promotional messages for shows, public service announcements, and the like.

cognitive dissonance (4) A state of psychological tension or postpurchase doubt that a consumer may experience after making a purchase decision. This tension often leads the consumer to try to reduce it by seeking supportive information.

cognitive processing (4) The process by which an individual transforms external information into meanings or patterns of thought and how these meanings are used to form judgments or choices about behavior.

cognitive responses (5) Thoughts that occur to a message recipient while reading, viewing, and/or hearing a communication.

collateral services (3) Companies that provide companies with specialized services such as package design, advertising production, and marketing research.

combination rates (12) A special space rate or discount offered for advertising in two or more periodicals. Combination rates are often offered by publishers who own both morning and evening editions of a newspaper in the same market.

commission system (3) A method of compensating advertising agencies whereby the agency receives a specified commission (traditionally 15 percent) from the media on any advertising time or space it purchases.

communication (5) The passing of information, exchange of ideas, or process of establishing shared meaning between a sender and a receiver.

communication objectives (1, 7) Goals that an organization seeks to achieve through its promotional program in terms of communication effects such as creating awareness, knowledge, image, attitudes, preferences, or purchase intentions.

communication task (7) Under the DAGMAR approach to setting advertising goals and objectives, something that can be performed by and attributed to advertising such as awareness, comprehension, conviction, and action.

comparative advertising (6, 9) The practice of either directly or indirectly naming one or more competitors in an advertising message and usually making a comparison on one or more specific attributes or characteristics.

compensatory decision rule (4) A type of decision rule for evaluating alternatives where consumers consider each brand with respect to how it performs on relevant or salient attributes and the importance of each attribute. This decision rule allows for a negative evaluation or performance on a particular attribute to be compensated for by a positive evaluation on another attribute.

competitive advantage (2) Something unique or special that a firm does or possesses that provides an advantage over its competitors.

competitive parity method (7) A method of setting the advertising and promotion budget based on matching the absolute level of percentage of sales expenditures of the competition.

compliance (6) A type of influence process where a receiver accepts the position advocated by a source to obtain favorable outcomes or to avoid punishment.

computer simulation models (7) Quantitative-based models that are used to determine the relative contribution of advertising expenditures on sales response.

concave downward function (7) An advertising/sales response function that views the incremental effects of advertising on sales as decreasing.

concentrated marketing (2) A type of marketing strategy whereby a firm chooses to focus its marketing efforts on one particular market segment.

concept testing (19) A method of pretesting alternative ideas for an advertisement or campaign by having consumers provide their responses and/or reactions to the creative concept.

conditioned response (4) In classical conditioning, a response that occurs as a result of exposure to a conditioned stimulus.

conditioned stimulus (4) In classical conditioning, a stimulus that becomes associated with an unconditioned stimulus and capable of evoking the same response or reaction as the unconditioned stimulus.

conjunctive decision rule (4) A type of decision rule for evaluating alternatives where consumers establish minimally acceptable levels of performance for each important product attribute and accept an alternative only if it meets the cutoff level for each attribute.

consent order (21) A settlement between a company and the Federal Trade Commission whereby an advertiser agrees to

stop the advertising or practice in question. A consent order is for settlement purposes only and does not constitute an admission of guilt.

consumer behavior (4) The process and activities that people engage in when searching for, selecting, purchasing, using, evaluating, and disposing of products and services so as to satisfy their needs and desires.

consumer franchise-building promotions (16) Sales promotion activities that communicate distinctive brand attributes and contribute to the development and reinforcement of brand identity.

consumer juries (19) A method of pretesting advertisements by using a panel of consumers who are representative of the target audience and provide ratings, rankings, and/or evaluations of advertisements.

consumer-oriented sales promotion (16) Sales promotion techniques that are targeted to the ultimate consumer such as coupons, samples, contests, rebates, sweepstakes, and premium offers.

consumer socialization process (22) The process by which an individual acquires the skills needed to function in the marketplace as a consumer.

content sponsorship (15) The sponsor not only provides dollars in return for name association on the Internet but participates in the provision of content itself.

contest (16) A promotion whereby consumers compete for prizes or money on the basis of skills or ability, and winners are determined by judging the entries or ascertaining which entry comes closest to some predetermined criteria.

continuity (10) A media scheduling strategy where a continuous pattern of advertising is used over the time span of the advertising campaign.

contribution margin (7) The difference between the total revenue generated by a product or brand and its total variable costs.

controlled circulation basis (12) Distribution of a publication free to individuals a publisher believes are of importance and responsible for making purchase decisions or are prescreened for qualification on some other basis.

cookie (15) An identifying string of text attached to a website visitor's computer for information-gathering purposes, such as how often they visit the site, what is looked at, and in what sequence.

cooperative advertising (2, 16) Advertising program in which a manufacturer pays a certain percentage of the expenses a retailer or distributor incurs for advertising the manufacturer's product in a local market area.

copy platform (8) A document that specifies the basic elements of the creative strategy such as the basic problem or issue the advertising must address, the advertising and communications objectives, target audience, major selling idea or key benefits to communicate, campaign theme or appeal, and supportive information or requirements.

copywriter (3, 8) Individual who helps conceive the ideas for ads and commercials and writes the words or copy for them.

corporate advertising (17) Advertising designed to promote overall awareness of a company or enhance its image among a target audience.

corrective advertising (21) An action by the Federal Trade Commission whereby an advertiser can be required to run advertising messages designed to remedy the deception or misleading impression created by its previous advertising.

cost per customer purchasing (14) A cost effectiveness measure used in direct marketing based on the cost per sale generated.

cost per order (CPO) (13) A measure used in direct marketing to determine the number of orders generated relative to the cost of running the advertisement.

cost per ratings point (10) A computation used by media buyers to compare the cost efficiency of broadcast programs that divides the cost of commercial time on a program by the audience rating.

cost per thousand (10) A computation used in evaluating the relative cost of various media vehicles that represents the cost of exposing 1,000 members of a target audience to an advertising message.

cost plus system (3) A method of compensating advertising agencies whereby the agency receives a fee based on the cost of the work it performs plus an agreed-on amount for profit.

Council of Better Business Bureaus (21) The parent office of local offices of the Better Business Bureau. The council assists in the development of codes and standards for ethical and responsible business and advertising practices.

counterargument (5) A type of thought or cognitive response a receiver has that is counter or opposed to the position advocated in a message.

coverage (10) A measure of the potential audience that might receive an advertising message through a media vehicle.

CPC (15) Cost-per-click is a marketing formula used to price ad banners. Some advertisers pay based on the number of clicks a specific banner gets.

creative boutique (3) An advertising agency that specializes in and provides only services related to the creative aspects of advertising.

creative execution style (9) The manner or way in which a particular advertising appeal is transformed into a message.

creative selling (18) A type of sales position where the primary emphasis is on generating new business.

creative strategy (8) A determination of what an advertising message will say or communicate to a target audience.

creative tactics (8) A determination of how an advertising message will be implemented so as to execute the creative strategy.

creativity (8) A quality possessed by persons that enables them to generate novel approaches, generally reflected in new and improved solutions to problems.

credibility (6) The extent to which a source is perceived as having knowledge, skill, or experience relevant to a communication topic and can be trusted to give an unbiased opinion or present objective information on the issue.

cross-media advertising (12) An arrangement where opportunities to advertise in several different types of media are offered by a single company or a partnership of various media providers.

cross/multimagazine deals (12) An arrangement where two or more publishers offer their magazines to an advertiser as one media package.

cross-ruff coupon (16) A coupon offer delivered on one product that is redeemable for the purchase of another product. The other product is usually one made by the same company but may involve a tie-in with another manufacturer.

cross sell (18) A term used in personal selling that refers to the sale of additional products and/or services to the same customer.

cultural values (20) Refers to beliefs and goals shared by members of a society regarding ideal end-states of life and modes of conduct.

culture (4) The complexity of learned meanings, values, norms, and customs shared by members of a society.

cume (11) A term used for cumulative audience, which is the estimated total number of different people who listened to a radio station for a minimum of five minutes during a particular daypart.

D

DAGMAR (7) An acronym that stands for defining advertising goals for measured advertising results. An approach to setting advertising goals and objectives developed by Russell Colley.

daily inch rate (10) A cost figure used in periodicals based on an advertisement placed one inch deep and one column wide (whatever the column inch).

database (14) A listing of current and/or potential customers for a company's product or service that can be used for direct-marketing purposes.

database marketing (14) The use of specific information about individual customers and/or prospects to implement more effective and efficient marketing communications.

day-after recall scores (19) A measure used in on-air testing of television commercials by various marketing research companies. The day-after recall score represents the percentage of viewers surveyed who can remember seeing a particular commercial.

dayparts (10, 11) The time segments into which a day is divided by radio and television networks and stations for selling advertising time.

decentralized organizational structure (20) A method of organizing for international advertising and promotion where managers in each market or country have decision-making authority.

decentralized system (3) An organizational system whereby planning and decision-making responsibility for marketing, advertising, and promotion lies with a product/brand manager or management team rather than a centralized department.

deception (21) According to the Federal Trade Commission, a misrepresentation, omission, or practice that is likely to mislead the consumer acting reasonably in the circumstances to the consumer's detriment.

decoding (5) The process by which a message recipient transforms and interprets a message.

demographic segmentation (2) A method of segmenting a market based on the demographic characteristics of consumers.

departmental system (3) The organization of an advertising agency into departments based on functions such as account services, creative, media, marketing services, and administration.

derived demand (19) A situation where demand for a particular product or service results from the need for other goods and/or services. For example, demand for aluminum cans is derived from consumption of soft drinks or beer.

designated market area (DMA) (11) The geographic areas used by the Nielsen Station Index in measuring audience size. DMAs are nonoverlapping areas consisting of groups of counties from which stations attract their viewers.

differentiated marketing (2) A type of marketing strategy whereby a firm offers products or services to a number of market segments and develops separate marketing strategies for each.

differentiation (22) A situation where a particular company or brand is perceived as unique or better than its competitors.

direct-action advertising (1) Advertising designed to produce an immediate effect such as the generation of store traffic or sales.

direct broadcast by satellite (DBS) (20) A television signal delivery system whereby programming is beamed from satellites to special receiving dishes mounted in the home or yard.

direct channel (2) A marketing channel where a producer and ultimate consumer interact directly with one another.

direct headline (9) A headline that is very straightforward and informative in terms of the message it is presenting and the target audience it is directed toward. Direct headlines often include a specific benefit, promise, or reason for a consumer to be interested in a product or service.

direct marketing (1, 14) A system of marketing by which an organization communicates directly with customers to generate a response and/or transaction.

direct-marketing media (14) Media that are used for direct-marketing purposes including direct mail, telemarketing, print, and broadcast.

direct-response advertising (1, 14) A form of advertising for a product or service that elicits a sales response directly from the advertiser.

direct-response agencies (3) Companies that provide a variety of direct-marketing services to their clients including database management, direct mail, research, media service, and creative and production capabilities.

direct selling (1, 14) The direct personal presentation, demonstration, and sale of products and services to consumers usually in their homes or at their jobs.

directional medium (13) Advertising media that are not used to create awareness or demand for products or services but rather to inform customers as to where purchases can be made once they have decided to buy. The Yellow Pages are an example of a directional medium.

display advertising (12) Advertising in newspapers and magazines that uses illustrations, photos, headlines, and other visual elements in addition to copy text.

dissonance/attribution model (5) A type of response hierarchy where consumers first behave, then develop attitudes or feelings as a result of that behavior, and then learn or process information that supports the attitude and behavior.

diverting (16) A practice whereby a retailer or wholesaler takes advantage of a promotional deal and then sells some of the product purchased at the low price to a store outside of their area or to a middleman who will resell it to other stores.

domain name (15) The unique name of an Internet site. There are six domains widely used in the U.S.: .com (commercial), .edu (education), .net (network operations), .gov (U.S. government), .mil (U.S. military), and .org (organization). Additional two letter domains specify a country, for example, .sp for Spain.

duplicated reach (10) Audience members' exposure to a message as a result of messages having appeared in two or more different media vehicles.

dyadic communication (18) A process of direct communication between two persons or groups such as a salesperson and a customer.

E

e-commerce (15) Direct selling of goods and services through the Internet.

economic infrastructure (20) A country's communications, transportation, financial, and distribution networks.

economies of scale (7, 22) A decline in costs with accumulated sales or production. In advertising, economies of scale often occur in media purchases as the relative costs of advertising time and/or space may decline as the size of the media budget increases.

effective reach (10) A measure of the percentage of a media vehicle's audience reached at each effective frequency increment.

elaboration likelihood model (ELM) (5) A model that identifies two processes by which communications can lead to persuasion—central and peripheral routes.

electrodermal response (19) A measure of the resistance the skin offers to a small amount of current passed between two electrodes. Used as a measure of consumers' reaction level to an advertisement.

electroencephalographic (EEG) measures (19) Measures of the electrical impulses in the brain that are sometimes used as a measure of reactions to advertising.

electronic teleshopping (14) Online shopping and information retrieval service that is accessed through a personal computer.

emotional appeals (6, 9) Advertising messages that appeal to consumers' feelings and emotions.

encoding (5) The process of putting thoughts, ideas, or information into a symbolic form.

ethics (22) Moral principles and values that govern the actions and decisions of an individual or group.

evaluative criteria (4) The dimensions or attributes of a product or service that are used to compare different alternatives.

event marketing (16) A type of promotion where a company or brand is linked to an event, or where a themed activity is developed for the purpose of creating experiences for consumers and promoting a product or service.

event sponsorship (17) A type of promotion whereby a company develops sponsorship relations with a particular event such as a concert, sporting event, or other activity.

evoked set (4) The various brands identified by a consumer as purchase options and that are actively considered during the alternative evaluation process.

exchange (1) Trade of something of value between two parties such as a product or service for money. The core phenomenon or domain for study in marketing.

exclusive (17) A public relations tactic whereby one particular medium is offered exclusive rights to a story.

expertise (6) An aspect of source credibility where a communicator is perceived as being knowledgeable in a given area or for a particular topic.

external analysis (1) The phase of the promotional planning process that focuses on factors such as the characteristics of an organization's customers, market segments, positioning strategies, competitors, and marketing environment.

external audiences (17) In public relations, a term used in reference to individuals who are outside of or not closely connected to the organization such as the general public.

external audits (17) Evaluations performed by outside agencies to determine the effectiveness of an organization's public relations program.

external search (4) The search process whereby consumers seek and acquire information from external sources such as advertising, other people, or public sources.

eye tracking (19) A method for following the movement of a person's eyes as he or she views an ad or commercial. Eye tracking is used for determining which portions or sections of an ad attract a viewer's attention and/or interest.

F

failure fee (16) A trade promotion arrangement whereby a marketer agrees to pay a penalty fee if a product stocked by a retailer does not meet agreed-upon sales levels.

Fairness Doctrine (21) A Federal Communications Commission program that required broadcasters to provide time for opposing viewpoints on important issues.

fear appeals (6) An advertising message that creates anxiety in a receiver by showing negative consequences that can result from engaging in (or not engaging in) a particular behavior.

Federal Trade Commission (FTC) (21) The federal agency that has the primary responsibility for protecting consumers and businesses from anticompetitive behavior and unfair and deceptive practices. The FTC regulates advertising and promotion at the federal level.

Federal Trade Commission Act (21) Federal legislation passed in 1914 that created the Federal Trade Commission and gave it the responsibility to monitor deceptive or misleading advertising and unfair business practices.

fee-commission combination (3) A type of compensation system whereby an advertising agency establishes a fixed monthly fee for its services to a client and media commissions received by the agency are credited against the fee.

feedback (5) Part of message recipient's response that is communicated back to the sender. Feedback can take a variety of forms and provides a sender with a way of monitoring how an intended message is decoded and received.

field of experience (5) The experiences, perceptions, attitudes, and values that senders and receivers of a message bring to a communication situation.

field tests (19) Tests of consumer reactions to an advertisement that are taken under natural viewing situations rather than in a laboratory.

financial audit (3) An aspect of the advertising agency evaluation process that focuses on how the agency conducts financial affairs related to serving a client.

first-run syndication (11) Programs produced specifically for the syndication market.

fixed-fee arrangement (3) A method of agency compensation whereby the agency and client agree on the work to be done and the amount of money the agency will be paid for its services.

flat rates (12) A standard newspaper advertising rate where no discounts are offered for large-quantity or repeated space buys.

Flesch formula (19) A test used to assess the difficulty level of writing based on the number of syllables and sentences per 100 words.

flighting (10) A media scheduling pattern in which periods of advertising are alternated with periods of no advertising.

focus groups (4)(8) A qualitative marketing research method whereby a group of 10–12 consumers from the target market are led through a discussion regarding a particular topic such as a product, service, or advertising campaign.

forward buying (16) A practice whereby retailers and wholesalers stock up on a product being offered by a manufacturer at a lower deal or off-invoice price and resell it to consumers once the marketer's promotional period has ended.

frequency (10) The number of times a target audience is exposed to a media vehicle(s) in a specified period.

frequency programs (16) A type of promotional program that rewards customers for continuing to purchase the same brand of a product or service over time (also referred to as continuity or loyalty programs).

full-service agency (3) An advertising agency that offers clients a full range of marketing and communications services including the planning, creating, producing, and placing of advertising messages and other forms of promotion.

functional consequences (4) Outcomes of product or service usage that are tangible and can be directly experienced by a consumer.

G

game (16) A promotion that is a form of sweepstakes because it has a chance element or odds of winning associated with it. Games usually involve game card devices that can be rubbed or opened to unveil a winning number or prize description.

gatefolds (12) An oversize magazine page or cover that is extended and folded over to fit into the publication. Gatefolds are used to extend the size of a magazine advertisement and are always sold at a premium.

general preplanning input (8) Information gathering and/or market research studies on trends, developments, and happenings in the marketplace that can be used to assist in the initial stages of the creative process of advertising.

geographical weighting (10) A media scheduling strategy where certain geographic areas or regions are allocated higher levels of advertising because they have greater sales potential.

geographic segmentation (2) A method of segmenting a market on the basis of different geographic units or areas.

global advertising (20) The use of the same basic advertising message in all international markets.

global marketing (20) A strategy of using a common marketing plan and program for all countries in which a company operates, thus selling the product or services the same way everywhere in the world.

green marketing (22) The marketing and promotion of products on the basis of environmental sensitivity.

gross ratings points (GRPs) (10) A measure that represents the total delivery or weight of a media schedule during a specified time period. GRPs are calculated by multiplying the reach of the media schedule by the average frequency.

group system (3) The organization of an advertising agency by dividing it into groups consisting of specialists from various departments such as creative, media, marketing services, and other areas. These groups work together to service particular accounts.

H

halo effect (19) The tendency for evaluations of one attribute or aspect of a stimulus to distort reactions to its other attributes or properties.

headline (9) Words in the leading position of the advertisement; the words that will be read first or are positioned to draw the most attention.

hemisphere lateralization (19) The notion that the human brain has two relatively distinct halves or hemispheres with each being responsible for a specific type of function. The right side is responsible for visual processing while the left side conducts verbal processing.

heuristics (4) Simplified or basic decision rules that can be used by a consumer to make a purchase choice, such as buy the cheapest brand.

hierarchy of effects model (5) A model of the process by which advertising works that assumes a consumer must pass through a sequence of steps from initial awareness to eventual action. The stages include awareness, interest, evaluation, trial, and adoption.

hierarchy of needs (4) Abraham Maslow's theory that human needs are arranged in an order or hierarchy based on their importance. The need hierarchy includes physiological, safety, social/love and belonging, esteem, and self-actualization needs.

hit (15) Each time a server sends a file to a browser it is recorded as a "hit." Hits are used to measure the traffic on a website.

horizontal cooperative advertising (16) A cooperative advertising arrangement where advertising is sponsored in common by a group of retailers or other organizations providing products or services to a market.

households using television (HUT) (11) The percentage of homes in a given area that are watching television during a specific time period.

I

identification (6) The process by which an attractive source influences a message recipient. Identification occurs when the receiver is motivated to seek some type of relationship with the source and adopt a similar position in terms of beliefs, attitudes, preferences, or behavior.

image advertising (8) Advertising that creates an identity for a product or service by emphasizing psychological meaning or symbolic association with certain values, lifestyles, and the like.

image transfer (11) A radio advertising technique whereby the images of a television commercial are implanted into a radio spot.

incentive-based system (3) A form of compensation whereby an advertising agency's compensation level depends on how well it meets predetermined performance goals such as sales or market share.

index numbers (10) A ratio used to describe the potential of a market. The index number is derived by dividing the percentage of users in a market segment by the percentage of population in the same segment and multiplying by 100.

indirect channels (2) A marketing channel where intermediaries such as wholesalers and retailers are utilized to make a product available to the customer.

indirect headlines (9) Headlines that are not straightforward with respect to identifying a product or service or providing information regarding the point of an advertising message.

in-flight advertising (13) A variety of advertising media targeting air travelers while they are in flight.

infomercials (11, 14) Television commercials that are very long, ranging from several minutes to an hour. Infomercials are designed to provide consumers with detailed information about a product or service.

information processing model (5) A model of advertising effects developed by William McGuire that views the receiver of a message as an information processor and problem solver. The model views the receiver as passing through a response hierarchy that includes a series of stages including message presentation, attention, comprehension, acceptance or yielding, retention, and behavior.

informational/rational appeals (9) Advertising appeals that focus on the practical, functional, or utilitarian need for a product or service and emphasize features, benefits, or reasons for owning or using the brand.

ingredient sponsored cooperative advertising (16) Advertising supported by raw material manufacturers with the objective being to help establish end products that include materials and/or ingredients supplied by the company.

inherent drama (8) An approach to advertising that focuses on the benefits or characteristics that lead a consumer to purchase a product or service and uses dramatic elements to emphasize them.

in-house agency (3) An advertising agency set up, owned, and operated by an advertiser that is responsible for planning and executing the company's advertising program.

ink-jet imaging (12) A printing process where a message is reproduced by projecting ink onto paper rather than mechanical plates. Ink-jet imaging is being offered by many magazines to allow advertisers to personalize their messages.

innovation-adoption model (5) A model that represents the stages a consumer passes through in the adoption process for an innovation such as a new product. The series of steps includes: awareness, interest, evaluation, trial, and adoption.

inquiry tests (19) Tests designed to measure advertising effectiveness on the basis of inquiries or responses generated from the ad such as requests for information, number of phone calls, or number of coupons redeemed.

inside cards (13) A form of transit advertising where messages appear on cards or boards inside of vehicles such as buses, subways, or trolleys.

instant coupon (16) Coupons attached to a package that can be removed and redeemed at the time of purchase.

in-store couponing (16) The distribution of coupons in retail stores through various methods such as tear-off pads, handouts, and on-shelf or electronic dispensers.

in-store media (13) Advertising and promotional media that are used inside of a retail store such as point-of-purchase displays, ads on shopping carts, coupon dispensers, and display boards.

integrated marketing communication objectives (7) Statements of what various aspects of the integrated marketing communications program will accomplish with respect to factors such as communication tasks, sales, market share, and the like.

integrated marketing communications (1) A concept of marketing communications planning that recognizes the added value of a comprehensive plan that evaluates the strategic roles of a variety of communication disciplines—for example, general advertising, direct response, sales promotion, and public relations—and combines these disciplines to provide clarity, consistency, and maximum communications impact.

integration processes (4) The way information such as product knowledge, meanings, and beliefs is combined to evaluate two or more alternatives.

interactive agency (3) An organization that specializes in the creation of interactive media such as CD-ROMs, kiosks, and websites.

interactive media (10) A variety of media that allows the consumer to interact with the source of the message, actively receiving information and altering images, responding to questions, and so on.

interconnects (11) Groups of cable systems joined together for advertising purposes.

internal analysis (1) The phase of the promotional planning process that focuses on the product/service offering and the firm itself including the capabilities of the firm and its ability to develop and implement a successful integrated marketing communications program.

internal audiences (17) In public relations, a term used to refer to individuals or groups inside of the organization or with a close connection to it.

internal audits (17) Evaluations by individuals within the organization to determine the effectiveness of a public relations program.

internalization (6) The process by which a credible source influences a message recipient. Internalization occurs when the receiver is motivated to have an objectively correct position on an issue and the receiver will adopt the opinion or attitude of the credible communicator if he or she believes the information from this source represents an accurate position on the issue.

internal search (4) The process by which a consumer acquires information by accessing past experiences or knowledge stored in memory.

international media (20) Advertising media that have multicountry coverage and can be used to reach audiences in various countries.

Internet (15) A worldwide means of exchanging information and communicating through a series of interconnected computers.

interstitial (15) An advertisement that appears in a window on your computer screen while you are waiting for a Web page to load.

J

jingles (9) Songs about a brand or company that usually carry the advertising theme and a simple message.

L

laboratory tests (19) Tests of consumer reactions to advertising under controlled conditions.

Lanham Act (21) A federal law that permits a company to register a trademark for its exclusive use. The Lanham Act was recently amended to encompass false advertising and prohibits any false description or representation including words or other symbols tending falsely to describe or represent the same.

layout (9) The physical arrangement of the various parts of an advertisement including the headline, subheads, illustrations, body copy, and any identifying marks.

lexicographic decision rule (4) A type of decision rule where choice criteria are ranked in order of importance and alternatives are evaluated on each attribute or criterion beginning with the most important one.

link (15) An electronic connection between two websites.

local advertising (11) Advertising done by companies within the limited geographic area where they do business.

localized advertising strategy (20) Developing an advertising campaign specifically for a particular country or market rather than using a global approach.

low-involvement hierarchy (5) A response hierarchy whereby a message recipient is viewed as passing from cognition to behavior to attitude change.

M

magazine networks (12) A group of magazines owned by one publisher or assembled by an independent network that offers advertisers the opportunity to buy space in a variety of publications through a package deal.

mailing list (14) A type of database containing names and addresses of present and/or potential customers who can be reached through a direct-mail campaign.

major selling idea (8) The basis for the central theme or message idea in an advertising campaign.

marginal analysis (7) A principle of resource allocation that balances incremental revenues against incremental costs.

market opportunities (2) Areas where a company believes there are favorable demand trends, needs, and/or wants that are not being satisfied, and where it can compete effectively.

market segmentation (2) The process of dividing a market into distinct groups that have common needs and will respond similarly to a marketing action.

market segments (2) Identifiable groups of customers sharing similar needs, wants, or other characteristics that make them likely to respond in a similar fashion to a marketing program.

marketing (1, 2) The process of planning and executing the conception, pricing, promotion, and distribution of ideas, goods, and services to create exchanges that satisfy individual and organizational objectives.

marketing channels (2) The set of interdependent organizations involved in the process of making a product or service available to customers.

marketing mix (1, 2) The controllable elements of a marketing program including product, price, promotion, and place.

marketing objectives (1, 7) Goals to be accomplished by an organization's overall marketing program such as sales, market share, or profitability.

marketing plan (1) A written document that describes the overall marketing strategy and programs developed for an organization, a particular product line, or a brand.

marketing public relations function (MPR) (17) Public relations activities designed to support marketing objectives and programs.

mass media (5) Nonpersonal channels of communication that allow a message to be sent to many individuals at one time.

materialism (22) A preoccupation with material things rather than intellectual or spiritual concerns.

media buying services (3) Independent companies that specialize in the buying of media, particularly radio and television time.

media objectives (10) The specific goals an advertiser has for the media portion of the advertising program.

media organizations (3) One of the four major participants in the integrated marketing communications process whose function is to provide information or entertainment to subscribers, viewers, or readers while offering marketers an environment for reaching audiences with print and broadcast messages.

media plan (10) A document consisting of objectives, strategies, and tactics for reaching a target audience through various media vehicles.

media planning (10) The series of decisions involved in the delivery of an advertising message to prospective purchasers and/or users of a product or service.

media strategies (10) Plans of action for achieving stated media objectives such as which media will be used for reaching a target audience, how the media budget will be allocated, and how advertisements will be scheduled.

media vehicle (10) The specific program, publication, or promotional piece used to carry an advertising message.

medium (10) The general category of communication vehicles that are available for communicating with a target audience such as broadcast, print, direct mail, and outdoor.

message (5) A communication containing information or meaning that a source wants to convey to a receiver.

missionary sales (18) A type of sales position where the emphasis is on performing supportive activities and services rather than generating or taking orders.

mnemonics (4) Basic cues such as symbols, rhymes, and associations that facilitate the learning and memory process.

mobile billboards (13) An out-of-home medium in which advertisements are able to be transported to different locations (signs painted on automobiles, trailers pulling billboards, and the like).

motivation research (4) Qualitative research designed to probe the consumer's subconscious and discover deeply rooted motives for purchasing a product.

motive (4) Something that compels or drives a consumer to take a particular action.

multiattribute attitude model (4) A model of attitudes that views an individual's evaluation of an object as being a function of the beliefs that he or she has toward the object on various attributes and the importance of these attributes.

multimagazine deals (12) Arrangements whereby two to more publishers offer advertisers the opportunity to buy space in their magazines with one single media buy.

multiplexing (11) An arrangement where multiple channels are transmitted by one cable network.

N

narrowcasting (11) The reaching of a very specialized market through programming aimed at particular target audiences. Cable television networks offer excellent opportunities for narrowcasting.

national advertisers (2) Companies that advertise their products or services on a nationwide basis or in most regions of the country.

National Advertising Review Board (NARB) (21) A part of the National Advertising Division of the Council of Better Business Bureaus. The NARB is the advertising industry's primary self-regulatory body.

National Advertising Review Council (NARC) (21) An organization founded by the Council of Better Business Bureaus and various advertising industry groups to promote high standards of truth, accuracy, morality, and social responsibility in national advertising.

National Association of Attorneys General (21) An organization consisting of state attorneys general that is involved in the regulation of advertising and other business practices.

national spot (11) All non-network advertising done by a national advertiser in local markets.

negotiated commission (3) A method of compensating advertising agencies whereby the client and agency negotiate the commission structure rather than relying on the traditional 15 percent media commission.

noise (5) Extraneous factors that create unplanned distortion or interference in the communications process.

noncompensatory integration strategies (4) Types of decision rules used to evaluate alternatives that do not allow negative evaluation or performance on a particular attribute to be compensated for by positive evaluation or performance on some other attribute.

nonfranchise-building promotions (16) Sales promotion activities that are designed to accelerate the purchase decision process and generate an immediate increase in sales but do little or nothing to communicate information about a brand and contribute to its identity and image.

nonmeasured media (13) A term commonly used in the advertising industry to describe support media.

nonpersonal channels (5) Channels of communication that carry a message without involving interpersonal contact between sender and receiver. Nonpersonal channels are often referred to as mass media.

nontraditional media (13) A term commonly used in the advertising industry to describe support media.

O

objective and task method (7) A build-up approach to budget setting involving a three-step process: (1) determining objectives, (2) determining the strategies and tasks required to attain these objectives, and (3) estimating the costs associated with these strategies and tasks.

off-invoice allowance (16) A promotional discount offered to retailers or wholesalers whereby a certain per-case amount or percentage is deducted from the invoice.

off-network syndication (11) Reruns of network shows bought by individual stations.

on-air tests (19) Testing the effectiveness of television commercials by inserting test ads into actual TV programs in certain test markets.

one-sided message (6) Communications in which only positive attributes or benefits of a product or service are presented.

one-step approach (14) A direct-marketing strategy in which the medium is used directly to obtain an order (for example, television direct-response ads).

open rate structure (12) A rate charged by newspapers in which discounts are available based on frequency or bulk purchases of space.

operant conditioning (instrumental conditioning) (4) A learning theory that views the probability of a behavior as being dependent on the outcomes or consequences associated with it.

opt-in-e-mail (15) Lists where Internet users have voluntarily signed up to receive commercial e-mail about topics of interest.

order taking (18) A personal selling responsibility in which the salesperson's primary responsibility is taking the order.

out-of-home advertising (13) The variety of advertising forms including outdoor, transit, skywriting, and other media viewed outside the home.

outside posters (13) Outdoor transit posters appearing on buses, taxis, trains, subways, and trolley cars.

P

PACT (Positioning Advertising Copy Testing) (19) A set of principles endorsed by 21 of the largest U.S. ad agencies aimed at improving the research used in preparing and testing ads, providing a better creative product for clients, and controlling the cost of TV commercials.

page views (15) Number of times a user requests a page that contains a particular ad. Used to indicate the number of times an ad was potentially seen, or "gross impressions."

participations (11) The situation where several advertisers buy commercial time or spots on network television.

pass-along rate (10) An estimate of the number of readers of a magazine in addition to the original subscriber or purchaser.

pass-along readership (12) The audience that results when the primary subscriber or purchaser of a magazine gives the publication to another person to read, or when the magazine is read in places such as waiting rooms in doctors' offices, etc.

pattern advertising (20) Advertisements that follow a basic global approach although themes, copy, and sometimes even visual elements may be adjusted.

payout plan (7) A budgeting plan that determines the investment value of the advertising and promotion appropriation.

people meter (11) An electronic device that automatically records a household's television viewing, including channels watched, number of minutes of viewing, and members of the household who are watching.

percentage charges (3) The markups charged by advertising agencies for services provided to clients.

percentage of projected future sales method (7) A variation of the percentage of sales method of budget allocation in which projected future sales are used as the base.

percentage of sales method (7) A budget method in which the advertising and/or promotions budget is set based on a percentage of sales of the product.

perception (4) The process by which an individual receives, selects, organizes, and interprets information to create a meaningful picture of the world.

perceptual map (2) A "map" of perceptions of the positions of brands or products as received by consumers.

peripheral route to persuasion (5) In the elaboration likelihood model, one of two routes to persuasion in which the receiver is viewed as lacking the ability or motivation to process information and is not likely to be engaging in detailed cognitive processing.

personal selling (1) Person-to-person communication in which the seller attempts to assist and/or persuade prospective buyers to purchase the company's product or service or to act on an idea.

personalization (15) Individuals can request that specific information they are interested in viewing be sent to their computers.

persuasion matrix (6) A communications planning model in which the stages of the response process (dependent variables) and the communications components (independent variables) are combined to demonstrate the likely effect that the independent variables will have on the dependent variables.

phased processing strategy (4) An information processing strategy in which more than one decision rule is applied during the purchase decision process.

planograms (16) A planning configuration of products that occupy a shelf section in a store that is used to provide more efficient shelf space utilization.

pop-ups (15) Advertisement windows on the Internet usually larger than a banner ad and smaller than a full screen.

portfolio tests (19) A laboratory methodology designed to expose a group of respondents to a portfolio consisting of both control and test print ads.

positioning (2) The art and science of fitting the product or service to one or more segments of the market in such a way as to set it meaningfully apart from competition.

positioning strategies (2) The strategies used in positioning a brand or product.

posttests (19) Ad effectiveness measures that are taken after the ad has appeared in the marketplace.

preferred position rate (12) A rate charged by newspapers that ensures the advertiser the ad will appear in the position required and/or in a specific section of the newspaper.

premium (16) An offer of an item of merchandise or service either free or at a low price that is used as an extra incentive for purchasers.

preprinted inserts (12) Advertising distributed through newspapers that is not part of the newspaper itself, but is printed by the advertiser and then taken to the newspaper to be inserted.

press release (17) Factual and interesting information released to the press.

pretests (19) Advertising effectiveness measures that are taken before the implementation of the advertising campaign.

price elasticity (2) The responsiveness of the market to change in price.

price-off deal (16) A promotional strategy in which the consumer receives a reduction in the regular price of the brand.

primacy effect (6) A theory that the first information presented in the message will be the most likely to be remembered.

primary circulation (12) The number of copies of a magazine distributed to original subscribers.

problem detection (8) A creative research approach in which consumers familiar with a product (or service) are asked to generate an exhaustive list of problems encountered in its use.

problem recognition (4) The first stage in the consumer's decision-making process in which the consumer perceives a need and becomes motivated to satisfy it.

problem-solver stage (18) A stage of personal selling in which the seller obtains the participation of buyers in identifying their problems, translates these problems into needs, and then presents a selection from the supplier's offerings that can solve those problems.

procreator stage (18) A stage of personal selling in which the seller defines the buyer's problems or needs and the solutions to those problems or needs through active buyer-seller collaboration, thus creating a market offering tailored to the customer.

product manager (3) The person responsible for the planning, implementation, and control of the marketing program for an individual brand.

product placement (13) A form of advertising and promotion in which products are placed in television shows and/or movies to gain exposure.

product-specific preplanning input (8) Specific studies provided to the creative department on the product or service, the target audience, or a combination of the two.

product symbolism (2) The meaning that a product or brand has to consumers.

program rating (11) The percentage of TV households in an area that are tuned to a program during a specific time period.

promotion (1) The coordination of all seller-initiated efforts to set up channels of information and persuasion to sell goods and services or to promote an idea.

promotional management (1) The process of coordinating the promotional mix elements.

promotional mix (1) The tools used to accomplish an organization's communications objective. The promotional mix includes advertising, direct marketing, sales promotion, publicity/public relations, and personal selling.

promotional plan (1) The framework for developing, implementing, and controlling the organization's communications program.

promotional products marketing (13) The advertising or promotional medium or method that uses promotional products such as ad specialties, premiums, business gifts, awards, prizes, or commemoratives.

promotional pull strategy (2) A strategy in which advertising and promotion efforts are targeted at the ultimate consumers to encourage them to purchase the manufacturer's brand.

promotional push strategy (2) A strategy in which advertising and promotional efforts are targeted to the trade to attempt to get them to promote and sell the product to the ultimate consumer.

prospector stage (18) A selling stage in which activities include seeking out selected buyers who are perceived to have a need for the offering as well as the resources to buy it.

Protestant ethic (22) A perspective of life which stresses hard work and individual effort and initiative and views the accumulation of material possessions as evidence of success.

psychoanalytic theory (4) An approach to the study of human motivations and behaviors pioneered by Sigmund Freud.

psychographic segmentation (2) Dividing the product on the basis of personality and/or lifestyles.

psychosocial consequences (4) Purchase decision consequences that are intangible, subjective, and personal.

public relations (1, 17) The management function that evaluates public attitudes, identifies the policies and procedures of an individual or organization with the public interest, and executes a program to earn public understanding and acceptance.

public relations firm (3) An organization that develops and implements programs to manage a company's publicity, image, and affairs with consumers and other relevant publics.

publicity (1, 17) Communications regarding an organization, product, service, or idea that is not directly paid for or run under identified sponsorship.

puffery (21) Advertising or other sales presentations that praise the item to be sold using subjective opinions, superlatives, or exaggerations, vaguely and generally, stating no specific facts.

pulsing (10) A media scheduling method that combines flighting and continuous scheduling.

pupillometrics (19) An advertising effectiveness methodology designed to measure dilation and constriction of the pupils of the eye in response to stimuli.

purchase intention (4) The predisposition to buy a certain brand or product.

push money (16) Cash payments made directly to the retailers' or wholesalers' sales force to encourage them to promote and sell a manufacturer's product.

push technology (15) Allows a company to "push" a message to the consumer through the Internet rather than waiting for them to find it.

Q

qualified prospects (18) Those prospects that are able to make the buying decision.

qualitative audit (3) An audit of the advertising agency's efforts in planning, developing, and implementing the client's communications programs.

qualitative media effect (6) The positive or negative influence the medium may contribute to the message.

R

ratings point (11) A measurement used to determine television viewing audiences in which one ratings point is the equivalent of 1 percent of all of the television households in a particular area tuned to a specific program.

rational appeal (6) Communications in which features and/or benefits are directly presented in a logical, rational method.

reach (10) The number of different audience members exposed at least once to a media vehicle (or vehicles) in a given period.

readers per copy (10) A cost comparison figure used for magazines that estimates audience size based on pass-along readership.

recall tests (19) Advertising effectiveness tests designed to measure advertising recall.

receiver (5) The person or persons with whom the sender of a message shares thoughts or information.

recency effect (6) The theory that arguments presented at the end of the message are considered to be stronger and therefore are more likely to be remembered.

recognition method (19) An advertising effectiveness measure of print ads that allows the advertiser to assess the impact of an ad in a single issue of a magazine over time and/or across alternative magazines.

reference group (4) A group whose perspectives, values, or behavior is used by an individual as the basis for his or her judgments, opinions, and actions.

refutational appeal (6) A type of message in which both sides of the issure are presented in the communication, with arguments offered to refute the opposing viewpoint.

regional networks (11) A network that covers only a specific portion of the country. Regional network purchases are based in proportion to the percentage of the country receiving the message.

reinforcement (4) The rewards or favorable consequences associated with a particular response.

relationship marketing (1, 18) An organization's effort to develop a long-term, cost-effective link with individual customers for mutual benefit.

relative cost (10) The relationship between the price paid for advertising time or space and the size of the audience delivered; it is used to compare the prices of various media vehicles.

reminder advertising (9) Advertising designed to keep the name of the product or brand in the mind of the receiver.

repositioning (2) The changing of a product or brand's positioning.

resellers (2) Intermediaries in the marketing channel such as wholesalers, distributors, and retailers.

response (5) The set of reactions the receiver has after seeing, hearing, or reading a message.

retail trading zone (12) The market outside the city zone whose residents regularly trade with merchants within the city zone.

rich media (15) A term for advanced technology used in Internet ads, such as a streaming video which allows interaction and special effects.

ROI budgeting method (return on investment) (7) A budgeting method in which advertising and promotions are considered investments, and thus measurements are made in an attempt to determine the returns achieved by these investments.

rolling boards (13) Advertising painted or mounted on cars, trucks, vans, trailers, etc., so the exposure can be mobile enough to be taken to specific target market areas.

run of paper (ROP) (12) A rate quoted by newspapers that allows the ad to appear on any page or in any position desired by the medium.

S

S-shaped response curve (7) A sales response model that attempts to show sales responses to various levels of advertising and promotional expenditures.

sales-oriented objectives (7) Budgeting objectives related to sales effects such as increasing sales volume.

sales promotion (1, 16) Marketing activities that provide extra value or incentives to the sales force, distributors, or the ultimate consumer and can stimulate immediate sales.

sales promotion agency (3) An organization that specializes in the planning and implementation of promotional programs such as contests, sweepstakes, sampling, premiums, and incentive offers for its clients.

sales promotion trap (16) A spiral that results when a number of competitors extensively use promotions. One firm uses sales promotions to differentiate its product or service and other competitors copy the strategy, resulting in no differential advantage and a loss of profit margins to all.

salient beliefs (4) Beliefs concerning specific attributes or consequences that are activated and form the basis of an attitude.

sampling (16) A variety of procedures whereby consumers are given some quantity of a product for no charge to induce trial.

scatter market (11) A period for purchasing television advertising time that runs throughout the TV season.

schedules of reinforcement (4) The schedule by which a behavioral response is rewarded.

script (9) A written version of the commercial that provides a detailed description of its video and audio content.

selective attention (4) A perceptual process in which consumers choose to attend to some stimuli and not others.

selective binding (12) A computerized production process that allows the creation of hundreds of copies of a magazine in one continuous sequence.

selective comprehension (4) The perceptual process whereby consumers interpret information based on their own attitudes, beliefs, motives, and experiences.

selective demand advertising (2) Advertising that focuses on stimulating demand for a specific manufacturer's product or brand.

selective exposure (4) A process whereby consumers choose whether or not to make themselves available to media and message information.

selective learning (5) The process whereby consumers seek information that supports the choice made and avoid information that fails to bolster the wisdom of a purchase decision.

selective perception (4) The perceptual process involving the filtering or screening of exposure, attention, comprehension, and retention.

selective retention (4) The perceptual process whereby consumers remember some information but not all.

selectivity (12) The ability of a medium to reach a specific target audience.

self-liquidating premiums (16) Premiums that require the consumer to pay some or all of the cost of the premium plus handling and mailing costs.

self-paced media (6) Media that viewers and/or readers can control their exposure time to, allowing them to process information at their own rate.

self-regulation (21) The practice by the advertising industry of regulating and controlling advertising to avoid interference by outside agencies such as the government.

semiotics (5) The study of the nature of meaning.

sensation (4) The immediate and direct response of the senses (taste, smell, sight, touch, and hearing) to a stimulus such as an advertisement, package, brand name, or point-of-purchase display.

shaping (4) The reinforcement of successive acts that lead to a desired behavior pattern or response.

share-of-audience (11) The percentage of households watching television in a special time period that are tuned to a specific program.

showing (13) The percentage of supplicated audience exposed to an outdoor poster daily.

similarity (6) The supposed resemblance between the source and the receiver of a message.

single-source tracking (19) A research method designed to track the behaviors of consumers from the television set to the supermarket checkout counter.

situational determinants (4) Influences originating from the specific situation in which consumers are to use the product or brand.

sleeper effect (6) A phenomenon in which the persuasiveness of a message increases over time.

slotting allowance (16) Fees that must be paid to retailers to provide a "slot" or position to accommodate a new product on the store shelves.

social class (4) Relatively homogeneous divisions of society into which people are grouped based on similar lifestyles, values, norms, interests, and behaviors.

source (5, 6) The sender—person, group, or organization—of the message.

source bolsters (5) Favorable cognitive thoughts generated toward the source of a message.

source derogations (5) Negative thoughts generated about the source of a communication.

source power (6) The power of a source as a result of his or her ability to administer rewards and/or punishments to the receiver.

spam (15) Unsolicited commercial e-mail.

specialized marketing communication services (3) Organizations that provide marketing communication services in their areas of expertise including direct marketing, public relations, and sales promotion firms.

specialty advertising (13) An advertising, sales promotion, and motivational communications medium that employs useful articles of merchandise imprinted with an advertiser's name, message, or logo.

split runs (12) Two or more versions of a print ad are printed in alternative copies of a particular issue of a magazine.

split run test (19) An advertising effectiveness measure in which different versions of an ad are run in alternate copies of the same newspaper and/or magazine.

split 30s (11) 30-second TV spots in which the advertiser promotes two different products with two different messages during a 30-second commercial.

sponsorship (11) When the advertiser assumes responsibility for the production and usually the content of a television program as well as the advertising that appears within it.

sponsorships (15) When advertisers sponsor content on a website, it is considered a sponsorship.

spot advertising (11) Commercials shown on local television stations, with the negotiation and purchase of time being made directly from the individual stations.

standard advertising unit (SAU) (12) A standard developed in the newpaper industry to make newspaper purchasing rates more comparable to other media that sell space and time in standard units.

standard learning model (5) Progression by the consumers through a learn-feel-do hierarchical response.

station reps (11) Individuals who act as sales representatives for a number of local stations and represent them in dealings with national advertisers.

storyboard (8) A series of drawings used to present the visual plan or layout of a proposed commercial.

strategic marketing plan (2) The planning framework for specific marketing activities.

subcultures (4) Smaller groups within a culture that possess similar beliefs, values, norms, and patterns of behavior that differentiate them from the larger cultural mainstream.

subheads (9) Secondary headlines in a print ad.

subliminal perception (4) The ability of an individual to perceive a stimulus below the level of conscious awareness.

superagencies (3) Large external agencies that offer integrated marketing communications on a worldwide basis.

superstations (11) Independent local stations that send their signals via satellite to cable operators that, in turn, make them available to subscribers (WWOR, WPIX, WGN, WSBK, WTBS).

support advertising (14) A form of direct marketing in which the ad is designed to support other forms of advertising appearing in other media.

support argument (5) Consumers' thoughts that support or affirm the claims being made by a message.

support media (13) Those media used to support or reinforce messages sent to target markets through other more "dominant" and/or more traditional media.

sweeps periods (10) The times of year in which television audience measures are taken (February, May, July, and November).

sweepstakes (16) A promotion whereby consumers submit their names for consideration in the drawing or selection of prizes and winners are determined purely by chance. Sweepstakes cannot require a proof of purchase as a condition for entry.

syndicated programs (11) Shows sold or distributed to local stations.

T

target marketing (2) The process of identifying the specific needs of segments, selecting one or more of these segments as a target, and developing marketing programs directed to each.

target ratings points (TRPs) (10) The number of persons in the primary target audience that the media buy will reach—and the number of times.

team approach (17) A method of measuring the effectiveness of public relations programs whereby evaluators are actually involved in the campaign.

teaser advertising (9) An ad designed to create curiosity and build excitement and interest in a product or brand without showing it.

telemarketing (14) Selling products and services by using the telephone to contact prospective customers.

tele-media (14) The use of telephone and voice information services (800, 900, 976 numbers) to market, advertise, promote, entertain, and inform.

television households (11) The number of households in a market that own a television set.

television network (11) The provider of news and programming to a series of affiliated local television stations.

terminal posters (13) Floor dislays, island showcases, electronic signs, and other forms of advertisements that appear in train or subway stations, airline terminals, etc.

testing bias (19) A bias that occurs in advertising effectiveness measures because respondents know they are being tested and thus alter their responses.

tests of comprehension and reaction (19) Advertising effectiveness tests that are designed to assess whether the ad conveyed the desired meaning and is not reacted to negatively.

theater testing (19) An advertising effectiveness pretest in which consumers view ads in a theater setting and evaluate these ads on a variety of dimensions.

top-down approaches (7) Budgeting approaches in which the budgetary amount is established at the executive level and monies are passed down to the various departments.

total audience (television) (11) The total number of homes viewing any five-minute part of a television program.

total audience/readership (12) A combination of the total number of primary and pass-along readers multiplied by the circulation of an average issue of a magazine.

tracking studies (19) Advertising effectiveness measures designed to assess the effects of advertising on awareness, recall, interest, and attitudes toward the ad as well as purchase intentions.

trade advertising (2) Advertising targeted to wholesalers and retailers.

trademark (2) An identifying name, symbol, or other device that gives a company the legal and exclusive rights to use.

trade-oriented sales promotion (16) A sales promotion designed to motivate distributors and retailers to carry a product and make an extra effort to promote or "push" it to their customers.

trade regulation rules (TRRs) (21) Industrywide rules that define unfair practices before they occur. Used by the Federal Trade Commission to regulate advertising and promotion.

trade show (16) A type of exhibition or forum where manufacturers can display their products to current as well as prospective buyers.

transformational advertising (9) An ad that associates the experience of using the advertised brand with a unique set of psychological characteristics that would not typically be associated with the brand experience to the same degree without exposure to the advertisement.

transit advertising (13) Advertising targeted to target audiences exposed to commercial transportation facilities, including buses, taxis, trains, elevators, trolleys, airplanes, and subways.

trustworthiness (6) The honesty, integrity, and believability of the source of a communication.

two-sided message (6) A message in which both good and bad points about a product or claim are presented.

two-step approach (14) A direct-marketing strategy in which the first effort is designed to screen or qualify potential buyers, while the second effort has the responsibility of generating the response.

U

undifferentiated marketing (2) A strategy in which market segment differences are ignored and one product or service is offered to the entire market.

unduplicated reach (10) The number of persons reached once with a media exposure.

unfairness (21) A concept used by the Federal Trade Commission to determine unfair or deceptive advertising practices. Unfairness occurs when a trade practice causes substantial physical or economic injury to consumers, could not be avoided by consumers, and must not be outweighed by countervailing benefits to consumers or competition.

unique selling proposition (8) An advertising strategy that focuses on a product or service attribute that is distinctive to a particular brand and offers an important benefit to the customer.

unique users (15) The number of different individuals who visit a site within a specific time period.

up-front market (11) A buying period that takes place prior to the upcoming television season when the networks sell a large part of their commercial time.

V

valid hits (15) The number of hits that deliver all of the information to a user (excludes error messages, redirects, etc.).

values and lifestyles program (VALS) (2) Stanford Research Institute's method for applying lifestyle segmentation.

vehicle option source effect (19) The differential impact the advertising exposure will have on the same audience member if the exposure occurs in one media option rather than another.

vertical cooperative advertising (16) A cooperative arrangement under which a manufacturer pays for a portion of the advertising a retailer runs to promote the manufacturer's product and its availability in the retailer's place of business.

video advertising (13) Advertisements appearing in movie theaters and on videotapes.

video news release (16) News stories produced by publicists so that television stations may air them as news.

visits (15) A sequence of requests made by one user at one site.

voiceover (9) Action on the screen in a commercial that is narrated or described by a narrator who is not visible.

W

want (4) A felt need shaped by a person's knowledge, culture, and personality.

waste coverage (10) A situation where the coverage of the media exceeds the target audience.

webcasting (15) A system for pushing out site information to Web users rather than waiting for them to find the site on their own. (Often referred to as push technologies.)

website (15) The information made available to users of the Internet by the provider.

Wheeler-Lea Amendment (21) An act of Congress passed in 1938 that amended section 5 of the FTC Act to read that unfair methods of competition in commerce and unfair or deceptive acts or practices in commerce are declared unlawful.

wireless (15) A communications network that allows access, as well as transmissions to and from the Internet to travel over the air waves, rather than fixed land lines.

word-of-mouth communications (5) Social channels of communication such as friends, neighbors, associates, coworkers, or family members.

World Wide Web (WWW) (15) Commonly referred to as the Web. The commercial component of the Internet.

Y

Yellow Pages advertising (13) Advertisements that appear in the various Yellow Pages–type phone directories.

Z

zapping (11) The use of a remote control device to change channels and switch away from commercials.

zero-based communications planning (7) An approach to planning the integrated marketing communications program that involves determining what tasks need to be done and what marketing communication functions should be used to accomplish them and to what extent.

zipping (11) Fast-forwarding through commercials during the playback of a program previously recorded on a VCR.

Endnotes

Chapter One

1. Robert J. Coen, *Insider's Report: Robert Coen Presentation on Advertising Expenditures* (New York: Universal McCann, McCann Erickson Worldwide, December 2002).
2. Ibid.
3. "AMA Board Approves New Marketing Definition," *Marketing News*, March 1, 1985, p. 1.
4. Richard P. Bagozzi, "Marketing as Exchange," *Journal of Marketing* 39 (October 1975), pp. 32–39.
5. Leonard L. Berry, "Relationship Marketing of Services—Growing Interest, Emerging Perspectives," *Journal of the Academy of Marketing Science* 23, no. 4, 1995, pp. 236–45; Jonathan R. Capulsky and Michael J. Wolfe, "Relationship Marketing: Positioning for the Future," *Journal of Business Strategy*, July–August 1991, pp. 16–26.
6. James H. Gilmore and B. Joseph Pine II, "The Four Faces of Customization," *Harvard Business Review*, 75 (1) (January–February 1997), pp. 91–101.
7. Robert J. Lavidge, "'Mass Customization' Is Not an Oxy-Moron," *Journal of Advertising Research*, (July–August 1999), pp. 70–72.
8. B. Joseph Pine II, Don Peppers, and Martha Rogers, "Do You Want to Keep Your Customers Forever?" *Harvard Business Review*, 73 (2) (March–April 1995), pp. 103–14.
9. Adrienne Ward Fawcett, "Integrated Marketing—Marketers Convinced: Its Time Has Arrived," *Advertising Age*, November 6, 1993, pp. S1–2.
10. "Do Your Ads Need a SuperAgency?" *Fortune*, April 27, 1991, pp. 81–85; Faye Rice, "A Cure for What Ails Advertising?" *Fortune*, December 16, 1991, pp. 119–22.
11. Scott Hume, "Campus Adopts 'New' Advertising," *Advertising Age*, September 23, 1991, p. 17.
12. Don E. Schultz, "Integrated Marketing Communications: Maybe Definition Is in the Point of View," *Marketing News*, January 18, 1993, p. 17.
13. Ibid.
14. Tom Duncan and Sandra E. Moriarty, "A Communication-Based Model for Managing Relationships," *Journal of Marketing* 62, (2), (April 1998), pp. 1–13.
15. Ronald Alsop, "The Best Corporate Reputations in America," *The Wall Street Journal*, September 29, 1999, pp. B1, 6.
16. Harlan E. Spotts, David R. Lambert, and Mary L. Joyce, "Marketing Déjà Vu: The Discovery of Integrated Marketing Communications," *Journal of Marketing Education*, Vol. 20, (3) (December 1998), pp. 210–18.
17. Kate Fitzgerald, "Beyond Advertising," *Advertising Age*, August 3, 1998, pp. 1, 14; Jane Smith, "Integrated Marketing," *Marketing Tools*, November/December 1995, pp. 63–70; Thomas R. Duncan and Stephen E. Everett, "Client Perception of Integrated Marketing Communications," *Journal of Advertising Research*, May/June 1993, pp. 30–39.
18. Anthony J. Tortorici, "Maximizing Marketing Communications through Horizontal and Vertical Orchestration," *Public Relations Quarterly*, Vol. 36, (1) (1991), pp. 20–22.
19. Robert H. Ducoffe, Dennis Sandler, and Eugene Secunda, "A Survey of Senior Agency, Advertiser, and Media Executives on the Future of Advertising," *Journal of Current Issues and Research in Advertising* 18, no. 1 (Spring 1996) pp. 1–19.
20. Earle Eldridge, "These cars want to be in pictures," *USA TODAY*, May 24, 2002, p. 3B.
21. Sergio Zyman, *The End of Marketing As We Know It* (New York: HarperBusiness, 1999); Joe Cappo, "Agencies: Change or Die," *Advertising Age*, December 7, 1992, p. 26.
22. Don E. Schultz, "Be Careful Picking Database for IMC Efforts," *Marketing News*, March 11, 1996, p. 14.
23. Kevin Lane Keller, "The Brand Report Card," *Harvard Business Review*, 78 (1) (January/February 2000) p. 3–10.
24. Kevin Lane Keller, "Conceptualizing, Measuring, and Managing Customer-Based Brand Equity," *Journal of Marketing*, Vol. 57 (January 1993), pp. 1–22.
25. Michael L. Ray, *Advertising and Communication Management* (Englewood Cliffs, NJ: Prentice Hall, 1982).
26. Ralph S. Alexander, ed., *Marketing Definitions* (Chicago: American Marketing Association, 1965), p. 9.
27. "Network Television Cost and CPM Trends," *Trends in Media*, Television Bureau of Advertising, New York. http://www.tvb.org
28. Richard Lewis, "Absolut Vodka Case History," *A Celebration of Effective Advertising: 30 Years of Winning EFFIE Campaigns* (New York: American Marketing Association, 1999), pp. 20–23.
29. Janis Maya, "Nike: Best Integrated Campaign," *Brandweek*, June 5, 2000, pp. IQ44–IQ47.
30. "Slow + Steady: Promo's Exclusive Annual Report of the U.S. Promotion Industry," *Promo*, April 2002.
31. Jefferson Graham, "Abs Machine Sales Go Flabby," *USA Today*, October 22, 1996, p. D1.
32. H. Frazier Moore and Bertrand R. Canfield, *Public Relations: Principles, Cases, and Problems*, 7th ed. (Burr Ridge, IL: Irwin, 1977), p. 5.
33. Jack Neff, "Ries' thesis: Ads don't build brands, PR does," *Advertising Age*, July 15, 2002, pp. 14–15; Art Kleiner, "The Public Relations Coup," *Adweek's Marketing Week*, January 16, 1989, pp. 20–23.
34. Ronald Alsop, "The Best Corporate Reputations in America," *The Wall Street Journal*, September 29, 1999, pp. B1, 6.

Chapter Two

1. Hillary Cassidy, "Chasing a Retail Brand," *Brandweek*, January 21, 2002, pp.18–21.
2. John Gaffney, "Shoe Fetish," *Business 2.0*, March 2002, pp. 98–99.
3. Dan Fost, "Growing Older, but Not Up," *American Demographics*, September 1998, pp. 58–65.
4. Eric N. Berkowitz, Roger A. Kerin, and William Rudelius, *Marketing*, 6th

ed. (Burr Ridge, IL: Irwin/McGraw-Hill, 2000).
5. Edward M. Tauber, "Research on Food Consumption Values Finds Four Market Segments: Good Taste Still Tops," *Marketing News*, May 15, 1981, p. 17; Rebecca C. Quarles, "Shopping Centers Use Fashion Lifestyle Research to Make Marketing Decisions," *Marketing News*, January 22, 1982, p. 18; and "Our Auto, Ourselves," *Consumer Reports*, June 1985, p. 375.
6. Judith Graham, "New VALS 2 Takes Psychological Route," *Advertising Age*, February 13, 1989, p. 24.
7. *Ayer's Dictionary of Advertising Terms* (Philadelphia: Ayer Press, 1976).
8. Davis A. Aaker and John G. Myers, *Advertising Management*, 3rd ed. (Englewood Cliffs, NJ: Prentice Hall, 1987), p. 125.
9. Jack Trout and Al Ries, "Positioning Cuts through Chaos in the Marketplace," *Advertising Age*, May 1, 1972, pp. 51–53.
10. Ibid.
11. David A. Aaker and J. Gary Shansby, "Positioning Your Product," *Business Horizons*, May–June 1982, pp. 56–62.
12. Aaker and Myers, *Advertising Management*.
13. Trout and Ries, "Positioning Cuts through Chaos."
14. Aaker and Myers, *Advertising Management.*
15. J. Paul Peter and Jerry C. Olson, *Consumer Behavior* (Burr Ridge, IL: Richard D. Irwin, 1987), p. 505.
16. Michael R. Solomon, "The Role of Products as Social Stimuli: A Symbolic Interactionism Perspective," *Journal of Consumer Research*, 10, (December 1983), pp. 319–29.
17. Don. E. Schultz, Stanley I. Tannenbaum, and Robert F. Lauterborn, *Integrated Marketing Communications* (Lincolnwood, IL: NTC Publishing Group 1993), p. 72.
18. Peter and Olson, *Consumer Behavior*, p. 571.
19. Paul W. Farris and David J. Reibstein, "How Prices, Ad Expenditures, and Profits Are Linked," *Harvard Business Review*, (November–December 1979), pp. 172–84.
20. Berkowitz, Kerin, and Rudelius, *Marketing*.
21. David W. Stewart, Gary L. Frazier, and Ingrid Martin, "Integrated Channel Management: Merging the Communication and Distribution Functions of the Firm," in *Integrated Communication: Synergy of Persuasive Voices*, pp. 185–215, Esther Thorson & Jeri Moore (eds), Lawrence Earlbaum Associates, 1996, Mahwah, NJ.

Chapter Three

1. Jack Neff, "P&G Redefines the Brand Manager," *Advertising Age*, October 13, 1997, pp. 1, 18, 20.
2. Thomas J. Cosse and John E. Swan, "Strategic Marketing Planning by Product Managers—Room for Improvement?" *Journal of Marketing* 47 (Summer 1983), pp. 92–102.
3. "Behind the Tumult at P&G," *Fortune*, March 7, 1994, pp. 74–82; "Category Management: New Tools Changing Life for Manufacturers, Retailers," *Marketing News*, September 25, 1989, pp. 2, 19.
4. Cosse and Swan, "Strategic Marketing Planning by Product Managers—Room for Improvement?"
5. Kathleen Kerwin, "GM Warms Up the Branding Iron," *BusinessWeek*, September 23, 1996, pp. 153–54; Jean Halliday, "GM's Brand Management Report Card," *Advertising Age*, March 9, 1998, pp. 1, 26.
6. Victor P. Buell, *Organizing for Marketing/Advertising Success* (New York: Association of National Advertisers, 1982).
7. M. Louise Ripley, "What Kind of Companies Take Their Advertising In-House?" *Journal of Advertising Research*, 31 (4) (October/November 1991), pp. 73–80.
8. Bruce Horovitz, "Some Companies Say the Best Ad Agency Is No Ad Agency at All," *Los Angeles Times,* July 19, 1989, Sec IV, p. 5.
9. Bradley Johnson and Alice Z. Cuneo, "Gateway 2000 Taps DMB&B," *Advertising Age*, March 24, 1997, p. 2.
10. Kate MacArthur, "Chicago Blues," *Advertising Age*, September 10, 2001, pp. 1, 12; Anthony Vagnoni, "Gotham Regains Some Lost Luster as Center of U.S. Agency Creativity," *Advertising Age*, April 12, 1999, pp. 1, 10.
11. Sally Goll Beatty, "Global Needs Challenge Midsize Agencies," *The Wall Street Journal*, December 14, 1995, p. B9.
12. Kate MacArthur and Laurel Wentz, "The Final 4: Publicis makes cut," *Advertising Age*, March 11, 2002, pp. 1, 43; Kathryn Kranhold, "Fallon McElligott to Be Part of Publics," *The Wall Street Journal,* February 3, 2000, p. B5.
13. Gordon Fairclough, "Pace of Ad Mergers Is Expected to Continue," *The Wall Street Journal*, April 23, 1999, p. B2.
14. Suzanne Vranica, "Ad Giant Interpublic Shops for Literacy, Talent Agencies," *The Wall Street Journal*, June 14, 2002, pp. B1, 3.
15. Bob Lammons, "A Good Account Exec Makes a Big Difference," *Marketing News*, June 3, 1996, p. 12.
16. Jack Feurer, "Universal McCann Wins Nestlé Buying Review," *http://www.adweek.com*, April 12, 2002.
17. Michael McCarthy, "Ads go Hollywood with short films," USA TODAY, June 20, 2002, p. 3B.
18. Patricia Sellers, "Do You Need Your Ad Agency?" *Fortune*, November 15, 1993, pp. 47–61.
19. Jack Neff, "Feeling the Squeeze," *Advertising Age*, June 4, 2001, pp. 1, 14.
20. Ibid.
21. Kate MacArthur, "McD's squeezes agency fees," November 11, 2002, *Advertising Age*, pp. 1, 45; Kathryn Kranhold, "P&G Expands Its Program to Tie Agency Pay to Brand Performance," *The Wall Street Journal*, September 16, 1999, p. B12.
22. Sally Beatty, "P&G to Test Ad Agency Pay Tied to Sales," *The Wall Street Journal*, November 9, 1998, p. B4.
23. Alice Z. Cuneo, "Nissan Ties TBWA's Pay to Car Sales," *Advertising Age*, June 7, 1999, pp. 1, 49.
24. Jean Halliday, "GM to Scrap Agency Commissions," *Advertising Age*, November 16, 1998, pp. 1, 57.
25. Joanne Lipman, "Study Shows Clients Jump Ship Quickly," *The Wall Street Journal*, May 21, 1992, p. B6.
26. Alice Z. Cuneo, "Bartle Bogle tapped to cure Levi's blues," *Advertising Age*, January 14, 2002, p. 6.
27. Alice Z. Cuneo and Jean Halliday, "Saturn's Entire $300 Million Account Goes To Goodby," *http://www.Adage.com*, January 31, 2002.
28. Fred Beard, "Marketing Client Role Ambiguity as a Source of Dissatisfaction in Client–Ad Agency Relationships," *Journal of Advertising Research*, (September/October 1996), pp. 9–20; Paul Michell, Harold Cataquet, and Stephen Hague, "Establishing the Causes of Disaffection in Agency-Client Relations," *Journal of Advertising Research*, 32, 2, 1992, pp. 41–48; Peter Doyle, Marcel Corstiens, and Paul Michell, "Signals of Vulnerability in Agency-Client Relations," *Journal of Marketing*, 44 (Fall 1980), pp. 18–23; and Daniel B. Wackman, Charles Salmon, and

Caryn C. Salmon, "Developing an Advertising Agency–Client Relationship," *Journal of Advertising Research 26*, no. 6 (December 1986/January 1987), pp. 21–29.
29. Suzanne Vranica, "Pinched Firms Woo Rivals' Happy Clients," *The Wall Street Journal*, March 4, 2002, p. B8.
30. Sally Goll Beatty, "Blockbuster Puts Agencies in a Permanent Shootout," *The Wall Street Journal*, October 2, 1996, pp. B1, 8; and "Big Agencies Starting to Call for End to Costly Free Pitches," *The Wall Street Journal*, February 22, 1989, p. B7.
31. Fred K. Beard, "Exploring the Use of Advertising Agency Review Consultants," *Journal of Advertising Research*, 42 (1) (January/February) 2002, pp. 39–50.
32. "A Potent New Tool For Selling: Database Marketing," *BusinessWeek*, September 5, 1994, pp. 56–62.
33. Jack Neff, "Ries' thesis: Ads don't build brands, PR does," *Advertising Age*, July 15, 2002, pp. 14–15; Prema Nakra, "The Changing Role of Public Relations in Marketing Communications," *Public Relations Quarterly*, 1 (1991) pp. 42–45.
34. Sally Beatty, "Interpublic Buying Stake in Icon Medialab," *The Wall Street Journal*, March 25, 1999, p. B2; Sally Goll Beatty, "Interpublic Diversifies Further with Purchase of Direct Marketer," *The Wall Street Journal*, May 17, 1996, p. B5.
35. Betsy Spethmann, "Sudden Impact," *Promo*, April 1999, pp. 42–48.
36. Quote in: Laura Q. Hughes and Kate MacArthur, "Soft boiled," *Advertising Age*, May 28, 2001, pp. 3, 54.
37. Philip J. Kitchen and Don E. Schultz, "A Multi-Country Comparison of the Drive for IMC," *Journal of Advertising Research*, January/February 1999, pp. 21–38.
38. Laura Q. Hughes and Kate MacArthur, "Soft boiled."
39. David N. McArthur and Tom Griffin, "A Marketing Management View of Integrated Marketing Communications," *Journal of Advertising Research*, 37, no. 5 (September/October) 1997, pp. 19–26; and Adrienne Ward Fawcett, "Integrated Marketing—Marketers Convinced: Its Time Has Arrived," *Advertising Age*, November 6, 1993, pp. S1–2.

Chapter Four

1. Russell W. Belk, "Possessions and the Extended Self," *Journal of Consumer Research*, 15 (2) (September 1988), pp. 139–68.
2. Eric N. Berkowitz, Roger A. Kerin, Steven W. Hartley, and William Rudelius, *Marketing*, 6th ed. (Burr Ridge, IL: Irwin/McGraw-Hill, 2000), p. 14.
3. A. H. Maslow, "'Higher' and 'Lower' Needs," *Journal of Psychology* 25 (1948), pp. 433–36.
4. Morton Deutsch and Robert M. Krauss, *Theories in Social Psychology* (New York: Basic Books, 1965).
5. Jeffrey Ball, "But How Does It Make You Feel?" *The Wall Street Journal*, May 3, 1999, p. B1.
6. Jagdish N. Sheth, "The Role of Motivation Research in Consumer Psychology" (Faculty Working Paper, University of Illinois, Champaign: 1974); Bill Abrams, "Charles of the Ritz Discovers What Women Want," *The Wall Street Journal*, August 20, 1981, p. 29; and Ernest Dichter, *Getting Motivated* (New York: Pergamon Press, 1979).
7. Ronald Alsop, "Advertisers Put Consumers on the Couch," *The Wall Street Journal*, May 13, 1988, p. 19.
8. Ball, "But How Does It Make You Feel?"
9. For an excellent discussion of memory and consumer behavior, see James R. Bettman, "Memory Factors in Consumer Choice: A Review," *Journal of Marketing*, 43 (2) (Spring 1979), pp. 37–53.
10. Gilbert Harrell, *Consumer Behavior* (San Diego: Harcourt Brace Jovanovich, 1986), p. 66.
11. Raymond A. Bauer and Stephen A. Greyser, *Advertising in America: The Consumer View* (Boston: Harvard Business School, 1968).
12. Neal Santelmann, "Color That Yells 'Buy Me'," *Forbes*, May 2, 1988, p. 110.
13. J. Paul Peter and Jerry C. Olson, *Consumer Behavior*, 2nd ed. (Burr Ridge, IL: Irwin/McGraw-Hill, 1990), p. 73.
14. Gordon W. Allport, "Attitudes," in *Handbook of Social Psychology*, ed. C. M. Murchison (Winchester, MA: Clark University Press, 1935), p. 810.
15. Robert B. Zajonc and Hazel Markus, "Affective and Cognitive Factors in Preferences," *Journal of Consumer Research,* 9 (2) (June 1982), pp. 123–31.
16. Alvin Achenbaum, "Advertising Doesn't Manipulate Consumers," *Journal of Advertising Research*, (April 1970) pp. 3–13.
17. William D. Wells, "Attitudes and Behavior: Lessons from the Needham Lifestyle Study," *Journal of Advertising Research*, (February–March 1985), pp. 40–44; and Icek Ajzen and Martin Fishbein, "Attitude-Behavior Relations: A Theoretical Analysis and Review of Empirical Research," *Psychological Bulletin*, (September 1977) pp. 888–918.
18. For a review of multiattribute models, see William L. Wilkie and Edgar A. Pessemier, "Issues in Marketing's Use of Multiattribute Models," *Journal of Marketing Research*, 20 (November 1983), pp. 428–41.
19. Joel B. Cohen, Paul W. Minniard, and Peter R. Dickson, "Information Integration: An Information Processing Perspective," in *Advances in Consumer Research*, vol. 7, ed. Jerry C. Olson (Ann Arbor, MI: Association for Consumer Research, 1980), pp. 161–70.
20. Peter and Olson, *Consumer Behavior*, p. 182.
21. Peter L. Wright and Fredric Barbour, "The Relevance of Decision Process Models in Structuring Persuasive Messages," *Communications Research*, July 1975, pp. 246–59.
22. James F. Engel, "The Psychological Consequences of a Major Purchase Decision," in *Marketing in Transition*, (ed.) William S. Decker (Chicago: American Marketing Association, 1963), pp. 462–75.
23. John A. Howard and Jagdish N. Sheth, *The Theory of Consumer Behavior* (New York: John Wiley & Sons, 1969).
24. Leon G. Schiffman and Leslie Lazar Kannuk, *Consumer Behavior*, 4th ed. (Englewood Cliffs, NJ: Prentice Hall, 1991), p. 192.
25. Ivan. P. Pavlov, *Conditioned Reflexes: An Investigation of the Physiological Activity of the Cerebral Cortex,* G. V. Anrep (trans ed) (London: The Oxford Press, 1927).
26. Gerald J. Gorn, "The Effects of Music in Advertising on Choice: A Classical Conditioning Approach," *Journal of Marketing* 46 (Winter 1982), pp. 94–101.
27. James J. Kellaris, Anthony D. Cox, and Dena Cox, "The Effect of Background Music on Ad Processing: A Contingency Explanation," *Journal of Marketing*, 57, (4) (Fall 1993), p. 114.
28. Brian C. Deslauries and Peter B. Everett, "The Effects of Intermittent and Continuous Token Reinforcement on Bus Ridership," *Journal of Applied Psychology*, 62 (August 1977), pp. 369–75.
29. Michael L. Rothschild and William C. Gaidis, "Behavioral Learning Theory: Its Relevance to Marketing and Promotions," *Journal of Marketing*

Research 45, (2) (Spring 1981), pp. 70–78.
30. For an excellent discussion of social class and consumer behavior, see Richard P. Coleman, "The Continuing Significance of Social Class to Marketing," *Journal of Consumer Research* 10, (3) (December 1983), pp. 265–80.
31. Lyman E. Ostlund, "Role Theory and Group Dynamics," in *Consumer Behavior: Theoretical Sources*, ed. Scott Ward and Thomas S. Robertson (Englewood Cliffs, NJ: Prentice Hall, 1973), pp. 230–75.
32. James Stafford and Benton Cocanougher, "Reference Group Theory," in *Perspectives in Consumer Behavior*, (ed.) H. H. Kassarjian and T. S. Robertson (Glenview, IL: Scott, Foresman, 1981), pp. 329–43.
33. Jagdish N. Sheth, "A Theory of Family Buying Decisions," in *Models of Buying Behavior*, (ed.) Jagdish N. Sheth (New York: Harper & Row, 1974), pp. 17–33.
34. Russell Belk, "Situational Variables and Consumer Behavior," *Journal of Consumer Research*, (December 1975), pp. 157–64.

Chapter Five

1. Wilbur Schram, *The Process and Effects of Mass Communications* (Urbana: University of Illinois Press, 1955).
2. Ibid.
3. Joseph Ransdell, "Some Leading Ideas of Peirce's Semiotic," *Semiotica* 19 (1977), pp. 157–78.
4. Michael Solomon, *Consumer Behavior*, 5th ed. (Upper Saddle River, NJ: Prentice-Hall, 2001), pp. 62–63.
5. Nina Munk, "Levi's Ongoing Quest for Street Cred," *Fortune*, February 1, 1999, p. 40.
6. For an excellent article on the application of semiotics to consumer behavior and advertising, see David G. Mick, "Consumer Research and Semiotics: Exploring the Morphology of Signs, Symbols, and Significance," *Journal of Consumer Research* 13, no. 2 (September 1986), pp. 196–213; see also Edward F. McQuarrie and David Glen Mick, "Figures of Rhetoric in Advertising Language," *Journal of Consumer Research* 22 (4) (March 1996), pp. 424–38.
7. Robert E. Smith and Christine A. Vogt, "The Effects of Integrating Advertising and Negative Word-of-Mouth Communications on Message Processing and Response," *Journal of Consumer Psychology*, 4 No. 2 (1995), pp. 133–51; Barry L. Bayus, "Word of Mouth: The Indirect Effect of Marketing Efforts," *Journal of Advertising Research*, 25 (3) (June/July 1985), pp. 31–39.
8. Quote by Gordon S. Bower in *Fortune*, October 14, 1985, p. 11.
9. Thomas V. Bonoma and Leonard C. Felder, "Nonverbal Communication in Marketing: Toward Communicational Analysis," *Journal of Marketing Research*, (May 1977), pp. 169–80.
10. Jacob Jacoby and Wayne D. Hoyer, "Viewer Miscomprehension of Televised Communication: Selected Findings," *Journal of Marketing*, 46 (4) (Fall 1982), pp. 12–26; Jacoby and Hoyer, "The Comprehension and Miscomprehension of Print Communications: An Investigation of Mass Media Magazines," *Advertising Education Foundation Study*, New York, 1987.
11. E. K. Strong, *The Psychology of Selling* (New York: McGraw-Hill, 1925), p. 9.
12. Robert J. Lavidge and Gary A. Steiner, "A Model for Predictive Measurements of Advertising Effectiveness," *Journal of Marketing* 24 (October 1961), pp. 59–62.
13. Everett M. Rogers, *Diffusion of Innovations* (New York: Free Press, 1962), pp. 79–86.
14. William J. McGuire, "An Information Processing Model of Advertising Effectiveness," in *Behavioral and Management Science in Marketing*, ed. Harry J. Davis and Alvin J. Silk (New York: Ronald Press, 1978), pp. 156–80.
15. Michael L. Ray, "Communication and the Hierarchy of Effects," in *New Models for Mass Communication Research*, ed. P. Clarke (Beverly Hills, CA: Sage, 1973), pp. 147–75.
16. Herbert E. Krugman, "The Impact of Television Advertising: Learning without Involvement," *Public Opinion Quarterly* 29 (Fall 1965), pp. 349–56.
17. Scott A. Hawkins and Stephen J. Hoch, "Low-Involvement Learning: Memory without Evaluation," *Journal of Consumer Research* 19, no. 2 (September 1992), pp. 212–25.
18. Harry W. McMahan, "Do Your Ads Have VIP?" *Advertising Age*, July 14, 1980, pp. 50–51.
19. Robert E. Smith, "Integrating Information from Advertising and Trial: Processes and Effects on Consumer Response to Product Information," *Journal of Marketing Research* 30 (May 1993), pp. 204–19.
20. DeAnna S. Kempf and Russell N. Laczniak, "Advertising's Influence on Subsequent Product Trial Processing," *Journal of Advertising*, Vol. 30, No. 3, Fall 2001, pp. 27–38.
21. Harold H. Kassarjian, "Low Involvement: A Second Look," in *Advances in Consumer Research*, vol. 8 (Ann Arbor: Association for Consumer Research, 1981), pp. 31–34; also see Anthony G. Greenwald and Clark Leavitt, "Audience Involvement in Advertising: Four Levels," *Journal of Consumer Research* 11, no. 1 (June 1984), pp. 581–92.
22. Judith L. Zaichkowsky, "Conceptualizing Involvement," *Journal of Advertising* 15, no. 2 (1986), pp. 4–14.
23. Richard Vaughn, "How Advertising Works: A Planning Model," *Journal of Advertising Research* 20, no. 5 (October 1980), pp. 27–33.
24. Richard Vaughn, "How Advertising Works: A Planning Model Revisited," *Journal of Advertising Research* 26, no. 1 (February/March 1986), pp. 57–66.
25. Jerry C. Olson, Daniel R. Toy, and Phillip A. Dover, "Mediating Effects of Cognitive Responses to Advertising on Cognitive Structure," in *Advances in Consumer Research*, vol. 5, ed. H. Keith Hunt (Ann Arbor, MI: Association for Consumer Research, 1978), pp. 72–78.
26. Anthony A. Greenwald, "Cognitive Learning, Cognitive Response to Persuasion and Attitude Change," in *Psychological Foundations of Attitudes*, ed. A. G. Greenwald, T. C. Brock, and T. W. Ostrom (New York: Academic Press, 1968); Peter L. Wright, "The Cognitive Processes Mediating Acceptance of Advertising," *Journal of Marketing Research* 10 (February 1973), pp. 53–62; Brian Wansink, Michael L. Ray, and Rajeev Batra, "Increasing Cognitive Response Sensitivity," *Journal of Advertising* 23, no. 2 (June 1994), pp. 65–76.
27. Peter Wright, "Message Evoked Thoughts, Persuasion Research Using Thought Verbalizations," *Journal of Consumer Research* 7, no. 2 (September 1980), pp. 151–75.
28. Scott B. Mackenzie, Richard J. Lutz, and George E. Belch, "The Role of Attitude toward the Ad as a Mediator of Advertising Effectiveness: A Test of Competing Explanations," *Journal of Marketing Research* 23 (May 1986), pp. 130–43; and Rajeev Batra and Michael L. Ray, "Affective Responses Mediating Acceptance of Advertising," *Journal of Consumer*

Research 13 (September 1986), pp. 234–49; Tim Ambler and Tom Burne, "The Impact of Affect on Memory of Advertising," *Journal of Advertising Research* 29, no. 3 (March/April 1999), pp. 25–34.

29. Ronald Alsop, "TV Ads That Are Likeable Get Plus Rating for Persuasiveness," *The Wall Street Journal*, February 20, 1986, p. 23.
30. David J. Moore and William D. Harris, "Affect Intensity and the Consumer's Attitude toward High Impact Emotional Advertising Appeals," *Journal of Advertising* 25, no. 2 (Summer 1996), pp. 37–50; Andrew A. Mitchell and Jerry C. Olson, "Are Product Attribute Beliefs the Only Mediator of Advertising Effects on Brand Attitude?" *Journal of Marketing Research* 18 (August 1981), pp. 318–32.
31. David J. Moore, William D. Harris, and Hong C. Chen, "Affect Intensity: An Individual Difference Response to Advertising Appeals," *Journal of Consumer Research* 22 (September 1995), pp. 154–64; Julie Edell and Marian C. Burke, "The Power of Feelings in Understanding Advertising Effects," *Journal of Consumer Research* 14 (December 1987), pp. 421–33.
32. Richard E. Petty and John T. Cacioppo, "Central and Peripheral Routes to Persuasion: Application to Advertising," in *Advertising and Consumer Psychology*, ed. Larry Percy and Arch Woodside (Lexington, MA: Lexington Books, 1983), pp. 3–23.
33. David A. Aaker, Rajeev Batra and John G. Myers, *Advertising Management*, 5th ed. (Upper Saddle River, NJ: Prentice Hall, 1996).
34. Richard E. Petty, John T. Cacioppo, and David Schumann, "Central and Peripheral Routes to Advertising Effectiveness: The Moderating Role of Involvement," *Journal of Consumer Research,* 10 (September 1983), pp. 135–46.
35. Demetrios Vakratsas and Tim Ambler, "How Advertising Works: What Do We Really Know?" *Journal of Marketing* 63 (January 1999), pp. 26–43.
36. Bruce F. Hall, "A New Model for Measuring Advertising Effects," *Journal of Advertising Research*, Vol. 42, No. 2, (March/April 2002) pp. 23–31.
37. William M. Weilbacher, "Point of View: Does Advertising Cause a 'Hierarchy of Effects'?," *Journal of Advertising Research*, 41, No. (6) (November/December 2001) pp. 19–26.

Chapter Six

1. William J. McGuire, "An Information Processing Model of Advertising Effectiveness," in *Behavioral and Management Science in Marketing,* ed. Harry J. Davis and Alvin J. Silk (New York: Ronald Press, 1978), pp. 156–80.
2. Garry Khermouch and Jeff Green, "Buzz Marketing," *BusinessWeek*, July 30, 2001, pp. 50–56; Daniel Eisenberg, "It's an Ad, Ad, Ad World," *Time*, September 2, 2002, pp. 38–41.
3. Herbert C. Kelman, "Processes of Opinion Change," *Public Opinion Quarterly* 25 (Spring 1961), pp. 57–78.
4. William J. McGuire, "The Nature of Attitudes and Attitude Change," in *Handbook of Social Psychology*, 2nd ed., ed. G. Lindzey and E. Aronson (Cambridge, MA: Addison-Wesley, 1969), pp. 135–214; Daniel J. O'Keefe, "The Persuasive Effects of Delaying Identification of High- and Low-Credibility Communicators: A Meta-Analytic Review," *Central States Speech Journal* 38 (1987), pp. 63–72.
5. Roobina Ohanian, "The Impact of Celebrity Spokespersons' Image on Consumers' Intention to Purchase," *Journal of Advertising Research*, 31 (1) (February/March 1991), pp. 46–54.
6. David P. Hamilton, "Celebrities Help 'Educate' Public on New Drugs," *The Wall Street Journal*, April 22, 2002, p. B1
7. "Business Celebrities," *BusinessWeek*, June 23, 1986, pp. 100–07.
8. Bruce Horovitz and Theresa Howard, "Wendy's Loses Its Legend," *USA TODAY*, January 9, 2002, pp. 1, 2B.
9. Frank Green, "Masters of the Pitch," *The San Diego Union-Tribune*," January 30, 2000, pp. 1, 6.
10. Erick Reidenback and Robert Pitts, "Not All CEOs Are Created Equal as Advertising Spokespersons: Evaluating the Effective CEO Spokesperson," *Journal of Advertising* 20, no. 3 (1986), pp. 35–50; Roger Kerin and Thomas E. Barry, "The CEO Spokesperson in Consumer Advertising: An Experimental Investigation," in *Current Issues in Research in Advertising*, ed. J. H. Leigh and C. R. Martin (Ann Arbor: University of Michigan, 1981), pp. 135–48; and J. Poindexter, "Voices of Authority," *Psychology Today*, August 1983.
11. Frank Green, "Masters of the Pitch."
12. A. Eagly and S. Chaiken, "An Attribution Analysis of the Effect of Communicator Characteristics on Opinion Change," *Journal of Personality and Social Psychology* 32 (1975), pp. 136–44.
13. For a review of these studies, see Brian Sternthal, Lynn Phillips, and Ruby Dholakia, "The Persuasive Effect of Source Credibility: A Situational Analysis," *Public Opinion Quarterly* 42 (Fall 1978), pp. 285–314.
14. Brian Sternthal, Ruby Dholakia, and Clark Leavitt, "The Persuasive Effects of Source Credibility: Tests of Cognitive Response," *Journal of Consumer Research* 4, no. 4 (March 1978), pp. 252–60; and Robert R. Harmon and Kenneth A. Coney, "The Persuasive Effects of Source Credibility in Buy and Lease Situations," *Journal of Marketing Research* 19 (May 1982), pp. 255–60.
15. For a review, see Noel Capon and James Hulbert, "The Sleeper Effect: An Awakening," *Public Opinion Quarterly* 37 (1973), pp. 333–58.
16. Darlene B. Hannah and Brian Sternthal, "Detecting and Explaining the Sleeper Effect," *Journal of Consumer Research* 11, (2) (September 1984), pp. 632–42.
17. H. C. Triandis, *Attitudes and Attitude Change* (New York: Wiley, 1971).
18. J. Mills and J. Jellison, "Effect on Opinion Change Similarity between the Communicator and the Audience He Addresses," *Journal of Personality and Social Psychology* 9, no. 2 (1969), pp. 153–56.
19. Arch G. Woodside and J. William Davenport, Jr., "The Effect of Salesman Similarity and Expertise on Consumer Purchasing Behavior," *Journal of Marketing Research* 11 (May 1974), pp. 198–202; and Paul Busch and David T. Wilson, "An Experimental Analysis of a Salesman's Expert and Referent Bases of Social Power in the Buyer-Seller Dyad," *Journal of Marketing Research* 13 (February 1976), pp. 3–11.
20. Denise Gellene, "Bionic Woman Wired for Success with Region's Ford Sales," *Los Angeles Times*, November 19, 1998, pp. C1, 7.
21. Valerie Folkes, "Recent Attribution Research in Consumer Behavior: A Review and New Directions," *Journal of Consumer Research* 14 (March 1988), pp. 548–65; John C. Mowen and Stephen W. Brown, "On Explaining and Predicting the Effectiveness of Celebrity Endorsers," in *Advances in Consumer Research*, vol. 8 (Ann Arbor, MI: Association for Consumer Research, 1981), pp. 437–41.

22. Bruce Horovitz, "Armstrong rolls to market gold," *USA TODAY*, May 4, 2000, pp. 1, 2B.
23. Stephen Rae, "How Celebrities Make Killings on Commercials," *Cosmopolitan*, January 1997, pp. 164–67.
24. Charles Atkin and M. Block, "Effectiveness of Celebrity Endorsers," *Journal of Advertising Research* 23, (1) (February/March 1983), pp. 57–61.
25. Ellen Neuborne, "Generation Y," *BusinessWeek*, February 15, 1999, pp. 81–88.
26. Richard Morin, *The Washington Post*, February 3, 2002, pp. B5; Brian D. Till and Terence A. Shimp, "Endorsers in Advertising: The Case of Negative Celebrity Information," *Journal of Advertising*, 27, no. 1, Spring 1998, pp. 67–82.
27. Greg Hernandez, "Carl's Jr. Execs Yank Rodman TV Ads, Again," *Los Angeles Times*, April 17, 1999, pp. C1, 8.
28. Mike Freeman, "Callaway Ends Deal with Golfer John Daly," *San Diego Union-Tribune*, September 16, 1999, pp. C1, 3.
29. Maureen Tracik, "Reebok's Iverson Shoe Line Strong, Despite NBA Star's Legal Woes," *The Wall Street Journal*, July 22, 2002, p. B3.
30. Betsy Cummings, "Star Power," *Sales and Marketing Management*, April 2001, pp. 52–59; Michael A. Kamins, "An Investigation into the 'Match-Up' Hypothesis in Celebrity Advertising," *Journal of Advertising* 19, no. 1 (1990), pp. 4–13.
31. Grant McCracken, "Who Is the Celebrity Endorser? Cultural Foundations of the Endorsement Process," *Journal of Consumer Research* 16, no. 3 (December 1989), pp. 310–21.
32. Ibid., p. 315.
33. B. Zafer Erdogan, Michael J. Baker and Stephen Tagg, "Selecting Celebrity Endorsers: The Practitioner's Perspective," *Journal of Advertising Research*, Vol. 41, No. 43 (May/June 2001), pp. 39–48.
34. For an excellent review of these studies, see Marilyn Y. Jones, Andrea J. S. Stanaland, and Betsy D. Gelb, "Beefcake and Cheesecake: Insights for Advertisers," *Journal of Advertising* 27, no. 2 (Summer 1998), pp. 32–51; and W. B. Joseph, "The Credibility of Physically Attractive Communicators," *Journal of Advertising* 11, no. 3 (1982), pp. 13–23.
35. Michael Solomon, Richard Ashmore, and Laura Longo, "The Beauty Match-Up Hypothesis: Congruence between Types of Beauty and Product Images in Advertising," *Journal of Advertising* 21, no. 4, pp. 23–34; M. J. Baker and Gilbert A. Churchill, Jr., "The Impact of Physically Attractive Models on Advertising Evaluations," *Journal of Marketing Research* 14 (November 1977), pp. 538–55.
36. Robert W. Chestnut, C. C. La Chance, and A. Lubitz, "The Decorative Female Model: Sexual Stimuli and the Recognition of the Advertisements," *Journal of Advertising* 6 (Fall 1977), pp. 11–14; and Leonard N. Reid and Lawrence C. Soley, "Decorative Models and Readership of Magazine Ads," *Journal of Advertising Research* 23, no. 2 (April/May 1983), pp. 27–32.
37. Amanda B. Bower, "Highly Attractive Models in Advertising and the Women Who Loathe Them: The Implications of Negative Affect for Spokesperson Effectiveness," *Journal of Advertising*, Vol. 30, No. 3, (Fall 2001), pp. 51–63; Amanda B. Bower and Stacy Landreth, "Is Beauty Best? Highly Versus Normally Attractive Models in Advertising," *Journal of Advertising*, Vol. 30, No. 1, pp. 1–12.
38. Herbert E. Krugman, "On Application of Learning Theory to TV Copy Testing," *Public Opinion Quarterly* 26 (1962), pp. 626–39.
39. C. I. Hovland and W. Mandell, "An Experimental Comparison of Conclusion Drawing by the Communicator and by the Audience," *Journal of Abnormal and Social Psychology* 47 (July 1952), pp. 581–88.
40. Alan G. Sawyer and Daniel J. Howard, "Effects of Omitting Conclusions in Advertisements to Involved and Uninvolved Audiences," *Journal of Marketing Research,* 28 (November 1991), pp. 467–74.
41. Paul Chance, "Ads without Answers Make Brain Itch," *Psychology Today* 9 (1975), p. 78.
42. George E. Belch, "The Effects of Message Modality on One- and Two-Sided Advertising Messages," in *Advances in Consumer Research*, vol. 10, ed. Richard P. Bagozzi and Alice M. Tybout (Ann Arbor, MI: Association for Consumer Research, 1983), pp. 21–26.
43. Robert E. Settle and Linda L. Golden, "Attribution Theory and Advertiser Credibility," *Journal of Marketing Research* 11 (May 1974), pp. 181–85; and Edmund J. Faison, "Effectiveness of One-Sided and Two-Sided Mass Communications in Advertising," *Public Opinion Quarterly* 25 (Fall 1961), pp. 468–69.
44. Joel A. Baglole, "Cough Syrup Touts 'Awful Taste' in U.S.," *The Wall Street Journal*, December 15, 1999, p. B10.
45. Alan G. Sawyer, "The Effects of Repetition of Refutational and Supportive Advertising Appeals," *Journal of Marketing Research* 10 (February 1973), pp. 23–37; and George J. Szybillo and Richard Heslin, "Resistance to Persuasion: Inoculation Theory in a Marketing Context," *Journal of Marketing Research* 10 (November 1973), pp. 396–403.
46. Andrew A. Mitchell, "The Effect of Verbal and Visual Components of Advertisements on Brand Attitudes and Attitude toward the Advertisement," *Journal of Consumer Research* 13 (June 1986), pp. 12–24; and Julie A. Edell and Richard Staelin, "The Information Processing of Pictures in Advertisements," *Journal of Consumer Research* 10, no. 1 (June 1983), pp. 45–60; Elizabeth C. Hirschmann, "The Effects of Verbal and Pictorial Advertising Stimuli on Aesthetic, Utilitarian and Familiarity Perceptions," *Journal of Advertising,* 15, no. 2 (1986), pp. 27–34.
47. Jolita Kisielius and Brian Sternthal, "Detecting and Explaining Vividness Effects in Attitudinal Judgments," *Journal of Marketing Research* 21, (1) (1984), pp. 54–64.
48. H. Rao Unnava and Robert E. Burnkrant, "An Imagery-Processing View of the Role of Pictures in Print Advertisements," *Journal of Marketing Research* 28 (May 1991), pp. 226–31.
49. Susan E. Heckler and Terry L. Childers, "The Role of Expectancy and Relevancy in Memory for Verbal and Visual Information: What Is Incongruency?" *Journal of Consumer Research* 18, no. 4 (March 1992), pp. 475–92.
50. Michael J. Houston, Terry L. Childers, and Susan E. Heckler, "Picture-Word Consistency and the Elaborative Processing of Advertisements," *Journal of Marketing Research*, 24 (November 1987), pp. 359–69.
51. William L. Wilkie and Paul W. Farris, "Comparative Advertising: Problems and Potential," *Journal of Marketing* 39 (1975), pp. 7–15.
52. For a review of comparative advertising studies, see Cornelia Pechmann and David W. Stewart, "The Psychology of Comparative Advertising," in *Attention, Attitude and Affect in Response to Advertising*, ed. E. M.

Clark, T. C. Brock, and D. W. Stewart (Hillsdale, NJ: Lawrence Erlbaum, 1994), pp. 79–96; and Thomas S. Barry, "Comparative Advertising: What Have We Learned in Two Decades?" *Journal of Advertising Research*, (33), no. 2 (1993), pp. 19–29.

53. Patrick Meirick, "Cognitive Responses to Negative and Comparative Political Advertising," *Journal of Advertising*, Vol. 31, No. 1, (Spring 2002), pp. 49–59.
54. Bruce E. Pinkleton, Nam-Hyun Um, and Erica Weintraub Austin, "An Exploration of the Effects of Negative Political Advertising on Political Decision Making," *Journal of Advertising*, 31, (1), (Spring 2002), pp. 13–25.
55. Bruce E. Pinkleton, "The Effects of Negative Comparative Political Advertising on Candidate Evaluations and Advertising Evaluations: An Exploration," *Journal of Advertising*, Vol. 26, No. 1, (1997), pp. 19–29.
56. Michael L. Ray and William L. Wilkie, "Fear: The Potential of an Appeal Neglected by Marketing," *Journal of Marketing* 34 (January 1970), pp. 54–62.
57. Brian Sternthal and C. Samuel Craig, "Fear Appeals Revisited and Revised," *Journal of Consumer Research* 1 (December 1974), pp. 22–34.
58. Punam Anand Keller and Lauren Goldberg Block, "Increasing the Persuasiveness of Fear Appeals: The Effect of Arousal and Elaboration," *Journal of Consumer Research* 22, no. 4 (March 1996), pp. 448–60.
59. John F. Tanner, Jr., James B. Hunt, and David R. Eppright, "The Protection Motivation Model: A Normative Mode of Fear Appeals," *Journal of Marketing* 55 (July 1991), pp. 36–45.
60. Ibid.
61. Sternthal and Craig, "Fear Appeals Revisited and Revised."
62. Herbert Jack Rotfeld, "The Textbook Effect: Conventional Wisdom, Myth and Error in Marketing," *Journal of Marketing* 64 (April 2000), pp. 122–27.
63. For a discussion of the use of humor in advertising, see C. Samuel Craig and Brian Sternthal, "Humor in Advertising," *Journal of Marketing* 37 (October 1973), pp. 12–18.
64. Yong Zhang, "Response to Humorous Advertising: The Moderating Effect of Need for Cognition," *Journal of Advertising* 25, no. 1 (Spring 1996), pp. 15–32; Marc G. Weinberger and Charles S. Gulas, "The Impact of Humor in Advertising: A Review," *Journal of Advertising* 21 (December 1992), pp. 35–59.
65. Marc G. Weinberger and Leland Campbell, "The Use of Humor in Radio Advertising," *Journal of Advertising Research* 31 (December/January 1990–91), pp. 44–52.
66. Thomas J. Madden and Marc G. Weinberger, "Humor in Advertising: A Practitioner View," *Journal of Advertising Research* 24, no. 4 (August/September 1984), pp. 23–26.
67. Harold C. Cash and W. J. E. Crissy, "Comparison of Advertising and Selling: The Salesman's Role in Marketing," *Psychology of Selling,* 12 (1965), pp. 56–75.
68. Marshall McLuhan, *Understanding Media: The Extensions of Man* (New York: McGraw-Hill, 1966).
69. Marvin E. Goldberg and Gerald J. Gorn, "Happy and Sad TV Programs: How They Affect Reactions to Commercials," *Journal of Consumer Research*, 14, no. 3 (December 1987), pp. 387–403.
70. Andrew B. Aylesworth and Scott B. MacKenzie, "Context Is Key: The Effect of Program-Induced Mood on Thoughts About the Ad," *Journal of Advertising*, 27, no. 2 (Summer 1998), pp. 17–32.
71. Michael T. Elliott and Paul Surgi Speck, "Consumer Perceptions of Advertising Clutter and Its Impact across Various Media," *Journal of Advertising Research*, 38, (1) (January/February 1998), pp. 29–41; and Peter H. Webb, "Consumer Initial Processing in a Difficult Media Environment," *Journal of Consumer Research*, 6, (3) (December 1979), pp. 225–36.
72. "AAAA/ANA Annual Study Shows TV Clutter Levels Up Across Dayparts," American Association of Advertising Agencies, *http://www.aaa.org/newsreleases*, February 14, 2002.
73. Chuck Ross, "TV Commercial Clutter Has Ad Buyers Worried," *Advertising Age*, December 6, 1999, p. 77.

Chapter Seven

1. Robert A. Kriegel, "How to Choose the Right Communications Objectives," *Business Marketing*, April 1986, pp. 94–106.
2. Christine Bittar, "Unilever Joins Colgate, P&G in Oral Encounter," *Brandweek,* May 13, 2002, p. 12
3. Laura Q. Hughes, "Measuring Up," *Advertising Age*, February 5, 2001, pp. 1, 34.
4. Stephanie Thompson, "Kellogg retakes lead," *Advertising Age*, May 13, 2002, pp. 3, 73; Debbie Howell, "Cereal selling in need of new promos," *Dsn retailing today*, May 20, 2002, p. S9
5. Donald S. Tull, "The Carry-Over Effect of Advertising," *Journal of Marketing*, (April 1965), pp. 46–53.
6. Darral G. Clarke, "Econometric Measurement of the Duration of Advertising Effect on Sales," *Journal of Marketing Research*, 23 (November 1976), pp. 345–57.
7. Philip Kotler, *Marketing Decision Making: A Model Building Approach* (New York: Holt, Rinehart & Winston, 1971), ch. 5.
8. John Gaffney, "Sweet Spot Awards," *Business 2.0*, May 2002, pp. 97–99.
9. For a more detailed discussion of this, see William M. Weilbacher, *Advertising*, 2nd ed. (New York: Macmillan, 1984), p. 112.
10. Stephanie Thompson, "Kelloggs retakes lead."
11. Courtland I. Bovee and William F. Arens, *Advertising*, 3rd ed. (Burr Ridge, IL: Richard D. Irwin, 1989).
12. Bob Francis, "Color My World, Boise," *Brandweek*, March 18, 2002, p. R17.
13. Russell H. Colley, *Defining Advertising Goals for Measured Advertising Results* (New York: Association of National Advertisers, 1961).
14. Ibid., p. 21.
15. Don E. Schultz, Dennis Martin, and William Brown, *Strategic Advertising Campaigns*, 2nd ed. (Lincolnwood, IL: Crain Books, 1984).
16. Howard Sherman, "Positioning a Brand for Long Term Growth," in *A Celebration of Effective Advertising: 30 Years of Winning EFFIE Awards,* American Marketing Association, 1998, pp. 54–57; Andy Wood, "Campaign of the Week: Foster's Ice," *Marketing,* February 13, 1997, p. 12.
17. Michael L. Ray, "Consumer Initial Processing: Definitions, Issues, Applications," in *Buyer/Consumer Information Processing*, (ed.) G. David Hughes (Chapel Hill: University of North Carolina Press, 1974); David A. Aaker and John G. Myers, Advertising Management, 2nd ed. (Englewood Cliffs, NJ: Prentice Hall, 1982), pp. 122–23.
18. Sandra Ernst Moriarty, "Beyond the Hierarchy of Effects: A Conceptual Framework," in *Current Issues and Research in Advertising*, ed. Claude R. Martin, Jr., and James H. Leigh (Ann Arbor, MI: University of Michigan, 1983), pp. 45–55.

19. Aaker and Myers, *Advertising Management*.
20. Kristian S. Palda, "The Hypothesis of a Hierarchy of Effects: A Partial Evaluation," *Journal of Marketing Research* 3 (February 1966), pp. 13–24.
21. Stewart H. Britt, "Are So-Called Successful Advertising Campaigns Really Successful?" *Journal of Advertising Research* 9, (2) (1969), pp. 3–9.
22. Steven W. Hartley and Charles H. Patti, "Evaluating Business-to-Business Advertising: A Comparison of Objectives and Results," *Journal of Advertising Research* 28 (April/May 1988), pp. 21–27.
23. Ibid., p. 25.
24. Study cited in Robert F. Lauterborn, "How to Know If Your Advertising Is Working," *Journal of Advertising Research* 25 (February/March 1985), pp. RC 9–11.
25. Don E. Schultz, "Integration Helps You Plan Communications from Outside-In," *Marketing News*, March 15, 1993, p. 12.
26. Thomas R. Duncan, "To Fathom Integrated Marketing, Dive!" *Advertising Age*, October 11, 1993, p. 18.
27. Robert L. Steiner, "The Paradox of Increasing Returns to Advertising," *Journal of Advertising Research*, February/March 1987, pp. 45–53.
28. Frank M. Bass, "A Simultaneous Equation Regression Study of Advertising and Sales of Cigarettes," *Journal of Marketing Research* 6 (3) (August 1969), p. 291.
29. David A. Aaker and James M. Carman, "Are You Overadvertising?" *Journal of Advertising Research* 22 (4) (August/September 1982), pp. 57–70.
30. Julian A. Simon and Johan Arndt, "The Shape of the Advertising Response Function," *Journal of Advertising Research* 20 (4) (1980), pp. 11–28.
31. Paul B. Luchsinger, Vernan S. Mullen, and Paul T. Jannuzzo, "How Many Advertising Dollars Are Enough?" *Media Decisions* 12 (1977), p. 59.
32. Paul W. Farris, "Determinants of Advertising Intensity: A Review of the Marketing Literature," *Report no. 77–109, Marketing Science Institute*, (Cambridge, MA, 1977).
33. Melvin E. Salveson, "Management's Criteria for Advertising Effectiveness," in *Proceedings 5th Annual Conference, Advertising Research Foundation*, (New York, 1959), p. 25.
34. Robert Settle and Pamela Alreck, "Positive Moves for Negative Times," *Marketing Communications*, January 1988, pp. 19–23.
35. James O. Peckham, "Can We Relate Advertising Dollars to Market Share Objectives?" in *How Much to Spend for Advertising*, ed. M. A. McNiven (New York: Association of National Advertisers, 1969), p. 30.
36. George S. Low and Jakki Mohr, "Setting Advertising and Promotion Budgets in Multi-Brand Companies," *Journal of Advertising Research*, 39 (1) (January/February 1999), pp. 667–78.
37. "Marketers Fuel Promotion Budgets," *Marketing and Media Decisions*, September 1984, p. 130.
38. Ibid.
39. Mary Welch, "Upbeat Marketers Wield Bigger Budgets, Shift Marketing Mix," *Business Marketing*, February 1993, p. 23.
40. John P. Jones, "Ad Spending: Maintaining Market Share," *Harvard Business Review*, 68 (1) (January/February 1990), pp. 38–42; and James C. Schroer, "Ad Spending: Growing Market Share," *Harvard Business Review*, 68 (1) (January/February 1990), pp. 44–48.
41. Randall S. Brown, "Estimating Advantages to Large-Scale Advertising," *Review of Economics and Statistics* 60 (August 1978), pp. 428–37.
42. Kent M. Lancaster, "Are There Scale Economies in Advertising?" *Journal of Business* 59, (3) (1986), pp. 509–26.
43. Johan Arndt and Julian Simon, "Advertising and Economics of Scale: Critical Comments on the Evidence," *Journal of Industrial Economics* 32, (2) (December 1983), pp. 229–41; Aaker and Carman, "Are You Overadvertising?"
44. George S. Low and Jakki J. Mohr, "The Budget Allocation between Advertising and Sales Promotion: Understanding the Decision Process," *AMA Educators' Proceedings, Summer 1991* (Chicago: American Marketing Association 1991), pp. 448–57.

Chapter Eight

1. Kate MacArthur, "BK flame-broils McCann," *Advertising Age*, October 1, 2001, pp. 1, 60.
2. Suzanne Vranica, "New Burger King Shop Hits the Grill," *The Wall Street Journal*, August 15, 2002, p. B2.
3. Joshua Levine, "Fizz, Fizz—Plop, Plop," *Fortune*, June 21, 1993, p. 139.
4. Jean Halliday and Alice Z. Cuneo, "Nissan Reverses Course to Focus on the Product," *Advertising Age*, February 16, 1998, pp. 1, 39.
5. Jean Halliday, "Nissan Launches New Brand Campaign," August 21, 2002, *http://www.adage.com/news.*
6. Brent Bouchez, "Trophies are meaningless," *Advertising Age*, July 30, 2001, p. 16; Vanessa O'Connell, "Ad Slump Deflates Awards Show," *The Wall Street Journal*, May 21, 2002, pp. B2; Bill Abrams, "What Do Effie, Clio, Addy, Andy and Ace Have in Common?" *The Wall Street Journal*, July 16, 1983, p. 1; Jennifer Pendleton, "Awards-Creatives Defend Pursuit of Prizes," *Advertising Age*, April 25, 1988, p. 1; David Herzbrun, "The Awards Awards," *Advertising Age*, May 2, 1988, p. 18.
7. Elizabeth C. Hirschman, "Role-Based Models of Advertising Creation and Production," *Journal of Advertising* 18, No. 4 (1989), pp. 42–53.
8. Ibid., p. 51.
9. Cyndee Miller, "Study Says 'Likability' Surfaces as Measure of TV Ad Success," *Marketing News*, January 7, 1991, pp. 6, 14; and Ronald Alsop, "TV Ads That Are Likeable Get Plus Rating for Persuasiveness," *The Wall Street Journal*, February 20, 1986, p. 23.
10. For an interesting discussion on the embellishment of advertising messages, see William M. Weilbacher, *Advertising*, 2nd ed. (New York: Macmillan, 1984), pp. 180–82.
11. David Ogilvy, *Confessions of an Advertising Man* (New York: Atheneum, 1963); and Hanley Norins, *The Compleat Copywriter* (New York: McGraw-Hill, 1966).
12. Hank Sneiden, *Advertising Pure and Simple* (New York: ANACOM, 1977).
13. Quoted in Valerie H. Free, "Absolut Original," *Marketing Insights*, Summer 1991, p. 65.
14. Jeff Jensen, "Marketer of the Year," *Advertising Age*, December 16, 1996, pp. 1, 16; Cathy Taylor, "Risk Takers: Wieden & Kennedy," *Adweek's Marketing Week*, March 23, 1992, pp. 26, 27.
15. Kate MacArthur and Stephanie Thompson, "Wrigley ads take on bite," *Advertising Age*, March 18, 2002, pp. 4, 70.
16. Arthur J. Kover, "Copywriters' Implicit Theories of Communication: An Exploration," *Journal of Consumer Research*, Vol. 21, (4) (March 1995), pp. 596–611.

17. James Webb Young, *A Technique for Producing Ideas*, 3rd ed. (Chicago: Crain Books, 1975), p. 42
18. Debra Goldman, "Origin of the Species: Has the Planner Finally Evolved into the Agency's Most Potent Creature?" *Adweek*, April 10, 1995, pp. 28–38.
19. Jon Steel, *Truth, Lies & Advertising: The Art of Account Planning* (New York: Wiley, 1998).
20. Sandra E. Moriarty, *Creative Advertising: Theory and Practice* (Englewood Cliffs, NJ: Prentice Hall, 1986).
21. E. E. Norris, "Seek Out the Consumer's Problem," *Advertising Age*, March 17, 1975, pp. 43–44.
22. Kathryn Kranhold, "Agencies Beefing Up on Brand Research," *The Wall Street Journal*, March 9, 2000, p. B14.
23. Thomas L. Greenbaum, "Focus Groups Can Play a Part in Evaluating Ad Copy," *Marketing News*, September 13, 1993, pp. 24–25.
24. Eric J. Arnould and Melanie Wallendorf, "Market-Oriented Ethnography: Interpretation Building and Marketing Strategy Formulation," *Journal of Marketing Research*, 31 (November 1994), pp. 388–396.
25. Gerry Khermouch, "Consumers in the Mist," *BusinessWeek*, February 26, 2001, pp. 92–94.
26. Paula Mergenhagen, "How 'Got Milk' Got Sales," *Marketing Tools*, September 1996, pp. 4–7.
27. A. Jerome Jeweler, *Creative Strategy in Advertising*, (Belmont, CA: Wadsworth, 1981).
28. John O'Toole, *The Trouble with Advertising*, 2nd ed. (New York: Random House, 1985), p. 131.
29. David Ogilvy, *Ogilvy on Advertising* (New York: Crown, 1983), p. 16.
30. Rosser Reeves, *Reality in Advertising* (New York: Knopf, 1961), pp. 47, 48.
31. Shelly Branch and Frances A. McMorris, "Irate Firms Take Comparisons to Court," *The Wall Street Journal*, December 22, 1999, p. B8.
32. Alecia Swasy, "How Innovation at P&G Restored Luster to Washed-Up Pert and Made It No. 1," *The Wall Street Journal,* December 6, 1990, p. B1.
33. Ogilvy, *Confessions*.
34. Martin Mayer, *Madison Avenue, U.S.A.* (New York: Pocket Books, 1958).
35. Al Ries and Jack Trout, *Positioning: The Battle for Your Mind*, New York: McGraw-Hill, 1985; "The Positioning Era Cometh," Jack Trout and Al Ries, *Advertising Age*, April 24, 1972, pp. 35–38; May 1, 1972, pp. 51–54; May 8, 1972, pp. 114–16.
36. Jean Halliday, "Sometimes oil and oil don't mix," *Advertising Age*, March 4, 2002, pp. 4, 62.
37. Rajeev Batra, John G. Myers, and David A. Aaker, *Advertising Management*, 5th ed. (Upper Saddle River, NJ: Prentice Hall, 1996).
38. Anthony Vagnoni, "They Might Be Giants," *Advertising Age*, April 27, 1998, pp. 1, 20, 24.
39. _____, "Goodby, Silverstein Do 'Intelligent Work' with a Sales Pitch," *Advertising Age*, April 27, 1998, pp. 20, 24.
40. _____, "Having Ad Bosses Focus on the Work Key to Cult of Clow," *Advertising Age*, April 27, 1998, pp. 22, 24.

Chapter Nine

1. Sandra E. Moriarty, *Creative Advertising: Theory and Practice*, 2nd ed. (Englewood Cliffs, NJ: Prentice Hall, 1991), p. 76.
2. William M. Weilbacher, *Advertising*, 2nd ed. (New York: Macmillan, 1984), p. 197.
3. William Wells, John Burnett, and Sandra Moriarty, *Advertising* (Englewood Cliffs, NJ: Prentice Hall, 1989), p. 330.
4. Stuart J. Agres, "Emotion in Advertising: An Agency Point of View," in *Emotion in Advertising: Theoretical and Practical Explanations*, ed. Stuart J. Agres, Julie A. Edell, and Tony M. Dubitsky (Westport, CT: Quorom Books, 1991).
5. Edward Kamp and Deborah J. Macinnis, "Characteristics of Portrayed Emotions in Commercials: When Does What Is Shown in Ads Affect Viewers?" *Journal of Advertising Research*, (November/December 1995), pp. 19–28.
6. For a review of research on the effect of mood states on consumer behavior, see Meryl Paula Gardner, "Mood States and Consumer Behavior: A Critical Review," *Journal of Consumer Research* 12, no. 3 (December 1985), pp. 281–300.
7. Cathy Madison, "Researchers Work Advertising into an Emotional State," *Adweek*, November 5, 1990, p. 30.
8. Louise Kramer, "McDonald's Ad Goal: 'Touch People,'" *Advertising Age*, November 15, 1999, p. 22.
9. Christopher P. Puto and William D. Wells, "Informational and Transformational Advertising: The Different Effects of Time," in *Advances in Consumer Research*, Vol. 11, ed. Thomas C. Kinnear (Ann Arbor, MI: Association for Consumer Research, 1984), p. 638.
10. Ibid.
11. David Ogilvy and Joel Raphaelson, "Research on Advertising Techniques That Work and Don't Work," *Harvard Business Review*, July/August 1982, p. 18.
12. *Topline,* no. 4 (September 1989), McCann-Erickson, New York.
13. Eric Schmuckler, "Plan of the Year: Best Campaign Spending between $10 Million and $25 Million," *MediaWeek*, May 24, 1999.
14. Dottie Enrico, "Teaser Ads Grab Spotlight on Madison Ave.," *USA TODAY*, July 6, 1995, pp. 1, 2B.
15. "Infiniti Ads Trigger Auto Debate," *Advertising Age*, January 22, 1990, p. 49.
16. Quote by Irwin Warren, cited in Enrico, "Teaser Ads Grab Spotlight."
17. Martin Mayer, *Madison Avenue, U.S.A.* (New York: Pocket Books, 1958), p. 64.
18. Sally Beatty, "P&G to Ad Agencies: Please Rewrite Our Old Formulas," *The Wall Street Journal*, November 5, 1998, pp. B1, 10; Alecia Swasy, "P&G Tries Bolder Ads—With Caution," *The Wall Street Journal*, May 7, 1990, pp. B1, 7.
19. *A Celebration of Effective Advertising: 30 Years of Winning EFFIE Campaigns* (New York: American Marketing Association, 1999), pp. 30–33.
20. Lynn Coleman, "Advertisers Put Fear into the Hearts of Their Prospects," *Marketing News*, August 15, 1988, p. 1.
21. Kevin Goldman, "Chips Ahoy! Ad Uses Spin on Claymation," *The Wall Street Journal*, February 9, 1994, p. B5.
22. Marla Matzer, "Alcohol Activists Want to Cage Bud's Lizards," *Los Angeles Times*, May 5, 1998, pp. D1, 17.
23. Sally Beatty, "Tobacco Industry Agrees to Ad Loopholes," *The Wall Street Journal*, November 17, 1998, p. B11.
24. Barbara B. Stern, "Classical and Vignette Television Advertising: Structural Models, Formal Analysis, and Consumer Effects," *Journal of Consumer Research* 20, no. 4 (March 1994), pp. 601–15; and John Deighton, Daniel Romer, and Josh McQueen, "Using Drama to Persuade," *Journal of Consumer*

Research 15, no. 3 (December 1989), pp. 335–43.
25. Moriarty, *Creative Advertising*, p. 77.
26. William F. Arens, *Contemporary Advertising*, 6th ed. (Burr Ridge, IL: Irwin/McGraw-Hill, 1998), p. 284.
27. W. Keith Hafer and Gordon E. White, *Advertising Writing*, 3rd ed. (St. Paul, MN: West Publishing, 1989), p. 98.
28. Carol Marie Cooper, "Who Says Talk Is Cheap," *New York Times*, October 22, 1998, pp. C1, 5; and Wendy Brandes, "Star Power Leaves Some Voice-Over Artists Speechless," *The Wall Street Journal*, June 2, 1995, p. B6.
29. Linda M. Scott, "Understanding Jingles and Needledrop: A Rhetorical Approach to Music in Advertising," *Journal of Consumer Research* 17, no. 2 (September 1990), pp. 223–36.
30. Ibid., p. 223.
31. Kineta Hung, "Framing Meaning Perceptions with Music: The Case of Teaser Ads," *Journal of Advertising*, Vol. 30, No. 3 (Fall 2001), pp. 39–49; Russell I. Haley, Jack Richardson, and Beth Baldwin, "The Effects of Nonverbal Communications in Television Advertising," *Journal of Advertising Research*, (July/August 1984) 24, no. 4, pp. 11–18.
32. Gerald J. Gorn, "The Effects of Music in Advertising on Choice Behavior: A Classical Conditioning Approach," *Journal of Marketing* 46 (Winter 1982), pp. 94–100.
33. Donna DeMarco, "TV Ads Go Pop: Advertisers marry modern music with their products," *Washington Times*, May 12, 2002, p. A1.
34. Todd Wasseman, "Nortel Taps Rank and File," *Brandweek*, January 3, 2000, p. 6; Stephanie N. Mehta, "Northern Telecom Plays Down Phone Roots, Embraces 'I Word,'" *The Wall Street Journal*, April 14, 1999, p. B10.
35. Stephanie Thompson, "Promotions: Nostalgia Bolognese," *Brandweek*, April 14, 1997.
36. Eleftheria Parpis, "Creative: Best Campaign," *Adweek*, January 24, 2000, p. 1.
37. Beatty, "P&G to Ad Agencies."
38. Kate MacArthur and Stephanie Thompson, "Wrigley ads take on bite," *Advertising Age*, March 18, 2002, pp. 4, 70.
39. Eva Pomice, "Madison Avenue's Blind Spot," *U.S. News & World Report*, October 3, 1988, p. 49.
40. Bruce Horowitz, "TV Spots for Light Bulbs, Diet Pepsi This Year's Big Clio Award Winners," *Los Angeles Times*, June 21, 1988, pt. IV, p. 6.
41. Bob Garfield, "1999—the Year in Ad Review," *Advertising Age*, December 20, 1999, pp. 18, 20; Alice Z. Cuneo, "Can an Agency Be Guilty of Malpractice?" *Advertising Age*, January 31, 2000, pp. 24, 25.

Chapter Ten

1. John P. Cortez, "Flowers Flourish through Interactive Media," *Advertising Age*, July 12, 1993, p. 12.
2. Stephanie Clifford, "Most Bang for the Buck," *Business 2.0*, May 2002, p. 102
3. Chuck Ross, "Study Finds for Continuity vs. Flights," *Advertising Age*, April 19, 1999, p. 2.
4. Michael J. Naples, *Effective Frequency: The Relationship between Frequency and Advertising Effectiveness* (New York: Association of National Advertisers, 1979).
5. Joseph W. Ostrow, "Setting Frequency Levels: An Art or a Science?" *Journal of Advertising Research* 24 (August/September 1984), pp. i9–11.
6. David Berger, "How Much to Spend," *Foote, Cone & Belding Internal Report*, in Michael L. Rothschild, Advertising (Lexington, MA: Heath, 1987), p. 468.
7. David W. Olson, "Real World Measures of Advertising Effectiveness for New Products," *Speech to the 26th Annual Conference of the Advertising Research Foundation*, New York, March 18, 1980.
8. Naples, *Effective Frequency.*
9. Joseph W. Ostrow, "What Level Frequency?" *Advertising Age*, November 1981, pp. 13–18.
10. Jack Myers, "More Is Indeed Better," *Media Week*, September 6, 1993, pp. 14–18; and Jim Surmanek, "One-Hit or Miss: Is a Frequency of One Frequently Wrong?" *Advertising Age*, November 27, 1995, p. 46.
11. Ostrow, "What Level Frequency?"
12. Louisa Ha, "Media Models and Advertising Effects: Conceptualization and Theoretical Implications," *Journal of Current Issues and Research in Advertising*, Fall 1995, pp. 1–15.
13. Ibid.
14. Erwin Ephron, "Meet TV Planning's Whiz-Kid Brother," *Television Bureau of Advertising*, New York, NY, 1999, pp. 1–6.

Chapter Eleven

1. *Radio Marketing Guide and Fact Book for Advertisers: 2002–2003 Edition*, New York: Radio Advertising Bureau.
2. "Nielsen Media Research Estimates 106.7 Million TV Households in the U.S.," *http://www.nielsenmedia.com/newsreleases/2002*, August 28, 2002.
3. "Network Television Cost and CPM Trends," Trends in Media, Television Bureau of Advertising, New York. *http://www.tvb.org/recentral/mediatrends/track/tv*
4. Lex van Meurs, "Zapp! A Study on Switching Behavior during Commercial Breaks," *Journal of Advertising Research* (January/February 1998), pp. 43–53; John J. Cronin, "In-Home Observations of Commercial Zapping Behavior," *Journal of Current Issues and Research in Advertising*, Vol. 17, No. 2 (Fall 1995), pp. 69–75.
5. "AAAA Survey Finds Three Percent Drop In Cost To Produce Thirty Second TV Commercials," *http://www.aaaa.org/news*, December 31, 2001.
6. Bruce Horovitz, "More Advertisers Are Tailoring TV Spots to Ethnicity of Viewers," *Los Angeles Times*, May 3, 1994, pp. D1, 3.
7. "Network Television Commercial Activity By Length of Commercial," Trends in Television, Television Bureau of Advertising, New York, *http://www.tvb.org/rcentral/mediatrendstrack/tv*.
8. Joe Flint, "Commercial Clutter on TV Networks Rises to Record," *The Wall Street Journal*, March 2, 2000, p. B18.
9. "AAAA/ANA Annual Study Shows TV Clutter Levels Up Across Dayparts," American Association of Advertising Agencies, *http://www.aaaa.org/news* February 14, 2002.
10. Dennis Kneal, "Zapping of TV Ads Appears Pervasive," *The Wall Street Journal*, April 25, 1988, p. 27.
11. John J. Cronin and Nancy Menelly, "Discrimination vs. Avoidance: 'Zipping' of Television Commercials," *Journal of Advertising*, Vol. 21, no. 2 (June 1992), pp. 1–7.
12. Cronin, "In-Home Observations of Commercial Zapping Behavior."
13. Carrie Heeter and Bradley S. Greenberg, "Profiling the Zappers," *Journal of Advertising Research*, April/May 1985, pp. 9–12; Fred S. Zufryden, James H. Pedrick, and Avu Sandaralingham, "Zapping and Its Impact on Brand Purchase Behavior," *Journal of Advertising Research*, Vol. 33 (January/February 1993), pp. 58–66; and Patricia Orsini, "Zapping: A Man's World," Spring Television Report, *Adweek's Marketing Week*, April 8, 1991, p. 3.
14. Lex van Meurs, "Zapp! A Study on Switching Behavior during Commer-

cial Breaks," *Journal of Advertising Research*, (January/February 1998) 38 (1), pp. 43–53.
15. Alan Ching Biu Tse and Rub P. W. Lee, "Zapping Behavior During Commercial Breaks," *Journal of Advertising Research*, 41, (3), (May/June 2001), pp. 25–29.
16. Marc Gunther, "The Future of Television," *Fortune,* April 1, 2002, pp. 106–112.
17. Linda F. Alwitt and Paul R. Prabhaker, "Identifying Who Dislikes Television Advertising: Not by Demographics Alone," *Journal of Advertising Research*, Vol. 32, no. 5 (1992), pp. 30–42.
18. Banwari Mittal, "Public Assessment of TV Advertising: Faint Praise and Harsh Criticism," *Journal of Advertising Research*, Vol. 34, No. 1 (1994), pp. 35–53; Ernest F. Larkin, "Consumer Perceptions of the Media and Their Advertising Content," *Journal of Advertising*, 8 (1979), pp. 5–7.
19. Lucy L. Henke, "Young Children's Perceptions of Cigarette Brand Advertising Symbols: Awareness, Affect, and Target Market Identification," *Journal of Advertising*, Vol. 24, no. 4 (Winter 1995), pp. 13–28.
20. David Goetzl and Wayne Friedman, "'Friends' tops ad price list," *Advertising Age*, September 30, 2002, pp. 1, 58.
21. Chris Pursell, "Syndicators prepped and stockpiling fare," *Advertising Age*, May 14, 2001, pp. S14–16.
22. "And Now, a Show from Your Sponsor," *BusinessWeek*, May 22, 1995, pp. 100–102.
23. *Cable TV Facts 2002* (New York: Cabletelevision Advertising Bureau, 2002).
24. Sally Goll Beatty, "MSNBC Already Waging Marketing War," *The Wall Street Journal*, July 9, 1996, p. B8.
25. Leslie Cauley, "Buyers Turn to Cable as Ratings Gap Slims," *The Wall Street Journal*, October 5, 1998, p. B7.
26. Leslie Cauley, "Cable-TV Firms Pledge a Tight Rein on Price Increases," *The Wall Street Journal*, April 1, 1999, p. B12.
27. Kathy Chen, "Measure to Let Satellite TV Air Network Fare," *The Wall Street Journal*, November 22, 1999, p. B8.
28. Tom Lowry, "ESPN's Full-Court Press," *BusinessWeek*, February 11, 2002, pp. 60–1.
29. Gary Levin, "Arbitron Exits from Ratings Race," *Advertising Age*, October 25, 1993, p. 4.
30. "Nielsen Media Research Estimates 106.7 Million TV Households In The U.S."
31. Chuck Ross, "Nielsen Defends Research Showing Drop in Key Demo," *Advertising Age*, January 18, 1999, pp. 3, 48; Elizabeth Jensen, "Networks Blast Nielsen, Blame Faulty Ratings for Drop in Viewership," *The Wall Street Journal*, November 22, 1996, pp. A1, 10.
32. David J. Wallace, "Changes at Oft-Maligned Nielsen," *Advertising Age*, July 22, 1996, p. S16. Chuck Ross, "Nielsen Explores Switch to Continuous Measurement," *Advertising Age*, April 8, 1996, p. 10.
33. Chuck Ross, "Nielsen Out to Expand People Meters," *Advertising Age*, January 11, 1999, pp. 3, 40.
34. "Nielsen People Meter Service Begins in Boston," *http://www nielsenmedia.com/newsreleases/2002*, April 25, 2002.
35. Chuck Ross, "Smart Demise Marks Setback for Nets, Shops," *Advertising Age*, May 31, 1999, pp. 3, 72.
36. Jack Neff and Wayne Friedman, "QVC, Comcast challenge Nielsen," *Advertising Age*, March 12, 2001, pp. 1, 42.
37. Doug Young, "New Audience Measurement Device Tested," *Los Angeles Times*, December 26, 2001, p. C2.
38. Hoag Levins and David Goetzl, "Nielsen Can Now Monitor TiVo," *AdAge.com*, August 7, 2002; Steve McClellan, "Nielsen wants to know a lot more about PVRs," *Broadcasting & Cable*, December 9, 2002, p. 22.
39. Dom Rossi, "Rethink 'prime time'," *Advertising Age*, April 29, 2002, p. 1.
40. Cristel Russell, Andrew T. Norman, and Susan E. Heckler, "People and Their Television Shows: An Exploration Into The Construct of Audience Connectedness," *Marketing Letters*, 10 (4), pp. 387–401.
41. *Radio Marketing Guide and Fact Book for Advertisers: 2002–2003 Edition*
42. Suein L. Hwang, "Old Media Get a Web Windfall," *The Wall Street Journal*, September 17, 1999, p. B1.
43. Verne Gay, "Image Transfer: Radio Ads Make Aural History," *Advertising Age*, January 24, 1985, p. 1.
44. Avery Abernethy, "Differences Between Advertising and Program Exposure for Car Radio Listening," *Journal of Advertising Research*, Vol. 31, no. 2 (April/May 1991), pp. 33–42.
45. Martin Peers, "Radio Produces Both Gains and Skeptics," *The Wall Street Journal*, January 1, 1999, p. B6.
46. Ibid.
47. Warren Cohen, "Radio Plays New Tricks," *U.S. News & World Report*, January 1, 2000, p. 42.
48. Doug Young, "New Audience Measurement Device Tested."
49. Katy Bachman, "Radio/A New Ratings Stream," *Mediaweek*, December 13, 1999, p. 8.

Chapter Twelve

1. Herbert E. Krugman, "The Measurement of Advertising Involvement," *Public Opinion Quarterly* 30 (Winter 1966–67), pp. 583–96.
2. *The Magazine Handbook: A Comprehensive Guide for Advertisers, Advertising Agencies and Consumer Marketers* 2002/2003 (New York: Magazine Publishers of America, www.magazine.org)
3. Ann Marie Kerwin, "Sports Spawns Most Magazines," *Advertising Age*, January 10, 2000, p. 42.
4. Ann-Christine P. Diaz, "Weider Spin-off Targets Women Weight Lifters," *Advertising Age*, November 8, 1999, p. 22.
5. Scott Donaton and Pat Sloan, "Ad 'Printaculars' under Scrutiny," *Advertising Age*, February 12, 1990, p. 3.
6. *The Magazine Handbook.*
7. Ibid.
8. Steve Fajen, "Numbers Aren't Everything," *Media Decisions* 10 (June 1975), pp. 65–69.
9. *A Study of Media Involvement*, Vol. 7 (New York: Magazine Publishers of America, 1996).
10. Ibid.
11. *The Magazine Handbook.*
12. Christine Larson, "Made to Order," *Adweek*, October 25, 1999, pp. 64–70.
13. Sally Goll Beatty, "Philip Morris Starts Lifestyle Magazine," *The Wall Street Journal*, September 16, 1996, pp. B1, 8.
14. Jon Fine, "Audit Bureau To Change How It Counts Circulation," *http://AdAge.com/news*, July 17, 2001.
15. Study cited in Jim Surmanek, *Media Planning: A Practical Guide* (Lincolnwood, IL: Crain Books, 1985).
16. "How Advertising Readership Is Influenced by Ad Size," Report no. 110.1, *Cahners Advertising Research*, Newton, MA; and "Larger Advertisements Get Higher Readership," *LAP Report no. 3102*, McGraw-Hill Research, New York; "Effect of Size, Color and Position on Number of Responses to Recruitment Advertising," *LAP Report no. 3116*, McGraw-Hill Research, New York.

17. "Almost Everything You Want to Know About Positioning in Magazines," study by Roper Starch Worldwide, Inc. 1999, *http://www.magazine.org/resources/research.*
18. "Readership by Advertising Unit Type," *Magazine Dimensions* 2001 Media Dynamics, Inc., *http://www.magazine.org/resources/fact_sheets/adv15_8_01.html.*
19. Kate Fitzgerald, "No Holding Back Rate Cuts," *Advertising Age*, March 4, 2002, p. S-2.
20. Jon Fine, "Stop the presses," *Advertising Age*, August 20, 2001, pp. 1, 45.
21. Jenna Schnuer, "Mags in a mail-storm of rate hikes," *Advertising Age*, October 22, 2001, p. S10.
22. Tony Case, "Special report: Overview-triumph of the niche," *Adweek*, March 4, 2002, pp. SR4-8.
23. Ann Marie Kerwin, "Magazine Study Links Circ Woes to Sweepstakes Fall," *Advertising Age*, November 8, 1999, p. 3.
24. Sheree R. Curry, "A Blessing in Disguise," *Advertising Age*, October 25, 1999, pp. S2, 20; Matthew Rose, "Deal May Help Magazines Add Subscribers," *The Wall Street Journal*, January 11, 1999, p. B8.
25. Richard Siklos and Catherine Yang, "Welcome to the 21st Century," *BusinessWeek*, January 24, 2000, pp. 37–44.
26. *The Magazine Handbook.*
27. Junu Bryan Kim, "Cracking the Barrier of Two Dimensions," *Advertising Age*, October 6, 1991, pp. 32, 34.
28. *Facts about Newspapers 2002* (Vienna, VA: Newspaper Assocation of America, www.naa.org).
29. Ann Marie Kerwin, "After a Long Lobbying Effort, 'New York Times' Wins New Ad Status," *Advertising Age*, February 22, 1999, p. 24.
30. Ann Marie Kerwin, "Big-City Dailies Eye National Stage," *Advertising Age*, February 22, 1999, p. 24.
31. Hanna Liebman, "NAA Network Ready to Roll," *Mediaweek*, December 13, 1993, p. 18.
32. Michele Marchetti, "Extras!" *Sales and Marketing Management*, March 1996, pp. 56–61.
33. Matthew Rose, "Publishers Take Nips and Tucks," *The Wall Street Journal*, March 18, 2002, pp. B1, 6.
34. Studies cited in *Facts About Newspapers 2002.*
35. "Brandy, Bon Jovi, Barbara Bush, Elway, Hill and Streep Return for Fourth Flight of NAA National Ad Campaign," news release, Newspaper Association of America, 1999 (*http://www.naa.org*).
36. Bruce Bigelow, "Newspapers Plot Ways to End Slide in Readership," *San Diego Union-Tribune*, April 27, 1999, pp. C1, 5; Newspaper Readership Initiative Information Site, *http://www.naa.org/readership.*
37. Ann Marie Kerwin, "Print's Power Play," *Advertising Age: The Next Century*, special issue, 1999.

Chapter Thirteen

1. "OAAA Special Report" (New York: Outdoor Advertising Association of America, 2002).
2. Ira Teinowitz, "Supreme Court's Inaction Opens Way for Outdoor Bans," *Advertising Age*, May 5, 1997, p. 58.
3. Maritz AmeriPoll, August 1998.
4. *Adweek*, August 25, 1997, p. 3.
5. Mukesh Bhargava and Naveen Donthu, "Sales Response to Outdoor Advertising," *Journal of Advertising Research*, August 1999, pp. 7–18.
6. Denise Henry, "Appeals on Wheels," *Business 99*, April/May 1999, pp. 28–31.
7. Amanda Beeter, "New Audit Gauges Impact of Truck-Side Advertising," *Advertising Age*, January 10, 2000, p. 43.
8. David Kalish, "Supermarket Sweepstakes," *Marketing & Media Decisions*, November 1988, p. 34.
9. Adam Snyder, "Outdoor Forecast: Sunny, Some Clouds," *Adweek's Marketing Week*, July 8, 1991, pp. 18–19.
10. American Public Transportation Association, 2002.
11. Eve Tahmincioglu, "Room at the Top," *Smart Business Magazine*, April 2002, p. 26
12. *Advertisers Take the City Bus to Work* (New York: Winston Network, 1988), p. 13.
13. *American Public Transit Authority*, 2002 (http://www.apta.com).
14. *Promotional Products Association International* (Irving, TX), 1996.
15. *Promotional Products Association International*, 2000.
16. George L. Herpel and Steve Slack, *Specialty Advertising: New Dimensions in Creative Marketing* (Irving, TX: Specialty Advertising Association, 1983), pp. 76, 79–80.
17. Ibid., p. 78.
18. M. J. Caballero and J. B. Hunt, "Smilin' Jack: Measuring Goodwill," unpublished research report from the Center for Professional Selling, Baylor University, 1989; M. J. Cooper and J. B. Hunt, *How Specialty Advertising Affects Goodwill, research report of Specialty Advertising Association* International (now PPAI), Irving, TX, 1992.
19. George L. Herpel and Steve Slack, *Specialty Advertising: New Dimensions in Creative Marketing* (Irving, TX: Specialty Advertising Association, 1983), p. 75.
20. *Yellow Pages Publishers Association*, 2002.
21. Carol Hall, "Branding the Yellow Pages," *Marketing & Media Decisions*, April 1989, p. 59.
22. Ibid., p. 3.
23. Ibid.
24. Ibid., p. 5.
25. Ibid.
26. *Yellow Pages Publishers Association*, 2002.
27. Ibid., p. 8.
28. Joel J. Davis, *Understanding Yellow Pages* (Troy, MI: Yellow Pages Publishers Association, 1995).
29. Pamela Paul, "Coming Soon: More Ads Tailored to Your Tastes," *American Demographics*, August 2001, pp. 28–31
30. Adam Snyder, "Are Spots on Home Video Badvertising?" *Brandweek*, January 29, 1996, p. 40.
31. Scott Hume, "Consumers Pan Ads on Video Movies," *Advertising Age*, May 28, 1990, p. 8.
32. Joanne Lipman and Kathleen A. Hughes, "Disney Prohibits Ads in Theaters Showing Its Movies," *The Wall Street Journal*, February 9, 1990, p. B1.
33. Snyder, "Are Spots on Home Video Badvertising?"
34. Ibid.
35. Sora Song, "For the Record," *Time*, January 14, 2002, p. 16
36. Motion Picture Association of America, 2002.
37. Betsy Baurer, "New Quick Flicks: Ads at the Movies," *USA Today*, March 13, 1986, p. D1.
38. Michael A. Belch and Don Sciglimpaglia, "Viewers' Evaluations of Cinema Advertising," *Proceedings of the American Institute for Decision Sciences*, March 1979, pp. 39–43.
39. Snyder, "Are Spots on Home Video Badvertising?"
40. Alice Cuneo, "Now Playing: Gap, Target Take Retail to the Movies," *Advertising Age*, June 9, 1997, p. 14.
41. "Hershey Befriends Extra-Terrestrial," *Advertising Age*, July 19, 1982, p. 1.
42. J. D. Reed, "Plugging Away in Hollywood," *Time*, January 2, 1998, p. 103.

43. Pola B. Gupta and Kenneth Lord, "Product Placement in Movies: The Effect of Prominence and Mode on Audience Recall," *Journal of Current Issues and Research in Advertising* 20, (1) (Spring 1998), pp. 1–29.
44. Pola B. Gupta and Stephen J. Gould, "Consumers' Perceptions of the Ethics and Acceptability of Product Placements in Movies: Product Category and Individual Differences," *Journal of Current Issues and Research in Advertising* 19, no. 1 (Spring 1997), pp. 40–49.
45. "Consumer Products Become Movie Stars," *The Wall Street Journal*, February 29, 1988, p. 23.
46. Damon Darlin, "Highbrow Hype," *Forbes*, April 12, 1993, pp. 126–27.
47. *Hemispheres Magazine*, 2002.
48. Jennifer Lawrence, "In-Flight Gets above Turbulence," *Advertising Age*, August 19, 1991, p. 32.
49. Jennifer Merin, "SkyMall has come up with a cure for boredom: Shopping," *USA Today*, April 9, 2002, p. 4E.
50. *Hemispheres Magazine*, 2002.
51. *American Way Magazine*, 2002.
52. Ibid.
53. Ira Teinowitz, "Channel One Criticized as 'Crass Commercialism,'" *Advertising Age*, May 21, 1999, p. 2.
54. Dean Takahashi, "Intel Plans a Major Blitz through Kiosks," *The Wall Street Journal*, August 30, 1996, p. B2.
55. "K-Mart's in-store kiosks now drive 20 percent of visitor traffic to Bluelight.com," *Internet Retailer*, October 30, 2001, p. 1.

Chapter Fourteen

1. Stan Rapp and Thomas I. Collins, *Maximarketing* (New York: McGraw-Hill, 1987).
2. Peter D. Bennett, ed., Dictionary of Marketing Terms (Chicago: American Marketing Association, 1988), p. 58.
3. *Direct Marketing Association Economic Impact*, 2002. (New York: Direct Marketing Association, 2002).
4. Ibid.
5. Daniel McGinn, "Maxed," *Newsweek*, August 27, 2001, pp. 34–40; Federal Reserve.
6. Jagdish N. Sheth, "Marketing Megatrends," *Journal of Consumer Marketing*, 1, (1) (June 1983), pp. 5–13.
7. "Women's share of labor force to edge higher by 2008," *Bureau of Labor Statistics*, February 14, 2000.
8. "A 15.6 Billion Home Shopping Spree by 2006," Response TV, December 1997, *http://www.Ads.com.*
9. Nancy Hatch Woodward, "Direct Mail Pushes the Recruiting Envelope," *HR Magazine*, May 2000, pp. 145–152
10. "Direct Mail by the Numbers," *U.S. Postal Service*, 1999.
11. "A Potent New Tool for Selling: Database Marketing," *BusinessWeek*, September 5, 1994, pp. 56–59.
12. Herbert Kanzenstein and William S. Sachs, *Direct Marketing*, 2nd ed. (New York: Macmillan, 1992).
13. "Direct Mail by the Numbers."
14. *Direct Marketing Association Economic Impact: U.S. Direct and Interactive Marketing Today Executive Summary*, 2002.
15. Ibid.
16. Ibid.
17. Cleveland Horton, "Porsche 300,000: The New Elite," *Advertising Age*, February 5, 1990, p. 8.
18. *Direct Marketing Association Economic Impact*, 2002.
19. Patricia O'Dell, "Mail's Last Call?" *Direct*, January 2000, pp. 63–64.
20. *Direct Marketing Association*, 2002.
21. Elaine Underwood, "Is There a Future for the TV Mall?" *Brandweek*, March 25, 1996, pp. 24–26.
22. *Direct Marketing Association*, 2002.
23. Shay Moftakhar, "Infomercial Media Billings," *http://www.response magazine.com*, September 24, 2002.
24. Marianna Morello, "Print Media + DRTV = Retail Success," *Response*, September 2002, p. 6.
25. Anne-Marie Crawford, "Peugeot Develops First TV Advertorials for Cars," *Marketing*, December 9, 1999, p. 9
26. Linda Moss "What Recession?" *Broadcasting & Cable*, July 15, 2002, p. 484.
27. "A 15.6 Billion Home Shopping Spree by 2006."
28. *Direct Marketing Association*, 2002.
29. Ibid.
30. Ibid.
31. Ibid.
32. Ibid.
33. Ibid.
34. Tom Eisenhart, "Tele-media: Marketing's New Dimension," *Business Marketing*, February 1991, pp. 50–53.
35. *Direct Marketing Association*, 2002.
36. _____, "QVC: The original e-tailer scores big on the web," *http://www. internetretailer.com*, August 9, 2002.
37. Bob Howard, "Successful K-Tel TV Strategy Doesn't Translate to Net," *Los Angeles Times*, January 31, 2000, p. C1.
38. *Direct Selling Association*, 2002, www.DSA.com.
39. *Direct Marketing Association*, 2002.
40. _____, "Jupiter Predicts Consumers to Receive Over 3,900 Spam E-mails Annually by 2007," *Direct Newsline*, *http://www. directmag.com*, September 18, 2002.
41. U.S. Postal Service, Postal News, September 6, 2002, Release No. 02–066.
42. Bear Market, *Direct*, December 1999, p. 1+.

Chapter Fifteen

1. "The World's Online Populations," *http://www.eMarketer.com*, March 21, 2002.
2. "Web Ad Industry Facing Down Problems," *http://www.Internet.com*, March 22, 2002, *eMarketer.com*, 2002.
3. Stephen Lason, "Gartner cuts its forecast for growth of b-to-b," *infoworld*, February 2001, p. 1.
4. Michael Shirer, "eMarket Places Will Lead U.S. Business eCommerce to $2.7 Trillion in 2004, According to Forrester," *http://www.individual. com*, February 8, 2000.
5. Laurie Freeman, "HP Gambles $100 M on Securing Its Net Position," *Business Marketing*, June 1999, pp. 1+.
6. Melinda Ligos, "Point, Click, Sell," *Sales and Marketing Management*, May 1999, pp. 51–55.
7. Ibid.
8. Karen Benezra, "Branding the Web," *Chief Executive*, January 2001, pp. 30–34.
9. Erwin Ephron, "Direct Response or Branding?" *Advertising Age*, November 5, 2001, p. 14.
10. Sean Callahan, "Branding: Is it worth it?" *B to B*, August 20, 2001, p. 1, 24.
11. _____, "Sears: Its 870 stores are 'little warehouses' for its web site," *http:www.Internet Retailer.com*, August 8, 2002, pp. 1–2.
12. _____ "Web Ad Industry Facing Down Problems," 2002.
13. Ibid.
14. Chad Kaydo, "You've Got Sales," *Sales and Marketing Management*, October 1999, pp. 29–39.
15. _____ "Sifting through Spam and e-Mail Marketing," *eMarketer.com*, September 24, 2002.
16. *eMarketer.com*, 2002.
17. Chana R. Shoenberger, "Web, what Web?" *Forbes*, June 10, 2002, p. 136.
18. _____, "Catalogers Seeing Returns from Web," *http:www.internetnews. com*, June 12, 2002, p. 1.

19. "November brings increase in e-commerce activity," *Cyberatlas* Cyberatlas.com, December 2001, p. 1.
20. *eMarketer,* 2002.
21. Quentin Hardy, "Window Shopping," *Forbes*, January 24, 2000, p. 62.
22. Ellen Neuborne and Robert D. Hof, "Branding on the Net," *Business-Week*, November 9, 1998, pp. 76–86.
23. Alexa Bezjian-Avery, "New Media Interactive Advertising vs. Traditional Advertising," *Journal of Advertising Research*, 37 (3), (August 1998), pp. 23–32; Qimel Chen and William D. Wells, "Attitude toward the Site," *Journal of Advertising Research*, 38, (4) (September 1999), pp. 27–38; Kim Bartel Sheehan and Sally J. McMillan, "Response Variation in E-Mail Surveys," *Journal of Advertising Research*, 38 (3) (July 1999), pp. 45–54; and John Eighmey, "Profiling User Responses to Commercial Websites," *Journal of Advertising Research*, 36 (2) (May 1997), pp. 59–66.
24. "Pluggin' in and Logging on: Simultaneous TV and Internet Usage," *eMarketer* Issue 181, September 12, 2002, p. 1.
25. San Brekke, "Jumpin' Jupiter," *Business 2.0*, October 1999, pp. 154–61.
26. Joseph Menn, "Web Firms May Vastly Inflate Claims of 'Hits'," *Los Angeles Times*, April 17, 2000, pp. 1–8.
27. Beth Cox, "Top 50 Web Sites Get 95 Percent of All Ad Dollars," *http://internetnews.com*, June 17, 1999.
28. _____, "Ad-Heavy Sites Spur Consumer Ire," *http://internetnews.com*, September 3, 2002.
29. Jeffrey Graham, "Spyware, Pop-Ups, TiVo, and Spam, _____ August 7, 2002, pp. 1–2.
30. Tamara Chuang, "Pop-ups are going to keep popping up," *San Diego Union-Tribune*, July 1, 2002, p. E1.
31. Jeffrey Graham, "Spyware Pop-Us, TiVo and Spam."
32. Marc Weingarten, "It's an Ad! It's a Game! It's Both!" *Business 2.0*, March 2002, p. 102.
33. _____, "New SRI Study Reveals Cloudy ITV Picture; VOD, IPG's Are Bright Spots," *http://www.statisticalresearch.com*, August 28, 2001, p. 1.
34. Sean Carton, " The Future of Interactive Television: Report From Two Alternative Universes," *http://www.clickz.com*, March 13, 2002, p. 1–2.
35. Thom Weidlich, "Online spots—a new generation," *Advertising Age*, July 30, 2001.
36. _____, "Toyota Gets Interactive with New 4Runner Campaign," *http://www.internetnews.com*, September 23, 2002, p. 1.
37. Michael Pastore, "U.S. Consumers Still Not Sold on iTV," *http://www.cyberatlas.internet.com*, August 30, 2001, pp. 1–2.
38. Amanda Wilkinson, "Open verdict on Sky interactive Shopping," *Marketing Week*, February 15, 2001, pp. 18–19.

Chapter Sixteen

1. Louis J. Haugh, "Defining and Redefining," *Advertising Age*, February 14, 1983, p. M44.
2. Scott A. Nielsen, John Quelch, and Caroline Henderson, "Consumer Promotions and the Acceleration of Product Purchases," in *Research on Sales Promotion: Collected Papers*, ed. Katherine E. Jocz (Cambridge, MA: Marketing Science Institute, 1984).
3. J. Jeffrey Inman and Leigh McAlister, "Do Coupon Expiration Dates Affect Consumer Behavior?" *Journal of Marketing Research*, Vol. 31, August 1994, pp. 423–28.
4. "Slow + Steady: Promo's Exclusive Annual Report of the U.S. Promotion Industry," *Promo*, April 2002.
5. Ibid.
6. Betsy Spethmann, "Is Promotion a Dirty Word?" *Promo*, March 2001, pp. 64–72.
7. "Clutter: Extras, Extras!" *http://promomagazine.com*, August 1, 2001.
8. Ibid.
9. Betsy Spethmann, "Sudden Impact," *Promo*, April 1999, pp. 42–48; _____, "Is Advertising Dead?" *Promo*, September 1998, pp. 32–36.
10. Richard Sale, "Evaluation in Evolution," *Promo*, September 1998, pp. 79–84.
11. _____, "Attack," *Promo*, September 1999, pp. 79–84.
12. "The Effects of Promotion Stimuli on Consumer Purchase Behavior," (Glenview, IL: FSI Council, 1999).
13. "1996 Trend Report," Actmedia, Inc., Anaheim, CA.
14. Leigh McAlister, "A Model of Consumer Behavior," *Marketing Communications*, April 1987.
15. "Too Many Choices," *The Wall Street Journal*, April 20, 2001, p. B1.
16. Betsy Spethmann, "Trading Newsprint for Pepperoni," *Promo*, August 1999, pp. 51–52.
17. Al Urbanski, "Techno Promo," *Promo*, August 1998, pp. 48–52, 146, 147.
18. Richard Gibson, "How Products Check Out Helps Determine Pay," *The Wall Street Journal*, August 1, 1991, p. B1.
19. Betsy Spethmann, "Account Specific Comes Due," *Promo*, November 1996, pp. 39–48.
20. *NCH Reporter, no. 1* (Nielsen Clearing House, 1983).
21. *The Magazine Handbook*, no. 59 (New York: Magazine Publishers of America, 1991).
22. "Clutter: Extra, Extras!"
23. Judann Dagnoli, "Jordan Hits Ad Execs for Damaging Brands," *Advertising Age*, November 4, 1991, p. 47.
24. R. M. Prentice, "How to Split Your Marketing Funds Between Advertising and Promotion Dollars," *Advertising Age*, January 10, 1977, pp. 41–42, 44.
25. Betsy Spethmann, "Money and Power," *Brandweek*, March 15, 1993, p. 21.
26. "Calling All Shoppers," *Promo Special Report*, April 1998, pp. S5, 6.
27. "Trial and Conversion VI: Consumers' Reactions to Samples and Demonstrations," *Promotional Marketing Association, Inc.* 2002.
28. *2002 Trend Report*, (Lincolnshire, IL: NCH Promotional Services).
29. J. Jeffrey Inman and Leigh McAlister, "Do Coupon Expiration Dates Affect Consumer Behavior?"
30. Jack Neff, "Coupons Get Clipped," *Advertising Age*, November 5, 2001, pp. 1, 47.
31. "Redeeming factors," *http://www.promomagazine.com*, February 1, 2001.
32. Raju Narisetti, "Many Companies Are Starting to Wean Consumers Off Coupons," *The Wall Street Journal,* January 22, 1997, pp. B1, 10.
33. Jack Neff, "Coupons Get Clipped."
34. Betsy Spethmann, "A Wake-Up Call at Breakfastime," *Promo*, December 1996, pp. 27–28.
35. Jack Neff, "P&G Extends Co-branded Coupons," *Advertising Age*, June 3, 1996, p. 9; Richard Sale, "Not Your Mother's Coupon," *Promo*, April 1999, pp. 56–61.
36. Survey by Oxtoby-Smith, Inc., cited in "Many Consumers View Rebates as a Bother," *The Wall Street Journal*, April 13, 1989, p. B1.
37. William R. Dean, "Irresistible but Not Free of Problems," *Advertising Age*, October 6, 1980, pp. S1–12.

38. Eric Schmuckler, "Two Action Figures to Go, Hold the Burger," *Brandweek*, April 1, 1996, pp. 38–39.
39. "Mickey May Be the Big Winner in Disney–McDonald's Alliance," *The Wall Street Journal*, May 24, 1996, p. B5; Louise Kramer, "McD's Steals Another Toy from BK," *Advertising Age*, November 15, 1999, pp. 1, 74.
40. William A. Robinson, "What Are Promos' Weak and Strong Points?" *Advertising Age*, April 7, 1980, p. 54.
41. Richard Sale, "Serving Up Sweeps," *Promo*, August 1999, pp. 70–78; "Sweepstakes Fever," *Forbes*, October 3, 1988, pp. 164–66.
42. Bob Woods, "Picking a Winner," *Promo*, August 1998, pp. 57–62.
43. Richard Sale, "Sweeping the Courts," *Promo*, May 1998, pp. 422–45, 148–52.
44. Maxine S. Lans, "Legal Hurdles Big Part of Promotions Game," *Marketing News*, October 24, 1994, pp. 15–16.
45. Survey by Oxtoby-Smith, Inc., "Many Consumers View Rebates."
46. Peter Tat, William A. Cunningham III, and Emin Babakus, "Consumer Perceptions of Rebates," *Journal of Advertising Research*, 28 (4) (August/September 1988), pp. 45–50.
47. Martha Graves, "Mail-In Rebates Stirring Shopper, Retailer Backlash," *Los Angeles Times*, January 11, 1989, pt. IV, p. 1.
48. Edward A. Blair and E. Lair Landon, "The Effects of Reference Prices in Retail Advertisements," *Journal of Marketing*, Vol. 45, no. 2 (Spring 1981), pp. 61–69.
49. Betsy Spethman, "Switching Loyalty," *Promo*, July 2002, pp. 40–45.
50. "Calling All Shoppers," *Promo Special Report*, April 1998, pp. S5, 6.
51. Betsy Spethman, "Switching Loyalty."
52. Adapted from Terrence A. Shimp, *Advertising, Promotion, and Supplemental Aspects of Integrated Marketing Communication,* 4th ed. (Fort Worth, TX: Dryden Press, 1997), p. 487.
53. William L. Wilkie, Debra M. Desrochers, and Gregory T. Gundlach, "Marketing Research and Public Policy: The Case of Slotting Fees," *Journal of Marketing & Public Policy*, Vol. 21, (2), (Fall 2002) pp. 275–288; Frank Green, "Battling for Shelf Control," *San Diego Union-Tribune*, November 19, 1996, pp. C1, 6, 7.
54. "Want Shelf Space at the Supermarket? Ante Up," *BusinessWeek*, August 7, 1989, pp. 60–61.
55. Ira Teinowitz, "Senators Berate Industry Abuse of Slotting Fees," *Advertising Age*, September 20, 1999, pp. 3, 66.
56. Paul N. Bloom, Gregory T. Gundlach, and Joseph P. Cannon, "Slotting Allowances and Fees: Schools of Thought and Views of Practicing Managers," *Journal of Marketing,* 64, April 2000, pp. 92–108.
57. Melissa Campanelli, "What's in Store for EDLP?" *Sales & Marketing Management*, August 1993, pp. 56–59; "Procter & Gamble Hits Back," *BusinessWeek*, July 19, 1993, pp. 20–22.
58. Amy Barone and Laurel Wentz, "Artz Steering Barilla into EDLP Strategy," *Advertising Age*, February 26, 1996, p. 10.
59. Kerry J. Smith, "Procter Move the Market Again," *Promo,* July 1999, p. 6; "Make It Simple," *BusinessWeek*, September 6, 1996, pp. 96–104.
60. "Crunching the Numbers," *Promo*, May 1, 2001, pp. 49–50.
61. Matthew Kinsman, "No Pain, No Gain," *Promo*, January 2002, pp. 26–28.
62. Tom Steinhagen, "Space Management Shapes Up with Planograms," *Marketing News*, November 12, 1990, p. 7.
63. Srinath Gopalakrishna, Gary L. Lilien, Jerome D. Williams, and Ian K. Sequeria, "Do Trade Shows Pay Off?" *Journal of Marketing,* Vol. 59, July 1995, pp. 75–83.
64. Cynthia Rigg, "Hard Times Means Growth for Co-op Ads," *Advertising Age*, November 12, 1990, p. 24.
65. Edwin L. Artzt, "The Lifeblood of Brands," *Advertising Age*, November 4, 1991, p. 32.
66. "Everyone Is Bellying Up to This Bar," *BusinessWeek*, January 27, 1992, p. 84.
67. Jack Neff, "The New Brand Management," *Advertising Age*, November 8, 1999, pp. S2, 18; Benson P. Shapiro, "Improved Distribution with Your Promotional Mix," *Harvard Business Review*, (March/April 1977), p. 116; and Roger A. Strang, "Sales Promotion—Fast Growth, Faulty Management," *Harvard Business Review*, (July/August 1976), p. 119.
68. Quote by Thomas E. Hamilton, director of sales promotion service, William Esty Advertising, cited in Felix Kessler, "The Costly Couponing Craze," *Fortune*, June 9, 1986, p. 84.
69. Priya Raghubir and Kim Corfman, "When Do Price Promotions Affect Pretrial Brand Evaluations?" *Journal of Marketing Research* 36 (May 1999), pp. 211–22.
70. Alan G. Sawyer and Peter H. Dickson, "Psychological Perspectives on Consumer Response to Sales Promotion," in *Research on Sales Promotion: Collected Papers*, ed. Katherine E. Jocz (Cambridge, MA: Marketing Science Institute, 1984).
71. William E. Myers, "Trying to Get Out of the Discounting Box," *Adweek*, November 11, 1985, p. 2.
72. Leigh McAlister, "Managing the Dynamics of Promotional Change," in *Looking at the Retail Kaleidoscope, Forum IX* (Stamford, CT: Donnelley Marketing, April 1988).
73. "Promotions Blemish Cosmetic Industry," *Advertising Age*, May 10, 1984, pp. 22–23, 26.
74. Cliff Edwards, "Everyone Loves A Freebie—Except Dell's Rivals," *BusinessWeek*, July 22, 2002, p. 41.

Chapter Seventeen

1. Raymond Simon, *Public Relations, Concept and Practices*, 2nd ed. (Columbus, OH: Grid Publishing, 1980), p. 8.
2. Scott M. Cutlip, Allen H. Center, and Glen M. Broom, *Effective Public Relations,* 8th ed., (Upper Saddle River, N.J.: Prentice Hall, 2000).
3. William N. Curry, "PR Isn't Marketing," *Advertising Age*, December 18, 1991, p. 18.
4. Martha M. Lauzen, "Imperialism and Encroachment in Public Relations," *Public Relations Review* 17, (3) (Fall 1991), pp. 245–55.
5. Cutlip, Center, and Broom, *Effective Public Relations.*
6. Philip Kotler and William Mindak, "Marketing and Public Relations," *Journal of Marketing* 42 (4) (October 1978), pp. 13–20.
7. Thomas L. Harris, "How MPR Adds Value to Integrated Marketing Communications," *Public Relations Quarterly*, (Summer 1993), pp. 13–18.
8. Jack Neff, Cara Dipasquale, and Jean Halliday, "Ries' thesis: Ads don't build brands, PR does," *Advertising Age*, July 15, 2002, pp. 14–15.
9. Alice Z. Cuneo, "Victoria's Secret Web Plan Cuts Superbowl for Cannes," *Advertising Age*, November 22, 1999, p. 3.
10. Thomas L. Harris, "Marketing PR—The Second Century," *Reputation Management, http://www.prcentral.com*, (January/February 1999), pp. 1–6.

11. Neff, Dipasquale, and Halliday, "Ries' thesis: Ads don't build brands, PR does."
12. Simon, Public Relations, Concepts and Practices, p. 164.
13. Bob Donath, "Corporate Communications," *Industrial Marketing*, July 1980, pp. 53–57.
14. Scott M. Cutlip, Allen H. Center, and Glenn M. Broom, *Effective Public Relations*, 8th ed. (Englewood Cliffs, NJ: Prentice Hall, 2000), p. 200.
15. John E. Marston, *Modern Public Relations* (New York: McGraw-Hill, 1979).
16. Joe Agnew, "Marketers Find the Antidrug Campaign Addictive," *Marketing News*, October 9, 1987, p. 12.
17. Michael J. McCarthy, "Inside the Beer Industry's Political Machine," *The Wall Street Journal*, August 18, 1997, pp. B1–2.
18. Susie Stoughton, "Recovering from Floyd," *Virginian-Pilot*, December 5, 1999, p. 6.
19. Tina Moore, "Pilgrim's Pride issues nationwide recall of cooked deli products, largest in U.S. history," *http://www.SFGate.com*, October 15, 2002, pp. 1–3.
20. Shel Holtz, *Public Relations on the Internet* (New York: American Management Association, 1998).
21. Raymond Serafin, "Cars Squeeze Mileage from Awards," *Advertising Age*, June 4, 1990, p. 36.
22. Raymond Simon, *Public Relations, Concepts and Practices*, 3rd ed. (New York: John Wiley & Sons, 1984), p. 291.
23. Harold Mendelsohn, "Some Reasons Why Information Campaigns Can Succeed," *Public Opinion Quarterly*, (Spring 1973), p. 55.
24. Walter K. Lindenmann, "An Effectiveness Yardstick to Measure Public Relations Success," *Public Relations Quarterly* 38, no. 1 (Spring 1993), pp. 7–10.
25. Deborah Holloway, "How to Select a Measurement System That's Right for You," *Public Relations Quarterly*, 37 (3) (Fall 1992), pp. 15–18.
26. Brian Lambert, "Sugarcoating television news," *Electronic Media*, May 6, 2002, pp. 9–10.
27. "Cooking Martha's Goose," *The Economist*, September 14, 2002, pp. 75–77.
28. Jaye S. Niefeld, "Corporate Advertising," *Industrial Marketing*, July 1980, pp. 64–74.
29. Tom Garbett, "What Companies Project to Public," *Advertising Age*, July 6, 1981, p. 51.
30. Ed Zotti, "An Expert Weighs the Prose and Yawns," *Advertising Age*, January 24, 1983, p. M-11.
31. Bob Seeter, "AMA Hopes New Ads Will Cure Image Problem," *Los Angeles Times*, August 14, 1991, p. A5.
32. John Burnett, "Shopping for Sponsorships? Integration Is Paramount," *Brandweek*, February 14, 1994, p. 18.
33. Ed Zotti, "An Expert Weighs the Prose and Yawns."
34. Ronald Alsop, "The Best Corporate Reputations in America," *The Wall Street Journal*, September 29, 1999, p. B1.
35. David Caraviello, "Racing fuel: tobacco money makes motorsports go," *The Post and Courier*, May 18, 2002, p. 1A.
36. Brian Trusdell, "Will a Cigarette Ban Stall Nascar's Growth?" *Sales & Marketing Management*, February 1997, pp. 67–75.
37. David Caraviello, "Racing fuel; Tobacco money makes motorsports go," *The Post and Courier*, May 18, 2002, p1A.
38. Erica Bulman, "FIA wants Tobacco Sponsors Banned," *http://www.dailynews.yahoo.com*, Novermber 21, 2002, pp. 1–2.
39. Raymond Sefafin, "Upscale Drivers," *Advertising Age*, February 26, 1996, pp. 30–31.
40. Prakash Sethi, *Advertising and Large Corporations* (Lexington, MA: Lexington Books, 1977), pp. 7–8.
41. Janet Myers, "JWT Anti-Japan Ad Is a Bomb," *Advertising Age*, April 2, 1990, p. 4.
42. Harvey Meyer, "When the Cause Is Just," *Journal of Business Strategy*, (November/December 1999), pp. 27–31.
43. Ibid., p. 28.
44. Ibid., p. 29.
45. Karen Benezra, "Cause and Effects Marketing," *Brandweek*, April 22, 1996, p. 38.
46. Donath, "Corporate Communications," p. 52.
47. Ibid., p. 53.
48. Ibid., p. 52.

Chapter Eighteen

1. Ginger Conlon, "Cornering the Market," *Sales & Marketing Management*, March 1997, pp. 74–76.
2. Carl G. Stevens and David P. Keane, "How to Become a Better Sales Manager: Give Salespeople How to, Not Rah Rah," *Marketing News*, May 30, 1980, p. 1.
3. Tom Wotruba and Edwin K. Simpson, *Sales Management* (Boston: Kent Publishing, 1989).
4. Cahners Publishing Co., "Evaluating the Costs of Sales Calls in Business to Business Markets," *http:www.cahners.com/research*, 2002.
5. Thomas R. Wotruba, "The Evolution of Personal Selling," *Journal of Personal Selling & Sales Management,* 11, (3) (Summer 1991), pp. 1–12.
6. James Champy, "Selling to Tomorrow's Customer," *Sales & Marketing Management*, March 1999, p. 28.
7. Kevin Hoffberg and Kevin J. Corcoran, "Selling at the Speed of Change," *Customers 2000*, pp. S22–26.
8. Jonathan R. Copulsky and Michael J. Wolf, "Relationship Marketing: Positioning for the Future," *Journal of Business Strategy*, (July/August 1990), pp. 16–20.
9. Don Pepper and Martha Rogers, "In Vendors They Trust," *Sales & Marketing Management*, November 1999, pp. 30–32.
10. Cahners Publishing Co., "Evaluating the Costs of Sales Calls in Business to Business Markets," *http://www.cahners.com/research, 2002.*
11. Thayer C. Taylor, "A Letup in the Rise of Sales Call Costs," *Sales & Marketing Management*, February 25, 1980, p. 24.
12. Melinda Ligos, "Gimme, gimme, gimme," *Sales & Marketing Management*, March 2002, pp. 32–40.
13. Erin Strout, "Spy games," *Sales & Marketing Management*, February 2002, pp. 30–3.
14. Theodore Levitt, "Communications and Industrial Selling," *Journal of Marketing,* 31 (April 1967), pp. 15–21.
15. John E. Morrill, "Industrial Advertising Pays Off," *Harvard Business Review*, (March/April 1970), p. 4.
16. "Salespeople Contact Fewer than 10 Percent of Purchase Decision Makers over a Two-Month Period," *McGraw-Hill LAP Report no. 1029.3* (New York: McGraw-Hill, 1987).
17. *Direct Marketing Association, 2000.*
18. Peggy Moretti, "Telemarketers Serve Clients," *Business Marketing*, April 1994, pp. 27–29.
19. Ginger Conlon, "Just Another Channel," *Wired Executive*, January 2000, pp. 23–26.
20. Rolph E. Anderson, Joseph F. Hair, and Alan J. Bush, *Professional Sales Management* (New York: McGraw-Hill 1988).

Chapter Nineteen

1. Mary Tolan, "Holidays Are Here and So Is Ad Puzzle," *Advertising Age*, November 16, 1998, p. 36.
2. Ibid.

3. Noreen O'Leary, "Does Creativity Count?" *Adweek*, December 11, 2000, pp. 30–34.
4. Barbara Lippert, "Party Pooper," *Adweek*, September 9, 2002, p. 18
5. Laura Bird, "Loved the Ad. May (or May Not) Buy the Product," *The Wall Street Journal*, April 7, 1994, p. B1.
6. Bruce Horowitz, "TV Ads the Public Will Never See," *Los Angeles Times*, August 3, 1988, p. 1.
7. McGraw-Hill Lab Report no. 3151 (New York: McGraw-Hill, 1988); Alan D. Fletcher, *Target Marketing through the Yellow Pages* (Troy, MI: Yellow Pages Publishers Association, 1991), p. 23.
8. Personal interview with Jay Khoulos, president of World Communications, Inc., 1988.
9. David A. Aaker and John G. Myers, *Advertising Management*, 3rd edition, (Englewood Cliffs, NJ: Prentice Hall, 1987), p. 474.
10. Joel N. Axelrod, "Induced Moods and Attitudes toward Products," *Journal of Advertising Research* 3 (June 1963), pp. 19–24; Lauren E. Crane, "How Product, Appeal, and Program Affect Attitudes toward Commercials," *Journal of Advertising Research,* 4 (March 1964), p. 15.
11. Robert Settle, "Marketing in Tight Times," *Marketing Communications* 13 (1) (January 1988), pp. 19–23.
12. "What Is Good Creative?" *Topline, no. 41* (New York: McCollum Spielman Worldwide, 1994), p. 4.
13. James R. Hagerty, "Tests Lead Lowe's to Revamp Strategy," *The Wall Street Journal*, March 11, 1999, p. B18.
14. "21 Ad Agencies Endorse Copy-Testing Principles," *Marketing News* 15, (February 19, 1982), p. 1.
15. Ibid.
16. John M. Caffyn, "Telepex Testing of TV Commercials," *Journal of Advertising Research* 5 (2) (June 1965), pp. 29–37; Thomas J. Reynolds and Charles Gengler, "A Strategic Framework for Assessing Advertising: The Animatic vs. Finished Issue," *Journal of Advertising Research*, (October/November 1991), pp. 61–71; Nigel A. Brown and Ronald Gatty, "Rough vs. Finished TV Commercials in Telepex Tests," *Journal of Advertising Research*, 7, (4) (December 1967), p. 21.
17. Charles H. Sandage, Vernon Fryburger, and Kim Rotzoll, *Advertising Theory and Practice*, 10th ed. (Burr Ridge, IL: Richard D. Irwin, 1979).
18. Lyman E. Ostlund, "Advertising Copy Testing: A Review of Current Practices, Problems and Prospects," *Current Issues and Research in Advertising*, 1978, pp. 87–105.
19. Jack B. Haskins, "Factual Recall as a Measure of Advertising Effectiveness," *Journal of Advertising Research*, 4 (1) (March 1964), pp. 2–7.
20. John Philip Jones and Margaret H. Blair, "Examining 'Conventional Wisdoms' about Advertising Effects with Evidence from Independent Sources," 36 (6) *Journal of Advertising Research*, (November/December 1996), pp. 37–52.
21. Paul J. Watson and Robert J. Gatchel, "Autonomic Measures of Advertising," *Journal of Advertising Research*, 19 (June 1979), pp. 15–26.
22. Priscilla A. LaBarbera and Joel D. Tucciarone, "GSR Reconsidered: A Behavior-based Approach to Evaluating and Improving the Sales Potency of Advertising," *Journal of Advertising Research*, 35 (3) (September/October 1995), pp. 33–40.
23. Flemming Hansen, "Hemispheric Lateralization: Implications for Understanding Consumer Behavior," *Journal of Consumer Research* 8 (1988), pp. 23–36.
24. Kevin Lane Keller, Susan E. Heckler, and Michael J. Houston, "The Effects of Brand Name Suggestiveness on Advertising Recall," *Journal of Marketing*, 62 (20) (January 1998), pp. 48–57.
25. Jan Stapel, "Recall and Recognition: A Very Close Relationship," *Journal of Advertising Research*, July/August 1998, pp. 41–45.
26. Hubert A. Zielske, "Does Day-after Recall Penalize 'Feeling Ads'?" *Journal of Advertising Research*, 22, (1) (1982), pp. 19–22.
27. Arthur J. Kover, "Why Copywriters Don't Like Advertising Research—and What Kind of Research Might They Accept," *Journal of Advertising Research*, 36 (March/April 1996), pp. RC8–RC10; Gary Levin, "Emotion Guides BBDO's Ad Tests," *Advertising Age*, January 29, 1990, p.12.
28. Terry Haller, "Day-after Recall to Persist Despite JWT Study; Other Criteria Looming," *Marketing News*, May 18, 1979, p. 4.
29. Ravi Chandiramani, "Reckitt launches debut iTV campaign for Finish," *Marketing*, January 10, 2002, p. 9.
30. Kipp Cheng, "IPG platform gains major advertisers," *Adweek*, July 23, 2001, p. 5.
31. Dave Kruegel, "Television Advertising Effectiveness and Research Innovations," *Journal of Consumer Marketing,* 5 (3) (Summer 1988), pp. 43–52.
32. Gary Levin, "Tracing Ads' Impact," *Advertising Age*, November 12, 1990, p. 49.
33. John Philip Jones, "Single-source Research Begins to Fulfill Its Promise," *Journal of Advertising Research*, 35 (May/June 1995), pp. 9–16.
34. Jeffrey L. Seglin, "The New Era of Ad Measurement," *Adweek's Marketing Week*, January 23, 1988, p. 24.
35. James F. Donius, "Marketing Tracking: A Strategic Reassessment and Planning Tool," *Journal of Advertising Research* 25 (1) (February/March 1985), pp. 15–19.
36. Russell I. Haley and Allan L. Baldinger, "The ARF Copy Research Validity Project," *Journal of Advertising Research*, (April/May 1991) pp. 11–32.
37. Glenn Heitsmith, "Something for Nothing," *Promo*, September 1993, pp. 30, 31, 93.
38. Ibid.
39. "Journeying Deeper into the Minds of Shoppers," *BusinessWeek*, February 4, 1991, p. 85.
40. Elizabeth Gardener and Minakshi Trivedi, "A Communications Framework to Evaluate Sales Promotion Strategies," *Journal of Advertising Research*, 38 (3) (May/June 1998), pp. 67–71.
41. David W. Schumann, Jennifer Grayson, Johanna Ault, Kerri Hargrove, Lois Hollingsworth, Russell Ruelle, and Sharon Seguin, "The Effectiveness of Shopping Cart Signage: Perceptual Measures Tell a Different Story," *Journal of Advertising Research*, (February/ March 1991), pp. 17–22.
42. June Bryan Kim, "Research Makes Ski Run Easier," *Advertising Age*, August 18, 1991, p. 30.
43. Bettina Cornwell and Isabelle Maignan, "An International Review of Sponsorship Research," *Journal of Advertising,* 27 (1) (March 1998), pp. 1–23.
44. Michel Tuan Pham, "The Evaluation of Sponsorship Effectiveness: A Model and Some Methodological Considerations," *Gestion 2000*, pp. 47–65.

Chapter Twenty

1. David A. Aaker and Erich Joachimsthaler, "The Lure of Global Branding," *Harvard Business Review*, (November/December 1999), pp. 137–144.

2. Dana James, "Mixed Messages," *Marketing News*, July 22, 2002, pp. 1, 7–8.
3. Deborah Game, "Match Game," *Marketing News*, November 11, 2002, pp. 1, 11–12; John A. Byrne, "Philip Morris: Inside America's Most Reviled Company," *BusinessWeek*, November 29, 1999, pp. 176–92.
4. Hillay Chura, "Beer Giant SAB Wins Approval for Miller Acquisition," *http://www.AdAge.com*, July 1, 2002.
5. "Drop in travel forces review of Aussie ads," *Marketing News*, September 16, 2002, p. 46.
6. Paula Lyon Andruss, "Slow Boat To China," *Marketing News*, September 10, 2001, pp. 1,11–12; Normandy Madden, "China Ad Opportunities to Grow with WTO Deal," *Advertising Age International*, January 2000, p. 6.
7. Colgate-Palmolive 2001 Annual Report, *http://www.colgate palmolive.com.*
8. Stacy Holmes, Drabe Bennett, Kate Carlisle and Chester Dawson, "Planet Starbucks, *BusinessWeek*, September 9, 2002, pp. 100–110.
9. General Mills 2002 Annual Report; Christoper Knowles, "Europe Cooks Up a Cereal Brawl," *Fortune*, June 3, 1991, pp. 175–78.
10. Insiders' Report, Robert Coen Presentation on Advertising Expenditures (New York: Universal McCann, McCann-Erickson Worldwide, December 2002).
11. Ibid.
12. *Top Global Ad Markets, http:AdAge global.com.*
13. Vern Terpstra, International Marketing, 4th ed. (New York: Holt, Rinehart & Winston/Dryden Press, 1987), p. 427.
14. "Asian Horizons," *Sales & Marketing Management*, August 1996, pp. 64–68.
15. Laurel Wentz and Charles Newbery, "Argentina Ad Industry in Crisis," *http://AdAge.com*, July 29, 2002; "Argentina: From Bad To Worse," *adageglobal*, February 2002, p. 25.
16. Claudia Penteado, "Latin America Report: Breaking Brazil's Barriers," *http://adageglobal.com*, February 11, 2002.
17. Paula Lyon Andruss, "Slow Boat To China."
18. Miriam Jordan, "Selling Birth Control to India's Poor," *The Wall Street Journal*, September 21, 1999, pp. B1, 4.
19. Anne Moncreiff Arrarte, "Advertisers Find Latin American Children's Media a Growing Market," *Miami Herald*, December 17, 1997.
20. G. Pascal Zachary, "Major U.S. Companies Expand Efforts to Sell to Consumers Abroad," *The Wall Street Journal*, June 13, 1996, pp. A1, 6.
21. George E. Belch and Michael A. Belch, "Toward Development of a Model and Scale for Assessing Consumer Receptivity to Foreign Products and Global Advertising," in *European Advances in Consumer Research*, vol. 1, ed. Gary J. Bamossy and W. Fred van Raaij (Provo, UT: Association for Consumer Research, 1993), pp. 52–57.
22. Subhash Sharma, Terrence Shimp, and Jeongshin Shin, "Consumer Ethnocentrism: A Test of Antecedents and Moderators," *Journal of the Academy of Marketing Science* (Winter 1995), pp. 26–37.
23. Shelly Pannill, "The Road to Richesse," *Sales & Marketing Management*," November 1999, pp. 89–96.
24. "They all want to be like Mike," *Fortune*, July 21, 1997, pp. 51–53.
25. For an excellent discussion of various elements of Japanese culture such as language and its implications for promotion, see John F. Sherry, Jr., and Eduardo G. Camargo, "May Your Life Be Marvelous: English Language Labelling and the Semiotics of Japanese Promotion," *Journal of Consumer Research*, 14 (September 1987), pp. 174–88.
26. Barbara Mueller, "Reflections on Culture: An Analysis of Japanese and American Advertising Appeals," *Journal of Advertising Research*, June/July 1987, pp. 51–59.
27. Barbara Mueller, "Standardization vs. Specialization: An Examination of Westernization in Japanese Advertising," *Journal of Advertising Research*, 31 (1) (January/February 1992), pp. 15–24; and Johny K. Johanson, "The Sense of Nonsense: Japanese TV Advertising," *Journal of Advertising* 23, no. 1 (March 1994), pp. 17–26.
28. Michael L. Maynard and Charles R. Taylor, "Girlish Images across Cultures: Analyzing Japanese versus U.S. Seventeen Magazine Ads," *Journal of Advertising* 28, no. 1 (Spring 1999), pp. 39–49.
29. John B. Ford, Patricia Kramer Voli, Earl D. Honeycutt, Jr., and Susan L. Casey, "Gender Role Portrayals in Japanese Advertising: A Magazine Content Analysis," *Journal of Advertising* 27, no. 1 (Spring 1998).
30. Francis Hsu, *Americans and Chinese: Passage to Differences*, (Honolulu, HI: University Press of Hawaii 1981).
31. Carolyn A. Lin, "Cultural Values Reflected in Chinese and American Television Advertising," *Journal of Advertising*, Vol. 30, (4) pp. 83–94.
32. Don E. Schultz, "New systems make China next hot spot," *Marketing News*, January 7, 2002, p. 5.
33. Marian Katz, "No Women, No Alcohol; Learn Saudi Taboos before Placing Ads," *International Advertiser*, February 1986, pp. 11–12.
34. Safran S. Al-Makaty, G. Norman van Tubergen, S. Scott Whitlow, and Douglas S. Boyd, "Attitudes toward Advertising in Islam," *Journal of Advertising Research*, 36 (3) (May/June 1996), pp. 16–26.
35. Elizabeth Bryant, "P&G Pushes the Envelope in Egypt with TV Show on Feminine Hygiene," *Advertising Age International*, December 14, 1998, p. 2.
36. Dean M. Peebles and John K. Ryans, *Management of International Advertising* (Newton, MA: Allyn & Bacon, 1984).
37. "Malaysia bans 'sly' tobacco ads," *Marketing News*, September 1, 2002, p. 7.
38. Deborah James, "Match Game."
39. Simon Tegel, "Tobacco advertising on TV to end in Mexico," *www.adage global.com*, June 20, 2002.
40. Vanessa Fuhrmans, "In Europe, Prescription-Drug Ads Are Banned—and Health Costs Lower," *The Wall Street Journal*, March 15, 2002, pp. B1, 4.
41. Laurel Wentz, "Local Laws Keep International Marketers Hopping," *Advertising Age*, July 11, 1985, p. 20.
42. Jeremy Slate, "EC Lets Stand Toy Ad Ban," *Advertising Age International*, August 1999, pp. 1, 11.
43. Sam Loewenberg, "Effort in EU to Ban TV Ads Aimed at Kids Gains Steam," *Los Angeles Times*, July 9, 2001, p. C3.
44. Al-Makatay et al., "Attitudes Toward Advertising in Islam."
45. Naveen Donthu, "A Cross-Country Investigation of Recall of and Attitude toward Comparative Advertising," *Journal of Advertising* 27, no. 2 (Summer 1998), pp. 111–122.
46. Derek Turner, "Coke Pops Brazilian Comparative Ad," *Advertising Age*, September 9, 1991, p. 24.
47. J. Craig Andrews, Steven Lysonski, and Srinivas Durvasula, "Understanding Cross-Cultural Student Perceptions of Advertising in General: Implications for Advertising Educators and Practitioners," *Journal of Advertising* 20, no. 2 (June 1991), pp. 15–28.

48. J. Boddewyn and Iris Mohr, "International Advertisers Face Government Hurdles," *Marketing News*, May 8, 1987, pp. 21–22.
49. Tze Yee-Lin, "Malaysia May Allow Foreign Commercials," *Advertising Age International*, March 1997, p. i22.
50. Matthew Rose and Leslie Chang, "Chinese Officials Force Magazines to Go without Famous Names," *The Wall Street Journal*, February 2, 2000, p. B1.
51. Sam Loewenberg, "Effort in EU to Ban TV Ads Aimed at Kids Gains Steam."
52. Ali Qassim, "U.K. mounts kids advertising program," *http://adageglobal.com,* April 17, 2002.
53. Robert D. Buzzell, "Can You Standardize Multinational Marketing?" *Harvard Business Review*, (November/December 1968), pp. 102–13; and Ralph Z. Sorenson and Ulrich E. Wiechmann, "How Multinationals View Marketing," *Harvard Business Review*, (May/June 1975), p. 38.
54. Theodore Levitt, "The Globalization of Markets," *Harvard Business Review*, (May/June 1983), pp. 92–102; and Theodore Levitt, *The Marketing Imagination* (New York: Free Press, 1986).
55. Anne B. Fisher, "The Ad Biz Gloms onto Global," *Fortune*, November 12, 1984, p. 78.
56. Maduh Agrawal, "Review of a 40-Year Debate in International Advertising," *International Marketing Review*," Vol. 12 (1), pp. 26–48; William L. James and John S. Hill, "International Advertising Messages: To Adapt or Not to Adapt (That is the Question)," *Journal of Advertising Research*, 31, (June/July 1991), pp. 65–71; Keith Reinhard and W. E. Phillips, "Global Marketing: Experts Look at Both Sides," *Advertising Age*, April 15, 1988, p. 47; and Anthony Rutigliano, "The Debate Goes On: Global vs. Local Advertising," *Management Review*, June 1986, pp. 27–31.
57. Kevin Goldman, "Professor Who Started Debate on Global Ads Still Backs Theory," *The Wall Street Journal*, October 13, 1992, p. B8.
58. Example from speech by Eugene H. Kummel, chairman emeritus, McCann-Erickson Worldwide, and Koji Oshita, president and CEO, McCann-Erickson, Hakuhodo, Japan, in San Diego, California, October 19, 1988; Margo Sugarman, "Nescafé Israel Entry Redefines Coffee Market," *Advertising Age International*, April 1997, p. i12.
59. Joanne Lipman, "Marketers Turn Sour on Global Sales Pitch," *The Wall Street Journal*, May 12, 1988, p. 1.
60. Joseph M. Winski and Laurel Wentz, "Parker Pens: What Went Wrong?" *Advertising Age*, June 2, 1986, p. 1.
61. Lipman, "Marketers Turn Sour."
62. Sally Goll Beatty, "Global Needs Challenge Midsize Agencies," *The Wall Street Journal*, December 14, 1995, p. B9.
63. Criteria cited by Edward Meyer, CEO, Grey Advertising, in Rebecca Fannin, "What Agencies Really Think of Global Theory," *Marketing & Media Decisions*, December 1984, p. 74.
64. Quote cited in Reinhard and Phillips, "Global Marketing," p. 47.
65. Salah S. Hassan and Lea P. Katsansis, "Identification of Global Consumer Segments: A Behavioral Framework," *Journal of International Consumer Marketing* 3, (2), (1991) pp. 11–28.
66. Arundhati Parmar, "Global Youth United," *Marketing News*, October 28, 2002, pp.1, 49; "Ready to Shop until They Drop," *BusinessWeek*, June 22, 1998, pp. 104–110; "Teens Seen as the First Truly Global Consumers," *Marketing News*, March 27, 1995, p. 9; Shawn Tully, "Teens: The Most Global Market of All," *Fortune*, May 16, 1994, pp. 90–97.
67. Fannin, "What Agencies Really Think," p. 75.
68. William Echikson, "For Coke, Local Is It," *BusinessWeek*, July 2, 2000, p. 122.
69. Stephanie Thompson, "Coca-Cola Taps Local Pleasures to Push Classic," *Advertising Age*, January 17, 2000, p. 53.
70. Magz Osborne, "Testing Coke's Local vision," *http://www.adageglobal.com*, May 2001, p. 6.
71. Robert E. Hite and Cynthia L. Fraser, "International Advertising Strategies of Multinational Corporations," *Journal of Advertising Research,* 28 (4) (August/September 1988), pp. 9–17.
72. Ali Kanso, "International Advertising Strategies: Global Commitment to Local Vision," *Journal of Advertising Research*, January/February 1992, pp. 10–14.
73. Jan Jaben, "Ad Decision-Makers Favor Regional Angle," *Advertising Age International*, May 1995, pp. i3, 16.
74. Penelope Rowlands, "Global Approach Doesn't Always Make Scents," *Advertising Age International*, January 17, 1994, pp. i–1, 38.
75. Kevin Goldman, "Global Companies Hone Agency Rosters," *The Wall Street Journal*, July 25, 1995, p. B8.
76. Sally Goll Beatty, "Young & Rubicam Is Only One for Colgate," *The Wall Street Journal*, December 1, 1995, p. B6.
77. Kevin Goldman, "Global Companies Hone Agency Rosters."
78. Calmetta Y. Coleman, "U.S. Agencies Expand in Latin America," *The Wall Street Journal*," January 3, 1996, p. B8.
79. "Advertising Is Indeed Going Global," *Market Europe*, October 1997, pp. 8–10.
80. Anne-Marie Crawford, "Clients and agencies split over ad superstars," *adageglobal*, May 2001, p. 16.
81. Joseph T. Plummer, "The Role of Copy Research in Multinational Advertising," *Journal of Advertising Research*, October/November 1986, p. 15.
82. Erin White, "German Ads Get More Daring, But Some Firms Aren't Pleased," *The Wall Street Journal*, November 22, 2002, p. B6.
83. Larry Speer, "French government attacks 'sexist' ads," *adageglobal*, May 2001, p. 7.
84. Lawrence J. Speer and Ali Qassim, "Naked male ads stir controversy in Europe," *http://adageglobal.com,*, October 28, 2002.
85. Karen Yates, "Advertising's Heart of Darkness," *Advertising Age International*, March 1997, p. i22.
86. Kip D. Cassino, "The World of Advertising." *American Demographics*, November 1997, pp. 57–60.
87. Mir Maqbool Alam Kahn, "TV Ad Spending Could Suffer under Pro-India Politicking," *Advertising Age International*, March 1997, p. i22.
88. Rochell Burbury, "Australia Ends Ban on Cable TV Spots," *Advertising Age International*, March 1997, p. i22.
89. Michael Laris, "China: The World's Most Populous Market," *Advertising Age*, May 15, 1996, p. 111.
89. "Seeing Is Believing," Cable & Satellite Asia, January 1998, pp. 1, 40; Fara Warner, "Sofres Group Faces Daunting Task of Rating China's TV Audience," *The Wall Street Journal*, August 1, 1996, p. B7.
90. Leslie Chang, " Cracking China's Huge TV Market," *The Wall Street Journal*, August 1, 2000, pp. B1, 4.
91. Chuck Ross, "Global Rules Are Proposed for Measuring TV," *Advertising Age*, August 12, 1996, pp. 3, 28.
92. "Young Murdock's Asian Adventure," *adageglobal.com*, May 2001, pp. 30–31.
93. Leslie Chang, "A Phoenix Rises in China," *The Wall Street Journal*, May 26, 1999, pp. B1, 4.

94. Alam Khan, "TV Ad Spending Could Suffer."
95. Frank Rose, "Think Globally, Script Locally," *Fortune*, November 8, 1999, pp. 156–60.
96. "Over There: 'Below-the-Line' Is Coming on Strong," *Promo Magazine, Special Report*, August 1998, pp. S12–13.
97. Margret McGKegney, "Coke's good sports," *adageglobal,* March 2002, pp. 18–19.
98. Kamran Kashani and John A. Quelch, "Can Sales Promotion Go Global?" *Business Horizons*, May/June 1990, pp. 37–43.
99. "What You Should Know About Advertising in Japan," *Advertising World*, April 1985, pp. 18–42.
100. Lenard C. Huff and Dana L. Alden, "An Investigation of Consumer Response to Sales Promotion in Developing Markets: A Three Country Analysis," *Journal of Advertising Research*, May/June 1998, pp. 47–56.
101. Douglas J. Wood and Linda A. Goldstein, "A Lawyer's Guide to Going Global," *Promo Magazine*, Special Report, August 1998, p. S11.
102. Kashani and Quelch, "Can Sales Promotion Go Global?"
103. Andrew Tanzer, "Citibank Blitzes Asia," *Forbes*, May 6, 1995, p. 44.
104. Lisa Bertagnoli, "Selling overseas complex endeavor," *Marketing News*, July 30, 2001, p. 4.
105. Ibid.
106. "Foreign Ads Go Further with PR," *International Advertiser*, December 1986, p. 30.
107. Patricia Sellers, "Crunch Time for Coke," *Fortune*, July 19, 1999, pp. 72–78.
108. The World's Online Populations, *http://www.eMarketer.com*. March 21, 2002.
109. Ibid.

Chapter Twenty-one

1. Fred W. Morgan and Jeffrey J. Stoltman, "Advertising and Product Liability Litigation," *Journal of Advertising* 26, no. 2 (Summer 1997), pp. 63–75.
2. Ira Teinowitz, "Curb proposal raises tobacco markers' ire," *Advertising Age*, March 18, 2002, p. 70; Myron Levin, "U.S. to Pursue Lawsuit to Curb Cigarette Marketing," *Los Angeles Times*, March 12, 2002, pp. C1, 15.
3. Joe Flint and Shelly Branch, "In Face of Widening Backlash, NBC Gives Up Plan to Run Liquor Ads," *The Wall Street Journal*, March 21, 2002, pp. B1,4.
4. Alice Z. Cuneo, "Of Contracts and Claims; Agencies Face Liability Issues," *Advertising Age*, January 31, 2000, p. 25.
5. Steven W. Colford and Raymond Serafin, "Scali Pays for Volvo Ad: FTC," *Advertising Age*, August 26, 1991, p. 4.
6. Alice Z. Cuneo, "Can an Agency Be Guilty of Malpractice?" *Advertising Age*, January 31, 2000, pp. 24–25.
7. Ian P. Murphy, "Competitive Spirits: Liquor Industry Turns to TV Ads," *Marketing News*, December 2, 1996, pp. 1, 17.
8. Priscilla A. LaBarbera, "Analyzing and Advancing the State of the Art of Advertising Self-Regulation," *Journal of Advertising*, 9, no. 4 (1980), p. 30.
9. John F. Archer, "Advertising of Professional Fees: Does the Consumer Have a Right to Know?" *South Dakota Law Review* 21 (Spring 1976), p. 330.
10. *Bates v. State of Arizona*, 97 S.Ct. 2691. 45, *U.S. Law Week 4895*, (1977).
11. Charles Laughlin, "Ads on Trial," *Link*, May 1994, pp. 18–22; and "Lawyers Learn the Hard Sell—And Companies Shudder," *BusinessWeek*, June 10, 1985, p. 70.
12. Bruce H. Allen, Richard A. Wright, and Louis E. Raho, "Physicians and Advertising," *Journal of Health Care Marketing* 5 (Fall 1985), pp. 39–49.
13. Robert E. Hite and Cynthia Fraser, "Meta-Analyses of Attitudes toward Advertising by Professionals," *Journal of Marketing* 52, no. 3 (July 1988), pp. 95–105.
14. Laughlin, "Ads on Trial."
15. Shelly Branch, "Campbell Is in the Soup on V8 Ad," *The Wall Street Journal*, April 26, 2002, p. B4.
16. Jack Neff, "Household Brands Counterpunch," *Advertising Age*, November 1, 1999, p. 26.
17. Jean Halliday, "BMW to Appeal NAD Vindication of Volvo Spot," *Advertising Age*, August 19, 1996, pp. 4, 32.
18. "NAD Urges in Brawny Ads," *Advertising Age*, November 3, 1999, p. 2.
19. *NAD Case Reports*, 2002 Summary (National Advertising Division, Council of Better Business Bureaus) 33, no. 1 (January 2003), p. 1.
20. Dorothy Cohen, "The FTC's Advertising Substantiation Program," *Journal of Marketing* 44, no. 1 (Winter 1980), pp. 26–35.
21. Eric J. Lyman, "The True Colors of Toscani," *adageglobal*, September 2001, pp. 22–23.
22. Lynda M. Maddox and Eric J. Zanot, "The Suspension of the National Association of Broadcasters' Code and Its Effects on the Regulation of Advertising," *Journalism Quarterly*, 61 (Summer 1984), pp. 125–30, 156.
23. Joe Mandese, "ABC Loosens Rules," *Advertising Age*, September 9, 1991, pp. 2, 8.
24. Avery M. Abernethy and Jan LeBlanc Wicks, "Self-regulation and Television Advertising: A Replication and Extension," *Journal of Advertising Research*, Vol. 41, (3) (May/June 2001), pp. 31–37; Eric Zanot, "Unseen but Effective Advertising Regulation: The Clearance Process," *Journal of Advertising*, Vol. 14, (4) (1985), p. 48.
25. Joanne Voight and Wendy Melillo, "To see or not to see?" *Adweek*, March 11, 2002, p. 30.
26. Mandese, "ABC Loosens Rules."
27. Steven W. Colford, "Speed Up the NAD, Industry Unit Told," *Advertising Age*, May 1, 1989, p. 3.
28. *Virginia State Board of Pharmacy v. Virginia Citizens Consumer Council*, 425 U.S. 748, 96 S.Ct. 1817, 48 L. Ed. 2d 346 (1976).
29. *Bates v. State of Arizona*.
30. *Central Hudson Gas & Electric v. Public Service Commission*, 447 U.S. 557,100 S. Ct. 2343, 65 L. Ed. 2d 341 (1980).
31. *44 Liquormart, Inc. v. Rhode Island*, 517 U.S. 484 (1996).
32. Roger Parloff, "Can We Talk?" *Fortune*, September 2, 2002, pp. 102–110.
33. Robert S. Greenberger, "High Court to Hear Nike Case Involving Commercial Speech," *The Wall Street Journal*, January 13, 2003, p. B2.
34. *FTC v. Raladam Co.,* 258 U.S. 643 (1931).
35. Edward Cox, R. Fellmeth, and J. Schultz, *The Consumer and the Federal Trade Commission* (Washington, DC: American Bar Association, 1969); and *American Bar Association, Report of the American Bar Association to Study the Federal Trade Commission* (Washington, DC: The Association, 1969).
36. *FTC Staff Report on Advertising to Children* (Washington, DC: Government Printing Office, 1978).

37. *Federal Trade Commission Improvements Act of 1980*, P.L. No. 96-252, 94 Stat. 374 (May 28, 1980).
38. Bruce Silverglade, "Does FTC Have an 'Unfair' Future?" *Advertising Age*, March 26, 1994, p. 20.
39. Ivan L. Preston, *The Great American Blow-Up: Puffery in Advertising and Selling* (Madison: University of Wisconsin Press, 1975), p. 3.
40. Isabella C. M. Cunningham and William H. Cunningham, "Standards for Advertising Regulation," *Journal of Marketing* 41 (October 1977), pp. 91–97; and Herbert J. Rotfeld and Kim B. Rotzell, "Is Advertising Puffery Believed?" *Journal of Advertising*, 9 (3) (1980), pp. 16–20.
41. Herbert J. Rotfeld and Kim B. Rotzell, "Puffery vs. Fact Claims—Really Different?" in *Current Issues and Research in Advertising*, ed. James H. Leigh and Claude R. Martin, Jr. (Ann Arbor: University of Michigan, 1981), pp. 85–104.
42. Preston, *The Great American Blow-Up.*
43. Chuck Ross, "Marketers Fend Off Shift in Rules for Ad Puffery," *Advertising Age*, February 19, 1996, p. 41.
44. *Federal Trade Commission, "Policy Statement on Deception," 45 ATRR 689* (October 27, 1983), at p. 690.
45. For an excellent discussion and analysis of these three elements of deception, see Gary T. Ford and John E. Calfee, "Recent Developments in FTC Policy on Deception," *Journal of Marketing* 50, no. 3 (July 1986), pp. 86–87.
46. Ray O. Werner, ed., "Legal Developments in Marketing," *Journal of Marketing* 56 (January 1992), p. 102.
47. Ira Teinowitz, "FTC Strives to Clarify 'Made in USA' Rules," *Advertising Age*, April 29, 1996, p. 12.
48. Kalpana Srinivasan, "FTC Spells Out Tough Standards for 'Made in USA,'" *Marketing News*, January 18, 1999, p. 18.
49. Cohen, "The FTC's Advertising Substantiation Program."
50. *Trade Regulation Reporter*, Par. 20,056 at 22,033, 1970–1973 Transfer Binder, Federal Trade Commission, July 1972.
51. John E. Califee, "FTC's Hidden Weight-Loss Ad Agenda," *Advertising Age*, October 25, 1993, p. 29.
52. Michael J. McCarthy, "Abbott Will Settle FTC Charges Linked to Ensure Endorsement," *The Wall Street Journal,* January 2, 1997, p. B2.
53. For an excellent description of the Campbell Soup corrective advertising case, see Dick Mercer, "Tempest in a Soup Can," *Advertising Age*, October 17, 1994, pp. 25, 28–29.
54. William L. Wilkie, Dennis L. McNeill, and Michael B. Mazis, "Marketing's 'Scarlet Letter': The Theory and Practice of Corrective Advertising," *Journal of Marketing* 48 (Spring 1984), pp. 11–31.
55. *Warner-Lambert Co. v. Federal Trade Commission*, CCH P61, 563A-D.C., August 1977 and CCH P61, 646 CA-D.C., September 1977.
56. Bruce Ingersoll, "FTC Orders Novartis to Correct Claims," *The Wall Street Journal*, May 28, 1999, p. B2.
57. Ira Teinowitz, "Doan's Decision Worries Marketers," *Advertising Age*, May 31, 1999, p. 74.
58. "Deceptive Ads: The FTC's Laissez-Faire Approach Is Backfiring," *BusinessWeek*, December 2, 1985, p. 136.
59. Bruce Ingersoll, "FTC Action Snares Home Shopping, iMall," *The Wall Street Journal*, April 16, 1999, p. B2.
60. Ira Teinowitz, "Chairman Muris promises evolution at FTC," *Advertising Age*, June 25, 2001, pp. 3, 42.
61. Christopher Saunders, "FTC to Pursue Deceptive E-mail Advertisers," February 1, 2002, *http://www.internetnews/IAR/article/0,,12_967151,00.html.*
62. Ira Teinowitz, "Beales makes regulation academic as FTC director," *Advertising Age*, December 10, 2001, p. 66.
63. Ira Teinowitz, "FCC, FTC Vow 'Action' Against Phone Ads," *Advertising Age*, November 8, 1999, p. 129.
64. "The new team: marketers see different enforcement picture," *Marketing News*, March 4, 2002, pp. 13–14.
65. Ibid.
66. Sheryl Stolberg, "Clinton Imposes Wide Crackdown on Tobacco Firms," *Los Angeles Times*, August 24, 1996, pp. A1,10.
67. Joy Johnson Wilson, Summary of the Attorneys General Master Tobacco Settlement Agreement, National Conference of State Legislators, *http://academic.udayton.edu/health/syllabi/tobacco/summary.html.*
68. Charles King III, and Michael Siegel, "The Master Settlement Agreement with the Tobacco Industry and Cigarette Advertising in Magazines," *The New England Journal of Medicine*, Vol. 345, August 16, 2001, pp. 504–511.
69. Steven W. Colford, "$12 Million Bite," *Advertising Age*, December 2, 1991, p. 4.
70. Jan Joben, "A Setback for Competitive Ads?" *Business Marketing*, October 1992, p. 34.
71. Bruce Buchanan and Doron Goldman, "Us vs. Them: The Minefield of Comparative Ads," *Harvard Business Review*, May/June 1989, pp. 38–50.
72. Maxine Lans Retsky, "Lanham Have It: Law and Comparative Ads," *Marketing News*, November 8, 1999, p. 16.
73. Judann Pollack, "Prego Prevails in Battle Over Comparative Ad," *Advertising Age*, September 1, 1996, p. 12; Michael Fumento, "Free-a-the-Papa!" *Forbes*, February 21, 2000, p. 53.
74. Daniel Golden and Suzanne Vranica, "Duracell's Duck Will Carry Disclaimer," *The Wall Street Journal*, February 7, 2002, p. B7.
75. Michael J. Barone, Randall L. Rose, Paul W. Minniard, and Kenneth C. Manning, "Enhancing the Detection of Misleading Comparative Advertising," *Journal of Advertising Research*, 39 (5) (September/October 1999), pp. 43–50.
76. "Deceptive Ads: The FTC's Laissez-Faire Approach."
77. Jennifer Lawrence, "State Ad Rules Face Showdown," *Advertising Age,* November 28, 1988, p. 4.
78. Steven Colford, "ABA Panel Backs FTC over States," *Advertising Age*, April 10, 1994, p.1.
79. S. J. Diamond, "New Director Putting Vigor Back into FTC," *Los Angeles Times*, March 29, 1991, pp. D1, 4.
80. *Federal Trade Commission, "Trade Regulation Rule: Games of Chance in the Food Retailing and Gasoline Industries,"* 16 CFR, Part 419 (1982).
81. Richard Sale, "Sweeping the Courts," *Promo*, May 1998, pp. 42–45, 148–152.
82. Ira Teinowitz and Carol Krol, "Multiple States Scrutinize Sweepstakes Mailings," *Advertising Age*, February 9, 1998, p. 41.
83. Mark Pawlosky, "States Rein in Sweepstakes, Game Operators,"

The Wall Street Journal, July 3, 1995, pp. B1, 3.
84. *Children Advertising Review Unit Self Regulatory Guidelines for Children's Advertising*, Council of Better Business Bureaus, December 2001, *http://www.caru.org/carusubpgs/guidepg.asp*
85. Steven W. Colford, "Top Kid TV Offender: Premiums," *Advertising Age*, April 29, 1991, p. 52.
86. *Federal Trade Commission, "Guides for Advertising Allowances and Other Merchandising Payments and Services,"* 16 CFR, Part 240 (1983).
87. William L. Wilkie, Debra M. Desrochers, and Gregory T. Gundlach, "Marketing Research and Public Policy: The Case of Slotting Fees," *Journal of Marketing & Public Policy*," Vol. 21, (2), (Fall 2002), pp. 275–288.
88. Ira Teinowitz, "FTC, McCormick reach accord on slotting fees," *Advertising Age*, March 13, 2000, p. 75.
89. *Federal Trade Commission, "Trade Regulation Rule: Use of Negative Option Plans by Sellers in Commerce*, 16 CFR, Part 42 (1982).
90. For a more thorough discussion of legal aspects of sales promotion and mail-order practices, see Dean K. Fueroghne, *Law & Advertising* (Chicago: Copy Workshop, 1995).
91. Mary Lu Carnevale, "FTC Adopts Rules to Curb Telemarketing," *The Wall Street Journal*, September 18, 1992, pp. B1, 10.
92. Scott Hume, "900 Numbers: The Struggle for Respect," *Advertising Age*, February 18, 1991, p. S1.
93. *Federal Register*, "Rules and Regulations," August 9, 1993, 42364–42406.
94. "Commission to Seek Public Comment on 900-Number Rule Revisions," *Federal Trade Commission Press Release*, October 23, 1998; Russell N. Laczniak, Les Carlson, and Ann Walsh, "Antecedents of Mothers' Attitudes toward the FTC's Rule for 900-Number Advertising Directed at Children," *Journal of Current Issues and Research in Advertising* 21, no. 2 (Fall 1999) pp. 49–58.
95. "US FTC: FTC workshop to address proposed changes to its pay-per-call-rule," *M2 Presswire*, May 20, 1999.
96. Ira Teinowitz, "'Do not call' proposal sparks response," *Advertising Age*, April 8, 2002, p. 16; _____ "'Do not call' rule gains congressional support," *Advertising Age*, January 20, 2003, p. 14.
97. Ira Teinowitz, "FTC Chairman Seeking Voluntary Web Rules," *Advertising Age*, June 10, 1996, p. 42.
98. Ibid.
99. Ira Teinowitz and Jennifer Gilbert, "FTC Chairman: Stop Undisclosed Profiling on Net," *Advertising Age*, November 8, 1999, p. 2.
100. Andrea Petersen, "DoubleClick Reverses Course After Privacy Outcry," *The Wall Street Journal*, March 3, 2000, pp. B1, 6; Jennifer Gilbert and Ira Teinowitz, "Privacy Debate Continues to Rage," *Advertising Age*, February 7, 2000, pp. 44, 46.
101. "NAI Launches Privacy-awareness web site," *Adage.com*, May 28, 2001; "Online advertisers launch two consumer privacy tools," *Network Advertising Initiative*, May 23, 2001, *http://www.network advertising.org/aboutnai*.
102. James Heckman, "COPPA to Bring No Surprises, Hefty Violation Fines in April," *Marketing News*, January 31, 2000, p. 6.
103. Betsy Spethmann, "Private Eyes," *Promo*, January 2002, pp. 37–43.
104. "Protecting Consumers' Privacy: 2002 and Beyond," Remarks of FTC Chairman Timothy J. Muris at *The Privacy 2001 Conference*, Cleveland, Ohio, October 4, 2001, *http://www.ftc.gov/speeches/muris/privisp1002*.
105. Spethmann, "Private Eyes"; Lisa Takeuchi Cullen, "Some More Spam, Please," *Time*, November 11, 2002, pp. 58–62.
106. Maxine Lans Retsky, "At least one firm's willing to sue spammers," *Marketing News*, April 29, 2002, p. 11; Deborah Szynal, "Internet proposals await lawmakers," *Advertising Age*, January 7, 2002, p. 11

Chapter Twenty-two

1. Robert L. Heilbroner, "Demand for the Supply Side," *New York Review of Books* 38 (June 11, 1981), p. 40.
2. David Helm, "Advertising's Overdue Revolution," speech given to the *Adweek Creative Conference*, October 1, 1999.
3. Joan Voight, "The Consumer Rebellion," *Adweek*, January 10, 2000, pp. 46–50.
4. Eric N. Berkowitz, Roger A. Kerin, Steven W. Hartley, William Rudelius, et al., *Marketing*, 5th ed. (Burr Ridge, IL: Irwin/McGraw-Hill, 1997), p. 102.
5. Je Eun Lee, Meichum Kuo and Hang Lee, "College Binge Drinking in the 1990's: A Continuing Problem. Results of the Harvard School of Public Health 1999 College Alcohol Study," *Journal of American Collegiate Health*, 48 (5), 2000, pp. 199–210.
6. Jennifer Christie, Dan Fisher, John C. Kozup, Scott Smith, Scott Burton and Elizabeth H. Creyer, "The effects of bar-sponsored beverage promotions across binge and nonbinge drinkers," *Journal of Public Policy & Marketing*," 20 (2), (Fall 2001), pp. 240–253.
7. Ira Teinowitz, "BoozeHounded," *Advertising Age*, March 25, 2002, pp. 1, 27.
8. Jim O Hara, "New Study Shows Underage Youth a Target of Alcohol Marketing: Youth Are More Likely To See Alcohol Advertising Than Adults," *U.S. Newswire*, September 24, 2002.
9. Ibid.
10. "Calvin's World," *Newsweek*, September 11, 1995, pp. 60–66.
11. Stephanie Bentley, "Benetton Risks Fresh Outrage," *Marketing Week*, September 13, 1996, p. 9; Gary Levin, "Benetton Ad Lays Bare the Bloody Toll of War," *Advertising Age*, February 21, 1994, p. 38.
12. Jerry Della Famina, "Benetton Ad Models Are Dressed To Kill Sales," *The Wall Street Journal*, March 20, 2000, p. A34.
13. Stephanie O'Donohoe, "Attitudes to Advertising: A Review of British and American Research," *International Journal of Advertising* 14 (1995), pp. 245–61.
14. Banwari Mittal, "Public Assessment of TV Advertising: Faint Praise and Harsh Criticism," *Journal of Advertising Research* 34, no. 1 (January/February 1994), pp. 35–53.
15. Sharon Shavitt, Pamela Lowery, and James Haefner, "Public Attitudes toward Advertising; More Favorable Than You Might Think," *Journal of Advertising Research* 38 (4), (July/August 1998), pp. 7–22.
16. Gita Venkataramini Johar, "Consumer Involvement and Deception from Implied Advertising Claims," *Journal of Marketing Research* 32 (August 1995), pp. 267–79;

J. Edward Russo, Barbara L. Metcalf, and Debra Stephens, "Identifying Misleading Advertising," *Journal of Consumer Research* 8 (September 1981), pp. 119–31.
17. Shelby D. Hunt, "Informational vs. Persuasive Advertising: An Appraisal," *Journal of Advertising*, Summer 1976, pp. 5–8.
18. Banwari Mittal, "Public Assessment of TV Advertising: Faint Praise and Harsh Criticism"; J. C. Andrews, "The Dimensionality of Beliefs toward Advertising in General," *Journal of Advertising* 18, no. 1 (1989), pp. 26–35; Ron Alsop, "Advertisers Find the Climate Less Hostile Outside the U.S.," *The Wall Street Journal*, December 10, 1987, p. 29.
19. Helen Cooper, "CDC Advocates Use of Condoms in Blunt AIDS-Prevention Spots," *The Wall Street Journal*, January 5, 1994, p. B1.
20. David A. Aaker and Donald E. Bruzzone, "Causes of Irritation in Advertising," *Journal of Marketing*, Spring 1985, p. 47–57.
21. Stephen A. Greyser, "Irritation in Advertising," *Journal of Advertising Research* 13 (February 1973), pp. 3–10.
22. Ron Alsop, "Personal Product Ads Abound as Public Gets More Tolerant," *The Wall Street Journal*, April 14, 1986, p. 19.
23. Joan Voight and Wendy Melillo, "Rough Cut," *Adweek*, March 11, 2002, pp. 27–29; Joanne Lipman, "Censored Scenes: Why You Rarely See Some Things in Television Ads," *The Wall Street Journal*, August 17, 1987, p. 17.
24. For an interesting analysis of an interpretation of this ad from a literary theory perspective see Aaron C. Ahuvia, "Social Criticism of Advertising: On the Role of Literary Theory and the Use of Data," *Journal of Advertising* 27, no. 1 (Spring 1998), pp. 143–62.
25. John P. Cortez and Ira Teinowitz, "More Trouble Brews for Stroh Bikini Team," *Advertising Age*, December 9, 1991, p. 45.
26. Bob Garfield, "Miller Lite's latest is a return to the bad old days of beer ads," *Advertising Age*, January 20, 2003, p. 37.
27. Hillary Chura, "Lap dancer, toilet jokes hawk new whiskey," *http://www.AdAge.com*, July 9, 2001.
28. _____, Beer exec apologizes for sex show involvement," *http://www.AdAge.com*, August 27, 2002.
29. Michael McCarthy, "Shockvertising Jolts Ad Viewers," *USA TODAY*, February 23, 2000, p. 6B.
30. Leanne Potts, "Retailers, ads bare flesh for bottom line," *Albuquerque Journal*, December 20, 2002, p. D1.
31. Rebecca Quick, "Is Ever-So-Hip Abercrombie & Fitch Losing Its Edge with Teens?" *The Wall Street Journal*, February 22, 2000, pp. B1, 4.
32. David Lieberman, "Broadcasters Crowd the Playground," *USA TODAY*, February 7, 1996, pp. 1, 2B.
33. Scott Ward, Daniel B. Wackman, and Ellen Wartella, *How Children Learn to Buy: The Development of Consumer Information Processing Skills* (Beverly Hills, CA: Sage, 1979).
34. Thomas S. Robertson and John R. Rossiter, "Children and Commercial Persuasion: An Attribution Theory Analysis," *Journal of Consumer Research* 1, no. 1 (June 1974), pp. 13–20; and Scott Ward and Daniel B. Wackman, "Children's Information Processing of Television Advertising," in *New Models for Communications Research,* ed. G. Kline and P. Clark (Beverly Hills, CA: Sage, 1974), pp. 81–119.
35. Merrie Brucks, Gary M. Armstrong, and Marvin E. Goldberg, "Children's Use of Cognitive Defenses against Television Advertising: A Cognitive Response Approach," *Journal of Consumer Research* 14, no. 4 (March 1988), pp. 471–82.
36. For a discussion on consumer socialization, see Scott Ward, "Consumer Socialization," *Journal of Consumer Research* 1, no. 2 (September 1974), pp. 1–14.
37. Tamara F. Mangleburg and Terry Bristol, "Socialization and Adolescents' Skepticism toward Advertising," *Journal of Advertising* 27, no. 3 (Fall 1998), pp. 11–21.
38. *FTC Staff Report on Advertising to Children* (Washington, DC: Government Printing Office, 1978).
39. Ben M. Enis, Dale R. Spencer, and Don R. Webb, "Television Advertising and Children: Regulatory vs. Competitive Perspectives," *Journal of Advertising* 9, no. 1 (1980), pp. 19–25.
40. Richard Zoglin, "Ms. Kidvid Calls It Quits," *Time*, January 20, 1992, p. 52.
41. Elizabeth Jensen and Albert R. Karr, "Summit on Kids' TV Yields Compromise," *The Wall Street Journal,* July 30, 1996, p. B12.
42. Sally Goll Beatty, "White House Pact on TV for Kids May Prove a Marketing Bonanza," *The Wall Street Journal*, August 2, 1996, p. B2.
43. Ronald Alsop, "Watchdogs Zealously Censor Advertising Targeted to Kids," *The Wall Street Journal*, September 5, 1985, p. 35.
44. Deborah L. Vence, "Marketing to minors has changed," *Marketing News*, May 22, 2002, pp. 5–6.
45. Ibid.
46. Robert E. Hite and Randy Eck, "Advertising to Children: Attitudes of Business vs. Consumers," *Journal of Advertising Research*, October/ November 1987, pp. 40–53.
47. Dan Lippe, "What children say about media and advertising," *http://AdAge.com*, February 4, 2002.
48. Ronald Berman, *Advertising and Social Change* (Beverly Hills, CA: Sage, 1981), p. 13.
49. Quote in Voight, "The Consumer Rebellion."
50. John K. Galbraith, *The New Industrial State* (Boston: Houghton Mifflin, 1967), cited in Richard W. Pollay, "The Distorted Mirror: Reflections on the Unintended Consequences of Advertising," *Journal of Marketing*, August 1986, p. 25.
51. Raymond A. Bauer and Stephen A. Greyser, "The Dialogue That Never Happens," *Harvard Business Review*, January/February 1969, pp. 122–28.
52. Morris B. Holbrook, "Mirror Mirror on the Wall, What's Unfair in the Reflections on Advertising," *Journal of Marketing* 5 (July 1987), pp. 95–103; and Theodore Levitt, "The Morality of Advertising," *Harvard Business Review*, July/August 1970, pp. 84–92.
53. Stephen Fox, The Mirror Makers: A History of American Advertising and Its Creators (New York: Morrow, 1984), p. 330.
54. Richard W. Pollay, "The Distorted Mirror: Reflections on the Unintended Consequences of Advertising," *Journal of Marketing* 50 (April 1986), p. 33.
55. Jules Backman, "Is Advertising Wasteful?" *Journal of Marketing* 32 (January 1968), pp. 2–8.
56. Hunt, "Informational vs. Persuasive Advertising."
57. Ibid., p. 6.

58. Kevin Goldman, "Survey Asks Which 'Green' Ads Are Read," *The Wall Street Journal*, April 11, 1994, p. B5.
59. Geoffrey A. Fowler, "'Green' Sales Pitch Isn't Moving Many Products," *The Wall Street Journal*, March 6, 2002, pp. B1, 4.
60. Alice E. Courtney and Thomas W. Whipple, "Sex Stereotyping in Advertising," (Lexington, MA: Lexington Books, 1984).
61. Daniel J. Brett and Joanne Cantor, "The Portrayal of Men and Women in U.S. Television Commercials: A Recent Content Analysis and Trends of 15 Years," *Sex Roles 18*, no. 9/10 (1998), pp. 595–608; John B. Ford and Michael La Tour, "Contemporary Perspectives of Female Role Portrayals in Advertising," *Journal of Current Issues and Research in Advertising* 28, no. 1 (1996), pp. 81–93.
62. Beverly A. Browne, "Gender Stereotypes in Advertising on Children's Television in the 1990s: A Cross-National Analysis," *Journal of Advertising* 27, no. 1 (Spring 1998), pp. 83–96.
63. Richard H. Kolbe, "Gender Roles in Children's Advertising: A Longitudinal Content Analysis," in *Current Issues and Research in Advertising*, ed. James H. Leigh and Claude R. Martin, Jr. (Ann Arbor: University of Michigan, 1990), pp. 197–206.
64. Debra Merskin, "Boys Will Be Boys: A Content Analysis of Gender and Race in Children's Advertisements on the Turner Cartoon Network," *Journal of Current Issues and Research in Advertising*, 24, (1), (Spring 2002), pp. 51–60.
65. Cate Terwilliger, "'Love Your Body Day' Auraria Event Takes Aim at 'Offensive' Images, Ads," *Denver Post*, September 23, 1999, p. E3.
66. Steven M. Kates and Glenda Shaw-Garlock, "The Ever Entangling Web: A Study of Ideologies and Discourses in Advertising to Women," *Journal of Advertising* 28, no. 2 (Summer 1999), pp. 33–49.
67. Basil Englis, Michael Solomon, and Richard Ashmore, "Beauty before the Eyes of Beholders: The Cultural Encoding of Beauty Types in Magazine Advertising and Music Television," *Journal of Advertising,* June 1994, pp. 49–64.
68. Thomas H. Stevenson, "How Are Blacks Portrayed in Business Ads?" *Industrial Marketing Management* 20 (1991), pp. 193–99; Helen Czepic and J. Steven Kelly, "Analyzing Hispanic Roles in Advertising," in *Current Issues and Research in Advertising*, ed. James H. Leigh and Claude Martin (Ann Arbor: University of Michigan, 1983), pp. 219–40; R. F. Busch, Allan S. Resnik, and Bruce L. Stern, "A Content Analysis of the Portrayal of Black Models in Magazine Advertising," in *American Marketing Association Proceedings: Marketing in the 1980s*, ed. Richard P. Bagozzi (Chicago: American Marketing Association, 1980); and R. F. Busch, Allan S. Resnik, and Bruce L. Stern, "There Are More Blacks in TV Commercials," *Journal of Advertising Research* 17 (1977), pp. 21–25.
69. James Stearns, Lynette S. Unger, and Steven G. Luebkeman, "The Portrayal of Blacks in Magazine and Television Advertising," in AMA Educator's Proceedings, ed. Susan P. Douglas and Michael R. Solomon (Chicago: American Marketing Association, 1987).
70. Robert E. Wilkes and Humberto Valencia, "Hispanics and Blacks in Television Commercials," *Journal of Advertising* 18, no. 1 (1989), pp. 19–26.
71. Julia Bristor, Renee Gravois Lee, and Michelle Hunt, "Race and Ideology: African American Images in Television Advertising," *Journal of Public Policy and Marketing* 14 (Spring 1995), pp. 48–59.
72. Leon E. Wynter, "Minorities Play the Hero in More TV Ads as Clients Discover Multicultural Sells," *The Wall Street Journal*, December 24, 1993, pp. B1, 6.
73. Bob Garfield, "Ikea Again Furnishes Ad Breakthrough," *Advertising Age*, April 1, 1996, p. 61.
74. Corliss Green, "Ethnic Evaluations of Advertising: Interaction Effects of Strength of Ethnic Identification, Media Placement, and Degree of Racial Composition," *Journal of Advertising* 28, no. 1 (Spring 1999), pp. 49–64.
75. Charles R. Taylor and Barbara B. Stern, "Asian-Americans: Television Advertising and the 'Model Minority' Stereotype," *Journal of Advertising* 26, no. 2 (Summer 1997), pp. 47–61.
76. Jon Berry, "Think Bland," *Adweek's Marketing Week*, November 11, 1991, pp. 22–24.
77. Todd Pruzman, "Brewing New Ties with Gay Consumers," *Advertising Age*, April 8, 1996, p. 13.
78. Ronald Alsop, "Web Site Sets Gay-Themed Ad for Big, National Publications," *The Wall Street Journal*, February 17, 2000, p. B4.
79. Mike Wilke, "Commercial Closet: Millers Ads Get Gay Inclusive," *http://www.gfn.com/archives/story.html,* May 23, 2001.
80. Jef I. Richards and John H. Murphy, II, "Economic Censorship and Free Speech: The Circle of Communication between Advertisers, Media and Consumers," *Journal of Current Issues and Research in Advertising* 18, no. 1 (Spring 1996), pp. 21–33.
81. Lawrence C. Soley and Robert L. Craig, "Advertising Pressure on Newspapers: A Survey," *Journal of Advertising*, December 1992, pp. 1–10.
82. Mark Simon, "Mercury News Ad Dispute Cooling Off: Advertisers Return While Reporters Stew," *San Francisco Business Chronicle*, July 15, 1994, p. B1.
83. Soley and Craig, "Advertising Pressure on Newspapers."
84. David Shaw, "An Uneasy Alliance of News and Ads," *Los Angeles Times*, March 29, 1998, pp. A1, 28; Steven T. Goldberg, "Do the Ads Tempt the Editors?" *Kiplinger's*, May 1996, pp. 45–49.
85. Janet Guyon, "Do Publications Avoid Anti-Cigarette Stories to Protect Ad Dollars?" *The Wall Street Journal*, November 22, 1982, pp. 1, 20; Elizabeth M. Whelan, "When Newsweek and Time Filtered Cigarette Copy," *The Wall Street Journal*, November 1, 1984, p. 3; and "RJR Swears Off Saatchi and Nabisco Is in a Sweat," *Business-Week*, April 18, 1988, p. 36.
86. Joanne Lipman, "Media Content Is Linked to Cigarette Ads," *The Wall Street Journal*, January 30, 1992, p. B5.
87. Laurie Freman, "Pillsbury Re-evaluates Ads on Violent Shows," *Advertising Age*, January 15, 1996, p. B6.
88. David Shaw, "An Uneasy Alliance of News and Ads," *Los Angeles Times*, March 29, 1998, pp. A1,28.
89. Steven T. Goldberg, "Do the Ads Tempt the Editors?" *Kiplingers Personal Finance*, May 1996, pp. 45–49.
90. David E. Sumner, "Who Pays for Magazines? Advertisers or Con-

sumers?" *Journal of Advertising Research*, 41 (6), (November/December 2001), pp. 61–67.

91. Pamela Sebastian, "Boys & Girls Club Featuring Denzel Washington Is a Standout," *The Wall Street Journal*, July 8, 1996, p. B7.
92. For a discussion of monopolies in the cereal industry, see Paul N. Bloom, "The Cereal Industry: Monopolists or Super Marketers?" *MSU Business Topics*, Summer 1978, pp. 41–49.
93. Lester G. Telser, "Advertising and Competition," *Journal of Political Economy*, December 1964, pp. 537–62.
94. Robert D. Buzzell, Bradley T. Gale, and Ralph G. M. Sultan, "Market Share—A Key to Profitability," *Harvard Business Review*, (January/February 1975), pp. 97–106.
95. Robert D. Buzzell and Paul W. Farris, *Advertising Cost in Consumer Goods Industries*, Marketing Science Institute, Report no. 76, August 1976, p. 111; and Paul W. Farris and David J. Reibstein, "How Prices, Ad Expenditures, and Profits Are Linked," *Harvard Business Review*, (November/December 1979), pp. 173–84.
96. Thomas M. Buron, "Reining in Drug Advertising," *The Wall Street Journal*, March 13, 2002, pp. B1, 4.
97. Paul W. Farris and Mark S. Albion, "The Impact of Advertising on the Price of Consumer Products," *Journal of Marketing* 44, no. 3 (Summer 1980), pp. 17–35.
98. Buron, "Reining in Drug Advertising."
99. Farris and Albion, "The Impact of Advertising on the Price of Consumer Products."
100. Lee Benham, "The Effect of Advertising on the Price of Eyeglasses," *Journal of Law and Economics* 15 (October 1972), pp. 337–52.
101. Robert L. Steiner, "Does Advertising Lower Consumer Price?" *Journal of Marketing* 37, no. 4 (October 1973), pp. 19–26.
102. Farris and Albion, "The Impact of Advertising," p. 30.
103. James M. Ferguson, "Comments on 'The Impact of Advertising on the Price of Consumer Products,'" *Journal of Marketing* 46, no. 1 (Winter 1982), pp. 102–5.
104. Farris and Albion, "The Impact of Advertising."
105. Cyndee Miller, "The Marketing of Advertising," *Marketing News*, December 7, 1992, pp. 1, 2.

Credits and Acknowledgments

Chapter 1

Chapter opening photo: Courtesy of United States Army Recruiting Command and the Department of the Army. **Exhibit 1-1:** Courtesy of United States Army Recruiting Command and the Department of the Army. **Exhibit 1-2:** Courtesy of American Red Cross. **Exhibit 1-3:** Courtesy of Dell Computer Corp. **Exhibit 1-4:** Used with permission of Ben & Jerry's Homemade Holdings, Inc. 2000. **Exhibit 1-5:** Courtesy of Montblanc, Inc. **Exhibit 1-6:** Photo by David Allan Brandt. Courtesy of American Airlines®. **IMC Perspective 1-1:** AP/Wide World Photos. **IMC Perspective 1-2:** Courtesy of American Advertising Federation. **Exhibit 1-7:** Courtesy of V&S Vin and Spirit AB. Imported by the Absolut Spirits Company, New York, NY. **Exhibit 1-8:** Used by permission of Eveready Battery Company, Inc. Energizer® is a registered trademark of Eveready Battery Company. **Exhibit 1-9:** Courtesy of America's Dairy Farmers and Milk Processors. **Exhibit 1-10:** Courtesy of Bose Corp. **Exhibit 1-12:** Courtesy of NIKE, Inc. **Exhibit 1-13:** Courtesy of Johnson & Johnson Consumer Products, Inc. **Exhibit 1-14:** Courtesy of E. I. du Pont de Nemours and Company. **Exhibit 1-15:** Courtesy of Honeywell. **IMC Perspective 1-3:** Kenneth Cole Productions, Inc. in-house. **Figure 1-2:** Reprinted with permission from the June 24, 2002 issue of *Advertising Age,* © Crain Communications, Inc. 1999.

Chapter 2

Chapter opening photo: © Steven E. Frischling/CORBIS Sygma. **Exhibit 2-1:** Courtesy of Wolverine World Wide, Inc. **Exhibit 2-2:** Courtesy of Campbell Soup Company. **Exhibit 2-3:** AP/Wide World Photos. **Exhibit 2-4:** Courtesy of Grupo Modelo, A.A. de C.V. **Diversity Perspective 2-1:** Photo by David Allan Brandt. Courtesy of American Airlines®. **Figure 2-4:** Used with permission by *Marketing,* 7 ed., by Kerin, et al., © 2003 McGraw-Hill/Irwin. **Exhibit 2-5:** Courtesy of Big Red, Inc. **Exhibit 2-7:** Courtesy of Abercrombie & Fitch. **Exhibit 2-8:** Courtesy of AARP. **Exhibit 2-9:** Courtesy of Pfizer Inc. **Exhibit 2-10a:** Courtesy of Pfizer Inc. **Exhibit 2-10b:** Courtesy of Pfizer Inc. **Exhibit 2-11:** Courtesy of Maxwell Business Systems. **Exhibit 2-12:** Courtesy of Loro Piana. **Exhibit 2-13:** © The Coca-Cola Company. "PowerAde," "PowerAde Light," the design of the stylized "P" and "Andean Chill" are trademarks of The Coca-Cola Company. **Exhibit 2-14:** © 2002. Lands' End, Inc. Used with permission. **Exhibit 2-15:** Courtesy of Black & Decker. **Exhibit 2-16a:** Courtesy of Church & Dwight Company, Inc. **Exhibit 2-16b:** Courtesy of Church & Dwight Company, Inc. **Exhibit 2-17:** Courtesy of America's Dairy Farmers, National Dairy Board. **Exhibit 2-18:** Courtesy of The Valvoline Company, a division of Ashland Inc. **Exhibit 2-19:** Courtesy of The Pillsbury Company. **Exhibit 2-20:** Courtesy of Fallon-McElligott for Rolling Stone. **IMC Perspective 2-1:** Courtesy of JetBlue Airways and The Ad Store. Creative Director/Copywriter: Paul Cappelli; Copywriter: Brian Flatow; Art Director: Victor Anselmi; Producer/Editor Daniel Miller; Production Company: U Direct. **Exhibit 2-21:** © James Leynse/CORBIS SABA. **Exhibit 2-22:** Courtesy of Rado Watch Company Ltd. **Exhibit 2-23:** Courtesy of Pfizer Consumer Healthcare. **Exhibit 2-24:** Designs © by Tiffany and Company. **Exhibit 2-25:** Courtesy of McNeil Consumer Healthcare, 1999. **Exhibit 2-26:** Acushnet Company ©. Photography © Francine Zaslow.

Chapter 3

Chapter opening photo: © 2004 BMW of North America, LLC, used with permission. The BMW name and logo are registered trademarks. **Exhibit 3-1:** Courtesy of The History Channel, a programming service of A & E Television Networks. **Exhibit 3-2a:** © The Procter & Gamble Company. Used by permission. **Exhibit 3-2b:** © The Procter & Gamble Company. Used by permission. **Exhibit 3-3:** Courtesy of No Fear. **Exhibit 3-4:** Courtesy of Mentus. **IMC Perspective 3-1:** Courtesy of J. Walter Thompson. **Exhibit 3-5:** © The Coca-Cola Company. "Coca-Cola" and the Dynamic Ribbon device are registered trademarks of The Coca-Cola Company. **Exhibit 3-8:** DR PEPPER ® is a registered trademark of Dr. Pepper/Seven Up, Inc. © 2000 Dr. Pepper/Seven Up, Inc. **IMC Perspective 3-3:** Courtesy of Gateway, Inc. **Exhibit 3-9:** Courtesy of International Business Machines Corp. **Exhibit 3-10:** Courtesy of DVC. **Figure 3-6:** Reprinted with permission from the April 22, 2002 issue of *Advertising Age*. © Crain Communications, Inc. **Figure 3-9:** Used by permission of Association of National Advertisers: Trend in Compensation Survey: 2000. **Figure 3-10:** The Direct Marketing Association Direct Response Agency Report for 2001. www.the-dma.org. **Figure 3-11:** Reprinted with permission from the February 4, 2002 issue of *Adweek*.

Chapter 4

Chapter opening photo: Courtesy of Red Bull North America, Inc. **Exhibit 4-1:** Courtesy of Ashworth, Inc. **IMC Perspective 4-1:** Courtesy of Roxy. **Exhibit 4-2:** Courtesy of John Paul Mitchell Systems. **Exhibit 4-3:** Courtesy of Del Pharmaceuticals, Inc. a subsidiary of Del Laboratories. **Exhibit 4-4:** Courtesy of HiddenMind Technology, LLC. **Exhibit 4-5:** © The Procter & Gamble Company. Used by permission. **Exhibit 4-6:** Used with permission from DaimlerChrysler Corp. **Exhibit 4-7:** Courtesy of Puig Beauty and Fashion North America. **Exhibit 4-8:** © American Association of Advertising Agencies. **Exhibit 4-9:** Courtesy of Tropicana Products, Inc. **Exhibit 4-10:** Courtesy of The Spokesman-Review. Ad produced by Hanna & Associates Advertising Agency. **Ethical Perspective 4-1:** AP/Wide World Photos. **Exhibit 4-11:** Courtesy of Callaway Golf Company. **Exhibit 4-12:** Courtesy of Panasonic. **Exhibit 4-13:** Courtesy of The Pillsbury Company. **Exhibit 4-14:** Courtesy of Anheuser-Busch Companies, Inc. **Exhibit 4-15:** Courtesy of UUNET Technologies, Inc. a subsidiary of MCI WorldCom, Inc. **Exhibit 4-16:** Fidelity Investments. © 2002 FMR Corp. All rights reserved. Used with permission. **Exhibit 4-17:** Courtesy of Lancome, Paris. **Exhibit 4-18:** Used by permission of Eveready Battery Company, Inc. Energizer® is a registered trademark of Eveready Battery Company. **Exhibit 4-19a:** Courtesy of Kronos, The Optimal Health Company. **Exhibit 4-19b:** Courtesy of Seiko Watch Corp. **Exhibit 4-20:** Courtesy of The New York Palace. **Exhibit 4-21a:** United States Navy. **Exhibit 4-21b:** Courtesy of Shell Oil Company. **IMC Perspective 4-2:** The photograph of the PT Cruiser is used with permission from DaimlerChrysler Corp. Emotional Rescue ad—Mervin Franklin, photographer.

Chapter 5

Chapter opening photo: Courtesy of EDS Corp. **Diversity Perspective 5-1:** Courtesy of California Milk Processor Board. **Exhibit 5-1:** Courtesy of Rolex Watch U.S.A., Inc. **Exhibit 5-2:** Courtesy of Estee Lauder. **Exhibit 5-3:** © 1999 Time, Inc. Reprinted by permission. **Exhibit 5-4:** Courtesy of Johnson & Johnson Products, Inc. **Exhibit 5-5:** Courtesy of Zenith Electronics Corp. **Exhibit 5-6:** Courtesy Xerox Corp. **Exhibit 5-7:** Courtesy of Michelin North America. **Exhibit 5-8:** © H. J. Heinz Company, L.P. Used with permission. **IMC Perspective 5-2:** Courtesy of Whirlpool Corp. **Exhibit 5-9:** © The Procter & Gamble Company. Used by permission. **Exhibit 5-10:** Courtesy of Maxfli Golf. **Figure 5-7:** From the work of Richard Vaughn of Foote, Cone & Belding Advertising Agency. **Figure 5-10:** *Journal of Marketing* 663, "How Advertising Works: What Do We Really Know?" p. 26, by Demetrios Vakratas and Tim Ambler. © 1999 by The American Marketing Association. Used by Permission.

Chapter 6

Chapter opening photo: Courtesy of PONY. **Exhibit 6-1:** Courtesy of HEAD/Penn Racquet Sports. **Exhibit 6-2:** Courtesy of Lever Brothers Company. **Exhibit 6-3:** Courtesy of Wendy's International, Inc. **Exhibit 6-4:** Used with permission of General Motors Corp. **Exhibit 6-5:** Courtesy of The Coca-Cola Company. **Exhibit 6-6:** Courtesy of PowerBar. **Exhibit 6-7:** Courtesy of Revlon Consumer Products Corp. **Exhibit 6-8:** Courtesy of The Advertising Council. **Exhibit 6-9:** Courtesy of White Wave, Inc. **Exhibit 6-10:** Courtesy of W. K. Buckley Limited. **Exhibit 6-11:** Courtesy of The Almond Board of California. **Exhibit 6-12:** Courtesy of CamelBak Products, Inc. **Exhibit 6-13:** Courtesy of Savin Corp. **Exhibit 6-14:** Courtesy of SmithKline Beecham. **Exhibit 6-15:** PayDay is a registered trademark. Used with permission of Hershey Foods Corp. Photography © Howard Berman. **IMC Perspective 6-4:** Used with permission of Little Caesar Enterprises, Inc. © 1995, Little Caesar Enterprises, Inc. All rights reserved. **Exhibit 6-16:** Courtesy of *Travel & Leisure*. © 2002 by American Express Publishing Corp.

Chapter 7

Chapter opening photo: Courtesy Waterford Wedgwood USA, Inc. **Exhibit 7-1:** Courtesy of Toyota Motor North America, Inc. **Exhibit 7-2:** © State Farm Mutual Automobile Insurance Company, 1996. Used by permission. **IMC Perspective 7-1:** Courtesy of Microsoft Corp. **Exhibit 7-3:** © The Procter & Gamble Company. Used by permission. **Exhibit 7-4:** Courtesy of MINI USA. **Exhibit 7-5:** Courtesy SkyTel Communications, SkyTel an MCI WorldCom Company. **Exhibit 7-6:** Courtesy of Mattress Gallery. **Exhibit 7-7:** Courtesy of Hitachi America, Ltd. **Exhibit 7-8:** Courtesy of Foster's Brewing Group. **Exhibit 7-9:** Courtesy of the Zoological Society of San Diego. **Exhibit 7-10:** © American Association of Advertising Agencies. **Exhibit 7-11:** Courtesy of Palm Inc. Photography by Timothy Greenfield-Sanders. **IMC Perspective 7-2:** © Steven E. Frischling/CORBIS Sygma. **Figure 7-6:** Data from Subaru of America, Inc. **Figure 7-8:** Courtesy of San Diego Zoo. **Figure 7-15:** Schonfeld & Associates, Inc. **Figure 7-23:** Used with permission by eMarketer, Inc.

Chapter 8

Chapter opening photo: Courtesy of NIKE, Inc. **Exhibit 8-1:** © 2002 BMW of North America, LLC. Used with permission. The BMW name and logo are registered trademarks. **Exhibit 8-2:** Courtesy of Nissan North America, Inc. **Global Perspective 8-1:** Courtesy of NIKE, Inc. **Exhibit 8-3:** Courtesy of V&S Vin and Spirit AB. Imported by the Absolut Spirits Company, New York, NY. **Exhibit 8-4:** Courtesy of Wm. WRIGLEY Jr. Company. **IMC Perspective 8-2:** Courtesy of Norwegian Cruise Line and Goodby Silverstein & Partners. **Exhibit 8-5:** © Sharon Hoogstraten. **Exhibit 8-6:** Courtesy of Westin Hotels & Resorts. **Exhibit 8-7a–b:** Courtesy California Milk Processor Board. **Exhibit 8-8:** Courtesy of Skyy Spirits, LLC. **IMC Perspective 8-4:** Courtesy of Miller Brewing Company. **Exhibits 8-8a–c:** Courtesy of Polaroid Corp. **Exhibit 8-10:** Courtesy of United Technologies. **Exhibit 8-11:** Courtesy of Colgate-Palmolive Company. **Exhibit 8-12:** Courtesy of No Fear. **Exhibit 8-13:** Courtesy of Leo Burnett Company, Inc. as agent for Hallmark Cards, Inc. **Exhibit 8-14:** Courtesy of 3M. **Exhibit 8-15:** Courtesy of Pennzoil-Quaker State Company. **Exhibit 8-16:** Courtesy of Pennzoil Quaker State Company. **Figure 8-2:** Reprinted with permission of D'Arcy, Masius, Benton & Bowles from website, © 2000. **Figure 8-3:** www.adage.com/century/slogans.

Chapter 9

Chapter Opening Photo: Courtesy of Skyy Spirits, LLC. **Exhibit 9-1:** Courtesy of Nordica. **Exhibit 9-2:** Jeep. Used with permission from DaimlerChrysler Corp. **Exhibit 9-3:** Courtesy of the Quaker Oats Company. **Exhibit 9-4:** Courtesy of Bristol-Meyers Squibb Company. **Exhibit 9-5:** Nutri-Grain ® is a registered trademark of Kellogg Company. © 2002 Kellogg Company. **IMC Perspective 9-1:** Courtesy of Pepsi-Cola Company. Used with permission. **Exhibits 9-6a & b:** Courtesy of Norwegian Cruise Line. **Exhibit 9-7:** Courtesy of Team One Advertising for Lexus. **Exhibit 9-8:** Courtesy of MasterCard International, Inc. **Exhibit 9-9:** Courtesy of Leo Burnett Company, Inc. for Callard & Bowser-Suchard, Inc. **Exhibit 9-10:** Courtesy of Lee Jeans. **Exhibit 9-11:** Courtesy of Porsche Cars North America, Inc. **Exhibit 9-12:** Syntec © 1999 Castrol North America, Inc. **IMC Perspective 9-2:** Pets.com puppet © John Boehm. **Exhibit 9-13:** The Dermasil ad courtesy of Chesebrough-Pond's, USA Company. **Exhibit 9-14:** Courtesy DuPont. Teflon® is a registered trademark of DuPont. **Exhibit 9-15:** Courtesy of Apple Computer, Inc. **Exhibits 9-16a & b:** Courtesy of AT&T and Young & Rubicam. **Exhibit 9-17:** Courtesy of Hormel Foods, LLC. **Exhibit 9-18:** Courtesy of Starkist Seafood, Pittsburgh, PA. **Exhibit 9-19:** Courtesy of AFLAC, Inc., Columbus, GA. **Exhibit 9-20:** Courtesy of BASF Corp. **Exhibit 9-21:** Courtesy Thomson Multimedia. Product photo by Tomas Card. Model photo by Dominick Guillemot. **Exhibit 9-22:** Courtesy of Team One Advertising for LEXUS. Photo by Martin Oort. **Exhibit 9-23:** Courtesy of Cambridge SoundWorks. **Exhibit 9-24:** Courtesy of Sims. **Exhibits 9-25a–d:** Courtesy of Volkswagen of America, Inc. and Arnold Worldwide. **IMC Perspective 9-3:** Courtesy of Mitsubishi Motor Sales of America, Inc. **Exhibits 9-26 a & b:** Courtesy of Apple Computer, Inc. **IMC Perspective 9-4:** Courtesy of Savin Corp. **Exhibits 9-27 a–f:** Courtesy of Philips Lighting Company.

Chapter10

Chapter Opening Photo: AP/Wide World Photos. **IMC Perspective 10-2:** Dunkin Donuts "loosen up" logo. Courtesy of Allied Domecq Retailing USA. **Exhibit 10-1:** Courtesy of Scarborough Research. **Figure 10-1:** Reprinted with permission from the June 24, 2002 issue of *Advertising Age*, © Crain Communications, Inc., 2002. **Figure 10-4:** Simmons Market Research Bureau, Inc. 1997. **Figure 10-5:** MediaMark Research, Inc. **Figure 10-8:** www.adage.com/dataplace. **Figure 10-9:** Reprinted with permission from *Sales & Marketing Management*, © 2001, VNU Business Publications, USA. **Figure 10-10:** Reprinted with permission from *Sales & Marketing Management*, © 2001, VNU Business Publications, USA. **Figure 10-11:** Reprinted with permission from *Sales & Marketing Management*, © 2001, VNU Business Publications, USA. **Figure 10-12:** Reprinted with permission from *Sales & Marketing Management*, © 2001, VNU Business Publications, USA. **Figure 10-15:** Simmons Market Research Bureau, © 2002. **Figure 10-18:** Who watches ads? December-January ratings in New York Market R. C. Percy & Company. **Figure 10-28:** Reach and frequency analyses: San Diego Trust and Savings Bank. **Appendix A:** Adapted with permission from Arnold M. Bantam, Donald W. Jugenheimer, and Peter B. Burk, *Advertising Media Sourcebook*, 3/e (Lincolnwood, IL: NTC Business Books), pp. 8–9. **Appendix B:** Table on page 340: MRI Spring. Weighted by population © MRI. All rights reserved. Appendix G: Table Source: IMS Model reach and frequency report. Appendix B: IMS Net/Duplication Report © 1996 MRI. All rights reserved.

Chapter 11

Chapter Opening Photo: Courtesy of TiVo, Inc. **Exhibit 11-1:** Courtesy of Porsche Cars North America, Inc. **Exhibit 11-2:** Courtesy of Court TV. **IMC Perspective 11-1:** © AFP/CORBIS. **Exhibit 11-3:** Courtesy United Paramount Network & World Wrestling Federation Entertainment, Inc. **Diversity Perspective 11-2:** Courtesy of Univision. **Exhibits 11-4 a–d:** Courtesy of Superstation WGN. **Exhibit 11-5:** Courtesy of New York Interconnect. **Exhibit 11-6:** © 2000 National Broadcasting Company, Inc. Used by permission. All rights reserved. **IMC Perspective 11-3:** Courtesy of ESPN. **IMC Perspective 11-4:** © Tom Wagner/CORBIS SABA. **Exhibit 11-7:** © 1996 Cable News Network, Inc. A Time-Warner Company. All rights reserved. **Exhibit 11-8:** Courtesy of Nielsen Media Research. **Exhibit 11-9:** Courtesy of KFMB-TV. **Exhibit 11-10:** Courtesy of Radio Advertising Bureau. **Exhibit 11-12:** Banana Boat of California, Inc. **IMC Perspective 11-6:** Courtesy of XM Satellite Radio. **Exhibit 11-13:** KCEO Radio. **Figure 11-1:** Reprinted from the June 24, 2002 issue of *Advertising Age*, © Crain Communications, Inc. 2002. **Figure 11-2:** Reprinted from the June 24, 2002 issue of *Advertising Age*. © Crain Communications, Inc. 2002. **Figure 11-3:** Used with permission of Nielson Media Research. **Figure 11-6:** Reprinted with permission of the Radio Advertising Bureau, Radio Marketing Guide and Fact Book, 2002–2003, p. 34. **Figure 11-7:** Reprinted with permission of the Radio Advertising Bureau, Radio Marketing Guide and Fact Book, 2002–2003, p. 27. **Figure 11-9:** Courtesy of Station XHTZ-FM, Chula Vista, CA. **Figure 11-10:** Reprinted courtesy of Arbitron.

Chapter 12

Chapter Opening Photo: Photo by Sante D'Orazio from *Rolling Stone*, October 17, 2002. © 2002 Rolling Stone, LLC. Reprinted by permission. All rights reserved. **Exhibit 12-1:** Courtesy of Virgo Publishing, Inc. **Exhibit 12-2:** Courtesy of TransWorld Media. **Exhibit 12-3:** Courtesy of *Beef* Magazine. **Exhibit 12-4:** Courtesy of Weider Publications, Inc. **IMC Perspective 12-1:** Courtesy of TransWorld Media. **Exhibit 12-5:** Courtesy of Jones Agency. **Exhibit 12-6:** Courtesy of *Newsweek* Magazine. **Exhibit 12-7:** Courtesy of Nabisco and Intervisual Communications, Inc. Photo by Sharon Hoogstraten. **Exhibit 12-8:** Used by permission of WD-40 Company. **Exhibit 12-9:** Courtesy of Magazine Publishers of America. **IMC Perspective 12-2:** Courtesy of NIKE, Inc. **Exhibit 12-11:** Courtesy of SRDS. **Exhibit 12-12:** Courtesy of Ivy League Magazine Network. **Exhibit 12-13:** Cover image reproduced with permission of Fast Company Magazine. All rights reserved. **IMC Perspective 12-3:** Courtesy of Magazine Publishers of America. **Exhibit 12-14:** Courtesy of Newsweek, Inc. All rights reserved. **Exhibit 12-16:** © 2000 by the New York Times Company. Reprinted by permission. **Exhibit 12-17:** Courtesy of *The Daily Collegian*. **Exhibit 12-18:** Courtesy of *The San Diego-Union Tribune*. **Exhibit 12-19:** Courtesy of Chevrolet Division General Motors and Campbell-Ewald Advertising. **Exhibit 12-20:** Courtesy of the *Chicago Tribune*. **Exhibit 12-21:** Courtesy of *The San Diego-Union Tribune*. **Exhibit 12-22:** Courtesy of *The San Diego-Union Tribune*. **Exhibit 12-23:** Courtesy of Cathay Pacific Airways and McCann-Erickson. **Exhibit 12-24:** Courtesy of Newspaper National Network. **Exhibit 12-25:** Courtesy of the Miami Herald/El Nuevo Herald. **Exhibit 12-26:** Courtesy of Newsweek, Inc. All rights reserved. **Exhibit 12-27:** Courtesy of the Newspaper Association of America. **Figure 12-1:** Magazine Publisher of America, Fact Sheet, www.magazine.org. Used with permission by Audit Bureau of Circulations. **Figure 12-2:** Courtesy of Beta Research, Inc. **Figure 12-3:** Magazine Publisher of America, Fact Sheet, www.magazine.org. Used with permission by Audit Bureau of Circulations. **Figure 12-4:** Facts About Newspapers, 2002, Newspaper Association of America, www.naa.org. Used with permission by Scarborough Research. **Figure 12-5:** Courtesy of Newspaper Advertising Bureau, Inc.

Chapter 13

Chapter Opening Photo: AP/Wide World Photos. **Exhibit 13-1:** Courtesy of Outdoor Advertising Association of America, Inc. **Exhibit 13-2:** Courtesy of Inflatable Design Group, El Cajon, CA ™ and © 1999 Saban. All rights reserved. **Exhibit 13-4:** Courtesy of Sanyo. **Exhibit 13-5:** AP/Wide World Photos. **Exhibit 13-6b:** Courtesy of Outdoor Advertising Association of America, Inc. **Exhibit 13-7:** Courtesy of Outdoor Advertising Association of America, Inc. **Exhibit 13-8:** Courtesy of Vert, Inc. **Exhibit 13-9:** Courtesy of Outdoor Advertising Association of America, Inc. **Exhibit 13-10:** Courtesy of Promotional Products Association International. **Exhibit 13-11:** Courtesy of Bell Atlantic Directory Services, Bell Atlantic Corp. **Exhibit 13-12:** AP/Wide World Photos. **IMC Perspective 13-1:** The Kobal Collection/Outlaw/Warner Bros/Robert Zuckerman. **Exhibit 13-13:** Cover art by Paul Webb, May 2002, reprinted Courtesy of Hemispheres, the magazine of United Airlines. **Exhibit 13-14:** Courtesy of DKY Video, LLC. **IMC Perspective 13-2 a & b:** Courtesy of Princeton Video Image, Inc. **Exhibit 13-15:** AP/Wide World Photos. **Figure 13-1:** Courtesy of Outdoor Advertising Association of America, Inc. **Figure 13-2:** Courtesy of Outdoor Advertising Association of America, Inc. **Figure 13-3:** Courtesy of Outdoor Advertising Association of America, Inc. **Figure 13-5:** Courtesy of Outdoor Advertising Association of America, Inc. **Figure 13-7:** Used with permission by Promotional Products Association International. **Figure 13-11:** © 2001, Media Central a PRIMEDIA Company. All rights reserved. **Figure 13-12:** Reprinted by permission of Halsey Publishing Company.

Chapter 14

Chapter Opening Photo: Courtesy of KitchenAid Home Appliances. **Exhibit 14-2:** Courtesy of The San Diego Convention & Visitors Bureau, CA. **Exhibit 14-3:** © 1999 Hertz System, Inc. Hertz is a registered service mark and trademark of Hertz System, Inc. **Exhibit 14-4:** BLOCKBUSTER name, design and related marks are trademarks of Blockbuster, Inc. © 2003 Blockbuster, Inc. All rights reserved. **IMC Perspective 14-1:** Courtesy of PETCO Animal Supplies, Inc. **Exhibit 14-5:** Courtesy of Porsche Cars North America, Inc. **Exhibit 14-6:** Photo by Sharon Hoodstraten. **Exhibit 14-7:** VNU Business Media. **Exhibit 14-8:** Courtesy of Neiman Marcus. **Exhibit 14-9:** Courtesy of Cmedia. **Exhibit 14-10:** Courtesy of Volvo Cars of North America. **Exhibit 14-11:** Courtesy of Lenox, Inc. **Exhibit 14-12:** Courtesy of Cutco Cutlery Corp. **Figure 14-5:** Simmons Market Research Bureau. **Figure 14-6:** Used with permission by The After Market Company. **Figure 14-7:** Direct Marketing Association, 1996 Statistical Fact Book, p. 146. **Figure 14-8:** From DSA's 2002 National Sales Force Survey.

Chapter 15

Chapter Opening Photo: © 2001 FedEx. All rights reserved. **Exhibit 15-1:** Reprinted from *INC.*, October 1995, pp 84–85, with permission of Hot Hot Hot. **Exhibit 15-4:** Courtesy of General Mills, Inc. "Cheerios" is a registered trademark of General Mills. Used with permission. **Exhibits 15-8a & b:** Courtesy of Grantastic Designs, Inc. **Exhibit 15-13:** © 2002 Lands' End, Inc. Used with permission. **Exhibit 15-14:** Courtesy of WebTV Networks, Inc. **Figure 15-2:** Source: www.adres.com. Reprinted by permission of Ad Resource. **Figure 15-3:** Used with permission by eMarketer, Inc. **Figure 15-4:** *Two-Thirds Hit the Net,* Robyn Greenspan www.cyberatlas.com. **Figure 15-7:** Data reprinted with permission from the June 2002 issue of *Business. 2.0.*

Chapter 16

Chapter Opening Photo: Reprinted with permission of The Pillsbury Company. BAKE-OFF is a registered trademark of The Pillsbury Company. **Exhibit 16-1:** © Procter & Gamble. Used by permission. **Exhibit 16-2:** Used with permission of General Motors Corp. **Exhibit 16-3:** Courtesy of DVC Worldwide. **Exhibit 16-4:** KELLOGG'S® POP TARTS PASTRY SWIRLS® and POP TARTS SNAK-STIX® are registered trademarks of Kellogg Company. All rights reserved. Used with permission. **Diversity Perspective 16-1:** Courtesy of Mott's, Inc. **Exhibit 16-6:** Courtesy of DVC Worldwide. **Exhibit 16-7:** Courtesy of Ryan Partnership. **Exhibit 16-8:** Courtesy of WD-40 Company. **Exhibit 16-9:** Courtesy of Burson Marsteller for Church & Dwight Company, Inc. **Exhibit 16-10:** Reproduced with permission of PepsiCo, Inc. 1994, Purchase, NY. **Exhibit 16-11:** Courtesy of DVC Worldwide. **IMC Perspective 16-2:** Courtesy of Georgia-Pacific. **Exhibit 16-12:** Courtesy of *The San Diego-Union Tribune.* **Exhibit 16-14:** ArmorAll Products Corp. **IMC Perspective 16-3:** Courtesy of Valpak Direct Marketing Systems, Inc. **Exhibit 16-16:** Courtesy of Kellogg Company Eggo®, Common Sense® and Kellogg's® are registered trademarks of Kellogg Company. All rights reserved. **Exhibit 16-17:** Courtesy of Catalina Marketing. **Exhibit 16-19:** Used with permission from McDonald's Corp. **Exhibit 16-20:** Courtesy of American Airlines. **Exhibit 16-22:** Courtesy of Intuit. Quicken® and TurboTax® are registered trademarks of Intuit, Inc. **Exhibit 16-23:** ArmorAll Products Corp. **Exhibit 16-24:** Courtesy of Bristol Myers Company. **Exhibit 16-26:** Courtesy of Triarc Beverage Group. **Exhibit 16-27:** Courtesy of Van Camp Seafood Company. **Exhibit 16-28:** Courtesy of Van Camp Seafood Company. **Exhibit 16-29:** Courtesy of Wilson Sporting Goods Co. and Great Northern Corp. Display Group. **Exhibit 16-31:** Courtesy of New Balance Athletic Shoe, Inc. **Exhibit 16-32:** Courtesy of WD-40 Company. **Exhibit 16-33:** Courtesy of Lever Brothers Company. **Exhibit 16-34:** © Dell Computer Corp. **Figure 16-4:** NCH Marketing Services, 2002 Trend Report.

Chapter 17

Chapter Opening Photo: AP/Wide World Photos. **Exhibit 17-1:** AP/Wide World Photos. **Exhibit 17-2:** Courtesy of Bridgestone/Firestone Americas Holding, Inc. **Exhibit 17-3:** Courtesy of San Diego State University, College of Business Administration. **Exhibit 17-4:** ©2002. Lands' End, Inc. Used with permission. **Exhibit 17-5:** Reprinted with permission of Chevron Corp. **Exhibit 17-6:** Courtesy of KFMB-TV. **Exhibit 17-7:** Courtesy of Yellow Pages Publishers Assn. **Exhibit 17-9:** AP/Wide World Photos. **Exhibit 17-11:** CLIENT: Olympus America, Inc. AGENCY: McCaffrey & Ratner Gottlieb Lane. **Exhibit 17-12:** © 1991 Dow Jones & Company, Publisher of *The Wall Street Journal.* All rights reserved. **Exhibit 17-13:** Courtesy of Odwalla. **IMC Perspective 17-1:** AP/Wide World Photos. **Exhibit 17-14:** Used by permission of Tree Top, Inc. **Exhibit 17-15:** Courtesy of Tyco International. **Exhibit 17-16:** Courtesy Pharmaceutical Research and Manufacturers of America. **Exhibit 17-17:** Courtesy of KitchenAid Home Appliances. **IMC Perspective 17-2:** AP/Wide World Photos. **Exhibit 17-20:** Courtesy of American Civil Liberties Union. **Exhibit 17-21:** Courtesy of AT&T Advertising. **Figure 17-1:** www.prcentral.com. Reprinted by permission. **Figure 17-5:** Reprinted courtesy of Ketchum Public Relations. **Figure 17-6:** Data reprinted with permission from the March 4, 2002 issue of *Fortune* Magazine. **Figure 17-7:** Reprinted with permission from Business Ethics, Minneapolis, MN www.business-ethics.com. **Figure 17-8:** Annual sponsorship spending data from www.sponsorship.com.

Chapter 18

Chapter Opening Photo: Courtesy of Hobart Corp. **Exhibit 18-1:** Courtesy of PeopleSoft, Inc. **Exhibit 18-2:** Courtesy of CDW. **Exhibit 18-3:** Courtesy of Giltspur Inc./Haddon Advertising. **Exhibit 18-4:** Courtesy of Gateway. **Exhibit 18-5:** Courtesy of Gordon Publications, Inc. **Exhibit 18-6:** © 2003 EXPLANATIONS™ by EXPLANE.com®. **Exhibit 18-7:** Courtesy of GoldMine Software Corp. **Exhibit 18-8:** Courtesy of WebEx Communications, Inc. **IMC Perspective 18-1:** © ConAgra Brands, Inc. **IMC Perspective 18-2:** Overture Creative Services. **Figure 18-6:** *Sales and Marketing Management*, "The 20 Traits of Top Sales People," by Erica Rasmusson, August 1999. © 2003 by VNU Bus Pubs USA. Reprinted with permission through © Clearance Center. **Figure 18-7:** Botter Repping Survey Report, Berman Information Services, Inc. **Figure 18-8:** Adapted from Ted Pollock, "12 Ways to Use Your Advertising to Sell More," American Salesman, October, 2002.

Chapter 19

Chapter Opening Photo: Online Publishers Assn./MBIQ Media Mix Study, April 2002. **Exhibit 19-1:** Churchill & Klehr/Liaison Agency, Inc. **IMC Perspective 19-1:** Courtesy of Covering Kids. **Exhibit 19-2:** Courtesy of Chiat/Day/Mojo, Inc. Advertising. **Exhibit 19-3:** Courtesy Lowe's Companies, Inc. **IMC Perspective 19-2:** AP/Wide World Photos. **Exhibit 19-5:** Courtesy of Roper Starch Worldwide, Inc. **Exhibit 19-6:** Courtesy of Ipsos-ASI, Inc. **Exhibit 19-7:** Decision Analyst, Inc. **Figure 19-13:** Reprinted with permission from BUSINESS MARKETING, "Ad Response Methods," p. 41, March, 1999. © Crain Communications, Inc., 1999. All Rights Reserved. **Figure 19-21:** © 1994 ASM Communications. Used with permission from May 16, 1994 issue of *Brandweek.*

Chapter 20

Chapter Opening Photo: Courtesy of ACNeilsen Corp. **Exhibit 20-1:** Courtesy of The Australian Tourist Commission™ © The Brand Australia Trademark is the subject of copyright and is a trademark of the Australian Tourist Commission, 1995. **Exhibit 20-2:** Used by permission of WD-40 Company. **Global Perspective 20-1:** AP/Wide World Photos. **Exhibit 20-3:** Courtesy of Heineken Breweries. **Exhibit 20-4:** Courtesy of New Balance. **Exhibit 20-5:** Coca-Cola and Coca-Cola Light are registered trademarks of The Coca-Cola Company. Permission granted by The Coca-Cola Company. **Exhibit 20-6:** Illustrations appear with permission of The Gillette Company. **Exhibits 20-7 a & b:** Courtesy of Nestle. **Exhibit 20-8:** Courtesy of Nestlé. **Exhibit 20-9:** Courtesy of The Colgate-Palmolive Company. **Exhibit 20-10:** Courtesy of The Boeing Company. **Exhibits 20-11 a & b:** Courtesy of Continental Airlines. **Global Perspective 20-2:** © Tom Wagner/CORBIS SABA. **Exhibit 20-12:** Courtesy of The Coca-Cola Company. **Global Perspective 20-3:** © Macduff Everton/CORBIS. **Exhibit 20-14:** Central

Intelligence Agency. **Exhibit 20-15:** Courtesy of Haagen-Daz. **Exhibit 20-16:** Courtesy of PRESIDENT, Inc. **Exhibit 20-17:** Courtesy of Hearst Magazines International. **Exhibit 20-18:** STAR Creative Team. **Global Perspective 20-4:** Courtesy of MTV, a division of Viacom. **Exhibit 20-19:** Courtesy of WD-40 Company. Photo by Sharon Hoogstraten. **Exhibit 20-20:** Courtesy of DVC Worldwide. **Global Perspective 20-5:** AP/Wide World Photos. **Figure 20-1:** Reprinted with permission from www.AdAgeGlobal.com. **Figure 20-4:** NCH Marketing Services 2002 Trend Report.

Chapter 21

Chapter Opening Photo: Reprinted by permission of American Medical Assn., January 2003. **Exhibit 21-1:** Courtesy of Kinney & Lange. **IMC Perspective 21-1:** AP/Wide World Photos. **Exhibit 21-2** Courtesy of Luce, Forward, Hamilton & Scripps, LLP. **Exhibit 21-4:** Courtesy of Benetton Cosmetics Corp. Photo by O. Toscani. **Exhibit 21-5 a & b:** Courtesy of California Milk Processor Board. **IMC Perspective 21-2:** © Sharon Hoogstraten. **Exhibit 21-9:** Courtesy of Jenny Craig Weight Loss Centers, Inc. **Exhibit 21-10:** Courtesy of ExtendMedia. **Exhibit 21-11:** Courtesy of Van Kamp Seafood Company. **Exhibit 21-12:** Courtesy of American Legacy Foundation. **Exhibit 21-13:** Courtesy of Campbell Soup Company. **Exhibit 21-14:** © 1992. Wildcraft® Herbs, Santa Cruz, CA. **Exhibit 21-15:** Courtesy of Direct Selling Assn.

Chapter 22

Exhibit 22-1: Courtesy of Anheuser-Busch Company, Inc. **Exhibit 22-2:** Used by permission of Calvin Klein. **Exhibit 22-3:** Concept: O. Toscani. Courtesy of United Colors of Benetton. **Exhibit 22-4:** Courtesy of Ansell. **Exhibit 22-5:** Used by permission of Calvin Klein. **Exhibit 22-6:** Courtesy of Airwalk. **Exhibit 22-7:** © Sharon Hoogstraten. **Exhibit 22-8:** Courtesy of Bijan Designer for Men, Beverly Hills, CA. **Ethical Perspective 22-1:** Courtesy of a.k.a. Cartoon, Inc. **Ethical Perspective 22-2:** AP/Wide World Photos. **Exhibit 22-9:** Reprinted by permission of Rolls Royce Motor Cars, Inc. **Exhibit 22-10:** © America Association of Advertising Agencies. **Exhibit 22-11:** © America Association of Advertising Agencies. **Exhibit 22-12:** Courtesy of Maidenform, Inc./Agency-Levine, Huntley, Schmidt & Beaver; Creative-Rochelle Klein, Michael Vitello; Director—Mark Coppos, Coppos Films. **Exhibit 22-13:** Courtesy of IKEA and Deutsch, Inc. **Exhibit 22-14:** © The Procter & Gamble Company. Used by permission. **Exhibit 22-15:** Courtesy of gfn.com, the Gay Financial Network, Inc. **Exhibit 22-16:** Courtesy of International Advertising Assn. **Exhibit 22-17:** Courtesy of Boys & Girls Clubs of America. **IMC Perspective 22-3:** Source: Office of National Drug Control Policy. **Exhibit 22-18:** Courtesy of *ADWEEK*. **Exhibit 22-19:** © American Assn. of Advertising Agencies. **Exhibit 22-20:** Courtesy of Daewoo Motor America, Inc. **Exhibit 22-21:** © American Assn. of Advertising Agencies. **Exhibit 22-22:** Courtesy of International Advertising Assn. **IMC Perspective 22-4:** Courtesy of American Advertising Federation.

Name and Company Index

A

AAA Going Places, 403
Aaker, David A., 52, 54, 214, 485, 486, 493, 796, 799, 801, 802, 803, 811, 817
A.B. Zeller, 474
ABA Journal, 455
Abacus, 501
Abbot Laboratories, 730
ABC, 23, 30, 144, 174, 358, 359, 360, 365, 366, 368, 431, 508, 574, 710, 756, 759
ABC Radio Network, 383
ABC/Capital Cities, 369
Abercrombie & Fitch, 40, 46, 48, 106, 757–758
Abernethy, Avery, 382, 448, 805, 814
Abrams, Bill, 797, 802
Abrams, Lee, 381
Absolut, 17, 18, 241–242, 265, 266
A.C. Nielsen Co., 45, 226, 230, 372, 446, 645, 657, 658, 683, 685; *see also* Nielsen Media Research
Accenture, 585
Access Resources Services, Inc., 482
Achenbaum, Alvin, 797
Action for Children's Television (ACT), 761
ActMedia, 438, 534
Adams, Chris, 738
AdCenter at Virginia Commonwealth, 751
Addvantage Media Group, 438
Adidas, 165, 432, 458
ADLINK Digital Interconnect, 367
Adobe Systems, 477
Advanced Promotion Technologies, 438
Advertising Age, 17, 77, 103, 215, 240, 248, 252, 259, 287, 334, 414, 428, 448, 494, 553, 564, 565, 572, 583, 762, 779
Advertising Research Foundation, 619, 648
Advo Inc., 528, 531
Adweek, 248, 327, 774, 779
A&E Network, 365, 370
Affleck, Ben, 286
AFLAC, 281
Agassi, Andre, 117, 168
AGB, 373
AGENCY.COM, 95, 96
Agnew, Joe, 810
Agrawal, Maduh, 813
Agres, Stuart J., 803
Ahmed, Salim, 432
Ahuvia, Aaron C., 817
Aiello, Thomas L., 6
Air Products & Chemicals, 481
Airwalk, 756, 757
Ajzen, Icek, 797
akademiks, 486
Albion, Mark, 776, 777, 819
Alcone Marketing Group, 582
Alden, Dana L., 692, 814
Alexa, 503
Alexander, Jason, 178
Alexander, Ralph S., 795
Alka-Seltzer, 238, 245
Allen, Bruce H., 814
Allen, David, 375
Allen, Paul, 97
Alley, Kirstie, 178
Allianz, 585
Allport, Gordon, 117, 797
Allstate Insurance, 288
Allure, 752
Al-Makaty, Safran S., 812
Almay, 95
Almond Board of California, 181, 182
Alpine Promotions, 438
Alpo Petfoods, 470, 738
Alreck, Pamela, 802
Alsop, Ronald, 795, 797, 799, 802, 810, 817, 818
Altera, 615
Alternative Press, 391
Altoids, 274, 435, 779
Altria Group, Inc., 586; *see also* Philip Morris Cos.
Alwitt, Linda F., 805
Amara Raja, 663
Amazon.com, 62, 494, 503
Ambler, Tim, 161, 799
AMC Entertainment Inc., 449
America Online (AOL), 11, 223, 359, 411, 437, 440, 474, 496, 507, 691
American Airlines, 11, 12, 45, 72, 118, 454, 456, 512, 518, 536, 541–542, 589
American Business Press, 209
American Can Co., 295
American Cybercast, 97
American Express, 105, 173, 463, 473, 669, 688
American Family, 411, 538, 741
American Legacy Foundation, 736
American Legion Magazine, 403
American Movie Classics, 365
American Productivity and Quality Center, 615
American Way, 455
Ameritech, 456
Ameritrade, 276
Amicada, 495
Amoeba, 238
Amtrak, 53, 454
Amway, 20, 478, 479
Anderson, Rolph E., 810
And 1, 166
Andover Franchising, Inc., 223
Andrews, J. Craig, 812, 817
Andruss, Paula Lyon, 812
Anheuser-Busch, 30, 84, 104, 186, 223, 253, 281, 353, 356, 659, 752, 753, 769, 775
Animal Planet, 365
Anonymous Content, 67
Anrep, G.V., 797
Answerthink Interactive Marketing, 96
Anton, Susan, 625
ANZ Bank, 589
AOL-Time Warner, 17, 302, 352, 358, 411
Apple Computer, 52, 91, 230, 277–278, 286, 291, 407, 495, 558, 566, 577, 592, 659
Applied Industrial Technologies, 501
Arbitron Ratings Co., 329, 334, 372, 376, 385–386, 504
Arbor Mist Winery, 567
Archer, John F., 814
Archipelago, 327
Architectural Digest, 322, 400
Architectural Forum, 395
Arens, William F., 801, 804
Arm & Hammer, 53, 523
Armor All, 528
Armstrong, Gary M., 817
Armstrong, Lance, 173, 176, 235, 675
Arndt, Johan, 214, 802
Arnell Group, 91–92
Arnold Advertising, 84
Arnold Worldwide, 77
Arnould, Eric J., 803
Aronson, E., 799
Arrarte, Anne Moncreiff, 812
Arrid, 59
Arteaga, Erasmo, 45
Arthur Andersen, 589
Artzt, Edwin L., 809
Ashley, Morris, 518
Ashmore, Richard, 800, 818
Ashworth, 105
Aston Martin, 12
AstraZeneca, 581
Atkin, Charles, 800
AT&T, 17, 45, 91, 132, 223, 270, 279, 363, 376, 418, 433, 446, 448, 586, 590, 602, 616, 639
AT&T Wireless, 384
Attache, 407, 455
Audi, 384, 612
Audience Measurement by Market for Outdoor (AMMO), 439, 440
Audit Bureau of Circulation, 334, 394, 403, 405, 406, 504
Audits and Surveys, 230, 438
Ault, Johanna, 811
Aussie Home Loans, 589
Austin, Erica Weintraub, 801
Australian Tourist Commission, 63, 659
Autozone, 384
Aventis, 581, 585
Avis, 42, 54, 252, 256
Avon, 24, 62, 75, 478, 588
Axelrod, Joel N., 811
Aylesworth, Andrew, 188, 801

B

Baar, Aaron, 495
Babakus, Emin, 809
Bacall, Lauren, 749
Bacardi, 710
Bacharach, Burt, 673
Bachman, Katy, 305, 805
Backman, Jules, 817
Badu, Erykah, 518
Baglole, Joel A., 800
Bagozzi, Richard P., 795, 800, 818
Baker, Michael J., 800
Baldinger, Allan L., 811
Baldwin, Beth, 804
Ball, Jeffrey, 133, 797
Ballmer, Steve, 574
Bally Leather, 674
Bally's Health & Tennis Corp., 478
Bamossy, Gary J., 812
Banana Boat Suncare, 378–380
Banana Republic, 475
Bank of America, 586
Barbour, Fredric, 797

Barenaked Ladies, 289
Barkley, Charles, 165
BAR/LNA; *see* Competitive Media Reporting
Barnes & Noble, 62, 494
Barone, Amy, 809
Barone, Michael J., 739, 815
Barron's, 256
Barry, Thomas E., 799
Barry, Thomas S., 801
Bartle Bogle Hegarty, 68, 78, 90, 240, 245
BASF, 585
Baskin-Robbins, 327
Basney, Barbara, 612
Bass, Frank, 214, 802
Bates U.S.A., 13, 77
Bath & Body Works, 106
Batra, Rajeev, 798, 799, 803
Batt, Robert, 38
Bauer, Raymond, 765, 797, 817
Baurer, Betsy, 806
Bayer, 725
Bayus, Barry L., 798
BBC America, 365
BBC World Service, 381
BBDO, 248, 295, 435
BBDO Worldwide, 90, 230, 643
Bcom3 Group, 78
Bea Systems, 615
Beard, Fred K., 796, 797
Beardi, Cara, 539
The Beatles, 287, 288, 327
Beatrice Foods, 585
Beatty, Sally Goll, 253, 796, 797, 803, 804, 805, 813, 817
Bebe, 58
Beef, 394
Beeter, Amanda, 806
Beime, Mike, 470
Belch, George E., 798, 800, 812
Belch, Michael A., 450, 806, 812
Belk, Russell W., 797, 798
Belushi, Jim, 178
Ben & Jerry's, 10, 28, 500
Benetton, 75, 674, 719, 752–753, 757
Benezra, Karen, 493–494, 807, 810
Benham, Lee, 777, 819
Bennett, Drabe, 812
Bennett, John, 586
Bennett, Peter, 463, 807
Benson & Hedges, 465
Bentley, Stephanie, 816
Berger, David, 319, 804
Berkowitz, Eric N., 44, 795, 796, 797, 816
Berkshire Hathaway, 587
Berman, Ronald, 762, 817
Berman Information Services, 606
Bermuda Tourism, 63
Bernbach, William, 245, 275, 276
Berry, Jon, 818
Berry, Leonard L., 795
Bertagnoli, Lisa, 676, 814
Best Buy, 37
BET Networks, 365, 381
Beta Research, 401
Better Homes & Gardens, 394, 403
Bettman, James R., 797
Beyond.com, 276
Bezjian-Avery, Alexa, 808
Bhargava, Mukesh, 435, 806
Bible, Geoffrey, 586
Big Boy, 450
Big Chair, 84
Big Red, 46
Bigelow, Bruce, 92, 806
Bijan, 758
Bill Communications, 474
Billabong USA, 106
Billboard, 289
Bird, Laura, 811
Bittar, Christine, 738, 801
Black & Decker, 52, 53, 295
Black Enterprise, 518
Blair, Edward A., 809
Blair, Margaret H., 636, 811
Blasko, 224
Blender, 391, 392
Block, Lauren Goldberg, 185, 801
Block, M., 800
Blockbuster Entertainment, 465, 468, 469
Bloom, Paul, 549, 809, 819
Bloomberg News, 381
Blue Cross, 586, 738
BMW, 41, 46, 67–68, 88, 105, 118, 200–201, 237, 240, 249, 252, 277, 418, 465, 494, 591, 716, 725
Bobbie Dreams, 582
Boddewyn, J., 813
Bodine, Geoff, 477
Body Shop, 563
Boeing, 15, 132, 381, 672, 673
Boise Cascade, 205
Bon Jovi, 806
Bonoma, Thomas V., 798
Bose Corp., 20
Boston, 396
Boston Beer Co., 84, 757
Boucher, Geoff, 371
Bouchez, Brent, 245–246, 246, 802
Bouchez Kent and Company, 245
Bounds, Gwendolyn, 30, 410
Bove, Jose, 696
Bovee, Courtland I., 801
Bower, Amanda B., 800
Bower, Gordon S., 798
Bowie, David, 381
Boyd, Douglas S., 812
Boyle, John, 548
Boys & Girls Clubs of America, 772
Bozell & Jacobs Advertising, 592, 593
Bradford and Bingley, 589
Branch, Shelly, 658, 710, 803, 814
Brand Jordan, 404
Brand Keys, 193
Brand Marketing, 779
Brandes, Wendy, 804
Brandweek, 103, 193, 248, 449, 493–494, 779
Brandy, 806
Brann Worldwide, 94
Branson, Richard, 775
Bravo Network, 508
Brett, Daniel J., 818
Bridgestone/Firestone, 568, 577
Bristol, Terry, 760, 817
Bristor, Julia, 818
British Airways, 96, 301, 454, 669
British Satellite Broadcasting, 689
British Sky Broadcasting (BSkyB), 689
Britt, Stewart H., 209, 802
Broadcast Advertiser Reports, 334
Brock, T.C., 798, 801
Bronson, Charles, 179
Broom, Glen M., 565, 569, 809, 810
Brown, Dick, 137
Brown, Heidi, 38
Brown, Nigel A., 811
Brown, Randall S., 802
Brown, Stephen W., 799
Brown, William, 801
Browne, Beverly A., 818
Brown-Forman, 673
Brucks, Merrie, 817
Bruegger's Bagels, 84
Bruzzone, Donald E., 817
Bryant, Elizabeth, 812
Bryant, Kobe, 165
Brylcreem, 287
Buchanan, Bruce, 815
Bud Lite, 186
Budweiser, 120, 185, 186, 249, 281, 289, 452, 586, 779
Buell, Victor P., 796
Buick, 173, 625
Bulman, Erica, 810
Bumble Bee Tuna, 313, 314, 323, 335–347, 568
Burbury, Rochell, 813
Burger King, 193, 237–238, 353, 384, 518, 532, 536, 558, 582
Burke, Marian C., 799
Burne, Tom, 799
Burnett, Carol, 178
Burnett, John, 803, 810
Burnett, Leo, 258, 276, 778
Burnkrant, Robert E., 800
Buron, Thomas M., 819
Burros, Marian, 697
Burson-Marsteller, 563, 694
Burton, Scott, 816
Busch, Paul, 799
Busch, R. F., 818
Bush, Alan J., 810
Bush, Barbara, 806
Business 2.0, 504
Business Ethics, 588
Business Publications Audit of Circulation, 334, 405
Business Week, 256, 326, 395, 412, 572, 687
Buster Brown, 54
Butterball, 566
buy.com, 501
Buzzell, Robert D., 813, 819
Byrne, John A., 812

C

Caballero, M.J., 806
Cacioppo, John, 158, 799
Cadbury Schweppes, 104, 295
Cadillac, 41, 287, 288, 475, 590
Caffyn, John M., 811
Cahners Research, 600
Caldera, Louis, 3
Califee, John E., 815
California Kiwi Fruit Commission, 567
California Milk Advisory Board, 97, 759
California Milk Processor Board, 95, 140, 247, 250
California Raisin Advisory Board, 279
Callahan, Sean, 807
Callaway Golf, 117
Calvin Klein, 59, 75, 410, 431, 452, 659, 673, 752, 753, 756, 757
Calvo, David, 371
Camargo, Eduardo G., 812
Cambridge SoundWorks, 284
Camel, 588
Camelbak, 183
Campanelli, Melissa, 809
Campbell, Leland, 801
Campbell Mithun, 77
Campbell Soup Co., 41, 42, 88, 119, 287, 363, 418, 525, 645, 716, 728, 731–732, 739
Campbell-Ewald, 77, 622
Canfield, Bertrand R., 795
Cannon, Joseph, 549, 809
Canon, 37, 105, 183, 293, 690
Cantor, Joanne, 818
Capital One, 41–42
Capon, Noel, 799
Cappo, Joe, 795

Captivate Network, 327
Capulsky, Jonathan R., 795
Car & Driver, 580
Carat Interactive, 495
Caraviello, David, 810
Carlisle, Kate, 812
Carl's Jr., 175
Carlson, Les, 816
Carman, James, 214, 802
Carmichael Lynch, 91, 779
Carmike Cinemas Inc., 449
Carnevale, Mary Lu, 816
Cartier, 674
Carton, Sean, 808
Cartoon Network, 365
Case, Tony, 305, 806
Casey, Susan L., 812
Cash, Harold C., 801
Casison, Jeanie, 582
Cass Communications, 456
Cassidy, Hilary, 166, 236, 795
Cassino, Kip D., 813
Castrol, 275, 663
Catalina Marketing, 438, 528, 534, 535
Cataquet, Harold, 796
Cathay Pacific Airways, 421
Cauley, Leslie, 805
CBS, 30, 144, 169, 300, 355, 358, 359, 360, 364, 374, 451, 458, 465, 495, 532, 581, 710, 756, 759
Celebrated Living, 456
Center, Allen H., 565, 569, 809, 810
Center for Digital Democracy, 750
Center for Media Education, 505
Central Hudson Gas & Electric Corp., 722
Century Theatres, 449
Cereal Partners Worldwide (CPW), 660
Chaiken, S., 799
Champy, James, 810
Chan, Jackie, 427
Chance, Paul, 800
Chandiramani, Ravi, 197, 811
Chanel, Inc., 678
Chang, Il-Hyung, 38
Chang, Leslie, 813
Channel One, 456, 763
Charles Schwab, 314
Cheerwine, 46
Chemical Week, 395
Chemistri, 4
Chen, Hong C., 799
Chen, Kathy, 805
Chen, Qimel, 808
Cheng, Kipp, 811
Cher, 173
Chesney, Kenny, 470
Chestnut, Robert W., 800
Chevrolet, 256, 287, 288, 417, 515
Chevron, 49, 571
Chiat, Jay, 259
Chiat/Day, 78, 291, 624; *see also* TBWA/Chiat/Day
Chicago Cable Interconnect, 367
Chicago Tribune, 324, 325, 418
Chicken of the Sea, 545–546, 548, 566, 735
Childers, Terry L., 800
Children's Television Workshop, 492
China Central Television (CCTV), 685
China Sofres Media, 685
China Viewers Survey & Consulting Centre, 685
Ching, Alan, 805
Chiquita, 54
Ch'rewd Marketing, 582
Christian Science Monitor, 413
Christie, Jennifer, 816
Chrysler Corp., 171, 363, 499–500, 540, 576, 645; *see also* DaimlerChrysler
Chuang, Tamara, 808
Chura, Hillary, 30, 104, 144, 223, 812, 817
Churchill, Gilbert A., Jr., 800
Cigar Aficionado, 455
Cinemark USA Inc., 449
Cingular Wireless, 354, 384
Circuit City, 37, 193, 494
Cisco Systems, 490, 604
Citibank, 693–694
Citicorp, 473
Citigroup, 587
Clairol, 252, 448, 496
Claritas, 527
Clark, E.M., 800–801
Clarke, Darral G., 801
Clarke, P., 798, 817
Clifford, Stephanie, 804
Clinton, Bill, 588, 735
Clorox, 363
Clow, Lee, 259, 260
Club Libby Lu, 106
CMT (Country Music Television), 365
CNBC, 137, 365, 366, 367, 381
CNET, 381
CNN, 137, 167, 171, 174, 356, 365, 366, 368, 381, 411, 577
CNN International, 370
Coca-Cola, 15, 28, 42, 50, 51, 83, 104, 115, 141, 165, 184, 188, 197, 223, 237, 252, 286, 287, 352, 353, 363, 432, 448, 453, 456, 457, 458, 492, 498, 512, 518, 523–524, 657, 658, 659, 660, 661, 668, 669, 674, 675, 676, 679, 687, 690, 694–695, 763, 779
Cocanougher, Benton, 798
Coen, Robert J., 795, 812
Cohen, Andy, 616
Cohen, Dorothy, 814, 815
Cohen, Joel B., 797
Cohen, Marshal, 106
Cohen, Nina, 245, 246
Cohen, Warren, 805
Coleman, Calmetta Y., 813
Coleman, Lynn, 803
Coleman, Richard P., 798
Coleman, Ronald, 518
Colford, Steven W., 814, 815, 816
Colgate-Palmolive, 41, 88, 198, 257, 295, 440, 645, 660, 671–672, 680, 681
Colley, Russell, 206, 208, 209, 801
Collins, Thomas, 462, 807
Colman's Mustard, 431
Columbia Pictures, 12
Combs, "P. Diddy," 371
Comcast, 376
Comedy Central, 365
Commercial Alert, 452, 750, 763, 764
CommonHealth, 77
Compaq, 558
Competitive Media Reporting, 222, 310, 334, 414, 437
ConAgra, 592, 612–613
Condé Nast Publications, 305, 410
Condé Nast Traveler, 56, 63
Condon, George E., Jr., 116
Coney, Kenneth A., 799
Conlon, Ginger, 810
Connery, Sean, 178
Conseco, 589
Consoli, John, 458
Consumer Reports, 113, 580
Consumers Union, 456
Continental Airlines, 72, 674
Control G Software, 329
Converse, 759
Cook, Diane, 751
Cook, Rachel Lee, 773
Cooking Light, 403
Cooper, Carol Marie, 804
Cooper, Helen, 817
Cooper, M.J., 806
Coors Brewing Co., 253, 363, 568, 608–609, 659, 775
Coppertone, 436, 519
Copulsky, Jonathan R., 602, 810
Corcoran, Kevin, 601–602, 810
Corfman, Kim, 557, 809
Cornwell, Bettina, 811
Corra, Henry, 91
Corstiens, Marcel, 796
Cortez, John P., 804, 817
Cosby, Bill, 176, 178
Cosgrove, Julia, 271
CosmoGirl, 397
Cosmopolitan, 326, 394, 396, 403, 410, 498, 668, 687
Cosse, Thomas J., 796
Country Living, 403
Couples, Fred, 160
Courter, Eileen, 598
Courtney, Alice E., 818
CourtTV, 353, 365
Cox, Anthony D., 797
Cox, Beth, 808
Cox, Dena, 797
Cox, Edward, 814
Cox Target Media Inc., 466, 531, 532, 535
Cracker Jack, 511
Craftsman, 193
Craig, C. Samuel, 801
Craig, Robert, 770, 818
Crain, Rance, 564
Crane, Lauren E., 811
Crate & Barrel, 486
Crawford, Anne-Marie, 689, 807, 813
Crawford, Cindy, 177
Crayola, 566
Creative Artists Agency, 83
Cressey, Peter, 710
Creyer, Elizabeth, 816
Crissy, W.J.E., 801
Cronin, John, 356, 804
Cronkite, Walter, 169
Cross, Kim, 616
Cruise, Tom, 178, 451
C-Span, 381
Culver Franchising System, 84
Cummings, Betsy, 800
Cummins Engine, 588
Cuneo, Alice Z., 133, 246, 714, 796, 802, 804, 806, 809, 814
Cunningham, Isabella C.M., 815
Cunningham, William A., III, 809
Cunningham, William H., 815
Curry, Sheree, 613, 806
Curry, William N., 565, 809
Curtis, Ben, 174
Cutco, 479
Cutlip, Scott M., 565, 569, 809, 810
C.W. Post Co., 511, 529, 534–535
Czepic, Helen, 818

D

Daewoo Motor Co., 775–776
Daft, Douglas, 676
Dagnoli, Judann, 808
Dahlin Smith White, 553
The Daily Collegian, 414
Daimler-Benz, 12
DaimlerChrysler, 17, 112, 132, 268, 302
Daly, John, 175, 800
Darby, Ian, 300
D'Arcy Masius Benton & Bowles, 77, 78, 91, 132–133, 238, 241, 242, 271
Darlin, Damon, 453, 807
Datatec Industries, 649
Datatrak Systems Inc., 329
Davenport, J. William, Jr., 799

Davies, Jennifer, 452, 750
Davis, Harry J., 798, 799
Davis, Joel J., 806
Dawson, Chester, 812
DDB Chicago, 174
DDB Needham, 248
DDB Needham Worldwide, 90
DDB Worldwide Communications, 77, 249, 750
De Marc, Donna, 289
Dean, William R., 808
DeBeers, 252, 448
Decker, William S., 797
Dee, Sean, 142
Deighton, John, 803
Dell, Michael, 171
Dell Computer, 8, 20, 38, 171, 173, 174, 490, 558, 604, 659, 660, 697
Delta Air Lines, 454, 586
DeMarco, Donna, 804
DeNiro, Robert, 178
Den-Mat Corp., 49
Denny's, 319, 320, 384
Denstu Young & Rubicam Partnerships (DYR), 679
Dentropy Partners (Interpublic Group), 96
Dentsu, 78
Departures, 455
Deslauries, Brian C., 797
Desphande, Rohit, 675
Desrochers, Debra M., 809, 816
Destiny's Child, 500
Details, 266
Detroit News, 324, 325
Deutsch, 77, 95, 97, 238, 289
Deutsch, Morton, 797
Deutsche Telekom, 585
Dholakia, Ruby, 799
Diageo, 17, 238
Diagnostic Research Inc., 633, 644
Diamond, S.J., 815
Diaz, Ann-Christine P., 805
DiCaprio, Leonardo, 170
Dichter, Ernest, 110, 797
Dickson, Peter H., 557, 809
Dickson, Peter R., 797
Dietz, Jim, 223
Digitas, 94, 96
DiMassimo Brand Advertising, 91
Diners Club, 463
Dipasquale, Cara, 564, 809
Direct Marketing, 464
DirecTV, 170, 368, 370
Disa Records, 359
Discovery Channel, 193, 327, 365, 370, 381
Discovery Health Channel, 365
Discovery Network, 480
Discovery Toys, 20
Dish Network, 384
Distilled Spirits Council of the United States (DISCUS), 709–710, 714
DiversityInc.com, 518
D.L. Blair, 528
Doan's Pills, 733
Dobrow, Larry, 397
Dr. Pepper/Seven UP Inc., 51, 90, 114, 763
Dodge Dealer Association, 384
Dole, Bob, 737
Domain Chandon, 132–133
Domino's Pizza, 517
Donath, Bob, 602, 810
Donaton, Scott, 56, 805
Donius, James F., 811
Donnelley, 329, 439
Donnelly, Sally, 56
Donnelly Marketing, 438
Donthu, Naveen, 435, 476, 806, 812
Doordarshan Network, 689
Doritos, 452
DoubleClick, 745
Doug Flutie, Jr. Foundation, 591
Douglas, Susan P., 818
Dove, 169
Dover, Phillip A., 798
Dow Chemical, 230
Downy Wrinkle Releaser, 452
Doyle, Peter, 796
Doyle Dane Bernbach, 275
Draft Worldwide, 94
Dranhold, Katheryn, 156
DreamWorks, 327
Dreyer, Diane, 133
Dreyfuss, Richard, 286
Drug Store News, 395
Dubitsky, Tony M., 803
Dubow, Joel, 636
Ducoffe, Robert H., 795
Dufour, Francois, 696
Dun & Bradstreet, 230
Duncan, Thomas R., 10, 11, 210, 795, 802
Dunkin' Donuts, 327
DuPont, 23, 194, 277, 278, 552, 553
Duracell, 739
Durvasula, Srinivas, 812
DVC Worldwide, 95, 515, 524, 693
Dynamic Logic, Inc., 503, 619

E

E! Entertainment Television, 365, 370, 371
Eagly, A., 799
Earlbaum, Lawrence, 796
Earnest, Leslie, 106
Earthlink, 498
Eastman Kodak; *see* Kodak
Easy-Off, 59
eBay, 494, 616
Ebenkamp, Becky, 140
Ebony, 395, 403, 518
Echikson, William, 813
EchoStar, 370
Eck, Randy, 817
Eckert, Toby, 116
Economist, 103
Eddie Bauer, 475, 494
Edell, Julie A., 799, 800, 803
Edge Creative, 83
Edison Research, 382
Editor & Publisher Market Guide, 334
Edwards, Cliff, 809
Edwards, Jim, 728
Edwards Theatres Circuit, 449
Eighmey, John, 808
Eircom, 589
Eisenberg, Daniel, 432, 750, 799
Eisenhart, Tom, 477, 807
Eisman, Regina, 808
Eldridge, Earle, 795
Electronic Data Systems (EDS), 137–138, 141, 354, 673
Elkin, T., 92, 300, 350, 507, 554
Elle, 431, 567
Elliott, Jim, 407
Elliott, Michael T., 801
Elliott, Stuart, 271, 458, 710
Elway, John, 806
eMarketer, 488, 490, 504, 505, 508
Encyclopaedia Britannica, 479
Energizer Holdings, 186, 256, 566, 739, 779
Engel, James F., 797
Englis, Basil, 818
Enis, Ben M., 817
Enrico, Dottie, 186, 803
Enron Corp., 589
Entertainment Weekly, 266, 403
Entrepreneur, 223
Ephron, Erwin, 331, 494, 804, 807
Ephron, Papazian & Ephron, 331
Eppright, David R., 801
Epson, 384
Erdogan, B. Zafer, 800
Ericsson, 659
Erlbaum, Lawrence, 801
ESPN, 243, 356, 360, 365, 366, 367, 368–369, 370, 381, 457, 590, 709
ESPN The Magazine, 391, 397
ESPN.com, 619
Esquire, 396, 400, 668
Estée Lauder, 141
Estrostep, 49
Esty, William, 809
E-toys, 494
E*Trade Financial, 276–277, 314, 759
EuroRSCG, 77, 94, 95, 96
Evalucom, Inc., 205
Evangelista, Benny, 68
Eveready, 18, 125, 153, 186
Everett, Peter B., 797
Everett, Stephen E., 795
Everyday Picture, 404
Evian, 243, 457, 458
Excedrin, 269
Excite, 461, 495
The Experience Music Project, 97
Express, 473

F

Faber, Peggy J., 764
Fabergé, 453
The Faces, 289
Fairclough, Gordon, 796
Faison, Edmund J., 800
Fajen, Steve, 805
Fallon McElligott, 78, 81, 137, 274
Fallon Worldwide, 67–68, 91, 240, 327
Family Circle, 394, 403
Family PC, 409
Famina, Jerry Della, 816
Fannie Mae, 588
Fannin, Rebecca, 813
Farm Journal, 394
Farmer, Chad, 266
Farmer's Insurance, 402
Farris, Paul, 776, 777, 796, 800, 802, 819
Fast Company, 409, 504, 572
Fatsis, Stefan, 166
Fattal & Collins, 97
Fawcett, Adrienne Ward, 795, 797
FDNY, 625
Federated Department Stores, 301
FedEx, 185, 186, 279, 485, 582, 587, 589, 768
Feinstein, John, 368
Feiss, Ellen, 495
Felder, Leonard C., 798
Fellmeth, R., 814
Ferguson, James, 777, 819
Feurer, Jack, 796
FHM, 391, 397, 409
Fiat, 661
Fidelity Investments, 123
Field, Marshall, 599
Field & Stream, 420
Fila, 165
Fincher, David, 67
Fine, Jon, 305, 392, 397, 415, 805, 806
Fingerhut, 8, 474
Finish Line, 404
Firestone; *see* Bridgestone/Firestone
First Chicago Corp., 295
First for Women, 394
Fishbein, Martin, 797
Fisher, Anne B., 813
Fisher, Dan, 816
Fisher, Melissa L., 466, 532
Fishing World, 420
Fitzgerald, Kate, 710, 795, 806
Flagg, Michael, 680

Fleet Bank, 589
Fleishman-Hillard Inc., 98
Flesch, Rudolph, 634
Flint, Joe, 710, 804, 814
Flutie, Doug, 591
Foley, 224
Folkes, Valerie, 799
Food & Wine, 462
Food Network, 365
Foote, Cone & Belding, 77, 80, 81, 90, 112, 154–155, 245, 271, 319
Footstar, 714
Forbes, 395, 456, 779
Ford, Gary T., 815
Ford, Harrison, 170, 178
Ford, Henry, 50
Ford, John B., 812, 818
Ford Motor Co., 12, 13, 17, 42, 88, 96, 173, 211, 302, 352, 360, 363, 404, 452, 468, 506, 615, 645, 659, 660, 661
Forrester Research, 350, 504, 597
Fort James Corp., 716, 717
Fortune, 381, 395, 411, 456, 572, 587, 687
44 Liquormart Inc., 722
Fost, Dan, 795
Foster's Beer, 206–207
4-Wheel & Off Road, 576
Fowler, Geoffrey A., 818
Fox, Michael J., 91, 178
Fox, Stephen, 765, 817
Fox Broadcasting Co., 30, 327, 358, 359, 360, 365, 384, 710, 713, 759
Fox News, 381
Fox Sports, 368, 370, 457
Franchise Times, 223
Francis, Bob, 801
Franciscus Co., 574
Franeheimer, John, 67
Franklin, Ben, 463
Fraser, Cynthia L., 813, 814
Frazier, Gary L., 796
Free, Valerie H., 802
Freeman, Laurie, 807, 818
Freeman, Mike, 800
French Connection, 115
Freud, Sigmund, 110
Friedman, Wayne, 371, 805
The Friendly Review, 402
Frieswick, Kris, 194
Frito-Lay, Inc., 41
Fruit of the Loom, 271, 589
Fryburger, Vernon, 811
fubu, 486
Fueroghne, Dean K., 816
Fuhrmans, Vanessa, 812
Fujitsu, 37
Fulmer, Melinda, 266
Fumento, Michael, 728
Fusion Idea Lab, 84

G

Gaffney, John, 795, 801
Gaidis, William C., 126, 797
Galavision, 45, 359, 365
Galbraith, John K., 764, 817
Gale, Bradley T., 819
Gallo, 243
Gallup & Robinson, 448, 583, 634, 642, 643, 644, 646
Game, Deborah, 812
Game Show Network, 365
Gannett Company, 415
Gannett Transit, 441
Gap, 75, 84, 289, 448, 463, 475, 494, 762
Garbett, Tom, 810
Gardener, Elizabeth, 649, 811
Gardner, Meryl Paula, 803
Garfield, Bob, 116, 804, 817, 818
Gatchel, Robert, 636, 811
Gateway, 20, 76, 85, 90, 91–92, 171, 452, 586, 608
Gatorade, 137
Gatty, Ronald, 811
Gay, Verne, 805
Gay Financial Network, 769
Gear, 397
Gee, Carol, 194
Gelb, Betsy D., 800
Gellene, Denise, 799
Geller, Adam, 639
General Cinema Theatres, 449
General Electric, 15, 90, 132, 294, 295, 359, 363, 473, 508, 587, 615, 625, 660, 710
General Foods, 57–58, 530, 637, 645, 684; *see also* Kraft-General Foods
General Mills, 173, 194, 199, 252, 493, 534, 588, 637, 660, 763
General Motors, 17, 42, 46, 73–75, 80, 84, 88, 132, 137, 199, 211, 223, 230, 237, 301, 302, 352, 363, 376, 393, 418, 422, 425, 446, 458, 465, 470, 481, 498, 570, 576, 586, 602, 627, 660, 661, 679, 738
General Nutrition Center (GNC), 581
Gengler, Charles, 811
George Foreman Grill, 476
Georgia-Pacific Corp., 525, 563
Getz, David, 371
Gibney, Frank, Jr., 38
Gibson, Mel, 178
Gibson, Richard, 808
Gilbert, Jay, 166
Gilbert, Jennifer, 816
Gillette Co., 72, 249, 353, 563, 566, 657, 659, 660, 669, 670, 679, 687, 690, 697, 738–739
Gilliland, David, 476
Gilmore, James H., 795
Giltspur, 604
Girl Mania, 106
Girls, Inc., 106
Gladwell, Malcolm, 13
Glamour, 13, 394, 403, 410
GlaxoSmithKline, 352, 506
Glick, Shav, 810
Gobbles, 394
Godiva, 486, 674
Goetzl, David, 458, 805
Goldberg, Marvin E., 801, 817
Goldberg, Steven T., 818
Goldblum, Jeff, 286
Golden, Daniel, 815
Golden, Linda L., 800
Goldman, Abigail, 133
Goldman, Debra, 803
Goldman, Doron, 815
Goldman, Kevin, 186, 803, 813, 818
Goldmine, 611
Goldstein, Linda A., 814
Goldstine, Jonathan, 15
Goldwasser, Amy, 56
Golf, 580
Golf Channel, 365
Golf Digest, 403
Golin/Harris International, 98
Good Earth Teas, 741
Good Housekeeping, 394, 400, 403, 498, 532, 612, 719
Goodby, Jeff, 245, 259, 260
Goodby, Silverstein & Partners, 90, 245, 247, 254, 259, 759
Google, 496–498
Gopalakrishna, Srinath, 809
Gorn, Gerald, 124, 797, 801, 804
Gould, Stephen, 451, 807
Gourmet, 322
GQ, 13, 188, 400, 410
Graco, 573
Graham, Jefferson, 350, 795, 808
Graham, Judith, 796
Graves, Martha, 809
Grayson, Jennifer, 811
Great Foods of America, 735
Green, Corliss, 768, 818
Green, Frank, 799, 809
Green, Jeff, 13, 799
Green Giant, 54, 55, 279
Greenbaum, Thomas L., 803
Greenberg, Bradley S., 804
Greenberger, Robert S., 814
Greenspan, Alan, 498
Greenwald, Anthony G., 798
Greer, Margolis, Mitchell, Burns and Associates, 622
Gretzky, Wayne, 178
Grey Advertising, 498, 674
Grey Digital Marketing, 95, 96
Grey Direct Marketing, 94
Grey Global Group, 13, 199
Grey Worldwide, 77
Greyser, Stephen, 765, 797, 817
Grote, Dick, 615
Group Asia, 663
Grover, Ronald, 360
Grupo Modelo, 44
Grupo Televisa, 359
Guardian Life Insurance, 597–598
Gucci, 58
Guccione, Bob, Jr., 391
Guess, 407
Guideposts, 403
Guinto, Joseph, 369
Gulas, Charles S., 801
Gulf Oil, 586
Gundlach, Gregory, 549, 809, 816
Gunther, Marc, 805
Gupta, Pola, 451, 807
Guyon, Janet, 818

H

Ha, Louisa, 804
Häagen Dazs, 660, 684, 690
Haberstroh, Jack, 115, 116
Haefner, James, 816
Hafer, W. Keith, 804
Hagerty, James R., 811
Hague, Stephen, 796
Hair, Joseph F., 810
Hal Riney & Partners, 90, 259
Haley, Russell I., 804, 811
Hall, Bruce F., 161, 799
Hall, Carol, 806
Haller, Terry, 811
Halliday, Jean, 289, 470, 564, 796, 802, 803, 809, 814
Hallmark, 237, 258, 270, 321, 327, 363, 586
Hallward, John, 637
Hamilton, David P., 799
Hamilton, Thomas E., 809
Hammacher Schlemmer, 455, 475
Hammill, Dorothy, 737
Hancock, Greg, 407
Hanks, Tom, 178
Hannah, Darlene B., 799
Hansen, Flemming, 811
Hansen Beverage, 104
Hardy, Quentin, 808
Hargrove, Kerri, 811
Harley-Davidson, 41
Harmon, Robert R., 799
Harrell, Gilbert, 797
Harris, Thomas, 563, 566, 567, 809

Harris, William D., 799
Harris Interactive, 587
Harris Media Systems, 440
Harris-Donovan Media Systems, 439
Hartley, Steven W., 797, 802, 816
Harvard Business Review, 230, 455, 687
Haskins, Jack, 636, 811
Hassan, Salah, 673, 813
Hatfield, Stefano, 240
Haugh, Louis J., 808
Havrix, 185
Hawkins, Scott, 152, 798
Hay Group, 587
Hayden, Steve, 246
HBO, 451, 452, 488
Head, 168
Hearst Custom Publishing, 404
Hearst Magazines International, 687
Hearst Publications, 305
Heart-wear, 652, 653
Heckler, Susan, 377, 642, 800, 805, 811
Heckman, James, 816
Heeter, Carrie, 804
Heilbroner, Robert, 750, 816
Hein, Kenneth, 104, 194, 197, 266
Heineken, 664, 694
Heinz; *see* H.J. Heinz Co.
Heitsmith, Glenn, 811
Helm, David, 751, 816
Hemispheres, 453, 454, 455
Henderson, Caroline, 808
Henke, Lucy L., 805
Henry, Denise, 806
Herman Miller, 588
Hernandez, Greg, 800
Herpel, George L., 806
Hershey, 775
Hertz, 42, 54, 175, 256, 468, 469
Herzbrun, David, 802
Heslin, Richard, 800
Hewlett-Packard, 28, 247, 293, 477, 490, 558, 566, 579, 588, 673, 697
Hidden Mind, 108
High-Yield Marketing, 144
Hill, Grant, 165, 427, 806
Hill, Holliday, Connors, Cosmopulos, 77, 327
Hill, John S., 813
Hill & Knowlton, 98
Hilsenrath, Jon, 30
Hinustan Lever, 663
Hirschman, Elizabeth, 239–241, 800, 802
Hispanic Broadcasting, 359
History Channel, 70, 365
Hitachi, 37, 202
Hite, Robert E., 813, 814, 817
H.J. Heinz Co., 152, 280, 545, 564, 680
Hobart, 597
Hoch, Stephen, 152, 798
Hof, Robert D., 808
Hoffberg, Kevin, 601–602, 810
Holbrook, Morris B., 817
Hollingsworth, Lois, 811
Holloway, Deborah, 810
Hollywood Pictures, 97
Hollywood-Madison Avenue Group, 178
Holmes, Stacy, 812
Holstein, William J., 38
Holtz, Shel, 499, 575, 810
Home & Away, 403
Home & Garden Television, 365
Home Depot, 384, 586, 587
Home Shopping Network, 730
Honda Motor Co., 17, 41, 286, 407, 659
Honeycutt, Earl D., Jr., 812
Honeywell, 24
Hopper, Dennis, 170
Horizon.FCB, 80
Horovitz, Bruce, 796, 799, 800, 804, 811
Horton, Cleveland, 807
Hot Hot Hot, 491
House Beautiful, 322
Houston, Michael, 642, 800, 811
Hovland, C.I., 800
Howard, Bob, 807
Howard, Daniel J., 800
Howard, John A., 797
Howard, Theresa, 266, 404, 495, 799
Hoyer, Wayne D., 147, 798
Hoyts Cinema Corp., 449
H&R Block, 288, 532
Hsu, Francis, 812
Hueber, Graham, 584
Huff, Lenard C., 692, 814
Hughes, G. David, 801
Hughes, Kathleen A., 806
Hughes, Laura Q., 81, 797, 801
Hughes, Mike, 762
Hughes, Paul, 807
Hughes, Sarah, 178
Hulbert, James, 799
Hume, Scott, 795, 806, 816
Hung, 224
Hung, Kineta, 804
Hunt, H. Keith, 798
Hunt, James B., 801, 806
Hunt, Michelle, 818
Hunt, Shelby, 765–766, 817
Husni, Samir, 395
Hwang, Suein L., 277, 805
Hyundai, 384

I

I Can't Believe It's Not Butter!, 59
Iacocca, Lee, 171
IBM, 15, 37, 93, 137, 291, 363, 439, 553, 582, 586, 588, 592, 610, 639, 673, 680, 697, 769
IDC Collaborative Computing Services, 507
iDeutsch, 95, 96
IKEA, 402–403, 762, 768, 769
iMall, 501
Impact, 266
IMS, 329, 439
In Style, 403, 404
Industrial Engineering, 395
Industry Standard, 409
Infiniti, 275, 435
Information Resources Inc., 613, 636, 645
Ingersoll, Bruce, 815
Ingram, 602
Initiative Media, 85, 327
Inman, J. Jeffrey, 529, 808
Innova Marketing, 438
Institute of Outdoor Advertising, 437, 439
Institute of Practitioners, 653
In-Store Advertising, 438
InStyle, 266
Intel Corp., 15, 28, 117, 223, 256, 456, 552, 553–554, 587, 779
IntelliQuest, 502, 619
Interactive Advertising Bureau, 619
Interbrand Corp., 15
International Communications Group, 321
Internet Advertising Report, 504
Interpublic Group, 78, 80, 98, 199, 663
Interview, 266
Intuit, 496, 540
Invesco, 589
Ipsos-ASI, 503, 504, 634, 636, 642, 644, 646
Iron and Steelmaker, 395
ISkyB, 689
Isuzu, 245, 271
Iverson, Allan, 165, 166
Ivester, Douglas, 694
iVillage, 46, 48, 496, 498
Ivy, Jim, 293
Ivy League Magazine Network, 409
iXL, 97

J

J. Crew, 20
J. Walter Thompson, 77, 81, 199, 244, 404, 646
Jaben, Jan, 813
Jabra, 452
Jack Daniel's, 710
Jack in the Box, 574, 643
Jackson, Barry, 360
Jackson, Michael, 175
Jacobson, Aileen, 404
Jacobson Consulting Applications, 478
Jacoby, Jacob, 147, 798
Jager, Durk, 530, 534
Jaguar, 289, 450
James, Dana, 598, 664, 812
James, Deborah, 812
James, William L., 813
James G. Elliott Company, 407
Jameson, Jenna, 757
Jannuzzo, Paul T., 802
Japan Air Lines, 454, 456
Jared's Jewelers, 384
Jarvis, Steve, 30, 764
JCPenney Co., 17, 46, 51, 301, 354, 474
J.D. Edwards, 616
J.D. Powers & Associates, 576
Jeep, 110, 268, 452, 576, 673
Jellison, J., 799
Jenny Craig, 730
Jensen, Elizabeth, 805, 817
Jensen, Jeff, 802
Jet Set, 586
JetBlue Airways, 55, 56, 63
Jeter, Derek, 165
Jeweler, A. Jerome, 255, 803
Joachimsthaler, Erich, 811
Joben, Jan, 815
Jobs, Steven, 577
Jocz, Katherine E., 808, 809
Johanson, Johny K., 812
Johar, Gita Venkataramini, 816
John Brown Contract Publishing, 402
Johnson, Bradley, 796
Johnson, Greg, 46, 197, 589, 728
Johnson, Lady Bird, 434
Johnson & Johnson, 17, 22, 28, 148, 302, 352, 451, 579–580, 587, 592, 637
Johnston & Murphy, 468
Jones, Chris, 81
Jones, John Philip, 230–231, 636, 802, 811
Jones, Lafayette, 518
Jones, Marilyn Y., 800
Jones, Marion, 235, 236
Jordan, Michael, 165, 178, 235, 280, 675
Jordan, Miriam, 812
Joseph, W.B., 800
Jovi, Jon Bon, 427
Joyce, Mary L., 795
Joyce Julius & Associates, 650
Joyner-Kersey, Jackie, 178
J.P. Morgan Chase & Co., 15
Judd, Ashley, 286
Junior Mints, 452
Jupiter Media Metrix, 504, 597
Just For Feet, 84, 296, 712–714

K

Kahn, Gabriel, 432
Kahn, Mir Maqbool Alam, 813, 814
Kaiser Permanente, 477
Kal Kan, 470
Kalish, David, 806

Kamins, Michael A., 800
Kamp, Edward, 270, 803
Kanbar, Maurice, 265
Kannuk, Leslie Lazar, 797
Kanso, Ali, 813
Kanzenstein, Herbert, 807
Karr, Albert R., 817
Kashani, Kamran, 691, 692, 814
Kassarjian, Harold H., 798
Kates, Steven, 767, 818
Katsansis, Lea, 673, 813
Katz, Marian, 812
Kaydo, Chad, 807
KCBO, 385–386
Keane, David P., 810
Keebler, 54
Kellaris, James J., 125, 797
Keller, Kevin, 14, 15, 642, 795, 811
Keller, Punam Anand, 185, 801
Kellogg Company, 132, 199, 202, 258, 269, 281, 451, 517, 533, 534, 542
Kelly, J. Steven, 818
Kelman, Herbert, 168, 177, 799
Kempf, DeAnna S., 798
Kenneth Cole, 457
Kenny Roger's Roasted Chicken, 452
Kentucky Fried Chicken, 660, 675
Kerin, Roger A., 44, 795, 796, 797, 799, 816
Kerrigan, John, 46
Kerwin, Ann Marie, 805, 806
Kerwin, Kathleen, 796
Kessler, Felix, 809
Ketchum Public Relations, 573, 583, 584
Keyes, Alicia, 500
KFMB, 374
Khermouch, Gerry, 13, 15, 799, 803
Khoulos, Jay, 811
Kim, Joo-Ho, 620
Kim, June Bryan, 806, 811
Kimberly-Clark Corp., 491–492, 657
Kinetix, 566
King, B.B., 381
King, Charles, III, 815
Kinnear, Thomas C., 803
Kinney & Lange, 712
Kinsman, Matthew, 518, 525, 809
Kirin, 170
Kirsner, Scott, 350
Kisielius, Jolita, 800
Kitchen, Philip J., 797
KitchenAid, 461–462, 586
Kleiner, Art, 795
Kline, G., 817
Kmart, 37, 55, 62, 117, 360, 456, 485, 581
Kneal, Dennis, 804
Knight, Paul, 300
Knowles, Christopher, 812
Kodak, 41, 46, 49, 270, 321, 404, 678
Kohl's Department Stores, 384
Kolbe, Richard H., 818
Konica, 183
Koppel, Ted, 144
Kotler, Philip, 566, 801, 809
Kover, Arthur, 244, 802, 811
Kozup, John C., 816
Kraft Foods, 363, 425, 518, 519, 539, 542, 657, 721, 740, 770
Kraft-General Foods, 440, 468; *see also* General Foods
Kramer, Louise, 728, 803, 809
Kranhold, Kathryn, 81, 250, 277, 796, 803
Krauss, Robert M., 797
Kriegel, Robert A., 801
Krispy Kreme, 577, 580–581
Krol, Carol, 815
Kronos, 128
Kruegel, Dave, 811
Krugman, Herbert, 152, 798, 800, 805
K-Tel, Inc., 478
Kummel, Eugene H., 813
Kuo, Meichum, 816

L

La Chance, C.C., 800
La Tour, Michael, 818
LaBand, David, 448
LaBarbera, Priscilla, 636, 811, 814
LaBelle, Patti, 518
Laczniak, Russell N., 798, 816, 817
Ladies' Home Journal, 394, 396, 403
Lambert, Brian, 810
Lambert, David R., 795
Lambesis, 68, 266
Lammons, Bob, 796
Lancaster, 224
Lancaster, Kent, 231, 802
Lancôme, 124
Landeche, Dean, 597
Landon, E. Lair, 809
Landreth, Stacy, 800
Lands' End, 20, 21, 52, 53, 468, 475, 501, 570
Lane, David, 639
Lans, Maxine S., 809
Laris, Michael, 813
Larkin, Ernest E., 805
Larson, Christine, 805
Larson, Megan, 371
Lason, Stephen, 807
Lau, Debra, 170
Laughlin, Charles, 814
Lauterborn Robert F., 796, 802
Lauzen, Martha M., 809
Lavidge, Robert, 148, 202, 206, 795, 798
Lawrence, Jennifer, 807, 815
La-Z-Boy, 55, 59
Leach, Robin, 271
Leavitt, Clark, 798, 799
Led Zeppelin, 288
Lee, Ang, 67
Lee, Hang, 816
Lee, Je Eun, 816
Lee, Renee Gravois, 818
Lee, Richard, 144
Lee, Rub P.W., 805
Lee, Ruby, 357
Lee Jeans Company, 274
Legend Computers, 679
Lego, 132, 455
Leibman, Hanna, 806
Leibovitz, Annie, 391
Leigh, James H., 799, 801, 815, 818
Lenox, 477
Leo Burnett, 3–4, 6, 77, 78, 80, 81, 90, 249, 258, 260, 279, 643, 646
Lever Brothers, 523, 556
Levi Strauss & Co., 68, 90, 142, 237, 245, 277, 392, 498, 674, 678
Levin, Gary, 805, 811, 816
Levin, Myron, 482, 814
Levine, Joshua, 802
Levins, Hoag, 805
Levitt, Mark, 507
Levitt, Theodore, 608, 657, 669, 810, 813, 817
Lewinsky, Monica, 574
Lewis, Richard, 795
Lexus, 41, 272, 284, 437
Lieberman, David, 817
LifeStyles, 755
Lifetime Television, 365
Light, Larry, 15
Ligos, Melinda, 807, 810
Lilly's Kids, 468
Limbaugh, Rush, 383
Limited Too, 106
Lin, Carolyn A., 812
Lincoln, 41
Lindenmann, Walter, 579, 810
Lindzey, G., 799
Linnett, Richard, 92
Lipman, Joanne, 796, 806, 813, 817, 818
Lippert, Barbara, 811
Listerine, 51, 60, 733
Little Caesar's, 185, 186
Liz Claiborne, 45
L.L. Bean, 20, 475
Loewenberg, Sam, 812, 813
Loews Cineplex Entertainment, 449
Longo, Laura, 800
Lord, Kenneth, 451
L'Oreal, 17
Los Angeles Magazine, 243, 396
Los Angeles Times, 416, 495, 496
Lotus, 578
Low, George, 228, 232, 802
Low Healthcare Worldwide, 77
Lowe, Rob, 749
Lowe & Partners Worldwide, 77
Lowe Lintas & Partners, 84, 238, 663
Lowery, Pamela, 816
Lowe's Home Improvement Warehouse, 156, 574, 627
Lowry, Tom, 369, 805
Lubitz, A., 800
Lublin, Joann S., 807
Lucent Technologies, 585, 586
Luchsinger, Paul B., 802
Luczak, Laurie, 598
Ludacris, 625
Luebkeman, Steven G., 818
Lunman, Kim, 170
Lutz, Richard J., 798
Lycos, 440
Lyman, Eric J., 814
Lysonski, Steven, 812

M

McAlister, Leigh, 516, 529, 808, 809
McArthur, David N., 797
MacArthur, Kate, 4, 327, 539, 582, 796, 797, 802, 804
McCann-Erikson, 77, 80, 91, 112, 199, 230, 238, 273, 289, 663, 679
McCarthy, Michael, 4, 68, 174, 240, 253, 750, 796, 810, 815, 817
McClellan, Steve, 805
McCollum Spielman Worldwide; *see* MSW Group
McCormick & Co., 741
McCracken, Grant, 175–176, 800
McDonald, Marci, 45, 46
McDonald's, 6, 15, 17, 41, 62, 90, 96, 141, 193, 237, 258, 270, 287, 360, 363, 433, 448, 511, 512, 536, 539, 570, 582, 586, 659, 660, 671, 687, 696–697
McFarland, Ronald, 759
McGinn, Daniel, 807
McGkegney, Margret, 814
McGraw-Hill Corp., 608
McGuire, William, 148, 798, 799
Machlis, Sharon, 639
Macinnis, Deborah J., 270, 803
MacKenzie, Scott, 188, 798, 801
McLuhan, Marshall, 188, 801
McMahan, Harry, 153, 798
McMaster, Mark, 598
McMillan, Sally J., 808
McMorris, Frances A., 803
McNeill, Dennis L., 815
McNiven, M.A., 802
McPherson, Jennifer Gonzalez, 46
McQueen, Josh, 803
Macromedia, 604
Macy's, 498
Madden, John, 178
Madden, Normandy, 664, 680, 812

Madden, Thomas J., 801
Maddox, Lynda M., 814
Madison, Cathy, 803
Madonna, 175, 288–289, 691
Magellan's, 455
Maharaj, Davan, 728
Maidenform, 767
Maignan, Isabelle, 811
Major League Baseball, 201, 358, 360, 370, 457, 586, 649
Make-a-Wish Foundation, 586
Mandell, W., 800
Mandese, Joe, 814
Mangalindan, Mylene, 495
Mangleburg, Tamara, 760, 817
Mann, Aimee, 673
Manning, Jeff, 140
Manning, Kenneth C., 815
Manning Selvage & Lee, 78
March of Dimes, 58
Marchetti, Michele, 806
Marcus, Anne-Marie, 450
Maritz AmeriPoll, 434
Marker, 586
Marketing, 432
Marketing Evaluations/TVQ, Inc., 178, 179
Marketing Evolution, 619
Marketing News, 414
Marketmath, Inc., 439
MarketSource, 645, 649
Markus, Hazel, 797
Marlboro, 15, 90, 142, 208, 465, 537, 658, 672–673
Marley, Bob, 287
Marriott, 271, 542
Mars Inc., 657, 770
Marston, John, 569, 810
Martell, 456
Martha Stewart Living, 403, 532
Martin, Claude R., Jr., 799, 801, 815, 818
Martin, Dennis, 801
Martin, Ingrid, 796
Martin Agency, 762
Mary Beth's Beanies & More, 404
Mary Kay Cosmetics, 24, 62, 478
Maslow, A.H., 109–110, 766, 797
Mason, Margie, 582
Master Lock, 115
MasterCard, 45, 273, 463, 690
Mateschitz, Dietrich, 103–104
Matsushita, 37
Mattel, 8, 586–587, 768
Mattress Gallery, 201
Matzer, Marla, 803
Max Factor, 24
Maxfli, 160
Maxim, 326, 391, 397, 403, 409, 752
Maxwell Business Systems, 51
Maxwell House, 252
Maya, Janis, 795
Mayer, Martin, 275, 803
Maynard, Brian, 461
Maynard, Michael L., 812
Maytag, 85, 156, 258, 281, 490
Mazis, Michael B., 815
M&C Saatchi, 679
Media Market Guide (MMG), 439
Media One, Inc., 438
Media Plan, Inc., 329
Mediamark Research Inc. (MRI). 305, 306–309, 310, 328, 329, 334, 408, 422, 437, 448, 504
MediaMetrics, 504
Mediaweek, 779
Mehta, Stephanie N., 804
Meirick, Patrick, 801
Melillo, Wendy, 760, 814, 817
Mendelsohn, Harold, 579, 810
Mendelsohn Media Research, Inc., 334
Menelly, Nancy, 804
Menn, Joseph, 808
Men's Health, 397, 403
Mentus Communications, 78
Mercedes-Benz, 15, 41, 46, 49, 51, 118, 418, 461, 473, 581
Mercer, Dick, 815
Merck & Co., 17
Mercy Medical Center, 591
Mergenhagen, Paula, 803
Merin, Jennifer, 807
Merrell, 40
Merrill Lynch, 314, 669
Merskin, Debra, 818
Metcalf, Barbara L., 817
MetLife, 96
Metromail, 474, 531
Meurs, Lex van, 804
Meyer, Edward, 813
Meyer, Harvey, 810
MGM/United Artists, 12, 449
MH-18, 397
Miami Herald, 425
Michelin, 41, 58, 151, 249
Michell, Paul, 796
Mick, David Glen, 798
Micron Technology, 37
Microsoft, 15, 68, 97, 117, 197, 199, 240, 243, 287, 288, 299, 366, 508, 574, 582, 585, 587, 615, 619, 653
Microsoft Network, 11
Microvision, 527
Midwest Express Airlines, 56, 207
Miller, Chris, 410
Miller, Cyndee, 802, 819
Miller, James, III, 726
Miller, Liz, 589
Miller Brewing Co., 223, 250, 252, 253, 360, 433, 437, 659, 769, 775
Mills, J., 799
Millward Brown, 502, 619, 644, 646
Mindak, William, 566, 809
Mindtec, 115
Minnelli, Liza, 371
Minniard, Paul W., 797, 815
Miss Cleo, 482
Mita, 183
Mitchell, Andrew A., 799, 800
Mitsubishi, 95, 287, 289
Mittal, Banwari, 805, 816, 817
Mobile, 586
Modem Media (Interpublic Group), 96
Modern Maturity, 46, 394, 396, 403
Modern Media, 95
Modern Photography, 395
Modernista!, 84
Moftakhar, Shay, 807
Mohr, Iris, 813
Mohr, Jakki, 228, 232, 802
Mohr, Jay, 368
Molson, 589
Money, 403
Monster.com, 223, 461, 586
Montana, Joe, 178
Montana Farmer, 394
Montblanc, 10–11
Moore, David J., 799
Moore, Demi, 170
Moore, H. Frazier, 795
Moore, Jeri, 796
Moore, Timothy, 115, 116
Moore, Tina, 810
More.com, 377–378
Moretti, Peggy, 810
Morgan, Fred W., 814
Morgan Stanley Technology Research, 488
Moriarty, Sandra, 10, 11, 247, 282, 795, 801, 803, 804
Morin, Richard, 800
Morrill, John, 608, 810
Morris, Errol, 495
Morrisson, Fiona, 63
Morton Salt, 252
Moses, Elissa, 675
Moss, Linda, 807
Motor Trend, 113, 576
Motor Week, 576
Motorola, 37, 456, 481, 588, 625, 659
Motown Records, 518
Mott's Inc., 518
Mountain Dew, 452
Movie Channel, 451
Movieline, 266
Mowen, John C., 799
Moxie, 46
Mr. Clean, 153
Mr. T, 271
MRM Partners Worldwide, 94
Ms., 396, 767
MSN TV, 508
MSNBC, 365, 366
MSW Group, 627, 635, 636
MTV, 84, 356, 365, 366, 367, 368, 371, 381, 623, 675, 688–689, 709
Mueller, Barbara, 812
Mullen, Vernan S., 802
Munk, Nina, 798
Murdoch, Rupert, 689
Murphy, John H., II, 818
Murris, Timothy, 721, 734, 816
Muscle & Fitness Hers, 395–396
Muzak, 456
My Generation, 394, 403
Myers, Jack, 321, 804
Myers, Janet, 810
Myers, John G., 52, 54, 796, 799, 801, 802, 803, 811
Myers, William E., 809
Myers Reports, 321

N

Nabisco, 399, 537, 588
Nader, Ralph, 456, 590, 750, 763, 764
Nakra, Prema, 797
Naples, Michael J., 804
Narisetti, Raju, 294, 808
NASCAR, 354, 462, 477, 513, 627
National Amusements, 449
National Basketball Association (NBA), 359, 360, 368, 370
National Enquirer, 322, 394, 403
National Football League (NFL), 201, 355, 358, 370, 713
National Geographic, 394, 403, 687
National Geographic Channel, 365
National Geographic Society, 468
National Hog Farmer, 394
National Institute on Media & Family, 764
National Law Review, 395
National SemiConductor, 501
National Yellow Pages Monitor (NYPM), 448
Navistar, 592
NBC, 23, 30, 300, 358, 359, 360, 364, 366, 508, 710, 756
NCH Marketing Services, 531
NCH Nù World Marketing Ltd., 683
NCH Promotional Services, 529
Nebraska Farmer, 394
Nebraska Furniture Mart, 38
NEC, 37
Neff, Jack, 564, 795, 796, 797, 805, 808, 809, 814
Neiman Marcus, 51, 62, 475, 581
Nelson Communications Worldwide, 77, 328
Neoforma, 499
Nestlé, 72, 80, 310, 425, 440, 542, 645, 657, 659, 660, 661, 670–671, 679, 694, 725

Netherlands Institute of Public Opinion (NIPO), 643
Neuborne, Ellen, 800, 808
New Balance, 40, 552, 665, 728
New Product News, 516
New York Interconnect, 367
New York Palace, 129
New York Stock Exchange, 327, 495
New York Times, 137, 171, 322, 414, 415, 495, 500, 507, 572, 779
New York Times Sunday Magazine, 416
Newbery, Charles, 812
Newborne, Ellen, 81
News Corp., 689
News Network, 408–409
Newspaper National Network (NNN), 423
Newsweek, 301, 323, 324, 326, 393, 396–398, 403, 408, 411, 412, 426, 427, 687
Nextel Cellular Service, 384
Nickelodeon, 365
Niefeld, Jaye S., 810
Nielsen, Scott A., 808
Nielsen Interactive Group, 299
Nielsen Media Research, 305, 329, 330, 331, 334, 349, 352, 356, 359, 361, 373–376, 504, 636, 650; *see also* A.C. Nielsen Co.
Nihon Television (NTV), 63
Nike, 15, 21, 40, 41, 58, 85, 96, 117, 141, 165, 168, 173, 235–236, 237, 240, 243, 247, 252, 256, 277, 280, 288, 289, 404, 458, 568, 625, 659, 660, 674, 675, 690, 722–723
NikeGoddess, 236, 404
9-Lives, 281
Nintendo, 197
Nissan, 88, 237, 238, 239, 299, 407, 659, 660
Nivea, 452
Nixon, Richard, 733
No Boundaries, 404
No Fear, 75, 257
Nokia, 15, 659, 679, 688
Noonan, David, 104
Nordica, 267, 394
Nordstrom, 404, 465, 474
Norelco, 241
Norins, Hanley, 802
Norman, Andrew, 377, 805
Norris, E.E., 803
Nortel Networks, 287, 616
North American Hunter, 407
North American Philips Lighting Corp., 292, 294, 296
North Communications, 456
North Power, 589
Norwegian Cruise Lines, 245, 270–272
Novartis Consumer Health Corp., 733
NPDFashion-World, 106
NRTA/AARP Bulletin, 394, 403
Nudd, Tim, 589
Nuprin, 114
NuSkin, 586
NutraSweet, 478, 552, 572, 694
Nutri-Grain, 55, 269
NW Air World Traveler, 455
NW Ayer, 238

O

O, The Oprah Magazine, 403, 532
Oakley, 173
Ocean Spray, 732
O'Connell, Vanessa, 223, 271, 355, 760, 774, 802
O'Dell, Patricia, 807
O'Donnell, Rosie, 178
O'Donohoe, Stephanie, 816
Odwalla, 580
Office Depot, 457, 586
Ogilvy, David, 250, 256, 257, 259–260, 272, 275, 276, 622, 802, 803
Ogilvy & Mather, 77, 93, 250, 253, 663, 680, 773
Ogilvy Interactive, 95, 96
Ogilvy Outreach, 663
Ogilvy Worldwide, 246
OgilvyOne Worldwide Interactive, 94
Ohanian, Roobina, 169, 799
O'Hara, Jim, 816
O'Keefe, Daniel J., 799
Olavsrud, Thor, 582
Old Milwaukee, 756
Old Spice, 643
Olde Brooklyn Beverage Co., 46
Oldsmobile, 55, 643
O'Leary, Noreen, 811
Olson, David, 319, 804
Olson, Jerry, 117, 119, 796, 797, 798, 799
Olympus, 576
Omnicom Group, 78, 98
One and All Shop, 84
1-800-COLLECT long distance, 271
OpenTV, 508
Orajel, 108
Orbitz, 496
O'Reilly, Bill, 625
Orsini, Patricia, 804
Orton, Charles Wesley, 462
Orwell, George, 291
Osborne, Magz, 813
Osbourne family, 371
Oscar Mayer, 153, 270, 287, 485, 511
Oshita, Koji, 813
Ostlund, Lyman E., 798, 811
Ostrom, T.W., 798
Ostrow, Joseph, 318, 319, 326, 804
O'Toole, John, 255, 803
Outback Steak House, 586
Outerspace, 97
Outpost.com, 276
Ovaltine, 511
Owen, Clive, 67
Oxygen, 365

P

Pacific Sunwear, 106
Packard, Vance, 749
Palda, Kristian S., 802
Palm, 563
Palmeiro, Rafiel, 737
Palmer, Arnold, 175, 590
Pampers, 110, 658
Panasonic, 119
Pannill, Shelly, 812
Papa John's, 726, 727–728
Paper, 266
Parade, 305, 414
Paramount Pictures, 456
Paramount Television Groups, 363
Parenting Magazine, 403, 612
Parents, 403, 719
Parker Pen, 671, 678
Parloff, Roger, 814
Parmalat USA, 574
Parmar, Arundhati, 676, 813
Parpis, Eleftheria, 84, 277, 804
Partnership for a Drug Free America, 582, 772, 773
PartyLite Gifts, 479
Pascual, Aixa M., 360
Passikoff, Robert, 193
Pastore, Michael, 808
Patti, 224
Patti, Charles H., 802
Patton, Phil, 133
Paul, Pamela, 806
Paul Mitchell, 107
Pavlov, Ivan P., 123, 797
Pawlosky, Mark, 815
PayDay, 185
PC Flowers, 301
Pearsall, Jed, 589
Pechmann, Cornelia, 800
Peckham, James O., 226, 802
Pedrick, James H., 804
Peebles, Dean M., 812
Peers, Martin, 805
Pells, Richard, 665
Pendleton, Jennifer, 802
Pennzoil-Quaker State Co., 259, 260
Penteado, Claudia, 689, 812
Penthouse, 585–586
People, 393, 406, 411, 736
People Weekly, 394, 403
PeopleSoft, 602
Pepitone, Berkshire, Piaget Worldwide, 615
Pepitone, James S., 615
Pepper, Don, 602, 795, 810
PepsiCo, 17, 42, 51, 90, 120, 175, 184, 185, 186, 223, 237, 256, 271, 287, 302, 352, 448, 453, 458, 485, 495, 498, 499, 511–512, 523–524, 539, 625, 646, 657, 659, 660, 674, 675, 687, 763, 775
Pepsodent, 664–665
Pepto-Bismol, 114
Percy, Larry, 799
Perdue Farms, Inc., 524
Perez, Evan, 525
Performance Research, 589, 651
Perot, Ross, 137
Perrier, 694
Perrin, Jane, 658
Pessemier, Edgar A., 797
Petco, 470
Peter, J. Paul, 117, 119, 796, 797
Petersen, Andrea, 816
Peterson, Will, 178
Peterson Milla Hooks, 84
Pets.com, 276
PetsMart, 470
Petty, Richard, 158, 799
Peugot, 477
Pfizer, 17, 199, 302, 352, 581, 585, 737, 738
Pham, Alex, 197, 650
Pham, Michel Tuan, 811
Philadelphia, 396
Philadelphia Phillies, 457
Philip Morris Cos., 17, 252, 302, 352, 403, 536–537, 539, 586, 657, 659, 736
Philips Electronics, 37, 156, 178–179, 432, 660
Phillips, Lynn, 799
Phillips, W.E., 813
Phillips Beverage Co., 756–757
Phillips Petroleum, 585
Phoenix Satellite Television Co., 689
Piagio U.S.A., 13
Pilgrim's Pride, 575
Pillsbury, 54, 153, 512, 525, 542, 563, 566
Pine, B. Joseph, II, 795
Pinkleton, Bruce E., 801
Pitofsky, Robert, 734, 744
Pitt, Brad, 170
Pitts, Robert, 799
Pizza Hut, 175, 436, 625, 675, 726, 727–728, 763
Playboy, 396, 403
Plummer, Joseph T., 813
PNB, 589
Poindexter, J., 799
Point of Purchase Advertising Institute (POPAI), 437, 439, 550
PointCast, 495
Polaroid, 247, 254–255
Pollack, Judann, 815
Pollay, Richard, 765, 817
Pollock, Ted, 608–609
Poltrack, David, 300
Pomice, Eva, 804

Pontiac, 498, 576
Pony, 166
Popular Science, 407
Porsche, 41, 274–275, 351, 473, 495, 598
Porter, Eduardo, 360
Porter Novelli, 63
Post Cereal, 199
Pottery Barn, 452, 474
Potts, Leanne, 817
Powder, 394
Power Rangers, 434
Powerade, 51, 54
PowerBar, 173, 176
PR Data Systems, 453
Prabhaker, Parul R., 805
Prego, 739
Premiere Radio Network, 383
Prentice, R.M., 808
President, 686
Preston, Ivan, 725, 815
Prevention, 403
Priceline.com, 276
Prime Image Co., 382
Princess Cruises, 63
Princeton Video Image, 457
Printers Ink, 740
Procter & Gamble, 17, 46, 72, 73, 74, 75, 88, 103, 132, 198, 211, 230, 237, 241, 257, 278–279, 291, 301, 302, 310, 352, 363, 376, 393, 425, 431, 485, 511, 513, 529, 530, 534, 535, 549–550, 568, 585, 588, 592, 637, 645, 650, 657, 660, 661, 663, 666, 679, 688, 716, 770, 775
Profile Bread, 732
Progressive Farmer, 394
Progressive Grocer, 395
Progresso, 119
Promedia, 456
Promo, 588
Promotion Decisions, Inc., 516, 649
Provident Bank, 574
Providian Financial, 586
Proximity Worldwide, 94
Pruzman, Todd, 818
PS Productions, 651
PSA Peugeot Citroen, 661
PSINet, 589
Psychic Readers Network, Inc., 482
Public Citizen's Health Research Group, 737
Public Relations News, 564
Publicis Groupe, 78, 156, 694–695
Publicis U.S.A., 77
Publishers Clearing House, 411, 475, 741
Puck, Wolfgang, 437
Pulley, Brett, 689
Purex, 621
Purina, 470
Pursell, Chris, 805
Puto, Christopher, 270, 803

Q

Qassim, Ali, 813
Quaker Oats, 41, 268, 271
Quaker State, 259, 260
Qualcomm, 589
Quarles, Rebecca C., 796
Quelch, John, 691, 692, 808, 814
Quick, Rebecca, 817
Quicksilver Inc., 106
QVC, 376, 477, 501
Qwest, 586

R

RADAR (Radio's All-Dimension Audience Research), 386
Radio Advertising Bureau, 378, 379
Radio Shack, 470
Rado, 59
Rae, Stephen, 170, 800
Raghubir, Priya, 557, 809
Ragu, 739
Raho, Louis E., 814
Ralph Lauren, 257
Ralston Purina, 738
Ramos, Roberto, 45
Ransdell, Joseph, 798
Rapaille, G. Clotaire, 132
Raphaelson, Joel, 272, 803
Rapp, Stan, 462, 807
Rapp Collins Worldwide, 94
Ray, Michael, 150–151, 152, 273, 795, 798, 801
Ray-Ban, 451
Razorfish, 137
RC Cola, 543
RCA, 283
R.D. Percy & Co., 317
Reader's Digest, 45, 167, 322, 393, 394, 396, 401, 402, 403, 475, 672, 687, 719
Real Networks, 300
Reckitt, 645
Recupero, Linda, 563
Red Bull, 103–104
Redbook, 315, 403, 532
Redken Laboratories, 76
Redstone, Sumner, 688–689
Reebok, 13, 40, 165, 166, 175, 363, 574, 589
Reed, J.D., 806
Reese's Pieces, 450, 452
Reeves, Dan, 737
Reeves, Rosser, 256–257, 260, 276, 803
Regal Cinema, 449
Reibstein, David J., 615, 796, 819
Reid, Leonard N., 800
Reidenback, Erick, 799
Reinhard, Keith, 750, 813
Renault, 660
Reputation Institute, 587
Research Systems Corp., 186
Resnik, Allan S., 818
Restaurant Business, 395
Restoration Hardware, 463
Retail Alliance, 574
Retsky, Maxine Lans, 815, 816
Revlon, 24, 75, 177, 257, 431
Reyes, Sonia, 613
Reynolds, Thomas J., 811
R/GA, 95, 96
RHI Entertainment Inc., 363
Rice, Faye, 795
Rice, Jerry, 178
Richard Manville Research, 446
Richards, Jeff I., 818
Richardson, Jack, 804
Ricoh Corp., 105, 293
Ries, Al, 52, 54, 258–259, 553, 563, 565, 796, 803
Ries, Laura, 563, 565
Rigg, Cynthia, 809
Riney, Hal, 259
Ripken, Cal, Jr., 178, 417
Ripley, M. Louise, 76, 796
Ritchie, Guy, 68
R.J. Reynolds, 89, 281, 659
RJR Nabisco, 399, 537, 588
Road & Track, 112–113, 314, 315
Robb Report, 455
Robert Wood Johnson Foundation, 622
Robertson, Thomas S., 798, 817
Robinson, William A., 809
Rockport, 76, 567
Rodale Inc., 397
Rodman, Dennis, 165, 175
Rodman, Yank, 800
Rogaine, 107
Rogers, Everett M., 798
Rogers, Martha, 115, 602, 795
Rolex, 141
Rolling Stone, 55, 57, 266, 315, 391–392, 407, 410, 736
Rolling Stones, 288, 691
Rolls-Royce, 764
Romer, Daniel, 803
Roper ASW, 675, 766
Roper Starch Worldwide, 408, 641
Rose, Frank, 814
Rose, Josh, 97
Rose, Matthew, 806, 813
Rose, Pete, 165, 166
Rose, Randall L., 815
Rosie, 403
Roslow Research Group, 140
Ross, Chuck, 801, 804, 805, 813, 815
Rossi, Dom, 805
Rossignol, 394
Rossiter, John R., 817
Rotfeld, Herbert, 185, 801, 815
Rothschild, Michael L., 126, 797, 804
Rotzell, Kim B., 811, 815
Rowlands, Penelope, 813
Royal Crown Cola, 51
Rubel, Chad, 807
Rudelius, William, 44, 795, 796, 797, 816
Ruelle, Russell, 811
Ruido Group, 45
Ruskin, Gary, 452, 750, 763–764
Russell, Cristel, 377, 805
Russo, J. Edward, 817
Rutigliano, Anthony, 813
Ryan, Meg, 170
Ryan, Nolan, 175, 178
Ryan, Tom K., 92
Ryan Partnership, 521
Ryans, John K., 812

S

Saatchi & Saatchi, 77, 78, 112, 240, 713–714
Sachs, William S., 807
Saegart, Joel, 115
Safeguard, 59
Saks Fifth Avenue, 62, 475
Sale, Richard, 764, 808, 809, 815
Saleforce.com, 615
Sales & Marketing Management, 230, 310, 311, 334, 598, 603, 605, 607
Salmon, Caryn C., 797
Salmon, Charles, 796
Salomon, 394
Salveson, Melvin, 218, 802
Sampras, Pete, 235
Samsonite, 132
Samsung, 37–38, 62, 432
Samuel Adams Boston Lager, 757
San Augustine, 224
San Diego Gas & Electric, 571
San Diego Padres, 457
San Diego Union-Tribune, 416, 419
San Diego Zoological Society, 211, 212
San Francisco Examiner, 416
San Francisco Giants, 457
San Jose Mercury News, 770
Sandage, Charles H., 811
Sandaralingham, Avu, 804
Sandler, Dennis, 795
Santelmann, Neal, 797
Sanyo, 37, 436
SAP, 602
Satellite Television Asian Region (STAR TV), 689
Saturn Corp., 90
Saunders, Christopher, 38, 482, 815
Saurwein, Kristina, 179
Savin Corp., 183, 292, 293–294
Savvis Communications, 589

Sawyer, Alan, 557, 800, 809
SBC Communications, 384
Scarborough Reports, 328, 439
Schenker, Jonathan, 573
Schibsted, Evantheia, 462
Schiffer, Claudia, 265
Schiffman, Betsy, 764
Schiffman, Leon G., 797
Schmuckler, Eric, 327, 803, 809
Schnatter, John, 727
Schnucks, 649
Schnuer, Jenna, 806
Schram, Wilbur, 798
Schreiber and Associates, 446
Schroer, James, 231, 802
Schultz, Don, 9, 210, 795, 796, 797, 801, 802, 812
Schultz, J., 814
Schumann, David W., 799, 811
Schwab, Charles, 171
Schwartz, John, 495
Schwarzenegger, Arnold, 170
SCI FI Channel, 365
Scient, 137
Scientific American, 315
Scientific International, 490
Sciglimpaglia, Don, 450, 806
Scope, 51
Scorsese, Martin, 179
Scott, Linda, 286, 804
Screen Actors Guild, 78
Screen Vision, 450
Seagram, 645, 647, 709
Sean John, 493
Searle, 572
Sears, Roebuck & Co., 17, 45, 51, 55, 89, 106, 117, 360, 363, 446, 448, 494, 517, 602, 645, 753
Sears, Warren, 463
Seattle Mariners, 457
Sebastian, Pamela, 819
Secunda, Eugene, 795
Seeter, Bob, 810
Sega, 197, 247, 448
Seger, Bob, 288
Seglin, Jeffrey L., 811
Seguin, Sharon, 811
Segunda Juventud, 46, 48
Segway, 563, 567, 568
Seibel Systems, 602
Seiko, 128, 437, 586
Seiler, Christine A., 115
Seinfeld, Jerry, 176
Self, 314, 315, 396, 404
Sellers, Patricia, 796, 814
Sensormatic, 586
Sentara Health Systems Inc., 466
Sequeria, Ian K., 809
Serafin, Raymond, 810, 814
Sethi, Prakash, 810
Settle, Robert E., 800, 802, 811
Seventeen, 106, 315, 397, 403
Shakira, 574
Shanahan, Laura, 452
Shansby, J. Gary, 52, 796
Shape, 314, 315, 403, 407
Shapiro, Benson P., 809
Sharma, Subhash, 812
Sharp Electronics, 493
Sharper Image, 455, 475, 486
Shatner, William, 276
Shavitt, Sharon, 816
Shaw, David, 818
Shaw-Garlock, Glenda, 767, 818
Sheehan, Kim Bartel, 808
Sheen, Martin, 597
Shell, 130
Sherman, Howard, 801
Sherry, John F., Jr., 812
Sheth, Jagdish N., 797, 798, 807
Shields, Todd, 327
Shimp, Terence A., 800, 809, 812
Shin, Jeongshin, 812
Shirer, Michael, 807, 808
Shiver, Jube, Jr., 382
Shoenberger, Chana R., 807
Showtime, 451
Siebel Systems, 615, 616
Siegel, Michael, 815
Siemens, 660
Sierra Club, 480
Siklos, Richard, 806
Silk, Alvin J., 798, 799
Silk Soymilk, 181
Siltanen/Keehn, 91
Silverglade, Bruce, 815
Silverstein, Rich, 259, 260, 759
Simmons Market Research Bureau, 305, 306–309, 310, 314, 315, 328, 329, 334, 408, 422, 437, 448, 471, 472, 504, 650
Simon, Julian, 214, 802, 810
Simon, Mark, 818
Simon, Raymond, 579, 809, 810
Simon Marketing, 539
Simpson, Edwin K., 810
Simpson, O.J., 175
Sims Snowboards, 285, 286
Sirius Satellite Radio, 382
Skechers, 407, 642
Ski Magazine, 315
Skiing, 322
Skin Diver, 393
Sky Magazine, 455
Sky Television, 689
SkyTel, 201
SKY-TV, 454, 456
Skyy vodka, 68, 265–266, 277
Slack, Steve, 806
Slate, Jeremy, 812
Slatky, Tom, 97
Sloan, Pat, 805
Smirnoff, 710
Smith, Anna Nicole, 371
Smith, Greg, 495
Smith, Jane, 795
Smith, Kerry J., 809
Smith, Robert, 153, 798
Smith, Scott, 816
Smithsonian, 315, 403
Smitty's, 649
Snapple, 95, 104, 492, 725
Sneiden, Hank, 243, 802
Snoop Dog, 197, 381
Snowboarding, 394
Snyder, Adam, 449, 806
Snyder, Wally, 223, 779
Soap Opera Digest, 315, 612
Soley, Lawrence, 770, 800, 818
Solomon, Michael, 142, 796, 798, 800, 818
Song, Sora, 806
SONICblue, Inc., 349–350
Sony, 17, 37, 49, 51, 197, 507, 602, 679
Sony Ericsson, 431
Sony Pictures Entertainment, 300
Sorenson, Ralph Z., 813
SOUP (Students Opposed to Unfair Practices), 732
South African Breweries, 659
Southern California Edison, 589
Southern Living, 315, 396, 403
Southwest Airlines, 56, 63, 72, 118, 587
space, 402–403
SPAR Marketing Force, 438
Spears, Britney, 175, 197, 271, 495, 625, 675
Speck, Paul Surgi, 801
Speer, Lawrence, 697, 813
Spencer, Dale R., 817
Spethmann, Betsy, 452, 539, 797, 808, 809, 816
Spic and Span, 59
Spin, 266, 391, 736, 752
Spinner, 97
Sport, 314
Sporting Goods Dealer, 407
Sporting News, 315
Sports Afield, 188, 314, 315
Sports Channel America, 366
Sports Illustrated, 315, 326, 396, 397, 403, 736, 752
Sports Illustrated for Women, 404
Spotts, Harlan E., 795
Sprewell, Lattrell, 165–166
Springer, Jerry, 770
Sprit Corp., 17, 38
Srinivasan, Kalpana, 116, 815
St. Paul Cos., 588
Stabler, Ken, 165, 166
Staelin, Richard, 800
Stafford, James, 798
Stagg Chili, 279–280
Stamler, Bernard, 462
Stanaland, Andrea J.S., 800
Stance, 397
Standard Rate & Data Service, 334, 384, 393, 394, 395, 398, 405, 406, 408, 421, 422, 438, 471
Stanford Research Institute, 49
Stanley, T.L., 452
Stapel, Jan, 811
Star, 315, 394
Starbucks, 38, 249, 450, 563, 659, 660
Starch INRA Hooper, 334, 520
Starcom Media Vest Group, 78, 80
StarKist, 271, 280
State Farm Insurance, 195, 384
Statistical Research Inc. (SRI), 300, 376, 448
Stearns, James, 818
Steel, Jon, 247, 803
Stein, Nicholas, 415
Steiner, Gary, 148, 202, 206, 798
Steiner, Robert, 213, 777, 802, 819
Steinhagen, Tom, 809
Steortz, Eva, 453
Stephens, Debra, 817
Stereo Review, 395
Sterling Group, 354
Stern, 224
Stern, Barbara B., 803, 818
Stern, Bruce L., 818
Sternthal, Brian, 799, 800, 801
Stevens, Carl G., 810
Stevenson, Thomas H., 818
Stewart, David W., 62, 796, 800, 801
Stewart, Martha, 581
Stimler, Mike, 450
Sting, 288, 289
Stix, Louise, 294, 295
Stolberg, Sheryl, 815
Stolichnaya Vodka, 265, 266
Stoltman, Jeffrey J., 814
Stoughton, Susie, 810
STP Corp., 732
Strang, Roger A., 809
Strata Marketing, Inc., 329
Strategic Planning Institute, 61
Stratmar Systems, 438
Streep, Meryl, 427, 806
Street, Picabo, 141
Stroh Brewing Co., 756
Strong, E.K., 798
Strout, Erin, 223, 616, 810
Stuff, 391, 397, 409
Suave, 257
Subaru, 207
Successful Farming, 394
Sugarman, Margo, 813
Sultan, Ralph G.M., 819
Sumner, David F., 818

Sun Microsystems, 582, 615
Sunflower Group, 528
Sunkist, 222
Sunset, 315, 396
Sunsplash Amusement Park, 435
Suntory Ltd., 660
Super Valu, 649
Supermarket Communications Systems, 438
Surmanek, Jim, 321, 804, 805
Survey of Buying Power, 230
Susan G. Komen Breast Cancer Foundation, 586
Suzuki, 538
SW Airlines Spirit, 455
Swan, John E., 796
Swasy, Alecia, 803
Symantec, 407
Szybillo, George J., 800
Szynal, Deborah, 816

T

Taco Bell, 450
Tagg, Stephen, 800
Tahmincioglu, Eve, 806
Takahashi, Dean, 807
Tannenbaum, Stanley I., 796
Tanner, John F., Jr., 801
Tanzer, Andrew, 689, 814
TAPSCAN, 439
Target, 84, 448
Tat, Peter, 809
Tatum, Jack, 165, 166
Tauber, Edward M., 796
Taylor, Cathy, 802
Taylor, Charles R., 812, 818
Taylor, Thayer C., 810
Taylor-Made Golf Co., 674
TBWA, 78, 243
TBWA Worldwide, 77, 78
TBWA/Chiat/Day, 90, 91, 142, 241, 245, 259, 495; *see also* Chiat/Day
Ted Bates Agency, 256, 260
Teen, 397
Teen People, 106, 397, 403, 404, 652, 653
Teenage Research Unlimited, 397
Tegel, Simon, 812
Teinowitz, Ira, 415, 774, 806, 807, 809, 814, 815, 816, 817
Telefutura, 359–360
Tele-Lawyer, 478
Telemundo, 358, 359–360
Televisia, 359, 457
Television Production Partners, 363
Telmar, 328–329, 334, 439
Telser, Lester, 775, 819
Tennis, 315, 402
10-10-220 long distance, 271
Terhune, Chad, 525
Terpstra, Vern, 812
Territory Ahead, 486
Terwilliger, Cate, 818
Texaco, 586
Texas Instruments, 38
Texas Monthly, 396
Texas Pacific Group, 238
Thales Navigation, 525
Theus, Kathryn, 115, 116
Third Space, 236
Thomas, Blake, 449
Thomas, Dave, 171
Thomas, Jackie, 236
Thompson, Robert, 271
Thompson, Stephanie, 801, 802, 804, 813
Thorson, Esther, 796
3Com, 216
3M, 258–259, 437, 467
Tide, 513, 535, 621
Tiffany & Co., 60
Till, Brian D., 800
Tillamook Cheese, 45
Time, 301, 324, 325, 326, 393, 394, 396, 401–402, 403, 408, 411, 477, 687
Time, Inc., 645, 647
Time In-Store, 438
Time Warner, 358, 528
Times Mirror, 305
Timex, 67
Titleist, 61, 62
TiVo Inc., 300, 349–350, 376, 452, 750
T.J. Maxx, 450
TLC (The Learning Channel), 365, 370
TMP Worldwide, 77
TNN, 365
TNT, 365, 411
Toffler, Van, 371
Tolan, Mary, 810
Tommy Hilfiger, 762
Tortorici, Anthony J., 795
Toscani, Oliviero, 752–753
Total Research Corp., 193
Touchstone, 97
Tower Records, 664
Toy, Daniel R., 798
Toyota Motor Co., 17, 57, 195, 310, 407, 448, 457, 458, 495, 508, 645, 661
Tracik, Maureen, 800
Trade Show Bureau, 551
Traffic Audit Bureau (TAB), 437, 439, 650
Tragos, Bill, 243
TransWorld Media, 397
Travel, 322
Travel & Leisure, 188, 189, 315
Travel Channel, 365
Tree Top, 581
Trevino, Lee, 590
Triandis, H.C., 799
Tribal DDB (Omnicom Group), 96
TriStar, 498
Trivedi, Minakshi, 649, 811
Tropicana Products Inc., 114, 684
Trout, Jack, 52, 54, 99, 258–259, 553, 563, 796, 803
Trusdell, Brian, 810
TRW, 466
Tse, Alan, 357
Tse, Biu, 805
Tsingato, 679
Tubergen, G. Norman van, 812
Tucciarone, Joel, 636, 811
Tucker, Chris, 382
Tull, Donald S., 801
Tully, Shawn, 813
Tupperware, 20, 62, 478, 479
Turlington, Christy, 673
Turner, Derek, 812
Turner, Kathleen, 749
Turner Broadcasting System (TBS), 365, 370, 411, 458
Turner Cartoon Network, 767
TV Guide, 167, 291, 315, 393, 394, 401, 403, 612, 645
TV Guide Channel, 327
TV3, 574
TWA, 589
20th Century Fox Studio, 532
212 Men, 112
Ty, 566
Tybout, Alice M., 800
Tyco, 585
Tylenol, 60, 577, 579–580
Tyme ATMs, 456
Tyson, Mike, 175

U

U-Haul, 446
Um, Nam-Hyun, 801
Underhill, Paco, 133
Underwood, Elaine, 807
Unger, Lynette S., 818
UNICEF, 586
Unilever, 17, 88, 198, 310, 431, 452, 563, 619, 659, 660, 661, 663, 674, 679
Unisys, 592
United Airlines, 454, 456, 477, 490, 536, 586, 589, 769
United Artists Theatres, 449
United Negro College Fund, 518
U.S. Gymnastics Foundation, 586
U.S. News & World Report, 45, 403, 409
United Technologies Corp., 256
United Way, 58
Universal McCann, 80
Universal Pictures, 495
Universal Studios, 106
Univision, 358, 359–360
Univision Online, 359
UniWorld Group, Inc., 238
Unnava, H. Rao, 800
Unser, Al, Jr., 462
UPN (United Paramount Network), 358
Urbanski, Al, 808
Urschel, Joe, 289
US Airways, 407, 454
US Weekly, 315, 652, 653
USA Network, 365, 366
USA Today, 174, 305, 413, 414, 415, 454, 687, 779
USA Weekend, 305, 315, 414–416
USX, 585, 592
U2, 355
UUNET, 122
Uzzi, Don, 137–138

V

Vagnoni, Anthony, 68, 84, 246, 259, 796, 803
Vakratsas, Demetrios, 161, 799
Valencia, Humberto, 818
Valvoline, 54, 485
Van Den Bergh Foods, 739
van der Pool, Lisa, 714
van Meurs, Lex, 357, 804
van Raaij, W. Fred, 812
van Tubergen, G. Norman, 812
Vanity Fair, 56, 314, 326, 410
Vans, 456
Vaseline Research, 277
Vaughn, Richard, 154–155, 798
Velocity, 84
Vence, Deborah L., 817
Venesision, 359
Verified Audit Circulation Corp., 334
Verizon Communications, 17, 585
Verizon Wireless, 384
Vernors, 46
Versace, 58
Vert, Inc., 441
VFW Magazine, 403
VH1, 327, 365, 370, 371, 381
Via Magazine, 403
Viacom, 17, 371, 688–689
Viagra, 50
Viant, 137
Vibe, 391, 752
Vicary, James, 110, 115
Victoria's Secret, 463, 465, 468, 475, 566–567, 652, 653
Video Storyboard Tests, 186, 625
Virgin Atlantic Airways, 56, 775
Virgin Mobile, 299–300
Virginia Slims, 46
Visa, 463, 586, 591, 690–691
Vogt, Christine A., 798
Vogue, 13, 266, 410, 473, 567
Voight, Joan, 760, 814, 816, 817
Voli, Patricia Kramer, 812

Volkswagen, 51, 103, 289–290, 310, 410, 436, 566, 661
Volvo, 118, 418, 476, 494, 495, 508, 518, 716, 717, 740
Vons, 649
Vranica, Suzanne, 138, 174, 277, 355, 796, 797, 802, 815

W

Wackman, Daniel B., 796, 817
Wagner, Lindsay, 173
Wagner, Mary, 486
Waitt, Ted, 91, 171
The Wall Street Journal, 137, 138, 174, 248, 256, 305, 327, 413, 414, 415, 455, 456, 495, 578, 687, 779
Wallace, David J., 805
Wallas, Graham, 246
Wallendorf, Melanie, 803
Wal-Mart, 28, 37, 62, 106, 249, 519, 574, 587
Walsh, Ann, 816, 817
Walsh, David, 764
Walt Disney Co., 15, 17, 83, 97, 173, 302, 352, 360, 368, 369, 448, 449, 456, 508, 536
Walt Disney Pictures, 97
Walters, Barbara, 574
Walters, John P., 773
Wansink, Brian, 798
Ward, Montgomery, 463
Ward, Scott, 15, 817
Warner, Fara, 236, 813
Warner Communications, 688
Warner-Lambert, 733
Warren, Irwin, 803
Wartella, Ellen, 817
Wartzman, Rick, 140
Warwick, Dione, 461
Washington, Denzel, 178, 772
The Washington Post, 416, 426, 427
Wasseman, Todd, 804
Wasserman, Tom, 138
Water Bearer Films, 450
Waterford Crystal, 193
Watson, Paul, 636, 811
WB Network, 358, 411
WD-40 Co., 399, 521–522, 555, 660, 690
Weather Channel, 365
Webb, Don R., 817
Webb, Peter H., 801
Webex, 611
Weiden & Kennedy, 21
Weider Publications, 396
Weidlich, Thom, 495, 808
Weilbacher, William, 161–162, 266–267, 799, 801, 802, 803
Weinberger, Marc G., 801
Weingarten, Marc, 808
Weis, Michael J., 375
Weitzen, Jeff, 91
Welch, Jack, 615
Welch, Mary, 802
Weldon, Fay, 452
Wells, William, 270, 797, 803, 808
Wells Fargo, 384, 457, 602
Wendy's, 171, 252, 256, 363, 591
Wenner, Jan, 391
Wentz, Laurel, 240, 676, 796, 809, 812, 813
Werner, Ray O., 815
West, 224
Westin Hotels & Resorts, 248
Westways, 403
Westwood One, 383
WGN, 365, 366
Wheaties, 252
Whelan, Elizabeth M., 818
Whipple, Thomas W., 818
Whirlpool, 89, 155–156, 310, 645
White, Erin, 397, 813
White, Gordon E., 804
White Rabbit, 680
Whitlow, S. Scott, 812
Whittle, Chris, 763
Whittle Communications, 456
Wicks, Jan LeBlanc, 814
Wiechmann, Ulrich E., 813
Wieden, Dan, 259
Wieden & Kennedy, 84, 240, 243, 259
Wilke, Mike, 818
Wilkes, Robert E., 818
Wilkie, William L., 797, 800, 801, 809, 815, 816
Wilkinson, Amanda, 808
Wilkinson Sword, 738–739
Williams, Jerome D., 809
Wilsion, Joy Johnson, 815
Wilson, David T., 799
Wilson Sporting Goods Co., 551
Windigo, 496
Wine Institute, 714
Winski, Joseph M., 813
Winston, 287, 588
Winters, Rebecca, 166
Wirthlin Worldwide, 622
The Wiseguys, 289
W.K. Buckley Limited, 181, 182
Wolf, Michael J., 602, 795, 810
Woman's Day, 394, 403, 532, 668
Woman's World, 393, 394, 403
Women's National Basketball Association (WNBA), 359
Women's Wear Daily, 395
Wonderbra, 567
Wong, Edward, 236
Wood, Andy, 801
Wood, Douglas J., 814
Woodruff, David, 697
Woods, Bob, 809
Woods, Tiger, 117, 168, 173, 178, 235, 625, 675
Woodside, Arch G., 799
Woodward, Keith, 194
Woodward, Nancy Hatch, 807
Working Woman, 409, 767
World Bank, 683
Wotruba, Thomas, 600–601, 810
WPP Group, 78, 98, 663
Wright, Peter L., 797, 798
Wright, Richard A., 814
Wrigley, 153, 243–244, 287, 291, 470
Wrigley, Bill, Jr., 291
Wunderman, 94
Wynter, Leon E., 818

X

Xerox, 151, 183, 293, 501, 612, 669, 673, 697
XM Satellite Radio, 380, 381–382

Y

Yahoo!, 174, 249, 457
Yahoo! Internet Life, 409
Yalch, Richard, 125
Yang, Catherine, 806
Yankee, 396
Yankelovich Skelly & White, 593
Yates, Karen, 813
Yee-Lin, Tze, 813
YM, 106, 397, 403, 652, 653
Yoon, Sung-Joon, 620
York, 586
Young, Doug, 805
Young, James Webb, 244–246, 803
Young & Rubicam, 3, 90, 249, 318, 612, 680
Youth AIDS, 500
Y&R Advertising, 77

Z

Zachary, G. Pascal, 812
Zacson Corp., 610
Zagat, 56
Zaichkowsky, Judith, 154, 798
Zajonc, Robert B., 797
Zanot, Eric J., 814
ZapMe Corp., 763
Zelwegger, Renee, 286
Zenith, 37, 144, 149, 713
Zepeda, Teresa, 266
Zerex, 282
Zero One Design, 170
Zhang, Yong, 801
Zielske, Hubert A., 811
Zimmerman, Eilene, 616
Zoglin, Richard, 817
Zotti, Ed, 810
Zucker, Jeff, 300
Zufryden, Fred S., 804
Zyman, Sergio, 795

Subject Index

A

Ability, 159
Absolute cost, 323
Account executive, 79–80
Account planning, 246–247
Account-specific marketing, 519–520
Actual state, 107
Ad agency review consultants, 93
Ad click rate, 487
Ad clicks, 487
Ad execution-related thoughts, 158
Ad views (impressions), 487, 502
Adjacencies, 364
"Admazines," 402–403, 404
Advertainment, 68, 749–750
Advertiser-supported syndication, 362
Advertising, 16–18
  business-to-business, 19
  classifications of, 19
  cooperative, 552–554
  corporate; *see* Corporate advertising
  corrective, 730–733
  creative strategy; *see* Creative strategy
  creativity in; *see* Advertising creativity
  criticisms of, 753–772
    deception/untruthfulness, 754
    offensiveness/bad taste, 754–756
    sexual appeals, 756–757
    social/cultural impact; *see* Social/cultural impact, of advertising
  deceptive; *see* Deceptive advertising
  decline in, 12
  direct marketing combined with, 465
  direct-response, 20, 201, 475
  economic effects of, 772–779
  economies of scale in, 231–232, 775
  effectiveness of, 193–194
  global; *see* Global advertising
  growth of, 5–7
  image, 257, 265–266, 585–588
  IMC program development, 27
  international; *see* International advertising/promotion
  local, 19, 361, 383
  national, 19
  organizing for, 71–76
  personal selling combined with, 606–609
  primary-demand, 19
  product pricing and, 61–62
  professional, 19, 714–715
  promotional products combined with, 445
  public relations combined with, 609
  retail, 19
  sales promotion combined with, 554–556
  selective-demand, 19
  subliminal, 115–116
  teaser, 274–275
  trade, 19, 64
  youth bias in, 143–144
Advertising agencies, 69–70, 75–93
  account services, 79–80
  accountability of, 14, 87
  art department, 82
  billings, 77
  clients, gaining and losing, 90–93
  compensation systems, 85–88
  copywriters, 82
  creative boutiques, 83, 84
  creative services, 82
  departmental system, 82
  financial audits, 88
  full-service, 79
  group system, 82–83
  IMC capabilities, 81, 98–99
  in-house, 75–76
  for international marketing, 678–682
  management and finance, 82
  marketing services, 80–81
  media buying services, 83–85
  media department, 80
  organization and structure of, 79, 82–83
  performance evaluation, 88–93
  production department, 82
  qualitative audits, 88
  reasons for using, 78–79
  research department, 80
  self-regulation by, 712–714
  superagencies, 77–78
  traffic department, 82
  types of, 79–85
Advertising appeals, 183–187, 266–275; *see also* Creative execution styles
  combining, 272–273
  comparative; *see* Comparative advertising
  competitive advantage, 268
  emotional, 269–273
  favorable price, 268
  fear, 184–185
  feature, 268
  humor, 185–187, 282
  informational/rational, 267–269, 272–273
  news, 268
  nostalgic, 271
  product/service popularity, 268–269
  refutation, 181
  reminder advertising, 274
  sexual, 756–757
  teaser advertising, 274–275
  transformational ads, 270–272
Advertising campaign, 251–254
Advertising creativity, 237–243; *see also* Creative strategy
  defined, 241
  hard-sell advertising *vs.*, 245–246
  importance of, 237–239
  perspectives on, 239–243
  standards for, 242
Advertising Digital Identification (Ad-Id), 503
Advertising manager, 71–72
Advertising Research Foundation, 93, 250, 550
Advertising substantiation, 729–730
Advertorials, 477, 507
Advocacy advertising, 590
Aerial advertising, 436
Affect referral decision rule, 120
Affective stage, 150
Affiliates, 358
Affirmative disclosure, 726–728
Affordable method, 218
African-Americans
  sales promotion aimed at, 517–518
  stereotyping of, 768
Agency compensation, 85–88
  commission system, 85–87
  cost-plus system, 87
  fee-commission combination, 87
  fixed-fee method, 87
  future of, 88
  incentive-based system, 87–88
  negotiated commission, 86–87
  percentage charges, 88
AIDA model, 147–148
Alcoholic beverage advertising, 709–710
  to college/underage drinkers, 752
  sexual appeals, 756–757
Allocation models, 329
Alpha activity, 638
Alternative media, 432
Ambush marketing, 431
American Advertising Federation (AAF), 716
  advertising principles, 755
  Great Brands campaign, 16, 223
  value of advertising promotion, 779
American Association of Advertising Agencies (AAAA), 93, 716
  Ad-Id system, 503
  background research and, 248
  client-agency relationships, 90
  comparative advertising guidelines, 718
  IMC definition, 9
  responses to critics, 765, 766, 775, 776
  self-regulation by, 716, 718
  sweeps, 375
  value of advertising promotion, 113, 778, 779
American Association of Retired Persons (AARP), 45
American Bar Association (ABA), 714, 715, 724, 733, 740
American Family Association, 770
American Marketing Association (AMA), 466
  marketing definition, 7
American Medical Association (AMA), 585, 709, 710
American Red Cross, 7, 500
American Trucking Association, 437
Animatic, 251
Animation, 279–280
Arbitrary allocation, 218
Archetype research, 132–133
Art department, 82
Asian-Americans, 768–769
Aspirational reference groups, 129
Association of National Advertisers (ANA), 86, 88, 206, 503, 716
Association of Talent Agents, 78
Association tests, 111
Associative process, 123–124
Attitude toward the ad, 158
Attitudes, 117–119
Attractiveness, 172–177
Audimeter, 373
Audiotex, 446, 477–478
Average frequency, 321
Average quarter-hour (AQH), 385
Average quarter-hour rating (AQH RTG), 386
Average quarter-hour share (AQH SHR), 386
Awards, 240
  for media planning, 327
  Ogilvy Award, 622–623, 627, 648, 651

B

Balance-of-trade deficit, 660
Banner ads, 487, 496
Barrier to entry, 775
Barter syndication, 362
Behavioral stage, 150
Behavioristic segmentation, 49
Benchmark measures, 207–208
Benefit segmentation, 49
Better Business Bureau (BBB), 715
Big idea, 237, 255; *see also* Major selling idea
Billboards; *see* Outdoor advertising
Billings, 77
Bleed pages, 398–399
Body copy, 285
Bonus packs, 541
Boomerang, 160
Bounce-back coupon, 533
Brand development index (BDI), 310–312
Brand equity, 59, 520, 524–525
Brand identity, 14
Brand loyalty, 120, 121, 516
Brand manager, 72–75
Branding, 59–60
  brand strength research, 249–250
  emotional bonding, 273
  global, 657–658
  image advertising, 257, 265–266
  IMC role in, 14–16
  Internet and, 492–494
  power of, 15
  promotional perspective, 59
  sales promotion and, 516–517
Broadcast media, 348–389
  direct marketing and, 475
  radio; *see* Radio
  television; *see* Television
Budgeting, 211–232
  advertising-to-sales ratios by industry, 220–221
  affordable method, 218
  allocating budget, 229–232
  approaches to, 217–229
  arbitrary allocation, 218
  build-up approaches, 225–228
  client/agency policies and, 230
  competitive parity, 222–224
  computer simulation models, 228
  cutting budgets, 223
  economies of scale and, 231–232
  effectiveness measurement, 626
  establishing budget, 211–229
  factors influencing, 215–217
  IMC elements, 229–230
  marginal analysis, 213–214
  market potential and, 230
  market share goals and, 230–231
  market size and, 230
  media strategy, 323–326
  methods compared, 224
  methods summarized, 228–229
  objective and task method, 225–226
  organizational characteristics and, 232
  payout planning, 226–227
  percentage of sales, 218–222
  promotional planning process, 27, 31
  quantitative models, 228
  ROI method, 224
  sales promotion, 554–555
  sales response models, 214–215
  theoretical issues, 213–215
  top-down approaches, 217–225
Build-up budgeting approaches, 225–228
Bureau of Alcohol, Tobacco, and Firearms (BATF), 738
Business/Professional Advertising Association (B/PAA), 334
Business-to-business advertising, 19
  database contents, 468
  problem/solution approach, 279
Button, 487
Buying allowances, 547
Buzz marketing, 13

C

Cable television, 364–370
  advantages of, 367–369
  advertising on, 366–367
  future of, 369–370
  growth of, 364–366
  limitations of, 369
  major networks, 365
Campaign theme, 251–254
Cannes Lion Awards, 240
Carryover effect, 199–200
Cash system, 382–383
Catalogs, 474–475
Category development index (CDI), 311–312
Category management system, 73–75
Cause-related marketing, 590–592
Cease-and-desist order, 730
Celebrity endorsement
  audience receptivity, 173–175, 625
  controversial, 165–166
  Fame Index, 178–179
  involvement and, 160–161
  in Japan, 170
  meaning transfer model, 175–177
  overexposure, 173
  product overshadowing, 173
  Q ratings, 178–179
  risk in using, 175
  testimonials, 278
Center for Science in the Public Interest, 710, 716, 761
Center on Alcohol Marketing and Youth, 752
Centers for Disease Control and Prevention (CDC), 756
Central Hudson Test, 722
Central Intelligence Agency (CIA), 683
Central route to persuasion, 159–160
Centralized system, 71–72, 76, 677–678
Channel, 143, 167
Children; *see also* Teenagers
  advertising regulation, 717
  ethical issues, 758–762
  in-school marketing, 763–764
  online privacy, 746
  premium regulations, 742
  TV networks' guidelines, 720
  tweens (7-14 yr-olds), 106
Children's Advertising Review Unit (CARU), 716–718, 761
Children's Online Privacy Protection Act (COPPA), 746
Children's Television Act, 761
Circulation, magazine, 403, 405
City zone, 421
Classical conditioning, 123–125
Classified advertising, 416
Click, 502
Click-through, 502
Client server, 487
Clients, 69
  creative output evaluation/approval by, 291–296
  gaining and losing, 90–93
  organizing for advertising/promotion, 71–76
Clio Award, 240
Clipping service, 222
Close, 604–605
Clutter, 188–189, 356
  magazines, 402–403, 404
  newspapers, 421
  online, 505
  public relations and, 577
  radio, 382–383
  sales promotion, 520
  television, 188–189, 356
Cognitive dissonance, 121–122
Cognitive learning theory, 126–127
Cognitive orientation, 123
Cognitive responses, 157–158
Cognitive stage, 150
Collateral services, 70–71, 96–98
Comarketing, 519
Combination rates, 425
Commercial speech, 722
Commission system, 85–87
Common ground, 143
Communication, 136–163
  analysis of, 27
  audience aggregation, 146–147
  channel; *see* Communication channels
  cognitive processing of, 157–161
  decoding, 143–145
  dyadic, 599
  encoding, 141
  feedback, 145
  message, 141–143
  model of, 139–145
  nature of, 139
  noise, 145
  receiver, 143–147
  response, 145; *see also* Response process
  semiotics, 142–143
  source; *see* Source
Communication channels, 146, 167
  clutter, 188–189
  context/environment effects, 188
  information processing differences, 188
  media effects, 187–188
  personal *vs.* nonpersonal, 187
Communication objectives, 31, 202–206
Communications effect pyramid, 203–204
Communications situation, 130
Communications task, 206
Comparative advertising, 183–184, 277
  AAAA guidelines, 718
  in foreign markets, 667–668
  lawsuits arising from, 738–739
Competitive advantage, 41, 257
Competitive advantage appeals, 268
Competitive analysis, 29, 41–42
Competitive parity method, 222–224
Compliance, 177
Comprehension and reaction tests, 631
Computer simulation models, 228
Computers
  budget simulation models, 228
  in media planning, 326–331
  in media strategy development, 328–331
  optimizer software, 330–331
Conative stage, 150
Concave-downward function model, 214–215
Concentrated marketing, 51
Concept testing, 629–631
Conditioned response, 123–124
Conditioned stimulus, 123
Consent orders, 730
Consumer, family decision making, 129
Consumer behavior, 102–134
  alternative approaches, 131–133
  archetype research, 132–133
  attitudes, 117–119
  attribution theory, 557
  behavioral learning theory, 123–126
  classical conditioning, 123–125
  cognitive learning theory, 126–127
  culture and, 127–128
  decision-making; *see* Decision-making process
  environmental influences on, 127–131
  hypnosis, 132–133

learning process, 123–127
motives, 109–112
operant conditioning, 125–126
overview, 105–107
reference groups, 129
response process; *see* Response process
situational determinants, 130–131
social class and, 128–129
subcultures and, 128–129
Consumer franchise building (CFB) promotions, 520–522
Consumer juries, 631–633
Consumer magazines, 393–394
Consumer socialization process, 760
Consumer-oriented sales promotion, 22, 513, 514, 522–544
bonus packs, 541
building brand equity with, 524–525
contests, 525, 537–540, 740–742
coupons; *see* Coupons
defending current customers with, 524
event marketing, 543
frequency programs, 541–542
IMC enhancement with, 524–526
increasing consumption with, 523–524
objectives, 522–525, 543–544
obtaining trial/repurchase with, 522–523
premiums, 535–537
price-off deals, 541
problems with, 539
refunds/rebates, 540–541
sales promotion trap, 557–558
sampling, 526–529
sweepstakes, 537–540, 740–742
target marketing with, 524
techniques for, 526–544
Content sponsorship, 496
Contests, 537–540
building brand equity with, 525
regulation of, 740–742
trade-oriented, 546–547
Continuity, 314, 316
Continuity programs, 541–542
Continuous reinforcement schedule, 125
Contribution margin, 213
Controlled-circulation basis, 405
Convergence, 299–300
Cookie, 502
Cooperative advertising, 552–554
Copy, 285
Copy platform, 254–255
Copywriters, 82
Corporate advertising, 583–593
advantages/disadvantages, 592
advocacy advertising, 590
cause-related marketing, 590–592
effectiveness measurement, 593
event sponsorship, 588–590
financial support generation, 587–588
image advertising, 585–588
objectives, 585
recruiting, 586–587
sponsorship, 586
stadium naming, 589
types of, 585–592
Corrective advertising, 730–733
Cost per click (CPC), 487
Cost per order (CPO), 480
Cost per ratings point (CPRP), 323
Cost per thousand (CPM), 323–326, 487
Cost-plus system, 87
Council of Better Business Bureaus, 711, 715–716, 727
Counterarguments, 157–158
Coupons, 529–535
advantages/limitations, 529–530
cost calculations, 530
distribution methods, 531–534
in foreign markets, 691
online, 535
trends in, 534–535
Coverage, 301–303
Creative boutiques, 83, 84
Creative execution styles, 266, 275–283; *see also* Advertising appeals
animation, 279–280
combinations, 282–283
comparison, 277
demonstration, 277
dramatization, 281–282
evaluation/approval of, 291–296
fantasy, 281
humor, 282
print advertising tactics, 283–286
scientific/technical evidence, 277
slice-of-life, 278–279
straight sell/factual message, 275–277
television advertising tactics, 286–290
testimonials, 277–278
Creative selling, 603
Creative space buys, 399
Creative strategy, 31, 234–297
account planning, 246–247
advertising appeals; *see* Advertising appeals
advertising campaign, 251–254
background research, 247–248
brand image creation, 257, 265–266
campaign theme, 251–254
challenges, 243
copy platform, 254–255
creative process, 244–251
development of, 251–260
evaluation/approval of, 291–296
execution styles; *see* Creative execution styles
general preplanning input, 247–248
inherent drama, 258
international advertising, 683–684
for low involvement products, 152–153
major selling idea, 255–260
personnel considerations, 244
planning, 243–251
positioning; *see* Positioning
problem detection, 248
product/service-specific preplanning input, 248–250
qualitative research input, 250–251
risk taking, 243–244
slogans, top ten, 252
unique selling proposition, 256–257
verification/revision, 251
Creative tactics, 237; *see also* Creative execution styles
Creativity; *see* Advertising creativity; Creative strategy
Credibility, 168–172
Cross-media advertising, 411, 426
Cross-ruff coupon, 533
Cross-selling, 468, 470, 605
Cultural symbols, 54
Cultural values, 665
Culture, consumer behavior and, 127–128
Cume, 385–386
Custom publications, 402–403, 404
Custom Publishing Council, 404
Customer analysis, 29
Customer relationship management (CRM), 468–469, 602
Customers, lifetime value of, 8

D

DAGMAR model, 206–209
Daily inch rate, 323–324
Daily newspapers, 413
Database, 467
business-to-business, 468
consumer, 468–469
effectiveness measurement, 471
functions of, 468–469
information sources for, 469–471
Database marketing, 12–14, 411, 467–471
Day-after recall tests, 636, 643–644
Dayparts, 364, 384
Decentralized system, 72–75, 76, 678
Deception, 726
Deceptive advertising, 725–733, 754
advertising substantiation, 729–730
affirmative disclosure, 726–728
cease-and-desist orders, 730
complaint procedure, 731
consent orders, 730
corrective advertising, 730–733
defined, 726
FTC remedies for, 730–733
on the Internet, 507
puffery, 725–728
Decision maker, family decision making, 129
Decision-making process, 107–123
alternative evaluation, 114–117
attitudes and, 117–119
decision rules, 119–120
evaluative criteria, 116–117
evoked set, 116
family roles in, 129–130
information search, 112–114
integration processes, 119–120
model of, 105
perception, 113–114
postpurchase evaluation, 120–122
problem recognition, 107–109
purchase decision, 120
variations in, 122–123
Decoding, 143–145
Demographic segmentation, 46–47
Demographic selectivity, 396
Demonstration advertising, 277
Departmental system, ad agency, 82
Dependent variables, 166–167
Designated market areas (DMAs), 374
Differentiated marketing, 50–51
Differentiation, 774
Digital video recorders, 349–350
Direct broadcast satellite (DBS) services, 370, 689
Direct channels, 62
Direct headlines, 283–284
Direct mail, 471–474
characteristics of, 330
coupon delivery by, 531–533
Internet and, 474, 500–501
regulation of, 743
Direct marketing, 18–20, 460–483
advantages/disadvantages, 480–481
advertorials, 477, 507
broadcast media and, 475
catalogs, 474–475
database development, 467–471
defined, 463
direct mail; *see* Direct mail
direct selling, 478–480, 743–744
effectiveness measurement, 480
electronic teleshopping, 478
flowchart, 464
growth of, 463–465
infomercials, 11, 461–462, 475–477
Internet and, 478, 500–501
objectives, 467
one-step approach, 471
personal selling combined with, 610–611
print media and, 477
promotional products combined with, 445
regulation of, 742–744
role in IMC program, 27, 465–467
scam artists, 482
strategies/media, 471–480
telemarketing, 477–478, 610, 743

Direct marketing—*Cont.*
teleshopping, 477, 501
two-step approach, 471
Direct Marketing Association (DMA), 469, 471, 572, 743, 744
Direct selling, 478–480, 743–744
Direct Selling Association, 743–744
Direct source, 168
Directional medium, 446–447
Direct-response advertising, 20, 201, 475
Direct-response agencies, 94
Direct-response media, 463
Disassociative reference groups, 129
Display advertising, 416
Dissatisfaction
postpurchase, 121, 151
problem recognition and, 107
Dissonance/attribution model, 150, 151–152
Distribution channels, 62
Diverting, 549
Domain name, 487
Door-to-door sampling, 527
Dramatization, 281–282
Duplicated reach, 318
Dyadic communication, 599

E

E-commerce, 494, 501
Economic censorship, 769–771
Economic impact, of advertising, 772–779
competition, 775–776
consumer choice, 774–775
information, 777, 778
market power, 777–778
product costs/prices, 776–777
Economic infrastructure, 662
Economies of scale, 231–232, 775
Edward Davis Educational Foundation, 518
Effective reach, 320–321
Effectiveness measurement, 618–654
advertising, 193–194
arguments against, 623–625
arguments in favor of, 621–623
of budgeting decisions, 626
comprehensive measures, 644
concept testing, 629–631
consumer juries, 631–633
corporate advertising, 593
current methods, problems with, 647–648
database, 471
day-after recall tests, 643–644
diagnostics, 644
direct marketing, 480
dummy advertising vehicles, 634
effective testing essentials, 648
eye tracking, 638, 639
field tests, 626, 628
Flesch formula, 634
focus groups, 629–631
how to test, 628–629
IMC impact, 619–620, 651–653
inquiry tests, 640–641
Internet, 501–504, 619–620
laboratory tests, 626, 627–628
market testing, 638–647
media planning and, 305
media strategies, 625–626
message, 625
nontraditional media, 650
objectives and, 196
on-air tests, 636
PACT principles, 628, 647–648
personal selling, 613–616
persuasive measures, 644
physiological measures, 636–638
portfolio tests, 633
posttests, 626, 627
of broadcast commercials, 643–647
of print ads, 638–643
pretests, 626–627, 633–638
of broadcast ads, 634–638
of print ads, 633–634
public relations, 577–579, 584
publicity, 583, 584
readability tests, 634
recall tests, 642–643
recognition tests, 641–642
rough testing, 631–633
sales promotion, 648–650
single-source tracking studies, 645–646
of source factors, 625
sponsorships, 650–651
Starch readership studies, 641–642
television advertising, 619–620
test marketing, 644–645
testing bias, 627–628
theater tests, 635
tracking studies, 646–647
what to test, 625–626
when to test, 626–627
where to test, 627–628
Effies, 240
Eight-Sheet Outdoor Advertising Association, 438
80-20 rule, 49
Elaboration likelihood model (ELM), 158–161
Electrodermal response, 636
Electroencephalographic (EEG) measures, 638
Electronic mail (e-mail), 487
Electronic teleshopping, 478
Emotional appeals, 269–273
bases for, 269
rational appeals combined with, 272–273
transformational ads, 270–272
Emotional bonding, 273
Emotional integration, 270
Encoding, 141
Endorsement, 278; *see also* Celebrity endorsement
Environmental analysis, 29
Environmental Protection Agency, 728
Esteem needs, 109–110
Ethics, 751–753; *see also* Social/cultural impact, of advertising
AAF advertising principles, 755
advertising to children, 758–764
alcoholic beverage advertising, 709–710, 752, 756–757
deceptive Internet practices, 507
deceptive/untruthful advertising, 754
direct selling code of ethics, 744
in-school marketing, 763–764
network censors, 759–760
offensive advertising, 754–756
online privacy issues, 744–746
sexual appeals, 756–757
shock advertising, 757–758
stealth marketing, 431–432, 749–750
subliminal advertising, 115–116
Ethnocentrism, 665
Ethnographic research, 250
Evaluation models, 329
Evaluative criteria, 116–117
Event marketing, 543
Event sampling, 528
Event sponsorship, 543
corporate advertising, 588–590
effectiveness measurement, 650–651
Everyday low pricing (EDLP), 549–550
Evoked set, 116
Exchange, 7
Exclusive, 574
External analysis, 27, 28–29
External audiences, 569
External audits, 579
External search, 112–113
Externally paced information, 188
Eye tracking, 638, 639

F

Factual message advertising, 275–277
Failure fees, 549
Fame Index, 178–179
Family decision making, 129–130
Fantasy appeals, 281
Favorable price appeals, 268
FCB planning model, 154–155
Fear appeals, 184–185
Feature appeals, 268
Federal Bureau of Investigation (FBI), 440, 539
Federal Communications Commission (FCC), 115, 361, 382, 711, 734–735
Federal regulation
background on, 723
Bureau of Alcohol, Tobacco, and Firearms (BATF), 738
current status of, 733–734
Fairness Doctrine, 734
FCC; *see* Federal Communications Commission (FCC)
FDA (Food and Drug Administration), 268, 711, 735–738
First Amendment and, 722–723, 732–733
FTC; *see* Federal Trade Commission (FTC)
Lanham Act, 738–739
Postal Service; *see* U.S. Postal Service
prescription drug advertising, 737–738
Supreme Court; *see* U.S. Supreme Court
Federal Trade Commission Act, 723
Federal Trade Commission (FTC), 711, 722–734
advertising to children, 760–761
alcohol advertising to youth, 752
Bureau of Competition, 723
Bureau of Consumer Protection, 723–724, 740
Bureau of Economics, 723
comparative advertising, 183
complaint procedure, 731
country of origin claims, 728
current regulatory status of, 733–734
deceptive advertising; *see* Deceptive advertising
direct marketing, 482, 742–744
FTC Improvements Act, 724, 725, 733
Internet marketing, 744–746
900-Number Rule, 743
Pay-Per-Call Rule, 743
product placements, 453
professional advertising, 714
sales promotion regulation, 740–742
slotting fees, 549, 742
trade regulation rules, 724
unfairness interpretation, 724–725
uniqueness claims, 257
Wheeler-Lea Amendment, 723, 724
Federation Internationale de Football Association (FIFA), 432, 458
Fee-commission combination, 87
Feedback, 145
Field of experience, 143
Field tests, 626, 628
File transfer protocol (ftp), 487
Financial audits, 88
First-run syndication, 362
Fixed-fee method, 87
Flat rates, 424
Flesch formula, 634
Flighting, 314, 316
Florists' Transworld Delivery Association, 301
Focus groups, 111, 250, 629–631
Food and Drug Administration (FDA), 268, 711, 735–738
Forward buying, 549
Freestanding inserts, 531

Frequency, 303
average, 321
computer analysis of, 328–329
determining factors, 322
effective reach and, 320–321
effects of, 320
gross ratings points and, 318–320
level needed, 317–318
magazines and, 402
objectives, 318
Frequency programs, 541–542
Full-service agencies, 79
Functional consequences, 117

G

Galvanic skin response, 636
Game, 537
Gatefolds, 398
Gay consumers, 769
General advertising rates, 422–423
General preplanning input, 247–248
Generation Y, 13
Geographic segmentation, 46, 47
Geographic selectivity, 396
Global advertising, 668–677
advantages, 669
appropriate use of, 672–674
localization of, 674–677, 684, 688–689
problems with, 670–672
Global marketing, 669; *see also* Global advertising
Goodwill, 571
Gopher, 487
Gross ratings points (GRPs), 318–320
Group system, ad agency, 82–83
Guaranteed circulation, 405
Guerilla marketing, 431

H

Habit formation strategy, 155
Halo effect, 632
Headlines, 283–284
Hemispheric lateralization, 638
Heuristics, 119–120
Hierarchy of effects model, 147–148
Hierarchy of needs, 109–110
High involvement strategies, 155
Highway Beautification Act, 434
Hispanics
as market segment, 45–46
sales promotion aimed at, 517
Spanish-language TV networks, 359–360
stereotyping of, 768
teenagers, 140
Hit, 487, 502
Home shopping channels, 477, 478, 501
Horizontal cooperative advertising, 552
Households using television (HUT), 372
Humor appeals, 185–187, 282
Hypertext transfer protocol (http), 487
Hypnosis, 132–133

I

Ideal state, 107
Identification, 172
Image advertising, 257, 265–266, 585–588
Image transfer, 378
Incentive-based system, 87–88
Independent variables, 166–167
In-depth interviews, 111
Index number, 306–308
Indirect channels, 62
Indirect headlines, 284
Indirect source, 168
Industrial markets, segmentation variables for, 47
In-flight advertising, 453–456
Influencer, family decision making, 129
Infomercials, 11, 461–462, 475–477, 501
Information processing model, 147–148
Information provider, family decision making, 129
Information search, 112–114
Informational/rational appeals, 267–269, 272–273
Informative strategy, 155
Ingredient-sponsored cooperative advertising, 552
Inherent drama, 258
In-house agencies, 75–76
Initiator, family decision making, 129
Ink-jet imaging, 412
Innovation adoption model, 147–148
Inquiry tests, 640–641
Inserts, magazine, 399
Inside cards, 441
Inside-out planning, 210
Instant coupon, 533–534
In-store couponing, 534
In-store media, 437
In-store sampling, 527
Instrumental conditioning; *see* Operant conditioning
Integrated marketing communications (IMC), 4–5, 9–16
ad agencies shifting to, 9, 81, 98–99
agency compensation and, 88
in branding, 14–16
defined, 9
evolution of, 9–11
importance of, 11–14
objectives for, 198, 210–211
participants in process, 69–71
planning process; *see* Promotional planning process
promotional management, 24–25
promotional mix; *see* Promotional mix
pros and cons of, 98–99
responsibility for, 99
Integration processes, 119–120
Interaction models, 329
Interactive agencies, 95–96
Interactive marketing, 20–21; *see also* Internet
IMC program development, 27
iTV, 299–300, 506–508, 735
Wink-enhanced ads, 506
Interactive media, 20, 299–300
characteristics of, 330
wireless communications, 508
Interactive Services Association, 744
Interactive TV (iTV), 299–300, 506–508, 735
Interconnects, 367
Intermittent reinforcement schedule, 126
Internal analysis, 25–28, 29
Internal audiences, 569
Internal audits, 579
Internal search, 112
Internalization, 169
International Advertising Association (IAA), 771, 778
International advertising/promotion, 656–707; *see also* International marketing
agency selection, 678–682
centralization, 677–678
creative decisions, 683–684
decentralization, 677–678
global approach; *see* Global advertising
international markets, importance of, 659–660
international media, 687–689
legal restrictions by country, 700–707
local media, 686
localized strategy, 674–677, 684, 688–689
media selection, 685–689
organizing for, 677–678
research, 682–683
role of, 660–661
tobacco advertising, 667
top ten companies, by expenditure, 661
International marketing
advertising; *see* International advertising/promotion
anti-American sentiments, 696–697
in China, 663, 666, 679–680
cultural environment, 662, 664–666
demographic environment, 662, 664
in developing countries, 663–664
economic environment, 661–664, 691
Internet used in, 695–697
in Japan, 665
legal restrictions by country, 700–707
legal/political environment, 662, 666–668
personal selling, 693–694
public relations, 694–695
sales promotion, 690–693
International Trade Administration (ITA), 683
Internet, 484–509
advantages, 504–505
advertising on; *see* Internet advertising
business-to-business users, 489–490
catalogs, 475
characteristics of, 330
Children's Online Privacy Protection Act, 746
consumer market users, 488–489
cookies, 502
coupons on, 535
deceptive practices on, 507
defined, 486
direct mail, 474, 500–501
direct marketing and, 478, 500–501
disadvantages, 505–506
e-commerce, 494, 501
effectiveness measurement, 501–504, 619–620
audience measures, 501–502
data sources, 504
IAB guidelines for, 502
online measuring, 502–503
problems with, 505
features of, 487
growth of, worldwide, 695
IMC programs and, 496–501
infomercials, 501
international marketing and, 695–697
magazines on, 412–413
as marketing tool, 20–21
newspapers on, 428
objectives
awareness creation, 492
brand strengthening, 493–494
communications, 492–494
image creation, 493
information dissemination, 492–493
interest generation, 492
product trial, 494
website, 490–492
personal selling on, 498–499, 611
privacy issues, 744–746
program development, 488–494
public relations on, 499–500, 575
regulatory issues, 744–746
sales promotion on, 498
sampling via, 528
shopping channels on, 501
SPAM, 500–501, 507, 746
terminology, 487
users of, 488–489
website development/maintenance, 490–492
Internet advertising, 276–277, 496–498
advertainment, 67–68
advertorials, 507
banner ads, 496
effectiveness measurement, 639
"The Hire" campaign, 67–68
interactive agencies, 95–96
interstitials, 498

Internet advertising—*Cont.*
links, 498
online ad formats, 497
pop-ups/pop-unders, 496–498, 507
push (webcasting) technologies, 498
sponsorships, 496
Yellow Pages, 446
Internet Advertising Bureau (IAB), 502, 504, 505, 506, 507
Interstitials, 487, 498
Introductory allowances, 549
In-unit click, 502
Involvement, 123, 153–156, 160–161
magazines and, 400–401
newspapers and, 419
Island ads, 421

J

Jingles, 287

K

Kelley Awards, 240
Kiosks, 456

L

Laboratory tests, 626, 627–628
Lanham Act, 738–739
Layouts, 82, 285–286
Leads, 604
Links, 487, 498
Local advertising, 19, 361, 383
Local advertising rates, 422–423
Localized advertising strategy, 674–677, 684, 688–689
Low involvement hierarchy, 150, 152–153
Low involvement strategies, 155
Loyalty programs, 541–542

M

MADD, 710
Magazine advertising; *see also* Magazines
absolute/relative cost of, 401–402
buying space, 408–409
comparative costs, 324–326
creative tactics, 283–286
cross-magazine/media deals, 411
Magazine networks, 408–409
Magazine Publishers of America (MPA), 240, 248, 305, 334, 394, 400, 403, 410, 779
Magazines, 393–413; *see also* Magazine advertising
advantages of, 395–401
advertiser influence on, 769–771
advertising costs, 401–402
advertising regulation by, 719
business publications, 395
characteristics of, 330
circulation, 403, 405
circulation management, 409–411
classifications of, 393–395
clutter in, 402–403, 404
competition among, 402–403
consumer, 393–394
consumer receptivity/involvement, 400–401
coupons via, 533
creative flexibility of, 398–399
custom, 402–403, 404
database marketing, 411
disadvantages of, 401–403
editorial platform strength and, 409
farm publications, 394
future for, 409–413
in-flight, 453
lead time, 402
online delivery methods, 412–413
permanence of, 400
prestige of, 400
reach/frequency limitations of, 402
readership, 403, 405–406
reproduction quality of, 398
research, 406–408
role of, 393
sampling via, 528
selectivity of, 395–398
services offered by, 401
technological advances and, 411–412
for teens, 397
Mailing list, 473–474
Major selling idea, 255–260
Marginal analysis, 213–214
Market niches, 146
Market opportunities, 40–41
Market segmentation, 44–50
bases for, 46–49
behavioristic, 49
benefit, 49
demographic, 46–47
80-20 rule, 49
geographic, 46, 47
Hispanics, 45–46
market selection, 49–50
psychographic, 47, 48–49
Market segments, 40, 146
Marketer-induced problem recognition, 108
Marketing, 36–65
buzz, 13
competitive analysis, 41–42
concentrated, 51
database, 12–14, 411, 467–471
described, 7–8
differentiated, 50–51
event, 543
exchange concept and, 7
interactive/Internet, 20–21
opportunity analysis, 40–41
post 9/11, 30
process model, 39
program development/planning; *see* Marketing planning program
relationship, 7–8
revolution in, 12–14
strategy/analysis, 40–42
target marketing; *see* Target marketing process
undifferentiated, 50–51
Marketing channels, 62
Marketing mix, 8
Marketing objectives, 31, 196–198
Marketing plan, 25
Marketing planning program, 58–64
advertising and, 64
branding, 59
distribution channel decisions, 62
packaging, 59–60
price decisions, 60–62
product decisions, 58–60
promotion and, 64
push *vs.* pull strategies, 62–64
Marketing public relations (MPR), 566–567
Marketing research, 110–112, 682–683
Marketing research companies, 98
Mass customization, 7–8
Mass markets, 146–147
Mass media, 143, 146–147
broadcast media; *see* Broadcast media
information processing and, 187–188
print media; *see* Print media
Master recording, 287
Master Settlement Agreement, 735–736
Materialism, 764–765
Media
compared, 330
mass; *see* Mass media
nontraditional, 432, 650
relative costs of, 323–326
support; *see* Support media
Media buying services, 83–85
Media department, ad agency, 80
Media objectives, 301
Media organizations, 70
Media planning, 298–347
activities involved in, 304
awards for, 327
Bumble Bee Tuna case study, 335–347
computers in, 326–331
convergence, 299–300
creative aspects, 321
defined, 301
effectiveness measurement difficulties and, 305
evaluation/follow-up, 326
geographic considerations, 310–312
inconsistent terminologies and, 303
information sources, 334
insufficient information and, 303
internal/external factors, 309–310
market analysis, 306–312, 328
media buying department organization, 309
media characteristics, 330, 331
media services companies, 305
national advertisers ranked by spending, 302
objectives, 312
overview of, 301–305
problems in, 303–305
strategy development/implementation; *see* Media strategy
target market identification, 306–309
terminology, 301–303
time pressures and, 303
Media services companies, 305
Media strategy, 31, 301, 313–326
budget considerations, 323–326
computers in, 328–331
effectiveness measurement, 625–626
flexibility, 323
geographic coverage, 314
international advertising, 685–689
media mix, 313
mood, 322–323
reach *vs.* frequency, 316–321
scheduling, 314–316
target market coverage, 313–314
Media vehicle, 301
Medium, 301
Message, 141–143, 179–187
appeals; *see* Advertising appeals
conclusion drawing, 180–181
effectiveness measurement, 625
order of presentation, 179–180
persuasion matrix, 167–168
refutation, 181
sidedness of, 181
structure, 179–183
verbal *vs.* visual, 181–183
Missionary sales, 603
Mnemonics, 114
Mobile billboards, 436–437
Motion Picture Association of America, 714
Motivation, 109–112, 159
hierarchy of needs, 109–110
psychoanalytic theory, 110, 111
Motivation research, 110–112
Motives, 109
Mouse-over, 502
Movie theater advertising, 448–450
Multiattribute attitude model, 117–118
Multimagazine deals, 411
Multiplexing, 370
Music, in television advertising, 286–289
Musical composition, 287
Mystery ads, 274–275

N

Narrowcasting, 367
National advertising, 19
National Advertising Division (NAD), 716–718, 721, 727
National Advertising Review Board (NARB), 711, 716–718
National Advertising Review Council (NARC), 716–718
National Association of Attorneys General (NAAG), 740
National Association of Black School Educators, 518
National Association of Broadcasters (NAB), 248, 719
National Association of Theatre Owners, 449
National Center on Addiction and Substance Abuse, 710
National Highway Traffic Safety Administration, 518
National Inhalant Prevention Coalition, 582
National newspapers, 413–414, 415
National Organization for Marijuana Legalization, 774
National Organization for Women (NOW), 752, 767
National PTA, 582
National spot advertising, 361, 367
Needledrop, 286
Needs, 107, 109–110
Negotiated commission, 86–87
Network advertising, 358–361, 383
Network Advertising Initiative (NAI), 745
New needs/wants, problem recognition, 107
New products
  advertising for, 205
  problem recognition and, 108–109
New York Marketing Association, 93, 240
News appeals, 268
Newspaper advertising; *see also* Newspapers
  buying space, 422–425
  classified, 416
  comparative costs, 324–326
  creative tactics, 283–286
  display advertising, 416
  general *vs.* local rates, 422–423
  local, 416
  national/general, 416
  preprinted inserts, 416
  rate structures, 424–425
  units of measure for, 423–424
Newspaper Association of America (NAA), 334, 421, 423, 427
Newspaper Rates and Data, 421
Newspapers, 413–428; *see also* Newspaper advertising
  advantages of, 417–419
  advertiser influence on, 769–771
  advertising regulation by, 719
  audience information, 421–422
  characteristics of, 330
  clutter, 421
  competition from other media, 425–426
  coupons via, 533
  cross-media buys, 426
  daily, 413
  declining circulation, 426
  extensive penetration of, 417
  flexibility of, 417–418
  future for, 425–428
  geographic selectivity of, 418
  limitations of, 419–421
  national, 413–414, 415
  online, 428
  poor reproduction quality of, 419
  reader attraction/retention, 426–428
  reader involvement/acceptance, 419
  role of, 393
  sampling via, 528
  selectivity, lack of, 420
  services offered by, 419
  short life span of, 419–420
  special audience, 414
  supplements, 414–416
  types of, 413–416
  weekly, 413
Nielsen Television Index, 373
9/11 terrorist attack, marketers' response to, 30
Noise, 145
Non-franchise building (non-FB) promotions, 522
Nonmeasured media, 432
Nonpersonal channels, 143, 187
Nonprofit organizations, 7, 772–774
Nontraditional media, 432, 650

O

Objective and task method, 225–226
Objectives, 192–211
  benchmark measures, 207–208
  campaign coordination and, 195–196
  communications, 31, 202–206, 492–494
  concrete/measurable, 206–207
  DAGMAR model, 206–209
  decision making and, 196
  direct-marketing, 467
  effectiveness measurement and, 196
  good, characteristics of, 206–208
  IMC, 198, 210–211
  improving use of, 209–210
  marketing, 31, 196–198
  media planning, 312
  need for, 195–196
  planning and, 196
  problems in setting, 209–211
  promotional, determining, 196–198
  sales-oriented, 198–202
  target audience and, 207
  time period specification, 208
  website, 490–492
Office of National Drug Control Policy, 45
Off-invoice allowance, 547
Off-network syndication, 361
Ogilvy Award, 622–623, 627, 648, 651
On-air test, 636
One-sided message, 181
One-step approach, 471
Online Publishers Association, 619
On-package sampling, 528
Open-rate structure, 424
Operant conditioning, 125–126
Opportunity analysis, 40–41
Optimizers, 330–331
Opt-in-e-mail, 487
Order taking, 603
Organization for advertising/promotion, 71–76
  administration and execution, 72
  brand management system, 72–75
  category management system, 73–75
  centralized system, 71–72, 76, 677–678
  coordination with other departments, 72
  coordination with outside agencies/services, 72
  decentralized system, 72–75, 76, 678
  in-house agencies, 75–76
  international markets, 677–678
  media buying department, 309
  planning and budgeting, 72
  systems compared, 76
Out of stock, problem recognition, 107
Outdoor advertising, 433–436
  advantages/disadvantages, 435–436
  billings by category, 433
  characteristics of, 330
  mobile billboards, 436–437
Outdoor Advertising Association of America (OAAA), 433, 439
Out-of-home advertising, 432–443
  aerial advertising, 436
  audience measurement, 437–440
  in-store media, 437
  miscellaneous, 437, 439
  mobile billboards, 436–437
  outdoor advertising, 433–436
  transit advertising, 440–443
Outside posters, 441
Outside-in planning, 210

P

PACT (Positioning Advertising Copy Testing), 628, 647–648
Page views (impressions), 487, 502
Participations, 363
Pass-along rate, 326
Pass-along readership, 405–406
Pattern advertising, 674
Payout plan, 226–227
People meter, 373–374
Perceived concern, 177
Perceived control, 177
Perceived scrutiny, 177
Percentage charges, 88
Percentage-of-sales method, 218–222
Perception, 113–114
  information interpretation, 113–114
  information selection, 113
  selective, 114
  sensation and, 113
  subliminal, 114, 115–116
Peripheral route to persuasion, 160
Personal channels, 143, 187
Personal relevance, 154
Personal selling, 23–24, 596–617
  advantages/disadvantages, 606–608
  advertising combined with, 606–609
  closing, 604–605
  cost of, 600, 602–603
  creative selling, 603
  cross selling, 605
  described, 598
  direct marketing combined with, 465, 610–611
  effectiveness measurement, 613–616
  evaluation criteria, 613–614
  fire starting, 602
  in foreign markets, 693–694
  guiding, 602
  IMC program development, 27
  Internet and, 498–499, 611
  likes/dislikes of buyers, 606
  mapmaking, 601
  missionary sales, 603
  nature of, 600–606
  new role of, 601–602
  order taking, 603
  promotional mix and, 599–600
  promotional products combined with, 445
  prospecting, 603–604
  relationship marketing, 602
  responsibilities, 603–606
  role in IMC program, 599–606, 612–613
  sales force motivation, 597–598
  sales promotion combined with, 611
  scope of, 598
  stages of, 600–601
  surveying, 601
  top performers, traits of, 605
Personal video recorders (PVRs), 349–350
Personality symbols, 54, 153, 281
Personalization, 498
Persuader stage, 600, 601

Persuasion
central route to, 159–160
elaboration likelihood model, 158–161
peripheral route to, 160
Persuasion matrix, 166–168
Pharmaceutical Manufacturers Association, 714
Physiological needs, 109–110
Place-based media, 456
Planograms, 551
Point-of-Purchase Advertising International, 550
Point-of-purchase (POP) displays, 550–551
Political advertising, 184
Pop-unders, 496–498, 507
Pop-ups, 496–498, 507
Portable people meter (PPM), 376
Portfolio tests, 633
Positioning, 51–58
approaches to, 51–52
basic questions for, 52
by competitor, 54
competitor considerations, 55–57
consumer preferences and, 57
corporate image ads, 585–586
as creative strategy, 258–260
by cultural symbols, 54
monitoring, 58
positioning decision, 57–58
by price/quality, 52
by product attributes/benefits, 52
by product class, 53–54
by product user, 54
repositioning, 55
strategy determination, 55–58
strategy development, 52–55
by use or application, 52–53
Postpurchase dissonance, 151
Posttests, 626, 638–647
Preferred position rate, 424–425
Premiums, 535–537, 742
Preprinted inserts, 416
Prescription drug advertising, 737–738
Presentations, gaining clients by, 93
Press conference, 574
Press release, 573
Pretests, 626–627, 633–638
Price, positioning by, 52
Price-off deals, 541
Primacy effect, 179
Primary circulation, 405
Primary-demand advertising, 19
Print advertising
body copy, 285
creative tactics for, 283–286
direct/indirect headlines, 283–284
headlines, 283–284
layout, 285–286
posttests of, 638–643
pretests of, 633–634
subheads, 284
tracking studies, 646–647
visual elements, 285
Print media, 390–429
direct marketing and, 477
magazines; *see* Magazines
newspapers; *see* Newspapers
role of, 393
Printaculars, 399
PRIZM, 334
Problem detection, 248
Problem recognition, 107–109
Problem-solver stage, 601
Procreator stage, 601
Product manager, 73
Product placements, 12, 450–453
advantages of, 451
audience measurement, 453
disadvantages of, 451–453
virtual, 457–458
Product symbolism, 58
Production department, 82
Products, problem recognition and, 108
Product/service popularity appeals, 268–269
Product/service-specific preplanning input, 248–250
Professional advertising, 19, 714–715
Program rating, 372
Projective techniques, marketing research, 111
Promotion
client's role in organizing for; *see* Organization for advertising/promotion
defined, 16
growth of, 5–7
product pricing and, 61–62
push *vs.* pull strategies, 62–64
Promotion agencies, 556
Promotion Marketing Association (PMA), 68, 527
Promotional allowances, 547
Promotional management, 24–25
Promotional mix, 16–24
advertising; *see* Advertising
direct marketing; *see* Direct marketing
interactive marketing; *see* Interactive marketing; Internet
personal selling; *see* Personal selling
public relations; *see* Public relations
publicity; *see* Publicity
sales promotion; *see* Sales promotion
Promotional plan, 25
Promotional planning process
budgeting, 27, 31
communication process analysis, 27, 29–31
external analysis, 27, 28–29
IMC planning model, 26–27
IMC program development, 27, 31–32
integration/implementation, 27
internal analysis, 25–28, 29
marketing plan review, 25, 27
monitoring, evaluation, and control, 27, 32
persuasion matrix and, 166–168
situation analysis, 25–29
Promotional Products Association International (PPAI), 443, 446, 572
Promotional products marketing, 443–446
advantages/disadvantages, 443–445
audience measurement, 446
impact of, 445
product sales by category, 444
Promotional pull strategy, 64
Promotional push strategy, 64
Proprietary Association, 714
Prospecting, 603–604
Prospector stage, 600, 601
Prospects, 604
Protestant ethic, 764
Provider stage, 600, 601
Psychoanalytic theory, 110, 111
Psychographic segmentation, 47, 48–49
Psychosocial consequences, 117
Public relations, 23, 563–579; *see also* Corporate advertising; Publicity
advantages, 576–577
advertising combined with, 609
blunders, 582
clutter avoidance, 577
community involvement, 574
cost of, 576–577
credibility of, 576
disadvantages, 577
effectiveness measurement, 577–579, 584
exclusives, 574
in foreign markets, 694–695
gaining clients by, 93
image building with, 577
IMC program development, 27
in-studio media tours, 573
Internet and, 499–500, 575
interviews, 574
Ketchum Effectiveness Yardstick (KEY), 584
lead generation by, 577
marketing public relations (MPR), 566–567
new role of, 563–564, 565
press conferences, 574
press release, 573
process of, 568–575
plan evaluation, 569
planning, 569
program implementation, 573–575
public attitude evaluation, 568
target audience determination, 569–573
in promotional mix, 566
reaching specific groups with, 577
target audiences, 569–573
civic/business organizations, 572
community members, 570–571
educators, 572
employees, 570
external, 569
financial groups, 572–573
governments, 572
internal, 569
the media, 571–572
stockholders/investors, 570
suppliers/customers, 571
targeted newswire stories, 573
team approach to, 579
technological methods for, 573
telephone press conferences, 573
traditional definition, 564–565
value to marketing program, 567
video news releases (VNR), 573
Public relations firms, 95
Publicity, 22–23, 579–583
accuracy, 583
advantages/disadvantages, 583
control/dissemination of, 581–583
effectiveness measurement, 583, 584
IMC program development, 27
negative, 582
power of, 579–581
timing, 583
Puffery, 725–728
Pulsing, 314, 316
Pupillometrics, 636
Purchase intention, 120
Purchase situation, 130
Purchasing agent, family decision making, 129
Push money, 546–547
Push technologies, 498

Q

Q ratings, 178–179
Qualified prospects, 604
Qualitative audits, 88
Qualitative media effect, 188
Quality, positioning by, 52

R

RADAR (Radio's All-Dimension Audience Research), 386
Radio, 377–387
advantages of, 377–380
advertising regulation by, 719
audience information, 385–387
buying procedures, 380, 383–385
characteristics of, 330
clutter, 382–383
cost/efficiency of, 377–378

creative limitations of, 380
flexibility of, 378
fragmentation and, 380
IMC opportunities on, 378–380
limitations of, 380–382
limited research data for, 380–382
listener attention and, 382
mental imagery, 378
satellite, 381–382
selectivity of, 378
time classifications, 383–385
Ratings point, 372
Reach, 301–303
computer analysis of, 328–329
effective, 320–321
effects of, 320
gross ratings points and, 318–320
level needed, 316–317
of magazines, 402
objectives, 318
Readability tests, 634
Readers per copy, 326
Readership, magazine, 405–406
Reality programming, 371
Rebates, 540–541
Recall tests, 642–643
Receiver, 143–147, 167; *see also* Response process
Recency effect, 179
Recognition method, 641–642
Reference groups, 129
Referrals, gaining clients by, 92–93
Refunds, 540–541
Refutational appeal, 181
Regulation, 708–747
alcoholic beverage advertising, 709–710
contests, 740–742
direct marketing, 742–744
federal; *see* Federal regulation
in foreign markets, 666–668, 700–707
Internet marketing, 744–746
premiums, 742
sales promotion, 740–742
self-regulation; *see* Self-regulation
state and local, 740, 741–742
sweepstakes, 740–742
trade allowances, 742
Reinforcement, 125–126
Relationship marketing, 7–8, 468–469, 602
Relative cost, 323
Reminder advertising, 116, 274
Repetition, 124
Repositioning, 55
Republican National Committee, 115
Reputation, gaining clients by, 93
Research department, ad agency, 80
Resellers, 62
Response, 145
Response process, 147–162
advertising and, 161–162
alternative hierarchies, 150–153
dissonance/attribution, 150, 151–152
implications of, 153
low involvement, 150
standard learning, 150–151
cognitive approach, 157–158
elaboration likelihood model, 158–161
FCB planning model, 154–155
feedback methods, 149
involvement, 153–156
stages of, 150
traditional hierarchy models, 147–150
AIDA model, 147–148
evaluating, 150
hierarchy of effects, 147–148
implications of, 149–150
information processing, 147–148
innovation adoption, 147–148
Retail advertising, 19, 201–202
Retail advertising rates, 422–423
Retail trading zone, 421
RFM scoring method, 471
Rich media, 487
ROI budgeting method, 224
Rough testing, 631–633
Run of paper (ROP), 424

S

Safety needs, 109–110
Sales objectives, 198–202, 209
Sales promotion, 21–22, 510–560
abuse of, 557–558
accountability and, 519
account-specific, 519–520
advertising combined with, 554–556
brand equity and, 520, 524–525
brand loyalty and, 516
brand proliferation and, 516–517
budget allocation, 554–555
clutter and, 520
competition and, 519–520
concerns about, 520
consumer franchise building (CFB), 520–522
consumer market fragmentation and, 517–519
consumer-oriented; *see* Consumer-oriented sales promotion
defined, 513
direct marketing combined with, 465
effectiveness measurement, 648–650
in foreign markets, 690–693
growth of, 515–522
history of, 511–512
IMC program development, 27
increased sensitivity to, 516
Internet and, 498
media support/timing, 555–556
non-franchise building (non-FB), 522
overuse of, 557
personal selling combined with, 611
regulation of, 740–742
retailers' power and, 515–516
scope/role of, 513
short-term focus of, 519
theme coordination, 555
trade-oriented; *see* Trade-oriented sales promotion
Sales promotion agencies, 94–95
Sales promotion trap, 557–558
Sales response models, 214–215
Salient attributes, 52
Salient beliefs, 118
Sampling, 526–529
Satellite radio, 381–382
Satellite television, 370, 689
Satisfaction, customer, 120–121
Scatter market, 358
Schedules of reinforcement, 125–126
Scientific presentation advertising, 277
Script, 289–290
Securities and Exchange Commission (SEC), 581
Selective attention, 114
Selective binding, 411–412
Selective comprehension, 114
Selective exposure, 114
Selective learning, 151
Selective perception, 114
Selective retention, 114
Selective-demand advertising, 19
Selectivity, magazine, 395–398
Self-actualization needs, 109–110
Self-liquidating premiums, 536–537
Self-paced information, 188
Self-regulation, 712–721
by advertisers/agencies, 712–714
by advertising associations, 718
appraising, 721
by businesses, 715–716
direct marketing, 743–744
by media, 718–721
by trade associations, 714–715
Self-satisfaction strategy, 155
Semiotics, 142–143
Sensation, 113
Sets in use, 372
Sexual appeals, 756–757
Sexual Assault Prevention and Awareness Center, 767
Shaping, 126
Share of audience, 372–373
Shelter Advertising Association, 438
Shock advertising, 757–758
Showing, 435
Side panels, 496
Single-source tracking methods, 645–646
Situational determinants, 130–131
Skyscrapers, 496
Sleeper effect, 172
Slice-of-death advertising, 279
Slice-of-life advertising, 278–279
Slotting allowances, 547–549, 742
Small Business Administration, 549
Smart-TV, 376
Social class, consumer behavior and, 128–129
Social/cultural impact, of advertising, 762–772
anti-drug advertising, 773–774
consumer manipulation, 765–766
economic censorship, 769–771
materialism, 764–765
public service advertising, 772–774
stereotyping, 766–769
Social/love needs, 109–110
Solicitations, gaining clients by, 93
Source, 141, 168–179
attractiveness, 172–177
celebrities as; *see* Celebrity endorsement
corporate leaders as, 171
credibility, 168–172
decorative models, 177
direct, 168
effectiveness measurement, 625
expertise, 169
familiarity, 172
identification, 172
indirect, 168
likability, 172, 173–177
power of, 177–179
similarity, 172–173
trustworthiness, 169–171
Source bolsters, 158
Source derogations, 158
Source power, 177–179
SPAM, 500–501, 507, 746
Special audience newspapers, 414
Specialized marketing communications services, 70, 94–96
Specialty advertising, 443
Spiffs, 546–547
Split-run tests, 640
Split-runs, 401
Split-30s, 356
Sponsorship, 363
annual spending by property, 588
corporate advertising, 586
effectiveness measurement, 650–651
event, 543, 588–590
in foreign markets, 690–691
Internet advertising, 487, 496
Spot advertising, 361, 364, 367, 383

S-shaped response curve, 214–215
Standard advertising units (SAUs), 423–424
Standard Directory of Advertisers, 334
Standard Directory of Advertising Agencies, 77, 334
Standard learning model, 150–151
State and Metropolitan Area Data Book, 334
Station reps, 361
Stealth marketing, 431–432, 749–750
Stocking allowances, 549
Stopping power, 173
Storyboards, 82, 251
Straight sell advertising, 275–277
Strategic marketing plan, 40
Street money, 549
Study of Media and Markets, 408
Subcultures, consumer behavior and, 128–129
Subheads, 284
Subliminal perception, 114, 115–116
Super Bowl, 354–355
Superagencies, 77–78
Superstations, 365–366
Support advertising, 475
Support arguments, 157–158
Support media, 430–459
  direct marketing combined with, 467
  in-flight advertising, 453–456
  kiosks, 456
  miscellaneous, 456–458
  movie theater ads, 448–450
  out-of-home; *see* Out-of-home advertising
  place-based, 456
  product placements; *see* Product placements
  promotional products marketing, 443–446
  scope of, 432
  virtual advertising, 457–458
  Yellow Pages advertising, 446–448
Survey of buying power index, 310, 311
Sustainable competitive advantage, 257
Sweeps periods, 303, 374, 375
Sweepstakes, 537–540, 740–742
Syndicated programs, 361–362

T

Target audience, 146–147, 207
Target CPM, 325
Target marketing process, 43–58
  Internet and, 504–505
  market identification, 43–44
  market segmentation; *see* Market segmentation
  market selection, 42, 50–51
  media planning and, 306–309, 313–314
  positioning; *see* Positioning
Target ratings points (TRPs), 319–320
TargetTV, 376
Team approach, 579
Teaser advertising, 274–275
Technical evidence advertising, 277
Teenagers
  alcoholic beverage advertising and, 752
  bicultural, 140
  as global market segment, 675–676
  magazines and, 397
Telemarketing, 477–478, 610, 743
Telemedia, 477–478
Teleshopping, 477, 501
Television; *see also* Television advertising
  advantages of, 351–353
  advertiser influence on, 769–771
  advertising regulation by, 719–721
  attention and, 352, 356–357
  audience measurement, 370–377
    developments in, 374–377
    households using television (HUT), 372
    local audience information, 374
    network audience information, 373
    Nielsen Television Index, 373
    people meter, 373–374
    program rating, 372
    share of audience, 372–373
    sweeps ratings, 374, 375
    television households, 372
  cable, 364–370
  captivity of, 352
  characteristics of, 330
  clutter, 188–189, 356
  coverage/cost effectiveness of, 352
  creativity/impact of, 351
  distrust/negative evaluation of, 357
  fleeting message of, 355
  flexibility of, 352–353
  infomercials, 11, 461–462, 475–477
  interactive, 299–300, 506–508, 735
  limitations of, 353–357
  reality programs, 371
  satellite, 370, 689
  selectivity of, 352–355
  Spanish-language networks, 359–360
Television advertising; *see also* Television
  audio component, 286–289
  buying time, 357–364
    local advertising, 361
    methods of, 362–364
    network advertising, 358–361
    participations, 363
    sponsorship, 363
    spot advertising, 361, 367
    spot announcements, 364
    syndicated programs, 361–362
    time period/program selection, 364
  on cable television, 366–367
  clearance departments, 759–760
  clutter and, 188–189, 356
  comparative costs, 324–326
  cost of, 353–355, 360
  creative tactics for, 286–290
  effectiveness measurement, 619–620; *see also* Effectiveness measurement
  international, 685–686
  jingles, 287
  low involvement products and, 152–153
  music, 286–289
  needledrop, 286
  online, 495
  planning, 289–290
  posttests of, 643–647
  pretests of, 634–638
  production of, 290
  PVRs and, 349–350
  script, 289–290
  Super Bowl ads, 354–355
  tracking studies, 646–647
  video component, 286
  zipping/zapping of, 349–350, 356–357
Television households, 372
Television network, 358
Telnet, 487
Terminal posters, 441
Test marketing, 644–645
Testimonials, 277–278
Testing bias, 627–628
Text perspective/organization, 32–33
Theater testing, 635
Tobacco advertising, 667, 735–736
Top-down budgeting approaches, 217–225
Top-of-mind awareness, 116
Total audience, 373
  audience information, 406–408
  magazine, 405–406
Toy Manufacturers Association, 714
Tracking studies, 646–647
Trade advertising, 19, 64
Trade allowance, 547–550, 742
Trade associations, self-regulation by, 714–715
Trade regulation rules, 724
Trade shows, 445, 551
Trade-oriented sales promotion, 22, 513–514, 544–554
  for building retail inventories, 546
  buying allowances, 547
  contests, 546–547
  cooperative advertising, 552–554
  displays, 550–551
  for established brand retail display, 545–546
  for established brand trade support, 545
  everyday low pricing (EDLP) and, 549–550
  incentives, 546–547
  for new product distribution, 544–545
  objectives, 544–546
  planograms, 551
  point-of-purchase materials, 550–551
  promotional allowances, 547
  slotting allowances, 547–549, 742
  targeted to reseller salespeople, 547
  trade allowances, 547–550, 742
  trade shows, 445, 551
  types of, 546–554
Traffic department, 82
Transformational ads, 270–272
Transit advertising, 440–443
  advantages/disadvantages, 442
  audience measurement, 443
  inside cards, 441
  outside posters, 441
  terminal posters, 441
Two-sided message, 181
Two-step approach, 471

U

Unconditioned response, 123–124
Unconditioned stimulus, 123–124
Undifferentiated marketing, 50–51
Unduplicated reach, 318
Unfairness, 725
Unique selling proposition (USP), 256–257
Unique users, 487, 502
United Nations Statistical Yearbook, 683
U.S. Air Force, 619
U.S. Army, 3–5, 6, 130, 256
U.S. Brewers Association, 714
U.S. Census Bureau, 469
U.S. Commerce Department, 683
U.S. Consumer Products Safety Commission, 582
U.S. Government, 17
U.S. Navy, 622
U.S. Office of National Drug Control Policy (ONDCP), 773
U.S. Postal Service, 173, 463, 471, 711, 736–738, 743
U.S. Supreme Court
  commercial speech restrictions, 722
  corrective advertising, 733
  professional advertising, 714
  puffery, 726, 727–728
Universal estimate (UE), 372
Up-front market, 358
Usage situation, 130
Usenet, 487

V

Valid hits, 487
VALS program, 49
Vehicle option source effect, 626
Vertical cooperative advertising, 552

Verticals, 496
Video news release (VNR), 581
Virtual advertising, 457–458
Visits, 487, 502
Visual image personality (VIP), 153
Voice-over, 286

W

Want, 107
Waste coverage, 313
Web films, 67–68
Webcasting, 498
Website, 490–492
Weekly newspapers, 413
Wheeler-Lea Amendment, 723, 724
Wide Area Information Server (WAIS), 487
Wireless communications, 508
Women, stereotyping of, 766–767
Women Against Pornography, 752
Word-of-mouth communication, 143
World Health Organization, 667
World Trade Organization, 679, 696
World Wide Web (WWW), 486, 487; *see also* Internet
  webcast listenership measurement, 386
  website development/maintenance, 490–492

Y

Yellow Pages, 426, 446–448
  advantages/disadvantages, 447–448
  audience measurement, 448
  forms of, 446
Yellow Pages Publishers Association (YPPA), 448–450, 572

Z

Zapping, 349–350, 356–357
Zero-based communications planning, 210
Zipping, 349–350, 356